# Social Psychology

**NINTH EDITION**

# Social Psychology

## SAUL KASSIN • STEVEN FEIN • HAZEL ROSE MARKUS

John Jay College    Williams College    Stanford University

© Keren Su/China Span

**WADSWORTH**
CENGAGE Learning·

Australia • Brazil • Japan • Korea • Mexico • Singapore • Spain • United Kingdom • United States

**WADSWORTH**
CENGAGE Learning·

*Social Psychology*, **Ninth Edition**
Saul Kassin, Steven Fein, and
Hazel Rose Markus

Publisher: Jon-David Hague

Executive Editor: Jon-David Hague

Developmental Editor: Thomas Finn, Tangelique
    Williams

Assistant Editor: Jessica Alderman

Editorial Assistant: Amelia Blevins

Media Editor: Jasmin Tokatlian

Brand Manager: Elizabeth Rhoden

Market Development Manager: Chris Sosa

Content Project Manager: Carol Samet

Art Director: Vernon Boes

Manufacturing Planner: Karen Hunt

Rights Acquisitions Specialist: Tom McDonough

Production Service: Lachina Publishing Services

Photo Researcher: Roman Barnes

Text Researcher: Pablo D'Stair

Copy Editor: Lachina Publishing Services

Text and Cover Designer: Diane Beasley

Cover Image: Keren Su/China Span

Compositor: Lachina Publishing Services

For product information and technology assistance, contact us at
**Cengage Learning Customer & Sales Support, 1-800-354-9706**.

For permission to use material from this text or product,
submit all requests online at **www.cengage.com/permissions**.
Further permissions questions can be e-mailed to
**permissionrequest@cengage.com**.

Library of Congress Control Number: 2012943547

Student Edition:

ISBN-13: 978-1-133-95775-1

ISBN-10: 1-133-95775-7

Loose-leaf Edition:

ISBN-13: 978-1-133-95774-4

ISBN-10: 1-133-95774-9

**Wadsworth**
20 Davis Drive
Belmont, CA 94002-3098
USA

Cengage Learning is a leading provider of customized learning solutions
with office locations around the globe, including Singapore, the United
Kingdom, Australia, Mexico, Brazil, and Japan. Locate your local office at
**www.cengage.com/global**.

Cengage Learning products are represented in Canada by Nelson Education, Ltd.

To learn more about Wadsworth, visit **www.cengage.com/Wadsworth**.

Purchase any of our products at your local college store or at our preferred
online store **www.CengageBrain.com**.

Printed in Canada
1 2 3 4 5 6 7  17 16 15 14 13

*We dedicate this book to Bob Zajonc,*
*an inspiration to us all.*

# BRIEF CONTENTS

# CONTENTS

# 5  Stereotypes, Prejudice, and Discrimination    150

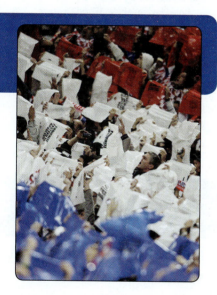

# PART 3  Social Influence

## 6  Attitudes   204

## 7  Conformity   252

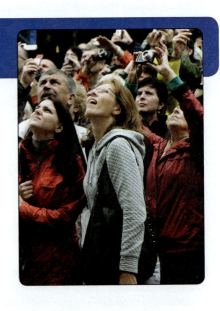

# 8 Group Processes 294

# PART 4 Social Relations

# 9 Attraction and Close Relationships 338

# 10  Helping Others   390

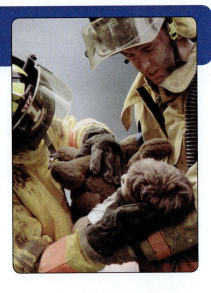

**Putting *Common Sense* to the Test   392**

# 11  Aggression  432

# PART 5  Applying Social Psychology

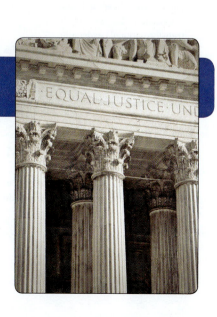

# 12  Law  484

# 13 Business   530

# 14 Health and Well-Being 570

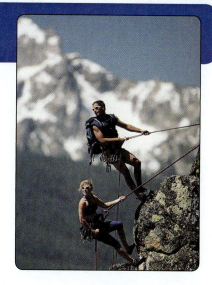

**The world of the twenty-first century** is an exciting and tumultuous place right now—more so, it seems, than any time in recent memory. On the one hand, thanks to Twitter, Skype, YouTube, and other social media, it has never been easier to talk or share information, opinions, pictures, music, and footage of live events as they occur with people from all corners of the world. On the other hand, deep social and political divisions, religious and ethnic conflicts all over the world, economic turmoil, and an ever-present threat of terrorism surround us. As Charles Dickens (1859) said in *A Tale of Two Cities*, "It was the best of times, it was the worst of times."

Encircled by its place in science and by current world events, social psychology—its theories, research methods, and basic findings—has never been more relevant or more important. We used to think of social psychology as a discipline that is slow to change. As in other sciences, we thought, knowledge builds in small increments, one brick at a time. Social psychology has no "critical" experiments, no single study can "prove" a theory, and no single theory can fully explain the complexities of human social behavior. While all this remains true, the process of revising this textbook always seems to shows us how complex, dynamic, and responsive our field can be. As the world around us rapidly changes—socially, politically, technologically, and in other disciplines—so too does social psychology.

At the same time, social psychology was recently rocked by scandal and controversy. In 2011, a well-known social psychologist in the Netherlands was found to have falsified data that had appeared in several dozen articles. That case was followed by two other instances of fraud. In addition, an article purporting to provide evidence of extrasensory perception, or ESP, was published in social psychology's top journal until questions were raised about the methods and statistical analyses. Then a controversy erupted over the question of whether social psychology research was inadvertently biased by political ideology. As a result of these recent events, the discipline is now undergoing a process of self-examination. Noting that crisis can beget opportunity, the Society of Personality and Social Psychology (SPSP) has initiated new workshops, policies, and standards of responsible conduct—all designed to prevent future instances of intentional and unintentional bias.

## Goals for This Edition

We had three main goals for this revision.

1. Our first goal was to present the most important and exciting perspectives in the field as a whole. To communicate the breadth and depth of social psychology, we have self-consciously expanded our coverage to include not only the classics but also the most recent developments in the field—developments that capture new thinking about social neuroscience, embodied cognition, evolutionary theory, implicit processes, and cultural influences.

2. In light of the fraud scandals that have surfaced, our second goal was to try to vet brand new findings in an effort to ensure that the social psychology we present will prove accurate over time. No method of vetting is perfect. But as a departure from

past practice, we have chosen to exclude from this edition any research presented at professional conferences or reported in the news that has not been published in a peer-reviewed journal. For articles newly published, we sought to determine if the findings were consistent with other research.

3. Finally, we want this book to serve as a good teacher outside the classroom. While speaking the student's language, we always want to connect social psychology to current events in politics, sports, business, law, entertainment, the use of social networking sites, and other life domains. We will say more about this later in the preface, in a section on "Connections with Current Events."

# What's New in This Edition

As in the past, we have tried to capture some subtle but important shifts within the field so that the reader can feel the pulse of social psychology *today* in each and every page of this textbook.

## ❯ The Content

**Comprehensive, Up-to-Date Scholarship** Like its predecessors, the ninth edition offers a broad, balanced, mainstream look at social psychology. Thus, it includes detailed descriptions of classic studies from social psychology's historical warehouse as well as the latest research findings from hundreds of new references. In particular, we draw your attention to the following topics, which are either new to this edition or have received expanded coverage:

- Introductions to social neuroscience, evolutionary, and cultural perspectives (Chapter 1)
- Introductions to behavioral economics, embodied cognition, and other interdisciplinary approaches (Chapter 1)
- The challenges of doing research across cultures (Chapter 2)
- New ways of conducting research online (Chapter 2)
- Discussion of recent cases of academic fraud (Chapter 2)
- God, religion, and self-awareness (Chapter 3)
- The evolution of self-deception (Chapter 3)
- Generational differences in the self (Chapter 3)
- Mind perception (Chapter 4)
- Embodiment effects in social cognition (Chapter 4)
- New research on motivated "wishful seeing" (Chapter 4)
- Racism as seen in the Trayvon Martin shooting and other news events (Chapter 5)
- Evolutionary perspectives on intergroup perception biases (Chapter 5)
- Social neuroscience perspectives on intergroup perception biases (Chapter 5)
- Benefits of extended contact and intergroup friendships (Chapter 5)
- Effects of being stigmatized (Chapter 5)
- Political attitudes and the "political brain" (Chapter 6)

- Attitude embodiment effects (Chapter 6)
- Perceptual consequences of cognitive dissonance (Chapter 6)
- Digital social influence, as seen in the Arab Spring (Chapter 7)
- Imitation in nonhumans and infants (Chapter 7)
- fMRI images of conformity and exclusion (Chapter 7)
- Cultural influences on group cohesiveness (Chapter 8)
- Culture and diversity in groups (Chapter 8)
- Group dynamics challenges posed by "virtual teams" (Chapter 8)
- The phenomenon of online dating (Chapter 9)
- The speed-dating phenomenon and research paradigm (Chapter 9)
- Gender differences in the expression of romantic love (Chapter 9)
- Evolutionary psychology of conspicuous consumption (Chapter 9)
- Prosocial media effects (Chapter 10)
- The evolution of empathy (Chapter 10)
- Applications of bystander research to bullying (Chapter 10)
- The struggle for self-control in aggression (Chapter 11)
- Social neuroscience perspectives on aggression and its control (Chapter 11)
- Effects of social rejection and ostracism on aggression (Chapter 11)
- Policy research on how to improve eyewitness justice (Chapter 12)
- Post–9/11 research on lie detection and intelligence gathering (Chapter 12)
- Cultural perspectives on law and justice (Chapter 12)
- The Progress Principle of motivation in the workplace (Chapter 13)
- The symbolic power of money (Chapter 13)
- The psychological consequences of unemployment (Chapter 13)
- The link between socioeconomic status and health (Chapter 14)
- Cultural differences in social support seeking as a means of coping (Chapter 14)
- The emerging science on how to increase happiness (Chapter 14)

As this nonexhaustive list shows, this ninth edition contains a good deal of new material. In particular, you will see that we have zeroed in on developments within five important domains: social neuroscience, embodied cognition, evolutionary theory, implicit processes, and cultural perspectives. Across chapters, as always, we have also made it a point to illustrate the relevance of social psychology to current events and to ask students to reflect on their commonsense conceptions.

**Social Neuroscience**   The first domain concerns social neuroscience and the fMRI brain-imaging studies that are poised to enlighten our understanding of the human social experience. Social neuroscience has not fully arrived, and researchers are still raising questions about how to interpret the newly observed links between brain activity and self-referential thoughts, social perceptions, motives, emotions, and behavior. While we acknowledge the current limitations, we also want to provide students with a glimpse of this exciting new fusion of social psychology and neuroscience.

**Embodied Cognition**    More and more, social psychologists are finding that human thought is "embodied"—that the way we view ourselves and others is influenced by the physical position, orientation, sensations, and movements of our bodies. By varying whether people nod or shake their heads, stretch their arms inward or outward, stand on a surface that is hard or soft, or hold an object that is hot or cold, a number of new studies illustrate *embodiment effects* in self and other perceptions, beliefs, evaluations, and attitudes.

**Evolutionary Theory**    We continue in this edition to represent various evolutionary perspectives on human nature, at the heart of which is the notion that we humans, like other species, have an ancestral past that predisposes us, albeit flexibly, to behave in ways that are adapted to promote survival and reproduction. Evolutionary psychologists today seek to explain a wide range of social phenomena—such as snap judgments in social perception, prejudice, helping, aggression, beauty, mate selection, and romantic jealousy. To some extent, this perspective is still controversial. To another extent, it has become part of the mainstream, with respected journals filled with studies and critiques of evolutionary psychology. This edition fully integrates the approach, its findings, and its limitations with the rest of social psychology.

**Implicit Processes**    More and more, social psychologists across a range of research areas are finding it informative to use both implicit and explicit processes, especially for the purpose of supplementing self-report measures of beliefs and preferences. In matters relating to the unconscious, psychology owes a debt of gratitude to Freud. After some resistance, social psychologists have also come to realize the value of the conscious–unconscious distinction in the study of self-esteem, priming, stereotyping, prejudice, attitudes, ambivalence, social influence, attraction, and other core topics. Hence, we describe recent work involving the Implicit Association Test, or IAT, and the ongoing debate about what it measures, what it means, and what behaviors it predicts.

**Cultural Perspectives**    On the heels of our highly expanded coverage over the past two editions, we have continued in this edition not only to cover but also to fully integrate current research on cultural influences in social behavior. Social psychologists have long been fascinated by similarity and difference—among cultural groups and between racial and ethnic groups within cultures. As the people of the world have come into closer contact, researchers have broadened their scope from the situational snapshot to a fuller account of people in their cultural milieu. Cultural phenomena, once marginalized, are now fully integrated into social psychology. As in our previous edition, every chapter now contains one, two, or three sections on the role of culture. These sections appear within the body of the text and are richly accompanied by photographs, not boxed or set apart.

As social psychology is now a truly international discipline, this book also includes many new citations to research conducted throughout Europe, Asia, Australia, and other parts of the world. We believe that the study of human diversity—from the perspectives of researchers who themselves are a diverse lot—can help students become better informed about social relations as well as about ethics and values.

**Connections with Current Events**    To cover social psychology is one thing; to use its principles to explain events in the real world is quite another. More than a decade ago, the events of 9/11 changed the world. In different ways not fully discernible, so did the recent and severe economic recession in the United States and Europe; the presidential election of Barack Obama; the change that has swept through the Arab world; and the increasing ease with which people meet and interact through online social networking sites. More than ever, we are convinced that connecting theory to real life is the best way to heighten student interest and involvement. Over the years, teachers and students have told us how much they value the "newsy" features of our book.

The ninth edition, like its predecessors, is committed to making social psychology *relevant.* Almost every page includes a passage, a quote, a figure, a table, a photo, or a cartoon that refers to people, places, events, social trends, and issues that are prominent in contemporary culture. The reader will find stories about the killing of Osama Bin Laden; the near economic collapse and its aftermath; the shooting in Florida of Trayvon Martin; the sex abuse scandal and coverup at Penn State University; the trials of Amanda Knox in Italy; the 2012 presidential election; *The Hunger Games*; ongoing political debates over health care reform, gay marriage, and immigration policy; and the role of Facebook, Twitter, and YouTube during the revolutions of the Arab Spring.

As in our last edition, you will also find—in the margins—various quotations, song lyrics, public opinion poll results, "factoids," and website addresses. These high-interest items are designed to further illustrate the connectedness of social psychology to a world that extends beyond the borders of a college campus.

**Social Psychology and Common Sense**   In an earlier edition, we introduced a feature that we remain excited about. Building on a discussion in Chapter 1 about the links (and lack thereof) between social psychology and common sense, each substantive chapter opens with *Putting Common Sense to the Test,* a set of true–false questions designed to assess the student's intuitive beliefs about material later contained in that chapter. Some examples: "Sometimes the harder you try to control a thought, feeling, or behavior, the less likely you are to succeed," "People often come to like what they suffer for," "Opposites attract," and "Groups are less likely than individuals to invest more in a project that is failing." The answers to these questions are revealed in a marginal box after the topic is presented in the text. These answers are then explained at the end of each chapter. We think that students will find this exercise engaging. It will also enable them, as they read, to check their intuitive beliefs against the findings of social psychology and to notice the discrepancies that exist.

## ❯ The Organization

Of all the challenges faced by teachers and textbooks, perhaps the greatest is to put information together in a way that is both accurate and easy to understand. A strong organizational framework helps in meeting this challenge. There is nothing worse for a student than having to wade through a "laundry list" of studies whose interconnections remain a profound mystery. A strong structure thus facilitates the development of conceptual understanding.

But the tail should not wag the dog. Since organizational structure is a means to an end, not an end in itself, we want to keep it simple and unobtrusive. Look through the Table of Contents, and you will see that we present social psychology in five major parts—a heuristic structure that instructors and students have found sensible and easy to follow through eight editions. The book opens with two *Introduction* chapters on the history, subject matter, and research methods of social psychology (Part I). As before, we then move to an intraindividual focus on *Social Perception* (Part II), shift outward to *Social Influence* (Part III) and *Social Relations* (Part IV), and conclude with *Applying Social Psychology* (Part V). We realize that some instructors like to reshuffle the deck to develop a chapter order that better fits their own approach. There is no problem in doing this. Each chapter stands on its own and does not require that others be read first.

## The Presentation

Even when the content of a textbook is accurate and up to date, and even when its organization is sound, there is still the matter of presentation. As the "teacher outside the classroom," a good textbook should facilitate learning. Thus, every chapter contains the following pedagogical features:

- A narrative preview, chapter outline, and commonsense quiz (beginning with Chapter 3).

- Key terms highlighted in the text, defined in the margin, listed at the end of the chapter, and reprinted in an alphabetized glossary at the end of the book. Both the list and the glossary provide page numbers for easy location of each term.

- Numerous bar graphs, line graphs, tables, sketches, photographs, flowcharts, and cartoons that illustrate, extend, enhance, and enliven material in the text. Some of these depict classic images and studies from social psychology's history; others, new to the ninth edition, are contemporary and often "newsy."

- At the end of each chapter, a comprehensive bulleted review summarizing the major sections and points.

# Teaching and Learning Support Package

## For the Instructor

**Instructor's Resource Manual with Test Bank**   Every chapter includes learning objectives, a detailed chapter outline, lecture and discussion ideas, classroom activities, handouts, multimedia resources, and multiple-choice and essay questions.

**PowerLecture with ExamView**   This one-stop lecture and class preparation tool contains ready-to-use PowerPoint® slides that enable you to assemble, edit, publish, and present custom lectures for your course. PowerLecture lets you bring together text-specific lecture outlines and art from the ninth edition along with videos or your own materials, culminating in a powerful, personalized media-enhanced presentation. The DVD-ROM also includes the ExamView® assessment and tutorial system, which guides you step by step through the process of creating tests.

**CourseMate**   Interested in a simple way to complement your text and course content with study and practice materials? Psychology CourseMate includes an interactive eBook with highlighting and note-taking features and an interactive glossary, as well as interactive learning tools like quizzes, flashcards, videos, and more! Engagement Tracker, a first-of-its-kind tool, monitors student engagement in the course.

**WebTutor**   WebTutor™ offers a full array of text-specific online study tools, including learning objectives, glossary flashcards, practice quizzes, and web links. All content is assignable and feeds into the gradebook in your learning management system where you can track student grades and progress.

***Revealing Psychology***   These social psychology video segments are informative, engaging, and fun. Hidden cameras reveal people's surprising and amusing reactions when social forces conspire against them. How do you behave when people invade your personal space? Do you help a person who lies sprawled on a busy street? How often do you lie in a 10-minute conversation? These real-world vignettes reveal human foibles and at the same time dramatically illustrate underlying psychological principles. They are available to instructors on DVD for classroom presentation.

***Social Psych in Film DVD***   This DVD, with closed captioning, contains more than 25 clips from popular films and classic experiments that illustrate key concepts in social psychology. Clips from films like *Apollo 13, Schindler's List, Snow Falling on Cedars,* and *In the Name of the Father* are combined with overviews and discussion questions to help bring psychology alive for students and to demonstrate its relevance to contemporary life and culture.

***ABC Video: Social Psychology, Volumes I & II***   ABC Videos feature short, high-interest clips from current news events as well as historic raw footage going back 40 years. Perfect for discussion starters or to enrich your lectures and spark interest in the material in the text, these brief videos provide students with a new lens through which to view the past and present, one that will greatly enhance their knowledge and understanding of significant events and open up to them new dimensions in learning. Clips are drawn from such programs as *World News Tonight, Good Morning America, This Week, PrimeTime Live, 20/20,* and *Nightline,* as well as numerous ABC News specials and material from the Associated Press Television News and British Movietone News collections.

***Research in Action, Volumes I & II***   *Research in Action* features the work of research psychologists to give students an opportunity to learn about cutting-edge research—not just who is doing it, but also how it is done, and how and where the results are being used. By taking students into the laboratories of both established and up-and-coming researchers, and by showing research results being applied outside of the laboratory, these videos offer insight into both the research process and the many ways in which real people's lives are affected by research in the fields of psychology and neuroscience.

## ▶ For the Student

***Readings in Social Psychology: The Art and Science of Research, Fifth Edition***   This item contains original articles, each with a brief introduction, and questions to stimulate critical thinking about "doing" social psychology. The articles represent some of the most creative and accessible research, both classic and contemporary, on topics of interest to students.

***CourseMate***   The more you study, the better the results. Make the most of your study time by accessing everything you need to succeed in one place. Psychology CourseMate includes an interactive eBook with highlighting and note-taking features and an interactive glossary, as well as interactive learning tools like quizzes, flashcards, videos, and more!

***WebTutor***   WebTutor™ offers a full array of text-specific online study tools, including learning objectives, glossary flashcards, practice quizzes, and web links.

# Acknowledgments

Textbooks are the product of a team effort. We are grateful to Cengage Learning for its commitment to quality as the first priority. First, we want to thank Thomas Finn and Tangelique Williams, our developmental editors. We also want to express our gratitude to Roman Barnes, our photo researcher, who has helped to make this book so photographically interesting. Finally, we want to thank all those whose considerable talents and countless hours of hard work can be seen on every page: Carol Samet and Pat Waldo, Senior Project Managers; Lachina Publishing Services, Copyediting; Matthew Orgovan, Lachina Publishing Services, Project Manager; Jessica Alderman, Assistant Editor; Jasmin Tokatlian, Media Editor; and Amelia Blevins, Editorial Assistant. We also thank Publisher Jon-David Hague; Senior Brand Manager, Liz Rhoden; and Market Development Manager, Chris Sosa.

Several colleagues have guided us through their feedback on this and all prior editions. Every one of these teachers and scholars has helped to make this a better book. For their invaluable insights, comments, and suggestions, we thank reviewers of the ninth edition:

William Adler, *Collin County College*
Craig Anderson, *Iowa State University*
Lorraine Benuto, *University of Nevada, Las Vegas*
Kimberly Coffman, *Florida International University*
Jean Egan, *Asnuntuck Community College*
Rebecca Francis, *West Virginia State University*
Mike Mangan, *University of New Hampshire, Durham*
Margo Monteith, *Purdue University*
Paul Paulus, *University of Texas at Arlington*
William Pedersen, *California State University, Long Beach*
Michele Reich, *Drexel University*
Nicole Shelton, *Princeton University*
Jennifer Shibley, *Columbia College, Chicago*
Arlene Stillwell, *SUNY College at Potsdam*
Eric Stocks, *University of Texas at Tyler*
Elizabeth Williford, *Belhaven University*

We also thank past edition reviewers:

Shelley N. Aikman, *Syracuse University*
Scott Allison, *University of Richmond*
Thomas William Altermatt, *Hanover College*
Sowmya Anand, *The Ohio State University*
Robin A. Anderson, *St. Ambrose University*
Austin Baldwin, *Southern Methodist University*
C. Daniel Batson, *University of Kansas*
Arnold James Benjamin, Jr., *Oklahoma Panhandle State University*
Lisa M. Bohon, *California State University*
Bryan Bonner, *The University of Utah*

Jennifer K. Bosson, *The University of Oklahoma*
Martin Bourgeois, *University of Wyoming*
Nyla Branscombe, *University of Kansas*
Brad J. Bushman, *University of Michigan*
Melissa A. Cahoon, *University of Dayton*
Nathaniel Carter, *Lane College*
Serena Chen, *University of California, Berkeley*
Nicholas Christenfeld, *University of California, San Diego*
James E. Collins, *Carson Newman College*
Eric Cooley, *Western Oregon University*
Keith E. Davis, *University of South Carolina*

Jack Dovidio, *Yale University*
Richard Ennis, *University of Waterloo*
Leandre R. Fabrigar, *Queen's University*
Mark A. Ferguson, *University of Kansas*
Joseph R. Ferrari, *DePaul University*
J. H. Forthman, *San Antonio College*
Donelson Forsyth, *University of Richmond*
Paul A. Franco, *Calumet College of St. Joseph*
Timothy M. Franz, *St. John Fisher College*
Traci Giuliano, *Southwestern University*
Diana Odom Gunn, *McNeese State University*
MarYam G. Hamedani, *Stanford University*
Karen L. Harris, *Western Illinois University*
Lora D. Haynes, *University of Louisville*
James Hobbs, *Ulster County Community College*
L. Rowell Huesmann, *University of Michigan*
Karen Huxtable-Jester, *University of Texas at Dallas*
Alisha Janowsky, *University of Central Florida*
Robert D. Johnson, *Arkansas State University*
Warren H. Jones, *University of Tennessee*
Cheryl Kaiser, *Michigan State University*
Steven J. Karau, *Southern Illinois University*
Suzanne C. Kieffer, *University of Houston*
William M. Klein, *University of Pittsburgh*
LaRue Kobrin, *College of the Redwoods*
Vladimir J. Konecni, *University of California, San Diego*
Doug Krull, *Northern Kentucky University*
Kevin Lanning, *Florida Atlantic University*
Patrick Laughlin, *University of Illinois*
Herbert L. Leff, *University of Vermont*
Margaret A. Lloyd, *Georgia Southern University*

David C. Lundgren, *University of Cincinnati*
Rusty McIntyre, *Wayne State University*
Judith McIlwee, *Mira Costa College*
Roque V. Mendez, *Southwest Texas State University*
Daniel Molden, *Northwestern University*
Richard Moreland, *University of Pittsburgh*
Cynthia R. Nordstrom, *Illinois State University*
Randall E. Osborne, *Indiana University East*
Patricia A. Oswald, *Iona College*
Carol K. Oyster, *University of Wisconsin, La Crosse*
David Pillow, *University of Texas at San Antonio*
Louis H. Porter, *Westchester University of Pennsylvania*
Margaret M. Pulsifer, *Harvard Medical School*
Sally Radmacher, *Missouri Western State University*
Chris Robert, *University of Missouri*
Todd Shackelford, *Florida Atlantic University*
Laura S. Sidorowicz, *Nassau Community College*
Paul Silvia, *University of North Carolina at Greensboro*
Anthony Stahelski, *Central Washington University*
Charles Stangor, *University of Maryland*
Nicole M. Stephens, *Northwestern University, Kellogg School of Management*
Jeffrey Stone, *University of Arizona*
JoNell Strough, *West Virginia University*
Kari Terzino, *Iowa State University*
Courtney von Hippel, *University of Queensland*
William von Hippel, *University of Queensland*
Kipling D. Williams, *Purdue University*
Ann Zak, *College of St. Rose*

*Saul Kassin*
*Steven Fein*
*Hazel Rose Markus*

# About the Authors

**SAUL KASSIN** is Distinguished Professor of Psychology at John Jay College of Criminal Justice, in New York, and Massachusetts Professor of Psychology at Williams College, Williamstown, Massachusetts. Born and raised in Brooklyn, New York, he received his Ph.D. from the University of Connecticut followed by a postdoctoral fellowship at the University of Kansas, a U.S. Supreme Court Fellowship, and a visiting professorship at Stanford University. In addition to authoring textbooks, he has co-authored and edited *Confessions in the Courtroom, The Psychology of Evidence and Trial Procedure, The American Jury on Trial,* and *Developmental Social Psychology.* Several years ago, Kassin pioneered the scientific study of false confessions, an interest that continues to this day. He has also studied the impact of this and other evidence on the social perceptions and verdicts of juries. Kassin is past president of the American Psychology-Law Society and is a Fellow of APS, APA, and Divisions 8 and 41. He has testified as an expert witness; lectures frequently to judges, lawyers, and law enforcement groups; and has appeared as a media consultant on national and syndicated news programs.

**STEVEN FEIN** is Professor of Psychology at Williams College, Williamstown, Massachusetts. Born and raised in Bayonne, New Jersey, he received his A.B. from Princeton University and his Ph.D. in social psychology from the University of Michigan. He has been teaching at Williams College since 1991, with time spent teaching at Stanford University in 1999. His edited books include *Emotion: Interdisciplinary Perspectives, Readings in Social Psychology: The Art and Science of Research,* and *Motivated Social Perception: The Ontario Symposium.* He has served on the executive committee of the Society of Personality and Social Psychology and as the social and personality psychology representative at the American Psychological Association. His research interests concern stereotyping and prejudice, suspicion and attributional processes, social influence, and self-affirmation theory.

**HAZEL ROSE MARKUS** is the Davis-Brack Professor in the Behavioral Sciences at Stanford University. She also co-directs the Research Institute of the Stanford Center for Comparative Studies in Race and Ethnicity. Before moving to Stanford in 1994, she was a professor at the University of Michigan, where she received her Ph.D. Her work focuses on how the self-system, including current conceptions of self and possible selves, structures and lends meaning to experience. Born in England to English parents and raised in San Diego, California, she has been persistently fascinated by how nation of origin, region of the country, gender, ethnicity, race, religion, and social class shape self and identity. With her colleague Shinobu Kitayama at the University of Michigan, she has pioneered the experimental study of how culture and self influence one another. Markus was elected to the American Academy of Arts and Sciences in 1994 and is a Fellow of APS, APA, and Division 8. Some of her recent co-edited books include *Culture and Emotion: Empirical Studies of Mutual Influence, Engaging Cultural Differences: The Multicultural Challenge in Liberal Democracies, Just Schools: Pursuing Equal Education in Societies of Difference,* and *Doing Race: 21 Essays for the 21st Century.*

# What Is Social Psychology?

This chapter introduces you to the study of social psychology. We begin by defining social psychology and identifying how it is distinct from but related to some other areas of study, both outside and within psychology. Next, we review the history of the field. We conclude by looking forward, with a discussion of the important themes and perspectives that are propelling social psychology into a new century.

# 1

© Yuri Arcurs/Shutterstock

**A few years from now,** you may receive a letter in the mail inviting you to a high school or college reunion. You'll probably feel a bit nostalgic, and you'll begin to think about those old school days. What thoughts will come to mind first? Will you remember the poetry you finally began to appreciate in your junior year? Will you think about the pride you felt when you completed your first chemistry lab? Will a tear form in your eye as you remember how inspiring your social psychology class was?

Perhaps. But what will probably dominate your thoughts are the people you knew in school and the interactions you had with them—the long and intense discussions about everything imaginable; the loves you had, lost, or wanted so desperately to experience; the time you made a fool of yourself at a party; the effort of trying to be accepted by a fraternity, sorority, or clique of popular people; the day you sat in the pouring rain with your friends while watching a football game.

We focus on these social situations because we are social beings. We forge our individual identities not alone but in the context of other people. We work, play, and live together. We hurt and help each other. We define happiness and success for each other. And we don't fall passively into social interactions; we actively seek them. We visit family, make friends, have parties, build networks, go on dates, pledge an enduring commitment, decide to have children. We watch others, speculate about them, and predict who will wind up with whom, whether in real life or on "reality" TV shows such as *The Real World* or *The Bachelor*. Many of us text or tweet each other about everything we're up to, or we spend lots of time on social networking sites such as Facebook, interacting with countless peers from around the world, adding hundreds or even thousands of "friends" to our social networks.

You've probably seen or at least heard about the movie *It's a Wonderful Life*. When the hero, George Bailey, was about to kill himself, the would-be angel Clarence didn't save him by showing him how much personal happiness he'd miss if he ended his life. Instead, he showed George how much his life had touched the lives of others and how many people would be hurt if he was not a part of their world. It was these social relationships that saved George's life, just as they define our own.

One of the exciting aspects of learning about social psychology is discovering how basic and profoundly important these social relationships are to the human animal. And research continues to find new evidence for and point to new implications of our social nature. Consider, for example, this set of conclusions from recent research:

> *"You carry [your friends and family] with you in your heart, your mind, your stomach, because you do not just live in a world but a world lives in you."*
>
> —Frederick Buechner

Millions of people tune in to watch strangers relate to each other on popular "reality" shows. Pictured here is a group who appeared in a recent season of *The Bachelorette*, as viewers wondered which man might get engaged to the featured bachelorette. The enormous popularity of shows like these illustrates part of the appeal of social psychology—people are fascinated with how we relate to one another.

- Having close friends and staying in contact with family members is associated with health benefits such as protecting against heart disease, infection, diabetes, and cancer, and with living longer and more actively (Hawkley & Cacioppo, 2013; Luo et al., 2012).

- Children who are socially excluded from activities by their peers are more likely than other children to suffer academically as well as socially in school even several years later (Buhs et al., 2010; Rodkin & Ryan, 2012).

- Experiencing a social rejection or loss is so painful that it produces activity in the same parts of the brain as when we feel physical pain. Being treated well and fairly by other people, on the other hand, activates parts of the brain associated with physical rewards such as desirable food and drink (Eisenberger, 2012; Eisenberger & Cole, 2012).

Craig Sjodin/ABC via Getty Images

- As many doctors can tell you, there is something very real about a "broken heart." For example, a person is more than 20 times more likely than usual to suffer a heart attack within one day of the death of a loved one (Mostofsky et al., 2012).

Precisely because we need and care so much about social interactions and relationships, the social contexts in which we find ourselves can influence us profoundly. You can find many examples of this kind of influence in your own life. Have you ever laughed at a joke you didn't get just because those around you were laughing? Do you present yourself in one way with one group of people and in quite a different way with another group? The power of the situation can also be much more subtle, and yet more powerful, than in these examples, as when another's unspoken expectations about you literally seem to cause you to become a different person.

The relevance of social psychology is evident in everyday life, of course, such as when two people become attracted to each other or when a group tries to coordinate its efforts on a project. Dramatic events can heighten its significance all the more, as is evident in people's behavior during and after war, terrorist attacks, or natural disasters. In these traumatic times, a spotlight shines on how people help or exploit each other, and we witness some of the worst and best that human relations have to offer. These events invariably call attention to the kinds of questions that social psychologists study—questions about hatred and violence, about intergroup conflict and suspicion, as well as about heroism, cooperation, and the capacity for understanding across cultural, ethnic, racial, religious, and geographic divides. We are reminded of the need for a better understanding of social psychological issues as we see footage of death and destruction in the Middle East or Congo or are confronted with the reality of an all-too-violent world as nearby as our own neighborhoods and campuses. We also appreciate the majesty and power of social connections as we recognize the courage of a firefighter, read about the charity of a donor, or see the glow in the eyes of a new parent. These are all—the bad and the good, the mundane and the extraordinary—part of the fascinating landscape of social psychology.

Egyptian youth post video to Facebook and Twitter of footage they shot earlier that day of revolutionary protests in Tahrir Square in 2011 (left). Social networking sites played a key role in protests for social and economic reform that broke out throughout the world that year, including in this "Occupy" protest at the University of California, Davis, in which a police officer sprays pepper spray into the face of a student (right). Social psychologists study important issues such as the ones raised here, including about the expanding role of social networking and technology in our lives, and how people deal with conflict.

Not only will you learn interesting and relevant research findings throughout the book, you also will learn *how* social psychologists have discovered this evidence. It is an exciting process and one that we are enthusiastic about sharing with you. The purpose of this first chapter is to provide you with a broad overview of the field of social psychology. By the time you finish it, you should be ready and (we hope) eager for what lies ahead.

# What Is Social Psychology?

We begin by previewing the new territory you're about to enter. Then we define social psychology and map out its relationship to sociology and some other disciplines within the field of psychology.

## Defining Social Psychology

**Social psychology** is the scientific study of how individuals think, feel, and behave in a social context. Let's look at each part of this definition.

Our social relationships and interactions are extremely important to us. Most people seek out and are profoundly affected by other people. This social nature of the human animal is what social psychology is all about.

IT Stock/Jupiter Images

**Scientific Study**   There are many approaches to understanding how people think, feel, and behave. We can learn about human behavior from novels, films, history, and philosophy, to name just a few possibilities. What makes social psychology different from these artistic and humanistic endeavors is that social psychology is a science. It applies the *scientific method* of systematic observation, description, and measurement to the study of the human condition. How, and why, social psychologists do this is explained in Chapter 2.

**How Individuals Think, Feel, and Behave**   Social psychology concerns an amazingly diverse set of topics. People's private, even nonconscious beliefs and attitudes; their most passionate emotions; their heroic, cowardly, or merely mundane public behaviors—these all fall within the broad scope of social psychology. In this way, social psychology differs from other social sciences such as economics and political science. Research on attitudes offers a good illustration. Whereas economists and political scientists may be interested in people's economic and political attitudes, respectively, social psychologists investigate a wide variety of attitudes and contexts, such as individuals' attitudes toward particular groups of people or how their attitudes are affected by their peers or their mood. In doing so, social psychologists strive to establish general principles of attitude formation and change that apply in a variety of situations rather than exclusively to particular domains.

Note the word *individuals* in our definition of social psychology. This word points to another important way in which social psychology differs from some other social sciences. Sociology, for instance, typically classifies people in terms of their nationality, race, socioeconomic class, and other *group factors*. In contrast, social psychology typically focuses on the psychology of the *individual*. Even when social psychologists study groups of people, they usually emphasize the behavior of the individual in the group context.

**social psychology**   The scientific study of how individuals think, feel, and behave in a social context.

**A Social Context**   Here is where the "social" in social psychology comes into play and how social psychology is distinguished from other branches of psychology. As a whole, the discipline of psychology is an immense, sprawling enterprise, the 800-pound gorilla of the social sciences, concerned with everything from the actions of neurotransmitters in the brain to the actions of music fans in a crowded club. What makes <mark>social psychology unique is its emphasis on the social nature of individ</mark>uals.

However, the "socialness" of social psychology varies. In attempting to establish general principles of human behavior, social psychologists sometimes examine nonsocial factors that affect people's thoughts, emotions, motives, and actions. For example, they may study whether hot weather causes people to behave more aggressively (Anderson & DeLisi, 2011). What is social about this is the behavior: people hurting each other. In addition, social psychologists sometimes study people's thoughts or feelings about nonsocial things, such as people's attitudes toward Nike versus Adidas basketball shoes. How can attitudes toward basketball shoes be of interest to social psychologists? One way is if these attitudes are influenced by something social, such as whether LeBron James's endorsement of Nike makes people prefer that brand. Both examples—determining whether heat causes an increase in aggression or whether LeBron James causes an increase in sales of Nike shoes—are *social* psychological pursuits because the thoughts, feelings, or behaviors either (a) *concern other people* or (b) *are influenced by other people.*

The "social context" referred to in the definition of social psychology does not have to be real or present. Even the implied or imagined presence of others can have important effects on individuals (Allport, 1985). For example, if people imagine receiving positive or negative reactions from others, their self-esteem can be affected significantly (Libby et al., 2012; Smart Richman & Leary, 2009). If children imagine having contact with a child from another country, their attitudes toward individuals from that country can become more positive (Vezzali et al., 2012). And if college students imagine living a day in the life of a professor, they are likely to perform better later on an analytic test; if they imagine instead being a cheerleader, however, they perform worse (Galinsky et al., 2008)!

## Social Psychological Questions and Applications

For those of us fascinated by social behavior, social psychology is a dream come true. Just look at Table 1.1 and consider a small sample of the questions you'll explore in this textbook. As you can see, the social nature of the human animal is what social psychology is all about. Learning about social psychology is learning about ourselves and our social worlds. And because social psychology is scientific rather than anecdotal, it provides insights that would be impossible to gain through intuition or experience alone.

The value of social psychology's perspective on human behavior is widely recognized. Courses in social psychology are often required or encouraged for students interested in careers in business, education, medicine, law, and journalism as well as in psychology and sociology. Although many advanced graduates with a Ph.D. in social psychology hold faculty appointments in colleges or universities, others work in medical centers, law firms, government agencies, the military, and a variety of business settings involving investment banking, marketing, advertising, human resources, negotiating, and social networking.

The number and importance of these applications continue to grow. Judges are drawing on social psychological research to render landmark decisions, and lawyers are depending on it to select juries and to support or refute evidence. Businesses are

Danny Moloshok/Landov

A well-liked celebrity such as Oprah Winfrey can influence the attitudes and behaviors of millions of people. For many years, when Oprah recommended a book, for example, sales of the book were likely to skyrocket.

**TABLE 1.1**
**Examples of Social Psychological Questions**

---

**Social Perception: What Affects the Way We Perceive Ourselves and Others?**

- Why do people sometimes sabotage their own performance, making it more likely that they will fail? (Chapter 3)
- How do people in East Asia often differ from North Americans in the way they explain people's behavior? (Chapter 4)
- Where do stereotypes come from, and why are they so resistant to change? (Chapter 5)

**Social Influence: How Do We Influence Each Other?**

- Why do we often like what we suffer for? (Chapter 6)
- How do salespeople sometimes trick us into buying things we never really wanted? (Chapter 7)
- Why do people often perform worse in groups than they would have alone? (Chapter 8)

**Social Interaction: What Causes Us to Like, Love, Help, and Hurt Others?**

- How similar or different are the sexes in what they look for in an intimate relationship? (Chapter 9)
- When is a bystander more or less likely to help you in an emergency? (Chapter 10)
- Does exposure to TV violence or to pornography trigger aggressive behavior? (Chapter 11)

**Applying Social Psychology: How Does Social Psychology Help Us Understand Questions About Law, Business, and Health?**

- Can interrogators really get people to confess to serious crimes they did not commit? (Chapter 12)
- How can business leaders most effectively motivate their employees? (Chapter 13)
- How does stress affect one's health, and what are the most effective ways of coping with stressful experiences? (Chapter 14)

© Cengage Learning

using cross-cultural social psychological research to operate in the global marketplace, and they are consulting research on group dynamics to foster the best conditions for their work forces. Health care professionals are increasingly aware of the role of social psychological factors in the prevention and treatment of disease. Indeed, we can think of no other field of study that offers expertise that is more clearly relevant to so many different career paths.

## The Power of the Social Context: An Example of a Social Psychology Experiment

The social nature of people runs so deep that even very subtle clues about our social connection with others can have a profound effect on our lives. Think about your first weeks of high school or college. If you're like most students, there probably were times when you felt insecure and wondered if you fit in there. For some groups of students, however, these fears are especially frequent and strong. Students from underrepresented racial or ethnic minority groups are especially vulnerable to such doubts about social belonging on campus. Social psychological research suggests that these concerns can interfere with the academic performance.

Gregory Walton and Geoffrey Cohen are among the social psychologists who have studied this issue. They wondered if they could improve the academic success of African American students at a selective, predominately European American university by protecting them against the heightened "belonging uncertainty" that often plagues these students. To test this idea, Walton and Cohen (2011) conducted an experiment in which they provided some students in their first semester at college with a brief bit of information suggesting how typical it is that most students—regardless of their gender, race, or ethnicity—go through periods of social stress and uncertainty during their freshman year, and that these struggles tend to go away soon after their first year. Walton and Cohen wanted to assess how these students would do during their four years of college compared to other students who did not receive any information about social belonging concerns.

Walton and Cohen found that giving this information to African American students raised their grade-point averages (GPAs) significantly higher relative to other African American students who were not given this information. Take a look at ● Figure 1.1. The bars in this graph illustrate the spring-term senior year GPAs of African American students who either did not (the left bar) or did (the right bar) receive the information about social belonging in the fall term of their first year in college. As the difference in height of these two bars indicate, the African American students who read about how common and temporary these social doubts are got better grades than those who did not read this information. And keep in mind that they read this information in their first semester at college, and the GPAs reflected in Figure 1.1 are from the spring term of their senior year!

Walton and Cohen found that the information about social belonging concerns did not affect the GPAs of white students. The researchers believe that the white students were much less likely to have persistent doubts about their social connection to the majority of students at their campus, and therefore providing them information about social belonging did not have much impact on them. For the African American students, on the other hand, the information they received about how typical and temporary these doubts are in one's first year may have come as great relief, reduced their fears about being outsiders, and enabled them to reach their academic potential. The social context—or *perceived* social context—had a significant effect on the students' success at college. You'll learn more about this and related research by Walton and Cohen in Chapter 5.

According to social psychological research described in this chapter and elsewhere in the book, how socially connected students feel with their fellow students can have a significant effect on their academic success.

##  Social Psychology and Related Fields: Distinctions and Intersections

Social psychology is sometimes confused with certain other fields of study. Before we go on, it is important to clarify how social psychology is distinct from these other fields. At the same time, it is important to illustrate some of the ways that interesting and significant questions can be addressed through interactions between social psychology and these other fields (see Table 1.2 on page 10).

**Social Psychology and Sociology**   Sociologists and social psychologists share an interest in many issues, such as violence, prejudice, cultural differences, and marriage. As noted, however, sociology tends to focus on the group level, whereas social psychology tends to focus on the individual level. For example, sociologists might track the racial attitudes of the middle class in the United States, whereas social psychologists might examine some of the specific factors that make individuals more or less likely to behave in a racist way toward members of some group.

In addition, although there are many exceptions, social psychologists are more likely than sociologists to conduct experiments in which they manipulate some variable and determine the effects of this manipulation using precise, quantifiable measures.

Despite these differences, sociology and social psychology are clearly related. Indeed, many sociologists and social psychologists share the same training and publish in the same journals. When these two fields intersect, the result can be a more complete understanding of important issues. For example, interdisciplinary research

### ● FIGURE 1.1
**Social Belonging and GPA**

In a 2011 experiment by Gregory Walton and Geoffrey Cohen, some students during their first semester at college were given information designed to reduce their doubts about fitting in and socially belonging at their school, and other students were not given this information. For African American students, this manipulation had a significant effect on their grade point averages (GPAs) through their subsequent college years. In this graph, the bars represent the average GPAs of the African American students in the second term of their senior year who either did not (the left bar) or did (the right bar) receive this information designed to reduce uncertainty about belonging.
Adapted from Walton & Cohen, 2011. © Cengage Learning

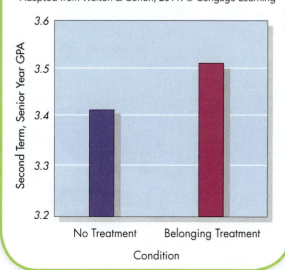

on stereotyping and prejudice has examined the dynamic roles of both societal and immediate factors, such as how particular social systems or institutional norms and beliefs affect individuals' attitudes and behaviors (Eagly & Wood, 2012; Jost & van der Toorn, 2012; Levy et al., 2010; Sidanius & Pratto, 2012).

**Social Psychology and Related Areas of Psychology** Tell people not very familiar with psychology that you are taking a social psychology class, and they may say things like "Oh, great, now you're going to start psychoanalyzing me" or "Finally, maybe you can tell me why everyone in my family is so messed up." The assumption underlying these reactions, of course, is that you are studying clinical, or abnormal, psychology. If you base your impressions of psychology primarily by how it's portrayed in popular culture, you're likely to miss how incredibly broad and diverse the field is. Although social psychology is related to other areas of psychology, each has a very different focus.

Clinical psychologists, for example, seek to understand and treat people with psychological difficulties or disorders. Social psychologists do not focus on disorders; rather, they focus on the more typical ways in which individuals think, feel, behave, and influence each other. Personality psychology is another area that is often confused with social psychology. However, personality psychology seeks to understand stable differences between individuals, whereas social psychology seeks to understand how social factors affect most individuals *regardless of* their different personalities. In other words, a personality psychologist may ask, "Is this person outgoing and friendly almost all the time, in just about any setting?" A social psychologist may ask, "Are people in general more likely to seek out friends when they are made anxious by a situation than when they are made to feel relaxed?"

Cognitive psychologists study mental processes such as thinking, learning, remembering, and reasoning. Social psychologists are often interested in these same processes. More specifically, though, social psychologists are interested in how people think, learn, remember, and reason with respect to social information and in how these processes are relevant to social behavior.

These examples show the contrast between the fields, but, in fact, social psychological theory and research often intersect with these other

Do provocative, sexualized images in advertisings, such as on the billboard seen here (near the sign about "student body cards"), make people more sexist or prone to sexual aggression? This is one of the questions that social psychology addresses.

© Michael Newman/Photo Edit, Inc.

areas quite a bit. For example, both clinical and social psychology may address how people cope with anxiety or pressure in social situations, or how being bullied or stereotyped by others can affect individuals' physical and mental health (Bijleveld et al., 2012; Brodish et al., 2011; Crocker et al., 2010; Gibbons et al., 2012; Greenland et al., 2012; Huynh et al., 2012).

Personality and social psychology are especially closely linked because they complement each other so well. For example, some social psychologists examine how receiving negative feedback (a social factor) can have different effects on people as a function of their self-esteem (a personality factor), or whether playing violent video games (a social factor) is especially likely to trigger aggressiveness in particular types of children (a personality factor) (Bosson & Swann, 2009; Thomas & Levant, 2012; Zeigler-Hill et al., 2011).

Cognitive and social psychology are also closely connected. The last few decades have seen an explosion of interest in the intersection of cognitive and social psychology. The study of *social cognition* is discussed in more detail later in this chapter, and it is a focus throughout this text, especially in Part II on Social Perception.

**Social Psychology and Other Fields of Study**   Social psychologists today are doing research that spans across traditional boundaries between fields more than ever. The intersections of social psychology with disciplines such as neuroscience, biology, economics, political science, public health, environmental studies, law, and medicine are increasingly important to contemporary social psychology. We will discuss a bit more about some of these intersections later in this chapter, but you should see these connections throughout this book, most especially in Part V on Applying Social Psychology.

## Social Psychology and Common Sense

After reading about a theory or finding of social psychology, you may sometimes think, "Of course. I knew that all along. Anyone could have told me that." This "knew-it-all-along" phenomenon often causes people to question how social psychology is different from common sense, or traditional folk wisdom. After all, why would any of the following social psychological findings be surprising?

- Beauty and brains don't mix. Physically attractive people tend to be seen as less smart than physically unattractive people.

- People will like an activity more if you offer them a large reward for doing it, causing them to associate the activity with the positive reinforcement.

- People think that they're more unique than they really are. They tend to underestimate the extent to which others share the same opinions or interests.

- Playing contact sports or violent video games releases aggression and makes people less likely to vent their anger in violent ways.

In a minute, we will have more to say about each of these statements.

Common sense may seem to explain many social psychological findings after the fact. The problem is distinguishing commonsense fact from commonsense myth. After all, for many commonsense notions, there is an equally sensible-sounding notion that says the opposite. Is it "Birds of a feather flock together" or "Opposites attract"? Is it "Two heads are better than one" or "Too many cooks spoil the broth"? Which are correct? We have no reliable way to answer such questions through common sense or intuition alone.

Social psychology, unlike common sense, uses the scientific method to put its theories to the test. How it does so will be discussed in greater detail in the next chapter. But before we leave this section, one word of caution: Those four "findings" listed above? *They are all false.* Although there may be sensible reasons to believe each of the statements to be true, research indicates otherwise. Therein lies another problem with relying on common sense: Despite offering very compelling predictions and explanations, it is sometimes wildly inaccurate. And even when it is not completely wrong, common sense can be misleading in its simplicity. Often there is no simple answer to a question such as "Does absence make the heart grow fonder?" In reality, the answer is more complex than common sense would suggest, and social psychological research reveals how such an answer depends on a variety of factors.

To emphasize these points and to encourage you to think critically about social psychological issues *before* as well as after learning about them, this textbook contains a feature called "Putting Common Sense to the Test." Beginning with Chapter 3, each chapter opens with a few statements about social psychological issues that will be covered in that chapter. Some of the statements are true, and some are false. As you read each statement, make a prediction about whether it is true or false and think about why this is your prediction. Marginal notes throughout the chapter will tell you whether the statements are true or false. In reading the chapter, check not only whether your prediction was correct but also whether your reasons for the prediction were appropriate. If your intuition wasn't quite on the mark, think about what the right answer is and how the evidence supports that answer. There are few better ways of learning and remembering than through this kind of critical thinking.

# A Brief History of Social Psychology

> *"Psychology has a long past, but only a short history."*
>
> —Herman Ebbinghaus, *Summary of Psychology*

People have probably been asking social psychological questions for as long as humans could think about each other. Certainly early philosophers such as Plato offered keen insights into many social psychological issues. But no systematic and scientific study of social psychological issues developed until the end of the nineteenth century. The field of social psychology is therefore a relatively young one. Recent years have marked a tremendous interest in social psychology and an injection of many new scholars into the field. As social psychology is now in its second century, it is instructive to look back to see how the field today has been shaped by the people and events of its first century.

## The Birth and Infancy of Social Psychology: 1880s–1920s

Like most such honors, the title "founder of social psychology" has many potential recipients, and not everyone agrees on who should prevail. Over the years, most have pointed to the American psychologist Norman Triplett, who is credited with having published the first research article in social psychology at the end of the nineteenth century (1897–1898). Triplett's work was noteworthy because after observing that bicyclists tended to race faster when racing in the presence of others than when simply racing against a clock, he designed an experiment to study this phenomenon in a carefully controlled, precise way. This scientific approach to studying the effects of the social context on individuals' behavior can be seen as marking the birth of social psychology.

A case can also be made for the French agricultural engineer Max Ringelmann. Ringelmann's research was conducted in the 1880s but wasn't published until 1913. In an interesting coincidence, Ringelmann also studied the effects of the presence of others on the performance of individuals. In contrast to Triplett, however, Ringelmann noted that individuals often performed worse on simple tasks such as pulling rope when they performed the tasks with other people. The issues addressed by these two early researchers continue to be of vital interest, as will be seen later in Chapter 8.

Some scholars (Haines & Vaughan, 1979; Stroebe, 2012) suggest a handful of other possible examples of the first social psychology studies, including research that Triplett himself cited. These studies also were conducted in the 1880s and 1890s, which seems to have been a particularly fertile time for social psychology to begin to spring roots.

AP Photo/Christophe Ena

Despite their place in the history of social psychology, these late-nineteenth-century studies did not truly establish social psychology as a distinct field of study. Credit for this creation goes to the writers of the first three textbooks in social psychology: the English psychologist William McDougall (1908) and two Americans, Edward Ross (1908) and Floyd Allport (1924). Allport's book in particular, with its focus on the interaction of individuals and their social context and its emphasis on the use of experimentation and the scientific method, helped establish social psychology as the discipline it is today. These authors announced the arrival of a new approach to the social aspects of human behavior. Social psychology was born.

> Racers from around the world compete in one stage of the Tour de France in July 2012. Would these cyclists have raced faster or slower if they were racing individually against the clock rather than racing simultaneously with their competitors? More generally, how does the presence of others affect an individual's performance? The earliest social psychology experiments ever done sought to answer questions such as these. Chapter 8 on group processes brings you up to date on the latest research in this area.

## A Call to Action: 1930s–1950s

What one person would you guess has had the strongest influence on the field of social psychology? Various social psychologists, as well as psychologists outside of social psychology, might be mentioned in response to this question. But someone who was not a psychologist at all may have had the most dramatic impact on the field: Adolf Hitler.

Hitler's rise to power and the horrendous consequences that followed caused people around the world to become desperate for answers to social psychological questions about what causes violence, prejudice, genocide, conformity and obedience, and a host of other social problems and behaviors. In addition, many social psychologists living in Europe in the 1930s fled to the United States and helped establish a critical mass of social psychologists who would give shape to the rapidly maturing field. The years just before, during, and soon after World War II marked an explosion of interest in social psychology.

In 1936, Gordon Allport (younger brother of Floyd, author of the 1924 textbook) and a number of other social psychologists formed the Society for the Psychological Study of Social Issues. The name of the society illustrates these psychologists' concern for making important, practical contributions to society. Also in 1936, a social psychologist named Muzafer Sherif published groundbreaking experimental research on social influence. As a youth in Turkey, Sherif had witnessed groups of Greek soldiers brutally killing his friends. After immigrating to the United States, Sherif drew on this experience and began to conduct research on the powerful influences groups can exert on their individual members. Sherif's research was crucial for the development of social psychology because it demonstrated that it is possible to study complex social processes such as conformity and social influence in a rigorous, scientific manner. This innovation laid the foundation for what was to become one of the major topics in social psychology. Research and theory on social influence are discussed throughout this text, particularly in Part III on Social Influence.

Another great contributor to social psychology, Kurt Lewin, fled the Nazi onslaught in Germany and immigrated to the United States in the early 1930s. Lewin was a bold and creative theorist whose concepts have had lasting effects on the field (e.g., Lewin, 1935, 1947). One of the fundamental principles of social psychology that Lewin helped establish was that behavior is a function of the interaction between the person and the environment. This position, which later became known as the interactionist perspective (Blass, 1991), emphasized the dynamic interplay of internal and external factors, and it marked a sharp contrast from other major psychological paradigms during his lifetime: psychoanalysis, with its emphasis on internal motives and fantasies; and behaviorism, with its focus on external rewards and punishments.

Lewin also profoundly influenced the field by advocating for social psychological theories to be applied to important, practical issues. Lewin researched a number of practical issues, such as how to persuade Americans at home during the war to conserve materials to help the war effort, how to promote more economical and nutritious eating habits, and what kinds of leaders elicit the best work from group members. Built on Lewin's legacy, applied social psychology flourishes today in areas such as advertising, business, education, environmental protection, health, law, politics, public policy, religion, and sports. Throughout this text, we draw on the findings of applied social psychology to illustrate the implications of social psychological principles for our daily lives. In Part V, three prominent areas of applied social psychology are discussed in detail: law, business, and health. One of Lewin's statements can be seen as a call to action for the entire field: "No research without action, no action without research."

During World War II, many social psychologists answered Lewin's call as they worked for their government to investigate how to protect soldiers from the propaganda of the enemy, how to persuade citizens to support the war effort, how to select officers for various positions, and other practical issues. During and after the war, social psychologists sought to understand the prejudice, aggression, and conformity the war had brought to light. The 1950s saw many major contributions to the field of social psychology. For example, Gordon Allport (1954) published *The Nature of Prejudice,* a book that continues to inspire research on stereotyping and prejudice more than a half century later. Solomon Asch's (1951) demonstration of how willing people are to conform to an obviously wrong majority amazes students even today. Leon Festinger (1954, 1957) introduced two important theories—one concerning how people try to learn about themselves by comparing themselves to other people, and one about how people's attitudes can be changed by their own behavior—that remain among the most influential theories in the field. These are just a sample of a long list of landmark contributions made during the 1950s. With this remarkable burst of activity and impact, social psychology was clearly, and irrevocably, on the map.

Lawrence Migdale/Photo Researchers, Inc.

What determines whether people are likely to act to conserve their environment, as these individuals did by volunteering to clean up a beach in California on Earth Day? Built on the legacy of Kurt Lewin, applied social psychology contributes to the solution of numerous social problems, such as environmental degradation.

**interactionist perspective**   An emphasis on how both an individual's personality and environmental characteristics influence behavior.

## Confidence and Crisis: 1960s–Mid-1970s

In spectacular fashion, Stanley Milgram's research in the early and middle 1960s linked the post–World War II era with the coming era of social revolution. Milgram's research was inspired by the destructive obedience demonstrated by Nazi officers and ordinary citizens in World War II, but it also looked ahead to the civil disobedience that was beginning to challenge institutions in many parts of the world. Milgram's experiments, which demonstrated individuals' vulnerability to the destructive commands of authority, became the most famous research in the history of social psychology. This research is discussed in detail in Chapter 7.

With its foundation firmly in place, social psychology entered a period of expansion and enthusiasm. The sheer range of its investigations was staggering. Social psychologists considered how people thought and felt about themselves and others. They studied interactions in groups and social problems, such as why people fail to help others in distress. They also examined aggression, physical attractiveness, and stress. For the field as a whole, it was a time of great productivity.

Ironically, it was also a time of crisis and heated debate. Many of the strong disagreements during this period can be understood as a reaction to the dominant research method of the day: the laboratory experiment. Critics of this method asserted that certain practices were unethical, that experimenters' expectations influenced their participants' behavior, and that the theories being tested in the laboratory were historically and culturally limited (Gergen, 1973; Kelman, 1967; Rosenthal, 1976). Those who favored laboratory experimentation, on the other hand, contended that their procedures were ethical, their results were valid, and their theoretical principles were widely applicable (McGuire, 1967). For a while, social psychology seemed split in two.

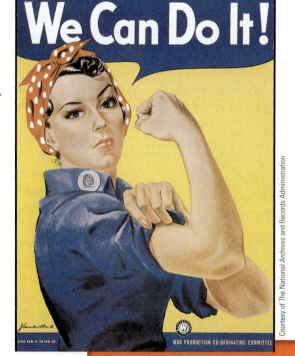

*Courtesy of The National Archives and Records Administration*

This World War II poster featuring Rosie the Riveter was part of the U.S. government's campaign to encourage women to take jobs in traditionally male-dominated occupations, such as welding. When the war was over and the men who had served in the military returned to the work force, new advertisements were designed to encourage women to leave these jobs and concentrate on raising families.

## An Era of Pluralism: Mid-1970s–1990s

Fortunately, both sides won. As we will see in the next chapter, more rigorous ethical standards for research were instituted, more stringent procedures to guard against bias were adopted, and more attention was paid to possible cross-cultural differences in

*Lorne Resnick/Stone/Getty Images*

Social psychologists are becoming increasingly interested in cross-cultural research, which helps us break out of our culture-bound perspective. Many of our behaviors differ across cultures. In some cultures, for example, people are expected to negotiate about the price of the products they buy, as in this market in Tunisia. In other cultures, such bargaining would be highly unusual and cause confusion and distress.

behavior. Laboratory experiments continued to dominate, but often with more precise methods. Laboratory experiments did, however, get some company. A pluralistic approach emerged as a wider range of research techniques and questions became established.

Pluralism in social psychology extends far beyond its methods. There are also important variations in what aspects of human behavior are emphasized. For example, social psychologists became more and more interested in processes relevant to (as well as to adapt methods from) cognitive psychology. A new subfield was born called **social cognition**, the study of how we perceive, remember, and interpret information about ourselves and others. Social cognition research continues to thrive today and examines issues important to virtually every major area in social psychology.

Another source of pluralism in social psychology is its development of international and multicultural perspectives. Although individuals from many countries helped establish the field, social psychology achieved its greatest professional recognition in the United States and Canada. At one point, it was estimated that 75% to 90% of social psychologists lived in North America (Smith & Bond, 1993; Triandis, 1994). However, this aspect of social psychology began to change rapidly in the 1990s, reflecting not only the different geographic and cultural backgrounds of its researchers and participants but also the recognition that many social psychological phenomena once assumed to be universal may actually vary dramatically as a function of culture. You can find evidence of this new appreciation of the role of culture in every chapter of this book.

# Social Psychology in a New Century: What Is Trending Today?

As we began the twenty-first century, social psychology began its second hundred years. The field today continues to grow in the number and diversity of researchers and research topics, areas of the world in which research is conducted, and industries that hire social psychologists and apply their work.

Throughout this text, we emphasize the most current, cutting-edge research in the field, along with the classic findings of the past. In the remainder of the chapter, we focus on a few of the exciting themes and perspectives emerging from current research.

## Integration of Emotion, Motivation, and Cognition

In the earlier days of social cognition research in the 1970s and 1980s, the dominant perspective was called "cold" because it emphasized the role of cognition and de-emphasized the role of emotion and motivation in explaining social psychological issues. This was contrasted with a "hot" perspective, focusing on emotion and motivation as determinants of our thoughts and actions. Today there is growing interest in integrating both "hot" and "cold" perspectives, as researchers study how individuals' emotions and motivations influence their thoughts and actions, and vice versa. For example, researchers today examine how motivations we aren't even consciously aware of (such as being motivated to treat others fairly, or being motivated to feel superior to others) can bias how we interact with or interpret information about another person (Moskowitz et al., 2011; Rydell et al., 2012; Spencer et al., 2003; Wyer, 2012).

**social cognition**  The study of how people perceive, remember, and interpret information about themselves and others.

One issue illustrating the integration of "hot" and "cold" variables concerns the conflict between wanting to be *right* and wanting to *feel good* about oneself, and how these different motivations influence how we process information. On the one hand, we want to be accurate in our judgments about ourselves and others. On the other hand, we don't want to be accurate if it means we will learn something bad about ourselves or those closest to us. These goals can pull our cognitive processes in very different directions. How we perform the required mental gymnastics is an ongoing concern for social psychologists.

Another theme running through many chapters of this book is the growing interest in distinguishing between automatic and controllable processes and in understanding the relationship between them (Monteith et al., 2010; Payne & Iannuzzi, 2012; Trawalter & Shapiro, 2010). How much do we have control over our thoughts and actions, and how vulnerable are we to influences beyond our awareness or control? Are we sometimes influenced by stereotypes even if we don't want to believe them? Can we train ourselves to regulate ourselves against automatic impulses? These are among the questions that social psychologists are studying today.

"On the one hand, eliminating the middleman would result in lower costs, increased sales, and greater consumer satisfaction; on the other hand, we're the middleman."

Our desire to be accurate in our judgments can sometimes interfere with our desire to feel good about ourselves.

## Biological and Evolutionary Perspectives

As the technology available to researchers evolves, biological perspectives are increasingly being integrated into all branches of psychology, and this integration should continue to grow in social psychology. We are, of course, biological organisms, and it is clear that our brains and bodies influence, and are influenced by, our social experiences. This interaction between the physical and the social is the focus of more research than ever before in the field, and examples can be found throughout the textbook, such as in studies demonstrating the cardiovascular effects of being the target of discrimination, and research examining the role of hormones and neurotransmitters in human aggression (Kaholokula et al., 2012; Mendes & Jamieson, 2012).

A particularly exciting recent development is the emergence of the subfield of social neuroscience—the study of the relationship between neural and social processes. This intersection of social psychology and neuroscience is addressing a rapidly growing number of fascinating issues, such as how playing violent video games can affect brain activity and subsequent acts of aggression, or how different patterns of activity in parts of the brain relates to how people are likely to perceive themselves or members of a different racial group (Amodio, 2013; Beer, 2012; Engelhardt et al., 2011).

Recent advances in behavioral genetics—a subfield of psychology that examines the effects of genes on behavior—has triggered new research to investigate such matters as the extent to which political attitudes are at least partially inherited and the roles that genes play in individuals' sexual orientation or identity (Kim, 2009; Rhee & Waldman, 2011).

Evolutionary psychology, which uses the principles of evolution to understand human behavior, is another growing area that is sparking new research in social psychology. According to this perspective, to understand a social psychological issue such as jealousy, we should ask how tendencies and reactions underlying jealousy today may have evolved from the natural-selection pressures our ancestors faced. Evolutionary

**social neuroscience** The study of the relationship between neural and social processes.

**behavioral genetics** A subfield of psychology that examines the role of genetic factors in behavior.

**evolutionary psychology** A subfield of psychology that uses the principles of evolution to understand human social behavior.

psychological theories can then be used to explain and predict gender differences in jealousy, the situational factors most likely to trigger jealousy, and so on (Buss, 2012; DelPriore et al., 2012; Perilloux et al., 2012; Shackelford et al., 2012). This perspective is discussed in many places throughout the textbook, especially in Part IV on Social Relations.

## Cultural Perspectives

Because of the fantastic advancements in communication technologies in recent years and the globalization of the world's economies, it is faster, easier, and more necessary than ever before for people from vastly different cultures to interact with one another. Thus, our need and desire to understand how we are similar to and different from one another are greater than ever as well. Social psychology is currently experiencing tremendous growth in research designed to give us a better understanding and appreciation of the role of culture in all aspects of social psychology.

What is meant by "culture" is not easy to pin down, as many researchers think of culture in very different ways. Broadly speaking, culture may be considered to be a system of enduring meanings, beliefs, values, assumptions, institutions, and practices shared by a large group of people and transmitted from one generation to the next. Whatever the specific definition, it is clear that how individuals perceive and derive meaning from their world are influenced profoundly by the beliefs, norms, and practices of the people and institutions around them.

Increasing numbers of social psychologists are evaluating the universal generality or cultural specificity of their theories and findings by conducting cross-cultural research, in which they examine similarities and differences across a variety of cultures. More and more social psychologists are also conducting multicultural research, in which they examine racial and ethnic groups within cultures.

These developments are already profoundly influencing our view of human behavior. For example, cross-cultural research has revealed important distinctions between the collectivist cultures (which value interdependence and social harmony) typically found in Africa, Asia, and Latin America and the individualistic ones (which value independence and self-reliance) more commonly found in North America and Europe. The implications of these differences can be seen throughout the textbook. Consider, for instance, our earlier discussion of the integration of "hot" and "cold" variables in contemporary social psychology, in which we mentioned the conflict people have between wanting to be right and wanting to feel good about themselves. Cross-cultural research has shown that how people try to juggle these two goals can differ dramatically across cultures.

Several researchers have found, for example, that people from individualistic cultures are more likely than people from collectivist cultures to seek out or focus on information that makes them feel good about themselves rather than information that points to the need for improvement (Heine, 2007). In one such study, Carl Falk and others (2009) asked Japanese or European-Canadian individuals to indicate which of a variety of desirable and undesirable traits characterized themselves. ● Figure 1.2 illustrates the results of the study, demonstrating that European-Canadian participants were far more likely to choose desirable than undesirable traits as characteristic of themselves, but the Japanese participants were much more balanced between desirable and undesirable traits.

In this text, we describe studies conducted in dozens of countries, representing every populated continent on earth. As our knowledge expands, we should be able to see much more clearly both the behavioral differences among cultures and the similari-

**culture** A system of enduring meanings, beliefs, values, assumptions, institutions, and practices shared by a large group of people and transmitted from one generation to the next.

**cross-cultural research** Research designed to compare and contrast people of different cultures.

**multicultural research** Research designed to examine racial and ethnic groups within cultures.

ties we all share. But it is important to note that even within a particular society, people are often treated differently as a function of social categories such as gender, race, physical appearance, and economic class. They may be raised differently by their parents, confronted with different expectations by teachers, exposed to different types of advertising and marketing, and offered different kinds of jobs. In a sense, then, even people within the same town or region may develop and live in distinct subcultures, and these differences can have profound effects on people's lives.

Some social psychology textbooks devote a separate chapter to culture or to culture and gender. We chose not to do so. Because we believe that cultural influences are inherent in *all* aspects of social psychology, we chose instead to integrate discussions of the role of culture and gender in every chapter of the textbook.

## Behavioral Economics, Embodied Cognition, and Other Interdisciplinary Approaches

One of us taught a new course just before working on this edition of the textbook. It was called Interdisciplinary Approaches to Social Psychology and the reading list was packed with fascinating studies that were at the intersection of social psychology and other disciplines, such as economics, environmental studies, political science, and so forth. What may be especially noteworthy about this was that of the more than 40 readings assigned for the semester, almost all of them were published within a year or two of the semester in which the course was taught. And it would have been easy to choose another 40 readings from the same time period that would have been similarly interesting and relevant.

The point of this is that there is a rapidly growing number of social psychologists today who are asking questions and using methodologies that cross traditional academic boundaries. We've already discussed intersections of social psychology with neuroscience, evolutionary theory, and cultural psychology. Other topics are beginning to trend in increasing numbers. For example, one relatively new area of study that has received a great deal of attention is known as **behavioral economics**. This subfield focuses on how psychology—particularly social and cognitive psychology—relates to economic decision making. Behavioral economics research has revealed that the traditional economic models were inadequate because they failed to account for the powerful—and often seemingly irrational—role that psychological factors have on people's economic behavior. For example, Nathan Pettit and Niro Sivanathan (2011) found that if people experienced a threat to their self-esteem, such as by receiving negative feedback about their cognitive abilities, they became more likely to make purchases based on the status of the item and to use credit rather than cash. This reaction could result in a short-term burst of satisfaction at the risk of longer-term debt.

Another interdisciplinary area of research attracting increasing interest among social psychologists today is known as **embodied cognition**, which focuses on the close links between our minds and the positioning, experiences, and actions of our bodies. According to this perspective, people's perceptions and judgments reflect and can influence their bodily experiences. For example, recent studies have found that people's feelings of guilt for having done something morally wrong were reduced if they washed their hands with soap, and that people found the face of a stranger to be more trustworthy if they were induced to pull their arms toward themselves when viewing the

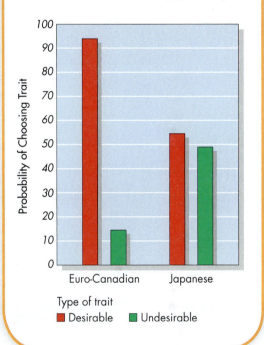

● **FIGURE 1.2**

**Self-Descriptions Across Cultures**

Japanese or European-Canadian research participants were presented with a list of desirable (e.g., sincere, intelligent) and undesirable (e.g., cruel, indecisive) traits and asked which traits were characteristic of themselves. The European-Canadian participants (the two bars on the left) were much more likely to choose desirable than undesirable traits, but the Japanese participants (the two bars on the right) chose a much more balanced mix of traits. Based on Falk et al. (2009). © Cengage Learning

**behavioral economics**   An interdisciplinary subfield that focuses on how psychology—particularly social and cognitive psychology—relates to economic decision making.

**embodied cognition**   An interdisciplinary subfield that examines the close links between our minds and the positioning, experiences, and actions of our bodies.

stranger's picture (thereby moving in a way symbolic of encouraging the stranger to approach) than if they pushed their arms away from them (Meier et al., 2012; Slepian et al., 2012; Zhong & Liljenquist, 2006).

There is a longer history of social psychology research that intersects with political science, but interest continues to expand, and some of it now also includes social-cognitive and social-neuroscience approaches. For example, a number of researchers have found provocative differences between liberals and conservatives in how they attend to and process different kinds of social information, and even in their patterns of brain activity (Jost & Amodio, 2012). Social psychological research can help inform the public about vitally important matters such as whether prejudice may play a role in attitudes toward political policies or candidates, or how the reactions of the audience at a presidential debate can be even more important in affecting viewers' attitudes about the candidates' performance than the actual content of what the candidates said (Fein et al., 2007; Knowles et al., 2010; Levin et al., 2012).

## New Technologies and the Online World

Advances in technologies that allow researchers to see images of the brain at work through noninvasive procedures have had a profound effect on several areas of psychology, including social psychology. A growing number of social psychologists are using techniques such as *positron emission tomography (PET), event-related potential (ERP), transcranial magnetic stimulation (TMS),* and *functional magnetic resonance imaging (fMRI)* to study the interplay of the brain and discrete thoughts, feelings, and behaviors. Social psychology research today benefits from other technological advances as well, such as new and better techniques to measure hormone levels, to code people's everyday dialogue into quantifiable units, and to present visual stimuli to research participants at fractions of a second and then record the number of milliseconds it takes the participants to respond to these stimuli. Some researchers are using virtual reality technology to examine a number of social psychological questions. James Blascovich and others created the Research Center for Virtual Environments and Behavior at the University of California at Santa Barbara and are conducting fascinating research on issues such as conformity, group dynamics, aggression and altruism, social support, and eyewitness testimony (e.g., Blascovich & McCall, 2010; Kane et al., 2012). Because participants in these experiments are immersed in a virtual reality that the experimenters create for them, the researchers can test questions that would be impractical, impossible, or unethical without this technology.

*Awesome* is an overused word, but it surely describes the revolution that is taking place in how we access information and communicate with each other. The waves of this revolution have carried social psychology research along with it. Social psychologists around the world can now not only communicate and collaborate much more easily but can also gain access to research participants from populations that would otherwise never have been available. These developments have sparked the field's internationalization, perhaps its most exciting course in this new century. World War II triggered an explosion of social psychological research in the United States; the Internet is extending this research to the rest of the world. Just within the last few years there has been an exponential increase in the number of studies that are conducted

Advances in technology enable social psychologists to extend their research in exciting new directions, such as by using functional magnetic resonance imaging (fMRI) to study activity in the brain in response to various thoughts or stimuli.

Jeff Miller/University of Wisconsin, Madison

online, providing access to vastly more diverse samples of research participants than had been possible even just a decade before.

The Internet itself is also becoming a provocative topic of study. As more people interact with each other through social networking sites, online dating services, and communications services such as Skype or FaceTime, there is growing interest in studying how attraction, prejudice, group dynamics, and a host of other social psychological phenomena unfold online versus offline. Other important, and potentially troubling, questions raised by our increasingly online lives are the subject of new research, such as: What factors contribute to or protect against cyberbullying? Can too much time on social networking sites lead to depression or loneliness? Does the habit of frequent texting or checking to see who has commented on one's most recent shared photo lead to attentional and social problems offline?

We would be presumptuous, and probably naive, to try to predict how new communication and new technologies will influence the ways that people will interact in the coming years, but it probably is safe to predict that their influence will be great. As more and more people fall in love online, or fall into social isolation, or react with anxiety or violence to the loss of individual privacy, social psychology will explore these issues. We expect that some of the students reading this textbook today will be among those explorers in the years to come.

Joe Raedle/Getty Images

**Together, and apart.** Even when interacting in a group, many of us today are also pulled away by our individual phones, electronic games, iPods, laptops or tablets, and so on. How new technologies and living so much of our lives online affect human interaction is becoming increasingly important to social psychology.

# REVIEW

## What Is Social Psychology?

### Defining Social Psychology
- Social psychology is the scientific study of how individuals think, feel, and behave in a social context.
- Like other sciences, social psychology relies on the systematic approach of the scientific method.
- Distinctive characteristics of social psychology include a focus on the individual as well as a broad perspective on a variety of social contexts and behaviors.
- The "socialness" of social psychology varies, as social psychologists sometimes examine how nonsocial factors affect social thoughts, feelings, and behaviors and sometimes study how social factors influence nonsocial thoughts, feelings, and behaviors.

### Social Psychological Questions and Applications
- Social psychologists study a large variety of fascinating questions about people and their social worlds. The scope and relevance of these questions to so many important aspects of our lives make social psychology applicable to many careers and interests.

### The Power of the Social Context: An Example of a Social Psychology Experiment
- In one experiment that illustrates the power of the social context, African American students achieved greater academic success if their concerns about fitting in and belonging at their predominately European American university were reduced by information received during their first semester at college that indicated how typical and temporary these concerns are for most students.

### Social Psychology and Related Fields: Distinctions and Intersections
- Social psychology is related to a number of different areas of study, including sociology, clinical psychology, personality psychology, and cognitive psychology. Important work is being done at the intersection of social psychology and each of these fields.
- Social psychology tends to focus on individuals, whereas sociology tends to focus on groups. In addition, social psychology is less likely than sociology to study the relation between broad societal variables and people's behaviors and is more likely to use experimentation.

- In contrast to clinical psychology, social psychology focuses not on disorders but rather on the more typical ways that individuals think, feel, behave, and interact.
- Personality psychology focuses on differences between individuals that remain relatively stable across a variety of situations; social psychology focuses on how social factors affect most individuals, regardless of their different personalities.
- Cognitive and social psychologists share an interest in mental processes such as thinking, learning, remembering, and reasoning, but social psychologists focus on the relevance of these processes to social behavior.

### Social Psychology and Common Sense

- Many social psychological theories and findings appear to be like common sense. One problem with common sense, however, is that it may offer conflicting explanations and provide no way to test which is correct. Another problem is that common sense is often oversimplified and therefore misleading.

# A Brief History of Social Psychology

### The Birth and Infancy of Social Psychology: 1880s–1920s

- Early research by Triplett and Ringelmann established an enduring topic in social psychology: how the presence of others affects an individual's performance.
- The first social psychology textbooks in 1908 and 1924 began to give the emerging field of social psychology its shape.

### A Call to Action: 1930s–1950s

- Social psychology began to flourish because the world needed an explanation for the violence of war and solutions to it.
- Sherif's work laid the foundation for later studies of social influence, and the legacy of Kurt Lewin is still evident throughout much of social psychology.
- The 1940s and 1950s saw a burst of activity in social psychology that firmly established it as a major social science.

### Confidence and Crisis: 1960s–Mid-1970s

- Stanley Milgram's experiments demonstrated individuals' vulnerability to the destructive commands of authority.
- While social psychology was expanding in many new directions, there was also intense debate about the ethics of research procedures, the validity of research results, and the generalizability of conclusions drawn from research.

### An Era of Pluralism: Mid-1970s–1990s

- During the 1970s, social psychology began to take a pluralistic approach to its research methods, the integration of perspectives such as social psychology and cognitive psychology into a subfield called social cognition, and the development of international and multicultural perspectives.

# Social Psychology in a New Century: What Is Trending Today?

- Several exciting themes and perspectives are helping to shape the beginning of social psychology's second century.

### Integration of Emotion, Motivation, and Cognition

- Researchers are becoming more interested in how emotion, motivation, and cognition can operate together in influencing individuals' thoughts, feelings, and behaviors.
- Individuals sometimes are faced with a conflict between two motivations that can affect cognitive processes: wanting to be right and wanting to feel good about oneself.
- A great deal of recent social psychological research has explored the automatic versus controllable nature of a number of processes, such as stereotyping.

### Biological and Evolutionary Perspectives

- Biological perspectives, including perspectives based on neuroscience, genetics, and evolutionary principles, are being applied to the study of social psychological issues such as gender differences, relationships, and aggression.

### Cultural Perspectives

- Increasing numbers of social psychologists are evaluating the universal generality or cultural specificity of their theories and findings by examining similarities and differences across cultures as well as between racial and ethnic groups within cultures.
- For example, in one experiment Canadian participants chose more desirable than undesirable traits as characteristic of themselves, whereas Japanese participants chose a balance of desirable and desirable traits.

### Behavioral Economics, Embodied Cognition, and Other Interdisciplinary Approaches

- The emerging subfield of behavioral economics studies how psychology—particularly social and cognitive psychology—relates to economic decision making.
- Research on embodied cognition focuses on the connections between the mind and the body, such as in how body gestures or movements can influence and be influenced by our thoughts and feelings.

- Social psychological research that intersects with political science can offer valuable insights into a variety of important contemporary issues, such as whether prejudice affects people's attitudes toward political policies or candidates, or how learning about other people's reactions to a presidential debate influences an individual's own judgments about the candidates.

### New Technologies

- Advances in technology, such as improved brain-imaging techniques, have given rise to groundbreaking research in social psychology.

- Virtual reality technology enables researchers to test questions that otherwise would be impractical, impossible, or unethical.
- The Internet has fostered communication and collaboration among researchers around the world, enabled researchers to study participants from diverse populations, and inspired researchers to investigate whether various social psychological phenomena are similar or different online versus offline.
- As rapidly advancing technologies change how individuals communicate and access information, the ways that they interact are also likely to change. The social psychology of the next era will explore these issues.

## KEY TERMS

behavioral economics (19)

behavioral genetics (17)

cross-cultural research (18)

culture (18)

embodied cognition (19)

evolutionary psychology (17)

interactionist perspective (14)

multicultural research (18)

social cognition (16)

social neuroscience (17)

social psychology (6)

## MEDIA RESOURCES

Go to CengageBrain.com to access Psychology CourseMate, where you will find an interactive eBook, glossaries, flashcards, quizzes, videos, and more.

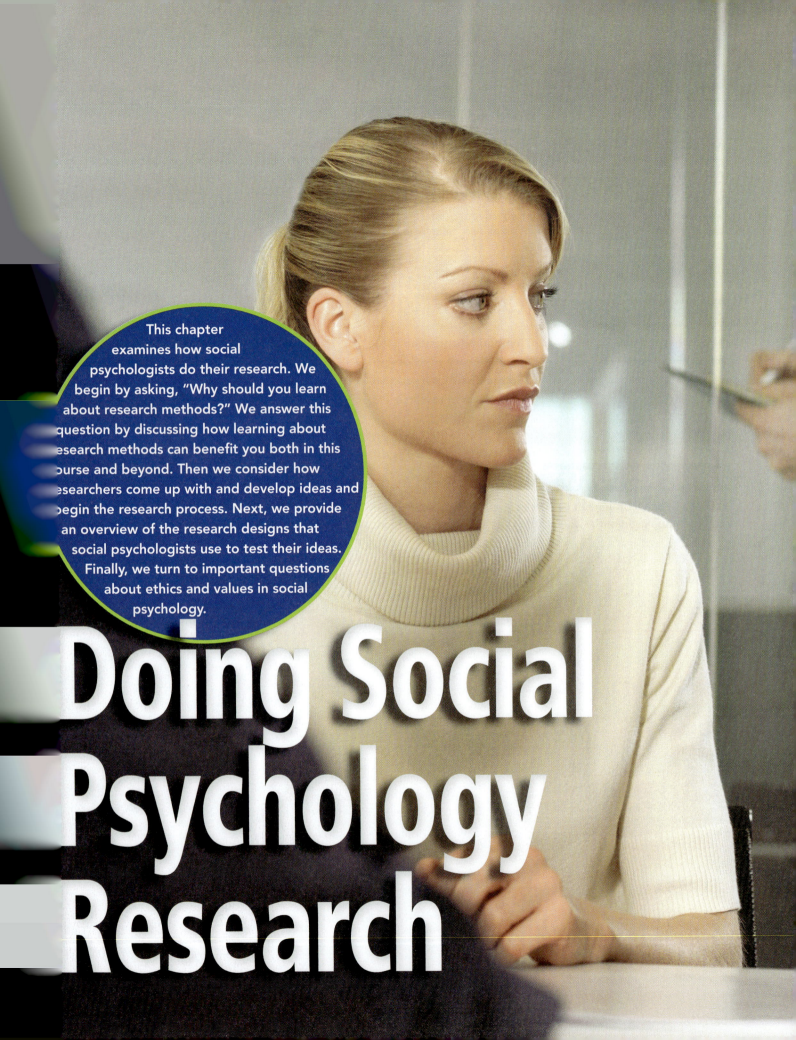

This chapter examines how social psychologists do their research. We begin by asking, "Why should you learn about research methods?" We answer this question by discussing how learning about research methods can benefit you both in this course and beyond. Then we consider how researchers come up with and develop ideas and begin the research process. Next, we provide an overview of the research designs that social psychologists use to test their ideas. Finally, we turn to important questions about ethics and values in social psychology.

# Doing Social Psychology Research

# 2

© Matthias Tunger/Corbis

**It's a familiar situation.** You're starting a new semester or quarter at school, and you're just beginning to settle into a new schedule and routine. You're looking forward to your new courses. In general, it's an exciting time. But there's one major catch: As you spend more and more time with your new classmates and new responsibilities, you're leaving someone behind. It could be a boyfriend or girlfriend, a spouse, or a close friend—someone who is not involved in what you are doing now. You may now live far apart from each other or your new commitments in school may be keeping you apart from each other much more than you'd like. The romantic in you says, "Together forever." Or at least, "No problem." But the realist in you worries a bit. Will your love or friendship be the same? Can it survive the long distance, or the new demands on your time, or the new people in your respective environments? Your friends or family may have advice to offer in this situation. Some might smile and reassure you: "Don't worry. Remember what they say, 'Absence makes the heart grow fonder.' This will only strengthen your relationship." Others might call you aside and whisper, "Don't listen to them. Everybody knows, 'Out of sight, out of mind.' You'd better be careful."

Taking your mind off this problem, you begin to work on a class project. You have the option of working alone or as part of a group. Which should you do? You consult the wisdom of common sense. Maybe you should work in a group. After all, everyone knows that "two heads are better than one." As some members of your group begin to miss meetings and shirk responsibilities, though, you remember that "too many cooks spoil the broth." Will you regret having been so quick to decide to join this group? After all, haven't you been taught to "look before you leap"? Then again, if you had waited and missed the chance to join the group, you might have regretted your inaction, recalling that "he who hesitates is lost."

Questions about the course of relationships, the efficiency of working in groups, and the regret from action versus inaction are social psychological questions. And because we all are interested in predicting and explaining people's behaviors and their thoughts and feelings about each other, we all have our own opinions and intuitions about social psychological matters. If the discipline of social psychology were built on the personal experiences, observations, and intuitions of everyone who is interested in social psychological questions, it would be full of interesting theories and ideas, but it would also be a morass of contradictions, ambiguities, and relativism. Instead, social psychology is built on the scientific method.

Scientific? It's easy to see how chemistry is scientific. When you mix two specific compounds in the lab, you can predict exactly what will happen. The compounds will act the same way every time you mix them if the general conditions in the lab are the same. But what happens when you mix together two chemists, or any two people, in a social context? Sometimes you get great chemistry between them; other times you get apathy or even repulsion. How, then, can social behavior, which seems so variable, be studied scientifically?

To many of us in the field, that's the great excitement and challenge of social psychology—the fact that it *is* so dynamic and diverse. Furthermore, in spite of these characteristics, social psychology can, and should, be studied according to scientific principles. Social psychologists develop specific, quantifiable hypotheses that can be tested empirically. If these hypotheses are wrong, they can be proven wrong. In addition, social scientists report the details of how they conduct their tests so that others can try to replicate their findings. They integrate evidence from across time and place. And slowly but steadily they build a consistent and ever more precise understanding of human nature. How social psychologists investigate social psychological questions scientifically is the focus of this chapter. Before we explain the methodology they use, we first explain why it's important and interesting for you to learn about these matters.

*"The most exciting phrase to hear in science, the one that heralds new discoveries, is not 'Eureka!' (I found it!) but 'That's funny. . . .'"*
—Isaac Asimov

# Why Should You Learn About Research Methods?

One important benefit for learning about research methods is that it can make you a better, more sophisticated consumer of information. Training in research methods in psychology can improve your reasoning about real-life events and problems (Lehman et al., 1988; Leshowitz et al., 2002; VanderStoep & Shaughnessy, 1997). We are constantly bombarded with "facts" from the media, from sales pitches, and from other people. Much of this information turns out to be wrong or, at best, oversimplified and misleading. We are told about the health benefits of eating certain kinds of food, the college entrance exam score benefits of certain preparation courses, or the social status benefits of driving a certain kind of car or wearing a certain kind of shoe. To each of these pronouncements, we should say, "Prove it." What is the evidence? What alternative explanations might there be?

For example, a commercial tells us that most doctors prefer a particular brand of aspirin. So should we buy this brand? Think about what it was compared with. Perhaps the doctors didn't prefer that brand of aspirin more than other (and cheaper) brands of aspirin but rather were asked to compare that brand of aspirin with several nonaspirin products for a particular problem. In that event, the doctors may have preferred *any* brand of aspirin more than nonaspirin products for that need. Thinking like a scientist while reading this text will foster a healthy sense of doubt about claims such as these. You will be in a better position to critically evaluate the information to which you're exposed and separate fact from fiction.

More immediately, learning about research methods should help you better understand the research findings reported in the rest of this book, which will in turn help you on tests and in subsequent courses. If you simply read a list of social psychological findings without knowing and understanding the evidence that social psychologists have produced to support the findings, you may discover later that the task of remembering which were the actual findings and which merely sound plausible can be difficult. Being able to understand, and therefore remember, the research evidence on which social psychological principles are based should provide you with a deeper comprehension of the material.

AP Photo/Chuck Zoeller

We are bombarded with information in our everyday lives, such as in the countless advertisements designed to persuade us to buy particular products or adopt particular opinions or attitudes. Learning the methods used in social psychology research can help students become more sophisticated consumers of this information.

# Developing Ideas: Beginning the Research Process

The research process involves coming up with ideas, refining them, testing them, and interpreting the meaning of the results obtained. This section describes the first stage of research—coming up with ideas. It also discusses the role of hypotheses and theories and of basic and applied research.

## Getting Ideas and Finding Out What's Been Done

Every social psychology study begins with a question. And the questions come from everywhere. As discussed in Chapter 1, one of the first social psychology experiments published was triggered by the question "Why do bicyclists race faster in the presence of other bicyclists?" (Triplett, 1897–1898). Or consider a much more recent example— social psychologist Dylan Selterman has been conducting fascinating studies examining the connection between people's dreams about romantic partners and their actual patterns of emotions and behaviors in personal relationships (Selterman & Drigotas, 2009; Selterman et al., 2012). Where did this idea come from? It was inspired in part by the dreams some of his ex-girlfriends told him about!

Questions can come from a variety of sources, from something tragic, such as a controversial interracial shooting of an unarmed man; to something perplexing, such as the underrepresentation of women in math and science; to something amusing, such as the lyrics of a country song suggesting that female patrons seem more attractive to the men in a bar as closing time approaches (Good et al., 2012; Payne & Iannuzzi, 2012; Pennebaker et al., 1979).

Ideas also come from reading about research that has already been done. The most important research not only answers some pressing questions but raises new questions, inspiring additional research. The most reliable way to get ideas for new research, therefore, is to read about research already published. Even if you already have an idea, you'll need to search the social psychological literature to find out what's been published already. How do you find these published studies? Textbooks such as this one offer a good starting point. You also can find information about many research findings by searching the Internet, of course, but general searches on the Internet can be wildly variable in the relevance, quality, and accuracy of the information presented. Instead, scholars in the field rely on electronic databases of published research, typically available via college or university library systems. Some of these databases, such as PsycINFO, are specific to the psychology literature; others are more general. These databases allow one to instantly search hundreds of thousands of published articles and books.

## Hypotheses and Theories

An initial idea for research may be so vague that it amounts to little more than a hunch or an educated guess. Some ideas vanish with the break of day. But others can be shaped into a **hypothesis**—an explicit, testable prediction about the conditions under which an event will occur. Based on observation, existing theory, or previous research findings, one might test a hypothesis such as "Teenage boys are more likely to be aggressive toward others if they have just played a violent video game for an hour than if they played a nonviolent video game for an hour." This is a specific prediction, and it can be tested empirically. Formulating a hypothesis is a critical step toward planning and conducting research. It allows us to move from the realm of common sense to the rigors of the scientific method.

As hypotheses proliferate and data are collected to test the hypotheses, a more advanced step in the research process may take place: the proposal of a **theory**—an organized set of principles used to explain observed phenomena. Social psychologists aspire to do more than collect a list of findings. The goal is to explain these findings, to articulate the connections between the variables that are studied, and to thereby predict and more completely understand our social worlds. All else being equal, the best theories are efficient and precise; encompass all of the relevant information; and

*"Education is not the filling of a pail, but the lighting of a fire."*
—William Butler Yeats

*"The currency of science is not truth, but doubt."*
—Dennis Overbye

**hypothesis** A testable prediction about the conditions under which an event will occur.

**theory** An organized set of principles used to explain observed phenomena.

lead to new hypotheses, further research, and better understanding. Good social psychological theories inspire subsequent research designed to test various aspects of the theories and the specific hypotheses that are derived from them. Whether it truly is accurate or not, a theory has little worth if it cannot be tested. One of the chief criticisms of many of Freud's theories of personality in the early twentieth century, for example, was that they could not be tested sufficiently.

A theory may make an important contribution to the field even if it turns out to be wrong. The research it inspires may prove more valuable than the theory itself, as the results shed light on new truths that might not have been discovered without the directions suggested by the theory. Indeed, the best theorists want their ideas to be debated and even doubted, to inspire others in the field to put their ideas to the test. The goal is for these theories to evolve, to become more and more accurate and complete.

 ## Basic and Applied Research

Is testing a theory the purpose of research in social psychology? For some researchers, yes. **Basic research** seeks to increase our understanding of human behavior and is often designed to test a specific hypothesis from a specific theory. **Applied research** has a different purpose: to enlarge our understanding of naturally occurring events and to contribute to the solution of social problems.

Despite their differences, basic and applied research are closely connected in social psychology. Some researchers switch back and forth between the two—today basic, tomorrow applied. Some studies test a theory and examine a real-world phenomenon simultaneously. Keith Payne, Joshua Correll, and several other social psychologists, for example, have tested theories about automaticity and nonconscious stereotyping while studying the real-world problem of police officers mistakenly perceiving a weapon in the hands of an unarmed suspect (Ma & Correll, 2011; Payne & Iannuzzi, 2012). Carol Dweck (2012) has tested theories about the effects of people's beliefs about human abilities while addressing important problems such as the underrepresentation of women in math and science. As a pioneer in both basic and applied approaches, Kurt Lewin (1951) set the tone when he encouraged basic researchers to be concerned with complex social problems and urged applied researchers to recognize that "there is nothing so practical as a good theory."

*"Give people facts and you feed their minds for an hour. Awaken curiosity and they feed their own minds for a lifetime."*

—Ian Russell

*"Close cooperation between theoretical and applied psychology can be accomplished . . . if the theorist does not look toward applied problems with highbrow aversion or with a fear of social problems, and if the applied psychologist realizes that there is nothing so practical as a good theory."*

—Kurt Lewin

 # Refining Ideas: Defining and Measuring Social Psychological Variables

To test their hypotheses, researchers always must decide how they will define and measure the variables in which they are interested. This is sometimes a straightforward process. For example, if you are interested in comparing how quickly people run a 100-meter dash when alone and when racing against another person, you're all set if you have a stopwatch and runners who can race alone or in pairs. Many other times, however, the process is less straightforward. For example, imagine you are interested in studying the effects of mood on altruistic (helpful) behavior. Sounds simple, right?

**basic research**  Research whose goal is to increase the understanding of human behavior, often by testing hypotheses based on a theory.

**applied research**  Research whose goals are to enlarge the understanding of naturally occurring events and to find solutions to practical problems.

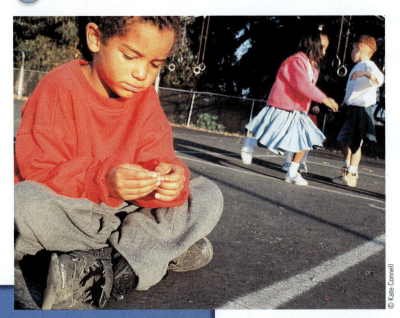

© Kate Connell

From this picture, we can guess that the boy sitting by himself on the playground is lonely, but how do researchers precisely define and measure conceptual variables such as loneliness? Researchers may use any of a number of approaches, such as asking people how they feel and observing their behavior.

But wait. You need to step back and ask yourself, "What do I mean by mood? How would I measure or manipulate it? What do I mean by altruistic behavior?" You will need to define these concepts, and there may be countless ways to do this. Which ones should you pick?

## From the Abstract to the Specific: Conceptual Variables and Operational Definitions

When a researcher first develops a hypothesis, the variables typically are in an abstract, general form. These are *conceptual variables*. Examples of conceptual variables include prejudice, conformity, attraction, love, group pressure, and social anxiety. In order to test specific hypotheses, we must then transform these conceptual variables into variables that can be manipulated or measured in a study. The specific way in which a conceptual variable is manipulated or measured is called the **operational definition** of the variable. For example, "conformity" in a particular study may be defined as the number of times a participant indicated agreement with the obviously wrong judgments made by a group of confederates. Part of the challenge and fun of designing research in social psychology is taking an abstract conceptual variable such as love or group pressure and deciding how to operationally define it so as to manipulate or measure it.

Imagine, for example, wanting to conduct a study on the effects of alcohol intoxication on aggression. One of the conceptual variables might be whether or not participants are intoxicated. There are several ways of measuring this variable, most of which are relatively straightforward. For instance, one researcher might operationally define intoxication as when a participant has a blood alcohol level of .10 or more, whereas another might define it as when a participant says that he or she feels drunk. A second conceptual variable in this study would be aggression. Measuring aggression in experiments is particularly difficult because of ethical and practical issues—researchers can't let participants in their studies attack each other. Researchers interested in measuring aggression are thus often forced to measure relatively unusual behaviors, such as administering shocks or blasts of noise to another person as part of a specific task.

Often there is no single best way to transform a variable from the abstract (conceptual) to the specific (operational). A great deal of trial and error may be involved.

**operational definition** The specific procedures for manipulating or measuring a conceptual variable.

"Clemson here, how may I disappoint you?"

This person would probably score low on the Rosenberg Self-Esteem Scale.

However, sometimes there are systematic, statistical ways of checking how valid various manipulations and measures are, and researchers spend a great deal of time fine-tuning their operational definitions to best capture the conceptual variables they wish to study.

Researchers evaluate the manipulation and measurement of variables in terms of their **construct validity**. Construct validity refers to the extent to which (1) the manipulations in an experiment really manipulate the conceptual variables they were designed to manipulate, and (2) the measures used in a study (experimental or otherwise) really measure the conceptual variables they were designed to measure.

## Measuring Variables: Using Self-Reports, Observations, and Technology

Social psychologists measure variables in many ways, but most can be placed into one of two categories: self-reports and observations. We discuss each of these methods in the next sections, along with how advances in technology are enabling social psychologists to measure variables in new ways.

**Self-Reports**   Collecting *self-reports*—in which participants disclose their thoughts, feelings, desires, and actions—is a widely used measurement technique in social psychology. Self-reports can consist of individual questions or sets of questions that together measure a single conceptual variable. One popular self-report measure, the Rosenberg Self-Esteem Scale, consists of a set of questions that measures individuals' overall self-esteem. For example, respondents are asked the extent to which they agree with statements such as "I feel that I have a number of good qualities," and "All in all, I am inclined to feel that I'm a failure." This scale, first developed by Morris Rosenberg in the 1960s, continues to be used today in a wide variety of settings in countries from around the world because many researchers consider it to have good construct validity (Huang & Dong, 2012; Supple & Plunkett, 2011; Vasoncelos-Rapaso et al., 2012).

Self-reports give the researcher access to an individual's beliefs and perceptions. But self-reports are not always accurate and can be misleading. For example, the desire to look good to ourselves and others can influence how we respond. This is evident in the results of research using the **bogus pipeline technique**—a procedure in which participants are led to believe that their responses will be verified by an infallible lie detector. When participants believe their lies will be detected, they report facts about themselves more accurately and endorse socially unacceptable opinions more frequently. The bogus pipeline is, in fact, bogus; no such infallible device exists. But belief in its powers discourages people from lying (Grover & Miller, 2012; Jones & Sigall, 1971; Mann & Kawakami, 2012; Myers & Ziegler-Hill, 2012).

Self-reports are also affected by the way that questions are asked, such as how they are worded or in what order or context they are asked (Betts & Hartley, 2012; Schwarz & Oyserman, 2011). For instance, although "global warming" and "climate change" mean the same thing to most Americans, Jonathon Schuldt and others (2011) found that Republican respondents to a survey in the United States were much less likely to indicate that they believe in the issue if it was referred to as "global warming" rather than "climate change" (see ● Figure 2.1). In another study, a large majority (88%) of participants indicated that they thought condoms were effective in stopping AIDS when condoms were said to have a "95 percent success rate." However, when condoms were said to have a "5 percent failure rate" (which is merely another way of saying the same thing

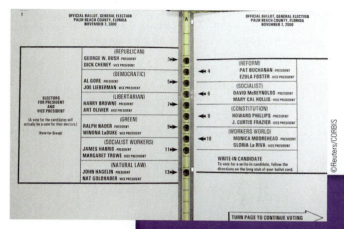

The importance of well-designed questions and response options may never have been more evident than in the aftermath of the U.S. presidential election of November 2000. The positioning of the choices on the "butterfly" ballot design confused voters in Palm Beach County, Florida, apparently causing thousands of people to mistakenly vote for Pat Buchanan when they had intended to vote for Al Gore. This confusion may well have caused Gore to lose the presidency to George W. Bush.

**construct validity**   The extent to which the measures used in a study measure the variables they were designed to measure and the manipulations in an experiment manipulate the variables they were designed to manipulate.

**bogus pipeline technique**   A procedure in which research participants are (falsely) led to believe that their responses will be verified by an infallible lie detector.

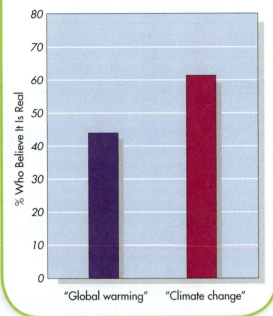

● **FIGURE 2.1**

**"Global Warming" or "Climate Change"?**

Although most people think of "global warming" and "climate change" as the same thing, a majority of Republican respondents to a survey in the United States indicated that they did not believe that the phenomenon was happening when it was labeled as "global warming" (the bar on the left), but a majority of Republican respondents reported that they did believe it was happening if it was labeled as "climate change" (the bar on the right). (Although not shown in this figure, it may be worth noting that the wording manipulation did not significantly affect the attitudes reported by non-Republicans.)

Based on Schuldt et al., 2011. © Cengage Learning

**interrater reliability** The degree to which different observers agree on their observations.

as a 95% success rate), less than half (42%) of the participants indicated that they thought condoms were effective (Linville et al., 1992)! There are theoretical explanations that can account for the seemingly irrational results reported in these two studies, but the point here is that subtle factors can have significant effects on the attitudes and opinions that people report.

Indeed, even the exact same question can elicit very different responses depending on the context in which the question occurs. For example, all individuals contacted in one telephone survey were asked how important the issue of skin cancer was in their lives, but this question was asked either before or after a series of questions about other health concerns. Even though the wording of the question was identical, respondents rated skin cancer as significantly more important if the question was asked first than if it came after the other health questions (Rimal & Real, 2005). In another example of the impact of previous questions, Kimberly Rios Morrison and Adrienne Chung (2011) found that white college students indicated significantly less support for multiculturalism if they had earlier marked their race/ethnicity as "White" on a questionnaire than if the questionnaire used the term "European American" instead.

Another reason self-reports can be inaccurate is that they often ask participants to report on thoughts or behaviors from the past, and people's memory of their thoughts or behaviors is very prone to error, particularly if how they feel *now* about things is different from how they felt in the past. To minimize this problem, psychologists have developed ways to reduce the time that elapses between an actual experience and the person's report of it. For example, some use *interval-contingent* self-reports, in which respondents report their experiences at regular intervals, usually once a day. Researchers may also collect *signal-contingent* self-reports. Here, respondents report their experiences as soon as possible after being signaled to do so, usually by means of a text message or a special app. Finally, some researchers collect *event-contingent* self-reports, in which respondents report on a designated set of events as soon as possible after such events have occurred. For example, the Rochester Interaction Record (RIR) is an event-contingent self-report questionnaire used by respondents to record every social interaction lasting 10 minutes or more that occurs during the course of the study, usually a week or two (Nezlek et al., 2012).

**Observations**   Self-reports are but one tool social psychologists use to measure variables. Researchers also observe people's actions. Sometimes these observations are very simple, as when a researcher notes which of two items a person selects. At other times, however, the observations are more elaborate and require that interrater reliability be established. **Interrater reliability** refers to the level of agreement among multiple observers of the same behavior. Only when different observers agree can the data be trusted.

The advantage of observational methods is that they avoid our sometimes-faulty recollections and distorted interpretations of our own behavior. Actions can speak louder than words. Of course, if individuals know they are being observed, their behaviors, like their self-reports, may be biased by the desire to present themselves in a favorable light. Therefore, researchers sometimes make observations much more subtly. For example, in experiments concerning interracial interactions, researchers may record participants' eye contact and seating distance to demonstrate biases that would not be revealed using more overt measures (Goff, Steele, & Davies, 2008; Todd et al., 2011).

**Technology** Social psychologists use more than merely their eyes and ears to observe their subjects, of course. Advances in technology offer researchers exciting new tools that enable them to make extremely precise, subtle, and complex observations that were beyond the dreams of social psychologists just a generation or so ago. Various kinds of equipment are used to measure physiological responses such as changes in heart rate, levels of particular hormones, and sexual arousal. Computers are used to record the speed with which participants respond to stimuli, such as how quickly they can identify the race of people in photographs or the presence of a weapon in the hands of a white or black man (Bishara & Payne, 2009; Klauer et al., 2011). Eye-tracking technology is used to measure exactly where and for how long participants look at particular parts of a stimulus, such as an advertisement or a video (Crosby et al., 2008; DeWall et al., 2009).

Most recently, social psychologists have begun opening a window into the live human brain—fortunately, without having to lift a scalpel. Brain-imaging technologies take and combine thousands of images of the brain in action. As mentioned in Chapter 1, many social psychology studies today use fMRI (functional magnetic resonance imaging) scans to provide researchers with visual images of activity in parts of the brain while the research subject is thinking, making decisions, responding to audio or visual stimuli, and so on. These images can show researchers what parts of the brain seem to "light up"—or show increased activity—in response to a particular stimulus or situation. For example, although participants in a study may show no signs of any racial or sexist biases on their self-reports or through easily observable behavior in the lab, these same participants may show increased activity in parts of their brain associated with feelings of threat or strong emotion when they see pictures of or think about people from a particular racial group or gender (Amodio, 2013; Jenkins & Mitchell, 2011; Van Bavel & Cunningham, 2010).

Joanne Pasila/one2

Computerized video technology, such as this Perception Analyzer™, allows researchers to track participants' moment-to-moment reactions to events on the screen (in this case, a comedian's performance). It can also simultaneously display the average ratings of groups of participants in a graph superimposed over the video. This technology can help researchers study the dynamics of social influence.

# Testing Ideas: Research Designs

Social psychologists use several different methods to test their research hypotheses and theories. Although methods vary, the field generally emphasizes objective, systematic, and quantifiable approaches. Social psychologists do not simply seek out evidence that supports their ideas; rather, they test their ideas in ways that could very clearly prove them wrong. We can divide these types of tests into three categories: descriptive, correlational, and experimental.

## Descriptive Research: Discovering Trends and Tendencies

One obvious way of testing ideas about people is simply to record how frequently or how typically people think, feel, or behave in particular ways. The goal of *descriptive research* in social psychology is, as the term implies, to describe people and their thoughts, feelings, and behaviors. This method can test questions such as: Do most people support capital punishment? What percentage of people who encounter a person lying on the sidewalk would offer to help that person? What do men and women say are the things most likely to make them jealous of their partner? Particular methods of doing descriptive research include observing people, studying records of past events and behaviors, and surveying people. We discuss each of these methods in this section.

*"You can observe a lot just by watching."*

—Yogi Berra

**Observational Studies**    We can learn about other people simply by observing them, of course, and some social psychological questions can be addressed through observational studies. For example, although researchers around the world who study bullying among schoolchildren often use self-report measures to ask children and teachers about the frequency and severity of bullying, some researchers have gotten a more direct look at the problem by spending time in playgrounds and schoolyards carefully watching and taking notes on the children's interactions, sometimes using hidden cameras and microphones (with the schools and parents' consent) to record incidents of bullying (Frey et al., 2009; Hawkins et al., 2001).

**Archival Studies**    Archival research involves examining existing records of past events and behaviors, such as newspaper articles, medical records, diaries, sports statistics, personal ads, crime statistics, or hits on a web page. A major advantage of archival measures is that because the researchers are observing behavior secondhand, they can be sure that they did not influence the behavior by their presence. A limitation of this approach is that available records are not always complete or sufficiently detailed, and they may have been collected in a nonsystematic manner.

Archival measures are particularly valuable for examining cultural and historical trends. In Chapter 11 on Aggression, for example, we report a number of trends concerning the rate of violent crime in the United States and how it has changed in recent years, and we report differences in homicide rates in countries around the world. These data come from archival records, such as the records of police stations, the Federal Bureau of Investigation (FBI), and the United Nations. Recent examples of archival research include a study that analyzed how black and white defendants in death-penalty cases were described in newspaper articles over a 20-year period and a study that examined whether the wording of job advertisements was biased as a function of gender stereotypes (Gaucher et al., 2011; Goff, Eberhardt et al., 2008).

Observational research can reveal some fascinating—and sometimes disturbing!—insights into social behavior.

"Just as we suspected—they're beginning to form a boy band."

**Surveys**    It seems that nobody in politics these days sneezes without first conducting an opinion poll. Surveys have become increasingly popular in recent years, and they are conducted on everything from politics to attitudes about social issues to the percentages of people who think the best cure for hiccups is to drink a glass of water or hold your breath (OK, we'll tell you: According to a May 2012 poll on Yahoo.com with almost 60,000 responses, 52% say drink water, 37% say hold your breath—and 12% say have someone scare you). Conducting surveys involves asking people questions about their attitudes, beliefs, and behaviors. Surveys can be conducted in person, over the phone, by mail, or via the Internet. Many social psychological questions can be addressed only with surveys because they involve variables that are impossible or unethical to observe directly or manipulate, such as people's sexual behaviors or their optimism about the future.

Although anyone can conduct a survey (and sometimes it seems that everyone does), there is a science to designing, conducting, and interpreting the results of surveys. Like other self-report measures, surveys can be affected strongly by subtle aspects of the wording and context of questions, and good survey researchers are trained to consider these issues and to test various kinds of wording and question ordering before conducting their surveys.

One of the most important issues that survey researchers face is how to select the people who will take part in the survey. The researchers first must identify the *population* in which they are interested. Is this survey supposed to tell us about the attitudes of North Americans in general, shoppers at Wal-Mart, or students in an Introduction to Social Psychology course at University X, for example? From this general population, the researchers select a subset, or *sample*, of individuals. For a survey to be accurate, the sample must be similar to, or representative of, the population on important characteristics such as age, sex, race, income, education, and cultural background. The best way to achieve this representativeness is to use **random sampling**, a method of selection in which everyone in a population has an equal chance of being selected for the sample. Survey researchers use randomizing procedures, such as randomly distributed numbers generated by computers, to decide how to select individuals for their samples.

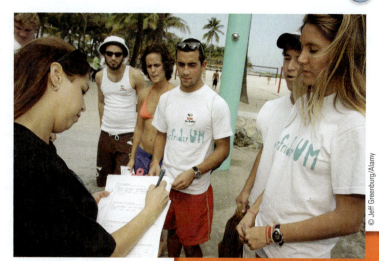

Many social psychological questions are addressed using surveys, which can be conducted over the phone, by mail, via the Internet, or face to face in field settings

To see the importance of random sampling, consider a pair of U.S. presidential elections (Rosnow & Rosenthal, 1993). Just before the 1936 election, a magazine called the *Literary Digest* predicted that Alfred Landon, the Republican governor of Kansas, would win by 14 percentage points over Franklin Roosevelt. The *Digest* based its prediction on a survey of more than 2 million Americans. In fact, though, Landon *lost* the election by 24 percentage points. The magazine, which had been in financial trouble before the election, declared bankruptcy soon after.

Twenty years later, the Gallup survey's prediction of Dwight Eisenhower's victory was almost perfect—it was off by less than 2%. The size of its sample? Only about 8,000. How could the 1936 survey, with its much larger sample of 2 million people, be so wrong and the 1956 survey be so right? The answer is that the 1936 sample was not randomly selected. The *Digest* contacted people through sources such as phone books and club membership lists. In 1936, many people could not afford to have telephones or belong to clubs. The people in the sample, therefore, tended to be wealthier than much of the population, and wealthier people preferred Landon. In 1956, by contrast, Gallup pollsters randomly selected election districts throughout the country and then randomly selected households within those districts. Today, because of improved sampling procedures, surveys conducted on little more than 1,000 Americans can be used to make accurate predictions about the entire U.S. population.

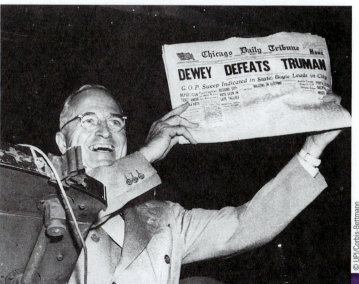

In the 1948 U.S. presidential election, pollsters nationwide predicted that Thomas Dewey would defeat Harry Truman by a wide margin. As Truman basked in his victory, pollsters realized that their predictions were based on nonrandom samples of voters. Random sampling would have led to much more accurate predictions.

**random sampling** A method of selecting participants for a study so that everyone in a population has an equal chance of being in the study.

## Correlational Research: Looking for Associations

Although there is much to learn from descriptive research, social psychologists typically want to know more. Most research hypotheses in social psychology concern the relationship between variables. For example, is there a relationship between people's gender and their willingness to ask for help from others or between how physically attractive people are and how much money they make?

One way to test such hypotheses is with correlational research. Like descriptive research, **correlational research** can be conducted using observational, archival, or survey methods. Unlike descriptive research, however, correlational approaches measure the *relationship* between different variables. The extent to which variables relate to each other, or correlate, can suggest how similar or distinct two different measures are (for example, how related people's self-esteem and popularity are) and how well one variable can be used to predict another (for example, how well we can predict academic success in college from college entrance exam scores). It is important to note that researchers doing correlational research typically do not manipulate the variables they study; they simply measure them.

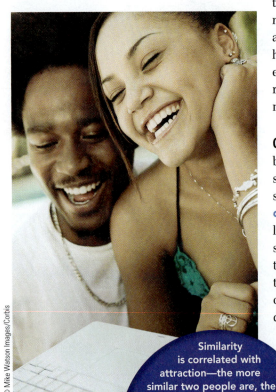

© Mike Watson Images/Corbis

Similarity is correlated with attraction—the more similar two people are, the more attractive they are likely to find each other. But a correlation cannot identify the cause of this attraction. Chapter 9 on Attraction and Close Relationships discusses correlational and experimental research on the role of similarity in the attraction process.

**Correlation Coefficient**   When researchers examine the relationship between variables that vary in quantity (such as temperature or degree of self-esteem), they can measure the strength and direction of the relationship between the variables and calculate a statistic called a **correlation coefficient**. Correlation coefficients can range from +1.0 to −1.0. The absolute value of the number (the number itself, without the positive or negative sign) indicates how strongly the two variables are associated. The larger the absolute value of the number, the stronger the association between the two variables, and thus the better either of the variables is as a predictor of the other. Whether the coefficient is positive or negative indicates the direction of the relationship. A positive correlation coefficient indicates that as one variable increases, so does the other. For example, college entrance exam scores correlate positively with grades. The positive direction of this relationship indicates higher entrance exam scores are associated with higher grades and lower entrance exam scores are associated with lower grades. This correlation is not perfect; some people with high entrance exam scores have poor grades and vice versa. Therefore, the correlation is less than +1.0, but it is greater than 0 because there is some association between the two. A negative coefficient indicates that the two variables go in opposite directions: As one goes up, the other tends to go down. For example, number of classes missed and GPA are likely to be negatively correlated. And a correlation close to 0 indicates that there is no consistent relationship at all. These three types of patterns are illustrated in ● Figure 2.2. Because few variables are perfectly related to each other, most correlation coefficients do not approach +1.0 or −1.0 but have more moderate values, such as +.39 or −.57.

Some correlational studies involve a variable that does not vary in quantity, such as race, gender, political affiliation, or whether Italian, Mexican, or Thai food is their favorite. In this case, researchers cannot compute a typical correlation coefficient but instead use different kinds of statistical analysis. The same point applies, though, as the researchers can determine if there is a relationship between the two variables.

**correlational research**   Research designed to measure the association between variables that are not manipulated by the researcher.

**correlation coefficient**   A statistical measure of the strength and direction of the association between two variables.

● **FIGURE 2.2**

**Correlations: Positive, Negative, and None**

Correlations reveal a systematic association between two variables. Positive correlations indicate that variables are in sync: Increases in one variable are associated with increases in the other; decreases, with decreases. Negative correlations indicate that variables go in opposite directions: Increases in one variable are associated with decreases in the other. When two variables are not systematically associated, there is no correlation.

© Cengage Learning

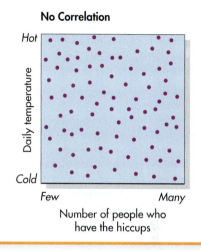

### Advantages and Disadvantages of Correlational Research

Correlational research has many advantages. It can study the associations of naturally occurring variables that cannot be manipulated or induced—such as gender, race, ethnicity, and age. It can examine phenomena that would be difficult or unethical to create for research purposes, such as love, hate, and abuse. And it offers researchers a great deal of freedom in where variables are measured. Participants can be brought into a laboratory specially constructed for research purposes or they can be approached in a real-world setting (often called "the field") such as a shopping mall or airport.

Despite these advantages, however, correlational research has one very serious disadvantage. And here it is in bold letters: **Correlation is not causation**.

In other words, a correlation cannot demonstrate a cause-and-effect relationship. Instead of revealing a specific causal pathway from one variable, A, to another variable, B, a correlation between variables A and B contains within it three possible causal effects: A could cause B; B could cause A; or a third variable, C, could cause both A and B. For example, imagine learning that the number of hours per night one sleeps is negatively correlated with the number of colds one gets. This means that as the amount of sleep increases, colds decrease in frequency; conversely as sleep decreases, colds become more frequent. One reasonable explanation for this relationship is that lack of sleep (variable A) causes people to become more vulnerable to colds (variable B). Another reasonable explanation, however, is that people who have colds can't sleep well, and so colds (variable B) cause lack of sleep (variable A). A third reasonable explanation is that some other variable (C) causes both lack of sleep and greater frequency of colds. This third variable could be stress. Indeed, stress has many effects on people, as will be discussed in Chapter 14 on Health. ● Figure 2.3 describes another correlation that can be explained in many ways—the correlation between playing violent video games and aggression.

We can guarantee you this: There will be many, many times in your life when you'll encounter reports in the media that suggest cause-and-effect relationships based on

● **FIGURE 2.3**

**Explaining Correlations: Three Possibilities**

The correlation between one variable (A) and another variable (B) could be explained in three ways. Variable A could cause changes in variable B, or variable B could cause changes in variable A, or a third variable (C) could cause similar changes in both A and B, even if A and B did not influence each other. For example, a correlation between how much children play violent video games and how aggressively they behave could be explained in the following ways:

1. Playing violent video games causes aggressive behavior.
2. Children who behave aggressively like to play a lot of violent video games.
3. Children who have family troubles, such as parents who are not very involved in the children's development, tend both to play a lot of violent video games and to behave aggressively.

© Cengage Learning

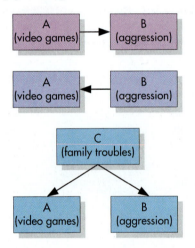

**experiment** A form of research that can demonstrate causal relationships because (1) the experimenter has control over the events that occur and (2) participants are randomly assigned to conditions.

**random assignment** A method of assigning participants to the various conditions of an experiment so that each participant in the experiment has an equal chance of being in any of the conditions.

correlational research. Even the most respectable news sources are guilty of this repeatedly. If you look for it, you can find numerous examples on a weekly basis. One of the great benefits of learning and gaining experience with the material in this chapter is that you can see the flaws in media reports such as these and are less likely to be taken in by them. Correlation is not causation.

Do we learn nothing, then, from correlations? To say that would be to take caution too far. Correlations tell researchers about the strength and direction of relationships between variables, thus helping them understand these variables better and allowing them to use one variable to predict the other. Correlations can be extremely useful in developing new hypotheses to guide future research. And by gathering large sets of correlations and using complicated statistical techniques to crunch the data, we can develop highly accurate predictions of future events.

## Experiments: Looking for Cause and Effect

Social psychologists often do want to examine cause-and-effect relationships. Although it is informative to know, for example, that playing a lot of violent video games is correlated with violent behavior in real life, the inevitable next question is whether playing these video games *causes* an increase in violent behavior. If we want to examine cause-and-effect relationships, we need to conduct an **experiment**. Experiments are the most popular method of testing ideas in social psychology, and they can range from the very simple to the incredibly elaborate. All of them, however, share two essential characteristics.

1. The researcher has *control* over the experimental procedures, manipulating the variables of interest while ensuring uniformity elsewhere. In other words, all participants in the research are treated in exactly the same manner—except for the specific differences the experimenter wants to create.

2. Participants in the study are *randomly* assigned to the different manipulations (called "conditions") included in the experiment. If there are two conditions, who goes where may be determined by simply flipping a coin. If there are many conditions, a computer program may be used. But however it's done, **random assignment** means that participants are not assigned to a condition on the basis of their personal or behavioral characteristics. Through random assignment, the experimenter attempts to ensure a level playing field. *On average, the participants randomly assigned to one condition are no different from those assigned to another condition.* Differences that appear between conditions after an experimental manipulation can therefore be attributed to the impact of that manipulation and not to any preexisting differences between participants.

Because of experimenter control and random assignment of participants, an experiment is a powerful technique for examining cause and effect. Both characteristics serve the same goal: to eliminate the influence of any factors other than the experimental manipulation. By ruling out alternative explanations for research results, we become more confident that we understand just what has, in fact, caused a certain outcome to occur. Table 2.1 summarizes the distinctions between correlational and experimental research.

**TABLE 2.1**
**Correlations Versus Experiments**

| | Correlational Research | Experimental Research |
|---|---|---|
| *What does it involve?* | Measuring variables and the degree of association between them | Random assignment to conditions and control over the events that occur; determining the effects of manipulations of the independent variable(s) on changes in the dependent variable(s) |
| *What is the biggest advantage of using this method?* | Enables researchers to study naturally occurring variables, including variables that would be too difficult or unethical to manipulate | Enables researchers to determine cause-and-effect relationships—that is, whether the independent variable can cause a change in the dependent variable |

© Cengage Learning

**Random Sampling Versus Random Assignment**   You may recall that we mentioned random sampling earlier, in connection with surveys. It's important to remember the differences between random *sampling* and random *assignment*. Table 2.2 summarizes these differences. Random sampling concerns how individuals are selected to be in a study. It is important for generalizing the results obtained from a sample to a broader population, and it is therefore very important for survey research. Random assignment concerns not who is selected to be in the study but rather how participants in the study are assigned to different conditions, as explained above. Random assignment is essential to experiments because it is necessary for determining cause-and-effect relationships; without it, there is always the possibility that any differences found between the conditions in a study were caused by preexisting differences among participants. Random sampling, in contrast, is not necessary for establishing causality. For that reason, and because random sampling is difficult and expensive, very few experiments use random sampling. We consider the implications of this fact later in the chapter.

**TABLE 2.2**
**Random Sampling Versus Random Assignment**

| | Random Sampling | Random Assignment |
|---|---|---|
| *What does it involve?* | Selecting participants to be in the study so that everyone from a population has an equal chance of being a participant in the study | Assigning participants (who are already in the study) to the various conditions of the experiment so that each participant has an equal chance of being in any of the conditions |
| *What is the biggest advantage of using this procedure?* | Enables researchers to collect data from samples that are representative of the broader population; important for being able to generalize the results to the broader population | Equalizes the conditions of the experiment so that it is very unlikely that the conditions differ in terms of preexisting differences among the participants; essential to determine that the independent variable(s) caused an effect on the dependent variable(s) |

© Cengage Learning

**Laboratory and Field Experiments**   Most experiments in social psychology are conducted in a *laboratory* setting, usually located in a college or university, so that the environment can be controlled and the participants carefully studied. Social psychology labs do not necessarily look like stereotypical laboratories with liquid bubbling in beakers or expensive equipment everywhere (although many social psychology labs are indeed very high-tech). They can resemble ordinary living rooms or even game

© Gideon Mendel/Corbis

In field research, people are observed in real-world settings. Field researchers may observe children in a schoolyard, for example, to study any of a variety of social psychological issues, such as friendship patterns, group dynamics, conformity, helping, aggression, and cultural differences.

rooms. The key point here is that the laboratory setting enables researchers to have control over the setting, measure participants' behaviors precisely, and keep conditions identical for participants.

*Field* research is conducted in real-world settings outside the laboratory. Researchers interested in studying helping behavior, for example, might conduct an experiment in a public park. The advantage of field experiments is that people are more likely to act naturally in a natural setting than in a laboratory in which they know they are being studied. The disadvantage of field settings is that the experimenter often has less control and cannot ensure that the participants in the various conditions of the experiment will be exposed to the same things.

Because of the important role that experiments play in social psychology, let's take a closer look at the elements of experiments by focusing on two recent experiments.

### Experiment 1: Can Video Games Make You More or Less Aggressive?

As we will see in Chapter 11 on Aggression, a growing number of studies demonstrate that playing violent videos can lead to real-life aggression. But can playing video games that feature helping others, rather than hurting them, lead to the opposite effect—that is, of making people become *less* aggressive? Tobias Greitemeyer and others (2012) conducted a series of experiments to address this question. In one of their experiments with college students in Germany, they randomly assigned one-third of the students to play a violent video game (*Mortal Kombat*—a game involving violent fighting), another third to play a neutral video game (pinball), and a third to play a helping-oriented game (helping characters escape from burning buildings). After playing the assigned video game for 15 minutes, the students were then given the opportunity to act aggressively toward another person by blasting them with noise while this person tried to complete a task.

As ● Figure 2.4 shows, the students who had played the violent game were more aggressive (that is, selected louder levels of noise) than the students who had played the neutral game. On the other hand, the students who had played the helpful game were *less* aggressive than the students who had played the neutral game.

### Experiment 2: Mood and Culture

Imagine that someone shows you a handful of pens. Most of the pens are of one color (e.g., black), and a minority of

● **FIGURE 2.4**

**Effects of Violent vs. Helpful Video Games**

Participants in Greitemeyer et al.'s experiment played either a violent, neutral, or helping-oriented video game, and they later had the chance to deliver annoying blasts of noise to another person as this person tried to complete a task. (This "noise blast" procedure has been a successful measure of aggression in a number of experiments.) This graph shows that the students who played the helpful game were the least aggressive, and the students who played the violent game were the most aggressive. Based on Greitemeyer et al., 2012. © Cengage Learning

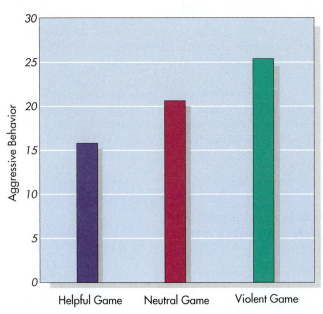

the pens are of a different color (e.g., blue). You can choose to keep one of the pens. Do you choose a color from the majority or the minority? Believe it or not, there is a consistent cultural difference in how people make this choice. People from Western cultures, such as the United States, tend to choose the uncommon pen color, whereas people from East Asian cultures, such as Korea, tend to choose the majority pen color.

This cultural difference was explored in an interesting way in an experiment by Claire Ashton-James and others (2009). The researchers hypothesized that being in a positive mood makes people more open to new experiences, which can result in their acting in ways that are inconsistent with how people in their culture typically behave. Would being in a good mood, therefore, cause people to become more likely to defy their cultural norm, making Westerners more interested in the common color pen and East Asians more interested in the uncommon color pen? The researchers tested this idea by presenting participants from either Western (European, Euro-Canadian) or East Asian background with the pen choice described above. Before looking at the pens, though, the participants were randomly assigned to be placed into a positive or negative mood. How was mood manipulated? The participants in the positive-mood condition listened to a very pleasant, upbeat piece of classical music (by Mozart), and those in the negative-mood condition listened to a much more serious, rather depressing piece (by Rachmaninov). Table 2.3 summarizes the design of this experiment.

● Figure 2.5 depicts the results of this study. The bars in this graph depict what percentage of participants in each condition chose the uncommon pen. Among the Western participants, as can be seen in the left half of the graph, those put in a positive mood were *less* likely to choose the uncommon pen compared to those in the

> ### TABLE 2.3
> **Mood and Culture: The Conditions**
>
> In Ashton-James et al.'s experiment, participants from Western or East Asian backgrounds were put in a positive or negative mood. Combining these two variables—culture and the manipulation of mood—creates the four conditions displayed here.
>
> |  | Western | East Asian |
> |---|---|---|
> | **Positive Mood** | Condition 1<br>Western/Positive | Condition 2<br>East Asian/Positive |
> | **Negative Mood** | Condition 3<br>Western /Negative | Condition 4<br>East Asian/ Negative |
>
> Based on Vandello & Cohen (2003). © Cengage Learning

negative-mood condition. The opposite was true for the East Asian participants: Those put in a positive mood were *more* likely to choose the uncommon pen compared to those in the negative-mood condition. The results, therefore, supported the researchers' predictions: Positive moods did make individuals more likely to act in ways that deviated from the norms of their cultures.

**Independent and Dependent Variables**   Now that we've looked at a couple experiments, let's focus on some of the specific elements. In an experiment, researchers manipulate one or more **independent variables** and examine the effect of these manipulations on one or more **dependent variables**. In the first experiment above, some participants were randomly assigned to play a violent video game, others to play a neutral video game, and others to play a helping-oriented video game. This was the independent variable. The dependent variable in that experiment was how much noise the participants chose to deliver to another person. It was the dependent variable because the researchers were interested in seeing if it would *depend* on (that is, be influenced by) the manipulation of the independent variable.

**Subject Variables**   Some experiments include variables that are neither dependent nor truly independent. The gender, ethnicity, and prior political leanings of the participants may vary, for example, and researchers may be interested in examining some of these differences. These variables cannot be manipulated and randomly assigned, so

**independent variable**   In an experiment, a factor that experimenters manipulate to see if it affects the dependent variable.

**dependent variable**   In an experiment, a factor that experimenters measure to see if it is affected by the independent variable.

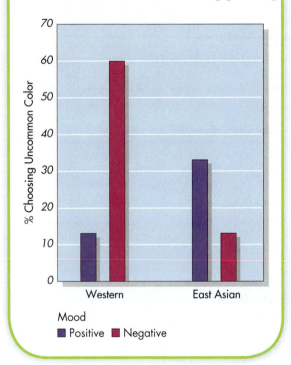

● **FIGURE 2.5**

**Mood and Culture**

Research participants from Western or East Asian backgrounds were put in a positive or negative mood and then were given a choice to keep one of several pens. Most of the pens were in one color, but one or two were in a different color. Western participants were more likely to choose the uncommon color when in a negative mood than a positive mood, whereas East Asian participants showed the opposite pattern. These results supported the hypothesis that positive moods can make individuals act in ways that are inconsistent with their cultural norms.

Based on Ashton-James et al., 2009. © Cengage Learning

**subject variable**  A variable that characterizes preexisting differences among the participants in a study.

they are not true independent variables, and they are not influenced by the independent variables, so they are not dependent variables. Variables such as these are called **subject variables** because they characterize preexisting differences among the subjects, or participants, in the experiment. If a study includes subject variables but no true, randomly assigned independent variable, it is not a true experiment. But experiments often include subject variables along with independent variables so that researchers can test whether the independent variables have the same or different effects on different kinds of participants. The second experiment described above, by Ashton-James and colleagues on mood and culture, is an example of an experiment with one true independent variable and one subject variable. The randomly assigned independent variable was the manipulation of mood—some were placed into a good mood, others into a bad mood. The subject variable was the participants' cultural background—some were of Western background, some were of East Asian background. The dependent variable in this study was which pen the participants chose to keep.

**Statistical Significance and Replications**  In the Ashton-James experiment, 60% of the Western participants chose the uncommon color pen when in a negative mood, but only 13% did so when in a positive mood. Is the difference between 60% and 13% large enough to be meaningful, or could this difference simply be due to chance (that is, just random variation, like flipping a coin ten times and getting heads six times and tails four)? The answer is that you can't tell just by looking at these numbers alone. Results obtained in an experiment are examined with statistical analyses that allow the researcher to determine how likely it is that the results could have occurred by random chance. The standard convention is that if the results could have occurred by chance five or fewer times in 100 possible outcomes, then the result is *statistically significant* and should be taken seriously.

The fact that results are statistically significant does not mean, however, that they are absolutely certain. In essence, statistical significance is an attractive betting proposition. The odds are quite good (at least 95 out of 100) that the effects obtained in the study were due to the experimental manipulation of the independent variable. But there is still the possibility (as high as 5 out of 100) that the findings occurred by chance. This is one reason why it is important to try to *replicate* the results of an experiment—to repeat the experiment and see if similar results are found. If similar results are found, the probability that these results could have occurred by chance both times is less than 1 out of 400. Very recently there has been a growing emphasis in psychology (and some other disciplines, such as medicine) on the importance of both replicating research findings and developing and using statistical techniques that serve as alternatives to the focus on statistical significance. We will return to this issue in the final section of this chapter.

Statistical significance is relevant not only for the results of experiments but also for many other kinds of data as well, such as correlations. A correlation between two variables may be statistically significant or not, depending on the strength of the correlation and the number of participants or observations in the data.

When the results of some research are reported in the media or an advertisement, it's not always clear from the reporting whether the results are statistically significant, so it is important to be very cautious when learning about them. You can be sure, however, that whenever we report in this textbook that there is a difference between conditions of an experiment or that two variables are correlated, these results are statistically significant.

### Internal Validity: Did the Independent Variable Cause the Effect?

When an experiment is properly conducted, its results are said to have **internal validity**: There is reasonable certainty that the independent variable did, in fact, cause the effects obtained on the dependent variable (Cook & Campbell, 1979). As noted earlier, both experimenter control and random assignment seek to rule out alternative explanations of the research results, thereby strengthening the internal validity of the research. If some other factor varies consistently along with the manipulation, this other factor is called a **confound**. A confound is a serious threat to internal validity and, therefore, makes the issue of cause and effect in the experiment uncertain. For example, if the students who played the violent video game in Greitemeyer's study always did so in a very hot room, and the students who played the helping-oriented game did so in a cool room, then this would be a confound, and it would be impossible to know if the different games or the different temperatures caused the effect on aggressive behavior. Fortunately, Greitemeyer and his colleagues knew to avoid this problem.

Experiments sometimes include *control groups* for purposes of internal validity. Typically, a control group consists of participants who experience all of the procedures except the experimental treatment. In Greitemeyer's study, for example, the participants in the condition in which the video game content was neutral could be considered a control group, which provided a baseline against which to compare the behavior of participants who played a violent or helping-oriented game.

Outside the laboratory, creating control groups in natural settings that examine real-life events raises many practical and ethical problems. For example, researchers testing new medical treatments for deadly diseases face a terrible dilemma. Individuals randomly assigned to the control group receive the standard treatment, but they are excluded for the duration of the study from what could turn out to be a life-saving new intervention. Yet without such a comparison, it is extremely difficult to determine which new treatments are effective and which are useless.

In assessing internal validity, researchers need to consider their own role as well. Unwittingly, they can sometimes sabotage their own research. For example, imagine you are a researcher and you know which participants are in which conditions of your experiment. You will no doubt have expectations (and possibly even strong hopes) about how your participants will respond differently between conditions. Because of these expectations, and without realizing it, you may treat the participants a little differently between conditions. It turns out that even very subtle differences in an experimenter's behavior can influence participants' behavior (Rosenthal, 1976). Therefore, because of these **experimenter expectancy effects**, the results you find in your experiment may be produced by your own actions rather than by the independent variable!

The best way to protect an experiment from these effects is to keep experimenters uninformed about assignments to conditions. This often is called being "blind to the conditions" in a study. If the experimenters do not know the condition to which a participant has been assigned, they cannot treat participants differently as a function of their condition. In their experiment, Greitemeyer and his colleagues wisely decided to use one experimenter in the first part of the study (when the participants played the video games) and a different experimenter for the second part (when the participants chose the noise level to use on another person). The second experimenter did not know which video game the participants had played and therefore could not bias the results through experimenter expectancy effects.

---

**internal validity** The degree to which there can be reasonable certainty that the independent variables in an experiment caused the effects obtained on the dependent variables.

**confound** A factor other than the independent variable that varies between the conditions of an experiment, thereby calling into question what caused any effects on the dependent variable.

**experimenter expectancy effects** The effects produced when an experimenter's expectations about the results of an experiment affect his or her behavior toward a participant and thereby influence the participant's responses.

Of course, there may be times when keeping experimenters uninformed is impossible or impractical. In such cases, the opportunity for experimenter expectancy effects to occur can at least be reduced somewhat by minimizing the interaction between experimenters and participants. For example, rather than receiving instructions directly from an experimenter, participants can be asked to read the instructions on a computer screen.

**External Validity: Do the Results Generalize?**  In addition to guarding internal validity, researchers are concerned about **external validity**, the extent to which the results obtained under one set of circumstances would also occur in a different set of circumstances (Berkowitz & Donnerstein, 1982). When an experiment has external validity, its findings can be assumed to generalize to other people and to other situations. Both the participants in the experiment and the setting in which it takes place affect external validity.

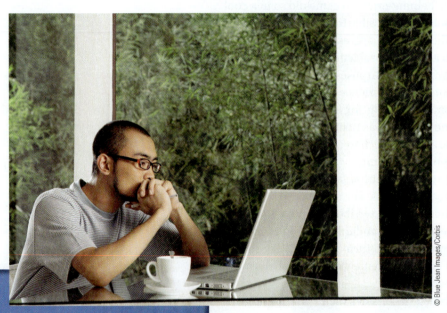

To help increase external validity, social psychologists would love to conduct their experiments with huge samples of participants that are representative of the general population. Usually, however, they must rely on convenience samples drawn from populations that are readily available to them, which explains why so much of social psychological research is conducted on college students. There are very practical reasons for the use of convenience samples. Representative samples are fine for surveys that require short answers to a short list of questions. But what about complex, time-consuming experiments? The costs and logistical problems associated with this would be staggering. Advocates of convenience samples contend that the more basic the principle, the less it matters who participates in the research.

© Blue Jean Images/Corbis

Many individuals earn money at home by participating in online research projects through a service provided by Amazon called *Mechanical Turk*. Online services like this now allow social psychologists to reach out to vastly more diverse samples of people from around the world to participate in their studies.

For example, people from different cultures, regions, and ages might differ in the *form* of aggression they typically exhibit when angry, but the situational factors that cause people to be *more likely to* aggress—in whatever way that aggression is expressed—may be similar for most individuals across time and place. Yet in spite of these arguments, having the most diverse, representative samples of research participants as possible is ideal. The growing interest in cross-cultural research in the field is certainly one step in the right direction.

Another promising development is the rapidly increasing use of the Internet to collect data, which allows for far more diverse sets of participants. There are numerous challenges associated with this approach as well, however, such as having less control over what participants are seeing or doing as they participate in the study from afar. Fortunately, recent research testing the data collected via of one of most popular online services, called Mechanical Turk, suggests that the data are at least as reliable as data collected through traditional methods and offer a much greater diversity of participants (Buhrmester et al., 2011; Mason & Suri, 2012).

The external validity of an experiment may also depend in part on how realistic the study is for the participants. But what is meant by realistic is not as straightforward as one might think. Two types of realism can be distinguished: mundane versus experimental (Aronson & Carlsmith, 1968). **Mundane realism** refers to the extent to which the research setting resembles the real-world setting of interest. In order to

**external validity**  The degree to which there can be reasonable confidence that the results of a study would be obtained for other people and in other situations.

**mundane realism**  The degree to which the experimental situation resembles places and events in the real world.

study interpersonal attraction, Theodore Newcomb (1961) set up an entire college dormitory—a striking example of mundane realism. Advocates of mundane realism contend that if research procedures are more realistic, research findings are more likely to reveal what really goes on. In contrast, **experimental realism** refers to the degree to which the experimental setting and procedures are real and involving to the participant, regardless of whether they resemble real life or not. According to those who favor experimental realism, if the experimental situation is compelling and real to the participants while they are participating in the study, their behavior in the lab—even if the lab is in the basement of the psychology building—will be as natural and spontaneous as their behavior in the real world. The majority of social psychologists who conduct experiments emphasize experimental realism.

**Deception in Experiments**　Researchers who strive to create a highly involving experience for participants often rely on **deception**, providing participants with false information about experimental procedures. Toward this end, social psychologists sometimes employ **confederates**, people who act as though they are participants in the experiment but are really working for the experimenter. For example, in Solomon Asch's (1956) classic research on conformity, research participants made judgments about the lengths of lines while in the midst of a number of confederates—who were pretending to be ordinary participants—who at various times all gave wrong answers. The researchers wanted to see if the real participants would conform to the confederates and give the obviously wrong answer that the confederates had given. Although it was a very odd setting, the situation was a very real one to the participants (and therefore was high in experimental realism), and many of the participants clearly struggled with the decision about whether or not to conform.

Deception not only strengthens experimental realism but also provides other benefits: It allows the experimenter to create situations in the laboratory that would be difficult to find in a natural setting, such as a regulated, safe environment in which to study a potentially harmful behavior such as aggression or discrimination. Studies have shown that participants are rarely bothered by deception and often particularly enjoy studies that use it (Smith & Richardson, 1983). Nevertheless, the use of deception creates some serious ethical concerns, leading to debate about whether and how it should be used (Hertwig & Ortmann, 2008; Kimmel, 2012). Fortunately, as we will see a bit later in the chapter, procedures have been put in place to try to ensure the ethical integrity of research today.

## ❯ Meta-Analysis: Combining Results Across Studies

We have seen that social psychologists conduct original descriptive, correlational, and experimental studies to test their hypotheses. Another way to test hypotheses in social psychology is to use a set of statistical procedures to examine, in a new way, relevant research that has already been conducted. This technique is called **meta-analysis**. By "meta-analyzing" the results of a number of studies that have been conducted in different places and by different researchers, researchers can measure precisely how strong and reliable particular effects are. For example, studies published concerning the effects of alcohol on aggression may sometimes contradict each other. Sometimes alcohol increases aggression; sometimes it doesn't. By combining the data from all the studies that are relevant to this hypothesis and conducting a meta-analysis, a researcher can determine what effect alcohol typically has, how strong that effect typically is, and perhaps under what specific conditions that effect is most likely to occur. This technique is being used with increasing frequency in social psychology today, and we report the results of many meta-analyses in this textbook.

**experimental realism**　The degree to which experimental procedures are involving to participants and lead them to behave naturally and spontaneously.

**deception**　In the context of research, a method that provides false information to participants.

**confederate**　Accomplice of an experimenter who, in dealing with the real participants in an experiment, acts as if he or she is also a participant.

**meta-analysis**　A set of statistical procedures used to review a body of evidence by combining the results of individual studies to measure the overall reliability and strength of particular effects.

## Culture and Research Methods

The study by Ashton-James and others (2009) on the effects of mood on Western and East Asian participants' pen choices is but one example of the growing interest in studying culture in social psychology. One of the advantages of this approach is that it provides better tests of the external validity of research that has been conducted in any one setting. By examining whether the results of an experiment generalize to a very different culture, social psychologists can begin to answer questions about the universality or cultural specificity of their research. It is important to keep in mind that when a finding in one culture does not generalize well to another culture, this should be seen not simply as a failure to replicate but also as an opportunity to learn about potentially interesting and important cultural differences and about how and why these differences affect the issue being studied.

The setting in which children attend school can vary dramatically across cultures. Here students sit outside in a class in Imbabura, Ecuador. Recognizing cultural variation has become increasingly important in social psychology today, and social psychologists are conducting their research across a wider range of cultures and contexts than ever before.

As important and exciting as these cultural investigations are, however, they offer special challenges to researchers. For example, cultural differences have been found in how affected people are by the context of questions as they complete a survey, or about the assumptions respondents make about what the researchers have in mind for a given question (Schwarz et al., 2010). It also can be difficult for researchers to translate materials from one language into another. Although it is relatively easy to create literal translations, it can be surprisingly challenging to create translations that have the same meaning to people from various cultures. Table 2.4 presents examples—from signs displayed around the world—of what can go wrong when simple sentences are poorly translated.

An even more subtle point about language is that multilingual people may think or act differently as a function of what language is being used in a particular setting. A study by Nairán Ramírez-Esparza and others (2008) illustrates this point. They found that how agreeable a sample of bilingual Mexican American participants appeared to be—either on a self-report questionnaire or in their behavior in an interview—varied significantly as a function of whether the study was conducted in Spanish or in English.

---

**TABLE 2.4**

**Lost in Translation**

- "Drop your trousers here for best results." (a dry cleaner in Thailand)
- "You are invited to take advantage of the chambermaid." (a hotel in Japan)
- "Ladies are requested not to have children in the bar." (a cocktail lounge in Mexico)
- "Take one of our horse-driven city tours—we guarantee no miscarriages." (a tourist agency in the former Czechoslovakia)
- "We take your bags and send them in all directions." (an airline in Denmark)

Source: Triandis (1994). © Cengage Learning

# Ethics and Values in Social Psychology

Regardless of where research is conducted and what method is used, ethical issues must always be considered. Researchers in all fields have a moral and legal responsibility to abide by ethical principles. In social psychology the use of deception has caused some concern about ethics, as we indicated earlier. In addition, several studies have provoked fierce debate about whether the procedures used in the studies went beyond the bounds of ethical acceptability. The most famous of these controversial studies was designed by Stanley Milgram in the early 1960s. Milgram (1963) designed a series of studies to address the question "Would people obey orders to harm an innocent person?" To test this question, he put volunteers into a situation in which an experimenter commanded them to administer painful electric shocks to someone they thought was another volunteer participant. (In fact, the other person was a confederate who was not actually receiving any shocks.) The experiment had extremely high experimental realism—many of the participants experienced a great deal of anxiety and stress as they debated whether they should disobey the experimenter or continue to inflict pain on another person. The details and results of this experiment will be discussed in Chapter 7 on Conformity, but suffice it to say that the results of the study made people realize how prevalent and powerful obedience can be.

Milgram's research was inspired by the obedience displayed by Nazi officers in World War II. No one disputes the importance of his research question. What has been debated, however, is whether the significance of the research topic justified exposing participants to possibly harmful psychological consequences. Even though no one in Milgram's studies actually received the electric shocks, the participants were quite stressed during the study because they *thought* they were harming another person, until the experimenter finally told them the truth at the conclusion of the experiment. Under today's provisions for the protection of human participants, Milgram's classic experiments probably could not be conducted in their original form. (In an interesting twist, even though conducting an experiment like Milgram's might be impossible now, in popular culture today individuals endure far greater stress and even humiliation in numerous unscripted TV shows for the entertainment of viewers at home.)

Several studies in the history of social psychology have sparked ethical debate or controversy, including a famous study in which Philip Zimbardo and others simulated a prison environment in the basement of Stanford University's psychology department building to study how ordinary people can be affected in extraordinary ways by the roles they are assigned in a prison environment (Haney et al., 1973). This study is discussed in detail in Chapter 12 on Law. Although the controversial studies such as Milgram's and Zimbardo's have received the most public attention, today virtually every social psychology study is evaluated for its ethics by other people before the study can be conducted. In the following sections, we describe current policies and procedures as well as continuing concerns about ethics and values in social psychological research.

## Institutional Review Boards and Informed Consent: Protecting Research Participants

In 1974, the agency then called the United States Department of Health, Education, and Welfare established regulations designed to protect human participants in research.

These regulations created institutional review boards (IRBs) at all institutions seeking federal funding for research involving human participants. IRBs became a key safeguard for research, taking on the responsibility of reviewing research proposals to ensure that the welfare of participants is adequately protected.

Besides submitting their research to IRBs, researchers must also abide by their profession's code of ethics. The American Psychological Association (APA), for example, requires psychologists to follow its *Ethical Principles of Psychologists and Code of Conduct* (2002, 2010), which considers a wide range of ethical issues, including those related to research procedures and practices. The APA code stipulates that researchers are obligated to guard the rights and welfare of all those who participate in their studies.

One such obligation is to obtain **informed consent**. Individuals must be asked whether they wish to participate in the research project and must be given enough information to make an informed decision. Participants must also know that they are free to withdraw from participation in the research at any point. The APA code also recognizes that research "involving only anonymous questionnaires, naturalistic observations, or certain kinds of archival research" may not require informed consent.

One reason for the use of deception in an experiment is so that the participants will act more naturally when they are not aware of what is being studied. In these cases, it is especially important for the researchers to provide a full and thorough debriefing.

"What if these guys in white coats who bring us food are, like, studying us and we're part of some kind of big experiment?"

## Debriefing: Telling All

Just as participants should receive informed consent before they begin their participation in a study, they should receive a **debriefing** at the end of it, especially if deception was used. Debriefing is a process of disclosure in which researchers fully inform their participants about the nature of the research in which they have participated. During a debriefing, the researcher goes over all procedures, explaining exactly what happened and why. The researcher discusses the purpose of the research, reveals any deceptions, and makes every effort to help the participant feel good about having participated. A skillful debriefing takes time and requires close attention to the individual participant. Indeed, we have known students who became so fascinated by what they learned during a debriefing that it sparked their interest in social psychology, and eventually they became social psychologists themselves!

## Values and Science: Points of View and New Controversies

**informed consent**  An individual's deliberate, voluntary decision to participate in research, based on the researcher's description of what will be required during such participation.

**debriefing**  A disclosure, made to participants after research procedures are completed, in which the researcher explains the purpose of the research, attempts to resolve any negative feelings, and emphasizes the scientific contribution made by the participants' involvement.

Ethical principles are based on moral values. These values set standards for and impose limits on the conduct of research, but do values affect science in other ways as well? Although many people hold science to a standard of complete objectivity, science can probably never be completely unbiased and objective because it is a human enterprise. Scientists choose what to study and how to study it; their choices are affected by personal values as well as by professional rewards. Indeed, some think that values *should* fuel scientific research and that scientists would be not only naive but also irresponsible to try to keep values out of the picture. Most social psychologists, however, strive to use the scientific methods described in this chapter to free themselves of their preconceptions and, thereby, to see reality more clearly and objectively, even if never perfectly.

One value on which the entire field agrees is that researchers must conduct and report their research with complete honesty. It is therefore both shocking and deeply disturbing when a case of academic fraud is revealed. One such example rocked the field toward the end of 2011, when a Dutch social psychologist was caught—and soon confessed to—having committed a massive amount of dishonesty, involving the fabrication of data published in dozens of studies for about a decade (Bartlett, 2011). The news of this scandal, together with a few other events during this period of time, caused some social psychologists to question the field's practices. One such event was the publication of a set of studies that claimed to find evidence for the seemingly outrageous idea that a future outcome can influence a past action (Bem, 2011). Not surprisingly, this publication set off a firestorm of criticism and controversy. Also around this time, social psychologist Jonathan Haidt made news criticizing the lack of diversity of political ideologies represented by social psychologists today and suggesting that this could bias research (Tierney, 2011). This too triggered a good deal of criticism and controversy.

With all this in the air, a wave of suggestions for how the field should better protect itself against intentional or unintentional bias or dishonesty emerged. These suggestions included utilizing more advanced and precise statistical methods to better and more fairly test researchers' ideas, demanding researchers to be more open for public scrutiny of their materials and data, and instituting much more emphasis on replicating each other's research (Bartlett, 2012; John et al., 2012; Young, 2012). It is important to note that these concerns are by no means specific to social psychology. High-profile cases of fraud, for example, span across all fields, including physics, medicine, history, literature, and journalism (Coscarelli, 2012; Deer, 2011; Rayner, 2010; Sovacool, 2008). It is also important to note that the strong reaction by the social psychology community to these issues is a testament to how much it cares about its integrity and will work diligently to reassert and protect it in the years to come.

Your introduction to the field of social psychology is now complete. In these first two chapters, you have gone step by step through a definition of social psychology, a review of its history and discussion of its future, an overview of its research methods, and a consideration of ethics and values. As you study the material presented in the coming chapters, the three of us who wrote this book invite you to share our enthusiasm. You can look forward to information that overturns commonsense assumptions, to lively debate and heated controversy, and to a better understanding of yourself and other people. Welcome to the world according to social psychology. We hope you enjoy it!

> *"[Objectivity in science] is willingness (even the eagerness in truly honorable practitioners) to abandon a favored notion when testable evidence disconfirms key expectations."*
>
> —Stephen Jay Gould

# REVIEW

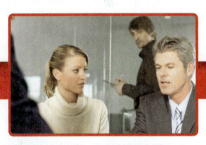

## Why Should You Learn About Research Methods?

- Studying research methods in psychology improves people's reasoning about real-life events and information presented by the media and other sources.

- Understanding the scientific evidence on which social psychological theories and findings are based will help you better understand the research that is reported throughout this book, which in turn will help you learn the material more deeply.

## Developing Ideas: Beginning the Research Process

### Getting Ideas and Finding Out What's Been Done

- Ideas for research in social psychology come from everywhere—personal experiences and observations, events in the news, and other research.
- Before pursuing a research idea, it is important to see what research has already been done on that idea and related topics.

- Electronic databases provide access to a wealth of information, both in the psychology literature and in more general sources.

### Hypotheses and Theories

- Formulating a hypothesis is a critical step toward planning and conducting research.

- Theories in social psychology attempt to explain and predict social psychological phenomena. The best theories are precise, explain all the relevant information, and generate research that can support or disconfirm them. They should be revised and improved as a result of the research they inspire.

### Basic and Applied Research

- The goal of basic research is to increase understanding of human behavior.
- The goal of applied research is to increase understanding of real-world events and contribute to the solution of social problems.

# Refining Ideas: Defining and Measuring Social Psychological Variables

### From the Abstract to the Specific: Conceptual Variables and Operational Definitions

- Researchers often must transform abstract, conceptual variables into specific operational definitions that indicate exactly how the variables are to be manipulated or measured.
- Construct validity is the extent to which the operational definitions successfully manipulate or measure the conceptual variables to which they correspond.

### Measuring Variables: Using Self-Reports, Observations, and Technology

- In self-reports, participants indicate their thoughts, feelings, desires, and actions.
- Self-reports can be distorted by efforts to make a good impression as well as by the effects of the wording and context of questions.

- In studies using the bogus pipeline technique, participants' self-reports tend to be more accurate and less socially desirable when they are led to believe that a machine can tell whether or not they are telling the truth.
- To increase the accuracy of self-reports, some approaches emphasize the need to collect self-reports as soon as possible after participants experience the relevant thoughts, feelings, or behaviors.
- Observations are another way for social psychologists to measure variables.
- Interrater reliability, or the level of agreement among multiple observers of the same behavior, is important when measuring variables using observation.
- New and improved technologies enable researchers to measure physiological responses, reaction times, eye movements, and activity in regions of the brain.

# Testing Ideas: Research Designs

- Most social psychologists test their ideas by using objective, systematic, and quantifiable methods.

### Descriptive Research: Discovering Trends and Tendencies

- In descriptive research, social psychologists record how frequently or typically people think, feel, or behave in particular ways.
- One form of descriptive research is observational research, in which researchers observe individuals systematically, often in natural settings.
- In archival research, researchers examine existing records and documents such as newspaper articles, diaries, and published crime statistics.
- Surveys involve asking people questions about their attitudes, beliefs, and behaviors.
- Survey researchers identify the population to which they want the results of the survey to generalize, and they select a sample of people from that population to take the survey.
- To best ensure a sample that is representative of the broader population, researchers should randomly select people from the population to be in the survey.

### Correlational Research: Looking for Associations

- Correlational research examines the association between variables.
- A correlation coefficient is a measure of the strength and direction of the association between two variables.
- Positive correlations indicate that as scores on one variable increase, scores on the other variable increase, and that as scores on one variable decrease, scores on the other decrease.
- Negative correlations indicate that as scores on one variable increase, scores on the other decrease.

- Correlation does not indicate causation; the fact that two variables are correlated does not necessarily mean that one causes the other.
- Correlations can be used for prediction and for generating hypotheses.

### Experiments: Looking for Cause and Effect

- Experiments require (1) control by the experimenter over events in the study and (2) random assignment of participants to conditions.
- Random sampling concerns how people are selected to be in a study, whereas random assignment concerns how people who are in the study are assigned to the different conditions of the study.
- Experiments are often conducted in a laboratory so that the researchers can have control over the context and can measure variables precisely.
- Field experiments are conducted in real-world settings outside the laboratory.
- A recent experiment found that compared to playing a neutral video game, playing a violent video game made participants behave more aggressively but playing a helping-oriented video game made them behave less aggressively.
- Participants in another experiment were more likely to act in ways that deviated from cultural norms if they were put in a positive rather than a negative mood.
- Experiments examine the effects of one or more independent variables on one or more dependent variables.
- Subject variables are variables that characterize preexisting differences among the participants.
- Results that are statistically significant could have occurred by chance 5 or fewer times in 100 possible outcomes.

- Experimental findings have internal validity to the extent that changes in the dependent variable can be attributed to the independent variables.
- A confound is a serious problem to internal validity, as it means that some other factor varied along with the independent variable and therefore makes it impossible to know if the independent variable caused the effect on the dependent variable.
- Control groups strengthen internal validity; experimenter expectancy effects weaken it.
- Research results have external validity to the extent that they can be generalized to other people and other situations.
- Although using a representative sample would strengthen a study's external validity, most social psychology studies use convenience samples.
- The rapidly increasing use of the Internet to collect data allows for far more diverse sets of participants in social psychological research today.

- Mundane realism is the extent to which the research setting seems similar to real-world situations.
- Experimental realism is the extent to which the participants experience the experimental setting and procedures as real and involving.
- Deception is sometimes used to increase experimental realism.
- Confederates act as though they are participants in an experiment but actually work for the experimenter.

## Meta-Analysis: Combining Results Across Studies

- Meta-analysis uses statistical techniques to integrate the quantitative results of different studies.

## Culture and Research Methods

- There is growing interest in studying the role of culture in social psychology.
- As important and exciting as these cultural investigations are, they offer special challenges to researchers.

# Ethics and Values in Social Psychology

- Ethical issues are particularly important in social psychology because of the use of deception in some research.

## Institutional Review Boards and Informed Consent: Protecting Research Participants

- Established by the federal government, IRBs are responsible for reviewing research proposals to ensure that the welfare of participants is adequately protected.
- The American Psychological Association's code of ethics requires psychologists to secure informed consent from research participants.

## Debriefing: Telling All

- During a debriefing at the end of a study the researchers disclose the facts about the study and make sure that the participant does not experience any distress. This is especially important if deception was used.

## Values and Science: Points of View and New Controversies

- Moral values set standards for and impose limits on the conduct of research.
- Various views exist on the relation between values and science. Few believe that there can be a completely value-free science, but some advocate trying to minimize the influence of values on science, whereas others argue that values should be recognized and encouraged as an important factor in science.
- Recent controversies in social psychology have led to a variety of suggestions for how the field should better protect itself against intentional or unintentional bias or dishonesty, including more openness to scrutiny, use of different statistical analyses, and greater emphasis on replication.

## KEY TERMS

applied research (29)
basic research (29)
bogus pipeline technique (31)
confederate (45)
confound (43)
construct validity (31)
correlation coefficient (36)
correlational research (36)
debriefing (48)
deception (45)

dependent variables (41)
experiment (38)
experimental realism (45)
experimenter expectancy effects (43)
external validity (44)
hypothesis (28)
independent variables (41)
informed consent (48)
internal validity (43)

interrater reliability (32)
meta-analysis (45)
mundane realism (44)
operational definition (30)
random assignment (38)
random sampling (35)
subject variables (42)
theory (28)

## MEDIA RESOURCES

Go to CengageBrain.com to access Psychology CourseMate, where you will find an interactive eBook, glossaries, flashcards, quizzes, videos, and more.

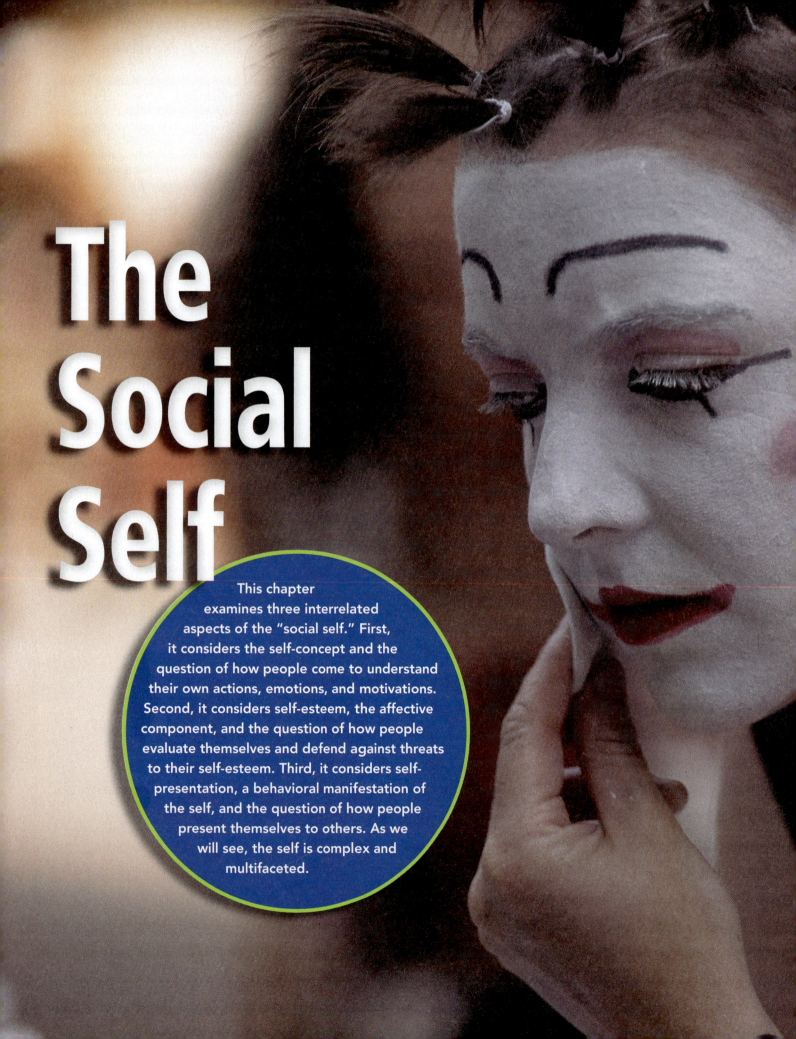

# The Social Self

This chapter examines three interrelated aspects of the "social self." First, it considers the self-concept and the question of how people come to understand their own actions, emotions, and motivations. Second, it considers self-esteem, the affective component, and the question of how people evaluate themselves and defend against threats to their self-esteem. Third, it considers self-presentation, a behavioral manifestation of the self, and the question of how people present themselves to others. As we will see, the self is complex and multifaceted.

© Gail Mooney/Corbis

# 3

# Putting *Common Sense* to the Test

### Circle Your Answer

**T  F**  Humans are the only animals who recognize themselves in the mirror.

**T  F**  Smiling can make you feel happier.

**T  F**  Sometimes the harder you try to control a thought, feeling, or behavior, the less likely you are to succeed.

**T  F**  People often sabotage their own performance in order to protect their self-esteem.

**T  F**  It's more adaptive to alter one's behavior than to stay consistent from one social situation to the next.

**Can you imagine** living a meaningful or coherent life without a clear sense of who you are? In *The Man Who Mistook His Wife for a Hat*, neurologist Oliver Sacks (1985) described such a person—a patient named William Thompson. According to Sacks, Thompson suffered from an organic brain disorder that impairs a person's memory of recent events. Unable to recall anything for more than a few seconds, Thompson was always disoriented and lacked a sense of inner continuity. The effect on his behavior was startling. Trying to grasp a constantly vanishing identity, Thompson would construct one tale after another to account for who he was, where he was, and what he was doing. From one moment to the next, he would improvise new identities—a grocery store clerk, a minister, or a medical patient, to name just a few. In social settings, Thompson's behavior was especially intriguing. As Sacks (1985) observed,

> The presence of others, other people, excite and rattle him, force him into an endless, frenzied, social chatter, a veritable delirium of identity-making and -seeking; the presence of plants, a quiet garden, the nonhuman order, making no social demands upon him, allow this identity-delirium to relax, to subside. (p. 110)

Thompson's plight is unusual, but it highlights two important points—one about the private "inner" self, the other about the "outer" self we show to others. First, the capacity for self-reflection is necessary for people to feel as if they understand their own motives and emotions and the causes of their behavior. Unable to ponder his own actions, Thompson appeared vacant and without feeling—"desouled," as Sacks put it. Second, the self is heavily influenced by social factors. Thompson himself seemed compelled to put on a face for others and to improvise characters for the company he kept. We all do, to some extent. We may not create a kaleidoscope of multiple identities as Thompson did, but the way we manage ourselves is influenced by the people around us.

This chapter examines the ABCs of the self: A for *affect*, B for *behavior*, and C for *cognition*. First, we ask a cognitive question: How do people come to know themselves, develop a self-concept, and maintain a stable sense of identity? Second, we explore an affective, or emotional, question: How do people evaluate themselves, enhance their self-images, and defend against threats to their self-esteem? Third, we confront a behavioral question: How do people regulate their own actions and present themselves to others according to interpersonal demands? As we'll see, the self is a topic that in recent years has attracted unprecedented interest among social psychologists (Leary & Tangney, 2003; Sedikides & Spencer, 2007; Swann & Bosson, 2010; Vohs & Finkel, 2006).

# The Self-Concept

Have you ever been at a noisy gathering—holding a drink in one hand and a spring roll in the other, struggling to have a conversation over music and the chatter of voices—and yet managed to hear someone at the other end of the room say your name? If so, then you have experienced the "cocktail party effect"—the tendency of people to pick a personally relevant stimulus, like a name, out of a complex and noisy environment

(Cherry, 1953; Wood & Cowan, 1995). Even infants who are too young to walk or talk exhibit this tendency (Newman, 2005). To the cognitive psychologist, this phenomenon shows that human beings are selective in their attention. To the social psychologist, it also shows that the self is an important object of our own attention.

The term **self-concept** refers to the sum total of beliefs that people have about themselves. But what specifically does the self-concept consist of? According to Hazel Markus (1977), the self-concept is made up of cognitive molecules she called **self-schemas**: beliefs about oneself that guide the processing of self-relevant information. Self-schemas are to an individual's total self-concept what hypotheses are to a theory or what books are to a library. You can think of yourself as masculine or feminine, as independent or dependent, as liberal or conservative, as introverted or extroverted. Indeed, any specific attribute may have relevance to the self-concept for some people but not for others. The self-schema for body weight is a good example. Men and women who regard themselves as extremely overweight or underweight, or for whom body image is a conspicuous aspect of the self-concept, are considered *schematic* with respect to weight. For body-weight schematics, a wide range of otherwise mundane events—a trip to the supermarket, new clothing, dinner at a restaurant, a day at the beach, or a friend's eating habits—may trigger thoughts about the self. In contrast, those who do not regard their own weight as extreme or as an important part of their lives are *aschematic* on that attribute (Markus et al., 1987).

 ## Rudiments of the Self-Concept

Clearly the self is a special object of our attention. Whether you are mentally focused on a memory, a conversation, a foul odor, the song in your head, your growling stomach, or this sentence, consciousness is like a "spotlight." It can shine on only one object at a point in time, but it can shift rapidly from one object to another and process information outside of awareness. In this spotlight, the self is front and center. But is the self so special that it is uniquely represented in the neural circuitry of the brain? And is the self a uniquely human concept, or do other animals also distinguish the self from everything else?

**Is the Self Specially Represented in the Brain?**　As illustrated by the story of William Thompson that opened this chapter, our sense of identity is biologically rooted. In *The Synaptic Self: How Our Brains Become Who We Are*, neuroscientist Joseph LeDoux (2002) argues that the synaptic connections in the brain provide the biological base for memory, which makes possible the sense of continuity that is needed for a normal identity. In *The Lost Self: Pathologies of the Brain and Identity*, Todd Feinberg and Julian Keenan (2005) describe how the self can be transformed and even completely destroyed by severe head injuries, brain tumors, diseases, and exposure to toxic substances that damage the brain and nervous system.

Social neuroscientists are starting to explore these possibilities. Using PET scans, fMRI, and other imaging techniques that can capture the brain in action, these researchers are finding that certain areas become more active when laboratory participants see a picture of themselves rather than a picture of another person (Platek et al., 2008), when they viewed self-relevant words such as their own name or street address rather than other-relevant words (Moran et al., 2009), and when they take a first-person perspective while playing a video game as opposed to a third-person perspective (David et al., 2006). As we will see throughout this chapter, the self is a frame of reference that powerfully influences our thoughts, feelings, and behaviors. Not all aspects of the self are housed in a single structure of the brain. However, the bulk of research does seem to suggest that various self-based processes can be traced to activities occurring in certain areas (Northoff & Panskepp, 2008; Heatherton, 2011).

**self-concept** The sum total of an individual's beliefs about his or her own personal attributes.

**self-schema** A belief people hold about themselves that guides the processing of self-relevant information.

**Do Nonhuman Animals Show Self-Recognition?**   When you stand in front of a mirror, you recognize the image as a reflection of yourself. But what about dogs, cats, and other animals—how can we possibly know what nonhumans think about mirrors? In a series of studies, Gordon Gallup (1977) placed different species of animals in a room with a large mirror. At first, they greeted their own images by vocalizing, gesturing, and making other social responses. After several days, only great apes (chimpanzees, gorillas, and orangutans)—but not other animals—seemed capable of self-recognition, using the mirror to pick food out of their teeth, groom themselves, blow bubbles, and make faces for their own entertainment. From all appearances, the apes recognized themselves.

In other studies, Gallup anesthetized the animals, then painted an odorless red dye on their brows and returned them to the mirror. Upon seeing the red spot, only the apes spontaneously reached for their own brows—proof that they perceived the image as their own (Povinelli et al., 1997; Keenan et al., 2003). Among the apes, this form of self-recognition emerges in young adolescence and is stable across the life span, at least until old age (de Veer et al., 2003). By using a similar red dye test (without anesthetizing the infants), developmental psychologists have found that most humans begin to recognize themselves in the mirror between the ages of 18 and 24 months (Lewis & Brooks-Gunn, 1979).

Many researchers believe that self-recognition among great apes and human infants is the first clear expression of the concept "me" (Boysen & Himes, 1999). Recent research suggests that certain intelligent non-primates can also recognize themselves. In one study, researchers at a New York aquarium found that two bottlenose dolphins marked with black ink often stopped to examine themselves in a mirror (Reiss & Marino, 2001). In a second study, researchers found that three Asian elephants placed in front of a jumbo-sized mirror used the mirror to inspect themselves—as when they moved their trunks to see the insides of their mouths, a part of the body they usually cannot see (Plotnik et al., 2006).

It's important not to assume from this research that mirror test is a pure measure of self-recognition or that it emerges at the same age throughout the world. Tanya Broesch and others (2011) tested children between the ages of 33 and 72 months in a number of countries. In line with past research, 88% of American children and 77% of Canadian children "passed" the test. Yet elsewhere it was only 58% in Saint Lucia, 52% in Peru, and 51% in Grenada; only two children passed in Kenya and none did so in Fiji. Based on their observations, the researchers speculated that the children in these non-Western

Researchers found that elephants placed in front of the jumbo-sized mirror pictured here used the mirror to inspect themselves. This observation suggests that elephants join human beings, great apes, and bottlenose dolphins as animal species that exhibit self-recognition (Plotnik et al., 2006).

Joshua Plotnik/PA Photos/Landov

countries did not lack self-recognition. They knew it was their image in the mirror but—having been raised for compliance, and trained not to ask questions—they did not dare to touch or remove the mark. Whatever the interpretation, this cross-cultural research raises questions as to whether the mirror test can be used to measure the self-concept (Broesch et al., 2011).

Humans are the only animals who recognize themselves in the mirror. **F**ALSE.

**What Makes the Self a Social Concept?**    The ability to see yourself as a distinct entity in the world may be a necessary first step in the evolution and development of a self-concept. The second step involves social factors. Sociologist Charles Horton Cooley (1902) introduced the term *looking-glass self* to suggest that other people serve as a mirror in which we see ourselves. Expanding on this idea, George Herbert Mead (1934) added that we often come to know ourselves by imagining what significant others think of us and then incorporating these perceptions into our self-concepts.

Picking up where the classic sociologists left off, Susan Andersen and Serena Chen (2002) theorized that the self is "relational"—that we draw our sense of who we are from our past and current relationships with the significant others in our lives. It is interesting that when Gallup tested his apes, those that had been raised in isolation—without exposure to peers—did not recognize themselves in the mirror. Only after such exposure did they begin to show signs of self-recognition. Among human beings, our self-concepts match our *perceptions* of what others think of us. Illustrating our capacity for "meta-insight," research also shows that people can distinguish between how they perceive themselves—for example, how smart, funny, or outgoing—and how others see them (Carlson et al., 2011).

In recent years, social psychologists have broken new ground in the effort to understand the social self. People are not born thinking of themselves as reckless, likable, shy, or outgoing. So where do their self-concepts come from? In the coming pages, the following sources are considered: introspection, perceptions of our own behavior, other people, autobiographical memories, and the cultures in which we live.

## > Introspection

Let's start at the beginning: How do people achieve insight into their own beliefs, attitudes, emotions, and motivations? Common sense makes this question seem ludicrous. After all, don't you know what you think because *you* think it? And don't you know how you feel because *you* feel it? Look through popular books on how to achieve self-insight, and you'll find the unambiguous answers to these questions to be yes. Whether the prescribed technique is yoga, meditation, psychotherapy, religion, dream analysis, or hypnosis, the advice is basically the same: Self-knowledge is derived from introspection, a looking inward at one's own thoughts and feelings.

If these how-to books are correct, it stands to reason that no one can know you as well as you know yourself. Thus, people tend to assume that for others to know you at all, they would need information about your private thoughts, feelings, and other inner states—not just your behavior. But is this really the case? Most social psychologists are not sure that this faith in introspection is justified. Several years ago, Richard Nisbett and Timothy Wilson (1977) found that research participants often cannot accurately explain the causes or correlates of their own behavior. This observation forced researchers to confront a thorny question: Does introspection provide a direct pipeline to self-knowledge?

In *Strangers to Ourselves*, Wilson (2002) argues that it does not. In fact, he finds that introspection can sometimes impair self-knowledge. In a series of studies, he found that the attitudes people reported having about different objects corresponded closely to their behavior toward those objects. The more participants said they enjoyed a task, the more time they spent on it; the more attractive they found a scenic landscape, the more pleasure they revealed in their facial expressions; the happier they said they were with a current dating partner, the longer the relationship with that partner ultimately lasted. Yet after participants were told to analyze the reasons for how they felt, the attitudes that they reported no longer corresponded to their behavior. There are two problems. The first, as described by Wilson, is that human beings are mentally busy processing information, which is why we so often fail to understand our own thoughts, feelings, and behaviors. Apparently, it is possible to think too much and be too analytical, only to get confused.

**In some ways, our sense of self is malleable and subject to change.**

"Look, babe. At this point, you've reinvented yourself so many times you're back to who you were at the start."

In *Self-Insight: Roadblocks and Detours on the Path to Knowing Thyself*, David Dunning (2005) points to a second type of problem in self-assessment: that people overestimate the positives. Most people, most of the time, think they are better than average, even though it is statistically impossible for this to happen. As we will see in our later discussion of self-enhancement, people from all walks of life tend to overrate their own skills, their prospects for success, the accuracy of their opinions, and the impressions they form of others—sometimes with dire consequences for their health and well-being.

People also have difficulty projecting forward and predicting how they would feel in response to future emotional events—a process referred to as **affective forecasting**. Imagine that you have a favorite candidate in an upcoming political campaign. Can you anticipate how happy you would be one month after the election if this candidate were to win? How unhappy would you be if he or she were to lose? Closer to home, how happy would you be six months after winning a million-dollar lottery? Or how unhappy would you be if you were injured in an automobile accident?

In a series of studies, Timothy Wilson and Daniel Gilbert (2003; 2005) asked research participants to predict how they would feel after various positive and negative life events and compared their predictions to how others experiencing those events said they actually felt. Consistently, they found that people overestimate the strength and duration of their emotional reactions, a phenomenon they call the *impact bias*. In one study, junior professors predicted that receiving tenure would increase their happiness levels for several years, yet professors who actually received tenure were no happier several years later than those not granted tenure. In a second study, voters predicted they would be happier a month after an election if their candidate won than if he or she lost. In actuality, supporters of the winning and losing candidates did not differ in their happiness levels one month after the election.

There are two possible reasons for the impact bias in affective forecasting. First, when it comes to negative life events—such as an injury, illness, or big financial loss—people do not fully appreciate the extent to which our psychological coping mechanisms help us to cushion the blow. In the face of adversity, human beings can be remarkably resilient—and not as devastated as we fear we will be (Gilbert et al., 1998). In fact, people are even more likely to overlook the coping mechanisms that *others* use. The result is a self–other difference by which we tend to predict that others will suffer even longer than we will (Igou, 2008). A second reason for these overestimates is that when we introspect about the emotional impact on us of a future event—say, the breakup of a close relationship—we become so focused on that single event that we neglect to take into account the effects of other life experiences. To become more accurate in our predictions, then, we need to force ourselves to think more broadly, about *all* the events that impact us. In one study, college students were asked to predict their emotional reactions to their school

**affective forecasting** The process of predicting how one would feel in response to future emotional events.

football team's winning or losing an important game. As usual, they tended to overestimate how long it would take them to recover from the victory or defeat. This bias disappeared, however, when the students first completed a "prospective diary" in which they estimated the amount of future time they will spend on everyday activities like going to class, talking to friends, studying, and eating meals (Wilson & Ross, 2000).

## ❯ Self-Perception

Regardless of what we can learn from introspection, Daryl Bem (1972) proposed that people can learn about themselves the same way outside observers do—by watching their own behavior. Bem's **self-perception theory** is simple yet profound. To the extent that internal states are weak or difficult to interpret, people infer what they think or how they feel by observing their own behavior and the situation in which that behavior takes place. Have you ever listened to yourself arguing with someone in an e-mail exchange, only to realize with amazement how angry you were? Have you ever devoured a sandwich in record time, only then to conclude that you must have been incredibly hungry? In each case, you made an inference about yourself by watching your own actions.

There are limits to self-perception, of course. According to Bem, people do not infer their own internal states from behavior that occurred in the presence of compelling situational pressures such as reward or punishment. If you argued vehemently or wolfed down a sandwich because you were paid to do so, you probably would not assume that you were angry or hungry. In other words, people learn about themselves through self-perception only when the situation alone seems insufficient to have caused their behavior.

Over the years, a good deal of research has supported self-perception theory. When people are gently coaxed into saying or doing something and when they are not otherwise certain about how they feel, they often come to view themselves in ways that are consistent with their public statements and behaviors (Chaiken & Baldwin, 1981; Kelly & Rodriguez, 2006; Schlenker & Trudeau, 1990). In one study, participants induced to describe themselves in flattering terms scored higher on a later test of self-esteem than did those who were led to describe themselves more modestly (Jones et al., 1981; Rhodewalt & Agustsdottir, 1986). Similarly, those who were maneuvered by leading questions into describing themselves as introverted or extroverted—whether or not they really were—came to define themselves as such later on, unless they were certain of this aspect of their personality (Fazio & Zanna, 1981; Swann & Ely, 1984). British author E. M. Forster long ago anticipated the theory when he asked, "How can I tell what I think 'til I see what I say?"

Self-perception theory may have even more reach than Bem had anticipated. Bem argued that people sometimes learn about themselves by observing their *own* freely chosen behavior. But might you also infer something about yourself by observing the behavior of *someone else* with whom you completely identify? In a series of studies, Noah Goldstein and Robert Cialdini (2007) demonstrated this phenomenon, which they call *vicarious self-perception*. In one experiment, for example, they asked college students to listen to an interview with a fellow student who had agreed afterward to spend a few extra minutes helping out on a project on homelessness. Before listening to the interview, all participants were fitted with an EEG recording device on their foreheads that allegedly measured brain activity as they viewed a series of images and words. By random assignment, some participants but not others were then told that their brain-wave patterns closely resembled that of the person whose interview they would soon hear—a level of resemblance, they were told, that signaled genetic similarity and relationship closeness. Would participants in this similarity feedback condition draw inferences about themselves by observing the behavior of a fellow student? Yes. In a post-interview questionnaire, these participants (compared to those in the no-feedback control group) rated themselves as more sensitive

**self-perception theory**  The theory that when internal cues are difficult to interpret, people gain self-insight by observing their own behavior.

and as more self-sacrificing if the student whose helpfulness they observed was said to be similar, biologically. What's more, when the session was over, 93% of those in the similarity condition agreed to spend some extra time themselves helping the experimenter—compared to only 61% in the no-feedback control group.

Introspection and self-perception theory make different predictions about the extent to which people can know themselves. If self-knowledge derives from introspection, then clearly you know yourself better than anyone else can. If self-knowledge derives solely from observations of behavior, then it should be possible for others to know us as well as we know ourselves. Assuming that self-knowledge is gained from both sources, then the truth lies somewhere in the middle. But wait. Is it ever possible for others to know us *better* than we know ourselves?

Simine Vazire (2010) asked this very question and came up with a surprising answer. Vazire proposed a Self–Other Knowledge Asymmetry (SOKA) model in which she predicts that we know ourselves better than others do when it comes to traits that are "internal" and hard to observe (such as how optimistic, anxious, or easily upset a person is) and that there is no self-other difference when it comes to traits that are "external" and easy to observe (such as how quiet, sociable, or messy a person is). She also predicts that others may actually know us *better* than we know ourselves when it comes to observable traits that can be so touchy for self-esteem purposes that we have motivated "blind spots" (such as how smart, creative, or rude a person is). In these latter instances, Vazire predicts, others can be more objective than we are about ourselves.

To test these predictions, Vazire asked college students to rate themselves—and then had their friends rate the participants—on a number of personality traits. Three types of traits were studied: (1) high in observability (talkativeness, dominance, and leadership), (2) low in observability and not evaluative (self-esteem and anxiety), and (3) low in observability and highly evaluative (intelligent and creative). To determine accuracy, Vazire then measured how participants fared on objective measures of these traits using various laboratory exercises and paper-and-pencil tests. The results provided strong support for the SOKA model. ● Figure 3.1 shows that self- and friend-ratings were equally accurate for highly observable traits, that self-ratings were more accurate for internal non-evaluative traits, but that friend-ratings were more accurate for internal evaluative traits. Clearly, to know thyself requires a combination of information and objectivity (see Vazire & Carlson, 2011).

● **FIGURE 3.1**

**The Self–Other Knowledge Asymmetry (SOKA) Model**

Participants rated themselves and were rated by friends on personality traits for which they took various objective tests. As shown, self-ratings were more accurate for internal/non-evaluative traits (left) and self- and friend-ratings were equally accurate for observable/non-evaluative traits (center). Interestingly, however, friend-ratings were more accurate for internal/evaluative traits. Supporting SOKA, this pattern shows that "know thyself" requires a combination of information and objectivity.

From Vazire, S., "Who knows what about a person? The self–other knowledge asymmetry (SOKA) model," *Journal of Personality and Social Psychology* vol 98 (pp. 281–300). Copyright © 2010 American Psychological Association. Reprinted with permission.

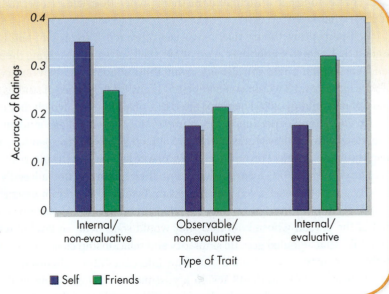

**Self-Perceptions of Emotion**    Draw the corners of your mouth back and up and tense your eye muscles. Okay, relax. Now raise your eyebrows, open your eyes wide, and let your mouth drop open slightly. Relax. Now pull your brows down and together and clench your teeth. Relax. If you followed these directions, you would have appeared to others to be feeling first happy, then fearful, and finally angry. The question is "How would you have appeared to yourself?"

Social psychologists who study emotion have asked precisely that question. Viewed within the framework of self-perception theory, the **facial feedback hypothesis** states that changes in facial expression can trigger corresponding changes in the subjective experience of emotion. In the first test of this hypothesis, James Laird (1974) told participants that they were taking part in an experiment on activity of the facial muscles. After attaching electrodes to their faces, he showed them a series of cartoons. Before each one, the participants were instructed to contract certain facial muscles in ways that created either a smile or a frown. As Laird predicted, participants rated what they saw as funnier when they were smiling than when they were frowning. In follow-up research, people were similarly induced through posed expressions to experience fear, anger, sadness, and disgust (Dimberg & Söderkvist, 2011; Duclos et al., 1989).

Facial feedback can evoke and magnify certain emotional states. It's important to note, however, that the face is not *necessary* to the subjective experience of emotion. When neuropsychologists recently tested a young woman who suffered from bilateral facial paralysis, they found that despite her inability to outwardly *show* emotion, she reported *feeling* various emotions in response to positive and negative visual images (Keillor et al., 2003).

How does facial feedback work? With 80 muscles in the human face that can create over 7,000 expressions, can we actually vary our own emotions by contracting certain muscles and wearing different expressions? Research suggests that we can, though it is not clear what the results mean. Laird argues that facial expressions affect emotion through a process of self-perception: "If I'm smiling, I must be happy." Consistent with this hypothesis, Chris Kleinke and others (1998) asked people to emulate either the happy or angry facial expressions depicted in a series of photographs. Half the participants saw themselves in a mirror during the task; the others did not. Did these manipulations affect mood states? Yes. Compared to participants in a no-expression control group, those who put on happy faces felt better, and those who put on angry faces felt worse. As predicted by self-perception theory, the differences were particularly pronounced among participants who saw themselves in a mirror.

Other researchers believe that facial movements spark emotion by producing physiological changes in the brain (Izard, 1990). For example, Robert Zajonc (1993) argues that smiling causes facial muscles to increase the flow of air-cooled blood to the brain, a process that produces a pleasant state by lowering brain temperature. Conversely, frowning decreases blood flow, producing an unpleasant state by raising temperature. To demonstrate, Zajonc and his colleagues (1989) conducted a study in which they asked participants to repeat certain vowels 20 times each, including the sounds *ah*, *e*, *u*, and the German vowel *ü*. In the meantime, temperature changes in the forehead were measured and participants reported on how they felt. As it turned out, *ah* and *e* (sounds that cause people to mimic smiling) lowered forehead temperature and elevated mood, whereas *u* and *ü* (sounds that cause us to mimic frowning) increased temperature and dampened mood. In short, people need not infer how they feel. Rather, facial expressions evoke physiological changes that produce an emotional experience.

"I don't sing because I am happy. I am happy because I sing."

**As suggested by self-perception theory, we sometimes infer how we feel by observing our own behavior.**

**facial feedback hypothesis**    The hypothesis that changes in facial expression can lead to corresponding changes in emotion.

Other expressive behaviors, such as body posture, can also provide us with sensory feedback and influence the way we feel. When people feel proud, they stand erect with their shoulders raised, chest expanded, and head held high (*expansion*). When dejected, however, we slump over with shoulders drooping and head bowed (*contraction*). Clearly, your emotional state is revealed in the way you carry yourself. But is it also possible that the way you carry yourself affects your emotional state? Can people lift their spirits by expansion or lower their spirits by contraction? Yes. Sabine Stepper and Fritz Strack (1993) arranged for people to sit in either a slumped or an upright position by varying the height of the table they had to write on. Those forced to sit upright reported feeling more pride after succeeding at a task than did those placed in a slumped position. In another study, participants who were asked to lean forward with their fists clenched during the experiment reported feeling anger, whereas those who sat slumped with their heads down said they felt sadness (Duclos et al., 1989; Flack et al., 1999).

**Self-Perceptions of Motivation**    Without quite realizing it, the author Mark Twain was a self-perception theorist. In *The Adventures of Tom Sawyer*, written in the late 1800s, he quipped, "There are wealthy gentlemen in England who drive four-horse passenger coaches 20 or 30 miles on a daily line, in the summer, because the privilege costs them considerable money; but if they were offered wages for the service that would turn it into work then they would resign." Twain's hypothesis—that reward for an enjoyable activity can undermine interest in that activity—seems to contradict both our intuition and the results of psychological research. After all, aren't we all motivated by reward, as B. F. Skinner and other behaviorists have declared? The answer depends on how *motivation* is defined.

As a keen observer of human behavior, Twain anticipated a key distinction between intrinsic and extrinsic motivation. *Intrinsic motivation* originates in factors within a person. People are said to be intrinsically motivated when they engage in an activity for the sake of their own interest, the challenge, or sheer enjoyment. Eating a fine meal, listening to music, spending time with friends, and having a hobby are among the activities that you might find intrinsically motivating. In contrast, *extrinsic motivation* originates in factors outside the person. People are said to be extrinsically motivated when they engage in an activity as a means to an end, for tangible benefit. It might be to acquire money, grades, or recognition; to fulfill obligations; or to avoid punishment. Clearly, people strive for reward. The question is "What happens to the intrinsic motivation once that reward is no longer available?"

From the standpoint of self-perception theory, Twain's hypothesis makes sense. When someone is rewarded for listening to music, playing a game, or eating a tasty food, his or her behavior becomes *over*justified, or *over*rewarded, which means that it can be attributed to extrinsic as well as intrinsic motives. By creating ambiguity about a person's motivation, can the **overjustification effect** have unintended consequences? When athletes are paid millions of dollars to play their sport, does the money overwhelm their love of the game, making play feel like work? Once paid, do people begin to wonder if the activity was ever worth pursuing in its own right?

Research has shown that when people start getting rewarded for a task they already enjoy, they sometimes lose interest in it. In an early demonstration of this phenomenon, Mark Lepper and his colleagues (1973) gave preschool children an opportunity to play with colorful felt-tipped markers—an opportunity most could not resist. By observing how much time the children spent on the activity, the researchers were able to measure their intrinsic motivation. Two weeks later, the children were divided into three groups, all about equal in terms of initial levels of intrinsic motivation. In one, the children were simply asked to draw some pictures with the markers. In the second, they were

---

Smiling can make you feel happier. **T**RUE.

---

**overjustification effect**   The tendency for intrinsic motivation to diminish for activities that have become associated with reward or other extrinsic factors.

told that if they used the markers, they would receive a "Good Player Award," a certificate with a gold star and a red ribbon. In a third group, the children were not offered a reward for drawing pictures, but—like those in the second group—they received a reward when they were done.

About a week later, the teachers placed the markers and paper on a table in the classroom while the experimenters observed through a one-way mirror. Since no rewards were offered on this occasion, the amount of free time the children spent playing with the markers reflected their intrinsic motivation. As predicted, those who had expected and received a reward for their efforts were no longer as interested in the markers as they had been. Children who had not received a reward were not adversely affected, nor were those who had received the unexpected reward. Having played with the markers without the promise of tangible benefit, these children remained intrinsically motivated (see ● Figure 3.2).

The paradox that reward can undermine rather than enhance intrinsic motivation has been observed in many settings and with both children and adults (Deci & Ryan, 1985; Pittman & Heller, 1987; Tang & Hall, 1995). Accept money for a leisure activity, and before you know it, what used to be "play" comes to feel more like "work." In the long run, this can have negative effects on the quality of your performance. In a series of studies, Teresa Amabile (1996) and others had participants write poems, draw or paint pictures, make paper collages, and generate creative solutions to business dilemmas. Consistently, they found that people are more creative when they feel interested and challenged by the work itself than when they feel pressured to make money, fulfill obligations, meet deadlines, win competitions, or impress others. When Amabile had art experts rate the works of professional artists, she found that their commissioned work (art they were contracted for) was judged as lower in quality than their noncommissioned work. People are likely to be more creative when they are intrinsically motivated in relation to the task, not compelled by outside forces.

But wait. If extrinsic benefits serve to undermine intrinsic motivation, should teachers and parents *not* offer rewards to their children? Are the employee incentive programs that are so often used to motivate workers in the business world doomed to fail, as some (Kohn, 1993) have suggested? It all depends on how the reward is perceived and by whom. If a reward is presented in the form of verbal praise that is perceived to be sincere or as a special "bonus" for superior performance, then it can *enhance* intrinsic motivation by providing positive feedback about competence—as when people win competitions, scholarships, or a pat on the back from people they respect (Cameron & Pierce, 1994; Cameron et al., 2005; Eisenberger & Cameron, 1996; Henderlong & Lepper, 2002).

The notion that intrinsic motivation is undermined by some types of reward but not others was observed even among 20-month-old babies. In a clever study, Felix Warneken and Michael Tomasello (2008) brought babies into the lab, where the experimenter accidentally dropped a pen or crumpled paper onto the floor and appeared unable to reach it. The child could help by picking up the object and handing it to the experimenter. Most of the babies helped in this situation. In a treatment phase, the researchers responded to the assistance by giving the child a toy cube ("For this you get a cube"),

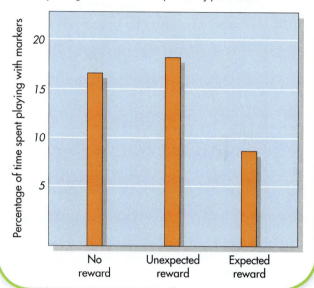

● **FIGURE 3.2**

**Paradoxical Effects of Reward on Intrinsic Motivation**

In this study, an expected reward undermined children's intrinsic motivation to play with felt-tipped markers. Children who received an unexpected reward or no reward did not lose interest.

From Lepper, M.R., Greene, D., and Nisbett, K.E., "Undermining children's intrinsic interest with extrinsic reward: A test of the 'overjustification' hypothesis," *Journal of Personality and Social Psychology* vol 28 (pp. 129–137). Copyright © 1973 by the American Psychological Association. Reprinted by permission.

● **FIGURE 3.3**

In front of 20-month-old babies on the floor of a laboratory, an experimenter accidentally dropped a pen or crumpled paper. Most of the babies helped pick up the fallen object in this situation—a positive act that was met with a tangible reward, verbal praise, or nothing at all. Would the babies help the experimenter again if needed? As shown, babies in the no-response and verbal praise conditions continued to help at high rate. However, those who had received a reward became less likely to help later when that reward was no longer available, suggesting that tangible rewards undermined altruistic tendencies.

Warneken & Tomasello, 2008. © Cengage Learning

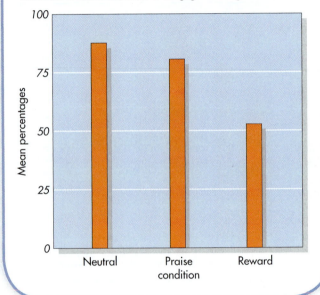

verbal praise ("Thank you, that's really nice!"), or nothing at all. Would these same children continue to help? ● Figure 3.3 shows that in a later test phase, when presented with a number of helping opportunities, those in the no-response condition continued to help 89% of the time and that this tendency remained high at 81% in the verbal praise condition. Yet among children who had earlier received a reward, helping in the test phase dropped to 53% when that reward was no longer available.

Individual differences in people's motivational orientation toward work must also be considered. For intrinsically oriented people who say, "What matters most to me is enjoying what I do" and "I seldom think about salary and promotions," reward may be unnecessary and may even be detrimental (Amabile et al., 1994). Yet for people who are highly focused on the achievement of certain goals—whether at school, at work, or in sports—inducements such as grades, scores, bonuses, awards, trophies, and the sheer thrill of competition, as in team sports, tend to boost intrinsic motivation (Durik & Harackiewicz, 2007; Harackiewicz & Elliot, 1993).

## Influences of Other People

As we noted earlier, Cooley's (1902) theory of the looking-glass self emphasized that other people help us define ourselves. In this section, we will see the importance of this proposition to our self-concepts.

**Social Comparison Theory** Suppose a stranger were to ask, "Who are you?" If you had only a minute or two to answer, would you mention your religion or your ethnic background? What about your hometown? Would you describe your talents and your interests or your likes and dislikes? When asked this question, people tend to describe themselves in ways that set them apart from others in their immediate vicinity (McGuire & McGuire, 1988). Among children, boys are more likely to cite their gender when they grow up in families that are predominantly female; girls do the same when living in families that are predominantly male (McGuire et al., 1979). Similarly, on the college campus, "nontraditional" older students are more likely to mention their age than are traditional younger students (Kite, 1992). Regardless of whether the unique attribute is gender, age, height, or eye color, this pattern is basically the same. The implication is intriguing: Change someone's social surroundings, and you can change that person's spontaneous self-description.

This reliance on distinguishing features in self-description indicates that the self is "relative," a social construct, and that each of us defines ourselves in part by using family members, friends, acquaintances, and others as a benchmark (Mussweiler & Rüter, 2003; Mussweiler & Strack, 2000). At least temporarily, our standards of self-comparison can even be influenced by our fleeting, everyday exposure to strangers (Mussweiler et al., 2004). Indeed, that is what Leon Festinger (1954) proposed in his **social comparison theory**. Festinger argued that when people are uncertain of their abilities or opinions—that is, when objective information is not readily available—they evaluate themselves through comparisons with similar others. The theory seems reasonable, but is it valid? Over the years, social psychologists have put social comparison theory to the test, focusing on two key questions: (1) *When* do people turn to others for comparative information? (2) Of all the people who inhabit the Earth, *with whom* do we choose to compare ourselves? (Suls & Wheeler, 2000).

As Festinger proposed, the answer to the "when" question appears to be that people engage in social comparison in states of uncertainty, when more objective means of self-evaluation are not available. It's not clear whether Festinger understated the importance of social comparison processes. Some research suggests that people judge themselves in relation to others even when more objective standards really are available (Klein, 1997). Yet other research supports Festinger's theory that people are less influenced by social comparison information when objective information is available—for example, through our personal histories of success and failure (Steyn & Mynhardt, 2008).

The "with whom" question has also been the subject of many studies. The answer seems to be that when we evaluate our own taste in music, value on the job market, or athletic ability, we look to others who are similar to us in relevant ways (Goethals & Darley, 1977; Wheeler et al., 1982). If you are curious about your flair for writing, for example, you're more likely to compare yourself with other college students than with high schoolers or best-selling authors. There are exceptions to this rule, of course. Later in this chapter, we will see that people often cope with personal inadequacies by focusing on others who are *less* able or *less* fortunate than themselves.

**Two-Factor Theory of Emotion**   People seek social comparison information to evaluate their abilities and opinions. Do they also turn to others to determine something as personal and subjective as their own emotions? In classic experiments on affiliation, Stanley Schachter (1959) found that when people were frightened into thinking they would receive painful electric shocks, most sought the company of others who were in the same predicament. Nervous and uncertain about how they should be feeling, participants wanted to affiliate with similar others, presumably for the purpose of comparison. Yet when they were not fearful and expected only mild shocks or when the "others" were not taking part in the same experiment, participants preferred to be alone. As Schachter put it, "Misery doesn't just love any kind of company; it loves only miserable company" (p. 24).

Intrigued by the possibilities, Schachter and his research team took the next step. Could it be, they wondered, that when people are uncertain about how they feel, their emotional state is actually determined by the reactions of others around them? In answer to this question, the researchers proposed that two factors are necessary to feel a specific emotion. First, the person must experience the symptoms of physiological arousal—such as a racing heart, perspiration, rapid breathing, and tightening of the stomach. Second, the person must make a *cognitive interpretation* that explains the source of the arousal. And that is where the people around us come in: Their reactions help us interpret our own arousal.

To test this provocative **two-factor theory of emotion**, Schachter and Singer (1962) injected male volunteers with epinephrine, a drug that heightens physiological arousal. Although one group was forewarned about the drug's effects, a second group was not. Members of a third group were injected with a harmless placebo. Before the drug (which was described as a vitamin supplement) actually took effect, participants were left alone with a male confederate introduced as another participant who had received the same injection. In some sessions, the confederate behaved in a euphoric manner. For 20 minutes, he bounced around happily, doodling on scratch paper, sinking jump shots into the wastebasket, flying paper airplanes across the room, and playing with a Hula-Hoop. In other sessions, the confederate displayed anger, making fun of a questionnaire they were filling out and, in a fit of rage, ripping it up and hurling it into the wastebasket.

**two-factor theory of emotion**   The theory that the experience of emotion is based on two factors: physiological arousal and a cognitive interpretation of that arousal.

Think for a moment about these various combinations of situations. As the drug takes effect, participants in the *drug-informed* group will begin to feel their hearts pound, their hands shake, and their faces flush. Having been told to expect these symptoms, however, they need not search for an explanation. Participants in the *placebo* group will not become aroused in the first place, so they will have no symptoms to explain. But now consider the plight of those in the *drug-uninformed* group, who suddenly become aroused without knowing why. Trying to identify the sensations, these participants, according to the theory, should take their cues from someone else in the same predicament—namely, the confederate.

In general, the experimental results supported Schachter and Singer's line of reasoning. Drug-uninformed participants reported feeling relatively happy or angry depending on the confederate's performance. In many instances, they even exhibited similar kinds of behavior. One participant, for example, "threw open the window and, laughing, hurled paper basketballs at passersby." In the drug-informed and placebo groups, however, participants were, as expected, less influenced by these social cues.

Schachter and Singer's two-factor theory has attracted a good deal of controversy, as some studies have corroborated their findings but others have not. In one experiment, for example, participants who were injected with epinephrine and not forewarned about the symptoms later exhibited more fear in response to a scary film, but they were not more angry or amused while seeing films that tend to elicit these other emotions (Mezzacappa et al., 1999). Overall, it now appears that one limited but important conclusion can safely be drawn: When people are unclear about their own emotional states, they sometimes interpret how they feel by watching others (Reisenzein, 1983). The "sometimes" part of the conclusion is important. For other people to influence your emotion your level of physiological arousal cannot be too intense or else it will be experienced as aversive, regardless of the situation (Maslach, 1979; Zimbardo et al., 1993). Also, research shows that other people must be present as a possible explanation for arousal *before* its onset. Once people are aroused, they turn for an explanation to events that preceded the change in their physiological state (Schachter & Singer, 1979; Sinclair et al., 1994).

In subsequent chapters, we will see that the two-factor theory of emotion has far-reaching implications for passionate love, anger and aggression, and other affective experiences.

## Autobiographical Memories

Philosopher James Mill once said, "The phenomenon of the Self and that of Memory are merely two sides of the same fact." If the story of patient William Thompson at the start of this chapter is any indication, Mill was right. Without autobiographical memories—recollections of the sequences of events that have touched your life (Bernsten, 2009; Fivush et al., 2003; Rubin, 1996; Thompson et al., 1998)—you would have no coherent self-concept. After all, who would you be if you could not remember your parents or your childhood playmates, your successes and failures, the places you lived, the schools you attended, the books you read, and the teams you played for? Clearly, memories shape the self-concept. In this section, we'll see that the self-concept shapes our personal memories as well (Conway & Pleydell-Pearce, 2000).

When people are prompted to recall their own experiences, they typically report more events from the recent past than from the distant past. There are, however, two consistent exceptions to this simple recency rule. The first is that older adults tend to retrieve a large number of personal memories from their adolescence and early adulthood years—a "reminiscence bump" found across many cultures that may occur because these are busy and formative years in one's life (Conway et al., 2005; Fitzgerald,

1988; Jansari & Parkin, 1996). A second exception is that people tend to remember transitional "firsts." Reflect for a moment on your own college career. What events pop to mind—and when did they occur? Did you come up with the day you arrived on campus or the first time you met your closest friend? What about notable classes, parties, or sports events? When David Pillemer and his colleagues (1996) asked college juniors and seniors to recount the most memorable experiences of their first year, 32% of all recollections were from the transitional month of September. When college graduates were given the same task, they too cited a disproportionate number of events from the opening two months of their first year, followed by the next major transitional period, the last month of their senior year. Among students, these busy transitional periods are important regardless of whether their schools follow a semester calendar or some other academic schedule (Kurbat et al., 1998).

Obviously, not all experiences leave the same impression. Ask people old enough to remember November 22, 1963, and they probably can tell you exactly where they were, who they were with, and what was happening the moment they heard the news that President John F. Kennedy had been shot. Roger Brown and James Kulik (1977) coined the term *flashbulb memories* to describe these enduring, detailed, high-resolution recollections and speculated that humans are biologically equipped for survival purposes to "print" dramatic events in memory. These flashbulb memories are not necessarily accurate or even consistent over time. Still, these recollections "feel" special and serve as prominent landmarks in the biographies that we tell about ourselves (Conway, 1995; Talarico & Rubin, 2007).

By linking the present to the past and providing us with an inner sense of continuity, autobiographical memory is a vital part of—and can be shaped by—our identity. Perhaps that is why people are often motivated to distort the past in ways that are self-inflated. According to Anthony Greenwald (1980), "The past is remembered as if it were a drama in which the self was the leading player" (p. 604).

To illustrate this bias, let's turn the clock back to a momentous event in American history: the Senate Watergate hearings of 1973. The witness was John Dean, former counsel to President Richard Nixon. Dean had submitted a 245-page statement in which he recounted word for word the details of many conversations. Dean's memory seemed so impressive that he was called "the human tape recorder." But then, in an ironic twist of fate, investigators discovered that Nixon had taped the meetings that Dean recalled. Was Dean accurate? A comparison of his testimony with the actual tapes revealed that although he correctly remembered the gist of his White House meetings, he consistently exaggerated his own role and importance in these events. Cognitive psychologist Ulric Neisser (1981), who analyzed Dean's testimony, wondered, "Are we all like this? Is everyone's memory constructed, staged, self-centered?" The answer is yes and no. To be sure, everyone's memories are centered on the self. But people differ in their self-esteem and in the extent to which they skew the past in ways that portray the self in a favorable light (Conner Christensen et al., 2003).

In other ways, too, people tend to revise their fading personal histories to reflect favorably on the self. In one study, Harry Bahrick and others (1996) had 99 college students try to recall all of their high school grades and then checked their reports against the actual transcripts. Overall, the majority of grades were recalled correctly. But most of the errors in memory were grade *inflations*—and most of these were made when the actual grades were *low* (see ● Figure 3.4). In a second study, Simone Schlagman and others (2006) talked to young and old volunteers for a period of one week and then analyzed the autobiographical memories that they spontaneously recounted—about births, deaths, holidays, accidents, school events, special occasions, and the like. Both groups recalled plenty of positive events, but older adults recalled fewer negative memories. These findings bring to mind sociologist George

*"The nice thing about having memories is that you can choose."*
—William Trevor

Although adults recall more events from the recent than distant past, people are filled with memories from late adolescence and early adulthood. These formative years are nicely captured by high school yearbook photos, such as those of American actresses Angelina Jolie (top) and Jennifer Aniston (bottom).

● **FIGURE 3.4**

**Distortions in Memory of High School Grades**

College students were asked to recall their high school grades, which were then checked against their actual transcripts. These comparisons revealed that most errors in memory were grade inflations. Lower grades were recalled with the least accuracy (and the most inflation). It appears that people sometimes revise their own past to suit their current self-image.

From Bahrick et al., "Accuracy and distortion in memory for high school grades," *Psychological Science* vol 7 (pp. 265–271). Copyright © 1996 Sage Publications, Inc. Reprinted by permission.

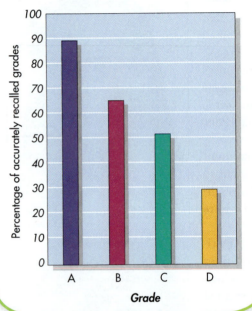

Herbert Mead's (1934) contention that our visions of the past are like pure "escape fancies . . . in which we rebuild the world according to our hearts' desires" (pp. 348–349).

Our autobiographies are so interconnected with our sense of who were are that as our self-concept changes, so does our visual perspective on the past. Think about an important way in which you have changed. Once you were a kid, now you are in college or working. Or maybe you were a smoker and stopped, or obese and lost weight. Or maybe you underwent a religious conversion, or had cancer and survived—and now you feel "reborn." Theorizing that our current self-concept colors how we see our past selves, Lisa Libby and Richard Eibach (2002) asked college students to write about one aspect of themselves that had changed a lot and another that had not changed since high school. Analyzing the language used to describe these recollections, these researchers found that participants used more third-person pronouns to describe past actions that no longer fit their current selves—and they rated themselves as more detached from these actions.

## ▶ Culture and the Self-Concept

The self-concept is also heavily influenced by cultural factors. In America, it is said that "the squeaky wheel gets the grease"; in Japan, it is said that "the nail that stands out gets pounded down." Thus, American parents try to raise their children to be independent, self-reliant, and assertive (a "cut above the rest"), whereas Japanese children are raised to fit into their groups and community.

The preceding example illustrates two contrasting cultural orientations. One values *individualism* and the virtues of independence, autonomy, and self-reliance. The other orientation values *collectivism* and the virtues of interdependence, cooperation, and social harmony. Under the banner of individualism, one's personal goals take priority over group allegiances. In collectivist cultures, by contrast, a person is first and foremost a loyal member of a family, team, company, church, and state, motivated to be part of a group—not different, better, or worse (Triandis, 1994). In what countries are these orientations the most extreme? In a worldwide study of 116,000 employees of IBM, Geert Hofstede (1980) found that the most fiercely individualistic people were from the United States, Australia, Great Britain, Canada, and the Netherlands—in that order. The most collectivist people were from Venezuela, Colombia, Pakistan, Peru, Taiwan, and China.

Individualism and collectivism are not mere opposites on a continuum and that the similarities and differences between countries do not fit a simple pattern. Daphna Oyserman and others (2002) conducted a meta-analysis of thousands of respondents in 83 studies. Within the United States, they found that African Americans were the most individualistic subgroup and that Asian Americans and Latino Americans were the most collectivistic. Comparing nations, they found that collectivist orientations varied within Asia, as the Chinese were more collectivistic than Japanese and Korean respondents.

Individualism and collectivism are so deeply ingrained in a culture that they mold our very self-conceptions and identities. According to Hazel Markus and Shinobu Kitayama (1991), most North Americans and Europeans have an *independent* view of the self. In this view, the self is an entity that is distinct, autonomous, self-contained, and endowed with unique dispositions. Yet in much of Asia, Africa, and Latin America, people hold an *interdependent* view of the self. Here, the self is part of a larger network that includes one's family, co-workers, and others with whom one is socially connected. People with an independent view say that "the only person you can count on is yourself" and "I enjoy being unique and different from others." In contrast, those with an interdependent view are more likely to agree that "I'm partly to blame if one of my family members or co-workers fails" and "my happiness depends on the happiness of those around me" (Rhee et al., 1995; Singelis, 1994; Triandis et al., 1998). These contrasting orientations—one focused on the personal self, the other on a collective self—are depicted in ● Figure 3.5.

Research of various sorts confirms the close link between cultural orientation and conceptions of the self. In one study, David Trafimow and others (1991) had North American and Chinese college students complete 20 sentences beginning with "I am...." Americans were more likely to fill in the blank with trait descriptions ("I am shy"), whereas the Chinese were more likely to identify themselves by group affiliations ("I am a college student"). Consistent with this finding, a second study showed that compared to American children who tend to recall autobiographical events that feature personal aspects of themselves, Chinese children tend to recall relationships, group memberships, and other social aspects of themselves (Q. Wang, 2006). A third study has shown that when Chinese participants—but not Americans—think about themselves areas of the brain are activated that are also activated when they think about their mothers (Zhu et al., 2007a).

Our cultural orientations can color the way people perceive, evaluate, and present themselves in relation to others. Markus and Kitayama (1991) identified two interesting differences between East and West. The first is that people in individualistic cultures strive for personal achievement, whereas those living in collectivist cultures derive more satisfaction from the status of a valued group. Thus, whereas North Americans tend to overestimate their own contributions to a team effort, seize the credit for success, and blame others for failure, people from collectivist cultures tend to underestimate

● **FIGURE 3.5**

**Cultural Conceptions of Self**

As depicted here, different cultures foster different conceptions of the self. Many Westerners have an *independent view* of the self as an entity that is distinct, autonomous, and self-contained. Yet many Asians, Africans, and Latin Americans hold an *interdependent view* of the self that encompasses others in a larger social network.
From Marcus, H.R. and Kitayama, S., "Culture and the self: Implications for cognition, emotion, and motivation," *Psychological Review* vol 98 (p. 226). Copyright © 1991 by the American Psychological Association. Reprinted by permission.

A. Independent View of Self

Mother    Father    Sibling    Self    Friend    Friend    Co-worker

B. Interdependent View of Self

Mother    Father    Sibling    Self    Friend    Friend    Co-worker their own role and present themselves in more modest, self-effacing terms in relation to other members of the group (Akimoto & Sanbonmatsu, 1999; Heine et al., 2000).

A second consequence of these differing conceptions of the self is that American college students see themselves as less similar to other people than do Asian Indian students. This difference reinforces the idea that individuals with independent self-conceptions believe they are unique. In fact, our cultural orientations toward conformity or independence may lead us to favor similarity or uniqueness *in all things*. In a study that illustrates the point, Heejung Kim and Hazel Markus (1999) showed abstract figures to subjects from the United States and Korea. Each figure contained nine parts. Most of the parts were identical in shape, position, and direction. One or more were different. Look at ● Figure 3.6. Which of the nine subfigures within each group do you like most? The American subjects liked the subfigures that were unique or in the minority, while Korean subjects preferred those that "fit in" as part of the group. In another study, these same researchers approached pedestrians of American and East Asian heritage at San Francisco's airport and had them fill out a questionnaire. Afterward, as a gift, they offered the participants a choice of one pen from a handful of pens, three or four of which had the same color barrel, green or orange. The result: 74% of the Americans chose a uniquely colored pen, and 76% of the East Asians selected a commonly colored pen! It seems that culturally ingrained orientations to conformity and independence leave a mark on us, leading us to form preferences for things that "fit in" or "stand out."

Are people from disparate cultures locked into thinking about the self in either personal or collective terms, or are both aspects present in everyone, to be expressed according to the situation? Reconsider the study noted above, where American students described themselves more in terms of personal traits and Chinese students cited more group affiliations. In a follow-up to that study, Trafimow and others (1997) tested students from Hong Kong, all of whom spoke English as a second language. One half of the students were given the "Who am I?" test in Chinese, and the other half took the test in English. Did this variation influence the results? Yes. Students who took the test in English focused more on personal traits, whereas those who took the test in Chinese focused more on group affiliations. It appears that each of us have both personal and collective aspects of the self to draw on—and that the part that comes to mind depends on the situation we are in.

The more closely social psychologists examine cultures and their impact on how people think, the more complex is the picture that emerges. Clearly, research documents the extent to which self-conceptions are influenced by the individualist and collectivist impulses within a culture. But there are other core differences as well. Kaiping Peng and Richard Nisbett (1999) note that people in East Asian cultures think in dialectical terms about contradictory characteristics—accepting, for example, that apparent opposites (such as black and white, friend and enemy, and strong and weak) can coexist within a single person either at the same time or as a result of changes over time. Grounded in Eastern

Reflecting an independent view of the self, children in Japan are taught to fit into the community. Reflecting a more independent view of the self, children in the United States are encouraged to express their individuality.

BLOOMimages/Getty Images

© Ariel Skelley/Corbis

traditions, **dialecticism** is a system of thought characterized by the acceptance of such contradictions through compromise, as implied by the Chinese proverb "Beware of your friends, not your enemies." This thought style contrasts sharply with the American and European perspective, grounded in Western logic, by which people differentiate seeming opposites on the assumption that if one is right, the other must be wrong.

Wondering if a dialectical style of thought has implications for the self, Tammy English and Serena Chen (2007) conducted a series of studies in which they questioned American college students who were of European or Asian descent about what kind of person they are in such different everyday situations as a classroom, a cafeteria, a party, or the gym. Overall, they found that compared to European Americans who portray their "true selves" as stable across the board, Asian Americans vary their self-concepts more to suit different relationship situations—though they are consistent within these situations. Other research too has shown that East Asians are more willing than Americans to see and accept contradictory aspects of themselves (Spencer-Rodgers et al., 2009)—as seen in their willingness to accept both positive and negative aspects of themselves at the same time (Boucher et al., 2009).

The study of cultural aspects of the self is also expanded by social psychologists interested in Latin American cultures, where social and emotional relationships are a particularly important part of the collectivist orientation. According to Renee Holloway and others (2009), Latino cultures prize the concept of *simpatico*, which emphasizes expressive displays of personable charm, graciousness, and hospitality. Does this cultural value become part of the Latino self-concept? Clearly, no two individuals are the same. But when these researchers presented Latino and white Americans with the "Who am I?" task described earlier, they found that the Latino participants on average were more likely to describe themselves using simpatico-related terms such as likable, friendly, sympathetic, amiable, and gracious.

Before we conclude our discussion of cultural influences, it is important to realize that cultures themselves change over time, from one generation to another. American children who grew up in the 1940s and 1950s, a generation known as "baby boomers," grew up in a very different culture than those who grew up in the 1960s and 1970s, a group commonly referred to as "GenX'ers," and those who grew up in the 1980s and 1990s, a group known as "Millenials." Analyzing questionnaire data collected from 9.2 million American high school seniors and college students from 1966 to 2009, Jean Twenge and her colleagues (2012) found that compared to boomers, subsequent generations were more focused on money, fame, and self-image and less concerned with affiliation, community, and civic engagement (see ● Figure 3.7). This change in values— described as a shift from "Generation We" to "Generation Me"—suggests that American culture is more individualistic today than it was a half century ago.

● **FIGURE 3.6**

**What's Your Preference: Similarity or Uniqueness?**

Which subfigure within each set do you prefer? Kim and Markus (1999) found that Americans tend to like subfigures that "stand out" as unique or in the minority, while Koreans tend to like subfigures that "fit in" with the surrounding group.

From Kim, H. and Marcus, H.R., "Deviance or uniqueness, harmony or conformity? A cultural analysis," *Journal of Personality and Social Psychology* vol 77 (pp. 785–800). Copyright © 1999 by the American Psychological Association. Reprinted by permission.

**dialecticism**   An Eastern system of thought that accepts the coexistence of contradictory characteristics within a single person.

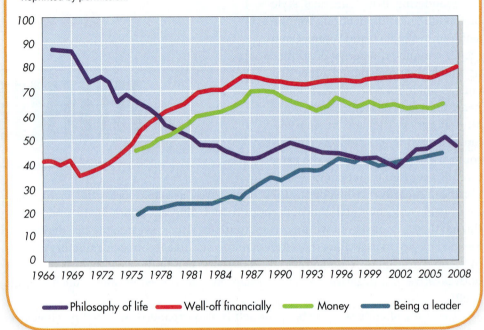

● **FIGURE 3.7**

**Generational Differences in American Cultural Orientation**

Over the years, surveys have been administered to millions of Americans who grew up in the 1940s–1950s ("baby boomers"), 1960s–1970s ("GenX'ers"), and 1980s–1990s ("Millennials"). From the responses of high school and college students from 1966 to 2009, it seems that compared to boomers, later generations were more focused on money, fame, and self-image, and less concerned with affiliation, community, and civic engagement. These changes suggest that American culture is more individualistic today than it was a half century ago.

From Twenge, J. M., Campbell, W. K., & Freeman, E. C., "Generational differences in young adults' life goals, concern for others, and civic orientation, 1966–2009," *Journal of Personality and Social Psychology* vol 102 (pp. 1045–1062). Copyright © 2012 by the American Psychological Association. Reprinted by permission.

## Self-Esteem

How do you feel about yourself? Are you generally satisfied with the way you look, your personality, academic and athletic abilities, your accomplishments, and your friendships? Are you optimistic about your future? When it comes to the self, people are not cool, objective, dispassionate observers. Rather, we are judgmental, motivated, emotional, and highly protective of our **self-esteem**—an affectively charged component of the self.

The word *esteem* comes from the Latin *aestimare*, which means "to estimate or appraise." Self-esteem thus refers to our positive and negative evaluations of ourselves (Coopersmith, 1967). Some individuals have a higher self-esteem than others do—an attribute that can have a profound impact on the way they think about, feel about, and present themselves. It's important to keep in mind, however, that although some of us have higher self-esteem than others, a feeling of self-worth is not a single trait etched permanently in stone. Rather, it is a state of mind that fluctuates up and down in response to success, failure, social relations, and other life experiences (Heatherton & Polivy, 1991).

With the self-concept made up of many self-schemas, people typically view parts of the self differently: Some parts they judge more favorably or see more clearly or as more

**self-esteem** An affective component of the self, consisting of a person's positive and negative self-evaluations.

important than other parts (Pelham, 1995). Indeed, just as individuals differ according to how high or low their self-esteem is, they also differ in the extent to which their self-esteem is stable or unstable. As a general rule, self-esteem stays roughly the same from childhood through old age (Trzesniewski et al., 2003). Yet for some people in particular, self-esteem seems to fluctuate in response to daily experiences, which makes them highly responsive to praise and overly sensitive to criticism (Baldwin & Sinclair, 1996; Kernis & Waschull, 1995; Schimel et al., 2001).

## The Need for Self-Esteem

You, me, and just about everyone else on the planet seem to have a need for self-esteem, wanting to see ourselves in a positive light. As a result of who we are and the culture we live in, each of us may value different attributes and pursue this need in different ways. Some people derive a sense of worth from their appearance; others value physical strength, professional accomplishments, wealth, people skills, or group affiliations. Whatever the source, it is clear that the pursuit of self-worth is an aspect of human motivation that runs deep. But let's step back for a moment and ask, why? Why do we seem to need self-esteem the way we need food, air, sleep, and water?

At present, there are two social psychological answers to this question. Sociometer Theory, proposed by Mark Leary and Roy Baumeister (2000), maintains that people are inherently social animals and that the desire for self-esteem is driven by a more primitive need to connect with others and gain their approval. As a result of this social connection for survival, people may have evolved a "sociometer"—a mechanism that enables us to detect acceptance and rejection and then translate these perceptions into high and low self-esteem. In this way, self-esteem serves as a rough indicator of how we're doing in the eyes of others. The threat of social rejection thus lowers self-esteem, which activates the need to regain approval and acceptance. In an experiment aimed at identifying a "neural sociometer," participants underwent fMRI while viewing positive and negative feedback words that a confederate ostensibly used to describe them (words such as *interesting* and *boring*). Participants also rated their self-esteem in response to each feedback word. Results showed that increased activity in rejection-related brain regions was associated with lowered self-esteem (Eisenberger et al., 2011).

There is a second important theory. Jeff Greenberg, Sheldon Solomon, and Thomas Pyszczynski (1997) proposed **Terror Management Theory** to help explain our relentless need for self-esteem. According to this provocative and influential theory, we humans are biologically programmed for life and self-preservation. Yet we are conscious of—and terrified by—the inevitability of our own death. To cope with this paralyzing, deeply rooted fear, we construct and accept cultural worldviews about how, why, and by whom the Earth was created; religious explanations of the purpose of our existence; and a sense of history filled with heroes, villains, and momentous events. These world views provide meaning and purpose and a buffer against anxiety. In a series of experiments, these investigators found that people react to graphic scenes of death or to the thought of their own death with intense defensiveness and anxiety. When people are given positive feedback on a test, however, which boosts their self-esteem, that reaction is muted. Other research has since confirmed this type of result (Schmeichel et al., 2009). As we'll see in later chapters, this theory has been used to explain how Americans are likely to cope with the trauma of 9/11 and the terror that it triggered (Pyszczynski et al., 2002).

**Terror Management Theory** The theory that humans cope with the fear of their own death by constructing worldviews that help to preserve their self-esteem.

As for the need for self-esteem, Pyszczynski and his colleagues (2004) put it this way:

> Self-esteem is a protective shield designed to control the potential for terror that results from awareness of the horrifying possibility that we humans are merely transient animals groping to survive in a meaningless universe, designed only to die and decay. From this perspective, each individual human's name and identity, family and social identifications, goals and aspirations, occupation and title, and humanly created adornments are draped over an animal that, in the cosmic scheme of things, may be no more significant or enduring than any individual potato, pineapple, or porcupine. (p. 436)

Confirming folk wisdom, a good deal of research shows that high and low self-esteem can color our outlook on life. People with positive self-images tend to be happy, healthy, productive, and successful. They also tend to be confident, bringing to new challenges a winning attitude that leads them to persist longer at difficult tasks, sleep better at night, maintain their independence in the face of peer pressure, and suffer from fewer ulcers. In contrast, people with negative self-images tend to be more depressed, pessimistic about the future, and prone to failure. Lacking confidence, they bring to new tasks a losing attitude that traps them in a vicious, self-defeating cycle. Expecting to fail and fearing the worst, they become anxious, exert less effort, and "tune out" on important challenges.

People with low self-esteem don't trust their own positive self-appraisals (Josephs et al., 2003). And when they fail, they tend to blame themselves, which makes them feel even less competent (Brockner, 1983; Brown & Dutton, 1995). Low self-esteem may even be hazardous to your health. Some research suggests that becoming aware of one's own negative attributes lessens the activity of certain white blood cells in the immune system, thus compromising the body's capacity to ward off disease (Strauman et al., 1993; 2004).

Does high self-esteem ensure good life outcomes? This seemingly simple question is now the subject of debate. On the one hand, based on an extensive review of the research, Roy Baumeister and others (2003) conclude that although high self-esteem leads people to feel good, take on new challenges, and persist through failure, the correlational evidence does not clearly support the strong conclusion that boosting self-esteem *causes* people to perform well in school or at work, to be socially popular, or to behave in ways that foster physical health. What's more, Jennifer Crocker and Lora Park (2004) argue that the process of pursuing self-esteem itself is costly. Specifically, they point to research showing that in trying hard to boost and maintain their self-esteem, people often become anxious, avoid activities that risk failure, neglect the needs of others, and suffer from stress-related health problems. Self-esteem has its benefits, they concede, but striving for it can also be costly. Challenging the conclusion that self-esteem is not worth striving for, William Swann and others (2007) note that although a person's overall, or *global*, sense of self-worth may not be predictive of positive life outcomes, people with specific domains of self-esteem benefit in more circumscribed ways. In other words, research suggests that individuals with high self-esteem specifically for public speaking, mathematics, or social situations will outperform those who have less self-confidence in the domains of public speaking, math, and social situations, respectively.

## Are There Gender and Race Differences?

Just as individuals differ in their self-esteem, so too do social and cultural groups. If you were to administer a self-esteem test to thousands of people all over the world, would you find that some segments of the population score higher than others? Would you expect to see differences in the averages of men and women, blacks and whites, or inhabitants of different cultures? Believing that self-esteem promotes health, happiness, and success and concerned that some groups are disadvantaged in this regard, researchers have indeed made these types of comparisons.

Are there gender differences in self-esteem? Over the years, a lot has been written in the popular press about the inflated but fragile "male ego," the low self-regard among adolescent girls and young women, and the resulting gender-related "confidence gap" (Orenstein, 1994). Does the research support this assumption? To find out, Kristin Kling and others (1999) statistically combined the results of 216 studies involving 97,000 respondents and then analyzed the surveys of 48,000 American students conducted by the National Center for Education Statistics. The result: Among adolescents and adults, males outscored females on various general measures of self-esteem. Contrary to popular belief, however, the difference was very small, particularly among older adults.

Researchers have also wondered if low self-esteem is a problem for members of stigmatized minority groups who historically have been victims of prejudice and discrimination. Does membership in a minority group, such as African Americans, deflate one's sense of self-worth? Based on the combined results of studies involving more than half a million respondents, Bernadette Gray-Little and Adam Hafdahl (2000) reported that black American children, adolescents, and adults consistently score higher—not lower—than their white counterparts on measures of self-esteem.

In a meta-analysis of hundreds of studies that compared all age groups and different American minorities, Jean Twenge and Jennifer Crocker (2002) confirmed the African American advantage in self-esteem relative to whites but found that Hispanic, Asian, and Native American minorities have lower self-esteem scores. This self-esteem advantage is not easy to interpret. Surprised by the high African American scores, some researchers have suggested that perhaps African Americans—more than other minorities—are able to preserve their self-esteem in the face of adversity by attributing negative outcomes to the forces of discrimination and using this adversity to build a sense of group pride. In this regard, Twenge and Crocker found that self-esteem scores of black Americans, relative to those of whites, have risen over time from the pre–civil rights days of the 1950s to the present.

## Self-Discrepancy Theory

What determines how people feel about themselves? According to E. Tory Higgins (1989), our self-esteem is defined by the match or mismatch between how we see ourselves and how we want to see ourselves. To demonstrate, try the following exercise. On a blank sheet of paper, write down 10 traits that describe the kind of person you think you *actually* are (smart? easygoing? sexy? excitable?). Next, list 10 traits that describe the kind of person you think you *ought* to be, characteristics that would enable you to meet your sense of duty, obligation, and responsibility. Then make a list of traits that describe the kind of person you *would like* to be, an *ideal* that embodies your hopes, wishes, and dreams. If you follow these instructions, you should have three lists: your actual self, your ought self, and your ideal self.

Research has shown that these lists can be used to predict your self-esteem and your emotional well-being. The first list is your self-concept. The others represent your personal standards, or *self-guides*. To the extent that you fall short of these standards, you will experience lowered self-esteem, negative emotion, and, in extreme cases, a serious affective disorder. The specific consequence depends on which self-guide you fail to achieve. If there's a discrepancy between your actual and ought selves, you will feel guilty, ashamed, and resentful. You might even suffer from excessive fears and anxiety-related disorders. If the mismatch is between your actual and ideal selves, you'll feel disappointed, frustrated, unfulfilled, and sad. In the worst-case scenario you might even become depressed (Boldero & Francis, 2000; Higgins, 1999; Strauman, 1992). Our self-discrepancies may even set into motion a self-perpetuating process. Participating in a study of body images, college women with high rather than low discrepancies between their actual and ideal selves were more likely to compare themselves with thin models in TV commercials, which further increased their body dissatisfaction and depression (Bessenoff, 2006).

Each and every one of us must cope with some degree of self-discrepancy. Nobody's perfect. Yet we do not all suffer from the emotional consequences. The reason, according to Higgins, is that self-esteem depends on a number of factors. One is simply the amount of discrepancy. The more of it there is, the worse we feel. Another is the importance of the discrepancy to the self. The more important the domain in which we fall short, again, the worse we feel. A third factor is how much we focus on our self-discrepancies. The more focused we are, the greater the harm. This last observation raises an important question: What causes us to be more or less focused on our personal shortcomings? For an answer, we turn to self-awareness theory.

## The Self-Awareness "Trap"

If you carefully review your daily routine—classes, work, errands, sports, leisure activities, social interactions, and meals—you will probably be surprised at how little time you actually spend thinking about yourself. In a study that illustrates this point, more than a hundred people, ranging in age from 19 to 63, were equipped for a week with electronic beepers that sounded every two hours or so between 7:30 a.m. and 10:30 p.m. Each time the beepers went off, participants interrupted whatever they were doing, wrote down what they were thinking at that moment, and filled out a brief questionnaire. Out of 4,700 recorded thoughts, only 8% were about the self. For the most part, attention was focused on work and other activities. In fact, when participants were thinking about themselves, they reported feeling relatively unhappy and wished they were doing something else (Csikszentmihalyi & Figurski, 1982).

*"I have the true feeling of myself only when I am unbearably unhappy."*

—Franz Kafka

**State of Self-Awareness**   The finding that people may be unhappy while they think about themselves is interesting, but what does it mean? Does self-reflection bring out our personal shortcomings the way staring into a mirror draws our gaze to every blemish on the face? Is self-awareness an unpleasant mental state from which we need to retreat?

Many years ago, Robert Wicklund and his colleagues theorized that the answer is yes (Duval & Wicklund, 1972; Silvia & Duval, 2001; Wicklund, 1975). According to their **self-awareness theory**, most people are not usually self-focused, but certain situations predictably force us to turn inward and become the objects of our own attention. When we talk about ourselves, glance into a mirror, stand before an audience or in front of a camera, watch ourselves on videotape, or behave in a socially conspicuous manner, we enter into a state of heightened self-awareness that leads us naturally to compare our behavior to some high standard. This comparison often results in a negative discrepancy and a temporary reduction in self-esteem as we discover that we fall short. Thus, research participants who are seated in front of a mirror tend to react more negatively to their self-discrepancies, often slipping into a negative mood state (Hass & Eisenstadt, 1990; Phillips & Silvia, 2005). Interestingly, Japanese people—whose culture already leads them to be highly concerned about their public "face"—are unaffected by the added presence of a mirror (Heine et al., 2008).

The real-life consequences can be substantial. The more self-focused people are in general, the more likely they are to find themselves in a bad mood (Flory et al., 2000) or

**self-awareness theory**   The theory that self-focused attention leads people to notice self-discrepancies, thereby motivating either an escape from self-awareness or a change in behavior.

depressed (Pyszczynski & Greenberg, 1987). People who are self-absorbed are also more likely to suffer from alcoholism, anxiety, and other clinical disorders (Mor & Winquist, 2002) and have self-destructive, suicide-related thoughts when they fail to meet their own standards (Chatard & Selimbegović, 2011).

Is there a solution? Self-awareness theory suggests two basic ways of coping with such discomfort: (1) "shape up" by behaving in ways that reduce our self-discrepancies or (2) "ship out" by withdrawing from self-awareness. According to Charles Carver and Michael Scheier (1981), the solution chosen depends on whether people think they can reduce their self-discrepancy and whether they're pleased with the progress they make once they try (Duval et al., 1992). If so, they tend to match their behavior to personal or societal standards; if not, they tune out, look for distractions, and turn attention away from the self. This process is depicted in ● Figure 3.8.

In general, research supports the prediction that when people are self-focused, they are more likely to behave in ways that are consistent either with their own personal values or with socially accepted ideals. Two interesting field studies illustrate this point. In one, Halloween trick-or-treaters—children with masks, costumes, and painted faces—were greeted at a researcher's door and left alone to help themselves from a bowl of candy. Although the children were asked to take only one piece, 34% violated the request. When a full-length mirror was placed behind the candy bowl, however, that number dropped to 12%. Apparently, the mirror forced the children to become self-focused, leading them to behave in a way that was consistent with public standards of desirable conduct (Beaman et al., 1979). In a second study, in England, customers at a lunch counter were trusted to pay for their coffee, tea, and milk by depositing money into an unsupervised "honesty box." Hanging on the wall behind the counter was a poster that featured a picture of flowers or a pair of eyes. By calculating the ratio of money deposited to drinks consumed, researchers observed that people paid nearly three times more money in the presence of the eyes (Bateson et al., 2006).

Self-awareness theory states that if a successful reduction of self-discrepancy seems unlikely, individuals will take a second route: escape from self-awareness. Roy Baumeister (1991) speculates that drug abuse, sexual masochism, spiritual ecstasy, binge eating, and suicide all serve this escapist function. Even television may serve as a form of escape. Sophia Moskalenko and Steven Heine (2003) brought college students into a laboratory and tested their actual–ideal self-discrepancies twice. Half watched a brief

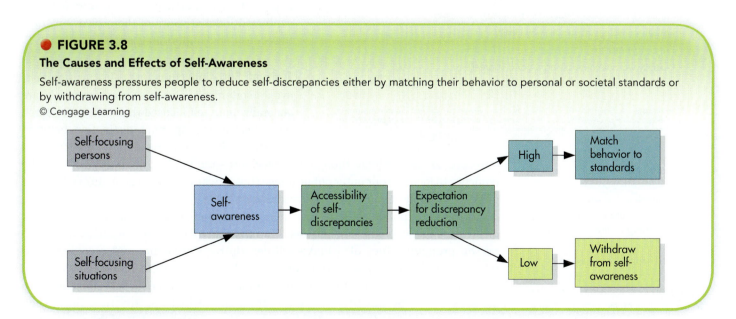

● **FIGURE 3.8**

**The Causes and Effects of Self-Awareness**

Self-awareness pressures people to reduce self-discrepancies either by matching their behavior to personal or societal standards or by withdrawing from self-awareness.

© Cengage Learning

TV show on nature before the second test. In a second study, students were sent home with the questionnaire and instructed to fill it out either before or after watching TV. In both cases, those who watched TV had lower self-discrepancies on the second measure. In yet a third study, students who were told they had done poorly on an IQ test spent more time watching TV while waiting in the lab than those who were told they had succeeded. Perhaps TV and other forms of entertainment enable people to "watch their troubles away."

One particularly disturbing health implication concerns the use of alcohol. According to Jay Hull, people often drown their sorrows in a bottle as a way to escape the negative implications of self-awareness. To test this hypothesis, Hull and Richard Young (1983) administered what was supposed to be an IQ test to male participants and gave false feedback suggesting that they had either succeeded or failed. Supposedly as part of a separate study, those participants were then asked to taste and rate different wines. As they did so, experimenters kept track of how much they drank during a 15-minute tasting period. As predicted, participants who were prone to self-awareness drank more wine after failure than after success, presumably to dodge the blow to their self-esteem. Among participants not prone to self-awareness, there was no difference in alcohol consumption. These results come as no surprise. Indeed, many of us expect alcohol to grant this form of relief (Leigh & Stacy, 1993) and help us manage our emotional highs and lows (Cooper et al., 1995).

Claude Steele and Robert Josephs (1990) believe that alcoholic intoxication offers more than just a means of tuning out on the self. By causing people to lose touch with reality and shed their inhibitions, it also evokes a state of "drunken self-inflation." In one study, for example, participants rated their actual and ideal selves on various traits—some important to self-esteem, others not important. After drinking either an 80-proof vodka cocktail or a harmless placebo, they re-rated themselves on the same traits. As measured by the perceived discrepancy between actual and ideal selves, participants who were drinking expressed inflated views of themselves on traits they considered important (Banaji & Steele, 1989).

**Trait of Self-Consciousness**   Just as *situations* evoke a state of self-awareness, some *individuals* are generally more self-focused than others. Research has revealed an important distinction between **private self-consciousness**—the tendency to introspect about our inner thoughts and feelings—and **public self-consciousness**—the tendency to focus on our outer public image (Buss, 1980; Fenigstein et al., 1975). Table 3.1 presents a sample of items used to measure these traits.

Private and public self-consciousness are distinct traits. People who score high on a test of private self-consciousness tend to fill in incomplete sentences with first-person pronouns. They also make self-descriptive statements and recognize self-relevant words more quickly than other words (Mueller, 1982; Eichstaedt & Silvia, 2003). In contrast, those who score high on a measure of public self-consciousness are sensitive to the way they are viewed from an outsider's perspective. Thus, when people were asked to draw a capital letter E on their foreheads, 43% of those with high

---

**TABLE 3.1**

**How Self-Conscious Are You?**

These sample items appear in the Self-Consciousness Scale. How many of these statements indicating private or public self-consciousness would you use to describe yourself?

**Items That Measure Private Self-Consciousness**

- I'm always trying to figure myself out.
- I'm constantly examining my motives.
- I'm often the subject of my fantasies.
- I'm alert to changes in my mood.
- I'm aware of the way my mind works when I work on a problem.

**Items That Measure Public Self-Consciousness**

- I'm concerned about what other people think of me.
- I'm self-conscious about the way I look.
- I'm concerned about the way I present myself.
- I usually worry about making a good impression.
- One of the last things I do before leaving my house is look in the mirror.

From Fenigstein, A., Scheier, M. F., and Buss, A. H., "Public and private self-consciousness: Assessment and theory," *Journal of Consulting and Clinical Psychology* vol 43 (pp. 522–527). Copyright © 1975 by the American Psychological Association. Reprinted by permission.

---

**private self-consciousness**   A personality characteristic of individuals who are introspective, often attending to their own inner states.

**public self-consciousness**   A personality characteristic of individuals who focus on themselves as social objects, as seen by others.

levels of public self-consciousness, compared with only 6% of those with low levels, oriented the E so that it was backward from their own standpoint but correct for an outside observer (Hass, 1984). People who are high in public self-consciousness are also particularly sensitive to the extent to which others share their opinions (Fenigstein & Abrams, 1993).

The distinction between private and public self-awareness has implications for the ways in which we reduce self-discrepancies. According to Higgins (1989), people are motivated to meet either their own standards or the standards held for them by significant others. If you're privately self-conscious, you listen to an inner voice and try to reduce discrepancies relative to your own standards; if you're publicly self-conscious, however, you try to match your behavior to socially accepted norms. As illustrated in ● Figure 3.9, there may be "two sides of the self: one for you and one for me" (Scheier & Carver, 1983, p. 123).

● **FIGURE 3.9**

**Revolving Images of Self**

According to self-awareness theory, people try to meet either their own standards or standards held for them by others— depending, perhaps, on whether they are in a state of private or public self-consciousness (Snyder et al., 1983). As Scheier and Carver (1983, p. 123) put it, there are "two sides of the self: one for you and one for me."

Snyder et al., 1983. © Cengage Learning

**God: Like a Camera in the Sky?**    Across nations, cultures, and religions, more than 90% of the people on Earth believe in God or some other omnipotent force. In most religions, people believe that God watches, evaluates, rewards, and punishes people for their moral and immoral behavior (Atran & Norenzayan, 2004).

For people of faith, thinking about God should trigger a state of self-focus—in the way that cameras, microphones, and other forms of surveillance do. As we saw, self-awareness theory predicts that self-focus should heighten a concern for our standards of good behavior. Does thinking about God have this effect? In a series of experiments, Will Gervais and Ara Norenzayan (2012) administered a religiosity scale to sort people into groups of high believers and low believers. All participants were then randomly assigned to complete a word task that required them to think about God, the presence of others, or something neutral. One study showed that high believers who were primed to think about God—but not low believers—became more self-aware, as if they were being observed by other people. A second study showed that thinking about God, as opposed to something neutral, led high believers to answer various questions in ways that were socially desirable—claiming, for example, that they are always good listeners and that they were never irritated by people who ask for favors (see ● Figure 3.10). For individuals of faith, note Gervais and Norenzayan, God is "like a camera in the sky."

As you might expect from this finding, other research has shown that thoughts of God can lead people of faith to behave more prosocially toward others. In one study, reported in an article entitled "God Is Watching You," participants were given ten $1 coins to keep or donate to an anonymous stranger. Before engaging in this "economic decision-making task," participants were instructed to unscramble sentences containing words that were neutral or religious (*God, divine, spirit, prophet, sacred*). How much of the $10 did the participants then leave for the stranger? Those who had worked with neutral words left an average of $1.84; those primed with God-related words left more than twice that amount, an average of $4.44 (Shariff & Norenzayan, 2007). Reasoning that thoughts of an all-knowing God should reduce people's sense of anonymity, and increase their sense of accountability, other researchers have found that reminders of God increase resistance to temptation—as measured, for example, by the number of bite-sized chocolate chip cookies participants ate in a taste-testing experiment (Laurin et al., 2012).

● **FIGURE 3.10**

**Does Thinking About God Produce Self-Awareness Effects?**

Participants classified as High or Low Believers completed a word task that led them to think about God or something neutral. Afterward, they answered questions about themselves. Consistent with self-awareness theory, thinking about God—as opposed to something neutral—led High Believers (but not Lows) to answer the questions in ways that were more socially desirable.

From Gervais, W. M., & Norenzayan, A., "Like a camera in the sky? Thinking about God increases public self-awareness and socially desirable responding," *Journal of Experimental Social Psychology* vol 48 (pp. 298–302). Copyright © 2012 Sage Publications, Inc. Reprinted with permission.

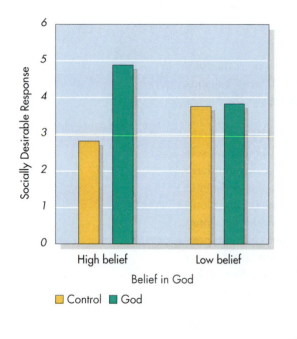

## Self-Regulation and Its Limits

To this point, we have seen that self-focused attention can motivate us to control our behavior and strive toward personal or social ideals. Achieving these goals—which enables us to reduce the self-discrepancies that haunt us—means that we must constantly engage in **self-regulation**—the processes by which we seek to control or alter our thoughts, feelings, behaviors, and urges in order to live an acceptable social life. From lifting ourselves out of bed in the early morning to dieting, running the extra mile, limiting how much we drink at a party, practicing safe sex, smiling politely at people we really don't like, and working when we have more fun things to do, the exercise of self-control is something we do all the time (Baumeister & Vohs, 2004; Carver & Scheier, 1998; Forgas et al., 2009; Heatherton, 2011).

Conflicts between our desires and need for self-control are constant. When a sample of 205 adults wore Blackberry beepers for a week and reported their current states on cue, they indicated 7,827 episodes of *desire*—including, in order, biological desires to eat, sleep, and drink, followed by desires for media use, leisure activities, social contact, grooming and hygiene, sex, work, and sports activities. In nearly half of all instances, the desire was described as posing a conflict with other of the participants' motivations, goals, and values (Hofmann et al., 2012).

Although the need is constant, Mark Muraven and Roy Baumeister (2000) theorized that self-control is a limited inner resource that can temporarily be depleted by usage. There are two components to their theory. The first is that all self-control efforts draw from a single common reservoir. The second is that exercising self-control is like flexing a muscle: Once used, it becomes fatigued and loses strength, making it more difficult to re-exert self-control—at least for a while, until the resource is replenished. Deny yourself the ice cream sundae that tickles your sweet tooth, and you'll find it more difficult to hold your temper when angered. Try to conceal your stage fright as you stand before an audience, and you'll find it harder to resist the urge to watch TV when you should be studying.

Research has supported this provocative hypothesis. Muraven and Baumeister (1998) had participants watch a brief clip from an upsetting film that shows scenes of sick and dying animals exposed to radioactive waste. Some of the participants were instructed to stifle their emotional responses to the clip, including their facial expressions; others were told to amplify or exaggerate their facial responses; a third group received no special instructions. Both before and after the movie, self-control was measured by the length of time participants were able to squeeze a handgrip exerciser without letting go. As predicted, those who had to inhibit or amplify their emotions during the film—but not those in the third group—lost their willpower in the handgrip task from the first time they tried it to the second (see ● Figure 3.11). Other studies have since confirmed the point: After people exert self-control in one task, their capacity for self-regulation is weakened—causing them to talk too much, disclose too much, or brag too much in a later social situation (Vohs et al., 2005).

**self-regulation** The process by which people control their thoughts, feelings, or behavior in order to achieve a personal or social goal.

● **FIGURE 3.11**

**Self-Control as a Limited Inner Resource**

Participants were shown an upsetting film and told to amplify or suppress their emotional responses to it (a third group received no self-control instruction). Before and afterward, self-control was measured by persistence at squeezing a handgrip exerciser. As shown, the two groups that had to control their emotions during the film—but not those in the third group—later lost their willpower on the handgrip.

Muraven & Baumeister, 1998. © Cengage Learning

It appears that we can control ourselves only so much before self-regulation fatigue sets in, causing us to "lose it." What might this mean, then, for people who constantly regulate their behavior? To find out, Kathleen Vohs and Todd Heatherton (2000) showed a brief and dull documentary to individual female college students, half of whom were chronic dieters. Placed in the viewing room—either within arm's reach (high temptation) or 10 feet away (low temptation)—was a bowl filled with Skittles, M & Ms, Doritos, and salted peanuts that participants were free to sample. After watching the movie, they were taken to another room for an ice-cream taste test and told they could eat as much as they wanted. How much ice cream did they consume? The researchers predicted that dieters seated within reach of the bowl would have to fight the hardest to avoid snacking—an act of self-control that would cost them later. The prediction was confirmed. As measured by the amount of ice cream consumed in the taste test, dieters in the high-temptation condition ate more ice cream than did all nondieters and dieters in the low-temptation situation. What's more, a second study showed that dieters who had to fight the urge in the high-temptation situation were later less persistent and quicker to give up on a set of impossible cognitive problems they were asked to solve.

Additional research suggests that self-regulation fatigue sets in because exerting self-control is physically taxing, as measured by the extent to which it consumes glucose, a vital source of bodily energy. Across a range of experiments, Matthew Gailliot and others (2007) had participants engage in an act of self-control—such as suppressing a word, thought, or emotion—before and after which blood samples were taken. Consistently, they found that acts of self-control—relative to similar acts not requiring self-control—were followed by reduced blood glucose levels and a lessened capacity for additional self-control. What's more, these researchers were able to counteract these adverse effects merely by feeding participants sugared lemonade between tasks, which restored glucose to the bloodstream.

Is it possible to counteract self-regulation fatigue through psychological intervention alone, without the calories associated with glucose consumption? Brandon Schmeichel and Kathleen Vohs (2009) reasoned that people may be able to restore their capacity for self-control by stopping to mentally bolster or "affirm" their sense of who they are. To test this hypothesis, they asked participants to write a short story. To vary the exercise of self-control, some but not others were prohibited from using certain letters of the alphabet (try writing even a short paragraph without using the letters *a* or *n* and you will appreciate the discipline that is needed!). Afterward, all participants were administered a classic pain tolerance task that required them to soak one hand in a tub of circulating ice-cold water for as long as they could, until it was too painful to continue. Between the two tasks, "self-affirmation" participants were given a chance to express a core value by writing an essay about the one personal characteristic they find most important (such as family relations, friendships, creativity, or athletics). Others wrote about some less important characteristic. Can a small act of self-affirmation counteract the effects of self-regulation fatigue on cold tolerance? Yes. Among participants in the no-affirmation condition, the prior act of self-control sharply reduced their tolerance to cold pain from an average of 78 seconds to 27 seconds. Among those who were prompted to self-affirm, however, the adverse effect of the first self-control task on pain tolerance was erased.

## > Ironic Mental Processes

There's another possible downside to self-control that is often seen in sports when athletes become so self-focused under pressure that they stiffen up and "choke." Although many athletes rise to the occasion, the pages of sports history are filled with stories of basketball players who lose their touch in the final minute of a championship game, of golfers who cannot sink a routine final putt to win a tournament, and of tennis players who lose their serve, double-faulting when it matters most. "Choking" in these ways seems to be a paradoxical type of failure caused by trying too hard and thinking too much. When you learn a new motor activity like how to throw a curve ball or land a jump, you must think through the mechanics in a slow and cautious manner. As you get better, however, your movements become automatic, so you do not have to think about timing, breathing, the position of your head and limbs, or the distribution of your weight. You relax and just do it. Unless trained to perform while self-focused, athletes under pressure often try their hardest not to fail, become self-conscious, and think too much—all of which disrupts the fluid and natural flow of their performance (Baumeister, 1984; Beilock & Carr, 2001; Gray, 2004; Lewis & Linder, 1997).

The paradoxical effects of attempted self-control are evident in other situations, too. Studying what he calls *ironic processes*, Daniel Wegner (1994) has found that,

*"The highest possible stage in moral culture is when we recognize that we ought to control our thoughts."*

—Charles Darwin

Why do some athletes choke under pressure and others rise to the occasion? Heading into the 2006 Winter Olympics in Turin, Italy, American downhill racer Bode Miller, a daredevil from New Hampshire, was favored to win several gold medals. Yet after slipping, falling, and missing gates, he failed to win a single medal, gold or otherwise (left). In contrast, American beach volleyball players Misty May-Treanor and Kerri Walsh Jennings were the twice-reigning gold medalists when they entered the 2012 Summer Olympics in London. Despite the pressure to defend their title, they turned in a series of clutch performances and won gold for the third straight Olympics (right).

at times, the harder you try to inhibit a thought, feeling, or behavior, the less likely you are to succeed. Try not to think about a white bear for the next 30 seconds, he finds, and that very image intrudes upon consciousness with remarkable frequency. Instruct the members of a jury to disregard inadmissible evidence, and the censored material is sure to pop to mind as they deliberate. Try not to worry about how long it's taking to fall asleep, and you'll stay awake. Try not to laugh in class, think about the chocolate cake in the fridge, or scratch the itch on your nose—well, you get the idea.

According to Wegner, every conscious effort at maintaining control is met by a concern about failing to do so. This concern automatically triggers an "ironic operating process" as the person, trying hard *not* to fail, searches his or her mind for the unwanted thought. The ironic process will not necessarily prevail, says Wegner. Sometimes we can put the imaginary white bear out of mind. But if the person is cognitively busy, tired, distracted, hurried, or under stress, then the ironic process, because it "just happens," will prevail over the intentional process, which requires conscious attention and effort. As Wegner (1997) put it, "Any attempt at mental control contains the seeds of its own undoing" (p. 148).

Ironic processes have been observed in a wide range of behaviors. In an intriguing study of this effect on motor behavior, Wegner and his colleagues (1998) had participants hold a pendulum (a crystalline pendant suspended from a nylon fishing line) over the center of two intersecting axes on a glass grid, which formed a +. Some participants were instructed simply to keep the pendulum steady; others were pointedly told not to allow it to swing back and forth along the horizontal axis. Try this yourself and you'll see that it's not easy to prevent all movement. In this experiment, however, the pendulum was more likely to swing horizontally when this direction was specifically forbidden. To further examine the role of mental distraction, the researchers had some participants count backward from a thousand by sevens while trying to control the pendulum. In this situation, the ironic effect was even greater. Among those who tried to prevent horizontal movement but could not concentrate fully on the task, the pendulum swayed freely back and forth in the forbidden direction (see ● Figure 3.12). Applying this logic to keeping secrets, other researchers have found that instructing word-game players to conceal hidden clues from a fellow player increased rather than decreased their tendency to leak that information (Lane et al., 2006). It may seem both comic and tragic, but at times our efforts at self-control backfire, thwarting even the best of intentions.

● **FIGURE 3.12**

**Ironic Effects of Mental Control**

In this study, participants tried to hold a pendulum motionless over a grid. As illustrated in the tracings shown here, they were better at the task when simply instructed to keep the pendulum steady (a) than when specifically told to prevent horizontal movement (c). Among participants who were mentally distracted during the task, this ironic effect was even greater (b and d). Wegner et al., 1998. © Cengage Learning

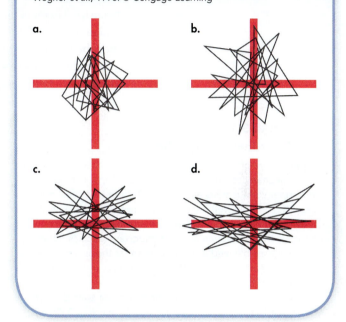

Sometimes the harder you try to control a thought, feeling, or behavior, the less likely you are to succeed. **T**RUE.

## Mechanisms of Self-Enhancement

We have seen that self-awareness can lower self-esteem by focusing attention on self-discrepancies. We have seen that people often avoid focusing on themselves and turn away from unpleasant truths but that such avoidance is not always possible. And we have seen that efforts at self-regulation often fail and sometimes even backfire. How, then, does the average person cope with his or her faults, inadequacies, and uncertain future?

**The Better-Than-Average Effect** At least in Western cultures, most people most of the time think highly of themselves. Consistently, and across a broad range of life domains, people see positive traits as more self-descriptive than negative traits, rate themselves more highly than they do others, rate themselves more highly than they are rated *by* others, exaggerate their control over life events, and predict that they have a bright future (Dunning et al., 2004; Sedikides & Gregg, 2008; Taylor, 1989).

The list of self-enhancement biases is long and impressive. Research shows that people overrate their effectiveness as speakers to an audience (Keysar & Henly, 2002); overestimate their own contributions to a group and how much they would be missed if absent (Savitsky et al., 2003); selectively recall positive feedback while neglecting the negative (Green et al., 2008); believe that they will achieve more in the future than they had in the past (Johnson, 2009); recognize themselves in self-portraits that were digitally morphed with 10% of another face that is highly attractive (Eply & Whitchurch, 2008); and credit themselves but not others for future but yet unrealized potential (Williams et al., 2012). Relative to others and across a wide range of domains, it seems that people in general believe they are better, more honorable, more capable, and more compassionate. This pattern is known as the "better-than-average" effect.

What is particularly interesting is that people are more likely to see themselves as better than average when it comes to personal traits that are important. Jonathon Brown (2012) presented participants with a list of characteristics and, for each one, he asked them to rate how important it is, how well it describes the self, and how well it describes most other people. ● Figure 3.13 shows that the effect is greater for traits that were rated as high in importance (such as *honest, kind, responsible,* and *intelligent*) than for traits of lesser importance (such as *conscientious, agreeable, imaginative,* and *outgoing*).

**Implicit Egotism** It is clear and perhaps not surprising that people tilt positive when asked explicitly to evaluate themselves relative to other people. Other research suggests that people also exhibit **implicit egotism**—an unconscious and subtle expression of self-esteem. Implicit egotism is illustrated in various types of research—such as studies showing that people are *quicker* to associate "self" words with positive traits than with negative traits. Particularly interesting is the finding that people evaluate the letters contained within their own names more favorably than other letters of the alphabet (Hoorens & Nuttin, 1993). This name-letter effect is also found in people's preferences for their own birthday numbers (Jones et al., 2004).

In an article entitled "Why Susie Sells Seashells by the Seashore," Brett Pelham and his colleagues (2002) theorized that the positive associations people form with the sight and sound of their own name may draw them toward other people, places, and entities that share this most personal aspect of "self." In a thought-provoking series of studies, these researchers examined several important life choices that we make and found that people exhibit a small but statistically detectable tendency to gravitate toward things that contain the letters of their own name. For example, men and women are more

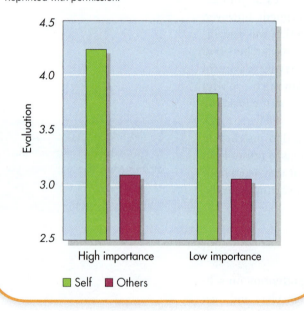

● **FIGURE 3.13**

**The Better-Than-Average Effect**

In general, people see themselves as better than others on a range of characteristics. In this study, participants rated how important various traits are, how well these traits describe the self, and how well they describe most other people. As shown, the better-than-average effect was more prominent for traits that were seen as more important (such as *honest, kind, responsible,* and *intelligent*) than for those seen as less important (such as *conscientious, agreeable, imaginative,* and *outgoing*).

From Brown, J. D., "Understanding the better than average effect: Motives (still) matter," *Personality and Social Psychology Bulletin* vol 38 (pp. 209–219). Copyright © 2012 Sage Publications, Inc. Reprinted with permission.

**implicit egotism** A nonconscious form of self-enhancement.

likely than would be predicted by chance to live in places (Mike in Michigan, George in Georgia), attend schools (Kari from the University of Kansas, Preston from Penn State University), and choose careers (Dennis and Denise as dentists) whose names resemble their own. Marriage records found on various genealogical websites also indicate that people are disproportionately likely to marry others with first or last names that resemble their own (Jones et al., 2004). Perhaps in a subtle but remarkable way, we unconsciously seek out reflections of the self in our surroundings (Pelham et al., 2005).

Uri Simonsohn (2011) is not so sure. Although impressed with evidence for implicit egotism in the laboratory, Simonsohn re-analyzed the real-life data and concluded that too often the links resulted from a statistical fluke. Consider the finding that people are more likely than expected to marry others whose names resemble their own. A closer look at these numbers reveals that the name effect results from an "ethnic bias" so that people often marry others who share the same Hispanic, Asian, or other group's last name. As for women named Georgia from that state, birth records show that more babies born in Georgia are named after the state of Georgia. To sum up: It's clear that people prefer the letters of their own name and the number of their own birthday. What is less clear is whether these preferences influence the highest stakes decisions we make with regard to a marriage partner, or career, or a place to live.

Research on implicit egotism shows that people hold themselves in high regard. We can't all be perfect, however, nor can we all be better than average. So what supports this common illusion? In this section, we examine four methods that people use to rationalize or otherwise enhance their self-esteem: self-serving beliefs, self-handicapping, basking in reflected glory, and downward social comparisons.

**Self-Serving Beliefs**    How well did you do on the SAT? When James Shepperd (1993b) asked college students about their performance on this infamous college entrance test, he uncovered two interesting patterns. First, the students overestimated their actual scores by an average of 17 points. This inflationary distortion was most pronounced among those with relatively low scores, and it persisted somewhat even when students knew that the experimenter would check their academic files. Second, a majority of students whose SAT scores were low described their scores as inaccurate and the test in general as invalid. In fact, the SATs for the group as a whole were predictive of their grade point averages. It's not that people are delusional. But as memories fade, which can occur with the passage of time, the potential for self-enhancing recollections of test scores is increased (Willard & Gramzow, 2008).

> *"We don't see things as they are, we see them as we are."*
> —Anaïs Nin

When students receive exam grades, those who do well take credit for the success; those who do poorly complain about the instructor or test questions. When researchers have articles accepted for publication, they credit the quality of their work; when articles are rejected, they blame the editors and reviewers. When gamblers win a bet, they marvel at their skillfulness; when they lose, they blame fluke events that transformed near-victory into defeat. Whether people have high or low self-esteem, explain their own outcomes publicly or in private, and try to be honest or to make a good impression, there is bias. Across a range of cultures, people tend to take credit for success and distance themselves from failure (Mezulis et al., 2004; Schlenker et al., 1990)—all while seeing themselves as objective, not biased (Pronin et al., 2004).

Most of us are also unrealistically optimistic about the future. College students who were asked to predict their own futures compared with that of the average peer believed that they would graduate higher in their class, get a better job, have a happier marriage, and bear a gifted child. They also believed that they were less likely to get

Don Murray/Getty Images

In casinos, racetracks, and lotteries, gamblers lose billions of dollars a year. This self-defeating behavior persists in part because people exaggerate their control over random events. For example, craps players often blow on the dice, or throw hard, or throw soft, as if they can control the outcome.

**self-handicapping** Behaviors designed to sabotage one's own performance in order to provide a subsequent excuse for failure.

fired or divorced, have a car accident, become depressed, be victimized by crime, or suffer a heart attack (Weinstein, 1980). In sports, politics, health, and social issues, people exhibit an optimistic bias—essentially a case of wishful thinking—about their own future, judging desirable events as more likely to occur than undesirable events (Krizan & Windschitl, 2007; Lench, 2009).

Perhaps one reason that people are eternally optimistic is that they harbor illusions of control, overestimating the extent to which they can influence personal outcomes that are not, in fact, within their power to control (Thompson, 1999). In a series of classic experiments on the illusion of control, Ellen Langer (1975) found that college students bet more money in a chance game of high-card when their opponent seemed nervous rather than confident and were more reluctant to sell a lottery ticket if they'd chosen the number themselves than if it was assigned. Emily Pronin and others (2006) tested the related hypothesis that imagining an event before it occurs can lead people to think they had influenced it. In one study, for example, participants watched a trained confederate shoot hoops on a basketball court. Before each shot, they were instructed to visualize his success ("the shooter releases the ball and it swooshes through the net") or an irrelevant event ("the shooter's arm curls to lift a dumbbell"). After the confederate's successful shooting spree, spectators rated the extent of their influence over his performance. As if linking thoughts to outcomes, they exhibited an illusion of mental causation, taking more credit when they had visualized the shooter's success than when they had not.

**Self-Handicapping** "My dog ate my homework." "I had a flat tire." "My alarm didn't go off." "My computer crashed." "I had a bad headache." "The referee blew the call." On occasion, people make excuses for their past performance. Sometimes they even come up with excuses in anticipation of future performance. Particularly when people are afraid that they might fail in an important situation, they use illness, shyness, anxiety, pain, trauma, and other complaints as excuses (Kowalski, 1996; Snyder & Higgins, 1988). The reason people do this is simple: By admitting to a limited physical or mental weakness, they can shield themselves from what could be the most shattering implication of failure—a lack of ability.

One form of excuse-making that many of us can relate to is procrastination—a purposive delay in starting or completing a task that is due at a particular time (Ferrari et al., 1995). Some people procrastinate chronically, whereas others do so only in certain situations. The phenomenon itself is found in a number of cultures—including Spain, Peru, Venezuela, England, Australia, and the United States, where nearly 15% of men and women identify themselves as chronic procrastinators (Ferrari et al., 2007). There are many reasons why someone might put off what needs to get done—whether it's studying for a test, shopping for Christmas, or preparing for the April 15 tax deadline. According to Joseph Ferrari (1998), one "benefit" of procrastinating is that it helps to provide an excuse for possible failure.

Making excuses is one way to cope with the threatening implications of failure. Under certain conditions, this strategy is taken one step further, as when people actually sabotage their own performance. It seems like the ultimate paradox, but there are times when we purposely set ourselves up for failure in order to preserve our precious self-esteem. As first described by Stephen Berglas and Edward Jones (1978), **self-handicapping** refers to actions people take to handicap their own performance in order to build an excuse for anticipated failure. To demonstrate, Berglas and Jones recruited college students for an experiment supposedly concerning the effects of drugs on intellectual performance. All the participants worked on a 20-item test of analogies and were told that they had done well, after which they expected to work on a second, similar test. For one group, the problems in the first test were relatively easy, leading participants to expect more success in the second test; for a second group, the problems were insoluble, leaving participants confused about their initial success and worried about possible failure. Before seeing or taking the second test, participants were given a choice of two drugs: Actavil, which was supposed to improve performance, and Pandocrin, which was supposed to impair it.

Although no drugs were actually administered, most participants who were confident about the upcoming test selected the Actavil. In contrast, most males (but not females) who feared the outcome of the second test chose the Pandocrin. By handicapping themselves, these men set up a convenient excuse for failure—an excuse, we should add, that may have been intended more for the experimenter's benefit than for the benefit of the participants themselves. A follow-up study showed that although self-handicapping occurs when the experimenter witnesses the participants' drug choice, it is reduced when the experimenter is not present while that choice is being made (Kolditz & Arkin, 1982).

Some people use self-handicapping as a defense more than others do—and in different ways (Rhodewalt, 1990). For example, some men self-handicap by taking drugs (Higgins & Harris, 1988) or neglecting to practice (Hirt et al., 1991), whereas women tend to report stress and physical symptoms (Smith et al., 1983). Another tactic is to set one's goals too high, as perfectionists like to do, which sets up failure that is not interpreted to reflect a lack of ability (Hewitt et al., 2003). Yet another paradoxical tactic used to reduce performance pressure is for people to play down their own ability, lower expectations, and publicly predict that they will fail—a self-presentation strategy called *sandbagging* (Gibson & Sachau, 2000). People also differ in their reasons for self-handicapping. Dianne Tice (1991) found that people who are low in self-esteem use self-handicapping to set up a defensive, face-saving excuse in case they fail, whereas those who are high in self-esteem use it as an opportunity to claim extra credit if they succeed.

Whatever the tactics and whatever the goal, self-handicapping seems like an ingenious strategy: With the odds seemingly stacked against us, the self is insulated from failure and enhanced by success. Of course, this strategy is not without a cost. Sabotaging ourselves—by not practicing or by drinking too much, faking illness, or setting goals too high—objectively increases the risk of failure. What's worse, it does not exactly endear us to others. Frederick Rhodewalt and his colleagues (1995) found that participants did not like their partners in an experiment when they thought that these partners had self-handicapped by claiming they did not care, were anxious, or were medically impaired. Women in particular are suspicious and critical of people who self-handicap (Hirt et al., 2003).

**People often sabotage their own performance in order to protect their self-esteem.  T**RUE.

**Basking in Reflected Glory**    To some extent, your self-esteem is influenced by individuals and groups with whom you identify. According to Robert Cialdini and his colleagues (1976), people often **bask in reflected glory (BIRG)** by showing off their connections to successful others. Cialdini's team first observed BIRGing on the university campuses of Arizona State, Louisiana State, Notre Dame, Michigan, Pittsburgh, Ohio State, and Southern California. On the Monday mornings after football games, they counted the number of school sweatshirts worn on campus and found that more of them were worn if the team had won its game on the previous Saturday. In fact, the larger the margin of victory was, the more school shirts they counted.

**bask in reflected glory (BIRG)**  To increase self-esteem by associating with others who are successful.

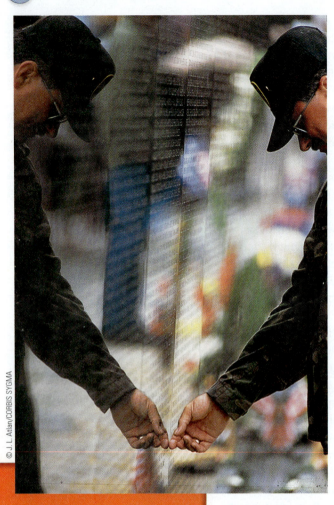

© J. L. Atlan/CORBIS SYGMA

When Vietnam veterans returned home without victory some 40 years ago, they were neglected, even scorned, by the American public. It seems that the tendency to bask in reflected glory is matched by an equally powerful need to cut off reflected failure.

**downward social comparison** The defensive tendency to compare ourselves with others who are worse off than we are.

To evaluate the effects of self-esteem on BIRGing, Cialdini gave students a general-knowledge test and rigged the results so half would succeed and half would fail. The students were then asked to describe in their own words the outcome of a recent football game. In these descriptions, students who thought they had just failed a test were more likely than those who thought they had succeeded to share in their team's victory by exclaiming that "we won" and to distance themselves from defeat by lamenting how "*they* lost." In another study, participants coming off a recent failure were quick to point out that they had the same birth date as someone known to be successful—thus BIRGing by a merely coincidental association (Cialdini & De Nicholas, 1989).

If self-esteem is influenced by our links to others, how do we cope with friends, family members, teammates, and co-workers of low status? Again, consider sports fans, an interesting breed. They loudly cheer their team in victory, but they often turn and jeer their team in defeat. This behavior seems fickle, but it is consistent with the notion that people derive part of their self-esteem from associations with others. In one study, participants took part in a problem-solving team that then succeeded, failed, or received no feedback about its performance. Participants were later offered a chance to take home a team badge. In the success and no-feedback groups, 68% and 50%, respectively, took badges; in the failure group, only 9% did (Snyder et al., 1986). For die-hard sports fans—male and female alike—the tendency to bask in reflected glory is matched by an equally powerful tendency to CORF—that is, to cut off reflected failure (Ware & Kowalski, 2012).

**Downward Social Comparisons** Earlier, we discussed Festinger's (1954) theory that people evaluate themselves by comparison with similar others. But contemplate the implications. If the people around us achieve more than we do, what does that do to our self-esteem? Perhaps adults who shy away from class reunions in order to avoid having to compare themselves with former classmates are acting out an answer to that question.

Festinger fully realized that people don't always seek out objective information and that social comparisons are sometimes made in self-defense. When a person's self-esteem is at stake, he or she often benefits from making **downward social comparisons** with others who are less successful, less happy, or less fortunate (Wills, 1981; Wood, 1989). Research shows that people who suffer some form of setback or failure adjust their social comparisons in a downward direction (Gibbons et al., 2002) and that these comparisons have an uplifting effect on their mood and on their outlook for the future (Aspinwall & Taylor, 1993; Gibbons & McCoy, 1991).

Although Festinger never addressed the issue, Anne Wilson and Michael Ross (2000) note that in addition to making social comparisons between ourselves and similar others, we make *temporal* comparisons between our past and present selves. In one study, these investigators had college students describe themselves; in another, they analyzed the autobiographical accounts of celebrities appearing in popular magazines. In both cases, they counted the number of times the self-descriptions contained references to past selves, to future selves, and to others. The result was that people made more comparisons to their own past selves than to others, and most of these temporal comparisons were favorable. Other research has confirmed the basic point. Keenly aware of how "I'm better today than when I was in the past," people use downward temporal comparisons the way they use downward social comparisons as a means of self-enhancement (Zell & Alicke, 2009).

Whether people make upward or downward social comparisons can have striking health implications. When victimized by tragic life events (perhaps a crime, an accident, a disease, or the death of a loved one), people like to *affiliate* with others in the same predicament who have adjusted well, role models who offer hope and guidance. But they tend to *compare* themselves with others who are worse off, a form of downward social comparison (Taylor & Lobel, 1989).

Clearly it helps to know that life could be worse, which is why most cancer patients tend to compare themselves with others in the same predicament but who are adjusting less well than they are. In a study of 312 women who had early-stage breast cancer and were in peer support groups, Laura Bogart and Vicki Helgeson (2000) had the patients report every week for seven weeks on instances in which they talked to, heard about, or thought about another patient. They found that 53% of all the social comparisons made were downward, to others who were worse off; only 12% were upward, to others who were better off (the rest were "lateral" comparisons to similar or dissimilar others). Bogart and Helgeson also found that the more often patients made these social comparisons, the better they felt. Downward social comparison is also associated with an ability to cope with the kinds of life regrets that sometimes haunt people as they get older. Adult development researchers have observed that aging adults often experience intense feelings of regret over decisions made, contacts lost, opportunities passed up, and the like—and these regrets can compromise the quality of their lives. Isabelle Bauer and others (2008) asked adults ranging from 18 to 83 years old to disclose their biggest regret and then indicate whether their same-age peers had regrets that were more or less severe. Among the older adults in the sample, those who tended to see others as having more severe regrets than their own felt better than those who saw their others as less regretful.

## > Are Positive Illusions Adaptive?

Psychologists used to maintain that an accurate perception of reality is vital to mental health. In recent years, however, this view has been challenged by research on the mechanisms of self-enhancement. Consistently, as we have seen, people preserve their self-esteem by deluding themselves and others with biased beliefs, self-handicapping, BIRGing, and downward comparisons. The result: Most people see themselves as better than average. Are these strategies a sign of health and well-being or are they symptoms of disorder?

When Shelley Taylor and Jonathon Brown (1988) first reviewed the research, they found that individuals who are depressed or low in self-esteem actually have more realistic views of themselves than do most others who are better adjusted. Their self-appraisals are more likely to match appraisals of them made by neutral observers, they make fewer self-serving attributions to account for success and failure, they are less likely to exaggerate their control over uncontrollable events, and they make more balanced predictions about their future. Based on these results, Taylor and Brown reached the provocative conclusion that positive illusions promote happiness, the desire to care for others, and the ability to engage in productive work—hallmark attributes of mental health: "These illusions help make each individual's world a warmer and more active and beneficent place in which to live" (p. 205). People with high self-esteem thus appear to be better adjusted in personality tests and in interviews rated by friends, strangers, and mental health professionals (Taylor et al., 2003).

Drawing on evolutionary theory, William von Hippel and Robert Trivers (2011) have offered a new and provocative perspective on the adaptive advantages of self-deception. Over the years, evolutionary psychologists have noted that deceit is a communication skill that animals use to curry favor, attract a mate, and influence others to share food, shelter, and other resources. Just as humans have evolved ways to deceive others, we have also evolved ways to detect deception in others. The more skilled we are in these interactions, the more we flourish. The problem is that when people lie, they become nervous, try to suppress the nervousness, and work hard to make the lie sound believable—especially when talking to others who know them. Here's the hitch: If deceivers can convince themselves that their deception is true, they will not be as nervous, not have to suppress, not have to work so hard at the presentation, and, therefore, be more successful. As *Seinfeld* character George Costanza advised Jerry, who was scheduled to take a lie-detector test, "It's not a lie if *you* believe it."

When it comes to the illusion of control, unrealistic optimism, and the other self-enhancement biases that enable people to see themselves as better than average, von Hippel and Trivers (2011) extend their argument: By deceiving ourselves in ways that create positive illusions, we are able to display greater confidence in public than we may actually feel, making us more successful our social relations. Perhaps this explains the research finding that people tend to overestimate the self-esteem of other people—independent of how well we know them (Kilianski, 2008).

Not everyone agrees with the notion that it is adaptive in the long run to wear rose-colored glasses. Roy Baumeister and Steven Scher (1988) warned that positive illusions can give rise to chronic patterns of self-defeating behavior, as when people escape from self-awareness through alcohol and other drugs, self-handicap themselves into failure and underachievement, deny health-related problems until it's too late for treatment, and rely on the illusion of control to protect them from the inescapable odds of the gambling casino. Others have noted that people sometimes need to be self-critical in order to improve. In a study on success and failure feedback, Heine and others (2001) found that whereas North American college students persisted less on a task after an initial failure than after success, Japanese students persisted more in this situation. Sometimes we have to face up to our shortcomings in order to correct them.

From an interpersonal standpoint, C. Randall Colvin and others (1995) found that people with inflated rather than realistic views of themselves were rated less favorably on certain dimensions by their own friends. In their studies, self-enhancing men were seen as boastful, condescending, hostile, and less considerate of others; self-enhancing women were seen as more hostile, more defensive and sensitive to criticism, more likely to overreact to minor setbacks, and less well liked. People with inflated self-images may make a good first impression on others, but they are liked less and less as time wears on (Paulhus, 1998).

In a study that illustrates this possible dark side of high self-esteem, Todd Heatherton and Kathleen Vohs (2000) administered a self-esteem test to pairs of unacquainted college students and then brought them together for a brief conversation. Just before meeting, one student within each pair took a "Remote Associates Test," which involved finding one word that connects sets of three seemingly unrelated words (for example, *lick, sprinkle,* and *mines* were linked by the word *salt*). For half of these target students, the test was pitched as experimental, and the problems given to them were easy to solve. Others were told that the test measured achievement potential and were given very difficult problems, leading them to perform, supposedly, worse than average. Did this ego-threatening feedback affect the students' behavior—and the impressions they made on their interaction partners? In the no-ego-threat group, the high and low self-esteem students were equally well liked. In the ego-threat situation, however, students with high self-esteem became less likable; in fact, they were rated by their partners as rude, unfriendly, and arrogant.

Realism or illusion—which orientation is more adaptive? As social psychologists debate the short-term and long-term effects of positive illusions, and their evolutionary advantages, it seems that there is no simple answer. For now, the picture that has emerged is this: People who harbor positive illusions of themselves are likely to enjoy the benefits and achievements of high self-esteem and social influence. But these same individuals may pay a price in other ways, as in their relations with others. Do positive illusions motivate personal achievement but alienate us socially from others? Is it adaptive to see oneself in slightly inflated terms but maladaptive to take a view that is too biased? It will be interesting to see how this thorny debate is resolved in the years to come.

## Culture and Self-Esteem

Earlier we saw that inhabitants of individualistic cultures tend to view themselves as distinct and autonomous, whereas those in collectivist cultures view the self as part of an interdependent social network. Do these different orientations have implications for self-esteem? This turns out to be a tricky question.

Steven Heine and his colleagues (1999) argued that cultures have differing effects on the pursuit of self-esteem. Comparing the distribution of self-esteem test scores in Canada and Japan, they found that whereas most Canadians' scores clustered in the high-end range, a majority of Japanese respondents scored in the center of that same range. In other studies, they also observed that Japanese respondents can sometimes be quite self-critical, talking about themselves in negative, self-effacing terms.

Do Japanese people have a less positive self-esteem compared to North Americans? Or do Japanese respondents have a positive self-esteem but feel compelled to present themselves modestly *to others* (as a function of the collectivist need to "fit in" rather than "stand out")? To answer this question, some researchers have used indirect, subtle, "implicit" tests of self-esteem—tests that would enable them to measure a person's self-esteem without his or her awareness. In a timed word-association study, researchers found that despite their lower scores on overt self-esteem tests, Asian Americans—just like their European American counterparts—are quicker to associate themselves with positive words like *happy* and *sunshine* than with negative words such as *vomit* and *poison* (Greenwald & Farnham, 2000; Kitayama & Uchida, 2003). In keeping with the Eastern dialectical perspective described earlier, other implicit self-esteem research has shown that although East Asians, like Westerners, are quick to associate the self with positive traits, they are more likely to associate the self with contradictory negative traits as well (Boucher et al., 2009).

Drawing on these results, Constantine Sedikides and his colleagues (2003) maintain that people from individualist and collectivist cultures are similarly motivated to think highly of themselves—that the burning need for positive self-regard is universal, or "pancultural." The observed differences, they argue, stem from the fact that cultures influence *how* we seek to fulfill that need: Individualists present themselves as unique and self-confident, whereas collectivists present themselves as modest, equal members of a group. From this perspective, people are tactical in their self-enhancements, exhibiting self-praise or humility depending on what is desirable within their cultural surroundings (J. D. Brown, 2003; Lalwani et al., 2006; Sedikides et al., 2005). As for what is desirable—when Japanese and American students evaluated a fictitious person on the basis of his or her high or low responses on a self-esteem questionnaire, Americans showed a stronger preference for the high-self esteem person (Brown, 2010).

Heine and his colleagues agree only in part with this interpretation of the research. They too argue that all people have a need for positive self-regard, wanting to become "good selves" within their own culture. They note, however, that in the effort to achieve this goal, Westerners and other individualists tend to use self-enhancement tactics to stand out, confirm, and express themselves, whereas East Asians and other collectivists tend to maintain face in order to fit in, improve the self, and adjust to the standards set by their groups. In short, the underlying need for positive self-regard is universal, but the specific drive toward self-enhancement is culturally ingrained (Heine, 2005; Heine & Hamamura, 2007).

# Self-Presentation

The human quest for self-knowledge and esteem tells us about the inner self. The portrait is not complete, however, until we paint in the outermost layer, the behavioral expression of the social self. Most people are acutely concerned about the image they present to others. The fashion industry, cosmetic surgeries designed to reshape everything from eyelids and noses to buttocks and breasts, and the endless search for miracle drugs that grow hair, remove hair, whiten teeth, freshen breath, and smooth out wrinkles all exploit our preoccupation with physical appearance. In a similar manner, we are concerned about the impressions we convey through our public behavior both in person and on Facebook, LinkedIn, and other social networking sites.

These days, people self-consciously present a public self to others on Facebook and other online social-networking sites.

Thomas Gilovich and others (2000) found that people are so self-conscious in public settings that they are often subject to the *spotlight effect*, a tendency to believe that the social spotlight shines more brightly on them than it really does. In one set of studies, participants were asked to wear a T-shirt with a flattering or embarrassing image into a room full of strangers, after which they estimated how many of those strangers would be able to identify the image. Demonstrating that people self-consciously feel as if all eyes are upon them, the T-shirted participants overestimated by 23% to 40% the number of observers who had noticed and could recall what they were wearing. Follow-up studies have similarly shown that when people commit a public social blunder, they later overestimate the negative impact of their behavior on those who had observed them (Savitsky et al., 2001).

John Moore/Getty Images

In *As You Like It*, William Shakespeare wrote, "All the world's a stage, and all the men and women merely players." This insight was first put into social science terms by sociologist Erving Goffman (1959), who argued that life is like a theater and that each of us acts out certain *lines*, as if from a script. Most important, said Goffman, is that each of us assumes a certain *face*, or social identity, that others politely help us maintain. Inspired by Goffman's theory, social psychologists study **self-presentation**—the process by which we try to shape what other people think of us and what we think of ourselves (Schlenker, 2003). An act of self-presentation may take many different forms. It may be conscious or unconscious, accurate or misleading, or intended for an external audience or for ourselves. In this section, we look at the various goals of self-presentation and the ways that people try to achieve these goals.

**self-presentation** Strategies people use to shape what others think of them.

## Strategic Self-Presentation

There are basically two types of self-presentation, each serving a different motive. *Strategic self-presentation* consists of our efforts to shape others' impressions in specific ways in order to gain influence, power, sympathy, or approval. Prominent examples of strategic self-presentation are everywhere: in personal ads, in online message boards, in political campaign promises, in defendants' appeals to the jury. The specific goals vary and include the desire to be seen as likable, competent, moral, dangerous, or helpless. Whatever the goal may be, people find it less effortful to present themselves in ways that are accurate rather than contrived (Vohs et al., 2005).

To illustrate this point, Beth Pontari and Barry Schlenker (2000) instructed research participants who tested as introverted or extroverted to present themselves to a job interviewer in a way that was consistent or inconsistent with their true personality. Without distraction, all participants successfully presented themselves as introverted or extroverted, depending on the task they were given. But could they present themselves as needed if, during the interview, they also had to keep an eight-digit number in mind for a memorization test? In this situation, cognitively busy participants self-presented successfully when asked to convey their true personalities but not when asked to portray themselves in a way that was out of character.

The specific identities that people try to present may vary from one person and situation to another. However, two strategic self-presentation goals are very common. The first is *ingratiation*, a term used to describe acts that are motivated by the desire to "get along" with others and be liked. The other is *self-promotion*, a term used to describe acts that are motivated by a desire to "get ahead" and gain respect for one's competence (Arkin, 1981; Jones & Pittman, 1982). As shown in Table 3.2, observations of employment interviews reveal that ingratiation and self-promotion are the most common self-presentation tactics that job applicants use (Stevens & Kristof, 1995) and that these tactics lead recruiters to form positive impressions (Higgins & Judge, 2004).

---

**TABLE 3.2**

**Strategic Self-Presentation in the Employment Interview**

In studies of the influence tactics that job applicants report using in employment interviews, the following uses of ingratiation and self-promotion were commonly reported.

**Ingratiation**

- I complimented the interviewer or organization.
- I discussed interests I shared in common with the recruiter.
- I indicated my interest in the position and the company.
- I indicated my enthusiasm for working for this organization.
- I smiled a lot or used other friendly nonverbal behaviors.

**Self-Promotion**

- I played up the value of positive events that I took credit for.
- I described my skills and abilities in an attractive way.
- I took charge during the interview to get my main points across.
- I took credit for positive events even if I was not solely responsible.
- I made positive events I was responsible for appear better than they actually were.

Higgins & Judge, 2004; Stevens & Kristof, 1995. © Cengage Learning

On the surface, it seems easy to achieve these goals. When people want to be liked, they put their best foot forward, smile a lot, nod their heads, express agreement, and, if necessary, use favors, compliments, and flattery. When people want to be admired for their competence, they try to impress others by talking about themselves and immodestly showing off their status, knowledge, and exploits. In both cases, there are trade-offs. As the term brown-nosing graphically suggests, ingratiation tactics need to be subtle or else they will backfire (Jones, 1964). People also do not like those who relentlessly trumpet and brag about their own achievements (Godfrey et al., 1986) or who exhibit a "slimy" pattern of being friendly to their superiors but not to subordinates (Vonk, 1998).

Self-presentation may give rise to other problems as well. Suggesting that "Self-Presentation Can Be Hazardous to Your Health," Mark Leary and his colleagues (1994) reviewed evidence suggesting that the need to project a favorable public image can lure us into unsafe patterns of behavior. For example, self-presentation concerns can increase the risk of AIDS (as when men are too embarrassed to buy condoms and talk openly with their sex partners), skin cancer (as when people bake under the sun to get an attractive tan), eating disorders (as when women over-diet or use amphetamines, laxatives, and forced vomiting to stay thin), drug abuse (as when teenagers smoke, drink, and use drugs to impress their peers), and accidental injury (as when young men drive recklessly to look fearless to others).

## Self-Verification

In contrast to strategic self-presentation is a second motive, *self-verification*: the desire to have others perceive us as we truly perceive ourselves. According to William Swann (1987), people are highly motivated in their social encounters to confirm or verify their existing self-concept in the eyes of others. Swann and his colleagues have gathered a great deal of evidence for this hypothesis and have found, for example, that people selectively elicit, recall, and accept personality feedback that confirms their self-conceptions. In fact, people sometimes bend over backward to correct others whose impressions are positive but mistaken. In one study, participants interacted with a confederate who later said that they seemed dominant or submissive. When the comment was consistent with the participant's self-concept, it was accepted at face value. Yet when it was inconsistent, participants went out of their way to prove the confederate wrong: Those who perceived themselves as dominant but were labeled submissive later behaved more assertively than usual; those who viewed themselves as submissive but were labeled dominant subsequently became even more docile (Swann & Hill, 1982).

Self-verification seems desirable, but do people who harbor a negative self-concept want others to share that impression? Nobody is perfect, and everyone has some faults. But do we really want to verify these faults in the eyes of others? Do those of us who feel painfully shy, socially awkward, or insecure about an ability want others to see these weaknesses? Or would we prefer to present ourselves in public as bold, graceful, or competent? What happens when the desire for self-verification clashes with the need for self-enhancement?

Seeking to answer this question, Swann and his colleagues (1992) asked each student participant in a laboratory study to fill out a self-concept questionnaire and then choose an interaction partner from two other participants—one who supposedly had evaluated them favorably and a second who had supposedly evaluated them unfavorably. The result? Although participants with a positive self-concept chose partners who viewed them in a positive light, a majority of those with a negative self-concept preferred partners who confirmed their admitted shortcomings. In a later study, 64% of participants with low self-esteem (compared with only 25% with high self-esteem) sought clinical feedback about their weaknesses rather than strengths when given a choice (Giesler et al., 1996). Indeed, research suggests that people also prefer to interact with others who verify their group memberships, an aspect of their collective self (Chen et al., 2009).

If people seek self-verification from laboratory partners, it stands to reason that they would want the same from their close relationships. In a study of married couples, husbands and wives separately answered questions about their self-concepts, their spouse, and their commitment to the marriage. As predicted, people who had a positive self-concept expressed more commitment to partners who appraised them favorably, whereas those with a negative self-concept felt more committed to partners who appraised them unfavorably (Swann et al., 1992).

On important aspects of the self-concept, research shows that people would rather reflect on and learn more about their positive qualities than negative ones. Still, it appears that the desire for self-verification is powerful and can even, at times, trump the need for self-enhancement. We all want to make a good impression, but we also want others in our lives to have an accurate impression (Swann & Bosson, 2010). Studying online social-networking sites, Mitja Back and others (2010) found strong support for this proposition. These researchers studied 236 Facebook users in the United States and Germany and found that the impressions conveyed by their posted profiles correlated highly with a combination of objective personality tests, self-reports, and reports from a sample of well-acquainted friends.

"I don't want to be defined by who I am."

## Self-Monitoring

Although self-presentation is a way of life for all of us, it differs considerably among individuals. Some people are generally more conscious of their public image than others. Also, some people are more likely to engage in strategic self-presentation, whereas others seem to prefer self-verification. According to Mark Snyder (1987), these differences are related to a personality trait he called **self-monitoring**: the tendency to regulate one's own behavior to meet the demands of social situations.

Individuals who are high in self-monitoring appear to have a repertoire of selves from which to draw. Sensitive to strategic self-presentation concerns, they are poised, ready, and able to modify their behavior as they move from one setting to another. As measured by the Self-Monitoring Scale (Snyder, 1974; Snyder & Gangestad, 1986), they are likely to agree with such statements as "I would probably make a good actor" and "In different situations and with different people, I often act like very different persons." In contrast, low self-monitors are self-verifiers by nature, appearing less concerned about the social acceptability of their behavior. Like character actors always cast in the same role, they express themselves in a consistent manner from one situation to the next, exhibiting what they regard as their true and honest self. On the Self-Monitoring Scale, low self-monitors say that "I can only argue for ideas which I already believe" and "I have never been good at games like charades or improvisational acting" (see Table 3.3).

**self-monitoring** The tendency to change behavior in response to the self-presentation concerns of the situation.

## TABLE 3.3
### Self-Monitoring Scale

Are you a high or low self-monitor? For each statement, answer *True* or *False*. When you are done, give yourself one point if you answered *T* to items 4, 5, 6, 8, 10, 12, 17, and 18. Then give yourself one point if you answered *F* to items 1, 2, 3, 7, 9, 11, 13, 14, 15, and 16. Count your total number of points. This total represents your Self-Monitoring Score. Among North American college students, the average score is about 10 or 11.

1. I find it hard to imitate the behavior of other people.
2. At parties and social gatherings, I do not attempt to do or say things that others will like.
3. I can only argue for ideas which I already believe.
4. I can make impromptu speeches even on topics about which I have almost no information.
5. I guess I put on a show to impress or entertain others.
6. I would probably make a good actor.
7. In a group of people I am rarely the center of attention.
8. In different situations and with different people, I often act like very different persons.
9. I am not particularly good at making other people like me.
10. I'm not always the person I appear to be.
11. I would not change my opinions (or the way I do things) in order to please someone or win their favor.
12. I have considered being an entertainer.
13. I have never been good at games like charades or improvisational acting.
14. I have trouble changing my behavior to suit different people and different situations.
15. At a party I let others keep the jokes and stories going.
16. I feel a bit awkward in company and do not show up quite as well as I should.
17. I can look anyone in the eye and tell a lie with a straight face (if for a right end).
18. I may deceive people by being friendly when I really dislike them.

From Snyder, M., and Gangstad, S., "On the nature of self-monitoring: Matters of assessment, matters of validity," *Journal of Personality and Social Psychology* vol 51 (pp. 125–139). Copyright © 1986 by the American Psychological Association. Reprinted by permission.

Social psychologists disagree on whether the Self-Monitoring Scale measures one global trait or a combination of two or more specific traits. They also disagree about whether high and low self-monitors represent two discrete types of people or just points along a continuum. Either way, the test scores do appear to predict important social behaviors (Gangestad & Snyder, 2000).

Concerned with public image, high self-monitors go out of their way to learn about others with whom they might interact and about the rules for appropriate conduct. Then, once they have the situation sized up, they modify their behavior accordingly. If a situation calls for conformity, high self-monitors conform; if the same situation calls for autonomy, they refuse to conform. By contrast, low self-monitors maintain a relatively consistent posture across a range of situations (Snyder & Monson, 1975). Unconsciously adapting to social situations, high self-monitors are likely to mimic the demeanor of others in subtle ways that facilitate smooth social interactions (Cheng & Chartrand, 2003). They are also more likely to switch dialects according to their local surroundings, facilitating "linguistic adaptation" (Blank et al., 2012). Consistent with the finding that high self-monitors are more concerned than lows about what *other people* think of them, research conducted in work settings shows that high self-monitors receive higher performance ratings and more promotions and that they are more likely to emerge as leaders (Day et al., 2002).

It's more adaptive to alter one's behavior than to stay consistent from one social situation to the next. **F**ALSE.

Throughout this textbook, we see that because so much of our behavior is influenced by social norms, self-monitoring is relevant to many aspects of social psychology. There are also interesting developmental implications. A survey of 18- to 73-year-olds revealed that self-monitoring scores tend to drop with age, presumably because people become more settled and secure about their personal identities as they get older (Reifman et al., 1989). For now, however, ponder this question: Is it better to be a high or low self-monitor? Is one orientation inherently more adaptive than the other?

The existing research does not enable us to make this kind of value judgment. Consider high self-monitors. Quite accurately, they regard themselves as *pragmatic*, flexible, and adaptive and as able to cope with the diversity of life's roles. But they could also be described as fickle or phony opportunists, more concerned with appearances than with reality and willing to change colors like a chameleon just to fit in. Now think about low self-monitors. They describe themselves as *principled* and forthright; they are without pretense, always speaking their minds so others know where they stand. Of course, they could also be viewed as stubborn, insensitive to their surroundings, and unwilling to compromise in order to get along. Concerning the relative value of these two orientations, then, it is safe to conclude that neither high nor low self-monitoring is necessarily undesirable—unless carried to the extreme. Goffman (1955) made the same point many years ago, when he wrote:

> Too little perceptiveness, too little savoir faire, too little pride and considerateness, and the person ceases to be someone who can be trusted to take a hint about himself or give a hint that will save others embarrassment. . . . Too much savoir faire or too much considerateness and he becomes someone who is too socialized, who leaves others with the feeling that they do not know how they really stand with him, nor what they should do to make an effective long-term adjustment. (p. 227)

# Reflections: The Multifaceted Self

Throughout human history, writers, poets, philosophers, and personality theorists have portrayed the self as an enduring aspect of personality, as an invisible "inner core" that is stable over time and slow to change. The struggle to find your "true self" is based on this portrait. Indeed, when people older than 85 years were asked to reflect on their lives, almost all said that despite having changed in certain ways, they had remained essentially the same person (Troll & Skaff, 1997). In recent years, however, social psychologists have focused on change. In doing so, they have discovered that at least part of the self is malleable—molded by life experiences and varying from one situation to the next. From this perspective, the self has many different faces.

When you look into the mirror, what do you see, one self or many? Do you see a person whose self-concept is enduring or one whose identity seems to change from time to time? Do you see a person whose strengths and weaknesses are evaluated with an objective eye or one who is insulated from unpleasant truths by mechanisms of self-defense? Do you see a person who has an inner, hidden self that is different from the face shown to others?

Based on the material presented in this chapter, the answer to such questions seems always to be the same: The self has all these characteristics. Long before social psychology was born, William James (1890) said that the self is not simple but complex and multifaceted. Based on current theories and research, we can now appreciate just how right James was. Sure, there's an aspect of the self-concept that we can come to know only through introspection and that is stable over time. But there's also an aspect that changes with the company we keep and the information we get from others. When it comes to self-esteem, there are times when we are self-focused enough to become acutely aware of our shortcomings. Yet there are also times when we guard ourselves through self-serving cognitions, self-handicapping, BIRGing, and downward social comparisons. Then there is the matter of self-presentation. It's clear that each of us has a private self that consists of our inner thoughts, feelings, and memories. But it is equally clear that we also have an outer self, portrayed by the roles we play and the masks we wear in public. As you read through the pages of this text, you will see that the cognitive, affective, and behavioral components of the self are not separate and distinct but interrelated. They are also of great significance for the rest of social psychology.

# Review

## The Self-Concept

- The self-concept is the sum total of a person's beliefs about his or her own attributes. It is the cognitive component of the self.

### Rudiments of the Self-Concept

- Using brain scans, social neuroscientists find that certain areas become relatively more active when people process self-relevant information.
- Recognizing oneself as a distinct entity is the first step in the development of a self-concept.
- Human beings and apes are the only animals to recognize their mirror-image reflections as their own.
- Cooley's "looking-glass" self suggests that social factors are a necessary second step.

> **Putting *Common Sense* to the Test**
>
> **Humans are the only animals who recognize themselves in the mirror.**
>
> **False.** *Studies have shown that the great apes (chimpanzees, gorillas, and orangutans) are also capable of self-recognition.*

### Introspection

- People believe that introspection is a key to knowing the true self.
- But research shows that introspection sometimes diminishes the accuracy of self-reports.
- People also tend to overestimate their emotional reactions to future positive and negative events.

### Self-Perception

- Bem's self-perception theory holds that when internal states are difficult to interpret, we infer our inner states by observing our own behavior and the surrounding situation.
- Based on self-perception theory, the facial feedback hypothesis states that facial expressions can produce—not just reflect—an emotion state (smiling can cause us to feel happy).
- But it's unclear if the emotion occurs via self-perception or because facial expressions trigger physiological changes that produce the emotional response.
- Also derived from self-perception theory, the overjustification effect shows that people sometimes lose interest in activities for which they were rewarded.
- But if a reward is seen as a "bonus" for superior performance, then it can enhance intrinsic motivation by providing positive feedback.

> **Putting *Common Sense* to the Test**
>
> **Smiling can make you feel happier.**
>
> **True.** *Consistent with the facial feedback hypothesis, facial expressions can trigger or amplify the subjective experience of emotion.*

### Influences of Other People

- According to social comparison theory, people often evaluate their own opinions and abilities by comparing themselves to similar others.

- Schachter and Singer proposed that the experience of emotion is based on two factors: physiological arousal and a cognitive label for that arousal.
- Under certain conditions, people interpret their own arousal by watching others in the same situation.

## Autobiographical Memories
- Memory of one's life events is critical to the self-concept.
- When people recall life experiences, they typically report more events from the recent past than from the distant past, though some types of memories are generally more vivid and lasting than others.

- Autobiographical memories are shaped by self-serving motives, as people overemphasize their own roles in past events.

## Culture and the Self-Concept
- Cultures foster different conceptions of self.
- Many Europeans and North Americans hold an independent view of the self that emphasizes autonomy.
- People in certain Asian, African, and Latin American cultures hold an interdependent view of the self that encompasses social connections.
- These cultural differences influence the way we perceive, feel about, and present ourselves in relation to others.

# Self-Esteem

- Self-esteem refers to a person's positive and negative evaluations of the self.

## The Need for Self-Esteem
- People have a need for high self-esteem and want to see themselves in a positive light.
- People with low self-esteem often find themselves caught in a vicious cycle of self-defeating behavior.

## Are There Gender and Race Differences?
- Among adolescents and young adults, males have higher self-esteem than females do, though the difference is very small, particularly among older adults.
- African Americans outscore white Americans on self-esteem tests, indicating, perhaps, that stigmatized minorities focus on their positive attributes.

## Self-Discrepancy Theory
- Self-esteem can be defined by the match between how we see ourselves and how we want to see ourselves. Large self-discrepancies are associated with negative emotional states.
- Discrepancies between the actual and ideal selves are related to feelings of disappointment and depression.
- Discrepancies between the actual and the ought selves are related to shame, guilt, and anxiety.
- These emotional effects depend on the amount of discrepancy and whether we are consciously focused on it.

## The Self-Awareness "Trap"
- In general, people spend little time actually thinking about themselves.
- But certain situations (mirrors, cameras, audiences) increase self-awareness, and certain people are generally more self-conscious than others.
- Self-awareness forces us to notice self-discrepancies and can produce a temporary reduction in self-esteem.
- To cope, we either adjust our behavior to meet our standards or withdraw from the self-focusing situation.
- Heavy drinking can be viewed as a means of escaping from self-awareness.

- For people of faith, thinking about God can have the same effects as other triggers of self-awareness.

## Self-Regulation and Its Limits
- Requiring effort, self-control can temporarily be depleted by usage.
- This depletion effect can be reversed, enabling additional self-control, by the consumption of glucose and by self-affirmation.

## Ironic Mental Processes
- Due to the operation of ironic processes, our efforts at self-control may also backfire, causing us to think, feel, and act in ways that are opposite to our intentions.
- Choking under pressure is an ironic phenomenon often seen in sports.

### Putting *Common Sense* to the Test
**Sometimes the harder you try to control a thought, feeling, or behavior, the less likely you are to succeed.**
**True.** *Research on ironic processes in mental control have revealed that trying to inhibit a thought, feeling, or behavior often backfires.*

## Mechanisms of Self-Enhancement
- Most people think highly of themselves and have unconscious positive associations with things related to the self.
- People protect their self-esteem in four major ways: through self-serving cognitions, such as taking credit for success and denying the blame for failure; self-handicapping, in order to excuse anticipated failure; basking in reflected glory, which boosts their self-esteem through associations with successful others; and downward social comparisons to others who are less well off.

### Putting *Common Sense* to the Test
**People often sabotage their own performance in order to protect their self-esteem.**
**True.** *Studies have shown that people often handicap their own performance in order to build an excuse for anticipated failure.*

- When others surpass us in ways that are important to us, we become jealous and distance ourselves from them. When surpassed in ways that are not self-relevant, we feel pride and seek closeness.

### Are Positive Illusions Adaptive?

- Recent research suggests that certain positive illusions may foster high self-esteem and mental health and may be adaptive from an evolutionary standpoint.
- An alternative view is that such illusions promote self-defeating behavior patterns and that people with inflated views of themselves are liked less by others.

### Culture and Self-Esteem

- Cross-cultural comparisons indicate that people from collectivist cultures present themselves as modest in their self-esteem relative to people from individualistic cultures.
- Researchers are seeking to determine whether collectivists have a less inflated self-esteem or simply feel compelled to present themselves modestly to others.
- Everyone has a need for positive self-regard; individualists and collectivists seek to fulfill that need in different ways.

# Self-Presentation

- We care deeply about what others think of us and often believe that the social spotlight shines more brightly on us than it really does.
- Self-presentation is the process by which we try to shape what others think of us and even what we think of ourselves. There are two general motives in self-presentation: strategic self-presentation and self-verification.

### Strategic Self-Presentation

- Strategic self-presentation is the process by which we try to shape others' impressions of us.
- In social encounters, people often try to get others to see them in a positive light, as likable or competent, for example.

### Self-Verification

- Apart from the desire to be seen in a positive light, people seek self-verification, a process by which we try to get others to perceive us "accurately," as we see ourselves.

- Research shows that self-verification motives often trump the desire to be seen in a positive light.

### Self-Monitoring

- Individuals differ in their tendency to regulate their behavior to meet the demands of social situations.
- High self-monitors modify their behavior, as appropriate, from one situation to the next.
- Low self-monitors express themselves in a more consistent manner, exhibiting at all times what they see as their true self.

---

**Putting *Common Sense* to the Test**

**It's more adaptive to alter one's behavior than to stay consistent from one social situation to the next.**

**False.** *High and low self-monitors differ in the extent to which they alter their behavior to suit the situation they are in, but neither style is inherently more adaptive.*

---

# Reflections: The Multifaceted Self

- As this chapter has shown, the self is not simple but complex and multifaceted.

## KEY TERMS

affective forecasting (58)

bask in reflected glory (BIRG) (87)

dialecticism (71)

downward social comparisons (88)

facial feedback hypothesis (61)

implicit egotism (84)

overjustification effect (62)

private self-consciousness (78)

public self-consciousness (78)

self-awareness theory (76)

self-concept (55)

self-esteem (72)

self-handicapping (86)

self-monitoring (95)

self-perception theory (59)

self-presentation (92)

self-regulation (80)

self-schema (55)

social comparison theory (64)

Terror Management Theory (73)

two-factor theory of emotion (65)

## MEDIA RESOURCES

Go to CengageBrain.com to access Psychology CourseMate, where you will find an interactive eBook, glossaries, flashcards, quizzes, videos, and more.

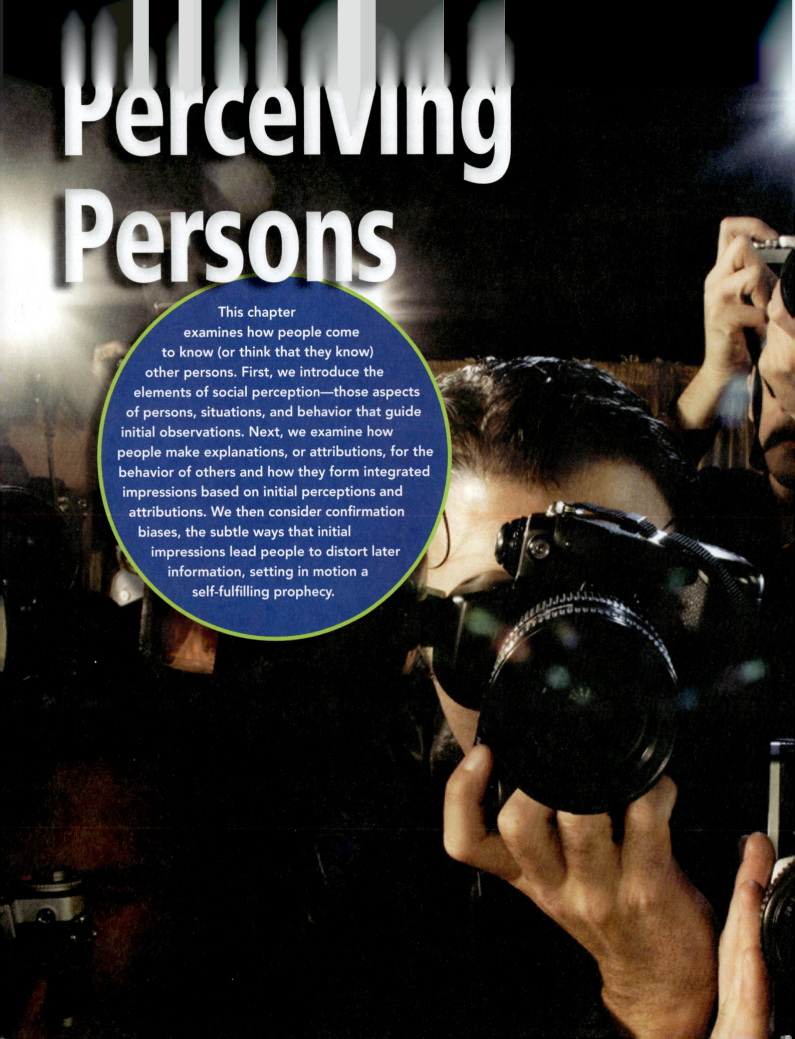

# Perceiving Persons

This chapter examines how people come to know (or think that they know) other persons. First, we introduce the elements of social perception—those aspects of persons, situations, and behavior that guide initial observations. Next, we examine how people make explanations, or attributions, for the behavior of others and how they form integrated impressions based on initial perceptions and attributions. We then consider confirmation biases, the subtle ways that initial impressions lead people to distort later information, setting in motion a self-fulfilling prophecy.

4

© Patrik Giardino/Corbis

103

**On February 26, 2012,** Trayvon Martin, a 17-year-old African American, was shot and killed on a street in Sanford, Florida. The gunman was 28-year-old George Zimmerman, a multiracial Hispanic American who occasionally patrolled the area for a community watch group. What happened, exactly, that led to the shooting is a matter of dispute.

Suspicious of Martin's presence in the neighborhood, Zimmerman called the local police department at about 7 p.m. to report his sighting. "This guy looks like he is up to no good or he is on drugs or something," he said. Two minutes into the call, Zimmerman said that Martin was running and complained in frustration that "they always get away." Zimmerman then started to follow Martin on foot, leading the dispatcher to say, "We don't need you to do that." At that same time, Martin was talking on the cell phone to his girlfriend who later reported that Martin had told her that a "crazy and creepy" man was watching him from a car and then following him. All of a sudden she heard a verbal exchange and a scuffle, at which point she lost the connection.

A police officer arrived moments later and saw Zimmerman standing near Martin, who was face down in the grass and motionless. Zimmerman, armed with a 9mm semi-automatic pistol, admitted that he had shot Martin. His back was covered with wet grass. He was bleeding from a broken nose and from the back of his head. Shortly afterward, Martin was pronounced dead, and Zimmerman was taken to the police station for questioning. Witnesses saw the two men scuffle but gave varying accounts of who did what to whom. In recordings of the 911 call, one man can be heard crying for help. According to Zimmerman, that voice was his, and he shot Martin in self-defense.

Why did George Zimmerman shoot Trayvon Martin? Does he have a violent streak he cannot control? Is he racist? Was he temporarily frustrated by a rash of break-ins in the neighborhood? Did Martin attack or do something to provoke him? As news of this event broke, people quickly formed opinions based on a combination of facts, rumors, and speculation. At first, Zimmerman was released; then he was arrested and charged. That Zimmerman shot Martin is not in dispute. But why did he do it? Was it something about him or the situation he was in? And should he be held responsible in the eyes of the law?

Four years earlier, in the fall of 2008, former NASDAQ chairman Bernie Madoff was arrested for running an elaborate $50 billion Ponzi scheme that fooled and claimed more than 14,000 individual and institutional victims. It was the largest fraud of its kind ever, completely draining individual fortunes and retirement nest eggs, destroying charitable foundations, and even pushing one investor to commit suicide. The 70-year-old Madoff had first started this scheme many years ago. Yet remarkably, despite servicing an elite group of clients who were intelligent and motivated by their high-stakes investments, Madoff demonstrated what research to be described later has shown: that people are notoriously inept at distinguishing truths and lies. Why did Madoff, a respected financial leader and

## Putting *Common Sense* to the Test

*Circle Your Answer*

**T F** The impressions we form of others are influenced by superficial aspects of their appearance.

**T F** Adaptively, people are skilled at knowing when someone is lying rather than telling the truth.

**T F** Like social psychologists, people are sensitive to situational causes when explaining the behavior of others.

**T F** People are slow to change their first impressions on the basis of new information.

**T F** The notion that we can create a "self-fulfilling prophecy" by getting others to behave in ways we expect is a myth.

**T F** People are more accurate at judging the personalities of friends and acquaintances than of strangers.

Trayvon Martin, a 17-year-old African American, was shot and killed in Sanford, Florida (left). The gunman was 28-year-old George Zimmerman, who patrolled the area for a community watch group (right). How people interpret this event raises core questions about social perception.

millionaire, perpetrate this fraud? Was he a narcissist, or what clinical psychologists would call a "white-collar psychopath" who harms others with calloused and vicious indifference? Or were his actions triggered by life circumstances? Is it possible that once he started, Madoff was unable to stop, having put himself into a gradually escalating trap from which he could not escape without punishment? Whatever the explanation, Madoff was sentenced for his offenses to 150 years in prison.

Whatever the topic—crime, business, sports, politics, entertainment, or personal events closer to home—we are all engaged and interested participants in social perception, the processes by which people come to understand one another. This chapter is divided into four sections. First we look at the "raw data" of social perception: persons, situations, and behaviors. Second, we examine how people explain and analyze behavior. Third, we consider how people integrate their observations into a coherent impression of other persons. Fourth, we discuss some of the subtle ways that our impressions create a distorted picture of reality, often setting in motion a self-fulfilling prophecy. As you read this chapter, you will notice that the various processes are considered from a perceiver's vantage point. Keep in mind, however, that in the events of life, you are both a *perceiver* and a *target* of others' perceptions.

# Observation: The Elements of Social Perception

As our opening examples suggest, understanding others may be difficult, but it's a common and vital part of everyday life. How do we do it? What kinds of evidence do we use? We cannot actually "see" someone's mental or emotional state or his or her motives or intentions any more than a detective can see a crime that has already been committed. So like a detective who tries to reconstruct events by turning up witnesses, fingerprints, blood samples, and other evidence, the social perceiver comes to know others by relying

**social perception** A general term for the processes by which people come to understand one another.

on indirect clues—the elements of social perception. These clues arise from an interplay of three sources: persons, situations, and behavior.

 ## A Person's Physical Appearance

Have you ever met someone for the first time and formed a quick impression based only on a quick "snapshot" of information? As children, we were told that we should not judge a book by its cover, that things are not always what they seem, that surface appearances are deceiving, and that all that glitters is not gold. Yet as adults we can't seem to help ourselves.

To illustrate the rapid-fire nature of the process, Janine Willis and Alexander Todorov (2006) showed college students photographs of unfamiliar faces for one-tenth of a second, half a second, or a full second. Whether the students judged the faces for how attractive, likable, competent, trustworthy, or aggressive they were, their ratings— even at the briefest exposure—were quick and were highly correlated with judgments that other observers made without time-exposure limits (see Table 4.1). In fact, research has shown that people evaluate spontaneously and unconsciously whether a face indicates that a person is dominant or submissive, and trustworthy or untrustworthy (Stewart et al., 2012). Flip quickly through the pages of an illustrated magazine, or browse the internet, and you may see for yourself that sometimes it takes a mere fraction of a second for you to form certain impressions of a stranger from his or her face.

If first impressions are quick to form, then on what are they based? In 500 B.C.E., the mathematician Pythagoras looked into the eyes of prospective students to determine if they were gifted. At about the same time, Hippocrates, the founder of modern medicine, used facial features to make diagnoses of life and death. In the nineteenth century, Viennese physician Franz Gall introduced a carnival-like science called phrenology and claimed that he could assess people's character by the shape of their skulls. And in 1954, psychologist William Sheldon concluded from flawed studies of adult men that there is a strong link between physique and personality.

People may not measure each other by bumps on the head, as phrenologists used to do, but first impressions are influenced in subtle ways by a person's height, weight, skin color, hair color, tattoos, piercings, eyeglasses, and other aspects of physical appearance.

As social perceivers, we also form impressions of people that are often accurate based on a host of indirect telltale cues. In *Snoop: What Your Stuff Says About You*, Sam Gosling (2008) describes research he has conducted showing that people's personalities can be revealed in the knick-knacks found in their offices and dormitory rooms, the identity claims they make on Facebook pages, the books that line their shelves, and the types of music that inhabit their iPods. Other superficial cues also lead us to form quick impressions of others. In one study, fictional characters with "old-generation" names such as Harry, Walter, Dorothy, and Edith were judged to be less popular and less intelligent than those with younger-generation names such as Kevin, Michael, Lisa, and Michelle (Young et al., 1993). In a second study, both men and women were seen as more feminine when they spoke in high-pitched voices than in lower-pitched voices (Ko et al., 2006). In a third study, cleverly entitled "I

**TABLE 4.1**

**First Impressions in a Fraction of a Second**

Participants rated unfamiliar faces based on pictures they saw for one-tenth of a second, half a second, or a full second. Would their impressions stay the same or change with unlimited time? As measured by the correlations of these ratings with those made by observers who had no exposure time limits, the results showed that ratings were highly correlated even at the briefest exposure times. Giving participants more time did not increase these correlations.

| Traits Being Judged | 0.10 sec | 0.50 sec | 1 sec |
| --- | --- | --- | --- |
| Trustworthy | .73 | .66 | .74 |
| Competent | .52 | .67 | .59 |
| Likable | .59 | .57 | .63 |
| Aggressive | .52 | .56 | .59 |
| Attractive | .69 | .57 | .66 |

Willis &Todorov, 2006. © Cengage Learning

like you but I don't know why," people rated new computer-generated faces more positively when these faces—unbeknownst to them—were created to resemble a boyfriend or girlfriend in a satisfying relationship (Günaydin et al., 2012).

The human face in particular attracts more than its share of attention. Since the time of ancient Greece, human beings have attended to physiognomy—the art of reading character from faces. Although we may not realize it, this tendency persists today. For example, Ran Hassin and Yaacov Trope (2000) found that people prejudge others in photographs as kind-hearted rather than mean-spirited based on such features as a full, round face, curly hair, long eyelashes, large eyes, a short nose, full lips, and an upturned mouth. Interestingly, these researchers also found that just as people read traits from faces, at times they read traits into faces based on prior information. In one study, for example, participants who were told that a man was kind—compared to those told he was mean—later judged his face to be fuller, rounder, and more attractive.

In social perception studies of the human face, researchers have found that adults who have baby-faced features—large, round eyes; high eyebrows; round cheeks; a large forehead; smooth skin; and a rounded chin—tend to be seen as warm, kind, naive, weak, honest, and submissive. In contrast, adults who have mature features—small eyes, low brows and a small forehead, wrinkled skin, and an angular chin—are seen as stronger, more dominant, and more competent (Berry & Zebrowitz-McArthur, 1986). In small claims court, judges are more likely to favor baby-faced defendants who are accused of intentional wrongdoing but rule against them when accused of negligence. In the work setting, baby-faced job applicants are more likely to be recommended for employment as day-care teachers, whereas mature-faced adults are considered to be better suited for work as bankers. Recent research even shows that a link between baby-faced appearance and personal characteristics is perceived not only in Western cultures but also among the Tsimané people living in a Bolivian rainforest (Zebrowitz et al., 2012). Results like these have led Leslie Zebrowitz and Joann Montepare (2005) to conclude that baby-facedness "profoundly affects human behavior in the blink of an eye" (p. 1565).

What accounts for these findings? And why, in general, are people so quick to judge others by appearances? To begin with, human beings are programmed by evolution to respond gently to infantile features so that real babies are treated with tender loving care. Many years ago, animal behaviorist Konrad Lorenz noted that infantile features in many animal species seem to trigger a special nurturing response to cuteness. Recently, this old idea derived new support from a brain-imaging study showing that a frontal brain region associated with love and other positive emotions is activated when people are exposed, even fleetingly, to pictures of babies' faces but not to pictures of the faces of other adults (Kringelbach et al., 2008).

Our reflex-like response to babies is understandable. But do we really respond in the same way to baby-faced adults and, if so, why? Leslie Zebrowitz believes that we do—that we associate infantile features with helplessness traits and then overgeneralize this expectation to baby-faced adults. Consistent with this point, she and her colleagues found in a recent brain-imaging study that the region of the brain that was activated by pictures of babies' faces was also activated by pictures of baby-faced men (Zebrowitz et al., 2009).

Other researchers also believe that people as social perceivers have a tendency to overgeneralize in making snap judgments. Alexander Todorov and others (2008)

Look at these two office cubicles. Do these images lead you to form any impressions of their inhabitants? If so, do you suppose these impressions would be accurate or misleading?

*"Our faces, together with our language, are social tools that help us navigate the social encounters that define our "selves" and fashion our lives."*

—Alan J. Fridlund

find that people are quick to perceive unfamiliar faces as more or less trustworthy—an important judgment we must often make—and that we do so by focusing on features that resemble the expressions of happiness and anger (a trustworthy face has a U-shaped mouth and raised eyebrows; in an untrustworthy face, the mouth curls down and the eyebrows form a V). In other words, faces are seen as trustworthy if they look happy, an emotion that signals a person who is safe to approach, and untrustworthy if they look angry, an emotion that signals danger to be avoided. Facial expressions may be temporary, but they too can influence our perceptions. When people smile, their faces look lighter and brighter than when they frown (Song et al., 2012).

The impressions we form of others are influenced by superficial aspects of their appearance. **T**RUE.

## Perceptions of Situations

In addition to the beliefs we hold about persons, each of us has preset notions about certain types of situations—"scripts" that enable us to anticipate the goals, behaviors, and outcomes that are likely to occur in a particular setting (Abelson, 1981; Read, 1987). Based on past experience, people can easily imagine the sequences of events likely to unfold in a typical greeting or at a shopping mall, the dinner table, or a tennis match. The more experience you have in a given situation, the more detail your scripts will contain.

In *Do's and Taboos Around the World*, Roger Axtell (1993) describes many scripts that are culture specific. In Bolivia, dinner guests are expected to fully clean their plates to prove that they enjoyed the meal. Eat in an Indian home, however, and you'll see that many native guests will leave some food on the plate to show the host that they had enough to eat. Social scripts of this nature can influence perceptions and behavior. As we'll see in Chapter 11 on aggression, in places that foster a "culture of honor," men are expected to defend against insult, women are expected to remain modest and loyal, and indications of female infidelity can trigger domestic violence (Vandello & Cohen, 2003).

Behavioral scripts can be quite elaborate. Studying the "first date" script, John Pryor and Thomas Merluzzi (1985) asked U.S. college students to list the sequence of events that take place in this situation. From these lists, a picture of a typical American first date emerged. Sixteen steps were identified, including (1) male arrives; (2) female greets male at door; (3) female introduces date to parents or roommate; (4) male and female discuss plans and make small talk; (5) they go to a movie; (6) they get something to eat or drink; (7) male takes female home; (8) if interested, he remarks about a future date; (9) they kiss; (10) they say good night. Sound familiar? Pryor and Merluzzi then randomized their list of events and asked participants to arrange them into the appropriate order. They found that those with extensive dating experience were able to organize the statements more quickly than those who had less dating experience. For people who are familiar with a script, the events fall into place like pieces of a puzzle. In fact, almost 30 years later, despite changes in gender and dating norms, research shows that this basic script has remained essentially the same (Morr Serewicz & Gale, 2008).

Knowledge of social settings provides an important context for understanding other people's verbal and nonverbal behavior. For example, this knowledge leads us to expect someone to be polite during a job interview, playful at a picnic, and rowdy at a NASCAR rally. Often our expectations for how situations affect us can influence the way we interpret other people's facial expressions. In one study, participants looked at photographs of human faces that had ambiguous expressions. When told that the person in the photo was being threatened by a vicious dog, they saw the facial expression as fearful; when told that the individual had just won money, participants interpreted

Observation: The Elements of Social Perception

the same expression as a sign of happiness (Trope, 1986). In other studies, scowling faces were seen as afraid when the surrounding situation was described as dangerous or as determined when said to be in a race for the gold medal on an Olympic rowing team (Carroll & Russell, 1996). Context effects on the perception of joy, anger, fear, pride, disgust, surprise, and other emotions in the face are quick and automatic (Aviezer et al., 2008; Barrett et al., 2011). ● Figure 4.1 illustrates this point.

## Behavioral Evidence

An essential first step in social perception is recognizing what someone is doing at a given moment. Identifying actions from movement is surprisingly easy. Even when actors dressed in black move about in a dark room with point lights attached only to the joints of their bodies, people quickly and easily recognize such complex acts as walking, running, jumping, exercising, and falling (Johansson et al., 1980). This ability is found in people of all cultures (Barrett et al., 2005) and enables us to recognize specific individuals, such as friends, strictly on the basis of their movements (Loula et al., 2005).

More interesting, perhaps, is that people derive *meaning* from their observations by dividing the continuous stream of human behavior into discrete "units." By having participants observe someone on videotape and press a button whenever they detect a meaningful action, Darren Newtson and his colleagues (1987) found that some perceivers break the behavior stream into a large number of fine units, whereas others break it into a small number of gross units. While watching a baseball game, for example, you might press the button after each pitch, after each batter, after every inning, or only after runs are scored. The manner in which people divide a stream of behavior can influence their perceptions in important ways. Research participants who were told to break an event into fine units rather than gross units attended more closely, detected more meaningful actions, and remembered more details about the actor's behavior than did participants who were told to break events into gross units (Lassiter et al., 1988).

In a new and developing area of research, social psychologists are now interested in mind perception, the process by which people attribute humanlike mental states to various animate and inanimate objects, including other people. Studies show that people who identify someone's actions in high-level terms rather than low-level terms (for example, by describing the act of "painting a house" as "trying to make a house look new," not just "applying brush strokes") are also more likely to attribute humanizing thoughts, feelings, intentions, consciousness, and other states of mind to that actor (Kozak et al., 2006).

Although people do not tend to attribute mental states to inanimate objects, in general the more humanlike a target object is, the more likely we are to attribute to it qualities of "mind." In a series of studies, Carey Morewedge and others (2007) found that whether people are asked to rate different animals in nature (such as a sloth, turtle, housefly, deer, wolf, and hummingbird); cartoon robots or human beings whose motion was presented in slow, medium, and fast speeds; or a purple blob oozing down a city street at the same, slower, or faster pace than the people around it, the result is always the same: People see inner qualities of mind in target objects that superficially resemble humans in their speed of movement.

Asking "What kinds of things have minds?" Heather Gray and her colleagues (2007) conducted an online survey in which they presented more than 2,000 respondents with

### ● FIGURE 4.1
**Judging Emotions in Context**

Look at the face of tennis star Serena Williams (left). How is she feeling—angry, perhaps, or in agony? Now look at her in a fuller context (right). You can see that Williams was actually euphoric, clenching her fist in victory at the 2008 U.S. Open.

Timothy A. Clary/AFP/Getty Images

**mind perception** The process by which people attribute humanlike mental states to various animate and inanimate objects, including other people.

an array of human and nonhuman characters such as a 7-week-old fetus, a 5-month-old infant, an adult man, a man in a vegetative state, a dead woman, a frog, the family dog, a chimpanzee, God, and a sociable robot. They then asked respondents to rate the extent to which each character possessed various mental capacities such as pleasure, pain, fear, pride, embarrassment, memory, self-control, and morality. Once statistically combined, the results showed that people perceive minds along two dimensions: agency (a target's ability to plan and execute behavior) and experience (the capacity to feel pleasure, pain, and other sensations). Overall, the more "mind" respondents attributed to a character, the more they liked it, valued it, wanted to make it happy, and wanted to rescue it from destruction.

In recent years, social psychologists have found that the perception of mind is an important aspect in how we perceive, connect with, and behave toward one another; that we sometimes see human mind-like qualities in nonhuman beings, and in certain inanimate objects; and that people are more likely to ascribe mind to others with whom they share a social connection than to distant others (Waytz et al., 2010). In a series of studies, for example, Adam Waytz and Nicholas Epley (2012) found that research participants who were asked to reflect on someone in their lives to whom they are close—say, a good friend, significant other, or family member—were then less likely to attribute humanizing mental qualities to other people.

What about the gadgets we tuck into our pockets? Does an iPhone have qualities of mind? In 2012, Apple introduced a series of television commercials for the iPhone that are focused on Siri, the virtual assistant that is programmed to answer questions. In one commercial, actor John Malkovich asks Siri about the meaning of life. At one point, she advises him to be nice to people, avoid eating fat, and read a good book every now and then. "And try to live together in peace and harmony with people of all creeds and nations." Malkovich thanks Siri for the advice: "I enjoyed this chat immensely. You are very eloquent." "That's nice of you to say," Siri responds.

### The Silent Language of Nonverbal Behavior

Behavioral cues are used not only to identify someone's physical actions but also to determine his or her inner states. Knowing how another person is feeling can be tricky because people often try to conceal their true emotions from others. Have you ever had to suppress your rage at someone, mask your disappointment after failure, feign surprise, make excuses, or pretend to like something just to be polite? Sometimes people come right out and tell us how they feel. At other times, however, they do not tell us, they are themselves not sure, or they actively try to hide their true feelings. For these reasons, we often tune in to the silent language of nonverbal behavior.

What kinds of nonverbal cues do people use in judging how someone else is feeling? In *The Expression of the Emotions in Man and Animals*, Charles Darwin (1872) proposed that the face expresses emotion in ways that are innate and understood by people all over the world. Contemporary research supports this notion. Many studies have shown that when presented with photographs similar to those on page 111, people can reliably identify at least six "primary" emotions: happiness, sadness, anger, fear, surprise, and disgust. In one study, participants from 10 different countries—Estonia, Germany, Greece, Hong Kong, Italy, Japan, Scotland, Sumatra, Turkey, and the United States—exhibited high levels of agreement in their recognition of these emotions (Ekman et al., 1987).

In this episode of the hit comedy *The Big Bang Theory*, Raj looks adoringly at his iPhone while having a "conversation" with Siri, its virtual assistant. Indicating that people can perceive a "mind" in gadgets, Raj begins to fall in love with Siri and fantasizes about dating her.

Monty Brinton/CBS via Getty Images

**nonverbal behavior** Behavior that reveals a person's feelings without words, through facial expressions, body language, and vocal cues.

From one end of the world to the other, it is clear that a smile is a smile and a frown is a frown and that just about everyone knows what they mean, even when the expressions are "put on" by actors and are not genuinely felt. But do the results fully support the claim that basic emotions are "universally" recognized from the face, or is the link culturally specific? (Russell, 1994) To answer this question, Hillary Elfenbein and Nalini Ambady (2002) meta-analyzed 97 studies involving a total of 22,148 social perceivers from 42 different countries. As shown in ● Figure 4.2, they found support for both points of view. On the one hand, people all over the world are able to recognize the primary emotions from photographs of facial expressions. On the other hand, people are 9% more accurate at judging faces from their own national, ethnic, or regional groups than from members of less familiar groups—indicating that we enjoy an "in-group advantage" when it comes to knowing how those who are closest to us are feeling.

In a study that illustrates the point, Elfenbein and Ambady (2003) showed pictures of American faces to groups with varying degrees of exposure to Americans. As predicted, more life exposure was associated with greater accuracy, from a low of 60% among Chinese participants living in China up to 83% among Chinese living in the United States and 93% among non–Chinese Americans. When it comes to recognizing emotions in the face, it appears that familiarity breeds accuracy.

Darwin believed that the ability to recognize emotion in others has survival value for all members of a species. This hypothesis suggests that it is more important to identify some emotions than others. For example, it may be more adaptive to be wary of someone who is angry, and hence prone to lash out in violence, than of someone who is happy, a nonthreatening emotion. Indeed, studies have shown that angry faces arouse us and cause us to frown even when presented subliminally and without our awareness (Dimberg & Ohman, 1996; Dimberg et al., 2000). Illustrating what Christine and Ranald Hansen (1988) called the "anger superiority effect," researchers have found that people are quicker to spot—and slower to look away from—angry faces in a crowd than faces with neutral and less threatening emotions (Fox et al., 2002; Horstmann & Bauland, 2006). Of course, what people search for may be conditioned by a current motivational state. In a visual search task resembling "Where's Waldo?" research participants who

● **FIGURE 4.2**

**How Good Are People at Identifying Emotions in the Face?**

A meta-analysis of emotion recognition studies involving 22,148 participants from 42 countries confirmed that people all over the world can recognize the six basic emotions from posed facial expressions.

From Elfenbein, H.A., and Ambady, N., "How good are people at identifying emotions in the face?" *Psychological Bulletin* vol 128 (pp. 203–235). Copyright © 2002 by the American Psychological Association. Reprinted by permission.

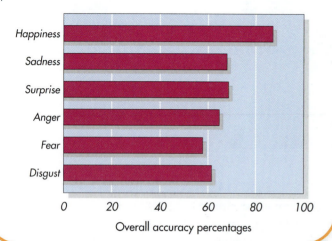

were led to fear social rejection and loneliness were quicker to spot faces in diverse crowds that wore welcoming smiles than other expressions (DeWall et al., 2009).

Disgust is another basic emotion that has adaptive significance. When confronted with an offensive stimulus such as a foul odor, spoiled food, feces, rotting flesh, or the sight of mutilation, people react with an aversion that shows in the way they wrinkle the nose, raise the upper lip, and gape. This visceral reaction is often accompanied by nausea; in the case of bad food, this can facilitate gagging and vomiting (Rozin & Fallon, 1987). In nature, food poisoning is a real threat, so it is adaptive for us to recognize disgust in the face of others. To illustrate, Bruno Wicker and others (2003) had 14 men watch video clips of people smelling pleasant, disgusting, or neutral odors. Afterward, these same men were exposed to the odors themselves. If you've ever inhaled the sweet, floury aroma of a bakery or inserted your nose into a carton of soured milk, you'll appreciate the different reactions that would appear on your face. Using fMRI, researchers monitored activity in the participants' brains throughout the experiment. They found that a structure in the brain known as the *insula* was activated not only when participants sniffed the disgusting odor but also when they watched *others* sniffing it. This result suggests that people more than recognize the face of disgust; they experience it at a neural level.

The social value of the human face is evident when we communicate by text, twitter, or e-mail. When e-mail first became popular, the written word was often misinterpreted, especially when the writer tried to be funny or sarcastic, because we lacked the nonverbal cues that normally animate and clarify live interactions. To fill in this gap, e-mailers created smiley faces and other "emoticons" (emotion icons) from standard keyboard characters. A sampling of routinely used emoticons, which are meant to be viewed with one's head tilted 90 degrees to the left, are shown in ● Figure 4.3. To simplify the task, Gmail, Hotmail, Yahoo!, and other e-mail providers now offer a choice of still and animated emoticon faces to communicate an assortment of emotions and other mental states.

Other nonverbal cues can also influence social perception, enabling us to make quick and sometimes accurate judgments of others based on "thin slices" of expressive behavior (Ambady & Rosenthal, 1993). "Thin slicing is not an exotic gift," notes Malcolm Gladwell (2005), author of the best seller *Blink*. "It is a central part of what it means to be human" (p. 43). In one study, for example, research participants were able to judge the intelligence of strangers accurately, as measured by standardized test scores, based only on hearing them read short sentences (Borkenau et al., 2004). In another study, 100 college students rated the faces of CEOs from the top- and bottom-ranked Fortune 1000 companies on key leadership traits related to power (competent, dominant, mature-faced) and warmth (likable, trustworthy). As it turned out, the CEOs whose faces the students had rated as more powerful—based on nothing more than cropped head shots—were in fact more successful, as measured by their company's most recent profits (Rule & Ambady, 2008). It's no wonder that Nalini Ambady (2010) has come to describe quick thin-slice judgments as "intuitive" and "efficient."

Eye contact, or *gaze*, is another powerful form of nonverbal communication. As social beings, people are highly attentive to eyes, often following the gaze of others. Look up, down, left, or right, and someone observing you will likely follow the direction

## FIGURE 4.3

### Some Common E-mail "Emoticons"

In order to clarify meaning of their written words, e-mailers often add smiles, winks, and other face-like symbols, or emoticons, to their electronic messages. One set of emoticons is shown here; you may be familiar with others.

Reprinted with permission from "Smileys" © 1996 O'Reilly & Associates, Inc. All rights reserved. www.oreilly.com

| Wink | Smirk | Said smiling | Said frowning | Sardonic incredulity |
|------|-------|--------------|---------------|----------------------|
| '-)  | :-,   | :-)          | :-(           | ;-)                  |

| Disgusted | Kiss, kiss | Clowning around | Said late at night | Said tongue-in-cheek |
|-----------|------------|-----------------|--------------------|----------------------|
| :-l       | :-X        | :-*)            | l-(                | :-J                  |

of your eyes (Langton et al., 2000). Even one-year-old infants tend to follow gaze, looking toward or pointing at the object of an adult researcher's attention (Brooks & Meltzoff, 2002). Clearly, each of us is drawn like a magnet to another person's direct gaze. Controlled laboratory studies of this "eye contact effect" show that people who look us straight in the eye quickly draw and then hold our attention, increase arousal, and activate key "social" areas of the brain and that this sensitivity is present at birth (Senju & Johnson, 2009).

Eyes have been called the "windows of the soul." In many cultures, people tend to assume that someone who avoids eye contact is evasive, cold, fearful, shy, or indifferent; that frequent gazing signals intimacy, sincerity, self-confidence, and respect; and that the person who stares is tense, angry, and unfriendly. If you've ever conversed with someone who kept looking away, as if uninterested, then you would understand why people might form negative impressions from "gaze disengagement" (Mason et al., 2005). Sometimes eye contact is interpreted in light of a preexisting relationship. If two people are friendly, frequent eye contact elicits a positive impression. If a relationship is not so friendly, that same eye contact is seen in negative terms. Hence, it is said that if two people lock eyes for more than a few seconds, they will either make love or kill each other (Kleinke, 1986).

Another powerful and primitive form of nonverbal signal is *touch*—as in the congratulatory high-five, the fist bump, the bear hug, the sympathetic pat on the back, the joking elbow in the ribs, the painfully strong handshake, and the lingering tender loving embrace. Physical touching has long been regarded as an expression of friendship, nurturance, and sexual interest. But it may also serve other functions. Many years ago,

Joe Burbank/Orlando Sentinel/MCT via Getty Images

After the 9/11 terrorist attacks in 2001, the Transportation Security Administration (TSA) has trained its agents to observe the facial expressions and demeanor of airport passengers in an effort to detect signs of malintent. Thus far, there is little evidence that the judgments they make by this type of observations are accurate.

Nancy Henley (1977) observed that men, older persons, and those of high socioeconomic status were more likely to touch women, younger persons, and individuals of lower status than the other way around. Henley's interpretation is that touching may be an expression not only of intimacy but also of dominance and control. Is social touching reserved for those in power? It appears that the answer is no. After an exhaustive review of past research, Judith Hall and her colleagues (2005) found that although we tend to believe that people touch others more when they are dominant than when they are subordinate, there is no behavioral support for this hypothesis (though dominant people are more facially expressive, encroach more on others' personal space, speak louder, and are more likely to interrupt).

As described by Axtell (1993), nonverbal communication norms vary a great deal from one culture to the next. So watch out! In Bulgaria, nodding your head means "no," and shaking your head sideways means "yes." In Germany and Brazil, the American "okay" sign (forming a circle with your thumb and forefinger) is an obscene gesture. Personal-space habits also vary across cultures. Japanese people like to maintain a comfortable distance while interacting. But in Puerto Rico and much of Latin America, people stand very close and backing off is considered an insult. Also beware of what you do with your eyes. In Latin America, locking eyes is a must, yet in Japan, too much eye contact shows a lack of respect. If you're in the habit of stroking your cheek, you should know that in Italy, Greece, and Spain it means that you find the person you're talking to attractive. And whatever you do, don't ever touch someone's head in predominantly Buddhist countries, especially Thailand. The head is sacred there.

Different cultures also have different rules for the common greeting. In Finland, you should give a firm handshake; in France, you should loosen the grip; in Zambia, you should use your left hand to support the right; and in Bolivia, you should extend your arm if your hand is dirty. In Japan, people bow; in Thailand, they put both hands together in a praying position on the chest; and in Fiji, they smile and raise their eyebrows. In certain parts of Latin America, it is common for people to hug, embrace, and kiss upon meeting. And in most Arab countries, men greet one another by saying *salaam alaykum*, then shaking hands, saying *kaifhalak*, and kissing each other on the cheek.

"I knew the suspect was lying because of certain telltale discrepancies between his voice and nonverbal gestures. Also his pants were on fire."

## Distinguishing Truth From Deception

Social perception is tricky because people often try to hide or stretch the truth about themselves. Poker players bluff to win money, witnesses lie to protect themselves, public officials make campaign promises they don't really intend to keep, and acquaintances pass compliments to each other to be polite and supportive. On occasion, everyone tells something less than "the truth, the whole truth, and nothing but the truth." Can social perceivers tell the difference? Can *you* tell when someone is lying?

Sigmund Freud, the founder of psychoanalysis, once said that "no mortal can keep a secret. If his lips are silent, he chatters with his fingertips; betrayal oozes out of him at every pore" (1905, p. 94). Paul Ekman and Wallace Friesen (1974) later revised Freud's observation by pointing out that some pores "ooze" more than others. Ekman and Friesen proposed that some channels of communication are difficult for deceivers to control, whereas others are relatively easy. To test this hypothesis, they showed a series of films—some pleasant, others disgusting—to a group of female nurses. While watching, the nurses were instructed either to report their honest impressions of these films or to conceal their true feelings. Through the use of hidden cameras, these participants were videotaped. Others, acting as observers, then viewed the tapes and judged whether the participants had been truthful or deceptive. The results showed that judgment accuracy rates were influenced by which types of nonverbal cues the observers were exposed to. Observers who watched tapes that focused on the body were better at detecting deception than were those who saw tapes focused on the face. The face can communicate emotion but is relatively easy for deceivers to control, unlike nervous movements of the hands and feet. Clearly, there is nothing like the wooden Pinocchio's nose to reveal whether someone is lying or telling the truth.

This study was the first of hundreds. In all this research, one group of participants makes truthful or deceptive statements, while another group reads the transcripts, listens to audiotapes or watches videotapes, and then tries to judge the statements. Consistently, in laboratories all over the world, results show that people are only about 54% accurate in judging truth and deception, too often accepting what others say at face value (Bond & DePaulo, 2006; Vrij, 2008). In fact, a good deal of research shows that professionals who are specially trained and who regularly make these kinds of judgments for a living—such as police detectives, judges, psychiatrists, customs inspectors, and those who administer lie-detector tests for the CIA, the FBI, and the military—are also highly prone to error (Ekman & O'Sullivan, 1991; Granhag & Strömwall, 2004; Meissner & Kassin, 2002; Vrij, 2008; see Table 4.2).

What seems to be the problem? One common hypothesis is that there is a mismatch between the behavioral cues that signal deception and those we use to detect deception (Zuckerman et al., 1981; DePaulo et al., 2003). Think about it. There are four channels of communication that provide potentially relevant information: the spoken word, the face, the body, and the voice. Yet when people have a reason to lie, the words they choose cannot be trusted, and they are generally able to control both the face and body (the voice is the most telling channel; when people lie, they tend to hesitate, then speed up and raise the pitch of their voice). In a survey of approximately 2,500 adults in 58 countries, an international team of researchers found that more than 70% believed that liars tend to avert their eyes—a cue that is not supported by any research. Similarly, most survey respondents believed that people squirm, stutter, fidget, and touch themselves when they lie—also cues that are not supported by the research (Global Deception Research Team, 2006).

Perhaps people rely on the wrong behavioral cues to deception, but a recent analysis of this same literature shows that the problem should be somewhat differently stated: It's not that people make truth and lie judgments on the basis of the wrong cues, but rather the problem is that none of the behavioral cues people look for are very telling (Hartwig & Bond, 2011). Throughout history, people have tended to assume that the way to spot a liar is to watch for signs of stress in

© Everett Collection

Research on lying and its detection has shown that there is no one behavioral cue, like Pinocchio's growing wooden nose, that can be used to signal deception.

### TABLE 4.2

**Can the "Experts" Distinguish Truth and Deception?**

Lie-detection experts with experience at making judgments of truth and deception were shown brief videotapes of 10 women telling the truth or lying about their feelings. Considering that there was a 50–50 chance of guessing correctly, the accuracy rates were remarkably low. Only a sample of U.S. Secret Service agents posted a better-than-chance performance.

| Observer Groups | Accuracy Rates (%) |
|---|---|
| College students | 52.82 |
| CIA, FBI, and military | 55.67 |
| Police investigators | 55.79 |
| Trial judges | 56.73 |
| Psychiatrists | 57.61 |
| U.S. Secret Service agents | 64.12 |

From Ekman, P., and O'Sullivan, M., "Who can catch a liar?" *American Psychologist* vol 46 (pp. 913–920). Copyright © 1991 by the American Psychological Association. Reprinted by permission.

© David Becker/NewSport/Corbis

Pius Heinz is a professional poker player from Bonn, Germany. At the age of 22, he won the Main Event at the 2011 World Series of Poker and received $8.7 million for his first place finish. As with all successful players, Heinz wears the proverbial "poker face" while playing so as not to betray how he feels about his hand.

Adaptively, people are skilled at knowing when someone is lying rather than telling the truth. **F**ALSE.

his or her behavior. Yet in important real-life situations—for example, at a high-stakes poker table, the security screening area of an airport, or a police interrogation room—truth tellers are also likely to exhibit signs of stress. For this reason, researchers today are seeking a different approach. Most notably, Aldert Vrij and his colleagues theorize that lying is harder to do and requires more thinking than telling the truth (Vrij et al., 2010; Vrij & Granhag, 2012). Therefore, they argue, we should focus on behavioral cues that betray cognitive *effort*.

This realization has led researchers to create more challenging types of interviews that could outsmart liars, force them to think harder, and thereby expose their deception. In one study, for example, they asked truth tellers and liars to recount their stories in reverse chronological order. This task was more effortful for the deceivers to do, which made the interviewers better able to distinguish between truths and lies (Vrij et al., 2008). In a second study, truth tellers and liars were instructed to maintain eye contact with their interviewer. This added burden taxed those who were lying more it did those who were telling the truth, which enabled observers to better distinguish between the two groups (Vrij et al., 2010).

In the wake of the September 11 terrorist attacks and heightened worldwide concerns about security, the ability to distinguish truths and lies is essential, potentially a matter of life and death. Yet research shows that social perceivers tune in to the wrong channels. Too easily seduced by the silver tongue, the smiling face, and the restless body, we often fail to notice the quivering voice. Too focused on how stressed a person seems while speaking—an emotional state that afflicts not only guilty liars but innocent truth tellers who stand falsely accused—we fail to notice the amount of effort it takes someone to recite their story or answer a question. With social psychologists in hot pursuit of ways to improve upon human lie-detection skills, stay tuned for further developments in years to come.

# Attribution: From Elements to Dispositions

To interact effectively with others, we need to know how they feel and when they can be trusted. But to understand people well enough to predict their future behavior, we must also identify their inner *dispositions*—stable characteristics such as personality traits, attitudes, and abilities. Since we cannot actually see dispositions, we infer them indirectly from what a person says and does. In this section, we look at the processes that lead us to make these inferences.

## ❯ Attribution Theories

Do you ever think about the influence you have on other people? What about the roles of heredity, childhood experiences, and social forces? Do you wonder why some people succeed while others fail? Individuals differ in the extent to which they feel a need to explain the uncertain events of human behavior (Weary & Edwards, 1994). Although there are vast differences among us, people in general tend to ask "why?" when they confront events that are important, negative, or unexpected (Weiner, 1985)—and when understanding these events has personal relevance (Malle & Knobe, 1997).

To make sense of our social world, we try to understand the causes of other people's behavior. But what kinds of explanations do we make, and how do we go about making them? In a classic book entitled *The Psychology of Interpersonal Relations*, Fritz Heider (1958) took the first step toward answering these questions. To Heider, we are all scientists of a sort. Motivated to understand others well enough to manage our social lives, we observe, analyze, and explain their behavior. The explanations we come up with are called *attributions,* and the theory that describes the process is called attribution theory. The questions posed at the beginning of the chapter regarding the behavior of George Zimmerman, Trayvon Martin, and Wall Street criminal Bernie Madoff are all questions of attribution.

Ask people to explain why their fellow human beings behave as they do—why they succeed or fail, laugh or cry, work or play, or help or hurt others—and you'll see that they come up with complex explanations often focused on whether the behavior is intentional or unintentional (Malle et al., 2000). Interested in how people answer these kinds of *why* questions, Heider found it particularly useful to group the explanations people give into two categories: *personal* and *situational*. In the 2012 shooting incident, everyone wanted to know what caused Zimmerman to follow Martin. Immediately, some observers pointed the finger of blame at Zimmerman, an overly suspicious community patrolman (a personal attribution). Yet others speculated that his actions were provoked by a rash of recent crimes in the neighborhood or something specific about Martin's appearance or behavior (a situational attribution). The same questions were asked about why Zimmerman then shot Martin: Was his finger on the trigger and ready to shoot or did he act in self-defense?

The task for the attribution theorist is not to determine the true *causes* of such an event but rather to understand people's *perceptions* of causality. Heider's insights provided an initial spark for a number of formal models that together came to be known as attribution theory (Weiner, 2008). For now, we describe two of these theories.

"It's not you, Frank, it's me—I don't like you."

**People make personal and situational attributions all the time in an effort to make sense of their social world. But what kind of attribution is being made here?**

**Jones's Correspondent Inference Theory**  According to Edward Jones and Keith Davis (1965), each of us tries to understand other people by observing and analyzing their behavior. Jones and Davis's *correspondent inference theory* predicts that people try to infer from an action whether the act corresponds to an enduring personal trait of the actor. Is the person who commits an act of aggression a beast? Is the person who donates money to charity an altruist? To answer these kinds of questions, people make inferences on the basis of three factors.

The first factor is a person's degree of *choice*. Behavior that is freely chosen is more informative about a person than behavior that is coerced. In one study, participants read

**attribution theory**  A group of theories that describe how people explain the causes of behavior.

**personal attribution**  Attribution to internal characteristics of an actor, such as ability, personality, mood, or effort.

**situational attribution**  Attribution to factors external to an actor, such as the task, other people, or luck.

● **FIGURE 4.4**

**What Does This Speechwriter Really Believe?**

As predicted by correspondent inference theory, participants who read a student's speech (behavior) were more likely to assume that it reflected the student's true attitude (disposition) when the position taken was freely chosen (left) rather than assigned (right). But also note the evidence for the fundamental attribution error. Even participants who thought the student had been assigned a position inferred the student's attitude from the speech. From Jones, E.G. and Harris, K.E., "The attribution of attitudes," *Journal of Experimental Social Psychology* vol 3 (pp. 1–24). Copyright © 1967 Elsevier. Reprinted with with permission.

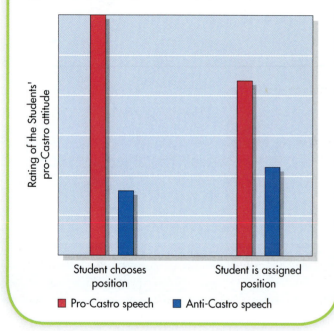

a speech, presumably written by a college student, that either favored or opposed Fidel Castro, then the communist leader of Cuba. Some participants were told that the student had freely chosen this position and others were told that the student had been assigned the position by a professor. When asked to judge the student's true attitude, participants were more likely to assume a correspondence between the essay (behavior) and the student's attitude (disposition) when the student had had a choice than when he or she had been assigned to the role (Jones & Harris, 1967; see ● Figure 4.4). Keep this study in mind. It supports correspondent inference theory, but as we will see later, it also demonstrates one of the most tenacious biases of social perception.

The second factor that leads us to make dispositional inferences is the *expectedness* of behavior. As previously noted, an action tells us more about a person when it departs from the norm than when it is typical, part of a social role, or otherwise expected under the circumstances (Jones et al., 1961). Thus, people think they know more about a student who wears three-piece suits to class or a citizen who openly refuses to pay taxes than about a student who wears blue jeans to class or a citizen who dutifully files tax returns on April 15.

Third, social perceivers take into account the intended *effects* or consequences of someone's behavior. Acts that produce many desirable outcomes do not reveal a person's specific motives as clearly as acts that produce only a single desirable outcome (Newtson, 1974). For example, you are likely to be uncertain about exactly why a person stays on a job that is enjoyable, high paying, and in an attractive location—three highly desirable outcomes, each sufficient to explain the behavior. In contrast, you may feel more certain about why a person stays on a job that is tedious and low paying but is in an attractive location—only one desirable outcome.

**Kelley's Covariation Theory** Correspondent inference theory seeks to describe how perceivers try to discern an individual's personal characteristics from a slice of behavioral evidence. However, behavior can be attributed not only to personal factors but to situational factors as well. How is this distinction made? In the opening chapter, we noted that the causes of human behavior can be derived only through experiments. That is, one has to make more than a single observation and compare behavior in two or more settings in which everything stays the same except for the independent variables. Like Heider, Harold Kelley (1967) theorized that people are much like scientists in this regard. They may not observe others in a controlled laboratory, but they too search for clues, make comparisons, and think in terms of "experiments."

According to Kelley, people make attributions by using the **covariation principle**: In order for something to be the cause of a behavior, it must be present when the behavior occurs and absent when it does not. Three kinds of covariation information in particular are useful: consensus, distinctiveness, and consistency. To illustrate these concepts, imagine you are standing on a street corner one hot, steamy evening minding your own business, when all of a sudden a stranger comes out of a cool air-conditioned movie theater and blurts out, "Great flick!" Looking up, you don't recognize the movie title, so

**covariation principle** A principle of attribution theory that holds that people attribute behavior to factors that are present when a behavior occurs and are absent when it does not.

you wonder what to make of this "recommendation." Was the behavior (the rave review) caused by something about the person (the stranger), the stimulus (the film), or the circumstances (say, the comfortable theater)? If you are possibly interested in spending a night at the movie, how would you proceed to explain what happened? What kinds of information would you want to obtain?

Thinking like a scientist, you might seek out *consensus information* to see how different persons react to the same stimulus. In other words, what do other moviegoers think about this film? If others also rave about it, then this stranger's behavior is high in consensus and is attributed to the stimulus. If others are critical of this film, however, then the behavior is low in consensus and is attributed to the person.

Still thinking like a scientist, you might also want *distinctiveness information* to see how the same person reacts to different stimuli. In other words, what does this moviegoer think of other films? If the stranger is generally critical of other films, then the target behavior is high in distinctiveness and is attributed to the stimulus. If the stranger raves about everything he or she sees, however, then the behavior is low in distinctiveness and is attributed to the person.

Finally, you might want to seek *consistency information* to see what happens to the behavior at another time when the person and the stimulus both remain the same. How does this moviegoer feel about this film on other occasions? If the stranger raves about the film on video as well as in the theater, regardless of surroundings, then the behavior is high in consistency. If the stranger does not always enjoy the film, the behavior is low in consistency. According to Kelley, behavior that is consistent is attributed to the stimulus when consensus and distinctiveness are also high and to the person when they are low. In contrast, behavior that is low in consistency is attributed to transient circumstances, such as the temperature of the movie theater.

Kelley's theory and the predictions it makes are represented in ● Figure 4.5. Does this model describe the kinds of information you seek when you try to determine what causes people to behave as they do? Often it does. Research shows that people who are

● **FIGURE 4.5**

**Kelley's Covariation Theory**

For behaviors that are high in consistency, people make personal attributions when there is low consensus and distinctiveness (top row) and stimulus attributions when there is high consensus and distinctiveness (bottom row). Behaviors that are low in consistency (not shown) are attributed to passing circumstances.

© Cengage Learning

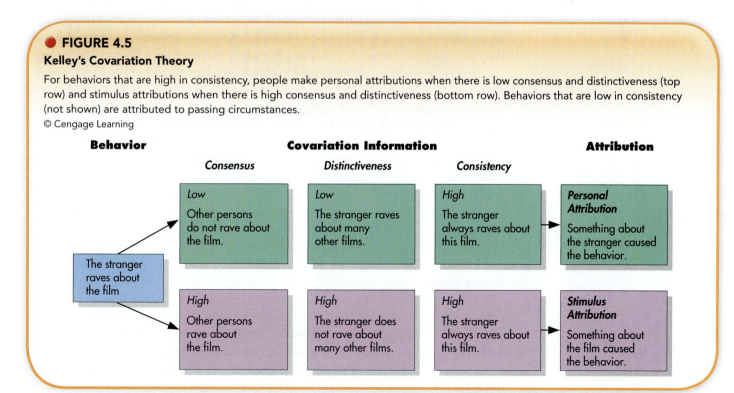

asked to make attributions for various events do tend to follow the logic of covariation (Cheng & Novick, 1990; Fosterling, 1992; McArthur, 1972). However, this research also shows that individuals have their own attributional styles, so people often disagree about what caused a particular behavior (Robins et al., 2004). There are two ways in which social perceivers differ. First, individuals vary in the extent to which they believe that human behaviors are caused by personal characteristics that are fixed ("Everyone is a certain kind of person; there is not much that can be done to really change that") or by characteristics that are malleable ("People can change even their most basic qualities") (Dweck, 2012). Second, some individuals are more likely than others to process new information in ways that are colored by self-serving motives (von Hippel et al., 2005).

## Attribution Biases

Daniel Kahneman won a Nobel Prize in Economics for work on the psychology of judgment and decision making. In his newest book, *Thinking, Fast and Slow*, Kahneman (2011) summarizes a lifetime of research showing that the human mind operates by two different systems of thought. System 1 is quick, easy, and automatic—using a process that one might call "intuitive." Determining which of two objects is more distant, detecting anger in someone's face, adding 2 + 2, and understanding a simple sentence are the kinds of automatic activities engaged by this system. In contrast, System 2 is slow, controlled, and requires attention and effort—using a process that feels more reasoned. Looking for a specific face in a crowd, parking in a narrow space, counting the number of letters on a page, figuring out how a magic trick works, and filling out taxes are the kinds of activities that require your focused and undivided attention. According to Kahneman, Systems 1 and 2 are both active when people are awake. System 1 runs automatically and guides us until it runs into difficulty, as when something unexpected happens. At that point the more effortful System 2 is activated.

When the theories of attribution were first proposed, they were represented by elaborate flow charts, formulas, and diagrams, leading many social psychologists to wonder: Do people really analyze behavior in the way that one might expect of scientists, or computers? Do people have the time, the motivation, or the cognitive capacity for such elaborate, mindful, System 1 processes? The answer is sometimes yes, sometimes no.

As social perceivers, we are limited in our ability to process all relevant information, or we may lack the kinds of training needed to employ fully the principles of attribution theory. More important, we often don't make an effort to think carefully about the attributions we make. With so much to explain and not enough time in a day, people take mental shortcuts, cross their fingers, hope for the best, and get on with life. The problem is that speed brings bias and perhaps even a loss of accuracy. In this section, we examine some of these shortcuts and their consequences.

**Cognitive Heuristics** According to Kahneman, Tversky, and others, people often make attributions and other types of social judgments by using "cognitive heuristics"—information-processing rules of thumb that enable us to think in ways that are quick and easy but that often lead to error (Gilovich et al., 2002; Kahneman et al., 1982; Nisbett & Ross, 1980).

One rule of thumb that has particularly troublesome effects on attribution is the availability heuristic, a tendency to estimate the odds that an event will occur by how easily instances of it pop to mind. To demonstrate this phenomenon, Tversky and Kahneman (1973) asked research participants: Which is more common, words that start with the letter *r* or words that contain *r* as the third letter? In actuality, the English language has many more words with *r* as the third letter than as the first. Yet most people guessed that more words begin with *r*. Why? Because it's easier to bring to mind words in which

**availability heuristic** The tendency to estimate the likelihood that an event will occur by how easily instances of it come to mind.

*r* appears first. Apparently, our estimates of likelihood are heavily influenced by events that are readily available in memory (MacLeod & Campbell, 1992). Sadly, the availability heuristic can lead us astray in two ways. First, it gives rise to the **false-consensus effect**, a tendency for people to overestimate the extent to which others share their opinions, attributes, and behaviors. This bias is pervasive. Regardless of whether people are asked to predict how others feel about military spending, abortion, gun control, Campbell's soup, certain types of music, or norms for appropriate behavior, they exaggerate the percentage of others who behave similarly or share their views (Krueger, 1998; Ross et al., 1977).

To illustrate the effect, Joachim Krueger (2000) asked participants in a study to indicate whether or not they had certain personality traits. Then they were asked to estimate the percentage of people in general who have these same traits. As shown in Table 4.3, participants' beliefs about other people's personalities were biased by their own self-perceptions. In part, the false-consensus bias is a by-product of the availability heuristic. We tend to associate with others who are like us in important ways, so we are more likely to notice and recall instances of similar rather than dissimilar behavior (Deutsch, 1989).

| TABLE 4.3 |
| :--- |
| **The False-Consensus Effect** |
| In this study, participants who did and participants who did not rate various personality traits as descriptive of themselves estimated the percentage of other people who had these traits. As shown below, participants' estimates of the population consensus were biased by their own self-perceptions. |

| Traits | Self Yes (%) | Self No (%) |
| --- | --- | --- |
| Alert | 75 | 65 |
| Discontented | 48 | 33 |
| Loud | 46 | 43 |
| Meticulous | 52 | 41 |
| Sly | 36 | 28 |
| Smug | 41 | 33 |

Krueger (2000) © Cengage Learning

A second consequence of the availability heuristic is that social perceptions are influenced more by one vivid life story than by hard statistical facts. Have you ever wondered why so many people buy lottery tickets despite the astonishingly low odds or why so many travelers are afraid to fly even though they are more likely to perish in a car accident? These behaviors are symptomatic of the **base-rate fallacy**—the fact that people are relatively insensitive to numerical base rates, or probabilities; they are influenced more by graphic, dramatic events such as the sight of a multimillion-dollar lottery winner celebrating on TV or a photograph of bodies being pulled from the wreckage of a plane crash.

The base-rate fallacy can thus lead to various misperceptions of risk. Indeed, people overestimate the number of those who die in shootings, fires, floods, and terrorist bombings and underestimate the death toll caused by heart attacks, strokes, diabetes, and other mundane events. Perceptions of risk seem more relevant now than in the past by newly acquired fears of terrorism, or economic collapse, and research shows that such perceptions are affected more by fear, anxiety, and other emotions than by cold and objective probabilities (Loewenstein et al., 2001; Slovic, 2000). At times the result can be capricious and downright irrational. Consistent with the fact that people tend to fear things that sound unfamiliar, participants in one study rated fictional food additives as more hazardous to health when the names were difficult to pronounce, such as Hnegripitrom, than when they were easier to pronounce, such as Magnalroxate (Song & Schwarz, 2009).

Every day, we are besieged by both types of information: We read and hear about the unemployment rate, and we watch personal interviews with people who were recently laid off; we read the casualty figures of war, and we witness the agony of a parent who has lost a child in combat. Logically, statistics that summarize the experiences of large numbers of people are more informative than a single and perhaps atypical case, but perceivers march to a different drummer. As long as the personal anecdote is seen as relevant (Schwarz et al., 1991) and the source as credible (Hinsz et al., 1988), it seems that one vivid image is worth a thousand numbers.

*"A single death is a tragedy; a million is a statistic."*

—Joseph Stalin

**false-consensus effect**   The tendency for people to overestimate the extent to which others share their opinions, attributes, and behaviors.

**base-rate fallacy**   The finding that people are relatively insensitive to consensus information presented in the form of numerical base rates.

**Counterfactual Thinking** Interestingly, people can also be influenced by how easy it is to imagine events that did *not* occur. As thoughtful and curious beings, we are often not content to accept what happens to us or to others without wondering, at least in private, "What if . . . ?"

According to Kahneman and Miller (1986), people's emotional reactions to events are often colored by counterfactual thinking, a tendency to imagine alternative outcomes that might have occurred but did not. There are different types of counterfactual thoughts. If we imagine a result that is better than the actual result, then we're likely to experience disappointment, regret, and frustration. If the imagined result is worse, then we react with emotions that range from relief and satisfaction to elation. Thus, the psychological impact of positive and negative events depends on the way we think about "what might have been" (Roese, 1997; Roese & Olson, 1995).

What domains of life trigger the most counterfactual thinking—and the regret that may follow? Summarizing past research, Neal Roese and Amy Summerville (2005) found that people's top three regrets center, in order, on education ("I should have stayed in school"), career ("If only I had applied for that job"), and romance ("If only I had asked her out")—all domains that present us with opportunities that we may or may not realize. Of course, counterfactual thinking does not necessarily lead people into a sense of regret. In fact, Laura Kray and others (2010) note that reflecting on "what might have been" can sometimes help us to define ourselves as well as the meaning in our lives. Think about it. What would you be like today if you had chosen to attend a different school, or if you had not met your best friend? These researchers found that participants who were asked to reflect on these counterfactual "what if" questions later saw their college choices and friendships as more meaningful than those who did not stop to ask these questions. Perhaps by thinking about what might have been, people can more fully appreciate what they have.

Obviously, people don't immerse themselves in counterfactual thought after every experience. Research shows that we are more likely to think about what might have been—often with feelings of regret—after negative outcomes that result from actions we take rather than from actions we don't take (Byrne & McEleney 2000). Consider an experience that may sound all too familiar: You take a multiple-choice test, and after reviewing an item you struggled over, you want to change the answer. What do you do? Research has shown that most changes in test answers are from incorrect to correct. Yet most college students harbor the "first instinct fallacy" that it is best to stick with one's original answer. Why? Justin Kruger and his colleagues (2005) found that this myth arises from counterfactual thinking: that students are more likely to react with regret and frustration ("If only I had . . .") after changing a correct answer than after failing to change an incorrect answer.

According to Victoria Medvec and Kenneth Savitsky (1997), certain situations—such as being on the *verge* of a better or worse outcome, just above or below some cutoff point—also make it especially easy to conjure up images of what might have been. The implications are intriguing. Imagine, for example, that you are an Olympic athlete and have just won a silver medal—a remarkable feat. Now imagine that you have just won the bronze medal. Which situation would make you feel better? Rationally speaking, you should feel more pride and satisfaction with a silver medal. But what if your achievement had prompted you to engage in counterfactual thinking? What alternative would haunt your mind if you had finished in second place? Where would your focus be if you had placed third? Is it possible that the athlete who is better off objectively will feel worse?

Country singer Lee Brice wrote a song about counterfactual thinking. In *A Woman Like You*, his girlfriend asks, "Honey, what would you do if you'd never met me?" Here's part of his response:

*I'd do a lot more offshore fishin'*
*I'd probably eat more drive-thru chicken*
*Take a few strokes off my golf game*
*If I'd have never known your name*
*I'd still be driving that old green Nova*
*I probably never would have heard of yoga*
*Be a better football fan*
*But if I was a single man*
*Alone and out there on the loose*
*Well I'd be looking for a woman like you.*

Rick Diamond/Getty Images

**counterfactual thinking** The tendency to imagine alternative events or outcomes that might have occurred but did not.

To examine this question, Medvec and others (1995) videotaped 41 athletes in the 1992 summer Olympic Games at the moment they realized that they had won a silver or a bronze medal and again, later, during the medal ceremony. Then they showed these tapes, without sound, to people who did not know the order of finish. These participants were asked to observe the medalists and rate their emotional states on a scale ranging from "agony" to "ecstasy." The intriguing result, as you might expect, was that the bronze medalists, on average, seemed happier than the silver medalists. Was there any more direct evidence of counterfactual thinking? In a second study, participants who watched interviews with many of these same athletes rated the silver medalists as more negatively focused on finishing second rather than first and the bronze medalists as more positively focused on finishing third rather than fourth. For these world-class athletes, feelings of satisfaction were based more on their thoughts of what might have been than on the reality of what was.

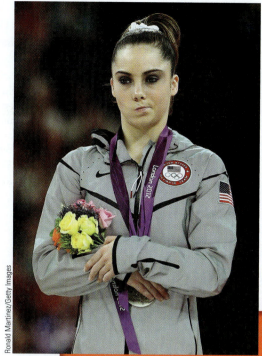

Ronald Martinez/Getty Images

Entering the 2012 Summer Olympics in London, U.S. gymnast McKayla Maroney was the best female vaulter in the world. She went on to win a silver medal. In what fast became an iconic image, here she is during the podium ceremony. Thinking about what might have been, Maroney, clearly, was focused on not winning gold.

**The Fundamental Attribution Error**    By the time you finish reading this textbook, you will have learned the cardinal lesson of social psychology: People are profoundly influenced by the *situational* contexts of their behavior—or, as Samuel Sommers (2011) put it, *Situations Matter*. This point is not as obvious as it may seem. For instance, parents are often surprised to hear that their mischievous child, the family monster, is a perfect angel in the classroom. And students are often surprised to observe that their favorite professor, so eloquent in the lecture hall, may stumble over words in less formal gatherings. These reactions are symptomatic of a well-documented aspect of social perception. When people explain the behavior of others, they tend to overestimate the role of personal factors and overlook the impact of situations. Because this bias is so pervasive (and sometimes so misleading) it has been called the **fundamental attribution error** (Ross, 1977).

Evidence of the fundamental attribution error was first reported in the Jones and Harris (1967) study described earlier, in which participants read an essay presumably written by a student. In that study, participants were more likely to infer the student's true attitude when the position taken had been freely chosen than when they thought that the student had been assigned to it. But look again at Figure 4.4, and you'll notice that even when participants thought that the student had no choice but to assert a position, they still used the speech to infer his or her attitude. This finding has been repeated many times. Whether the essay topic is nuclear power, abortion, drug laws, or the death penalty, the results are essentially the same (Jones, 1990).

People fall prey to the fundamental attribution error even when they are fully aware of the situation's impact on behavior. In one experiment, the participants were themselves assigned to take a position, whereupon they swapped essays and rated each other. Remarkably, they still jumped to conclusions about each other's attitudes (Miller et al., 1981). In another experiment, participants inferred attitudes from a speech even when they were the ones who had assigned the position to be taken (Gilbert & Jones, 1986).

A fascinating study by Lee Ross and his colleagues (1977) demonstrates the fundamental attribution error in a familiar setting, the TV quiz show. By a flip of the coin, participants in this study were randomly assigned to play the role of either the questioner or the contestant in a quiz game while spectators looked on. In front of the contestant and spectators, the experimenter instructed each questioner to write 10 challenging questions from his or her own store of general knowledge. If you are a trivia buff, you can imagine how esoteric such questions can be: Who was the founder of e-Bay? What team won the NHL Stanley Cup in 1976? It is no wonder that contestants correctly answered only about 40% of the questions asked. When the game was over, all participants rated the questioner's and contestant's general knowledge on a scale of 0 to 100.

*"During the 1996 Olympics, Nike ran a counterfactual (and controversial) ad: 'You don't win silver, you lose gold.'"*

**fundamental attribution error**
The tendency to focus on the role of personal causes and underestimate the impact of situations on other people's behavior.

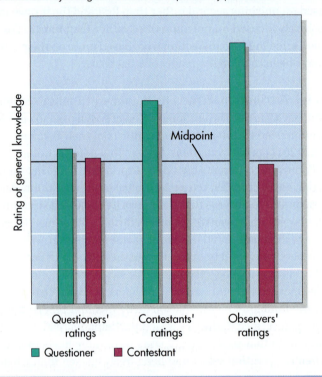

● **FIGURE 4.6**

**Fundamental Attribution Error and the TV Quiz Show**

Even though the simulated quiz show situation placed questioners in an obvious position of advantage over contestants, observers rated the questioners as more knowledgeable (right). Questioners did not overrate their general knowledge (left), but contestants rated themselves as inferior (middle) and observers rated them as inferior as well. These results illustrate the fundamental attribution error.

From Ross, L., Amabile, T.M, and Steinmetz, J.L., "Social roles, social control, and biases in social perception process," *Journal of Personality and Social Psychology* vol 35 (pp. 485–494). Copyright © 1977 by the American Psychological Association. Reprinted by permission.

Picture the events that transpired. The questioners appeared more knowledgeable than the contestants. After all, they knew all the answers. But a moment's reflection should remind us that the situation put the questioner at a distinct advantage (there were no differences between the two groups on an objective test of general knowledge). Did participants take the questioner's advantage into account, or did they assume that the questioners actually had greater knowledge? The results were startling. Spectators rated the questioners as above average in their general knowledge and the contestants as below average. The contestants even rated themselves as inferior to their partners. Like the spectators, they too were fooled by the loaded situation (see ● Figure 4.6).

What's going on here? Why do social perceivers consistently make assumptions about persons and fail to appreciate the impact of situations? According to Daniel Gilbert and Patrick Malone (1995), the problem stems in part from *how* we make attributions. Attribution theorists used to assume that people survey all the evidence and then decide on whether to make a personal or a situational attribution. Instead, it appears that social perception is a two-step process: First, we identify the behavior and make a quick personal attribution; then we correct or adjust that inference to account for situational influences. At least for those raised in a Western culture, the first step is simple and automatic, like a reflex; the second requires attention, thought, and effort. At present, social neuroscience researchers are beginning to use neuroimaging to probe the brain for evidence of this model (Lieberman et al., 2004).

Several research findings support this hypothesis. First, without realizing it, people often form impressions of others based on a quick glimpse at a face or fleeting sample of behavior (Newman & Uleman, 1989; Todorov & Uleman, 2004). Second, perceivers are *more* likely to commit the fundamental attribution error when they are cognitively busy, or distracted, as they observe the target person than when they pay full attention (Gilbert et al., 1992; Trope & Alfieri, 1997). Since the two-step model predicts that personal attributions are automatic but that the later adjustment for situational factors requires conscious thought, it makes sense to suggest that when attention is divided, when the attribution is made hastily, or when perceivers lack motivation, the second step suffers more than the first. As Gilbert and his colleagues (1988) put it, "The first step is a snap, but the second one's a doozy" (p. 738).

Why is the first step such a snap, and why does it seem so natural for people to assume a link between acts and personal dispositions? One possible explanation is based on Heider's (1958) insight that people see others' dispositions in behavior because of a perceptual bias, something like an optical illusion. When you listen to a speech or watch a quiz show, the actor is the conspicuous *figure* of your attention; the situation fades into the *background* ("out of sight, out of mind," as they say). According to Heider, people attribute events to factors that are perceptually conspicuous, or *salient*. To test this hypothesis, Shelley Taylor and Susan Fiske (1975) varied the seating arrangements of observers who watched as two actors engaged in a carefully staged conversation. In each session, the participants were seated so that they faced actor A, actor B, or both actors. When later questioned about their observations, most participants rated the actor they faced as the more dominant member of the pair, the one who set the tone and direction.

## Culture and Attribution

In the fifth century B.C.E., Herodotus, a Greek historian, argued that Greeks and Egyptians thought differently because the Greeks wrote from left to right and the Egyptians from right to left. Many years later, inspired by anthropologist Edward Sapir, Benjamin Lee Whorf (1956) theorized that the language people speak—the words, the rules, and so on—can influence the way they conceptualize the world. To illustrate, he pointed to cultural variations in the use of words to represent reality. He noted that the Hanunoo of the Philippines have 92 different terms for rice, in contrast to the crude distinction North Americans make between "white rice" and "brown rice." Similarly, while English speakers have one word for snow, Eskimos have several words, which, Whorf argued, enables them to make distinctions that others may miss between "falling snow, snow on the ground, snow packed hard like ice, slushy snow, wind-driven flying snow—whatever the situation may be" (p. 216).

As a result of many years of research, it is now clear that language and culture can influence the way people think about time, space, objects, and other aspects of the physical world around them (Bloom, 1981; Hardin & Banaji, 1993). Consider perceptions of color. The rainbow is a continuum of light varying smoothly between the shortest and longest wavelengths of the visible spectrum. Yet when we look at it, we see distinct categories of color that correspond to "red," "orange," "yellow," "green," "blue," and so on. Languages differ in the parts of the color spectrum that are named. In Papua, New Guinea, where Berinmo speakers distinguish between green and brown (they single out a form of "khaki" as the color of dead leaves), an object reflecting light at 450 nanometers would be called green. Yet many English speakers, who distinguish between colors that cross the blue-green part of the spectrum, might see that same object as blue (Özgen, 2004).

Just as culture influences the way we perceive the physical world, so it also influences the way we view individuals and their place in the social world around them.

How knowledgeable is this man? Alex Trebek has hosted the TV quiz show *Jeopardy!* since 1984. As host, Trebek reads questions to contestants and then reveals the correct answers. In light of the quiz show study by Ross and others (1977), which illustrates the fundamental attribution error, viewers probably see Trebek as highly knowledgeable, despite knowing that the answers he recites are provided to him as part of his job.

Like social psychologists, people are sensitive to situational causes when explaining the behavior of others. **F**ALSE.

Hence, although attribution researchers used to assume that people all over the world explained human behavior in the same ways, it is now clear that cultures shape in subtle but profound ways the kinds of attributions we make about people, their behavior, and social situations (Nisbett, 2003).

Consider the contrasting orientations between Western "individualist" cultures (whose members tend to believe that persons are autonomous, motivated by internal forces, and responsible for their own actions) and non-Western "collectivist" cultures (whose members take a more holistic view that emphasizes the relationship between persons and their surroundings). Do these differing world views influence the attributions we make? Is it possible that the fundamental attribution error is a uniquely Western phenomenon?

To answer these questions, Joan Miller (1984) asked Americans and Asian Indians of varying ages to describe the causes of positive and negative behaviors they had observed in their lives. Among young children, there were no cultural differences. With increasing age, however, the American participants made more personal attributions, while the Indians made more situational attributions (see ● Figure 4.7). Testing this hypothesis in different ways, other studies as well have revealed that people form habits of thought, learning to make attributions according to culturally formed beliefs about the causes of human behavior (Lieberman et al., 2005; Miller et al., 2011; Miyamoto & Kitayama, 2002; Na & Kitayama, 2011).

On this point, Ara Norenzayan and Richard Nisbett (2000) argue that cultural differences in attribution are founded on varying folk theories about human causality. Western cultures, they note, emphasize the individual person and his or her attributes,

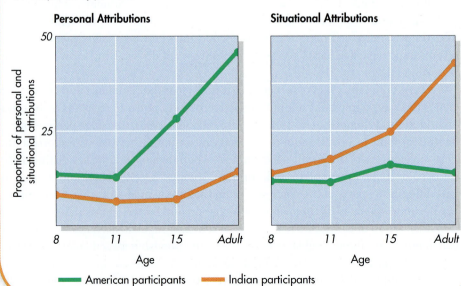

● **FIGURE 4.7**

**Fundamental Attribution Error: A Western Bias?**

American and Asian Indian participants of varying ages described the causes of negative actions they had observed. Among young children, there were no cultural differences. With increasing age, however, Americans made more personal attributions and Indian participants made more situational attributions. Explanations for positive behaviors followed a similar pattern. This finding suggests that the fundamental error is a Western phenomenon.

From Miller, J.G., "Culture and the development of everyday social explanation," *Journal of Personality and Social Psychology* vol 46 (pp. 961–978). Copyright © 1984 by the American Psychological Association. Reprinted by permission.

whereas East Asian cultures focus on the background or field that surrounds that person. To test this hypothesis, they showed American and Japanese college students underwater scenes featuring a cast of small fish, small animals, plants, rocks, and coral and one or more large, fast-moving *focal* fish, the stars of the show. Moments later, when asked to recount what they had seen, both groups recalled details about the focal fish to a nearly equal extent, but the Japanese reported far more details about the supporting cast in the background. Other researchers have also observed cultural differences in the extent to which people notice, think about, and remember the details of focal objects and their contexts (Ishii et al., 2003; Kitayama et al., 2003; Masuda & Nisbett, 2001).

Look at this tropical underwater scene, then turn away and try to recount as much of it as you can. What did you notice? What did you forget? When researchers showed American and Japanese students underwater scenes, they found that even though both groups recalled the focal fish (like the large blue one shown here), the Japanese recalled more about the elements of the background.

These cultural differences can also be observed in naturally occurring settings outside a psychology laboratory. In an article entitled "Going for the Gold," Hazel Rose Markus and her colleagues (2006) compared the way Olympic performances were described in the United States and Japan. By analyzing the newspaper and TV coverage in these countries, these researchers discovered that although everyone attributed victory and defeat to the athletes, American media were more likely to focus on each athlete's unique personal attributes (such as strength, speed, health, and determination). "I just stayed focused," said Misty Hyman, American gold medalist swimmer. "It was time to show the world what I could do." In addition to reflecting on personal attributes, Japanese media were also more likely to report more wholly on an athlete's background, his or her mental state, and the role of others such as parents, coaches, and competitors. Woman's marathon gold medalist Naoko Takahashi explained her own success this way: "Here is the best coach in the world, the best manager in the world, and all of the people who support me—all of these things were getting together and became a gold medal."

Clearly, the world is becoming a global village characterized by increasing racial and ethnic diversity within countries. Many people who migrate from one country to another become *bicultural* in their identity, retaining some ancestral manners of thought while adopting some of the lifestyles and values of their new homeland. How might these bicultural individuals make attributions for human behavior? Is it possible that they view people through one cultural frame or the other, depending on which one is brought to mind? It's interesting that when shown a picture of one fish swimming ahead of a group, and asked why, Americans see the lone fish as *leading* the others (a personal attribution), while Chinese see the same fish as being *chased* by the others (a situational attribution). But what about bicultural social perceivers? In a study of China-born students attending college in California, researchers presented images symbolizing one of the two cultures (such as the U.S. and Chinese flags), administered the fish test, and found that compared to students exposed to the American images, those who saw the Chinese images made more situational attributions, seeing the lone fish as being chased rather than as leading (see ● Figure 4.8). Apparently, it is possible for us to hold differing cultural worldviews at the same time and to perceive others through either lens, depending on which culture is brought to mind (Hong et al., 2000; Oyserman & Lee, 2008).

## Motivational Biases

As objective as we try to be, our social perceptions are sometimes colored by personal needs, wishes, and preferences. This tendency shows itself in the officiating controversies of the Olympics every four years, in other competitive sports, and in talent contests such as *American Idol* and *The Voice*.

● **FIGURE 4.8**

**Attributions Within Cultural Frames**

When one fish swims ahead of the others in a group, Americans see that fish as leading the others (a personal attribution), while Chinese see it as being chased by the others (a situational attribution). In a study of bicultural Chinese students attending college in California, Ying-yi Hong and others (2000) displayed visual images that symbolized the United States or China before administering the fish test. As you can see, compared to students who were not shown any images (center), the tendency to make situational attributions was more common among those exposed to Chinese images (right) and less common among those exposed to American images (left). It appears that social perceptions are fluid for people who are familiar with more than one worldview and that their perceptions depend on which culture is brought to mind.

From Hong, Y., Morris, M.W., Chiu, C., and Benet-Martinez, V., "Multicultural minds: A dynamic constructivist approach to culture and cognition," *American Psychologist*, vol 55 (pp. 709–720). Copyright © 2000 by the American Psychological Association. Reprinted by permission.

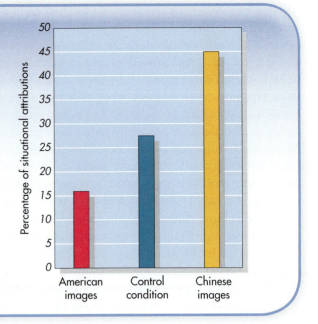

**Wishful Seeing** To illustrate wishful seeing in action, look at the object in ● Figure 4.9. What do you see? In a series of studies, Emily Balcetis and David Dunning (2006) showed stimuli like this one to college students who thought that they were participating in a taste-testing experiment. The students were told that they would be randomly assigned to taste either freshly squeezed orange juice or a greenish, foul-smelling "organic" drink—depending on whether a letter or a number was flashed on a laptop computer. For those told that a letter would assign them to the orange juice condition, 72% saw the letter *B*. For those told that a number would assign them to the orange juice, 61% saw the number *13*. In another study, research participants in a laboratory were quicker to identify rapidly presented food words on a computer screen when they were hungry than when they had recently eaten (Radel & Clement-Guillotin, 2012). In some very basic ways, people have a tendency to see what they want to see.

In a particularly ingenious program of research on "wishful seeing," Balcetis and Dunning (2010) wondered if people would judge objects that they want to be physically closer than more neutral objects. In one study, college students who were thirsty (fed pretzels without water) compared to those who were quenched (drank as much water as they wanted) estimated that a bottle of water across a table was 3 inches closer to them. In a second study, students estimated their distance in a room from a $100 bill as 8 inches closer when they thought they could win it than when it had no potential value. In a third study, participants took part in a beanbag toss in which they tried to hit a target on the floor that was 13 feet away. When the target was said to be worth $25 compared to when it had $0 value, participants underthrew the beanbag by an average of 9 inches—suggesting that they perceived the target to be closer than it was.

**Need for Self-Esteem** Motivations can bias our social perceptions in other ways as well. In Chapter 3, we saw that people have a strong need for self-esteem, a motive that can lead us to make favorable, self-serving, and one-sided attributions for our own behavior. Research with students, teachers, parents, workers, athletes, and others shows that people tend to take more credit for success than blame for failure. Similarly, people seek more information about their strengths than about weaknesses, overestimate their contributions to group efforts, exaggerate their control, and predict a rosy future. The false-consensus effect described earlier also has a self-serving side to it. It seems that we overestimate the extent to which others think, feel, and behave as we do, in part to assure ourselves that our ways are correct, normal, and socially appropriate (Alicke & Largo, 1995). This positivity bias in attributions is ubiquitous. Through a meta-analysis of 266 studies involving thousands of participants, Amy Mezulis and others (2004) found that except in some Asian cultures, "the self-serving bias is pervasive in the general population" (p. 711).

According to Dunning (2005), the need for self-esteem can bias social perceptions in other subtle ways too, even when we don't realize that the self is implicated. For example, do you consider yourself to be a "people person," or are you more of a "task-oriented" type? And which of the two styles do you think makes for great leadership? It turns out that students who describe themselves as people-oriented see social skills as necessary for good leadership, whereas those who are more task-focused see a task orientation as better for leadership. Hence, people tend to judge favorably others who are similar to themselves rather than different on key characteristics (McElwee et al., 2001).

Sometimes *ideological motives* can color our attributions for the behavior of others. In the United States, it is common for political conservatives to blame poverty, crime, and other social problems on an "underclass" of people who are uneducated, immoral, lazy, or self-indulgent; in contrast, liberals often attribute these same problems to social and economic institutions that favor powerful groups over others. Do conservatives and liberals think differently about the causes of human behavior, or do the attributions they make depend on whether the particular behavior they're trying to explain fits with their ideology? In a series of studies, Linda Skitka and others (2002) had college students who identified themselves as conservative or liberal make attributions for various events. They found that even though participants in general made personal attributions, as Westerners reflexively tend to do, they corrected for situational factors when ideologically motivated to do so. To explain why a prisoner was paroled, conservatives were more likely to believe that the facility was overcrowded (a situational attribution) than that the prisoner had reformed (a personal attribution); to explain why a man lost his job, liberals were more likely to blame the company's finances (a situational attribution) than the worker's poor performance (a personal attribution).

**Belief in a Just World**   At times, personal defensive motives lead us to blame others for their misfortunes. Consider the following classic experiment. Participants thought they were taking part in an emotion-perception study. One person, actually a confederate, was selected randomly to take a memory test while the others looked on. Each time the confederate made a mistake, she was jolted by a painful electric shock (actually, there was no shock; what participants saw was a staged videotape). Since participants knew that only the luck of the draw had kept them off the "hot seat," you might think they would react with sympathy and compassion. Not so. In fact, they belittled the hapless confederate (Lerner & Simmons, 1966).

Melvin Lerner (1980) argues that the tendency to be critical of victims stems from our deep-seated **belief in a just world**. According to Lerner, people need to view the world as a just place in which we "get what we deserve" and "deserve what we get"—a world where hard work and clean living always pay off and where laziness and a sinful lifestyle are punished. To believe otherwise is to concede that we, too, are vulnerable to the cruel twists and turns of fate. A good deal of research supports this theory (Hafer & Begue, 2005). Research also suggests that the belief in a just world can help victims cope and serves as a buffer against stress. But how might this belief system influence

● **FIGURE 4.9**

**Motivated Visual Perception: How People See What They Want to See**

Look at the image below. What do you see, the letter *B* or the number *13*? The stimulus itself is ambiguous and can plausibly be seen either way. Research participants who thought they were in a taste-testing experiment were told that they would be assigned to taste orange juice or a foul-smelling green drink depending on whether a letter or a number was flashed on a laptop computer. For those told that a *letter* would yield orange juice, 72% saw the image as *B*. For those told that a *number* would yield orange juice, 61% saw a *13*. This difference shows that sometimes people see what they *want* to see.
From Balcetis, E., & Dunning, D., "See what you want to see: Motivational influences on visual perception," *Journal of Personality and Social Psychology* vol 91 (pp. 612–625). Copyright © 2006 by the American Psychological Association. Reprinted by permission.

**belief in a just world**   The belief that individuals get what they deserve in life, an orientation that leads people to disparage victims.

perceptions of *others*? If people cannot help or compensate the victims of misfortune, they turn on them. Thus, it is often assumed that poor people are lazy, that crime victims are careless, that battered wives provoke their abusive husbands, and that gay men and women with AIDS are promiscuous. As you might expect, cross-national comparisons reveal that people in poorer countries are less likely than those in more affluent countries to believe in a just world (Furnham, 2003).

The tendency to disparage victims may seem like a symptom of the fundamental attribution error: too much focus on the person and not enough on the situation. But the conditions that trigger this tendency suggest there is more to it. Over the years, studies have shown that accident victims are held more responsible for their fate when the damages from the accident are severe rather than mild (Walster, 1966), when the victim's situation is similar to the perceiver's (Shaver, 1970), when the perceiver is generally anxious about threats to the self (Thornton, 1992), and when the perceiver identifies with the victim (Aguiar et al., 2008). Apparently, the more threatened we feel by an apparent injustice, the greater is the need to protect ourselves from the dreadful implication that it could happen to us, an implication we defend by disparaging the victim. Ironically, recent research shows that people may also satisfy their belief in a just world by *enhancing* members of disadvantaged groups—for example, by inferring that poor people are happy and that obese people are sociable, both attributes that restore justice by compensation (Kay & Jost, 2003; Kay et al., 2005).

In a laboratory experiment that reveals part of this process at work, participants watched a TV news story about a boy who was robbed and beaten. Some were told that the boy's assailants were captured, tried, and sent to prison. Others were told that the assailants fled the country, never to be brought to trial—a story that strains one's belief in a just world. Afterward, participants were asked to name as quickly as they could the colors in which various words in a list were typed (for example, the word *chair* may have been written in blue, *floor* in yellow, and *wide* in red). When the words themselves were neutral, all participants—regardless of which story they had seen—were equally fast at naming the colors. But when the words pertained to justice (words such as *fair* and *unequal*), those who had seen the justice-threatened version of the story were more distracted by the words and hence slower to name the colors. In fact, the more distracted they were, the more they derogated the victim. With their cherished belief in a just world threatened, these participants became highly sensitive to the concept of "justice" and quick to disparage the innocent victim (Hafer, 2000).

> Attributions of blame are often biased by self-serving motivations.

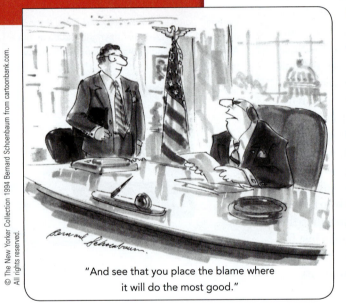

"And see that you place the blame where it will do the most good."

# Integration: From Dispositions to Impressions

When behavior is attributed to situational factors, we do not make strong inferences about the actor. However, personal attributions often lead us to infer that a person has a certain disposition—that the leader of a failing business is incompetent, for example, or that the enemy who extends an olive branch wants peace. Human beings are not one-dimensional, however, and one trait does not a person make. To have a complete picture of someone, social perceivers must assemble the various bits and pieces into a unified impression.

## Information Integration: The Arithmetic

Once personal attributions are made, how are they combined into a single coherent picture of a person? How do we approach the process of impression formation? Do we simply add up all of a person's traits and calculate a mental average, or do we combine the information in more complicated ways? Anyone who has written or received letters of recommendation will surely appreciate the practical implications. Suppose you're told that an applicant is friendly and intelligent, two highly favorable qualities. Would you be more or less impressed if you then learned that this applicant was also prudent and even-tempered, two moderately favorable qualities? If you are more impressed, then you are intuitively following a *summation* model of impression formation: The more positive traits there are, the better. If you are less impressed, then you are using an *averaging* model: The higher the average value of all the various traits, the better.

To quantify the formation of impressions, Norman Anderson (1968) had research participants rate the desirability of 555 traits on a 7-point scale. By calculating the average ratings, he obtained a *scale value* for each trait (*sincere* had the highest scale value; *liar* had the lowest). In an earlier study, Anderson (1965) used similar values and compared the summation and averaging models. Specifically, he asked a group of participants to rate how much they liked a person described by two traits with extremely high scale values (*H, H*). A second group received a list of four traits that included two that were high and two that were moderately high in their scale values (*H, H, M1, M1*). In a third group, participants received two extremely low, negative traits (*L, L*). In a fourth group, they received four traits, including two that were low and two that were moderately low (*L, L, M2, M2*). What effect did the moderate traits have on impressions? As predicted by an averaging model, the moderate traits diluted from rather than added to the impact of the highly positive and negative traits. The practical implication for those who write letters of recommendation is clear. Applicants are better off if their letters include only the most glowing comments and omit favorable remarks that are somewhat more guarded in nature.

After extensive amounts of research, it appears that although people do tend to combine traits by averaging, the process is somewhat more complicated. Consistent with Anderson's (1981) information integration theory, impressions formed of others are based on a combination, or integration, of (1) personal dispositions and the current state of the perceiver and (2) a *weighted* average, not a simple average, of the target person's characteristics (Kashima & Kerekes, 1994). Let's look more closely at these two sets of factors.

## Deviations From the Arithmetic

Like other aspects of our social perceptions and attributions, impression formation does not follow the rules of cold logic. Weighted averaging may describe the way most people combine different traits, but the whole process begins with a warm-blooded human perceiver, not a computer. Thus, certain deviations from the "arithmetic" are inevitable.

**Perceiver Characteristics** To begin with, each of us differs in terms of the kinds of impressions we form of others. Some people seem to measure others with an intellectual yardstick; others look for physical beauty, a warm smile, a good sense of humor, or

**impression formation** The process of integrating information about a person to form a coherent impression.

**information integration theory** The theory that impressions are based on (1) perceiver dispositions and (2) a weighted average of a target person's traits.

a firm handshake. Whatever the attribute, each of us is more likely to notice and recall certain traits than others (Bargh et al., 1988; Higgins et al., 1982). Thus, when people are asked to describe a group of target individuals, there's typically more overlap between the various descriptions provided by the same perceiver than there is between those provided for the same target (Dornbusch et al., 1965; Park, 1986). Part of the reason for differences among perceivers is that we tend to use ourselves as a standard, or frame of reference, when evaluating others. Compared with the inert couch potato, for example, the serious jock is more likely to see others as less active and athletic. As we saw earlier, people also tend to see their own skills and traits as particularly desirable for others to have (McElwee et al., 2001).

A perceiver's current mood state can also influence the impressions formed of others (Forgas, 2000). In a classic experiment, Joseph Forgas and Gordon Bower (1987) told research participants that they had performed very well or poorly on a test of social adjustment. This positive feedback not only altered their moods but affected their view of other people. When presented with behavioral information about various characters, participants spent more time attending to positive facts and formed more favorable impressions when they were happy than when they were sad. Follow-up research has shown that people who are induced into a happy mood are also more optimistic, more lenient, and less critical in the attributions they make for others who succeed or fail (Forgas & Locke, 2005). In a positive mood, we are also more likely to interpret another person's smile as genuine and heartfelt (Forgas & East, 2008b), more trusting and gullible in judging someone who is lying (Forgas & Rebekah, 2008), and more likely to form a quick impression of someone based on the first information we receive (Forgas, 2011).

Our current mood is one aspect of our temporary state that can influence how we perceive other people. More and more, social psychologists are also finding that human thought is "embodied"—that the way we view ourselves and others is influenced by the physical position, orientation, sensations, and movements of our bodies (Lakoff & Johnson, 1999; Niedenthal et al., 2005). A number of new studies illustrate *embodiment effects* in social perception. Consider the physical sensation of warmth. Research has shown that warm–cold is one of the two most powerful dimensions in terms of the way we judge others (the other dimension is competent–incompetent). As we will see shortly, once we see a person as warm versus cold we assume that this person is also trustworthy, friendly, caring, and helpful. Of course, warmth is also a physical sensation that because of early life experiences we tend to associate with shelter, safety, and nourishment. Would feeling warm influence social perception? To find out, Lawrence Williams and John Bargh (2008) asked research participants to hold a cup of hot or iced coffee just before they read about and evaluated a fictitious target person. Compared to those who held the iced coffee, those who held the hot drink described the target as warmer, more generous, and more caring.

If this result seems far-fetched, other studies have also demonstrated embodiment effects in social perception. In one study, participants made harsher moral judgments about the behavior of other people when they were given a bitter herbal mix rather than a sweet berry punch or water to drink during the experiment (Eskine et al., 2011). In a second study, participants on a computer judged people in photographs to be more trustworthy when they were induced to pull the palm of their hand up against the underside of the desk (a motion that we associate with approach) than when they were induced to press that same palm down against the top of the desk (a motion we associate with avoidance) (Slepian et al., 2012).

**Priming Effects**    The combined effects of stable perceiver differences, fluctuating moods, and bodily sensations point to an important conclusion: To some extent, impression formation is in the eye of the beholder. The characteristics we tend to see in other people also change from time to time, depending on recent experiences. Have you ever noticed that once a seldom-used word slips into a conversation or appears on a blog, it is often repeated over and over again? If so, then you have observed **priming**, the tendency for frequently or recently used concepts to come to mind easily and influence the way we interpret new information.

The effect of priming on person impressions was first demonstrated by E. Tory Higgins and others (1977). Research participants were presented with a list of trait words, ostensibly as part of an experiment on memory. In fact, the task was designed as a priming device to plant certain ideas in their minds. Some participants read words that evoked a positive image: *brave, independent, adventurous*. Others read words that evoked a more negative image: *reckless, foolish, careless*. Later, in what they thought to be an unrelated experiment, participants read about a man named Donald who climbed mountains, drove in a demolition derby, and tried to cross the Atlantic Ocean in a sailboat. As predicted, their impressions of Donald were shaped by the trait words they had earlier memorized. Those exposed to positive words later formed more favorable impressions of him than those exposed to negative words. All the participants read exactly the same description, yet they formed different impressions depending on what concept was already on their minds to be used as a basis for comparison (Mussweiler & Damisch, 2008). In fact, priming seems to work best when the prime words are presented so rapidly that people are not even aware of the exposure (Bargh & Pietromonaco, 1982).

Additional research has shown that our motivation and even our social behavior are also subject to the automatic effects of priming without awareness. In one provocative study, John Bargh and Tanya Chartrand (1999) gave participants a "word search" puzzle that contained either neutral words or words associated with achievement motivation (*strive, win, master, compete, succeed*). Afterward, the participants were left alone and given 3 minutes to write down as many words as they could form from a set of Scrabble letter tiles. When the 3-minute limit was up, they were signaled over an intercom to stop. Did these participants, who were driven to obtain a high score, stop on cue or continue to write? Through the use of hidden cameras, the experimenters observed that 57% of those primed with achievement-related words continued to write after the stop signal, compared to only 22% in the control group.

Looking at priming effects on social behavior, Bargh, Chen, and Burrows (1996) gave people 30 sets of words presented in scrambled order ("he it hides finds instantly") and told them to use some of the words in each set to form grammatical sentences. After explaining the test, which would take 5 minutes, the experimenter told participants to locate him down the hall when they were finished so he could administer a second task. So far so good. But when participants found the experimenter, he was in the hallway immersed in conversation, and he stayed in that conversation for 10 full minutes without acknowledging their presence. What's a person to do, wait patiently or interrupt? The participants didn't know it, but some had worked on a scrambled word test that contained many "politeness" words (*yield, respect, considerate, courteous*), whereas others had been exposed to words related to rudeness (*disturb, intrude, bold, bluntly*). Would these test words secretly prime participants, a few minutes later, to behave in one way or the other? Yes. Compared with those given the neutral words to unscramble, participants primed for rudeness were more likely—and those primed for politeness were less likely—to break in and interrupt the experimenter (see ● Figure 4.10).

What accounts for this effect of priming, not only on our social perceptions but also on our behavior? The link between perception and behavior is automatic; it happens like a mindless reflex. Present scrambled words that prime the "elderly" stereotype (*old, bingo*) and research participants walk out of the experiment more slowly as if mimicking an elderly person (Dijksterhuis & Bargh, 2001). But why? Joseph Cesario and others

**priming** The tendency for recently used or perceived words or ideas to come to mind easily and influence the interpretation of new information.

● **FIGURE 4.10**

**The Priming of Social Behavior Without Awareness**

Would waiting participants interrupt the busy experimenter? Compared with those who had previously been given neutral words to unscramble (center), participants given politeness words were less likely to cut in (left), and those given rudeness words were more likely to cut in (right). These results show that priming can influence not only our social judgments but our behavior as well.

From Bargh, J.A., Chen, M., and Burrows, L., "Automaticity of social behavior: direct effects of trait construct and stereotype activation on action," *Journal of Personality and Social Psychology* vol 71 (pp. 23–244). Copyright © 1996 by the American Psychological Association. Reprinted by permission.

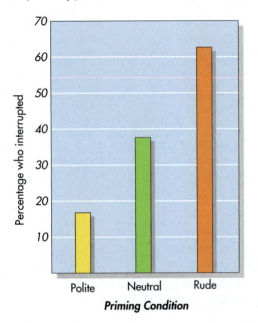

(2006) suggest that the automatic priming of behavior is an adaptive social mechanism that helps us to prepare for upcoming encounters with a primed target—if we are so motivated. After measuring participants' attitudes toward the elderly, these researchers predicted and found that those who liked old people walked more slowly after priming (as if synchronizing with a slow friend), while those who disliked old people walked more quickly (as if fleeing from such an interaction).

**Target Characteristics**    Just as not all social perceivers are created equal, neither are all traits created equal. In recent years, personality researchers have discovered, across cultures, that individuals can reliably be distinguished from one another along five broad traits, or factors: extroversion, emotional stability, openness to experience, agreeableness, and conscientiousness (De Raad, 2000; McCrae & Costa, 2003; Wiggins, 1996). Some of these factors are easier to judge than others. Based on their review of 32 studies, David Kenny and others (1994) found that social perceivers are most likely to agree in their judgments of a target's extroversion: that is, the extent to which he or she is sociable, friendly, fun-loving, outgoing, and adventurous. It seems that this characteristic is easy to spot, and different perceivers often agree on it even when rating a target person whom they are seeing for the first time.

The valence of a trait—whether it is considered good or bad—also affects its impact on our final impressions. Over the years, research has shown that people exhibit a *trait negativity bias*, the tendency for negative information to weigh more heavily on our impressions than positive information (Rozin & Royzman, 2001; Skowronski & Carlston, 1989). This means that we form more extreme impressions of a person who is said to be dishonest than of one who is said to be honest. When you think about it, this makes sense. We tend to view others favorably, so we are quick to take notice and pay careful attention when this expectation is violated (Pratto & John, 1991). As a result, one bad trait may be enough to tarnish a person's reputation, regardless of other qualities. In light of this research, Baumeister and others (2001) have concluded that bad is stronger than good in a "disappointingly relentless pattern" (p. 362).

Our positive expectations of others are so strong that the absence of a favorable evaluation may lead us to assume the worst. If you've ever read or written letters of recommendation, you will understand this next study. In evaluating people—whether it's for school or a job or membership in a social group—it is customary to comment on two characteristics of that person—warmth and competence. What if you're reading a letter that raves about how competent an applicant is but says nothing about how nice he or she is as a person? Or what if a letter comments on how nice the applicant is but says nothing about competence? No negative information is stated, but is it implied by omission? Yes. In a series of studies, Nicolas Kervyn and others (2012) found that when research participants read brief but praiseworthy evaluations of a person that focused only on competence ("seems like a very smart, hardworking, and competent person") or only on warmth ("seems like a very nice, sociable, and outgoing person"), they drew negative inferences about the dimension that was omitted. Illustrating the expression, "Damned by faint praise," Kervyn et al. referred to this result as the innuendo effect.

When you think about it, it's probably adaptive for people to stay alert for negative, potentially threatening information. Recent research suggests that people are quicker to sense their exposure to subliminally presented negative words such as *bomb, thief, shark,* and *cancer* than to positive words such as *baby, sweet, friend,* and *beach* (Dijksterhuis & Aarts, 2003). This sensitivity to negative information is found in infants less than a year old (Vaish et al., 2008). It can also be "seen" in the brain (N. K. Smith et al., 2003). In one study, Tiffany Ito and others (1998) exposed research participants to slides that depicted images that were positive (a red Ferrari, people enjoying a roller coaster), negative (a mutilated face, a handgun pointed at the camera), or neutral (a plate, a hair dryer). Using electrodes attached to participants' scalps, these researchers recorded electrical activity in different areas of the brain during the presentation. Sure enough, certain types of activity were more pronounced when participants saw negative images than when they saw stimuli that were positive or neutral. It appears, as these researchers commented, that "negative information weighs more heavily on the brain" (p. 887).

Brain research shows that when people are exposed to negative emotional images—such as the car bomb on the right as opposed to the beach scene on the left—activity in certain parts of the brain is more pronounced.

The impact of trait information on our impressions of other people depends not only on characteristics of the perceiver and target but on context as well. Think, for example, about a time when you met a person for the first time who was in the company of someone you like or dislike, or find attractive or unattractive. Would your impression of the target person be colored by this relationship? In studies of "stigma by association," John Pryor and his colleagues (2012) found that the answer is yes. Even when a target person's relationship to the positive or negative other comes about by chance, not as a matter of choice, our first impressions are influenced by it. Two other contextual factors are also particularly important: (1) implicit theories of personality and (2) the order in which we receive information about one trait relative to other traits.

**Implicit Personality Theories**    Whether we realize it or not, each of us harbors an implicit personality theory—a network of assumptions about the relationships among various types of people, traits, and behaviors. Knowing that someone has one trait leads us to infer that he or she has other traits as well (Bruner & Tagiuri, 1954; Schneider, 1973; Sedikides & Anderson, 1994). For example, you might assume that a person who is unpredictable is probably also dangerous or that someone who speaks slowly is also slow-witted. You might also assume that certain traits and behaviors are linked together (Reeder, 1993; Reeder & Brewer, 1979)—that a celebrity with a sweet and beloved persona, for example, could not possibly have skeletons in the closet.

Solomon Asch (1946) was the first to discover that the presence of one trait often implies the presence of other traits. Asch told one group of research participants that an individual was "intelligent, skillful, industrious, warm, determined, practical and cautious." Another group read an identical list of traits, except that the word *warm* was replaced by *cold.* Only the one term was changed, but the two groups formed very different impressions. Participants inferred that the warm person was also happier and more generous, good-natured, and humorous than the cold person. Yet when two other words were varied (*polite* and *blunt*), the differences were less pronounced. Why? Asch concluded that *warm* and *cold* are central traits, meaning that they imply the presence of certain other traits

**implicit personality theory**    A network of assumptions people make about the relationships among traits and behaviors.

**central traits**    Traits that exert a powerful influence on overall impressions.

and exert a powerful influence on final impressions. In fact, when college students in different classes were told ahead of time that a guest lecturer was a warm or cold person, their impressions after the lecture were consistent with these beliefs, even though he gave the same lecture to everyone (Kelley 1950; Widmeyer & Loy 1988).

Is there something magical about the traits warm and cold? To learn more about the structure of implicit personality theories, Seymour Rosenberg and his colleagues (1968) handed research participants 60 cards, each with a trait word written on it, and asked them to sort the cards into piles that represented specific people, perhaps friends, co-workers, acquaintances, or celebrities. The traits were then statistically correlated to determine how often they appeared together in the same pile. The results were plotted to display the psychological distance between the various characteristics. The "map" shown in ● Figure 4.11 shows that the traits—positive and negative alike—were best captured by two dimensions: social and intellectual. More recent research has since

● **FIGURE 4.11**

**Universal Dimensions of Social Cognition**

Rosenberg and others (1968) asked people to sort 60 cards, each with a trait word on it, into piles that depicted specific individuals. Through a statistical procedure used to plot how frequently the various traits appeared together, an implicit personality theory "map" emerged. This map shows that both positive and negative traits can be ordered along two dimensions: social (warmth) and intellectual (competent). Since this study, other research has confirmed that warmth and competence are universal dimensions by which people perceive each other.

From Rosenberg, S., Nelson, C., & Vivekananthan, P. S., "A multidimensional approach to the structure of personality impressions," *Journal of Personality and Social Psychology* vol 9 (pp. 283–294). Copyright © 1968 by the American Psychological Association. Reprinted by permission.

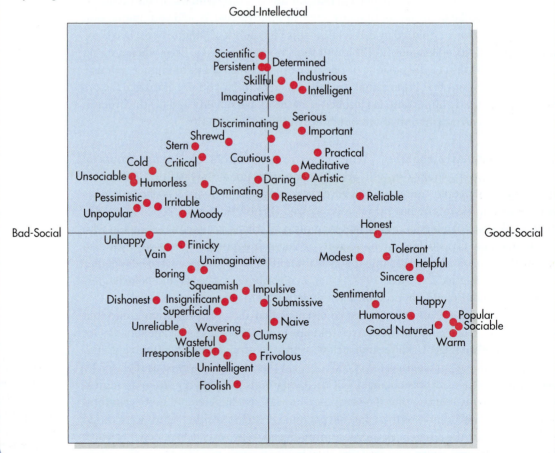

confirmed this basic point that people differentiate each other first in terms of warmth (*warm* is seen in such traits as friendly, helpful, and sincere), and second in terms of their competence (*competent* is seen in such traits as smart, skillful, and determined). According to Susan Fiske and her colleagues (2007), warmth and competence are "universal dimensions of social cognition."

**The Primacy Effect** The order in which a trait is discovered can also influence its impact. It is often said that first impressions are critical, and social psychologists are quick to agree. Studies show that information often has greater impact when presented early in a sequence rather than late, a common phenomenon known as the **primacy effect**.

In another of Asch's (1946) classic experiments, one group of participants learned that a person was "intelligent, industrious, impulsive, critical, stubborn, and envious." A second group received exactly the same list but in reverse order. Rationally speaking, the two groups should have felt the same way about the person. But instead, participants who heard the first list in which the more positive traits came first formed more favorable impressions than did those who heard the second list. Similar findings were obtained among participants who watched a videotape of a woman taking an SAT-like test. In all cases, she correctly answered 15 out of 30 multiple-choice questions. But participants who observed a pattern of initial success followed by failure perceived the woman as more intelligent than did those who observed the opposite pattern of failure followed by success (Jones et al., 1968). There are exceptions, but as a general rule, people tend to be more heavily influenced by the "early returns."

What accounts for this primacy effect? There are two basic explanations. The first is that once perceivers think they have formed an accurate impression of someone, they tend to pay less attention to subsequent information. Thus, when research participants read a series of statements about a person, the amount of time they spent reading each of the items declined steadily with each succeeding statement (Belmore, 1987).

Does this mean we are doomed to a life of primacy? Not at all. If we are unstimulated or mentally tired, our attention may wane. But if perceivers are sufficiently motivated to avoid tuning out and are not pressured to form a quick first impression, then primacy effects are diminished (Anderson & Hubert, 1963; Kruglanski & Freund, 1983). In one study, college students "leaped to conclusions" about a target person on the basis of preliminary information when they were mentally fatigued from having just taken a two-hour exam but not when they were fresh, alert, and motivated to pay attention (Webster et al., 1996). In addition, Arie Kruglanski and Donna Webster (1996) found that some people are more likely than others to "seize" upon and "freeze" their first impressions. Apparently, individuals differ in their **need for closure**, the desire to reduce ambiguity. People who are low in this regard are open-minded, deliberate, and perhaps even reluctant to draw firm conclusions about others. In contrast, those who are high in the need for closure tend to be impulsive and impatient and to form quick and lasting judgments of others.

More unsettling is the second reason for primacy, known as the *change-of-meaning hypothesis*. Once people have formed an impression, they start to interpret inconsistent information in light of that impression. Asch's research shows just how malleable the meaning of a trait can be. When people are told that a kind person is *calm*, they assume that he or she is gentle, peaceful, and serene. When a cruel person is said to be *calm*, however, the same word is interpreted to mean cool, shrewd, and calculating. There are many examples to illustrate the point. Based on your first impression, the word *proud* can mean self-respecting or conceited, *critical* can mean astute or picky, and *impulsive* can mean spontaneous or reckless.

**primacy effect** The tendency for information presented early in a sequence to have more impact on impressions than information presented later.

**need for closure** The desire to reduce cognitive uncertainty, which heightens the importance of first impressions.

It is remarkable just how creative we are in our efforts to transform a bundle of contradictions into a coherent, integrated impression. For example, the person who is said to be "good" but also "a thief" can be viewed as a Robin Hood–like character (Burnstein & Schul, 1982). Asch and Henri Zukier (1984) presented people with inconsistent trait pairs and found that they used different strategies to reconcile the conflicts. For example, a brilliant-foolish person may be seen as "very bright on abstract matters, but silly about day-to-day practical tasks," a sociable-lonely person has "many superficial ties but is unable to form deep relations," and a cheerful-gloomy person may simply be someone who is "moody."

# Confirmation Biases: From Impressions to Reality

"Please your majesty," said the knave, "I didn't write it and they can't prove I did; there's no name signed at the end." "If you didn't sign it," said the King, "that only makes the matter worse. You must have meant some mischief, or else you'd have signed your name like an honest man."

This exchange, taken from Lewis Carroll's *Alice's Adventures in Wonderland*, illustrates the power of existing impressions.

**confirmation bias** The tendency to seek, interpret, and create information that verifies existing beliefs.

It is striking but often true: Once people make up their minds about something—even if they have incomplete information—they become more and more unlikely to change their minds when confronted with new evidence.

People can be quite intellectually stubborn. Political leaders often refuse to withdraw support for government programs that don't work and scientists often steadfastly defend their pet theories in the face of contradictory research data. These instances are easy to explain. Politicians and scientists have personal stakes in their opinions, as votes, pride, funding, and reputation may be at risk. But what about people who more innocently fail to revise their opinions, often to their own detriment? What about the baseball manager who clings to old strategies that don't work or the trial lawyer who consistently selects juries according to false stereotypes? Why are they often slow to face the facts? As we will see, people are subject to various **confirmation biases**—tendencies to interpret, seek, and create information in ways that verify existing beliefs.

## Perseverance of Beliefs

Imagine you are looking at a slide that is completely out of focus. Gradually, it becomes focused enough so that the image is less blurry. At this point, the experimenter wants to know if you can recognize the picture. The response you're likely to make is interesting. Participants in experiments of this type have more trouble making an identification if they watch the gradual focusing procedure than if they simply view the final, blurry image. In the mechanics of the perceptual process, people apparently form early impressions that interfere with their subsequent ability to "see straight" once presented with improved evidence (Bruner & Potter, 1964). As we will see in this section, social perception is subject to the same kind of interference, which is another reason why first impressions often stick like glue even after we are forced to confront information that discredits them.

Consider what happens when you're led to expect something that does not materialize. In one study, John Darley and Paget Gross (1983) asked participants to evaluate the academic potential of a 9-year-old girl named Hannah. One group was led to believe that Hannah came from an affluent community in which both parents were well-educated professionals (high expectations). A second group thought that she was from a run-down urban neighborhood and that both parents were uneducated blue-collar workers (low expectations). As shown in ● Figure 4.12, participants in the first group were slightly more optimistic in their ratings of Hannah's potential than were those in the second group. In each of these groups, however, half the participants then watched a videotape of Hannah taking an achievement test. Her performance on the tape seemed average. She correctly answered some difficult questions but missed others that were

relatively easy. Look again at Figure 4.12 and you'll see that even though all participants saw the same tape, Hannah now received much lower ratings of ability from those who thought she was poor and higher ratings from those who thought she was affluent. Apparently, presenting an identical body of mixed evidence did not extinguish the biasing effects of beliefs; it *fueled* these effects.

Events that are ambiguous enough to support contrasting interpretations are like inkblots: We see or hear in them what we expect to see or hear. Illustrating the point, one group of researchers had people rate from photographs the extent to which pairs of adults and children resembled each other. Interestingly, the participants did not see more resemblance in parents and offspring than in random pairs of adults and children. Yet when told that certain pairs were related, they did "see" a resemblance, even when the relatedness information was false (Bressan & Martello, 2002). In another study, participants listened to noisy, more or less "degraded" tape recordings of two people talking—not unlike what is often heard in wiretaps

● **FIGURE 4.12**

**Mixed Evidence: Does It Extinguish or Fuel First Impressions?**

Participants evaluated the potential of a schoolgirl. Without seeing her test performance, those with high expectations rated her slightly higher than did those with low expectations. Among the participants who watched a tape of the girl taking a test, the expectations effect was even greater.

From Darley, J. M., and Gross, P. H., "A hypothesis-confirming bias in labeling effects," *Journal of Personality and Social Psychology* vol 44 (pp. 20–33). Copyright © 1983 by the American Psychological Association. Reprinted by permission.

and 9-1-1 dispatch recordings. Some participants were told that the interviewee was a crime suspect; others were told that he was a job applicant. When the speech recordings were degraded, interpretations of what was said were influenced by expectations: Participants were more likely to hear incriminating statements in degraded recordings when they thought that the interviewee was a criminal suspect than a job applicant (Lange et al., 2011).

What about information that plainly disconfirms our beliefs? What then happens to our first impressions? Craig Anderson and his colleagues (1980) addressed this question by supplying participants with false information. After they had time to think about it, they were told that it was untrue. In one experiment, half the participants read case studies suggesting that people who take risks make better firefighters than do those who are cautious. The others read cases suggesting the opposite conclusion. Next, participants were asked to come up with a theory for the suggested correlation. The possibilities are easy to imagine: "He who hesitates is lost" supports risk-taking, whereas "You have to look before you leap" supports caution. Finally, participants were led to believe that the session was over and were told that the information they had received was false, manufactured for the sake of the experiment. Participants, however, did not abandon their theories about firefighters. Instead, they exhibited belief perseverance, sticking to initial beliefs even after these had been discredited. Apparently, it's easier to get people to build a theory than to convince them to tear it down. Thus, five full months after the terrorist attack on the World Trade Center, the Gallup Organization interviewed some 10,000 residents of nine Muslim countries and found that 61% did *not* believe—despite hard evidence—that the attacks were carried out by Arab men (Gallup Poll Editors, 2002).

Why do beliefs often outlive the evidence on which they are supposed to be based? The reason is that when people conjure up explanations that make sense, those explanations take on a life of their own. In fact, once people form an opinion, that opinion becomes strengthened when they merely *think* about the topic, even if they do not articulate the reasons for it (Tesser, 1978). And therein lies a possible solution. By asking people to consider why an *alternative* theory might be true, we can reduce or eliminate the belief perseverance effects to which they are vulnerable (Anderson & Sechler, 1986).

> ## Confirmatory Hypothesis Testing

Social perceivers are not passive recipients of information. Like detectives, we ask questions and actively search for clues. But do we seek information objectively or are we inclined to confirm the suspicions we already hold?

Mark Snyder and William Swann (1978) addressed this question by having pairs of participants who were strangers to one another take part in a getting-acquainted interview. In each pair, one participant was supposed to interview the other. But first, that participant was falsely led to believe that his or her partner was either introverted or extroverted (actually, participants were assigned to these conditions on a random basis) and was then told to select questions from a prepared list. Those who thought they were talking to an introvert chose mostly introvert-oriented questions ("Have you ever felt left out of some social group?"), whereas those who thought they were talking to an extrovert asked extrovert-oriented questions ("How do you liven up a party?"). Expecting a certain kind of person, participants unwittingly sought evidence that would confirm their expectations. By asking loaded questions, in fact, the interviewers actually gathered support for their beliefs. Thus, neutral observers who later listened to the tapes were also left with the mistaken impression that the interviewees really were as introverted or extroverted as the interviewers had assumed.

This last part of the study is powerful but in hindsight not all that surprising. Imagine yourself on the receiving end of an interview. Asked about what you do to liven up parties, you would probably talk about organizing group games, playing dance music, and telling jokes. On the other hand, if you were asked about difficult social situations, you might talk about being nervous before oral presentations or about what it feels like to be the new kid on the block. In other words, simply by going along with the questions that are asked, you supply evidence confirming the interviewer's beliefs. Thus, perceivers set in motion a vicious cycle: Thinking someone has a certain trait, they engage in a one-sided search for information. In doing so, they create a reality that ultimately supports their beliefs (Zuckerman et al., 1995).

Sadly, the fact that people can be blinded by their existing beliefs is a pervasive phenomenon with consequences. In one study, research participants reviewed a mock police file on a crime investigation into a home invasion and shooting case. The file contained weak circumstantial evidence pointing to a possible suspect. At that point,

---

People are slow to change their first impressions on the basis of new information. **T**RUE.

---

*"It is a capital mistake to theorize before you have all the evidence. It biases the judgment."*
—Arthur Conan Doyle

---

**belief perseverance** The tendency to maintain beliefs even after they have been discredited.

some participants but not others were asked to form and state an initial hypothesis as to the likely offender. As predicted, those who did went on to search for additional evidence and then interpret that evidence in ways that confirmed their hypothesis. In these ways, a weak suspect became the *prime* suspect (O'Brien, 2009). In a second study, researchers presented psychiatrists and medical students with an experimental patient file and found that 13% of psychiatrists and 25% of students who had made a preliminary diagnosis exhibited confirmation biases in searching for new information—and those who did were less likely than others to make the correct diagnosis and prescribed treatment (Mendel et al., 2011).

Let's stop for a moment and contemplate what all this research means for the broader question of why we often seem to resist changing our negative but mistaken impressions of others more than our positive but mistaken impressions. Jerker Denrell (2005) argues that even when we form a negative first impression on the basis of all available evidence and even when we interpret that evidence accurately, our impression may be misleading. The reason is *biased experience sampling*. Meet someone who seems likable and you may interact with that person again. Then if he or she turns out to be twisted, dishonest, or self-centered, you'll be in a position to observe these traits and revise your impression. But if you meet someone you don't like, you will try to avoid that person in the future, cutting yourself off from new information and limiting the opportunity to revise your opinion. Attraction breeds interaction, which is why our negative first impressions in particular tend to persist.

## The Self-Fulfilling Prophecy

In 1948, sociologist Robert Merton told a story that is particularly instructive for us today in light of the recent economic downturn. The story was about Cartwright Millingville, president of the Last National Bank during the Great Depression of the 1930s. The bank was solvent, yet a rumor began to spread that it was floundering. Within hours, hundreds of depositors were lined up to withdraw their savings before no money was left to withdraw. The rumor was false, but the bank eventually failed. Using stories such as this, Merton proposed what seemed like an outrageous hypothesis: that a perceiver's expectation can actually lead to its own fulfillment, a **self-fulfilling prophecy**.

Merton's hypothesis lay dormant within psychology until Robert Rosenthal and Lenore Jacobson (1968) published the results of a study in a book entitled *Pygmalion in the Classroom.* Noticing that teachers had higher expectations for better students, they wondered if teacher expectations *influenced* student performance rather than the other way around. To address the question, they told teachers in a San Francisco elementary school that certain pupils were on the verge of an intellectual growth spurt. The results of an IQ test were cited, but in fact, the pupils had been randomly selected. Eight months later, when real tests were administered, the "late bloomers" exhibited an increase in their IQ scores compared with children assigned to a control group. They were also evaluated more favorably by their classroom teachers.

When the Pygmalion study was first published, it was greeted with chagrin. If positive teacher expectations can boost student performance, can negative expectations have the opposite effect? What about the social implications? Could it be that affluent children are destined for success and disadvantaged children are doomed to failure because educators hold different expectations for them? Many researchers were critical of the study and skeptical about the generality of the results. Unfortunately though, these findings cannot be swept under the rug. In a review of additional studies, Rosenthal (1985) found that teachers' expectations significantly predicted students' performance 36% of the time. Fortunately, teachers are less and less able to make these accurate predictions as children graduate from one grade to the next (A. Smith et al., 1999).

**self-fulfilling prophecy** The process by which one's expectations about a person eventually lead that person to behave in ways that confirm those expectations.

How might teacher expectations be transformed into reality? There are two points of view. According to Rosenthal (2002), the process involves covert communication. The teacher forms an initial impression of students early in the school year based, perhaps, on their background or reputation, physical appearance, initial classroom performance, and standardized test scores. The teacher then alters his or her behavior in ways that are consistent with that impression. If initial expectations are high rather than low, the teacher gives the student more praise, more attention, more challenging homework, and better feedback. In turn, the student adjusts his or her own behavior. If the signals are positive, the student may become energized, work hard, and succeed. If negative, there may be a loss of interest and self-confidence. The cycle is thus complete, and the expectations are confirmed.

While recognizing that this effect can occur, Lee Jussim (2012) has long questioned whether teachers in real life are so prone in the first place to form erroneous impressions of their students. It's true that in many naturalistic studies, occurring in real classrooms, the expectations teachers have at the start of a school year are ultimately confirmed by their students—a result that is consistent with the notion that the teachers had a hand in producing that outcome. But wait. That same result is also consistent with a more innocent possibility—that perhaps the expectations that teachers form of their students are *accurate*. In other words, sometimes teachers can accurately *predict* how their students will perform in the future without necessarily *influencing* that performance (Alvidrez & Weinstein, 1999).

Jussim admits that there are times when teachers may stereotype a student and without realizing it behave in ways that create a self-fulfilling prophecy. But his review of the research literature suggests that evidence for *bias* is not nearly as strong as it appears on the surface. Addressing this question in a longitudinal study of mothers and their children, Stephanie Madon and others (2003) found that underage adolescents are more likely to drink when their mothers had earlier expected them to. Statistical analyses revealed that this prophecy was fulfilled in part because the mothers *influence* their sons and daughters, as Rosenthal's work would suggest, but also in part because the mothers are able to *predict* their children's behavior, as Jussim's model would suggest. In fact, a follow-up study suggests that the link between a mother's expectations and her adolescent's later alcohol consumption did not strengthen or weaken over time, remaining stable as the child moved from the seventh grade through the twelfth (Madon et al., 2006).

It is clear that self-fulfilling prophecies are at work, to a greater or lesser degree, not only in schools but also in a wide range of organizations, including the military (Kierein & Gold, 2000; McNatt, 2000). In a study of 1,000 men assigned to 29 platoons in the Israel Defense Forces, Dov Eden (1990) led some platoon leaders but not others to expect that groups of trainees they were about to receive had great potential (in fact, these groups were of average ability). After 10 weeks, the trainees assigned to the high-expectation platoons scored higher than the others on written exams and on the ability to operate a weapon. The process may also be found in the criminal justice system when police interrogate suspects. To illustrate, Kassin and others (2003) had some college students but not others commit a mock crime, stealing $100 from a laboratory. All suspects were then questioned by interrogators who were led to believe that their suspect was probably guilty or innocent. Interrogators who presumed guilt asked more incriminating questions, conducted more coercive interrogations, and tried harder to get the suspect to confess. In turn, this more aggressive style made the suspects sound defensive and led observers who later listened to the tapes to judge them guilty, even when they were innocent. Follow-up research has confirmed this process in the police interrogation room (Hill et al., 2008; Narchet et al., 2011).

On a more personal level, the self-fulfilling prophecy is a process that can have particularly sad and ironic effects on people who are insecure about their social relationships. Studying what they have called the rejection prophecy, Danu Stinson, Jessica Cameron, and others have found that (1) people who are insecure are fearful of rejection, which makes them tense and awkward in the social situations; (2) their resulting behavior is off-putting to others, which (3) increases the likelihood of rejection and reinforces their initial insecurity (Stinson et al., 2009; Cameron et al., 2010). Fortunately, there is a way to break this vicious cycle. In a three-phased study that spanned 8 weeks, Stinson and others (2011) found that participants who were provided with an early opportunity to affirm the self—by writing about values that were important to them—became more secure over time and more relaxed in their social interactions.

The self-fulfilling prophecy is a powerful phenomenon (Darley & Fazio, 1980; Harris & Rosenthal, 1985). But how does it work? How do social perceivers transform their expectations of others into reality? Research indicates that the phenomenon occurs as a three-step process. First, a perceiver forms an impression of a target person, which may be based on interactions with the target or on other information. Second, the perceiver behaves in a manner that is consistent with that first impression. Third, the target person unwittingly adjusts his or her behavior to the perceiver's actions. The net result is behavioral confirmation of the first impression (see ● Figure 4.13).

Now let's straighten out this picture. It would be a sad commentary on human nature if each of us were so easily molded by others' perceptions into appearing brilliant or stupid, introverted or extroverted, competitive or cooperative, warm or cold. The effects are well established, but there are limits. By viewing the self-fulfilling prophecy as a three-step process, social psychologists can identify the links in the chain that can be broken to prevent the vicious cycle.

Consider the first step, the link between one's expectations and one's behavior toward the target person. In the typical study, perceivers try to get to know the target on only a casual basis and are not necessarily driven to form an accurate impression. But when perceivers are highly motivated to seek the truth (as when they are considering the target as

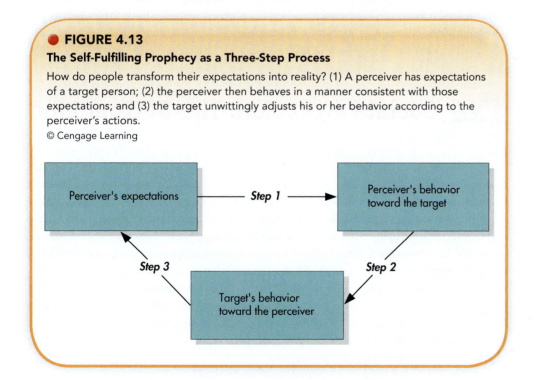

● **FIGURE 4.13**

**The Self-Fulfilling Prophecy as a Three-Step Process**

How do people transform their expectations into reality? (1) A perceiver has expectations of a target person; (2) the perceiver then behaves in a manner consistent with those expectations; and (3) the target unwittingly adjusts his or her behavior according to the perceiver's actions.

© Cengage Learning

Perceiver's expectations

Step 1

Perceiver's behavior toward the target

Step 3

Step 2

Target's behavior toward the perceiver

a possible teammate or opponent), they become more objective and often do not confirm prior expectations (Harris & Perkins, 1995; Hilton & Darley 1991).

The link between expectations and behavior depends in other ways as well on a perceiver's goals and motivations in the interaction (Snyder & Stukas, 1999). In one study, John Copeland (1994) put either the perceiver or the target into a position of relative power. In all cases, the perceiver interacted with a target person who was said to be introverted or extroverted. In half the pairs, the perceiver was given the power to accept or reject the target as a teammate for a money-winning game. In the other half, it was the target who was empowered to choose a teammate. The two participants interacted, the interaction was recorded, and neutral observers listened to the tapes and rated the target person. So did perceivers cause the targets to behave as introverted or extroverted, depending on initial expectations? Yes and no. Illustrating what Copeland called "prophecies of power," the results showed that high-power perceivers triggered the self-fulfilling prophecy, as in past research, but that low-power perceivers did not. In the low-power situation, the perceivers spent less time getting to know the target person and more time trying to be liked.

Now consider the second step, the link between a perceiver's behavior and the target's response. In the designs of much of the past research (as in much of life), target persons were not aware of the false impressions held by others. Thus, it is unlikely that Rosenthal and Jacobson's (1968) "late bloomers" knew of their teachers' high expectations or that Snyder and Swann's (1978) "introverts" and "extroverts" knew of their interviewers' misconceptions. But what if they had known? How would *you* react if you found yourself being cast in a particular light? When it happened to participants in one experiment, they managed to overcome the effect by behaving in ways that forced the perceivers to abandon their expectations (Hilton & Darley, 1985).

As you may recall from the discussion of self-verification in Chapter 3, this result is most likely to occur when the expectations of perceivers clash with a target person's own self-concept. When targets who viewed themselves as extroverted were interviewed by perceivers who believed they were introverted (and vice versa), what changed as a result of the interaction were the perceivers' beliefs, not the targets' behavior (Swann & Ely, 1984). Social perception is a two-way street; the persons we judge have their own prophecies to fulfill.

> The notion that we can create a "self-fulfilling prophecy" by getting others to behave in ways we expect is a myth.  **FALSE.**

## Social Perception: The Bottom Line

Trying to understand people—whether they are crime suspects, celebrities, professional athletes, world leaders, trial lawyers, or loved ones closer to home—is no easy task. As you reflect on the material in this chapter, you will notice that there are two radically different views of social perception. One suggests that the process is quick and relatively automatic. At the drop of a hat, without much thought, effort, or awareness, people make rapid-fire snap judgments about others based on physical appearance, preconceptions, cognitive heuristics, or just a hint of behavioral evidence. According to a second view, however, the process is far more mindful. People observe others carefully and reserve judgment until their analysis of the target person, behavior, and situation is complete. As suggested by theories of attribution and information integration, the process is eminently logical. In light of recent research, it is now safe to conclude that both accounts of social perception are correct. Sometimes our judgments are made instantly; at other times, they are based on a more painstaking analysis of behavior. Either way, we often steer our interactions with others along a path that is narrowed by first impressions, a process that can set in motion a self-fulfilling prophecy. The various aspects of social perception, as described in this chapter, are summarized in ● Figure 4.14.

At this point, we must confront an important question: How *accurate* are our impressions of each other? For years, this question has proved provocative but hard to answer (Cronbach, 1955; Kenny, 1994; West & Kenny, 2011). Granted, people often depart from the ideals of logic and exhibit bias in their social perceptions. In this chapter alone, we have seen that perceivers typically focus on the wrong cues to judge if someone is lying, use cognitive heuristics without regard for numerical base rates, overlook the situational influences on behavior, disparage victims whose misfortunes threaten their sense of justice, form premature first impressions, and interpret, seek, and create evidence in ways that support these impressions.

To make matters worse, we often have little awareness of our limitations, leading us to feel *overconfident* in our judgments. In a series of studies, David Dunning and his colleagues (1990) asked college students to predict how a target person would react in various situations. Some made predictions about a fellow student whom they had just met and interviewed, and others made predictions about their roommates. In both cases, participants reported their confidence in each prediction, and accuracy was determined by the responses of the target persons themselves. The results were clear: Regardless of whether they judged a stranger or a roommate, the students consistently overestimated the accuracy of their predictions. In fact, Kruger and Dunning (1999) found that people who scored low on tests of spelling, logic, grammar, and humor appreciation were later the most likely to overestimate their own performance. Apparently, poor performers are doubly cursed: They don't know what they don't know (Dunning et al., 2003)—and they don't know they are biased (Ehrlinger et al., 2005).

Standing back from the material presented in this chapter, you may find the list of our shortcomings, punctuated by the problem of overconfidence, to be long and depressing. How can this list be reconciled with the triumphs of civilization? Or, to put it another way, "If we're so dumb, how come we made it to the moon?" (Nisbett & Ross, 1980, p. 249).

It is true that people fall prey to the biases identified by social psychologists and probably even to some that have not yet been noticed. It is also true that we often get

---

● **FIGURE 4.14**

**The Processes of Social Perception**

Summarizing Chapter 4, this diagram depicts the processes of social perception. As shown, it begins with the observation of persons, situations, and behavior. Sometimes we make snap judgments from these cues. At other times, we form impressions only after making attributions and integrating these attributions. Either way, our impressions are subject to confirmation biases and the risk of self-fulfilling prophecy.

© Cengage Learning

fooled by con artists such as Bernie Madoff, misjudge our partners in marriage, and hire the wrong job applicants, and that our biases can have harmful consequences—sometimes giving rise, as we'll see in Chapter 5, to stereotypes, prejudice, and discrimination. Despite our imperfections, there are reasons to be guardedly optimistic about our competence as social perceivers:

1. The more experience people have with each other, the more accurate they are. For example, although people have a limited ability to assess the personality of strangers they meet in a laboratory, they are generally better at judging their own friends and acquaintances (Kenny & Acitelli, 2001; Levesque, 1997; Malloy & Albright, 1990). By observing nonverbal behavior, people are also more accurate at judging the true emotional state—happy, sad, or angry—of friends than of strangers (Sternglanz & DePaulo, 2004).

2. Although we are not good at making global judgments of others (that is, at knowing what people are like across a range of settings), we are able to make more precise circumscribed predictions of how others will behave in our own presence. You may well misjudge the personality of a roommate or co-worker, but to the extent that you can predict your roommate's actions at home or your co-worker's actions on the job, the mistakes may not matter (Swann, 1984).

3. People can form more accurate impressions of others when they are motivated by concerns for accuracy and open-mindedness (Biesanz & Human, 2010; Kruglanski & Webster, 1996). Many of the studies described in this chapter have shown that people exhibit less bias when there is an incentive for accuracy within the experiment, as when participants are asked to judge a prospective teammate's ability to facilitate success in a future task (Fiske & Neuberg, 1990) or a future dating partner's social competence (Goodwin et al., 2002).

4. Not everyone suffers from high levels of error and bias. Some people are more accurate than others in their social perceptions. In particular, people who are psychologically well adjusted (Human & Biesanz, 2011).

To summarize, research on the accuracy of social perceptions offers a valuable lesson: To the extent that we observe others with whom we've had time to interact, make judgments that are reasonably specific, are motivated to form an accurate impression, and are reasonably well adjusted, the problems that plague us can be minimized. Indeed, just being aware of the biases described in this chapter may well be a necessary first step toward a better understanding of others and our perceptions of them.

People are more accurate at judging the personalities of friends and acquaintances than of strangers. **T**RUE.

# Review

## Observation: The Elements of Social Perception

- To understand others, social perceivers rely on indirect clues—the elements of social perception.

### A Person's Physical Appearance

- People often make snap judgments of others based on physical appearances (for example, adults with baby-faced features are seen as having childlike qualities).

### Perceptions of Situations

- People have preconceptions, or "scripts," about certain types of situations. These scripts guide our interpretations of behavior.

### Behavioral Evidence

- People derive meaning from behavior by dividing it into discrete, meaningful units.
- Nonverbal behaviors are often used to determine how others are feeling.
- From facial expressions, people all over the world can identify the emotions of happiness, fear, sadness, surprise, anger, and disgust.
- Body language, gaze, and touch are also important forms of nonverbal communication.

### Distinguishing Truth From Deception

- People use nonverbal cues to detect deception but are often not accurate in making these judgments because they pay too much attention to the face and neglect cues that are more revealing.

---

**Putting *Common Sense* to the Test**

**The impressions we form of others are influenced by superficial aspects of their appearance.**

**True.** *Research shows that first impressions are influenced by height, weight, clothing, facial characteristics, and other aspects of appearance.*

**Adaptively, people are skilled at knowing when someone is lying rather than telling the truth.**

**False.** *People frequently make mistakes in their judgments of truth and deception, too often accepting what others say at face value.*

---

## Attribution: From Elements to Dispositions

- Attribution is the process by which we explain people's behavior.

### Attribution Theories

- People begin to understand others by making personal or situational attributions for their behavior.
- Correspondent inference theory states that people learn about others from behavior that is freely chosen, that is unexpected, and that results in a small number of desirable outcomes.
- From multiple behaviors, we base our attributions on three kinds of covariation information: consensus, distinctiveness, and consistency.

### Attribution Biases

- People depart from the logic of attribution theory in two major ways.
- First, we use cognitive heuristics—rules of thumb that enable us to make judgments that are quick but often in error.
- Second, we tend to commit the fundamental attribution error—overestimating the role of personal factors and underestimating the impact of situations.

### Culture and Attribution

- Cultures differ in their implicit theories about the causes of human behavior.
- Studies show, for example, that East Asians are more likely than Americans to consider the impact of the social and situational contexts of which they are a part.

### Motivational Biases

- Our attributions for the behavior of others are often biased by our own self-esteem motives.
- Needing to believe in a just world, people often criticize victims and blame them for their fate.

---

**Putting *Common Sense* to the Test**

**Like social psychologists, people are sensitive to situational causes when explaining the behavior of others.**

**False.** *In explaining the behavior of others, people overestimate the importance of personal factors and overlook the impact of situations, a bias known as the fundamental attribution error.*

---

# Integration: From Dispositions to Impressions

### Information Integration: The Arithmetic
- The impressions we form are usually based on an averaging of a person's traits, not on a summation.
- According to information integration theory, impressions are based on perceiver predispositions and a weighted average of individual traits.

### Deviations From the Arithmetic
- Perceivers differ in their sensitivity to certain traits and in the impressions they form.
- Differences stem from stable perceiver characteristics, priming from recent experiences, implicit personality theories, and the primacy effect.

# Confirmation Biases: From Impressions to Reality

- Once an impression is formed, people become less likely to change their minds when confronted with nonsupportive evidence.
- People tend to interpret, seek, and create information in ways that confirm existing beliefs.

### Perseverance of Beliefs
- First impressions may survive in the face of inconsistent information.
- Ambiguous evidence is interpreted in ways that bolster first impressions.
- The effect of evidence that is later discredited perseveres because people formulate theories to support their initial beliefs.

### Confirmatory Hypothesis Testing
- Once perceivers have beliefs about someone, they seek further information in ways that confirm those beliefs.

### The Self-Fulfilling Prophecy
- As shown by the effects of teacher expectancies on student achievement, first impressions set in motion a self-fulfilling prophecy.

- This is the product of a three-step process: (1) A perceiver forms an expectation of a target person; (2) the perceiver behaves accordingly; and (3) the target adjusts to the perceiver's actions.
- This self-fulfilling prophecy effect is powerful but limited in important ways.

> **Putting *Common Sense* to the Test**
>
> **People are slow to change their first impressions on the basis of new information.**
> **True.** *Studies have shown that once people form an impression of someone, they become resistant to change even when faced with contradictory new evidence.*
>
> **The notion that we can create a "self-fulfilling prophecy" by getting others to behave in ways we expect is a myth.**
> **False.** *In the laboratory and in the classroom, a perceiver's expectation can actually lead to its own fulfillment.*

# Social Perception: The Bottom Line

- Sometimes people make snap judgments; at other times, they evaluate others by carefully analyzing their behavior.
- Research suggests that our judgments are often biased and that we are overconfident.
- Still, there are conditions under which we are more competent as social perceivers.

> **Putting *Common Sense* to the Test**
>
> **People are more accurate at judging the personalities of friends and acquaintances than of strangers.**
> **True.** *People often form erroneous impressions of strangers but tend to be more accurate in their judgments of friends and acquaintances.*

# KEY TERMS

attribution theory (117)

availability heuristic (120)

base-rate fallacy (121)

belief in a just world (129)

belief perseverance (140)

central traits (135)

confirmation bias (138)

counterfactual thinking (122)

covariation principle (118)

false-consensus effect (121)

fundamental attribution error (123)

implicit personality theory (135)

impression formation (131)

information integration
  theory (131)

mind perception (109)

need for closure (137)

nonverbal behavior (110)

personal attribution (117)

primacy effect (137)

priming (133)

self-fulfilling prophecy (141)

situational attribution (117)

social perception (105)

# MEDIA RESOURCES

Go to CengageBrain.com to access Psychology CourseMate, where you will find an interactive eBook, glossaries, flashcards, quizzes, videos, and more.

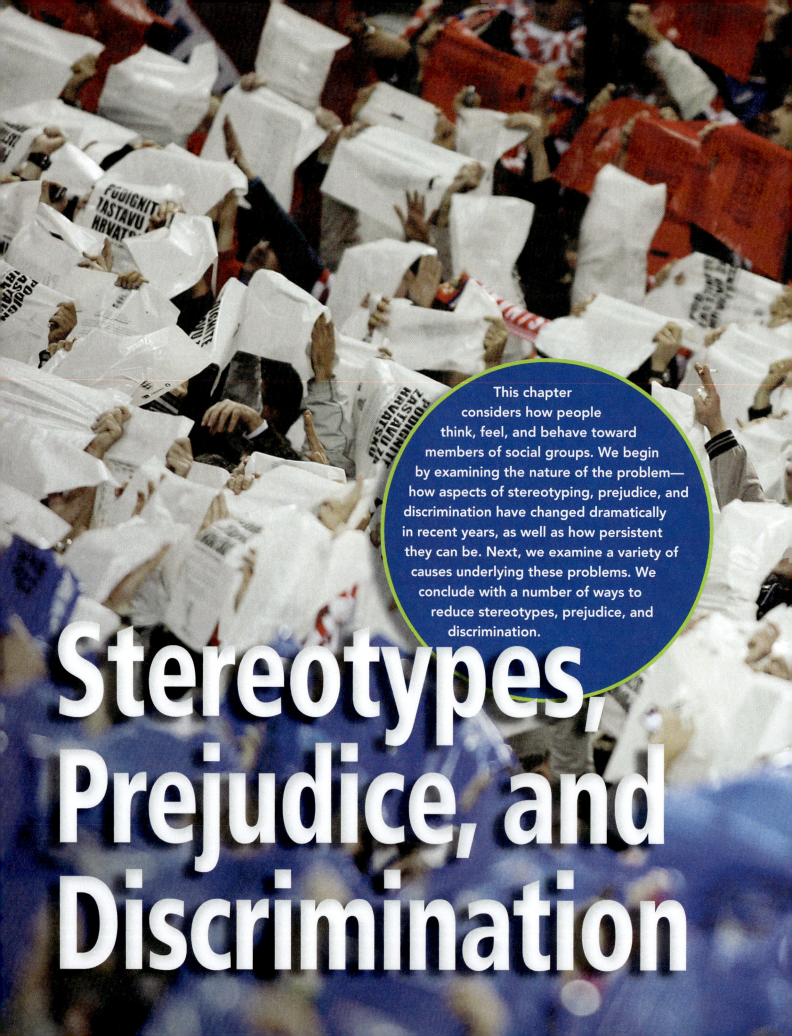

This chapter considers how people think, feel, and behave toward members of social groups. We begin by examining the nature of the problem—how aspects of stereotyping, prejudice, and discrimination have changed dramatically in recent years, as well as how persistent they can be. Next, we examine a variety of causes underlying these problems. We conclude with a number of ways to reduce stereotypes, prejudice, and discrimination.

# Stereotypes, Prejudice, and Discrimination

# 5

**151**

**In the spring of 2012,** the president of the United States and the chancellor of Germany engaged in tense and important discussions about the economic crisis in the European Union. The fact that this meeting of the leaders of two of the most powerful nations on earth was between an African American and a woman was not at all noteworthy. And the fact that it was not at all noteworthy is, itself, noteworthy—given that it would have been unimaginable a generation or two ago. The progress that has been made on issues of civil rights and discrimination during the past 70 years or so has been stunning.

But consider these stories, all of which took place within a few months of the meeting between President Barack Obama and Chancellor Angela Merkel:

- Star baseball player Delmon Young was arrested after a drunken tirade in which he yelled hateful things about Jews outside a hotel in New York City (Kemp & Lemire, 2012).

- A huge wave of fans of the popular book, *The Hunger Games*, posted their outrage on Twitter at the casting of African American actors to play some of the supporting characters in the movie version. Many were especially angry that one beloved character (Rue) would be African American—despite the fact that she is described in the book as having "dark brown skin" (Stewart, 2012).

- A Georgia high school student was removed from his position as student government president by faculty who were upset at his suggestion that same-sex couples should be eligible to be voted for honors at the prom (Garcia, 2012).

- Pete Hoekstra, a candidate for the U.S. Senate, ran a controversial commercial during the 2012 Super Bowl featuring an Asian woman talking in stereotypical broken English, thanking Hoekstra's opponent for practices making the American "economy get very weak, ours get very good; we take your jobs" (Schultz, 2012).

- A man who claimed to have links to an Islamic extremist group shot and killed a rabbi and three children at a school in France (Associated Press, 2012).

- Racist chants, animal noises, and people dancing around in banana suits were directed at African American and Latino high school and college basketball players in a variety of games in several states (Peralta, 2012; C. Smith, 2012a, 2012b).

- A law passed in St. Petersburg, Russia, criminalized public actions that could be seen as promoting homosexuality (Elder, 2012).

These were just a sample of stories from only three months in 2012. They reflect the troubling persistence of stereotyping, prejudice, and discrimination targeting various groups today.

Consider, also, your wardrobe. The chances are good that somewhere in it you have a divisive, controversial symbol of stereotyping, prejudice, racism, and aggression. And if you don't have it, then certainly some of your best friends do. What is this sinister sartorial item? A hoodie.

# Putting *Common Sense* to the Test

*Circle Your Answer*

**T    F**    Children do not tend to show biases based on race; it is only after they become adolescents that they learn to respond to people differently based on race.

**T    F**    Interracial interactions tend to go better and to reduce the perceptions of racism if a colorblind mentality is used, which denies or minimizes any acknowledgment of racial differences.

**T    F**    An African American student is likely to perform worse on an athletic task if the task is described as one reflecting sports intelligence than if it is described as reflecting natural athletic ability.

**T    F**    Being reminded of one's own mortality makes people put things into greater perspective, thereby tending to reduce ingroup–outgroup distinctions and hostilities.

**T    F**    People's very quick judgments are not influenced by a stereotype unless they actually believe the stereotype to be true.

A hoodie, of course, is simply a hooded sweatshirt, a casual, comfortable, and cheap staple of just about any young (and many older) person's wardrobe. Typically it is as noncontroversial a fashion statement as one can make. It's the comfort food of your closet. It's like macaroni and cheese—cheap, no fuss, and just about everybody likes it on a chilly spring day. But in the spring of 2012, the hoodie became hotly debated on news shows, blogs, and Twitter. Professional basketball players and student protestors wore them as symbols of defiant protest. Fox News Channel host Geraldo Rivera urged parents, particularly of black and Latino youngsters, to not let their children out of the house wearing them (Lee, 2012).

The hoodie uncharacteristically burst into the national consciousness that spring when news began to spread of the fatal shooting of an unarmed African American 17-year-old named Trayvon Martin. The details of this tragedy are discussed in the opening to Chapter 4. In addition to illustrating questions at the core of that chapter on Perceiving Persons, such as how people explain the causes of others' behaviors, the Martin shooting speaks to key issues concerning stereotypes, prejudice, and discrimination. For example, did race play a role in why George Zimmerman, the man who shot Martin, thought Martin looked suspicious? Zimmerman, of multiracial background including a father identified as white and a mother identified as Hispanic, called the police when he saw Martin and, according to the transcript, said that he "looks like he's up to no good, or he's on drugs or something." According to the transcript, when told that the police were on their way, Zimmerman said, "These ***holes they always get away." Would Zimmerman have been as suspicious of a white teenager walking in the neighborhood?

This story of an interracial shooting of an unarmed victim is by no means unique, unfortunately, but occasionally one of these stories captures wide attention and elicits tremendous controversy. This was one of those times. Of all the issues debated in the barrage of commentary during the spring of 2012, one of the odder ones was about the hoodie that Treyvon Martin was wearing. To many people following the case, the hoodie was not merely a nondescript and commonplace piece of apparel but was instead a symbol of a thuggish, dangerous culture, primarily associated with African American and Latino young men. When news commentator Geraldo Rivera urged parents not to let their children wear hoodies because they were so closely associated with violent criminal behavior, he said that the hoodie was as much to blame for Martin's death as George Zimmerman. Rivera was by no means alone in blaming Martin for wearing a hoodie and thereby looking like a criminal. Indeed, some communities around the world have adopted "hoodie-free zones" or have banned them from schools because of these associations with violence. Why do people make these associations despite the fact that hoodies are worn frequently and innocently by countless people from across all racial, ethnic, and class divisions? In the Treyvon Martin case, the hoodie took on significance because of a combination of stereotypes concerning race, class, and gender.

U.S. President Barack Obama talks with German Chancellor Angela Merkel at Camp David, Maryland, in May 2012 (top). An African American and a woman leading two of the most powerful nations in the world signify tremendous progress in civil rights. How far we still need to go, however, is suggested in the photo on the bottom, as players from the 2012 Miami Heat basketball team wear hoodies in protest of the Trayvon Martin tragedy and the negative attitudes expressed by some in the media about his hooded sweatshirt.

What all this reflects are some subtle but important truths about stereotypes, prejudice, and discrimination, which is the focus of this chapter. We begin by taking a close look at the nature of the problem of intergroup bias in contemporary life, including a focus on the different levels on which these biases operate today. Later in the chapter we address some of the key causes and important consequences of intergroup biases, and we close by discussing some of the most promising directions in efforts to reduce these problems.

# The Nature of the Problem: Persistence and Change

Even more than the tragedy itself, the frenzied debate about the role of race in Trayvon Martin's death is a testament to the complexity and contradictions that are at the core of contemporary intergroup relations. On the encouraging side, numerous surveys and other measures indicate tremendous progress in civil rights and in the reduction of prejudice and discrimination compared to previous generations.

On the other hand, examples of blatant, overt prejudice and discrimination remain all too prevalent—although relatively few people may know about them. Look back again at the troubling news stories from three months in 2012 listed in the opening of this chapter. And consider also a few reports published that spring. The Southern Poverty Law Center released a report detailing the sharp rise from 2000 to 2011 of the number of hate groups in the United States targeting people based on race, religion, and sexuality (Severson, 2012). Amnesty International (2012) released a report indicating that discrimination due to religion, especially Islam, is considered relatively acceptable in the various European countries it studied. The Anti-Defamation League (2012) released a report documenting "disturbingly high levels" of anti-Jewish attitudes in ten European countries, including large increases in these attitudes just since 2009 (see Table 5.1).

These stories and reports show that despite the progress that has been made, the problems of stereotypes, prejudice, and discrimination endure. What is even more persistent, however, are more subtle examples of bias. Like germs lurking beneath a seemingly clean countertop, stereotypes, prejudice, and discrimination in contemporary life live on under the surface to a much, much greater extent than most people realize. And like germs, their existence can have a profound effect on us, despite how hidden they may be.

In this section, we discuss some of the progress that has been made along with the persistence of more subtle forms of bias. To provide a focus and to reflect the topics that have most dominated the research literature, we will concentrate in this section

**TABLE 5.1**

**Unfavorable Views Toward Jews in Europe**

This table reports the percentages of survey respondents from each of several countries in Europe who agreed with a set of anti-Semitic stereotypes (for example, "Jews have too much power in the business world"). For most of these countries, these percentages in 2012 increased compared to a similar survey conducted in 2009.

| | |
|---|---|
| Austria | 28% |
| France | 24% |
| Hungary | 63% |
| Italy | 35% |
| The Netherlands | 10% |
| Poland | 48% |
| Spain | 53% |
| United Kingdom | 17% |

Anti-Defamation League, 2012. © Cengage Learning

on racism and sexism in particular—even though many of the points hold true across a wide variety of targets of stereotypes, prejudice, and discrimination.

## Defining Our Terms

Given the complexity of these issues, defining concepts such as prejudice or racism is no simple matter. Debates persist about how best to define the terms—how broad or specific they should be, whether they should focus on individual or institutional levels, and so on. For example, one way to define **racism** is as prejudice and discrimination based on a person's racial background. It is important to realize, however, that racism exists at several different levels. At the individual level, as this definition reflects, any of us can be racist toward anyone else. At the institutional and cultural levels, in contrast, some people are privileged while others are disadvantaged. For example, institutions may unwittingly perpetuate racism by tending to accept or hire individuals similar or connected to the people who already are in the institution. Therefore, another way to define racism is as institutional and cultural practices that promote the domination of one racial group over another (Jones, 1997b). Similarly, **sexism** may be defined as prejudice and discrimination based on a person's gender or as institutional and cultural practices that promote the domination of one gender (typically men) over another (typically women).

For the purposes of this chapter, we define **stereotypes** as beliefs or associations that link whole groups of people with certain traits or characteristics. **Prejudice** consists of negative feelings about others because of their connection to a social group. Whereas stereotypes concern associations or beliefs and prejudice concerns feelings, **discrimination** concerns behaviors—specifically, negative behaviors directed against persons because of their membership in a particular group. Stereotypes, prejudice, and discrimination can operate somewhat independently, but they often influence and reinforce each other.

## Racism: Current Forms and Challenges

A close examination of legislation, opinion polls, sociological data, and social psychological research indicates that racial prejudice and discrimination have been decreasing in the United States over the last 70 years (Dovidio et al., 2002; Pew Research Center for People and the Press, 2009), although elements of it may once again be on the rise, particularly in Western Europe. In a classic study of ethnic stereotypes published in 1933, Daniel Katz and Kenneth Braly found that white college students viewed the average white American as smart, industrious, and ambitious, and they saw the average African American as superstitious, ignorant, lazy, and happy-go-lucky. In multiple follow-up surveys with demographically similar samples of white students conducted from 1951 through 2001, these negative images of blacks largely faded and were replaced by more favorable images (Dovidio et al., 1996; Madon et al., 2001). Similarly, public opinion polls have indicated that racial prejudice in the United States has dropped sharply since World War II. Table 5.2 reports some of the changes in racial prejudice illustrated by these and other studies.

The election of Barack Obama as the first African American president of the United States in 2008 was a significant sign of racial progress. As Obama pointed out when he was inaugurated on January 20, 2009, his own father would not have been served in many restaurants in the nation's capital 60 years before, and now that father's son was being sworn in to the highest office in the land. That amount of progress in a person's lifetime is staggering. However, when those of us who study stereotypes, prejudice, and discrimination saw story after story in the popular media at the time heralding

**racism** Prejudice and discrimination based on a person's racial background, or institutional and cultural practices that promote the domination of one racial group over another.

**sexism** Prejudice and discrimination based on a person's gender, or institutional and cultural practices that promote the domination of one gender over another.

**stereotype** A belief or association that links a whole group of people with certain traits or characteristics.

**prejudice** Negative feelings toward persons based on their membership in certain groups.

**discrimination** Behavior directed against persons because of their membership in a particular group.

## TABLE 5.2
### Changes in Overt Racism

The results of many studies and surveys like these demonstrate that overt negative stereotyping and racism have declined dramatically over the years. Although these results are encouraging, research on more subtle modern racism reveals that the picture is more complex than these self-reports suggest.

**Percentage of White Participants Who Selected a Trait to Describe Black Americans**

| Trait | 1933 | 1967 | 1993 |
|---|---|---|---|
| Superstitious | 84% | 13% | 1% |
| Lazy | 75% | 26% | 5% |
| Happy-Go-Lucky | 38% | 27% | 2% |
| Ignorant | 38% | 11% | 5% |
| Musical | 26% | 47% | 12% |
| Very Religious | 24% | 8% | 17% |
| Stupid | 22% | 4% | 0% |

**Percentage of White Participants Who Report Being Willing to Admit Blacks into Various Relationships with Them**

| | 1949 | 1968 | 1992 |
|---|---|---|---|
| Willing to Admit Blacks to: | | | |
| Employment in my occupation | 78% | 98% | 99% |
| My club as personal friends | 51% | 97% | 96% |
| My street as neighbors | 41% | 95% | 95% |
| Close kinship by marriage | 0% | 66% | 74% |

**Percentage of Adult Participants Who Agree with the Statement "It's All Right for Blacks and Whites to Date Each Other"**

| | 1987 | 2012 |
|---|---|---|
| Agree | 48% | 86% |

Sources: Dovidio et al., 1996; Peterson, 1997; Pew, 2012. © Cengage Learning

**modern racism** A form of prejudice that surfaces in subtle ways when it is safe, socially acceptable, and easy to rationalize.

the dawn of a "postracial America," we knew how naive and wrong such notions were.

In sum, then, there are legitimate reasons to celebrate racial progress. Racism, however, remains a fact of life and is by no means limited merely to the actions of some fringe individuals or groups. And as we will see in the following section, it exists in ways that escape the recognition of most people.

**Modern Racism**  Consider two stories from the world of sports:

1. As the first half ended during a high school basketball game near Pittsburgh, fans of a predominately white high school ran onto the court in full body banana suits, surrounded the players from the predominately African-American opposing team, and "allegedly began making monkey noises and hurling racial epithets" at the players (Smith, 2012a). A few months later in Poland and Croatia, black members of the Dutch and Italian national soccer teams were allegedly the targets of racial abuse—including being on the receiving end of monkey chants and a flung banana—during the Euro2012 championships. Indeed, the 2012 tournament was marred by a variety of charges of racist taunting by players and fans from multiple European nations (Brown, 2012; Cue, 2012).

2. Christopher Parsons and others (2009) analyzed every pitch from four Major League Baseball seasons from 2004 through 2008—more than 3.5 million pitches in all—and found a fascinating set of results. Umpires were more likely to call strikes for pitchers who were of the same race/ethnicity as they were. Even more interesting is the fact that this bias emerged only under three conditions: (1) if the game was played in the subset of ballparks that did not have a computerized monitoring system the league uses to review umpires' performance in calling balls and strikes; (2) if the number of people attending the game was relatively low; and (3) if the call would not be the final ball or strike of the player at bat. In other words, the racial/ethnic bias was evident only under the conditions when there would be the least accountability or public outcry.

The first of these examples—concerning racist taunting—illustrates what some call old-fashioned racism. It is blatant, explicit, and unmistakable. The second—concerning the bias in umpiring—is what some call **modern racism**, a subtle form of prejudice that tends to surface when it is safe, socially acceptable, or easy to rationalize. Modern racism is far more subtle and most likely to be present under the cloud of ambiguity. According to theories of modern racism, many people are racially ambivalent. They want to see themselves as fair, but they still harbor feelings of anxiety and discomfort about other racial groups (Hass et al., 1992). There are several specific theories of modern racism, but they all emphasize contradictions and tensions that lead to subtle, often unconscious forms of prejudice and discrimination (Gawronski et al., 2008; Levy et al., 2006; Sears & Henry, 2005; Son Hing et al., 2008). For example, Samuel Gaertner and John Dovidio (1986; Hodson et al., 2010) proposed the related concept of *aversive racism*, which concerns the ambivalence between individuals' sincerely fair-minded attitudes and beliefs, on the one hand, and their largely unconscious and unrecognized negative

AP Photo/Manu Fernande

An opponent tries to prevent Barcelona's Samuel Eto from leaving the game after he was targeted by racist taunts from Spanish League fans.

feelings and beliefs about blacks, on the other hand. Some scholars today use the term *microaggression* to characterize the everyday, typically rather subtle but hurtful forms of discrimination that are experienced quite frequently by members of targeted groups (Torres-Harding et al., 2012).

In these forms of racism, prejudice surfaces primarily under circumstances when the expression of prejudice is safe, socially acceptable, and easy to rationalize because of its ambiguity. For example, several studies have found that white participants playing the role of jurors may be more likely to convict a black than a white defendant for a crime when the evidence is rather ambiguous, and thus one can justify either a guilty or not-guilty verdict for reasons having nothing to do with race. If, on the other hand, race is made to seem to be an important aspect of the case, then this bias may be eliminated or even reversed (Bucolo & Cohn, 2010; Fein et al., 1997; Sommers & Ellsworth, 2009).

These modern, ambivalent forms of racism are often evident in the "but some of my best friends are . . ." excuse. That is, people establish their *moral credentials* of not being racist by demonstrating—to others or even to themselves—that they have good friends from the racial or ethnic group in question or they have behaved in ways that were quite fair to members of this group (Effron et al., 2012; Merritt et al., 2010). Having such good behavior to their credit gives people the license to take actions that might otherwise put them at risk for seeming prejudiced. Indeed, Anna Merritt and others (2012) found that people sometimes go out of their way to try to establish such credits, such as by rating an African American job candidate more positively if they anticipated being in a later situation in which they might be judged as racist.

**Implicit Racism**    Modern racism sometimes operates consciously and sometimes it operates outside people's conscious awareness. Scholars call racism that operates unconsciously and unintentionally **implicit racism**. Undetected by individuals who want to be fair and unbiased, implicit racism—along with other forms of implicit prejudice—can skew judgments, feelings, and behaviors—without inducing the guilt that more conscious, explicit forms of racism would trigger.

Implicit racism may be subtle, but its effects can be profound. For example, Jennifer Eberhardt and others (2006) studied predictors of whether a criminal defendant was likely to be sentenced to death. They examined more than 600 death-penalty-eligible cases tried in Philadelphia, Pennsylvania, between 1979 and 1999. In cases involving

**implicit racism** Racism that operates unconsciously and unintentionally.

a white victim and a black male defendant, the more the defendant's physical appearance was stereotypically black, the more likely he would be sentenced to death. In a more recent study of more than 12,000 adult black women imprisoned in North Carolina from 1995 to mid-2009, Jill Viglione and others (2011) found that black women with lighter skin color received on average about 12% less prison time than black women with darker skin (see ● Figure 5.1). Finally, a nationally representative sample of white Americans in another study recommended significantly more severe sentences for juveniles convicted of a crime if the participants were subtly primed with the word "black" than "white" when reading about a previous example of a guilty juvenile (Rattan et al., 2012). It is very likely that most of the judges, jurors, and participants whose decisions were assessed in these studies were consciously unaware of these biases, just as it is likely that the umpires in Major League Baseball were unaware of the bias in how they called strikes, but the evidence in both cases reveals significant discrimination.

The question of how to detect and measure implicit racism is a challenging one. Because of its implicit nature, it can't be assessed by simply asking people to answer some questions about their attitudes. Rather, much more subtle, indirect measures typically are used. By far the most well-known measure of this kind is the Implicit Association Test (IAT), first developed and tested by Anthony Greenwald and others (1998). The IAT measures the extent to which two concepts are associated. It measures implicit racism toward African Americans, for example, by comparing how quickly or slowly participants associate African American cues (such as a black face) with negative and positive concepts compared to how quickly or slowly they make the same kinds of associations with European American cues. Other IATs focus on associations concerning older versus younger people, men versus women, and so on. The IAT is discussed in more detail in Chapter 6 on Attitudes. It has sparked an explosion of research, with more than 700 scientific publications already, along with some controversy about its validity and uses (Blanton et al., 2009; Nosek & Smyth, 2011). The IAT has been so popular that between October 1998 and August 2012 more than 14 *million* IATs were completed by visitors to the IAT website (Nosek, 2012).

Implicit racial bias as measured by the IAT has been found between groups around the world and even among children as young as 6 and 7 years old (Baron & Banaji, 2006; Dunham et al., 2008; Newheiser & Olson, 2012). And as can be seen in ● Figure 5.2, whereas older children and adults begin to control or change their explicit prejudices and show less bias on explicit measures, they continue to show implicit racism as measured by the IAT.

Implicit racism correlates with a variety of attitudes and behaviors. For example, higher implicit racism by white participants in several studies predicted negative, unfriendly nonverbal behaviors in interracial interactions, such as physical distancing or lack of eye contact—actions that can make the other person feel uncomfortable, disliked and that can lead to, for instance, poor performance in a job interview (Greenwald

## ● FIGURE 5.1

### Facial Features and Prison Sentences

According to a study by Jill Viglione and others (2011) of more than 12,000 adult black women imprisoned in North Carolina, the chances are good that if the two women depicted here were each found guilty of a crime, the woman on the left (whose face would be considered more "stereotypically black") would receive a longer prison sentence than the woman on the right.

© Peter Dresse/Blend Images/Corbis

© Rob Lewine/Tetra Images/Corbis

Children do not tend to show biases based on race; it is only after they become adolescents that they learn to respond to people differently based on race. **FALSE.**

## ● FIGURE 5.2

### Development of Explicit Versus Implicit Racial Preferences

On an explicit attitude measure (left), 6-year-old children showed a strong preference for a white child over a black child. This preference was reduced in 10 year olds and completely eliminated in adults. However, implicit attitudes, as measured by the Implicit Association Test (right), showed a consistent pro-white bias across all three age groups.
Based on Baron & Banaji, 2006; Dunham et al., 2008. © Cengage Learning

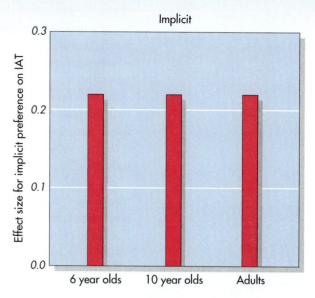

et al., 2009). Implicit racism has been found in several studies to be associated with negative attitudes toward President Obama and his policies (Hehman et al., 2011; Knowles et al., 2010). A particularly disturbing, and growing, set of findings concerns the link between doctors' and other health care providers' implicit racism and their treatment of patients from racial and ethnic minority groups (Penner et al., 2010; Shavers et al., 2012). For example, Lisa Cooper and others (2012) found that higher implicit racism among clinicians was related to poorer communication and less warmth toward black but not white patients. Janice Sabin and Anthony Greenwald (2012) found that doctors with stronger pro-white bias on the IAT were more likely to recommend prescribing pain-relieving medication after surgery for white patients, and less likely to do so for black patients, compared to physicians with less of a pro-white IAT score.

**Interracial Interactions**   The divides between racial and ethnic groups tend to be more vast and may promote stronger feelings of hostility, fear, and distrust than the divides based on other social categories, such as those based on gender, appearance, and age. One factor that can keep these negative feelings strong is the relative lack of contact between people of different racial and ethnic groups. In addition, in contemporary society, the stigma of being perceived as racist is especially troubling for most people (Crandall & Eshleman, 2003). This combination of stronger negative emotions, less contact, and greater anxiety about appearing racist makes interracial interaction particularly challenging and fraught with emotion and tension.

When engaging in interracial interactions, whites may be concerned about a number of things, including not wanting to be, or to appear to be, racist. They may therefore try to regulate their behaviors, be on the lookout for signs of distrust or dislike from their interaction partners, and so on. Because of these concerns, what should ideally be a smooth-flowing normal interaction can become awkward and even exhausting. This, in turn, can affect their partner's perceptions of them, possibly leading to the ironic outcome of their appearing to be racist because they were trying not to be. A number of researchers have been examining such phenomena (e.g., Hebl et al., 2009; Richeson & Shelton, 2012; Toosi et al., 2012). For example, Jennifer Richeson, Nicole Shelton, and their colleagues have found that white participants high in implicit racism are more likely to perform worse on a simple cognitive task after interacting with a black than a white confederate—evidence that the interaction was cognitively draining for them (Richeson & Shelton, 2010, 2012; Shelton et al., 2010).

According to Jacquie Vorauer (2003; Vorauer et al., 2009), individuals engaging in intergroup interactions often activate *metastereotypes*, or thoughts about the outgroup's stereotypes about them, and worry about being seen as consistent with these stereotypes. Indeed, this kind of concern about interracial interactions can lead to cardiovascular reactions associated with feelings of threat (Mendes et al., 2002). These potentially harmful physiological stress responses may not be isolated instances—Sophie Trawalter and others (2012) have found that they can endure over the course of an academic year among white students concerned about appearing prejudiced across repeated interracial interactions during the year.

It should not be surprising, then, that people sometimes try to avoid interracial interaction for fear of appearing racist or being treated in a racist way, and this avoidant behavior can have the ironic effect of making things all the worse. Ashby Plant and David Butz (2006), for example, found that when nonblack participants with this avoidant concern interacted with a black confederate, they had shorter and less pleasant interactions. Philip Goff, Claude Steele, and Paul Davies (2008) found that white male students sat farther away from black students than white students in an interaction—but only if they thought they would be engaged in a conversation about a racially sensitive topic.

In a clever demonstration of the kind of anxiety whites sometimes feel about race, Michael Norton and others (2006) paired white participants with either a white or black confederate in a game (similar to the children's board game *Guess Who?*) that required the participants to ask the confederate questions so they could guess which of a series of photographs the confederate had been given. As can be seen in ● Figure 5.3, participants were significantly less likely to ask about the race of the person in the photograph when playing the game with a black confederate than a white confederate, even though this hurt their ability to win the game. It seemed that the white participants would rather lose the game than run the risk of appearing racist by paying any attention to the race of the people in the photographs.

An interesting follow-up to this study examined the performance of children in this task (Apfelbaum et al., 2008). On a race-neutral version of the game, older children (10 and 11 year olds), not surprisingly, outperformed younger children (8 and 9 year olds). However, when race was a relevant category, the older children were much more likely to avoid asking about race, presumably because they are more aware of the sensitivities surrounding race. The result of this was that in the race-relevant version of the game, the younger children significantly outperformed the older children!

White adults in an interracial interaction often try to adopt a "colorblind" mentality and demeanor, acting—or trying to act—as if race is so unimportant to them that they may not even perceive their interaction partner's race. Often this attempt is sincere and with the best of intentions, but a variety of research findings has accumulated suggesting that

● **FIGURE 5.3**

**Colorblind?**

When white participants played a face-matching game in which they had to ask questions of a confederate to guess which of a series of photographs the confederate had, they were much less likely to ask about the race of the people in the photographs if they were interacting with a black confederate than a white confederate, even though this hurt their performance in the game.

Based on Norton et al., 2006. © Cengage Learning

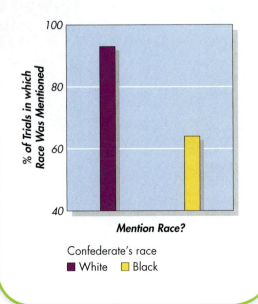

this approach often backfires and makes members of racial minority groups more, rather than less, uncomfortable. A multicultural approach that acknowledges and positively values racial and ethnic differences is often more effective in promoting better intergroup attitudes and behaviors (Holoien & Shelton, 2012; Plaut et al., 2009; Rattan & Ambady, 2012).

Anxieties and challenges associated with intergroup interactions are not limited to those between whites and blacks, of course, despite the fact that the majority of research has focused on this particular intergroup dynamic. Feelings of threat and anxiety in the face of intergroup interaction or relations play an important role in people's prejudice toward a variety of groups (Davis & Stephan, 2011; Stephan et al., 2009). For example, social psychological research has addressed these issues concerning intergroup interactions involving gay and lesbian individuals, overweight people, and native peoples of Canada (Blair et al., 2003; Everly et al., 2012; Hebl et al., 2009; Madera & Hebl, 2012).

> Interracial interactions tend to go better and to reduce the perceptions of racism if a colorblind mentality is used, which denies or minimizes any acknowledgment of racial differences. **F**ALSE.

## Sexism: Ambivalence, Objectification, and Double Standards

As with racism, old-fashioned blatant displays of sexism are less socially accepted than in years past, although they continue to exist at a frequency and with an intensity that would surprise many. As with racism, researchers have been documenting and studying modern and implicit forms of sexism that tend to escape the notice of most people but that can exert powerful discriminatory effects (Swim & Hyers, 2009).

There are some ways that sexism is different, however. Gender stereotypes are distinct from virtually all other stereotypes in that they often are *prescriptive* rather than merely *descriptive*. In other words, they indicate what many people in a given culture believe men and women *should* be. Few Americans, for example, think that gays *should* be artistic and sensitive or that old people *should* be forgetful and conservative, but many think that women *should* be nurturing and that men *should* be unemotional. Even though ambition and drive are valued in our society, women who exhibit such traits may be viewed in especially harsh terms, contributing to the double standards that are a hallmark of sexism (Brescoll et al., 2010; Prentice & Carranza, 2002; Rudman et al., 2012).

Another way that sexism is unique concerns the degree to which the ingroup and outgroup members interact. Men and women are intimately familiar with each other. They typically (although certainly not always) come from the same families, grow up together, are attracted to one another, live together, and produce and raise children together. Because of this, sexism involves more of an overt ambivalence between positive and negative feelings and beliefs than is typical of racism and other forms of prejudice and discrimination.

In this section, we will focus on this ambivalence and on some of the double standards that exist in sexism in degrees that are not as evident in most other forms of discrimination. Later in the chapter, we explore the related issues of gender stereotypes and how they are perpetuated.

**Ambivalent Sexism**  It may surprise you to learn that, overall, stereotypes of women tend to be more positive than those of men (Eagly et al., 1994). However, the positive traits associated with women are less valued in important domains such as the business world than the positive traits associated with men.

These contradictions are reflected in Peter Glick and Susan Fiske's (2001, 2011) concept of **ambivalent sexism**. Ambivalent sexism consists of two elements: *hostile sexism*, characterized by negative, resentful feelings about women's abilities, value, and ability to challenge men's power (e.g., "Once a woman gets a man to commit to her, she usually

**ambivalent sexism**  A form of sexism characterized by attitudes about women that reflect both negative, resentful beliefs and feelings and affectionate and chivalrous but potentially patronizing beliefs and feelings.

tries to put him on a tight leash"), and *benevolent sexism*, characterized by affectionate, chivalrous feelings founded on the potentially patronizing belief that women need and deserve protection (e.g., "Women should be cherished and protected by men"). Benevolent sexism, on the surface, does not strike many women or men as terribly troubling, but the two forms of sexism are positively correlated. Benevolent sexism is associated in particular with negative reactions toward women who defy traditional gender roles and stereotypes (Durán et al., 2011; Masser et al., 2010; Viki et al., 2004).

Glick, Fiske, and others (2000) conducted an ambitious study of 15,000 men and women in nineteen nations across six continents and found that ambivalent sexism was prevalent around the world. Among their most intriguing findings was that people from countries with the greatest degree of economic and political inequality between the sexes tended to exhibit the most hostile and benevolent sexism. ● Figure 5.4 depicts the average hostile sexism scores for each of several countries.

**Objectification** Women are all too often treated in objectifying ways. That is, they are viewed or treated more as mere bodies or objects and less as fully functioning human beings. The advertising industry specifically, and the popular media more generally, are filled with imagery of women represented as sexual objects or just parts of a body (Kilbourne, 2003). For example, Julie Stankiewicz and Francine Rosselli (2008) examined almost 2,000 advertisements depicting women from 58 popular magazines in the United States and found that half of them featured women as sex objects. Women also experience being treated and seen as objects in numerous interactions in their real lives. Although men are objectified in the media as well (and this appears to be a growing trend), and men are sometimes objectified in real interactions, it is still the case that women experience this much more frequently, and a good deal of research documents a variety of negative effects of this objectification on women, including on their mental and physical health, their academic performance, and how they behave in social interactions (Calogero et al., 2011; Fredrickson et al., 1998; Saguy et al., 2010; Tiggemann & Williams, 2012).

### Sex Discrimination: Double Standards and Pervasive Stereotypes

Many years ago, Philip Goldberg (1968) asked students at a small women's college to evaluate the content and writing style of some articles. When the material was supposedly written by John McKay rather than Joan McKay it received higher ratings, a result that led Goldberg to wonder if even women were prejudiced against women. Certain other studies showed that people often devalue the performance of women who take on tasks usually reserved for men (Lott, 1985) and attribute women's achievements to luck rather than ability (Deaux & Emswiller, 1974; Nieva & Gutek, 1981). These studies generated a lot of attention, but it now appears that this kind of devaluation of women is not commonly found in similar studies. More than a hundred studies modeled after Goldberg's indicate that people are

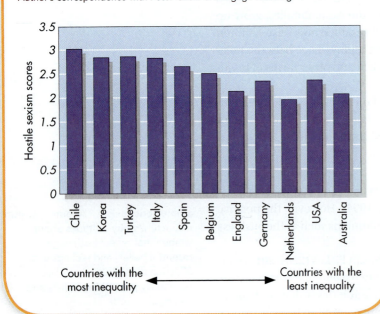

● **FIGURE 5.4**

**Hostile Sexism Across Countries**

Respondents from 19 countries completed measures of hostile and benevolent sexism. The average hostile sexism scores for male respondents from 11 of these countries are depicted here. The countries are listed from left to right in order of how equal the sexes are in terms of political and economic power as defined by United Nations criteria. It is clear both from this figure and from the data more generally that hostile sexism is positively correlated with gender inequality.

Author's correspondence with Peter Glick. © Cengage Learning

Countries with the most inequality ←→ Countries with the least inequality not generally biased by gender in the evaluation of performance (Swim & Sanna, 1996; Top, 1991).

This does not mean, however, that sex discrimination no longer exists. In many parts of the world blatant sexism is still quite evident, of course. For example, in parts of the Middle East, recent attempts at reforms to benefit women have been met by some with great support, but by others with hostile, sometimes violent, resistance. Women in some countries are pressured to have abortions if they are pregnant with girls (Goldberg & Dooley, 2011). A law in Morocco that enables rapists to escape prosecution by marrying their victim came under fire recently when a 16-year-old girl committed suicide after a court ordered her to marry the man who raped her (Hirsch, 2012). Other examples are less dramatic but still important.

Look at ● Figure 5.5 and Table 5.3, for instance, and you'll notice some striking sex differences in occupational choice. How many female airline pilots have you met lately? What about male dental hygienists? (It's interesting to note that 98% of the dental hygienists in the United States in 2011 were women, but only 22% of the dentists were.) The question is, of course, what explains these differences? Decades of social science

● **FIGURE 5.5**

**Percentage of Women in Specific Occupations in the United States, 2011**

Recent labor statistics reveal that men and women occupy very different positions in the U.S. work force. U.S. Bureau of Labor Statistics, 2012. © Cengage Learning

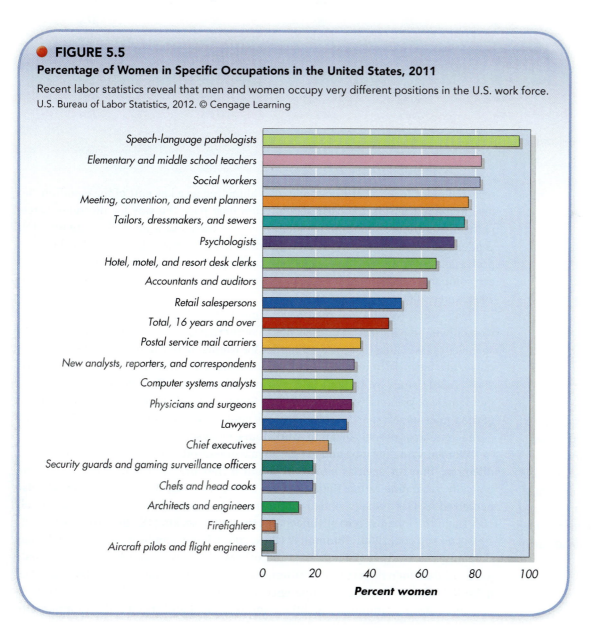

## TABLE 5.3
**Women in Work Settings in Selected Countries Around the World**

These international labor statistics show the percentage of workers in each category who are women in each of several countries. These data show some of the differences between nations, as well as some similarities concerning which types of jobs women are more or less likely to occupy around the world.

| Country | Total Workforce | Clerks | Craft and Trade Workers | Legislators, Senior Officials, Managers | Sales and Service Workers |
|---|---|---|---|---|---|
| Australia | 45% | 67% | 5% | 37% | 68% |
| Canada | 47% | 77% | 8% | 37% | 63% |
| Columbia | 39% | 58% | 19% | 46% | 61% |
| Costa Rica | 37% | 57% | 14% | 27% | 54% |
| Egypt | 21% | 29% | 3% | 11% | 10% |
| Iran | 18% | 24% | 23% | 13% | 11% |
| Israel | 46% | 74% | 5% | 30% | 60% |
| Italy | 39% | 59% | 14% | 33% | 57% |
| Republic of Korea | 42% | 52% | 15% | 9% | 63% |
| Mexico | 37% | 61% | 24% | 31% | 54% |
| Morocco | 27% | 25% | 19% | 12% | 6% |
| Netherlands | 45% | 69% | 5% | 28% | 69% |
| United Kingdom | 46% | 78% | 8% | 34% | 76% |

Data from International Labour Office, 2008. © Cengage Learning

research point to sexist attitudes and discrimination as a key part of the equation. Sex discrimination during the early school years may pave the way for diverging career paths in adulthood. Then, when equally qualified men and women compete for a job, gender considerations enter in once again, as some research indicates that business professionals favor men for so-called masculine jobs (such as a manager for a machinery company) and women for so-called feminine jobs (such as a receptionist) (Eagly 2004; Kmec, 2005).

Even when women and men have comparable jobs, the odds are good that the women will be paid less than their male counterparts and will be confronted with a so-called glass ceiling that makes it harder for women to rise to the highest positions of power in a business or organization (Barreto et al., 2009; Gorman & Kmec, 2009; Leicht, 2008). A 2011 study by Anthony Lo Sasso and others found that the starting salaries of new female physicians trained in New York State averaged almost $17,000 less than that of their male counterparts! (This difference could not be accounted for by things such as different areas of specialization, work hours, or setting.)

Women vying for jobs and career advancement often face a virtually impossible dilemma: They are seen as more competent if they present themselves with stereotypically masculine rather than feminine traits, yet when they do this, they are also perceived as less socially skilled and attractive—a perception that may ultimately cost them the job or career advancement they were seeking (Eagly, 2004; Fiske et al., 1991; Jackson et al., 2001; Rudman & Glick, 2001). For example, male and female participants in a study by Julie Phelan and others (2008) read about a male or female job candidate for a managerial position. Some candidates emphasized their "agentic" qualities—that is, technical competence, independence, and leadership ability. Others emphasized "communal" qualities—interpersonal and social skills. Compared to

*According to a 2011 national survey by Gallup, 40% of Americans would prefer to have a boy compared to 28% preferring a girl, if they could have only one child (the rest indicated no preference). These percentages are almost identical to those from a similar survey in 1941.*

agentic male candidates, agentic female candidates were perceived as high in competence but low in social skills. In addition, when judging how hirable the candidates were, participants tended to weigh perceptions of the candidates' competence more than their judgments about their social skills—except when judging agentic women! For agentic women, the participants deemphasized these candidates' strong suit—their competence—and instead weighed their (lack of) social skills more heavily.

For both women and men, being in a job that is traditionally seen as more typical of the other gender can be especially challenging. Consistent with this idea are the results of a study by Victoria Brescoll and others (2010). These researchers found that men and women were judged more harshly for a mistake made on a job traditionally held by the other sex than for the same kind of mistake on a job in which their gender was the majority. In another study Brescoll and others (2012) found that men were perceived as less masculine if they worked for a female supervisor in a traditionally masculine occupation. Examples like these show that even with all the great strides that have been made over the decades it is clear that defying traditional gender roles can still be daunting.

## Beyond Racism and Sexism: Age, Weight, Sexuality, and Other Targets

We have focused in this section on racism and sexism not only because of their historic significance but also because they have been dominant in social psychological research. It is important to note that other forms of bias and discrimination are, of course, quite important and are the subject of contemporary social psychological research. In fact, social psychologists today are studying a wider variety of stereotypes, prejudices, and targets of discrimination than ever. It is probably no coincidence, for example, that as our population ages and people tend to live longer, more researchers are studying ageism—prejudice and discrimination targeting the elderly (Nelson, 2009; North & Fiske, 2012). One of the interesting things about ageism is how much attitudes and behaviors toward the elderly vary so greatly across cultures. Another interesting aspect of ageism is that it is the rare prejudice held by people who will one day—if they are lucky to live that long—become members of the group they once were prejudiced against. Other forms of discrimination that are getting recent attention include those targeting people's physical disabilities or disfigurements, political ideology, economic class, being unmarried, or religion (or the lack of religious beliefs) (DePaulo, 2011; Gervais et al., 2011; Hewstone et al., 2011; Madera & Hebl, 2012; Smith & Redington, 2010).

Although it is much less socially acceptable to display obvious prejudice and discrimination of many kinds today, some forms of these biases appear to be considered more acceptable by many people. Among these are prejudice based on weight and based on sexuality. Although what is considered ideal body types can vary dramatically in some ways across times and cultures, it is clear that in some cultures today, particularly among white Americans, jokes, negative attitudes, and insensitive behaviors directed toward those who are perceived to be overweight can be pervasive and hurtful (Brochu & Esses, 2011; Crandall et al., 2009; Hebl et al., 2009; Schafer & Ferraro, 2011).

Prejudice and discrimination based on sexuality remain unusually overt and blatant, often being among the most divisive social issues in a society. For example, national polls in the United States show that 42% of Americans surveyed believe that homosexuality is morally wrong, and about a third believe that gay or lesbian relations between consenting adults should be legal (Gallup, 2012). Anti-gay groups have loudly protested at the funerals of American military personnel killed during the wars in Afghanistan and Iraq (Nelson, 2012). In addition to these overt examples, there are many more ways in which

● **FIGURE 5.6**

**Gay Pride and Spare Change**

Individuals in a parking lot near a shopping center in southern England were approached by someone who politely asked, "Excuse me, can you help me please, I am short of change and need 10 pence to pay my parking fee, could you check to see if you have a 10-pence piece I could have?" Requestors wearing a T-shirt with the words "Gay Pride" on the front were significantly less likely to be offered the change than requestors wearing a blank T-shirt.

Based on Hendren & Blank, 2009. © Cengage Learning

these prejudices and discrimination can operate more subtly. For example, in one field experiment, Amy Hendren and Hartmut Blank (2009) found that people at a parking lot at a shopping center in England were less likely to help someone who asked for some small change for a parking meter if the person was wearing a gay pride T-shirt than a blank T-shirt (see ● Figure 5.6). More troubling are the results of a study by András Tilcsik (2011). Tilcsik sent pairs of resumes in response to almost 1,800 job postings in seven states across the United States. The resumes in each pair were virtually identical except that in one of them, the job candidate indicated having volunteered time for a gay campus organization. Would these (fictitious) job applicants get invited to interview for the jobs? Even though the job-relevant skills and experiences were identical, the applicant with the experience in the gay campus organization was about 40% less likely to be invited for an interview than the other applicant.

## Being Stigmatized

We are all targets of other people's stereotypes and prejudices. These may be based on how we look, how we talk, how we dress, where we come from, and so on. None of us is immune from having our work evaluated in a biased way, our motives questioned, or our attempts at making new friends rejected because of stereotypes and prejudices. But for the targets of some stereotypes and prejudices, these concerns are relentless and profound. For them, there seem to be few safe havens. Social psychologists often refer to these targets as **stigmatized**—individuals who are targets of negative stereotypes, perceived as deviant, and devalued in society because they are members of a particular social group or because they have a particular characteristic (Major & Crocker, 1993). What are some of the effects of being stigmatized by stereotypes and prejudice?

In *Color-Blind*, writer Ellis Cose (1997), who is African American, tells a story about how he was treated in a job interview 20 years earlier. He was an award-winning newspaper reporter at the time and was hoping to land a job with a national magazine. The editor he met with was pleasant and gracious, but he said that the magazine didn't have many black readers. "All the editor saw was a young black guy, and since *Esquire* was not in need of a young black guy, they were not in need of me. . . . He had been so busy focusing on my race that he was incapable of seeing me or my work" (p. 150). Then, a few years later, and in light of affirmative action policies, Cose was asked if he was interested in a position in a firm as corporate director of equal opportunity. "I was stunned, for the question made no sense. I was an expert neither on personnel nor on equal employment law; I was, however, black, which seemed to be the most important qualification" (p. 156).

The targets of stigmatizing stereotypes frequently wonder whether and to what extent others' impressions of them are distorted through the warped lens of social categorization. On some occasions these suspicions can actually serve a self-protective function. For example, in a study by Jennifer Crocker and her colleagues (1991), black students who received negative interpersonal feedback from a white student suffered less of a blow to their self-esteem if they could easily attribute the white student's negative reaction to racism than if they could not. On the other hand, the self-esteem of black students was actually *reduced* by positive feedback from a white student if they could suspect that this feedback may have been due to their race.

Although attributing negative feedback to discrimination can protect one's overall self-esteem, it can also make people feel as if they have less personal control over their lives. Individuals from low-status groups may be threatened by this vulnerability

**stigmatized** Being persistently stereotyped, perceived as deviant, and devalued in society because of membership in a particular social group or because of a particular characteristic.

to discrimination and thus feel worse about themselves when they perceive that they were discriminated against, especially when they have reason to think that the discrimination against them could persist over time (Schmitt et al., 2002).

There has been a surge of troubling research findings in recent years concerning how stigmatized targets are at increased risk for serious and long-term physical and mental health problems. A meta-analysis by Elizabeth Pascoe and Laura Smart Richman (2009) of 134 studies concluded that perceived discrimination significantly predicts negative mental and physical health outcomes. Since then, even more studies have supported this link. For example, recent studies examining a wide variety of targeted groups have shown significant associations between degree of discrimination that people report experiencing and increased blood pressure, depression, breast cancer rates, diabetes, stroke, respiratory problems, chronic pain, and substance abuse (Brody et al., 2012; Dailey & Humphreys, 2011; Matheson & Anisman, 2012; Mereish et al., 2012; Smedley, 2012). Even simply anticipating interacting with someone who one thinks is prejudiced can trigger cardiovascular stress responses (Sawyer et al., 2012).

## Stereotype Threat

One of the more tragic effects of stereotyping in contemporary life is its effects on the intellectual performance and identity of its targets. An enormous wave of research on this issue was generated when social psychologist Claude Steele began writing about this problem in the 1990s. Steele proposed that in situations where a negative stereotype can apply to certain groups, members of these groups can fear being seen "through the lens of diminishing stereotypes and low expectations" (1999, p. 44). Steele (1997) called this predicament **stereotype threat**, for it hangs like "a threat in the air" when the individual is in the stereotype-relevant situation. The predicament can be particularly threatening for individuals whose identity and self-esteem are invested in domains where the stereotype is relevant. Steele argued that stereotype threat plays a crucial role in influencing the intellectual performance and identity of stereotyped group members. Steele and his colleagues (2002) later broadened the scope of their analysis to include *social identity threats* more generally. These threats are not necessarily tied to specific stereotypes but instead reflect a more general devaluing of a person's social group.

According to Steele's theory, stereotype threat can hamper achievement in academic domains in two ways. First, reactions to the "threat in the air" can directly interfere with performance—for example, by increasing anxiety and triggering distracting thoughts. Second, if this stereotype threat is chronic in the academic domain, it can cause individuals to *disidentify* from that domain—to dismiss the domain as no longer relevant to their self-esteem and identity.

To illustrate, imagine a black student and a white student who enter high school equally qualified in academic performance. Imagine that while taking a particularly difficult test at the beginning of the school year, each student struggles on the first few problems. Both students may begin to worry about failing, but the black student may have a whole set of additional worries about appearing to confirm a negative stereotype. Even if the black student doesn't believe the stereotype at all, the threat of being reduced to a stereotype in the eyes of those around her can trigger anxiety and distraction, impairing her performance. And if she experiences this threat in school often—perhaps because she stands out as one of only a few black students in the school or because she is treated by others in a particular way—the situation may become too threatening to her self-esteem. To buffer herself against the threat, she may disidentify with school. If she does this, her academic performance will become less relevant to her identity and self-esteem, and she will therefore work less hard and perform worse.

**stereotype threat** The experience of concern about being evaluated based on negative stereotypes about one's group.

**The Original Experiments**   Steele and others conducted a series of experiments in which they manipulated factors likely to increase or decrease stereotype threat as students took academic tests. For example, Steele and Joshua Aronson (1995) had black and white students from a highly selective university take a very difficult standardized verbal test. To some participants, it was introduced as a test of intellectual ability; to others, it was introduced as a problem-solving task unrelated to ability. Steele and Aronson reasoned that because of the difficulty of the test, *all* the students would struggle with it. If the test was said to be related to intellectual ability, however, the black students would feel the threat of a negative stereotype in addition to the stress of struggling with the test. In contrast, if the test was described simply as a research task and not a real test of intelligence, then negative stereotypes would be less applicable and the stereotype threat would be reduced. In that case, black students would be less impaired while taking the test. As shown in ● Figure 5.7, the results supported these predictions.

Thus, a seemingly minor change in the setting—a few words about the meaning of a test—had a powerful effect on the black students' performance. In a second study, the researchers used an even more subtle manipulation of stereotype threat: whether or not the students were asked to report their race just before taking the test. Making them think about race for a few seconds just before taking the test impaired the performance of black students but had no effect on white students. Think about the implications of such findings for important real-world contexts. (After years of conducting this research, social psychologists were finally able to convince the College Board and Educational Testing Service in June 2012 to agree to discontinue the practice of asking students demographic questions immediately before they begin high-stakes testing such as Advanced Placement exams.)

Because negative stereotypes concerning women's advanced math skills are prevalent, women may often experience stereotype threat in settings relevant to these skills. Reducing stereotype threat in these settings, therefore, should reduce the underperformance that women tend to exhibit in these areas. To test this idea, Steven Spencer and others (1999) recruited male and female students who were good at math and felt that math was important to their identities. The researchers gave these students a very difficult standardized math test, one on which all of them would perform poorly. Before taking the test, some students were told that the test generally showed no gender differences, thereby implying that the negative stereotype of women's ability in math was *not* relevant to this particular test. Other students were told that the test *did* generally show gender differences. As Steele's theory predicted, women performed worse than men when they were told that the test typically produced gender differences, but they performed as well as men when they were told that the test typically did not produce gender differences.

**The Prevalence and Diversity of Threats**   Since these original studies, research inspired by the theory of stereotype threat grew at a stunningly fast pace. The evidence for underperformance due to stereotype threat is quite strong and broad (Steele, 2010). It has been found both in the laboratory and in real-world settings, including schools and businesses. Although much of the research has documented the power of the effects of

● **FIGURE 5.7**

**Stereotype Threat and Academic Performance**

Before taking a very difficult standardized verbal test, some students were told that it was a test of their intellectual ability, but others were told that it was simply a research task unrelated to intellectual ability. All students' scores on this test were adjusted based on their scores from standardized college entrance verbal examinations. Despite this adjustment, black students did significantly worse than white students on the test if it was introduced as a test of intellectual ability (left). In contrast, among the students who had been told the test was unrelated to ability, black students and white students performed equally well (right).

From Steele, C.M. and Aronson, J., "Stereotype threat and the intellectual test performance of African Americans," *Journal of Personality and Social Psychology* vol 69 (pp. 797–781). Copyright © 1995 American Psychological Association. Reprinted by permission.

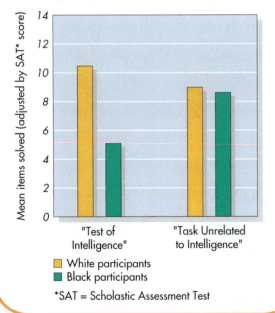

stereotype threat on African Americans and women, the scope of the research extends much further. Stereotype threats can affect any group for which strong, well-known negative stereotypes are relevant in particular settings. Social identity threats can be more general than that, affecting groups that may be devalued even in the absence of specific negative stereotypes about a particular domain.

The examples of these threats run far and wide. For instance, many white athletes feel stereotype threat whenever they step onto a court or playing field where they constitute the minority. Will the white athlete feel the added weight of this threat while struggling against the other athletes in a game? To address this question, Jeff Stone and others (1999) had black and white students play miniature golf. When the experimenters characterized the game as diagnostic of "natural athletic ability," the white students did worse. But when they characterized it as diagnostic of "sports intelligence," the black students did worse.

It should be pointed out that a person can be affected by stereotype threat even if he or she does not believe in the negative stereotype. Just knowing about the stereotype seems to be enough, particularly if the individual identifies strongly with the targeted group and cares about performing well. This last point is particularly poignant—the performance of people who have had success at something and who care the most may be most affected by stereotype threat effects. (An interesting side note: The first experiment to show that students who most identify with and care about success in school may be the most vulnerable to stereotype threat effects was conducted in an inner-city Los Angeles high school by a Stanford University undergraduate student named Mikel Jollet. Jollet soon after formed and became lead singer and songwriter of the very successful rock group, The Airborne Toxic Event.)

Here is a small sample of groups whose performance in various domains was hurt by stereotype threat, as demonstrated in experiments around the world:

- Low-socioeconomic-status students in France and the United States on a verbal test when the test was said to be diagnostic of intellectual ability (Croizet & Claire, 1998)

- European American men on a math test when compared with Asians (Aronson et al., 1999)

- Women on a math test in a co-ed rather than an all-female setting (Ben-Zeev et al., 2005; Sekaquaptewa & Thompson, 2003)

- Women playing chess on the computer when they were told that their opponent was male (Maass et al., 2008)

- White participants taking an IAT when they thought the test was diagnostic of racism (Frantz et al., 2004)

- Individuals with a history of mental illness on a test of reasoning ability when asked about their illness before taking the test (Quinn et al., 2004)

- Women on a negotiation task when success on the task was said to be associated with masculine traits; men on a negotiation task when success on the task was said to be associated with feminine traits (Kray et al., 2002)

An African American student is likely to perform worse on an athletic task if the task is described as one reflecting sports intelligence than if it is described as reflecting natural athletic ability. **T**RUE.

© Carin Perilloux

Three scholars who have done research on stereotype threat reunite backstage after an Airborne Toxic Event concert. Can you guess which one became the rock star?

- Student athletes primed to think about their identity as athletes before taking a difficult math test (Yopyk & Prentice, 2005)

- Overweight individuals primed to think about weight-related stereotypes (Seacat & Mickelson, 2009)

- Older adults on a memory test when it was presented as a memory test rather than an impression formation task (Chasteen et al., 2005)

- Women driving after being reminded of demeaning stereotypes about female drivers (causing women in a driving simulator to crash into jaywalkers!) (Yeung & von Hippel, 2008)

**Causes of Stereotype Threat Effects**   Stereotype threat exerts its effects in multiple ways (Inzlicht & Schmader, 2012; Schmader & Beilock, 2012; Ståhl et al., 2012). Stereotype threat has been shown to do each of the following to people: triggers physiological arousal and stress; drains cognitive resources; causes a loss of focus to the task at hand because of attempts to suppress thoughts about the relevant stereotype; impairs working memory; activates negative thoughts, worry, feelings of dejection, and concerns about trying to avoid failure than trying to achieve success. Think about trying to do your best on a difficult test that is important to you while all of these things are happening to you—you'd get some sense of how stereotype threat can undermine people's performance and ambitions.

Even though stereotype threat effects are widespread, the growing body of research on this subject also gives us reason to hope. Social psychologists have been uncovering ways that people can be better protected against these threats. We will focus on these promising ways in the final section of this chapter. Before we get to that point, however, we will first examine the social psychological causes at the root of the problems we have been discussing.

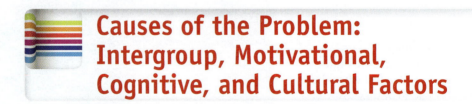

# Causes of the Problem: Intergroup, Motivational, Cognitive, and Cultural Factors

One of the reasons that stereotypes, prejudice, and discrimination continue to persist is because they are caused by more than just a few factors. There are many sources fueling these problems, and they operate both independently and in tandem. Some stem from the ways that humans cognitively process and remember information. Others can be traced to motivations and goals that drive us to see or react to our social worlds in particular ways. Still others concern how groups of people are represented or valued in one's culture. In this section we turn to look at some of the most important of these causes underlying stereotyping, prejudice, and discrimination.

## Social Categories and Intergroup Conflict

At the root of stereotyping, prejudice, and discrimination is the fact that we divide our social world into groups. As perceivers, we routinely sort each other into groups on the basis of gender, race, age, and other common attributes in a process called

**social categorization**. In some ways, social categorization is natural and adaptive. It allows us to form impressions quickly and use experience to guide new interactions. With so many things to pay attention to in our social worlds, we can save time and effort by using people's group memberships to make inferences about them. The time and energy saved through social categorization does come at a cost, however. Categorizing people leads us to overestimate the differences between groups and to underestimate the differences within groups (Krueger & DiDonato, 2008; Wyer et al., 2002). Indeed, even basic perception is affected by categorization. For example, studies have shown that people see racially ambiguous faces as darker if they are labeled racially black than white (Levin & Banaji, 2006).

Each of us is a member of multiple social categories, but some categorizations—particularly race, gender, and age—are more likely to quickly dominate our perceptions than others (Ito & Urland, 2003; Yzerbyt & Demoulin, 2010). The distinctions between some of these social categories may be seen as more rigid, even more biologically rooted, than they actually are. Many people assume, for example, that there is a clear genetic basis for classifying people by race. The fact is, however, that numerous biologists, anthropologists, and psychologists note that there is more genetic variation *within* races than *between* them and emphasize that race is more of a social conception than a genetic reality (Marks, 2011; Markus, 2008; Plaks et al., 2012). Indeed, how societies make distinctions between races can change dramatically as a function of historical contexts. For instance, it was fairly common for Americans in the early part of the twentieth century to consider Irish Americans as a racial group distinct from whites, but today such thinking is quite rare. As people today increasingly identify themselves in multiracial ways, or in ways that defy the traditional binary distinction between men and women, a greater recognition of the role of factors beyond biology in social categorization becomes all the more relevant.

Whether individuals think of various social categories as fixed and biologically rooted or not can be important (Sanchez & Garcia, 2009). For example, Melissa Williams and Jennifer Eberhardt (2008) found that people who tend to think of race as a stable, biologically determined entity are less likely to interact with racial outgroup members and are more likely to accept racial inequalities than are people who see race as more socially determined. Other research has found that biracial individuals are more vulnerable to some effects of stereotypes if they think of race as stable and biological (Sanchez & Garcia, 2009; Shih et al., 2007).

Just as race is a blurrier category than many people realize, so too are nationalities. A series of studies by Thierry Devos and others demonstrated how various ethnic minority groups such as Latino Americans, Asian Americans, and African Americans are not seen as truly American, but some situational factors—such as presenting individuals with examples of positive stereotypic traits of one of these groups—can reduce this tendency (Devos et al., 2010; Huynh et al., 2011; Rydell et al., 2010). As immigration battles intensify throughout much of the world, a variety of social, historical, economic, and political factors all play a role in who is categorized as "foreign."

Diana Sanchez and Julie Garcia (2012) have reported a number of ways in which racial categorization is also affected by people's social and economic status. For example, perceivers are more likely to categorize others as racially black if they are of lower socioeconomic status, if they are incarcerated, or if they are unemployed. These same factors may have similar effects on how people categorize themselves racially. Elirea Bornman (2010) has found that since apartheid ended in South Africa around 1994, blacks have strengthened their sense of national identity while Afrikan-speaking whites' national identification has weakened in favor of a greater emphasis on their racial identification.

*"In the 2010 census of the population of the United States, more than 21.7 million Americans did not believe the government's traditional categories of race fit them."*
—Yen (2012)

**social categorization** The classification of persons into groups on the basis of common attributes.

**Ingroups Versus Outgroups** Although categorizing humans is much like categorizing objects, there is a key difference. When it comes to *social* categorization, perceivers themselves are members or nonmembers of the categories they use. Groups that we identify with—our country, religion, political party, even our hometown sports team—are called **ingroups**, whereas groups other than our own are called **outgroups**. We see people in fundamentally different ways if we consider them to be part of our ingroup or as part of an outgroup.

One cognitive consequence is that we exaggerate the differences between our ingroup and other outgroups, and this exaggeration of differences helps to form and reinforce stereotypes. Another consequence is a phenomenon known as the **outgroup homogeneity effect**, whereby perceivers assume that there is a greater similarity among members of outgroups than among members of one's own group. In other words, there may be many and subtle differences among "us," but "they" are all alike (Linville & Jones, 1980). It is easy to think of real-life examples. People from China, Korea, Taiwan, and Japan see themselves as quite distinct from one another, of course, but to many Westerners they are seen simply as Asian. English majors see themselves as dissimilar to history majors, but science majors often lump them together as "humanities types." Californians proclaim their tremendous cultural, ethnic, and economic diversity, whereas outsiders talk of the "typical Californian." To people outside the group, outgroup members even *look* alike: People are less accurate in distinguishing and recognizing the faces of members of racial outgroups than of ingroups (Correll, Lemoine, & Ma, 2011; Marcon et al., 2010; Meissner et al., 2005; Young et al., 2012).

Why do people tend to perceive outgroups as homogeneous? One reason is that people tend to have less personal contact and familiarity with individual members of outgroups. Indeed, the more familiar people are with an outgroup, the less likely they are to perceive it as homogeneous. Second, people often do not encounter a representative sample of outgroup members. A student from one school who encounters students from a rival school only when they cruise into town for a Saturday football game, screaming at the top of their lungs, sees only the most avid rival fans—hardly a diverse lot.

Lack of familiarity and lack of diversity of experiences with outgroup members are two reasons why "*they* all look alike," but there's more to the story than that. Research using brain imaging or cognitive methods has found that as soon as we categorize an unfamiliar person as a member of our ingroup or an outgroup, we immediately process information about them differently at even the most basic levels. For example, student participants in experiments by Kurt Hugenberg and Olivier Corneille (2009) were exposed to unfamiliar faces of people who were the same race as the participants. These faces were categorized as ingroup members (from the same university as the participants) or outgroup members (from a rival university). The students processed faces more holistically (that is, they integrated the features of the faces into a global representation of the overall face) when they had been categorized as being from their ingroup than they did when they had been categorized as members of the outgroup. Jay Van Bavel, William Cunningham, and their colleagues (2008; 2011; 2012) have found related results in a series of recent studies, revealing greater activation in particular areas of perceivers' brains, such as the fusiform face area and the orbitofrontal cortex, upon exposure to unfamiliar faces labeled as ingroup members than outgroup members (see ● Figure 5.8).

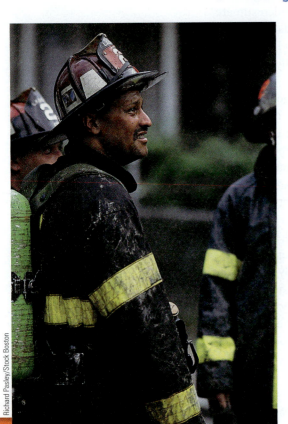

Richard Pasley/Stock Boston

Whether people are likely to immediately categorize this person by his race, gender, or occupation depends on a combination of cognitive, cultural, and motivational factors.

**ingroups** Groups with which an individual feels a sense of membership, belonging, and identity.

**outgroups** Groups with which an individual does not feel a sense of membership, belonging, or identity.

**outgroup homogeneity effect** The tendency to assume that there is greater similarity among members of outgroups than among members of ingroups.

**Dehumanizing Outgroups**    Perceivers may not only process outgroup faces more superficially but also sometimes process them more like objects than like fellow human beings. This was a conclusion suggested by Lasana Harris and Susan Fiske (2006). When participants in their research saw pictures of people from a variety of groups, fMRI showed activation in their medial prefrontal cortex, which is thought to be necessary for social cognition. However, this activation was not evident in response to images of either nonhuman objects or people from psychologically distant outgroups, such as addicts or the homeless.

Many social psychologists have illustrated both the subtle and not-so-subtle ways that people see or treat outgroup members as less than fully human (Demoulin et al., 2009; Harris & Fiske, 2009; Haslam & Loughnan, 2012; Landau et al., 2012). As but one example, Amy Cuddy and others (2007) conducted a study two weeks after Hurricane Katrina devastated the lives of numerous people in the southeastern United States in 2005. The researchers found that participants were less likely to infer that racial outgroup members were experiencing complex emotions considered uniquely human, such as remorse and mourning, than were racial ingroup members. Those who did infer such humanizing emotions, however, were more likely to report that they intended to take actions to help the victims of the hurricane.

Dehumanization has played a role in atrocities throughout history, such as in the Nazi propaganda that characterized the Jews in Germany as disease-spreading rats and blacks as half-apes. The continued presence of some of this kind of imagery in contemporary life is chilling, as in the examples discussed in the introduction of this chapter of black athletes in numerous countries being taunted with monkey chants. The strength and persistence of such dehumanization of African Americans were illustrated in a series of studies by Phillip Goff, Jennifer Eberhardt, and their colleagues that have demonstrated how participants in their studies automatically but nonconsciously associated black men with apes (Goff, Eberhardt, et al., 2008; Rattan & Eberhardt, 2010).

● **FIGURE 5.8**
**Neural Activity and Ingroup Bias**
Participants saw photographs of unfamiliar white and black faces. When the faces were said to be members of their ingroup, participants showed greater neural activity in particular areas of the brain, including the two areas highlighted here, the fusiform gyrus and the orbitofrontal cortex. Greater activation in the orbitofrontal cortex was also associated with stronger self-reported preference for ingroup faces.
Van Bavel et al., 2008; 2011.

*Psychological Science, 19, 1131–1139 Van Bavel et al., 2008*

**Fundamental Motives Between Groups**    The roots of dividing into ingroups and outgroups run quite deep in our evolutionary history, as early humans' survival depended on forming relatively small groups of similar others. A fundamental motive to protect one's ingroup and be suspicious of outgroups is therefore likely to have evolved. Consistent with this idea are the results of experiments that demonstrate that when people's basic motivations of self-protection are activated—such as in response to facing a threatening situation, seeing a scary movie, or even being in a completely dark room—people are more prone to exhibit prejudice toward outgroups or to be especially hesitant to see possible outgroup members as part of one's ingroup (Maner et al., 2003; 2012; Miller et al., 2010; Schaller & Neuberg, 2012).

From time to time our fundamental motivation for self-protection and preservation runs smack into the ultimate obstacle: thoughts about death and mortality. According to *Terror Management Theory*, which was discussed in Chapter 3, people cope with the fear of their own death by constructing worldviews that help preserve their self-esteem and important values. According to this perspective, favoring ingroups over outgroups is one important way that people preserve their cultural worldviews and, by doing so, try to attain a kind of immortality. This theory has been supported by numerous studies that demonstrate that when individuals are made to think about mortality—such as by presenting them with images of cemeteries or making them think about decomposing

Being reminded of one's own mortality makes people put things into greater perspective, thereby tending to reduce ingroup–outgroup distinctions and hostilities. **F**ALSE.

bodies—they become more likely to exhibit various ingroup biases, including negatively stereotyping and exhibiting prejudice toward a variety of outgroups (Greenberg & Arndt, 2012; Greenberg et al., 2009). Male students in an experiment by Russell Webster and Donald Saucier (2011), for example, indicated a variety of significantly more negative attitudes toward gay men if they had just written about what they thought would happen to them when they die than if they had written about the pain of going to the dentist.

**Motives Concerning Intergroup Dominance and Status**    Some people are especially motivated to preserve inequities between groups of people in society. For example, people with a **social dominance orientation** have a desire to see one's ingroups as dominant over other groups and a willingness to adopt cultural values that facilitate the oppression of other groups. Individuals with this orientation tend to endorse sentiments such as "If certain groups stayed in their place, we would have fewer problems" and to disagree with statements such as "Group equality should be our ideal." Research in numerous countries throughout the world has found that ingroup identification and outgroup derogation can be especially strong among people with a social dominance orientation (Kteily et al., 2012; Levin et al., 2012; Sidanius & Pratto, 2012).

Sean Delonas/Splash News

The image in this cartoon from the *New York Post* of February 18, 2009, referred to a chimpanzee that was shot to death by police in Connecticut after it had mauled a woman. However, the reference in the cartoon's text to the stimulus bill, which President Obama had just signed and championed during his first month in office, implied that the cartoon was depicting Obama as the chimpanzee.

Social dominance orientations promote self-interest. But some ideologies support a social structure that may actually oppose one's self-interest, depending on the status of one's groups. John Jost and his colleagues (Jost, 2011; Jost & van der Toorn, 2012) have focused on what they call **system justification theory**, which proposes that people are motivated (at least in part) to defend and justify the existing social, political, and economic conditions. System-justifying beliefs protect the status quo. Groups with power, of course, may promote the status quo to preserve their own advantaged position. But although some disadvantaged groups might be able to improve their circumstances if they were to challenge an economic or political system, members of disadvantaged groups with a system justification orientation think that the system is fair and just, and they may admire and even show outgroup favoritism to outgroups that thrive in this system.

**Stereotype Content Model**    The relative status and relations between groups in a culture influence the content of the culture's stereotypes about these groups. This is a central point in the **stereotype content model** (Cuddy et al., 2008; Fiske, 2012). According to this model, many group stereotypes vary along two dimensions: warmth and competence. Groups may be considered high on both dimensions, low on both, or high on one dimension but low on the other. For example, the elderly may be stereotyped as high on warmth but low on competence.

The stereotype content model proposes that stereotypes about the competence of a group are influenced by the relative *status* of that group in society—higher relative status is associated with higher competence. Stereotypes about the warmth of a group are influenced by perceived *competition* with the group—greater perceived competition is associated with lower warmth. For example, groups that are of low status but that remain compliant and do not try to upset the status quo are likely to be stereotyped as low in competence but high in warmth. A wave of immigrants who enter a country with low status but compete for jobs and resources, on the other hand, may be seen as low in both competence and warmth. For groups that are seen as high on one dimension but low on the other, there may be a perceived tradeoff between competence and warmth. A woman climbing up the corporate ladder by demonstrating strong competence, for

**social dominance orientation**    A desire to see one's ingroup as dominant over other groups and a willingness to adopt cultural values that facilitate oppression over other groups.

**system justification theory**    A theory that proposes that people are motivated (at least in part) to defend and justify the existing social, political, and economic conditions

**stereotype content model**    A model proposing that the relative status and competition between groups influence group stereotypes along the dimensions of competence and warmth.

example, may be seen as much less warm. If she tries to demonstrate warmth, however, she may be seen as less competent.

Researchers have found support for the stereotype content model both with experiments—in which perceived status and intergroup competition are manipulated—and from correlational studies conducted around the world (Cuddy et al., 2009; de Paula Couto & Koller, 2012).

**Robbers Cave: A Field Study in Intergroup Conflict**   Robbers Cave State Park in Oklahoma was the unlikely setting for one of the most classic field experiments in social psychology. In the summer of 1954, a small group of 11-year-old boys—all white middle-class youngsters, all strangers to one another—arrived at a 200-acre camp located in a densely wooded area of the park. The boys spent the first week or so hiking, swimming, boating, and camping out. After a while, they gave themselves a group name and printed it on their caps and T-shirts. At first, the boys thought they were the only ones at the camp. Soon, however, they discovered that there was a second group and that tournaments had been arranged between the two groups.

What these boys didn't know was that they were participants in an elaborate study conducted by Muzafer Sherif and his colleagues (1961). Parents had given permission for their sons to take part in an experiment for a study of competitiveness and cooperation. The two groups were brought in separately, and only after each had formed its own culture was the other's presence revealed. Now, the "Rattlers" and the "Eagles" were ready to meet. They did so under tense circumstances, competing against each other in football, a treasure hunt, tug of war, and other events. For each event, the winning team was awarded points; the tournament winner was promised a trophy, medals, and other prizes. Almost overnight, the groups turned into hostile antagonists, and their rivalry escalated into a full-scale war. Group flags were burned, cabins were ransacked, and a food fight that resembled a riot exploded in the mess hall. Keep in mind that the participants in this study were well-adjusted boys. Yet as Sherif (1966) noted, a naive observer would have thought the boys were "wicked, disturbed, and vicious" (p. 85).

Creating a monster through competition was easy. Restoring the peace, however, was not. First the experimenters tried saying nice things to the Rattlers about the Eagles and vice versa, but the propaganda campaign did not work. Then the two groups were brought together under noncompetitive circumstances, but that didn't help either. What did eventually work was the introduction of **superordinate goals**, mutual goals that could be achieved only through cooperation between the groups. For example, the experimenters arranged for the camp truck to break down, and both groups were needed to pull it up a steep hill. This strategy worked like a charm. By the end of camp, the two groups were so friendly that they insisted on traveling home on the same bus. In just 3 weeks, the Rattlers and Eagles experienced the kinds of changes that often take generations to unfold: They formed close-knit groups, went to war, and made peace.

The events of Robbers Cave mimicked the kinds of conflict that plague people all over the world. The simplest explanation for this conflict is competition. Assign strangers to groups, throw the groups into contention, stir the pot, and soon there's conflict. Similarly, the intergroup benefits of reducing the focus on competition by activating superordinate goals are also evident around the world. Consider, for example, the aftermath of natural disasters that befell Greece and Turkey in 1999, two nations that for many generations had often been in conflict and mistrusted each other. Greek–Turkish relations improved dramatically in the wake of earthquakes that rocked both countries. Television images of Turkish rescue workers pulling a Greek child from under a pile of rubble in Athens generated an outpouring of goodwill. Uniting against a shared threat,

**superordinate goal**   A shared goal that can be achieved only through cooperation among individuals or groups.

as the boys in Robbers Cave did when the camp truck broke down, the two nations began to bridge a deep divide (Kinzer, 1999).

**Realistic Conflict Theory**    The view that direct competition for valuable but limited resources breeds hostility between groups is called **realistic conflict theory** (Levine & Campbell, 1972). As a simple matter of economics, one group may fare better in the struggle for land, jobs, or power than another group. The losing group becomes frustrated and resentful, the winning group feels threatened and protective—and, before long, conflict heats to a rapid boil. It is likely that a good deal of prejudice in the world is driven by the realities of competition (Duckitt & Mphuthing, 1998; Stephan et al., 2005; Zárate et al., 2004). For example, Marcel Coenders and others (2008) found that support for discrimination against ethnic minority groups tended to increase in the Netherlands when the unemployment level had recently risen. David Butz and Kuma Yogeeswaran (2011) found that non–Asian American students indicated more prejudice against Asian Americans if they had just read information about serious economic problems and growing competition for scare resources in the United States. Kimberly Rios Morrison and Oscar Ybarra (2008) demonstrated a similar effect of this kind of threat on prejudice against Asian Americans, and found that this effect was particularly strong among European Americans whose racial identity was important to them.

But there is much more to prejudice than real competition. "Realistic" competition for resources may in fact be imagined—a perception in the mind of an individual who is not engaged in any real conflict. In addition, people may become resentful of other groups not because of their conviction that their own security or resources are threatened by these groups but because of their sense of **relative deprivation**, the belief that they fare poorly compared with others. What matters to the proverbial Smiths is not the size of their house per se but whether it is larger than the Jones's house next door (Pettigrew et al., 2008; Walker & Smith, 2002).

## > Social Identity Theory

People all over the world believe that their own nation, culture, language, and religion are better and more deserving than others. Part of the reason for that is even more basic than real or perceived competition for finite resources. Rather, it stems from something more subtle and psychological. A classic study of high school boys in Bristol, England, conducted by Henri Tajfel and his colleagues (1971) begins to reveal this point. The boys in this study were shown a series of dotted slides, and their task was to estimate the number of dots on each. The slides were presented in rapid-fire succession so the dots could not be counted. Later, the experimenter told the participants that some people are chronic "overestimators" and that others are "underestimators." As part of a second, entirely separate task, participants were divided into two groups—one that was said to consist of overestimators and the other of underestimators. (In fact, they were divided randomly.) Participants were then told to allocate points to other participants that could be cashed in for money.

This procedure was designed to create *minimal groups* in which people are categorized on the basis of trivial, minimally important similarities. Tajfel's overestimators and underestimators were not long-term rivals, did not have a history of antagonism, were not frustrated, did not compete for a limited resource, and were not even acquainted with each other. Still, participants consistently allocated more points to members of their own group than to members of the other group. This pattern of discrimination, called **ingroup favoritism**, has been found in studies performed in many countries and

**realistic conflict theory**    The theory that hostility between groups is caused by direct competition for limited resources.

**relative deprivation**    Feelings of discontent aroused by the belief that one fares poorly compared with others.

**ingroup favoritism**    The tendency to discriminate in favor of ingroups over outgroups.

using a variety of different measures (Capozza & Brown, 2000; Pinter & Greenwald, 2011; Scheepers et al., 2006).

To explain ingroup favoritism, Tajfel (1982) and John Turner (1987) proposed **social identity theory**. According to this theory, which is illustrated in ● Figure 5.9, each of us strives to enhance our self-esteem, which has two components: (1) a *personal* identity and (2) various collective or *social* identities that are based on the groups to which we belong. In other words, people can boost their self-esteem through their own personal achievements or through affiliation with successful groups. What's nice about the need for social identity is that it leads us to derive pride from our connections with others even if we don't receive any direct benefits from these others. What's sad, however, is that we often feel the need to belittle "them" in order to feel secure about "us." Religious fervor, racial and ethnic conceit, and aggressive nationalism may all fulfill this more negative side of our social identity. Even gossiping can play this role; Jennifer Bosson and others (2006; Weaver & Bosson, 2011) found that when people shared negative attitudes about a third party, they felt closer to each other.

Two basic predictions arose from social identity theory: (1) Threats to one's self-esteem heighten the need for ingroup favoritism, and (2) expressions of ingroup favoritism enhance one's self-esteem. Research generally supports these predictions (Ellemers & Haslam, 2012; Postmes & Branscombe, 2010).

American fans bask in the glory of their team's success at a World Cup soccer game.

**social identity theory** The theory that people favor ingroups over outgroups in order to enhance their self-esteem.

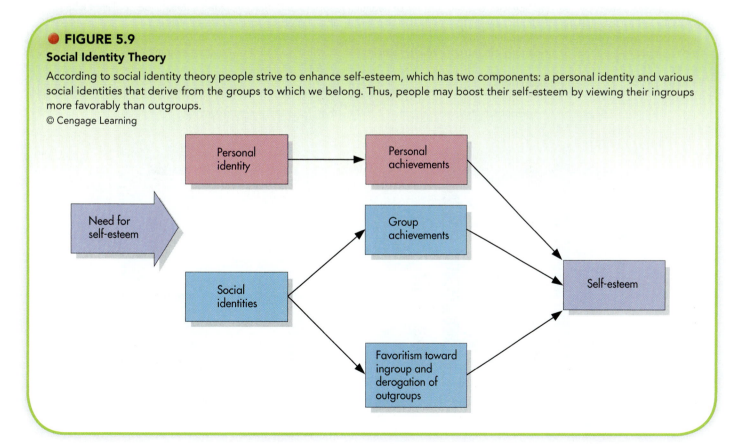

● **FIGURE 5.9**

**Social Identity Theory**

According to social identity theory people strive to enhance self-esteem, which has two components: a personal identity and various social identities that derive from the groups to which we belong. Thus, people may boost their self-esteem by viewing their ingroups more favorably than outgroups.

© Cengage Learning

Personal identity → Personal achievements

Need for self-esteem

Social identities → Group achievements

Favoritism toward ingroup and derogation of outgroups

Self-esteem

Steven Fein and Steven Spencer (1997) proposed that threats to one's self-esteem can lead individuals to use available negative stereotypes to derogate members of stereotyped groups, and that by derogating others they can feel better about themselves. In one study, for example, Fein and Spencer gave participants positive or negative feedback about their performance on a test of social and verbal skills—feedback that temporarily bolstered or threatened their self-esteem. These participants then took part in what was supposedly a second experiment in which they evaluated a job applicant. All participants received a photograph of a young woman, her résumé, and a videotape of a job interview. Half the participants were given information that suggested that the woman (named Julie Goldberg) was Jewish. The other half was given information that suggested that the woman (named Maria D'Agostino) was not Jewish. On the campus where the study was held, there was a popular negative stereotype of the "Jewish American Princess" that often targeted upper-middle-class Jewish women from the New York area.

As predicted, there were two important results (see ● Figure 5.10). First, among participants whose self-esteem had been lowered by negative feedback, they rated the woman more negatively if she seemed to be Jewish than if she did not, even though the videotaped job interview and credentials of the two women were the same. Second, participants who had received negative feedback and were given an opportunity to belittle the Jewish woman later exhibited a post-experiment increase in self-esteem—the more negatively they evaluated the Jewish woman, the better these participants felt about themselves. In sum, the results of this experiment suggests that a blow to one's self-image evokes prejudice and the expression of prejudice helps restore self-image.

● **FIGURE 5.10**

**Self-Esteem and Prejudice**

Participants in a study by Fein and Spencer received positive or negative feedback and then evaluated a female job applicant who was believed to be either Jewish or not Jewish. This study had two key results: (1) Participants whose self-esteem had been lowered by negative feedback evaluated the woman more negatively if they thought she was Jewish than if they thought she was not (left); and (2) negative-feedback participants given the opportunity to belittle the Jewish woman showed a post-experiment increase in self-esteem (right).

Fein and Spencer, 1997. © Cengage Learning

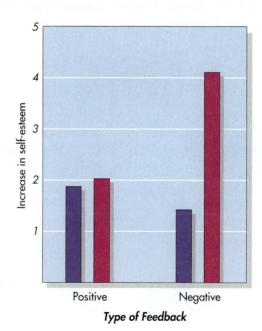

## Culture and Social Identity

Individuals' social identities are clearly important to people across cultures. Collectivists are more likely than individualists to value their connectedness and interdependence with the people and groups around them, and their personal identities are tied closely with their social identities. Collectivists do show some biases favoring their ingroups—indeed, being oriented strongly toward one's ingroup may be considered a highly desired and valued way of being (Capozza et al., 2000; Chen et al., 2002; Ruffle & Sosis, 2006). Some research indicates that collectivists draw sharper distinctions between ingroup and outgroup members than individualists do (Gudykunst & Bond, 1997).

However, a number of researchers have found that people from collectivist cultures are less likely to enhance their ingroups in order to boost their own self-esteem (Heine, 2005; Lehman et al., 2004; Snibbe et al., 2003; Yuki, 2003). For example, Kenichiro Nakashima and others (2008) reported that when participants' self-esteem was threatened, those with individualistic self-concepts showed more ingroup favoritism, whereas those with collectivistic self-concepts did not. In addition, people from the collectivist cultures of East Asia tend to have higher tolerance for what Westerners would consider contradictions (such as that something can be both good and bad at the same time), and this may explain why East Asianers are more likely to see their ingroups as having positive and negative qualities compared to Westerners, who tend to emphasize the positive aspects of their ingroups much more exclusively (Spencer-Rogers et al., 2012).

Mark Graham/AP/Wide World Photos

Being part of a small, close-knit group can be an important, rewarding part of one's personal identity.

## Culture and Socialization

The list of familiar stereotypes is quite long. Athletes are dumb, math majors are geeks, Americans are loud, Italians are emotional, Californians are laid back, white men can't jump, used-car salesmen can't be trusted as far as you can throw them. And on and on it goes. Dividing people into social categories, including ingroups and outgroups, certainly is a key factor in the formation of stereotypes and prejudices. But with so many well-known stereotypes and prejudices, many of which are shared around the world, it is clear that at some level we are somehow taught these stereotypes from our culture. We turn now to examine those processes.

Socialization refers to the processes by which people learn the norms, rules, and information of a culture or group. We learn a tremendous amount of information (often without even realizing it) by absorbing what we see around us in our culture, groups, and families. These lessons include what various stereotypes are, how valued or devalued various groups are, and which prejudices are acceptable to have.

Consider the story of something that happened to one of the authors of this book. When he was about 8 years old, his two best friends one day turned on him and derisively called him a "Jew ball." They had never thought of him as different from them or categorized him as Jewish before, and yet on this day, suddenly Jewishness was relevant—and negative to them. But why *then*, and how did they come up with "Jew ball"?! Only much later did it become clear that they had misheard their father say "Jew boy." Trying to model their father's values, they used an approximation of this expression against their friend, and thereafter they saw him in a different way. The biased lens through which the father saw people was passed down to the next generation.

Although it certainly isn't always the case, the stereotypes and prejudices of a parent can shape the stereotypes and prejudices of a child, often in implicit ways (Castelli et al., 2009). More generally, and more pervasively, the stereotypes and prejudices exhibited by peers, the popular media, and one's culture are part of the air each of us breathes as we develop, and these influences can be profound.

To narrow our discussion of these cultural and socialization processes, we will focus on gender stereotypes and sexism, but it is important to recognize that these processes are relevant to all kinds and targets of stereotypes, prejudice, and discrimination.

### Gender Stereotypes: Blue for Boys, Pink for Girls

We begin with what are often the first words uttered when a baby is born: "It's a boy!" or "It's a girl!" In many hospitals, the newborn boy is immediately given a blue hat and the newborn girl a pink hat. The infant receives a gender-appropriate name and is showered with gender-appropriate gifts. Over the next few years, the typical boy is supplied with toy trucks, baseballs, pretend tools, toy guns, and chemistry sets; the typical girl is furnished with dolls, stuffed animals, pretend make-up kits, kitchen and tea sets, and dress-up clothes. As they enter school, many expect the boy to earn money by mowing lawns and to enjoy violent superhero movies, while they expect the girl to earn money by babysitting and to enjoy sweet stories about friendship or love.

These distinctions persist in college, as more male students major in economics and the sciences and more female students major in the arts, languages, and humanities. In the work force, more men become doctors, construction workers, auto mechanics, airplane pilots, investment bankers, and engineers. In contrast, more women become secretaries, schoolteachers, nurses, flight attendants, bank tellers, and housewives. Back on the home front, the life cycle begins again when a couple has their first baby and discover that "It's a girl!" or "It's a boy!"

The traditional pinks and blues are not as distinct today as they used to be. Many gender barriers of the past have broken down, and the colors have somewhat blended together. Nevertheless, the stereotypes—and, as we discussed earlier, sexism—persists.

What do people say when asked to describe the typical man and woman? Males are said to be more adventurous, assertive, aggressive, independent, and task-oriented; females are thought to be more sensitive, gentle, dependent, emotional, and people-oriented. Young children distinguish men from women well before their first birthday, identify themselves and others as boys

The Blues and the Pinks. Even a very quick look at a toy store illustrates dramatic differences in how boys and girls are socialized. For example, boys are encouraged to play active, loud, and violent games (top), whereas girls are encouraged to engage in quieter, nurturing role play (bottom).

© UrbanZone/Alamy

AP Photo/Nick Ut

or girls by 3 years of age, form gender-stereotypic beliefs and preferences about stories, toys, and other objects soon after that, and then use their simplified stereotypes in judging others and favoring their own gender over the other in intergroup situations (Golombok & Hines, 2002; Knobloch et al., 2005; Leinbach & Fagot, 1993; Ruble & Martin, 1998).

Gerianne Alexander (2003) proposes that children's preferences about sex-based toys, although partly due to gender socialization, also have neurobiological and evolutionary roots. She based this conclusion from data about children exposed prenatally to atypical levels of sex hormones and data about sex differences in toy preferences among nonhuman primates. For example, one intriguing study reported that vervet monkeys showed sex differences in toy preferences similar to those seen in human children (Alexander & Hines, 2002).

Although biological and evolutionary factors may play a role in some of these preferences, it is clear that children have ample opportunity to learn gender stereotypes and roles from their parents and other role models (Montañés et al., 2012; Tenenbaum & Leaper, 2002). Beliefs about males and females are so deeply ingrained that they influence the behavior of adults literally the moment a baby is born. In one fascinating study, the first-time parents of 15 girls and 15 boys were interviewed within 24 hours of the babies' births. There were no differences between the male and female newborns in height, weight, or other aspects of physical appearance. Yet the parents of girls rated their babies as softer, smaller, and more finely featured. The fathers of boys saw their sons as stronger, larger, more alert, and better coordinated (Rubin et al., 1974). Could it be there really were differences that only the parents were able to discern? Doubtful. In another study, Emily Mondschein and others (2000) found that mothers of 11-month-olds underestimated their infants' crawling ability if they were girls but overestimated it if they were boys.

As they develop, boys and girls receive many divergent messages in many different settings. Barbara Morrongiello and Tess Dawber (2000) conducted a study that reflects this point. They showed mothers videotapes of children engaging in somewhat risky activities on a playground and asked them to stop the tape and indicate whatever they would ordinarily say to their own child in the situation shown. Mothers of daughters intervened more frequently and more quickly than did mothers of sons. As shown in Table 5.4, mothers of daughters were more likely to caution the child about getting hurt, whereas mothers of sons were more likely to encourage the child's risky playing. Another study by Morrongiello and others (2000) revealed that although boys typically experience more injuries from risky playing than girls, children by the age of 6 tend to think that girls are at greater risk of injury than boys.

### TABLE 5.4
### What Mothers Would Say

Mothers of young boys or girls watched a videotape of another child engaging in somewhat risky behavior on a playground. The mothers were instructed to stop the videotape whenever they would say something to the child if the child were theirs and to indicate what they would say. Mothers of daughters stopped the tape much more often than mothers of sons to express caution ("Be careful!"), worry about injury ("You could fall!"), and directives to stop ("Stop that this instant!"). In contrast, mothers of sons were more likely to indicate encouragement ("Good job! Let me see you go higher!").

| Context of Statement | Frequency of Statement by | |
| --- | --- | --- |
| | Mothers of Girls | Mothers of Boys |
| Caution | 3.9 | 0.7 |
| Worry about injury | 9.2 | 0.2 |
| Directive to stop | 9.3 | 0.6 |
| Encouragement | 0.5 | 3.0 |

Adapted from Morrongiello & Dawber, 2000. © Cengage Learning

**Social Role Theory**   As children develop, they begin to look at the larger culture around them and see who occupies what roles in society as well as how these roles are valued. According to Alice Eagly's (1987; Eagly & Wood, 2012) **social role theory**, although the perception of sex differences may be based on some real differences, it is magnified by the unequal social roles men and women occupy.

**social role theory**   The theory that small gender differences are magnified in perception by the contrasting social roles occupied by men and women.

The process involves three steps. First, through a combination of biological and social factors, a division of labor between the sexes has emerged over time, both at home and in the work setting. Men are more likely to work in construction or business; women are more likely to care for children and to take lower-status jobs. Second, since people behave in ways that fit the roles they play, men are more likely than women to wield physical, social, and economic power. Third, these behavioral differences provide a continuing basis for social perception, leading us to perceive men as dominant and women as domestic "by nature," when in fact the differences may reflect the roles they play. In short, sex stereotypes are shaped by—and often confused with—the unequal distribution of men and women into different social roles. According to this theory, perceived differences between men and women are based on real behavioral differences that are mistakenly assumed to arise from gender rather than from social roles.

Social role theory and socialization processes more generally can, of course, be extended beyond gender stereotypes and sexism. Seeing that some groups of people occupy particular roles in society more than other people do can fuel numerous stereotypes and prejudices. One extremely important factor in determining what kinds of people we see in what kinds of roles is the popular media. We examine some of the effects associated with media exposure next.

Although images of attractive people sell magazines and many consumers enjoy looking at them, they do raise the question of whether exposure to so many of these kinds of images also produce negative consequences. For example, does repeated exposure to such images perpetuate stereotypes or cause some people to engage in dangerous behaviors to try to achieve what are often impossible and unhealthy standards of masculinity and femininity?

**Media Effects**    More than ever, children, adolescents, and adults seem to be immersed in popular culture transmitted via the mass media. Watching TV shows on our phones or iPads while on the stationary bike at the gym, checking out the latest viral video sweeping the Internet while taking a break at work or the coffee shop, seeing advertisements popping up on our computer screens like weeds, glancing at the tabloid cover shots of the latest starlet hounded by relentless paparazzi—there often seems no escape. Through the ever-present media, we are fed a steady diet of images of people. These images have the potential to perpetuate stereotypes and discrimination.

Fortunately, the days when the media portrayed women and people of color in almost exclusively stereotypical, powerless roles are gone. Still, research in numerous countries around the world examining such varied content as music videos, commercials and print ads, TV programs, and children's books reveals that some stereotyping persists (Furnham & Paltzer, 2010; McCabe et al., 2011; Michelle, 2012; Wallis, 2011).

More to the point is the fact that media depictions can influence viewers, often without the viewers realizing it (Ward & Friedman, 2006). Studies have shown, for example, that female college students who had just watched a set of commercials in which the female characters were portrayed in stereotypical fashion tended to express lower self-confidence, less independence, and fewer career aspirations, and even performed more poorly on a math test, than did those who viewed stereotype-irrelevant or counter-stereotypical ads (Davies et al., 2002; Geis et al., 1984; Jennings et al., 1980).

Media images of impossibly thin or proportioned female models are implicated in the near-epidemic incidence of eating disorders and debilitating anxiety over physical appearance, particularly among young European American women (Henderson-King et al., 2001; Moradi et al., 2005; Ward & Friedman, 2006). The media's impact may be especially negative among individuals who already have concerns about their appearance or are particularly concerned with other people's opinions (Henderson-King & Henderson-King, 1997; Ricciardelli et al., 2000). Men's body images may also be affected by the media (Barlett et al., 2008). Indeed, graphic images of muscular and lean male models have become increasingly prevalent of late. More and more cases come to light every year of boys and young men copying star athletes by taking steroids and other drugs that can make them look more like their role models but that can seriously threaten their health (Hanc, 2006; Hobza & Rochlen, 2009; Martin & Govender, 2011; McCreary, 2011).

## How Stereotypes Distort Perceptions and Resist Change

Social categorization helps give rise to stereotypes, which offer us quick and convenient summaries of social groups. Dividing into ingroups and outgroups gives rise to seeing and treating each other in biased ways. Being socialized in a particular culture teaches us many of the stereotypes and prejudices that we carry with us in our lives. But once these stereotypes and prejudices are in place due to these types of factors, why are they often so resistant to change? Although some stereotypes may be accurate (Jussim, 2012; Madon et al., 1998), some certainly are false, and many are at least oversimplifications. Why, then, do inaccurate stereotypes defy evidence that should discredit them? In this section we turn to some of the mechanisms that help perpetuate stereotypes.

**Confirmation Biases and Self-Fulfilling Prophecies**  Imagine learning that a mother yelled at a 16-year-old girl, that a lawyer behaved aggressively, and that a Boy Scout grabbed the arm of an elderly woman crossing the street. Now imagine that a construction worker yelled at a 16-year-old girl, that a homeless man behaved aggressively, and that an ex-con grabbed the arm of an elderly woman crossing the street. Do very different images of these actions come to mind? This is a fundamental effect of stereotyping: Stereotypes of groups influence people's perceptions and interpretations of the behaviors of group members. This is especially likely when a target of a stereotype behaves in an ambiguous way; perceivers reduce the ambiguity by interpreting the behavior as consistent with the stereotype (Dunning & Sherman, 1997; Kunda et al., 1997). For example, black and white sixth-grade boys in one study saw pictures and descriptions of ambiguously aggressive behaviors (such as one child bumping into another). Both the black and the white boys judged the behaviors as more mean and threatening if the behaviors were performed by black boys than if they were done by white boys (Sagar & Schofield, 1980).

The effect of stereotypes on individuals' perceptions is a type of confirmation bias, which, as we saw in Chapter 4, involves people's tendencies to interpret, seek, and create information that seems to confirm their expectations. Jeff Stone and his colleagues (1997) demonstrated how people interpret information to confirm their stereotype-based expectancies in a study in which they had students listen to a radio broadcast of a college basketball game. Some were led to believe that a particular player was white; others were led to believe he was black. After listening to the game, all of the students were asked to evaluate how the player had performed in the game. Consistent with racial stereotypes, those students who believed the player was black rated him as having played better and more athletically, whereas those who thought he was white rated him as having played with more intelligence and hustle (see ● Figure 5.11).

Stereotypes typically are held not just by individuals but by many people within a culture, and they are often perpetuated through repeated communications. In a classic demonstration, Gordon Allport and Leo Postman (1947) showed participants a picture of a subway train filled with passengers. In the picture were a black man dressed in a suit and a white man holding a razor. One participant viewed the scene briefly and then described it to a second participant who had not seen it. The second participant communicated the description to a third participant and so on, through six rounds of communication. The result: In more

● **FIGURE 5.11**

**"White Men Can't Jump"?**

Students listened to a radio broadcast of a college basketball game and evaluated one particular player. Half of the students were led to believe the player was black; the other half, that he was white. Consistent with their stereotypes, the students perceived the player as having more physical ability if they thought he was black and as having more "court smarts" if they thought he was white.

Stone et al., 1997. © Cengage Learning

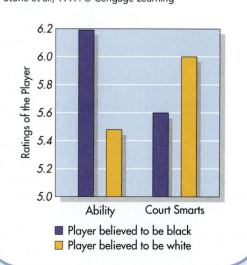

than half the sessions, the final participant's report indicated that the black man, not the white man, held the razor.

In a more recent demonstration of a similar point, Anthony Lyons and Yoshihisa Kashima (2001) had Australian students read a story about an Australian Rules Football player. The students were put in groups of four. One person read the story, and after a delay of a few minutes transmitted the story to the next student, and so on down the four-person chain. The students were supposed to relay the story as accurately as possible. Some of the information in the story was consistent with stereotypes about Australian Rules Football players (e.g., "On the way, Gary and his mate drank several beers in the car"), and some of it was inconsistent with the stereotype (e.g., "He switched on some classical music"). Although the first student in the chain was likely to communicate both stereotype-consistent and stereotype-inconsistent information, as the story went from person to person the stereotype-inconsistent information was progressively screened out. By the time the fourth person told the story, the football player seemed much more clearly stereotypical than he had seemed in the original story.

Confirmation biases are bad enough. But even more disturbing are situations in which stereotyped group members are led to actually behave in stereotype-confirming ways. In other words, stereotypes can create self-fulfilling prophecies (Madon et al., 2011; Rosenthal, 2002). As noted in Chapter 4, a self-fulfilling prophecy occurs when a perceiver's false expectations about a person cause the person to behave in ways that confirm those expectations. Stereotypes can trigger such behavioral confirmation. Consider a classic experiment by Carl Word and others (1974) involving a situation of great importance in people's lives: the job interview. White participants, without realizing it, sat farther away, made more speech errors, and held shorter interviews when interviewing black applicants than they did when interviewing white applicants. This colder interpersonal style, in turn, caused the black applicants to behave in a nervous and awkward manner. In short, the whites' racial stereotypes and prejudice actually hurt the interview performance of the black candidates. Since the black candidates' interview performance tended to be objectively worse than that of the white candidates, it seemed to confirm the interviewers' negative stereotypes—but this poor performance was caused by the interviewers, not the interviewees.

*"Not everyone's life is what they make it. Some people's life is what other people make it."*
—A character in Alice Walker's short story "You Can't Keep a Good Woman Down"

**Illusory Correlations**  One way that stereotypes endure is through the **illusory correlation**, a tendency for people to overestimate the link between variables that are only slightly or not at all correlated (Meiser & Hewstone, 2006; Risen et al., 2007; Sherman et al., 2009; Stroessner & Plaks, 2001). Illusory correlations result from two different processes. First, people tend to overestimate the association between variables that are *distinctive*: variables that capture attention simply because they are novel or deviant. When two relatively unusual events happen together, that combination may stick in people's minds, and this can lead people to overestimate an association between the two events. For example, if people see a story on the news about a person who was recently released from a mental institution (a rarely encountered category of person) committing a brutal murder (an uncommon behavior), they may remember the link between mental patient and murder better than if a more commonly encountered type of person committed the murder or than if a former mental patient did something more common. The implications for stereotyping are important. First, unless otherwise motivated, people overestimate the association between distinctive variables such as minority groups and deviant acts. Even children in second grade may perceive these false associations (Johnston & Jacobs, 2003).

**illusory correlation**  An overestimate of the association between variables that are only slightly or not at all correlated.

Second, people tend to overestimate the association between variables they already expect to go together (Hamilton & Rose, 1980; Susskind, 2003). The implications for stereotyping are important here as well: People overestimate the joint occurrence of variables they expect to be associated with each other, such as stereotyped groups and stereotypic behaviors. For example, if perceivers witness 10 men from a group of 100 men get into car accidents, and they also witness 10 women from a group of 100 women get into car accidents, perceivers who believe that women are worse drivers than men are likely to remember more of the women and fewer of the men getting into accidents.

**Attributions and Subtyping**    People also maintain their stereotypes through how they explain the behaviors of others. Chapter 4 discusses how perceivers make attributions, or explanations, about the causes of other people's behaviors and how these attributions can sometimes be flawed. One key finding discussed in that chapter is that people often don't take into account the context that someone was in when they try to explain his or her behavior. This can help perpetuate negative stereotypes by, for example, people failing to recognize how a poor performance by a member of a stereotyped group may be due to the effects of these stereotypes rather than a lack of actual ability.

On the other hand, when people see others acting in ways that seem to contradict a stereotype, they may be *more* likely to think about situational factors in order to explain the surprising behavior. Rather than accept a stereotype-disconfirming behavior at face value, such as a woman defeating a man in an athletic contest, perceivers imagine the situational factors that might explain away this apparent exception to the rule, such as random luck, ulterior motives, or other special circumstances. In this way, perceivers can more easily maintain their stereotypes of these groups (Karpinski & von Hippel, 1996; Sekaquaptewa et al., 2003; Sherman et al., 2005).

If we encounter someone's behavior that clearly contradicts our stereotypes and we can't easily explain it away as due to some situational factor, we may unwittingly pull out another trick to preserve our stereotypes: We consider the action or the person a mere exception to the rule. Confronted with a woman who does not seem particularly modest and nurturing, for example, people can either develop a more diversified image of females or toss the mismatch into a special *subtype*—say, "career women." To the extent that people create this subtype, their existing image of women in general will remain relatively intact (Carnaghi & Yzerbyt, 2007; Hewstone & Lord, 1998; Wilder et al., 1996).

© Ben Curtis/AP/Corbis

The United States women's soccer team celebrates winning the Gold Medal at the 2012 Olympics in London. People who believe that women are not tough and athletic may maintain this stereotype even in the face of examples like these young women who defy it. One way they do this is by subtyping such individuals as exceptions who don't truly represent the general category of women.

## Automatic Stereotype Activation

Part of the power of stereotypes is they can bias our perceptions and responses even if we don't personally agree with them. In other words, we don't have to believe a stereotype for it to trigger illusory correlations and self-fulfilling prophecies or to bias how we think, feel, and behave toward group members. Sometimes just being aware of stereotypes in one's culture is enough to cause these effects. Moreover, stereotypes can be activated without our awareness.

In a very influential line of research, Patricia Devine (1989) distinguished between automatic and controlled processes in stereotyping. She argued that people have become highly aware of the content of many stereotypes through socialization from their culture. Because of this high awareness people may automatically activate stereotypes whenever they are exposed to members of groups for which popular stereotypes exist. Thus, just as many of us are automatically primed to think *eggs* after hearing *bacon and*, we are also primed to think of concepts relevant to a stereotype when we think of a stereotyped group.

> People's very quick judgments are not influenced by a stereotype unless they actually believe the stereotype to be true. **FALSE.**

To demonstrate this point Devine exposed white participants in one study to subliminal presentations on a computer monitor. For one group, these presentations consisted of words relevant to stereotypes about black people, such as *Africa*, *ghetto*, *welfare*, and *basketball*. Subliminally presented information is presented so quickly that perceivers do not even realize that they have been exposed to it. Thus, these students were not consciously aware that they had seen these words. Those who were subliminally primed with many of these words activated the African American stereotype and saw another person's behavior in a more negative, hostile light. Especially noteworthy is the fact that these effects occurred *even among participants who did not consciously believe in the stereotypes in question.*

Devine's theory sparked an explosion of interest in these issues. The conclusions from the ensuing research is that it is clear that stereotype activation can be triggered implicitly and automatically, influencing subsequent thoughts, feelings, and behaviors even among perceivers who are relatively low in prejudice. But it also is clear that several factors can make such activation more or less likely to happen.

For example, some stereotypes are much more prevalent than others in a particular culture, and with more exposure to a stereotype comes a greater likelihood of automatic activation. Another factor is how prejudiced the perceiver is. Although stereotypes can be activated automatically even among perceivers very low in prejudice, the threshold for what triggers stereotype activation may be lower for those relatively high in prejudice (Kawakami et al., 1998; Lepore & Brown, 1997; 2002; Wittenbrink et al., 1997). Motivation can also play an important role. For example, when their self-esteem is threatened, people may become motivated to stereotype others so that they will feel better about themselves, and this can make them more likely to activate stereotypes automatically (Spencer et al., 1998). What about being motivated to control oneself from activating or applying stereotypes? Is this effective? People who are motivated for intrinsic reasons (that is, they really don't want to *be* prejudiced, rather than just not wanting to *be seen by others* as prejudiced) tend to be somewhat more successful at this kind of self-regulation. We will return to this issue in more detail in the final section of the chapter, on Reducing Stereotypes, Prejudice, and Discrimination.

## ❯ "41 Shots": A Focus on the Tragic Shooting of Amadou Diallo

The issue of automatic activation of stereotypes and its effects can be seen in concrete terms by focusing on one particular tragedy that sparked not only controversy but also a wave of social psychological research. In New York City on February 4, 1999, just after midnight, a West African immigrant named Amadou Diallo was killed in a hail of 41 bullets in the vestibule of his apartment building. He had been spotted by four white police officers who thought he was acting suspiciously and that he matched the general description of a suspected rapist they were searching for. As they approached him, Diallo reached into his pocket and began pulling out his wallet. One of the officers yelled, "Gun!" The police fired at Diallo 41 times, hitting him with 19 of the bullets. Diallo lay dead in the vestibule. Diallo did not have a weapon.

**subliminal presentation** A method of presenting stimuli so faintly or rapidly that people do not have any conscious awareness of having been exposed to them.

Chris Hondros/Getty Images

Protesters against police violence walk down Broadway in New York City on April 5, 2000. At the center is a photo of Amadou Diallo, an unarmed African immigrant who was killed in a burst of 41 gunshots by New York City police.

Protesters held rallies in the days that followed, chanting "forty-one shots" and holding up wallets. Others defended the police officers, noting how difficult it is to make life-or-death decisions in the blink of an eye. In March 2000 all four officers were found not guilty of any criminal charges. A central question, of course, was whether stereotypes associated with the color of Diallo's skin made the officers more likely to misperceive the wallet as a gun. Although none of us can ever know whether this was the case in the Diallo tragedy, it is possible to apply social psychology research to answer related questions, such as whether, in general, a black man is more likely than a white man to be misperceived as holding a gun when they are actually holding a wallet, and whether making such a mistake signals that a perceiver is prejudiced.

Keith Payne (2001) was the first to publish a study directly inspired by these questions. The participants in his study were undergraduate students, not police officers, but their task was to try to make the kind of decision the police had to make: very quickly identify an object as a weapon or not. Pictures of these objects (such as guns or tools) were presented on a computer screen, immediately preceded by a quick presentation of a black or a white male face. The pictures were presented for fractions of a second. Payne found that the participants were more likely to mistake a harmless object for a weapon if it was preceded by a black face than if the object was preceded by a white face. In other words, a quick glimpse of a black male face primed the participants to see a threatening object more than seeing a white male face.

Joshua Correll and others (2002) designed a video game for their experiment in which they had participants decide whether or not to "shoot" a target person who appeared on their computer screen (see ● Figure 5.12). Some of these targets were white men and others were black men. Some of them held guns and others held harmless objects (such as a black cell phone or a wallet). If the target held a gun, the participants were supposed to hit a "shoot" key as quickly as possible. If he held a harmless object, they were to hit a "don't shoot" key as quickly as they could.

As in the Payne study, these participants showed a bias consistent with racial stereotypes. If the target held a gun, they were quicker to press the "shoot" key if he was black than if he was white. If the target held a harmless object, they took longer to press the "don't shoot" key if he was black than if he was white. In addition, participants were more likely to mistakenly "shoot" an unarmed target if he was black than if he was white.

● **FIGURE 5.12**

**Shoot or Not?**

These are examples of scenes from the video game that Joshua Correll and his colleagues created to investigate whether perceivers, playing the role of police officers, would be biased by the target's race when trying to determine very quickly whether they should shoot him because he is holding a weapon or refrain from shooting because he is holding a harmless object.

Correll et al., 2002. © Cengage Learning

*"Police receive training to make them more sensitive to weapons, but they don't get training to undo unconscious race stereotypes or biases."*

—Anthony Greenwald

Since these first publications, a rapidly growing number of others followed to examine the processes involved more closely (e.g., Bradley & Kennison, 2012; Correll, Wittenbrink, et al., 2011). For example, Debbie Ma and Joshua Correll (2011) found that this racial bias in decisions to shoot were significantly stronger if the targets looked more stereotypic of their respective races (as rated by samples of participants) than if they did not. In a study targeting a different stereotype, Christian Unkelbach and others (2008) found that Australian participants were more likely to shoot at targets wearing Muslim headgear than bareheaded targets who did not appear Muslim.

Taken together the results of these studies suggest that when the decision must be made very quickly, members of some groups are more likely to be mistakenly perceived as holding a gun than members of other groups. It is important to note, though, that the participants in the initial studies were not police officers; they were undergraduate students or individuals from a community sample. Police officers receive extensive training in these kinds of tasks. But as the quote in the margin by social psychologist Anthony Greenwald indicates, the police may not be trained to avoid activating racial stereotypes, and given the prevalence and power of these stereotypes in our society, there is good reason to suspect that they would be influenced by them in split-second decisions.

Fortunately, several researchers have conducted these experiments with police officers as participants (Correll et al., 2007b; Ma & Correll, 2011; Peruche & Plant, 2006). In some of this research, the police have shown a similar bias to mistakenly "shoot" a black than white target, and in some they have shown less of this racial bias than civilians. Even in the studies in which the police officers' decisions were not as racially biased as the civilians' decisions were, however, some racial biases often were relevant. In the study by Ma and Correll (2011), for example, police officers' shooting decisions were less affected by whether the target was black or white than were the decisions of civilians. However, the officers were as strongly affected as the civilians were by whether the targets were racially stereotypic or not.

Some encouraging news comes from studies by Ashby Plant and her colleagues. In one experiment with 50 police officers, Michelle Peruche and Ashby Plant (2006) found that in initial trials the officers were more likely to erroneously decide to "shoot" an unarmed target when the target was black than if the target was white. With more and more trials, however, this racial bias was eventually reduced. This greater accuracy with practice is consistent with the encouraging results of another series of studies using undergraduate students playing the role of police officers (Plant et al., 2005). The students showed the typical racial bias in the decision to shoot or not, but the researchers also found that training the participants by exposing them to repeated trials in which the race of the target was unrelated to criminality eliminated this bias both immediately after the training and 24 hours later.

In addition to the question about whether racial bias may exist in perceptions of a weapon or the decision to shoot, a second question we posed above was whether exhibiting racial bias in the decision to shoot means that a perceiver has racist attitudes and beliefs. The evidence thus far suggests that this may not be the case. For example, Correll and others (2002) found that the magnitude of the racial bias in the decision to shoot was not related to participants' levels of racial prejudice as measured by a series of questionnaires. In addition, these researchers also found that African American participants showed the same bias against black targets as white participants did, again suggesting that racial prejudice is not necessarily reflected in this bias. Consistent with much of the research we've reported in this chapter, *awareness* of the stereotype was a necessary factor, but endorsing it was not. Indeed, Correll and others (2007a) found that by manipulating the accessibility of stereotypes that associate blacks with danger in perceivers' minds (such as by having them first read newspaper articles about black or white criminals), they could strengthen or weaken this bias.

"You look like this sketch of someone who is thinking about committing a crime."

## The Hoodie and the Gun: Revisiting the Trayvon Martin Killing

Now that we are at the end of the section of the chapter on the causes underlying stereotyping, prejudice, and discrimination, it is an appropriate time to consider for a moment how these factors could help explain the story discussed in the beginning of the chapter concerning the killing of Trayvon Martin. Although there are several very important differences between these cases, the results of the shooter bias research inspired by the Diallo tragedy adds some support to the idea that negative stereotypes about African American young men may have played a role (although, as with the Diallo killing, we can never be sure about any one case). More generally, it is quite likely that many of the factors that we have discussed in this chapter played roles here—factors such as social categorization, distrust of outgroup members, prevalence of particular stereotypes in the culture and through the media, confirmation biases, illusory correlations, and automatic stereotype activation. Each of these could have triggered not only Zimmerman's initial suspicions of Martin that eventually led to the confrontation but also to many of the negative reactions people posted online or discussed in the media about Martin, such as how his wearing a hoodie was a signal of his being thuggish or dangerous. Just as the Diallo case did, the Martin case is quite likely to spur social psychologists to design new research to examine more directly the questions raised by this tragedy.

# Reducing Stereotypes, Prejudice, and Discrimination

We have discussed the persistence of stereotypes, prejudice, and discrimination today, as well as numerous factors at the root of these problems. In this final section, we focus on some of the approaches that have been suggested for combating stereotypes, prejudice, and discrimination.

## Intergroup Contact

One of the many enduring ideas in Gordon Allport's (1954) classic book, *The Nature of Prejudice*, was the **contact hypothesis**, which states that under certain conditions, direct contact between members of rival groups will reduce intergroup prejudice.

Around the time of the publication of this book, the U.S. Supreme Court ruled in the historic 1954 case of *Brown v. Board of Education of Topeka* that racially separate schools were inherently unequal and violated the U.S. Constitution. In part, the decision was informed by empirical evidence supplied by 32 eminent social scientists on the harmful effects of segregation on both race relations and the self-esteem and academic achievement of black students (Allport et al., 1953). The Supreme Court's decision propelled the nation into a large-scale social experiment. What would be the effect?

Despite the Court's ruling, desegregation proceeded slowly. There were stalling tactics, lawsuits, and vocal and even violent opposition. Many schools remained untouched until the early 1970s. Then, as the dust began to settle, research brought the grave realization that contact between black and white schoolchildren was not having the intended effect on intergroup attitudes. Walter Stephan (1986) reviewed studies conducted during and after desegregation and found that although 13% of the studies reported a decrease in prejudice among whites, 34% reported no change, and 53% reported an *increase*. These findings forced social psychologists to challenge the wisdom of their testimony to the Supreme Court and to reexamine the contact hypothesis that had guided that advice in the first place.

Is the original contact hypothesis wrong? No. Although desegregation did not immediately produce the desired changes, it's important to realize that the ideal conditions for successful intergroup contact did not exist in the public schools that desegregated. Nobody ever said that deeply rooted prejudices could be erased just by throwing groups together. According to the contact hypothesis, four conditions are ideal for contact to succeed. These conditions are summarized in Table 5.5.

Thomas Pettigrew and Linda Tropp have extensively reviewed the research relevant to the contact hypothesis, and their conclusions have been very encouraging (Pettigrew et al., 2011; Tropp, 2013; Tropp & Page-Gould, 2013). In a series of meta-analyses involving more than 500 studies and a quarter of a million participants in 38 nations Pettigrew and Tropp (2000, 2006, 2008) found reliable support for the benefits of intergroup contact in reducing prejudice, particularly when the contact satisfies at least some of the

> *"'See that man over there?'*
> *'Yes.'*
> *'Well, I hate him.'*
> *'But you don't know him.'*
> *'That's why I hate him.'"*
>
> —Gordon Allport

**TABLE 5.5**

**The Contact Hypothesis: Conditions**

Four conditions are deemed ideal for intergroup contact to serve as a treatment for racism.

1. *Equal status.* The contact should occur in circumstances that give the two groups equal status.

2. *Personal interaction.* The contact should involve one-on-one interactions among individual members of the two groups.

3. *Cooperative activities.* Members of the two groups should join together in an effort to achieve superordinate goals.

4. *Social norms.* The social norms, defined in part by relevant authorities, should favor intergroup contact.

© Cengage Learning

**contact hypothesis** The theory that direct contact between hostile groups will reduce intergroup prejudice under certain conditions.

AP/Wide World Photos

AP/Wide World Photos

conditions in Table 5.5. These researchers propose that contact reduces prejudice by (1) enhancing knowledge about the outgroup; (2) reducing anxiety about intergroup contact; and (3) increasing empathy and perspective taking.

One of the most successful demonstrations of desegregation took place on the baseball diamond. On April 15, 1947, Jackie Robinson played for baseball's Brooklyn Dodgers and became the first black man to break the color barrier in a major American sport. Robinson's opportunity came through Dodgers owner Branch Rickey, who felt that integrating baseball was both moral and good for the game (Pratkanis & Turner, 1994). Rickey knew all about the contact hypothesis and was assured by a social scientist friend that a team could furnish the conditions needed for it to work: equal status among teammates, personal interactions, dedication to a common goal, and a positive climate from the owner, managers, and coaches. The rest is history. Rickey signed Robinson and tried to create the situation necessary for success. Although Robinson did face a great deal of racism, he endured, and baseball was integrated. At the end of his first year, Jackie Robinson was named rookie of the year, and in 1962 he was elected to the Baseball Hall of Fame. At his induction ceremony, Robinson asked three people to stand beside him: his mother, his wife, and his friend Branch Rickey.

Another potential cause for optimism, although perhaps tinged with some regret, is the finding by Nicole Shelton and Jennifer Richeson (2005) that both whites and blacks would like to have more contact with each other but believe that the other group does not want to have contact with them! This may be a case in which education about the problem can be an important tool in correcting it.

## Intergroup Friendships and Extended Contact

Developing friendships across groups is one of the best ways to experience many of the optimal conditions for contact that are listed in Table 5.5. Friendships typically involve equal status, meaningful one-on-one interactions that extend across time and settings, and cooperation toward shared goals. It therefore makes sense that one of the most encouraging lines of research on improving intergroup relations has focused on cross-group friendships. A recent meta-analysis by Kristin Davies and others (2011) on 135 studies supports the idea that cross-group friendships are associated with more positive attitudes and behaviors toward outgroup members.

*"A friendship is bonding capital, but when that friendship is multiracial, it is also bridging capital."*

—Emerson et al., 2002, p. 70.

The link between friendship and better intergroup relations has been examined in multiple ways. Numerous surveys have found that cross-group friendship is associated with less intergroup anxiety and prejudice (Davies et al., 2011; Page-Gould & Mendoza-Denton, 2011). To establish that cross-group friendship can *cause* improvement in intergroup attitudes and behaviors, however, it is important to have experimental evidence. Fortunately, a growing number of experiments have done just that, including a particularly impressive series of experiments by Elizabeth Page-Gould, Rodolfo Mendoza-Denton, and their colleagues (Mendoza-Denton & Page-Gould, 2008; Page-Gould et al., 2008; 2010).

For example, in one of these studies Page-Gould and others (2008) had pairs of Latinos/as and whites interact across three friendship-building meetings. The researchers created friendships by guiding the participants to ask questions of each other that cause them to increasingly disclose things about themselves (e.g., "How close and warm is your family? Do you feel your childhood was happier than most other people's?").

Levels of the hormone cortisol were measured in participants during the course of the study as a way to assess how threatened and stressed the participants felt during the interactions. The researchers found that in the initial meeting between the cross-group pairs, participants who were relatively high in implicit prejudice toward the other group showed increased levels of cortisol—indicating more experience of anxiety and threat—compared to participants lower in prejudice. By the second friendship meeting, however, the cortisol levels of the high-prejudice participants dropped to the level of the participants low in implicit prejudice (see ● Figure 5.13). Even more impressively, these initially high-prejudice participants also began to initiate more social interactions with outgroup members outside the laboratory after the final friendship meeting had taken place.

In a more recent correlational study Page-Gould (2012) tracked the social interactions of 60 participants in Toronto, Canada, for 10 days. She found that if individuals who had no or very few close cross-group friends experienced an intergroup conflict on a particular day, they became less likely to initiate intergroup interactions the next day. This reduction in initiating intergroup contact after an intergroup conflict did not

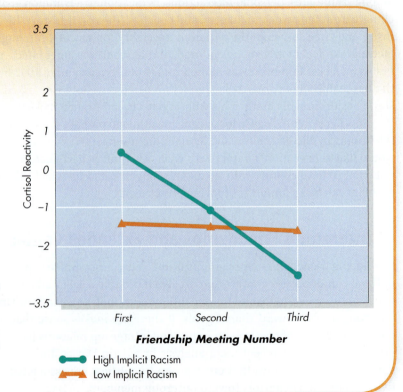

● **FIGURE 5.13**

**With A Little Help From My Cross-Group Friends**

Pairs of Latinos/as and whites interacted across three meetings designed to build friendships between them. During the first meeting participants relatively high in implicit racism showed greater cortisol reactivity—a measure of hormonal stress response—than did participants low in implicit racism, indicating that the former participants were made more anxious by interacting with a member of the other group. By the second friendship meeting, however, the stress of the high-racist participants was no longer higher than that of the low-racist participants, and it remained no higher through the third meeting. (In fact, during the third meeting the high-prejudice participants showed somewhat lower reactivity than the low-prejudice participants, but this was not a significant difference.) From Page-Gould, E., Mendoza-Denton, R., & Tropp, L. R., "With a little help from my cross-group friend: Reducing anxiety in intergroup contexts through cross-group friendship," *Journal of Personality and Social Psychology* vol 95 (pp. 1080–1094). Copyright © 2008 American Psychological Association. Reprinted with permission.

occur, however, among individuals who did have close cross-group friends. Having these cross-group friends seemed to buffer the individuals against any lingering effects of an intergroup conflict experience.

Of course there's often even greater contact—psychologically as well as physically—between romantic partners than friends, and some research has examined whether cross-group dating is associated with more positive intergroup attitudes. For example, a longitudinal study of dating in college by Shana Levin and others (2007) revealed that white, Asian American, and Latino students who dated outside their group more during college showed less ingroup bias and intergroup anxiety at the end of college than students who did not date outside their own racial group.

Jason LaVeris/WireImage/Getty Images

Even people who do not have a friend from an outgroup can benefit from having ingroup friends who do. A number of studies have found evidence for what is known as the *extended contact effect*, or the *indirect contact effect*—knowing that an ingroup friend has a good and close relationship with a member of an outgroup can produce positive intergroup benefits in ways similar to direct contact. Why would this happen? Several causes are involved, such as reducing ignorance and anxiety about outgroup members and providing individuals with positive examples of outgroup members (Cameron et al., 2011; Dovidio et al., 2011; Eller et al., 2011; Wright et al., 2008).

Although Charleston High School in Mississippi has been integrated for decades, it was not until 2008 that the school board allowed a racially integrated senior prom, although some at the school organized a "white prom" as an alternative. Pictured here are two of the students who attended the prom standing in front of a poster for the movie *Prom Night in Mississippi*, an award-winning documentary about this story. Some integrated schools in the United States still hold racially separate proms.

## The Jigsaw Classroom

As the third condition in Table 5.5 indicates, cooperation and shared goals are ideal for intergroup contact to be successful. Yet the typical classroom is filled with competition—exactly the wrong ingredient. Picture the scene. The teacher stands in front of the class and asks a question. Many children wave their hands, each straining to catch the teacher's eye. Then, as soon as one student is called on, the others groan in frustration. In the competition for the teacher's approval, they are losers—hardly a scenario suited to positive intergroup contact. To combat this problem in the classroom, Elliot Aronson and his colleagues (1978) developed a cooperative learning method called the **jigsaw classroom**. In newly desegregated public schools in Texas and California, they assigned fifth graders to small racially and academically mixed groups. The material to be learned within each group was divided into subtopics, much the way a jigsaw puzzle is broken into pieces. Each student was responsible for learning one piece of the puzzle, after which all members took turns teaching their material to one another. In this system, everyone—regardless of race, ability, or self-confidence—needs everyone else if the group as a whole is to succeed.

The method produced impressive results (Aronson, 2004). Compared with children in traditional classes, those in jigsaw classrooms grew to like each other more, liked school more, were less prejudiced, and had higher self-esteem. What's more, academic test scores improved for minority students and remained the same for white students. The jigsaw classroom offers a promising way to create a truly integrated educational experience.

**jigsaw classroom** A cooperative learning method used to reduce racial prejudice through interaction in group efforts.

## Shared Identities

One important consequence of the jigsaw classroom technique is that individuals became more likely to classify outgroup members as part of their own ingroup. Instead of seeing racial or ethnic "others" within the classroom, the students now see fellow classmates. Students feel that they are all in the same boat together. More generally, intergroup contact that emphasizes shared goals and fates can effectively reduce prejudice and discrimination—specifically by changing how group members categorize each other (Bettencourt & Dorr, 1998; Brewer & Gaertner, 2004; Ray et al., 2008; Van Bavel & Cunningham, 2009).

The Common Ingroup Identity Model developed by Samuel Gaertner and John Dovidio (2010; 2012) proposes that if members of different groups recategorize themselves as members of a more inclusive superordinate group, intergroup attitudes and relations can improve. By recognizing their shared categorization, just as the Rattlers and Eagles did when they changed from competitors to collaborators in Robbers Cave State Park, "they" become "we," and a common ingroup identity can be forged. Researchers have induced a common ingroup identity among participants in their studies in a variety of ways, such as by having different groups share a common label, dispersing them around a table so that they are not separated according to group, or having them wear similar t-shirts. For example, Blake Riek and others (2010) put Democrats and Republicans together into two-person groups. When their different political party memberships were highlighted, the participants rated the other group more negatively. When their shared identity as Americans was highlighted, however, such as by having them wear shirts with the American flag printed on the front and calling their group the America Group, their intergroup ratings were significantly more positive.

It is worth noting that at least in some contexts, individuals from minority groups or groups that have less power in a society tend to not feel as positively as majority group members do about recategorizing their groups into one common ingroup. A group with smaller numbers or less power may feel overwhelmed and a sense of lost identity if they merge completely with a larger or more powerful group. Instead, members of these groups sometimes prefer or benefit more from dual-identity categorizations, in which their distinctiveness as a member of their specific group is preserved but in which they recognize their connection and potential for cooperation with the majority or more powerful group (Dovidio et al., 2013). A key point remains, though, that seeing connections between the groups and ways in which their identities are shared is essential.

*"The many factors which divide us are actually much more superficial than those we share. Despite all of the things that differentiate us—race, language, religion, gender, wealth and so on—we are all equal concerning our fundamental humanity."*

—Dalai Lama

## Trust, Belonging, and Reducing Stereotype Threat

Claude Steele's theory of stereotype threat discussed earlier in the chapter received a great deal of attention because it not only helped explain causes underlying some profound social problems—such as the underperformance or reduced interests of large groups of people in various academic and career pursuits—but also offered encouragement rather than pessimism. It illustrated that making even small changes in the situational factors that give rise to stereotype threat can reduce the tremendous weight of negative stereotypes, allowing the targets of stereotypes to perform to their potential.

Dozens and dozens of experiments on stereotype threat were published soon after the theory was introduced in the mid-1990s, and in virtually each of them the negative effects of stereotype threat were reduced significantly or eliminated completely in some conditions of the study. Often this was achieved with seemingly very minor—but important—changes in the setting. Table 5.6 lists a sample of these ways.

A theme running through many of the successful interventions against stereotype threat effects is that the individuals feel a sense of trust and safety in the situation. That is, in this particular setting they feel that they are not the target of others' low expectations and they do not have to be concerned with unfairness or other obstacles that would otherwise distract, worry, or discourage them. The importance of establishing this trust is evident in the results of an experiment by Geoffrey Cohen and others (1999). Students in this study performed a writing task and then received criticism of their writing from a reviewer who presumably was white. Compared to white students, black students tended to respond less constructively and were more likely to dismiss the criticism as biased against them. These negative reactions to the criticism were eliminated, however, if the reviewer who gave the criticism added two elements: (1) he made it clear that he had high standards, and (2) he assured the students that he was confident that they had the capacity to achieve those standards. This combination of factors made the students trust the criticism and gave them the sense that they had a fair shot at succeeding at the task.

Geoffrey Cohen, Gregory Walton, and their colleagues have applied these ideas from experiments on stereotype threat to create interventions outside the lab that have had truly remarkable success with students in a number of schools (G. Cohen et al., 2008: 2009; Cook et al., 2012; Walton & Cohen, 2011). One example was a set of studies conducted by Geoffrey Cohen and others (2006; 2008; 2009) with seventh-graders from lower-middle-class and middle-class families in a school in the United States. When they were first measured, the grades of the African American students tended to be significantly lower than those of the European American students. Early in the school year all of the students performed a relatively brief writing task. For a randomly assigned half of the students, the task involved their writing about values and aspects of their lives they cared deeply about. Social psychologists call this type of task an *affirmation* procedure because it affirms individuals' images of themselves as good, valued people, and it helps reduce the effects of various kinds of psychological threats. The other half of the students were in a control condition in which they wrote about values and aspects of life they did not care much about.

African American students performed significantly better in the class if they were in the affirmation condition than if they had written about things they didn't care about. The affirmation manipulation had no effect on the European American students. Cohen and his colleagues reported that this subtle, simple manipulation reduced the racial achievement gap among these students by 40%!

One of the most powerful ways in which stereotype threat undermines students is that it reduces their sense of *belonging*. That is, targeted students are likely to feel that *people like me do not belong here*, such as in a particular major, school, career, or some other domain (Cook et al., 2012; Walton & Cohen, 2007). One of the reasons the brief affirmation task was so successful in the study at the middle school is because affirmation helped protect students' sense of belonging. Without the affirmation manipulation, African American students tended to feel a decreasing sense of belonging during middle school. This decline in the sense of belonging did not occur among the students who had written about values they cared about (Good et al., 2012).

---

**TABLE 5.6**

**Combating Stereotype Threat Effects**

Researchers have reduced or eliminated the negative effects of stereotype threat in particular settings in a variety of ways. Here is a sample of these successful interventions.

- Describing the task as not indicative of individuals' intellectual capabilities (Steele & Aronson, 1995)
- Informing individuals that their group typically does not perform worse than other groups on the task (Spencer et al., 1999)
- Giving individuals reason to attribute their anxiety while taking a test to irrelevant factors (Ben-Zeev et al., 2005)
- Getting individuals to think of intelligence as not a fixed trait but instead as something that is malleable and can be improved (Good et al., 2003)
- Exposing individuals to a member of their group who is said to be an expert in the domain in question (Stout et al., 2011)
- Having individuals think about values and interests that are very important to them that are not under threat (Taylor & Walton, 2011; von Hippel et al., 2011)
- Highlighting other aspects of individuals' identities that are associated with positive performance on the task at hand (Shih et al., 2012; Yopyk & Prentice, 2005)
- Excluding the presence of members of outgroups (Sekaquaptewa & Thompson, 2003)

© Cengage Learning

The issue of belonging was addressed more directly in a study by Walton and Cohen (2011) that was discussed in Chapter 1. In this study some African American students at a predominately European American college were given information during their first semester at the school designed to reduce feelings of uncertainty about their sense of belonging at the university. They read that it is quite typical of most students—regardless of their gender, race, or ethnicity—to go through periods of social stress and uncertainty during their freshman year, and that these struggles tend to go away soon after their first year. Walton and Cohen found that giving this information to African American students raised their grade-point averages significantly higher relative to other African American students who were not given this information. (You can see this effect illustrated in Figure 1.1 on p. 9 of Chapter 1.)

This was but one of several studies that illustrate how vulnerable some groups are to feeling uncertain about their belonging, and how affirming one's sense of belonging in an environment can serve as a powerful antidote against threats based on stereotyping and prejudice (Murphy & Taylor, 2012; Walton & Carr, 2012; Walton et al., 2012).

## Exerting Self-Control

A key point in this chapter is that people often stereotype and show prejudice toward others even when they would rather not. For example, we have reported research indicating that people often activate negative stereotypes about groups even if they do not believe them. Can we learn to control and rise above these impulses?

One of the obstacles to this is that trying to suppress stereotyping or to control prejudiced actions can take mental effort, and engaging in this effort can drain individuals of cognitive resources for some period of time (Richeson & Trawalter, 2005). Some factors make people less likely to have sufficient cognitive resources for successful control. For example, older people have a harder time suppressing stereotypes than younger people, which may explain in part why older people often appear more prejudiced than younger people (von Hippel & Henry, 2011). Being intoxicated makes even younger people have a difficult time with suppressing thoughts or inhibiting impulses (for example, consider the dreaded drunk dialing or texting). It may come as little surprise, therefore, that intoxication impairs people's ability to control stereotype activation and application (Bartholow et al., 2006; Schlauch et al., 2009).

Being physically tired or being affected by strong emotion or arousal can sap perceivers of the cognitive resources necessary to avoid stereotyping. In an intriguing demonstration of this, Galen Bodenhausen (1990) ran an experiment with two types of people: "morning people" (who are most alert early in the morning) and "night people" (who peak much later, in the evening). By random assignment, participants took part in an experiment that was scheduled at either 9 p.m. or 8 p.m. The result? Morning people were more likely to use stereotypes when tested at night; night owls were more likely to do so early in the morning.

Being intoxicated robs people of cognitive resources, making them less able to inhibit impulses and control expressions of stereotyping and prejudice.

© Martin Thomas Photography/Alamy

Matthew Gailliot and others (2007; 2009) proposed that trying to control automatic stereotyping can consume glucose—a source of energy—in people's blood. Consistent with this idea, they found that participants in one of their studies who were relatively high in anti-gay prejudice made fewer derogatory statements when writing about a gay man if they had consumed a high-glucose drink than did those who consumed a drink with no glucose. In other words, the sugar-boost from the high-glucose drink gave them the extra resources needed to exert self-control successfully. Some researchers are more skeptical about whether self-control in these types of situations truly consumes glucose, so more research will certainly be done to clarify the issue (Beedie & Lane, 2012; Molden et al., 2012). It is clear, however, that trying to control otherwise automatic stereotyping can be very challenging, and if people are tired, busy, or otherwise cognitively compromised, they will be less successful at exerting this control.

Researchers have distinguished between two kinds of motivation to control prejudiced responses and behaviors. One kind is *externally* driven—not wanting to *appear* to others to be prejudiced. A second type is *internally* driven—not wanting to *be* prejudiced, regardless of whether or not others would find out (Dunton & Fazio, 1997; Plant & Devine, 1998, 2009). Internally motivated individuals are likely to be more successful at controlling stereotyping and prejudice, even on implicit measures, but even they are vulnerable to the strong power of automatic stereotyping and implicit biases.

According to the *self-regulation of prejudiced responses model* proposed by Margo Monteith and others (2002; Monteith & Mark, 2009), internally motivated individuals in particular may learn to control their prejudices more effectively over time. According to this model, people who are truly motivated to be fair and unprejudiced are often confronted with the sad reality that they have failed to live up to that goal. These realizations lead to unpleasant emotions such as guilt. As individuals experience such feelings of guilt repeatedly, they begin to develop expertise at recognizing the situations and stimuli that tend to trigger these failures, and therefore they can exert more control over them. In so doing, they begin to interrupt what had been automatic stereotype activation.

A great example of this process is reflected in the quotes of one student in a study by Margo Monteith and others (2010). The student described how close he once came to describing a classmate in a racist way, and how terrible he felt about it. "I don't know why I was going to say it. It was kind of scary how it had been programmed into my head by those people around me." Later, this participant indicated how often he is reminded of that experience: "When I see people say stuff like that I think about it a lot. . . . It kind of quiets me down and makes me think about what I'm doing and makes me think about what I'm thinking, what I'm saying. It makes me feel that I should be more careful about what I say" (pp. 193–194).

Just as people who are internally motivated to control prejudice tend to become more successful at self-regulation than people who are motivated for external reasons, anti-prejudice messages that are designed to appeal more to people's internal motivations may be more effective than messages that seem more externally focused. To study this issue, Lisa Legault and others (2011) developed a pair of prejudice-reduction brochures. One of these brochures was designed to appeal to internal motivations. This brochure emphasized the personal as well as societal benefits of tolerance and diversity. For example, one line read, "When we let go of prejudice, the rich diversity of society is ours to enjoy." The other brochure appealed to external motivations, emphasizing the obligations that compel individuals and organizations to act in nonprejudiced ways. For example, an excerpt from this brochure included, "Teachers and students caught displaying racist attitudes and behavior can face serious consequences, such as termination and expulsion."

Students at a Canadian university were randomly assigned to read either of the two brochures, or they received no brochure at all. Later these students completed a measure of their prejudice toward black people (no black students were included in the study). The researchers found that these students exhibited significantly less prejudice if they received the brochure that appealed to internal motivations to control prejudice than if they received no brochure. On the other hand, the students who received the brochure appealing to external factors exhibited significantly *more* prejudice than the students who received no brochure (see ● Figure 5.14). The brochure that emphasized the external rather than internal reasons to control prejudice likely came across to the students as very controlling and made students rebel against it somewhat. People don't like to be told how they must think and not think, and so antiprejudice messages that are perceived in that way can be counterproductive.

## Changing Cognitions, Cultures, and Motivations

We have just discussed some of the challenges involved in trying *not* to think about stereotypes or act in a prejudiced way. There are several ways of thinking that can be more productive. Social–cognitive factors that research has shown can reduce stereotyping and prejudice include:

- Being exposed to and thinking about examples of group members that are inconsistent with the stereotype (Columb & Plant, 2011).

- Learning about the variability that exists among the people in a group (Brauer & Er-rafiy, 2011; Brauer et al., 2012).

- Being induced to take the perspective of a person from a stereotyped group (Todd et al., 2012).

- Being encouraged to pay attention to instances of discrimination (Becker & Swim, 2011).

- Believing that prejudice can be learned and unlearned and is therefore malleable rather than a fixed, unchanging reality (Carr et al., 2012; Neel & Shapiro, 2012).

- Learning that race is more ambiguous and socially determined than simply a genetic, fixed category (Williams & Eberhardt, 2008).

- Taking a multicultural view that not only recognizes but values group differences, rather than pretending to not see race and ethnicity or that distinctions between groups don't exist (Apfelbaum et al., 2008; Holoien & Shelton, 2012; Plaut et al., 2009; Rattan & Ambady, 2012).

- Thinking of multiculturalism as an approach that is inclusive of everyone, including the majority group, rather than as one that excludes the majority group to benefit only minority groups (Plaut et al., 2011).

How can these types of thinking be promoted? One important factor may be education. More generally, it is at the cultural level that much potential for

● **FIGURE 5.14**

**Productive and Counterproductive Antiprejudice Messages**

Students read an antiprejudice brochure that emphasized either internally driven motivations to not be prejudiced (such as why one would benefit by promoting diversity) or externally driven motivations (such as how one could get in trouble if caught doing or saying something racist). A control group of students did not receive any antiprejudice brochure. Compared to the no-brochure control group (the middle bar), the students who read the brochure that appealed to internal motivations subsequently exhibited significantly less prejudice on a measure of prejudice toward black people, but the students who received the brochure that appealed to external factors exhibited significantly more prejudice. From Legault, L, Gutsell, J.N., and Inzlicht, M., "Ironic effects of antiprejudice messages: How motivational interventions can reduce (but also increase) prejudice," *Psychological Science* vol 22:12 (pp. 1472–1477). Copyright © 2012 Sage Publications, Inc. Reprinted with permission.

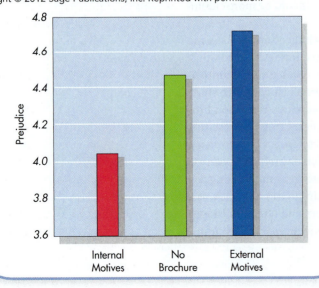

positive change can be found. Exposure to images and individuals that reflect the diversity within social groups, for example, can help weaken stereotypes and combat their automatic activation. These images might also change people's tendency to see groups as relatively fixed entities and help them see groups as dynamic entities with less rigid borders.

Motivations, norms, and values can and often do change over time. Here again popular culture is a key player. People—especially younger people—look to images in popular culture as well as to their peers and role models for information about what attitudes and behaviors are in fashion or out of date. We also look to our peers to get a sense of the local norms around us, including norms about stereotypes and prejudice (e.g., Fein et al., 2003; Nelson et al., 2012; Oyamot et al., 2012; Stangor et al., 2001). In a particular high

school, a senior might feel comfortable calling a friend a "fag" and mean little by it and think nothing of it. Yet several months later as a first-semester college student, this student might realize how wrong that is and feel guilty for ever having done so. If this lesson is learned, it's more likely to have been learned by watching and interacting with one's peers than from having been lectured to about diversity and sensitivity by a campus speaker. Learning these norms can motivate us to adopt them. Legislating against hate speech, unequal treatment, and hostile environments can also be an important weapon, of course. Although they can create resistance and backlashes, laws and policies that require behavior change can—if done right, with no suggestion of compromise and with important leaders clearly behind them—cause hearts and minds to follow (Aronson, 1992).

Elizabeth Levy Paluck (2011) has conducted some fascinating field studies showing the power of peer and cultural influences. In one study, students in several high schools were trained to be "peer leaders" who would confront expressions of intergroup prejudice. These students not only engaged in more antiprejudice behaviors, but these behaviors spread to their friends. Paluck (2009) also examined the role of the media in promoting positive norms in an unusual yearlong field experiment in Rwanda, which has been the site of terrible war, genocide, and intergroup conflict, particularly between the Hutus and Tutsis. She had Rwandans listen to a radio soap opera (radio being the most important form of mass media there) over the course of a year. She randomly assigned half to listen to a soap opera about conflicts that paralleled real conflicts in the country but that were solved in ways that modeled intergroup cooperation and communication, nonviolence, and opposition to prejudice. The other half of the participants listened to a soap opera about health issues. At the end of the year, those Rwandans who listened to the soap opera promoting positive intergroup norms had significantly more positive feelings about intergroup cooperation, trust, and interactions.

Studies like these show that a source for much positive change stems from what is at the very core of social psychology: the social nature of the human animal. Some of our baser instincts, such as intergroup competition that breeds intergroup biases, may always be present, but we also can learn from each other the thoughts, values, and goals that make us less vulnerable to perpetuating or being the targets of stereotypes, prejudice, and discrimination.

Soccer players from Mexico and Argentina line up with an antiracism banner before their match in Hanover, Germany, in response to the racist taunts and other actions by fans that had been plaguing the sport during international tournaments.

Andreas Rentz/Bongarts/Getty Images

# Review

- A sample of stories from the news illustrates both the progress and the persistent challenges regarding stereotyping, prejudice, and discrimination in contemporary life.

## The Nature of the Problem: Persistence and Change

### Defining Our Terms

- At the individual level, racism and sexism are forms of prejudice and discrimination based on a person's racial or gender background. At the institutional and cultural level, racism and sexism involve practices that promote the domination of one racial group or gender over another.
- Stereotypes are beliefs or associations that link groups of people with certain characteristics; prejudice refers to negative feelings toward persons based on their membership in certain groups; discrimination is negative behavior directed against persons because of their membership in a particular group.

### Racism: Current Forms and Challenges

- Over the years, various data show a decline in negative views of black Americans.
- However, modern forms of racism are more subtle and surface in less direct ways, particularly in situations where people can rationalize racist behavior.
- People's ambivalence concerning race can lead them to exhibit biases in favor of or against particular groups, depending on the context.
- Racism often works implicitly, as stereotypes and prejudice can fuel discrimination without conscious intent or awareness on the part of perceivers.
- Several studies illustrate subtle ways that racial bias can have serious effects on sentencing and verdicts of convicted criminals or suspects.
- Researchers use covert measures to detect and measure modern and implicit racism and other subtle forms of prejudice and discrimination.
- Implicit racism is associated with poorer treatment by doctors and health care providers of patients from racial and ethnic minority groups.
- Interracial interactions can feel threatening, can provoke anxiety, and can drain cognitive resources, particularly among people relatively high in implicit racism.
- Worried about appearing racist in these interactions, whites in particular may try to avoid interracial interactions or they may go out of their way to avoid any mention of race even when it is relevant.

### Sexism: Ambivalence, Objectification, and Double Standards

- Although similar in many other ways, sexism differs from other forms of prejudice and discrimination in part because gender stereotypes are more than just descriptive: They also indicate what the majority of people in a society believe men and women should be. Sexism is also unusual in that ingroup and outgroup members are so intimately familiar with each other.

- Ambivalent sexism reflects both hostile sexism, characterized by negative and resentful feelings toward women, and benevolent sexism, characterized by affectionate, chivalrous, but potentially patronizing feelings toward women.
- Individuals from countries with the greatest degree of economic and political inequality between men and women tend to exhibit high levels of both hostile and benevolent sexism.
- Women are often treated or presented in the popular media in objectifying ways in which they are viewed more as mere bodies and objects and less as fully functioning human beings.
- There are some striking sex differences in occupational choices and in the treatment individuals experience in the workplace.
- Women often face a difficult dilemma: If they behave consistently with gender stereotypes, they may be liked more but respected less.
- For both women and men, being in a job that is traditionally seen as more typical of the other gender can be especially challenging.

### Beyond Racism and Sexism: Age, Weight, Sexuality, and Other Targets

- A wide variety of forms of bias and discrimination exist, including those based on dimensions such as age, weight, and sexuality.
- Prejudice and discrimination based on people's bodies and their sexuality are especially overt today.
- Studies of biased treatment of people presumed to be gay illustrate some of the more subtle ways that people are discriminated against based on their sexual orientation.

### Being Stigmatized

- People are stigmatized when they are targets of negative stereotypes, perceived as deviant, and devalued in society because they are members of a particular social group or because they have a particular characteristic.
- When members of stigmatized groups perceive others' reactions to them as discrimination, they experience both benefits and drawbacks to their self-esteem and feelings of control.
- Stigmatized targets are at increased risk for serious and long-term physical and mental health problems.

### Stereotype Threat

- Situations that activate stereotype threat cause individuals to worry that others will see them in negative and stereotypical ways.
- Stereotype threat can impair the performance and affect the identity of members of stereotyped or devalued groups. Slight changes in a setting can reduce stereotype threat and its negative effects significantly.

- Stereotype threat can cause African American and female students to fail to perform to their potential in academic settings.
- Research has documented a huge and growing list of groups whose members show underperformance and performance-impairing behaviors when a negative stereotype about their abilities is made relevant.
- Stereotype threat causes its effects through multiple processes. Stereotype threat can lead to increased arousal, trigger attempts to suppress negative stereotypes, impair working memory, and cause individuals to feel dejection-related emotions or to engage in negative thinking.

---

### Putting *Common Sense* to the Test

**Children do not tend to show biases based on race; it is only after they become adolescents that they learn to respond to people differently based on race.**
**False.** *Children learn about social categories quite early and use stereotypes when they are very young. Children show biases in favor of their racial ingroup on both explicit and implicit measures.*

**Interracial interactions tend to go better and to reduce the perceptions of racism if a colorblind mentality is used, which denies or minimizes any acknowledgment of racial differences.**
**False.** *Research has shown that that this approach often backfires and makes members of racial minority groups more, rather than less, uncomfortable; a multicultural approach that acknowledges and positively values racial and ethnic differences is often more effective.*

**An African American student is likely to perform worse on an athletic task if the task is described as one reflecting sports intelligence than if it is described as reflecting natural athletic ability.**
**True.** *Research suggests that African American students are likely to experience stereotype threat and therefore underperform if the task is described as one that is diagnostic of their sports intelligence. White students tend to show the opposite effect: Their performance is worse if the task is described as reflecting natural athletic ability.*

---

## Causes of the Problem: Intergroup, Motivational, Cognitive, and Cultural Factors

### Social Categories and Intergroup Conflict

- The tendency for people to group themselves and others into social categories is a key factor in stereotype formation and prejudice.
- Social categories can be energy-saving devices that allow perceivers to make quick inferences about group members, but these categories can lead to inaccurate judgments.
- People who tend to think of race as a stable, biologically determined entity are less likely to interact with racial outgroup members and are more likely to accept racial inequalities than are people who see race as more socially determined.
- Ingroups are groups we identify with; we contrast these with outgroups.
- People tend to exaggerate the differences between ingroups and outgroups.
- The outgroup homogeneity effect is the tendency to assume that there is more similarity among members of outgroups than there is among members of ingroups.
- Research using brain imaging and cognitive methods has found that merely categorizing people as outgroup members can lead perceivers to process information about outgroup members less deeply.
- Perceivers sometimes dehumanize outgroups in a variety of ways.
- The tendency in people to divide the world into ingroups and outgroups—"us" versus "them"—and to favor the former over the latter in numerous ways is likely to be an evolved tendency due to the social nature of our species.
- When people's motives for self-protection are aroused, they show stronger biases against threatening outgroups.
- Being reminded about mortality triggers various ingroup biases, including negative stereotypes, and behavior that demonstrates prejudice toward a variety of outgroups.
- People with a social dominance orientation exhibit a desire to see their ingroups as dominant over other groups, and they tend to identify more strongly with their ingroup and to be more likely to disparage members of outgroups.
- People who tend to endorse and legitimize existing social arrangements can show signs of outgroup favoritism even when their group holds a relatively disadvantaged position in society.
- Many group stereotypes vary along two dimensions: warmth and competence.
- The stereotype content model proposes that stereotypes about the competence of a group are influenced by the relative status of that group in society and that stereotypes about the warmth of a group are influenced by perceived competition with the group.
- In the Robbers Cave study, boys divided into rival groups quickly showed intergroup prejudice. This prejudice was reduced when the boys were brought together through tasks that required intergroup cooperation.
- Realistic conflict theory maintains that direct competition for resources gives rise to prejudice. This competition can be real or imagined.

## Social Identity Theory

- Participants categorized into arbitrary minimal groups discriminate in favor of the ingroup.
- Social identity theory proposes that self-esteem is influenced by the fate of social groups with which we identify.
- Research shows that threats to the self cause individuals to derogate outgroups and that this behavior in turn increases self-esteem.

## Culture and Social Identity

- Cultural differences can influence social identity processes. Although people from collectivist cultures do show ingroup biases, individualists are more likely than collectivists to try to boost their self-esteem through overt ingroup-enhancing biases.

## Culture and Socialization

- We learn information relevant to stereotypes, prejudice, and discrimination without even realizing it by absorbing what we see around us in our culture, groups, and families.
- Boys and girls tend to show gender-stereotypical preferences for things like toys at very early ages.
- Gender stereotypes are so deeply ingrained that they bias perceptions of males and females from the moment they are born.
- Perceived differences between men and women are magnified by the contrasting social roles they occupy.
- The mass media foster stereotypes of various groups.
- Portrayals of men and women in advertising and other forms of media can influence the behavior and attitudes of men and women.

## How Stereotypes Distort Perceptions and Resist Change

- A fundamental effect of stereotyping is that it influence people's perceptions and interpretations of the behaviors of group members, causing them to perceive confirmation of their stereotype-based expectancies.
- The stereotypes that people hold about group members can lead them to behave in biased ways toward those members, sometimes causing the latter to behave consistently with the stereotypes. The stereotypes thus produce a self-fulfilling prophecy.
- People perceive illusory correlations between groups and traits when the traits are distinctive or when the correlations fit prior notions.
- People tend to make attributions about the causes of group members' behaviors in ways that help maintain their stereotypes.
- Group members who do not fit the mold are often subtyped, leaving the overall stereotype intact.

## Automatic Stereotype Activation

- Stereotypes—even ones in which we don't believe—are often activated without our awareness or intention and can influence our perceptions and reactions.
- Stereotype activation can be influenced by a number of factors, including how accessible various stereotypes are in perceivers' minds and how prejudiced the perceivers are.
- Some motivations make stereotype activation more likely to occur, and others make it less likely. For example, when perceivers are highly motivated to feel better about themselves, they may become more likely to activate some stereotypes and suppress others. On the other hand, people who are intrinsically motivated to not be prejudiced may be able to control stereotype activation and application more than other people.

## "41 Shots": A Focus on the Tragic Shooting of Amadou Diallo

- The shooting of an unarmed African man by New York City police officers triggered a great deal of controversy and inspired social psychology experiments designed to contribute to an understanding of the issues involved.
- Several studies have found that perceivers tend to be more biased toward seeing an unarmed man as holding a weapon and posing a threat if he is black than if he is white.
- Training may be effective in reducing the tendency of civilians or police officers to exhibit this bias.
- This bias is evident even among perceivers who do not endorse negative stereotypes or prejudiced attitudes. Awareness of the stereotype seems to be a key factor.

## The Hoodie and the Gun: Revisiting the Trayvon Martin Killing

- Social categorization, distrust of outgroup members, prevalence of particular stereotypes in the culture and through the media, confirmation biases, illusory correlations, and automatic stereotype activation all may have contributed to the killing of Trayvon Martin and to some of the reactions to the case.

### Putting *Common Sense* to the Test

**Being reminded of one's own mortality makes people put things into greater perspective, thereby tending to reduce ingroup–outgroup distinctions and hostilities.**

**False.** *Research has shown that when people feel threatened by thoughts of their own mortality, they tend to seek greater affiliation with their ingroups and exhibit greater prejudice against outgroups, in part to reaffirm their sense of place and purpose in the world.*

**People's very quick judgments are not influenced by a stereotype unless they actually believe the stereotype to be true.**

**False.** *Even very brief exposure to a member of a stereotyped group can activate the stereotype about the group, even if they do not believe the stereotype.*

# Reducing Stereotypes, Prejudice, and Discrimination

## Intergroup Contact

- According to the contact hypothesis, direct contact between members of rival groups will reduce intergroup prejudice, particularly if the contact involves equal status between the groups, there are personal interactions between members of the different groups, the groups have a shared superordinate goal, and social norms favor intergroup contact.
- The results of extensive reviews of the contact hypothesis indicate that intergroup contact tends to reduce prejudice, especially if the ideal conditions for contact are met.

## Intergroup Friendships and Extended Contact

- Having friends from outgroups is associated with decreased intergroup anxiety and prejudice. This link has been established in both correlational and experimental studies.
- Research on the *extended contact effect*, also known as the *indirect contact effect*, demonstrates that having an ingroup friend who has a good and close relationship with a member of an outgroup can reduce one's prejudice toward the outgroup.

## The Jigsaw Classroom

- Schools often fail to meet the conditions for reducing prejudice, in part because competition is too high. One program that is designed to foster intergroup cooperation and interdependence suggests that the right kinds of contact can improve attitudes and behaviors in a school setting.

## Shared Identities

- Research on the Common Ingroup Identity Model has found that if members of different groups recategorize themselves as members of a more inclusive superordinate group, intergroup attitudes and relations tend to improve.
- Members of minority groups or groups that have less power in a society may prefer and benefit more from dual-identity categorizations that allow them to preserve their smaller group identity but to recognize their connection with the majority or more powerful group.

## Trust, Belonging, and Reducing Stereotype Threat

- Even small changes in the situational factors that give rise to stereotype threat can reduce or eliminate their effects in particular settings.
- Individuals tend to be more protected against stereotype threats when they are made to feel a sense of trust and safety in the situation.
- A study of middle schoolers showed that the simple intervention of asking students to think about values that were important to them dramatically improved the performance of African American students.

- Stereotype threat can undermine an individual's sense of belonging in a particular setting, such as in a school. Interventions that promote feelings of belonging have been effective in reducing stereotype threat effects.

## Exerting Self-Control

- Trying to suppress stereotyping can be cognitively tiring. When age, fatigue, intoxication, or other cognitive impairment reduces people's cognitive resources, they are less able to control their stereotypes.
- People's whose motivation to control their prejudice is *externally* driven—that is, not wanting to *appear* to others to be prejudiced, tend to be less successful at exerting control than people whose motivation is *internally* driven—that is not wanting to *be* prejudiced, regardless of whether or not others would find out.
- Some individuals can become relatively expert at regulating prejudiced responses because they recognize the situational factors that have caused them to fail to live up to their egalitarian ideals in the past.
- A recent experiment suggests that antiprejudice messages that appeal more to internal reasons to control prejudice than external reasons are more effective. Appeals to externally driven factors, such as not wanting to get into trouble for appearing racist, can even backfire and increase expressions of prejudice.

## Changing Cognitions, Cultures, and Motivations

- Recent research suggests several changes to how people think that can reduce stereotypes, prejudice, and discrimination—such as thinking of examples that counter stereotypes, taking the perspective of others, learning that race is more ambiguous and socially determined than simply a genetic, fixed category, and taking a multicultural rather than colorblind approach to intergroup relations.
- Changes in the kinds of information perpetuated in one's culture can alter how one perceives social groups.
- Recent field experiments at American high schools and with a sample of people in Rwanda demonstrate the positive effects that peers and the media can have in promoting anti-prejudice norms.

## KEY TERMS

ambivalent sexism (161)
contact hypothesis (190)
discrimination (155)
illusory correlation (184)
implicit racism (157)
ingroup favoritism (176)
ingroups (172)
jigsaw classroom (193)
modern racism (156)

outgroup homogeneity effect (172)
outgroups (172)
prejudice (155)
racism (155)
realistic conflict theory (176)
relative deprivation (176)
sexism (155)
social categorization (171)
social dominance orientation (174)

social identity theory (177)
social role theory (181)
stereotype (155)
stereotype content model (174)
stereotype threat (167)
stigmatized (166)
subliminal presentation (186)
superordinate goal (175)
system justification theory (174)

## MEDIA RESOURCES

Go to CengageBrain.com to access Psychology CourseMate, where you will find an interactive eBook, glossaries, flashcards, quizzes, videos, and more.

# Attitudes

This chapter examines social influences on attitudes. We define attitudes and then discuss how they are measured and when they are related to behavior. Then we consider two methods of changing attitudes. First, we look at source, message, and audience factors that win persuasion through the media of communication. Second, we consider theories and research showing that people often change their attitudes as a consequence of their own actions.

# 6

Adam Kazmierski/Getty Images

205

**Al Qaeda. Abortion rights.** The death penalty. Gay marriage. Rush Limbaugh. Gun control. Israelis and Palestinians. Taxes. Anyone who has followed recent events in the United States—or anywhere else in the world, for that matter—knows how passionately people feel about the issues of the day. Attitudes and the mechanisms of attitude change, or persuasion, are a vital part of human social life. This chapter addresses three sets of questions: (1) What is an attitude, how can it be measured, and what is its link to behavior? (2) What kinds of persuasive messages lead people to change their attitudes? (3) Why do we often change our attitudes as a result of our own actions?

# The Study of Attitudes

Are you a Democrat, Republican, or Independent? Should smoking be banned in public places? Would you rather listen to alternative rock, country-western, or hip-hop? Do you prefer drinking Coke or Pepsi, working on a PC or Mac, and using an iPhone, Droid, or BlackBerry? Should terrorism be contained by war or conciliation?

As these questions suggest, each of us has positive and negative reactions to various persons, objects, and ideas. These reactions are called **attitudes**. Skim the chapters in this book, and you'll see just how pervasive attitudes are. You'll see, for example, that self-esteem is an attitude we hold about ourselves, that attraction is a positive attitude toward another person, and that prejudice is a negative attitude often directed against certain groups. Indeed, the study of attitudes—what they are, where they come from, how they can be measured, what causes them to change, and how they interact with behavior—is central to the whole field of social psychology (Bohner & Dickel, 2011; Crano & Prislin, 2008; Fazio & Petty, 2008; Perloff, 2010).

An attitude is a positive, negative, or mixed evaluation of an object that is expressed at some level of intensity—nothing more, nothing less. *Like, love, dislike, hate, admire,* and *detest* are the kinds of words that people use to describe their attitudes.

It's important to realize that attitudes cannot simply be represented along a single continuum ranging from wholly positive to wholly negative—as you might expect if attitudes were like the volume button on a remote control unit or the lever on a thermostat that raises or lowers temperature. Rather, as depicted in ● Figure 6.1, our attitudes can vary in strength along both positive and negative dimensions. In other words, we can react to something with positive affect, with negative affect, with ambivalence (strong but mixed emotions), or with apathy and indifference (Cacioppo et al., 1997). Some people more than others are troubled by this type of inconsistency (Newby-Clark et al., 2002). In fact, at times people can have both positive and negative reactions to the same attitude object without feeling conflict,

**attitude** A positive, negative, or mixed reaction to a person, object, or idea.

as when we are conscious of one reaction but not the other. Someone who is openly positive toward racial minorities but harbors unconscious prejudice is a case in point (Wilson et al., 2000).

Everyone routinely forms positive and/or negative evaluations of the people, places, objects, and ideas they encounter. This process is often immediate and automatic—much like a reflex action (Bargh et al., 1996; Ferguson, 2007). It now appears, however, that individuals differ in the extent to which they tend to react to things in strong positive and negative terms. What about you—do you form opinions easily? Do you have strong likes and dislikes? Or do you tend to react in more non-evaluative ways? People who describe themselves as high rather than low in the *need for evaluation* are more likely to view their daily experiences in judgmental terms. They are also more opinionated on a whole range of social, moral, and political issues (Bizer et al., 2004; Jarvis & Petty, 1996).

Before we examine the elusive science of attitude measurement, let's stop for a moment and ponder this question: Why do human beings bother to form and have attitudes? Does forming a positive or negative judgment of people, objects, and ideas serve any useful purpose? Over the years, researchers have found that attitudes serve important functions—such as enabling us to judge quickly and without much thought whether something we first encounter is good or bad, helpful or hurtful, and to be sought or avoided (Maio & Olson, 2000). The downside is that having preexisting attitudes toward persons, objects, and ideas can lead us to become closed-minded, bias the way we interpret new information, and make us more resistant to change. For example, Russell Fazio and others (2000) found that people who were focused on their positive or negative attitudes toward computerized faces, compared to those who were not, were later slower to notice when the faces were "morphed" and no longer the same.

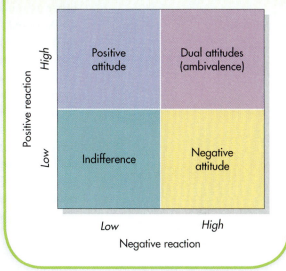

**● FIGURE 6.1**

**Four Possible Reactions to Attitude Objects**

As shown, people evaluate objects along both positive and negative dimensions. As a result, our attitudes can be positive, negative, ambivalent, or indifferent.

Cacioppo et al., 1997. © Cengage Learning

## How Attitudes Are Measured

In 1928, Louis Thurstone published an article entitled "Attitudes Can Be Measured." What Thurstone failed to anticipate, however, is that attitude measurement is tricky business. One review of research uncovered more than 500 different methods of determining an individual's attitudes (Fishbein & Ajzen, 1972).

**Self-Report Measures** The easiest way to assess a person's attitude about something is to ask. All over the world, public opinions are recorded on a range of issues in politics, the economy, health care, foreign affairs, science and technology, sports, entertainment, religion, and lifestyles. Simply by asking, Harris polls conducted in the United States in 2011 and 2012 have revealed that Americans prefer to watch football over baseball and like to eat chocolate ice cream more than vanilla and other flavors; that more than half say they surf the Internet while watching TV; that one in five adults now has a tattoo; that most would choose Hawaii, California, and Florida,

As seen in this "Occupy Wall Street" rally for economic justice, people can be very passionate about the attitudes they hold.

as states to live in other than their own; that Italy is the favorite foreign travel destination, followed by Great Britain, Australia, Ireland, and France; and that Christmas is America's favorite holiday, followed by Thanksgiving and Halloween (*http://www.harris interactive.com/*).

*Self-report* measures are direct and straightforward. But attitudes are sometimes too complex to be measured by a single question. As you may recall from Chapter 2, one problem recognized by public opinion pollsters is that responses to attitude questions can be influenced by their wording, the order and context in which they are asked, and other extraneous factors (Sudman et al., 2010; Tourangeau et al., 2000). In one survey, the National Opinion Research Center asked hundreds of Americans if the U.S. government spent too little money on "assistance to the poor" and 65% said yes. Yet when the very same question was asked using the word "welfare" instead, only 20% said the government spent too little (Schneiderman, 2008). In a second survey, researchers asked more than two thousand registered voters about their belief in the politically controversial phenomenon of "global warming" or "climate change." Although Democrats uniformly endorsed the proposition at a high rate, the number of Republicans who did so increased markedly from 44% when asked about global warming to 60% when asked about climate change (Schuldt et al., 2011).

Recognizing the shortcomings of single-question measures, researchers who study people's social and political opinions often use multiple-item questionnaires known as **attitude scales** (Robinson et al., 1991; 1998). Attitude scales come in different forms, perhaps the most popular being the Likert Scale, named after its inventor, Rensis Likert (1932). In this technique, respondents are presented with a list of statements about an attitude object and are asked to indicate on a multiple-point scale how strongly they agree or disagree with each statement. Each respondent's total attitude score is derived by summing his or her responses to all the items. However, regardless of whether attitudes are measured by one question or a full-blown scale, the results should be taken with caution. All self-report measures assume that people honestly express their true opinions. Sometimes this assumption is reasonable and correct, but often it is not. Wanting to make a good impression on others, people are often reluctant to admit to their failures, vices, weaknesses, unpopular opinions, and prejudices.

"What I drink and what I tell the pollsters I drink are two different things."

Pollsters and attitude researchers are well aware that self-reports cannot always be trusted, especially on sensitive topics.

One approach to this problem is to increase the accuracy of self-report measures. To get respondents to answer attitude questions more truthfully, researchers have sometimes used the **bogus pipeline**, an elaborate mechanical device that supposedly records our true feelings physiologically, like a lie-detector test. Not wanting to get caught in a lie, respondents tend to answer attitude questions more honestly, and with less positive spin, when they think that deception would be exposed by the bogus pipeline (Jones & Sigall, 1971; Roese & Jamieson, 1993). In one study, for example, people were more likely to admit to drinking too much, using cocaine, having frequent oral sex, and not exercising enough when the bogus pipeline was used than when it was not (Tourangeau et al., 1997). In another study, adolescents were more likely to admit to smoking when the bogus pipeline was used than when it was not (Adams et al., 2008).

**attitude scale** A multiple-item questionnaire designed to measure a person's attitude toward some object.

**bogus pipeline** A phony lie-detector device that is sometimes used to get respondents to give truthful answers to sensitive questions.

**Covert Measures** A second general approach to the self-report problem is to collect indirect, covert measures of attitudes that cannot be controlled. One possibility in this regard is to use observable behavior such as facial expressions, tone of voice, and body language. In one study, Gary Wells and Richard Petty (1980) secretly videotaped college students as they listened to a speech and noticed that when the speaker took a position that the students agreed with (that tuition costs should be lowered), most made vertical head movements. But when the speaker took a contrary position (that tuition costs should be raised), head movements were in a horizontal direction. Without realizing it, the students had signaled their attitudes by nodding and shaking their heads.

Although behavior provides clues, it is far from perfect as a measure of attitudes. Sometimes we nod our heads because we agree; at other times, we nod to be polite. The problem is that people monitor their overt behavior just as they monitor self-reports. But what about internal physiological reactions that are difficult if not impossible to control? Does the body betray how we feel? In the past, researchers tried to divine attitudes from involuntary physical reactions such as perspiration, heart rate, and pupil dilation. The result, however, was always the same: Measures of arousal reveal the intensity of one's attitude toward an object but not whether that attitude itself is positive or negative. On the physiological record, love and hate look very much the same (Petty & Cacioppo, 1983).

Although physiological arousal measures cannot distinguish between positive and negative attitudes, some exciting alternatives have been discovered. One is the **facial electromyograph (EMG)**. As shown in ● Figure 6.2, certain muscles in the face contract when we are happy and different facial muscles contract when we are sad. Some of the muscular changes cannot be seen with the naked eye, however, so the facial EMG is used. To determine whether the EMG can be used to measure the affect associated with attitudes, John Cacioppo and Richard Petty (1981) recorded facial muscle activity of college students as they listened to a message with which they agreed or disagreed. The agreeable message increased activity in the cheek muscles—the facial pattern that is characteristic of happiness. The disagreeable message sparked activity in the forehead and brow area—the facial patterns that are associated with sadness and distress. Outside observers who later watched the participants were unable to see these subtle changes. Apparently, the muscles in the human face reveal smiles, frowns, feelings of disgust, and other reactions to attitude objects that might otherwise be hidden from view (Cacioppo et al., 1986; Larsen et al., 2003; Tassinary & Cacioppo, 1992).

From a social neuroscience perspective, electrical activity in the brain may also assist in the measure of attitudes. In 1929, Hans Burger invented a machine that could detect, amplify, and record "waves" of electrical activity in the brain using electrodes pasted to the surface of the scalp. The instrument is called an *electroencephalograph*, or EEG, and the information it provides takes the form of line tracings called *brain waves*. Based on an earlier discovery that certain patterns of electrical brain activity are triggered by exposure to stimuli that are novel or unexpected, Cacioppo and others (1993) had participants list 10 items they liked and 10 they did not like within various object categories (fruits, sports, movies, universities, etc.). Later, these participants were brought into the laboratory, wired to an EEG, and presented with a list of category words that depicted objects they liked and disliked. The result: Brain-wave patterns that are normally triggered by inconsistency increased more when a disliked stimulus appeared after a string of positive items or when a liked stimulus was shown

● **FIGURE 6.2**

**The Facial EMG: A Covert Measure of Attitudes?**

The facial EMG makes it possible to detect differences between positive and negative attitudes. Notice the major facial muscles and recording sites for electrodes. When people hear a message with which they agree rather than disagree, there is a relative increase in EMG activity in the depressor and zygomatic muscles but a relative decrease in corrugator and frontalis muscles. These changes cannot be seen with the naked eye.

From Cacioppo, J.T and Petty, R.E., "Electromyograms as measures of extent and affectivity of information processing," *American Psychologist* vol 36 (pp. 441–456). Copyright © 1981 by the American Psychological Association. Reprinted by permission.

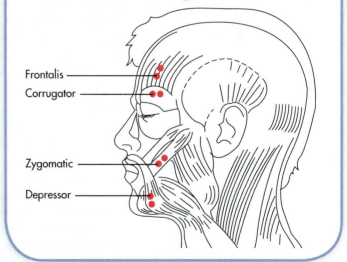

Frontalis
Corrugator
Zygomatic
Depressor

**facial electromyograph (EMG)**  An electronic instrument that records facial muscle activity associated with emotions and attitudes.

after a string of negative items than when either stimulus evoked the same attitude as the items that preceded it.

Today, social psychologists are also starting to use new forms of brain imaging in the measurement of attitudes. In one study, researchers used fMRI to record brain activity in participants as they read names of famous—and infamous—figures such as Bill Cosby and Adolf Hitler. When the names were read, they observed greater activity in the amygdala, a structure in the brain associated with emotion, regardless of whether or not participants were asked to evaluate the famous figures (Cunningham et al., 2003). In a study focused on political attitudes, other researchers used fMRI to record brain activity in opinionated men during the 2004 presidential election as they listened to positive and negative statements about the candidate of their choice. Although the brain areas associated with cognitive reasoning were unaffected during these presentations, activity increased in areas that are typically associated with emotion (Westen et al., 2006). Together, this new research suggests that people react automatically to positive and negative attitude objects. Although more work is needed, it appears that attitudes may be measurable by electrical activity in the brain.

**The Implicit Association Test (IAT)**   When it comes to covert measurement, one particularly interesting development is based on the notion that each of us has all sorts of **implicit attitudes** that we cannot self-report in questionnaires because we are not aware of having them (Fazio & Olson, 2003). To measure these unconscious attitudes, a number of indirect methods have been developed (De Houwer et al., 2009; Nosek et al., 2011). The most important of these is the **Implicit Association Test (IAT)** created by Anthony Greenwald, Mahzarin Banaji, Brian Nosek, and others. As we saw in Chapter 5, the IAT measures the speed with which people associate pairs of concepts (Greenwald et al., 1998). To see how it works, visit the IAT website by searching "Implicit Association Test" or typing *https://implicit.harvard.edu/implicit/* in your browser window.

To take a test that measures your implicit racial attitudes, you go through a series of stages. First, you are asked to categorize black or white faces as quickly as you can, for example, by pressing a left-hand key in response to a black face and a right-hand key for a white face. Next, you are asked to categorize a set of words, for example, by pressing a left-hand key for positive words (*love, laughter, friend*) and a right-hand key for negative words (*war, failure, evil*). Once you become familiar with the categorization task, the test combines faces and words. You may be asked, for example, to press the left-hand key if you see a black face or positive word and a right-hand key for a white face or negative word. Then, in the fourth stage, the opposite pairings are presented—black or negative, white or positive. Black and white faces are then interspersed in a quick sequence of trials, each time paired with a positive or negative word. In rapid-fire succession, you have to press one key or another in response to stimulus pairs such as *black-wonderful, black-failure, white-love, black-laughter, white-evil, white-awful, black-war,* and *white-joy*. As you work through the list, you may find that some pairings are harder and take longer to respond to than others. In general, people are quicker to respond when liked faces are paired with positive words and disliked faces are paired with negative words than the other way around. Using the IAT, your implicit attitudes about African Americans can thus be detected by the speed it takes you to respond to *black-bad/white-good* pairings relative to *black-good/white-bad* pairings. The test takes only 10–15 minutes to complete. When you're done, you receive the results of your test and an explanation of what it means (see ● Figure 6.3).

From 1998 to the present, visitors to the IAT website completed more than five million tests. In questionnaires, interviews, public opinion polls, and Internet surveys, people don't tend to express stereotypes, prejudices, or other unpopular attitudes. Yet

Researchers can tell if someone has a positive or negative attitude by measuring physiological arousal. **F**ALSE.

**implicit attitude**   An attitude, such as prejudice, that one is not aware of having.

**Implicit Association Test (IAT)**   A covert measure of unconscious attitudes derived from the speed at which people respond to pairings of concepts—such as black or white with good or bad.

● **FIGURE 6.3**

**The Implicit Association Test**

Through a sequence of tasks, the IAT measures implicit racial attitudes toward, for example, African Americans, by measuring how quickly people respond to *black-bad/white-good* word pairings relative to *black-good/white-bad* pairings. Most white Americans are quicker to respond to the first type of pairings than to the second, which suggests that they do not as readily connect *black-good* and *white-bad*.

From Kassin, S. *Essentials of psychology*. Copyright © 2004. Reprinted by permission of Pearson Education, Inc., Upper Saddle River, NJ.

on the IAT, respondents have exhibited a marked implicit preference for self over other, white over black, young over old, straight over gay, able over disabled, thin over obese, and the stereotype that links males with careers and females with family (Greenwald et al., 2003; Nosek et al., 2002). Because more and more researchers are using these kinds of indirect measures, social psychologists who study attitudes find themselves in the midst of a debate over what IAT scores mean, how the implicit attitudes revealed in the IAT are formed and then changed, how these attitudes predict or influence behavior, and how they differ from the more explicit attitudes that we consciously hold and report (Blanton et al., 2009; Gawronski & Bodenhausen, 2006; Petty et al., 2009; Wittenbrink & Schwarz, 2007).

Do implicit attitudes matter? Do millisecond differences in response times on a computerized test really predict behavior in real-world settings of consequence? And what does it mean when one's implicit and explicit attitudes clash? The importance of these questions cannot be overstated. If the IAT reveals unconscious prejudices that people do not self-report, should individuals be scrutinized in the laboratory for hidden motives underlying various potentially unlawful behaviors—as when a police officer shoots a black suspect, fearing that he or she is armed; as when an employer hires a male applicant over a female applicant, citing his credentials as opposed to discrimination; or as when a jury chooses to convict a Latino defendant on the basis of ambiguous evidence?

Kristin Lane and others (2007) have speculated about the relevance of implicit attitudes in law. But is their speculation justified? Some researchers are critical of strong claims concerning the predictive validity of the IAT, citing the need for more behavioral evidence (Blanton et al., 2009). Based on a meta-analysis of 122 IAT studies involving 15,000 participants, Greenwald and others (2009) conceded that people's implicit attitudes are generally less predictive of behavior than their explicit attitudes. They also found, however, that IAT measures are better when it comes to socially sensitive topics for which people often conceal or distort their self reports. In a poignant illustration of this point, one research team administered to a large group of psychiatric patients an IAT that measured their implicit associations between self and suicide. Over the next 6 months, patients appearing in the emergency room because of a suicide attempt had a stronger implicit association between self and suicide than those who appeared with other types of psychiatric emergencies (Nock et al., 2010).

## How Attitudes Are Formed

How did you become liberal or conservative in your political values? Why do you favor or oppose gay marriage? What draws you toward or away from organized religion?

**Are Attitudes Inherited?**   One hypothesis, first advanced by Abraham Tesser (1993), is that strong likes and dislikes are rooted in our genetic makeup. Research shows that on some issues the attitudes of identical twins are more similar than those of fraternal twins and that twins raised apart are as similar to each other as those who are raised in the same home. This pattern of evidence suggests that people may be predisposed to hold certain attitudes. Indeed, Tesser found that when asked about attitudes for which there seems to be a predisposition (such as attitudes toward sexual promiscuity, religion, and the death penalty), research participants were quicker to respond and less likely to alter their views toward social norms.

Tesser speculated that individuals are disposed to hold certain strong attitudes as a result of inborn physical, sensory, and cognitive skills, temperament, and personality traits. Other twin studies, too, as well as complex comparisons within extended families, have supported the notion that people differ in their attitudes toward a range of social and political issues in part because of genetically rooted differences in their biological makeup (Hatemi et al., 2010; Olson et al., 2001). There are different ways in which a person's inborn tendencies may influence social and political attitudes. In one study, for example, researchers brought 40 adults with strong political views into the lab for testing and found that those who physiologically were highly reactive to sudden noise and other unpleasant stimuli were more likely to favor capital punishment, the right to bear arms, defense spending, and other policies seen as protective against domestic and foreign threats (Oxley et al., 2008).

Chances are, these identical twins have more in common than being firefighters. Research suggests that people may be genetically predisposed to hold certain attitudes.

T. K. Wanstal/The Image Works

**Are Attitudes Learned?**    Whatever dispositions nature provides to us, our most cherished attitudes often form as a result of our exposure to attitude objects; our history of rewards and punishments; the attitudes that our parents, friends, and enemies express; the social and cultural context in which we live; and other types of experiences. In a classic naturalistic study, Theodore Newcomb (1943) surveyed the political attitudes of students at Bennington College in Vermont. At the time, Bennington was a women's college that drew its students from conservative and mostly affluent families. Once there, however, the students encountered professors and older peers who held more liberal views. Newcomb found that as the women moved from their first year to graduation, they became progressively more liberal. (In the 1936 presidential election, 62% of first-year Bennington students preferred the Republican Landon to the Democrat Roosevelt, compared to only 43% of sophomores and 15% of juniors and seniors.) This link between cultural environment and attitudes is particularly evident in the current political landscape of America—a "house divided" into red states and blue states by geography, culture, and ideology (Seyle & Newman, 2006).

Clearly, attitudes are formed through basic processes of learning. For example, a number of studies have shown that people can form strong positive and negative attitudes toward neutral objects that somehow are linked to emotionally charged stimuli. At the start of the twentieth century, Russian physiologist Ivan Pavlov (1927) discovered that dogs would naturally and reflexively salivate in response to food in the mouth. He then discovered that by repeatedly ringing a bell—a neutral stimulus—before the food was placed in the mouth, the dog would eventually start to salivate at the sound of the bell itself. This process by which organisms learn to associate a once neutral stimulus with an inherently positive or negative response is a basic and powerful form of learning.

It is now clear that this form of learning can help to explain the development of social attitudes. In a classic first study, college students were presented with a list of adjectives that indicate nationality (*German, Swedish, Dutch, Italian, French,* and *Greek*), each of which was repeatedly presented with words that were known to have very pleasant (*happy, gift, sacred*) or unpleasant (*bitter, ugly, failure*) connotations. When the participants later evaluated the nationalities by name, they were more positive in their ratings of those that had been paired with pleasant words than with unpleasant words (Staats & Staats, 1958).

More recent studies of **evaluative conditioning** have shown that implicit and explicit attitudes toward neutral objects can form by their association with positive and negative stimuli, even in people who are not conscious of this association (Hofmann et al., 2010; Olson & Fazio, 2001; Walther et al., 2011). That's why political leaders all over the world wrap themselves in a national flag to derive a benefit from positive associations, while advertisers strategically pair their products with sexy models, uplifting music, beloved celebrities, nostalgic images, and other positive emotional symbols. In a series of laboratory studies, researchers found that people came to prefer brands of a consumer product that were paired with humorous ads more than those that were associated with nonhumorous ads (Strick et al., 2009).

## The Link Between Attitudes and Behavior

People take for granted the notion that attitudes influence behavior. We assume that voters' opinions of opposing candidates predict the decisions they make on Election Day, that consumers' preference for one product rather than competing products influence the purchases they make, and that feelings of prejudice trigger bad acts of discrimination. Yet as sensible as these assumptions seem, the link between attitudes and behavior is far from perfect.

**evaluative conditioning**    The process by which we form an attitude toward a neutral stimulus because of its association with a positive or negative person, place, or thing.

Sociologist Richard LaPiere (1934) was the first to notice that attitudes and behavior don't always go hand in hand. In the 1930s, during the height of the Great Depression, LaPiere took a young Chinese American couple on a 3-month, 10,000-mile car trip, visiting 250 restaurants, campgrounds, and hotels across the United States. Although prejudice against Asians was widespread at the time, the couple was refused service only once. Yet when LaPiere wrote back to the places they had visited and asked if they would accept Chinese patrons, more than 90% of those who returned an answer said they would not. Self-reported attitudes did not correspond with behavior.

This study was provocative but seriously flawed. LaPiere measured attitudes several months after his trip, and during that time the attitudes may have changed. He also did not know whether those who responded to his letter were the same people who had greeted the couple in person. It was even possible that the Chinese couple were served wherever they went because they were accompanied by LaPiere—or because businesses were desperate during hard economic times.

Despite these limitations, LaPiere's study was the first of many to reveal a lack of correspondence between attitudes and behavior. In 1969, Allan Wicker reviewed the applicable research and concluded that attitudes and behavior are correlated only weakly, if at all. Sobered by this conclusion, researchers were puzzled: Could it be that the votes we cast do *not* follow from our political opinions, that consumers' purchases are *not* based on their attitudes toward a product, or that discrimination is *not* related to underlying prejudice? Is the study of attitudes useless to those interested in human social behavior? Not at all. During subsequent years, researchers went on to identify the conditions under which attitudes and behavior are correlated. Thus, when Stephen Kraus (1995) meta-analyzed all of this research, he concluded that "attitudes significantly and substantially predict future behavior" (p. 58). In fact, he calculated that there would have to be 60,983 new studies reporting a zero correlation before this conclusion would have to be revised. Based on a meta-analysis of 41 additional studies, Laura Glasman and Dolores Albarracín (2006) went on to identify some of the conditions under which attitudes most clearly predict future behavior.

**Attitudes in Context**   One important condition is the level of *correspondence*, or similarity, between attitude measures and behavior. Perhaps the reason that LaPiere (1934) did not find a correlation between self-reported prejudice and discrimination was that he had asked proprietors about Asians in general but then observed their actions toward only one couple. To predict a single act of discrimination, he should have measured people's more specific attitudes toward a young, well-dressed, attractive Chinese couple accompanied by an American professor.

Icek Ajzen and Martin Fishbein (1977) analyzed more than 100 studies and found that attitudes correlate with behavior only when attitude measures closely match the behavior in question. Illustrating the point, Andrew Davidson and James Jaccard (1979) tried to use attitudes to predict whether women would use birth control pills within the next 2 years. Attitudes were measured in a series of questions ranging from very general ("How do you feel about birth control?") to very specific ("How do you feel about using birth control pills during the next two years?"). The more specific the initial attitude question was, the better it predicted the behavior. Other researchers as well have replicated this finding (Kraus, 1995).

The link between our feelings and our actions should also be placed within a broader context. Attitudes are one determinant of social behavior, but there are other determinants as well. This limitation formed the basis for Fishbein's (1980) theory of reasoned action, which Ajzen (1991) later expanded into his **theory of planned behavior**. According to these theories, our attitudes influence our behavior through a process of deliberate decision making, and their impact is limited in four respects (see ● Figure 6.4).

**theory of planned behavior**   The theory that attitudes toward a specific behavior combine with subjective norms and perceived control to influence a person's actions.

First, as just described, behavior is influenced less by general attitudes than by attitudes toward a specific behavior. Second, behavior is influenced not only by attitudes but by *subjective norms*—our beliefs about what others think we should do. As we'll see in Chapter 7, social pressures to conform often lead us to behave in ways that are at odds with our inner convictions. Third, according to Ajzen, attitudes give rise to behavior only when we perceive the behavior to be within our *control*. To the extent that people lack confidence in their ability to engage in some behavior, they are unlikely to form an intention to do so. Fourth, although attitudes (along with subjective norms and perceived control) contribute to an *intention* to behave in a particular manner, people often do not or cannot follow through on their intentions.

A good deal of research now supports the theories of reasoned action and planned behavior (Ajzen & Fishbein, 2005). Indeed, this general approach, which places the link between attitudes and behaviors within a broader context, has successfully been used to predict a wide range of practical behaviors—such as using condoms, obeying speed limits, washing hands and other food safety habits, donating blood, and registering to become an organ donor (Albarracín et al., 2001; Conner et al., in press; Elliott et al., 2003; Hyde & White, 2009; Milton & Mullan, 2012).

● **FIGURE 6.4**
**Theory of Planned Behavior**
According to the theory of planned behavior, attitudes toward a specific behavior combine with subjective norms and perceived behavior control to influence a person's intentions. These intentions, in turn, guide but do not completely determine behavior. This theory places the link between attitudes and behavior within a broader context.
From Ajzen, *Organizational Behavior and the Human Decision Process*, vol 50, pp. 179–211. Copyright © 1991 Elsevier. Reprinted with permission.

**Strength of the Attitude**    According to the theories of reasoned action and planned behavior, specific attitudes combine with social factors to produce behavior. Sometimes attitudes have more influence on behavior than do the other factors; sometimes they have less influence. In large part, it depends on the importance, or *strength*, of the attitude. Each of us has some views that are nearer and dearer to the heart than others. Computer jocks often become attached to PCs or Macs, religious fundamentalists care deeply about issues pertaining to life and death, and political activists have fiery passions for one political party or policy over others. In each case, the attitude is held with great confidence and is difficult to change (Petty & Krosnick, 1995).

Why are some attitudes stronger than others? David Boninger and others (1995) identified three psychological factors that consistently seem to distinguish between our strongest and weakest attitudes. These investigators asked people to reflect on their views toward defense spending, gun control, the legalization of marijuana, abortion rights, and other issues. They found that the attitudes people held most passionately were those that concerned issues that (1) directly affected their own self-interests; (2) related to deeply held philosophical, political, and religious values; and (3) were of concern to their close friends, family, and social ingroups. This last, highly social, point is important. Research shows that when people are surrounded by others who are like-minded, the attitudes they hold are stronger and more resistant to change (Visser & Mirabile, 2004).

Several factors indicate the strength of an attitude and its link to behavior. One is that people tend to behave in ways that are consistent with their attitudes when they are well informed. For example, college students were asked which of two candidates they preferred in an upcoming local election for mayor. Those who knew the factual campaign issues were later the most likely to actually vote for their favored candidate (Davidson et al., 1985). In another study, college students were questioned about their views on various environmental issues and later were asked to take action—to sign petitions, participate in a recycling project, and so on. Again, the more informed the students were, the more consistent their attitudes about the environment were with their behavior (Kallgren & Wood, 1986).

The strength of an attitude is indicated not only by the *amount* of information on which it is based but also by *how* that information was acquired. Research shows that attitudes are more stable and more predictive of behavior when they are born of direct personal experience than when based on indirect, secondhand information. In a series of experiments, for example, Russell Fazio and Mark Zanna (1981) introduced two groups of participants to a set of puzzles. One group worked on sample puzzles; the other group merely watched someone else work on them. All participants were then asked to rate their interest in the puzzles (attitude) and were given an opportunity to spend time on them (behavior). As it turned out, attitudes and behaviors were more consistent among participants who had previously sampled the puzzles.

Third, an attitude can be strengthened, ironically, by an attack against it from a persuasive message. According to Zakary Tormala and Richard Petty (2002), people hold attitudes with varying degrees of certainty, and they become more confident in their positions after they successfully resist changing that attitude in response to a persuasive communication. In one study, researchers confronted university students with an unpopular proposal to add senior comprehensive exams as a graduation requirement. Each student read a pro-exam argument that was described as strong or weak, after which they were asked to write down counterarguments and indicate their attitude toward the policy. The result: Students who continued to oppose the policy despite reading what they thought to be a strong argument became even more certain of their opinion.

Additional studies have shown that this effect depends on how satisfied people are with their own resistance. When people resist a strong message and believe that they have done so in a compelling way, they become more certain of their attitude and more likely to form a behavioral intention that is consistent with it. When people resist a persuasive message "by the skin of their teeth," however, and see their own counterarguments as weak, they become less certain of their initial attitude and more vulnerable to subsequent attack (Tormala et al., 2006). Even if a person's belief in his or her own thoughtful response is incorrect, it can influence the strength of the attitude in question (Barden & Petty, 2008).

A fourth key factor is that strong attitudes are highly accessible to awareness, which means that they are quickly and easily brought to mind (Fazio, 1990). To return to our earlier examples, computer jocks think often about their computer preferences, and political activists think often about their allegiances to political parties. It turns out that many attitudes—not just those we feel strongly about—easily pop to mind by the mere sight or even just the mention of an attitude object (Bargh et al., 1992). When this happens, the attitude can trigger behavior in a quick, spontaneous way or by leading us to think carefully about how we feel and how to respond (Fazio & Towles-Schwen, 1999).

To sum up, research on the link between attitudes and behavior leads to an important conclusion. Our evaluations of an object do not always determine our actions because other factors must be taken into account. However, when attitudes are strong and specific to a behavior, the effects are beyond dispute. Under these conditions, voting is influenced by political opinions, consumer purchasing is affected by product attitudes, and racial discrimination is rooted in feelings of prejudice. Attitudes are important determinants of behavior. The question now is How can attitudes be changed?

# Persuasion by Communication

On a day-to-day basis, we are all involved in the process of changing attitudes. On TV, on Facebook pages, in magazines, and on billboards, advertisers flood consumers with ad campaigns designed to sell cars, soft drinks, MP3 players, credit cards, sneakers, new movies, and travel destinations. Likewise, politicians make speeches, run commercials, pass out bumper stickers, and kiss babies to win votes. Attitude change is sought whenever parents socialize their children, scientists advance theories, religious groups seek converts, financial analysts recommend stocks, or trial lawyers argue cases to a jury. Some appeals work; others do not. Some are soft and subtle; others are hard and blatant. Some serve the public interest, whereas others serve commercial interests. The point is, there is nothing inherently evil or virtuous about changing attitudes, a process known as **persuasion**. We do it all the time.

If you wanted to change someone's attitude on an issue, you'd probably try to do it by making a persuasive *communication*. Appeals made in person and through the mass media rely on the spoken word, the written word, and the image that is worth a thousand words. What determines whether an appeal succeeds or fails? To understand why certain approaches are effective whereas others are not, social psychologists have for many years sought to understand *how* and *why* persuasive communications work. For that, we need a road map of the persuasion process.

 ## Two Routes to Persuasion

It's a familiar scene in American politics: Every 4 years, two or more presidential candidates launch extensive—and expensive—campaigns for office. In a way, if you've seen one election, you've seen them all. The names and dates may change, but over and over again, opposing candidates accuse each other of ducking the substantive issues and turning the election into a flag-waving or mud-slinging popularity contest.

True or not, these accusations show that politicians are keenly aware that they can win votes through two different methods. They can stick to policy, issues, and rational argumentation using the power of words or they can base their appeals on other grounds. Interestingly, these "other grounds" can well determine who wins an election. In *The Political Brain*, Drew Westen (2007) presents a wealth of research evidence indicating that in the marketplace of politics, emotions trump reason. Based on a combination of laboratory experiments and public opinion polls, other political psychologists agree (Brader, 2006; Neuman et al., 2007). Outside the realm of politics too, influence can be quick and automatic. In *Split-Second Persuasion*, Kevin Dutton (2010) described how Buddhist monks, magicians, advertisers, con men, hostage negotiators, and other "super-persuaders" use simplicity, empathy, an air of self-confidence and other disarming tactics to effect instant persuasion.

To account for the two alternative approaches to persuasion, Richard Petty and John Cacioppo (1986) proposed a dual-process model. This model assumes that we do not always process communications the same way. When people think critically about the contents of a message, they are said to take a **central route to persuasion** and are influenced by the strength and quality of the arguments. When people do not think critically about the contents of a message but focus instead on other cues, they take a **peripheral route to persuasion**. As we'll see, the route taken depends on whether one is willing and able to scrutinize the information contained in the message itself.

**persuasion**   The process by which attitudes are changed.

**central route to persuasion**   The process by which a person thinks carefully about a communication and is influenced by the strength of its arguments.

**peripheral route to persuasion** The process by which a person does not think carefully about a communication and is influenced instead by superficial cues.

In U.S. presidential politics, candidates try to win votes by addressing the issues, as in debates and speeches delivered from a podium (the central route) or through the use of banners, balloons, music, and other theatrics (the peripheral route).

Over the years, this model has provided an important framework for understanding the factors that elicit persuasion (Petty & Wegener, 1998).

**The Central Route** In the first systematic attempt to study persuasion, Carl Hovland and colleagues (1949, 1953) started the Yale Communication and Attitude Change Program. They proposed that for a persuasive message to have influence, the recipients of that message must learn its contents and be motivated to accept it. According to this view, people can be persuaded only by an argument they attend to, comprehend, and retain in memory for later use. Regardless of whether the message takes the form of a live personal appeal, a newspaper editorial, a Sunday sermon, a TV commercial, or a pop-up window on a website, these basic requirements remain the same.

A few years later, William McGuire (1969) reiterated the information-processing steps necessary for persuasion and like the Yale group before him distinguished between the learning, or *reception*, of a message, a necessary first step, and its later *acceptance*. In fact, McGuire (1968) used this distinction to explain the surprising finding that a recipient's self-esteem and intelligence are unrelated to persuasion. In McGuire's analysis, these characteristics have opposite effects on reception and acceptance. People who are smart or high in self-esteem are better able to learn a message, but are less likely to accept its call for a change in attitude. People who are less smart or low in self-esteem are more willing to accept the message, but they may have trouble learning its contents. Overall, then, neither group is generally more vulnerable to persuasion than the other—a prediction that is supported by a good deal of research (Rhodes & Wood, 1992).

Anthony Greenwald (1968) and others then argued that persuasion requires a third, intermediate step: **elaboration**. To illustrate, imagine you are offered a job and your prospective employer tries to convince you over lunch to accept. You listen closely, learn the terms of the offer, and understand what it means. But if it's a really important interview, your head will spin with questions as you weigh all the pros and cons and contemplate the implications: What would it cost to move? Is there potential for advancement? Am I better off staying where I am? When confronted with personally significant messages, we don't listen just for the sake of collecting information, we think about that information. When this happens, the message is effective to the extent that it leads us to focus on favorable rather than unfavorable thoughts.

**elaboration** The process of thinking about and scrutinizing the arguments contained in a persuasive communication.

These theories of attitude change all share the assumption that the recipients of persuasive appeals are attentive, active, critical, and thoughtful of every word spoken. This assumption is correct—some of the time. When it is and when people consider a message carefully, their reaction to it depends on the strength of its contents. In these instances, messages have greater impact when they are easily learned rather than difficult, when they are memorable rather than forgettable, and when they stimulate favorable rather than unfavorable elaboration. Ultimately, strong arguments are persuasive and weak arguments are not.

On the central route to persuasion, the process is eminently rational. It's important to note, however, that thinking carefully about a persuasive message does not guarantee that the process is objective or that it necessarily promotes truth seeking. At times, each of us prefers to hold a particular attitude and become biased in the way we process information (Petty & Wegener, 1998). Among college students who were politically conservative or liberal, the tendency to agree with a social welfare plan was influenced more—rapidly, strongly, and persistently—by whether it was said to have the support of Democrats or Republicans than by the logical merits of the policy itself (Cohen, 2003; Smith et al., 2012). Similarly, college students were less likely to be persuaded by a proposed tuition hike to fund campus improvements when the increase would take effect in 1 year, thus raising the personal stakes, than by a proposal to raise tuition in 8 years (Darke & Chaiken, 2005). To further complicate matters, people who want to hold the right attitudes may fear that they are biased or overly influenced by nonrelevant factors and then try to correct for that bias, sometimes with an ironic result: *overcorrection*. In one study, for example, audience members who were forewarned that people are prone to agree with speakers they like later exhibited more attitude change in response to a speaker who was clearly not likable (Petty et al., 1998).

**The Peripheral Route**   "The receptive ability of the masses is very limited, their understanding small; on the other hand, they have a great power of forgetting." The author of this statement was Adolf Hitler (1933, p. 77). Believing that human beings are incompetent processors of information, Hitler relied in his propaganda on the use of slogans, uniforms, marching bands, swastika-covered flags, a special salute, and other symbols. For Hitler, "meetings were not just occasions to make speeches; they were carefully planned theatrical productions in which settings, lighting, background music, and the timing of entrances were devised to maximize the emotional fervor of an audience" (Qualter, 1962, p. 112).

Do these ploys work? Can the masses be handily manipulated into persuasion? History shows that they can. Audiences are not always thoughtful. Sometimes people do not follow the central route to persuasion but instead take a shortcut through the peripheral route. Rather than try to learn about a message and think through the issues, they respond with little effort on the basis of superficial peripheral cues.

On the peripheral route to persuasion, people will often evaluate a communication by using simple-minded heuristics, or rules of thumb (Chaiken, 1987; Chen & Chaiken, 1999). If a communicator has a good reputation, speaks fluently, or writes well, we tend to assume that his or her message must be correct. And when a speaker has a reputation for being honest, people think less critically about the specific contents of his or her communication (Priester & Petty, 1995). Likewise, we assume that a message must be correct if it contains a long litany of arguments or statistics or an impressive list of supporting experts, if it's familiar, if it elicits cheers from an audience, or if the speaker seems to be arguing against his or her own interests. In some cases, people will change their attitudes simply because they know that an argument has majority support (Giner-Sorolla & Chaiken, 1997).

On the mindless peripheral route, people are also influenced by a host of factors that are not relevant to attitudes, such as cues from their own body movements. Increasingly, social psychologists are coming to appreciate the extent to which human thought is embodied—that the way we think and feel about things is influenced by the physical position, orientation, and movements of our bodies (Lakoff & Johnson, 1999; Niedenthal et al., 2005). A number of studies illustrate *attitude embodiment effects*. In one study, participants were coaxed into nodding their heads up and down (as if saying yes) or shaking them from side to side (as if saying no) while listening via headphones to an editorial, presumably to test whether the headphones could endure the physical activity. Those coaxed into nodding later agreed more with the arguments than those coaxed into shaking their heads from side to side (Wells & Petty, 1980). In other studies, participants viewed graphic symbols or word-like stimuli (*surtel, primet*) while using an exercise bar to either stretch their arms out (which mimics what we do to push something away) or flex their arms in (which we do to bring something closer). Participants later judged these stimuli to be more pleasant when they were associated with the flexing of the arm than when they were associated with the stretching-out motion (Cacioppo et al., 1993; Priester et al., 1996). Even our attitudes toward consumer products can be influenced by bodily sensations. In one study, for example, participants evaluated the appearance of vases, flowers, and other products placed at a distance as more appealing when they stood on a soft, comfortable carpet than on a hard tile floor (Meyers-Levy et al., 2010).

**Route Selection** Thanks to Petty and Cacioppo's (1986) two-track distinction between the central and peripheral routes, it is easy to understand why the persuasion process seems so logical on some occasions yet so illogical on others—why voters may select candidates according to issues or images, why juries may base their verdicts on evidence or a defendant's appearance, and why consumers may base their purchases on marketing reports or product images. The process that is engaged depends on whether the recipients of a persuasive message have the *ability* and the *motivation* to take the central route or whether they rely on peripheral cues instead.

To understand the conditions that lead people to process information on one route or the other, it's helpful to view persuasive communication as the outcome

**FIGURE 6.5**

**Two Routes to Persuasion**

Based on aspects of the source, message, and audience, recipients of a communication take either a central or peripheral route to persuasion. On the central route, people are influenced by strong arguments and evidence. On the peripheral route, persuasion is based more on heuristics and other superficial cues. This two-process model helps explain how persuasion can seem logical on some occasions and illogical on others.

© Cengage Learning

of three factors: a *source* (who), a *message* (says what and in what context), and an *audience* (to whom). Each of these factors steers a recipient's approach to persuasive communication. If a source speaks clearly, if the message is important, if there is a bright, captive, and involved audience that cares deeply about the issue and has time to absorb the information, then audience members will be willing and able to take the effortful central route. But if the source speaks at a rate too fast to comprehend, if the message is trivial or too complex to process, or if audience members are distracted, pressed for time, or uninterested, then the less strenuous peripheral route is taken.

● Figure 6.5 presents a road map of persuasive communication. In the next three sections, we will follow this map from the input factors (source, message, and audience) through the central or peripheral processing routes to reach the final destination: persuasion.

> In reacting to persuasive communications, people are influenced more by superficial images than by logical arguments. **F**ALSE.

## The Source

Golfer Tiger Woods is a living legend, one of the most gifted athletes of our time. Until recently, he was also paid more millions of dollars per year than just about anyone else—to endorse Nike, American Express, and other products. Woods was considered a highly effective spokesman until his marriage and reputation were destroyed in 2009 by various extramarital affairs. He has struggled in his golf game since that time and is no longer the top-ranked golfer in the world or the most highly sought spokesperson. What does the story of Tiger Woods tells us about source effects in persuasion? More specifically, what makes some communicators in general more effective than others? As we'll see, there are two key attributes: credibility and likeability.

**Credibility** Imagine you are waiting in line in a supermarket and you catch a glimpse of a swollen headline: "Doctors Discover Cure for AIDS!" As your eye wanders across the front page, you discover that you are reading a supermarket tabloid that features aliens from another planet. What would you think? Next, imagine that you are reading through scientific periodicals in a library and you come across a similar article, but this time it appears in the *New England Journal of Medicine*. Now what would you think?

Born in 1930, in Omaha Nebraska, Warren Buffett is considered the most successful investor of our time. He is also among the world's wealthiest people. Nicknamed the "Oracle of Omaha," Buffett is an expert in matters of investment. His actions in the stock market draw attention and influence other investors.

Chances are, you'd react with more excitement to the medical journal than to the tabloid, even though both sources report the same news item. In a study conducted during the Cold War era of the 1950s, American participants read a speech that advocated for the development of nuclear submarines. The speech elicited more agreement when it was attributed to an eminent American physicist than when the source was said to be the Soviet government–controlled newspaper (Hovland & Weiss, 1951). Likewise, when participants read a lecture favoring more lenient treatment of juvenile offenders, they changed their attitudes more when they thought the speaker was a judge than when they believed the speaker was a convicted drug dealer (Kelman & Hovland, 1953). Now, after decades of research, it is clear that high-credibility sources are generally more persuasive than low-credibility sources (Pornpitakpan, 2004).

Why are some sources more believable than others? Why were the medical journal, the physicist, and the judge more credible than the tabloid, government-controlled newspaper, and drug dealer? For communicators to be seen as credible, they must have two characteristics: competence and trustworthiness. *Competence* refers to a speaker's ability. People who are knowledgeable, smart, or well spoken or who have impressive credentials are persuasive by virtue of their expertise (Hass, 1981). Experts can have a disarming effect on us. We assume they know what they're talking about. So when they speak, we listen. And when they take a position, even one that is extreme, we often yield. Recent research has shown that people attend more closely to experts than to non-experts and scrutinize their arguments more carefully (Tobin & Raymundo, 2009). This tendency is especially true when experts state a position that we oppose and do not like (Clark et al., 2012).

For various reasons, each of us is confronted by plenty of experts in life whose opinions do not sway us. The reason is that expertise alone is not enough. To have credibility, sources must also be *trustworthy*—that is, they must be seen as willing to report what they know truthfully and without compromise. What determines whether we trust a communicator? To some extent, we make these judgments on the basis of stereotypes. In 2011, for example, the Gallup Organization asked 1,000 Americans to rate how honest people were in various occupational categories. As shown in Table 6.1, nurses topped the list as the most trusted occupational group. Car salesmen, members of congress, and lobbyists, were the least trusted.

In judging the credibility of a source, common sense arms us with a simple rule of caution: Beware of people who have something to gain from successful persuasion. If a speaker has been paid off, has an ax to grind, or is simply telling us what we want to hear, we suspect some degree of bias. This rule sheds light on a classic dilemma in advertising concerning the value of celebrity spokespersons: The more products a celebrity endorses, the less trustworthy he or she appears to consumers (Tripp et al., 1994). In the courtroom, the same rule of caution can be used to evaluate witnesses. In one study, research participants served as jurors in a mock trial in which a man claimed that his exposure to an industrial chemical at work had caused him to contract cancer. Testifying in support of this claim was a biochemist who was paid either $4,800 or $75 for his expert testimony. You might think that jurors would be more impressed by the scientist who commanded the higher fee. Yet while he was highly paid, the expert was perceived to be a "hired gun" and was as a result less believable and less persuasive (Cooper & Neuhaus, 2000).

The self-interest rule has other interesting implications. One is that people are impressed by others who take unpopular stands or argue against their own interests. When research participants read a political speech accusing a large corporation of polluting a local river, those who thought that the speechmaker was a pro-environment candidate addressing a staunch environmentalist group perceived him to be biased, whereas those who thought he was a pro-business candidate talking to company supporters assumed he was sincere (Eagly et al., 1978). Trust is also established by speakers who are not purposely trying to change our views. Thus, people are influenced more when they think that they are accidentally overhearing a communication than when they receive a sales pitch

## TABLE 6.1
### Who Do You Trust?

At the end of 2011, a Gallup poll was conducted to determine the level of honesty attributed to people from various occupational groups. Indicated below are the percentages of respondents who rated each group as "high" or "very high" in honesty.

| Occupation | Honest? |
| --- | --- |
| Nurses | 84% |
| Pharmacists | 73% |
| Medical doctors | 70% |
| High school teachers | 62% |
| Clergy | 52% |
| Police officers | 54% |
| Accountants | 43% |
| Journalists | 26% |
| Bankers | 25% |
| Real estate agents | 20% |
| Lawyers | 19% |
| Business executives | 18% |
| Stockbrokers | 12% |
| Members of congress | 7% |
| Car salespersons | 7% |

© Cengage Learning

clearly intended for their ears (Walster & Festinger, 1962). That's why advertisers sometimes use the "overheard communicator" trick, in which the source tells a buddy about a new product that really works. As if eavesdropping on a personal conversation, viewers assume that what one friend says to another can be trusted. The self-interest rule also has great relevance in law, which is why people are far more likely to believe a crime suspect's admissions of guilt than his or her denials (Levine et al., 2010).

**Likeability**   More than anything else, the celebrity power of Tiger Woods was based on his athletic dominance, his popularity, and his winning smile. Before the revelations that destroyed Woods' marriage and derailed his game, he was a likeable person. But does that quality enhance someone's impact as a communicator? Yes. In his classic bestseller, *How to Win Friends and Influence People*, Dale Carnegie (1936) said that being liked and being persuasive go hand in hand. The question is, what makes a communicator likable? As we'll see in Chapter 9, two factors that spark attraction are *similarity* and *physical attractiveness*.

A study by Diane Mackie and others (1990) illustrates the persuasive power of similarity. Students enrolled at the University of California, Santa Barbara read a strong or a weak speech that argued against continued use of the SATs in college admissions. Half the participants were led to believe that the speech was written by a fellow UCSB student; the other half thought the author was a student from the University of New Hampshire. Very few participants were persuaded by the weak arguments. In contrast, many of those who read the strong message did change their attitudes, but only when they believed it was given by a fellow UCSB student.

Just as source similarity can spark persuasion, dissimilarity can have the opposite inhibiting effect. In a study of people's taste in music, Clayton Hilmert and others (2006) introduced participants to a confederate who seemed to like the same or different kinds of music, such as rock, pop, country, or classical. Others did not meet a confederate. When later asked to rate a particular song, participants were positively influenced by the similar confederate's opinion and negatively influenced by the dissimilar confederate's opinion. In fact, although the effect is more potent when the points of similarity seem relevant to the attitude in question (Berscheid, 1966), the participants in this study were also more or less persuaded by a confederate whose similarities or differences were wholly unrelated to music—for example, when the confederate had similar or different interests in shopping, world politics, museums, trying new foods, or surfing the Internet.

When he was just out of high school, basketball star LeBron James (left) signed a multimillion dollar contract with Nike. NASCAR racer Danica Patrick, the only woman ever to win in the IndyCar series, has lucrative contracts with GoDaddy.com, Coca Cola, Chevrolet, and other companies. Can celebrities sell products? Targeting the peripheral route to persuasion, the advertising industry seems to think so.

The effect of source similarity on persuasion has obvious implications for those who wish to exert influence. We're all similar to one another in some respects. We might agree in politics, share a common friend, have similar tastes in food, or enjoy spending summers on the same beach. If aware of the social benefits of similarity and the social costs of dissimilarity, the astute communicator can use common bonds to enhance his or her impact on an audience.

Advertising practices presuppose that beauty is also persuasive. After all, billboards, magazine ads, popup ads, and TV commercials routinely feature young and glamorous "supermodels" who are tall and slender (for women) or muscular (for men) and who have hard bodies, glowing complexions, and radiant smiles. Sure, these models can turn heads, you may think, but can they change minds? In a study that addressed this question, Shelly Chaiken (1979) had male and female college students approach others on campus. They introduced themselves as members of an organization that wanted the university to stop serving meat during breakfast and lunch. In each case, these student assistants gave reasons for the position and then asked respondents to sign a petition. The result: Attractive sources were able to get 41% of respondents to sign the petition, whereas those who were less attractive succeeded only 32% of the time. Additional research has shown that attractive male and female salespersons elicit more positive attitudes and purchasing intentions from customers then less attractive salespersons, even when they are up front about their desire to make a sale (Reinhard et al., 2006).

Image courtesy of The Advertising Archives

Advertisers are so convinced that beauty sells products that they pay millions of dollars for supermodels to appear in their ads. Shown here, supermodel Kate Moss appears in an ad for Italian fashion house Versace.

**When What You Say Is More Important Than Who You Are** To this point, it must seem as if the source of a persuasive communication is more important than the communication itself. Is this true? Certainly there are enough real-life examples—as when books used to skyrocket to the top of the best-seller list because Oprah Winfrey recommended them. The advertising industry has long debated the value of high-priced celebrity endorsements. David Ogilvy (1985), who was called "the king of advertising," used to say that celebrities are not effective because viewers know they've been bought and paid for. Ogilvy was not alone in his skepticism. Still, many advertisers scramble furiously to sign up famous entertainers and athletes. From Tiger Woods to Derek Jeter, Tina Fey, LeBron James, Peyton Manning, Taylor Swift, Scarlett Johansson, Jerry Seinfeld, Bono, Danica Patrick, and Beyonce, TV commercials regularly feature a parade of stars. The bigger the star, they say, the more valuable the testimonial.

Compared with the contents of a message, does the source really make the big difference that advertisers pay for? Are we so impressed by the expert, so enamored of the physical talent, and so drawn to the charming face that we embrace whatever they have to say? And are we so scornful of ordinary or unattractive people that their presentations fall on deaf ears? In light of what is known about the central and peripheral routes to persuasion, the answer to these questions is "it depends."

First, a recipient's level of involvement plays an important role. When a message has personal relevance to your life, you pay attention to the source and think critically about the message, the arguments, and the implications. When a message does not have personal relevance, however, you may take the source at face value and spend little time scrutinizing the information. In a classic study, Richard Petty and others (1981) had students listen to a speaker who proposed that all seniors should be required to take comprehensive exams in order to graduate. Three aspects of the communication situation were varied. First, participants were led to believe that the speaker was either an education professor at Princeton University or a high school student. Second, participants heard either well-reasoned arguments and hard evidence or a weak message based only on anecdotes and personal opinion. Third, participants were told either that the proposed exams might be used the following year (Uh oh, that means me!) or that they would not take effect for another 10 years (Who cares, I'll be long gone by then!).

As predicted, personal involvement determined the relative impact of the expertise of the source and the quality of speech. Among participants who would not be affected by the proposed change, attitudes were based largely on the speaker's credibility: The professor was persuasive; the high school student was not. Among participants who thought that the proposed change would affect them directly, attitudes were based on the quality of the speaker's proposal. Strong arguments were persuasive; weak arguments were not. As depicted in ● Figure 6.6, people followed the source rather than the message under low levels of involvement, illustrating the peripheral route to persuasion. But message factors did outweigh source characteristics under high levels of involvement, when participants cared enough to take the central route to persuasion. Likewise, research has shown that the tilt toward likable and attractive communicators is reduced when recipients take the central route (Chaiken, 1980).

There is a second limit to source effects. It is often said that time heals all wounds. Well, time may also heal the effects of a bad reputation. Hovland and Weiss (1951) varied communicator credibility (for example, the physicist versus the Soviet-controlled newspaper) and found that the change had a large and immediate effect on persuasion. But when they measured attitudes again 4 weeks later, the effect had vanished. Over time, the attitude change produced by the high-credibility source had decreased and the change caused by the low-credibility source had increased. This finding of a delayed persuasive impact of a low-credibility communicator is called the **sleeper effect**.

To explain this unforeseen result, the Hovland research group proposed the *discounting cue hypothesis.* According to this hypothesis, people immediately discount the arguments made by noncredible communicators, but over time, they dissociate what was said from who said it. In other words, we tend to remember the message but forget the source (Pratkanis et al., 1988). To examine the role of memory in this process, Kelman and Hovland (1953) reminded a group of participants of the source's identity before reassessing their attitudes. If the sleeper effect was caused by forgetting, they reasoned, then it could be

● **FIGURE 6.6**

**Source Versus Message: The Role of Audience Involvement**

People who were high or low in their personal involvement heard a strong or weak message from an expert or non-expert. For high-involvement participants (left), persuasion was based on the strength of arguments, not on source expertise. For low-involvement participants (right), persuasion was based more on the source than on the arguments. Source characteristics have more impact on those who don't care enough to take the central route.

Reprinted by permission from Richard E. Petty.

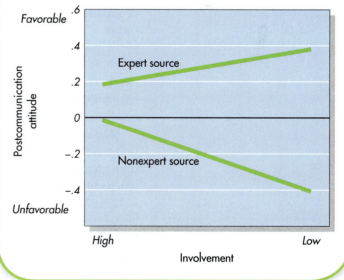

**sleeper effect**   A delayed increase in the persuasive impact of a noncredible source.

● **FIGURE 6.7**

**The Sleeper Effect**

In Experiment 1, participants changed their immediate attitudes more in response to a message from a high-credibility source than from a low-credibility source. When attitudes were measured again after 3 weeks, the high-credibility source had lost impact and the low-credibility source had gained impact—the sleeper effect. In Experiment 2, the sleeper effect disappeared when participants were reminded of the source.

Kelman & Hovland, 1953. © Cengage Learning

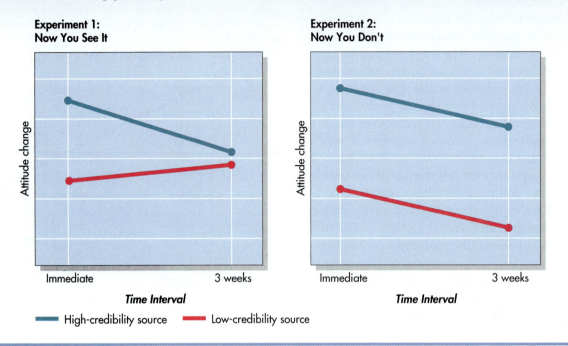

*"The truth is always the strongest argument."*

—Sophocles

eliminated through reinstatement of the link between the source and the message. As shown in ● Figure 6.7, they were right. When attitudes were measured after 3 weeks, participants who were not reminded of the source showed the usual sleeper effect. Yet those who did receive a source reminder did not. For these latter participants, the effects of high and low credibility endured. Recent studies by cognitive psychologists have confirmed that over time, people "forget" the connection between information and its source (Underwood & Pezdek, 1998).

The sleeper effect generated a good deal of controversy. There was never a doubt that credible communicators lose some impact over time. But researchers had a harder time finding evidence for delayed persuasion by noncredible sources. Exasperated at one point by their own failures to obtain this result, Paulette Gillig and Anthony Greenwald (1974) wondered, "Is it time to lay the sleeper effect to rest?" As it turned out, the answer was no. More recent research showed that the sleeper effect is reliable provided that participants do not learn who the source is until *after* they have received the original message (Greenwald et al., 1986; Kumkale & Albarracín, 2004).

To appreciate the importance of timing, imagine that you're surfing the Internet and you come across what appears to be a review of a new CD. Before you begin reading, however, you notice in the fine print that this so-called review is really an advertisement. Aware that you can't always trust what you read, you skim the ad and reject it. Now imagine the same situation, except that you read the entire ad before realizing what it is. Again you reject it. But notice the difference. This time, you have read the message with an open mind. You may still reject it but after a few weeks, the information will have sunk in to influence your evaluation of the music. This scenario illustrates the sleeper effect.

## The Message

On the peripheral route to persuasion, audiences are influenced heavily, maybe too heavily, by various source characteristics. But when people care about an issue, the strength of a message determines its impact. On the central route to persuasion, what matters most is whether a scientist's theory is supported by the data or whether a company has a sound product. Keep in mind, however, that the target of a persuasive appeal comes to know a message only through the medium of communication—*what* a person has to say and *how* that person says it.

**Informational Strategies**    Communicators often struggle with how to structure and present an argument to maximize its impact. Should a message be long and crammed with facts or short and to the point? Is it better to present a highly partisan, one-sided message or to take a more balanced, two-sided approach? How should arguments be ordered—from strongest to weakest or the other way around? These are the kinds of questions often studied by persuasion researchers—including those interested in marketing, advertising, and consumer behavior (Loken, 2006).

Often the most effective strategy to use will depend on whether members of the audience process the message on the central or the peripheral route. Consider the length of a communication. When people process a message lazily, with their eyes and ears half-closed, they often fall back on a simple heuristic: The longer a message, the more valid it must be. In this case, a large number of words gives the superficial appearance of factual support regardless of the quality of the arguments (Petty & Cacioppo, 1984; Wood et al., 1985). Thus, as David Ogilvy (1985) concluded from his years of advertising experience, "The more facts you tell, the more you sell" (p. 88).

When people process a communication carefully, however, length is a two-edged sword. If a message is long because it contains lots of supporting information, then longer does mean better. The more supportive arguments you can offer or the more sources you can find to speak on your behalf, the more persuasive your appeal will be (Harkins & Petty, 1981). But if the added arguments are weak or if the new sources are redundant, then an alert audience will not be fooled by length alone. When adding to the length of a message dilutes its quality, an appeal might well *lose* impact (Friedrich et al., 1996; Harkins & Petty, 1987).

When two opposing sides try to persuade the same audience, order of presentation becomes a relevant factor as well. During the summer of 2012, before the November presidential election, the Republicans held their national convention a few days before the incumbent Democrats held theirs. These events were watched on television by millions of voters. Do you think the order in which they were scheduled gave one party an advantage? If you believe that information that is presented first has more impact, you'd predict *a primacy effect* (advantage to the Republicans). If you believe that the information presented last has the edge, you'd predict a *recency effect* (advantage to the Democrats).

There are good reasons for both predictions. On the one hand, first impressions are important. On the other hand, memory fades over time, and people often recall only the last argument they hear before making a decision. In light of these contrasting

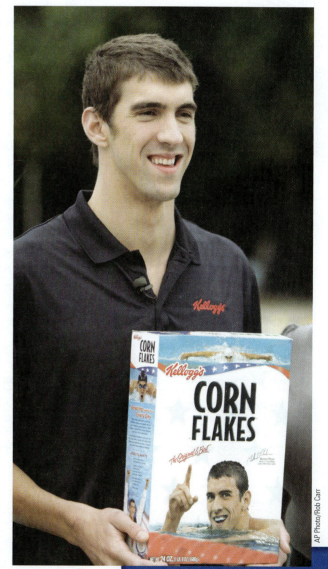

In the 2012 summer Olympics in London, Michael Phelps won 4 gold and 2 silver medals, giving him a total of 16 gold medals and 22 overall after three successive Olympics games. Being the most decorated Olympian ever, Phelps has earned a number of commercial endorsements.

AP Photo/Rob Carr

"It is a superb vision of America, all right, but I can't remember which candidate projected it."

**Research on the sleeper effect shows that people often remember the message but forget the source.**

predictions, Norman Miller and Donald Campbell (1959) searched for the "missing link" that would determine the relative effects of primacy and recency. They discovered that the missing link is *time*. In a study of jury simulations, they had people (1) read a summary of the plaintiff's case; (2) read a summary of the defendant's case; and (3) make a decision. The researchers varied how much time separated the two messages and then how much time elapsed between the second message and the decisions. When participants read the second message right after the first and then waited a whole week before reporting their opinion, a primacy effect prevailed and the side that came first was favored. Both messages faded equally from memory, so only the greater impact of first impressions was left. Yet when participants made a decision immediately after the second message but a full week after the first, there was a recency effect. The second argument was fresher in memory, thus favoring the side that went last. Using these results as a guideline, let's return to our original question: What is the impact on Election Day of how the national conventions are scheduled? Think for a moment about the placement and timing of these events. The answer appears in Table 6.2.

**Message Discrepancy** Persuasion is a process of changing attitudes. This objective is not easy to achieve. As a general rule, people are motivated to defend their opinions and attitudes, which they do, in part, through selective exposure to information that supports their views (Hart et al., 2009). Given an opportunity to advocate for attitude change, communicators confront what is perhaps the most critical strategic question: How extreme a position should they take? How *discrepant* should a message be from the audience's existing position in order to have the greatest impact? Common sense suggests two opposite answers. One approach is to take an extreme position in the hope that the more change you advocate, the more you will get. Another approach is to exercise caution and not push for too much change so that the audience will not reject the message outright. Which approach seems more effective? Imagine trying to convert your politically conservative friends into liberals or the other way around. Would you stake out a radical position in order to move them toward the center or would you preach moderation so as not to be cast aside?

Research shows that communicators should adopt the second, more cautious approach. To be sure, some discrepancy is needed to produce a change in attitude. But the relationship to persuasion can be pictured as an upside-down U with the most change being produced at moderate amounts of discrepancy (Bochner & Insko, 1966). A study by Kari Edwards and Edward Smith (1996) helps explain why taking a more extreme position is counterproductive. These investigators first measured people's attitudes on a number of hot social issues—for example, whether lesbian and gay couples should adopt children, whether employers should give preference in hiring to minorities, and whether the death penalty should be abolished. Several

---

**TABLE 6.2**

**Effects of Presentation Order and Timing on Persuasion**

A study by Miller and Campbell (1959) demonstrated the effect of presentation order and the timing of opposing arguments on persuasion. As applied to our example, the Democratic and Republican conventions resemble the fourth row of this table. From these results, it seems that the scheduling of such events is fair, promoting neither primacy nor recency.

| | | Conditions | | | | Results |
|---|---|---|---|---|---|---|
| 1. Message 1 | Message 2 | One week | Decision | | | **Primacy** |
| 2. Message 1 | One week | Message 2 | Decision | | | **Recency** |
| 3. Message 1 | Message 2 | Decision | | | | **None** |
| 4. Message 1 | One week | Message 2 | One week | Decision | | **None** |

© Cengage Learning

weeks later, they asked the same people to read, think about, and rate arguments that were either consistent or inconsistent with their own prior attitudes. The result: When given arguments to read that preached attitudes that were discrepant from their own, the participants spent more time scrutinizing the material and judged the arguments to be weak. Clearly, people tend to refute and reject persuasive messages they don't agree with. In fact, the more personally important an issue is to us, the more stubborn and resistant to change we become (Zuwerink & Devine, 1996).

**Fear Appeals**   Many trial lawyers say that to win cases they have to appeal to jurors through the heart rather than through the mind. The evidence is important, they admit, but what matters most is whether the jury reacts to their client with anger, disgust, sympathy, or sadness. Of course, very few messages are entirely based on rational argument or on emotion.

Fear is a particularly primitive and powerful emotion, serving as an early warning system that signals danger. Neuroscience research shows that fear is aroused instantly in response to pain, stimulation from noxious substances, or threat, enabling us to respond quickly without having to stop to think about it (LeDoux, 1996). The use of fear-based appeals to change attitudes is common. Certain religious cults have used scare tactics to indoctrinate new members. So do public health organizations that graphically portray the damage done to those who smoke cigarettes, use illicit drugs, eat too much junk food, and engage in unprotected sex.

Negative campaigning in American politics is prevalent, though the effects on voters are not clear (Lau & Rovner, 2009). From the large number of attack ads that flooded the 2012 presidential primaries and election, it would certainly seem that candidates, their consultants, and Super PACS strongly believe in the power of attacking their opponents by arousing fear about the consequences of voting for them. Presidential campaign ads have never been more negative. Yet the most hard-hitting and controversial ever was a TV commercial that aired just once, on September 7, 1964. In an ad to reelect Democratic president Lyndon Johnson, who was running against Republican Barry Goldwater, a young girl pictured in a field counted to 10 as she picked the petals off a daisy. As she reached 9, an adult voice broke in to count down from 10 to 0, followed by a blinding nuclear explosion and this message: "Vote for President Johnson on November 3. The stakes are too high for you to stay home."

The effects of fear arousal in politics are evident. Guided by Terror Management Theory (Greenberg et al., 1997; Pyszczynski et al., 2004; see Chapter 3) and the prediction that a deeply rooted fear of death motivates people to rally around their leaders as a way to ward off anxiety, Mark Landau and others (2004) found that college students expressed more support for former president George W. Bush and his policies when they were reminded of their own mortality or subliminally exposed to images of 9/11 than when they were not. This result is not limited to the laboratory. Analyzing patterns of government-issued terror warnings and Gallup polls, Robb Willer (2004) found that increased terror alerts were predictably followed by increases in presidential approval ratings.

Is fear similarly effective for commercial purposes? What about using fear to promote health and safety? If you're interested in public service advertising, visit the website of the Ad Council, the organization that created Smokey the Bear ("Only you can prevent forest fires") and the crash test dummies ("Don't be a dummy—buckle up"). In recent years,

© Courtesy of The Centers for Disease Control and Prevention

Public health organizations often use fear, or scare tactics, to change health-related attitudes and behavior.

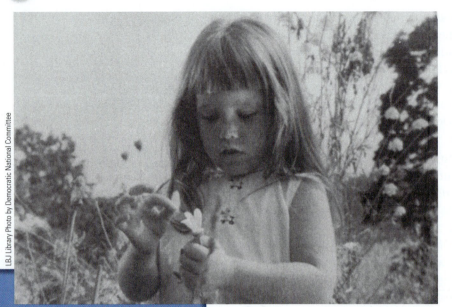

In a highly controversial appeal to fear, a TV commercial that aired only once during the 1964 presidential campaign, pictured this young girl in an open field, a blinding nuclear explosion, and the message: "Vote for President Johnson on November 3. The stakes are too high for you to stay home."

the Ad Council has run campaigns on a range of issues, including the use of steroids, flu prevention, AIDS prevention, cyber bullying, and the online sexploitation of youth. To get people to change behavior in these domains, is it better to arouse a little nervousness or a full-blown anxiety attack? To answer this question, social psychologists over the years have compared communications that vary in the levels of fear they arouse. In the first such study, Irving Janis and Seymour Feshbach (1953) found that high levels of fear did not generate increased agreement with a persuasive communication. Since then, however, research has shown that appeals that arouse high levels of fear can be highly effective (de Hoog et al., 2007).

Fear arousal increases the incentive to change for those who do not actively resist it, but its ultimate impact depends on the strength of the arguments and on whether the message also contains clear and reassuring advice on how to cope with the threatened danger (Keller, 1999; Leventhal, 1970; Rogers, 1983). This last point is important. Without specific instructions on how to cope, people feel helpless, and they panic and tune out the message. In one study, for example, participants with a chronic fear of cancer were less likely than others to detect the logical errors in a message that called for regular cancer checkups (Jepson & Chaiken, 1990). When clear instructions are included, however, high dosages of fear can be effective. In the past, research had shown that antismoking films elicit more negative attitudes toward cigarettes when they show gory lung-cancer operations than when they show charts filled with dry statistics (Leventhal et al., 1967) and that films about driving safety are more effective when they show bloody accident victims than when they show plastic crash test dummies (Rogers & Mewborn, 1976). In a meta-analysis of 105 studies, however, Natascha de Hoog and others (2007) found that communications that arouse fear do not have to be gruesome to be effective. The more personally vulnerable people feel about a threatened outcome, the more attentive they are to the message and the more likely they are to follow its recommendations.

**Positive Emotions** It's interesting that just as fear helps induce a change in attitude, so does positive emotion. In one study, people were more likely to agree with a series of controversial arguments when they snacked on peanuts and soda than when they did not eat (Janis et al., 1965). In another study, participants liked a television commercial more when it was embedded within a program that was upbeat rather than sad (Mathur & Chattopadhyay, 1991). Research shows that people are "soft touches" when they're in a good mood. Depending on the situation, food, drinks, a soft reclining chair, warm and tender memories, a success experience, breathtaking scenery, laughter, and good music can lull us into a positive emotional state and ripe for persuasion (Schwarz et al., 1991).

According to Alice Isen (1984), people see the world through rose-colored glasses when they are in a good mood. Filled with high spirits, we become more sociable, more generous, and generally more positive in our outlook. We also make decisions more quickly and with relatively little thought. The result: Positive feelings activate the peripheral route to persuasion, facilitating change and allowing superficial cues to take on added importance (Petty et al., 1993; Worth & Mackie, 1987).

What is it about feeling good that leads us to take shortcuts to persuasion rather than the more effortful central route? There are three possible explanations. One is that a positive emotional state is cognitively distracting, causing the mind to wander and impairing our ability to think critically about the persuasive arguments (Mackie & Worth, 1989; Mackie et al., 1992). A second explanation is that when people are in a good mood, they assume that all is well, let down their guard, and become somewhat lazy processors of information (Schwarz, 1990). A third explanation is that when people are happy, they become motivated to savor the moment and maintain their happy mood rather than spoiling it by thinking critically about new information (Wegener & Petty, 1994).

This last notion raises an interesting question: What if happy people are presented with a positive and uplifting persuasive message? Would they still appear cognitively distracted, or lazy, or would they pay close attention in order to prolong the rosy glow? To find out, Duane Wegener and others (1995) showed some college students a funny segment from *The Late Show with David Letterman*. Others, less fortunate, watched a somber scene from an HBO movie called *You Don't Have to Die*. The students were then asked to read and evaluate either an uplifting article they agreed with about a new plan to cut tuition or a distressing article they disagreed with about a new plan to raise tuition. In half the cases, the article they read contained strong arguments; in the other cases, the arguments were weak. Did the students read the material carefully enough to distinguish between the strong and weak arguments? Those in the somber condition clearly did. Among those in the happy condition, however, the response depended on whether they expected the message to be one they wanted to hear. When the happy students read about a tuition increase, they tuned out and were equally persuaded by the strong and weak arguments. When they read about the proposal to cut tuition, however, they were persuaded more when the arguments were strong than when they were weak. Because they were in a good mood and were receiving an agreeable message that would not spoil it, these happy students took the effortful central route to persuasion.

**Subliminal Messages**  In 1957, Vance Packard published *The Hidden Persuaders*, an exposé of Madison Avenue. As the book climbed the best-seller list, it awakened in the public a fear of being manipulated by forces they could not see or hear. What had Packard uncovered? In the 1950s, amid growing fears of communism and the birth of rock 'n' roll, a number of advertisers were said to have used *subliminal advertising*, the presentation of commercial messages outside of conscious awareness. It all started in a drive-in movie theater in New Jersey, where the words "Drink Coke" and "Eat popcorn" were secretly flashed on the screen during intermissions for a third of a millisecond. Although the audience never noticed the message, Coke sales were said to have increased 18% and popcorn sales 58% over a 6-week period (Brean, 1958).

This incident was followed by several others. A Seattle radio station presented subaudible anti-TV messages during its programs ("TV is a bore"), and department stores played music tapes over public address systems that contained subaudible warnings about theft ("If you steal, you'll get caught"). Later, in books entitled *Subliminal Seduction* (1973) and *The Age of Manipulation* (1989), William Bryan Key charged that advertisers routinely sneak faint sexual images in visual ads to heighten the appeal of their products. Several years ago, concerns were also raised about subliminal messages in rock music. In one case, the families of two boys who committed suicide blamed the British rock group Judas Priest for subliminal lyrics ("Do it") that promoted Satanism and suicide (*National Law Journal*, 1990). Although the families lost their case, it's clear that many people believe in the power of hidden persuaders.

At the time the story about the New Jersey theater broke, research on the topic was so sketchy and the public so outraged by the sinister implications that the matter was

Suggesting that a fear of death leads people to rally around their leaders, public opinion polls have shown that as terror threat levels increase, so do presidential approval ratings.

## PEOPLE HAVE BEEN TRYING TO FIND THE BREASTS IN THESE ICE CUBES SINCE 1957.

The advertising industry is sometimes charged with sneaking seductive little pictures into ads.

Supposedly, these pictures can get you to buy a product without your even seeing them.

Consider the photograph above. According to some people, there's a pair of female breasts hidden in the patterns of light refracted by the ice cubes.

Well, if you really searched you probably *could* see the breasts. For that matter, you could also see Millard Fillmore, a stuffed pork chop and a 1946 Dodge.

The point is that so-called "subliminal advertising" simply doesn't exist. Overactive imaginations, however, most certainly do.

So if anyone claims to see breasts in that drink up there, they aren't in the ice cubes.

They're in the eye of the beholder.

**ADVERTISING**
ANOTHER WORD FOR FREEDOM OF CHOICE.
American Association of Advertising Agencies

For years, advertisers have defended against the charge that they embed suggestive and sexual images in print ads. This piece by the American Association of Advertising Agencies defends against this claim.

quickly dropped. But soon there was renewed interest in subliminal influences and new research developments. In one recent field study, for example, researchers played traditional German or French music on alternating days for 2 weeks at a supermarket display of wines. Keeping track of sales, the researchers found that of the total number of wines bought, 83% were German on German-music days and 65% were French on French-music days. Yet when asked the reasons for their choices, customers did not cite the music as a factor, suggesting that they were not aware of the effect it had on them (North et al., 1999).

Current uses of subliminal influence are varied. In what is now a multimillion-dollar industry, companies today sell self-help CDs, DVDs, and MP3 downloads that play New Age music or nature images and sounds—and also contain fleeting messages or "affirmations" that promise to help you relax, lose weight, make friends, raise self-esteem, make money, improve athletic performance, and even improve your sex life. Can subliminal messages reflexively trigger behavior without our awareness? In 1982, Timothy Moore reviewed the existing research and concluded that "what you see is what you get"—nothing, "complete scams." Moore was right. The original story about the Coke-and-popcorn messages at the New Jersey theater was later exposed as a publicity stunt and hoax (Pratkanis, 1992). To further complicate matters, controlled experiments using subliminal self-help CDs that promise to raise self-esteem, improve memory, or lose weight show that these products offer no therapeutic benefits (Greenwald et al., 1991; Merikle & Skanes, 1992).

If there is no solid evidence of subliminal influence, why, you may wonder, does research demonstrate perception without awareness in studies of priming (described elsewhere in this book) but not in studies of subliminal persuasion? If you think about it, the two sets of claims are different. In the laboratory, subliminal exposures have a short-term effect on simple judgments and actions. But in claims of subliminal persuasion, the exposure is presumed to have long-term effects on eating, drinking, consumer purchases, voter sentiment, or even the most profound of violent acts, suicide. Psychologists agree that people can process information at an unconscious level, but they're quick to caution that this processing is "analytically limited" (Greenwald, 1992).

Perhaps people *perceive* subliminal cues but are not *persuaded* into action unless they are motivated to do so. To test this hypothesis, Erin Strahan and others (2002) brought thirsty college students into the laboratory for a marketing study and provided drinking water to some but not to others. Then, as part of a test administered by computer, they subliminally exposed these students to neutral words (*pirate*, *won*) or to thirst-related words (*thirst*, *dry*). Did the subliminal "thirsty" message later lead the students, like automatons, to drink more in a taste test of Kool-Aid beverages? Yes and no. ● Figure 6.8 shows that the subliminal thirst primes had little impact on students whose thirst had just been quenched, but they quite clearly increased consumption among those who were thirsty and had been deprived of water. For a subliminal message to influence behavior, it has to strike "while the iron is hot."

Other researchers have since extended this interesting effect in important ways. In one study, participants who were subliminally presented with the name of a specific soft drink, Lipton Ice, were later more likely to report that they would select that particular brand over others—provided they were thirsty (Karremans et al., 2006). In a second study, participants were subliminally presented with a logo for one brand of dextrose (a sugar pill) or another, after which they worked on a cognitive task that required intense concentration. The results showed that when given an opportunity to enhance their concentration, participants were more likely to select and consume the subliminally advertised brand than the other brand—provided they were mentally tired and in need of a boost (Bermeitinger et al., 2009).

> **People are most easily persuaded by commercial messages that are presented without their awareness. FALSE.**

## The Audience

Although source and message factors are important, the astute communicator must also take his or her audience into account. Presentation strategies that succeed with some people fail with others. Audiences on the central route to persuasion, for example, bear little resemblance to those found strolling along the peripheral route. In this section, we'll see that the impact of a message is influenced by two additional factors: the recipient's personality and his or her expectations.

Right from the start, social psychologists tried to identify types of people who were more or less vulnerable to persuasion. But it turned out that very few individuals are *consistently* easy or difficult to persuade. Based on this insight, the search for individual and group differences is now guided by an "interactionist" perspective. Assuming that each of us can be persuaded more in some settings than in others, researchers look for an appropriate match between characteristics of the message and the audience. So, what kinds of messages turn *you* on?

**The Need for Cognition**   Earlier, we saw that people tend to process information more carefully when they are highly involved. Involvement can be determined by the importance and self-relevance of a message. According to Cacioppo and Petty (1982), however, there are also individual differences in the extent to which people become involved and take the central route to persuasion. Specifically, they have found that individuals differ in the extent to which they enjoy and participate in effortful cognitive activities, or, as they call it, the **need for cognition (NC)**. People who are high rather than low in their need for cognition like to work on hard problems, search for clues, make fine distinctions, and analyze situations. These differences can be identified by the items contained in the Need for Cognition Scale, some of which appear in Table 6.3.

The need for cognition has interesting implications for changing attitudes. If people are prone to approach or avoid effortful cognitive activities, then a communicator could prepare messages unique to a particular audience. In theory, the high-NC audience should receive information-oriented appeals and the low-NC audience should be treated to appeals that rely on the use of peripheral cues. The theory is fine, but does it work? Can a message be customized to fit the information-processing style of its recipients?

In a test of this hypothesis, participants read an editorial that consisted of either a strong or a weak set of arguments. As predicted, the higher their NC scores were, the

● **FIGURE 6.8**
**Subliminal Influence**

Thirsty and nonthirsty research participants were subliminally exposed to neutral or thirst-related words. Afterward they participated in a beverage taste test in which the amount they drank was measured. You can see that the subliminal thirst cues had little impact on nonthirsty participants but that they did increase consumption among those who were thirsty. Apparently, subliminal cues can influence our behavior when we are otherwise predisposed.

Strahan et al., 2002. © Cengage Learning

**need for cognition (NC)**  A personality variable that distinguishes people on the basis of how much they enjoy effortful cognitive activities.

## TABLE 6.3
### Need for Cognition Scale: Sample Items

**Are you high or low in the need for cognition? These statements are taken from the NC Scale. If you agree with items 1, 3, and 5 and disagree with items 2, 4, and 6, you would probably be regarded as high in NC.**

1. I really enjoy a task that involves coming up with new solutions to problems.

2. Thinking is not my idea of fun.

3. The notion of thinking abstractly is appealing to me.

4. I like tasks that require little thought once I've learned them.

5. I usually end up deliberating about issues even when they do not affect me personally.

6. It's enough for me that something gets the job done; I don't care how or why it works.

From Cacioppo, J. T., and Petty, R. E., "The need for cognition," *Journal of Personality and Social Psychology* vol 42 (pp. 116–131). Copyright © 1982 by the American Psychological Association. Reprinted by permission.

more the participants thought about the material, the better they later recalled it, and the more persuaded they were by the strength of its arguments (Cacioppo et al., 1983). In contrast, people who are low in the need for cognition are persuaded by cues found along the peripheral route, such as a speaker's reputation and physical appearance, the overt reactions of others in the audience, and a positive mood state (Cacioppo et al., 1996). At times, they are mindlessly influenced by a reputable source even when his or her arguments are weak (Kaufman et al., 1999).

**Self-Monitoring** Just as people high in the need for cognition crave information, other personality traits are associated with an attraction to other kinds of messages. Consider the trait of *self-monitoring*. As described in Chapter 3, high self-monitors regulate their behavior from one situation to another out of concern for public self-presentation. Low self-monitors are less image conscious and behave instead according to their own beliefs, values, and preferences. In the context of persuasion, high self-monitors may be particularly responsive to messages that promise desirable social images. Whether the product is beer, soda, blue jeans, or cars, this technique is common in advertising, where often the image is the message.

To test the self-monitoring hypothesis, Mark Snyder and Kenneth DeBono (1985) showed image- or information-oriented print ads to high and low self-monitors. In an ad for Irish Mocha Mint coffee, for example, a man and woman were depicted as relaxing in a candlelit room over a steamy cup of coffee. The image-oriented version promised to "Make a chilly night become a cozy evening," while the informational version offered "a delicious blend of three great flavors—coffee, chocolate, and mint." As predicted, high self-monitors were willing to pay more for products after reading imagery ads, whereas low self-monitors were influenced more by information-oriented appeals. Smidt and DeBono (2011) found a similar result for energy drinks. They found that high self-monitors rated the drinks more favorably when they had an image-oriented name; low self-monitors preferred the drinks more when they had a self-descriptive name. Imagery can even influence the way that high self-monitors evaluate a product, independent of its quality. DeBono and others (2003) presented people with one of two perfume samples packaged in more or less attractive bottles. Whereas low self-monitors preferred the more pleasant-scented fragrance, high self-monitors preferred whatever scent came from the more attractive bottles.

**Regulatory Fit** Setting aside your political views, do you find yourself drawn to some *types* of speeches, arguments, editorials, and television commercials more than others? Joseph Cesario and others (2004) proposed that people are more likely to be influenced by messages that fit their frame of mind and "feel right." In particular, they noted that in an effort to regulate their own emotion state, some individuals are promotion-oriented (drawn to the pursuit of success, achievement, and their ideals), whereas others are more prevention-oriented (protective of what they have, fearful of failure, and vigilant about avoiding loss). Do these differing outlooks on life make people more responsive to some types of persuasive messages than others? To find out, these researchers presented two versions of an article advocating for a new after-school children's program. They found that promotion-motivated participants were more persuaded by the article when the arguments in it were framed in promotional terms ("because it will *advance* children's education and *support* more children to *succeed*"), while prevention-motivated participants were persuaded more when the very same arguments were framed in more defensive terms ("because it will *secure* children's education and *prevent* more children from *failing*").

In a follow-up study, Cesario and Higgins (2008) found that audience members are also influenced when a speaker's nonverbal style fits their motivational orientations. Watching a high school teacher deliver the same communication concerning a new after-school program, promotion-motivated participants were more receptive when the speaker exhibited an "eager" delivery style (fast, animated, and forward leaning, with hand gestures projecting outward), whereas prevention-oriented participants were more receptive when he displayed a cautious style (slow, precise, and backward leaning, with hand gestures pushing in).

There are plenty of other ways that you may be more comfortable with some types of messages than others. We saw earlier that some of us are high in the need for cognition, enjoying effortful forms of reasoning and problem solving. Some of us are also high in the need for affect, seeking out and enjoying feelings of strong emotion. In matters of persuasion, these traits lead people to be more receptive to messages that are presented in primarily cognitive or emotional terms (Haddock et al., 2008).

**Forewarning and Resistance**  When our attitudes or values come under attack, we can succumb to the challenge and change the attitude or we can resist it and maintain the attitude. There are different means of resistance. In a series of studies, Julia Jacks and Kimberly Cameron (2003) asked people to describe and rate the ways that they manage to resist persuasion in their attitudes on abortion or the death penalty. They identified seven strategies, the most common being attitude bolstering ("I think about all the reasons I believe the way I do") and the least common being source derogation ("I look for faults in the person who challenges my belief"). These means of resistance are listed in Table 6.4.

What leads people to invoke these mechanisms of resistance? Does it help to be forewarned that your attitude is about to come under attack? Perhaps the toughest audience to persuade is the one that knows you're coming. When people are aware that someone is trying to change their attitude, they become more likely to resist. All they need is some time to collect their thoughts and come up with a good defense. Jonathan Freedman and David Sears (1965) first discovered this when they told high school seniors to expect a speech on why teenagers should not be allowed to drive (an unpopular position, as you can imagine). The students were warned either 2 or 10 minutes before the talk began or not at all. Those who were the victims of a sneak attack were the most likely to succumb to the speaker's position. Those who had a full 10 minutes' warning were the least likely to agree. To be forewarned is to be forearmed. But why?

At least two processes are at work here. To understand them, let's take a closer look at what forewarning does. Participants in the Freedman and Sears (1965) study were put on notice in two ways: (1) They were informed of the position the speaker would take, and (2) they were told that the speaker intended to change their opinion. Psychologically, these two aspects of forewarning have different effects. The first effect is purely cognitive. Knowing in advance what position a speaker

| TABLE 6.4 **Strategies for Resisting Persuasion** | |
|---|---|
| **Strategy** | **Example** |
| Attitude bolstering | "I reassure myself of facts that support the validity of my belief." |
| Counterarguing | "I would talk to myself and play devil's advocate." |
| Social validation | "I also rely on others with the same opinion to be there for me." |
| Negative affect | "I tend to get angry when someone tries to change my beliefs." |
| Assertions of confidence | "I doubt anybody could change my viewpoint." |
| Selective exposure | "Most of the time I just ignore them." |
| Source derogation | "I look for faults in the person presenting the challenging belief." |

© Cengage Learning

will take enables us to come up with counterarguments and, as a result, to become more resistant to change. To explain this effect, William McGuire (1964) drew an analogy: Protecting a person's attitudes from persuasion, he said, is like inoculating the human body against disease. In medicine, injecting a small dose of infection into a patient stimulates the body to build up a resistance to it. According to this **inoculation hypothesis**, an attitude can be immunized the same way. As with flu shots and other vaccines, our defenses can be reinforced by exposure to weak doses of the opposing position before we actually encounter the full presentation. Studies of negative political ads show that inoculation can be used to combat the kinds of attack messages that sometimes win elections (Pfau et al., 1990).

Simply knowing that someone is trying to persuade us also sparks a motivational reaction as we brace ourselves to resist the attempt regardless of what position is taken. As a TV viewer, you have no doubt heard the phrase "And now, we pause for a message from our sponsor." What does this warning tell us? Not knowing yet who the sponsor is, even the grouchiest among us is in no position to object. Yet imagine how you would feel if an experimenter said to you, "In just a few minutes, you will hear a message prepared according to well-established principles of persuasion and designed to induce you to change your attitudes." If you are like the participants who actually heard this warning, you might be tempted to reply, "Oh yeah? Try me!" Indeed, participants rejected that message without counterargument and without much advance notice (Hass & Grady, 1975).

When people think that someone is trying to change their attitude or otherwise manipulate them, a red flag goes up. That red flag is called **psychological reactance**. According to Jack Brehm's theory of psychological reactance, all of us want the freedom to think, feel, and act as we (not others) choose. When we sense that a cherished freedom is being threatened, we become motivated to maintain it. And when we sense that a freedom is slipping away, we try to restore it (Brehm & Brehm, 1981). One possible result is that when a communicator comes on too strongly, we may react with *negative attitude change* by moving in the direction that is the opposite of the one being advocated—even, ironically, when the speaker's position agrees with our own (Heller et al., 1973). Sometimes, the motive to protect our freedom to think as we choose trumps our desire to hold a specific opinion. Reactance can trigger resistance to persuasion in two ways. Once aroused, the reactant target of attempted persuasion may simply shut down in a reflex-like response or disagree in a more thoughtful manner by questioning the credibility of the source and counterarguing the message (Silvia, 2006).

It's important to realize that forewarning does not always increase resistance to persuasion because the effects are not that simple. Based on a meta-analysis of 48 experiments, Wendy Wood and Jeffrey Quinn (2003) found that when people are forewarned about an impending persuasive appeal on a topic that is personally not that important, they start to agree before they even receive the message so as not to appear vulnerable to influence. Yet when people are forewarned about a persuasive appeal on a topic of personal importance, they feel threatened and think up counterarguments to bolster their attitude. This cognitive response strengthens their resistance to change once that appeal is delivered. It takes mental effort to resist a persuasive appeal. When people know that someone will try to influence them, they conserve their energy and generate the necessary counterarguments (Janssen et al., 2010).

> ## Culture and Persuasion

A communication is persuasive to the extent that the source is favorable and the message, however it is presented, meets the psychological needs of its audience. In this regard, cultural factors also play a subtle but important role.

---

*"To do just the opposite is also a form of imitation."*

—Lichtenberg

---

**inoculation hypothesis** The idea that exposure to weak versions of a persuasive argument increases later resistance to that argument.

**psychological reactance** The theory that people react against threats to their freedom by asserting themselves and perceiving the threatened freedom as more attractive.

In earlier chapters, we saw that cultures differ in the extent to which people are oriented toward individualism or collectivism. In light of these differences, Sang-Pil Han and Sharon Shavitt (1994) compared the contents of magazine advertisements in the United States, an individualistic country, and Korea, a country with a more collectivistic orientation. They found that American advertising campaigns were focused more on personal benefits, individuality, competition, and self-improvement ("She's got a style all her own"; "Make your way through the crowd"), and that Korean ads appealed more to the integrity, achievement, and well-being of one's ingroups ("An exhilarating way to provide for your family"; "Celebrating a half-century of partnership"). Clearly, there are different ways to appeal to the members of these two cultures.

In a second study, Han and Shavitt created two sets of ads for various products. One set portrayed individuals ("Treat yourself to a breath-freshening experience"), and the other set featured groups ("Share this breath-freshening experience"). Both sets were presented to American and Korean participants. The result: Americans were persuaded more by individualistic ads, and Koreans preferred collectivistic ads. Similar differences are found in the way celebrity endorsements are used in the two cultures. In the United States, celebrities tend to portray themselves using or talking directly about a product; in Korean commercials that appeal to belongingness, family, and traditional values, celebrities are more likely to play the role of someone else without being singled out (Choi et al., 2005).

As people from all over the world come into contact with each other through travel, satellite television, international trade agreements, and the Internet, cultural values begin to change. Just as humans develop as they get older, cultures sometimes change over time from one generation to the next. Recent and substantial modernization efforts in China—home to roughly one out of every five people on the planet—illustrate the point. There is so much recent change that Zhang and Shavitt (2003) sought to compare the contents of television commercials, which are primarily directed at the traditional mass market, with advertisements in new magazines that specifically target 18- to 35-year-old, educated, high-income citizens who constitute China's "X-generation." Based on their analysis of 463 ads, they found that although traditional and collectivist values predominated on mainstream TV, magazine ads were characterized by more modern and individualistic impulses. To be persuasive, a message should appeal to the culturally shared values of its audience.

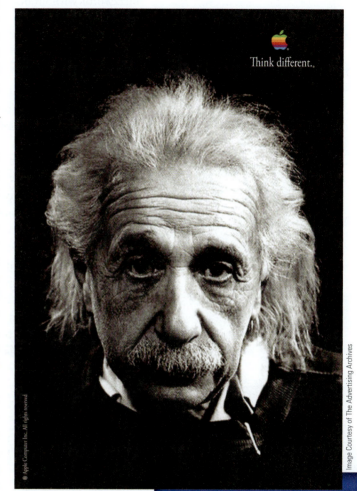

Think different.

In a series of print ads, Apple Computer featured Albert Einstein and other creative geniuses throughout history who dared to "think different." In a marketing campaign that paid tribute to individualism, Apple saluted "The crazy ones. The misfits. The rebels. The troublemakers. The round pegs in the square holes. The ones who see things differently."

## Persuasion by Our Own Actions

Anyone who has ever acted on stage knows how easy it is to become so absorbed in a role that the experience seems real. Feigned laughter can make an actor feel happy, and crocodile tears can turn into sadness. Even in real life, the effect can be dramatic.

In 1974, Patty Hearst, a sheltered college student from a wealthy California family, was kidnapped. By the time she was arrested months later, she was a gun-toting revolutionary who called herself Tania. How could someone be so totally converted? In Hearst's own words, "I had thought I was humoring [my captors] by parroting their clichés and buzzwords without believing in them . . . In trying to convince them I convinced myself" (Hearst, 1982).

## Role Playing: All the World's a Stage

The Patty Hearst case illustrates the powerful effects of *role playing*. Of course, you don't have to be kidnapped or terrorized to know how it feels to be coaxed into behavior that is at odds with your sense of who you are. People frequently engage in attitude-discrepant behavior as part of a job, for example, or to fit into a group. As commonplace as this seems, it raises a profound question. When we play along, saying and doing things that are privately discrepant from our own attitudes, do we begin to change those attitudes as a result? How we feel can determine the way we act. Is it also possible that the way we act can determine how we feel?

Many years ago, Irving Janis (1968) theorized that attitude change would persist more when it is inspired by our own behavior than when it stems from a passive exposure to a persuasive communication. Janis conducted a study in which one group of participants listened to a speech that challenged their positions on a topic and others were handed an outline and asked to give the speech themselves. As predicted, participants changed their attitudes more after giving the speech than after listening to it (Janis & King, 1954). According to Janis, role playing works to change attitudes because it forces people to learn the message. Hence, people tend to remember arguments they come up with on their own better than they remember arguments provided to them by other people (Slamecka & Graff, 1978). In fact, attitude change is more enduring even when people who read a persuasive message merely *expect* that they will later have to communicate it to others (Boninger et al., 1990).

But there's more to role playing than improved memory. The effects of enacting a role can be staggering, in part because it is so easy to confuse what we do or what we say with how we really feel. Think about the times you've dished out compliments you didn't mean or flashed a smile at someone you didn't like or nodded your head in response to a statement you disagreed with. We often shade what we say just to please a particular listener. What's fascinating is not that we make adjustments to suit others but that this role playing has such powerful effects on our own private attitudes. For example, participants in one study read about a man and then described him to someone else, who supposedly liked or disliked him. As you might expect, they described the man in more positive terms when their listener was favorably disposed. In the process, however, they also convinced themselves. At least to some extent, "saying is believing" (Higgins & Rholes, 1978).

Posing as a revolutionary named Tania, Patty Hearst was converted by the role her captors forced her to play. "In trying to convince them I convinced myself," she said.

Consider the implications. We know that attitudes influence behavior, as when people help those whom they like and hurt those whom they dislike. But research on role playing emphasizes the flip side of the coin—that behavior can change attitudes. Perhaps we come to like people because we have helped them and blame people whom we have hurt. To change people's inner feelings, then, maybe we should begin by focusing on their behavior. Why do people experience changes of attitude in response to changes in their own behavior? One answer to this question is provided by the theory of cognitive dissonance.

 ## Cognitive Dissonance Theory: The Classic Version

Many social psychologists believe that people are strongly motivated by a desire for cognitive consistency—a state of mind in which one's beliefs, attitudes, and behaviors are compatible with each other (Abelson et al., 1968). Cognitive consistency theories seem to presuppose that people are generally logical. However, Leon Festinger (1957) turned this assumption on its head. Struck by the irrationalities of human behavior, Festinger proposed **cognitive dissonance theory**, which states that a powerful motive to maintain cognitive consistency can give rise to irrational, sometimes maladaptive behavior.

According to Festinger, all of us hold many cognitions about ourselves and the world around us. These cognitions include everything we know about our own beliefs, attitudes, and behavior. Although generally our cognitions coexist peacefully, at times they clash. Consider some examples. You say you're on a diet, yet you just dove headfirst into a tub of chocolate fudge brownie ice cream. Or you waited in line for hours to get into a concert, and then the band proved to be disappointing. Or you baked for hours under the hot summer sun while listening to your iPod even though you knew the health risks. Each of these scenarios harbors inconsistency and conflict: You've already committed yourself to a course of action, yet you realize that the action is inconsistent with your attitude.

Under certain conditions, discrepancies such as these can evoke an unpleasant state of tension known as cognitive dissonance. But discrepancy doesn't always produce dissonance. If you broke a diet for a Thanksgiving dinner with family, your indiscretion would not lead you to experience dissonance. Or if you mistakenly thought the ice cream you ate was low in calories only to find out the truth later, then, again, you would not experience much dissonance. As we'll see, what really hurts is the knowledge that you committed yourself to an attitude-discrepant behavior freely and with some knowledge of the consequences. When that happens, dissonance is aroused, and you become motivated to reduce it. As shown in Table 6.5, there are many possible ways to reduce dissonance—such as rationalizing that others in one's ingroup are also hypocrites (McKimmie et al., 2009), denying personal responsibility for the behavior (Gosling et al., 2006), and trivializing the issue in question (Starzyk et al., 2009). Of course, sometimes the easiest way to reduce dissonance is to change your attitude to bring it in line with your behavior.

Right from the start, cognitive dissonance theory captured the imagination of social psychology. Festinger's basic proposition is simple, yet its implications are far-reaching. In this section, we examine three research areas that demonstrate the breadth of what dissonance theory has to say about attitude change.

*"Man is the only animal that learns by being hypocritical. He pretends to be polite and then, eventually, he becomes polite."*

—Jean Kerr

**TABLE 6.5**
**Ways to Reduce Dissonance**

"I need to be on a diet, yet I just dove head first into a tub of chocolate fudge brownie ice cream." If this were you, how would you reduce dissonance aroused by the discrepancy between your attitude and your behavior?

| Techniques | Examples |
|---|---|
| Change your attitude. | "I don't really need to be on a diet." |
| Change your perception of the behavior. | "I hardly ate any ice cream." |
| Add consonant cognitions. | "Chocolate ice cream is very nutritious." |
| Minimize the importance of the conflict. | "I don't care if I'm overweight—life is short!" |
| Reduce perceived choice. | "I had no choice; the ice cream was served for this special occasion." |

© Cengage Learning

**cognitive dissonance theory** The theory holding that inconsistent cognitions arouses psychological tension that people become motivated to reduce.

### Justifying Attitude-Discrepant Behavior: When Doing Is Believing 
Imagine for a moment that you are a participant in the classic study by Leon Festinger and J. Merrill

Carlsmith (1959). As soon as you arrive, you are greeted by an experimenter who says that he is interested in various measures of performance. Wondering what that means, you all too quickly find out. The experimenter hands you a wooden board containing 48 square pegs in square holes and asks you to turn each peg a quarter turn to the left, then a quarter turn back to the right, then back to the left, then back again to the right. The routine seems endless. After 30 minutes, the experimenter comes to your rescue. Or does he? Just when you think things are looking up, he hands you another board, another assignment. For the next half-hour, you are to take 12 spools of thread off the board, put them back, take them off, and put them back again. By now, you're just about ready to tear your hair out. As you think back over better times, even the first task begins to look good.

Finally, you're done. After one of the longest hours of your life, the experimenter lets you in on a secret: There's more to this experiment than meets the eye. You were in the control group. To test the effects of motivation on performance, other participants are being told that the experiment will be fun and exciting. You don't realize it, but you are now being set up for the critical part of the study. Would you be willing to tell the next participant that the experiment is enjoyable? As you hem and haw, the experimenter offers to pay for your services. Some participants are offered $1; others are offered $20. In either case, you agree to help out. Before you know it, you find yourself in the waiting room trying to dupe an unsuspecting fellow student (who is really a confederate).

By means of this elaborate staged presentation, participants were goaded into an attitude-discrepant behavior, an action that was inconsistent with their private attitudes. They knew how dull the experiment really was, yet they raved about it. Did this conflict arouse cognitive dissonance? It depends on how much the participants were paid. Suppose you were one of the lucky ones offered $20 for your assistance. By today's standards, that payment would be worth $80—surely a sufficient justification for telling a little white lie, right? Feeling well compensated, these participants experienced little if any dissonance. But wait. Suppose you were paid only $1. Surely your integrity is worth more than that, don't you think? In this instance, you have **insufficient justification** for going along, so you need a way to cope. According to Festinger (1957), unless you can deny your actions (which is not usually possible), you'll feel pressured to change your attitude about the task. If you can convince yourself that the experiment wasn't that bad, then saying it was interesting is all right.

The results were as Festinger and Carlsmith had predicted. When the experiment was presumably over, participants were asked how they felt about the peg-board tasks. Those in the control group who did not mislead a confederate openly admitted that the tasks were boring. So did those in the $20 condition, who had ample justification for what they did. However, participants who were paid only $1 rated the experiment as somewhat enjoyable. Having engaged in an attitude-discrepant act without sufficient justification, these participants reduced cognitive dissonance by changing their attitude. The results can be seen in ● Figure 6.9.

Two aspects of this classic study are noteworthy. First, it showed the phenomenon of self-persuasion: When people behave in ways that contradict their attitudes, they sometimes go on to change those attitudes without any exposure to a persuasive communication. Demonstrating the power of this phenomenon, Michael Leippe and Donna Eisenstadt (1994) found that white college students who were coaxed into writing essays in favor of new scholarship funds only for black students later reported more favorable attitudes in general toward African Americans. The second major contribution of

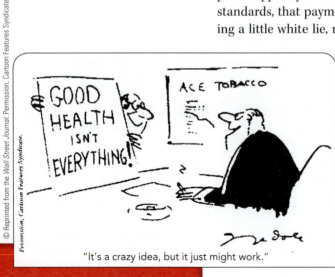

GOOD HEALTH ISN'T EVERYTHING!

ACE TOBACCO

*Permission, Cartoon Features Syndicate.*

"It's a crazy idea, but it just might work."

One way to reduce dissonance is to minimize the importance of the conflict.

**insufficient justification** A condition in which people freely perform an attitude-discrepant behavior without receiving a large reward.

Festinger and Carlsmith's results is that they contradicted the time-honored belief that big rewards produce greater change. In fact, the more money participants were offered for their inconsistent behavior, the more justified they felt and the less likely they were to change their attitudes.

Just as a small reward provides insufficient justification for attitude-discrepant behavior, mild punishment is **insufficient deterrence** for attitude-discrepant nonbehavior. Think about it. What happens when people refrain from doing something they really want to do? Do they devalue the activity and convince themselves that they never really wanted to do it in the first place? In one study, children were prohibited from playing with an attractive toy by being threatened with a mild or a severe punishment. All participants refrained. As cognitive dissonance theory predicts, however, only those faced with the mild punishment—an insufficient deterrent—later showed disdain for the forbidden toy. Those who confronted the threat of severe punishment did not (Aronson & Carlsmith, 1963). Once again, cognitive dissonance theory turned common sense on its head: The less severe the threatened punishment, the greater the attitude change produced.

### Justifying Effort: Coming to Like What We Suffer For

Have you ever spent tons of money or tried really hard to achieve something, only to discover later that it wasn't worth all the effort? This kind of inconsistency between effort and outcome can arouse cognitive dissonance and motivate a change of heart toward the unsatisfying outcome. The hypothesis is simple but profound: We alter our attitudes to justify our suffering.

In a classic test of this hypothesis, Elliot Aronson and Judson Mills (1959) invited female students to take part in a series of group discussions about sex. But there was a hitch. Because sex is a sensitive topic, participants were told that they would have to pass an "embarrassment test" before joining the group. The test consisted of reading sexual material aloud in front of a male experimenter. One group of participants experienced what amounted to a *severe* initiation in which they had to recite obscene words and lurid passages taken from paperback novels. A second group underwent a *mild* initiation in which they read a list of more ordinary words pertaining to sex. A third group was admitted to the discussions without an initiation test.

Moments later, all participants were given headphones and permitted to eavesdrop on the group they would soon be joining. Actually, what they heard was a tape-recorded discussion about "secondary sex behavior in the lower animals." It was dreadfully boring. When it was over, participants were asked to rate how much they liked the group members and their discussion. Keep in mind what dissonance theory predicts: The more time or money or effort you choose to invest in something, the more anxious you will feel if the outcome proves disappointing. One way to cope with this inconsistency is to alter your attitudes. That's exactly what happened. Participants who had endured a severe initiation rated the discussion group more favorably than did those who had endured little or no initiation.

Social embarrassment is not the only kind of "effort" we feel we need to justify to ourselves. As a general rule, the more you pay for something—whether you pay in physical exertion, pain, time, or money—the more you will come to like it. This principle

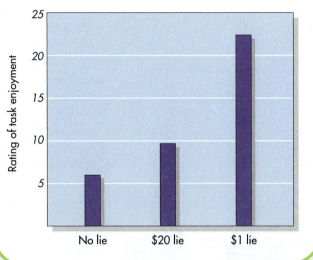

**● FIGURE 6.9**

**The Dissonance Classic**

Participants in a boring experiment (attitude) were asked to say that it was enjoyable (behavior) to a fellow student. Those in one group were paid $1 to lie; those in a second group were offered $20. Members of a third group, who did not have to lie, admitted that the task was boring. So did the participants paid $20, which was ample justification for telling a lie. Participants paid only $1, however, rated the task as more enjoyable. Behaving in an attitude-discrepant manner without justification, these latter participants reduced dissonance by changing their attitude.

From Festinger, L. and Carlsmith, J. M., "Cognitive Consequences and Forced Compliance," *Journal of Abnormal and Social Psychology* vol 58 (pp. 203–210). Copyright © 1959 by the American Psychological Association. Reprinted by permission.

> The more money you pay people to tell a lie, the more they will come to believe it. **F**ALSE.

**insufficient deterrence** A condition in which people refrain from engaging in a desirable activity, even when only mild punishment is threatened.

People often come to like what they suffer for.    **T**RUE.

has provocative implications for hazing practices in fraternities and sororities, on sports teams, and in the military. Research even suggests that the harder psychotherapy patients have to work at their own treatment, the more likely they are to feel better when that treatment is over (Axsom, 1989; Axsom & Cooper, 1985).

**Justifying Difficult Decisions: When Good Choices Get Even Better**    Whenever we make difficult decisions—whether to marry, what school to attend, where to live, or what job to accept—we feel dissonance. By definition, a decision is difficult when the alternative courses of action are about equally desirable. Marriage offers comfort and stability; staying single enables us to seek out exciting new relationships. One job might pay more money; the other may offer more interesting work. Once people make tough decisions like these, they are at risk because as negative aspects of the chosen alternatives and positive aspects of the unchosen alternatives are at odds with their decisions. According to dissonance theory, people rationalize whatever they decide by exaggerating the positive features of the chosen alternative and the negative features of the unchosen alternative.

In an early test of this hypothesis, Jack Brehm (1956) asked female participants to evaluate various consumer products, presumably as part of a marketing research project. After rating a toaster, a coffee pot, a radio, a stopwatch, and other products, participants were told that they could take one home as a gift. In the high-dissonance condition, they were offered a difficult choice between two items they found equally attractive. In the low-dissonance group, they were offered an easier choice between a desirable and an undesirable item. After receiving the gift, participants read a few research reports and then reevaluated all the products. The results provided strong support for dissonance theory. In the low-dissonance group, the participants' post-decision ratings were about the same as their pre-decision ratings. But in the high-dissonance condition, ratings increased for the chosen item and decreased for the item that was not chosen. Participants torn between two equivalent alternatives coped by reassuring themselves that they had made the right choice.

This phenomenon appears in a wide range of settings. For example, Robert Knox and James Inskter (1968) took dissonance theory to the racetrack and found that bettors who had already placed $2 bets on a horse were more optimistic about winning than were those still standing in line. This type of optimism may even begin to set in once a thoughtful decision is made, even before the bet is placed (Brownstein et al., 2004). Similarly, Dennis Regan and Martin Kilduff (1988) visited several polling stations on Election Day and found that voters were more likely to think that their candidates would win when they were interviewed after submitting their ballots than when they were interviewed before they submitted them. Since bets and votes cannot be taken back, people who had committed to a decision were motivated to reduce post-decision dissonance. So they convinced themselves that the decision they made was right.

Suggesting that people need to justify difficult irrevocable decisions to quell the dissonance they arouse, researchers found that gamblers who had already bet on a horse rated themselves as more certain of winning than those who were still waiting to place a bet.

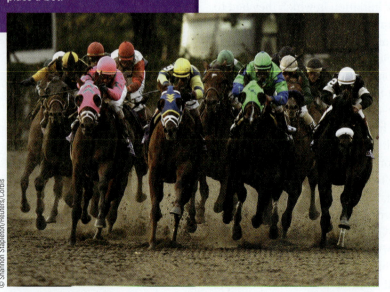

© Shannon Stapleton/Reuters/Corbis

> ## Cognitive Dissonance Theory: A New Look

Following in Festinger's bold footsteps, generations of social psychologists have studied and refined the basic theory (Cooper, 2007; Harmon-Jones & Mills, 1999). Nobody disputes the fact that when people are gently coaxed into performing an attitude-discrepant behavior, they often go on to change their attitudes. In fact, people will feel discomfort and change their attitudes when they disagree with others in a group (Matz & Wood, 2005) or even when they observe inconsistent behavior from others with whom they identify—a process of vicarious dissonance (Cooper & Hogg, 2007).

Researchers have also examined possible perceptual consequences of cognitive dissonance. In one study, Emily Balcetis and David Dunning (2007) took college students to the crowded center of campus and asked them to put on—and walk around in—a costume consisting of a grass skirt, a coconut bra, a flower lei around the neck, and a plastic fruit basket on the head. Embarrassing as it was to appear this way in public, all the participants walked across campus in this costume. In a high-choice condition, they were led to believe that they could decline in favor of a different task (insufficient justification). In a low-choice condition, they were told that no alternative tasks were available (sufficient justification). How bad was it? Afterward, all the students were asked to estimate the distance they had walked from one point to the other. Needing to justify their embarrassing antics, those in the high-choice condition underestimated how far they had walked relative to those in the low-choice condition. Apparently, the motivation to reduce dissonance can alter our visual representations of the natural environment.

Through systematic research, it became evident early on that Festinger's (1957) original theory was not to be the last word. People do change their attitudes to justify attitude-discrepant behavior, effort, and difficult decisions. But for dissonance to be aroused, certain specific conditions must be present. Thanks to Joel Cooper and Russell Fazio's (1984) "new look" at dissonance theory, we now have a pretty good idea of what those conditions are.

According to Cooper and Fazio, four steps are necessary for both the arousal and reduction of dissonance. First, the attitude-discrepant behavior must produce unwanted *negative consequences*. Recall the initial Festinger and Carlsmith (1959) study. Not only did participants say something they knew to be false but they also deceived a fellow student into taking part in a painfully boring experiment. Had these participants lied without causing hardship, they would *not* have changed their attitudes to justify the action (Cooper et al., 1974). To borrow an expression from schoolyard basketball, "no harm, no foul." In fact, negative consequences can arouse dissonance even when people's actions are consistent with their attitudes, as when college students who wrote against fee hikes were led to believe that their essays had backfired, prompting a university committee to favor an increase (Scher & Cooper, 1989).

The second necessary step in the process is a feeling of *personal responsibility* for the unpleasant outcomes of behavior. Personal responsibility consists of two factors. The first is the freedom of *choice*. When people believe they had no choice but to act as they did, there is no dissonance and no attitude change (Linder et al., 1967). Had Festinger and Carlsmith coerced participants into raving about the boring experiment, the participants would not have felt the need to further justify what they did by changing their attitudes. But the experimental situation led participants to think that their actions were voluntary and that the choice was theirs. Participants were pressured without realizing it and believed that they did not have to comply with the experimenter's request.

For people to feel personally responsible, they must also believe that the potential negative consequences of their actions were *foreseeable* at the time (Goethals et al., 1979). When the outcome could not realistically have been anticipated, then there is no dissonance and no attitude change. Had Festinger and Carlsmith's participants lied in private and found out only later that their statements had been tape-recorded for subsequent use, then, again, they would not have felt the need to further justify their behavior.

The third necessary step in the process is physiological *arousal*. Right from the start, Festinger viewed cognitive dissonance as a state of discomfort and tension that people seek to reduce—much like hunger, thirst, and other basic drives. Research has shown that this emphasis was well placed. In a study by Robert Croyle and Joel Cooper (1983), participants wrote essays that supported or contradicted their own attitudes. Some were ordered to do so, but others were led to believe that the choice was theirs. During the session, electrodes were attached to each participant's fingertips to record levels of physiological arousal. As predicted by cognitive dissonance theory, those who freely wrote attitude-discrepant essays were the most aroused, an observation made by other researchers as well (Elkin & Leippe, 1986). In fact, participants who write attitude-discrepant essays in a "free-choice" situation report feeling high levels of discomfort—which subside once they change their attitudes (Elliot & Devine, 1994).

The fourth step in the dissonance process is closely related to the third. It isn't enough to feel generally aroused. A person must also make an *attribution* for that arousal to his or her own behavior. Suppose you just lied to a friend or studied for an exam that was canceled or made a tough decision that you might soon regret. Suppose further that although you are upset, you believe that your discomfort is caused by some external factor, not by your dissonance-producing behavior. Under these circumstances, will you exhibit attitude change as a symptom of cognitive dissonance? Probably not. When participants were led to attribute their dissonance-related arousal to a drug they had supposedly taken (Zanna & Cooper, 1974), to the anticipation of painful electric shocks (Pittman, 1975), or to a pair of prism goggles that they had to wear (Losch & Cacioppo, 1990), attitude change did not occur. ● Figure 6.10 summarizes these four steps in the production and reduction of dissonance.

To this day, social psychologists continue to debate the "classic" and "new look" theories of cognitive dissonance. On the one hand, research has shown that attitude-discrepant actions do not always produce dissonance, in part because not everyone cares about being cognitively consistent (Cialdini et al., 1995) and in part because a change in attitude often seems to require the production of negative consequences (Johnson et al., 1995). On the other hand, some researchers have found that mere inconsistency can trigger cognitive dissonance, even without negative consequences. For example, Eddie Harmon-Jones and others (1996) had people drink a Kool-Aid beverage that was mixed with sugar or vinegar. They either told the participants (no choice) or asked them (high choice) to state in writing that they liked the beverage and then toss these notes, which were not really needed, into the wastebasket. Afterward, they rated how much they really liked the drink. You may have noticed that this experiment parallels the Festinger and

● **FIGURE 6.10**

**Necessary Conditions for the Arousal and Reduction of Dissonance**

Research suggests that four steps are necessary for attitude change to result from the production and reduction of dissonance.
© Cengage Learning

Carlsmith study with one key exception: For participants in the high-choice situation who consumed vinegar and said they liked it, the lie—although it contradicted their true attitudes—did not cause harm to anyone. Did they experience dissonance that they would have to reduce by overrating the vinegar Kool-Aid? Yes. Compared with participants who lied about the vinegar in the no-choice situation, those in the high-choice situation rated its taste as more pleasant. The lie was harmless, but the feeling of inconsistency still forced a change in attitude.

 ## Alternative Routes to Self-Persuasion

It is important to distinguish between the empirical facts uncovered by dissonance researchers and the theory that is used to explain them. The facts themselves are clear: Under certain conditions, people who behave in attitude-discrepant ways go on to change their attitudes. Whether this phenomenon reflects a human need to reduce dissonance, however, is a matter of some controversy. Over the years, three other explanations have been proposed.

**Self-Perception Theory**    Daryl Bem's (1965) *self-perception theory*, described in Chapter 3, posed the first serious challenge to dissonance theory. Noting that we don't always have firsthand knowledge of our own attitudes, Bem proposed that we infer how we feel by observing ourselves and the circumstances of our own behavior. This sort of self-persuasion is not fueled by the need to reduce tension or justify our actions. Instead, it is a cool, calm, and rational process in which people interpret ambiguous feelings by observing their own behavior. But can Bem's theory replace dissonance theory as an explanation of self-persuasion?

Bem confronted this question head-on. What if neutral observers who are not motivated by the need to reduce dissonance were to read a step-by-step description of a dissonance study and predict the results? This approach to the problem was ingenious. Bem reasoned that observers can have the same behavioral information as the participants themselves but not experience the same personal conflict. If observers generate the same results as real participants, it shows that dissonance arousal is not necessary for the resulting changes in attitudes.

To test his hypothesis, Bem (1967) described the Festinger and Carlsmith study to observers and had them guess participants' attitudes. Some were told about the $1 condition, some were told about the $20 condition, and others read about the control group procedure. The results closely paralleled the original study. As observers saw it, participants who said the task was interesting for $20 didn't mean it; they just went along for the money. But those who made the claim for only $1 must have been sincere. Why else would they have gone along? As far as Bem was concerned, the participants themselves reasoned the same way. No conflict, no arousal—just inference by observation.

So should we conclude that self-perception, not dissonance, is what's necessary to bring about attitude change? That's a tough question. It's not easy to come up with a critical experiment to distinguish between the two theories. Both predict the same results, but for different reasons. And both offer unique support for their own points of view. On the one hand, Bem's observer studies show that dissonance-like results can be obtained without arousal. On the other hand, the participants of dissonance studies *do* experience arousal, which seems necessary for attitude change to take place. Can we say that one theory is right and the other wrong?

Fazio and others (1977) concluded that both theories are right but in different situations. When people behave in ways that are strikingly at odds with their attitudes, they feel the unnerving effects of dissonance and change their attitudes to rationalize their actions. When people behave in ways that are not terribly discrepant from how they feel, however, they experience relatively little tension and form their attitudes as a matter of inference. In short, highly discrepant behavior produces attitude change through dissonance, whereas slightly discrepant behavior produces change through self-perception.

**Impression-Management Theory**   Another alternative to a dissonance view of self-persuasion is *impression-management theory*, which says that what matters is not a motive to be consistent but a motive to *appear* consistent. Nobody wants to be called fickle or be seen by others as a hypocrite. So we calibrate our attitudes and behaviors publicly in order to present ourselves to others in a particular light (Baumeister, 1982; Tedeschi et al., 1971). Or perhaps we are motivated not by a desire to appear consistent but by a desire to avoid being held responsible for the unpleasant consequences of our actions (Schlenker, 1982). Either way this theory places the emphasis on our concern for self-presentation. According to this view, participants in the Festinger and Carlsmith study mostly did not want the experimenter to think they had sold out for a paltry sum of money.

If the impression-management approach is correct, then cognitive dissonance does not produce attitude change at all—only reported change. In other words, if research participants were to state their attitudes anonymously or if they were to think that the experimenter could determine their true feelings through covert measures, then dissonance-like effects should vanish. Sometimes the effects do vanish, but other times they do not. In general, studies have shown that although self-persuasion can be motivated by impression management, it can also occur in situations that do not clearly arouse self-presentation concerns (Baumeister & Tice, 1984).

**Self-Esteem Theories**   A third competing explanation relates self-persuasion to the self. According to Elliot Aronson, acts that arouse dissonance do so because they threaten the self-concept, making the person feel guilty, dishonest, or hypocritical, and motivating a change in attitude or future behavior (Aronson, 1999; Stone et al., 1997). This being the case, perhaps Festinger and Carlsmith's participants needed to change their attitudes toward the boring task in order to repair damage to the self, not to resolve cognitive inconsistency.

If cognitive dissonance is aroused only by behavior that lowers self-esteem, then people with already low expectations of themselves should not be affected: "If a person conceives of himself as a 'schnook,' he will expect to behave like a schnook" (Aronson, 1969, p. 24). In fact, Jeff Stone (2003) found that when college students were coaxed into writing an essay in favor of a tuition increase (a position that contradicted their attitude) and into thinking about their own standards of behavior, those who had high self-esteem changed their attitude to meet their behavior, as dissonance theory would predict, more than those who had low self-esteem.

Claude Steele (1988) took this notion two steps further. First, he suggested that a dissonance-producing situation—engaging in attitude-discrepant behavior, exerting wasted effort, or making a tough decision—sets in motion a process of *self-affirmation* that serves to revalidate the integrity of the self-concept. Second, this revalidation can be achieved in many ways, not just by resolving dissonance. Self-affirmation theory makes a unique prediction: If the active ingredient in dissonance situations is a threat to the self, then people who have an opportunity to affirm the self in other ways will not suffer from the effects of dissonance. Give Festinger and Carlsmith's $1 participants a chance to donate money, help a victim in distress, or solve a problem, and their self-concepts should bounce back without further need to justify their actions.

Research provides support for this hypothesis. For example, Steele and others (1993) gave people positive or negative feedback about a personality test they had taken. Next, they asked them to rate 10 popular music CDs and then offered them a choice of keeping either their fifth- or sixth-ranked CD. Soon after making the decision, the participants were asked to rate the CDs again. As predicted by dissonance theory, most inflated their ratings of the chosen CD relative to the unchosen one. The key word, however, is *most*. The ratings of the participants who had received positive feedback did not change. Why not? According to Steele, it was because they had just enjoyed a self-affirming experience that was enough to overcome the need to reduce dissonance.

Steele's research suggests that there are many possible ways for people to repair a dissonance-damaged self. But if these efforts at indirect self-affirmation fail, would cognitive dissonance return and create pressure to make a change in attitude? Yes. In one study, college students were asked (high-choice) or told (low-choice) to deliver an attitude-discrepant speech advocating that a popular campus tradition (running nude on the evening of the first snowfall) be banned. For those in the basic high-choice condition, cognitive dissonance was aroused, creating pressure on them to change their attitude favoring the ban. Students in another high-choice group who were subsequently given an opportunity to self-affirm by expressing some cherished values felt less discomfort and exhibited less attitude change. For them, self-affirmation provided the necessary relief. However, among students in a fourth group (also high in choice) who self-affirmed but then received negative feedback about the values they expressed, cognitive dissonance returned, creating pressure to change their attitude toward the ban. In essence, cognitive dissonance and its impact on attitudes reemerged from the failed attempt at self-affirmation (Galinsky et al., 2000; see ● Figure 6.11).

To summarize, dissonance theory states that people change their attitudes to justify their attitude-discrepant behaviors, efforts, and decisions. Self-perception theory argues that the change occurs because people infer how they feel by observing their own

● **FIGURE 6.11**

**When Self-Affirmation Fails**

Students gave a dissonant speech advocating a ban on a popular campus tradition. Compared to those in a low-choice situation, students in a high-choice group changed their attitude more to favor the ban. As self-affirmation theory predicts, those given a chance to express their values afterward did not then favor the ban—unless their values were poorly received. Self-affirmation can repair the dissonance-damaged self. When it fails, however, cognitive dissonance returns to pressure the change in attitude.

Galinsky et al., 2000. © Cengage Learning

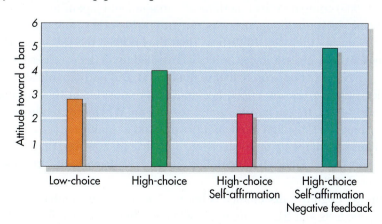

● **FIGURE 6.12**

**Theories of Self-Persuasion: Critical Comparisons**

Here we compare the major theories of self-persuasion. Each alternative challenges a different aspect of dissonance theory. Self-perception theory assumes that attitude change is a matter of inference, not motivation. Impression-management theory maintains that the change is more apparent than real, reported for the sake of public self-presentation. Self-affirmation theory contends that the motivating force is a concern for the self and that attitude change will not occur when the self-concept is affirmed in other ways.

|  | Theories | | | |
|  | Cognitive Dissonance | Self-Perception | Impression Management | Self-Affirmation |
|---|---|---|---|---|
| Is the attitude change motivated by a desire to reduce discomfort? | Yes | No | Yes | Yes |
| Does a person's private attitude really change? | Yes | Yes | No | Yes |
| Must the change be directly related to the attitude-discrepant behavior? | Yes | Yes | Yes | No |

behavior. Impression-management theory claims that the attitude change is spurred by concerns about self-presentation. And self-affirmation theory says that the change is motivated by threats to the self-concept (see ● Figure 6.12).

## Cultural Influences on Cognitive Dissonance

Over the years, social psychologists have presumed that the cognitive dissonance effects uncovered in 50 years of research and described in this chapter are universal and characteristic of human nature. More and more, however, it appears that cultural context may influence both the arousal and reduction of cognitive dissonance.

In Western cultures, individuals are expected to make decisions that are consistent with their personal attitudes and to make those decisions free from outside influences. In East Asian cultures, however, individuals are also expected to make decisions that benefit their ingroup members and to take the well-being of others into account in making those decisions. In light of these differences, Etsuko Hoshino-Browne and colleagues (2005) compared the reactions of Canadian and Japanese research participants in a post-decision dissonance experiment in which they rank-ordered items on a menu by choosing their top 10 dishes. Then they ranked the list again: Half made the choices for themselves, and the others were asked to imagine a close friend whose tastes they knew and choose on behalf of that friend. Did participants show the classic post-decision justification effect, becoming more positive in their ratings of the chosen items relative to nonchosen items? Yes and no. When they made decisions for themselves, only the Canadian participants exhibited a significant justification effect. When Japanese participants made decisions for a friend, however, they exhibited the stronger effect (see ● Figure 6.13). Similar results have been found in other studies (Kitayama et al., 2004).

To sum up: Cognitive dissonance is both universal and dependent on culture. At times everyone feels and tries to reduce dissonance, but cultures influence the conditions under which these processes occur.

**FIGURE 6.13**

**Cognitive Dissonance as Both Universal and Culturally Dependent**

Researchers compared Canadian and Japanese research participants in a post-decision dissonance study in which they rank ordered items on a menu, chose their top dishes, then ranked the list again. Half made the choices for themselves; the others were asked to imagine a close friend. When deciding for themselves, only the Canadians exhibited a significant justification effect; when deciding for a friend, however, Japanese participants exhibited the stronger effect.
Hoshino-Browne et al., 2005. © Cengage Learning

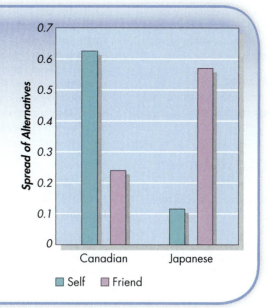

# Changing Attitudes

Attitudes and attitude change are an important part of social life. In this chapter, we have seen that persuasion can be achieved in different ways. The most common approach is through communication from *others*. Faced with newspaper editorials, junk mail, books, TV commercials, blogs, websites, and other messages, we take one of two routes to persuasion. On the central route, attitude change is based on the merits of the source and his or her communication. On the peripheral route, it is based on superficial cues. Either way, the change in attitude often precipitates a change in behavior.

A second, less obvious means of persuasion originates within *ourselves*. When people behave in ways that run afoul of their true convictions, they often go on to change their attitudes. Once again, there are many routes to change, not just one. Cognitive dissonance, self-perception, impression management, and self-esteem concerns are among the possible avenues. From attitudes to behavior and back again, the processes of persuasion are complex and interwoven.

# Review

## The Study of Attitudes

- An attitude is an affective, evaluative reaction toward a person, place, issue, or object.

### How Attitudes Are Measured
- The most common way to measure attitudes is through self-reports, such as attitude scales.
- To get respondents to answer questions honestly, the bogus pipeline may be used.

- Covert measures may also be used. Such measures include nonverbal behavior, the facial electromyograph (EMG), brain-wave patterns, and the Implicit Association Test (IAT).

### How Attitudes Are Formed
- Twin studies suggest that people may be genetically predisposed to hold certain attitudes.

- However, research shows that attitudes are formed by experience and evaluative conditioning—when people develop strong attitudes toward neutral objects because of their association with positive and negative stimuli.

### The Link Between Attitudes and Behavior

- Attitudes do not necessarily correlate with behavior, but under certain conditions, there is a high correlation.

# Persuasion by Communication

- The most common approach to changing attitudes is through a persuasive communication.

### Two Routes to Persuasion

- When people think critically about a message, they take the central route to persuasion and are influenced by the strength of the arguments.
- When people do not think carefully about a message, they take the peripheral route to persuasion and are influenced by peripheral cues.
- The route taken depends on whether people have the ability and the motivation to fully process the communication.

### The Source

- Attitude change is greater for messages delivered by a source that is credible (competent and trustworthy).
- Attitude change is also greater when the source is likable (similar and attractive).
- When an audience has a high level of personal involvement, source factors are less important than the quality of the message.
- The sleeper effect shows that people often forget the source but not the message, so the effects of the credibility of the source dissipate over time.

### The Message

- On the peripheral route, lengthy messages are persuasive. On the central route, length works only if the added information does not dilute the message.
- Whether it is best to present an argument first or second depends on how much time elapses—both between the two arguments and between the second argument and the final decision.
- Messages that are moderately discrepant from an audience's attitudes will inspire change, but highly discrepant messages will be scrutinized and rejected.
- High-fear messages motivate attitude change when they contain strong arguments and instructions about how to avoid the threatened danger.
- Positive emotion also facilitates attitude change because people are easier to persuade when they're in a good mood.

- Attitudes predict behavior best when they're specific rather than general and strong rather than weak.
- Attitudes compete with other influences on behavior.

> **Putting *Common Sense* to the Test**
>
> **Researchers can tell if someone has a positive or negative attitude by measuring physiological arousal.**
>
> **False.** *Measures of arousal can reveal how intensely someone feels, but not whether the person's attitude is positive or negative.*

- Research shows that subliminal messages do not produce meaningful or lasting changes in attitudes.

### The Audience

- People are not consistently difficult or easy to persuade. Rather, different kinds of messages influence different kinds of people.
- People who are high in the need for cognition are persuaded more by the strength of the arguments.
- People who are high in self-monitoring are influenced more by appeals to social images.
- Messages are persuasive to the extent that they are presented in a way that "feels right," fitting the individual orientations of audience members.
- Forewarning increases resistance to persuasive influence. It inoculates the audience by providing the opportunity to generate counterarguments, and it arouses psychological reactance.

### Culture and Persuasion

- Communications are successful to the extent that they appeal to the cultural values of an audience.
- Research shows that North Americans are persuaded more by individualistic ads, whereas East Asians prefer collectivistic ads.

> **Putting *Common Sense* to the Test**
>
> **In reacting to persuasive communications, people are influenced more by superficial images than by logical arguments.**
>
> **False.** *As indicated by the dual-process model of persuasion, people can be influenced by images or arguments, depending on their ability and motivation to think critically about the information.*
>
> **People are most easily persuaded by commercial messages that are presented without their awareness.**
>
> **False.** *There is no research evidence to support the presumed effects of subliminal ads.*

# Persuasion by Our Own Actions

## Role Playing: All the World's a Stage
- The way people act can influence how they feel because behavior can determine attitudes.

## Cognitive Dissonance Theory: The Classic Version
- Under certain conditions, inconsistency between attitudes and behavior produces an unpleasant psychological state called cognitive dissonance.
- Motivated to reduce the tension, people often change their attitudes to justify (1) attitude-discrepant behavior; (2) wasted effort; and (3) difficult decisions.

## Cognitive Dissonance Theory: A New Look
- According to the "new look" version of cognitive dissonance theory, four conditions must be met for dissonance to be aroused: (1) an act with unwanted consequences; (2) a feeling of personal responsibility; (3) arousal or discomfort; and (4) attribution of the arousal to the attitude-discrepant act.
- Social psychologists continue to debate whether dissonance can be aroused by cognitive inconsistency when no unwanted consequences are produced.

## Alternative Routes to Self-Persuasion
- Alternative explanations of dissonance-related attitude change have been proposed.
- Self-perception theory states that people logically infer their attitudes by observing their own behavior.

- Impression-management theory says that people are motivated to change their attitudes only to appear consistent to others.
- Self-esteem theories state that dissonance is triggered by threats to the self-concept and can be reduced indirectly, without a change in attitude, through self-affirming experiences.

## Cultural Influences on Cognitive Dissonance
- Recently, social psychologists have wondered whether cognitive dissonance effects are universal or specific to Western cultures.
- Research suggests that people all over the world will try to reduce dissonance when it arises but that the conditions that arouse it are influenced by cultural context.

### Putting *Common Sense* to the Test

**The more money you pay people to tell a lie, the more they will come to believe it.**
**False.** *Cognitive dissonance studies show that people believe the lies they are underpaid to tell as a way to justify their own actions.*

**People often come to like what they suffer for.**
**True.** *Studies show that the more people work or suffer for something, the more they come to like it as a way to justify their effort.*

# Changing Attitudes

- Through persuasive communications and the mechanisms of self-persuasion, the processes of changing attitudes and behavior are complex and interwoven.

## KEY TERMS

attitude (206)
attitude scale (208)
bogus pipeline (208)
central route to persuasion (217)
cognitive dissonance theory (239)
elaboration (218)
evaluative conditioning (213)

facial electromyograph (EMG) (209)
Implicit Association Test (IAT) (210)
implicit attitude (210)
inoculation hypothesis (236)
insufficient deterrence (241)
insufficient justification (240)
need for cognition (NC) (233)

peripheral route to persuasion (217)
persuasion (217)
psychological reactance (236)
sleeper effect (225)
theory of planned behavior (214)

## MEDIA RESOURCES

Go to CengageBrain.com to access Psychology CourseMate, where you will find an interactive eBook, glossaries, flashcards, quizzes, videos, and more.

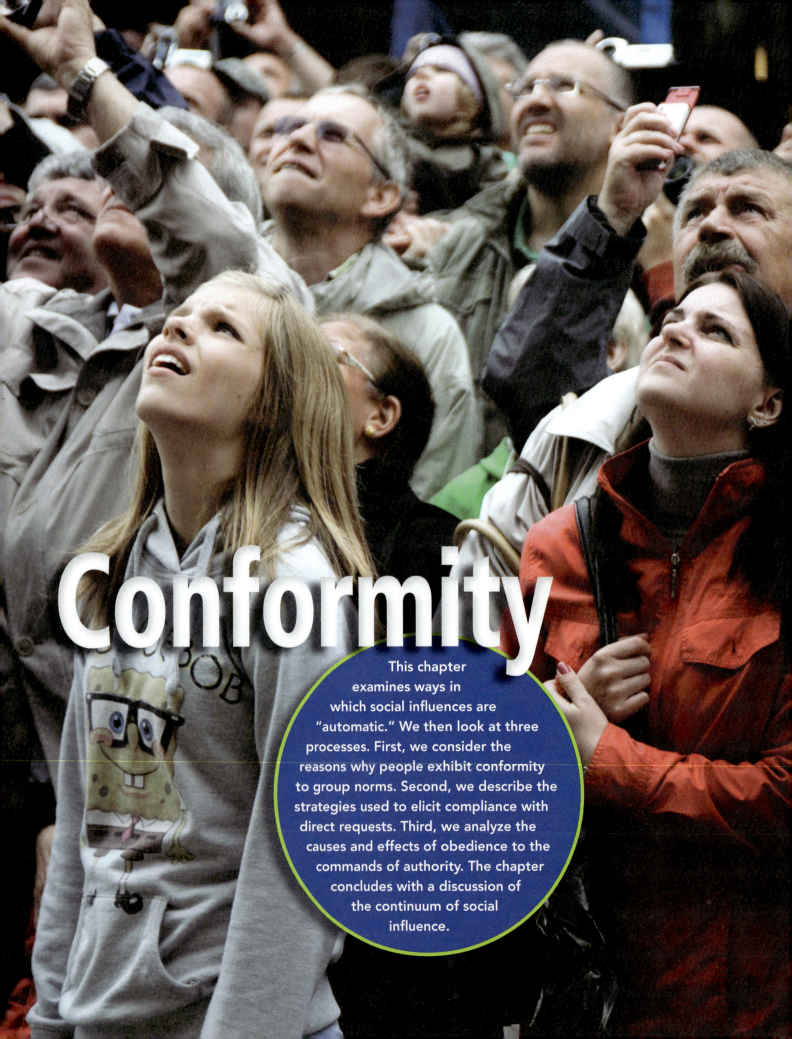

# Conformity

This chapter examines ways in which social influences are "automatic." We then look at three processes. First, we consider the reasons why people exhibit conformity to group norms. Second, we describe the strategies used to elicit compliance with direct requests. Third, we analyze the causes and effects of obedience to the commands of authority. The chapter concludes with a discussion of the continuum of social influence.

# 7

Krzysztof Dydynski/Getty Images

...

**On a Thursday evening in the summer of 2009,** a couple hundred ordinary people who were strangers to one another showed up in San Francisco's Union Square. At precisely 6 p.m., on cue, the impromptu group belted out the Beatles' song "With a Little Help from My Friends." Earlier that week, in York, England, feathers flew outside of the well-known Yorkshire Museum and Gardens when 500 happy Facebook users appeared, pillows in hand, for a mass pillow fight that lasted 5 minutes. In both cases, participants had received instructions on the Internet, gathered voluntarily at a set time and place, performed a silly but harmless action, and quickly dispersed. Illustrating the viral power of the Internet to serve as a vehicle for social influence, other "flash mobs" have formed in New York, Rome, Paris, Amsterdam, Berlin, Oslo, Melbourne, Budapest, Boston, Chicago, Los Angeles, Denver, Houston, and other cities.

Sometimes the social influences that move us are not entertaining and funny but potentially hazardous to our health. Consider the unusual events that occurred a while back in a Tennessee high school. It started when a teacher noticed a gas-like smell in her classroom and then came down with a headache, nausea, shortness of breath, and dizziness. Word spread. Others soon reported the same symptoms, and the school was evacuated. Eighty students and several staff members were taken to a local emergency room. Nothing showed up in blood tests, urine tests, or other medical procedures, nor were gases, pesticides, or other toxins detected. What the investigation did turn up was that students who reported feeling ill that day were more likely than others to have seen or heard about someone with symptoms. Reporting in the *New England Journal of Medicine*, researchers concluded that the problem stemmed from "mass psychogenic illness"—a profound, almost contagious form of social influence (Jones et al., 2000).

In *Outbreak! The Encyclopedia of Extraordinary Social Behavior*, Hilary Evans and Robert Bartholomew (2009) note that these types of incidents have occurred throughout human history, causing people to break out in rashes, vomit, bark, twirl, faint, strip naked, or laugh uncontrollably. The behaviors may vary. Recently, in Le Roy High School in Western New York, 6 girls—a number that grew to 18—developed a number of mysterious motor tics, uncontrollably writhing, shaking, twitching, head jerking, arms swinging, grimacing, and stuttering (Dominus, 2012).

*"We are discreet sheep; we wait to see how the drove is going and then go with the drove."*
—Mark Twain

Flash mobs and mass psychogenic illnesses reveal the awesome power of social influence. The effects that people have on each other can also be seen in mundane human events. Thus, sports fans spread the "wave" around massive stadiums, sing in unison, or chant "de-fense" in a spectacular show of unison. TV producers insert canned laughter into sitcoms to increase viewer responsiveness. Politicians trumpet the inflated results of their own favorable public opinion polls to attract voters. And bartenders, waiters, waitresses, and street musicians stuff dollar bills into their tip jars as a way to get others to follow suit. As they say, "Monkey see, monkey do."

You don't need to be a social psychologist to know that people have an impact on each other's behavior. The

# Putting *Common Sense* to the Test

### Circle Your Answer

T  F    When all members of a group give an incorrect response to an easy question, most people most of the time conform to that response.

T  F    An effective way to get someone to do you a favor is to make a first request that is so large the person is sure to reject it.

T  F    In experiments on obedience, most participants who were ordered to administer severe shocks to an innocent person refused to do so.

T  F    As the number of people in a group increases, so does the group's impact on an individual.

T  F    Conformity rates vary across different cultures and from one generation to the next.

trickier question is, How and with what effect? The term *social influence* refers to the ways that people are affected by the real and imagined pressures of others (Cialdini & Goldstein, 2004; Kiesler & Kiesler, 1969). The kinds of influences brought to bear on an individual come in different shapes and sizes. In this chapter, we look at social influences that are mindless and automatic. Then we consider three forms of influence that vary in the degree of pressure exerted on an individual—*conformity*, *compliance*, and *obedience*. As depicted in ● Figure 7.1, conformity, compliance, and obedience are not distinct, qualitatively different "types" of influence. In all three cases, the influence may emanate from a person, a group, or an institution. And in all instances, the behavior in question maybe constructive (helping oneself or others) or destructive (hurting oneself or others) or neutral. It is useful to note, once again, that social influence varies as points along a continuum according to the degree of pressure exerted on the individual. It is also useful to note that we do not always succumb under pressure. People may conform or maintain their independence from others, they may comply with direct requests or react with assertiveness, or they may obey the commands of authority or oppose powerful others in an act of defiance. In this chapter, we examine the factors that lead human beings to yield to or resist social influence.

# Social Influence as "Automatic"

Before we consider the explicit forms of social influence depicted in Figure 7.1, whereby individuals choose whether or not to "go along," it's important to note that as social animals humans are vulnerable to a host of subtle, almost reflex-like influences. Without realizing it, we often crack open an involuntary yawn when we see others yawning, laugh aloud when we hear others laughing, and grimace when we see others in pain. In an early demonstration, Stanley Milgram and others (1969) had research confederates stop on a busy street in New York City, look up, and gawk at the sixth-floor window of a nearby building. Films shot from behind the window indicated that about 80% of passersby stopped and gazed up when they saw the confederates.

Rudimentary forms of automatic imitation have been observed in various animal species, such as pigeons, monkeys, hamsters, and fish (Heyes, 2011; Zentall, 2012). There is even evidence to suggest that "cultures" are transmitted through imitation in groups of whales, as when humpback whales off the coast of Maine use lobtail feeding, a technique in which they slam their tail flukes onto the water, then dive and exhale, forming clouds of bubbles that envelop schools of prey fish. This complex behavior was first

● **FIGURE 7.1**

**Continuum of Social Influence**

Social influences vary in the degree of pressure they bring to bear on an individual. People may (1) conform to group norms or maintain their independence, (2) comply with requests or be assertive, and (3) obey or defy the commands of authority.
© Cengage Learning

**Yielding to Influence**                                                                 **Resisting Influence**

Obedience     Compliance     Conformity          Independence    Assertiveness     Defiance

Among humpback whales off the coast of Maine, "lobtail feeding" (a complex behavior that traps prey fish) was first observed in 1981. Through imitation, it soon spread across the entire whale population in the region.

observed in 1981. By 1989 it was measurably adopted by 50% of the whale population in that area (Rendell & Whitehead, 2001). Similar observations in other species have led animal scientists to suggest that many nonhuman animals form and transmit cultures to succeeding generations (Laland & Galef, 2009).

Do humans similarly imitate one another automatically, without thought, effort, or conflict? It appears that we do. In recent years, controlled studies of human infants have shown that sometimes shortly after birth, babies not only look at faces but (to the delight of parents all over the world) often they mimic simple gestures such as moving the head, pursing the lips, and sticking out the tongue (Meltzoff & Moore, 1977; Ray & Heyes, 2010). Studying 162 infants from 6 to 20 months old, Susan Jones (2007) found that imitation developed at different rates for different behaviors. Using parents as models, she found, for example, that infants mimicked opening the mouth wide, tapping their fingers on a table, and waving bye-bye before they mimicked clapping hands, flexing their fingers, or putting their hands on the head.

You may not realize it, but human adults unwittingly mimic each other all the time. To demonstrate, Tanya Chartrand and John Bargh (1999) set up participants to work on a task with a partner, a confederate who exhibited the habit of rubbing his face or shaking his foot. Hidden cameras recording the interaction revealed that without realizing it, participants mimicked these motor behaviors, rubbing their face or shaking a foot to match their partner's behavior. Chartrand and Bargh dubbed this phenomenon the "chameleon effect," after the lizard that changes colors according to its physical environment (see ● Figure 7.2).

There are two possible reasons for this nonconscious form of imitation. Chartrand and Bargh speculated that such mimicry serves an important *social* function, that being "in sync" in their pace, posture, mannerisms, facial expressions, tone of voice, accents, speech patterns, and other behaviors enables people to interact more smoothly with one another. Accordingly, Chartrand and Bargh (1999) turned the tables in a second study in which they instructed their confederate to match in subtle ways the mannerisms of some participants but not others. Sure enough, participants who had been mimicked liked the confederate more than those who had not. Further demonstrating the social aspect of mimicry, research shows that people mimic others more when they are highly motivated to affiliate—say, because they are similar to these others or are feeling excluded—than when they are not (Chartrand & van Baaren, 2009; Guéguen & Martin, 2009; Huntsinger et al., 2009; Lakin et al., 2008).

Social mimicry is so powerful that it can influence us even when the mimicker is not a real person. In a study entitled "digital chameleons," Jeremy Bailenson and Nick Yee (2005) immersed college students, one at a time, in a virtual reality environment in which they found themselves seated at a table across from a human-like person that looked something like a three-dimensional cartoon character. This character proceeded to argue that students should be required to carry identification cards at all times for security purposes. In half the sessions, this virtual speaker's back-and-forth head movements perfectly mimicked the participant's head movements at a four-second delay. In the other half, the speaker repeated the head movements of an earlier recorded participant. Very few of the students who were mimicked were aware of it. Yet when later asked about the experience, they rated the virtual character as more likable and were persuaded by its speech more if it imitated their head movements than if it imitated the movements of the previous participant.

● **FIGURE 7.2**

**The Chameleon Effect**

This graph shows the number of times per minute participants rubbed their face or shook their foot when they were with a confederate who was rubbing or shaking his foot.

From Kassin, S., *Psychology* 3rd ed. Copyright © 1997. Reprinted by permission of Pearson Education, Inc., Upper Saddle River, NJ.

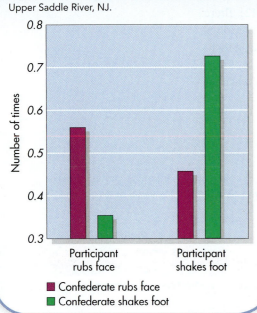

The human impulse to mimic others may have adaptive social value, but these types of effects can also be found in *nonsocial* situations. In one study, Roland Neumann and Fritz Strack (2000) had people listen to an abstract philosophical speech that was recited on tape in a happy, sad, or neutral voice. Afterward, participants rated their own mood as more positive when they heard the happy voice and as more negative when they heard the sad voice. Even though the speakers and participants never interacted, the speaker's emotional state was infectious, an automatic effect that can be described as a form of "mood contagion." The same can be true about the way we mimic the language we hear in other people's expressions and speech styles. To illustrate, Molly Ireland and James Pennebaker (2010) found that college students answering essay questions or working from excerpts of fictional writing tended in subtle ways to match the language style of the target material to which they were exposed—for example, in terms of their use of personal pronouns (such as *I, you*), conjunctions (such as *but, while*), and quantifiers (such as *many, few*).

Often we are not aware of the influence other people have on our behavior.

It is also important to realize that mimicry is a dynamic process, as when two people who are walking together or dancing become more and more coordinated over time. To demonstrate, Michael Richardson and others (2005) sat pairs of college students side by side to work on visual problems while swinging a handheld pendulum as "a distraction task." The students did not need to be synchronized in their swinging tempo in order to get along or solve the problems. Yet when each could see the other's pendulum (and even without speaking), their tempos gradually converged over time—like two hearts beating as one.

# Conformity

It is hard to find behaviors that are not in some way affected by exposure to the actions of others. When social psychologists talk of **conformity**, they specifically refer to the tendency of people to change their perceptions, opinions, and behavior in ways that are consistent with group norms.

Using this definition, would you call yourself a conformist or a nonconformist? How often do you feel inclined to follow what others are saying or doing? At first, you may deny the tendency to conform and, instead, declare your individuality and uniqueness. But think about it. When was the last time you attended a formal wedding dressed in blue jeans or remained seated during the national anthem at a sports event? People find it difficult to breach social norms. In an early demonstration of this point, research assistants were recruited to ask subway passengers to give up their seats—a conspicuous violation of the norm of acceptable conduct. Many of the assistants could not carry out their assignment. In fact, some of those who tried it became so anxious that they pretended to be ill just to make their request appear justified (Milgram & Sabini, 1978).

Because conformity is so widespread, it is interesting and ironic that research participants in North America who are coaxed into following a group norm will often not admit to being influenced. Instead, they try to reinterpret the task and rationalize their behavior as a way to see themselves in as independent (Hornsey & Jetten, 2004). This

**conformity** The tendency to change our perceptions, opinions, or behavior in ways that are consistent with group norms.

resistance to the conformity label is particularly characteristic of individuals who have high status and seniority within a group (Jetten et al., 2006). But there is a second reason why people do not see themselves as conformist. In a series of studies, Emily Pronin and others (2007) found that people perceive others to be more conforming than themselves in all sorts of domains—from why they bought an iPad to why they hold a popular opinion. Part of the reason for this asymmetry is that whereas people judge others by their overt behavior and the degree to which it matches what others do, they tend to judge themselves by focusing inward and introspecting about their thought processes, which blinds them to their own conformity.

People understandably have mixed feelings about conformity After all, some degree of it is essential if individuals are to maintain communities and coexist peacefully, as when people assume their rightful place in a waiting line. Yet at other times, conformity can have harmful consequences, as when people drink too heavily at parties, cheat on their taxes, or tell offensive jokes because they believe others are doing the same. For the social psychologist, the goal is to understand the conditions that promote conformity or independence and the reasons for these behaviors.

## The Early Classics

In 1936, Muzafer Sherif published a classic laboratory study of how norms develop in small groups. His method was ingenious. Male students, who believed they were participating in a visual perception experiment, sat in a totally darkened room. Fifteen feet in front of them, a small dot of light appeared for 2 seconds, after which participants were asked to estimate how far it had moved. This procedure was repeated several times. Although participants didn't realize it, the dot of light always remained motionless. The movement they thought they saw was merely an optical illusion known as the *autokinetic effect*: In darkness, a stationary point of light appears to move, sometimes erratically, in various directions.

At first, participants sat alone and reported their judgments to the experimenter. After several trials, Sherif found that they settled in on their own stable perceptions of movement, with most estimates ranging from 1 to 10 inches (although one participant gave an estimate of 80 feet!). Over the next 3 days, people returned to participate openly in three-person groups. As before, lights were flashed and the participants, one by one, announced their estimates. As shown in ● Figure 7.3, initial estimates varied considerably, but participants later converged on a common perception. Eventually, each group established its own set of norms.

Some 15 years after Sherif's demonstration, Solomon Asch (1951) constructed a very different task for testing how people's beliefs affect the beliefs of others. To appreciate what Asch did, imagine yourself in the following situation. You sign up for a psychology experiment, and when you arrive, you find six other students waiting around a table. Soon after you take an empty seat, the experimenter explains that he is interested in the ability to make

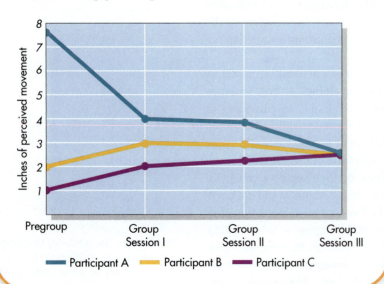

● **FIGURE 7.3**

**A Classic Case of Suggestibility**

This graph, taken from Sherif's study, shows how three participants' estimates of the apparent movement of light gradually converged. Before they came together, their perceptions varied considerably. Once in groups, however, participants conformed to the norm that had developed. Sherif, 1936. © Cengage Learning visual discriminations. As an example, he asks you and the others to indicate which of three comparison lines is identical in length to a standard line.

That seems easy enough. The experimenter then says that after each set of lines is shown, you and the others should take turns announcing your judgments out loud in the order of your seating position. Beginning on his left, the experimenter asks the first person for his judgment. Seeing that you are in the next-to-last position, you patiently await your turn. The opening moments pass uneventfully. The task and discriminations are clear and everyone agrees on the answers. On the third set of lines, however, the first participant selects what is quite clearly the wrong line. Huh? What happened? Did he suddenly lose his mind, his eyesight, or both? Before you have the chance to figure this one out, the next four participants choose the same wrong line. Now what? Feeling as if you have entered the twilight zone, you wonder if you misunderstood the task. And you wonder what the others will think if you have the nerve to disagree. It's your turn now. You rub your eyes and take another look. What do you see? More to the point, what do you do?

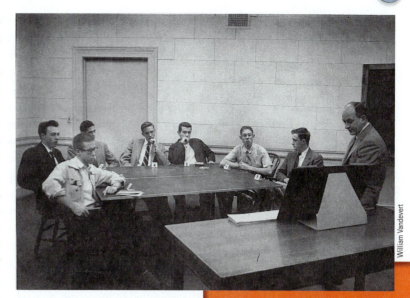

William Vandevert

After two uneventful rounds in Asch's study, the participant (seated second from the right) faces a dilemma. The answer he wants to give in the third test of visual discrimination differs from that of the first five confederates, who are all in agreement. Should he give his own answers or conform to theirs?

● Figure 7.4 gives you a sense of the bind in which Asch's participants found themselves—caught between the need to be right and the desire to be liked (Insko et al., 1982; Ross et al., 1976). As you may suspect by now, the other "participants" were actually confederates and had been trained to make incorrect judgments on 12 out of 18 presentations. There seems little doubt that the real participants knew the correct answers. In a control group, where they made judgments in isolation, they made almost no errors. Yet Asch's participants went along with the incorrect majority 37% of the time—far more often than most of us would ever predict. Not everyone conformed, of course. About 25% refused to agree on any of the incorrect group judgments. Yet 50% went along on at least half of the critical presentations and remaining participants conformed on an occasional basis. Similarly high levels of conformity were observed when Asch's study was repeated 30 years later and in recent studies involving other cognitive tasks. For example, recent research demonstrates strong conformity effects on memory—as when an eyewitness is influenced by the report of a co-witness (Gabbert et al., 2003; Horry et al., 2012). Recent research also shows Asch-like conformity effects on the perceptual judgments of 3- and 4-year-old children (Corriveau et al., 2009; Corriveau & Harris, 2010).

Let's compare Sherif's and Asch's classic studies of social influence. Obviously, both demonstrate that our visual perceptions can be heavily influenced by others. But how similar are they, really? Did Sherif's and Asch's participants exhibit the same kind of conformity and for the same reasons or was the resemblance in their behavior more apparent than real?

● **FIGURE 7.4**

**Line Judgment Task Used in Asch's Conformity Studies**

Which comparison line—A, B, or C—is the same in length as the standard line? What would you say if you found yourself in the presence of a unanimous majority that answered A or C? The participants in Asch's experiments conformed to the majority about a third of the time. Asch, 1955. © Cengage Learning

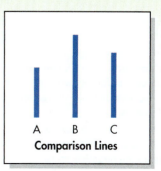

From the start, it was clear that these studies differed in some important ways. In Sherif's research, participants were quite literally "in the dark," so they naturally turned to others for guidance. When physical reality is ambiguous and we are uncertain of our own judgments, as in the autokinetic situation, others can serve as a valuable source of information (Festinger, 1954). Asch's participants found themselves in a much more awkward position. Their task was relatively simple, and they could see with their own eyes which answers were correct. Still, they often followed the incorrect majority. In interviews, many of Asch's participants reported afterward that they went along with the group even though they were not convinced that the group was right. Many who did not conform said they felt "conspicuous" and "crazy," like a "misfit" (Asch, 1956, p. 31).

Worldwide, 2.27 billion people, accounting for almost 33% of the planet's population, have access to the Internet (Internet World Stats, 2011). This being the case, you may wonder: Do the social forces that influence people in the face-to-face encounters studied by Sherif and Asch also operate in virtual groups whose members are nameless, faceless, and anonymous? The answer is yes. McKenna and Bargh (1998) observed behavior in various online blogs in which people with common interests posted and responded to messages on a whole range of topics, from obesity and sexual orientation to money and the stock market. The social nature of the medium in this virtual situation was "remote." Still, these researchers found that in newsgroups that brought together people with "hidden identities" (such as gays and lesbians who had concealed their sexuality), members were highly responsive to social feedback. Those who posted messages that were met with approval rather than disapproval later became more active participants of the newsgroup. When it comes to social support and rejection, even remote virtual groups have the power to shape our behavior (Bargh & McKenna, 2004; Williams et al., 2000).

## Why Do People Conform?

The Sherif and Asch studies demonstrate that people conform for two very different reasons: one informational, the other normative (Crutchfield, 1955; Deutsch & Gerard, 1955).

**A Need to Be Right**  Through **informational influence**, people conform because they want to make good and accurate judgments of reality and assume that when others agree on something, they must be right. In Sherif's autokinetic task, as in other difficult or ambiguous tasks, it's natural to assume that four eyes are better than two. Hence, research shows that eyewitnesses trying to recall a crime or some other event will alter their recollections and even create false memories in response to what they hear other witnesses report (Gabbert et al., 2003).

When people are in a state of uncertainty, following the collective wisdom of others may prove to be an effective strategy. In the popular TV game show *Who Wants to Be a Millionaire?* contestants who are stumped on a question can invoke one of two human forms of assistance: (1) calling a friend or relative who serves as a designated "expert"; or (2) polling the studio audience, which casts votes by computer for instant feedback. Overall, the "experts" are useful, as they offered the correct answer 65% of the time. Illustrating the wisdom of crowds, however, the studio audiences were even more useful, picking the right answer 91% of the time (Surowiecki, 2005).

**A Fear of Ostracism**  In contrast to the informational value of conformity, **normative influence** leads people to conform because they fear the consequence of rejection that follows deviance. It's easy to see why. Early on, research showed that individuals who

---

When all members of a group give an incorrect response to an easy question, most people most of the time conform to that response. **F**ALSE.

---

**informational influence**  Influence that produces conformity when a person believes others are correct in their judgments.

**normative influence**  Influence that produces conformity when a person fears the negative social consequences of appearing deviant.

stray from a group's norm tend to be disliked, rejected, ridiculed, and outright dismissed (Schachter, 1951). Although some people are more resilient than others, these forms of interpersonal rejection can be hard to take (Smart Richman & Leary, 2009).

In a series of controlled studies, people who were socially *ostracized*—for example, by being neglected, ignored, and excluded in a live or online chatroom conversation—react with various types of emotional distress, feeling alone, hurt, angry, and lacking in self-esteem (Williams et al., 2002; Gerber & Wheeler, 2009). Even being left out of a three-way text-messaging conversation on a cell phone can have this effect on us (Smith & Williams, 2004). Kipling Williams and Steve Nida (2011) note that the research on this point is clear: Some people become so distressed when they are rejected, ignored, or excluded from a group, even one that is newly and briefly formed, that they begin to feel numb, sad, angry, or some combination of these emotions. Over time, ostracism becomes a form of social death, making it difficult to cope.

Why does being ostracized hurt so much? Increasingly, social psychologists are coming to appreciate the extent to which human beings, over the course of evolution, have needed each other in order to survive and flourish. According to Geoff MacDonald and Mark Leary (2005), this need is so primitive that rejection can inflict a social pain that feels just like physical pain. You can sense the connection in the way people describe their emotional reactions to social loss using such words as "hurt," "brokenhearted," and "crushed." Recent research lends provocative support to this linkage. In brain-imaging studies, for example, young people who were left out by other players in a three-person Internet ball tossing game called "Cyberball" exhibited elevated neural activity in a part of the brain that is normally associated with physical pain (Eisenberger et al., 2003).

If there is a silver lining, it is that social pain can have positive motivating effects. Once feeling rejected, people seek to re-affiliate with others, which should increase their sensitivity to social perception cues that signal opportunities for inclusion. In a study that tested this hypothesis, Michael Bernstein and others (2008) found that research participants who were led to feel socially rejected or excluded became more accurate in their ability to distinguish between true smiles, which betray happiness and an openness to interaction, and "masking" smiles, which do not express a genuine emotion.

**Distinguishing Types of Conformity**   In group settings, both informational and normative influences are typically at work. Consider the Asch experiment. Even though many of his participants said they had conformed just to avoid being different, others said that they came to agree with their group's erroneous judgments. Is that possible? At the time, Asch had to rely on what his participants reported in interviews. Thanks to recent developments in social neuroscience, however, researchers can now peer into the socially active brain. In an ingenious medical school study that illustrates the point, Gregory Berns and others (2005) put 32 adults into a visual-spatial perception experiment in which they were asked to "mentally rotate" two geometric objects to determine if they were the same or different (see ● Figure 7.5). As in the original Asch study, participants were accompanied by four confederates who unanimously made incorrect judgments on certain trials. Unlike in the original study, however, participants were placed in an fMRI scanner while engaged in the task. There were two noteworthy results. First, participants conformed to 41% of the group's incorrect judgments. Second, these conforming judgments were accompanied by heightened activity in a part of the brain that controls spatial awareness—not in areas associated with conscious decision making. These results suggest that the group altered perceptions, not just behavior.

The distinction between the two types of social influence—informational and normative—is important, not just for understanding why people conform but because

● **FIGURE 7.5**

**Conformity Effects on Perception**

In this study, participants tried to determine if pairs of geometric objects were the same or different after observing the responses of four unanimous confederates. Participants followed the incorrect group 41% of the time. Suggesting that the group had altered perceptions, not just behavior, fMRI results showed that these conforming judgments were accompanied by increased activity in a part of the brain that controls spatial awareness.

Berns et al., 2005. Courtesy of Gregory Berns. © Cengage Learning

the two sources of influence produce different types of conformity: private and public (Allen, 1965; Kelman, 1961). Like beauty, conformity may be skin deep or it may penetrate beneath the surface. **Private conformity**, also called true acceptance or conversion, describes instances in which others cause us to change not only our overt behavior but our minds as well. To conform at this level is to be truly persuaded that others in a group are correct. In contrast, **public conformity** (sometimes called *compliance*, a term used later in this chapter to describe a different form of influence) refers to a more superficial change in behavior. People often respond to normative pressures by pretending to agree even when privately they do not. This often happens when we want to curry favor with others. The politician who tells constituents whatever they want to hear is a case in point.

How, you might be wondering, can social psychologists ever tell the difference between the private and public conformist? After all, both exhibit the same change in their observable behavior. The difference is that compared with someone who merely acquiesces in public, the individual who is truly persuaded maintains that change long after the group is out of the picture. When this distinction is applied to Sherif's and Asch's research, the results come out as expected. At the end of his study, Sherif (1936) retested participants alone and found that their estimates continued to reflect the norm previously established in their group—even among those who were retested a full year after the experiment (Rohrer et al., 1954). In contrast, when Asch (1956) had participants write their answers privately, so that others in the group could not see, their level of conformity dropped sharply (Deutsch & Gerard, 1955; Mouton et al., 1956).

In a study that demonstrated both processes, Robert S. Baron and others (1996) had people in groups of three (one participant and two confederates) act as eyewitnesses: First, they would see a picture of a person, then they would try to pick that person out of a lineup. In some groups, the task was difficult, like Sherif's, since participants saw each picture only once for half a second. For other groups, the task was easier, like Asch's, in that they saw each picture twice for a total of 10 seconds. How often did participants conform when the confederates made the wrong identification? It depended on how motivated they were. When the experimenter downplayed the task as only a "pilot study," the conformity rates were 35% when the task was difficult and 33% when it was easy. But when participants were offered a financial incentive to do well, conformity went up to 51% when the task was difficult and down to 16% when it was easy (see ● Figure 7.6). With pride and money on the line, the Sherif-like participants conformed more and the Asch-like participants conformed less.

**private conformity** The change of beliefs that occurs when a person privately accepts the position taken by others.

**public conformity** A superficial change in overt behavior without a corresponding change of opinion that is produced by real or imagined group pressure.

Table 7.1 summarizes the comparison of Sherif's and Asch's studies and the depths of social influence that they demonstrate. Looking at this table, you can see that the difficulty of the task is crucial. When reality cannot easily be validated by physical evidence, as in the autokinetic situation, people turn to others for information and conform because they are truly persuaded by that information. When reality is clear, however, the cost of dissent becomes the major issue. As Asch found, it can be difficult to depart too much from others even when you know that they—not you—are wrong. So you play along. Privately you don't change your mind. But you nod your head in agreement anyway.

## Majority Influence

Realizing that people often succumb to pressure from peers is only a first step in understanding the process of social influence. The next step is to identify the situational and personal factors that make us more or less likely to conform. We know that people tend to conform when the social pressure is intense and that they are insecure about how to behave. But what creates these feelings of pressure and insecurity? Here, we look at four factors: the size of the group, a focus on norms, the presence of an ally, and gender.

**Group Size: The Power in Numbers**   Common sense would suggest that as the number of other people in a majority increases, so should their impact. Actually, it is not that simple. Asch (1956) varied the size of groups, using 1, 2, 3, 4, 8, or 15 confederates, and he found that conformity increased with group size—but only up to a point. Once there were 3 or 4 confederates, the amount of *additional* influence exerted by the rest was negligible. Other researchers have obtained similar results (Gerard et al., 1968).

Beyond the presence of three or four others, additions to a group are subject to the law of "diminishing returns" (Knowles, 1983; Mullen, 1983). As we will see later, Bibb Latané (1981) likens the influence of people on an individual to the way lightbulbs illuminate a surface. When a second bulb is added to a room, the effect is dramatic. When

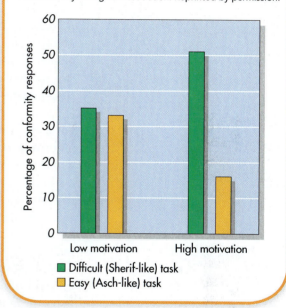

● **FIGURE 7.6**

**Distinguishing Types of Conformity**

People made judgments under conditions in which they had a high or low level of motivation. Regardless of whether the judgment task was difficult or easy, there were moderate levels of conformity when participants had low motivation (left). But when they were highly motivated (right), participants conformed more when the task was difficult (as in Sherif's study) and less when it was easy (as in Asch's study).

From Baron, R. et al., *Journal of Personality and Social Psychology* vol 71 (pp. 915–927). Copyright © 1996 by the American Psychological Association. Reprinted by permission.

**TABLE 7.1**

**Two Types of Conformity**

A comparison of Sherif's and Asch's studies suggests different kinds of conformity for different reasons. Sherif used an ambiguous task, so others provided a source of information and influenced the participants' true opinions. Asch used a task that required simple judgments of a clear stimulus, so most participants exhibited occasional public conformity in response to normative pressure but privately did not accept the group's judgments.

| Experimental Task | Primary Effect of Group | Depth of Conformity Produced |
|---|---|---|
| Sherif 's ambiguous autokinetic effect | Informational influence | Private acceptance |
| Asch's simple-line judgments | Normative influence | Public conformity |

© Cengage Learning

the tenth bulb is added, however, its impact is barely felt, if at all. Economists say the same about the perception of money. An additional dollar seems greater to the person who has only three dollars than it does to the person who has 300.

Another possible explanation is that as more and more people express the same opinion, an individual is likely to suspect that they are acting either in "collusion" or as "spineless sheep." According to David Wilder (1977), what matters is not the actual number of others in a group but one's perception of how many distinct others who are thinking independently the group includes. Indeed, Wilder found that people were more influenced by two groups of two than by one four-person group and by two groups of three than by one six-person group. Conformity increased even more when people were exposed to three two-person groups. When faced with a majority opinion, we do more than just count the number of warm bodies—we try to assess the number of independent minds.

**A Focus on Norms**   The size of a majority may influence the amount of pressure that is felt, but social norms give rise to conformity only when we know the norms and focus on them. This may sound like an obvious point, yet we often misperceive what is normative, particularly when others are too afraid or too embarrassed to publicly present their true thoughts, feelings, and behaviors.

One common example of this "pluralistic ignorance" concerns perceptions of alcohol usage. In a number of college-wide surveys, Deborah Prentice and Dale Miller (1996) found that most students overestimated how comfortable their peers were with the level of drinking on campus. Those who most overestimated how others felt about drinking at the start of the school year eventually conformed to this misperception in their own attitudes and behavior. In contrast, students who took part in discussion sessions that were designed to correct these misperceptions actually consumed less alcohol 6 months later. These findings are important. Additional research has shown that both male and female students tend to overestimate how frequently their same-sex peers use various substances and the quantities they consume. Whether the substance in question is alcohol, tobacco, or marijuana, the more normative students perceive peer usage to be, the more they consume (Henry et al., 2011).

Knowing how others are behaving in a situation is necessary for conformity, but these norms will influence us only when they are brought to our awareness, or "activated." Robert Cialdini (2003) and his colleagues have demonstrated this point in studies on littering. In one study, researchers had confederates pass out handbills to amusement park visitors and varied the amount of litter that appeared in one section of the park (an indication of how others behave in that setting). The result: The more litter there was,

In sports stadiums, restaurants, and other settings, social norms influence us when they are brought to awareness by the current or past behavior of others.

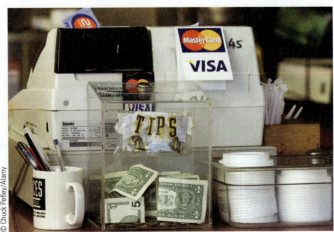

the more likely visitors were to toss their handbills to the ground (Cialdini et al., 1990). A second study showed that passersby were most influenced by the prior behavior of others when their attention was drawn to the existing norm. In this instance, people were observed in a parking garage that was either clean or cluttered with cigarette butts, candy wrappers, paper cups, and trash. In half of the cases, the norm that was already in place—clean or cluttered—was brought to participants' attention by a confederate who threw paper to the ground as he walked by. In the other half, the confederate passed by without incident. As participants reached their cars, they found a "Please Drive Safely" handbill tucked under the windshield wiper. Did they toss the paper to the ground or take it with them? The results showed that people were most likely to conform (by littering more when the garage was cluttered than when it was clean) when the confederate had littered—an act that drew attention to the norm (Cialdini et al., 1991).

**An Ally in Dissent: Getting by With a Little Help**   In Asch's initial experiment, unwitting participants found themselves pitted against unanimous majorities. But what if they had an ally, a partner in dissent? Asch investigated this issue and found that the presence of a single confederate who agreed with the participant reduced conformity by almost 80%. This finding, however, does not tell us why the presence of an ally was so effective. Was it because he or she *agreed with the participant* or because he or she *disagreed with the majority*? In other words, were the views of the participants strengthened because a dissenting confederate offered validating information or because dissent per se reduced normative pressures?

   A series of experiments explored these two possibilities. In one, Vernon Allen and John Levine (1969) led participants to believe that they were working together with four confederates. Three of these others consistently agreed on the wrong judgment. The fourth then followed the majority, agreed with the participant, or made a third judgment, which was also incorrect. This last variation was the most interesting: Even when the confederate did not validate their own judgment, participants conformed less often to the majority. In another experiment, Allen and Levine (1971) varied the competence of the ally. Some participants received support from an average person. In contrast, others found themselves supported by someone who wore very thick glasses and complained that he could not see the visual displays. Not a very reassuring ally, right? Wrong. Even though participants derived less comfort from this supporter than from one who seemed more competent at the task, his presence still reduced their level of conformity.

   Two important conclusions follow from this research. First, it is substantially more difficult for people to stand alone for their convictions than to be part of even a tiny minority. Second, *any* dissent—whether it validates an individual's opinion or not—can break the spell cast by a unanimous majority and reduce the normative pressures to conform. In an interesting possible illustration of how uncommon it is for individuals to single-handedly oppose a majority, researchers examined voting patterns on the U.S. Supreme Court from 1953 to 2001. Table 7.2 shows that out of 4,178 decisions in which all nine justices voted, the 8-to-1 split was the least frequent, occurring in only 10% of all decisions (Granberg & Barrels, 2005).

**Gender Differences**   Are there gender differences in conformity? Based on Asch's initial studies, social psychologists used to think that women, once considered the "weaker" sex, conform more than men. In light of all the research, however, it appears that two additional factors have to be considered. First, sex differences depend on how comfortable people are with the experimental task. Frank Sistrunk and John McDavid (1971) had male and female participants answer questions on stereotypically masculine, feminine, and gender-neutral topics. Along with each question, participants were told the percentage of others who agreed or disagreed. Although females conformed to the contrived majority more on masculine items, males conformed more on feminine items. There were no sex differences on the neutral questions. This finding suggests that one's familiarity with the issue at hand, not gender, is what affects conformity (Eagly & Carli, 1981).

A second factor is the type of social situation people face. As a general rule, gender differences are weak and unreliable. But there is an important exception: In face-to-face encounters, where people must disagree with each other openly, small differences do emerge. In fact, when participants think they are being observed, women conform more and men conform less than they do in a more private situation. Why does being "in public" create such a divergence in behavior? Alice Eagly (1987) argues that in front of others, people worry about how they come across and feel pressured to behave in ways that are viewed as acceptable according to traditional gender-role constraints. At least in public, men behave with fierce independence and autonomy, whereas women play a gentler, more harmonious role. From an evolutionary perspective, Vladas Griskevicius and others (2006) add that people are most likely to behave in gender-stereotyped ways when motivated to attract someone of the opposite sex. Consistent with research showing that women tend to like men who are independent, whereas men prefer women who are agreeable, their research shows that women conform more and that men conform less when primed to think about themselves in a romantic situation.

---

**TABLE 7.2**

**On Being a Lone Dissenter: Voting Patterns on the U.S. Supreme Court**

Out of 4,178 U.S. Supreme Court decisions handed down from 1953 to 2001, the 8-to-1 breakdown involving a lone dissenter was the least common type of vote. This historical observation is consistent with conformity research showing the power of the majority over an individual who lacks an ally

| Vote Breakdowns | Frequency |
|---|---|
| 9 to 0 | 35% |
| 8 to 1 | 10% |
| 7 to 2 | 14% |
| 6 to 3 | 20% |
| 5 to 4 | 21% |

Granberg & Bartels, 2005. © Cengage Learning

---

## Minority Influence

In a book entitled *Dissent in Dangerous Times*, Austin Sarat (2005) notes that while the freedom to dissent is highly valued in the American national psyche, individual dissenters are often vilified for their beliefs—especially in today's post-9/11 war on terrorism.

The fact is, it has never been easy for individuals to express unpopular views and enlist support for these views from others. Philosopher Bertrand Russell once said, "Conventional people are roused to frenzy by departure from convention, largely because they regard such departure as criticism of themselves." He may have been right. Although people who assert their beliefs against the majority are generally seen as competent and honest, they are also disliked and roundly rejected (Bassili & Provencal, 1988; Levine, 1989). It's no wonder that most people think twice before expressing unpopular positions. In a series of survey studies of what he called the "minority slowness effect," John Bassili (2003) asked people about their attitudes on social policy issues such as affirmative action or about their likes and dislikes for various celebrities, sports, foods, places, and activities. Consistently, and regardless of the topic, respondents who held minority opinions were slower to answer the questions than those in the majority.

Resisting the pressure to conform and maintaining one's independence may be socially difficult, but it is not impossible. History's famous heroes, villains, and creative minds are living proof: Joan of Arc, Jesus Christ, Charles Darwin, Mahatma Gandhi, and Nelson Mandela, to name just a few, were dissenters of their time who continue to capture the imagination. Then there is human behavior in the laboratory. Social psychologists have been so intrigued by Asch's initial finding that participants conformed 37% of the time that textbooks such as this one routinely refer to "Asch's conformity study." Yet the overlooked flip side of the coin is that Asch's participants refused to acquiesce

63% of the time—thus also indicating the power of independence, truth telling, and a concern for social harmony (Friend et al., 1990; Hodges & Geyer, 2006).

*Twelve Angry Men*, a classic film starring Henry Fonda, illustrates how a lone dissenter can resist the pressure to conform and convince others to follow. Almost as soon as the door of the jury room closes, the jury in this film takes a show-of-hands vote. The result is an 11-to-1 majority in favor of conviction with Fonda the lone holdout. Through 90 minutes of heated deliberation, Fonda works relentlessly to plant a seed of doubt in the minds of his peers. In the end, the jury reaches a unanimous verdict: *not* guilty.

Sometimes art imitates life; sometimes it does not. In this instance, Henry Fonda's heroics are highly atypical. When it comes to jury decision making, as we'll see in Chapter 12, the majority usually wins. Yet in trial juries, as in other small groups, there are occasional exceptions where minorities prevail—as when someone from the majority faction defects (Clark, 2001). Thanks to Serge Moscovici and others, we now know quite a bit about **minority influence** and the strategies that astute nonconformists use to act as agents of social change (Gardikiotis, 2011; Maass & Clark, 1984; Moscovici et al., 1985; Mugny & Perez, 1991).

**Moscovici's Theory**    According to Moscovici, majorities are powerful by virtue of their sheer *numbers*, whereas nonconformists derive power from the *style* of their behavior. It is not just what nonconformists say that matters but how they say it. To exert influence, says Moscovici, those in the minority must be forceful, persistent, and unwavering in support of their position. Yet at the same time, they must appear flexible and open-minded. Confronted with a consistent but evenhanded dissenter, members of the majority will sit up, take notice, and rethink their own positions.

Why should a consistent behavioral style prove effective? One possible reason is that unwavering repetition draws attention from those in the mainstream, which is a necessary first step to social influence. Another possibility is that consistency signals that the dissenter is unlikely to yield, which leads those in the majority to feel pressured to seek compromise. A third possible reason is that when confronted with someone who has the self-confidence and dedication to take an unpopular stand without backing down, people assume that he or she must have a point. Unless a dissenter is perceived in negative terms—as biased, obstinate, or just plain crazy—this situation stimulates others to re-examine their own views (Moskowitz, 1996). Of course, it helps to be seen as part of "us" rather than "them." Research shows that dissenters have more influence when people identify with them and perceive them to be similar in ways that are relevant and desirable (Turner, 1991; Wood et al., 1996).

Based on a meta-analysis of 97 experiments investigating minority influence, Wendy Wood and her colleagues (1994) concluded that there is strong support for the consistency hypothesis. In one classic study, for example, Moscovici and others (1969) turned Asch's procedure on its head by confronting people with a *minority* of confederates who made incorrect judgments. In groups of six, participants took part in what was supposed to be a study of color perception. They viewed a series of slides that all were blue but varied in intensity. For each slide, the participants took turns naming the color. The task was simple, but two confederates announced that the slides were green. When the confederates were *consistent*—that is, when both made incorrect green judgments for all slides—they had a surprising degree of influence. About a third of all participants incorrectly reported seeing at least one green slide, and 8% of all responses were incorrect. Subsequent research confirmed that the perception of consistency increases minority influence (Clark, 2001; Crano, 2000).

Noting that dissent often breeds hostility, Edwin Hollander (1958) recommended a different approach. Hollander warned that people who seek positions of leadership or

**minority influence**  The process by which dissenters produce change within a group.

challenge a group without first becoming accepted full-fledged members of that group run the risk that their opinions will fall on deaf ears. As an alternative to Moscovici's consistency strategy, Hollander suggested that to influence a majority, people should first conform in order to establish their credentials as competent insiders. By becoming members of the mainstream, they accumulate **idiosyncrasy credits**, or "brownie points." Once they have accumulated enough goodwill within the group, a certain amount of their deviance will then be tolerated. Several studies have shown that this "first conform, then dissent" strategy, like the "consistent dissent" approach, can be effective (Bray et al., 1982; Lortie-Lussier, 1987).

**Processes and Outcomes of Minority Influence**   Regardless of which strategy is used, minority influence is a force to be reckoned with. But does it work just like conformity, or is there something different about the way that minorities and majorities effect change? Some theorists believe that a *single process* accounts for both directions of social influence—that minority influence is like a "chip off the old block" (Latané & Wolf, 1981; Tanford & Penrod, 1984). Others have taken a *dual-process* approach (Moscovici, 1980; Nemeth, 1986). In this second view, majorities and minorities exert influence in different ways and for different reasons. Majorities, because they have power and control, elicit *public* conformity by bringing stressful normative pressures to bear on the individual. But minorities, because they are seen as seriously committed to their views, produce a deeper and more lasting form of *private* conformity, or *conversion*, by leading others to become curious and rethink their original positions.

To evaluate these single- and dual-process theories, researchers have compared the effects of majority and minority viewpoints on participants who are otherwise neutral on an issue in dispute. On the basis of this research, two conclusions can be drawn. First, the relative impact of majorities and minorities depends on whether the judgment that is being made is objective or subjective, a matter of fact or opinion. In a study conducted in Italy, Anne Maass and others (1996) found that majorities have greater influence on factual questions, for which only one answer is correct ("What percentage of its raw oil does Italy import from Venezuela?"), but that minorities exert equal impact on opinion questions, for which there is a range of acceptable responses ("What percentage of its raw oil *should* Italy import from Venezuela?"). People feel freer to stray from the mainstream on matters of opinion, when there is no right or wrong answer.

The second conclusion is that the relative effects of majority and minority points of view depend on how and when conformity is measured. To be sure, majorities have a decisive upper hand on direct or public measures of conformity. After all, people are reluctant to oppose a group norm in a conspicuous manner. But on more indirect or private measures of conformity, on attitude issues that are related but not focal to the point of conflict, or after the passage of time—all of which softens the extent to which majority participants would appear deviant—minorities exert a strong impact (Clark & Maass, 1990; Crano & Seyranian, 2009; Moscovici & Personnaz, 1991; Wood et al., 1996). As Moscovici cogently argued, each of us is changed in a meaningful but subtle way by minority opinion. Because of social pressures, we may not openly admit to influence, but sometimes the change is unmistakable (Wood et al., 1994).

According to Charlan Nemeth (1986), dissenters in a group serve a valuable purpose regardless of whether their views are correct. Dissenters spark innovation (De Dreu & De Vries, 2001). Simply by their willingness to stay firmly independent, minorities can force other group members to think more carefully, more openly, in new and different ways, and more creatively about a problem, enhancing the quality of a group's output. In one study, participants exposed to a minority viewpoint on how to solve anagram problems later found more novel solutions themselves (Nemeth & Kwan, 1987). In a

**idiosyncrasy credits** Interpersonal "credits" that a person earns by following group norms.

second study, those exposed to a consistent minority viewpoint on how to recall information later recalled more words from a list they were trying to memorize (Nemeth et al., 1990). In a third study, interacting groups with one dissenting confederate produced more original analyses of complex business problems (Van Dyne & Saavedra, 1996). Interestingly, Nemeth and others (2001) found that to have influence over a group, lone individuals must exhibit "authentic dissent," not merely play "devil's advocate," a tactic that actually bolsters a majority's position.

## Culture and Conformity

We humans are a heterogeneous and diverse lot. As a matter of *geography*, some of us live in large, heavily populated cities whereas others live in small towns, affluent suburbs, rural farming or fishing communities, hot and humid jungles, expansive deserts, high-altitude mountains, tropical islands, and vast arctic plains. Excluding dialects, more than 6,800 different *languages* are spoken. There are also hundreds of *religions* that people identify with—the most common being Christianity (33%), Islam (21%), Hinduism (14%), and Buddhism (6%), with Judaism (0.22%) and others claiming fewer adherents. Roughly 16% of the world's population is not affiliated with a religion (Adherents.com, 2012).

Linked together by historical time and geographical space, each culture has its own ideology, music, fashions, foods, laws, customs, and manners of expression. As many tourists and exchange students traveling abroad have come to learn, sometimes the hard way, the social norms that influence human conduct can vary in significant ways from one part of the world to another.

In *Do's and Taboos Around the World*, R. E. Axtell (1993) warns world travelers about some of these differences. Dine in an Indian home, he notes, and you should leave food on the plate to show the host that the portions were generous and you had enough to eat. Yet as a dinner guest in Bolivia, you would show your appreciation by cleaning your plate. Shop in an outdoor market in Iraq, and you should expect to negotiate the price of everything you buy. Plan an appointment in Brazil, and the person you're scheduled to meet is likely to be late; it's nothing personal. In North America, it is common to sit casually opposite someone with your legs outstretched. Yet in Nepal, as in many Muslim countries, it is

Cultures differ in their unique, often colorful norms. In Ecuador, many men wear handwoven Panama hats (top). In India, brightly colored powders are sold for the Hindu religious festival of Holi, which marks the beginning of spring (bottom left). In Spain, revelers in Pamplona hold up their bandanas before the start of the festival of San Fermin, during which six bulls run through crowded streets in the center of town (bottom right).

an insult to point the bottoms of your feet at someone. Even the way we space ourselves from each other is influenced by culture. Americans, Canadians, British, and northern Europeans keep a polite distance between themselves and others and feel "crowded" by the touchier, nose-to-nose style of the French, Greeks, Arabs, Mexicans, and people of South America. In the affairs of day-to-day living, each culture operates by its own rules of conduct.

Just as cultures differ in their social norms, so too they differ in the extent to which people are expected to adhere to those norms. As we saw in Chapter 3, there are different cultural orientations toward persons and their relationships to groups. Some cultures primarily value **individualism** and the virtues of independence, autonomy, and self-reliance, whereas others value **collectivism** and the virtues of interdependence, cooperation, and social harmony. Under the banner of individualism, personal goals take priority over group allegiances. Yet in collectivistic cultures, the person is first and foremost a loyal member of a family, city, team, company, church, and state.

What determines whether a culture becomes individualistic or collectivistic? Speculating on the origins of these orientations, Harry Triandis (1995) suggests that there are three key factors. The first is the *complexity* of a society. As people come to live in more complex industrialized societies (compared, for example, with a simpler life of food gathering among desert nomads), there are more groups to identify with, which means less loyalty to any one group and a greater focus on personal rather than collective goals. Second is the *affluence* of a society. As people prosper, they gain financial independence from each other, a condition that promotes social independence as well as mobility and a focus on personal rather than collective goals. The third factor is *heterogeneity*. Societies that are homogeneous or "tight" (where members share the same language, religion, and social customs) tend to be rigid and intolerant of those who veer from the norm. Societies that are culturally diverse or "loose" (where two or more cultures coexist) tend to be more permissive of dissent, thus allowing for more individual expression. According to Edward Sampson (2000), cultural orientations may also be rooted in religious ideologies, as in the link between Christianity and individualism.

Early research across nations showed that autonomy and independence are most highly valued in the United States, Australia, Great Britain, Canada, and the Netherlands, in that order. In contrast, other cultures value social harmony and "fitting in" for the sake of community, the most collectivist people being from Venezuela, Colombia, Pakistan, Peru, Taiwan, and China (Hofstede, 1980). Although it now appears that cultures differ in other more complicated ways and that individuals differ even within cultures (Oyserman et al., 2002), it is clear that nations on average vary in their orientations on the dimension of individualism (Schimmack et al., 2005). The difference can be seen in a host of basic institutions—such as the content of the stories told in school textbooks (Imada, 2012).

Do cultural orientations influence conformity? Among the Bantu of Zimbabwe, an African people in which deviance is scorned, 51% of participants who were placed in an Asch-like study conformed—more than the number typically seen in the United States (Whittaker & Meade, 1967). When John Berry (1979) compared participants from 17 cultures, he found that conformity rates ranged from a low of 18% among Inuit hunters of Baffin Island to a high of 60% among village-dwelling Temne farmers of West Africa. Additional analyses have shown that conformity rates are generally higher in cultures that are collectivistic rather than individualistic in orientation (Bond & Smith, 1996). Hence, many anthropologists—interested in human culture and its influence over individuals—study the processes of conformity and independence (Spradley & McCurdy 2012).

**individualism** A cultural orientation in which independence, autonomy, and self-reliance take priority over group allegiances.

**collectivism** A cultural orientation in which interdependence, cooperation, and social harmony take priority over personal goals.

# Compliance

In conformity situations, people follow implicit or explicit group norms. But another common form of social influence occurs when others make *direct requests* of us in the hope that we will comply. Situations calling for **compliance** take many forms. These include a friend's plea for help, sheepishly prefaced by the question "Can you do me a favor?" They also include the pop-up ads on the Internet designed to lure you into a commercial site and the salesperson's pitch for business prefaced by the dangerous words "Have I got a deal for you!" Sometimes, the request is up front and direct; what you see is what you get. At other times, it is part of a subtle and more elaborate manipulation.

How do people get others to comply with self-serving requests? How do police interrogators get crime suspects to confess? How do political parties draw millions of dollars in contributions from voters? How do *you* exert influence over others? Do you use threats, promises, politeness, deceit, or reason? Do you hint, coax, sulk, negotiate, throw tantrums, or pull rank whenever you can? To a large extent, the compliance strategies we use depend on how well we know the person we target, our status within a relationship, our personality, our culture, and the nature of the request.

By observing the masters of influence—advertisers, fund-raisers, politicians, and business leaders—social psychologists have learned a great deal about the subtle but effective strategies that are commonly used. What we see is that people often get others to comply with their requests by setting traps. Once caught in these traps, the unwary victim often finds it difficult to escape.

##  Mindlessness and Compliance

Sometimes people can be disarmed by the simple phrasing of a request, regardless of its merit. Consider, for example, requests that sound reasonable but offer no real basis for compliance. Ellen Langer and her colleagues (1978) have found that words alone can sometimes trick us into submission. In their research, an experimenter approached people who were using a library copying machine and asked to cut in. Three different versions of the request were used. In one, participants were simply asked, "Excuse me. I have five pages. May I use the Xerox machine?" In a second version, the request was justified by the added phrase "because I'm in a rush." As you would expect, more participants stepped aside when the request was justified (94%) than when it was not (60%). A third version of the request, however, suggests that the reason offered had little to do with the increase in compliance. In this case, participants heard the following: "Excuse me. I have five pages. May I use the Xerox machine because I have to make some copies?" If you read this request closely, you'll see that it really offered no reason at all. Yet 93% in this condition complied! It was as if the appearance of a reason, triggered by the word *because*, was all that was necessary. Indeed, Langer (1989) finds that the mind is often on "automatic pilot"—we respond *mindlessly* to words without fully processing the information they are supposed to convey. At least for requests that are small, "sweet little nothings" may be enough to win compliance.

It is interesting that although a state of mindlessness can make us vulnerable to compliance, it can also have the opposite effect. For example, many city dwellers will automatically walk past panhandlers on the street looking for a handout. Perhaps the way to increase compliance in such situations is to disrupt this mindless refusal

**compliance** Changes in behavior that are elicited by direct requests.

Con artists prosper from the tendency for people to respond mindlessly to requests that sound reasonable but offer no real basis for compliance.

response by making a request that is so unusual that it piques the target person's interest. To test this hypothesis, researchers had a confederate approach people on the street and make a request that was either typical ("Can you spare a quarter?") or atypical ("Can you spare 17 cents?"). The result: Atypical pleas elicited more comments and questions from those who were targeted—and produced a 60% increase in the number of people who gave money (Santos et al., 1994). In another study, researchers who went door to door selling holiday cards gained more compliance when they disrupted the mindless process and reframed the sales pitch. They sold more cards when they said the price was "three hundred pennies—that's three dollars, it's a bargain" than when they simply asked for three dollars (Davis & Knowles, 1999).

## The Norm of Reciprocity

A simple, unstated, but powerful rule of social behavior known as the *norm of reciprocity* dictates that we treat others as they have treated us (Gouldner, 1960). On the negative side, this norm can be used to sanction retaliation against those who cause us harm—"an eye for an eye." On the positive side, it leads us to feel obligated to repay others for acts of kindness. Thus, whenever we receive gifts, invitations, and free samples, we usually go out of our way to return the favor.

The norm of reciprocity contributes to the predictability and fairness of social interaction. However, it can also be used to exploit us. Dennis Regan (1971) examined this possibility in the following laboratory study. Individuals were brought together with a confederate who was trained to act in a likable or unlikable manner for an experiment on "aesthetics." In one condition, the confederate did the participant an unsolicited favor. He left during a break and returned with two bottles of Coca-Cola, one for himself and the other for the participant. In a second condition, he returned from the break empty-handed. In a third condition, participants were treated to a Coke, but by the experimenter, not the confederate. The confederate then told participants in all conditions that he was selling raffle tickets at 25 cents apiece and asked if they would be willing to buy any. On average, participants bought more raffle tickets when the confederate had earlier brought them a soft drink than when he had not. The norm of reciprocity was so strong that they returned the favor even when the confederate was not otherwise a likable character. In fact, participants in this condition spent an average of 43 cents on raffle tickets. At a time when soft drinks cost less than a quarter, the confederate made a handsome quick profit on his investment!

It's clear that the norm of reciprocity can be used to trap us, unwittingly, into acts of compliance. For example, research conducted in restaurants shows that waiters and waitresses can increase their tip percentages by writing, "Thank you" on the back of the customer's check, by drawing a happy face on it, or by placing candy on the check tray (Rind & Strohmetz, 2001; Strohmetz et al., 2002). But does receiving a favor make us feel indebted forever or is there a time limit to the social obligation that is so quietly unleashed? In an experiment designed to answer this question, Jerry Burger and others (1997) used Regan's soft drink favor and had the confederate try to "cash in" with a request either immediately or one week later. The result: Compliance levels increased in the immediate condition but not after a full week had passed. People may feel compelled to reciprocate, but that feeling—at least for small acts of kindness—is relatively short-lived.

Some people are more likely than others to trigger and exploit the reciprocity norm. According to Martin Greenberg and David Westcott (1983), individuals who use reciprocity to elicit compliance are called "creditors" because they always try to keep others in their debt so they can cash in when necessary. On a questionnaire that measures *reciprocation ideology*, people are identified as creditors if they endorse such statements as "If someone does you a favor, it's good to repay that person with a greater favor." On the receiving end, some people try more than others not to accept favors that might later set them up to be exploited. On a scale that measures *reciprocation wariness*, people are said to be wary if they express the suspicion, for example, that "asking for another's help gives them power over your life" (Eisenberger et al., 1987).

Cultures may also differ in terms of their reciprocation wariness—with interesting consequences for social behavior. Imagine that you bump into a casual friend at the airport, stop for a drink, and the friend offers to pay for it. Would you let the friend pay? Or, suppose a sales clerk in a supermarket offered you a free sample of soup to taste. Would you accept the offer? Theorizing that the norm of reciprocity operates with particular force in collectivist cultures that foster interdependence, Hao Shen and others (2011) conducted a series of studies in which they posed these kinds of questions to Chinese college students from Hong Kong and to European American students from Canada. As you can see in ● Figure 7.7, the students from China were consistently less willing to accept the favor. Additional questioning revealed that these participants were more likely to see the gift giver's motives as self-serving and to feel uncomfortably indebted by the situation.

## Setting Traps: Sequential Request Strategies

People who raise money or sell for a living know that it often takes more than a single plea to win over a potential donor or customer. Social psychologists share this knowledge and have studied several compliance techniques that are based on making two or more related requests. *Click!* The first request sets the trap. *Snap!* The second captures the prey. In a fascinating book entitled *Influence: Science and Practice*, Robert Cialdini (2009) describes a number of sequential request tactics in vivid detail. Other social psychologists have continued in this tradition (Kenrick et al., 2012). Some of these methods are presented in the following pages.

**The Foot in the Door** Folk wisdom has it that one way to get a person to comply with a sizable request is to start small. First devised by traveling salespeople peddling vacuum cleaners, hairbrushes, cosmetics, magazine subscriptions, and encyclopedias, the trick is to somehow get your "foot in the door." The expression need not be taken literally, of course. The point of the **foot-in-the-door technique** is to break the ice with a small initial request that the customer can't easily refuse. Once that first commitment is elicited, the chances are increased that another, larger request will succeed.

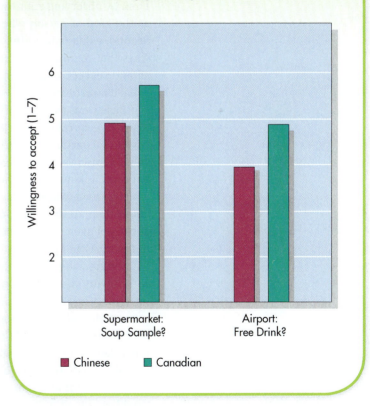

● **FIGURE 7.7**

People from China and Canada rated the likelihood that they would accept a free sample of soup in a supermarket (left) or a free drink from a casual friend at an airport (right). Feeling a greater burden to reciprocate, Chinese participants in both cases said they were less likely to accept the gift.

Shen et al., 2011. © Cengage Learning

**foot-in-the-door technique** A two-step compliance technique in which an influencer sets the stage for the real request by first getting a person to comply with a much smaller request.

Jonathan Freedman and Scott Fraser (1966) tested the impact of this technique in a series of field experiments. In one, an experimenter pretending to be employed by a consumer organization telephoned a large number of female homemakers in Palo Alto, California, and asked if they would be willing to answer some questions about household products. Those who consented were then asked a few quick and innocuous questions and thanked for their assistance. Three days later, the experimenter called back and made a considerable, almost outrageous, request. He asked the women if they would allow a handful of men into their homes for two hours to rummage through their drawers and cupboards so they could take an inventory of their household products.

The foot-in-the-door technique proved to be very effective. When the participants were confronted with only the very intrusive request, 22% consented. Yet the rate of agreement among those who had been surveyed earlier more than doubled, to 53%. This basic result has now been repeated over and over again. People are more likely to donate time, money, food, blood, the use of their home, and other resources once they have been induced to go along with a small initial request. Although the effect is not always as dramatic as that obtained by Freedman and Fraser, it does appear in a wide variety of circumstances, and it increases compliance rates, on average, by about 13% (Burger, 1999).

The practical implications of the foot-in-the-door technique are obvious. But why does it work? Over the years, several explanations have been suggested. One that seems plausible is based on self-perception theory—that people infer their attitudes by observing their own behavior. This explanation suggests that a two-step process is at work. First, by observing your own behavior in the initial situation, you come to see yourself as the kind of person who is generally cooperative when approached with a request. Second, when confronted with the more burdensome request, you seek to respond in ways that maintain this new self-image. By this logic, the foot-in-the-door technique should succeed only when you attribute an initial act of compliance to your own personal characteristics.

Based on a review of dozens of studies, Jerry Burger (1999) concludes that the research generally supports the self-perception account. Thus, if the first request is too trivial or if participants are paid for the first act of compliance, they won't later come to view themselves as inherently cooperative. Under these conditions, the technique *does not* work. Likewise, the effect occurs only when people are motivated to be consistent with their self-images. If participants are unhappy with what the initial behavior implies about them, if they are too young to appreciate the implications, or if they don't care about behaving in ways that are personally consistent, then again the technique does not work. Other processes may be at work, but it appears that the foot opens the door by altering self-perceptions, leading people who agree to the small initial request—without any compensation—to see themselves as helpful (Burger & Caldwell, 2003). In fact, this process can still occur even when a person tries to comply with the initial small request but fails. In a series of studies, Dariusz Dolinski (2000) found that when people were asked if they could find directions to a nonexistent street address or decipher an unreadable message—small favors that they could not satisfy—they, too, become more compliant with the next request.

Knowing that a foot in the door increases compliance rates is both exciting and troubling—exciting for the owner of the foot, troubling for the owner of the door. As Cialdini (2007) put it, "You can use small commitments to manipulate a person's self-image; you can use them to turn citizens into 'public servants,' prospects into 'customers,' prisoners into 'collaborators.' And once you've got a man's self-image where you want it, he should comply *naturally* with a whole range of your requests that are consistent with this view of himself" (p. 74).

**Lowballing**    Another two-step trap, arguably the most unscrupulous of all compliance techniques, is also based on the "start small" idea. Imagine yourself in the following situation. You're at a local car dealership. After some negotiation, the salesperson offers a great price on the car of your choice. You cast aside other considerations and shake hands on the deal and as the salesperson goes off to "write it up," you begin to feel the thrill of owning a new car. Absorbed in fantasy, you are suddenly interrupted by the return of the salesperson. "I'm sorry," he says. "The manager would not approve the sale. We have to raise the price by another $450. I'm afraid that's the best we can do." As the victim of an all-too-common trick known as **lowballing**, you are now faced with a tough decision. On the one hand, you really like the car; and the more you think about it, the better it looks. On the other hand, you don't want to pay more than you bargained for and you have an uneasy feeling in the pit of your stomach that you're being duped. What do you do?

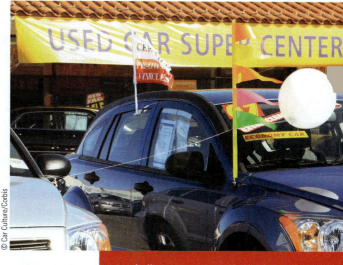

Lowballing is a common technique used in selling cars. For consumer advice on how to buy a car without falling into this and other compliance traps often set by dealers. Visit the Edmunds Automobile Buyer's Guide (*www.Edmunds.com*).

Salespeople who use this tactic are betting that you'll make the purchase despite the added cost. If the way research participants behave is any indication, they are often right. In one study, experimenters phoned introductory psychology students and asked if they would be willing to participate in a study for extra credit. Some were told up front that the session would begin at the uncivilized hour of 7 a.m. Knowing that, only 31% volunteered. But other participants were lowballed. Only *after* they agreed to participate did the experimenter inform them of the 7 a.m. starting time. Would that be okay? Whether or not it was, the procedure achieved its objective—the signup rate rose to 56% (Cialdini et al., 1978).

Disturbing as it may be, lowballing is an interesting technique. Surely, once the lowball offer has been thrown, many recipients suspect that they were misled. Yet they go along. Why? The reason appears to be based on the psychology of commitment (Kiesler, 1971). Once people make a particular decision, they justify it to themselves by thinking of all its positive aspects. As they get increasingly committed to a course of action, they grow more resistant to changing their mind, even if the initial reasons for the action have been changed or withdrawn entirely. In the car dealership scenario, you might very well have decided to purchase the car because of the price. But then you would have thought about its sleek appearance, the scent of the leather interior, the iPod dock, and the brand-new satellite radio. By the time you learned that the price would be more than you'd bargained for, it would be too late—you would already have been hooked.

Lowballing also produces another form of commitment. When people do not suspect duplicity, they feel a nagging sense of unfulfilled obligation to the person with whom they negotiated. Even though the salesperson was unable to complete the original deal, you might feel obligated to buy anyway, having already agreed to make the purchase. This commitment to the other person may account for why lowballing works better when the second request is made by the same person than by someone else (Burger & Petty, 1981). It may also explain why people are most vulnerable to the lowball when they make their commitment in public rather than in private (Burger & Cornelius, 2003).

**The Door in the Face**    Although shifting from an initial small request to a larger one can be effective, as in the foot-in-the-door and lowball techniques, oddly enough the opposite is also true. Cialdini (2007) describes the time he was approached by a Boy Scout and asked to buy two five-dollar tickets to an upcoming circus. Having better things to do with his time and money, he declined. Then the boy asked if he would be

**lowballing**    A two-step compliance technique in which the influencer secures agreement with a request but then increases the size of that request by revealing hidden costs.

interested in buying chocolate bars at a dollar apiece. Even though he does not particularly like chocolate, Cialdini—an expert on social influence—bought two of them. After a moment's reflection, he realized what had happened. Whether the Boy Scout planned it that way or not, Cialdini had fallen for what is known as the **door-in-the-face technique**.

The technique is as simple as it sounds. An individual makes an initial request that is so large it is sure to be rejected and then comes back with a second, more reasonable request. Will the second request fare better after the first one has been declined? Plagued by the sight of uneaten chocolate bars, Cialdini and others (1975) tested the effectiveness of the door-in-the-face technique. They stopped college students on campus and asked if they would volunteer to work without pay at a counseling center for juvenile delinquents. The time commitment would be forbidding: roughly two hours a week for the next two years! Not surprisingly, everyone who was approached politely slammed the proverbial door in the experimenter's face. But then the experimenter followed up with a more modest proposal, asking the students if they would be willing to take a group of kids on a two-hour trip to the zoo. The strategy worked like a charm. Only 17% of the students confronted with only the second request agreed. But of those who initially declined the first request, 50% said yes to the zoo trip. Importantly, the door-in-the-face technique does not elicit mere empty promises. Most research participants who comply subsequently do what they've agreed to do (Cialdini & Ascani, 1976).

Why is the door-in-the-face technique such an effective trap? One possibility involves the principle of *perceptual contrast*: To the person exposed to a very large initial request, the second request "seems smaller." Two dollars' worth of candy bars is not bad compared with ten dollars for circus tickets. Likewise, taking a group of kids to the zoo seems trivial compared with two years of volunteer work. As intuitively sensible as this explanation seems, Cialdini and others (1975) concluded that perceptual contrast is only partly responsible for the effect. When participants only heard the large request without actually having to reject it, their rate of compliance with the second request (25%) was only slightly larger than the 17% rate of compliance exhibited by those who heard only the small request.

A more compelling explanation for the effect involves the notion of *reciprocal concessions*. A close cousin of the reciprocity norm, this refers to the pressure to respond to changes in a bargaining position. When an individual backs down from a large request to a smaller one, we view that move as a concession that we should match by our own compliance. Thus, the door-in-the-face technique does not work if the second request is made by a different person (Cialdini et al., 1975). Nor does it work if the first request is so extreme that it comes across as an insincere "first offer" (Schwarzwald et al., 1979). On an emotional level, refusing to help on one request may also trigger feelings of guilt, which we can reduce by complying with the second, smaller request (O'Keefe & Figge, 1997; Millar, 2002).

An effective way to get someone to do you a favor is to make a first request that is so large the person is sure to reject it. **TRUE.**

**That's Not All, Folks!** If the notion of reciprocal concessions is correct, then a person shouldn't actually have to refuse the initial offer in order for the shift to a smaller request to work. Indeed, another familiar sales strategy manages to use concession without first eliciting refusal. In this strategy, a product is offered at a particular price, but then, before the buyer has a chance to respond, the seller adds, "And that's not all!" At that point, either the original price is reduced or a bonus is offered to sweeten the pot. The seller, of course, intends all along to make the so-called concession.

This ploy, called the **that's-not-all technique**, seems transparent, right? Surely no one falls for it, right? Jerry Burger (1986) was not so sure. He predicted that people are more likely to make a purchase when a deal seems to have improved than when the same deal is offered right from the start. To test this hypothesis, Burger set up a booth at a campus fair and sold cupcakes. Some customers who approached the table were told that the cupcakes cost 75 cents each. Others were told that they cost a dollar, but then, before they could respond, the price was reduced to 75 cents. Rationally speaking, Burger's manipulation did not affect the ultimate price, so it should not have affected sales. But it did. When customers were led to believe that the final price represented a reduction, sales increased from 44% to 73%.

At this point, let's step back and look at the various compliance tactics described in this section. All of them are based on a two-step process that involves a shift from a request of one size to another. What differs is whether the small or large request comes first and how the transition between steps is made (see Table 7.3). Moreover, all these strategies work in subtle ways by manipulating a target person's self-image, commitment to the product, feelings of obligation to the seller, or perceptions of the real request. It is even possible to increase compliance by first asking "How are you feeling?" (Howard, 1990) or by claiming some coincidental similarity like having the same first name or birthday (Burger et al., 2004). When you consider these various traps, you have to wonder whether it's ever possible to escape.

##  Assertiveness: When People Say No

Cialdini (2009) opens his book with a confession: "I can admit it freely now. All my life I've been a patsy." As a past victim of compliance traps, he is not alone. Many people find it difficult to assert themselves in social situations. Faced with an unreasonable request from a friend, spouse, or stranger, they become anxious at the mere thought of putting a foot down and refusing to comply. There are times when it is uncomfortable for anyone to say no. However, just as we can maintain our autonomy in the face of conformity pressures, we can also refuse direct requests—even clever ones. The trap may be set, but you don't have to get caught.

---

**TABLE 7.3**

**Sequential Request Strategies**

Various compliance techniques are based on a sequence of two related requests. *Click!* The first request sets the trap. *Snap!* The second captures the prey. Research has shown that the four sequential request strategies summarized in this table are all effective.

| Request Shifts | Technique | Description |
| --- | --- | --- |
| From small to large | Foot-in-the-door | Begin with a very small request, secure agreement, then make a separate, larger request. |
| | Lowballing | Secure agreement with a request and then increase the size of that request by revealing hidden costs. |
| From large to small | Door-in-the-face | Begin with a very large request that will be rejected; then follow that up with a more modest request. |
| | That's-not-all | Begin with a somewhat inflated request, then immediately decrease the apparent size of that request by offering a discount or bonus. |

© Cengage Learning

According to Cialdini, being able to resist compliance pressures rests, first and foremost, on being vigilant. If a stranger hands you a gift and then launches into a sales pitch, you should recognize the tactic for what it is and not feel indebted by the norm of reciprocity. And if you strike a deal with a salesperson who later reneges on the terms, you should be aware that you're being lowballed and react accordingly. That is exactly what happened to one of the authors of this book. After a Saturday afternoon of careful negotiation at a local car dealer, he and his wife finally came to terms on a price. Minutes later, however, the salesman returned with the news that the manager would not approve the deal. The cost of a power moon roof, which was supposed to be included, would have to be added on. Familiar with the research, the author turned to his wife and exclaimed, "It's a trick; they're lowballing us!" She then became furious, went straight to the manager, and made such a scene in front of other customers that he backed down and honored the original deal.

What happened in this instance? Why did recognizing the attempted manipulation spark such anger and resistance? As this story illustrates, compliance techniques work smoothly only if they are hidden from view. The problem is, they are not only attempts to influence us, they are deceptive. Flattery, gifts, and other ploys often win compliance, but not if perceived as insincere (Jones, 1964) or if the target has a high level of reciprocity wariness (Eisenberger et al., 1987). Likewise, the sequential request traps are powerful only to the extent that they are subtle and cannot be seen for what they are (Schwarzwald et al., 1979). People don't like to be hustled. In fact, feeling manipulated typically leads us to react with anger, psychological reactance, and stubborn noncompliance—unless the request is a command and the requester is a figure of authority.

> "Knowledge is power, and if you know when a clever technique is being used on you, then it becomes easier to ignore."
>
> —Burke Leon

# Obedience

Allen Funt, the creator and producer of the original TV program *Candid Camera* (a forerunner of the show *Punk'd*), spent as much time observing human behavior in the real world as most psychologists do. When asked what he learned from all his people watching, Funt replied, "The worst thing, and I see it over and over, is how easily people can be led by any kind of authority figure, or even the most minimal signs of authority." He went on to cite the time he put up a road sign that read "Delaware Closed Today." The reaction? "Motorists didn't question it. Instead they asked, 'Is Jersey open?'" (Zimbardo, 1985, p. 47).

Funt was right about the way we react to authority. Taught from birth that it's important to respect legitimate forms of leadership, people think twice before defying parents, teachers, employers, coaches, and government officials. The problem is that mere symbols of authority—titles, uniforms, badges, or the trappings of success, even without the necessary credentials—can sometimes turn ordinary people into docile servants. Leonard Bickman (1974) demonstrated this phenomenon in a series of studies in which a male research assistant stopped passersby on the street and ordered them to do something unusual. Sometimes he pointed to a paper bag on the ground and said, "Pick up this bag for me!" At other times, he pointed to an individual standing beside a parked car and said, "This fellow is overparked at the meter but doesn't have any change. Give him a dime!" Would anyone really take this guy seriously? When he was dressed in street clothes, only a third of the people stopped followed his orders. But when he wore a security guard's uniform, nearly nine out of every ten people obeyed! Even when the uniformed assistant turned the corner and walked away after issuing his command, the vast majority of passersby followed his orders. Clearly, uniforms signify the power of authority (Bushman, 1988).

Blind **obedience** may seem funny, but if people are willing to take orders from a total stranger, how far will they go when it really matters? As the pages of history attest, the implications are sobering. In World War II, Nazi officials participated in the deaths of millions of Jews, as well as Poles, Russians, gypsies, and homosexuals. Yet when tried for these crimes, all of them raised the same defense: "I was following orders."

Surely, you may be thinking, the Holocaust was a historical anomaly that says more about the Nazis as a group of bigoted, hateful, and pathologically frustrated individuals than about the situations that lead people in general to commit acts of destructive obedience. In *Hitler's Willing Executioners*, historian Daniel Goldhagen (1996) argued on the basis of past records that many German officials were willing participants in the Holocaust—not mere ordinary people forced to follow orders. Citing historical records, others have similarly argued that Nazi killers knew, believed in, and celebrated their mission (Cesarani, 2004; Haslam & Reicher, 2007; Vetlesen, 2005).

Yet two lines of evidence suggest that laying blame on the German people is too simple as an explanation of what happened. First, interviews with Nazi war criminals and doctors who worked in concentration camps suggested, at least to some, the provocative and disturbing conclusion that these people were "utterly ordinary" (Arendt, 1963; Lifton, 1986; Von Lang & Sibyll, 1983). Second, the monstrous events of World War II do not stand alone in modern history. Even today, various crimes of obedience—which may include suicide bombings and torture—are being committed in ruthless regimes, militaries, and terrorist organizations throughout the world (Haritos-Fatouros, 2002; Kelman & Hamilton, 1989).

As seen in many recent Wall Street scandals, crimes of obedience are also found in the corporate world, where business leaders and their subordinates "morally disengage" from fraud and other unethical actions by denying personal responsibility, minimizing consequences, and dehumanizing victims (Beu & Buckley, 2004; Moore et al., 2012). On extraordinary but rare occasions, obedience is carried to its ultimate limit. In 1978, 900 members of the People's Temple cult obeyed a command from Reverend Jim Jones to kill themselves by drinking poison. In 1997, in California, Marshall Applewhite, the leader of the Heaven's Gate cult, killed himself and convinced 37 followers to do the same. Fanatic cult members had committed mass suicide before, and they will likely do so again (Galanter, 1999).

Taken to the extreme, blind obedience can have devastating results. Nazi officials killed millions during World War II, and many said they did it "because I was just following orders."

*"Far more, and far more hideous, crimes have been committed in the name of obedience than have ever been committed in the name of rebellion."*

—C. P. Snow

## Milgram's Research: Forces of Destructive Obedience

During the time that Adolf Eichmann was being tried in Jerusalem for his Nazi war crimes, Stanley Milgram (1963) began a dramatic series of 18 experiments that culminated in his 1974 book *Obedience to Authority*. Milgram did not realize it at the time—and neither did his research participants—but they were about to make history in one of the most famous psychology experiments ever conducted.

For many years, the ethics of this research has been the focus of much debate. Those who say it was not ethical point to the potential psychological harm to which Milgram's participants were exposed. In contrast, those who believe that these experiments met appropriate ethical standards emphasize the profound contribution it has made to our understanding of an important social problem. They conclude that on balance, the danger that destructive obedience poses for all humankind justified Milgram's unorthodox

**obedience** Behavior change produced by the commands of authority.

This is the shock generator Milgram used (left). It still exists and can be seen in the Archives of the History of American Psychology at the University of Akron. Participants in Milgram's studies believed they were shocking Mr. Wallace, the man being strapped into his chair (right).

methods. Consider both sides of the debate, which were summarized in Chapter 2, and make your own judgment. Now, however, take a more personal look. Imagine yourself as one of the approximately 1,000 participants who found themselves in the following situation.

The experience begins when you arrive at a Yale University laboratory and meet two men. One is the experimenter, a stern young man dressed in a gray lab coat and carrying a clipboard. The other is a middle-aged gentleman named Mr. Wallace, an accountant who is slightly overweight and average in appearance. You exchange quick introductions, and then the experimenter explains that you and your co-participant will take part in a study on the effects of punishment on learning. After lots have been drawn, it is determined that you will serve as the teacher and that Mr. Wallace will be the learner. So far, so good.

Soon, however, the situation takes on a more ominous tone. You find out that your job is to test the learner's memory and administer electric shocks of increasing intensity whenever he makes a mistake. You are then escorted into another room, where the experimenter straps Mr. Wallace into a chair, rolls up his sleeves, attaches electrodes to his arms, and applies "electrode paste" to prevent blisters and burns. As if that isn't bad enough, you may overhear Mr. Wallace telling the experimenter that he has a heart problem. The experimenter responds by conceding that the shocks will be painful but reassures Mr. Wallace that the procedure will not cause "permanent tissue damage." In the meantime, you can personally vouch for how painful the shocks are because the experimenter stings you with one that is supposed to be mild. The experimenter then takes you back to the main room, where you are seated in front of a "shock generator," a machine with 30 switches that range from 15 volts, labeled "slight shock," to 450 volts, labeled "XXX."

Your role in this experiment is straightforward. First you read a list of word pairs to Mr. Wallace through a microphone. Then you test his memory with a series of multiple-choice questions. The learner answers each question by pressing one of four switches that light up signals on the shock generator. If his answer is correct, you move on to the next question. If it is incorrect, you announce the correct answer and shock him. When you press the appropriate shock switch, a red light flashes above it, relay switches click inside the machine, and you hear a loud buzzing sound go off in the learner's room. After each wrong answer, you're told, the intensity of the shock should be increased by 15 volts.

You aren't aware, of course, that the experiment is rigged and that Mr. Wallace—who is actually a confederate—is never really shocked. As far as you know, he gets zapped each time you press one of the switches. As the session proceeds, the learner makes more and more errors, leading you to work your way up the shock scale. As you reach 75, 90, and 105 volts, you hear the learner grunt in pain. At 120 volts, he begins to shout. If you're still in it at 150 volts, you can hear the learner cry out, "Experimenter! That's all.

Get me out of here. My heart's starting to bother me now. I refuse to go on!" Screams of agony and protest continue. At 300 volts, he says he absolutely refuses to continue. By the time you surpass 330 volts, the learner falls silent and fails to respond—not to be heard from again. Table 7.4 lists his responses in grim detail.

Somewhere along the line, you turn to the experimenter for guidance. "What should I do? Don't you think I should stop? Shouldn't we at least check on him?" You might even confront the experimenter head-on and refuse to continue. Yet in answer to your inquiries, the experimenter—firm in his tone and seemingly unaffected by the learner's distress—prods you along as follows:

- Please continue (or please go on).

- The experiment requires that you continue.

- It is absolutely essential that you continue.

- You have no other choice; you must go on.

What do you do? In a situation that begins to feel more and more like a bad dream, do you follow your own conscience or obey the experimenter?

Milgram described this procedure to psychiatrists, college students, and middle-class adults, and he asked them to predict how they would behave. On average, these groups estimated that they would call it quits at the 135-volt level. Not a single person thought he or she would go all the way to 450 volts. When asked to predict the percentage of *other* people who would deliver the maximum shock, those interviewed gave similar estimates. The psychiatrists estimated that only one out of a thousand people would exhibit that kind of extreme obedience. They were wrong. In Milgram's initial study, involving 40 men from the surrounding New Haven community, participants exhibited an alarming degree of obedience, administering an average of 27 out of 30 possible shocks. In fact, 26 of the 40 participants—that's *65%*—delivered the ultimate punishment of 450 volts.

**The Obedient Participant**    At first glance, you may see these results as a lesson in the psychology of cruelty and conclude that Milgram's participants were seriously disturbed. But research does not support such a simple explanation. To begin with, those in a control group who were not prodded along by an experimenter refused to continue early into the shock sequence. What's more, Milgram found that virtually all participants, including those who had administered severe shocks, were tormented by the experience. Many of them pleaded with the experimenter to let them stop. When he refused, they went on. But in the process, they trembled, stuttered, groaned, perspired, bit

**TABLE 7.4**

**The Learner's Protests in the Milgram Experiment**

As participants administered progressively more intense shocks, they heard the learner moan, groan, protest, and complain. All participants heard the same programmed set of responses. Eventually, the learner fell silent and ceased to respond.

| | |
|---|---|
| 75 volts | Ugh! |
| 90 volts | Ugh! |
| 105 volts | Ugh! *(louder)* |
| 120 volts | Ugh! Hey, this really hurts! |
| 135 volts | Ugh!! |
| 150 volts | Ugh!!! Experimenter! That's all. Get me out of here. I told you I had heart trouble. My heart's starting to bother me now. Get me out of here, please. My heart's starting to bother me. I refuse to go on. Let me out. |
| 165 volts | Ugh! Let me out! *(shouting)* |
| 180 volts | Ugh! I can't stand the pain. Let me out of here! *(shouting)* |
| 195 volts | Ugh! Let me out of here. Let me out of here. My heart's bothering me. Let me out of here! You have no right to keep me here! Let me out! Let me out of here! Let me out! Let me out of here! My heart's bothering me. Let me out! Let me out! |
| 210 volts | Ugh!! Experimenter! Get me out of here. I've had enough. I won't be in the experiment any more. |
| 225 volts | Ugh! |
| 240 volts | Ugh! |
| 255 volts | Ugh! Get me out of here. |
| 270 volts | *(Agonized scream)* Let me out of here. Let me out of here. Let me out of here. Let me out. Do you hear? Let me out of here. |
| 285 volts | *(Agonized scream)* |
| 300 volts | *(Agonized scream)* I absolutely refuse to answer any more. Get me out of here. You can't hold me here. Get me out. Get me out of here. |
| 315 volts | *(Intensely agonized scream)* I told you I refuse to answer. I'm no longer part of this experiment. |
| 330 volts | *(Intense and prolonged agonized scream)* Let me out of here. Let me out of here. My heart's bothering me. Let me out, I tell you. *(Hysterically)* Let me out of here. Let me out of here. You have no right to hold me here. Let me out! Let me out! Let me out! Let me out of here! Let me out! Let me out! |

their lips, and dug their fingernails into their flesh. Some burst into fits of nervous laughter. On one occasion, said Milgram, "we observed a [participant's] seizure so violently convulsive that it was necessary to call a halt to the experiment" (1963, p. 375).

Was Milgram's 65% baseline level of obedience attributable to his unique sample of male participants? Not at all. Forty women who participated in a later study exhibited precisely the same level of obedience: 65% threw the 450-volt switch. Before you jump to the conclusion that something was amiss in New Haven, consider the fact that Milgram's basic finding has been obtained in several different cultures and with children as well as college students and older adults (Blass, 2012). Obedience in the Milgram situation is so universal that it led one author to ask, "Are we all Nazis?" (Askenasy, 1978).

The answer, of course, is no. An individual's character can make a difference, and some people, depending on the situation, are far more obedient than others. In the aftermath of World War II, a group of social scientists, searching for the root causes of prejudice, sought to identify individuals with an *authoritarian personality* and developed a questionnaire known as the F-Scale to measure it (Adorno et al., 1950; Stone et al., 1993). What they found is that people who get high scores on the F-Scale (F stands for "Fascist") are rigid, dogmatic, sexually repressed, ethnocentric, intolerant of dissent, and punitive. They are submissive toward figures of authority but aggressive toward subordinates. Indeed, people with high F scores are also more willing than low scorers to administer high-intensity shocks in Milgram's obedience situation (Elms & Milgram, 1966).

Although personality characteristics may make someone vulnerable or resistant to destructive obedience, what seems to matter most is the situation in which people find themselves. By carefully altering particular aspects of his basic scenario, Milgram was able to identify factors that increase and decrease the 65% baseline rate of obedience in more than 20 variations of the basic experiment (see ● Figure 7.8). Three factors

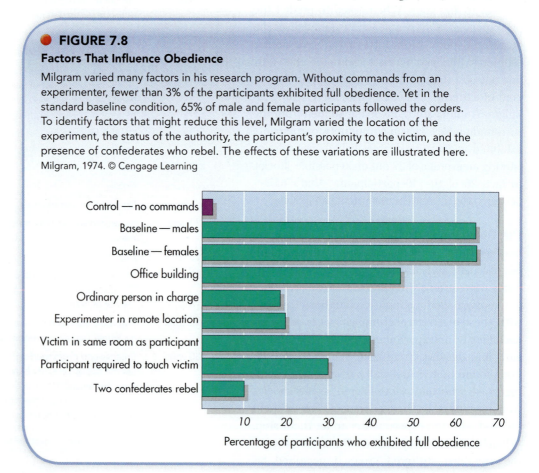

● **FIGURE 7.8**

**Factors That Influence Obedience**

Milgram varied many factors in his research program. Without commands from an experimenter, fewer than 3% of the participants exhibited full obedience. Yet in the standard baseline condition, 65% of male and female participants followed the orders. To identify factors that might reduce this level, Milgram varied the location of the experiment, the status of the authority, the participant's proximity to the victim, and the presence of confederates who rebel. The effects of these variations are illustrated here. Milgram, 1974. © Cengage Learning

Percentage of participants who exhibited full obedience

in particular are important: the authority figure, the proximity of the victim, and the experimental procedure (Blass, 1992; Miller, 1986).

**The Authority**    What is perhaps most remarkable about Milgram's findings is that a lab-coated experimenter is *not* a powerful figure of authority. Unlike a military superior, employer, coach, or teacher, the experimenter in Milgram's research could not ultimately enforce his commands. Still, his physical presence and his apparent legitimacy played major roles in drawing obedience. When Milgram diminished the experimenter's status by moving his lab from the distinguished surroundings of Yale University to a run-down urban office building in nearby Bridgeport, Connecticut, the rate of total obedience dropped to 48%. When the experimenter was replaced by an ordinary person—supposedly another participant—there was a sharp reduction to 20%. Similarly, Milgram found that when the experimenter was in charge but issued his commands by telephone, only 21% fully obeyed. (In fact, when the experimenter was not watching, many participants in this condition feigned obedience by pressing the 15-volt switch.) One conclusion, then, is clear. At least in the Milgram setting, destructive obedience requires the physical presence of a prestigious authority figure.

If an experimenter can exert such control over research participants, imagine the control wielded by truly powerful authority figures—whether they are present or not. An intriguing field study examined the extent to which hospital nurses would obey unreasonable orders from a doctor. Using a fictitious name, a male physician called several female nurses on the phone and told them to administer a drug to a specific patient. His order violated hospital regulations: The drug was uncommon, the dosage was too large, and the effects could have been harmful. Yet out of the 22 nurses who were contacted, 21 had to be stopped as they prepared to obey the doctor's orders (Hofling et al., 1966).

**The Victim**    Situational characteristics of the victim are also important factors in destructive obedience. Milgram noted that Nazi war criminal Adolf Eichmann felt sick when he toured concentration camps but only had to shuffle papers from behind a desk to play his part in the Holocaust. Similarly the B-29 pilot who dropped the atom bomb on Hiroshima in World War II said of his mission, "I had no thoughts, except what I'm supposed to do" (Miller, 1986, p. 228). These events suggest that because Milgram's participants were physically separated from the learner, they were able to distance themselves emotionally from the consequences of their actions.

To test the impact of a victim's proximity on destructive obedience, Milgram seated the learner in one of his studies in the same room as the participant. Under these conditions, only 40% fully obeyed. When participants were required to physically grasp the victim's hand and force it onto a metal shock plate, full obedience dropped to 30%. These findings represent significant reductions from the 65% baseline. Still, 3 out of 10 participants were willing to use brute force in the name of obedience.

**The Procedure**    Finally, there is the situation created by Milgram. A close look at the dilemma his participants faced reveals two important aspects of the experimental procedure. First, participants were led to feel relieved of any personal sense of *responsibility* for the victim's welfare. The experimenter said up front that he was accountable. When participants were led to believe that they were responsible, their levels of obedience dropped considerably (Tilker, 1970). The ramifications of this finding are immense. In the military and other organizations, individuals often occupy positions in a hierarchical chain of command. Eichmann was a middle-level bureaucrat who received orders from Hitler and transmitted them to others for implementation. Caught between individuals who make policy and those who carry it out, how personally responsible do those in the middle feel? Wesley Kilham and Leon Mann (1974) examined this issue in an obedience study that cast participants in one of two roles: the *transmitter* (who took orders from the experimenter and passed them on) and the *executant* (who actually pressed the shock levers). As they predicted, transmitters were more obedient (54%) than executants (28%).

The second feature of Milgram's scenario that promoted obedience is gradual escalation. Participants began the session by delivering mild shocks and then only gradually escalated to voltage levels of high intensity. After all, what's another 15 volts compared with the current level? By the time participants realized the frightening implications of what they were doing, it had become more difficult for them to escape (Gilbert, 1981). This sequence is much like the foot-in-the-door technique. In Milgram's words, people become "integrated into a situation that carries its own momentum. The subject's problem . . . is how to become disengaged from a situation which is moving in an altogether ugly direction" (1974, p. 73). We should point out that obedience by momentum is not unique to Milgram's research paradigm. As reported by Amnesty International, many countries still torture political prisoners, and those who are recruited for the dirty work are trained, in part, through an escalating series of commitments (Haritos-Fatouros, 2002).

> ## Milgram in the Twenty-First Century

When Stanley Milgram published the results of his first experiment in 1963, at the age of 28, a *New York Times* headline read: "Sixty-Five Percent in Test Blindly Obey Order to Inflict Pain." Milgram had pierced the public consciousness and was poised to become an important and controversial figure in psychology—and beyond. In a fascinating biography, Thomas Blass (2004) tells of how Milgram became interested in obedience and the impact his studies have had on social scientists, legal scholars, the U.S. military, and popular culture around the world (Milgram's book has been translated into 11 languages). Now, in an age filled with threats of global conflict, extremism, terrorism, economic desperation, and new forms of lethal weaponry, obedience to authority is an issue of such importance that social psychologists all over the world continue to ponder its ramifications (Benjamin & Simpson, 2009; Blass, 2009).

Today, a grainy black-and-white film that Milgram produced in 1965 in which a number of sessions were recorded from a hidden camera stands as visual proof of this phenomenon. It is clear from looking at this film that this experiment was conducted in another era, an era in which research participants called the young experimenter "sir." Would these results be repeated today? Would *you* obey the commands of Milgram's experimenter?

In an effort to answer this question, Dutch researchers Wim Meeus and Quinten Raaijmakers (1995) created a different but analogous situation. They constructed a moral dilemma much like Milgram's. Rather than order participants to inflict physical pain on someone, however, they ordered them to cause psychological harm. When participants arrived at a university laboratory, they met a confederate supposedly there to take a test as part of a job interview. If the confederate passed the test, he'd get the job; if he failed, he would not. As part of a study of performance under stress, the experimenter told participants to distract the test-taking applicant by making an escalating series of harassing remarks. On cue, the applicant pleaded with participants to stop, became angry, faltered, and eventually fell into a state of despair and failed. As in Milgram's research, the question was straightforward: How many participants would obey orders through the entire set of 15 stress remarks, despite the apparent harm caused to a real-life job applicant? In a control group that lacked a prodding experimenter, no one persisted. But when the experimenter ordered them to go on, 92% exhibited complete

In experiments on obedience, most participants who were ordered to administer severe shocks to an innocent person refused to do so. **FALSE.**

obedience despite seeing the task as unfair and distasteful. It appears that obedience is a powerful aspect of human nature brought about by the docile manner in which people relate to figures of authority—even today.

In a more recent—and even more direct—attempt to revisit Milgram, Jerry Burger (2009) conducted a "partial replication" for which he paid 50 dollars to 70 men and women, a diverse group that ranged from 20 to 81 years old, and used the same procedure. In the original experiment, the learner first protested and asked to stop at 150 volts, at which point nearly all participants paused and indicated a reluctance to continue. Some outright refused at this point. Of those participants who did continue, however, most went all the way (Packer, 2008). On the basis of this finding, Burger followed the Milgram protocol up to 150 volts in order to estimate the number of participants who would have pulled the switch at 450 volts. He also added a condition in which a defiant confederate posing as another participant refused to continue. In light of post-Milgram changes in standards for research ethics, he took additional precautions; he excluded from the study individuals he feared would experience too much stress and then informed and reminded participants three times that they could withdraw from the study at any time without penalty.

Despite all that has changed in 45 years, the obedience rate was not appreciably lower (see ● Figure 7.9). In the experiment that Burger modeled, 83% of Milgram's participants had continued past 150 volts. In Burger's more recent study, 70% did the

● **FIGURE 7.9**

### Obedience in the Twenty-First Century

In the version of the experiment that Burger modeled, 83% of Milgram's original participants continued past 150 volts. Forty-five years later, Burger saw a slight drop to 70%. Note too that the obedience rate dropped only slightly, to 63%, among participants who saw a defiant confederate refuse to continue. These results show that obedience to authority may have declined a bit over the years, but it has by no means extinguished. Burger, 2009. © Cengage Learning

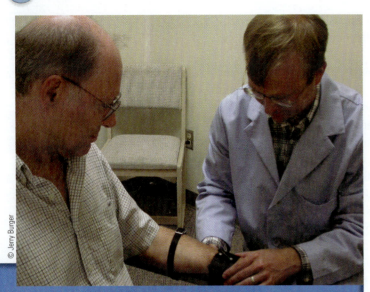

On January 3, 2007, ABC's *Primetime* news program aired a story titled "Basic Instincts: The Science of Evil." This story reported on Burger's (2009) re-creation of the Milgram obedience experiment.

Obedience to authority seems a timeless phenomenon. Just a few years ago, 18-year-old Louise Ogburn, working at a McDonald's in Kentucky, was accused of stealing money by a prank phone caller and taken into her manager's office. Posing as a police officer, the caller ordered several of the girl's co-workers to have her strip naked. For 4 hours, she was searched, spanked, and forced into humiliating positions on command. Surveillance footage showed that all but one co-worker obeyed the prank caller—and the girl obeyed the co-workers. Remarkably, 70 similar incidents were reported elsewhere. As seen here, Ms. Ogburn sued McDonald's and was awarded $6 million.

same (it can be estimated, therefore, that 55% would have exhibited full 450-volt obedience in the original experiment). Two additional results proved interesting: (1) Just as Milgram had found, there were no differences between men and women, and (2) the obedience rate declined only slightly, to 63%, among participants who saw a defiant confederate refuse to continue.

Already this new replication has drawn a good deal of interest and commentary. Alan Elms (2009), a graduate student and collaborator of Milgram's in the 1960s, is cautious about comparing Burger's "obedience lite" procedure to Milgram's but eager to see it revitalize the research program Milgram had initiated. Arthur Miller (2009), author of *The Obedience Experiments*, voices the same cautious excitement. Blass (2009), author of the Milgram biography, *The Man Who Shocked the World*, sees Burger's experiment as an important milestone and demonstrates the stability and resilience of obedience in human social behavior. In contrast, Jean Twenge (2009), author of *Generation Me*—a 2006 book on how Americans have become more self-centered, narcissistic, and wholly focused on personal rights—is skeptical of that conclusion that nothing has changed. Making precise comparisons, Twenge notes that relative to an obedience rate of 83% among Milgram's male participants, only 67% of Burger's men exhibited 150-volt obedience, a decline that is statistically comparable to the alarming change in U.S. obesity rates during that same period of time. Although impressed with the power of Milgram's situation, Twenge is hopeful that destructive obedience is less prevalent today, in the twenty-first century, than in the past.

Before leaving the Milgram studies, consider an important moral question: By providing a situational explanation for the evils of Nazi Germany or of modern-day terrorism, are social psychologists unwittingly excusing the perpetrators? Does blaming what they did on the situation let them off the hook of responsibility? In a series of studies, Miller and others (1999) found that after people were asked to come up with explanations for acts of wrongdoing, they tended to be more forgiving of the individuals who committed those acts and were seen as more forgiving by others. This appearance of forgiveness was certainly not Milgram's intent, nor is it the intent of other researchers today who seek to understand cruelty, even while continuing to condemn it. Miller and his colleagues are thus quick to caution, "To explain is not to forgive" (p. 265).

## Defiance: When People Rebel

History books will call it the "Arab Spring." On December 17, 2010, a young, unemployed, frustrated Tunisian man by the name of Mohamed Bouazizi set fire to himself in protest after police confiscated the fruits and vegetables he was selling on the street because he lacked a permit. Almost immediately, men and women took to the streets in protest. Despite the government's determination to suppress dissent, the crowds grew in size, marching, holding rallies, and demanding the resignation of the prime minister.

On January 14, 2011, the government was overthrown.

Across the Middle East, a region ruled in recent years by iron-fisted dictators who squashed all protest, an extraordinary year of pro-democracy rebellions erupted following this incident. Well-entrenched regimes were forced from power in Egypt, Libya, and Yemen. Huge uprisings broke out in Bahrain and Syria, which continue— and, to a lesser extent, in Algeria, Kuwait, Iran, Jordan, Morocco, and other countries as well. What exactly happened? In a region long characterized by population-wide obedience to oppressive authorities, how did a single incident empower millions of people into defiance and trigger a cascade of protests? To be sure, hard economic conditions accounted for a great deal of frustration. But how did one lone incident spread like a virus throughout Tunisia, and then instantly cross borders into other countries? By analyzing over 3 million Twitter feeds, YouTube videos, and Facebook posts, communication researchers concluded that the democracy movement was spread through the social media. Talk of revolution often preceded events on the ground; stories and images of protest then spread from one country to others. It's no wonder the regimes in power sought to censor and block the social media (Howard & Hussain, 2011).

Reading Milgram's research, it is easy to despair in light of the impressive forces that compel people toward blind obedience. But there's also good news. Just as

As part of the Arab spring of 2011, demonstrators held up the flags of Arab nations during a rally in Cairo's Tahrir Square (top). With protestors using social media to spread the word from one Arab country to another, governments in the region tried to block access to these media (bottom).

social influence processes can breed subservience to authority, social influence processes can also breed rebellion and defiance. The Arab Spring is a profound recent example. Few people realize it, but a similar phenomenon was seen during World War II. In *Resistance of the Heart*, historian Nathan Stoltzfus (1996) described a civil protest in Berlin in which the non-Jewish wives of 2,000 newly captured Jews congregated outside the prison. The women were there initially to seek information about their husbands. Soon they were filling the streets, chanting and refusing to leave. After 8 straight days of protest, the defiant women prevailed. Fearing the negative impact on public opinion, the Nazis backed down and released the men.

In addition to the new and evolving role of social networking media, recent studies indicate that for better or for worse, *synchrony* of behavior—for example, walking in step with others, clapping, singing, chanting, or raising arms in unison—can have a unifying effect on people, increasing the tendency to follow what others are doing. In one study, pairs of participants were seated in rocking chairs, side by side, and asked to rock in unison. Other pairs also rocked, but they could not see each other and were not in rhythm. Those in the synchrony condition were later more "in synch" when working jointly to move a steel ball through a wooden maze (Valdesolo et al., 2010). Other studies have shown that acting in unison with others can also increase our tendency to feel socially connected, cooperate for the common good, and even comply with a request to aggress against another person (Wiltermuth, 2012; Wiltermuth & Heath, 2010).

*"A little rebellion now and then is a good thing."*
—Thomas Jefferson

Are the actions of a whole group harder to control than the behavior of a single individual? Consider the following study. Pretending to be part of a marketing research firm, William Gamson and others (1982) recruited people to participate in a supposed discussion of "community standards." Scheduled in groups of nine, participants were told that their discussions would be videotaped for a large oil company that was suing the manager of a local service station who had spoken out against higher gas prices. After receiving a summary of the case, most participants sided with the station manager. But there was a hitch. The oil company wanted evidence to win its case, said the experimenter posing as the discussion coordinator. He told each of the group members to get in front of the camera and express the company's viewpoint. Then he told them to sign an affidavit giving the company permission to edit the tapes for use in court.

You can see how the obedience script was supposed to unfold. Actually, only 1 of 33 groups even came close to following the script. In all others, people became incensed by the coordinator's behavior and refused to continue. Some groups were so outraged that they planned to take action. One group even threatened to blow the whistle on the firm by calling the local newspapers. Faced with one emotionally charged mutiny after another, the researchers had to discontinue the experiment.

Why did this study produce such active, often passionate revolt when Milgram's revealed such utterly passive obedience? Could it reflect a change in values from the 1960s, when Milgram's studies were run? Many college students believe that people would conform less today than in the past, but an analysis of obedience studies has revealed that there is no correlation between the year a study was conducted and the level of obedience that it produced (Blass, 1999)—right up through Burger's (2009) recent effort. So what accounts for the contrasting results? One key difference is that people in Milgram's studies took part alone and those in Gamson's were in groups. Perhaps Michael Walzer was right: "Disobedience, when it is not criminally but morally, religiously, or politically motivated, is always a *collective act*" (quoted in Brown, 1986, p. 17).

Our earlier discussion of conformity indicated that the mere presence of one ally in an otherwise unanimous majority gives individuals the courage to dissent. The same may hold true for obedience. Notably, Milgram never had more than one participant present in the same session. But in one experiment, he did use two confederates who posed as co-teachers along with the real participant. In these sessions, one confederate refused to continue at 150 volts and the second refused at 210 volts. These models of disobedience had a profound influence on participants' willingness to defy the experimenter: In their presence, only 10% delivered the maximum level of shock (see Figure 7.8).

We should add that the presence of a group is not a guaranteed safeguard against destructive obedience. Groups can trigger aggression, as we'll see in Chapter 11. For example, the followers of Jim Jones were together when they collectively followed his command to die. And lynch mobs are just that—groups, not individuals. Clearly, there is power in sheer numbers. That power can be destructive, but it can also be used for constructive purposes. Indeed, the presence and support of others often provide the extra ounce of courage that people need to resist orders they find offensive.

# The Continuum of Social Influence

As we have seen, social influence on behavior ranges from the implicit pressure of group norms to the traps set by direct requests to the powerful commands of authority. In each case, people choose whether to react with conformity or independence, compliance or assertiveness, obedience or defiance. From all the research, it is tempting to conclude that the more pressure brought to bear on people, the greater the influence. Is it possible, however, that more produces less? In a series of conformity studies, Lucian Conway and Mark Schaller (2005) cast participants into a corporate decision-making task in which they were asked to choose between two business options after watching others make the same decision. Consistently, the participants followed the group more when its members had formed their opinions freely than when they were compelled by a leader. It appears that strong-arm tactics that force people to change their behavior may backfire when it comes to changing opinions.

At this point, let's step back and ask two important questions. First, although different kinds of pressure influence us for different reasons, is it possible to predict all effects with a single overarching principle? Second, what does all the theory and research on social influence say about human nature?

## ▶ Social Impact Theory

In 1981, Bibb Latané proposed that a common bond among the different processes involved in social influence leads people toward or away from such influence. Specifically, Latané proposed **social impact theory**, which states that social influence of any kind—the total impact of others on a target person—is a function of the others' strength, immediacy, and number. According to Latané, social forces act on individuals in the same way that physical forces act on objects. Consider, for example, how overhead lights illuminate a surface. The total amount of light cast on a surface depends on the strength of the bulbs, their distance from the surface, and their number. As illustrated in the left portion of ● Figure 7.10, the same factors apply to social impact.

The *strength* of a source is determined by his or her status, ability, or relationship to a target. The stronger the source, the greater the influence. When people view the other members of a group as competent, they are more likely to conform in their judgments. When it comes to compliance, sources enhance their strength by making targets feel obligated to reciprocate a small favor. And to elicit obedience, authority figures gain strength by wearing uniforms or flaunting their prestigious affiliations.

*Immediacy* refers to a source's proximity in time and space to the target. The closer the source, the greater its impact. Milgram's research offers the best example. Obedience rates were higher when the experimenter issued commands in person rather than from a remote location, and when the victim suffered in close proximity to the participant, he acted as a contrary source of influence and obedience levels dropped. Consistent with this hypothesis, Latané and others (1995) asked individuals to name up to seven people in their lives and to indicate how far away those people lived and how many memorable interactions they'd had with them. In three studies, the correlation was the same: The

"I invited a few friends over who think you should see a psychiatrist."

According to social impact theory, this "intervention" should prove persuasive.

**social impact theory** The theory that social influence depends on the strength, immediacy, and number of source persons relative to target persons.

● **FIGURE 7.10**

**Social Impact: Source Factors and Target Factors**

According to social impact theory, the total influence of other people, or "sources," on a target individual depends on three source factors: their strength (size of source circles), immediacy (distance from the target), and number (number of the source circles). Similarly, the total influence is diffused, or reduced, by the strength (size of target circles), immediacy (distance from source circle), and number of target persons.

From Latane, B., "The Psychology of Social Impact," *American Psychologist*, vol 36 (p. 344). Copyright © 1981 by the American Psychological Association. Reprinted by permission.

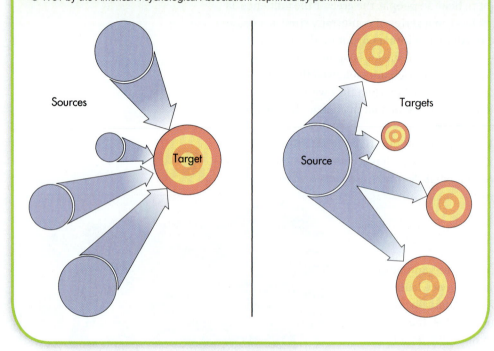

closer others are, geographically, the more impact they have on us.

Finally, the theory predicts that as the *number* of sources increases, so does their influence—at least up to a point. You may recall that when Asch (1956) increased the number of live confederates in his line-judgment studies from one to four, conformity levels rose, yet further increases had only a negligible additional effect.

Social impact theory also predicts that people sometimes resist social pressure. According to Latané, this resistance is most likely to occur when social impact is *divided* among many strong and distant *targets*, as seen in the right part of Figure 7.10. There should be less impact on a target who is strong and far from the source than on one who is weak and close to the source, and there should be less impact on a target who is accompanied by other target persons than on one who stands alone. Thus, we have seen that conformity is reduced by the presence of an ally and that obedience rates drop when people are in the company of rebellious peers.

Over the years, social impact theory has been challenged, defended, and refined on various grounds (Jackson, 1986; Mullen, 1985; Sedikides & Jackson, 1990). On the one hand, critics say that it does not enable us to *explain* the processes that give rise to social influence or answer *why* questions. On the other hand, the theory enables us to predict the emergence of social influence and determine *when* it will occur. Whether the topic is conformity, compliance, or obedience, this theory provides a stage for interesting new research in the years to come.

A number of social psychologists have recently argued that social impact is a fluid, dynamic, ever-changing process (Vallacher et al., 2002). Fifteen years before the Arab Spring became a reality, Latané and L'Herrou (1996) refined the theory in that vein. By having large groups of participants network through e-mail and by controlling their lines of communication, they found that the individuals within the network formed "clusters." Over time, neighbors (participants who were in direct e-mail contact with each other) became more similar to each other than did those who were more distant (not in direct e-mail contact) within the network. Referring to the geometry of social space, Latané and L'Herrou note that in the real world, immediacy cannot be defined strictly in terms of physical distance. Speculating on the role of technology, they noted that social impact theory has to account for the type of events that unfolded in the Middle East, in 2011, and that fact that remote social media may diminish the importance of physical proximity.

As the number of people in a group increases, so does the group's impact on an individual. **F**ALSE.

## Perspectives on Human Nature

From the material presented in this chapter, what general conclusions might you draw about human nature? Granted, social influence is more likely to occur in some situations than in others. But are people generally malleable or unyielding? Is there a tilt toward accepting influence or toward putting up resistance?

There is no single universal answer to these questions. As we saw earlier, some cultures value autonomy and independence; others place more emphasis on conformity to one's group. Even within a given culture, values may change over time. To demonstrate the point, ask yourself: If you were a parent, what traits would you like your child to have? When this question was put to American mothers in 1924, they chose "obedience" and "loy-alty," key characteristics of conformity. Yet when mothers were asked the same question in 1978, they cited "independence" and "tolerance of others," key characteristics of autonomy. Similar trends were found in surveys conducted not only in the United States but also in West Germany, Italy, England, and Japan (Alwin, 1990; Remley 1988) and in laboratory experiments, where conformity rates are somewhat lower today than in the past (Bond & Smith, 1996).

Is it possible that today's children—tomorrow's adults—will exhibit more resistance to the various forms of social influence? If so, what effects will this trend have on society as a whole? And what will be the future effects of Facebook, Twitter, and other social media? Cast in a positive light, conformity, compliance, and obedience are good and necessary human responses. They promote group solidarity and agreement—qualities that keep groups from being torn apart by dissension. Cast in a negative light, a lack of independence, assertiveness, and defiance are undesirable behaviors that lend themselves to narrow-mindedness, cowardice, and destructive obedience, often with terrible costs. For each of us and for society as a whole, the trick is to strike a balance.

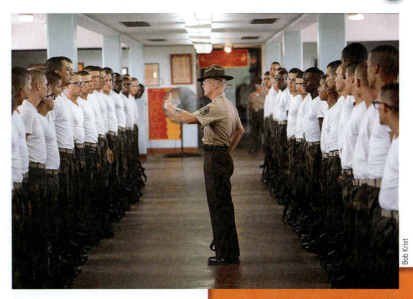

Bob Krist

According to social impact theory, a marine sergeant will exert influence to the extent that he is strong (in a position of power), immediate (physically close), and numerous (backed by others in the institution) relative to his trainees.

Conformity rates vary across different cultures and from one generation to the next. **T**RUE.

# Review

- Conformity, compliance, and obedience are three kinds of social influence, varying in the degree of pressure brought to bear on an individual.

## Social Influence as "Automatic"

- Sometimes we are influenced by other people without our awareness.

- Studies show that people mimic each other's behaviors and moods, perhaps as a way of smoothing social interactions.

# Conformity

- Conformity is the tendency for people to change their behavior to be consistent with group norms.

## The Early Classics

- Two classic experiments illustrate contrasting types of conformity.
- Sherif presented groups of participants with an ambiguous task and found that their judgments gradually converged.
- Using a simpler line-judgment task, Asch had confederates make incorrect responses and found that participants went along about a third of the time.

## Why Do People Conform?

- Sherif found that people exhibit private conformity, using others for information in an ambiguous situation.
- Asch's studies indicated that people conform in their public behavior to avoid appearing deviant.

## Majority Influence

- As the size of an incorrect unanimous majority increases, so does conformity—up to a point.
- People conform to perceived social norms when these norms are brought to mind.
- The presence of one dissenter reduces conformity, even when he or she disagrees with the participant and lacks competence at the task.
- Women conform more than men on "masculine" tasks and in face-to-face settings but not on "feminine" or gender-neutral tasks or in private settings.

## Minority Influence

- Sometimes minorities resist pressures to conform and are able to influence majorities.

- In general, minority influence is greater when the source is an ingroup member.
- According to Moscovici, minorities can exert influence by taking a consistent and unwavering position.
- Hollander claims that to exert influence, a person should first conform, then dissent.
- Majority influence is greater on direct and public measures of conformity, but minorities show their impact in indirect or private measures of conformity.
- By forcing other group members to think more openly about a problem, minorities enhance the quality of a group's decision making.
- People gain courage to resist conformity pressures after watching others do the same.

## Culture and Conformity

- Just as cultures differ in their social norms, so too they differ in the extent to which people are expected to adhere to those norms.
- Research shows that people from collectivist cultures conform more than people from individualistic cultures.

---

**Putting _Common Sense_ to the Test**

**When all members of a group give an incorrect response to an easy question, most people most of the time conform to that response.**

**False.** *In Asch's classic conformity experiments, respondents conformed only about a third of the time.*

---

# Compliance

- A common form of social influence occurs when we respond to direct requests.

## Mindlessness and Compliance

- People are more likely to comply when they are taken by surprise and when the request sounds reasonable.

## The Norm of Reciprocity

- We often comply when we feel indebted to a requester who has done us a favor.
- People differ in the extent to which they use reciprocity for personal gain and are wary of falling prey to this strategy.

## Setting Traps: Sequential Request Strategies

- Four compliance techniques are based on a two-step request: The first step sets a trap and the second elicits compliance.
- Using the foot-in-the-door technique, a person sets the stage for the "real" request by first getting someone to comply with a smaller request.
- In lowballing, one person gets another to agree to a request but then increases the size of the request by revealing hidden

costs. Despite the increase, people often follow through on their agreement.
- With the door-in-the-face technique, the real request is preceded by a large one that is rejected. People then comply with the second request because they see it as a concession to be reciprocated.
- The that's-not-all technique begins with a large request. Then the apparent size of the request is reduced by the offer of a discount or bonus.

## Assertiveness: When People Say No

- Many people find it hard to be assertive. Doing so requires that we be vigilant and recognize the traps.

---

**Putting _Common Sense_ to the Test**

**An effective way to get someone to do you a favor is to make a first request that is so large the person is sure to reject it.**

**True.** *This approach, known as the door-in-the-face technique, increases compliance by making the person feel bound to make a concession.*

# Obedience

- When the request is a command and the requester is a figure of authority, the resulting influence is called obedience.

## Milgram's Research: Forces of Destructive Obedience

- In a series of experiments, participants were ordered by an experimenter to administer increasingly painful shocks to a confederate.
- Sixty-five percent obeyed completely but felt tormented by the experience.
- Obedience levels are influenced by various situational factors, including a participant's physical proximity to both the authority figure and the victim.
- Two other aspects of Milgram's procedure contributed to the high levels of obedience: (1) Participants did not feel personally responsible; and (2) the orders escalated gradually.
- In more recent studies, people exhibited high rates of obedience when told to inflict psychological harm on another person.

## Milgram in the Twenty-First Century

- Milgram's studies have remained relevant and controversial into the twenty-first century.

- Researchers note that a situational explanation for acts of destructive obedience does not forgive them.
- A recent "partial replication" of Milgram's shock study suggests that most people are still fully obedient today.

## Defiance: When People Rebel

- Just as processes of social influence breed obedience, they can also support acts of defiance because groups are more difficult to control than individuals.
- Provision of a situational explanation for cruel behavior does not excuse that behavior.

> **Putting *Common Sense* to the Test**
>
> **In experiments on obedience, most participants who were ordered to administer severe shocks to an innocent person refused to do so.**
>
> **False.** *In Milgram's classic research, 65% of all participants obeyed the experimenter and administered the maximum possible shock.*

# The Continuum of Social Influence

## Social Impact Theory

- Social impact theory predicts that social influence depends on the strength, immediacy, and number of sources who exert pressure relative to target persons who absorb that pressure.

## Perspectives on Human Nature

- There is no single answer to the question of whether people are conformists or nonconformists.
- There are cross-cultural differences in social influence, and values change over time even within specific cultures.

> **Putting *Common Sense* to the Test**
>
> **As the number of people in a group increases, so does the group's impact on an individual.**
>
> **False.** *Increasing group size boosts the impact on an individual only up to a point, beyond which further increases have very little added effect.*
>
> **Conformity rates vary across different cultures and from one generation to the next.**
>
> **True.** *Research shows that conformity rates are higher in cultures that are collectivistic rather than individualistic in orientation and that values change over time even within cultures.*

## KEY TERMS

collectivism (270)

compliance (271)

conformity (257)

door-in-the-face technique (276)

foot-in-the-door technique (273)

idiosyncrasy credits (268)

individualism (270)

informational influence (260)

lowballing (275)

minority influence (267)

normative influence (260)

obedience (279)

private conformity (262)

public conformity (262)

social impact theory (289)

that's-not-all technique (276)

## MEDIA RESOURCES

Go to CengageBrain.com to access Psychology CourseMate, where you will find an interactive eBook, glossaries, flashcards, quizzes, videos, and more.

# Group Processes

This chapter examines social influence in a group context. First, we focus on the fundamentals of groups, in which we discuss issues such as why people are drawn to groups and how groups develop. We then turn to how the behavior of individuals is affected by the presence of others. Then we focus on group performance and discuss why the whole (the group decision or performance) so often is different from the sum of its parts (the attitudes and abilities of the group members). In the final section, on conflict, we examine how groups intensify or reconcile their differences.

# 8

**Around dawn on a summer Sunday morning,** July 22, 2012, workers dismantled and moved to a secret location the iconic statue of long-time Pennsylvania State University football coach, Joe Paterno, from in front of the football stadium. University officials hoped the early hour and lack of any announcement would mean few spectators would witness the controversial removal. Even so a small crowd watched, and soon the familiar chant of "We are . . . Penn State!" could be heard.

It was a stunning fall from grace. Only 9 months before, the beloved Joe Paterno coached Penn State to his 409th win, breaking the record for career wins by a Division I football coach. But this would be the last game for the 85-year-old legend. A week and a half later Paterno was fired in light of a child sex abuse scandal involving one of his former assistant coaches, Jerry Sandusky. Several thousand Penn State students demonstrated the night of Paterno's firing, and soon the increasingly unruly crowd knocked over light poles, overturned a news van, and hurled rocks at the police. Students loudly chanted "We are Penn State!" as they had done at so many Paterno-coached football games (Schweber, 2011). As if the stain on his previously untarnished reputation was too much for his body to bear, Paterno soon fell ill and died of lung cancer 2 months later.

An extensive investigation concluded that Paterno, along with Penn State's athletic director, vice president, and president together concealed information about these allegations from the police and community, effectively enabling Sandusky to continue to abuse numerous boys for years, including in university facilities such as the football team's shower room. Some reports alleged that after a decision was reached for the athletic director to alert child welfare authorities, he then changed his mind after a subsequent conversation with Paterno, deciding it would be better to try to handle the situation privately (Candiotti & Levitt, 2012).

This sad case illustrates some important points about the dynamics of groups. Groups all too often are overly concerned with protecting and promoting themselves and failing to think about the consequences for others or to seek outside opinions. Groups of intelligent and good people—and all accounts indicate that Paterno and the others involved in the decisions at Penn State were intelligent and good people—too often make decisions that are far worse than what any of the individual group members might have made on their own. Large groups of people sometimes lose their inhibitions and act out destructively and aggressively, in ways they typically would never endorse—just as the people who rioted at Penn State the night of Paterno's firing did.

The news about groups is not all bad, however, and this chapter will examine some of the benefits that groups produce. The Penn State students' pride in their school as reflected in their "We are Penn State!" rallying cry, for example, illustrates that people get a great deal of their identity and satisfaction by the groups of which they are a part.

In short, people are often at their best—and their worst—in groups. It is through groups that individuals form

# Putting *Common Sense* to the Test

*Circle Your Answer*

**T   F**   People will cheer louder when they cheer as part of a group than when they cheer alone.

**T   F**   People brainstorming as a group come up with a greater number of better ideas than the same number of people working individually.

**T   F**   Group members' attitudes about a course of action usually become more moderate after group discussion.

**T   F**   People and groups tend to do worse when they have "do your best" goals than when they have very specific, ambitious goals.

**T   F**   Large groups are more likely than small groups to exploit a scarce resource that the members collectively depend on.

**T   F**   When faced with the dilemma of whether to act in one's self-interest or cooperate with the greater good, women are more likely than men to cooperate.

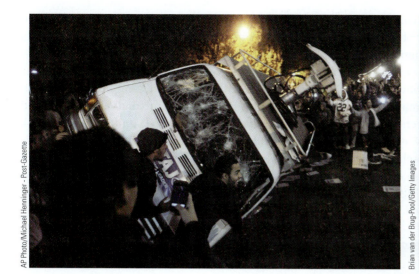

AP Photo/Michael Henninger - Post-Gazette

Brian van der Brug-Pool/Getty Images

Groups can have both negative and positive benefits. A group of Penn State students flips a TV news van during a riot after football coach Joe Paterno was fired on November 9, 2011 (left). NASA team members celebrate the extraordinary feat of successfully landing a rover onto the surface of Mars in August 2012 (right).

communities, pool resources, and share successes. But it is also through groups that stereotypes turn into oppression, frustrations turn into mob violence, and conflicts turn into wars. Clearly, it is important that we understand how groups work and how individuals influence, and are influenced by, groups. In this chapter, we first introduce the fundamentals of what groups are and how they develop, then we examine groups on several levels: At the individual level, we explore how individuals are influenced by groups; at the group level, we explore how groups perform; and at the intergroup level, we explore how groups interact with each other in cooperation and competition.

The research we report in this chapter reveals a fascinating fact: *Groups can be quite different from the sum of their parts.* When you think about that statement, it suggests something almost mystical or magical about groups, like quantum physics. How can a group be better—or worse—than its individual members? The math may not seem to add up, but the theory and research discussed in this chapter will help answer this question.

*"You think because you understand 'one,' you must understand 'two,' because one and one make two. But you must also understand 'and.'"*

—Ancient Sufi saying

# Fundamentals of Groups

We begin our exploration of groups by asking the basic questions: What is a group? Why do people join groups? We then focus on three important aspects of groups: roles, norms, and cohesiveness.

## What Is a Group? Why Join a Group?

**What Is a Group?**   The question might seem quite simple, but if you step back and think about it, the answer is less obvious. For example, many students are members of a variety of groups on Facebook. Are these really groups? You may be part of a large social psychology class: Is this a group identity that is meaningful to you?

A **group** may be characterized as a set of individuals who have direct interactions with each other over a period of time and share a common fate, identity, or set of goals. A

**group**   A set of individuals who interact over time and have shared fate, goals, or identity.

group can also consist of people who have joint membership in a social category based on sex, race, or other attributes; this characteristic is especially relevant for the issues discussed in Chapter 5 on Stereotypes, Prejudice, and Discrimination.

Groups vary in the extent to which they are seen as distinct *entities*, such as whether they have rigid boundaries that make them distinct from other groups. In other words, some groups seem more "groupy" (or in the unfortunate choice of word used by researchers on this issue: "entitative") than others (Hamilton et al., 2011). On the very low end of this dimension would be people attending a concert or working out near each other in a gym. These often are not considered real groups. Such assemblages are sometimes called *collectives*—people engaging in a common activity but having little direct interaction with each other (Milgram & Toch, 1969). Much more integrated groups include tight-knit clubs, sports teams, or work teams—groups that engage in very purposeful activities with a lot of interaction over time and clear boundaries of who is in and not in the group. People tend to identify more strongly with these more integrated, coherent groups and to get more satisfaction from them (Crawford & Salaman, 2011).

People join a group for any of several reasons, such as to affiliate with others, obtain social status, and interact with individual group members.

**Why Join a Group?** The complexity and ambitions of human life require that we work in groups. Much of what we hope to produce and accomplish can be done only through collective action. Lone individuals cannot play symphonies or football games, build cities or industries, or run governments or universities.

At a more fundamental level, humans may have an innate need to belong to groups stemming from evolutionary pressures that increased people's chances of survival and reproduction when they lived in groups rather than in isolation. Indeed, according to the *social brain hypothesis*, the unusually large size of primates' brains evolved because of their unusually complex social worlds (Dunbar, 2012; Van Vugt, 2012). As Mark Van Vugt and Mark Schaller (2008) state in their review of research on contemporary human group dynamics from an evolutionary perspective: "Humans may well have evolved a range of psychological mechanisms that promote an attraction to and capacity for living in groups" (p. 1).

For humans, attraction to group life serves not only to protect against threat and uncertainty in a physical sense but also to gain a greater sense of personal and social identity. According to *social identity theory*, which was discussed in Chapter 5, an important part of people's feelings of self-worth comes from their identification with particular groups, and so people care a great deal about being part of groups and about how their groups are valued (Ellemers & Haslam, 2012; Grant & Hogg, 2012; Swann et al., 2012). This is also at the root of why being rejected by a group is one of life's most painful experiences (Eisenberger, 2012; Williams, 2012).

*"The individuals which took the greatest pleasure in society would best escape various dangers, whilst those that cared least for their comrades, and lived solitary, would perish in greater numbers."*
—Charles Darwin, *The Descent of Man*

## ▶ Key Features of Groups: Roles, Norms, and Cohesiveness

Once an individual has joined a group, a process of adjustment takes place as the individual is socialized to how things work in the group. This socialization process may be formal and explicit, such as through an initiation or orientation program, mentoring or supervision, or documentation. The socialization may be primarily implicit, as newcomers observe how established members behave in the group. Effectively social-izing new members can produce short-term and long-term benefits for the group as a whole (Levine & Choi, 2010; Moreland & Levine, 2002).

Two of the things that are especially important for newcomers to learn—and for more established members of the group to continue to understand or revise—are the roles they are expected to play in the group, and what the norms of the group are. New-comers also often get socialized about how cohesive the group is. We focus on each of these three features of groups—roles, norms, and cohesiveness—in the following sections.

**Roles**   People's *roles* in a group—their set of expected behaviors—can be formal or informal. Formal roles are designated by titles: teacher or student in a class, vice presi-dent or account executive in a corporation. Informal roles are less obvious but still pow-erful. Robert Bales (1958) distinguished between two fundamental types of roles: an *instrumental* role to help the group achieve its tasks and an *expressive* role to provide emotional support and maintain morale. The same person can fill both roles, but often they are assumed by different individuals, and which of these roles is emphasized in groups may fluctuate over time depending on the needs of the group.

One problem that can seriously harm the performance of groups is when there is a mismatch between members' skills and what roles they occupy in the group. It is far too common in groups for members to be assigned or take on group roles in a way that is less than thoughtful and systematic. Members may be assigned roles simply based on who is available at a given point in time rather than who is best suited for the role. Groups function much better when members are assigned roles that best match their talents and personalities (Wool-ley et al., 2007).

Having a set of clear roles is beneficial to a group (Lu et al., 2008). Individuals are sometimes uncertain about exactly what their group roles are supposed to be. They may also find themselves in roles that conflict with other roles they have to play, either within the group (such as needing to be demanding while also being the source of emotional support) or between groups (such as between work and fam-ily). A meta-analysis of studies involving more than 11,000 individuals found a significant negative correlation between role ambiguity and job performance—the more role ambi-guity, the worse one's job performance is (Tubre & Collins, 2000). Role uncertainty, instability, and conflict are also associated with a variety of problems that go beyond job performance, including workplace bullying or emotional exhaustion and burnout (Brauchli et al., 2011; Hauge et al., 2011; Jawahar et al., 2012).

"I've had to be both hunter and gatherer."

When roles in a group are not distributed properly, group performance suffers.

Sometimes an opposite problem of role uncertainty or conflict develops: Group members can become so absorbed in their role that they lose themselves—and their personal beliefs and sense of morality—in their group role. Interrogators of a prisoner or suspect may get so lost in their role that they fail to recognize the ethical lines they are crossing. One of the most disturbing studies in the history of social psychology exam-ined this kind of issue, in what came to be known as The Stanford Prison Study (Haney et al., 1973). Participants in this study were randomly assigned to play the roles of pris-oners or guards in a simulated prison. The guards in particular got so into their roles as protectors of the "prison" and enforcer of the rules that they soon became cruel and sadistic. This fascinating but troubling study is discussed in detail in Chapter 12 on Law.

**Norms** In addition to roles for its members, groups also establish *norms*, rules of conduct for members. Like roles, norms may be either formal or informal. Fraternities and sororities, for example, usually have written rules for the behavior expected from their members. Informal norms are more subtle. What do I wear? How hard can I push for what I want? Who pays for this or that? What kind of language, joking, or socializing is typical? These norms provide individuals with a sense of what it means to be a good group member. Figuring out the unwritten rules of the group can take time and cause anxiety.

Groups often exert strong conformity pressures on individuals who deviate from group norms and perceive or treat these members very harshly, in part because deviations from group norms can threaten group members' sense of uniformity and social identity with the group (Hutchison et al., 2011). One way that low-status or new group members may try to establish a stronger position in the group is to be especially punishing of members who break group norms—especially if high-status group members would witness their harsh reaction to norm violators (Jetten et al., 2010). On the other hand, group members who are highly identified with the group and care about its collective success may be willing to deviate from a group norm if they think that the norm is likely to harm the group (Packer & Chasteen, 2010; Packer & Miners, 2012).

How tolerant groups are to violations of norms can be, itself, a kind of norm. Some groups, for example, pride themselves on how heterogeneous and free-thinking its members are. Others strongly value uniformity. Researchers have been able to experimentally manipulate individualist or collectivist norms through instructions and goals given to the members, and these norms in turn influence how much the group members value conformity to group norms (Jetten et al., 2010; McAuliffe et al., 2003). When a group develops a strong norm of individualism, it can cause members to conform to the norm of not conforming!

In a recent study by Paul Hutchison and others (2011), some British students answered questions about their university that were designed to highlight how the students at their university have uniform backgrounds and attitudes. For example, they were asked what percentage of the students preferred popular music over classical music, and what percentage liked to watch movies. Because the large majority of the students would prefer popular music and would like movies, questions like these would prime the students to see their similarities. Other students were asked questions induced to make them see their school as full of diverse backgrounds and attitudes. They were asked to estimate the percentages of students who most preferred dance, rock, hip-hop, pop, or classical, and what percentages most preferred movies featuring science fiction, love stories, comedy, martial arts, and so on. These questions would highlight the wide variety of opinions and tastes that were accepted at their university.

The students then read about a student who expressed an attitude about a war that was either typical or atypical of the students there. How would the participants react to this student? Participants in general rated the student with the typical attitude toward the war positively. If the student expressed an atypical attitude, however, they disliked him more if they were induced to see their university as very uniform than if they were induced to see their university as diverse

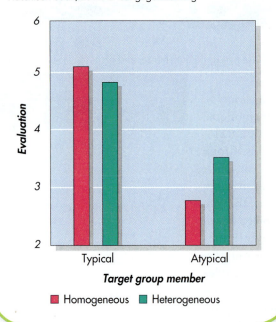

● **FIGURE 8.1**

**Tolerance for Deviating from the Norm**

Some students were primed to think of their university as being fairly homogenous (similar in backgrounds and tastes), and others were primed to think it was heterogeneous (a wide variety of backgrounds and tastes). They then evaluated a fellow student who expressed an attitude that was either typical or atypical for their university. In general, the student expressing the typical attitude was evaluated more positively than the atypical student. But if they had been primed to see their university as heterogeneous, they were less negative toward the atypical student than were the students who had been primed to see their university as homogenous.

Hutchison et al., 2011. © Cengage Learning

and heterogeneous (see ● Figure 8.1). In other words, a deviation from a group norm was met with more tolerance if the participants saw the group as more variable than if they saw their group as typically sharing similar background and values.

**Cohesiveness**    Groups whose members share similar attitudes and closely follow the groups norms are more likely than other groups to be cohesive. **Group cohesiveness** refers to the forces exerted on a group that push its members closer together (Cartwright & Zander, 1960; Festinger, 1950). Members of cohesive groups tend to feel commitment to the group task, feel positively toward the other group members, feel group pride, and engage in many—and often intense—interactions in the group (Dion, 2000; Rosh et al., 2012).

An interesting question is whether cohesiveness makes groups perform better. It may seem obvious that it should. Indeed, groups often strive to achieve cohesiveness, and if they feel that they are not very cohesive they may take steps to improve it, such as ordering everyone to go through bonding exercises or hang out together at a rustic retreat. In fact, however, the relationship between cohesiveness and performance is not a simple one. The causal relationship works both ways: On the one hand, when a group is cohesive, group performance often improves; on the other hand, when a group performs well, it often becomes more cohesive. Many team athletes recognize that winning creates team chemistry even more than team chemistry creates winning. Consistent with this idea, some research points to the causal effect of success on cohesion as more reliable than the effect of cohesion on success.

Whatever the cause and effect, several meta-analyses and longitudinal studies have provided evidence showing that group cohesion is associated with better performance, but other variables tend to be important in predicting when and to what extent this relationship emerges, such as how large the group is, whether the cohesiveness is primarily about the group's attraction to the task (*task cohesion*) or to each other (*interpersonal cohesion*), and what type of task the group performs (Beal et al., 2003; Chiocchio & Essiembre, 2009; Gully et al., 1995; Mullen & Cooper, 1994; Tekleab et al., 2009). For example, a meta-analysis of 46 studies of cohesiveness in sports teams found not only a generally positive correlation between cohesiveness and team performance but also that the relationship was particularly strong for female sports teams—possibly because women tend to be more interdependent than men (Carron et al., 2002). And as we will discuss later in the chapter, highly cohesive groups may be especially vulnerable to making terrible decisions because members fear going against a leader or group norm.

A scene from the classic cult movie, *Office Space*, depicts frustrated employees from a work group that is anything but cohesive.

## ❯ Culture and Cohesiveness

Group cohesiveness can be affected in different ways as a function of cultural differences. For example, Norman Wright and Glyn Drewery (2006) found that if some group members came late to meetings or did not carry their share of the workload, group cohesiveness was more likely to suffer among Japanese and Pacific Islanders than among Anglos. In a study of 381 work teams in the United States and Hong Kong, Derak Man and Simon Lam (2003) found that increases in task complexity or autonomy improved group cohesiveness more for teams in the United States than in Hong Kong.

**group cohesiveness**    The extent to which forces push group members closer together, such as through feelings of intimacy, unity, and commitment to group goals.

The extent to which groups are comfortable with conflict and heated debate among its members also varies across culture. This was demonstrated in a study by Roger Nibler and Karen Harris (2003) involving five-person groups of strangers and friends in China and the United States. Each group had to decide how to rank 15 items to be taken aboard a lifeboat from a ship that was about to sink. This task tends to trigger a fair amount of initial disagreement among group members before a consensus can be reached. With the Chinese groups and the groups of American strangers, these kinds of disagreements tended to be perceived as troubling and interfered with group performance. To the groups of American friends, in contrast, these disagreements were more likely to be seen as simply part of a freewheeling debate, and the sense of freedom to exchange opinions and disagree with one another tended to improve rather than hurt performance on this task.

# Individuals in Groups: The Presence of Others

When we engage in activities in groups, we are in the presence (either physically or virtually) of others. It's an obvious point, but some of its consequences are profound and surprising. In this section we focus on three important effects that the presence of others can have on individuals: social facilitation, social loafing, and deindividuation.

## Social Facilitation: When Others Arouse Us

Social psychologists have long been fascinated by how the presence of others affects behavior. In Chapter 1, we reported that one of the founders of social psychology was Norman Triplett, whose article "The Dynamogenic Factors in Pacemaking and Competition" (1897–1898) is often cited as the earliest publication in the field. Triplett began his research by studying the official bicycle records from the Racing Board of the League of American Wheelmen for the 1897 season. He noticed that cyclists who competed against others performed better than those who cycled alone against the clock. After dismissing various theories of the day (our favorite is "brain worry"), he proposed his own hypothesis: The presence of another rider releases the competitive instinct, which increases nervous energy and enhances performance. To test this proposition, Triplett got 40 children to wind up fishing reels, alternating between performing alone and working in parallel. Triplett reported that children were more likely to perform better when they worked side by side than when they worked alone. (In an interesting contemporary twist on this classic, Michael Strube (2005) used modern statistical techniques to re-analyze Triplett's original data and found that the results were quite weak and not as straightforward as Triplett's report suggested.)

Later research following Triplett's studies proved mixed. Sometimes the presence of others (side by side or with an audience out front) enhanced performance; at other times, performance declined. It seemed that Triplett's promising lead had turned into a blind alley, and social psychologists had largely abandoned this research by World War II. But years later, Robert Zajonc (1965; 1980) saw a way to reconcile the contradictory results by integrating research from experimental psychology with social psychological research. Zajonc offered an elegant solution: The presence of others increases arousal, which can affect performance in different ways, depending on the task at hand. Let's see how this works.

**The Zajonc Solution**    Zajonc proposed a three-step process:

1. The presence of others creates general physiological *arousal*, which energizes behavior. Based on experimental psychology research and principles of evolution, Zajonc argued that all animals, including humans, tend to become aroused when in the presence of *conspecifics*—that is, members of their own species.

2. Increased arousal enhances an individual's tendency to perform the *dominant response*. The dominant response is the reaction elicited most quickly and easily by a given stimulus.

3. The quality of an individual's performance varies according to the type of *task*. On an easy task (one that is simple or well learned), the dominant response is usually correct or successful. But on a difficult task (one that is complex or unfamiliar), the dominant response is often incorrect or unsuccessful.

Putting these three steps together (see ● Figure 8.2) yields the following scenarios. Suppose you are playing the violin. If you're an excellent player and are performing a well-learned, familiar arrangement, having other people around should enhance your performance; the presence of others will increase your arousal, which will enhance your dominant response. Because this arrangement is so well learned, your dominant response will be to perform it well. However, if you are just learning to play the violin and you are unfamiliar with this arrangement, the presence of others is the last thing you'll want. The increase in arousal should enhance the dominant response, which in this case would be *unsuccessful* violin playing.

When you think about it, this makes intuitive sense. If you are just learning how to perform some complicated task, such as playing the violin or riding a bike, it helps if you are not aroused. In contrast, if you are already good at the task, you may need the extra "juice" that comes from performing in front of others to help you rise to new heights and perform even better than you would if performing alone. And physical performances are not the only ones influenced; the effects also hold for social judgment or cognitive tasks, such as forming impressions of others or solving math problems (Lambert et al., 2003; Park & Catrambone, 2007).

Taken as a package, these two effects of the presence of others—helping performance on easy tasks but hurting performance on difficult tasks—are known as **social facilitation**. Unfortunately this term has been a prime source of confusion for countless students. The trick is to remember that the presence of others facilitates the dominant response, not necessarily the task itself. This facilitation of the dominant response does, in effect, facilitate easy tasks, but it makes difficult tasks even more difficult.

Zajonc proposed that social facilitation is universal, occurring not only in human activities but also among other animals, even insects. Have you ever wondered, for

● **FIGURE 8.2**

**Social Facilitation: The Zajonc Solution**

According to Zajonc, the presence of others increases arousal, which strengthens the dominant response to a stimulus. On an easy task, the dominant response is usually correct, and thus the presence of others enhances performance. On a difficult task, the dominant response is often incorrect, and thus the presence of others impairs performance.

© Cengage Learning

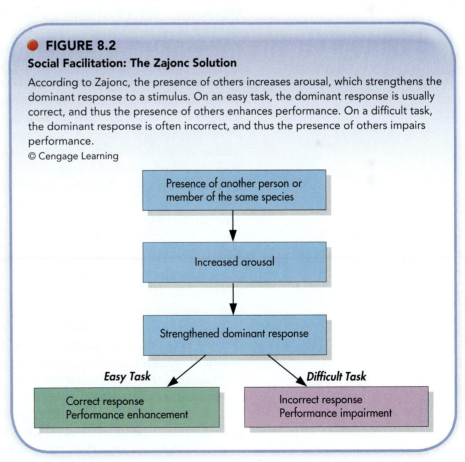

**social facilitation**    A process whereby the presence of others enhances performance on easy tasks but impairs performance on difficult tasks.

U.S. swimmer Michael Phelps surges to the lead on the way to one of his record-setting gold medals at the 2012 Olympics in London. Through social facilitation, some of the best athletes benefit from the presence of an audience and high pressure when performing well-learned routines.

Francois Xavier Marit/AFP/GettyImages

instance, how well a cockroach performs in front of other cockroaches? Neither did we—that is, we didn't until we first learned of Zajonc's creative research on the topic. Zajonc and his colleagues (1969) had cockroaches placed in a brightly lit start box connected to a darkened goal box. When the track was a simple one, with a straight runway between the start box and the goal box, cockroaches running in pairs ran more quickly toward the goal box than did those running alone. But in a more complex maze that required a right turn to reach the goal box, solitary cockroaches outraced pairs. In a particularly creative follow-up experiment, Zajonc and his colleagues found that cockroaches completed the easy maze faster, and the difficult maze slower, if they raced in front of a crowd of spectator cockroaches than if they raced with no audience. How did the researchers get cockroaches to participate as spectators? The researchers placed cockroaches in plexiglass "audience boxes" along either side of the maze, and this "audience" produced social facilitation.

**Social Facilitation Research Today**    Zajonc's formulation revived interest in the issues raised by Triplett's early research, and suddenly the inconsistent findings that had been reported began to make sense. The results of a meta-analysis of 241 studies were consistent with much of Zajonc's account (Bond & Titus, 1983). And despite its long history, research today continues to demonstrate new examples of social facilitation and to test its scope and limitations. Social facilitation effects have been demonstrated in settings where individuals are taking driving tests (a word of advice: Don't take your road test with another test-taker present in the car!), gambling electronically, and being given neuropsychological tests. The effects have also been found when the "others" present were merely a photograph of a favorite TV character or a computer display of a "virtual" person (Gardner & Knowles, 2008; Park & Catrambone, 2007; Rockloff & Dyer, 2007; Rosenbloom et al., 2007; Yantz & McCaffrey, 2007).

It is in part because of the effects of social facilitation that firefighters, police officers, military personnel, and others must train so much to be ready to make split-second decisions under highly arousing situations. They may seem to practice scenarios to the point of overtraining, but it is only through such repetition that their dominant response can be assured to typically be the correct one. When they are in the midst of a raging fire or military firefight, it is often impossible for them to think carefully, and so it's all the more essential that their dominant response be a good one (e.g., Gladwell, 2005).

**Alternative Explanations for Social Facilitation**    Social facilitation effects have been replicated across many domains, but not all of Zajonc's theory has received universal support. Zajonc proposed that the mere presence of others is sufficient to produce social facilitation. Some have argued, however, that a better explanation is the evaluation apprehension theory, which proposes that performance will be enhanced or impaired only in the presence of others who are in a position to evaluate that performance (Geen, 1991; Henchy & Glass, 1968). In other words, it's not simply because others are around that I'm so aroused and therefore inept as I try to learn to snowboard on a crowded mountain. Rather, it's because I worry that the others are watching and probably laughing at me, possibly uploading a video of my performance to YouTube. These concerns increase my dominant response, which, unfortunately, is falling.

"God, this is going to be all over YouTube."

**Fear of being evaluated by others can sometimes hurt performance.**

Another account of social facilitation, distraction–conflict theory, points out that being distracted while we're working on a task creates attentional conflict (Baron, 1986; Sanders, 1981). We're torn between focusing on the task and inspecting the distracting stimulus. When we are conflicted about where to pay attention, our arousal increases.

So is one of these theories right and the others wrong? Probably not. It seems likely that all three of the basic elements described by these theories (mere presence, evaluation, and attention) can contribute to the impact others have on our own performance (Uziel, 2007). But as we are about to see in the next section, there is even more to the story of how individuals are affected by the presence of others.

## Social Loafing: When Others Relax Us

The tasks that participants complete in research on social facilitation produce individually identifiable results. That is, individual behavior can be identified and evaluated. But on some tasks, efforts are pooled so that the specific performance of any one individual cannot be determined. It just so happens that research on these kinds of collective endeavors can also be traced back to Triplett's era of the late nineteenth century. In Chapter 1 we mentioned the French agricultural engineer Max Ringelmann as another contender for having conducted the first social psychology research. In research conducted during the 1880s, Ringelmann discovered that people's output declined when they worked together rather than alone on simple tasks like pulling a rope or pushing a cart (Kravitz & Martin, 1986; Ringelmann, 1913).

Why did individual output decline? One explanation is that the individuals exerted less effort when they acted collectively, but another explanation is that the individuals simply demonstrated poor coordination when working together—some pulled while others relaxed and vice versa. How can you distinguish lack of effort from poor coordination in a task like this? Nearly a hundred years after Ringelmann's research, Alan Ingham and his colleagues (1974) answered this question by using a rope-pulling machine and blindfolding participants. In one condition, participants were led to *think* that they were pulling with a bunch of other participants, and in another condition the participants were informed that they were pulling alone (which, in fact, they were). The researchers

**mere presence theory**    The proposition that the mere presence of others is sufficient to produce social facilitation effects.

**evaluation apprehension theory**    A theory that the presence of others will produce social facilitation effects only when those others are seen as potential evaluators.

**distraction–conflict theory**    A theory that the presence of others will produce social facilitation effects only when those others distract from the task and create attentional conflict.

**● FIGURE 8.3**
**Social Loafing: When Many Produce Less**

Social loafing is a group-produced reduction in individual output on simple tasks. In this study, college students were told to cheer or clap as loudly as they could. The noise produced by each of them decreased as the size of the group increased.

Based on Latané et al., 1979. © Cengage Learning

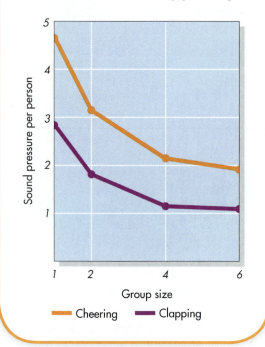

Cheering · Clapping

People will cheer louder when they cheer as part of a group than when they cheer alone. **F**ALSE.

**social loafing** A group-produced reduction in individual output on tasks where contributions are pooled.

**collective effort model** The theory that individuals will exert effort on a collective task to the degree that they think their individual efforts will be important, relevant, and meaningful for achieving outcomes that they value.

told the participants to pull as hard as they could. Ingham and colleagues were able to measure exactly how hard each individual participant pulled, and they observed that the participants pulled almost 20% harder when they thought they were pulling alone than when they thought they were pulling with others. Naoki Kugihara (1999) found a similar decline in rope-pulling among Japanese men (but not women) in a collective setting.

Bibb Latané and his colleagues (1979) found that group-produced reductions in individual output, which they called **social loafing**, are common in other types of tasks as well. For example, imagine being asked as part of a psychology experiment to cheer or clap as loudly as you can. Common sense might lead you to think that you would cheer and clap louder when doing this together with others in a group than when performing alone because you would be less embarrassed and inhibited if others were doing the same thing as you. But Latané and his colleagues found that when performing collectively, individual students loafed—they exerted less effort. The noise generated by each individual decreased as the size of the group increased (see ● Figure 8.3). This social loafing occurred even among cheerleaders, who are supposed to be experts at cheering and clapping with others!

Social loafing is not restricted to simple motor tasks. Sharing responsibility with others reduces the amount of effort that people put into more complex motor tasks, such playing team sports; cognitive tasks, such as completing memory, math, or verbal tests; and important, enduring real-world behaviors, such as working collaboratively on collective farms or team projects (Hoigaard & Ommundsen, 2007; Liden et al., 2004; Miles & Greenberg, 1993; Plaks & Higgins, 2000; Tan & Tan, 2008; Weldon et al., 2000). When others are there to pick up the slack, people slack off.

Most college students are quite familiar with having to work on group projects, and many have seen the pitfalls of social loafing in these settings. Praveen Aggarwal and Connie O'Brien (2008) studied several hundred college students to assess what factors can reduce the incidence of social loafing, and they offer these three strategies: (1) limit the scope of the project—projects that are very large and complex should be broken into smaller components; (2) keep the groups small; and (3) use peer evaluations.

Businesses have taken note of social loafing and have applied these research findings in an effort to reduce it in the workplace. For example, one form of social loafing at the workplace has come to be known as *cyberloafing*, which involves personal use of e-mail and the Internet at work; cyberloafing can be a huge drain on workers' productivity (Blanchard & Henle, 2008; Henle et al., 2009; Wagner et al., 2012). One result is that workers' actions on the job are coming under increasing surveillance as the number of computer keystrokes they make per hour or the content of their calls, e-mails, or Internet browsing can be recorded electronically.

**Collective Effort Model** Several researchers have constructed theoretical accounts to explain the findings about when social loafing is more or less likely to occur (e.g., Guerin, 2003; Shepperd & Taylor, 1999). The most influential of these is the **collective effort model** (Karau & Williams, 2001). This model asserts that individuals will try hard on a collective task when they think their efforts will help them achieve outcomes they personally value. If the outcome is important to individual members of the group *and* if they believe they can help achieve the desired outcome, they are less likely to socially loaf. In fact, in these cases they may even engage in *social compensation* by increasing their efforts on collective tasks to try to compensate for the antici-pated social loafing or poor performance of other group members.

Conversely, if the outcome is not personally important to indi-vidual members, if they believe that their contribution won't affect the outcome very much, or if they feel they are unable to compen-sate for the anticipated social loafing of other members, then they are likely to exert less effort. This is sometimes called the *sucker effect*: Nobody wants to be the "sucker" who does all the work while every-one else goofs off, so everyone withholds effort and the result is very poor group performance (Houldsworth & Mathews, 2000; Kerr, 1983; Shepperd, 1993a). The next time you work on a group project, such as a paper that you and several other students are supposed to write together, consider the factors that increase and decrease social loaf-ing. You might want to try to change aspects of the situation so that all group members are motivated to do their share of the work.

"We just haven't been flapping them hard enough."

Individuals often don't try as hard in groups as they do alone. If they can be convinced that their efforts will pay off, however, their output can soar.

## Culture and Social Loafing

Steven Karau and Kipling Williams (1993) conducted a meta-analysis of 78 studies and found social loafing to be a reliable phenomenon that is evident across numerous tasks and in countries around the world. Despite its prevalence around the world, some group and cul-tural differences in tendencies to socially loaf have been found.

Karau and Williams's meta-analysis found that social loafing was less prevalent among women than among men and less prevalent among people from East Asian, col-lectivist cultures (such as those in China, Japan, and Taiwan) than among people from Western, individualist cultures (such as those in Canada and the United States). With their tendencies to be more aware of their connections and mutual reliance on others, women and people from collectivist cultures may be relatively more concerned about the possible negative impact on others of their social loafing. If someone in the group does violate a norm of hard work, however, people from collectivist cultures may take more offense. That is the implication of research by Tsang-Kai Hung and others (2009), who found that workers in Taiwan who perceived co-workers as socially loafing were likely to be motivated to seek revenge toward their co-workers and even toward the organization.

Here, Chinese farmers cooperate on a task in which individual contributions cannot be identified. Social loafing on such tasks occurs less often in Eastern cultures than in Western ones.

In an interesting twist, Ying-yi Hong and others (2008) hypothesized that there are times when people from collectivist cultures may be especially likely to socially loaf. Because people from these cultures tend to be concerned with behaving consistently with group norms, they may be tempted to socially loaf if they are working in a group that has established a group norm of low productivity and effort. The researchers found support for this idea in a set of studies with Chinese students. When these students engaged in a task with a group of co-workers who were not being productive, the participants reduced their own efforts if they thought their effort would be evident to their co-workers. Not wanting to publicly deviate from the group norm, these students conformed to the norm of working less hard.

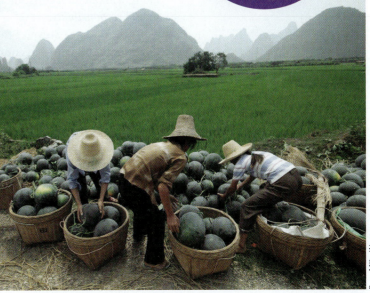

## Deindividuation

Being in the presence of others can lead to the relatively common effects of social facilitation and social loafing. But occasionally the presence of others can lead to extraordinary actions. A group of basketball fans excited at their home team's victory spills out of the arena onto the street, and soon a riot develops, complete with small fires, overturned cars, and looting. A conflict between two people late at night in a loud dance club suddenly turns to a raucous brawl, with bottles flying and punches thrown involving dozens of people. What turns an unruly crowd into a violent mob? No doubt many of the factors described in Chapter 11 on Aggression contribute to group violence as well as violence done by individuals. These include imitation of aggressive models, intense frustration, alcohol consumption, and the presence of weapons that trigger aggressive thoughts and actions. But there's also **deindividuation**, the loss of a person's sense of individuality and the reduction of normal constraints against deviant behavior. Most investigators believe that deindividuation is a collective phenomenon that occurs only in the presence of others (Diener et al., 1976; Festinger et al., 1952).

Philip Zimbardo (1969) observed that *arousal, anonymity,* and reduced feelings of individual *responsibility* together contribute to deindividuation. These elements certainly seemed to be in play during the rioting at Penn State the night that Joe Paterno was fired, as discussed in the opening of this chapter. Arousal, relative anonymity, and reduced feelings of individual responsibility in the midst of the large crowd facilitated the release of inhibitions and the destructiveness that followed. Consider another example at a college campus, but one involving a celebratory rather than resentful crowd. Immediately after the University of Kentucky's men's basketball team's beat its biggest rival, the University of Louisville, in the national championship tournament at the end of March 2012, thousands of rowdy fans gathered in the streets near Kentucky's campus, and the celebration took a destructive turn as couches were burned, cars were flipped, and beer bottles were thrown at police officers (Schreiner, 2012). It's important to note that the Kentucky fans were not frustrated and angry at a bitter loss; they were happy! So why would they—and the fans of many teams around the world after a big victory—act out destructively? All three elements that Zimbardo specified were present here: The fans were very *aroused* by their team's victory, the thousands of celebrating fans provided the individuals with relative *anonymity,* and these factors, quite possibly along with alcohol consumed during the game, contributed to reduced feelings of individual *responsibility.*

According to Steven Prentice-Dunn and Ronald Rogers (1982; 1983), two types of environmental cues—accountability cues and attentional cues—make deviant behaviors such as this rioting more likely to occur. *Accountability cues* affect the individual's cost–reward calculations. When accountability is low, those who commit deviant acts are less likely to be caught and punished, and people may deliberately choose to engage in gratifying but usually inhibited behaviors. Being in a large crowd or wearing a mask are two examples of instances when accountability may be low, and these factors are associated with more extreme and destructive behaviors.

*Attentional cues* focus a person's attention away from the self. In this state, the individual attends less to internal standards of conduct, reacts more to the immediate situation, and is less sensitive to long-term consequences of behavior (Diener, 1980). Behavior slips out from the bonds of cognitive control, and people act on impulse. When you are at a party with very loud music and flashing lights, you may be swept up with the pulsating crowd and feel your individual identity slipping away. In laboratory research,

> *"The sentiments and ideas of all the persons in the gathering take one and the same direction, and their conscious personality vanishes."*
>
> —Gustave Le Bon (1895)

**deindividuation** The loss of a person's sense of individuality and the reduction of normal constraints against deviant behavior.

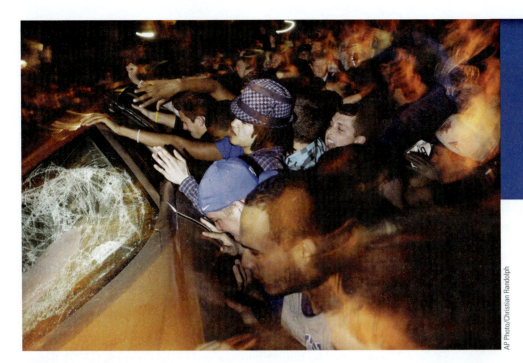

It has become fairly commonplace in recent years for celebrations by groups of fans after their team's victory in a championship to escalate from joy to mayhem and destruction. In this photo, University of Kentucky fans turn over a car as they celebrate Kentucky's win over archrival Louisville on March 31, 2012. In the midst of a crowd like this, people may feel deindividuated, which can lead to deviant behavior.

AP Photo/Christian Randolph

groups of participants placed in a highly stimulating environment (loud music, colorful video games) were more uninhibited, extreme, and aggressive in their actions (Diener, 1979; Spivey & Prentice-Dunn, 1990).

One context ripe for deindividuation is online behavior. If you've ever been part of an online community where people can post comments anonymously, there is a good chance that you've witnessed some of the nasty effects of deindividuation. Many well-intentioned sites or discussions or even the comments sections linked to online newspaper stories, videos, or celebrity gossip blogs soon devolve into a torrent of crude, hostile, and prejudiced venting and taunting that would never happen without the cloak of anonymity.

**Trick or Treat: Field Experiments on Halloween**   One particularly creative set of field experiments by Edward Diener and Arthur Beaman and their colleagues (Beaman et al., 1979; Diener et al., 1976) demonstrated how accountability cues and attentional cues can affect behavior on a night when many otherwise well-behaved individuals act in antisocial ways: Halloween. When you think about it, Halloween is a perfect time to study deindividuation: Children often wear costumes with masks, travel in large groups at night, and are highly aroused. In one study, the researchers unobtrusively observed more than 1,300 children who came trick-or-treating to 27 homes spread around Seattle. At each of these homes, a researcher met and greeted the children, who were either alone or in groups. In one condition, the researcher asked the children their names and where they lived; in another condition, the researcher did not ask them any questions about their identities. When asked to identify themselves, the children should have become more self-aware and more accountable for their actions. Children who were not asked to reveal their identities should have felt relatively deindividuated, safe, and anonymous in their costumes.

The children were then invited to take *one* item from a bowl full of candy and were left alone with the bowl. Hidden observers watched to see how many pieces of candy

● **FIGURE 8.4**

**Trick or Treat(s)**

Children trick-or-treating on Halloween were part of a field experiment. Some were alone and some were in groups with other trick-or-treaters. The experimenter who greeted them allowed a random half of the children to remain anonymous but asked the other half to indicate their names and where they lived. The experimenter instructed each child to take only one piece of candy, after which she left the children alone. The bars in this graph represent the percentage of children who took more than the one piece of candy. Consistent with predictions based on deindividuation, the children who were in a group and were anonymous were most likely to cheat by taking extra candy. Based on Diener et al., 1976. © Cengage Learning

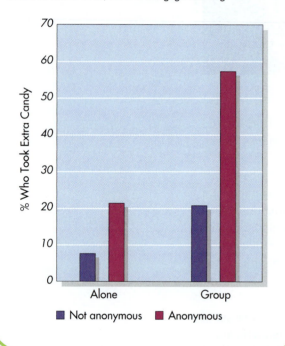

each child took. What did the observers see? As ● Figure 8.4 illustrates, children who were in a group were more likely to break the rule and take extra candy than were children who were alone. Add anonymity to the presence of a group, and children were even more likely to do so. In other words, the children were most likely to take extra candy when they were the most deindividuated: when they were in a group and had not been asked to identify themselves. In another experiment, the researchers placed a mirror behind the candy bowl in some conditions. As noted in Chapter 3, the presence of a mirror tends to increase people's self-awareness. Children who had been asked their names, especially older children, were much less likely to steal candy if there was a mirror present than if there wasn't. Older children are more likely to have internal standards against stealing, and making these children self-aware made them more likely to act according to those standards.

**Moving from Personal to Social Identity**    The loss of personal identity does not always produce antisocial behavior. In a study conducted by Robert Johnson and Leslie Downing (1979), female undergraduates donned garments resembling either robes associated with the Ku Klux Klan (a very racist hate group) or nurses' uniforms. Half of the participants were individually identified throughout the study; the others were not. All of the participants were then given the opportunity to increase or decrease the intensity of electric shocks delivered to a supposed other participant (actually, a confederate in the experiment) who had previously behaved in an obnoxious manner. Participants wearing Ku Klux Klan costumes increased shock levels in both the identified and anonymous conditions. However, among those in nurse's apparel, anonymous participants *decreased* shock intensity four times more frequently than did identified participants!

These findings support the **social identity model of deindividuation effects (SIDE)**, which proposes that whether deindividuation affects people for better or for worse reflects the characteristics and norms of the group immediately surrounding the individual as well as the group's power to act according to these norms (Cronin & Reicher, 2009; Klein et al., 2007; Lee, 2008; Postmes & Spears, 1998). As personal identity and internal controls are submerged, social identity emerges and conformity to the group increases. If a group defines itself in terms of prejudice and hatred against another group, deindividuation can ignite an explosion of violence. The occasional stories of horrendous violation of the human rights of prisoners of war may illustrate this. In these situations the intergroup hostilities the fighting has fueled and the numerous ways that the military depersonalizes its members may create a social identity that can overwhelm personal values of right and wrong. In contrast, if a group defines itself in terms of concern for the welfare of others, deindividuation can spark an expansion of goodness. Indeed, a group whose identity is tied to promoting positive social change can serve as a source for bold, prosocial collective action, such as protesting what they perceive to be a social injustice (Thomas et al., 2012; van Zomeren et al., 2008). The consequences of losing your personal identity, therefore, depend on what you lose it to.

**social identity model of deindividuation effects (SIDE)** A model of group behavior that explains deindividuation effects as the result of a shift from personal identity to social identity.

# Group Performance: Problems and Solutions

Social facilitation, social loafing, and deindividuation can all affect individuals whether they are working in real groups or are merely part of a collective or crowd. In this section, we examine processes that are specific to groups, where interaction among members is more direct and meaningful. We focus on how well groups perform, and in doing so, we address a fundamental question: Aren't two or more heads generally better than one? Although eight people typically can outproduce a lone individual, do eight people working together in a group typically outperform the sum of eight people working individually? You may be surprised to learn how often and in what ways groups perform worse than their potential would suggest. We also discuss when and how groups are more likely to perform well.

## Losses and Gains in Groups

According to Ivan Steiner (1972), when a group performs worse than its potential, it experiences **process loss**. Process loss refers to the reduction of group productivity due to problems in the dynamics of a group. According to Steiner, some types of group tasks are more vulnerable to process loss than others.

For instance, on an *additive* task, the group product is the *sum* of all the members' contributions. Donating to a charity is an additive task, as is making noise at a pep rally. Of course, for these tasks, the more the merrier in terms of overall output. A group typically will make more noise at the rally than an individual. However, as we have seen, people often indulge in social loafing during additive tasks, which creates process loss. In other words, each member's contribution may be less than it would be if that person worked alone. As a result the group performs less than its potential.

On a *conjunctive* task, the group product is determined by the individual with the *poorest* performance. Mountain-climbing teams are engaged in such a task; the "weakest link" will determine their success or failure. Because of this vulnerability to the poor performance of a single group member, group performance on conjunctive tasks tends to be worse than the performance of a single average individual.

On a *disjunctive* task, the group product is (or can be) determined by the performance of the individual with the *best* performance. Trying to solve a problem or develop a strategy may be a disjunctive task: What the group needs is a single successful idea or answer, regardless of the number of failures. In principle, groups have an edge on individuals in the performance of disjunctive tasks. The more people involved, the more likely it is that someone will make a breakthrough. In practice, however, group processes can interfere with coming up with ideas and getting them accepted, resulting in process loss. For example, groups may not realize which group members have the best ideas or are most expert. Unless the best solution for a particular problem is easily and clearly identifiable once it has been suggested, the group may fail to implement it; as a result, the group will perform worse than its best members (Soll & Larrick, 2009; Stasser et al., 1995; Straus et al., 2009). Have you ever had the experience of *knowing* you had the right idea but being unable to convince others in your group until it was too late? If so,

Just as the strength of a chain depends on its weakest link, the group product of a conjunctive task is determined by the individual with the poorest performance. In mountain climbing, for example, if one person slips or falls, the whole team is endangered.

**process loss** The reduction in group performance due to obstacles created by group processes, such as problems of coordination and motivation.

then you have experienced firsthand the problem of process loss on a disjunctive task. A bit later in this chapter, we will discuss strategies that help groups recognize and utilize expertise.

On some kinds of tasks, groups can even show **process gain**, in which they outperform even the best members. Patrick Laughlin and his colleagues (2008; Carey & Laughlin, 2012) have found that groups often perform better than the best individuals on tasks in which (1) the correct answer is clearly evident to everyone in the group once it is presented and (2) the work on the task can be divided up so that various subgroups work on different aspects of the task. In the business world, process gain may be known as *synergy*, and it is the ideal that business and organizational groups strive for (Hertel, 2011).

> ## Brainstorming

During the 1950s, advertising executive Alex Osborn developed a technique called **brainstorming** that was designed to enhance the creativity and productivity of problem-solving groups. The ground rules for brainstorming call for a freewheeling, creative approach:

- Express all ideas that come to mind even if they sound crazy.
- The more ideas, the better.
- Don't worry whether the ideas are good or bad, and don't criticize anyone's ideas; they can be evaluated later.
- All ideas belong to the group, so members should feel free to build on each other's work.

Osborn (1953) claimed that by using these procedures, groups could generate more and better ideas than could individuals working alone. The idea caught on. Brainstorming was soon a popular exercise in business, government, and education. In fact, it remains very popular today. But when the research caught up with the hype, it turned

*"A committee should consist of three men, two of whom are absent."*

—Herbert Beerbohm Tree

**process gain** The increase in group performance so that the group outperforms the individuals who comprise the group.

**brainstorming** A technique that attempts to increase the production of creative ideas by encouraging group members to speak freely without criticizing their own or others' contributions.

Small groups conducting brainstorming sessions in a board room. Despite its popularity, interactive group brainstorming suffers from several group dynamics problems. Fortunately, researchers have determined some ways to improve brainstorming.

Voices.com

out that Osborn's faith in the group process was unfounded. In fact, "nominal groups" (several individuals working alone) produce a greater number of better ideas than do real groups in which members interact with each other. Brainstorming can indeed be effective, but people brainstorming individually produce more and higher-quality ideas than the same number of people brainstorming together. One meta-analysis concluded that brainstorming groups are only about half as productive as an equal number of individuals working alone (Mullen et al., 1991). Rather than being inspired by each other and building on each other's ideas, people brainstorming in a group underperform (Diehl & Stroebe, 1987; Baruah & Paulus, 2011; Paulus, 2011; Stroebe et al., 2010).

The top half of Table 8.1 presents several explanations that have been proposed for why group brainstorming is ineffective. Recall our discussion of social loafing from earlier in the chapter, for example. As you can see in Table 8.1, social loafing is one factor that contributes to process loss in group brainstorming. The first obstacle listed in the table, production blocking, seems to be especially problematic for groups.

Despite the research evidence, brainstorming is still a popular device in many organizations. People who participate in interactive brainstorming groups typically think that it works wonderfully and evaluate their performance more favorably than do individuals in nominal groups. They also enjoy themselves more. And those who have not participated in an interactive brainstorming group believe that such groups are highly productive. Both the experienced and the inexperienced cling to the illusion that group brainstorming is much better than individual brainstorming (Nijstad & Stroebe, 2006).

Fortunately, after the initial shock at how poor group brainstorming really is, researchers have demonstrated a number of strategies that improve productivity while also preserving the enjoyment that group brainstorming can produce. For example, training people in effective brainstorming, alternating types of brainstorming sessions (such as by having members brainstorm alone and then together), giving the group a subset of categories to begin the brainstorming process, or using a trained facilitator during brainstorming sessions are each strategies than have been shown to improve group performance (Baruah & Paulus, 2011; Oxley et al., 1996; Paulus et al., 2006; Paulus & Brown, 2007).

Carsten De Dreu and others (2011) have found that a combination of two motivational factors can improve the number and creativity of ideas that groups produce when brainstorming: (1) being motivated for the collective success of the group, rather than for individual performance, and (2) being motivated to exert effort to achieve a thorough and accurate understanding of the group task or problem at hand. Groups comprised of individuals high in both of these motivations tend to outperform other groups. In addition, these motivations can be induced by situational factors, such as making the group more accountable for its performance or asking members to be ready to explain their decisions and handling of tasks.

Using computers to allow groups to engage in what is called electronic brainstorming can help group brainstorm more effectively. By allowing everyone in the group to enter ideas from their own laptops or keyboards and have the ideas appear on a central screen, electronic brainstorming combines the freedom of working alone and not having to take turns with the stimulation of seeing others' ideas. The bottom half of Table 8.1 presents some of the factors that make this type of brainstorming effective. A meta-analysis of research on electronic brainstorming reported encouraging results (DeRosa et al., 2007). Groups using electronic brainstorming tend to perform much better than other brainstorming groups, although the evidence is mixed concerning whether electronic brainstorming groups outperform nominal groups (Dornburg et al., 2009).

> People brainstorming as a group come up with a greater number of better ideas than the same number of people working individually. **F**ALSE.

##  Group Polarization

Imagine that you are given some information and based on it decide whether someone should behave in a risky or a cautious manner, such as whether an entrepreneur should risk trying to expand his or her business or whether an employee in a stable but boring job should quit and take a more creative job in a new but unproven Internet company. Imagine after you come to an initial opinion on this, you and a group of other people who have also arrived at initial opinions come together and discuss the case. What will be the result of the group discussion of the various opinions?

Common sense suggests two alternative predictions. Perhaps the most reasonable prediction is that there will be a compromise as group members move toward the average of all the individuals' attitudes. But common sense also suggests another prediction. Many people familiar with committees agree that forming a committee is a good way *not* to get something done. We think that as lone individuals we are willing to take risks and implement new ideas, but we recognize that groups tend to be cautious and slow moving. Wary of leading the group toward a risky decision, people often become more cautious in their views as they discuss them with other group members. So another prediction here would be that the people in your group would become more cautious in what they advocate.

So which prediction is the correct one: movement toward the average attitude or movement toward caution? It turns out that neither commonsense notion is correct. Rather, group discussion tends to enhance or exaggerate the initial leanings of the group. Thus, if most group members initially lean toward a risky position on a particular issue, the group members on average will move toward an even riskier position after the discussion. But if group members in general initially lean toward a cautious position, the group discussion leads to greater caution. This effect is called **group polarization**: the exaggeration through group discussion of initial tendencies in the thinking of group members (Moscovici & Zavalloni, 1969; Myers & Lamm, 1976).

Group polarization is not restricted to decisions involving risk versus caution. Any group decision can be influenced by group polarization, from serious decisions such as how to allocate scarce medical resources to more mundane decisions such as what theme a sorority should use at its next party (Chandrashekaran et al., 1996; Furnham et al., 2000).

What causes group polarization? According to *persuasive arguments theory*, the greater the number and persuasiveness of the arguments to which group members are exposed, the more extreme their attitudes become. If most group members favor a cautious decision, for example, most of the arguments discussed will favor caution, giving the members more and more reasons to think caution is the correct approach (Pavitt, 1994; Vinokur & Burnstein, 1974). A second explanation is based on *social comparison*

---

**TABLE 8.1**
**Brainstorming in Groups: Problems and Solutions**

**Factors That Reduce the Effectiveness of Group Brainstorming**

- *Production blocking.* When people have to wait for their turn to speak, they may forget their ideas, may be so busy trying to remember their ideas that they don't listen to others or generate additional ideas, or may simply lose interest.

- *Free riding.* As others contribute ideas, individuals may feel less motivated to work hard themselves. They see their own contributions as less necessary or less likely to have much impact. They therefore engage in social loafing.

- *Evaluation apprehension.* In the presence of others, people may be hesitant to suggest wild, off-the-wall ideas for fear of looking foolish and being criticized. Even if they are willing to suggest such ideas, they may spend time preparing to justify them that they otherwise could have spent coming up with more ideas.

- *Performance matching.* Group members work only as hard as they see others work. Once the other three factors have reduced the performance of a brainstorming group, performance matching can help maintain this relatively inferior performance.

**Why Electronic Brainstorming Is Effective**

- Production blocking is reduced because members can type in ideas whenever they come to mind.

- Free riding can be reduced by having the computer keep track of each member's amount of input.

- Evaluation apprehension is reduced because group members contribute their ideas anonymously.

- Performance matching is reduced because group members spend less time focusing on the performance of others as they type in their own ideas. In addition, performance matching is less of a problem because the initial performance of groups that brainstorm electronically is likely to be high.

- Group members can benefit by seeing the ideas of others, which can inspire new ideas that they might not otherwise have considered.

© Cengage Learning

---

*"A committee is a cul-de-sac down which ideas are lured and then quietly strangled."*

—Barnett Cocks

---

**group polarization** The exaggeration of initial tendencies in the thinking of group members through group discussion.

*theory*. As described in Chapter 3, individuals develop their view of social reality by comparing themselves with others. In the case of group discussions, as individuals learn that most of the other group members lean in one direction on some issue, they may adopt a more extreme attitude in this same direction. In other words, people who are members of a group that believes that X is good may be willing to state to the group that twice X is even better. By advocating for twice X, individuals can distinguish themselves in the group in a manner that is approved by the group (Lamm & Myers, 1978).

There are additional explanations for group polarization. For example, groups may polarize as a way to differentiate themselves from other groups (McGarty et al., 1992). Each of these accounts spotlights particular processes, but taken together they all seem to contribute to the emergence of group polarization. Now that you know about group polarization, you should be able to see evidence of it often as you observe the groups around you. It seems that political groups today have become more and more polarized, moving to extremes rather than toward moderation and compromise. On a smaller level, observe how the culture of a team may evolve over the course of a season or follow the attitudes of a group as it prepares for a debate against another group and you're likely to see group polarization develop through the processes we've just described.

> Group members' attitudes about a course of action usually become more moderate after group discussion. **F**ALSE.

## Groupthink

The processes involved in group polarization may set the stage for an even greater and perhaps more dangerous bias in group decision making. This bias can be seen in examples of very smart people collectively making very dumb decisions. For example, several days before the U.S. space shuttle *Columbia* disintegrated as it reentered the Earth's atmosphere on its way home on February 1, 2003, a team of engineers at the National Aeronautics and Space Administration (NASA) reviewed a video of foam breaking off the shuttle during launch and hitting the area near the left wing. The group speculated about whether the impact could have damaged the heat-shielding tiles located there. One engineer, Rodney Rocha, made more than half a dozen requests of NASA managers to go outside the agency and seek images from spy satellite photos or powerful telescopes that could provide a better look at the possible damage to the *Columbia* while it was in space. These requests were ignored or rejected. One manager said that he refused to be a "Chicken Little." The flight director e-mailed his rejection of the engineer's request with these chilling words: "I consider it to be a dead issue" (Glanz & Schwartz, 2003). The engineer's concerns about the tiles turned out to be justified, and all seven crew members on *Columbia* died in the ensuing tragedy.

Or consider one of the greatest fiascoes in U.S. history: the decision to invade Cuba in 1961. When John Kennedy became president of the United States, he assembled one of the most impressive, most highly educated groups of advisers in the history of American government. But this group devised a plan—inherited from the previous administration—to launch a small invasion of Cuba at the Bay of Pigs in order to spark a people's revolt that would overthrow Fidel Castro's government. Despite the intelligence of Kennedy and his group of advisers, their plan was hopelessly flawed. For example, once the invaders landed at the Bay of Pigs, they were to be supported by anti-Castro guerrillas camped in the mountains nearby. But had Kennedy and his advisers consulted a proper map, they might have noticed that the invaders were to land 80 miles away from these mountains and were separated from them by a huge swamp. Ultimately the invasion failed miserably. The invaders were quickly killed or captured, the world was outraged at the United States, and Cuba allied itself more closely with the Soviet Union—exactly the opposite of what Kennedy had intended. The United States was humiliated. After the fiasco, Kennedy himself wondered, "How could we have been so stupid?" (Janis, 1982).

According to Irving Janis (1982), the answer to this question lies in a particular kind of flawed group dynamic that he called **groupthink**, an excessive tendency to seek concurrence (that is, agreement or uniformity) among group members. Groupthink emerges when the need for agreement takes priority over the motivation to obtain accurate information and make appropriate decisions. ● Figure 8.5 outlines the factors that contribute to groupthink, along with its symptoms and consequences.

Janis believed that three characteristics contribute to the development of groupthink:

1. Since *highly cohesive groups* are more likely to reject members with deviant opinions, Janis thought they would be more susceptible to groupthink.

2. *Group structure* is also important. Groups that are composed of people from similar backgrounds, isolated from other people, directed by a strong leader, and lacking in systematic procedures for making and reviewing decisions should be particularly likely to fall prey to groupthink.

3. *Stressful situations* can provoke groupthink. Under stress, urgency can overrule accuracy and the reassuring support of other group members becomes highly desirable.

The idea that high cohesiveness contributes to groupthink got a lot of attention when Janis introduced the model because, as we indicated earlier, cohesiveness is something that most people view as something that groups should strive for and value. However, even though high cohesiveness in a group might feel great and make for smooth and easy interactions among group members, it can foster emphasis on preserving each other's feelings rather than an objective examination of the facts or an honest discussion of differences of opinion. Such a concern with agreement over accuracy is a hallmark of groupthink.

In Janis's formulation, groupthink is a kind of social disease, and infected groups display the behavioral symptoms indicated in the middle of Figure 8.5. For example, NASA's refusal to ask for outside help in obtaining images of the *Columbia* shuttle in space clearly illustrated the symptom of *closed-mindedness.* Another symptom, *pressures toward uniformity*, was evident in these examples. During the planning of the Bay of Pigs invasion, the president's brother, Robert Kennedy, served as a "mindguard" and warned dissenting members to keep quiet. A chilling example of this occurred during the debate about whether to go ahead with the launch of the space shuttle *Challenger* in 1986, 17 years before the *Columbia* disaster. When a vice-president for engineering voiced his objection to the *Challenger* being launched on schedule because of fear that the unusually cold weather could cause the O-ring seals in the rocket boosters to fail, a manager pressured him to change his vote by telling him to "take off your engineer hat and put on your management hat." Pressured to abandon one role and adopt the other, he changed his vote, and the tragic fate of the *Challenger* and its crew may have been sealed at that moment. In the end, this vice-president's decision helped foster an *illusion of unanimity* because top-level managers at NASA were unaware of all the dissent voiced by the engineers that morning.

● **FIGURE 8.5**

**Charting the Course of Groupthink**

Irving Janis depicted groupthink as a kind of social disease, complete with antecedents and symptoms, that increased the chance of making a bad decision.
Based on Janis, 1982. © Cengage Learning

**Antecedents**
- High cohesiveness
- Group structure
  *Homogeneous members*
  *Isolation*
  *Directive leadership*
  *Unsystematic procedures*
- Stressful situations

**Symptoms**
- Overestimation of the group
- Close-mindedness
- Increased pressures toward uniformity
  *Mindguards and pressure on dissenters*
  *Self-censorship*
  *Illusion of unanimity*
- Defective decision making
  *Incomplete survey of alternatives*
  *Incomplete survey of objectives*
  *Failure to examine risks of preferred choice*
  *Failure to reappraise initially rejected alternatives*
  *Poor information search*
  *Selective bias in processing information at hand*
  *Failure to work out contingency plans*

**High Probability of a Bad Decision**

**groupthink** A group decision-making style characterized by an excessive tendency among group members to seek concurrence.

More recently, some scholars have proposed that the group dynamics behind the decision to invade Iraq in 2003 led primarily by American and British forces reflected groupthink, particularly in the decision makers' serious failures in information gathering and analysis and in the underestimation of risks (Houghton, 2008; Rodrigues et al., 2005). Similarly, Jerrold Post (2011) argued that groupthink played a role in the torture of prisoners held at the Abu Ghraib prison in Iraq by U. S. Army personnel. And soon after the release of details about Penn State officials' failure to act on allegations of child sexual abuse, as described in the beginning of this chapter, *Time* magazine published an article with the headline: "Penn State Cover-Up: Groupthink in Action." The article was subtitled, "How do smart, principled men wind up defending a child abuser in their midst? Blame the phenomenon of groupthink" (Cohen & DeBenedet, 2012). Symptoms such as close-mindedness, incomplete survey of alternatives and objectives, and failure to examine the risks of the preferred choice are all apparent in the decision by Paterno and his colleagues to not report Sandusky to the proper authorities outside the university.

People may resist outside information that could improve their decisions even in low-stress situations and in very small groups. Indeed, Julia Minson and Jennifer Mueller (2012) found that when pairs of people made decisions collectively rather than individually, they became much more resistant to considering useful information offered by a peer from an outside viewpoint. Working collectively, individuals may be focused more on mutually reinforcing each other's judgments than arriving at the most accurate decisions.

When alternatives are not considered, the behavioral symptoms of groupthink can result in the defective decision making outlined in Figure 8.5. In turn, a defective decision-making process increases the likelihood that a group will make bad decisions.

**Preventing Groupthink**    To guard against groupthink, Janis urged groups to make an active effort to process information more carefully and accurately. He recommended that decision-making groups use the following strategies:

- To avoid isolation, groups should consult widely with outsiders.

- To reduce group pressures to conform, leaders should explicitly encourage criticism and not take a strong stand early in the group discussion.

- To establish a strong norm of critical review, subgroups should separately discuss the same issue, a member should be assigned to play devil's advocate and question all decisions and ideas, and a "second chance" meeting should be held to reconsider the group decision before taking action.

President Kennedy appeared to arrive at similar conclusions after the Bay of Pigs disaster. In the following year, 1962, the United States and the Soviet Union appeared to be at the brink of war after U.S. military intelligence discovered that Soviet missiles in Cuba were aimed at the United States. During this crisis, Kennedy stayed away from initial meetings about how to respond to the situation, he consulted with experts outside his inner circle of advisers, and he told his brother Robert to play "devil's advocate" and challenge all ideas—in sharp contrast to Robert's role of "mindguard" during the Bay of Pigs planning sessions. Unlike the Bay of Pigs invasion, the Cuban missile crisis ended exactly as Kennedy had hoped: The Soviet Union withdrew its missiles from Cuba, and a war was avoided.

Research has shown empirical support for the effectiveness of some strategies in curtailing groupthink tendencies. These include inserting someone in the group to play the role of a "reminder" who is responsible for informing the group about the dangers of biased decision making, making individual group members believe that they will be held personally responsible for the outcome of their group's decisions, increasing the diversity of group members, and creating a group norm that encourages critical thinking and discourages the search for concurrence (Kroon et al., 1991; Postmes et al., 2001; Schultz et al., 1995; t'Hart, 1998). And as we will see a bit later in the chapter, computer-based technology can be used during meetings to help avoid groupthink.

**Research on Groupthink: Myth or Reality?**   Groupthink is a rather distinctive theory in social psychology. On the one hand, its impact has been unusually broad: It is discussed in a variety of disciplines outside psychology including business, political science, and communication, and it has spawned numerous workshops, websites, and training videos. Yet on the other hand, there is not a great deal of empirical support for the model, certainly not in proportion to its fame. This may be partly due to the difficulty of experimentally testing such a broad set of variables in high-pressure group settings. In addition, many researchers disagree with Janis about the specific conditions that make groups vulnerable to groupthink (Baron, 2005; Choi & Kim, 1999; Henningsen et al., 2006; Kramer, 1998; Tetlock, 1998; t'Hart et al., 1995; Whyte, 1998). On the other hand, some researchers do believe that when multiple antecedents of groupthink are evident simultaneously, such as high cohesiveness, a strong and controlling leader, and a great deal of stress, groups are indeed vulnerable to the kinds of faulty decision making that Janis described (Esser, 1998; Mullen et al., 1994).

"On second thought, don't correct me if I'm wrong."

A controlling leader who discourages disagreement can promote groupthink, leading to bad decisions.

For now, the bottom line may be that even if one is skeptical about the details of Janis's theory of groupthink, as many and perhaps most scholars are, it does seem clear that many of the factors that Janis specified as antecedents and symptoms of groupthink can contribute to very faulty group decision making, and groups would be wise to be on the lookout for these traps. Perhaps most importantly, the steps that Janis advocated to avoid these traps should help most groups, regardless of the merits or problems with the theory of groupthink.

## Escalation Effects

A specific kind of trap that can be very costly to organizations and businesses is known as the **escalation effect** (sometimes referred to as *entrapment*). Escalation effects occur when commitment to a failing course of action is increased to justify investments already made (Haslam et al., 2006; Keil et al., 2007; Staw, 1997). Laboratory experiments show that groups are more likely to escalate commitment to a failing project and are likely to do so in more extreme ways than are individuals (Dietz-Uhler, 1996; Seibert & Goltz, 2001). Groups whose members are relatively homogenous or feel a strong psychological connection with each other are more prone to escalation effects (Greitemeyer et al., 2011; Gunia et al., 2009). In numerous instances outside the laboratory, groups, businesses, and governments have incurred huge costs because they continued to throw more money, time, and other resources into a project that should have been terminated long before (Ross & Staw, 1986; Schott et al., 2011). We will revisit this concept again in Chapter 13, when we discuss how businesses and individuals can fall into a "sunk cost" trap as they spend more and more money trying to justify an already bad investment.

A memorable example is the construction project in Boston known as the "Big Dig," which was designed to convert a congested stretch of highway into a high-speed underground tunnel. It was originally budgeted in 1983 for about $2.6 billion and was expected to be completed by 1995. Years of delays and increasing costs led to escalating commitments to try to salvage the troubled project. These 7.5 miles of road were costing

**escalation effect**   The condition in which commitments to a failing course of action are increased to justify investments already made.

millions of dollars a day, and many critics wanted to significantly reduce the project as a result, but with so much money already spent, commitments to completing the project only increased. As U.S. Congressman Barney Frank wryly suggested, it would have been cheaper to raise the city than to dig the tunnel (Roane, 2000). The project took more than a decade longer than planned to complete, and in 2008 its total cost was estimated to be a staggering $22 billion (Murphy, 2008).

*"Nor is the people's judgment always true: The most may err as grossly as the few."*

—John Dryden

## Communicating Information and Utilizing Expertise

One of the biggest flaws in how groups perform is that they often fail to use all the information or skills that group members have (Hackman & Katz, 2010). In this section we will explore some of the dynamics that cause this problem as well as some factors that can help groups better communicate and use important information.

**Information Sharing and Biased Sampling**  Imagine that you are part of a group that is discussing which of several candidates should be supported for an election. You have read some potentially damaging personal information about one of the candidates, and you incorrectly assume that the others are also aware of it. If you observe during group discussion that nobody else mentions this information, you may further assume that the others don't think the information is relevant or credible, so you may not mention it yourself. Other group members may also have unique bits of information known only to them. For similar reasons, these pieces of information fail to enter the discussion. In the end, the discussion is dominated by information everyone in the group already knew, while the unshared information never makes it to the table.

Or imagine another scenario that is not unusual in the business world. The chief executives of a company meet to decide whether to launch a risky expansion of their business. All of them share much of the same information about the potential costs and benefits, and the weight of this evidence suggests the risk is worth it. But one of the executives is an expert on some technical aspects of the stock market and knows a reason why this move might have bad stock implications. Another executive has special knowledge of one of their primary competitors and knows that the competitor might make a countermove that could be devastating. A third executive knows that the morale among the company's personnel could be hurt by the expansion more than the other executives realize. If these unique pieces of information made it into the discussion, the weight of the evidence would tip the other way, toward not expanding the company yet. But too often group members fail to share their uniquely held information, and bad decisions result.

These examples illustrate what Garold Stasser (1992; Stasser & Titus, 2003) termed **biased sampling**. Because of biased sampling, a group may fail to consider important information that is not common knowledge in the group. Inadequately informed, the group may make a bad decision. The results of a meta-analysis of 72 studies involving more than 17,000 people make clear how important sufficient information sharing is for group performance, and therefore biased sampling of information can be a significant problem (Mesmer-Magnus & DeChurch, 2009).

Sometimes biased sampling can have tragic consequences. The commission formed to investigate the 1986 explosion of the space shuttle *Challenger* concluded that inadequate sharing of information contributed to the disaster. For example, some engineers had information indicating that it would be unsafe to launch the shuttle that morning because of the low temperature, but this information was not shared with everyone. The people who ultimately made the decision to launch therefore were not aware of all the information that was relevant for their decision. The commission concluded,

**biased sampling**  The tendency for groups to spend more time discussing shared information (information already known by all or most group members) than unshared information (information known by only one or a few group members).

Reuters/Landov

The U.S. space shuttle *Challenger* explodes shortly after its launch on January 28, 1986, killing all seven crew members. Inadequate sharing of information and a flawed communication network were among the group dynamics problems that contributed to NASA's flawed, and ultimately fatal, decision to launch the shuttle that cold morning.

"If the decision-makers had known all the facts, it is highly unlikely that they would have decided to launch" (Presidential Commission on the Space Shuttle Challenger Accident, 1986, p. 82). Lessons learned after that tragedy appeared to have been forgotten 17 years later: Inadequate sharing of vital information also appeared to have contributed to the *Columbia* disaster in 2003.

Part of the problem in the NASA disasters was that the *communication network*, which defines who can speak with whom based on a group's structure, made it difficult for information to be distributed to all of the decision makers. In many organizations, information is passed up a chain of command through layers of middle management and only some of this information makes it all the way up to the executives who make the final decisions. This was the case at NASA. The engineers who were most familiar with the physical details of the shuttle could not communicate directly with the NASA officials at the top of the chain of command. According to Rodney Rocha, who was one of the engineers who most emphatically warned about the possible damage to the *Columbia*, "Engineers were often told not to send messages much higher than their own rung in the ladder" (Glanz & Schwartz, 2003). Because warnings were suppressed as the flow of information moved up the chain of command, the people at the top did not know the extent of the concerns of those lower in the chain.

Researchers have studied biased sampling of information in case studies of real groups, such as in the NASA disasters, as well as in laboratory experiments in which they give all the members of a group the same set of information but also give each individual or subsets of individuals unique pieces of information to see if these unique pieces find their way into the group discussion and decisions. Jessica Mesmer-Magnus and Leslie DeChurch (2009) conducted a meta-analysis of 72 studies involving almost 5,000 groups and found that biased sampling is a frequent and significant problem in groups. Groups that do a better job of sharing information tend to perform much better and are more cohesive.

Fortunately, researchers have discovered several conditions under which biased sampling is less likely to occur. For example, leaders who encourage a lot of group participation are more likely to elicit unshared (as well as shared) information during group discussions than are leaders who are more directive, and leaders who establish trust are also more effective in promoting information sharing (Larson et al., 1998; Lee et al., 2010). Another effective role that leaders can play is in shaping group members' understanding of their task. Wendy van Ginkel and Daan van Knippenberg (2008, 2012; van Ginkel et al., 2009) have found over a series of well-designed studies in the Netherlands and the United States how important it is for group members to have a particular understanding of their decision-making task. When groups share an understanding that the task requires a thorough exchange and critical discussion of ideas involving all the group members, they are much better at complete information sharing and making better decisions than when, for example, group members see their task more as involving finding common ground.

Van Ginkel and van Knippenberg (2012) hypothesized that groups that have leaders who try to instill a shared and productive understanding of the group task will tend to produce much better group performance than groups who do not have such a leader. To test this idea the researchers had business and economics students participate in three-person groups to make a series of decisions about managing a small market center. All of the group members were given a set of identical information relevant for their decision, but each member also received information unique to them that was crucial for the overall decision. In two-thirds of these groups, one of the members was randomly selected to be the group leader; in the remaining groups, no leader was selected. Among the groups with a leader, half of the leaders were given instructions that focused on the importance of thorough exchange of information, critical discussion, and avoiding prematurely reaching consensus. The other half of the leaders received instructions that emphasized the importance of seeking common ground in group decision making.

As can be seen in ● Figure 8.6, groups with a leader who was prompted to promote thorough information exchange were significantly more likely to discuss the unique pieces of information each group member had and to arrive at better decisions than the groups without a leader or the groups that had a leader who was prompted to encourage finding common ground.

**Information Processing and Transactive Memory**    Even if everyone in a group has all the available information, group members must process that information and use it to make judgments or perform tasks. How well do groups process information compared with individuals? In general, groups are susceptible to the same information-processing biases as individuals, only more so. In reviewing the research on group information processing, Verlin Hinsz and others (1997) concluded, "If some bias, error, or tendency predisposes individuals to process information in a particular way, then groups exaggerate this tendency. However, if this bias, error, or tendency is unlikely among individuals processing the information (e.g., less than half the sample), then groups are even less likely to process information in this fashion" (pp. 49–50). Individuals, for example, are prone to be more affected in their judgments by a few vivid examples than by statistics

● **FIGURE 8.6**

**Leadership and Information Sharing**

Groups made a series of decisions about managing a small market center. All the members of the group had a set of identical information relevant for the task, but each also had information that the others did not have. Some groups had a leader who was given information about the importance of a thorough and critical discussion of information, others had a leader who was given information about the importance of seeking common ground among the members, and others had no leader. Compared to the other two kinds of groups, the groups with a leader prompted to encourage thorough discussion did a better job discussing the unique information (graph on the left) and making better decisions (graph on the right).

Based on van Ginkel & van Knippenberg, 2012. © Cengage Learning

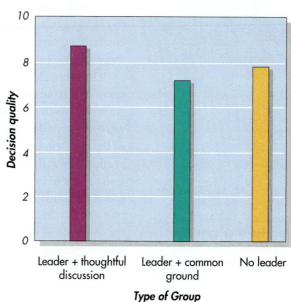

covering a much larger and more representative sample of information. Hinsz and others (2008) have found that groups are significantly more susceptible to this bias than individuals are.

One key advantage of groups is that they can divide a large body of information into smaller portions and delegate different members to remember these more manageable portions. Have you and a friend ever divided up a list of things to remember, such as which grocery items to remember to buy at the store or which sections of a textbook chapter each of you should be responsible for remembering before you study together? If so, you have tried to take advantage of a shared process known as **transactive memory**, which helps groups remember more information more efficiently than individuals (Argote & Ren, 2012; Wegner et al., 1991). But process loss can occur in this domain as well. Social loafing may occur, for example, when group members don't do their share of the work while expecting others to pick up the slack. A particularly important problem is that groups may not distribute the tasks and roles among group members in a rational or efficient manner, such as by matching individuals to tasks based on their skills, expertise, and preferences.

Groups that develop good transactive memory systems have enormous advantages over other groups (Argote & Ren, 2012; Lewis & Herndon, 2011; Liao et al., 2012; Zhong et al., 2012). Effective transactive memory systems involve a few key elements. First, the group must develop a division of knowledge, and the group members must be able to communicate and remember this information in the group; everyone must know *who knows what*. Second, the group members must be able to trust each other's specialized knowledge. And third, the group members need to coordinate their efforts so that they can work together on a task smoothly and efficiently.

## Goals and Plans in Groups

You've probably worked in many groups for which the goal was simply to "do your best." Despite the popularity of such goals, the research clearly shows that they are not as effective as specific goals. As Edwin Locke and Gary Latham (2002) concluded from their review of 35 years' worth of studies, "When people are asked to do their best, they do not do so" (p. 706). People are indeed capable of better than their vaguely defined "best." Groups, like individuals, tend to perform better on a task when they have specific, challenging, and reachable goals, particularly if the group members are committed to the goals and believe they have the ability to achieve them. In addition to having challenging and specific goals, groups are most likely to benefit when there are incentives in place for achieving these goals.

One benefit of groups over individuals is that group members can hold each other accountable and encourage each other to keep trying to achieve a goal. For example, Andrew Prestwich and others (2012) recruited a sample of British individuals who were interested in participating in a study on increasing their physical activity. Some of the participants were instructed to set specific plans for how to achieve their goal of increasing physical activity, including how they would respond in particular situations (*if we're in situation X, then we'll do Y*), and some were not asked to make these plans. In addition, some of these participants worked alone, and others worked with a partner. Participants who both had these plans and worked with a partner significantly increased their physical activity and lost significantly more weight than if they had no specific plans or if they had these plans but did not have a partner.

An experiment by Anita Williams Woolley and others (2008) demonstrated how important it is for groups to be induced to explicitly plan how to proceed so that they can properly utilize the expertise of its members. Four-person teams were given the task

---

People and groups tend to do worse when they have "do your best" goals than when they have very specific, ambitious goals. **T**RUE.

---

**transactive memory** A shared system for remembering information that enables multiple people to remember information together more efficiently than they could do so alone.

of solving a terrorist plot based on a set of information about suspects, potential locations, and planned activities. To solve the case, the teams would have to share and correctly use different sets of evidence. For some of the evidence, participants with strong verbal memory would be most likely to offer correct analyses. For some other evidence, participants with strong face-recognition ability would be most helpful.

Based on pre-testing of the participants' abilities, the teams were constructed so that some had experts and some did not. Specifically, half the teams had one verbal memory expert, one face-recognition expert, and two non-experts. The other half of the teams consisted of four non-experts. The researchers also manipulated whether or not the teams would receive a collaborative planning intervention. The teams that received this were required to discuss explicitly who would be responsible for which type of evidence and plan how they would integrate the various types of evidence they were given. The other teams did not receive this requirement and instead were able to launch immediately into their work.

As ● Figure 8.7 shows, groups with experts but no planning did no better (indeed, they even did somewhat worse) than groups without experts. Similarly, groups that engaged in planning but had no experts did no better than groups with no planning. Only the groups that had experts as well as the planning intervention did relatively well on the task. Requiring the groups to think about how they would use the available information and each other's skills enabled them to reap the benefits of the expertise of group members.

## > Training

We have discussed a variety of factors that can enhance group processes. Table 8.2 presents a set of the conditions that Ruth Wageman and her colleagues (2009) suggest are best for team effectiveness. These suggestions are consistent with the principles that we have addressed throughout this chapter, and they help illustrate the tremendous value that understanding the social psychology of groups can have in the business world or wherever group performance is essential. The last point in Table 8.2 concerns making technical assistance and training available to groups. Social psychologists often consult with businesses and organizations to offer these kinds of services.

Creating training programs and team interventions for groups can be a valuable investment of time and resources (Shuffler et al., 2011; van Ginkel et al., 2009). For example, Jane Prichard and Melanie Ashleigh (2007) found that the transactive memory and performance of groups improved with training programs that taught team skills such as problem solving, goal setting, and role allocation. A meta-analysis of the literature on group training involving 178 teams found reliable evidence supporting the value of training in improving group performance (Salas et al., 2007).

## > Computer Technology and Group Support Systems

Some of the obstacles that get in the way of good group discussion and decision making can be reduced through the use of interactive computer programs. Often referred to as **group support systems** (or *group decision support systems*), these programs help

● **FIGURE 8.7**

**Benefitting from Experts: The Role of Collaborative Planning**

Four-person teams sifted through different sets of evidence to try to solve a case. Some teams had two participants who had expert-level abilities relevant to some of the evidence, whereas other teams had no experts. In addition, half the teams were made to engage in collaborative planning before doing their task, and the other half did not. The bars on this graph reflect how well the groups performed on the task, with higher scores reflecting better performance. The only condition in which groups tended to perform well was when the group both had experts and engaged in collaborative planning.

Based on Woolley et al., 2008. © Cengage Learning

**group support systems** Specialized interactive computer programs that are used to guide group meetings, collaborative work, and decision-making processes.

remove communication barriers and provide structure and incentives for group discussions and decisions. Compared to groups that use more conventional face-to-face modes of discussion, groups that use these systems often do a better job of sampling information, communicating, and arriving at good decisions (Adla et al., 2011; Lim & Guo, 2008; Rains, 2005; Vathanophas & Liang, 2007). Table 8.3 lists some of the ways that computerized group support systems can help groups avoid groupthink.

## Virtual Teams

Teams consisting of people dispersed widely across the globe are a relatively recent and rapidly growing part of the business world. Recent estimates indicate that a majority of professional workers today spend time working in virtual teams (Cordery & Soo, 2008; Mathieu et al., 2008; Mesmer-Magnus et al., 2011). Virtual teams, sometimes also called dispersed teams, are "groups of people who work interdependently with shared purpose across space, time, and organization boundaries using technology to communicate and collaborate" (Kirkman et al., 2002, p. 67). Due to globalization and a variety of related factors, virtual teams will be increasingly important in businesses and organizations.

Most of the factors that contribute to process loss in groups apply as well to virtual groups, but virtual groups may be especially vulnerable to some of these. Given the physical distances between members and how little interaction they may have with each other, virtual groups may have a harder time building cohesiveness, keeping membership stable, socializing new members, keeping roles clear, sharing information, and developing transactive memory systems that enable the members to recognize or recall who has what knowledge or expertise in the group. Special attention must be paid to virtual groups, therefore, to offset these problems. For example, directories should be available and updated to allow members to access information about who knows what across the virtual team. Frequent teleconferencing sessions and occasional short visits to allow dispersed group members to spend some time together can also help (Cordery & Soo, 2008; Hackman & Katz, 2010; Oshri et al., 2008). The lack of cohesiveness in virtual groups can have some advantages, though, such as in helping these groups avoid some of the conformity pressures associated with groupthink-like problems.

## Culture and Diversity

One outgrowth of the surging use of virtual groups dispersed around the world is the creation of what are called multinational multicultural (MNMC) distributed teams. Even in face-to-face groups, though, groups are becoming increasingly diverse, most obviously in terms of sex, race, ethnicity, and cultural background. This diversity offers both unique challenges and opportunities to groups and how they perform.

How does diversity affect group performance? How can a group best use diversity to its advantage? The answers to such questions—and even the meaning of *diversity*—are likely to change as society changes in terms of its demographics and attitudes. In addition, diversity is not restricted to demographic differences among group members but can also mean differences in attitudes, personalities, skill levels, and so on. Thus, the issues surrounding diversity are particularly complex.

The evidence from empirical research concerning the effects of diversity on group performance is decidedly mixed (Hackman & Katz, 2010; Mannix & Neale, 2005; van Knippenberg & Schippers, 2007; Phillips, 2008). On the one hand, diversity often is associated with negative group dynamics. Miscommunications and misunderstandings are more likely to arise among heterogeneous group members, causing frustration and resentment and damaging group performance by weakening coordination, morale, and commitment to the group. Cliques often form in diverse groups, causing some group members to feel alienated.

On the other hand, research has also demonstrated positive effects of diversity, such as on patterns of socialization, classroom dynamics, and complexity and inclusiveness of group discussion (Antonio et al., 2004; Juvonen et al., 2006; Toosi et al., 2012). Samuel Sommers (2006) found that racially diverse juries exchanged a wider range of information, cited more facts about the case being decided, and made fewer errors in their deliberations than racially homogenous juries, at least when the defendant was black. Sommers and others (2008) also found that merely *anticipating* being in a racially mixed group made white individuals process information relevant to race more thoroughly.

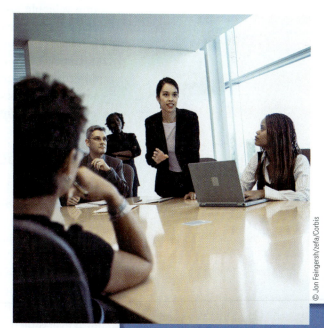

As more and more organizations try to attract customers and investors from diverse cultures, diversity in personnel should offer more and more advantages. Cedric Herring (2009) analyzed data from over 1,000 work establishments in the United States from 1996 to 1997 and found that racial diversity was associated with greater profits and market share. (Keep in mind, however, that this is a correlational finding and that the causality is ambiguous. For example, it could be the case that diversity contributed to success or that success made greater diversity possible.)

Because groups have become increasingly diverse in many settings, it is more important than ever that groups learn how to utilize the great benefits and minimize the costs of diversity in group processes.

Although the overall body of work on the effects of diversity on group performance remains quite mixed, newer research is focused on understanding specific factors that can help groups achieve the benefits of diversity while avoiding or reducing its problems. One set of recent findings is that multicultural groups perform better if their members or leaders have relatively high awareness of their own and others' cultural assumptions—what is sometimes called *cultural metacognition* (Chua et al., 2012; Crotty & Brett, 2012). People exhibit cultural metacognition to the extent that they often think about and check the accuracy of their cultural knowledge, particularly in cross-cultural interactions. In addition, culturally diverse groups whose members have a positive attitude toward learning new information tend to benefit from the diversity of their groups more than other groups (Nederveen Pieterse et al., 2013). Finally, Inga Hoever and others (2012) demonstrated that diverse groups who were encouraged to take each other's perspective as much as possible performed significantly better on a creativity task than did other homogenous groups or diverse groups not given special instructions to promote perspective taking.

Given trends in populations, globalization, business practices, and people's attitudes, we can predict that there will continue to be rapid acceleration in research dedicated to illuminating—and improving—the complex relationship between diversity and a variety of group processes.

# Conflict: Cooperation and Competition Within and Between Groups

Many of the most crucial issues confronting our world today involve conflicts between groups or between individuals and their groups. The desire of some individuals to consume valuable resources conflicts with the need to protect the environment for the greater good. A nation's claim to important territory or the right to nuclear arms conflicts with another nation's national security. In this section, we describe some of the dilemmas groups often must confront and what factors influence whether individuals and groups act cooperatively or competitively in dealing with them. We also look at some of the factors that cause conflicts between groups to escalate or be reduced, and we focus on an important mechanism for resolving group conflicts: negotiation.

## Mixed Motives and Social Dilemmas

Imagine that you have to choose between cooperating with others in your group versus pursuing your own self-interests, which can hurt the others. Examples of these mixed-motive situations are everywhere. An actor in a play may be motivated to try to "steal" a scene, a basketball player may be inclined to hog the ball, an executive may want to keep more of the company's profits, a family member may want to eat more than his fair share of the leftover birthday cake, and a citizen of the Earth may want to use more than her fair share of finite valuable resources.

In each case, the individual can gain something by pursuing his or her self-interests, but if everyone in the group pursues self-interests, all of the group members will ultimately be worse off than if they had cooperated with each other. Each option, therefore, has possible benefits as well as potential costs. When you are in a situation like this, you may feel torn between wanting to cooperate and wanting to compete, and these mixed motives create a difficult dilemma. The notion that the pursuit of self-interest can sometimes be self-destructive is the basis for what is called a **social dilemma**. In a social dilemma, what is good for one is bad for all. If everyone makes the most self-rewarding choice, everyone suffers the greatest loss. This section examines how people resolve the tension between their cooperative and competitive inclinations in social dilemmas.

**The Prisoner's Dilemma**    We begin with a crime story. Two partners in crime are picked up by the police for questioning. Although the police believe they have committed a major offense, there is only enough evidence to convict them on a minor charge. In order to sustain a conviction for the more serious crime, the police will have to convince one of them to testify against the other. Separated during questioning, the criminals

**social dilemma**  A situation in which a self-interested choice by everyone will create the worst outcome for everyone.

weigh their alternatives (see ● Figure 8.8). If neither confesses, they will both get light sentences on the minor charge. If both confess and plead guilty, they will both receive somewhat longer sentences. But if one confesses and the other stays silent, the confessing criminal will go free while the silent criminal will pay the maximum penalty.

This situation forms the basis for the research paradigm known as the **prisoner's dilemma**. In the two-person prisoner's dilemma, participants are given a series of choices that give them the option of cooperating or competing with each other, but either option has potential costs. Imagine that you're Prisoner A in Figure 8.8. You should see that no matter what Prisoner B does, you're better off if you compete with B and confess. If B doesn't confess to the police (in other words, if he cooperates with you by not ratting you

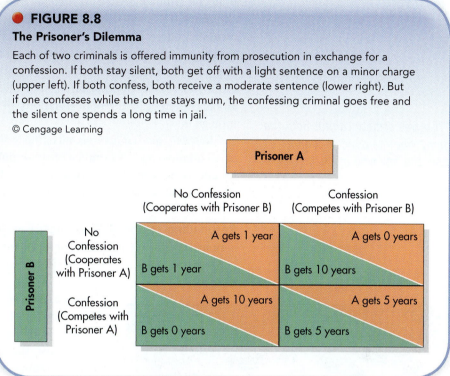

● **FIGURE 8.8**
**The Prisoner's Dilemma**
Each of two criminals is offered immunity from prosecution in exchange for a confession. If both stay silent, both get off with a light sentence on a minor charge (upper left). If both confess, both receive a moderate sentence (lower right). But if one confesses while the other stays mum, the confessing criminal goes free and the silent one spends a long time in jail.
© Cengage Learning

out), you will get a lighter penalty if you do confess than if you don't—no jail time versus one year in jail. If B confesses, you still get a lighter sentence if you confess than if you don't—5 versus 10 years. So clearly, you should confess, right? But here's the dilemma: If you *both* confess, each of you gets 5 years. If *neither* of you confesses, each of you gets only 1 year. In other words, each individual is better off selling out his or her partner, but if both individuals do this, they are worse off than if neither did. It's really a perplexing situation. What do you think you would do?

This kind of social dilemma is not limited to situations involving only two individuals at a time. Imagine, for example, being in a burning building or a sinking ship. Each individual might want to race for the exit or the lifeboats as quickly as possible and push others out of the way, but if everyone does that, more people will die in the panic. More lives will be saved if people leave in an orderly fashion. Soldiers engaged in combat may be better off individually if they take no chances and duck for cover, but if their comrades do the same thing, they all will be slaughtered by the enemy. Nations face such dilemmas as well. Two countries locked in an arms race would be better off if they stopped spending money and resources on weapons of mass destruction, but neither country wants to risk falling behind the other (Dawes, 1980).

**Resource Dilemmas**    One particular category of social dilemmas that people face frequently and in vitally important contexts is called **resource dilemmas**, which concern how two or more people share a limited resource. As with prisoner's dilemmas, attempts to gain a personal advantage will backfire if the other party also makes the competitive choice. Resource dilemmas come in two basic types: (1) commons dilemmas and (2) public goods dilemmas.

In the *commons dilemma*, if people take as much as they want of a limited resource that does not replenish itself, nothing will be left for anyone. One popular example of this dilemma is known as the "tragedy of the commons" (Hardin, 1968). In earlier times, people would let their animals graze on the town's lush grassy commons. But

*Would you like to try participating in a prisoner's dilemma game online? Simply search online with the phrase "Play Prisoner's Dilemma" and you should find several websites that offer a chance to do this.*

**prisoner's dilemma** A type of dilemma in which one party must make either cooperative or competitive moves in relation to another party. The dilemma is typically designed so that the competitive move appears to be in one's self-interest, but if both sides make this move, they both suffer more than if they had both cooperated.

**resource dilemmas** Social dilemmas involving how two or more people will share a limited resource.

if all the animals grazed to their hearts' content (and to their owners' benefit), the commons would be stripped, the animals' food supply would be diminished, and the owners' welfare would be threatened. Today, the tragedy of the commons is a clear danger on a global scale. Deforestation, air pollution, carbon emission, ocean dumping, massive irrigation, overfishing, commercial development of wilderness areas, a rapidly increasing population in some developing countries, and overconsumption of global resources by the richest nations all pit individual self-interest against the common good.

In *public goods dilemmas*, all of the individuals are supposed to *contribute* resources to a common pool. Examples of these public goods include the blood supply, public broadcasting, schools, libraries, roads, and parks. If no one gives, the service can't continue, and all will suffer. Again, self-interest conflicts with the public good.

### Responding to Social Dilemmas: Groups and Individuals

Social dilemmas pose serious threats to people's quality of life and even to life itself. How do people try to solve them? What factors make them more or less cooperative when faced with these dilemmas?

> "If a free society cannot help the many who are poor, it cannot save the few who are rich."
>
> —John F. Kennedy

Pollution from an oil refinery in Edmonton, Canada, glows in the dusk. A clean environment is a public resource that is vital for all of us, but protecting it often runs into conflict with the economic self-interest of individuals or groups.

© Dan Riedlhuber/Reuters/Corbis

Fear and greed are two critically important factors in determining reactions to these dilemmas—the fear of being exploited by others and the greedy desire to maximize one's own outcomes. Trust, therefore, is essential in promoting cooperation because it reduces the fear of being exploited. Similarly, a sense of belongingness and identity with the greater group also promotes cooperation, in part because this perspective can reduce fear and greed (Klapwijk & Van Lange, 2009; McLeish & Oxoby, 2011; Swann et al., 2012). In an interesting twist on this idea, Carsten de Dreu (2012) recently found that individuals who tend to feel that they can't depend on others were significantly more likely to cooperate on a social dilemma if they received a dose of oxytocin—a neurochemical that can increase people's feeling of bonding with another person and reduces their concerns of betrayal. Another important factor is threat of punishment (Mulder, 2008). Groups that punish members who exploit the rest of the group are more likely to thrive. Indeed, evolutionary psychologists point to how punishing those who do not cooperate with the group is an evolved psychological mechanism because cooperation was crucial for survival (O'Gorman et al., 2008).

These are just a few of the variables that help determine competition or cooperation in social dilemmas. Table 8.4 summarizes some of the factors that extensive research has identified as facilitating the best solutions to social dilemmas.

Groups tend to be more competitive than individuals in mixed-motive situations (Pinter & Wildschut, 2012; Wildschut et al., 2003). One reason for this is that it can be harder to establish trust between groups than between individuals (Naquin & Kurtzberg, 2009). Another reason is that members of a group feel that they are less identifiable by members of other groups. The greater anonymity that a group offers frees individual group members to act in a self-interested or aggressive manner. This is one reason why large groups are more likely to exploit scarce resources than small ones are (Pruitt, 1998; Seijts & Latham, 2000; Wildschut et al., 2003).

The fact remains that social dilemmas often do involve very large groups—a city, a state, a nation, the whole world. In these circumstances, the structural arrangements listed in Table 8.4 may be most appropriate.

Large groups are more likely than small groups to exploit a scarce resource that the members collectively depend on. **T**RUE.

**Individual and Gender Differences** Although all of us struggle with social dilemmas, people differ in their own tendencies toward cooperation and competition. One relevant dimension on which people differ is in their *social value orientation*. Individuals with a *prosocial, cooperative* orientation seek to maximize joint gains or achieve equal outcomes. Those with an *individualist* orientation seek to maximize their own gain. And people with a *competitive* orientation seek to maximize their own gain relative to that of others. Individuals with a cooperative orientation are less likely to behave in a competitive, resource-consuming fashion than are people with individualist or competitive orientations (Balliet et al., 2009; Emonds et al., 2011; van Dijk et al., 2009).

It is commonly believed that women are more cooperative and less individualistic than men, and so it would be a reasonable assumption that women behave more cooperatively than men in social dilemmas. It turns out this assumption is not supported by the data. A recent meta-analysis of 50 years of research on this topic found no overall sex difference on cooperation in social dilemmas (Bailliet et al., 2011). The meta-analysis did reveal that women tend to cooperate more than men in mixed-sex situations, but women cooperate less with other women than men cooperate with other men. One interesting sex difference reported by Mark Van Vugt and Wendy Iredale (2012) is that men contributed more in a public goods dilemma if women are present, but there was no parallel effect for women. The researchers explain these results based on evolutionary principles, suggesting that the men behaved generously in front of women to impress them, just as a peacock's display of his colorful tail for a peahen signals his health and genetic fitness.

## Culture and Social Dilemmas

Just as with gender differences, the relationship between cultural differences and responses to social dilemmas is less clear and straightforward than one might expect (Ishii & Kurzban, 2008; Kopelman, 2009; Takemura & Yuki, 2007; Yamagishi et al., 2005). The more complex reality is that collectivists may tend to cooperate more when dealing with friends or ingroup members but compete more aggressively when dealing with strangers or outgroup members; this difference tends not to be as strong among individualists (De Dreu et al., 2007; Oyserman et al., 2002). This point was supported in an interesting experiment by Rosana Yin-mei Wong and Ying-yi Hong (2005). Participants in this experiment were Hong Kong Chinese college students who could be considered bicultural; that is, they were exposed extensively throughout their lives to both Chinese and American cultures. These students played a prisoner's dilemma game with either a

---

**TABLE 8.4**
**Solving Social Dilemmas**

Behavior in a social dilemma is influenced by both psychological factors and structural arrangements. The characteristics listed here contribute to the successful solution of social dilemmas.

**Psychological Factors**

**Individual and Cultural Differences**

- Having a prosocial, cooperative orientation
- Trusting others
- Being a member of a collectivistic culture

**Situational Factors**

- Being in a good mood
- Having had successful experience managing resources and working cooperatively
- Being exposed to unselfish models
- Having reason to expect others to cooperate

**Group Dynamics**

- Acting as an individual rather than in a group
- Being in a small group rather than in a large group
- Sharing a social identity or superordinate goals

**Structural Arrangements**

- Creating a payoff structure that rewards cooperative behavior and/or punishes selfish behavior
- Removing resources from the public domain and handing them over to private ownership
- Establishing an authority to control the resources

© Cengage Learning

---

When faced with the dilemma of whether to act in one's self-interest or cooperate with the greater good, women are more likely than men to cooperate. **FALSE.**

"I'm running late—some people were waiting for my table so I had to take my sweet time."

People with a competitive social value orientation may go out of their way to prevent others from using a resource, even if in doing so, they hurt themselves in the long run as well.

friend or stranger. If the students were first primed with symbols associated with Chinese culture, they behaved much more cooperatively with a friend than with a stranger. If they were primed with American symbols, in contrast, they did not differentiate between friends and strangers (see ● Figure 8.9).

## Conflict Escalation and Reduction

Conflicts between groups are caused by many factors, including competition for scarce resources, stereotypes and prejudice, and competing ideologies. But once a conflict is in place, it can feed on itself. Indeed, *conflict spirals* are frequent, as one party annoys the other party, who retaliates, prompting a more extreme reaction from the first party, and so on (Brett et al., 1998; Rubin et al., 1994). Table 8.5 lists several factors that contribute to conflict escalation.

The final factor listed in Table 8.5—negative perceptions of "the other"—obviously is related to the issues of stereotypes and prejudice, including the favoring of ingroups over outgroups, that are discussed in Chapter 5. During conflict, the opposing group and its members are often perceived as "the other"—strange, foreign, alien. They are characterized in simplistic, exaggerated ways. Held at a psychological distance, the other becomes a screen on which it is possible to project one's worst fears. Indeed, groups often see each other as *mirror images*: They see in their enemies what their enemies see in them. As Urie Bronfenbrenner (1961) discovered when he visited the former Soviet Union during the Cold War, the Soviets saw Americans as aggressive, exploitative, and untrustworthy, just as the Americans saw them. The same is true of Israelis and Palestinians today.

Taken to extremes, negative views of the other can result in *dehumanization*, the perception that people lack human qualities or are "subhuman," and this can play a powerful role in escalating conflict and promoting prejudice or violence (Demoulin et al., 2009; Esses et al., 2008; Maoz & McCauley, 2008). As the Nazis began the Holocaust, they released propaganda that characterized Jews as less than human—as rats that spread disease and needed to be exterminated. During World War II, the United States portrayed the Japanese people as cold, identical robots. At the same time, the Japanese media portrayed Americans as bloodthirsty animals, as in cartoons depicting eagles flying off with bloodied Japanese citizens in their talons.

Dehumanization is the ultimate version of "us" versus "them," removing all religious and ethical constraints against the taking of human life. As George Orwell (1942) discovered during the Spanish Civil War, the cure for dehumanization is to restore the human connection. Sighting

● **FIGURE 8.9**

**Culture and the Prisoner's Dilemma**

Students from Hong Kong who were very familiar with both Chinese and American cultures played the prisoner's dilemma game with a friend or a stranger. Before playing, some participants were exposed to Chinese images and some were exposed to American images. When playing with a friend, students primed with Chinese images cooperated more than did students primed with American pictures. When playing with a stranger, there was no significant difference in cooperativeness as a function of which culture was primed.

Adapted from Wong & Hong, 2005. © Cengage Learning

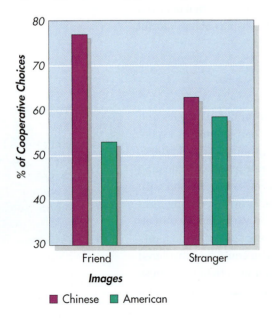

an enemy soldier holding up his trousers with both hands while running beside a nearby trench, Orwell was unable to take the easy shot: "I had come here to shoot at 'Fascists'; but a man who is holding up his trousers isn't a 'Fascist,' he is visibly a fellow creature, similar to yourself, and you don't feel like shooting at him" (p. 254).

A peacemaking strategy developed by Charles Osgood (1962) offers some hope for breaking a conflict between groups. In this strategy, called **graduated and reciprocated initiatives in tension-reduction (GRIT)**, one group takes the first move toward cooperation by making an initial concession. It then waits for the response from the other side and reciprocates that move: It responds to aggressiveness with aggressiveness and to cooperativeness with even more cooperativeness. There is not a great deal of research on GRIT, but what there is has been encouraging; even people with a competitive orientation tend to respond cooperatively to this strategy, and the positive effects of GRIT can be enduring (Lindskold & Han, 1988; Yamagishi et al., 2005).

> ## Negotiation

Unilateral concessions are useful for beginning the peace process, but extended negotiations are usually required to reach a final agreement. Negotiations on complex issues such as nuclear arms control, international environmental protection, and efforts to make peace in volatile regions such as the Middle East often go on for years or even decades. Negotiations are not restricted to the international scene. Unions and management engage in collective bargaining to establish employee contracts. Divorcing couples negotiate the terms of their divorce, by themselves or through their lawyers. Dating couples negotiate about which movie to attend. Families negotiate about who does which annoying household chores.

Successful negotiation can reduce these many conflicts, but it is important to ask this question: What constitutes a successful negotiation? You might think a 50–50 compromise is an ideal outcome for two negotiating parties. Here, the negotiators start at extreme positions and gradually work toward a mutually acceptable midpoint. In many situations, however, *both* sides can do better than this. The reason for this is that most negotiations are not simply fixed-sum situations in which each side can gain something only if the other side loses it (Bazerman & Neale, 1992). Instead, both sides often have the opportunity to reach an **integrative agreement**, in which both parties obtain outcomes that are superior to a 50–50 split.

A good way to understand this is to consider the tale of the two sisters and the orange (Follett, 1942). One sister wanted the juice to drink; the other wanted the peel for a cake. So they sliced the orange in half and each one took her portion. These sisters suffered from an advanced case of what is known as the *fixed-pie syndrome*, the belief that whatever one of them won, the other one lost. In fact, however, each of them could have had the whole thing: all of the juice for one, all of the peel for the other. An integrative

**TABLE 8.5**

**Factors That Promote and Sustain the Escalation of Between-Group Conflict**

- The group polarization process, which increases the extremity of group members' attitudes and opinions
- Pressures to conform, such as group cohesiveness and groupthink, that make it difficult for individuals to oppose the group's increasingly aggressive position
- Escalation of commitment, which seeks to justify past investments through the commitment of additional resources
- Premature use of threat capacity, which triggers aggressive retaliation
- Negative perceptions of "the other," which promote acceptance of aggressive behavior and enhance cohesiveness of the ingroup "us" against the outgroup "them"

© Cengage Learning

Group conflict is tragically hard to stop, as in the ongoing struggles between groups in the Middle East. In this photo, Palestinians hurl stones at Egyptian forces at the Egyptian border with the Gaza Strip during a clash in which a civilian was killed.

**graduated and reciprocated initiatives in tension-reduction (GRIT)** A strategy for unilateral persistent efforts to establish trust and cooperation between opposing parties.

**integrative agreement** A negotiated resolution to a conflict in which all parties obtain outcomes that are superior to what they would have obtained from an equal division of the contested resources.

agreement was well within their grasp, but they failed to see it. Unfortunately, research indicates that this happens all too often. Leigh Thompson and Dennis Hrebec (1996) conducted a meta-analysis of 32 experiments and found that in more than 20% of negotiations that could have resulted in integrative agreements, the participants agreed to settlements that were worse for both sides. Training in conflict-resolution techniques, using computerized negotiation support systems, and getting the parties to think about higher-order motives than just their preferred outcomes are among the ways that negotiations are more likely to end in better agreements (Davis & Hall, 2003; Kersten & Lai, 2007; Henderson, 2011; Taylor et al., 2008).

It is always difficult for participants in a dispute to listen carefully to each other and reach some reasonable understanding of each other's perspective. But communication in which both sides disclose their goals and needs is critically important in allowing each side to see opportunities for joint benefits (De Dreu et al., 2006). This may seem obvious and yet people in negotiations, just like the two sisters with the orange, very often fail to communicate their goals and needs. They may hold back information because of lack of trust in the other side, or because they think their goals are more clear to the other party than they actually are. If communication is improved, however, the outcomes can improve dramatically.

*Negotiating with car dealers is a form of negotiation that many of us engage in from time to time. Want some tips? Try the Tips & Advice section on the Edmunds website at www.edmunds.com.*

## Culture and Negotiation

As the world becomes smaller because of advances in technology, the globalization of business and the economy, and global threats concerning the environment and terrorism, the ability to negotiate effectively across cultures becomes increasingly important. Understanding cultural differences relevant to negotiation is therefore vital. Table 8.6 lists some common assumptions made by negotiators from Western, individualistic cultures that are not always shared by representatives from other cultures.

Consider, for example, our statement that good communication is a key ingredient in successful negotiation. Communication across cultures can present special challenges (Liu & Wilson, 2011; Liu et al., 2010; Thompson et al., 2010). Whereas an individualistic perspective emphasizes direct communication and confrontation, a collectivistic perspective emphasizes more indirect communication and a desire to avoid direct conflict. Individualistic negotiators may emphasize rationality, whereas a greater tolerance of contradiction and emotionality is characteristic of a collectivistic style—although collectivists prefer emotionality that is not confrontational. Negotiators from individualistic cultures are more likely to respond with a direct "no" to a proposal; negotiators from collectivistic cultures are more likely to refer to social roles and relationships.

According to Yunxia Zhu and others (2007a), for example, relationship building is an important part of the negotiation process among Chinese. Negotiators from individualistic cultures may need to be uncharacteristically patient with processes that may seem irrelevant to the task at hand because they are important in creating *guanxi*, a Chinese term for relationship. The initial sessions in negotiations with Chinese take on particular importance because they can set the tone for establishing *guanxi*.

Another difference concerns the timing of concessions. Individualists tend to prefer to make compromises and concessions toward the end of a negotiation, whereas collectivists may prefer to begin with generous concessions and gradually reduce their concessions later. Yet another factor

Representatives of nations from around the world meet in Geneva to try to negotiate agreements about nuclear policies. Negotiations across cultures and between groups with a history of conflict pose special challenges. They highlight the usefulness of social psychological research that has specified factors that make negotiations more or less likely to succeed.

AP Photo/Anja Niedringhaus, Pool

**TABLE 8.6**

**Cultural Assumptions About Negotiating**

People from different cultures make different assumptions about the negotiation process. This table summarizes some assumptions commonly made by U.S. and other Western negotiators. It also presents some alternative assumptions that negotiators from other cultures might hold. As you can see, such different assumptions could make it very difficult to reach a successful agreement.

| Assumptions of Negotiators from the United States and Other Western Countries | Assumptions of Negotiators from Non-Western Cultures |
| --- | --- |
| Negotiation is a business, not a social activity. | The first step in negotiating is to develop a trusting relationship between the individual negotiators. |
| Points should be made with rational, analytical arguments without contradiction. | Arguments may be more holistic, and emotionality and contradiction may be tolerated. |
| Communication is direct and verbal. | Some of the most important communication is nonverbal or indirect. |
| Written contracts are binding; oral commitments are not. | Written contracts are less meaningful than oral communications because the nonverbal context clarifies people's intentions. |
| Current information and ideas are more valid than historical or traditional opinions and information. | History and tradition are more valid than current information and ideas. Information must be understood in its greater context. |
| Time is very important; punctuality is expected; deadlines should be set and adhered to. | Building a relationship takes time and is more important than punctuality; setting deadlines is an effort to humiliate the other party. |

Based on Brett & Gelfand, 2006, De Dreu et al., 2007, Gelfand et al., 2007, Giebels & Taylor, 2009, and Kimmel, 1994, 2000.
© Cengage Learning

concerns "saving face"—feeling that others continue to respect you and that you have maintained honor. Although saving face in a negotiation is important across cultures, it may be of more central importance in collectivistic cultures (Oetzel et al., 2008; Rodriguez Mosquera et al., 2008; Tjosvold et al., 2004).

Emotional responses may hurt negotiations between members of different cultures if they are deemed inappropriate in one of the cultures. Expressions of pride are more likely to be received positively in individualistic cultures, whereas expressions of shame are more likely to be received positively in collectivistic cultures (Rodriguez Mosquera et al., 2004). Shirli Kopelman and Ashleigh Shelby Rosette (2008) conducted an experiment that illustrates cultural differences in sensitivity to particular emotions. Business students from Hong Kong and Israel participated in a negotiation exercise in which an American female business manager offered them a take-it-or-leave-it proposal by video. For half the students, the manager made the offer displaying positive emotion—she spoke in a friendly tone, smiled and nodded often, and appeared cordial. For the other half, the manager displayed negative emotion—she spoke in a more angry tone and appeared intimidating and irritated.

As the researchers had predicted, the students from Hong Kong responded very differently as a function of the emotion displayed. As can be seen in ● Figure 8.10, they were much more likely to accept the offer if it was made with a display of positive than negative emotions. Students from Israel, where direct and confrontational negotiations are more commonplace (and perhaps where an American woman would be seen less as an

**● FIGURE 8.10**

**Emotions During Negotiation: Cross-Cultural Differences**

Business students from Hong Kong and Israel participated in a negotiation exercise in which they received a take-it-or-leave-it proposal from an American business manager. The manager displayed either warm, positive emotion or angry, negative emotion while making the offer. Students from Hong Kong were much less likely to accept the offer if it was made with negative emotion rather than with positive emotion. The Israeli students' decisions were not strongly affected by the emotions displayed.

Based on Kopelman & Rosette, 2008. © Cengage Learning

outgroup), were relatively unaffected by the emotional display of the negotiator when deciding whether or not to accept the offer.

If negotiators are not aware of these kinds of cross-cultural differences or if they cannot respond effectively to them, misunderstandings are likely to prevent them from achieving a successful outcome. Wendi Adair and Jeanne Brett (2005) describe negotiation as a kind of dance. The partners move with each other according to various rhythms, and the dance will work only if they can synchronize their movements and work together. Negotiations across cultures can be challenging because the participants have different ways of performing these dances. As Adair and Brett put it, "Just as it will take time for a Cuban, who is accustomed to the rapid, staircase movements of Latin social dancing, and an American—accustomed to smooth walking dances like the waltz—to get in sync, it will take time for cross-cultural negotiators to synchronize their movements" (p. 46). It is in the best interest of negotiators, therefore, to learn each other's perspectives so they can work together more effectively and fluently without stepping on each other's toes.

## ▶ Finding Common Ground

Every conflict is unique, as is every attempt at conflict resolution. Still, all efforts to find a constructive solution to conflict require some common ground to build upon. Recognition of a *superordinate identity* is one way to establish common ground between groups in conflict. When group members perceive that they have a shared identity—a sense of belonging to something that is larger than and encompasses their own groups—the attractiveness of outgroup members increases, and interactions between the groups often become more peaceful. Those who would make peace, rather than stoke conflict, realize that it is in their own self-interest to find common ground and to understand that the cloak of humanity is large enough to cover a multitude of lesser differences.

# Review

## Fundamentals of Groups

### What Is a Group? Why Join a Group?

- Groups involve direct interactions among group members over a period of time and a shared common fate, identity, or set of goals.
- Groups vary in the extent to which they are seen as distinct entities.
- People join a group for a variety of reasons, including to perform tasks that can't be accomplished alone and to enhance self-esteem and social identity.
- Evolutionary scholars propose that attraction to groups is an evolved psychological mechanism.

### Key Features of Groups: Roles, Norms, and Cohesiveness

- Newcomers to groups typically go through a socialization process that may operate explicitly or implicitly.

- Establishing clear roles can help a group; but when members' roles are assigned poorly, are ambiguous, come in conflict with other roles, or undergo change, stress and poor performance can result.
- Groups often develop norms that group members are expected to conform to. Group members who go against the norm may be disliked, threatened, or rejected.
- Groups vary in how accepting they are of violations of their norms.
- One study found that participants were less harsh in their judgments of a student from their university who deviated from the university norm if they were led to perceive their university as consisting of people with very different backgrounds and attitudes rather than as fairly homogenous.
- Cohesiveness is related to group performance, but the causal direction of this relationship is not clear, and the relationship

depends on other factors such as the size of the group, the kind of task the group is performing, and even the gender of the group members.

### Culture and Cohesiveness
- What behaviors affect group cohesiveness can vary significantly across cultures.

- One study found that Chinese groups of friends or strangers and groups of American strangers felt troubled by heated debate on a group task, but groups of American friends seemed to react positively to the debate.

# Individuals in Groups: The Presence of Others

### Social Facilitation: When Others Arouse Us
- In an early experiment Triplett found that children were more likely to perform a simple motor task faster when they worked side by side rather than alone. Later research found the evidence for this type of effect was mixed.
- Robert Zajonc proposed an explanation to make sense of these results. According to his analysis, the presence of others creates arousal, and arousal increases tendencies to perform the dominant response.
- Social facilitation refers to two effects that occur when individual contributions are identifiable: The presence of others enhances performance on easy tasks but impairs performance on difficult tasks.
- Social facilitation effects have been found in a variety of domains. Even the "presence" of fictional TV characters or computerized images of people can trigger these effects.
- The theories of mere presence, evaluation apprehension, and distraction conflict give different explanations of the cause of social facilitation effects; all three explanations probably account for some of the social facilitation effects.

### Social Loafing: When Others Relax Us
- In early research on easy tasks involving pooled contributions, Ringelmann found that individual output declined when people worked with others. This social loafing effect has been replicated in numerous studies over the years.
- But social loafing is reduced or eliminated when people think that their individual efforts will be important, relevant, and meaningful. In such cases, individuals may engage in social compensation in an effort to offset the anticipated social loafing of others.

### Culture and Social Loafing
- Groups in collectivistic cultures may be more likely to have group norms that promote productive teamwork and discourage social loafing.

- People from collectivistic cultures may be likely to socially loaf if they are working in a group that has established a norm of low productivity and effort.

### Deindividuation
- Deindividuation diminishes a person's sense of individuality and reduces constraints against deviant behavior.
- Two types of environmental cues can increase deviant behavior: (1) Accountability cues, such as anonymity, signal to individuals that they will not be held responsible for their actions; and (2) attentional cues, such as intense environmental stimulation, produce a deindividuated state in which the individual acts impulsively.
- Large crowds can both increase anonymity and decrease self-awareness; together these two effects can increase violent or other deviant behavior.
- A field experiment of Halloween trick-or-treaters showed that when factors associated with deindividuation were highest—when children were anonymous and in a group—they were most likely to take more candy than permitted.
- The effects of deindividuation depend on the characteristics of the immediate group. In the context of an antagonistic social identity, antisocial behavior increases; in the context of a benevolent social identity, prosocial behavior increases.

**Putting *Common Sense* to the Test**

**People will cheer louder when they cheer as part of a group than when they cheer alone.**

**False.** *People tend to put less effort into collective tasks, such as group cheering, than into tasks where their individual performance can be identified and evaluated.*

# Group Performance: Problems and Solutions

### Losses and Gains in Groups
- Because of process loss, a group may perform worse than it would if every individual performed up to his or her potential.
- Group performance is influenced by the type of task (additive, conjunctive, or disjunctive).
- Among the factors that create process loss are social loafing, poor coordination, and failure to recognize the expertise of particular group members.
- Groups can experience process gain, in which they do better than even the best members of the group, on tasks that can be

divided among subgroups and when the correct approach is clearly demonstrable to the rest of the group members.

### Brainstorming
- Contrary to illusions about the effectiveness of interactive brainstorming, brainstorming interactive groups produce fewer creative ideas than the same number of people working alone.
- Computer-based technology can improve group brainstorming, as can some specific techniques or interventions.

## Group Polarization

- When individuals who have similar though not identical opinions participate in a group discussion, their opinions become more extreme.
- Explanations for group polarization emphasize the number and persuasiveness of arguments heard and social comparison with other group members.

## Groupthink

- Groupthink refers to an excessive tendency to seek concurrence among group members.
- The theory of groupthink proposes that groupthink is more likely to occur when groups are highly cohesive, have particular types of group structure, and are engaged in highly stressful situations.
- The symptoms of groupthink produce defective decision making, which can lead to a bad decision.
- Strategies that have been successful in helping groups avoid groupthink include consulting with outsiders, having the leader play a less controlling role, encouraging criticism and a thorough search for information, and having a group member play devil's advocate to challenge the consensus.
- Research to test the theory of groupthink has not produced as much evidence to support the theory as its fame might suggest, although the ideas behind the theory and how to avoid groupthink can prove valuable to groups.

## Escalation Effects

- Groups are susceptible to an escalation effect, which occurs when commitment to a failing course of action is increased to justify investments that have already been made. Instead of cutting its losses, groups essentially throw good money and time after bad.

## Communicating Information and Utilizing Expertise

- Biased sampling refers to the tendency for groups to pay more attention to information that is already known by all or most group members than to important information that is known by only one or a few group members.
- Information may not be communicated adequately in a group because of problems in the group's communication network, such as suppression of relevant information at some point in the decision-making chain.
- Group members encouraged to come to a shared understanding that their decision-making task should involve thorough and critical discussion tend to do a better job of information sharing and making good decisions.
- Groups can remember more information than individuals through transactive memory, a shared process by which the information can be divided among the group members.
- Groups with effective transactive memory systems develop a division of knowledge, know which group members know what information, trust each other's specialized knowledge, and coordinate their efforts well.

## Goals and Plans in Groups

- Setting specific and ambitious goals can improve group performance more than vague "do your best" goals.
- Having a specific plan and working with a partner can help people meet their goals.
- An experiment demonstrated that having experts in a group was not good enough to improve group performance unless their presence was coupled with an intervention that required the group to engage in collaborative planning.

## Training

- Training groups in better group dynamics, such as how set goals and allocate roles, can be effective.

## Computer Technology and Group Support Systems

- Computer technology can be used to guide group discussions and decision-making processes, which can help group avoid problems such as groupthink.

## Virtual Teams

- There is a growing trend in the business world toward teams that are dispersed geographically and that work interactively via technology, but such teams may be especially vulnerable to some of the factors that cause process loss. Therefore, special attention needs to be paid to virtual teams to offset these problems.

## Culture and Diversity

- Research on the effects of diversity on group performance is rather mixed; both positive and negative effects have been found thus far.
- Multicultural groups perform better if their members or leaders have relatively high awareness of their own and others' cultural assumptions.

---

### Putting *Common Sense* to the Test

**People brainstorming as a group come up with a greater number of better ideas than the same number of people working individually.**

**False.** *Groups in which members interact face to face produce fewer creative ideas when brainstorming than the same number of people brainstorming alone.*

**Group members' attitudes about a course of action usually become more moderate after group discussion.**

**False.** *Group discussion often causes attitudes to become more extreme as the initial tendencies of the group are exaggerated.*

**People and groups tend to do worse when they have "do your best" goals than when they have very specific, ambitious goals.**

**True.** *People and groups that have vague "do your best goals" don't tend to do their best. They can do better if they set specific, ambitious but reachable goals.*

---

# Conflict: Cooperation and Competition Within and Between Groups

## Mixed Motives and Social Dilemmas

- In mixed-motive situations, such as the prisoner's dilemma, there are incentives to compete as well as incentives to cooperate.
- In a social dilemma, personal benefit conflicts with the overall good.

- Resource dilemmas involve sharing limited resources. In the commons dilemma a group of people can take resources from a common pool, whereas in the public goods dilemma a group of people must make contributions to a shared resource.

- Behavior in a social dilemma is influenced by a number of psychological factors, including situational factors, group dynamics, and structural arrangements.
- Trust is important in promoting cooperation because it reduces the fear of being exploited.
- Groups tend to be more competitive than individuals in mixed-motive situations.
- Individuals with a prosocial, cooperative orientation are less likely to behave in a competitive, resource-consuming fashion than people with individualistic or competitive orientations are.
- A recent meta-analysis reports that there is no overall sex difference in cooperativeness or competitiveness on social dilemmas. Women tend to be more cooperative in these dilemmas with men than with other women. Men may sometimes act more generously in a public goods dilemma in the presence of women, perhaps in an attempt to impress them.

## Culture and Social Dilemmas

- The evidence concerning the relationship between cultural differences and responses to social dilemmas is somewhat mixed.
- Compared to individuals, collectivists may cooperate more when dealing with friends or ingroup members but compete more aggressively with strangers or outgroup members.
- In one experiment Chinese participants who were familiar with both American and Chinese cultures played a prisoner's dilemma with a friend or a stranger. If the participants were first primed with symbols associated with Chinese culture, they behaved much more cooperatively with a friend than with a stranger. If they were primed with American symbols, their behavior did not vary between friends and strangers.

## Conflict Escalation and Reduction

- Conflicts can escalate for many reasons, including conflict spirals and escalation of commitment.
- Perceptions of the other that contribute to conflict escalation include unfavorable mirror images and dehumanization.

- GRIT—an explicit strategy for the unilateral persistent pursuit of trust and cooperation between opposing parties—is a useful strategy for beginning the peace process.

## Negotiation

- Many negotiations have the potential to result in integrative agreements in which outcomes exceed a 50–50 split, but negotiators often fail to achieve such outcomes.
- Communication and an understanding of the other party's perspective are key ingredients of successful negotiation.

## Culture and Negotiation

- People from different cultures may have very different assumptions and styles concerning negotiations, such as whether direct or indirect communication is preferred, how important context and relationship-building is, and whether direct conflict should be avoided.
- One experiment found that business students from Hong Kong were much more affected by the emotion an American negotiator displayed than students from Israel were when deciding whether or not to accept the American's proposal.

## Finding Common Ground

- Recognition of a shared identity increases the likelihood of a peaceful resolution of differences.

---

### Putting *Common Sense* to the Test

**Large groups are more likely than small groups to exploit a scarce resource that the members collectively depend on.**

**True.** *Large groups are more likely to behave selfishly when faced with resource dilemmas, in part because people in large groups feel less identifiable and more anonymous.*

**When faced with the dilemma of whether to act in one's self-interest or cooperate with the greater good, women are more likely than men to cooperate.**

**False.** *Research suggests that there is no overall sex difference in cooperativeness or competitiveness on social dilemmas.*

---

## KEY TERMS

biased sampling (319)

brainstorming (312)

collective effort model (306)

deindividuation (308)

distraction-conflict theory (305)

escalation effect (318)

evaluation apprehension theory (305)

graduated and reciprocated initiatives in tension-reduction (GRIT) (331)

group (297)

group cohesiveness (301)

group polarization (314)

group support systems (323)

groupthink (316)

integrative agreement (331)

mere presence theory (305)

prisoner's dilemma (327)

process gain (312)

process loss (311)

resource dilemmas (327)

social dilemma (326)

social facilitation (303)

social identity model of deindividuation effects (SIDE) (310)

social loafing (306)

transactive memory (322)

---

## MEDIA RESOURCES

Go to CengageBrain.com to access Psychology CourseMate, where you will find an interactive eBook, glossaries, flashcards, quizzes, videos, and more.

# Attraction and Close Relationships

This chapter examines how people form relationships with each other. First, we describe the fundamental human need for being with others, why people affiliate, and the problem of loneliness. Then we consider various personal and situational factors that influence our initial attraction to specific others. Third, we examine different types of close relationships—what makes them rewarding, how they differ, the types of love they arouse, and the factors that keep them together or break them apart.

# 9

© Martin Meyer/Corbis

**No topic fascinates the people** of this planet more than interpersonal attraction. Needing to belong, we humans are obsessed about friendships, romantic relationships, dating, love, sex, reproduction, sexual orientation, marriage, and divorce. Playwrights, poets, and musicians write with eloquence and emotion about loves desired, won, and lost. In recent years, television has been filled with relationship-centered reality TV shows such as *The Bachelor, The Bachelorette, The Pickup Artist, Wife Swap, Bachelor Pad, Blind Date, elimiDATE, Here Come the Newlyweds, The Choice, Love In the Wild,* and *Cheaters.* More and more, people are meeting romantic partners online, not just in bars—on Facebook, in chat rooms, on Craigslist, and at dating service websites such as Match.com, eHarmony, and Compatible Partners. Both in our hearts and in our minds, the relationships we seek and enjoy with other people are more important than anything else.

At one time or another, each of us has been startled by our reaction to someone we have met. In general, why are human beings drawn to each other? Why are we so attracted to some people and yet indifferent to or repelled by others? What determines how our intimate relationships evolve over time? What does it mean to love someone, and what problems are likely to arise along the way? As these questions reveal, the processes of attraction among people—from the first spark through the flames of an intimate connection and the possibility of a cooling off—seem like a wild card in the deck of human behavior. This chapter unravels some of the mysteries.

# Need to Belong: A Fundamental Human Motive

Although born helpless, human infants are equipped with reflexes that orient them toward people. They are uniquely responsive to human faces, they turn their head toward voices, and they are able to mimic certain facial gestures on cue. Then, a few weeks later comes a baby's first smile, surely the warmest sign of all. Much to the delight of parents all over the world, the newborn seems an inherently social animal. But wait. If you reflect on the amount of time that you spend talking to, being with, flirting with, confiding in, pining for, or worrying about other people, you'll realize that we are all social animals. It seems that people need people.

According to Roy Baumeister and Mark Leary (1995), the need to belong is a basic human motive, "a pervasive drive to form and maintain at least a minimum quantity of lasting, positive, and significant interpersonal relationships" (p. 497). This general proposition is supported by everyday observation and a great deal of research. All over the world, people feel joy when they form new social

## Putting *Common Sense* to the Test

*Circle Your Answer*

T F People seek out the company of others, even strangers, in times of stress.

T F Infants do not discriminate between faces considered attractive and unattractive in their culture.

T F People who are physically attractive are happier and have higher self-esteem than those who are unattractive.

T F When it comes to romantic relationships, opposites attract.

T F Men are more likely than women to interpret friendly gestures by the opposite sex in sexual terms.

T F After the honeymoon period, there is an overall decline in levels of marital satisfaction.

attachments and react with anxiety and grief when these bonds are broken—as when separated from a loved one by distance, divorce, or death. The need to belong runs deep, which is why people get very distressed when they are neglected by others, rejected, excluded, stigmatized, or ostracized, all forms of "social death" (Leary, 2001; Smart Richman & Leary, 2009; Williams & Nida, 2011).

We care deeply about what others think of us, which is why we spend so much time and money to make ourselves presentable and attractive. In fact, some people are so worried about how they appear to others that they suffer from various symptoms of *social anxiety disorder* characterized by intense feelings of discomfort in situations that invite public scrutiny (Leary & Kowalski, 1995). One very familiar example is public-speaking anxiety, or "stage fright"—a performer's worst nightmare. If you've ever had to make a presentation only to feel weak in the knees and hear your voice quiver, you have experienced a hint of this disorder. When sufferers are asked what there is to fear, the most common responses are shaking and showing other signs of anxiety, going blank, saying something foolish, and being unable to continue (Stein et al., 1996). For people with high levels of social anxiety, the problem is also evoked by other social situations, such as eating at a public lunch counter, signing a check in front of a store clerk, and, for males, urinating in a crowded men's room. In extreme cases, the reaction can become so debilitating that the person just stays at home (Beidel & Turner, 1998; Crozier & Alden, 2005).

Our need to belong is a fundamental human motive. People who have a network of close social ties—in the form of lovers, friends, family members, and co-workers—have higher self-esteem and greater satisfaction with life compared to those who live more isolated lives (Denissen et al., 2008; Leary & Baumeister, 2000). People who are socially connected are also physically healthier and less likely to die a premature death (Cacioppo & Patrick, 2008; House et al., 1988; Uchino, 2006). Recent research shows that people can even draw the motivation to achieve success from their connections with others (Walton et al., 2012).

With regard to social networks, does it help to have a presence on Facebook and other online social media sites—which enable people to stay in touch, even if not in person? This medium is new but already it is sweeping through Western culture. In the United States, it is estimated that 90% of high school and college students have posted a profile on a social media site complete with a list of network "friends." ● Figure 9.1 shows that in 2006, the average network size among college students was 137; in 2007, it climbed to 185; in 2008, it climbed

ImagesBazaar/Getty Images

All over the world, for both men and women, the need to belong is a powerful human motive.

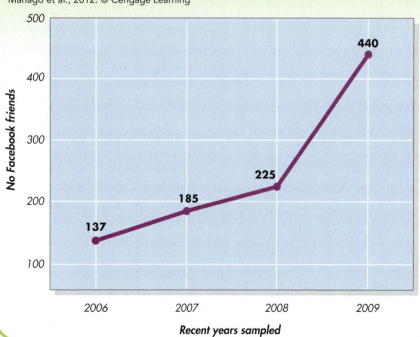

● **FIGURE 9.1**

**Social Media Networks: How Many Friends Do You Have?**

In the United States, the trend is clear: Since 2006, college students have exhibited a sharp increase in the number of network "friends" they have. Most of this growth comes from an increase in distant and superficial relationships.
Manago et al., 2012. © Cengage Learning

*No Facebook friends* (y-axis: 100, 200, 300, 400, 500)

- 2006: 137
- 2007: 185
- 2008: 225
- 2009: 440

*Recent years sampled* (x-axis)

"At this point, my privacy needs are interfering with my intimacy goals."

**People are motivated to establish and maintain an optimum level of social contact.**

again to 225. By 2009, the average number of network friends had soared to 440. It comes as no surprise that as Facebook friends lists have grown, most of the growth has come from an increase in distant and superficial relations. Importantly, it seems that the larger your online social network is, the more people there are to view your status updates and the more socially connected you are likely to feel (Manago et al., 2012).

## The Thrill of Affiliation

As social beings, humans are drawn to each other like magnets to metal. We work together, play together, live together, and often make lifetime commitments to grow old together. This social motivation begins with the **need for affiliation**, defined as a desire to establish social contact with others (McAdams, 1989). Individuals differ in the strength of their need for affiliation, but it seems that people are highly motivated to establish and maintain an *optimum* balance of social contact—sometimes craving the company of others, sometimes wanting to be alone—the way a body maintains a certain temperature level. In an interesting study, Bibb Latané and Carol Werner (1978) found that laboratory rats were more likely to approach others of their species after a period of isolation and were less likely to approach others after prolonged contact. These researchers suggested that rats, like many other animals, have a built-in "socio-stat" (social thermostat) to regulate their affiliative tendencies.

Is there evidence of a similar mechanism in humans? Shawn O'Connor and Lorne Rosenblood (1996) recruited college students to carry portable beepers for four days. Whenever the beepers went off (on average, every hour), the students wrote down whether at the time they were *actually* alone or in the company of other people and whether they *wanted* to be alone or with others. The results showed that students were in the state they desired two-thirds of the time. In fact, the situation they desired on one occasion (saying they wanted to be alone at 4 p.m.) predicted their actual situation the next time they were signaled (they would be alone at 5 p.m.). Whether it was solitude or social contact that the students sought, they successfully managed to regulate their own personal needs for affiliation.

People may well differ in the strength of their affiliative needs, but there are times when we all want to be with other people. Recall the scenes in Chicago, St. Louis, Dallas, New York, Pittsburgh, Philadelphia, Boston, Los Angeles, Miami, and other recent championship sports cities whenever the home team won the final championship game. From one city to the next, jubilant fans stayed long after the game had ended, milling about and exchanging high-fives, slaps on the back, and hugs and kisses. In each of these cities, it's clear that people wanted to celebrate together rather than alone.

Affiliating can satisfy us for other reasons as well, as others provide energy, attention, stimulation, information, and emotional support (Hill, 1987). One condition that strongly arouses our need for affiliation is stress. Have you ever noticed the way neighbors who never stop to say hello come together in snowstorms, hurricanes, power failures, and other major crises? Many years ago, Stanley Schachter (1959) theorized that an external threat triggers fear and motivates us to affiliate, particularly with others who face a similar threat. In a laboratory experiment that demonstrated the point, Schachter found that people who were expecting to receive painful electric shocks chose to wait with other nervous participants rather than alone. So far, so good. But when Irving Sarnoff and Philip Zimbardo (1961) led college students to expect that they would be engaging in an embarrassing behavior—sucking on large bottle nipples and pacifiers—their desire to be with others fell off. It seemed puzzling. Why do people in fearful misery love company while those in embarrassed misery seek solitude?

**need for affiliation** The desire to establish and maintain many rewarding interpersonal relationships.

Yacov Rofé (1984) proposed a simple answer: utility. Rofé argued that stress sparks the desire to affiliate only when being with others is seen as useful in reducing the negative impact of the stressful situation. Schachter's participants had good reason to believe that affiliation would be useful. They would have the opportunity to compare their emotional reactions with those of others to determine whether they really needed to be fearful. For those in the Sarnoff and Zimbardo study, however, affiliation had little to offer. When we face embarrassment, being with others is more likely to increase the stress than reduce it.

Let's return to Schachter's initial study. What specific benefit do people get from being in the presence of others in times of stress? Research suggests that people facing an imminent threat seek each other out in order to gain *cognitive clarity* about the danger they are in. In one study, James Kulik and Heike Mahler (1989) found that hospital patients waiting for open-heart surgery preferred to have as roommates other patients who were post-operative rather than pre-operative, presumably because they were in a position to provide information about the experience. Patients in a second study who had been assigned post-operative rather than pre-operative roommates became less anxious about the experience and were later quicker to recover from the surgery (Kulik et al., 1996).

Even in a laboratory setting, Kulik and others (1994) found that study participants anticipating the painful task of soaking a hand in ice-cold water preferred to wait with someone who had already completed the task rather than with someone who had not. They also asked more questions of these experienced peers than participants who did not know that the water would be painful. Under stress, we adaptively become motivated to affiliate with others who can help us cope with an impending threat. Summarizing his own work, Schachter (1959) noted that misery loves miserable company. Based on their more recent studies, Gump and Kulik (1997) further amended this assertion: "Misery loves the company of those in the same miserable situation" (p. 317).

When Spain won the World Cup soccer championship by beating the Netherlands in the summer of 2010, people all over the country poured into the streets to celebrate with one another.

Rafa Rivas/AFP/Getty Images

People seek out the company of others, even strangers, in times of stress. **T**RUE.

## The Agony of Loneliness

People need other people—to celebrate with, share news with, commiserate with, talk to, and learn from. But some people are painfully shy, socially awkward, inhibited, and reluctant to approach others (Bruch et al., 1989; Lane, 2007). Shyness itself is a common characteristic. Roughly 49% of all Americans describe themselves as shy, as do 31% in Israel, 40% in Germany, 55% in Taiwan, and 57% in Japan (Henderson & Zimbardo, 1998). People who are shy find it difficult to approach strangers, make small talk, telephone someone for a date, participate in small groups, or mingle at parties. Often they reject others, perhaps because they fear being rejected themselves. For people whose shyness is extreme, the result is a pattern of risk avoidance that can set them up for unpleasant and unrewarding interactions (Crozier, 2001).

Shyness can arise from different sources. In some cases, it may stem from an inborn personality trait. Jerome Kagan (1994) and others have found that some infants are highly sensitive to stimulation, inhibited, and cautious shortly after birth. In other cases, shyness develops as a learned reaction to failed interactions. Thus, interpersonal problems of the past can ignite social anxieties about the future (Leary & Kowalski, 1995). Not all shy infants grow up to become inhibited adults. But longitudinal research indicates

*"Loneliness and the feeling of being unwanted is the most terrible poverty."*

—Mother Teresa

that there is some continuity, that this aspect of our personalities may be predictable from our temperament and behavior as young children. Toddlers observed to be inhibited, shy, and fearful at age 3, for example, are more likely than toddlers who were more outgoing to be socially isolated at age 21 (Caspi, 2000). The differences can be seen in the adult brain. Using fMRI, researchers have recently observed that people who are shy, compared to those who are bold, exhibit greater activity in the amygdala—a region of the brain responsible for fear processing—when exposed to pictures of strangers (Beaton et al., 2008; Schwartz et al., 2003).

Whatever the source, shyness is a real problem, and it has painful consequences. Studies show that shy people evaluate themselves negatively, expect to fail in their social encounters, and blame themselves when they do. As a result, many shy people go into self-imposed isolation, which makes them feel lonely (Cheek & Melchior, 1990; Jackson et al., 2002). In part, the problem stems from a paralyzing fear of rejection, which inhibits people from making friendly or romantic overtures to those they are interested in. If you ever wanted to approach someone you liked but stopped yourself, you know that this situation often triggers an approach–avoidance conflict, pulling you between the desire for contact and a fear of being rejected. What's worse, research shows that people who fear rejection think that their friendly or romantic interest is transparent to others, which leads them to back off (Vorauer et al., 2003).

**Loneliness** is a sad and heart-wrenching emotional state. To be lonely is to feel deprived of human social connections (Cacioppo & Patrick, 2008). Some researchers maintain that loneliness is triggered by a discrepancy between the level of social contact a person has and the level he or she wants (Peplau & Perlman, 1982). Others find, more simply, that the less social contact people have, the lonelier they feel (Archibald et al., 1995). Unfortunately, people in some parts of the world are lonelier today than ever before. In *Bowling Alone*, Harvard professor of public policy Robert Putnam (2001) argued that Americans are more disconnected from their families, neighbors, co-workers, and communities than in the past. Not too long ago, he wrote, thousands of people belonged to bowling leagues. Today they are more likely to bowl alone. Lamenting the adverse effects, Putnam (2006) preaches: "You gotta have friends."

Who is lonely, and when? Loneliness is most likely to strike us during times of transition or disruption—as in the first year at college, after a romantic breakup, or when a loved one moves far away. Surveys show that people who are unattached are lonelier than those who have romantic partners, but that those who are widowed, divorced, and separated are lonelier than people who have never been married. Despite the stereotypic image of the lonely old man passing time on a park bench, the loneliest groups in American society are adolescents and young adults 18 to 30 years old. In fact, loneliness seems to decline over the course of adulthood—at least until health problems in old age limit social activities (Peplau & Perlman, 1982).

How do people cope with this distressing state? When college students were asked what behavioral strategies they use to combat loneliness, 96% said they often or sometimes try harder to be friendly to other people, 94% take their mind off the problem by reading or watching TV, and 93% try extra hard to succeed at another aspect of life. Others said that they distract themselves by running, shopping, washing the car, or staying busy at other activities. Still others seek new ways to meet people, try to improve their appearance, or talk to a friend, relative, or therapist about the problem. Though fewer in number, some are so desperate that they use alcohol or drugs to wash away feelings of loneliness (Rook & Peplau, 1982). Chapter 14 shows that as people age, loneliness becomes a risk factor—as toxic as smoking and obesity—for a broad range of physical and mental health problems, including physical inactivity and depression (Cacioppo et al., 2006; Hawkley et al., 2009).

**loneliness** A feeling of deprivation about existing social relations.

# The Initial Attraction

Affiliation is a necessary first step in the formation of a social relationship. But each of us is more drawn to some people than to others. If you've ever had a crush on someone, felt the tingly excitement of a first encounter, or enjoyed the first moments of a new friendship, then you know the meaning of the term *attraction*. When you meet someone for the first time, what do *you* look for? Does familiarity breed fondness or contempt? Do birds of a feather flock together or do opposites attract? Is beauty the object of your desire or do you believe that outward appearances are deceiving? And what is it about a situation or the circumstances of an initial meeting that draws you in for more?

According to one classic perspective, people are attracted to those with whom they can have a relationship that is rewarding (Byrne & Clore, 1970; Lott & Lott, 1974). The rewards may be direct, as when people provide us with attention, support, money, status, information, and other valuable commodities. Or the rewards may be indirect, as when it feels good to be with someone who is beautiful, smart, or funny, or who happens to be in our presence when times are good.

A second powerful perspective on attraction has also emerged in recent years—that of evolutionary psychology, the subdiscipline that uses principles of evolution to understand human social behavior. According to this view, human beings all over the world exhibit patterns of attraction and mate selection that favor the conception, birth, and survival of their offspring. This approach has a great deal to say about differences in this regard between men and women (Buss, 2011; Schaller et al., 2006).

Recognizing the role of rewards and the call of our evolutionary past provides broad perspectives for understanding human attraction. But there's more to the story—much more. Over the years, social psychologists have identified many important determinants of attraction and the development of intimate relationships (Berscheid & Regan, 2004; Miller & Perlman, 2009; Regan, 2011). It's important to note that most of the research has focused on heterosexuals, so we often do not know how well specific findings apply to the homosexual population. At the same time, it is important to realize that many of the basic processes described in this chapter affect the development of all close relationships—regardless of whether the individuals involved are gay, lesbian, or straight (Herek, 2006; Kurdek, 2005; Peplau & Fingerhut, 2007).

Finally, it is important to realize that way that people meet and become attracted is a process that is now in transition as a result of online dating services such as Match.com, eHarmony, Compatible Partners, OK Cupid, and HookUp.com—not to mention mobile phone dating apps such as Zoosk and Badoo, used by millions. Online dating is a new phenomenon, but it has exploded over the past decade. In a national survey, 4,002 adults were asked how they met their current partners. Among those who met between 2007 and 2009, the most recent time frame sampled, 22% of heterosexual couples had met on the Internet. The numbers were even higher for same-sex couples (Rosenfeld & Thomas, 2012). Why are online dating platforms so popular? Does meeting online rather than in person alter the attraction process? In a critical analysis of this phenomenon, Eli Finkel and others (2012) note that online dating promises three benefits: (1) exposure and access to profiles of potential romantic partners, (2) a means of communicating through e-mail, instant messaging, and live chat via webcams; and (3) a matching "algorithm" that brings together users who are likely to be attracted to one another. Thus far, note Finkel et al. (2012), there is no published research to support the claim that online dating produces romantic outcomes better than more traditional processes described in this chapter. Stay tuned. There is sure to be a surge of research on this topic in the years ahead.

# Familiarity: Being There

It seems so obvious that people tend to overlook it: We are most likely to become attracted to someone we have seen and become familiar with. So let's begin with two basic and necessary factors in the attraction process: proximity and exposure.

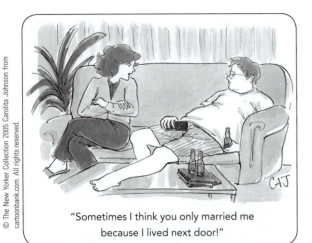

"Sometimes I think you only married me because I lived next door!"

**The Proximity Effect** It hardly sounds romantic, but the single best predictor of whether two people will get together is physical proximity or nearness. To be sure, we often interact at remote distances by telephone, e-mail, Twitter, blogs, and message boards. These days it's common for people to find friends, lovers, and sexual partners from a distance. Yet some of our most important social interactions still occur among people who find themselves in the same place at the same time (Latané et al., 1995).

To begin with, where we live influences the friends we make. Many years ago, Leon Festinger and his colleagues (1950) studied friendship patterns in married-student college housing and found that people were more likely to become friends with residents of nearby apartments than with those who lived farther away. More recent research has also shown that college students—who live in off-campus apartments, dormitories, fraternities and sorority houses—tend to date those who live either nearby (Hays, 1985) or in the same type of housing as they do (Whitbeck & Hoyt, 1994). In a field experiment on how people can become friends by chance, researchers randomly assigned first-year college students in an introductory psychology to their seats for the semester. ● Figure 9.2 shows that those who happened to be seated nearby or even in the same row were more likely to rate each other as friends one year later (Back et al., 2008).

## ● FIGURE 9.2

**Becoming Friends by Chance**

First-year college students were randomly assigned to specific seats for a semester-long class. Illustrating the proximity effect on attraction, those who happened to be seated nearby or in the same row were more likely to rate each other as friends one year later.

Back et al. (2008). © Cengage Learning

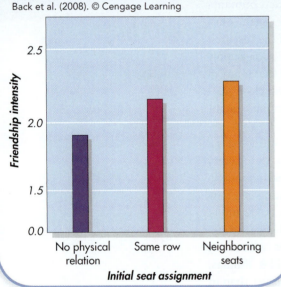

**The Mere Exposure Effect** Proximity does not necessarily spark attraction, but to the extent that it increases frequency of contact, it's a good first step. Folk wisdom often suggests a dim view of familiarity, which is said to "breed contempt." But in a series of experiments, Robert Zajonc (1968) found that the more often people saw a novel stimulus—whether it was a foreign word, a geometric form, or a human face—the more they came to like it. This phenomenon, which Zajonc called the **mere exposure effect**, has since been observed in more than 200 experiments (Bornstein, 1989).

People do not even have to be aware of their prior exposures for this effect to occur. In a typical study, participants are shown pictures of several stimuli, each for 1 to 5 milliseconds, which is too quick to register in awareness and too quick for anyone to realize that some stimuli are presented more often than others. After the presentation, participants are shown each of the stimuli and asked two questions: Do you like it, and have you ever seen it before? Perhaps you can predict the result. The more frequently the stimulus is presented, the more people like it. Yet when asked if they've ever seen the liked stimulus before, they say no. These results demonstrate that the mere exposure effect can influence us without our awareness (Kuntz-Wilson & Zajonc, 1980). In fact, the effect is stronger under these conditions (Bornstein & D'Agostino, 1992; Zajonc, 2001).

To appreciate the implications in a naturalistic situation, imagine yourself in a psychology class that is held in a large lecture hall. Three times a week, you trudge over to class, shake the cobwebs out of your head, and try your best to be alert. The room

**mere exposure effect** The phenomenon whereby the more often people are exposed to a stimulus, the more positively they evaluate that stimulus.

holds several hundred students. You come in and look down the tiered seats to the front where your instructor stands. During the semester, you're vaguely aware of another student who sits up front, but you never talk to her, and you probably would not recognize her if you saw her somewhere else. Then, at the end of the semester, you attend a special session where you are shown photographs of four women and asked some questions about them. Only then do you learn that you have participated in a study of the mere exposure effect.

Now view the same events from the perspective of Richard Moreland and Scott Beach (1992). These researchers selected four women who looked like typical students to be confederates in this study. One had a very easy job: She had her picture taken. But the other three also attended the class—5, 10, or 15 times. Did the frequency of exposure spark attraction among the real students in this situation? Yes. In questionnaires they completed after viewing pictures of all four women, students rated each woman on various traits (such as popularity, honesty, intelligence, and physical attractiveness) and recorded their beliefs about how much they would like her, enjoy spending time with her, and want to work with her on a mutual project. The results lined up like ducks in a row: The more classes a woman attended, the more attracted the students were to her.

In a well-controlled test of the familiarity hypothesis, Harry Reis and his colleagues (2011) recruited 110 same-sex pairs of college students who did not know each other to chat freely by e-mail, using anonymous screen names—once, twice, four times, six times, or eight times in a week. ● Figure 9.3 shows that when participants were asked to rate how much they liked their partner, ratings increased with the number of interactions they had. When asked if they would like to learn each other's identities so they could stay in contact, the percentages who said yes also increased with the number of interactions they had. There's no question about it: As a general rule, familiarity breeds attraction.

Familiarity can even influence our self-evaluations. Imagine that you had a portrait photograph of yourself developed into two pictures: one that depicted your actual appearance and the other a mirror-image copy. Which image would you prefer? Which would a friend prefer? Theodore Mita and others (1977) tried this interesting experiment with female college students and found that most

● **FIGURE 9.3**
**Virtual Familiarity Breeds Liking**

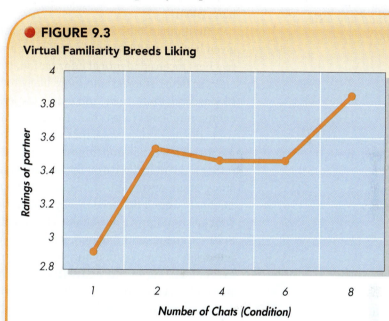

*Number of Chats (Condition)*

Same-sex pairs of college students were randomly assigned to chat by email varying times in a week. The more interactions the participants had, the more they liked their partner.

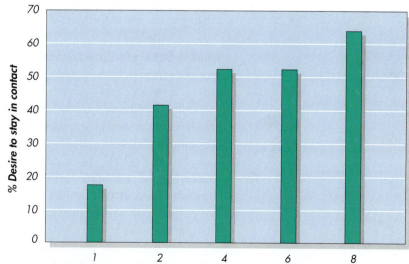

When participants were asked if they wanted to stay in contact after the experiment, the percentage who said yes also increased with the number of interactions they had.

Reiss et al. (2011). © Cengage Learning

preferred their mirror images, while their friends liked the actual photos. In both cases, the preference was for the view of the face that was most familiar.

## Physical Attractiveness: Getting Drawn In

What do you look for in a friend or romantic partner? Intelligence? Kindness? A sense of humor? How important, really, is a person's looks? As children, we were taught that "beauty is only skin deep" and that we should not "judge a book by its cover." Yet as adults, we react more favorably to others who are physically attractive than to those who are not. Over the years, studies have shown that in the affairs of our social world, beauty is a force to be reckoned with (Langlois et al., 2000; Patzer, 2006; Swami & Furnham, 2008).

The human bias for beauty is pervasive. In one study, fifth-grade teachers were given background information about a boy or girl, accompanied by a photograph. All teachers received identical information, yet those who saw an attractive child saw that child as being smarter and more likely to do well in school (Clifford & Walster, 1973). In a second study, male and female experimenters approached students on a college campus and tried to get them to sign a petition. The more attractive the experimenters were, the more signatures they were able to get (Chaiken, 1979). In a third study, Texas judges set lower bail and imposed smaller fines on suspects who were rated as attractive rather than unattractive on the basis of photographs (Downs & Lyons, 1991). In a fourth study, members of high-status sorority houses who glimpsed at pictures of prospective members were influenced by physical attractiveness in determining whether the young women would prove acceptable (Krendl et al., 2011). Finally, economists in the United States, Canada, and England, have discovered that within many occupational groups physically attractive men and women earn more pay than peers who are comparable except for being less attractive (Hamermesh & Biddle, 1994; Judge et al., 2009; Mobius & Rosenblat, 2006). There is no doubt about it: Across a range of settings, people fare better if they are attractive than if they are not (Hosoda et al., 2003).

It all seems so shallow, so superficial. But before we go on to accept the notion that people prefer others who are physically attractive, let's stop for a moment and consider a fundamental question: What constitutes beauty? Is it an objective and measurable human characteristic like height, weight, or hair color? Or is beauty a subjective quality, existing in the eye of the beholder? There are advocates on both sides.

**What Is Beauty?** No one would argue that there is a "gold standard" for beauty. However, some researchers do believe that certain faces are inherently more attractive than others. There are three sources of evidence for this proposition.

First, when people are asked to rate faces on a 10-point scale, there is typically a high level of agreement among children and adults, men and women, and people from the same or different cultures (Langlois et al., 2000). For example, Michael Cunningham and others (1995) asked Asian and Latino students and black and white American students to rate the appearance of women from all these groups. Overall, some faces were rated more attractive than others, leading these investigators to argue that people everywhere share an image of what is beautiful. It is interesting that people also tend to rate others similarly regardless of their attractiveness. By analyzing the 10-point ratings of pictures that people post of themselves on a rate-and-date website called HOTorNOT .com, Leonard Lee and others (2008) found that members tend to evaluate specific others similarly regardless of how high or low their own ratings were on the site.

People also tend to agree about what constitutes an attractive body. For example, men tend to be drawn to the "hourglass" figure often seen in women of average weight

*"Beauty is a greater recommendation than any letter of introduction."*

—Aristotle

© Luis Villota/CORBIS

Art Wolfe/Stone/Getty

John Callahan/Stone/Getty

The Kobal Collection at Art Resource, NY

Perceptions of facial beauty are largely consistent across cultures. Those regarded as good-looking in one culture also tend to be judged as attractive by people from other cultures. From left to right, the individuals pictured here are from Venezuela, Kenya, Japan, and the United States (the American is the actress Marilyn Monroe).

whose waists are a third narrower than their hips, a shape that is thought to be associated with reproductive fertility. In general, women with a 0.7 WHR (a waist-to-hip ratio where the waist circumference is 70% of the hip circumference) are rated as more attractive by men from European cultures. In fact, when shown photographs of women before and after they had microfat grafting surgery (where fat tissue is taken from the waist and implanted on the buttocks, which lowers the WHR), people rated the post-operative photographs as more attractive—independent of any changes in body weight (Singh & Randall, 2007). In contrast, women like men with a waist-to-hip ratio that forms a tapering V-shaped physique, signaling more muscle than fat (Singh, 1993, 1995). If marriage statistics are any indication, women also seem to prefer men with height. Comparisons made in Europe indicate that married men are a full inch taller, on average, than unmarried men (Pawlowski et al., 2000).

Second, a number of researchers have identified physical features of the human face that are reliably associated with ratings of attractiveness, such as smooth skin, a pleasant expression, and youthfulness (Rhodes, 2006). Particularly intriguing are studies showing that people like faces in which the eyes, nose, lips, and other features are not too different from the average. Judith Langlois and Lori Roggman (1990) showed college students both actual yearbook photos and computerized facial composites that "averaged" features from 4, 8, 16, or 32 of the photos. Time and again, they found that the students preferred the averaged composites to the individual faces and that the more faces used to form the composite, the more highly it was rated. Other studies have since confirmed this result (Jones et al., 2007; Langlois et al., 1994; Rhodes et al., 1999).

It seems odd that "averaged" faces are judged attractive when after all, the faces we find the most beautiful are anything but average. What accounts for these findings? Langlois and others (1994) believe that people like averaged faces because they are more prototypically face-like and have features that are less distinctive, so they seem more familiar to us. Consistent with this notion, research shows that just as people are more attracted to averaged human faces than to individual faces, they also prefer averaged dogs, birds, fish, wristwatches, and cars (Halberstadt & Rhodes, 2000; 2003).

Computerized averaging studies also show that people are drawn to faces that are symmetrical, where the paired features of the right and left sides line up and mirror each other (Grammer & Thornhill, 1994; Mealey et al., 1999). Why do we prefer symmetrical faces? Although support is mixed, evolutionary psychologists have speculated that our pursuit of symmetry is adaptive because symmetry is naturally associated with biological health, fitness, and fertility, qualities that are highly desirable in a mate (Rhodes et al., 2001; Shackelford & Larsen, 1999; Thornhill & Gangestad, 1993). Perhaps for that reason, people throughout the world try to enhance their appeal by wearing or painting symmetrical designs on their faces and bodies—designs that others find attractive (Cárdenas & Harris, 2006).

A third source of evidence for the view that beauty is an objective quality is that babies who are far too young to have learned their culture's standards of beauty exhibit a nonverbal preference for faces considered attractive by adults. Picture the scene in an infant laboratory: A baby, lying on its back in a crib, is shown a series of faces previously rated by college students. The first face appears and a clock starts ticking as the baby looks at it. As soon as the baby looks away, the clock stops and the next face is presented. The result: Young infants spend more time tracking and looking at attractive faces than at unattractive ones, regardless of whether the faces are young or old, male or female, or black or white (Game et al., 2003; Langlois et al., 1991). "These kids don't read *Vogue* or watch TV," notes Langlois, "yet they make the same judgments as adults" (Cowley, 1996, p. 66).

In contrast to this strong objective perspective, other researchers argue that physical attractiveness is subjective, and they point for evidence to the influences of culture, time, and the circumstances of our perception. When Johannes Hönekopp (2006) had large numbers of people rate the same faces, he found that although some faces were seen as more attractive than others, individuals differed a great deal in their private preferences. To some extent, beauty really is in the eye of the beholder.

One source of evidence for our variability in taste, first noted by Charles Darwin (1872), is that people from different cultures enhance their beauty in very different ways through face painting, makeup, plastic surgery, scarring, tattoos, hairstyling, the molding of bones, the filing of teeth, braces, and the piercing of ears and other body parts—all contributing to the "enigma of beauty" (Newman, 2000). In dramatic ways, what people find attractive in one part of the world may be seen as repulsive in another part of the world (Landau, 1989).

Ideals also vary when it comes to bodies. Looking at preferences for female body size in 545 cultures, Judith Anderson and others (1992) found that heavy women are judged more attractive than slender women in places where food is frequently in short supply. In one study, for example, Douglas Yu and Glenn Shepard (1998) found that Matsigenka men living in the Andes Mountains of southeastern Peru see female forms with "tubular" shapes—as opposed to hourglass shapes—as healthier, more attractive, and more desirable in a mate.

Differences in preference have also been found among racial groups within a given culture. Michelle Hebl and Todd Heatherton (1998) asked black and white female college students from the United States to rate thin, average, and overweight women from a set of magazine photographs. The result: The white students saw the heavy women as the least attractive, but the black students did not similarly discriminate. Follow-up studies showed the same difference in perceptions of black and white men (Hebl & Turchin, 2005). Why the difference? Based on the fact that white Americans are, on average, thinner than black Americans, one possible explanation is that they simply prefer a body type that is more typical of their group. Another possibility is that white Americans identify more with the "mainstream" weight-obsessed culture as portrayed in TV shows, magazine ads, and other media.

Standards of beauty also change over time, from one generation to the next. Many years ago, Brett Silverstein and others (1986) examined the measurements of female models appearing in women's magazines from the years 1901 to 1981, and

Computer-generated images that average the features of different faces are seen as more attractive than the individual faces on which they were based. In fact, up to a point, the more faces are represented in a composite, the more attractive it is. Shown here are sets of male and female composites that combine 2, 4, and 32 faces. Which do you prefer? (Langlois & Roggman, 1990.)

2-Face Composite    2-Face Composite

4-Face Composite    4-Face Composite

32-Face Composite    32-Face Composite

they found that "curvaceousness" (as measured by the bust-to-waist ratio) varied over time, with a boyish, slender look becoming particularly desirable in recent years. More recently, researchers took body measurements from all *Playboy* centerfolds, beginning with the first issue, in 1953, which featured Marilyn Monroe, through the last issue of 2001, with Eva Herzigova. The result: Over time, models became thinner and had lower bust-to-waist ratios—away from the ample "hourglass" to a more slender, athletic, stick-like shape (Voracek & Fisher, 2002).

Still other evidence for the subjective nature of beauty comes from various research laboratories. Time and again, social psychologists have found that our perceptions of someone's beauty can be inflated or deflated by various circumstances. Research shows, for example, that people often see others as more physically attractive if they have non-physical qualities that make them likable (Kniffin & Wilson, 2004). This link is illustrated in the student evaluations posted on www.RateMyPro-fessors.com, a popular website. An analysis of actual ratings on this site revealed that both male and female professors who were rated highly for their teaching were also more likely to be described as "hot" (Riniolo et al., 2006). Particularly interesting in this regard is that the more in love people are with their partners, the less attracted they are to others of the opposite sex (Johnson & Rusbult, 1989; Simpson et al., 1990).

When it comes to men's attraction to women, one particularly interesting context factor concerns color. The color red is routinely associated with sex. In many species of primates, females display red swelling on their genitals, chest, or face as they near ovulation. In human rituals that date back thousands of years, girls painted red ochre on their face and body at the emergence of puberty and fertility. Today, women use red lipstick and rouge to enhance their appeal, red hearts symbolize Valentine's Day, red lingerie is worn to entice, and red-light districts signal the availability of sex through prostitution.

Are men so conditioned by the color red that its presence boosts their perceptions of attractiveness? In a study of the "red-sex link," Andrew Elliot and Daniela Niesta (2008) had male and female research participants rate female photos that were set against a solid red or white background. Everyone saw the same photos, yet the attractiveness ratings were highest among the men in the red background condition (see ● Figure 9.4). In other studies, men continued to rate women as more attractive—and as more sexually desirable (but not generally more likable)—in the presence of red compared to women who were in the presence of gray, blue, or green. What is the process by which female red sparks male attraction? Follow-up research provides an answer: Women in red are perceived to be sexually receptive—and it's this receptivity that men find attractive (Pazda et al., 2012).

### Why Are We Blinded by Beauty?

Regardless of how beauty is defined, it's clear that people seen as physically attractive are at a social advantage. Perhaps that's why billions of dollars a year are spent on diets, shaving, waxing, makeup, hair gels, tattoos, body piercings, and cosmetic surgery designed to plump up sunken skin, peel and scrape wrinkles from the face, vacuum out fat deposits, lift faces, reshape noses, tuck in tummies, and enlarge or reduce breasts.

What creates the bias for beauty, and why are we drawn like magnets to people who are physically attractive? One possibility is that it is inherently rewarding to be in the company of people who are aesthetically appealing—that we derive pleasure from beautiful men and women the same way that we enjoy a breathtaking landscape or a

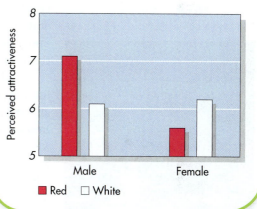

● **FIGURE 9.4**

**Romantic Red: The Color of Attraction?**

In this experiment, college students rated pictures of women that were set against a solid red or white background. Perhaps illustrating a learned association between the color red and romance, male students—but not their female counterparts—rated the pictured women as more attractive in the red background condition.

From Elliot, A. J., & Niesta, D., "Romantic red: Red enhances men's attraction to women," *Journal of Personality and Social Psychology* vol 95 (p. 1154). Copyright © 2008 by the American Psychological Association. Reprinted by permission.

Infants do not discriminate between faces considered attractive and unattractive in their culture. **F**ALSE.

*"There is no known culture in which people do not paint, pierce, tattoo, reshape or simply adorn their bodies."*

—Enid Schildkrout, anthropologist

magnificent work of art. In an fMRI study of men, for example, researchers found that areas of the brain known to respond to rewards such as food, money, and drugs such as cocaine are also activated by facial beauty (Aharon et al., 2001). Or perhaps the rewards are more extrinsic. Perhaps, for example, we expect the glitter of another's beauty to rub off on us. When average-looking men and women are seen alongside someone else of the same sex, they are rated as more attractive when the other person is good-looking and as less attractive when he or she is plain-looking (Geiselman et al., 1984).

A second possible reason for the bias toward beauty is that people tend to associate physical attractiveness with other desirable qualities, an assumption known as the **what-is-beautiful-is-good stereotype** (Dion et al., 1972). Think about children's fairy tales, where Snow White and Cinderella are portrayed as beautiful *and* kind, while the witch and stepsisters are said to be both ugly *and* cruel. This link between beauty and goodness can even be seen in Hollywood movies. Stephen Smith and others (1999) asked people to watch and rate the main characters who appeared in the 100 top-grossing movies between 1940 and 1990. They found that the more attractive the characters were, the more frequently they were portrayed as virtuous, romantically active, and successful. In this way, the entertainment industry unwittingly helps to perpetuate our tendency to judge people by their physical appearance.

It now appears that the stereotyped link between beauty and goodness can also be seen in the human brain. In a study using fMRI, Takashi Tsukiura and Roberto Capeza (2011) scanned the brains of participants while they evaluated the attractiveness of faces and the goodness of hypothetical actions. Both types of judgments increased activity in one region of the brain and decreased activity in another. Within each of these regions, the activations sparked by the two types of judgments were similar.

Studies have shown that good-looking people are judged to be smart, successful, happy, well-adjusted, sociable, confident, and assertive—but also vain (Eagly et al., 1991). Is this physical attractiveness stereotype accurate? Only to a limited extent. Research shows that good-looking people do have more friends, better social skills, and a more active sex life—and they are more successful at attracting a mate (Rhodes et al., 2005). But beauty is *not* related to objective measures of intelligence, personality, adjustment, or self-esteem. In these domains, popular perception appears to exaggerate the reality (Feingold, 1992b). It also seems that the specific nature of the stereotype depends on cultural conceptions of what is "good." When Ladd Wheeler and Youngmee Kim (1997) asked people in Korea to rate photos of various men and women, they found that people seen as physically attractive were also assumed to have "integrity" and "a concern for others"—traits that are highly valued in this collectivist culture. In contrast to what is considered desirable in more individualistic cultures, attractive people in Korea were not assumed to be dominant or assertive. What is beautiful is good, but what is good is (in part) culturally defined.

If the physical attractiveness stereotype is true only in part, why does it endure? One possibility is that each of us creates support for the bias via the type of *self-fulfilling prophecy* model described in Chapter 4. In a classic study of interpersonal attraction, Mark Snyder and others (1977) brought together unacquainted pairs of male and female college students. All the students were given biographical sketches of their partners. Each man also received a photograph of a physically attractive or unattractive woman, supposedly his partner. At that point, the students rated each other on several dimensions and had a phone-like conversation over headphones, conversations that were taped and later heard by uninvolved participants. The results were provocative. Men who thought they were interacting with a woman who was attractive (1) formed more positive impressions of her personality and (2) were friendlier in their conversational behavior. And now for the clincher: (3) the female students whose partners had seen the attractive picture were later rated by listeners to the conversation as warmer, more confident, and more

© Christie's Image/CORBIS

This painting depicts a Greek myth in which Pygmalion, the king of Cyprus, sculpted his ideal woman in an ivory statue he called Galatea, illustrating the power of a self-fulfilling prophecy. Pygmalion fell in love with his creation, caressed it, adorned it with jewelry, and eventually brought it to life.

**what-is-beautiful-is-good stereotype** The belief that physically attractive individuals also possess desirable personality characteristics.

animated. Fulfilling the prophecies of their own expectations, men who expected an attractive partner actually created one. These findings call to mind the Greek myth of Pygmalion, who fell in love with a statue he had carved and thus brought it to life.

**The Benefits and Costs of Beauty**    There's no doubt about it, good-looking people have a significant edge. As a result, they are more popular, more sexually experienced, more socially skilled, and more likely to attract a mate. In light of these advantages, it's remarkable that physical attractiveness is not a sure ticket to health, happiness, or high self-esteem (Diener et al., 1995; Feingold, 1992b; Langlois et al., 2000). The life of Marilyn Monroe is a case in point. A celebrity of the 1950s and 1960s, Monroe was considered the most ravishing woman of her time and one of the hottest actresses in Hollywood. Yet she was terribly vulnerable and insecure. Why?

One possible problem is that highly attractive people can't always tell if the attention and praise they receive from others is due to their talent or just their good looks. A study by Brenda Major and others (1984) illustrates the point. Male and female participants who saw themselves as attractive or unattractive wrote essays that were later positively evaluated by an unknown member of the opposite sex. Half the participants were told that their evaluator would be watching them through a one-way mirror as they wrote the essay; the other half were led to believe that they could not be seen. In actuality, there was no evaluator, and all participants received identical, very positive evaluations of their work. Participants were then asked why their essay was so favorably reviewed. The result: Those who saw themselves as unattractive felt better about the quality of their work after getting a glowing evaluation from someone who had seen them. Yet those who saw themselves as attractive and thought they had been seen attributed the glowing feedback to their looks, not to the quality of their work. For people who are highly attractive, positive feedback is sometimes hard to interpret (see ● Figure 9.5). This distrust may be well founded. In one study, many men and women openly admitted that if a prospective date was highly attractive, they would lie to present themselves well (Rowatt et al., 1999).

Another burden of physical attractiveness as a social asset is the pressure to maintain one's appearance. In today's American society, such pressure is particularly strong when it comes to the body. This focus on the human form can produce a healthy emphasis on nutrition and exercise. But it can also have unhealthy consequences, as when men pop steroids to build muscle and women overdiet to lose weight and inches. Particularly among young women, an obsession with thinness can give rise to serious eating disorders such as *bulimia nervosa* (food binges followed by purging) and *anorexia nervosa* (self-imposed starvation, which can prove fatal). Although estimates vary, recent studies indicate that less than 1% of women suffer from anorexia, that 2% to 3% have bulimia, and that these rates are higher among female college students than nonstudents (Fairburn & Brownell, 2002; Smolak & Thompson, 2009; Thompson, 2003).

Women are more likely than men to suffer from what Janet Polivy and others (1986) once called the "modern mania for slenderness." This slender ideal is regularly projected in the mass media. Studies have shown that young women who

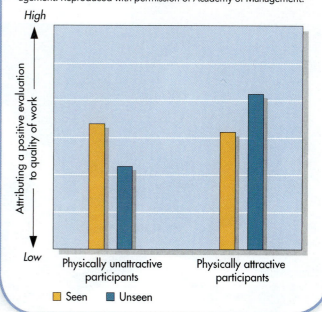

● **FIGURE 9.5**

**When Being Seen Leads to Disbelief**

People who believed they were physically unattractive were more likely to cite the quality of their work as the reason for receiving a positive evaluation when they thought they were seen by the evaluator. However, people who believed they were attractive were less likely to credit the quality of their work when they thought they were seen.

From Major, B., and Konar, E., "An investigation of sex differences in pay expectations and their possible causes," *Academy of Management Journal* vol 27 (pp. 777–791). Copyright © 1984 by Academy of Management. Reproduced with permission of Academy of Management.

see magazine ads or TV commercials that feature ultra-thin models become more dissatisfied with their own bodies than those who view neutral materials (Posavac et al., 1998). Trying to measure up to the multimillion-dollar supermodels can prove frustrating. What's worse, the cultural ideal for thinness may be set early in childhood. Several years ago, Kevin Norton and his colleagues (1996) projected the life-size dimensions of the original Ken and Barbie dolls that are popular all over the world. They found that both were unnaturally thin compared with the average young adult. In fact, the estimated odds that any young woman would have Barbie's original shape are approximately 1 in 100,000.

In sum, being beautiful may be a mixed blessing. There are some real benefits that cannot be denied, but there may be some costs as well. This tradeoff makes you wonder about the long-term effects. Some years ago, Ellen Berscheid and others (1972) compared the physical attractiveness levels of college students (based on yearbook pictures) to their adjustment when they reached middle age. There was little relationship between their appearance in youth and their later happiness. Those who were especially good-looking in college were more likely to be married, but they were not more satisfied with marriage or more content with life. Beauty may confer advantage, but it is not destiny.

> **People who are physically attractive are happier and have higher self-esteem than those who are unattractive. FALSE.**

## ❯ First Encounters: Getting Acquainted

Speed dating is a fascinating platform for men and women who are looking for a romantic relationship. In speed-dating events, individuals pay to have between 10 and 25 very brief "dates" lasting no more than 4 minutes. After rotating like clockwork from one partner to another, participants—who wear nametags—let the event hosts know which partners, if any, they'd be interested in seeing again. If two participants double-match, the host provides each with the other's contact information so they can schedule a real date (Finkel & Eastwick, 2008).

For a first encounter, does speed dating provide people with enough information? Is 4 minutes enough time for you to determine if you are romantically attracted to someone? To be sure, you get an up-close-and-personal look at a person's physical appearance. But then what other information would you want? Proximity boosts the odds that we will meet someone, familiarity puts us at ease, and beauty draws us in like magnets to a first encounter. But what determines whether sparks will fly in the early getting-acquainted stages of a relationship? In this section, we consider three characteristics of others who can influence our attraction: similarity, reciprocity, and being hard to get.

**Liking Others Who Are Similar** The problem with proverbial wisdom is that it often contradicts itself. Common sense tells us that "birds of a feather flock together." Yet we also hear that "opposites attract." So which is it? Before answering this question, imagine pulling out your laptop, meeting someone online, and striking up a conversation about school, sports, restaurants, movies, where you live, where you've traveled, or your favorite band—and you realize that the two of you have a lot in common. Now imagine the opposite experience of chatting with someone new who is very different in his or her background, interests,

Speed dating is a recent phenomenon that can be found all over the world. In London, pictured here, men and women gather for quick pairings in a round-robin series of "dates."

© Caroline Cortizo/Alamy

values, and outlook on life. Which of the two strangers would you want to meet, the one who is similar or the one who is different?

Over the years, research has consistently shown that people tend to associate with others who are similar to themselves (Montoya et al., 2008). The vast array of online dating sites illustrates the point. In addition to generic services such as Match.com, eHarmony, Compatible Partners, OK Cupid, and HookUp.com, all sorts of specialty services are specifically designed to bring together people of like backgrounds and minds—hence, ConservativeMatch.com, LiberalHearts.com, Jdate.com, Christian Cafe .com, and HappyBuddhist.com.

Four types of similarity are most relevant. The first is demographic. On a whole range of demographic variables—such as age, education, race, religion, height, level of intelligence, and socioeconomic status—people who go together as friends, dates, lovers, or partners in marriage tend to resemble each other more than randomly paired couples (Warren, 1966). These correlations cannot be used to prove that similarity causes attraction. A more compelling case could be made, however, by first measuring people's demographic characteristics and then determining whether these people, when they met others, liked those who were similar to them more than those who were dissimilar. This is what Theodore Newcomb did more than 50 years ago. In an elaborate study, Newcomb (1961) set up an experimental college dormitory and found that students who had similar backgrounds grew to like each other more than those who were dissimilar did. Is demographic similarity still a factor even today, with all the choices we have in our diverse and multicultural society? Yes. Commenting on the persistently magnetic appeal of similarity, sociologist John Macionis (2012) notes that "Cupid's arrow is aimed by society more than we like to think." One unfortunate result, as described in Chapter 5, is that by associating with similar others, people form social niches that are homogeneous and divided along the lines of race, ethnic background, age, religion, level of education, and occupation (McPherson et al., 2001).

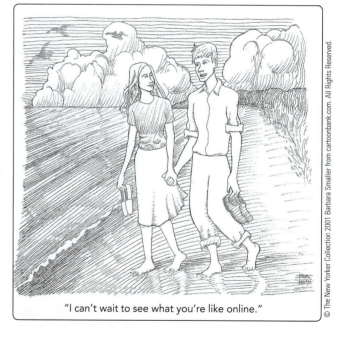

"I can't wait to see what you're like online."

People can also be similar in other ways, as when they share the same opinions, interests, and values. For example, what about *attitude* similarity and attraction? Here, the time course is slower because people have to get to know each other first. In Newcomb's study, the link between actual similarity and liking increased gradually over the school year. Laboratory experiments have confirmed the point. For example, Donn Byrne (1971) had people give their opinions on a whole range of issues and then presented them with an attitude survey that had supposedly been filled out by another person (the responses were rigged). In study after study, he found that participants liked this other person better when they perceived his or her attitudes as being more similar to theirs (Byrne, 1997).

The link between attitudes and attraction is evident among newly married couples. In a comprehensive study, Shanhong Luo and Eva Klohnen (2005) tested 291 newlywed couples and found that people tended to marry others who shared their political attitudes, religiosity, and values but who did not necessarily start out having similar personalities (for example, both being introverted or extroverted). Yet once in the relationship, similarities in personality became relevant: The more similar they were, the happier was the marriage. Clearly, birds of a feather both flock together and stay together. But wait. Does this necessarily mean that similarity breeds attraction, or might attraction breed similarity? In all likelihood, both mechanisms are at work. Luo and Klohnen compared couples who had been together for varying lengths of time before marriage and found that similarity was unrelated to the length of the relationship. Yet another study of dating couples showed that when partners who are close discover that they disagree on important moral issues, they bring their views on these issues into alignment and become more similar from that point on (Davis & Rusbult, 2001).

According to Milton Rosenbaum (1986), attraction researchers have overplayed the role of attitudinal similarity. Similarity does not spark attraction, he says. Rather, dissimilarity triggers repulsion: the desire to avoid someone. Rosenbaum maintains that people expect most others to be similar, which is why others who are different grab our attention. Taking this hypothesis one step further, Lykken and Tellegen (1993) argue that in mate selection, *all* forms of interpersonal similarity are irrelevant. After a person discards the 50% of the population who are least similar, they claim, a random selection process takes over.

So which is it: Are we turned on by others who are similar in their attitudes, or are we turned off by those who are different? As depicted in ● Figure 9.6, Byrne and his colleagues proposed a two-step model that takes both reactions into account. First, they claim, we avoid associating with others who are dissimilar; then, among those who remain, we are drawn to those who are most similar (Byrne et al., 1986; Smeaton et al., 1989). Our reactions may also be influenced by expectations. People expect similarity from ingroup members, like fellow Democrats or Republicans or fellow straights or gays. In a series of studies, Fang Chen and Douglas Kenrick (2002) found that research participants were particularly attracted to outgroup members who expressed similar attitudes, and they were most repulsed by ingroup members who expressed dissimilar attitudes.

In addition to demographics and attitudes, a third source of similarity and difference is also at work, at least in romantic relationships. Have you ever noticed the way people react to couples in which one partner is a knockout and the other is not? Typically, we are startled by "mismatches" of this sort, as if expecting people to pair off with others who are similarly attractive—not more, not less. This reaction has a basis in reality. Early on, laboratory studies showed that both men and women yearn for partners who are highly attractive. Thus, when incoming first-year students at the University of Minnesota were randomly coupled for a dance, their desire for a second date was influenced more by their partner's physical attractiveness than by any other variable (Walster et al., 1966). In real-life situations, however, where one can be accepted or rejected

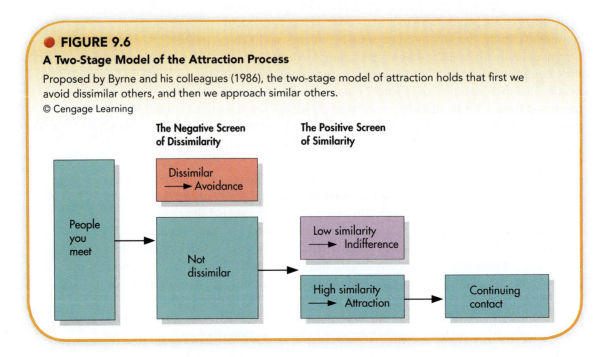

● **FIGURE 9.6**
**A Two-Stage Model of the Attraction Process**
Proposed by Byrne and his colleagues (1986), the two-stage model of attraction holds that first we avoid dissimilar others, and then we approach similar others.
© Cengage Learning

The Negative Screen of Dissimilarity

The Positive Screen of Similarity

People you meet

Dissimilar → Avoidance

Not dissimilar

Low similarity → Indifference

High similarity → Attraction

Continuing contact

by a prospective partner, people tend to shy away from making romantic overtures with others who seem "out of reach" (Berscheid et al., 1971; van Straaten et al., 2009). Correlational studies of couples who are dating, living together, or married support this "matching hypothesis": the idea that people tend to become involved romantically with others who are equivalent in their physical attractiveness (Feingold, 1988). Activity in a successful online dating site provides interesting new support. Based on activity logs, "popularity" was calculated for each user on the site. Sure enough, analysis of their interactions indicated popularity-based matching: Men and women tended to contact and be contacted by others whose relative popularity on the site was similar to their own (Taylor et al., 2011).

A fourth type of similarity can trigger attraction among strangers: a similarity in subjective experience. Imagine that a professor says something in class that strikes you as funny. You glance at the student next to you, who glances back, and the two of you burst out laughing, as if bonded by a private joke. Whenever two people who are at a common event laugh, cry, jump to their feet, cheer, shake their heads, or roll their eyes at the same time, they feel as if they have shared a subjective experience. Elizabeth Pinel and others (Pinel et al., 2006; Pinel & Long, 2012) called this experience "I-sharing" and theorized that people who I-share, even if they are otherwise dissimilar, feel a profound sense of connection to one another—like "kindred spirits." In a series of experiments, participants were asked to imagine themselves with a similar or dissimilar stranger with whom they did or did not react in the same way to an external event. Consistently, the participants liked the I-sharers more than everyone else, even when they had different backgrounds. The implications are intriguing: "A fundamentalist Christian and an atheist can find themselves enjoying the same sunset; a staunch Republican and an equally staunch Democrat can share a laugh. When two objectively different people I-share in these and other ways, their disliking for one another might lessen, if only for a moment" (Pinel et al., 2006, p. 245).

Before concluding that similarity is the key to attraction, what about the old adage that opposites attract? Many years ago, sociologists proposed the *complementarity hypothesis*, which holds that people seek others whose needs "oppose" their own—that people who need to dominate, for example, are naturally drawn to those who are submissive (Winch et al., 1954). Is there any support for this view? Surprisingly, the answer is no. Of course, most human beings are romantically attracted to others of the opposite sex. But when it comes to fitting mutual needs and personality traits the way keys fit locks, research shows that complementarity does not make for compatible attraction (Gonzaga et al., 2007; Luo & Klohnen, 2005; O'Leary & Smith, 1991). In an interview with the *Washington Post*, Gian Gonzaga—a researcher for eHarmony, the online dating service that matches people according to their similarities—debunked the complementarity hypothesis, noting that while opposites may seem exotic at first glance, over time the differences become difficult to negotiate (McCarthy, 2009).

**Liking Others Who Like Us**  Many years ago, Fritz Heider (1958) theorized that people prefer relationships that are psychologically "balanced" and that a state of imbalance causes distress. In groups of three or more individuals, a balanced social constellation exists when we like someone whose relationships with others parallel our own. Thus, we want to like the friends of our friends and the enemies of our enemies (Aronson & Cope, 1968). If you've ever had a good friend who dated someone you detested, then you know how awkward and unpleasant an unbalanced relationship can be. The fact is, we don't expect our friends and enemies to get along (Chapdelaine et al., 1994).

Between two people, a state of balance exists when a relationship is characterized by **reciprocity**: a mutual exchange between what we give and what we receive. Liking is mutual, which is why we tend to like others who indicate that they like us. In one

In 2012, eHarmony.com estimated that an average of 542 people a day get married in the United States as a result of meeting on their dating site—including Tanyalee and Joshua, pictured here. That number would account for nearly 5% of new U.S. marriages.

When it comes to romantic relationships, opposites attract. **F**ALSE.

**matching hypothesis**  The proposition that people are attracted to others who are similar in physical attractiveness.

**reciprocity**  A mutual exchange between what we give and receive—for example, liking those who like us.

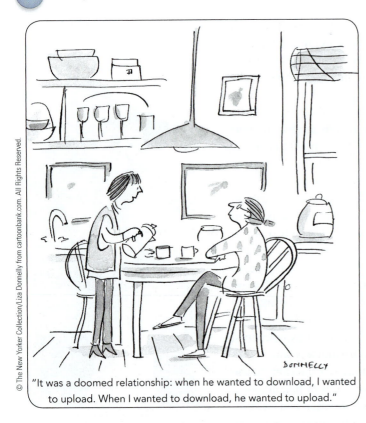

"It was a doomed relationship: when he wanted to download, I wanted to upload. When I wanted to download, he wanted to upload."

experiment, Rebecca Curtis and Kim Miller (1986) brought pairs of students into the laboratory, arranged for them to talk, and then "revealed" to one member in each pair that he or she was liked by the partner or disliked. When the students were later reunited for conversation, those who thought that they were liked were, in turn, warmer, more agreeable, and more self-disclosing. Feeling liked is important. When groups of men and women were asked to reflect on how they fell in love or developed friendships with specific people, many spontaneously said they had been turned on initially by the realization that they were liked (Aron et al., 1989).

But does reciprocity mean simply that the more people like us, the more we will like them back? Many years ago, Elliot Aronson and Darwyn Linder (1965) had female college students meet in pairs several times. In each pair, one student was a research participant; her partner was a confederate. After each meeting, the participant overheard a follow-up conversation between the experimenter and the confederate in which she was discussed and evaluated. Over time, the confederate's evaluation of the participant either was consistent or underwent a change—from negative to positive (gain) or from positive to negative (loss). Put yourself in the participant's shoes. All else being equal, in which condition would you like your partner most? In this study, participants liked the partner more when her evaluation changed from negative to positive than when it was positive all along. As long as the "conversion" is gradual and believable, people like others more when their affection takes time to earn than when it comes easily. Within a heterosexual speed-dating situation, Paul Eastwick and others (2007) confirmed the conversion point: People are drawn to members of the opposite sex who like them—but only when these others are selective in their liking and, hence, discriminating.

**Pursuing Those Who Are Hard to Get**   The Aronson and Linder (1965) finding suggests that we like others who are socially selective. This seems to support the popular notion that you can spark romantic interest by playing hard to get. Several years ago, Ellen Fein and Sherri Schneider (1996) wrote a book for women titled *The Rules: Time-Tested Secrets for Capturing the Heart of Mr. Right*. What were the rules? Here's one: "Don't call him and rarely return his calls." Here's another: "Let him take the lead." In all cases, the theme was that men are charmed by women who are hard to get. It's an interesting hypothesis.

Despite intuition, researchers found that the **hard-to-get effect** is harder to get than originally anticipated (Walster et al., 1973). One problem is that we are turned *off* by those who reject us because they are committed to someone else or have no interest in us (Wright & Contrada, 1986). Another problem is that we tend to prefer people who are moderately selective compared with those who are nonselective (they have poor taste or low standards) or too selective (they are snobs). In a study that well illustrates the point, researchers arranged for male and female college students to have 4-minute speed dates with 10 or so other students of the opposite sex, after which they all rated each other and indicated on a website if they were interested in meeting again. Analyses of the ratings showed that participants liked dates who selectively desired them more than others, but they did not like nondiscriminating dates who had indicated a desire for several of the men they encountered (Eastwick & Finkel, 2008). Additional research

**hard-to-get effect**   The tendency to prefer people who are highly selective in their social choices over those who are more readily available.

shows that we are drawn to others who seem hard to get because we are uncertain as to whether they like us (Whitchurch et al., 2011).

Now suppose that someone you are interested in is hard to get for external reasons. What if a desired relationship is opposed or forbidden by parents, as in the story of Romeo and Juliet? What about a relationship threatened by catastrophe, as in the love story portrayed in the 1997 hit movie *Titanic*, involving Leonardo DiCaprio and Kate Winslet—or a relationship threatened by parents over social class differences, as in the 2004 movie *The Notebook*, starring Ryan Gosling and Rachel McAdams? What about distance, a lack of time, or renewed interest from a partner's old flame? Chapter 6 describes the theory of psychological reactance, that people are highly motivated to protect their freedom to choose and behave as they please. When a valued freedom is threatened (not getting the object of one's affection), people reassert themselves, often by wanting that which is unavailable too much—like the proverbial forbidden fruit (Brehm & Brehm, 1981).

Consistent with reactance theory, studies conducted in bars like this have shown that men and women who are not in committed relationships see each other as more attractive as the night wears on.

Consider what happens when you think that your chance to get a date for the evening is slipping away. Is it true, to quote country-western musician Mickey Gilley, that "the girls all get prettier at closing time"? To find out, researchers entered some bars in Texas and asked patrons three times during the night to rate the physical attractiveness of other patrons of the same and opposite sex. As Gilley's lyrics suggested, people of the opposite sex were seen as more attractive as the night wore on (Pennebaker et al., 1979). The study is cute, but the correlation between time and attraction can be interpreted in other ways (perhaps attractiveness ratings rise with blood-alcohol levels!). In a follow-up study, Scott Madey and others (1996) also had patrons in a bar make attractiveness ratings throughout the night. They found that these ratings increased as the night wore on only among patrons who were not committed to a relationship. As reactance theory would predict, closing time posed a threat—which sparked desire—only to those on the lookout for a late-night date.

Another possible instance of passion fueled by reactance can be seen in "the allure of secret relationships." In a clever experiment, Daniel Wegner and others (1994) paired up male and female college students to play bridge. Within each foursome, one couple was instructed in writing to play footsie under the table, either secretly or in the open. Got the picture? After a few minutes, the game was stopped and the players were asked to indicate privately how attracted they were to their own partner and to the opposite-sex member of the other team. The result: Students who played footsie in secret were more attracted to each other than those who played in the open or not at all. This finding is certainly consistent with reactance theory. But there may be more to it. First, as we'll see later, the thrill of engaging in a forbidden act, or the sheer excitement of having to keep a secret, may help fan the flames of attraction. Second, however, it is important to realize that over time keeping a secret romance from others can become so much of a burden that the relationship itself will suffer (Foster & Campbell, 2005).

## Mate Selection: The Evolution of Desire

Before moving on to the topic of close relationships, let's stop and consider this question: When it comes to the search for a short-term or long-term mate, are men and women similarly motivated? If not, what are the differences? Later in this chapter, we'll see that most men appear to be more sex-driven than most women, desiring more frequent and more casual sex, more partners, and more variety, all of which leads some researchers in the area to conclude that "men desire sex more than women" (Baumeister et al., 2001, p. 270).

### Mate Selection Preferences

Why do these sex differences exist, and what do they mean? In *The Evolution of Desire*, David Buss (2003) argues that the answer can be derived from evolutionary psychology. According to this perspective, human beings all over the world exhibit mate-selection patterns that favor the conception, birth, and survival of their offspring—and women and men, by necessity, employ different strategies to achieve that common goal (Buss & Schmitt, 1993; Gangestad & Simpson, 2000; Trivers, 1972).

According to Buss, women must be highly selective because they are biologically limited in the number of children they can bear and raise in a lifetime. A woman must, therefore, protect her children and so searches for a mate who possesses (or has the potential to possess) economic resources and is willing to commit those resources to support her offspring. The result is that women should be attracted to men who are older and financially secure or who have ambition, intelligence, stability, and other traits predictive of future success.

In contrast, men can father an unlimited number of children and can ensure their reproductive success by inseminating many women. Men are restricted, however, by their ability to attract fertile partners and by their lack of certainty as to whether the babies born are actually their own. With these motives springing from their evolutionary past, men seek out women who are young and physically attractive (having smooth skin, full lips, lustrous hair, good muscle tone, and other youthful features)—attributes that signal health and reproductive fertility. To minimize their paternal uncertainty, men should also favor chastity, pursuing women they think will be sexually faithful rather than promiscuous.

In an initial test of this theory, Buss (1989) and a team of researchers surveyed 10,047 men and women in 37 cultures in North and South America, Asia, Africa, Eastern and Western Europe, and the Pacific. All respondents were asked to rank-order and rate the importance of various attributes in choosing a mate. The results were consistent with predictions. Both men and women gave equally high ratings to certain attributes, such as "having a pleasant disposition." In the vast majority of countries, however, "good looks" and "no previous experience in sexual intercourse" were valued more by men, whereas "good financial prospect" and "ambitious and industrious" were more important to women. Analyses of personal ads appearing in magazines and newspapers have similarly revealed that in the dating marketplace the "deal" is that women offer beauty, while men offer wealth (Feingold, 1992a; Rajecki et al., 1991; Sprecher et al., 1994). In the words of one investigator, the search for a heterosexual mate seems to feature "men as success objects and women as sex objects" (Davis, 1990).

Some researchers have suggested that these gendered preferences are not mere luxuries but are actually necessities in the mating marketplace. In Buss's (1989) study, men were more likely to prefer good looks, and women were more likely to prefer good financial prospects, but both sexes saw other characteristics—such

"Gee, but I miss the heightened eroticism of those five and a half years of conjugal visits."

This young man spies through his sunglasses at women on the beach. From an evolutionary perspective, his attraction is biologically (though not consciously) driven by the search for a fertile reproductive partner.

as being funny, dependable, and kind—as more important. But what happens in real life, where mate seekers who can't have it all must prioritize their desires? Studying "the necessities and luxuries in mate preferences," Norman Li and others (2002) asked participants to design their ideal marriage partner by purchasing different characteristics using "mate dollars." In some cases, they were granted a large budget to work with; in other cases, the budget was limited. In the large-budget condition, men spent somewhat more play money on physical attractiveness, and women spent somewhat more on social status, but both were just as interested in a partner who was kind, lively, and creative. In the low-budget condition, however, men spent even more of their play money on physical attractiveness, and women spent even more on social status. When mate seekers can't have it all and must therefore focus on what's most important, they prioritize their choices in the ways predicted by evolutionary theory (see ● Figure 9.7).

Also consistent with the evolutionary perspective is a universal tendency for men to seek younger women (who are most likely to be fertile) and for women to desire older men (who are most likely to have financial resources). Buss (1989) found this age-preference discrepancy in all the cultures he studied, with men on average wanting to marry women who were 2.7 years younger and women wanting men who were 3.4 years older. Based on their analysis of personal ads, Douglas Kenrick and Richard Keefe (1992) found that men in their twenties are equally interested in younger women and slightly older women still of fertile age. But men in their thirties seek out women who are 5 years younger, whereas men in their fifties prefer women 10 to 20 years younger. In contrast, girls and women of all ages are attracted to men who are older than they are. These patterns can also be seen in marriage statistics taken from different cultures and generations. There is one interesting exception: Teenage boys say they are most attracted to women who are slightly *older* than they are, women in their fertile twenties (Kenrick et al., 1996).

---

● **FIGURE 9.7**

**Sex Differences in Mate Preference: Evolutionary Necessities?**

In this study, participants built an ideal mate by "purchasing" characteristics. When they were given a large budget, men spent a somewhat higher percentage of money on physical attractiveness, and women spent somewhat more on social status than on other characteristics. On a low budget, however, men spent even more on physical attractiveness, and women spent even more on social status.

Li et al., 2002. © Cengage Learning

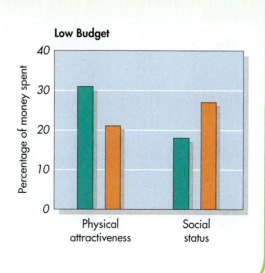

*"Men seek to propagate widely, whereas women seek to propagate wisely."*

—Robert Hinde

One might think that the mate preferences predicted by evolutionary theory would be limited to fertile men and women of youth. Not so. Recently, 600 Yahoo! personal ads were analyzed from four age groups: 20–34, 40–54, 60–74, and 75+ years. At all ages, men were more likely than women to offer information about their educational, employment, and income status. They were also more likely to seek indications of physical attractiveness. The older they were, the more the men wanted increasingly younger women. In contrast, women of all ages were more likely to seek out status information and men who were older (at least until the women were 75, at which point they sought men younger than themselves). Apparently, in the United States, the mate preferences predicted by evolutionary theory persist throughout the life span (Alterovitz & Mendelsohn, 2009).

**Conspicuous Consumption**   If women are drawn to men who have wealth or the ability to obtain it, then it stands to reason that men would flaunt their resources the way the male peacock displays his brilliantly colored tail. Showy displays of wealth are seen in cultures all over the world—from Iceland to Japan, Polynesia, and the Amazon jungle—leading evolutionary psychologists to speculate that *conspicuous consumption* may have evolved as a sexually selected mating signal (Miller, 2009; Saad, 2007). To see if it works, Jill Sundie and her colleagues (2011) briefly described to female participants a 32-year-old MBA graduate who made a good living as a financial analyst; who liked to bike, go to movies, and listen to music; and who just purchased a new car—either an expensive Porsche or a Honda Civic. Sure enough participants saw him as a more desirable date when he was said to have bought the flashier car.

If men flaunt their resources to attract women, then it stands to reason that the more competitive the reproductive landscape is for men, the more likely they are to spend money in conspicuous ways. Historically, the ratio of men to women in a population can vary over time and from one city to another. An abundance of women

● **FIGURE 9.8**

**Sex Ration Effects on Conspicuous Consumption**

After reading that the sex ratio on campus was biased toward more men or more women, male college students rated how much money they would spend on a Valentine's Day gift, a dinner date, and an engagement ring. In each case, the perception of competition led men to see more money as appropriate to spend on mating-related expenditures.
Griskevicius et al., 2012. © Cengage Learning

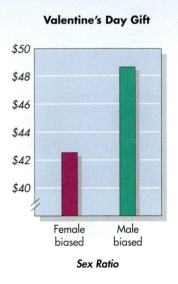

relative to men is associated with lower marriage rates and lower paternal investment; a relative abundance of men is associated with higher marriage rates and more paternal investment. To test "the financial consequences of too many men," Vladas Griskevicius and others (2012) presented male college students with one of two versions of a reputable local newspaper article concerning the ratio of men to women on their campus. One version indicated that the sex ratio was fast becoming female-biased (more women than men); a second version indicated that the sex ratio was male-biased (more men than women). Afterward, all participants were asked to rate how much money in dollars was appropriate to spend on a Valentine's Day gift, a dinner date, and an engagement ring. Across the board, the results strongly supported the prediction that the perception of competition among men would lead them to spend more money on mating-related expenditures (see ● Figure 9.8).

**Expressions of Love**   Chances are, common sense arms you to predict the male–female differences found in research on the evolution of desire. But what about romantic expressions of love and affection? Male and female stereotypes would suggest that whereas men are more likely to chase sex, women seek love. It comes as no surprise, therefore, that when Valentine's Day cards were analyzed for content, female authors were more likely than men to express love (Gonzalez & Koestner, 2006).

Saying "I love you" is a bold step for people seeking a mate because the words signal a marked shift in satisfaction and has implications for devotion, sacrifice, and commitment. Who normally professes their love first in a heterosexual relationship—the man or the woman? Have you ever been in love? If so, who broke the ice in *your* relationship? Interested in gender and expressions of love, Joshua Ackerman and his colleagues (2011) stopped pedestrians on a street corner and asked them to indicate which partner in general says it first. The result was consistent with expectations: 64% chose women. When asked who "gets serious" first, 84% chose women. Next, however, these researchers asked male and female college students who once had a past romantic relationship to recall who actually said "I love you" first. The result: 62% reported that the man said it first. In a third study, heterosexual couples from an online community sample were asked to report on their own relationship. Not all partners agreed on the answer—which is interesting. Among those who did agree, however, 70% reported that the man said it first (see ● Figure 9.9).

Does an evolutionary perspective shed light on why men would say "I love you" before women do? And do men and women react similarly to this heartfelt expression? Ackerman et al. (2011) predicted that timing matters—specifically, in relation to the onset of sexual activity. In an online study, they recruited male and female Craigslist posters who had received an "I love you" for the first and asked a number of questions about the experience—including whether the expression of love had come before or after sexual intercourse and how happy they were by the disclosure. Prior to sexual activity, men reported feeling happier and more positive about the expression of love than women did. After sexual activity, however, women reacted with somewhat more positive emotion. What does it all mean? As interpreted through the lens of an evolutionary perspective: "A presex confession may signal interest in advancing a relationship to include sexual activity, whereas a postsex confession may instead more accurately signal a desire for long-term commitment" (p. 1090).

**Jealousy**   Particularly supportive of evolutionary theory is research on *jealousy*, "the dangerous passion"—a negative emotional state that arises from a perceived threat to one's relationship. Although jealousy is a common and normal human reaction, men and women may be aroused by different triggering events. According to the theory, a man should be most upset by *sexual* infidelity because a wife's extramarital affair

● **FIGURE 9.9**

**Who's the First to Say "I Love You"?**

In one study, people were asked for their beliefs about which partner in a heterosexual relationship—the man or the woman—is more likely to say "I love you" first. In a second study, men and women who had a past romantic relationship were asked to recall who said "I love you" first. In a third study, both partners in heterosexual couples were asked to report on their own relationship. Contrary to our stereotypic belief (left), it appears that men are more likely to confess their love first (center and right).

Ackerman et al., 2011. © Cengage Learning

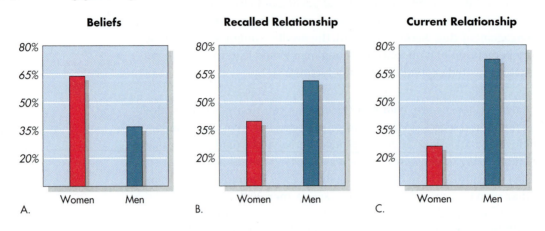

increases the risk that the children he supports are not his own. In contrast, a woman should feel threatened more by *emotional* infidelity because a husband who falls in love with another woman might leave and withdraw his financial support (Buss, 2000).

A number of studies support this hypothesis. In one, male and female college students were asked whether they would be more upset if their romantic partner were to form a deep emotional attachment or have sex with another person. Which situation would *you* find more distressing? The results revealed a striking gender difference: 60% of the men said they would be more upset by a partner's sexual infidelity, but 83% of the women felt that emotional infidelity was worse (Buss et al., 1992). This difference seems to reveal itself whenever men and women are asked which type of infidelity is more upsetting (Schützwohl, 2004; Shackelford et al., 2004). This gender difference also appeared when newly married husbands and wives were interviewed about how they would react if they suspected their partner of cheating. The men said they would use more "mate-retention" tactics (concealing or threatening the wife; taking action against the male rival) when their wives were young and attractive; women said they would use more mate-retention tactics (being watchful; enhancing their appearance) when married to men who strove for status and made more money (Buss & Shackelford, 1997).

In one study, researchers analyzed 398 individuals from various countries who had been clinically diagnosed with "morbid jealousy." Using information from published case histories, they found that whereas men were more likely to accuse their partners of sexual infidelity, women were more likely to be upset over emotional infidelity. Although only a few case histories contained details concerning the feared rival, jealous men were more likely to report that their rival had greater status and/or resources; jealous women were more likely to report that their rival was younger and/or more attractive (Easton et al., 2007).

**Sociocultural Perspectives** Although the gender differences are intriguing, critics of the evolutionary approach are quick to argue that some of the results can be interpreted in terms that are "psychological" rather than "evolutionary." One common argument is that women trade youth and beauty for money not for reproductive purposes but rather because they often lack *direct* access to economic power. With this hypothesis in mind, Steven Gangestad (1993) examined women's access to wealth in each of the countries in Buss's cross-cultural study. He found that the more economic power women had, the more important male physical attractiveness was to them. This result suggests that it may be the generally low social and economic status of women relative to men that leads them to care less about the physical attributes of a potential mate.

Another argument concerns the finding that men are more fearful of a mate's sexual infidelity (which threatens paternal certainty) and that women worry more about emotional infidelity (which threatens future support). The difference is consistent, but what does it mean? There are two criticisms. First, in contrast to the explanation evolutionary theory provides, some researchers have found that men get more upset over sexual infidelity not because of uncertain paternity but because they reasonably assume that a married woman who has a sexual affair is also likely to have intimate feelings for her extramarital partner. In other words, the man's concern, like the woman's, may be over the threats of loss, not about fatherhood issues (DeSteno & Salovey 1996; Harris & Christenfeld, 1996). Second, although men and women react differently when asked to imagine a partner's sexual or emotional infidelity, they are equally more upset by emotional infidelity when asked to recall actual experiences from a past relationship (Harris, 2002). At present, researchers continue to debate what the observed gender differences in romantic jealousy mean and the evolutionary model that is used to explain them (Harris, 2005; Sagarin, 2005).

A third argument is that the self-report differences typically found between the sexes are small compared to the similarities. This is an important point. In Buss's original cross-cultural study, both men and women gave their highest ratings to such attributes as kindness, dependability, a good sense of humor, and a pleasant disposition (physical attractiveness and financial prospects did not top the lists). In fact, research shows that women desire physical attractiveness as much as men do when asked about what they want in a short-term casual sex partner (Li & Kenrick, 2006; Regan & Berscheid, 1997).

Also limiting is the question of whether the *stated* preferences reported in the Buss (1989) surveys match the *actual* preferences when people find themselves face to face with real flesh-and-blood partners. In a recent study, Paul Eastwick and Eli Finkel (2008) recruited men and women for a speed-dating event. Beforehand, they asked participants about their preferences for an ideal partner. Replicating the usual effect, men were more likely to cite "physically attractive," and women were more likely to cite "earning prospects." Yet the romantic attraction ratings of partners during and after speed dating revealed that the differences among male and female participants about what traits were important had disappeared. In theory, men and women enacted the different roles cast by evolution; yet in practice, their attraction to each other was based on similar characteristics. These results can be seen in ● Figure 9.10.

Finally, the sex differences often observed are neither predictable nor universal. Human societies are flexible in terms of the ways people adapt to their environments, and there are revealing exceptions to the rules that are thought to govern human play on the evolutionary field. For example, David Geary (2000) points out that while human fathers spend less time doing child care than mothers do, they are unique among mammals—including baboons and chimpanzees, our evolutionary cousins—in the amount of care they give to their offspring. Geary speculates that human men care for their children in part because they enjoy more paternal certainty than do other male primates.

Abbas/Magnum Photos

The Bari tribeswomen of Venezuela are sexually promiscuous. The Bari believe that a baby can have multiple fathers, so being promiscuous enables a woman to secure child support from many men. This exception to the evolutionary norm illustrates that human behavior is flexible and that people can develop mating strategies to suit their cultural environment.

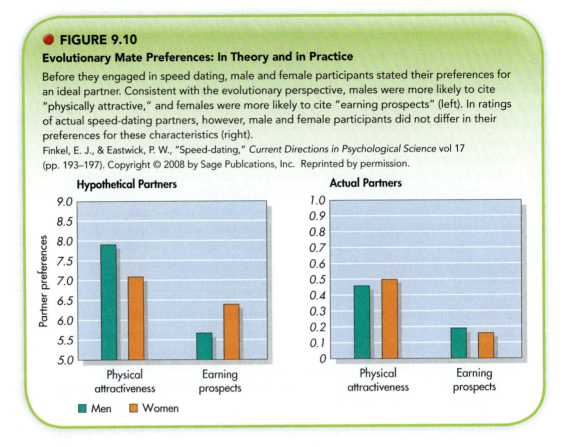

**FIGURE 9.10**

**Evolutionary Mate Preferences: In Theory and in Practice**

Before they engaged in speed dating, male and female participants stated their preferences for an ideal partner. Consistent with the evolutionary perspective, males were more likely to cite "physically attractive," and females were more likely to cite "earning prospects" (left). In ratings of actual speed-dating partners, however, male and female participants did not differ in their preferences for these characteristics (right).

Finkel, E. J., & Eastwick, P. W., "Speed-dating," *Current Directions in Psychological Science* vol 17 (pp. 193–197). Copyright © 2008 by Sage Publcations, Inc. Reprinted by permission.

Consider, too, the puzzling observation that women of the Bari tribe in Venezuela are highly promiscuous. From an evolutionary standpoint, this behavior does not seem adaptive since women who "sleep around" may scare off potential mates fearful of wasting their resources on children who are not their own. So why is female promiscuity the norm in this culture? In *Cultures of Multiple Fathers*, anthropologists Stephen Beckerman, Paul Valentine, and others note that the Bari and other aboriginal people in lowland South America believe that a baby can have multiple fathers and that all men who have sex with a pregnant woman make a biological contribution to her yet-to-be-born child (some groups believe that more than one father, or at least more than one insemination, are *required* to form a fetus). Thus, by taking many lovers a woman increases the number of men who will provide for her child. It appears that this strategy works. A multifathered Bari child is 16% more likely than a single-fathered child to survive to the age of 15 (Beckerman & Valentine, 2002).

**Summing Up**   The evolutionary perspective offers social psychologists an important and provocative perspective on relationships. The approach draws the criticism that the results are weak, limited, or explainable by nonevolutionary means (Harris, 2003; Hazan & Diamond, 2000; Pedersen et al., 2002). However, it also continues to generate new and interesting ideas. Currently, scientists in this area are studying a range of issues—such as the possible links between facial appearance and health and fertility (Geary, 2005; Grammer et al., 2005; Weeden & Sabini, 2005); the flexibility or "plasticity" of sexual orientation in men and women (Baumeister, 2000; Lippa, 2006); the potentially deadly link between sexual jealousy and violence (Buss, 2000); the reason that some men refuse to make child support payments (Shackelford et al., 2005); women's ability to detect and prefer men who are intelligent (Prokosch et al., 2009); the various sexual motives that can pull our attention toward attractive members of the opposite or same sex (Maner et al., 2007); and the conditions under which men and women would misperceive each other's sexual interest (Perilloux et al., 2012).

# Close Relationships

Being attracted to people can be exhilarating or frustrating, depending on how the initial encounters develop. How important is a good relationship to you? Several years ago, researchers asked 300 students to weigh the importance of having a satisfying romantic relationship against the importance of other life goals (such as getting a good education, having a successful career, or contributing to a better society) and found that 73% said they would sacrifice most other goals before giving up a good relationship (Hammersla & Frease-McMahan, 1990).

Intimate relationships often involve three basic components: (1) feelings of attachment, affection, and love; (2) fulfillment of psychological needs; and (3) interdependence between partners, each of whom has a meaningful influence on the other. Although people have many significant relationships in their lives that contain one or more of these components, social psychologists have concentrated their research on friends, dating partners, lovers, and married couples (Berscheid & Regan, 2005; Hendrick & Hendrick, 2000; Miller & Perlman, 2009; Regan, 2011; Sprecher et al., 2008).

Not all intimate relationships contain all three ingredients. A summer romance is emotionally intense, but in the fall, both partners resume their separate lives. An "empty shell" marriage revolves around coordinated daily activities, but emotional attachment is weak and psychological needs go unmet. Clearly, relationships come in different shapes and sizes. Some are sexual; others are not. Some involve partners of the same sex; others, partners of the opposite sex. Some partners commit to a future together; others drop by for a brief stay. Feelings run the gamut from joyful to painful and from loving to hateful, with emotional intensity ranging all the way from mild to megawatt.

How do we advance from our first encounters to the intimate relationships that warm our lives? Do we proceed gradually over time, in stages, step by step, or by leaps and bounds? According to one perspective, relationships progress in order through a series of stages. For example, Bernard Murstein's (1986) *stimulus–value–role (SVR) theory* says there are three: (1) the stimulus stage, in which attraction is sparked by external attributes such as physical appearance; (2) the value stage, where attachment is based on similarity of values and beliefs; and (3) the role stage, where commitment is based on the enactment of such roles as husband and wife. All three factors are important throughout a relationship, but each one is said to be first and foremost during only one stage.

In evaluating any stage theory, the critical issue is *sequence*. Does the value stage always precede the role stage or might a couple work out roles before exploring whether their values are compatible? Most researchers do not believe that intimate relationships progress through a fixed sequence of stages. What, then, accounts for how they change? One common answer is *rewards*. Love, like attraction, depends on the experience of positive emotions in the presence of a partner. Step by step, as the rewards pile up, love develops. Or, as rewards diminish, love erodes. In reward theories, quantity counts. But some would disagree. Think about your own relationships. Are your feelings for someone you love simply a more intense version of your feelings for someone you like? Is the love of a close friend the same as the love of a romantic partner? If not, then you appreciate that there are qualitative differences among relationships. The next section examines the reward-based approach to building a relationship. Then we consider differences among various types of relationships.

**intimate relationship** A close relationship between two adults involving emotional attachment, fulfillment of psychological needs, or interdependence.

## The Intimate Marketplace: Tracking the Gains and Losses

Earlier, we saw that people are initially attracted to others who provide them with direct or indirect rewards. But is "What's in it for me?" still important in a relationship that has blossomed and grown? Can an economic approach predict the future of a close relationship?

**Social Exchange Theory**   **Social exchange theory** is an economic model of human behavior according to which people are motivated by a desire to maximize profit and minimize loss in their social relationships just as they are in business (Homans, 1961; Thibaut & Kelley, 1959). The basic premise is simple: Relationships that provide more rewards and fewer costs will be more satisfying and endure longer. Between intimates, the rewards include love, companionship, consolation in times of distress, and sexual gratification if the relationship is of this nature. The costs include the work it takes to maintain a relationship, work though conflict, compromise, and sacrifice opportunities elsewhere.

"I've done the numbers, and I will marry you."

The development of an intimate relationship is clearly associated with the overall level of rewards and costs. Research has shown that dating couples who experience greater increases in rewards as their relationship progresses are more likely to stay together than are those who experience small increases or declines (Berg & McQuinn, 1986). People do not worry about costs during the honeymoon phase of a relationship (Hays, 1985). After a few months, however, both rewards and costs start to contribute to levels of satisfaction, both in married couples (Margolin & Wampold, 1981) and in gay and lesbian couples who are living together (Kurdek, 1991a).

Rewards and costs do not arise in a psychological vacuum. All people bring to a relationship certain expectations about the balance sheet to which they are entitled. John Thibaut and Harold Kelley (1959) coined the term *comparison level (CL)* to refer to this average expected outcome in relationships. A person with a high CL expects his or her relationships to be rewarding; someone with a low CL does not. Situations that meet or exceed a person's expectations are more satisfying than those that fall short. Even a bad relationship can look pretty good to someone who has a low CL.

According to Thibaut and Kelley, a second kind of expectation is also important. They coined the term *comparison level for alternatives* (*CLalt*) to refer to people's expectations about what they would receive in an alternative situation. If the rewards available elsewhere are believed to be high, a person will be less committed to staying in the present relationship (Drigotas & Rusbult, 1992). If people perceive that they have few acceptable alternatives (a low CLalt), they will tend to remain, even in an unsatisfying relationship that fails to meet expectations (CL).

Of course, just as these alternatives can influence our commitment, a sense of commitment can influence our perceptions of the alternatives. If you've ever been in love, you probably were not cold, calculating, and altogether objective in your perceptions of the alternatives. In close and intimate relationships, we tend to act like lovers, not like scientists, and harbor positive illusions. Research shows that people who are in love tend to see their partners and relationships through rose-colored glasses (Collins & Feeney 2000; Gagne & Lydon, 2001; Sanderson & Evans, 2001). They also tend to see other prospective partners as less appealing (Johnson & Rusbult, 1989; Simpson et al., 1990)—a motivated perception that enables people in

**social exchange theory**   A perspective that views people as motivated to maximize benefits and minimize costs in their relationships with others.

a committed relationship to resist temptation (Lydon, 2010). This generally positive perspective on one's own partner relative to others is conducive to a happy and stable relationship (Murray et al., 1996; Murray & Holmes, 1999)—except when people are in denial about their partners and incorrect in their perceptions (Neff & Karney, 2005).

A third element in the social exchange is investment. An *investment* is something a person puts into a relationship that he or she cannot recover if the relationship ends. If you don't like the way an intimate relationship is working out, you can pack your clothes, grab your laptop, and drive away. But what about all the time you put into trying to make the relationship last? What about all the romantic and career opportunities you sacrificed along the way? As you might expect, investments increase commitment. Because of those things we can't take with us, we're more likely to stay (Rusbult & Buunk, 1993).

Over the years, research has shown that the building blocks of the social exchange framework—as depicted in ● Figure 9.11 and as incorporated into Caryl Rusbult et al.'s (1998) investment model—can be used to determine the level of commitment partners bring to a relationship (Le & Agnew, 2003; Rusbult et al., 2012). This model is important because commitment levels predict how long relationships will last. In studies of dating and married couples, research shows that the best-adjusted ones are those in which each partner is committed and sees the other as mutually committed (Drigotas et al., 1999). Particularly important for the durability of a relationship, people who are committed are more likely to forgive and forget when their partners betray a relationship norm by flirting, lying, forgetting an anniversary, revealing a private and embarrassing story in public, or having an affair (Finkel et al., 2002). Unfortunately, there are times when commitment can be a trap. A study of battered women showed that the investment model can be used to predict whether battered women will remain in an abusive relationship (Rhatigan & Axsom, 2006).

*"Love looks not with the eyes, but with the mind; And therefore is wing'd Cupid painted blind."*
—William Shakespeare
*A Midsummer Night's Dream*

● **FIGURE 9.11**

**Relational Building Blocks**

The building blocks of social exchange are rewards, costs, comparison level for alternatives, and investments. These factors are strongly associated with the satisfaction and commitment partners experience in their relationship.
© Cengage Learning

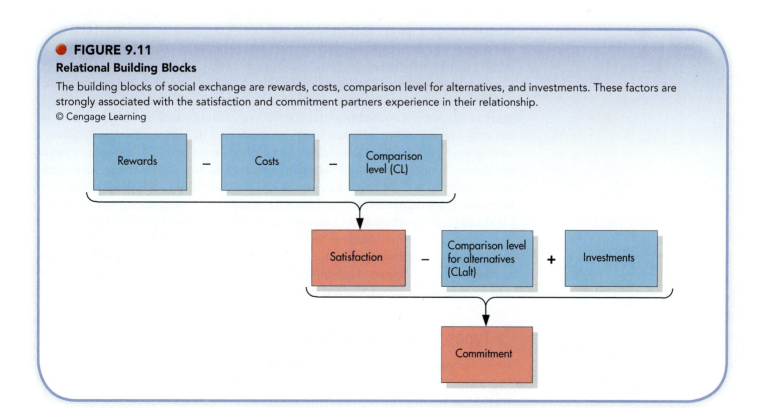

**Equity Theory**  **Equity theory** provides a special version of how social exchange operates in interpersonal interactions (Adams, 1965; Messick & Cook, 1983; Walster et al., 1978). According to this theory, an equitable relationship is a matter of social justice (Hatfield et al., 2008). All over the world, people are most content when the ratio between what they get out of a relationship (benefits) and what they put into it (contributions) is similar for both partners. Thus, the basic equity formula is

$$\frac{\text{Your Benefits}}{\text{Your Contributions}} = \frac{\text{Your Partner's Benefits}}{\text{Your Partner's Contributions}}$$

Equity is different from equality. According to equity theory, the balance is what counts. So if one partner benefits more from a relationship but also makes a greater contribution, then the situation is equitable. In an inequitable relationship, the balance is disturbed: One partner (called the *overbenefited*) receives more benefits than he or she deserves on the basis of contributions made, while the other partner (aptly called the *underbenefited*) receives fewer benefits than deserved.

Both overbenefit and underbenefit are unstable and often unhappy states. As you might expect, underbenefited partners feel angry and resentful because they are giving more than their partner for the benefits they receive, whereas overbenefited partners feel guilty because they are profiting unfairly. Both kinds of inequity are associated with negative emotions in dating couples (Walster et al., 1978), married couples (Schafer & Keith, 1981; Guerrero et al., 2008), and friendships among elderly widows (Rook, 1987). When it comes to satisfaction with a relationship, as you might expect, it is more unpleasant to feel underbenefited than overbenefited. People prefer to receive too much in life rather than too little, even if they feel bad about it (Grote & Clark, 2001; Hatfield et al., 1982; Sprecher, 2001).

If equity is so important, then any partner in a close relationship may at times feel a need to restore the balance sheet when he or she is feeling inferior as if he or she is falling short, or insecure. According to Sandra Murray and John Holmes (2008), people in relationships naturally and unconsciously maintain something of a "trust-insurance system" by which they keep a tally of costs and benefits in order to detect and then repair possible imbalances.

Murray and others (2009) went on to demonstrate the process in a series of studies of newlyweds. In one of these studies, more than 200 married couples, averaging 27 years of age, were recruited from local city clerk's offices when they applied for their marriage license. Each couple had been married for less than 6 months. All participants were given a personal digital assistant for keeping a daily diary by answering specific questions—about their feelings, behaviors, and doubts about the marriage—each night before going to bed. By tracking and statistically correlating each partner's answers over time, the researchers observed three steps of the trust-insurance system in action: (1) On days after participants anxiously felt that they were not good enough for their partner, they were more likely to make sacrifices—for example, by doing the dishes, making lunch, or picking up after the partner; (2) these restorative actions were accompanied by lowered feelings of inferiority that same day; and (3) on the next day, the partners who benefited from these actions expressed fewer doubts about their marriage.

## Types of Relationships

Social exchange models focus on quantity: The more (rewards, equity), the better (satisfaction, endurance). But is reward always necessary? What about qualitative differences among our relationships? Does more reward turn casual acquaintances into friends, and friends into lovers, or are these types of relationships different from each other?

**equity theory** The theory that people are most satisfied with a relationship when the ratio between benefits and contributions is similar for both partners.

**Exchange and Communal Relationships**   According to Margaret Clark and her colleagues, people operate by a reward-based model when they are in **exchange relationships**, which are characterized by an immediate tit-for-tat repayment of benefits. In these situations, people want costs to be quickly offset by compensation, leaving the balance at zero. But not all relationships fit this mold. Clark maintains that in **communal relationships**, partners respond to each other's needs and well-being over time and in different ways, without regard for whether they have given or received a benefit (Clark, 1984; Clark & Mills, 1979).

Exchange relationships typically exist between strangers and casual acquaintances and in certain long-term arrangements such as business partnerships. In contrast, strong communal relationships are usually limited to close friends, romantic partners, and family members (Clark & Mills, 1993). Based on fieldwork in West Africa, Alan Fiske (1992) is convinced that this distinction applies to human interactions all over the world. But the cynics among us wonder: Are communal relationships truly free of social exchange considerations? Can people really give without any desire to receive, or do partners in a communal relationship follow a more subtle version of social exchange, assuming that the benefits will balance out in the long run? Clark and Judson Mills (1993) believe that true communal relationships do exist—that once a communal norm has been adopted in a relationship, regardless of how it started, the motivation to respond to the other's needs becomes automatic.

**Secure and Insecure Attachment Styles**   Another interesting approach to understanding relationships is provided by Phillip Shaver, Cindy Hazan, and others who have theorized that just as infants display different kinds of attachment toward their parents, adults also exhibit specific **attachment styles** in their romantic relationships (Cassidy & Shaver, 1999; Mikulincer & Shaver, 2007; Rholes & Simpson, 2004).

For many years, child development psychologists had noticed that infants form intense, exclusive bonds with their primary caretakers. This first relationship is highly charged with emotion, and it emerges with regularity from one culture to the next. By observing the way babies react to both separations from and reunions with the primary caretaker, usually the mother, researchers also noticed that babies have different attachment styles. Those with *secure* attachments cry in distress when the mother leaves and then beam with sheer delight when she returns. Those with *insecure* attachments show one of two patterns. Some babies, described as anxious, cling and cry when the mother leaves but then greet her with anger or apathy upon her return. Others are generally more detached and *avoidant*, not reacting much on either occasion (Ainsworth et al., 1978).

How important is this first attachment? Does a secure and trusting bond in the first year of life set a foundation for close relationships later in life? John Bowlby (1988), a psychiatrist and influential theorist, has argued that there is a link—that infants form "internal working models" of attachment figures and that these models guide their relationships later in life. Research shows that infants classified as securely attached are later more positive in their outlook toward others (Cassidy et al., 1996). Other research has shown that adult relationship patterns are predictable from parent–child relations in adolescence (Nosko et al., 2011). Either way, whether adult attachment styles are rooted in infancy or traced from adolescence, the distinction among adults has proved to be a useful one (Dinero et al., 2008).

Read the descriptions of three attachment types in Table 9.1. Which fits you best? Hazan and Shaver (1987) presented this task initially in a "love quiz" that appeared in a Denver newspaper and then in a study of college students. As shown in Table 9.1, the distribution of responses was similar in the two samples, and it proved similar again in a later nationwide sample of 8,000 adults (Mickelson et al., 1997). In addition,

**exchange relationship**   A relationship in which the participants expect and desire strict reciprocity in their interactions.

**communal relationship**   A relationship in which the participants expect and desire mutual responsiveness to each other's needs.

**attachment style**   The way a person typically interacts with significant others.

**TABLE 9.1**

**Attachment Styles**

Question: Which of the following best describes your feelings?

| Answers and Percentages | Newspaper Sample | University Sample |
|---|---|---|
| **Secure** | 56 | 56 |
| I find it relatively easy to get close to others and am comfortable depending on them and having them depend on me. I don't often worry about being abandoned or about someone getting too close to me. | | |
| **Avoidant** | 25 | 23 |
| I am somewhat uncomfortable being close to others; I find it difficult to trust them completely and difficult to allow myself to depend on them. I am nervous when anyone gets too close, and often love partners want me to be more intimate than I feel comfortable being. | | |
| **Anxious** | 19 | 21 |
| I find that others are reluctant to get as close as I would like. I often worry that my partner doesn't really love me or won't want to stay with me. I want to merge completely with another person, and this desire sometimes scares people away. | | |

From Hazan, C., and Shaver, P., "Romantic love conceptualized as an attachment process," *Journal of Personality and Social Psychology* vol 52 (pp. 511–524). Copyright © 1987 by the American Psychological Association. Reprinted by permission.

the researchers found that people who have a secure attachment style report having satisfying relationships that are happy, friendly, based on mutual trust, and enduring. Cognitively, they see people as good-hearted, and they believe in romantic love. In contrast, avoidant lovers fear intimacy and believe that romantic love is doomed to fade; and anxious lovers report a love life full of emotional highs and lows, obsessive preoccupation, a greater willingness than others to make long-term commitments, and extreme sexual attraction and jealousy.

To some extent, our attachment styles can be seen in our everyday behavior. For example, Jeffrey Simpson and others (1996) videotaped dating couples as they tried to resolve various conflicts and then showed the tapes to outside observers. They found that men classified from a questionnaire as having an insecure-avoidant attachment style were the least warm and supportive and that women with an insecure-anxious style were the most upset and negative in their behavior. There is also reason to believe that people's attachment styles influence their physiological reactions to relationship conflict. In one study, Sally Powers and her colleagues (2006) brought 124 college-age dating couples into the laboratory to discuss a heated conflict they'd been having. Before and after this "conflict negotiation task," the researchers took saliva samples from all participants to measure levels of cortisol, a stress hormone. The results showed that boyfriends and girlfriends who were insecurely attached exhibited more physiological stress in response to the conflict task than did those who were securely attached.

What about the future? Does the attachment style you endorse today foretell relational outcomes tomorrow? On this question, the evidence is mixed. People who are secure do tend to have more lasting relationships. But the prognosis for those classified as insecure is harder to predict, with the results less consistent. What's important to realize is that although styles of attachment are modestly stable over time—perhaps as holdovers from infancy and childhood—they are not fixed, or set in stone. Lee Kirkpatrick and Cindy Hazan (1994) tracked down participants from a study that had taken place four years earlier and found that 30% had different attachment styles. In keeping with the central theme of social psychology—that we are profoundly shaped by the situations we are in—research suggests that people may continuously revise their own attachment styles in response to new relationship experiences.

## How Do I Love Thee? Counting the Ways

The poet Elizabeth Barrett Browning asked, "How do I love thee?" and then went on to "count the ways"—of which there are many. When college students were asked to list all kinds of love that came to mind, they produced 216 items, such as friendship, parental, brotherly, sisterly, romantic, sexual, spiritual, obsessive, possessive, and puppy love (Fehr & Russell, 1991).

Over the years, various schemes for classifying different types of love have been proposed (Berscheid, 2010; Sternberg & Weis, 2006). On the basis of ancient writings, sociologist John Alan Lee (1988) identified three primary love styles: *eros* (erotic love), *ludus* (game-playing, uncommitted love), and *storge* (friendship love). As with primary colors, Lee theorized, these three styles can be blended together to form new secondary types of love, such as *mania* (demanding and possessive love), *pragma* (pragmatic love), and *agape* (other-oriented, altruistic love). On a scale designed to measure these "colors of love," men tend to score higher than women on *ludus*, and women score higher on *storge*, *mania*, and *pragma* (Hendrick & Hendrick, 1995).

Another popular taxonomy is derived from Robert Sternberg's (1986) **triangular theory of love**. According to Sternberg, there are eight basic subtypes of love (seven different forms and an eighth combination that results in the absence of love)—and all can be derived from the presence or absence of three components. The combination can thus be viewed as the vertices of a triangle (see ● Figure 9.12). The components—and sample items used to measure each one—are described below:

*Intimacy*. The emotional component, which involves liking and feelings of closeness. ("I have a comfortable relationship with ___ .")

*Passion*: The motivational component, which contains drives that trigger attraction, romance, and sexual desire. ("Just seeing ___ is exciting for me.")

*Commitment*: The cognitive component, which reflects the decision to make a long-term commitment to a loved partner. ("I will always feel a strong responsibility for ___ .")

Research provides fairly good support for this tri-component model of love (Sternberg, 1999). In one study, Arthur Aron and Lori Westbay (1996) asked people to rate 68 prototypical features of love and found that all the various features fell into three categories: passion (*gazing at the other, euphoria, butterflies in the stomach*), intimacy (*feeling free to talk about anything, supportive, understanding*), and commitment (*devotion, putting the other first, long-lasting*). In a second study, Sternberg (1997) asked people to state what they see as important in different kinds of relationships and found that the results were consistent with the theory. For example, "ideal lover" scored high on all three components, "friend" scored high on intimacy and commitment but low on passion, and "sibling" scored high on commitment but low on intimacy and passion.

In light of theories involving infant attachment styles, colors, triangles, and other love classification schemes that have been proposed over the years, one wonders: How many types of love are there, really? It's hard to tell. But there are two basic types that are built into all models: *liking*, the type of feeling you would have for a platonic friend, and *loving*, the kind of feeling you would have for a romantic partner. According to Zick Rubin (1973), liking and loving are two distinct reactions to an intimate relationship. There is some question, however, about how sharp the difference is. Kenneth and Karen Dion (1976) questioned casual daters, exclusive daters, engaged couples, and married couples. Although casual daters reported more liking than loving, liking and loving did not differ among those in the more committed dating relationships. The two-pronged distinction Elaine Hatfield (1988) and her colleagues (Hatfield & Rapson, 1993) make between passionate and companionate love is even sharper. According to Hatfield, **passionate love** is an emotionally intense and *often erotic state* of absorption in another person, whereas **companionate love** is a secure, trusting, and stable partnership, similar to what Rubin called liking.

**triangular theory of love** A theory proposing that love has three basic components—intimacy, passion, and commitment—that can be combined to produce eight subtypes.

**passionate love** Romantic love characterized by high arousal, intense attraction, and fear of rejection.

**companionate love** A secure, trusting, stable partnership.

● **FIGURE 9.12**
**Sternberg's Triangular Theory of Love**

According to Sternberg, various combinations of passion, intimacy, and commitment give rise to seven different types of love. (Although it is not shown, the absence of all three components produces an eighth result, nonlove.)

From Sternberg, R., and Barnes, M. L. (eds.), *The Psychology of Love*, Yale University Press, 1986. Copyright © 1986 by Yale University Press. Reprinted by permission.

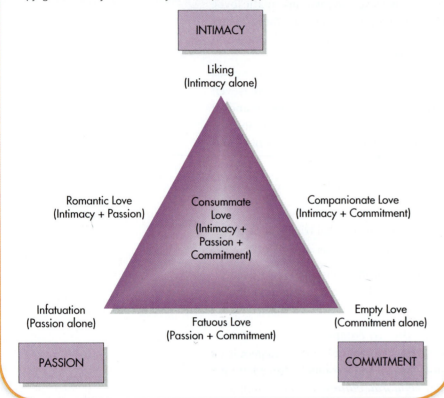

**Passionate Love**  Passionate love is an intense emotional, heart-thumping state of absorption in another person. From thrilling highs to agonizing lows, it is the bittersweet stuff of romance paperbacks, popular music, poems, and soap operas. What is passionate love, and where does it come from? According to Ellen Berscheid and Elaine Walster (later Hatfield) (1974), the key to understanding passionate love is to recognize that it is an emotion that can be analyzed like any other emotion. Drawing on Schachter's (1964) two-factor theory of emotion (see Chapter 3), they theorized that passionate love is fueled by two ingredients: (1) a heightened state of physiological arousal and (2) the belief that this arousal was triggered by the beloved person.

Sometimes, the arousal–love connection is obvious, as when a person feels a surge of sexual desire at the sight of a romantic partner. At other times, however, the symptoms of arousal—such as a pounding heart, sweaty palms, and weak knees—can be hard to interpret. When you're in the company of an attractive person, these symptoms may be attributed or "misattributed" to passionate love. Dolf Zillmann (1984) calls the process **excitation transfer**. According to Zillmann, arousal triggered by one stimulus can be transferred or added to the arousal from a second stimulus. The combined arousal is then perceived as having been caused only by the second stimulus.

Donald Dutton and Arthur Aron (1974) first tested this provocative hypothesis in a field study that took place on two bridges above British Columbia's Capilano River. One was a narrow, wobbly suspension bridge (450 feet long and 5 feet wide, with a low handrail) that sways 230 feet above rocky rapids—a nightmare for anyone the least bit afraid of heights. The other bridge was wide, sturdy, and only 10 feet from the ground. Whenever an unaccompanied young man walked across one of these bridges, he was met by an attractive young woman who introduced herself as a research assistant, asked him to fill out a brief questionnaire, and gave her phone number in case he wanted more information about the project. As predicted, men who crossed the scary bridge were later more likely to call her than those who crossed the stable bridge. In a study of "love at first fright" that took place in two amusement parks, Cindy Meston and Penny Frohlich (2003) similarly found that men and women who were not with a romantic partner rated a photographed person of the opposite sex as more attractive right after they rode on a roller coaster than they did before they began the ride. Perhaps terror can fan the hot flames of romance.

Or maybe not. Maybe it's just a relief to be with someone when we're in distress. To rule out the possibility that relief rather than arousal is what fuels attraction, Gregory White and his colleagues (1981) had to create arousal without distress. How? A little

**excitation transfer**  The process whereby arousal caused by one stimulus is added to arousal from a second stimulus and the combined arousal is attributed to the second stimulus.

exercise can do it. Male participants ran in place for either 2 minutes or 15 seconds and then saw a videotape of a woman they expected to meet. The woman had been made up to look physically attractive or unattractive. After watching the video, participants rated her appearance. The result: Those who exercised for 2 minutes as opposed to only 15 seconds saw the physically attractive woman as even more attractive and the unattractive woman as less attractive. This study and others like it (Allen et al., 1989) showed that arousal—even without distress—intensifies emotional reactions, positive or negative.

In June of 2011, after the Vancouver Canucks hockey team lost the Stanley Cup, a riot broke out in the city. Many people were injured; many others were arrested. Illustrating the intense state of absorption that defines passionate love, this young couple was photographed amidst the chaos kissing in the street. *Sports Illustrated* called this iconic image "the most compelling sports image of the year."

The implication of this research—that our passions are at the mercy of bridges, roller coasters, exercise, and anything else that causes the heart to race—is intriguing. It is certainly consistent with the common observation that people are vulnerable to falling in love when their lives are turbulent. But does the effect occur, as theorized, because people *mis*attribute their arousal to a person they have just met? Yes and no. Based on their review of 33 experiments, Craig Foster and others (1998) confirmed that the arousal–attraction effect does exist. They also found, however, that the effect occurs even when people know the actual source of their arousal—in other words, even without misattribution. According to these investigators, just being aroused, even if we know why, facilitates whatever is the most natural response. If the person we meet is good-looking and of the right sex, we become more attracted. If the person is not good-looking or is of the wrong sex, we become less attracted. No thought is required. The response is automatic.

It is now clear that passionate love is erotic and highly sexualized. In a book titled *Lust: What We Know About Human Sexual Desire*, Pamela Regan and Ellen Berscheid (1999) present compelling evidence for the proposition that intense sexual desire and excitement are a vital part of passionate love. In this regard, they note that "loving" is different from "being in love." To illustrate, Berscheid and Meyers (1996) asked college men and women to make three lists: people they loved, people they were in love with, and people they were sexually attracted to. As it turned out, only 2% of those in the "love" category also appeared in the sex list. Yet among those in the "in love" category, the overlap with sex was 85%. And when Regan and her colleagues (1998) asked people to list the characteristics of romantic love, two-thirds cited sexual desire—more than the number who put happiness, loyalty, communication, sharing, or commitment on the list.

Romantic ideals notwithstanding, many people doubt the staying power of passionate love. Does the fire within a relationship burn hot and bright over time, or is it just a passing infatuation? Comparisons of couples at different stages of their relationships and longitudinal studies that measure changes in the same couples over time have suggested that intense, sexual, passionate love does tend to diminish somewhat over time (Acker & Davis, 1992). Yet this decline is not clearly defined or inevitable. Bianca Acevedo and Arthur Aron (2009) meta-analyzed past survey research and asked couples who had been together for varying lengths of time questions about passionate love. They found that although the initial "obsessional" aspect of passionate love clearly diminishes in long-term relationships ("I sometimes find it difficult to concentrate on work

According to excitation transfer theory, bodily arousal triggered by one stimulus can be misattributed to another stimulus. This theory suggests that the energy that springs from dancing may intensify a person's feelings for his or her partner, fanning the flames of passion.

because thoughts of my partner occupy my mind"), there is a "romantic" aspect that often endures ("I would rather be with my partner than anyone else"). Acevedo and others (2012) next studied men and women who were married an average of 21 years—and who reported long-term, intense, romantic love for their partner. They had these participants undergo fMRI while viewing facial images of their partner; a highly familiar acquaintance; a close friend; and a low-familiar person. The scans revealed activity in regions of the brain that were specific to their partner—namely, in dopamine-rich reward areas and areas that are typically activated by maternal attachment. More research is needed, but these results support the self-report data that for some people, the intense love of their long-term partner may last for long periods of time.

**Companionate Love** In contrast to the intense, emotional, erotic, and sometimes obsessional nature of passionate love, companionate love is a form of affection that binds close friends as well as lovers. Companionate relationships rest on a foundation of mutual trust, caring, respect, friendship, and commitment—characteristics that John Harvey and Julie Omarzu (2000) see as necessary for "minding the close relationship."

Compared with the passionate form of love, companionate love is less intense but is in some respects deeper and more enduring. Susan Sprecher and Pamela Regan (1998) administered passionate and companionate love scales to heterosexual couples who had been together for varying amounts of time and found that the passionate love scores of both men and women initially rose over time but then peaked and declined somewhat during marriage. Companionate love scores, however, did not similarly decline. In fact, in couples that stay together, partners are likely to report that "I love you more today than yesterday" (Sprecher, 1999). Like the slow but steady tortoise in Aesop's fable, companionate love may seem to be outpaced by the flashier start of passionate love, but it can still cross the finish line well ahead.

Companionate love is characterized by high levels of **self-disclosure**, a willingness to open up and share intimate facts and feelings. In a way, self-disclosure is to companionate love what arousal is to passionate love. Think for a moment about your most embarrassing moment, your most cherished ambitions, or your sex life. Would you bare your soul on these private matters to a complete stranger? What about a casual acquaintance, date, friend, or lover? Whether or not to self-disclose—what, when, how much, and to whom—is a decision that each of us makes based on a consideration of what we stand to gain and lose in a relationship (Omarzu, 2000).

The willingness to disclose intimate facts and feelings lies at the heart of our closest and most intimate relationships (Derlega et al., 1993). Research shows that the more emotionally involved people are in a close relationship, the more they self-disclose to each other. Nancy Collins and Lynn Miller (1994) note three possible reasons for this correlation: (1) We disclose to people we like; (2) we like people who disclose to us; and (3) we like people to whom we have disclosed. Thus, among pairs of college students brought together in a laboratory for brief getting-acquainted conversations, the more they self-disclosed, the better they felt about each other afterward (Vittengl & Holt, 2000). In a longitudinal study of adult dating couples, partners who reported higher levels of self-disclosure also expressed more satisfaction, commitment, and love (Sprecher & Hendrick, 2004). When it comes to sex, too, partners who self-disclose their likes and dislikes to each other are more satisfied sexually than those who are less open (MacNeil & Byers, 2009).

Over the years, researchers have observed three patterns of self-disclosure in social relationships. One is that partners reveal more to each other as their relationship grows

*"True love never grows old."*

—Proverb

*"As soon as you cannot keep anything from a woman, you love her."*

—Paul Geraldy

**self-disclosure** Revelations about the self that a person makes to others.

over time. According to Irving Altman and Dalmas Taylor (1973), self-disclosure is a basic form of social exchange that unfolds as relationships develop. Their *social penetration theory* holds that relationships progress from superficial exchanges to more intimate ones. At first, people give relatively little of themselves to each other and receive little in return. If the initial encounters prove rewarding, however, the exchanges become both *broader* (covering more areas of their lives) and *deeper* (involving more sensitive areas). In short, social interaction grows from a narrow, shallow sliver to a wider, more penetrating wedge.

Recently, Tang and Wang (2012) conducted an online survey to explore the topics that 1,027 bloggers in Taiwan disclosed on their blogs and in the real world. Their results showed that bloggers self-disclose on a range of topics—including their attitudes, body, money, work, feelings, interests, and experiences. With regard to what is self-disclosed to three target audiences (online, best friend, and parents), bloggers expressed themselves to their best friends the most, followed by parents and online audiences, both in depth and in width. It appears that social penetration theory—proposed long before there was an Internet—provides a good description of self-disclosure, today, in online relationships.

A second observation is that patterns of self-disclosure change according to the state of a relationship. During a first encounter and in the budding stages of a new relationship, people tend to reciprocate another's self-disclosure with their own—at a comparable level of intimacy. If a new acquaintance opens up, it is polite to match that self-disclosure by revealing more of ourselves. Once a relationship is well established, however, strict reciprocity occurs less frequently (Altman, 1973; Derlega et al., 1976). Among couples in distress, two different self-disclosure patterns have been observed. For some, breadth and depth both decrease as partners withdraw and cease to communicate (Baxter, 1987). For others, the breadth of self-disclosure declines but depth increases as the partners express anger at each other (Tolstedt & Stokes, 1984). In this case, the social *de*penetration process resembles neither the sliver of a superficial affiliation nor the wedge of a close relationship but rather a long, thin dagger of discontent.

A third common observation is that individuals differ in the tendency to share private, intimate thoughts with others. For example, Kathryn Dindia and Mike Allen (1992) conducted a meta-analysis of 205 studies involving 23,702 white North Americans and found, on average, that women are more open than men—and that people in general are more self-disclosing to women than to men. This being the case, it comes as no surprise that women rate their same-sex friendships more highly than men rate theirs. At least in North America, male friends seem to bond more by taking part in common activities, whereas female friends engage more in a sharing of feelings (Duck & Wright, 1993). As Paul Wright (1982) put it, women tend to interact "face-to-face" but men go "side-by-side."

##  Culture, Attraction, and Close Relationships

In looking at attraction, desire, relationships, and love, one wonders: Are people all over the world similar or different? To what extent are these processes universal or different from one culture to another? In recent years, several social psychologists have raised these kinds of questions (Hatfield et al., 2007).

In his original cross-cultural study of mate selection, for example, Buss (1989) found that physical attractiveness is more important to men all over the world and that financial resources are more important to women—gender differences that appeared to be universal. Yet even Buss was struck by the powerful impact that culture had on mate preferences. In China, India, Indonesia, Iran, Taiwan, and the Palestinian territories of Israel, for example, people valued chastity in a mate. Yet in Finland, France, Norway,

Sweden, the Netherlands, and West Germany, chastity was either unimportant or negatively valued.

When it comes to close relationships, research has shown that passionate love is a widespread and universal emotion. In surveys conducted throughout the world, William Jankowiak and Edward Fischer (1992) detected indications of passionate love in 147 out of 166 cultures as varied as Indonesia, China, Turkey, Nigeria, Trinidad, Morocco, Australia, and Micronesia. Drawing on this universality, some researchers have begun to explore the underlying neuroscience. For example, anthropologist Helen Fisher (2004) believes that romantic love is hard-wired in the neurochemistry of the brain. In particular, Fisher argues that the neurotransmitter dopamine, which drives animals to seek rewards such as food and sex, is essential to the pleasure that is felt when these drives are satisfied. Hence, she argues, dopamine levels are associated with both the highs of romantic passion and the lows of rejection. Citing evidence from studies of humans and other animals, she also points to neurochemical parallels between romantic love and substance addiction.

Although most people in the world agree that sexual desire is what injects the passion into passionate love, not everyone sees it as necessary for marriage. Think about this question: If a man or woman had all other qualities you desired, would you marry this person if you were *not* in love? When American students were surveyed in 1967, 35% of men and 76% of women said yes. Twenty years later, only 14% of men and 20% of women said they would marry someone with whom they were not in love (Simpson et al., 1986). The shift among women may reflect the pragmatic point that marrying for love is an economic luxury that few women of the past could afford. As seen in the current popularity of prenuptial agreements, pragmatic considerations continue to influence marriage practices, even today.

The willingness to marry without love is also highly subject to cultural variation. In light of the different values that pervade individualist and collectivist cultures, the differences are not surprising. In many cultures, marriage is seen as a transaction between families that is influenced by social, economic, and religious considerations. Indeed, arranged marriages are still common in India, China, many Muslim countries, and sub-Saharan Africa. So, when Robert Levine and others (1995) asked college students from 11 countries about marrying without love, they found that the percentage who said they would do so ranged from 4% in the United States, 5% in Australia, and 8% in England, up to 49% in India, and 51% in Pakistan.

> "To an American in love, his/her emotions tend to overshadow everything else . . . to a Chinese in love, his/her love occupies a place among other considerations."
> —Hsu

In cultures in which love is not a sufficient basis for marriage, other factors play a role. In India, a historically entrenched caste system divides its citizens and holds sway over love and marriage (Singh, 2009). Indeed, even though the government legalized intercaste marriage more than 50 years ago and is now offering incentives for intercaste couples to marry, an invisible separation remains between the upper and lower castes that lasts from birth to death—and "honor killings" of couples who dare to cross these traditional lines are not uncommon (Wax, 2008). In China, where a cultural premium is placed on devotion, respect, and obedience of children to parents and other family elders, there is far less emphasis on the Western "fairytale ideals" of love and romance (Higgins et al., 2002; Jackson et al., 2006). In recent surveys, young adults in China, more than in the United States, said they would be influenced in their mate selection decisions by parents and close friends—for example, that they would try to persuade their parents to accept a dating partner and stop dating that partner if their parents did not approve (Zhang & Kline, 2009).

The influence of culture on love is interesting. On the one hand, it could be argued that the rugged individualism found in many Western cultures would inhibit the tendency to become intimate and interdependent with others. On the other hand, individualism leads people to give priority in making marital decisions to their own feelings rather than to family concerns, social obligations, religious constraints, income, and the like (Dion & Dion, 1996). In an illustration of this point, Fred Rothbaum and Bill Yuk-Piu Tsang (1998) compared popular love songs in the United States and China. They found that the American lyrics focused more on the two lovers as isolated entities, independent of social context ("There is nobody here, it's just you and me, the way I want it to be").

Tushar Agarwal and his bride Richa are married in a wedding ceremony in Bombay. Fulfilling a tradition that seems strange to most Americans, for whom being in love is essential, this Indian marriage was arranged.

## Relationship Issues: The Male–Female Connection

Browse the offerings of any real or online bookstore and you'll see one title after another on the general topic of gender. There are books for men and books for women, books that preach the masculine ideal and books that tell us how to be more feminine, books that portray men and women as similar and books that accentuate the differences. Is it true, to borrow John Gray's (1997) provocative book title, that *Men Are from Mars, Women Are from Venus*? If so, what are the implications when it comes to male–female relationships?

**Sexuality**   More than a hundred years ago, Sigmund Freud shocked the scientific community by proposing psychoanalytic theory, which placed great emphasis on sex as a driving force in human behavior. At the time, Freud's closest associates rejected this focus on sexual motivation. But was he wrong? Sexual images and themes pop up, quite literally, in our dreams, in the jokes we tell, in the TV shows we watch, in the novels we read, in the music we hear, and in the sex scandals that swirl around public figures in the news. It's no wonder that advertisers use sex to sell everything from blue jeans to perfume, soft drinks, and cars.

Sex, a most private aspect of human relations, is difficult to study systematically. During the 1940s, biologist Alfred Kinsey and his colleagues (1948; 1953) conducted the first large-scale survey of sexual practices in the United States. Based on confidential interviews of more than 17,000 men and women, these researchers sought for the first time to describe what nobody would openly talk about: sexual activity. Many of his results were shocking; reported sexual activity was more frequent and more varied than anyone had expected. Kinsey's books were instant bestsellers. Certain aspects of his methodology were flawed, however. For example, participants were mostly young, white, urban, and middle class— hardly a representative sample. He also asked leading questions to enable respondents to report on sexual activities—or make up stories (Jones, 1997a). Kinsey died in 1954, but his Institute for Sex Research at Indiana University remains to this day a major center for the study of human sexuality.

Since Kinsey's groundbreaking study, many sex surveys have been conducted, and they form part of the research history that has been chronicled, both seriously and with humor, in books with such titles as *Kiss and Tell: Surveying Sex in the Twentieth Century* (Ericksen & Steffen, 1999), and *Bonk: The Curious Coupling of Science and Sex* (Roach,

Pioneering sex researcher Alfred Kinsey.

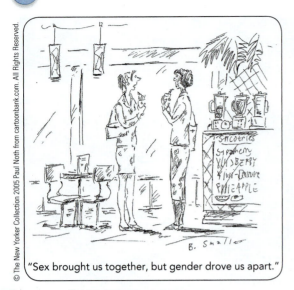

"Sex brought us together, but gender drove us apart."

2008). The limits of self-reports—regardless of whether they are taken in face-to-face interviews, telephone surveys, or on the Internet—is that we can never know for sure how accurate the results are. Part of the problem is that respondents may not be honest in their disclosures. Another limiting factor is that people differ in their interpretations of survey questions.

Researchers have used an array of methods to measure sexual attitudes and behavior. Studies of everyday interactions reveal that men view the world in more sexualized terms than women do. In 1982, Antonia Abbey arranged for pairs of male and female college students to talk for 5 minutes while other students observed the sessions. When she later questioned the actors and observers, Abbey found that the males were more sexually attracted to the females than vice versa. The males also rated the female actors as being more seductive and more flirtatious than the women had rated themselves as being. Among men more than women, eye contact, a compliment, a friendly remark, a brush against the arm, and an innocent smile are often interpreted as sexual come-ons (Kowalski, 1993). Despite all that has changed in recent years, these gender differences in perceptions of sexual interest still exist (Levesque et al., 2006). A recent speed-dating study showed that whereas men *over*perceive sexual interest, women tend to *under*perceive sexual interest (Perilloux et al., 2012).

Gender differences are particularly common in self-report surveys, where in contrast to women, men report being more promiscuous, more likely to think about sex, more permissive, more likely to enjoy casual sex without emotional commitment, and more likely to fantasize about sex with multiple partners (Oliver & Hyde, 1993). When asked to select 10 private wishes from a list, for example, most men and women similarly wanted love, health, peace on earth, unlimited ability, and wealth. But more men than women also wanted "to have sex with anyone I choose" (Ehrlichman & Eichenstein, 1992). In a large-scale study of 16,000 respondents from 52 countries all over the world, David Schmitt (2003) found that most men desire more sex partners and more sexual variety than most women do, regardless of their relationship status or sexual orientation. Based on this study and others, Roy Baumeister and others (2001) concluded that "men desire sex more than women" (p. 270).

**Men are more likely than women to interpret friendly gestures by the opposite sex in sexual terms. T**RUE.

*In an ABC* Primetime *survey of 1,501 American adults, a number of gender differences were found (Longer et al., 2004):*

|  | Men | Women |
| --- | --- | --- |
| *Think about sex every day* | *70%* | *34%* |
| *Have visited a sex website* | *34%* | *10%* |
| *Have fantasized about a threesome* | *33%* | *9%* |

**sexual orientation** A person's preference for members of the same sex (homosexuality), opposite sex (heterosexuality), or both sexes (bisexuality).

**Sexual Orientation**   At a time when policy makers, judges, religious leaders, scholars, and laypeople openly debate the topic of gay marriage, no discussion of human sexuality is complete without a consideration of differences in **sexual orientation**—defined as one's sexual preference for members of the same sex (homosexuality), the opposite sex (heterosexuality), or both sexes (bisexuality).

How common is homosexuality, and where does it come from? Throughout history and in all cultures, a vast majority of people have been heterosexual in their orientation. But how vast a majority is a subject of some debate. A 1970 survey funded by the Kinsey Institute revealed that 3.3% of American men sampled said that they had frequent or occasional homosexual sex (Fay et al., 1989). Between 1989 and 1992, the National Opinion Research Center reported that 2.8% of American men and 2.5% of women had exclusive homosexual activity. Together, large-scale surveys in the United States, Europe, Asia, and the Pacific suggest that the exclusively homosexual population in the world is 3% or 4% among men and about half that number among women (Diamond, 1993).

Although an exclusive homosexual orientation is relatively rare among humans and other animals, homosexual *behaviors* are more common. In *Biological Exuberance*, Bruce Bagemihl (1999) reports that sexual encounters among male–male and female–female pairs have been observed in more than 450 species, including giraffes, goats, birds, chimpanzees, and lizards. Among humans, the incidence of homosexual behavior varies from one generation and culture to the next, depending on prevailing attitudes. In *Same Sex, Different Cultures*, Gilbert Herdt (1998) notes that in parts of the world, stretching from Sumatra to Melanesia, it's common for adolescent males to engage in homosexual activities before being of age for marriage, even though homosexuality as a permanent trait is rare. It's important, then, to realize that sexual orientation cannot be viewed in black-or-white terms but should be seen along a continuum. In the center of that continuum, 1% of people describe themselves as actively bisexual.

To explain the roots of homosexuality, various theories have been proposed. The Greek philosopher Aristotle believed that it was inborn but strengthened by habit; post-Freud psychoanalysts argue that it stems from family dynamics, specifically a child's over-attachment to a parent of the same or opposite sex; social learning theorists point to rewarding sexual experiences with same-sex peers in childhood. Yet there is little hard evidence to support these claims. In a particularly comprehensive study, Alan Bell and others (1981) interviewed 1,500 homosexual and heterosexual adults about their lives. There were no differences in past family backgrounds, absence of a male or female parent, relationship with parents, sexual abuse, age of onset of puberty, or high school dating patterns. Except for the fact that homosexual adults described themselves as less conforming as children, the two groups could not be distinguished by past experiences. Both groups felt strongly that their sexual orientation was set long before it was "official."

Increasingly, there is scientific evidence of a biological disposition. In a highly publicized study, neurobiologist Simon LeVay (1991) autopsied the brains of 19 homosexual men who had died of AIDS, 16 heterosexual men (some of whom had died of AIDS), and 6 heterosexual women. LeVay examined a tiny nucleus in the hypothalamus that is involved in regulating sexual behavior and is known to be larger in heterosexual men than in women. The specimens were numerically coded, so LeVay did not know whether a particular donor he was examining was male or female, straight or gay. The result: In the male homosexual brains he studied, the nucleus was half the size as in male heterosexual brains and comparable in size to those found in female heterosexual brains. This research is described in Levay's (1993) book *The Sexual Brain*.

It's important to recognize that this study revealed only a correlation between sexual orientation and the brain and cannot be used to draw conclusions about cause and effect. More convincing support for the biological roots of sexual orientation comes from twin studies suggesting that there is a genetic predisposition. Michael Bailey and Richard Pillard (1991) surveyed 167 gay men and their twins and adopted brothers. Overall, 52% of the identical twins were gay, compared to only 22% of fraternal twins and 11% of adoptive brothers. Two years later, Bailey and others (1993) conducted a companion study of lesbians with similar results.

The origins of sexual orientation are complex for two reasons. First, it's not clear that sexual orientation for men and women is similarly rooted. In Australia, Bailey and others (2000) had hundreds of pairs of twins rate their own sexuality on a seven-point scale that ranged from "exclusively heterosexual" to "exclusively homosexual." Overall, 92% of both men and women saw themselves as exclusively heterosexual. Among the others, however, more women than men said that they had bisexual tendencies and more men than women said they were exclusively homosexual. In another study, a longitudinal investigation of 18- to 25-year-old women, Lisa Diamond (2003) found that more than a quarter of those who had initially identified themselves as lesbian or bisexual changed their orientation over the next 5 years—far more change than is ever reported among men.

Recent experiments in laboratory settings reinforce the point. In one study, Meredith Chivers and others (2004) recruited men and women who had identified themselves as heterosexual or homosexual in their orientation. In a private, dimly lit room, these participants watched a series of brief sex clips—some involving male couples, others involving female couples. While watching, the participants rated their subjective feelings of sexual attraction on a scale. At the same time, genital arousal was measured using devices that recorded penile erection (for males) and vaginal pulse (for females). Results showed that the women were genitally aroused by both male *and* female sex clips, regardless of whether they identified themselves as straight or lesbian in their orientation. Yet males exhibited more genital arousal in response to men *or* women, depending on their sexual orientation. In fact, although self-identified bisexual men reported an attraction to both sexes, most were genitally aroused by men or by women—but not both (Rieger et al., 2005). Although one study has since identified a group of men who are bisexual in their genital arousal (Rosenthal et al., 2012), a number of other findings too compel the conclusion that women are sexually more flexible than men, having more *erotic plasticity*. Simply put, women are more open and more likely to change sexual preferences over the course of a lifetime (Baumeister, 2000; Diamond, 2007; Peplau, 2003; Lippa, 2006).

A second complicating factor is that although there is strong evidence for a biological disposition, this does not necessarily mean that there's a "gay gene" (Hamer et al., 1999). Rather, Daryl Bem (1996; 2000) sees the development of sexual orientation as a *psycho*biological process. According to Bem, genes influence a person's temperament at birth, leading some infants and young children to be naturally more active, energetic, and aggressive than others. These differences in temperament draw some children to male playmates and "masculine" activities and others to female playmates and "feminine" activities. Bem refers to children who prefer same-sex playmates as gender conformists and to those who prefer opposite-sex playmates as gender nonconformists ("sissies" and "tomboys").

Activity preferences in childhood may be biologically rooted, but what happens next is the psychological part. According to Bem, gender-conforming children come to see members of the opposite sex as different, unfamiliar, arousing, and even exotic. Gender-nonconforming children, in contrast, come to see same-sex peers as different, unfamiliar, arousing, and exotic. Later, at puberty, as children become physically and sexually mature, they find that they are attracted to members of the same or opposite sex—depending on which is the more exotic. Bem describes his proposed chain of events as the "exotic becomes erotic" theory of sexual orientation.

At present, there is only sketchy support for this theory. It is true that genetic makeup can influence temperament and predispose a child to favor certain kinds of activities over others (Kagan, 1994). It is also true that gay men are likely to have been more feminine and lesbians to have been more masculine as children—differences seen not only in people's self-reported accounts from childhood (Bailey & Zucker, 1995) but also in their behavior, as memorialized in home videos (Rieger et al., 2008). It may even be true that people are genetically hard-wired to engage in gender-nonconforming behavior as children (Bailey et al., 2000). But do peer preferences in childhood alter adult sexual orientation, as Bem suggests, because the exotic becomes erotic? Or is there a "gay gene" that fosters gender nonconformity in childhood as well as homosexuality in adolescence and adulthood? And can a single theory explain homosexuality in both men and women or are separate theories needed, as some have suggested (Peplau et al., 1998)? At present, more research is needed to answer these questions and tease apart the biological and psychological influences. Either way, one point looms large:

On June 17, 2008, Sharon Papo and Amber Weiss exchanged wedding vows on the first full day of same-sex marriages in San Francisco. Nine states now legally permit gay marriage; a handful of others permit civil unions or domestic partnerships.

Erin Siegal/Reuters/Landov

People, especially men, do not seem to willfully choose their sexual orientation, nor can they easily change it.

Is there any reason to believe that the attraction process and the formation of intimate relationships are any different for same-sex couples? Not really. According to the U.S. Census Bureau, an estimated 650,000 same-sex couples were living together in the United States in 2010—up substantially from 10 years earlier. An estimated 132,000 reported that they were married. Recent research shows that gays and lesbians meet people in the same ways as straights, by seeking out others who are attractive and similar in their attitudes; that their satisfaction and commitment levels are affected by social exchange and equity concerns just as they are in heterosexual relationships; and that they report levels of liking and loving in their intimate relationships that are comparable to those in heterosexual couples. Same-sex couples differ from straight couples in two ways: They are more likely to retain friendships with former sex partners after breaking up, and they tend to divide chores more equally within a household (Kurdek, 2005; Peplau & Fingerhut, 2007). In light of these striking similarities, and with same-sex marriage now legal in six states, more research on gay and lesbian couples is sure to be conducted in the coming years.

*In 2001, the Netherlands became the first modern nation to grant same-sex marriages full legal status. Same-sex marriage has since become legal in Belgium (2003), Spain (2005), Canada (2005), South Africa (2006), Norway (2009), Sweden (2009), Portugal (2010), Iceland (2010), and Argentina (2010).*

**The Marital Trajectory**   Because we are social beings, having close relationships is important to us all—for our happiness and emotional well-being and even our physical health and longevity. As noted at the start of this chapter, 73% of American college students surveyed said they would sacrifice most other life goals rather than give up a satisfying relationship (Hammersla & Frease-McMahan, 1990). Yet sadly, if they live in the United States or Canada, these students live in a society in which roughly 40% of first marriages are likely to end in divorce. With just one previously divorced partner, the odds of divorce are even greater. This discrepancy between the stability most people want and the disruption they may have to confront is dramatic. Couples argue, break up, separate, and divorce. How do marriages evolve over time, and why do some last while others dissolve?

Ellen Berscheid and Harry Reis (1998) say that for social psychologists who study intimate relationships, this is the most frequently asked and vexing question. Is there a typical developmental pattern? No and yes. No, it's clear that all marriages are different and cannot be squeezed into a single mold. But yes, certain patterns do emerge when survey results are combined from large numbers of married couples that have been studied over long periods of time. Lawrence Kurdek (1999) reported on a longitudinal study of married couples in which he measured each spouse's satisfaction every year for 10 years (of the 522 couples he started with, 93 completed the study). ● Figure 9.13 shows that there was an overall decline in ratings of marital quality and that the ratings given by husbands and wives were very similar. There are two marked periods of decline. The first occurs during the first year of marriage. Newlyweds tend to idealize each other and to enjoy an initial state of marital bliss (Murray et al., 1996). However, this "honeymoon" is soon followed by a decline in satisfaction (Bradbury, 1998). After some stabilization, a second decline is observed at about the eighth year of marriage—a finding that is consistent with the popular belief in a "seven-year itch" (Kovacs, 1983).

This marital trajectory is interesting, but it represents a crude average of different types of marriages. There is no single mold, however, and one size does not fit all relationships. Realizing this limitation, researchers are actively seeking to plot more precise trend lines for specific marital situations. Thus far, these studies have shown that in heterosexual couples with a first child, the transition to parenthood hastens the sense of decline in both partners (Lawrence et al., 2008); that cohabiting gay and lesbian couples do not self-report the lowered satisfaction often seen in heterosexual couples (Kurdek, 2008);

● **FIGURE 9.13**

**Marital Satisfaction Over Time**

In a longitudinal study that spanned 10 years, married couples rated the quality of their marriages. On average, these ratings were high, but they declined among both husbands and wives. As you can see, there were two steep drops, occurring during the first and eighth years of marriage.

From Kurdek, L. A., "The nature and predictors of the trajectory of change in marital quality for husbands and wives over the first 10 years of marriage," *Developmental Psychology* vol 35 (pp. 1283–1296). Copyright © 1999 by the American Psychological Association. Reprinted by permission.

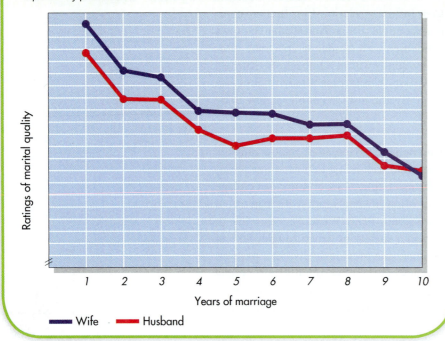

**Years of marriage**

— Wife  — Husband

and that, despite the initial dip, marital satisfaction increases again in middle age for parents whose children grow up, leave home, and empty the nest (Gorchoff et al., 2008).

Do specific factors predict future outcomes? To address this question, Benjamin Karney and Thomas Bradbury (1995) reviewed 115 longitudinal studies of more than 45,000 married couples and found only that certain positively valued variables (education, employment, constructive behaviors, similarity in attitudes) are somewhat predictive of positive outcomes. They did find, however, that the steeper the initial decline in satisfaction, the more likely couples are to break up later. This decline is, in part, related to the stress of having and raising children, a stress that is common among newly married couples. Boredom is also predictive of a loss in marital satisfaction. In a longitudinal study of 123 married couples, husbands and wives who felt like they were in a rut at one point in time were significantly less satisfied nine years later (Tsapelas et al., 2009).

Is there anything a couple can do to avoid a rut and keep the honeymoon alive? Perhaps there is. Arthur Aron and his colleagues (2000) have theorized that after the exhilaration of a new relationship wears off, partners can combat boredom by engaging together in new and arousing activities. By means of questionnaires and a door-to-door survey, these researchers found that the more new experiences spouses said they'd had together, the more satisfied they were with their marriages. To test this hypothesis in a controlled experiment, they brought randomly selected couples into the laboratory, spread gymnasium mats across the floor, tied the partners together at a wrist and ankle, and had them crawl on their hands and knees, over a barrier, from one end of the room to the other—all while carrying a pillow between their bodies. Other couples were given the more mundane task of rolling a ball across the mat, one partner at a time. A third group received no assignment. Afterward, all participants were asked about their relationships. As predicted, the couples that had struggled and laughed their way through the novel and arousing activity reported more satisfaction with the quality of their relationships than did those in the mundane and no-task groups. It's possible that the benefit of shared participation in this study was short-lived. But maybe, just maybe, a steady and changing diet of exciting new experiences can help keep the flames of love burning.

After the honeymoon period, there is an overall decline in levels of marital satisfaction. **T**RUE.

**Communication and Conflict** Disagreements about sex, children, money, in-laws, and other matters can stir conflict in close relationships. Of particular relevance during turbulent economic times, research shows that financial pressures can put enormous amounts of strain on marital relations (Conger et al., 1999). Whatever the cause, all couples experience some degree of friction. The issue is not whether it occurs but how we respond to it. One source of conflict is the difficulty some people have talking about their disagreements. When relationships break up, communication problems are among the most common causes cited by straight and gay couples alike (Kurdek, 1991b; Sprecher, 1994). But what constitutes "bad communication"? Comparisons between happy and distressed couples have revealed a number of communication patterns that often occur in troubled relationships (Fincham, 2003).

One common pattern is called *negative affect reciprocity*—a tit-for-tat exchange of expressions of negative feelings. Generally speaking, expressions of negative affect within a couple trigger more in-kind responses than do expressions of positive affect. But negative affect reciprocity, especially in nonverbal behavior, is greater in couples that are unhappy, distressed, and locked into a duel. For couples in distress, smiles pass by unnoticed, but every glare, every disgusted look, provokes a sharp reflex-like response. The result, as observed in unhappy couples around the world, is an inability to break the vicious cycle and terminate unpleasant interactions (Gottman, 1998).

Men and women react differently to conflict. Most women report more intense emotions and are more expressive than most men (Grossman & Wood, 1993). She tells him to "warm up"; he urges her to "calm down." Thus, many unhappy marriages are also characterized by a *demand/withdraw interaction pattern*, in which the wife demands that the couple discuss the relationship problems, only to become frustrated when her husband withdraws from such discussions (Christensen & Heavey, 1993). This pattern is not unique to married couples. When dating partners were asked about how they typically deal with problems, the same demand/withdraw pattern was found (Vogel et al., 1999). According to John Gottman (1994), there is nothing wrong with either approach to dealing with conflict. The problem lies in the discrepancy—that healthy relationships are most likely when both partners have similar styles of dealing with conflict.

Whatever one's style, there are two basic approaches to reducing the negative effects of conflict. The first is so obvious that it is often overlooked: Increase rewarding behavior in other aspects of the relationship. According to Gottman and Levenson (1992), marital stability rests on a "fairly high balance of positive to negative behaviors" (p. 230). If there's conflict over one issue, partners can and should search for other ways to reward each other. As the balance of positives to negatives improves, so should overall levels of satisfaction, which can reduce conflict (Huston & Vangelisti, 1991). A second approach is to try to understand the other's point of view. Being sensitive to what the partner thinks and how he or she feels enhances the quality of the relationship (Honeycutt et al., 1993; Long & Andrews, 1990). What motivates individuals in the heat of battle to make that effort to understand? For starters, it helps if they agree that there is a communication problem.

The attributions that partners make for each other's behaviors and the willingness to forgive are correlated with the quality of their relationship (Bradbury & Fincham, 1992; Fincham et al., 2007; Harvey & Manusov, 2001). As you might expect, happy couples make *relationship-enhancing attributions*: They see the partner's undesirable behaviors as caused by factors that are situational ("a bad day"), temporary ("It'll pass"), and limited in scope ("That's just a sore spot"). Yet they perceive desirable behaviors as caused by factors that are inherent in the partner, permanent, and generalizable to other aspects of the relationship. In contrast, unhappy couples flip the attributional coin on its tail by making the opposite *distress-maintaining attributions*. Thus, whereas happy couples minimize the bad and maximize the good, distressed couples don't give an inch. In light of these differing attributional patterns, it would seem that over time happy couples would get happier and miserable couples more miserable. Do they? Yes. By tracking married couples longitudinally, researchers have found that husbands and wives who made distress-maintaining attributions early in marriage reported less satisfaction at a later point in time (Fincham et al., 2000; Karney & Bradbury, 2000).

**Breaking Up** When an intimate relationship ends, as in divorce, the effect can be traumatic (Fine & Harvey, 2006)—and so stressful that people who get divorced are later 23% more likely to die early from all causes of death (Sbarra et al., 2011). As part of a longitudinal study of adults in Germany, Richard Lucas (2005) zeroed in on 817 men and women who at some point were divorced. Every year for 18 years, the participants were interviewed and asked to rate how satisfied they were with life on a scale of 0 to 10. On average, the divorcees were more than a half point less satisfied than their married counterparts. But did time heal the wound? ● Figure 9.14 shows three interesting patterns: (1) Participants had become less and less satisfied even before divorce; (2) satisfaction levels rebounded somewhat immediately after divorce; and (3) satisfaction levels never returned to original baseline levels. In short, people may adapt but often they do not fully recover from the experience.

People's ability to cope with divorce depends on the nature of the loss. One vital factor is the closeness of a relationship, or the extent to which the line between self and other becomes so blurred that mine and yours are one and the same.

Another important factor in this regard is interdependence, the social glue that binds us together. Research shows that the more interdependent couples are (as measured by the amount of time they spend together, the activities they share, and the influence each partner has over the other) and the more invested they are in the relationship, the longer it will likely last (Berscheid et al., 1989; Rusbult & Buunk, 1993) and the more devastated they will become when it ends (Fine & Sacher, 1997; Simpson, 1987). In trying to explain how people regulate the risks of forming close romantic relationships, Sandra Murray and others (2006) note that an ironic theme runs through much of the research: "The relationships that have the most potential to satisfy adult needs for interpersonal connection are the very relationships that activate the most

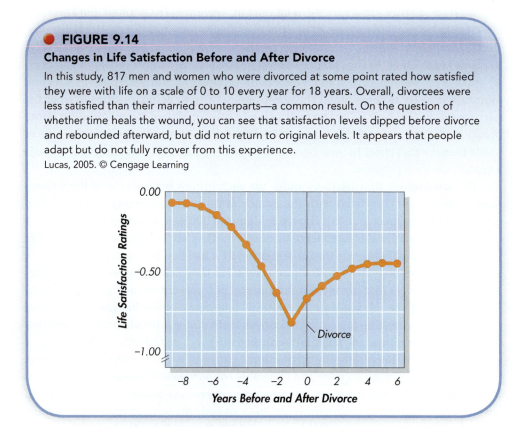

● **FIGURE 9.14**

**Changes in Life Satisfaction Before and After Divorce**

In this study, 817 men and women who were divorced at some point rated how satisfied they were with life on a scale of 0 to 10 every year for 18 years. Overall, divorcees were less satisfied than their married counterparts—a common result. On the question of whether time heals the wound, you can see that satisfaction levels dipped before divorce and rebounded afterward, but did not return to original levels. It appears that people adapt but do not fully recover from this experience.

Lucas, 2005. © Cengage Learning

anxiety about rejection" (p. 661). We are, to put it mildly, darned if we do and darned if we don't. The factors that contribute to the endurance of a relationship (closeness and interdependence) turn out to be the same factors that intensify the fear of rejection and make coping more difficult after a relationship ends. So, how do you balance making the psychological investment necessary for a lasting relationship against holding back enough for self-protection?

In the United States and other Western countries, various demographic markers indicate how problematic traditional forms of commitment have become: A high divorce rate, more single-parent families, more unmarried couples living together, and more never-married individuals. Yet the desire for long-term intimate relationships has never wavered or disappeared. On the contrary, people spend millions of dollars on online dating sites, gays and lesbians actively seek legal recognition of same-sex marriages, the vast majority of divorced individuals remarry, and stepfamilies forge a new sense of what it means to be a "family." It seems that we are in the midst of a great and compelling search as millions of men and women try to find ways to affiliate with, attract, get closer to, love, and commit themselves with permanence to other.

# Review

## Need to Belong: A Fundamental Human Motive

- The need to belong is a basic human motive, a pervasive drive to form and maintain lasting relationships.

### The Thrill of Affiliation
- This social motivation begins with the need for affiliation, a desire to establish social contact with others.
- People differ in the strength of their affiliative needs.
- Stressful situations in particular motivate us to affiliate with others who face a similar threat.

### The Agony of Loneliness
- Shyness is a pervasive problem that sets people up to have unrewarding interactions with others.

- People who are painfully shy are at risk for loneliness, a feeling of isolation and social deprivation.

> **Putting *Common Sense* to the Test**
>
> **People seek out the company of others, even strangers, in times of stress.**
>
> **True.** *Research has shown that external threat causes stress and leads people to affiliate with others who are facing or have faced a similar threat.*

## The Initial Attraction

- According to one perspective, people are attracted to others with whom the relationship is rewarding; rewards can be direct or indirect.
- Evolutionary psychologists argue that human beings exhibit patterns of attraction and mate selection that favor the passing on of their own genes.

### Familiarity: Being There
- Proximity sets the stage for social interaction, which is why friendships are most likely to form between people who live near each other.

- Supporting the mere exposure effect, studies show that the more often people see a stimulus, the more they come to like it.
- We do not have to be aware of our prior exposures for the increase in liking to occur.

### Physical Attractiveness: Getting Drawn In
- In a wide range of social settings, people respond more favorably to men and women who are physically attractive.
- Some researchers believe that certain faces (averaged and symmetrical) are inherently attractive—across cultures and to infants as well as adults.

- Others argue that beauty is in the eye of the beholder and point to the influences of culture, time, and context.
- One reason for the bias for beauty is that it's rewarding to be in the company of others who are attractive.
- A second reason is that people associate beauty with other positive qualities, a belief known as the what-is-beautiful-is-good stereotype.
- People seen as physically attractive are more popular, more sexually experienced, and more socially skilled. However, they are not happier or higher in self-esteem.
- One reason physically attractive people are not happier is that they often discount the praise they get for nonsocial endeavors.
- Another problem with having beauty as a social asset is that people, especially women, feel pressured to keep up their appearance and are often dissatisfied with how they look.

## First Encounters: Getting Acquainted
- People tend to associate with, befriend, and marry others whose demographic backgrounds, attitudes, and interests are similar to their own.
- People first avoid others who are dissimilar and then are drawn to those in the remaining group who are most similar to themselves.
- Supporting the matching hypothesis, people tend to become romantically involved with others who are equivalent in physical attractiveness.
- Contrary to popular belief, complementarity in needs or personality does not spark attraction.
- Illustrating the effects of reciprocity, we tend to like others who indicate that they like us.
- But people who are indiscriminate about who they like can be taken for granted and not be liked as much by others.

- Research on the hard-to-get effect shows that people like others best who are moderately selective in their social choices.

## Mate Selection: The Evolution of Desire
- Evolutionary psychologists say that women seek men with financial security or traits predictive of future success in order to ensure the survival of their offspring.
- In contrast, men seek women who are young and attractive (physical attributes that signal health and fertility) and are not promiscuous (an attribute that diminishes certainty of paternity).
- Cross-cultural studies tend to support these predicted sex differences, but critics note that many results are not that strong and can be viewed in terms that are more psychological than evolutionary.

---

### Putting *Common Sense* to the Test

**Infants do not discriminate between faces considered attractive and unattractive in their culture.**

**False.** *Two-month-old infants spend more time gazing at attractive than unattractive faces, indicating that they do make the distinction.*

**People who are physically attractive are happier and have higher self-esteem than those who are unattractive.**

**False.** *Attractive people are at an advantage in their social lives, but they are not happier, better adjusted, or higher in self-esteem.*

**When it comes to romantic relationships, opposites attract.**

**False.** *Consistently, people are attracted to others who are similar—not opposite or complementary—on a whole range of dimensions.*

---

# Close Relationships

- Intimate relationships include at least one of three components: feelings of attachment, fulfillment of psychological needs, and interdependence.
- Stage theories propose that close relationships go through specific stages, but evidence for a fixed sequence is weak.
- Two other views emphasize either a gradual accumulation of rewards or a sharp distinction between types of relationships.

## The Intimate Marketplace: Tracking the Gains and Losses
- According to social exchange theory, people seek to maximize gains and minimize costs in their relationships.
- Higher rewards, lower costs, and an outcome that meets or exceeds a partner's comparison level (CL) predict high levels of satisfaction.
- Lower expectations about alternatives (CLalt) and more investment in the relationship are associated with higher levels of commitment.
- Equity theory holds that satisfaction is greatest when the ratio between benefits and contributions is similar for both partners.
- Both overbenefit and underbenefit elicit negative emotions, but the underbenefited are usually less satisfied.

## Types of Relationships
- In exchange relationships, people are oriented toward reward and immediate reciprocity; in communal relationships, partners are responsive to each other's needs.
- People with secure attachment styles have more satisfying romantic relationships than do those with insecure (anxious or avoidant) styles.

## How Do I Love Thee? Counting the Ways
- According to the triangular theory of love, there are eight subtypes of love produced by the combinations of intimacy, passion, and commitment.
- Inherent in all classifications of love are two types: passionate and companionate.
- Passionate love is an intense, emotional, often erotic state of positive absorption in another person.
- In one theory, passionate love is sparked by physiological arousal and the belief that the arousal was caused by the loved person.
- Consistent with excitation transfer, arousal can increase or decrease attraction, depending on the initial attractiveness of the person whom one is with.

- Compared with passionate love, companionate love is less intense but in some respects deeper and more enduring.
- Companionate love rests on mutual trust, caring, friendship, commitment, and willingness to share intimate facts and feelings.
- Self-disclosure between partners often becomes broader and deeper over time, though self-disclosure varies with the state of the relationship.

## Culture, Attraction, and Relationships

- Although Buss identified universal gender differences in mate preference, he also found some striking cultural differences, for example in differing preferences for chastity.
- The universality of passionate love has led some researchers to explore the neuroscientific bases for this experience.
- Cultures differ in the extent to which romantic love is seen as necessary for marriage.

## Relationship Issues: The Male–Female Connection

- People vary in how they define what it means to "have sex."
- On average, men report being sexually more active than women and see opposite-sex interactions in more sexualized terms.
- An estimated 3 or 4% of men and 2% of women are exclusively homosexual in orientation.
- Both biological and environmental theories are used to explain the origins of homosexuality.
- When relationships break up, communication problems are among the most common causes.
- Unhappy couples often engage in negative affect reciprocity and exhibit a demand/withdraw interaction pattern.

- During conflict, women are more likely to be demanding and men are more likely to withdraw.
- Partners can reduce conflict by behaving in rewarding ways in other areas and by trying to understand each other's point of view.
- Happy couples make relationship-enhancing attributions, while unhappy couples make distress-maintaining attributions.
- On average, marital satisfaction starts high, declines during the first year, stabilizes, and then declines again at about the eighth year.
- Partners who are close and interdependent and for whom relationships are important to the self-concept (characteristics that normally promote stability) suffer more after breaking up.

### Putting *Common Sense* to the Test

**Men are more likely than women to interpret friendly gestures by the opposite sex in sexual terms.**

**True.** *Experiments have shown that men are more likely than women to interpret friendly interactions with members of the opposite sex as sexual come-ons.*

**After the honeymoon period, there is an overall decline in levels of marital satisfaction.**

**True.** *High marital satisfaction levels among newlyweds are often followed by a measurable decline during the first year and then, after a period of stabilization, by another decline at the eighth year—a pattern found among parents and nonparents alike.*

## KEY TERMS

attachment style (371)
communal relationship (371)
companionate love (373)
equity theory (370)
exchange relationship (371)
excitation transfer (374)
hard-to-get effect (358)

intimate relationship (367)
loneliness (344)
matching hypothesis (357)
mere exposure effect (346)
need for affiliation (342)
passionate love (373)
reciprocity (357)

self-disclosure (376)
sexual orientation (380)
social exchange theory (368)
triangular theory of love (373)
what-is-beautiful-is-good stereotype (352)

## MEDIA RESOURCES

Go to CengageBrain.com to access Psychology CourseMate, where you will find an interactive eBook, glossaries, flashcards, quizzes, videos, and more.

# Helping Others

This chapter describes the social psychology of giving and receiving help. We examine the evolutionary, motivational, situational, personal, and interpersonal factors that predict whether a potential helper will provide assistance to a person in need. In the concluding section, we discuss the helping connection, the role of social ties in promoting helpfulness to others.

# 10

**It was their bravery** that compelled them to risk their lives, but it was their compassion that ultimately saved them. Six firefighters from New York City's Ladder Company 6 were among the many rescue workers who courageously climbed up the stairs of the World Trade Center on September 11, 2001. The jets that had flown into each of the Twin Towers of the skyscraper were hemorrhaging fuel, causing an inferno of unprecedented proportion. A massive stream of people trying to flee raced down the narrow stairs, passing the firefighters who were going up. Awed by their courage and resolve, people yelled encouragement and blessings to the firefighters as they passed them. Under the burden of more than 100 pounds of equipment, the men of Ladder Company 6 had reached the 27th floor of the North Tower when they heard the horrifying sound of the South Tower collapsing. Their captain ordered them to turn back, realizing that if the other tower could collapse, so could theirs.

On their way down, around the 14th or 15th floor, they encountered a frail woman named Josephine Harris. She had walked down almost 60 flights already, and she was exhausted. The firefighters helped her walk, but she was slowing them down dangerously. Their captain, John Jonas, was growing more anxious: "I could hear the clock ticking in the back of my head. I'm thinking, 'C'mon, c'mon. We've got to keep moving.'" But none of the six men considered leaving her behind, so they slowly walked down together. Josephine didn't think she could go on, but one of the firefighters asked her about her family and told her that her children and grandchildren wanted to see her again. She continued but finally collapsed as they got near the fourth floor. On the fourth floor, they tried to find a chair to carry her in. And then, the 110-story skyscraper collapsed all around them.

Other rescue workers who had passed this slow-moving group on the stairs were killed on the floors below them. Virtually everyone who was still above them was killed. And yet somehow this group survived, trapped in an inexplicable pocket of safety amid the unimaginable wreckage, along with two other firefighters, a fire department chief, and a Port Authority police officer. After a harrowing search for a way out, they eventually found a small ray of light—a literal ray of hope—and followed it to safety.

The firefighters later called Josephine Harris their guardian angel and thanked *her* for saving *their* lives. They realized that had they not encountered her, they would have gone down the stairs faster, and had she not kept walking despite exhaustion, they would have been a few floors above. Either way, they would have been killed. But Josephine Harris knew that she owed her life to these brave men who risked not seeing their own children again so that she could see hers.

There were many other heroes that day, including ordinary citizens whose acts of self-sacrifice to help others were not part of their job descriptions. Some of the help was dramatically heroic, like that of the passengers aboard hijacked United Airlines Flight 93. They decided to fight the terrorists on their flight and sacrifice their own lives in order to try to prevent the terrorists from killing many more people on the ground. And much of the help was behind the scenes, as in the cases of people who volunteered endless hours to do the grueling work of cleaning up the disaster area, helping the injured and the grieving, and donating money, clothes, and other resources.

# Putting *Common Sense* to the Test

*Circle Your Answer*

**T F** People are more likely to help someone in an emergency if the potential rewards seem high and the potential costs seem low.

**T F** In an emergency, a person who needs help has a much better chance of getting it if three other people are present than if only one other person is present.

**T F** People are much more likely to help someone when they're in a good mood.

**T F** People are much less likely to help someone when they're in a bad mood.

**T F** Attractive people have a better chance than unattractive people of getting help when they need it.

**T F** Women seek help more often than men do.

When people read stories such as these, it is natural for them to wonder what they would have done: Would they have risked their lives to help others? What makes some people, at some times, act to help others? The wonderful acts of helping during the chaos of 9/11 are inspiring, to be sure. But there were also many stories that day of people who turned their backs on others, even on people who had just helped them.

Every day there are numerous unheralded acts of helping others and of failing to help others. A volunteer works tirelessly in a health clinic, a college student tutors a child, a congregation raises money for a charity, an older sister lets her little brother win at checkers. And yet every day someone ignores the screams outside his or her window, drives past motorists stranded on the side of a road, or tries to avoid making eye contact with a homeless person on the street.

Every few months we see a story like that of Lawrence Bowers, who dove into the waters off Coney Island, in New York City in June 2012 when he saw a man apparently drowning. "There were hundreds of people watching but no one was helping. . . . I said now I got to take action. I need to help this man." Bowers battled strong currents that kept pulling the drowning man away from him, but despite his exhaustion he continued his pursuit until finally a rescue team of scuba divers pulled them to safety. "I'm not a hero. I'm just a human being," Bowers later told reporters (Lysiak & Boyle, 2012).

And all too often we also learn stories like that of Angel Arce Torres, a 78-year-old man crossing the street in Hartford, Connecticut, in May 2008. From a video of the incident posted on the Internet, one can see a speeding car driving on the wrong side of the street hit Torres violently, sending him twisting in the air and crashing to the pavement. He lies there motionless. One car after another drives by, pausing only briefly before moving past the injured man. Numerous witnesses look on from the sidewalk. Several appear to consider checking on the man, but then something seems to hold them back. Eventually, finally, one man walks into the street to check on the victim, and only then do several others act as well. The victim, left paralyzed and unable to talk, died a year later. The police chief said, "It's incredible how people could be so inhuman. We no longer have a moral compass" (Cohen & De La Torre, 2009, p. A1).

These stories are by no means limited to the United States. For example, consider these two incidents from China's Guangdong province. In June 2012 a toddler fell through an opening in a window ledge on the fourth floor of his apartment building and dangled by his

Displaying bravery that seems to defy instinct, firefighter Mike Kehoe climbs the stairs of one of the towers of the World Trade Center to help with the rescue efforts during the terrorist attacks on the morning of September 11, 2001. This photograph became a famous symbol of the heroism exhibited by so many people on that horrific day. Kehoe was one of the fortunate ones who survived.

A two-year-old girl named Wang Yue lies on a narrow road in Guangdong, China, in October 2011, after getting run over by a van. For several horrifying minutes more than a dozen people passed by the gravely injured girl without checking on her, including the man seen in this photo. While lying in the street she was run over by a second vehicle. She died just over a week later. As discussed in this chapter, this kind of inaction by bystanders is all too common.

neck on the metal grating of a ledge used to hold plants. One of the residents of the building heard the boy's screams, climbed through a window on the floor below, and inched his way up until he could help relieve the pressure on the child's neck and wait for rescue workers to arrive. The fate of another toddler from the same province several months before was far, far worse, however. An absolutely horrifying video from a surveillance camera captured the scene of a 2-year-old girl run over by a van on a narrow road. As the girl lay under the van, the driver stopped the car for a few seconds and then drove on, running her over again with a back tire. More than a dozen people walked or drove past the gravely injured girl for about 7 minutes. A second vehicle—a truck—ran over her crushed body. Finally, a woman checked on her and pulled her away, just before the girl's mother arrived. The girl died more than a week later (Blanchard, 2011).

There is no simple answer to the question of why some people help and others don't or why some situations lead to quick assistance and others to shocking displays of inaction. The determinants of helping behavior are complex and multifaceted. But social psychologists have learned a great deal about these determinants—and therefore about human nature. As you will see in the pages to come, some of their findings are quite surprising.

In this chapter, we examine several questions about helping: *Why* do people help? *When* do they help? *Who* is likely to help? *Whom* do they help? The concluding section concentrates on a major recurring theme—social connection—that underlies much of the theory and research on helping.

# Evolutionary and Motivational Factors: Why Do People Help?

Although few individuals reach the heights of heroic helping, virtually everyone helps somebody sometime. People give their friends a ride to the airport; donate money, food, and clothing for disaster relief; babysit for a relative; work as a volunteer for charitable activities; pick up the mail for a neighbor who's out of town. The list of **prosocial behaviors**—actions intended to benefit others—is endless. But *why* do people help? Several factors have an impact.

## ❯ Evolutionary Factors in Helping

We begin with evolution. From an evolutionary perspective, what possible function can there be in helping others, especially at the risk of one's own life? Doesn't risking one's life for others fly in the face of evolutionary principles such as "survival of the fittest"?

**The "Selfish Gene"**  In fact, evolutionary perspectives emphasize not the survival of the fittest individuals but the survival of the individuals' genes (Dawkins, 1989; Hamilton, 1964). If a specific social behavior enhances reproductive success, then the genetic underpinnings of that behavior are more likely to be passed on to subsequent generations. In this way, the behavior can eventually become part of the common inheritance of the species. The behavior of helping others could have served the function of preserving individuals' genes by promoting the survival of those who share their genetic makeup. By means of this indirect route to genetic survival, the tendency to help genetic relatives, called **kin selection**, could become an innate characteristic of humans. In fact,

*According to a report by the Giving USA Foundation, Americans gave about $300 billion to charitable causes in 2011, despite a terrible economic recession. The large majority of this came from individuals rather than corporations, and a large majority of Americans donate.*

**prosocial behaviors** Actions intended to benefit others.

**kin selection** Preferential helping of genetic relatives, which results in the greater likelihood that genes held in common will survive.

kin selection is evident in the behavior of many organisms. For example, just as humans often risk their lives to save close relatives, ground squirrels, capuchin monkeys, and many other mammals and birds emit an alarm to warn nearby relatives of a predator. The alarm helps their relatives but makes the individual who sounds the alarm more vulnerable to attack (Hollén & Radford, 2009; Schel et al., 2009; Tórrez et al., 2012; Wheeler, 2008).

Because kin selection serves the function of genetic survival, preferential helping of genetic relatives should be strongest when the biological stakes are particularly high. This appears to be the case (Burnstein et al., 1994; Fitzgerald et al., 2010; Korchmaros et al., 2006; Stewart-Williams, 2007). For example, participants in a study by Carey Fitzgerald and Stephen Colarelli (2009) were asked how willing they would be to offer different kinds of help to a friend, a half-sibling, or a sibling. There were three levels of helping behavior: the lowest risk involved picking up items from a store for the person; the medium risk involved loaning the person $10,000; and the highest risk involved trying to rescue the person from a burning house.

As can be seen in ● Figure 10.1, for the lowest-risk helping scenario, participants rated themselves as likely to help a friend as a sibling. For the higher-risk scenarios, however, they were significantly more willing to help a sibling than a friend. Their willingness to help a half-sibling fell in between their willingness to help a friend and their willingness to help a sibling.

In a later study, Fitzgerald and others (2010) found that under low-risk scenarios participants were more likely to help romantic partners than siblings, and they were as willing to help romantic partners with whom they had no biological children as they were to help those with whom they did. Under high-risk situations, however, participants became more likely to help siblings and romantic partners with whom they had biological children, but less willing to help romantic partners with whom they had no children or had adopted children. In other words, under high-risk scenarios, genetic relatedness became more important in decisions about helping.

Participants in a series of studies by Elaine Madsen and others (2007) did more than speculate about what they thought they would do in different hypothetical scenarios—these participants actually suffered in order to help others. Participants in these studies were asked to hold a difficult position with their legs (from an isometric ski-training exercise). The longer they could hold the position, the more money would be earned for another person. However, the position became more and more painful to hold over time. Consistent with predictions based on kin selection, participants withstood the pain and held the position longer if they were doing so for a genetically close relative than for a more distant relative, a friend, or a charity. This effect was found among British students as well as among participants from Zulu populations in South Africa.

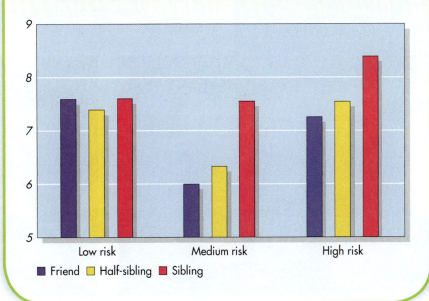

● **FIGURE 10.1**

**Helping Kin When Risks Are High**

Participants indicated how willing they would be to offer different types of help to a friend, a half-sibling, or a sibling. The help was either low risk, medium risk, or high risk. For the lowest-risk help, participants were as willing to help a friend as they were to help a sibling. For higher-risk helping, in contrast, participants were more willing to help a sibling than a friend, with willingness to help a half-sibling coming in the middle.

Based on Fitzgerald, 2009. © Cengage Learning

**Reciprocal Altruism** Kin selection provides only a partial explanation for helping. Relatives are not always helpful to each other. And even though relatives may get preferential treatment, most people help out non-kin as well. What's the reproductive advantage of helping someone who isn't related to you? The most common answer is reciprocity. Through *reciprocal altruism*, helping someone else can be in your best interests because it increases the likelihood that you will be helped in return (Krebs, 1987; Trivers, 1985). If A helps B and B helps A, both A and B increase their chances of survival and reproductive success. Over the course of evolution, therefore, individuals who engage in reciprocal altruism should survive and reproduce more than individuals who do not, thus enabling this kind of altruism to flourish.

Robert Trivers (1971) cited several examples of reciprocal altruism in animals. Many animals groom each other; for instance, monkeys groom other monkeys and cats groom other cats. Large fish (such as groupers) allow small fish (such as wrasses) to swim in their mouths without eating them; the small fish get food for themselves and at the same time remove parasites from the larger fish. And chimps who share with other chimps at one feeding are repaid by the other chimps at another feeding; those who are selfish are rebuffed, sometimes violently, at a later feeding (de Waal, 1996; 2008).

Frans de Waal (2003) observed a group of chimpanzees engaged in nearly 7,000 interactions and recorded their grooming and food-sharing behaviors. He noted striking evidence of reciprocal altruism among these chimps. If Chimp A groomed Chimp B, for instance, B became much more likely to then share his or her food with A. Moreover, if Chimp A groomed B but was not reciprocated in some way by B, A became unlikely to then share his or her food with B. Similar types of behaviors among capuchin monkeys have also been recorded (Tiddi et al., 2011).

It's interesting that these chimps and monkeys were able to negotiate this kind of reciprocity across acts: in grooming and food sharing. Chimpanzees have also been reported sharing plants and tools (Pruetz & Lindshield, 2012). It is as if these primates often operate under a norm of "You scratch my back, I'll scratch yours—or maybe I'll give you some of my apples." This more complicated reciprocation is not uncommon. For example, in a meta-analysis of studies involving 14 different primate species, Gabriele Schino (2007) found evidence that grooming is reciprocated with support in fights (against some other individual). You scratch my back and I'll have your back in a fight! A more charming type of reciprocation was reported by Barbara Tiddi and her colleagues (2010). They report that capuchin mothers allow other females to handle their infants (which young capuchin females apparently love to do) in exchange for being groomed by them.

*"Scratch my back and I'll scratch yours."*

—Proverb

Many animals groom each other, whether they are chimpanzees in Tanzania or young girls in the United States. According to evolutionary psychologists, such behavior often reflects reciprocal altruism.

© Keenan Ward/Corbis

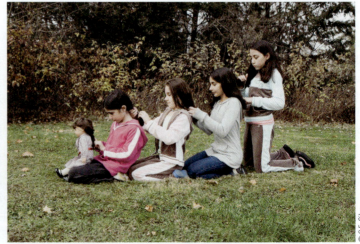

© C.E. Silva

Learning to cooperate, therefore, can be rewarding for both parties. One clever study that illustrates this was conducted by Frans de Waal and Michelle Berger (2000). They observed same-sex pairs of capuchin monkeys working cooperatively in a test chamber to obtain a tray of food. The two monkeys were separated from each other by a mesh partition. One monkey by itself could not pull the tray, but the two monkeys could accomplish the task if they cooperated. When successful, the monkey that wound up with the food consistently shared it with its helper. When they were rewarded in this way, the monkeys became even more likely to help each other on subsequent occasions.

In some human environments, reciprocal altruism is essential for survival even today. Consider, for example, the Northern Ache, who are indigenous peoples of northeastern Paraguay. Wesley Allen-Arave and others (2008) studied a group of Northern Ache who lived in households on a reservation and shared virtually all their food across households. The researchers found that households shared more food with other households that reciprocated in kind.

Reciprocal altruism is not restricted to basic needs such as food acquisition. Think of file sharing instead of food sharing. Swapping music and videos online through file-sharing services may be considered a form of reciprocal altruism, since an individual makes his or her own files available to others so that he or she can have access to theirs. (Of course, record companies and movie studios have other terms for these activities, such as *criminal* and *unethical*.) Strong norms often develop in these peer-to-peer networks. An individual who downloads songs or videos from others' computers but doesn't make his or her own files available is likely to be chastised quickly and emphatically.

## The Evolution of Empathy

Helping, of course, can go beyond assisting kin or members of one's own group. Consider the story of Binti Jua, for example. At the end of 1996, *People* magazine honored her as one of the 25 "most intriguing people" of the year, and *Newsweek* named her "hero of the year." Earlier that year while caring for her own 17-month-old daughter, Binti came across a 3-year-old boy who had fallen almost 20 feet onto a cement floor and been knocked unconscious. She picked up the boy and gently held him, rocking him softly, and then turned him over to paramedics. What was most "intriguing" about Binti? The fact that she was a gorilla.

When the boy climbed over a fence and fell into the primate exhibit at the Brookfield Zoo, near Chicago, witnesses feared the worst. One paramedic said, "I didn't know if she was going to treat him like a doll or a toy." With her own daughter clinging to her back the entire time, Binti "protected the toddler as if he were her own," keeping other gorillas at bay and eventually placing him gently at the entrance where zookeepers and paramedics could get to him. "I could not believe how gentle she was," observed a zoo director (O'Neill et al., 1996, p. 72).

Was this an act of kindness and compassion, or did the gorilla just do what she had been trained to do—pick up and fetch things

Binti Jua, a gorilla at the Brookfield Zoo, near Chicago, gently rocks a 3-year-old boy who had fallen 18 feet into the primate exhibit. The gorilla was acclaimed as a hero for her role in saving the boy. Did Binti Jua act out of kindness and empathy? Or did she simply do what she was taught—fetch objects that fall into her cage? This episode brings the altruism debate to life, even in the animal world.

AP Photo/WLS-TV

dropped into her cage? Cases like this raise the more fundamental question of whether concepts such as morality and empathy can apply to nonhuman animals. Most people think of these as qualities that allow humans to resist and rise above our more selfish, violent, "animal" nature, but instead they may reflect the social nature of many mammals, and particularly primates. In order to live successfully in small groups, it was important for social animals to develop some sense of the proper way to behave in groups and an ability to recognize and respond to danger or suffering in other group members. Humans certainly have much more highly developed moral reasoning and capacity for empathy, but their roots can be traced down the evolutionary chain (de Waal, 2006; de Waal & Ferrari, 2012; McCullough et al., 2008; Narvaez & Lapsley, 2009; Sinnott-Armstrong, 2008).

We will see in several places throughout this chapter the critically important role that **empathy** plays in helping. Unfortunately, the exact definition of empathy is much debated; for example, Dan Batson (2009b) has identified no fewer than eight distinct definitions of empathy that scholars use. Most researchers regard empathy as having both a cognitive component of understanding the emotional experience of another individual and an emotional experience that is consistent with what the other is feeling (Decety, 2011; de Waal, 2009; Eisenberg et al., 2010). A major cognitive component of empathy is *perspective taking*: using the power of imagination to try to see the world through someone else's eyes. A key emotional component of empathy is *empathic concern*, which involves other-oriented feelings, such as sympathy, compassion, and tenderness.

Although higher-order cognitive aspects of empathy are specific to humans, other animals show evidence of empathy in a variety of ways. Some of the examples we have already given offer some evidence of this. Frans de Waal (2008: 2012; Horner et al., 2011), among others, has cited numerous and startling examples of primates such as chimpanzees and bonobos seeming to show empathy. For example, ● Figure 10.2 depicts a juvenile chimpanzee putting an arm around an adult male who had just been defeated in a fight. This kind of consoling behavior is not uncommon in chimpanzees, and it has been shown to reduce the recipient's arousal. de Waal also reports examples of chimpanzees who risked their lives trying to save companions from drowning, even though they themselves were unable to swim. Less dramatically, young chimps have been seen helping to push an old and arthritic group member up onto a climbing frame for a grooming session. The examples de Waal has collected suggest at least some degree of perspective taking and sympathy among nonhuman primates.

Even rodents show evidence of being sensitive to the pain of other individuals of their species, and in some cases it may motivate them to engage in prosocial behavior.

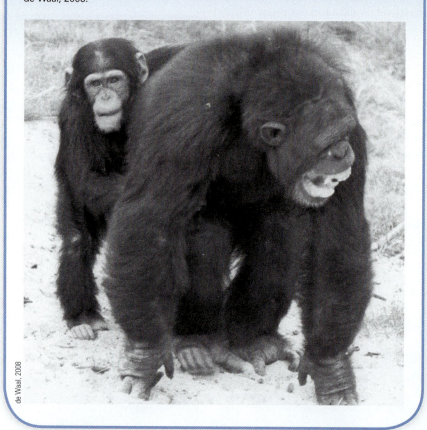

● **FIGURE 10.2**

**Consolation in Chimps**

A juvenile chimpanzee puts an arm around an adult male who has just lost a fight. Frans de Waal has observed many such acts of consoling behavior among apes.

de Waal, 2008.

de Waal. 2008

**empathy** Understanding or vicariously experiencing another individual's perspective and feeling sympathy and compassion for that individual.

For example, Inbal Ben-Ami Bartal and others (2011) found recently that rats intentionally worked to successfully open a restrainer to free a trapped cagemate who had been suffering inside, and they did this even when they could have ignored the cagemate to eat some chocolate contained in a different restrainer.

Paul MacLean (1985) proposed that empathy emerged with the evolutionary transition from reptiles to mammals. An important characteristic of mammals related to empathy is how much the young must be nurtured by the mother or parents. Caregivers must understand the emotional communications from their young and respond to its emotional needs. The gorilla Binti Jua very well may have been acting on maternal caregiving impulses as she gently held the little boy who had fallen into her area. Many scholars propose that once the capacity for empathy was established, it evolved beyond the parent–child relationship (Batson, 2011; Decety & Svetlova, 2012).

Very young human infants show signs of being affected by the distress of others and, by their first birthday, begin to comfort victims of distress (Decety et al., 2011). In one particularly interesting study, Felix Warneken and Michael Tomasello (2006) placed 18-month-old human infants with an adult experimenter. At various points in time, the experimenter appeared to have trouble reaching a goal. For example, he accidentally dropped a marker on the floor and tried unsuccessfully to reach it, or he couldn't put some magazines into a cabinet because the doors were closed. Twenty-two of the 24 infants tested in the study helped the experimenter in at least one of the tasks, and many infants helped on several tasks. In doing so, the infants apparently understood that the experimenter needed help—that is, that he was having trouble completing a task by himself.

Two additional details are worth noting about the study. First, the experimenter never requested help from the infants, nor did he praise or reward the infants when they did help. Second, for every task he needed help with, the experimenter created a similar situation in which he did not seem to have a problem. For example, rather than accidentally drop the marker on the floor and try to reach it, the experimenter sometimes intentionally threw the marker on the floor and did not try to retrieve it. In these situations, the infants were not likely to take action such as picking up the marker. This suggested that when they did help the experimenter, the infants did so because they understood he was trying to achieve some goal.

The researchers also tested three young chimpanzees using a similar procedure. The chimpanzees also helped the human experimenter when they saw that he appeared to need help reaching his goal, although not across as many tasks or as reliably as the human infants did.

Neuroscience research supports the idea that the capacity for empathy is part of our biology. A recent meta-analysis reported a strong body of evidence indicating that empathy for other's pain activates neural structures involved in the direct experience of pain (Lamm et al., 2011). In addition, the hormone oxytocin—which is well known as being involved in mother–infant attachment as well as in bonding between mating pairs—is implicated in empathy and prosocial behaviors. In fact, humans given a boost of oxytocin (through a nasal spray) in experiments behaved in more cooperative and trusting ways than did participants given a placebo (Israel et al., 2012).

*"Charity begins at home but shouldn't end there."*
—Scottish proverb

## Rewards of Helping: Helping Others to Help Oneself

Whether or not it can be traced to evolutionary and biological factors, one important reason why people help others is because it often is rewarding, even if the rewards are psychological rather than material. We all like the idea of being the hero, lifted onto the shoulders of our peers for coming to the rescue of someone in distress. Helping helps the helper. The potential rewards of helping, however, can be offset with significant costs.

People are more likely to help someone in an emergency if the potential rewards seem high and the potential costs seem low. **T**RUE.

A Peace Corps worker teaches English in Honduras. Volunteering one's time, energy, and skills to help others can make one feel good about oneself. Even if they are not financial, the rewards can be tremendous.

**arousal: cost–reward model** The proposition that people react to emergency situations by acting in the most cost-effective way to reduce the arousal of shock and alarm.

Indeed, people often seem to conduct a cost–benefit analysis not only when making deliberate decisions to behave prosocially, as when donating blood, but also in more impulsive, sudden decisions to intervene in an emergency. The empirical evidence on this point is clear: People are much more likely to help when the potential rewards of helping seem high relative to the potential costs.

The **arousal: cost–reward model** of helping stipulates that both emotional and cognitive factors determine whether bystanders to an emergency will intervene (Dovidio et al., 2006). Emotionally, bystanders experience the shock and alarm of personal distress; this unpleasant state of arousal motivates them to do something to reduce it. What they do, however, depends on the "bystander calculus," their computation of the costs and rewards associated with helping. When potential rewards (to self and victim) outweigh potential costs (to self and victim), bystanders will help. But raise those costs and lower those rewards and it is likely that the victims will not be helped (Fischer et al., 2011; Fritzsche et al., 2000; Piliavin et al., 1981).

**Feeling Good**    Helping often simply feels good. A growing body of research reveals a strong relationship between giving help and feeling better, including improvements in mental *and* physical health (Dillard et al., 2008; Omoto et al., 2009; Mojza et al., 2011; Piliavin, 2003; Post, 2005). Heidi Wayment (2004), for example, found that women who engaged in helping behaviors in the aftermath of the September 11, 2001, terrorist attacks in the United States showed greater reduction in their distress over time than women who did not do so. More recently, a longitudinal study by Jane Piliavin and Erica Siegl (2008) found that doing volunteer work was associated with improvements in psychological well-being and that volunteering for multiple organizations was associated with greater improvement.

In a provocative set of studies using brain-imaging techniques, James Rilling and others (2002) examined the brain activity of women playing a Prisoner's Dilemma game, which, as was discussed in Chapter 8, is a game in which individuals compete or cooperate with each other for individual and joint payoffs. The researchers found that when the women were engaged in mutual cooperation during the game, activation was observed in areas of the brain that are linked to the processing of rewards. Despite the fact that these individuals could have earned more money by competing with their partner after their partner had cooperated, their brain activity suggested that cooperation was intrinsically rewarding. This feeling could reinforce altruism and inhibit selfishness. Many studies more recently have similarly found a direct effect of prosocial behavior on these areas of the brain associated with material rewards (Moll et al., 2006; Rilling & Sanfey, 2011).

Even when the costs of helping are high enough that it doesn't feel good immediately, it can pay off in the long run. When parents reluctantly sacrifice relaxing with a good book or movie at the end of a hard day in order to help their child finish some homework, they might not feel immediate joy from giving help, but in the long run, they can expect to reap the benefits of their behavior (Salovey et al., 1991). In addition, people may feel good not only from their role of helper, but simply because of what is called *empathic joy*—the pleasure one has at seeing another person experience relief (Batson et al., 2008).

Children learn that helping others can be rewarding. Younger children focus on the rewards they get from parents and others, but as they develop into adolescents, they begin to reward themselves for helping, taking pride in their actions. Their helpful behavior can then be internally motivated, leading them to help even without the promise of immediate material or social rewards (Cialdini et al., 1981; Piliavin & Callero, 1991).

In their **negative state relief model**, Robert Cialdini and his colleagues (1987) propose that because of this positive effect of helping, people who are feeling bad may be inclined to help others in order to improve their mood. Indeed, after experiencing a traumatic event, some individuals seek out opportunities to help others in order to feel better about themselves instead of becoming bitter and antisocial (Staub & Vollhardt, 2008; Vollhardt, 2009; Vollhardt & Staub, 2011). Helping others may help one heal oneself.

> *"When you give to someone else, you get so much more."*
> —Former U.S. Secretary of State Colin Powell

**Being Good**   In addition to wanting to *feel* good, many of us also are motivated to *be* good—that is, to help because we recognize that "it's the right thing to do." Some situations are especially likely to call to mind norms that compel helpful behaviors. These may be everyday situations, as when encountering an elderly person in a parking lot who needs help getting grocery bags in her car. Sometimes norms can compel much more dramatic and risky action, particularly for individuals whose roles in a group or society give them responsibility in a situation. When the firefighters in Ladder Company 6 (described in the introduction of this chapter) risked their lives to stay with Josephine Harris, their actions were consistent with the idea of not leaving anyone behind who could be saved. Another example is that of Chesley "Sully" Sullenberger, pilot of US Airways Flight 1549 on the afternoon of January 15, 2009. When the jet hit a large flock of geese just after takeoff from LaGuardia Airport in New York City, it lost all power in its engines and was heading for catastrophe. Sullenberger somehow guided the jet to a safe landing in the Hudson River. As the plane began to fill up with water, the crew managed to get all 150 passengers out of the plane and onto the wings and rafts and eventually into various rescue crafts. Sullenberger refused to leave the sinking plane until he had walked up and down the cabin two final times to make sure no one was left behind. No matter what, he would be the last person off the plane as well as the last person off the rafts in the frigid river (McClam, 2009).

Rescue workers risk their lives regularly despite the potential costs involved in their jobs.

### The Cost of Helping or of Not Helping

Clearly helping has its rewards, but it has its costs as well. The firefighters in Ladder Company 6 who somehow survived the collapse of the North Tower of the World Trade Center while saving Josephine Harris were among the lucky ones. Many people were killed while helping others that day, such as Abraham Zelmanowitz, a computer programmer who refused to leave his quadriplegic friend who could not descend the stairs. And beyond 9/11, we often are moved by stories of the costs paid by those who offer help, such as Donald Liu, who in August 2012 saw two boys swept up by rip tides in Lake Michigan and swam in to save them, despite the protests from his own children about the dangerous

**negative state relief model**   The proposition that people help others in order to counteract their own feelings of sadness.

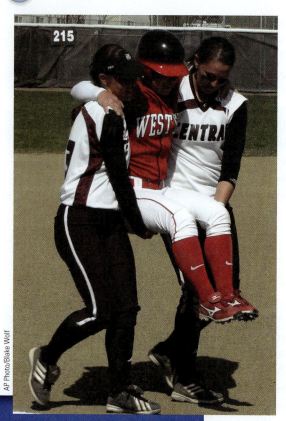

Liz Wallace and Mallory Holtman carry their opponent, Sara Tucholosky, around the bases in their college softball tournament game. After hitting the first home run of her career, Tucholosky injured her knee and could not run around the bases to complete the run, and her teammates and coaches were not allowed to help her and preserve the home run. Despite costing their own team a run, Wallace and Holtman volunteered to help her around the bases in an inspiring act of altruism.

*"The charity that hastens to proclaim its good deeds, ceases to be a charity, and is only pride and ostentation."*

—William Hutton

**egoistic**  Motivated by the desire to increase one's own welfare.

**altruistic**  Motivated by the desire to improve another's welfare.

conditions. The boys were saved, but the 50-year-old chief of pediatric surgery at the University of Chicago and father of three young children did not survive (Dizikes & Sobol, 2012).

Other helpers have done more sustained and deliberate helping, such as the people who helped hide runaway slaves in the nineteenth-century United States or the people who helped hide Jews during the Holocaust. Sharon Shepela and others (1999) call this type of thoughtful helping in the face of potentially enormous costs *courageous resistance*. And although giving help is often associated with positive affect and health, when the help involves constant and exhausting demands, which is often the case when taking long-term care of a very ill person, the effects on helpers' physical and mental health—as well as on their financial security—can be quite negative (Earle & Heymann, 2012; Fujino & Okamura, 2009; Miller, 2011; Mioshi et al., 2009).

To lower some of the costs of helping, some legislatures have created "Good Samaritan" laws that encourage bystanders to intervene in emergencies by offering them legal protection, particularly doctors who volunteer medical care when they happen upon emergencies (Cunningham, 2009; Oleson, 2009). Other kinds of Good Samaritan laws increase the costs of failing to help. Sometimes called "duty to rescue" laws, these laws require people to provide or summon aid in an emergency, so long as they do not endanger themselves in the process. In the United States, this kind of duty to rescue law is relatively rare, but they are more common in Europe and Canada.

## Altruism or Egoism: The Great Debate

We have documented some of the ways that helping others can help the helper. This raises a classic question, however: Are our helpful behaviors always **egoistic**—motivated by selfish concerns? Or are humans ever truly **altruistic**—motivated by the desire to increase another's welfare? Many psychological theories assume an egoistic, self-interested bottom line. It is not difficult to imagine egoistic interpretations for almost any acts of helping, even the most seemingly altruistic ones. Tutoring the disadvantaged? It will look good on your résumé or college application. Anonymously helping the homeless? It reduces your guilt. Donating blood to people you'll never know? It makes you feel a bit more noble. Risking your life for a stranger? Such heroism may benefit your reputation and status. So is all helping at some level egoistic?

Daniel Batson (2009a: 2011) thinks not. As we will see in the following section, he believes that the motivation behind some helpful actions is truly altruistic and that empathy plays a critically important role in it.

**The Empathy–Altruism Hypothesis**  Batson's model of altruism is based on his view of the consequences of empathy. According to Batson, if you perceive someone in need and imagine how *that person* feels, you are likely to experience other-oriented feelings of empathic concern, which in turn produce the altruistic motive to reduce the other person's distress. There are, however, instances in which people perceive someone in need and focus on their *own* feelings about this person or on how *they* would feel in that person's situation. Although many people (and some researchers) may think of this as "empathy," Batson contrasts this with instances in which people's concern is with how the *other person* is feeling. It's when your focus is on the other person that true altruism is possible.

A story that may illustrate empathy occurred during a college softball tournament game between Central Washington and Western Oregon in April 2008. In the second inning, a short, "really tiny" senior named Sara Tucholsky shocked everyone by hitting the first home run of her career. In her excitement she missed touching first base, and when she turned to go back and touch it, she tore a ligament in her knee and crumpled to the ground in agony. There was no way she could run around the bases, and therefore her home run would not be official. Her coach talked with officials about what to do. They said that no one from her team could help her around the bases and that she would have to be replaced and the home run would not count. Then someone stepped in and asked, "Excuse me, would it be OK if we carried her around and she touched each bag?"

It was the star hitter from the opposing team, Mallory Holtman. She and another player carried Tucholsky around the diamond, lowering her enough at each base to allow her to touch it so that she could preserve the one and only home run of her softball career. They did this despite the fact that it would cost their own team a run in a close and important game—a game they would ultimately lose by just two runs, thereby ending their season. According to Holtman, she didn't do it for any glory. Indeed, she couldn't understand why people made a fuss about it afterward. "Everyone else would have done it," she said (Hays, 2008). It is impossible to know from a story like this exactly what factors could have motivated the helping behavior, but clearly some degree of taking the other person's perspective and feeling sympathy for her were crucial elements behind Mallory Holtman's decision to help her fallen opponent.

The basic features of Batson's **empathy–altruism hypothesis** are outlined in ● Figure 10.3. The hard part, though, is this: How can we tell the difference between egoistic and altruistic motives? In both cases, people help someone else, but the helpers' reasons are different. Confronted with this puzzle, Batson came up with an elegant solution. It depends, he says, on whether one can obtain the relevant self-benefits without relieving the other's need. For example, when a person's motive is egoistic, helping should decline if it's easy for the individual to escape from the situation and therefore escape from his or her own feelings of distress. When a person's motive is altruistic, however, help will be given regardless of the ease of escape.

Based on this reasoning, Batson and others have conducted dozens of experiments that have found support for the empathy–altruism hypothesis. For example, Eric Stocks and his colleagues (2009) designed a very clever experiment in which student participants learned about a fellow student named Katie whose parents and sister had recently

> *"The great gift of human beings is that we have the power of empathy."*
>
> —Meryl Streep

**empathy–altruism hypothesis** The proposition that empathic concern for a person in need produces an altruistic motive for helping.

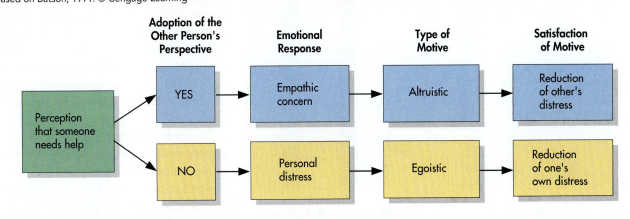

● **FIGURE 10.3**

**The Empathy–Altruism Hypothesis**

According to the empathy–altruism hypothesis, taking the perspective of a person in need creates feelings of empathic concern, which produce the altruistic motive to reduce the other person's distress. When people do not take the other's perspective, they experience feelings of personal distress, which produce the egoistic motive to reduce their own discomfort.

Based on Batson, 1991. © Cengage Learning

been killed in a car accident, leaving her to care for her younger brother and sister. At the conclusion of the study the students were given an opportunity to help Katie, such as by volunteering to help her with transportation or to babysit her siblings while she took night classes. Would the students offer to help Katie?

The researchers manipulated two variables before the students read about Katie's plight. One was a manipulation of empathy. Students in the low-empathy condition read that they should "try to remain as objective as possible about what has happened to the person described and how it has affected his or her life." Students in the high-empathy condition, in contrast, read that they should "try to imagine how the person described in the segment feels about what has happened and how it has affected his or her life." The researchers also manipulated whether or not the students would have an easy opportunity to not worry about the distress Katie was going through; in other words, could they psychologically escape the situation without lingering guilt? Students were informed that they would be using a memory training technique that would either enhance or eliminate their memory of the information they would be learning (that is, the information about Katie).

The key question: Would students help Katie if they could simply forget about her, or would they want to help her anyway? If they would only help her if they could not easily forget her plight, this would suggest an egoistic motivation. But if they would help her even if they were confident they would not have to remember her suffering, this would suggest altruism. The results supported the empathy–altruism hypothesis. In the low-empathy condition, students' helping decisions seemed to be governed by egoistic concerns—they agreed to help Katie only if they thought they would remember her problems. In the high-empathy condition, however, they agreed to help her regardless of whether they thought they would remember her or not (see ● Figure 10.4).

The empathy–altruism hypothesis does have its limits, however. For example, Batson has never claimed that *all* helping is altruistically motivated. There are multiple motives for helping, and many (and probably most) helpful acts are best explained in terms of the processes we consider elsewhere in this chapter. And any single helpful action can be the result of a mixture of egoistic and altruistic motives. Mark Snyder (1993) suggests, for example, that the most effective way to increase helping is to encourage people to recognize and feel comfortable with the convergence of self-oriented and other-oriented concerns. Another limit is created by the fact that motives do not guarantee behavior. Empathy leads to altruistic motivations but not necessarily to helpful behaviors. For example, someone with empathic concern for another might not help this person if he or she fears that the potential cost of offering the help will be very high (Batson et al.,

● **FIGURE 10.4**

**Empathy and Helping: Not Taking the Easy Way Out**

Students were induced to experience low or high empathy toward a suffering student named Katie. They were led to believe that they would remember or soon forget what they learned about Katie. The students were then given a chance to volunteer to help Katie. Students in the low-empathy condition tended to not offer their help if they thought they wouldn't remember Katie and her plight. Students in the high-empathy condition offered to help whether or not they thought they would forget her situation.

Based on Stocks et al., 2009. © Cengage Learning

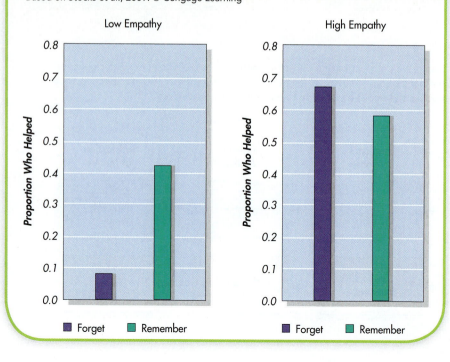

1983). And too much empathy can be overwhelming if it is not properly controlled. Doctors, nurses, and clinicians are often better able to help their patients if they can maintain some emotional distance and objectivity from them, and too much empathy can be a risk factor for depression (Decety & Svetlova, 2012).

**Convergence of Motivations: Volunteering**  People tend to engage in more long-term helping behavior, such as volunteerism, due to multiple motives. Some of these motives are associated with empathy, such as perspective taking and empathic concern, whereas other motives are more egoistic, such as wanting to enhance one's résumé, relieve negative emotions, or conform to prosocial norms (Hur, 2006; Penner et al., 2005; Piferi et al., 2006; Reeder et al., 2001). Allen Omoto and others (2009) have found that both other-focused motivation and self-focused motivation predicted volunteerism.

Table 10.1 lists five categories of motives that Allen Omoto and Mark Snyder (1995) determined were behind volunteers' decisions to help people with AIDS. One interesting finding was that volunteers who had initially endorsed self-oriented motives, such as gaining understanding and developing personal skills, remained active volunteers longer than did those who had initially emphasized other-oriented motives, such as humanitarian values and community concern. Why were the more egoistic goals associated with longer service? Snyder and Omoto (2008) observed that purely altruistic motives may not keep individuals motivated long enough to withstand the personal costs associated with some kinds of prolonged helping. As Mark Snyder noted, "The

The Newport News Daily Press

According to the empathy–altruism hypothesis, taking the perspective of someone in need is the first step toward altruism. When Sarah DeCristoforo returned to school after receiving chemotherapy for leukemia, her teacher and two friends actually put themselves in her place in one highly visible respect—they shaved their heads. Here, Sarah, wearing a scarf, is surrounded by her supporters.

---

### TABLE 10.1
**Motivations to Volunteer to Help People with AIDS**

Allen Omoto and Mark Snyder identified five categories of motivations underlying people's initial decisions to become volunteers to help people with AIDS. Within each category, three examples of specific statements representative of the general motive are presented.

| Values | Community Concern |
|---|---|
| Because of my humanitarian obligation to help others | Because of my sense of obligation to the gay community |
| Because I enjoy helping other people | Because I consider myself an advocate for gay-related issues |
| Because I consider myself a loving and caring person | Because of my concern and worry about the gay community |

| Understanding | Esteem Enhancement |
|---|---|
| To learn more about how to prevent AIDS | To feel better about myself |
| To learn how to help people with AIDS | To escape other pressures and stress in my life |
| To deal with my personal fears and anxiety about AIDS | To feel less lonely |

**Personal Development**

To get to know people who are similar to myself

To meet new people and make new friends

To gain experience dealing with emotionally difficult topics

From Omoto, A.M. and Snyder, M., "Sustained helping without obligation: Motivation, longevity of service, and perceived attitude change among AIDS volunteers," *Journal of Personality and Social Psychology* vol 68 (pp. 671–686). Copyright © 1995 by the American Psychological Association. Reprinted by permission.

*More than 27% of the U.S. population did at least some volunteer work between September 2010 and September 2011, according to the U.S. Bureau of Labor Statistics.*

*Interested in volunteering? One place to find information is Volunteermatch.org.*

good, and perhaps romanticized, intentions related to humanitarian concern simply may not be strong enough to sustain volunteers faced with the tough realities and personal costs of working with [persons with AIDS]" (Snyder, 1993, p. 258). When helping demands more of us, self-interest may keep us going.

Egoistic motives, therefore, can be put to good use. This was evident in a set of studies by Eamonn Ferguson and others (2008). They conducted a longitudinal study of blood donation in the United Kingdom and found that having other-oriented beliefs about blood donation (for example, *society* benefits from blood donation) and having self-oriented beliefs (for example, *the donor* would benefit by donating blood) each predicted people's later actual blood donation, but having the self-oriented beliefs was the stronger predictor.

# Situational Influences: When Do People Help?

Thus far, we have focused on *why* people help others. We now turn to the question of *when* people help. We begin by discussing a remarkably creative and provocative set of research findings that make a surprising point: If you need help in an emergency, you may be better off if there is only one witness to your plight than if there are several. We then focus on a wide range of other situational factors related to helping.

## The Bystander Effect

On January 15, 2008, a man named Rage Ibrahim was convicted for sexually assaulting a woman in the hallway of an apartment building in St. Paul, Minnesota, the previous summer. Surveillance video from the hallway showed several residents, as many as 10, opening their apartment doors, looking at the man beating and raping the screaming woman, and closing their doors as they went back into their apartments. At one point three men approached them, but they left after Ibrahim got off the woman and shoved one of them in the back. Despite the woman's cries for someone to call the police, no one called 911 for more than an hour. A police commander who saw the video said, "It was horrifying. I can't describe how it sent chills up my back, watching this woman getting assaulted and people turning their backs and doing nothing" (Gottfried, 2007, 2008).

The sad truth is that this kind of story of bystanders failing to act, while chilling, is not as uncommon as most people imagine. Two of the stories in the opening to this chapter—the hit-and-run incidents in Connecticut and China—are additional examples of this problem. The most famous of these stories occurred a half century ago. It has remained famous in large part because of the fascinating social psychology research it inspired.

The story begins at about 3:20 in the morning on March 13, 1964, in the New York City borough of Queens. Twenty-eight-year-old Kitty Genovese was returning home from her job as a bar manager. Suddenly, a man attacked her with a knife. She was stalked, stabbed, and sexually assaulted just 35 yards from her own apartment building. Lights went on and windows went up as she screamed, "Oh my God! He stabbed me! Please help me!" She broke free from her attacker twice, but only briefly. Newspaper reports indicated that 38 of her neighbors witnessed her ordeal, but not one intervened. Finally, after nearly 45 minutes of terror, one man called the police. But before they got her to the hospital, Genovese was dead.

The murder of Kitty Genovese shocked the nation. Were her neighbors to blame? It seemed unlikely that all 38 of them could have been moral monsters. Most of the media attention focused on the decline of morals and values in contemporary society and on the anonymity and apathy seen in large American cities such as New York. (Indeed, almost 50 years later in 2012 these very same problems were cited in the Chinese media about contemporary Chinese culture in response to the tragic hit-and-run incident that killed the toddler described in the beginning of the chapter.) A few days after the incident, John Darley and Bibb Latané discussed over dinner the events and the explanations being offered for it. They were not convinced that these explanations were sufficient to account for why Kitty Genovese didn't get the help she needed, and they wondered if other, more social psychological processes might have been at work. They speculated that because each witness to the attack could see that many other witnesses had turned on their lights and were looking out their windows, each witness may have assumed that others would, or should, take responsibility and call the police. To test their ideas, Darley and Latané (1968) set out to see if they could produce unresponsive bystanders under laboratory conditions. Let's take a look at one of their studies.

When a participant arrived, he or she was taken to one of a series of small rooms located along a corridor. Speaking over an intercom, the experimenter explained that he wanted participants to discuss personal problems college students often face. Participants were told that to protect confidentiality, the group discussion would take place over the intercom system and that the experimenter would not be listening. They were required to speak one at a time, taking turns. Some participants were assigned to talk with one other person, whereas other participants joined larger groups of three or six people.

Although one participant did mention in passing that he suffered from a seizure disorder that was sometimes triggered by study pressures, the opening moments of the conversation were uneventful. But soon, an unexpected problem developed. When the time came for this person to speak again, he stuttered badly, had a hard time speaking clearly, and sounded as if he were in very serious trouble:

> I could really-er-use some help so if somebody would-er-give me a little h-help-uh-er-er-er-er c-could somebody-er-er-help-er-uh-uh-uh [choking sounds] . . . . I'm gonna die-er-er-I'm . . . gonna die-er-help-er-er-seizure-er [chokes, then quiet].

Confronted with this situation, what would *you* do? Would you interrupt the experiment, dash out of your cubicle, and try to find the experimenter? Or would you sit there—concerned, but unsure how to react?

As it turns out, participants' responses to this emergency were strongly influenced by the size of their group. Actually all participants were participating alone, but tape-recorded material led them to believe that others were present. All the participants who thought that only they knew about the emergency quickly left the room to try to get help. In the larger groups, however, participants were less likely and slower to intervene. Indeed, 38% of the participants in the six-person groups never left the room at all during the 6 minutes before the experimenter would finally terminate the study! This research led Latané and Darley to a chilling conclusion: The more bystanders there are, the *less* likely the victim will be helped. This is the **bystander effect**, whereby the presence of others inhibits helping.

Before the pioneering work of Latané and Darley, most people would have assumed just the opposite. Isn't there safety in numbers? Don't we feel more secure rushing in to help when others are around to lend their support? Latané and Darley overturned this commonsense assumption and provided a careful, step-by-step analysis of the decision-making process involved in emergency interventions. In the following sections, we examine each of five steps in this process: noticing something unusual, interpreting it as

NY Times/Redux Stock

The murder of Kitty Genovese, pictured here, shocked the nation in 1964. How could 38 witnesses stand by and do nothing? Research conducted in the aftermath of this tragedy suggests that if there had been only one witness rather than almost 40, Kitty Genovese might have had a better chance of receiving help, and she might be alive today.

**bystander effect** The effect whereby the presence of others inhibits helping.

In an emergency, a person who needs help has a much better chance of getting it if three other people are present than if only one other person is present. **F**ALSE.

an emergency, taking responsibility for getting help, deciding how to help, and providing assistance. We also consider the reasons why people sometimes fail to take one of these steps and therefore do not help. These steps, and the obstacles along the way, are summarized in ● Figure 10.5.

**Noticing**   The first step toward being a helpful bystander is to notice that someone needs help or at least that something out of the ordinary is happening. Participants in the seizure study could not help but notice the emergency. In many situations, however, the problem isn't necessarily perceived. The presence of others can be distracting and can divert attention away from indications of a victim's plight. People who live in big cities and noisy environments may become so used to seeing people lying on sidewalks or hearing screams that they begin to tune them out, becoming susceptible to what Stanley Milgram (1970) called *stimulus overload*.

## ● FIGURE 10.5

### The Five Steps to Helping in an Emergency

On the basis of their analysis of the decision-making process in emergency interventions, Latané and Darley (1970) outlined five steps that lead to providing assistance. But obstacles can interfere, and if a step is missed, the victim won't be helped.
© Cengage Learning

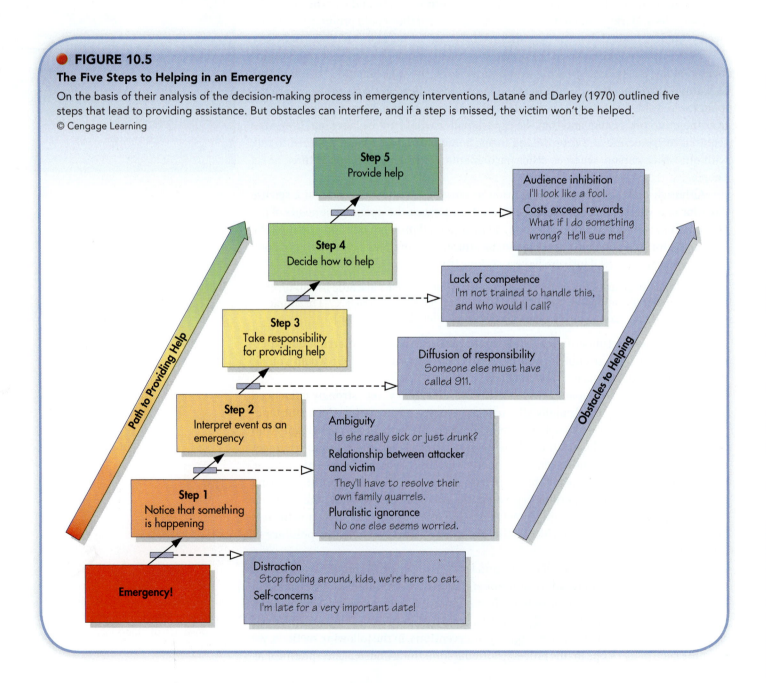

**Interpreting**  Noticing is a necessary first step toward helping, but then people must interpret the meaning of what they notice. Cries of pain can be mistaken for shrieks of laughter; a heart-attack victim can appear to be a sleeping drunk. So observers wonder: Does that person really need help? In general, the more ambiguous the situation is, the less likely it is that bystanders will intervene (Clark & Word, 1972).

Perhaps the most powerful information available during an emergency is the behavior of other people. Startled by a sudden, unexpected, possibly dangerous event, each person looks quickly to see what others are doing. As everyone looks at everyone else for clues about how to behave, the entire group is paralyzed by indecision. When this happens, the person needing help is a victim of **pluralistic ignorance**. In this state of ignorance, each individual believes that his or her own thoughts and feelings are different from those of other people, when in fact, many of the other people are thinking or feeling the same way. Each bystander thinks that other people aren't acting because somehow they know there isn't an emergency. Actually, everyone is confused and hesitant, but taking cues from each other's inaction, each observer concludes that help is not required.

Latané and Darley (1968) put this phenomenon to the test in an experiment in which participants completed a questionnaire in a room in which they were either (a) alone; (b) with two confederates who remained passive and took no action; or (c) with two other naive participants just like them. As the participants were working on the questionnaire, smoke began to seep into the room through a vent. Was this an emergency? How do you think you would respond? Within 4 minutes, half of the participants who were working alone took some action, such as leaving the room to report the smoke to someone. Within 6 minutes—the maximum time allotted before the researchers terminated the experiment—three-quarters of these participants took action. Clearly, they interpreted the smoke as a potential emergency.

But what about the participants working in groups of three? Common sense suggests that the chances that *somebody* will take action should be greater when more people are present. But only 1 of the 24 participants in this condition took action within 4 minutes, and only 3 did so before the end of the study—even though, at that point, the smoke was so thick they had to fan it away from their faces to see the questionnaire! The rate of action was even lower when participants were in a room with two passive confederates; in this condition, only 1 in 10 participants reported the smoke. If the participants in either of the two group conditions had interpreted the smoke as a potential emergency, they would have acted, because their own lives would have been at stake. But instead they looked at the reactions of the others in the room, and because of their individual attempts not to look panicky or uncool, they defined the situation for each other as nothing to be worried about.

**Taking Responsibility**  Noticing a victim and recognizing an emergency are crucial steps, but by themselves, they don't ensure that a bystander will come to the rescue. The issue of responsibility remains. When help is needed, who is responsible for providing it? If a person knows that others are around, it's all too easy to place the responsibility on *them*. People often fail to help because of the **diffusion of responsibility**: the belief that others will or should intervene. Presumably, each of those people who watched or

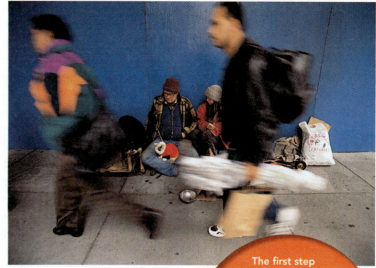

Bob Strong/The Image Works, Inc.

The first step toward providing help is to notice that someone needs assistance. Distracted by their own concerns or by the overwhelming stimuli of a big, bustling city, these people walking in midtown Manhattan may not even notice the homeless couple begging for spare change.

**pluralistic ignorance**  The state in which people in a group mistakenly think that their own individual thoughts, feelings, or behaviors are different from those of the others in the group.

**diffusion of responsibility**  The belief that others will or should take the responsibility for providing assistance to a person in need.

listened to Kitty Genovese's murder thought that someone else would do something to stop the attack. The witnesses to the hit-and-run in Hartford, Connecticut, in 2008 (described earlier in the chapter) also looked around and did nothing at first, presumably hoping that someone else would get involved. But remember those helpful participants in the seizure study who thought that they alone heard the other person's cry for help? Diffusion of responsibility cannot occur if an individual believes that only he or she is aware of the victim's need.

An interesting set of experiments by Stephen Garcia and others (2002) found that the presence of others can promote diffusion of responsibility even when those others are present only in one's mind! Garcia and his colleagues had participants simply *imagine* being in a crowd or being alone. Soon after, these participants were given an opportunity to help someone. The results indicated that participants who had just thought of being with many other people were less likely to help than were the participants who had imagined themselves alone.

Diffusion of responsibility usually takes place under conditions of anonymity. Bystanders who do not know the victim personally are more likely to see others as responsible for providing help. Accordingly, if the psychological distance between a bystander and the victim is reduced, there will be less diffusion of responsibility and more help. Reducing the psychological distance among bystanders can also counteract the diffusion of responsibility. Established groups in which the members know each other are usually more helpful than groups of strangers (Fischer et al., 2011). For example, Mark Levine and Simon Crowther (2008) replicated the inhibiting effect of bystanders on helping when the bystanders were strangers, but they found that the effect did not occur when the bystanders were all friends.

In addition, the diffusion of responsibility can be defeated by a person's role. A group leader, even if he or she has only recently been assigned to that position, is more likely than other group members to act in an emergency (Baumeister et al., 1988). And some occupational roles increase the likelihood of intervention. Registered nurses, for example, do not diffuse responsibility when confronted by a possible physical injury (Cramer et al., 1988). Recall Donald Liu, whose brave attempt to rescue two boys in Lake Michigan was described earlier the chapter. Liu was a pediatric surgeon, whose job was all about saving children.

**Deciding How to Help and Providing Help**    If a person has assumed the responsibility to help, he or she still must pass through the final two steps before taking action: deciding how to help and then deciding to provide help. Obstacles here include feeling a lack of competence in knowing how to help, or worrying that the potential costs of helping may too great to justify taking the risk. The presence of other witnesses can be obstacles in these two steps as well. Latané and Darley point out that people sometimes feel too socially awkward and embarrassed to act helpfully in a public setting. When observers do not act in an emergency because they fear making a bad impression on other observers, they are under the influence of **audience inhibition**.

This is a very common obstacle to helping, but sometimes it can be especially tragic. Melanie Carlson (2008) reports about a gang rape of an unconscious 15-year-old girl by four perpetrators in the presence of six bystanders at a party in 2002. The district attorney said that the bystanders did not intervene for fear of being considered "wusses" or being "made fun of" (p. 3). When Carlson interviewed young men from a university in California about how they would respond in situations like the gang rape, many of them raised similar concerns, indicating that their masculinity would be threatened if they intervened. This kind of concern about being embarrassed in front of friends and breaking perceived norms that promote minding one's own business plays a role in a tremendous amount of bystander inaction, involving everything from sexual assault to

**audience inhibition** Reluctance to help for fear of making a bad impression on observers.

bullying to abuse of animals (Arluke, 2012; Banyard, 2011). Adolescents in particular may be likely to think that the norm among their peers is more tolerant of aggression and bullying than it actually is, and this can make pluralistic ignorance and inaction all the more likely (Sandstrom & Bartini, 2010).

Worrying about how others will view us does not, however, always reduce helping. When people think they will be scorned by others for failing to help, the presence of an audience *increases* their helpful actions (Schwartz & Gottlieb, 1980).

**The Bystander Effect Online**  One relatively new application of the research on the bystander effect is in the world of electronic-based communication. Daniel Stalder (2008) reviewed studies on individuals' responses to e-mail or Internet-based requests for help. Even here, the bystander effect emerged, indicating that the virtual presence of others reduced the likelihood that any one individual would intervene. Abuse online, such as in the form of bullying via a social network site, or cries for attention and help from suicidal individuals may be met with the same kind of bystander inaction that we have seen in these real-world cases, and the diffusion of responsibility can be all the greater because of the additional physical and psychological distance the online world creates. Indeed, in multiple cases of people announcing on Facebook or an online group that they were going to kill themselves, the posts elicited many instances of taunting and indifference from online bystanders (Murphy, 2012; Wells, 2011).

**The Legacy of the Bystander Effect Research**  As you can see in Figure 10.5, providing help in an emergency is a challenging process. At each step along the way, barriers and diversions can prevent a potential helper from becoming an actual one. In 1981, Bibb Latané and Steve Nida conducted a meta-analysis of more than 50 studies on the bystander effect and concluded, "The original phenomenon discovered by Latané and Darley has a firm empirical foundation and has withstood the tests of time and replication" (p. 322). Thirty years later Peter Fischer and others (2011) conducted a new meta-analysis and similarly found strong support for the bystander effect model. This new review also found that the bystander effect is weaker in dangerous than non-dangerous situations. The researchers offer three reasons for this: (1) dangerous situations are more likely to be clearly interpreted to be emergencies where someone needs help; (2) the presence of other bystanders offers physical support, which is more necessary for dangerous situations; and (3) some dangerous situations can only be resolved through coordination among several bystanders.

The power and relevance of Latané and Darley's analysis are evident in the fact that newspapers around the world typically cite their work when reporting the latest shocking incident of bystander nonintervention. Virtually every such story mentions "Kitty Genovese" and many of them refer to the Latané and Darley research. Given its enduring legacy, it is interesting to note that some of the original details reported about the witnesses to the Kitty Genovese murder— accounts that have been repeated countless times over the years since then—may, in fact, be inaccurate. Rachel Manning and others (2008) recently published an article suggesting that some of the witnesses may have called the police

The legacy of the bystander intervention research lives on today as it is being applied to programs designed to encourage witnesses to destructive behaviors such as bullying and sexual assault to take action.

3 People Involved in Bullying

Bully

Victim

Bystander

well before the police finally arrived. These were in the days before "911" calls, and it is impossible to know whether or not these calls were made or what may have been said in them. Manning and her colleagues also question whether 38 was the correct number of witnesses and suggest that far fewer were likely to have actually seen the incident, although possibly even more than 38 heard it.

To us, these questions are interesting but beside the main point. Whether fully accurate or not, these original reports were what inspired John Darley and Bibb Latané to pursue the line of research we have reported in this section, and that research has yielded valuable insight concerning the social psychology of bystander intervention. In addition, we have cited several other more recent stories from the news of tragic inaction of bystanders, and for every one we cite, there are dozens more. Latané and Darley's theorizing continues to help people understand how these incidents can occur.

Many of us who teach social psychology have stories of former students who witnessed an emergency and jumped in to help while consciously thinking of the lessons they'd learned in their social psychology classes about Darley and Latané's bystander intervention research. Some research supports this point, finding that teaching participants about the research makes them less vulnerable to these effects (Beaman et al., 1978). Indeed, one of the authors of this book remembers being at a lecture in a room filled with social psychologists when a loud crash suddenly emanated from an adjacent room. After a few seconds of delay, dozens of social psychologists burst out of their chairs, almost trampling each other as they rushed to see if there was an emergency. And the only ones who were not explicitly thinking "Darley and Latané" while doing so were the ones thinking "Latané and Darley."

The legacy of the bystander research has recently been reaffirmed all the more by an explosion of interest in applying and extending the work to a constantly growing list of prevention and training programs aimed at reducing aggression, bullying, sexual assault, workplace violence, and other antisocial and dangerous behaviors that are often witnessed by bystanders (Banyard, 2011; Burn, 2009; Casey & Ohler, 2012; Pfetsch et al., 2011). This wave of research has found strong support for the applicability of the bystander research to understanding when and why bystanders are likely to fail to intervene in these situations, and researchers are beginning to find some positive results of training programs to reduce these effects. Numerous primary and secondary schools throughout the world have made "bystander" a buzzword as they try to educate and encourage students to intervene to reduce the prevalence and impacts of bullying.

**Getting Help in a Crowd: What Should You Do?**　So what do all these stories and experiments teach you about what to do if you need help in the presence of many people? Is there anything you can do to enhance the chances that someone will come to your aid? We can offer this advice: Try to counteract the ambiguity of the situation by making it very clear that you do need help and try to reduce diffusion of responsibility by singling out particular individuals for help, such as with eye contact, pointing, or direct requests (Markey, 2000; Moriarty, 1975; Shotland & Stebbins, 1980).

## Time Pressure

The presence of others can create obstacles at each step on the way toward helping in an emergency. Other factors, too, can affect multiple steps in this process. Our good intentions of helping those in need can sometimes conflict with other motivations. One such source of conflict is time pressure. When we are in a hurry or have a lot on our minds, we may be so preoccupied that we fail to notice others who need help, become less likely to accept responsibility for helping someone, or decide that the costs of helping are too high because of the precious time that will be lost. When we have other demands on us that seem very important, getting involved in someone else's problems may seem like a luxury we can't afford (Batson et al., 1978; Moore, 2005). John Darley and Daniel Batson (1973) examined the role of time pressure in an experiment that produced what may be the most ironic finding in the history of social psychology.

Their study was based on the parable of the Good Samaritan, from the Gospel of Luke. This parable tells the story of three different people—a priest, a Levite, and a Samaritan—each traveling on the road from Jerusalem to Jericho. Each encounters a man lying half-dead by the roadside. The priest and the Levite—both considered busy, important, and relatively holy people—pass by the man without stopping. The only one who helps is the Samaritan, a social and religious outcast of that time. A moral of the tale is that people with low status are sometimes more virtuous than those who enjoy high status and prestige. Why? Perhaps in part because high-status individuals tend to be busy people, preoccupied with their own concerns and rushing around to various engagements. Such characteristics may prevent them from noticing or deciding to help a victim in need of assistance.

Darley and Batson brought this ancient story to life. They asked seminary students to prepare to give a talk. Half of them were told that the talk was to be based on the parable of the Good Samaritan; the other half expected to discuss the jobs that seminary students like best. All participants were then instructed to walk over to a nearby building where the speech would be recorded. At this point, participants were told either that they were running ahead of schedule, that they were right on time, or that they were already a few minutes behind schedule. On the way to the other building, all participants passed a research confederate slumped in a doorway, coughing and groaning. Which of these future ministers stopped to lend a helping hand?

Perhaps surprisingly, the topic of the upcoming speech had little effect on helping. The pressure of time, however, made a real difference. Of those who thought they were ahead of schedule, 63% offered help—compared with 45% of those who believed they were on time and only 10% of those who had been told they were late. In describing the events that took place in their study, Darley and Batson noted that "on several occasions a seminary student going to give his talk on the parable of the Good Samaritan literally stepped over the victim as he hurried on his way!" These seminary students unwittingly demonstrated the very point that the parable they would be discussing warns against.

## ▶ Location and Helping

If the presence of others often inhibits helping, do individuals have a worse chance of being helped in an emergency in a big city, with its hectic pace and large crowds, than in a small town? Although place of residence does not seem to affect how much those in close relationships help each other (Franck, 1980; Korte, 1980), in general people are less likely to help strangers in urban areas than in rural ones. This relationship has been found in several countries around the world (Amato, 1983; Hedge & Yousif, 1992; Steblay, 1987).

In a similar vein, Robert Levine and his colleagues (2008) examined three kinds of spontaneous help offered to strangers in 24 U.S. cities. These measures of helping—all assessed in a downtown area during normal business hours on clear summer days—included picking up a pen that a stranger had apparently dropped accidentally, helping a stranger with a heavy limp pick up a pile of magazines that the stranger had dropped, and responding to a stranger's request for change for a quarter by at least checking to see if they had change.

As you can see in Table 10.2, Knoxville, Tennessee, wins the title of "Most Helpful City" among the 24 studied. You should also be able to see that the biggest cities tended to have the worst scores for helping. Overall, greater population size and population

**TABLE 10.2**

**Helping in the U.S.A.**

Three types of help offered to strangers, including helping them retrieve things they dropped or trying to make change for them, were studied in 24 U.S. cities. The top six and bottom six cities are listed in this table. Cities with the largest populations tended to have the least amount of helping. The economic well-being of a city was positively correlated with helping.

| Top Six Cities for Helping | | Bottom Six Cities for Helping | |
| --- | --- | --- | --- |
| **Overall Rank** | **Region** | **Overall Rank** | **Region** |
| 1. Knoxville, TN | South | 19. Youngstown, OH | North Central |
| 2. Kansas City, MO | North Central | 20. Atlanta, GA | South |
| 3. Louisville, KY | South | 21. Chicago, IL | North Central |
| 4. Indianapolis, IN | North Central | 22. Los Angeles, CA | West |
| 5. Dallas, TX | South | 23. San Francisco, CA | West |
| 6. Nashville, TN | South | 24. New York, NY | Northeast |

Based on data from Levine et al., 2008. © Cengage Learning

density (population per square mile) were associated with less helping. Levine and his colleagues also found that greater economic well-being of a city was associated with more helping. As we will see a bit later in this section, however, the picture of helping in the United States is different if one focuses specifically on charitable giving or volunteering.

 ## Culture and Helping

Around the world as well, some cities seem to have more helpful citizens than others. Robert Levine and others (2001) conducted similar field studies in a major city in each of 23 large countries around the world. Table 10.3 reports how the cities ranked in their propensity to help; pedestrians in Rio de Janeiro, Brazil, exhibited the highest rates of helping, and pedestrians in Kuala Lampur, Malaysia, exhibited the lowest rates. Levine and his colleagues examined a number of measures of each city to try to determine what factors predicted these differences in helping, such as how hectic the pace of life seemed to be (as determined by pedestrians' walking speed) or how individualistic or collectivistic the culture was. Only two measures correlated with helping rates. One was a measure of economic well-being—cities from countries with the greatest levels of economic well-being tended to exhibit the least helping, although this relationship was not very strong (and is inconsistent with the findings from the research of Levine and his colleagues in the United States).

The other variable that predicted helping concerned the notion of what is called *simpatía* in Spanish or *simpático* in Portuguese. Some researchers report that this is an important element of Spanish and Latin American cultures and involves a concern with the social well-being of others (Markus & Lin, 1999; Sanchez-Burks et al., 2000). The five cultures in the study conducted by Levine and colleagues that value *simpatía* did tend to show higher rates of helping than the *non-simpatía* cultures.

You may find it surprising that collectivism was not a predictor of helping, but the research on the relationship between individualism or collectivism and prosocial behavior is quite mixed at this time. This inconsistency may stem in part from differences in the kinds of helping studied. Compared to individualists, collectivists may be more likely to help ingroup members, but they are less likely to help outgroup members (Conway et al., 2001; Schwartz, 1990).

Lucian Conway and others (2001) proposed that collectivists are more responsive to the immediate needs of a person near them, but less responsive in more abstract situations. Consistent with this latter point, Markus Kemmelmeier and others (2006) found that people from the more individualistic states in the United States tended to exhibit greater charitable giving and volunteering than people from the more collectivistic states, particularly donations and volunteering that were not specific to one's ingroup affiliations. The authors propose that when helping involves this more abstract kind of giving—as opposed to, for example, helping someone from within one's ingroup—individualism may be associated with greater helping.

## Moods and Helping

Helping someone can put people in a better mood, but can being in a good mood increase people's likelihood of helping someone? Are we less likely to help if we're in a bad mood? What's your prediction?

**Good Moods and Doing Good**  Sunshine in Minneapolis, pleasant odors in Albany, and compliments in Sydney give us some clues about the relationship between good mood and helping. Over the course of a year, pedestrians in Minneapolis, Minnesota, were stopped and asked to participate in a survey of social opinions. When Michael Cunningham (1979) tabulated their responses according to the weather conditions, he discovered that people answered more questions on sunny days than on cloudy ones. Moving his investigation indoors, Cunningham found that sunshine is truly golden: The more the sun was shining, the more generous the tips left by restaurant customers were. Sunshine and helping seem to go together, but what's the connection? Probably it's the mood we're in, as a sunny day cheers us up and a cloudy day damps us down.

When the sun is not shining, many people head for the mall. One of the more powerful sensations you can count on experiencing while strolling through the mall comes when you pass a bakery or coffee shop, as the pleasant aroma of freshly baked chocolate chip cookies or freshly brewed French roast stops you in your tracks. Robert Baron (1997) believed that these pleasant scents put people in a good mood, and he wondered if this good mood would make them more likely to help someone in need. He tested this with passersby in a large shopping mall in Albany, New York. Each selected passerby was approached by a member of the research team and asked for change for a dollar. This interaction took place in a location containing either strong pleasant odors (such as near a bakery or a coffee-roasting café) or no discernible odor (such as near a clothing store).

## TABLE 10.3
### Helping Around the World

Three types of spontaneous helping of a stranger were examined in field experiments in a major city in each of 23 different countries around the world. The top six and bottom six cities are listed below, as are their respective ranks on a measure of economic prosperity. Cities with asterisks are considered to have *simpatía* cultural values, which are characterized by a concern with the social well-being of others.

**Top Six Cities for Helping**

| City | Helping Rank | Economic Rank |
|------|--------------|---------------|
| *Rio de Janeiro, Brazil | 1 | 16 |
| *San Jose, Costa Rica | 2 | 15 |
| Lilongwe, Malawi | 3 | 22 |
| Calcutta, India | 4 | 21 |
| Vienna, Austria | 5 | 4 |
| *Madrid, Spain | 6 | 9 |

**Bottom Six Cities for Helping**

| City | Helping Rank | Economic Rank |
|------|--------------|---------------|
| Taipei, Taiwan | 18 | (data unavailable) |
| Sofia, Bulgaria | 19 | 17 |
| Amsterdam, Netherlands | 20 | 6 |
| Singapore, Singapore | 21 | 2 |
| New York, United States | 22 | 1 |
| Kuala Lampur, Malaysia | 23 | 10 |

Based on Levine et al., 2001. © Cengage Learning

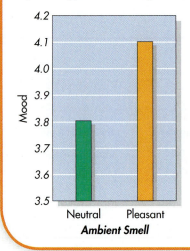

● **FIGURE 10.6**

**Scents and Sensibilities**

People walking in a mall were approached by someone who asked them for change. This encounter took place in areas of the mall with either pleasant ambient odors or no clear odors. The stranger also gave the individuals a questionnaire that measured their mood on a 5-point scale, ranging from 1 (very bad) to 5 (very good). As shown on the left, the people approached in a pleasant-smelling area were in a better mood than those approached in neutral-smelling locations. In addition (right), people were more likely to help the stranger by giving him change if they were in a pleasant-smelling area than if they were in a neutral-smelling area.
From Baron, R. A., "The sweet smell of...helping: Effects of pleasant ambient fragrance on prosocial behavior in shopping malls," *Personality and Social Psychology Bulletin*, vol 23 (pp. 498–503). Copyright © 1997 by Sage Publications, Inc. Reprinted by permission of Sage Publications, Inc.

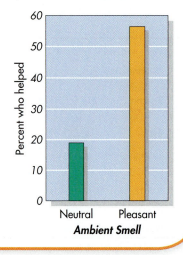

People are much more likely to help someone when they're in a good mood. **TRUE.**

As can be seen in ● Figure 10.6, people approached in a pleasant-smelling location were much more likely to help than people approached in a neutral-smelling location. Baron also found that people were in a better mood when they were in the pleasant-smelling environments. This effect on their mood appears to have caused their greater tendency to help. (Very similar results were found by Nicolas Guéguen (2012) in a recent replication in a mall in Rennes, France.)

Shoppers are not the only people at the mall affected by mood—the sales staff is affected too. Joseph Forgas and others (2008) conducted a field experiment at four department stores in Sydney, Australia. The moods of salespersons were manipulated by having a confederate approach them and say either very complimentary things (e.g., "I am so impressed with the service at this store"), negative things (e.g., "I am so disappointed with the service at this store"), or neutral things. A few seconds later, a second confederate approached the salesperson and asked for help finding an item that did not really exist. How much did the salesperson attempt to help this confederate?

The researchers predicted that the mood manipulation would not have much effect on the most experienced salespersons, as they would have a well-rehearsed set of responses to customer questions and would therefore respond accordingly. For the less-experienced staff, however, Forgas and his colleagues expected that they would exert greater effort to help the customer if they had been put in a good mood. As ● Figure 10.7 illustrates, this is exactly what the results indicated.

It is clear, then, that good moods increase helping. The next question is: Why? There seem to be several factors at work. Table 10.4 summarizes some of the reasons why feeling good often leads to doing good, and it also describes some of the detours in this road that can lead away from helping.

● **FIGURE 10.7**

**May I Help You?**

Salespersons at department stores in Sydney, Australia, were approached by a confederate who put them in a positive, negative, or neutral mood by saying either very positive, negative, or neutral things to them. A few seconds later a different confederate asked the salespersons for help in finding an item that didn't exist. How hard did the staff try to help the confederate? Among the less-experienced staff, those who had been put in a positive mood were much more helpful than were the other salespersons.
Data from Forgas et al., 2008. © Cengage Learning

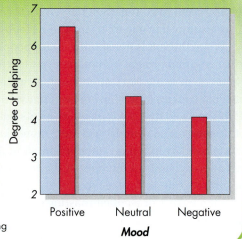

**Bad Moods and Doing Good**   Since a good mood increases helping, does a bad mood decrease it? Not necessarily. Under many circumstances, negative feelings can elicit positive behavior toward others (Cryder et al., 2012; Niesta Kayser et al., 2010; Vollhardt & Staub, 2011; Xu & Shankland, 2011; Zemack-Rugar et al., 2007).

Why might a bad mood promote prosocial behavior? As noted earlier, people know that helping makes them feel good. This point underlies the negative state relief model, which we described earlier as proposing that people who are feeling bad are motivated to repair their mood and they realize that one way to do it is by helping others. Remove the likelihood of feeling better by helping, however, and helping becomes less likely. This is what Daniela Niesta Kayser and others found (2010) in a series of studies. They found that both positive and negative moods did increase low-cost helping, but neither mood led to increased helping in a situation in which the helper could anticipate that it could be difficult and stressful.

Although negative moods can often boost helping, it is not as strong and consistent a relationship as that between good moods and helping. As Table 10.5 indicates, there are several limits to this effect. For example, one important variable is whether people accept responsibility for their bad feelings. If we blame others for our feeling lousy, we're less likely to be generous in our behavior toward others. If, instead, we feel guilty for something bad that we have caused to happen, we are more likely to act prosocially (Rogers et al., 1982; Zemack-Rugar et al., 2007).

> People are much less likely to help someone when they're in a bad mood.   **F**ALSE.

---

**TABLE 10.4**

**Good Moods Lead to Helping: Reasons and Limitations**

Research shows that people in positive moods are more likely to help someone in need than are people in neutral moods. There are several explanations for this effect as well as some limiting conditions that can weaken or reverse the help-promoting effects of good moods.

**Why Feeling Good Leads to Doing Good**

- *Desire to maintain one's good mood.* When we are in a good mood, we are motivated to maintain that mood. Helping others makes us feel good, so it can help maintain a positive mood.
- *Positive thoughts and expectations.* Positive moods trigger positive thoughts, and if we have positive thoughts about others, we should like them more and should have positive expectations about interacting with others, and these factors should make us more likely to help them.

**When Feeling Good Might Not Lead to Doing Good**

- *Costs of helping are high.* If the anticipated costs of helping in a particular situation seem high, helping would put our good mood at risk. In this case, if we can avoid getting involved and thus maintain our good mood, we are less likely to help.
- *Positive thoughts about other social activities that conflict with helping.* If our good mood makes us want to go out and party with our friends, our motivation to engage in this social activity may prevent us from taking the time to notice or take responsibility for helping someone in need.

© Cengage Learning

---

**TABLE 10.5**

**Bad Moods and Helping: When Does Feeling Bad Lead to Doing Good, and When Doesn't It?**

Research shows that people in negative moods are often more likely to help someone in need than are people in neutral moods. However, there are several limitations to this effect. This table summarizes some of the factors that make it more or less likely for people to do good when they feel bad.

**When Negative Moods Make Us More Likely to Help Others**

- If we take responsibility for what caused our bad mood ("I feel guilty for what I did.")
- If we focus on other people ("Wow, those people have suffered so much.")
- If we think about our personal values that promote helping ("I really shouldn't act like such a jerk next time; I have to be nicer.")

**When Negative Moods Make Us Less Likely to Help Others**

- If we blame others for our bad mood ("I feel so angry at that jerk who put me in this situation.")
- If we become very self-focused ("I am so depressed.")
- If we think about our personal values that do not promote helping ("I have to wise up and start thinking about my own needs more.")

© Cengage Learning

## Prosocial Media Effects

Politicians, educators, researchers, and parents have voiced strong concerns for decades about the negative effects of the media, such as TV, movies, and music lyrics and videos, and more recently video games, on the attitudes and behaviors of adolescents and young adults. And as is discussed in Chapter 11 on Aggression, there is very good reason for these concerns. But what has garnered far less attention is that popular media also can have positive effects, including on promoting prosocial attitudes and behaviors.

Douglas Gentile and others (2009) conducted a series of studies, using very different methods and across different cultures, to test the idea that playing video games featuring characters who help and support each other in nonviolent ways can make people more likely to behave in prosocial ways. In a correlational study, the researchers found that middle-school students in Singapore who played more prosocial games tended to behave more prosocially in their real lives (such as by being more likely to indicate that they share things with others or spend time or money to help others in need). In longitudinal studies of Japanese children and adolescents, playing prosocial games at one point in time predicted increases several months later in prosocial behavior. Finally, in an experiment involving undergraduates in the United States, students randomly assigned to play prosocial video games behaved more prosocially than students assigned to play either neutral or violent games.

In the experiment, students were randomly assigned to play specific parts of a prosocial game (Super Mario Sunshine or Chibi Robo), a violent game (Ty2 or Crash Twinsanity), or a neutral game (Pure Pinball or Super Monkey Ball Deluxe) for 20 minutes. (We've never played any of these ourselves, but we must admit to being intrigued by the title, Super Monkey Ball Deluxe.) In the prosocial games, the player tries to get "happy points" by cleaning up a house or to help the people of an island that has been polluted by others.

After playing the game, the students then had the task of assigning a fellow student puzzles to complete. Successful completion of these puzzles would earn this other student some money. Some puzzles were easy and others were difficult, but either way the other student would earn the same money for successfully completing them. Therefore, it would be most helpful for the participants to assign relatively easy puzzles to their partner. As can be seen in ● Figure 10.8, participants were more likely to assign easy puzzles to their partner if they had just played the prosocial video game than if they had played a neutral or a violent video game.

Jodi Whitaker and Brad Bushman (2012) found that even playing a merely relaxing, rather than prosocial, video game (such as a fishing game) led college students to donate more time to help the experimenter with a menial task after the apparent conclusion of the study) than if they had played a neutral or violent video game. Why did a relaxing game have this effect? The relaxing game put the students into a more positive mood, and this in turn led to more helpful behavior.

Seeing characters act in helpful, cooperative ways in popular media can serve to model prosocial behavior, particularly if the behavior is rewarded or associated with a well-liked character. Supporting this idea are the results of a meta-analysis of 34 studies involving more than 5,000 children. This analysis found a reliable positive effect of prosocial television on children's prosocial behavior, especially when specific acts of altruism were modeled on TV (Mares & Woodard, 2005).

● **FIGURE 10.8**

**Super Mario Makes You Super Nice? Effects of Prosocial Video Games**

College students played a video game in which the characters acted either in helpful, cooperative ways (prosocial game), violent ways (violent game), or neither (neutral game). They later had the opportunity to either help a partner's chances of earning money in a puzzle-solving task by assigning them easy puzzles or to hurt his or her chances by assigning difficult puzzles. Students were significantly more likely to help the partner by assigning an easier set of puzzles if they had played a prosocial video game than if they had played a neutral or violent game.

Adapted from Gentile et al., 2009. © Cengage Learning

## Role Models and Social Norms

The finding about the relation between prosocial television and children's real prosocial behavior illustrates the power of role models. Helpful models are important not only for children but for all of us. Observing helpful models increases helping in a variety of situations (Hearold, 1986; Ng & van Dyne, 2005; Sechrist & Milford, 2007; Siu et al., 2006).

Marlone Henderson and others (2012) proposed that learning about individuals who engage in acts of helping others who are very psychologically and perhaps physically distant from them can capture people's attention and inspire them to act in kind. (The Batman quote in the margin is related to this point.) In one of their studies to test this idea, students at the University of Texas at Austin read about a group of students from Peking University in Beijing, China, who donated their time helping disadvantaged children who were said to be either in Beijing (small-distance condition) or in Istanbul, Turkey (large-distance condition). After reading this information, the Texas students were given the chance to buy a t-shirt to raise money for these children. The students were significantly more likely to buy the shirt if they had read a model of large-distance than small-distance helping (see left side of ● Figure 10.9). In another study with the same manipulations, the Texas students were instead given the chance to donate money to a charity raising money for victims of a tornado in a Midwestern city in the United States. As you can see on the right side of Figure 10.9, the students were willing to donate more money after reading the large-distance than small-distance examples of helping by the Beijing students.

Why do people who exemplify helping inspire us to help? Three reasons stand out. First, they provide an example of behavior for us to imitate directly. Second, when they are rewarded for their helpful behavior, people who model helping behavior teach us that helping is valued and rewarding, which strengthens our own inclination to be helpful. Third, the behavior of these models makes us think about and become more aware of the standards of conduct in our society.

General rules of conduct established by society are called **social norms**. These norms embody standards of socially approved and disapproved behavior. Two sets of social norms bear directly on when people are likely to help. The first consists of norms based on fairness. As we mentioned in Chapter 7, the *norm of reciprocity* establishes a strong socially approved standard: People who give to you should be paid back. We discussed reciprocal altruism earlier in this chapter; many animals, including humans, help those who have helped them. Equity is the basis of another norm that calls for fairness in our treatment of others. The *norm of equity* prescribes that when people are in a situation in which they feel overbenefited (receiving more benefits than earned), they should help those who are underbenefited (receiving fewer benefits than earned).

> *"People need dramatic examples to shake them out of apathy."*
> —Bruce Wayne (Batman) in *Batman Begins*
> (quoted by Henderson et al. 2012)

● **FIGURE 10.9**
**Modeling Helping of Distant Others**

Students at the University of Texas read about students from Beijing who dedicated time to helping disadvantaged children. The children were psychologically and physically close (children in Beijing) or far (children in Turkey) from the helpers. Texas students were subsequently given the chance to buy a shirt to raise money for these children (left graph) or to donate money to help victims of the destructive impact of a tornado in a Midwestern city in the United States (right graph). In both cases, the Texas students were significantly more charitable after reading about a model of more distant rather than closer helping by the Beijing students.

Based on Henderson et al., 2012. © Cengage Learning

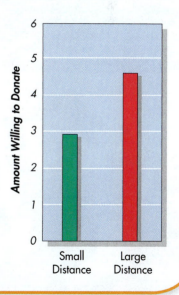

**social norm** A general rule of conduct reflecting standards of social approval and disapproval.

Other social norms related to help go beyond an immediate sense of fairness to a larger sense of what is right. The *norm of social responsibility* dictates that people should help those who need assistance. When people are more motivated by concerns about *justice or fairness*, however, their intentions to help someone will be driven more by their belief that this person *deserves* their assistance than by their belief that he or she simply needs it (Lerner, 1998). Norms based on religion are also important to many people and can influence attitudes and behavior about helping. In a sample of college students in Thailand, for example, Paul Yablo and Nigel Field (2007) found relatively high rates of self-reported altruistic behaviors, and the researchers attributed this to the fact that the Thai students were very likely to cite norms and values based on religion to explain why they would help in various situations.

# Personal Influences: Who Is Likely to Help?

As we have just seen, social psychological research addressing the question "When do people help?" has been quite productive. What about the question "Who is likely to help?" In this section, we consider some of the individual differences between people that address this question.

## Are Some People More Helpful Than Others?

Although situational factors clearly can overwhelm individual differences in influencing helping behaviors in many contexts (Latané & Darley, 1970), researchers have found some evidence that people who are more helpful than others in one situation are likely to be more helpful in other situations as well (Hampson, 1984; Hay & Cook, 2007; Rushton, 1981b). In addition, longitudinal research suggests that this individual difference may be relatively stable over time (Dovidio et al., 2006). For example, Nancy Eisenberg and others (2002) found that the degree to which preschool children exhibited spontaneous helping behavior predicted how helpful they would be in later childhood and early adulthood.

As with so many other individual differences, recent research suggests that differences in helpfulness appears to be partly based on genetics. Genetically identical (monozygotic) twins are more similar to each other in their helpful behavioral tendencies and their helping-related emotions and reactions, such as empathy, than are fraternal (dizygotic) twins, who share only a portion of their genetic makeup. These findings suggest that there may be a heritable component to helpfulness (Ebstein et al., 2010; Gregory et al., 2009; Knafo & Plomin, 2006). Joan Chiao (2011) estimates that between 56% and 72% of prosocial behavior can be attributed to genetic effects.

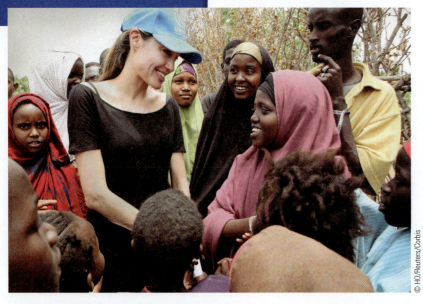

Movie star Angelina Jolie has used her celebrity as well as her own time and energy to raise awareness and resources for impoverished and malnourished children around the world. In this photo she is at a refugee camp on the Kenya-Somalia border.

© HO/Reuters/Corbis

## What Is the Altruistic Personality?

Some people are more helpful than others, but can we predict who is likely to be altruistic by looking at people's overall personalities? If so, what are the various components of *the altruistic personality*?

Consider, for example, Oskar Schindler, the wealthy German businessman during the Nazi regime who became the hero of the book and movie *Schindler's List*. Schindler was a shady operator, cheating in business and marriage, partying with sadistic German military officers. From his overall personality, could anyone have predicted his altruistic actions of risking his own life to save over 4,000 Jews during the Holocaust? It is doubtful. What about more recent models of altruism? Consider these people: Bill Gates, a computer geek who cofounded Microsoft and became the richest man in the world; Bono, the extraverted Irish rock star; Ted Turner, an eccentric American from the South who started the first 24-hour news cable station (CNN); Dikembe Mutombo, a 7-foot, 2-inch former professional basketball player originally from the Congo; Mother Teresa, a Roman Catholic nun from Macedonia. Gates and his wife Melinda have pledged *billions* of dollars to charity, much of it to target health issues around the world. Bono has worked tirelessly to raise money and awareness about the plight of poor African nations. Turner pledged a personal donation of $1 billion to the United Nations. Mutombo raised millions of dollars for the construction of hospitals in the Congo. Mother Teresa devoted her life to the poor in India. These well-known figures seem *quite* different from each other in overall personality—except for their concern with helping others.

The quest to discover the altruistic personality has not been an easy one. Much of the research conducted over the years has failed to find consistent, reliable personality characteristics that predict helping behavior across situations. Some researchers have changed the nature of the quest, however, focusing on personality variables that predict helping in some specific situations rather than across all situations; and their studies have been more successful in identifying traits that predict such behavior (Carlo et al., 2005; Finkelstein, 2009; Penner, 2004).

Research has found that people who tend to be very agreeable, and people who are relatively humble, are more likely to be helpful than people who are disagreeable or lack humility (Caprara et al., 2012; LaBouff et al., 2012). The two individual difference factors

> *"The purpose of human life is to serve and to show compassion and the will to help others."*
> —Albert Schweitzer

Rock star Bruce Springsteen (left) may not seem to have a lot in common with the Dalai Lama (seen in the photo on the right serving lunch at a soup kitchen in 2009) and many of the other people mentioned on this page as models of altruism, but like them, he donates a tremendous amount of time and money to helping others. At every stop on his concert tours in recent years, Springsteen has raised money for local causes, such as food banks, youth centers, and shelters.

that perhaps most of the research has focused on as predictors of helpfulness are empathy and advanced moral reasoning (Albiero et al., 2009; Carlo et al., 2011; Eisenberg et al., 2010; Malti et al., 2010; Roth-Hanania et al., 2011). We've already discussed empathy in this chapter, such as in the context of Batson's empathy–altruism hypothesis. Being able to take the perspective of others and experience empathy clearly is associated positively with helping and other prosocial behaviors in children and adults. The second characteristic associated with helping is moral reasoning. Children and adults who exhibit internalized and advanced levels of moral reasoning behave more altruistically than others. Such reasoning involves adhering to moral standards independent of external social controls and taking into account the needs of others when making decisions about courses of action. In contrast, people whose reasoning is focused on their own needs or on the concrete personal consequences that their actions are likely to have tend not to engage in many helping behaviors.

Elizabeth Midlarsky, Stephanie Fagin-Jones, and their colleagues (Fagin-Jones & Midlarsky, 2007; Midlarsky et al., 2005) have conducted one fascinating line of research that suggests the importance of both empathy and moral reasoning. They contrasted the personalities of "non-Jewish heroes of the Holocaust"—people who risked their lives to help Jews despite having no expectation of any extrinsic rewards—with bystanders who did not help during the Holocaust. The researchers found that rescuers did indeed tend to differ from bystanders on a combination of several variables associated with prosocial behavior, particularly empathic concern and moral reasoning. Both of these qualities are reflected in the quote of one woman who sheltered 30 Jews in her home in Poland: "Helping to give shelter was the natural thing to do, the human thing. When I looked into those eyes, how could I not care? Of course I was afraid—always afraid—but there was no choice but to do the only decent thing" (Midlarsky et al., 2005, p. 908).

"It's always poor you, isn't it, Albert?"

Someone relatively low in empathic concern for another.

*"True kindness presupposes the faculty of imagining as one's own the suffering and joy of others."*
—André Gide

# Interpersonal Influences: Whom Do People Help?

We have just seen how some people are more helpful than others, but now we turn to the question of whether some people are more likely to *receive* help than others, at least in certain situations. We also explore some of the interpersonal aspects of helping.

## Perceived Characteristics of the Person in Need

Although many characteristics of a person in need might affect whether that individual is helped, researchers have paid special attention to two: the personal attractiveness of the person in need and whether or not the person seems responsible for being in the position of needing assistance.

**Attractiveness**    In Chapter 9, we described the social advantages physically attractive individuals enjoy. The bias toward beauty also affects helping. Attractive people are more likely to be offered help and cooperation across a number of different settings, whether it be asking for directions on campus, playing a game that could be either competitive or cooperative, or requesting money in a health emergency (Farrelly et al., 2007; West & Brown, 1975; Wilson, 1978). In addition to physical attractiveness, interpersonal attractiveness is also related to receiving more help (Stürmer et al., 2005).

Certainly one explanation for some of these findings is that people help attractive others in the hope of establishing some kind of relationship with an attractive person. Not many people would be shocked to learn, for example, that male motorists in France were more likely to stop their cars and offer a ride to female hitchhikers whose bust size was enhanced (by a bra worn by a confederate) or who were smiling (Guéguen, 2007; Guéguen & Fischer-Lokou, 2004). (For whatever it's worth, Guéguen and Lamy (2009) have also found that female hitchhikers wearing a blonde wig are more likely to be helped by male motorists than those wearing brown or black wigs.)

What may be surprising, however, is that attractive people receive more help even when the helper does it anonymously, with no chance for any reward. One demonstration of this was a study by Peter Benson and his colleagues (1976) in a large metropolitan airport. Darting into a phone booth to make a call (these were the days long before cell phones), each of 604 travelers discovered some materials supposedly left behind accidentally by the previous caller (but actually planted by the experimenters): a packet containing a completed graduate school application form, a photograph of the applicant, and a stamped, addressed envelope. In some packets, the photo depicted a physically attractive individual; in others, the person was relatively unattractive. What was a busy traveler to do? When the researchers checked their mail, they found that people were more likely to send in the materials of the good-looking applicants than those of the less attractive applicants.

> Attractive people have a better chance than unattractive people of getting help when they need it. **T**RUE.

**Attributions of Responsibility**    People are more likely to help someone in need if they think the person shouldn't be held responsible for his or her predicament. If they think—even unjustifiably—that the person can be blamed for his or her situation, they are less likely to help. These effects can be seen on fairly mundane issues, such as requests to take notes for a fellow student (Barnes et al., 1979), or in life-and-death matters, such as intervening in an instance of domestic violence (Gracia et al., 2009) or helping someone very ill. This latter case was illustrated in research by Michelle Lobchuk and others (2008), who found that caregivers of people with lung cancer had more negative emotions and gave less supportive help if they believed the patient was largely responsible for his or her disease. Similarly, Nadine Mackay and Christine Barrowclough (2005) report that the medical and nursing staff at an emergency room felt more negative about and were less helpful to patients whose injuries they felt were more controllable and avoidable.

Participants in an experiment by Pamela Dooley (1995) read scenarios about someone who had just been diagnosed with AIDS. If the participants read that the person had contracted the disease through a blood transfusion rather than through sexual activity or drug use, they considered the situation less controllable, felt more pity for the person, and indicated a greater desire to engage in helping behaviors. More recently Jean Decety and others (2010) using fMRI technology found that participants showed brain activity indicating greater sensitivity when learning about the pain of individuals who had contracted AIDS as a result of a blood transfusion rather than drug use.

## A Little Help for Our Friends, and Others Like Us

As we would expect, people are usually more helpful to those they know and care about than to strangers or superficial acquaintances (Bell et al., 1995; Clark & Mills,

1993; Stewart-Williams, 2008). People in a *communal* relationship, such as close friends or romantic partners, feel mutual responsibility for each other's needs. People in an *exchange* relationship, such as acquaintances or business associates, give help with the expectation of receiving comparable benefits in return—"If I help you move your furniture, you'd better give me a ride to the airport." When people are, or desire to be, in a communal relationship with each other, they attend more to each other's needs, are more likely to help, and are less likely to be concerned with keeping track of rewards and costs than people in an exchange relationship are. People in a communal relationship also feel better about having helped the other, and they feel worse if they are unable to help (Williamson et al., 1996).

Whether they are friends or strangers, we are more likely to help others who are similar to us. All kinds of similarity—from dress to attitudes to nationality—increase our willingness to help, and signs of dissimilarity decrease it (Batson et al., 2005; Dovidio, 1984). There are probably several reasons underlying this effect. For one thing, as seen in Chapter 9, we are more likely to be attracted to and develop relationships with people who are similar to ourselves. In addition, people tend to empathize more with similar others or with people in their ingroups (Xu et al., 2009). The influence of similarity could even be a form of kin selection, as people may use similarity in appearance as a signal of potential kinship.

People are much more likely to help fellow ingroup members than they are to help members of an outgroup (Bernhard et al., 2006; Kogut & Ritov, 2007; Levine & Cassidy, 2010; Stürmer et al., 2006). Mark Levine and others (2005) demonstrated this point in a clever field experiment based on the bystander intervention research discussed earlier in the chapter. Participants were British university students who were supporters of a particular popular football (soccer) team. After completing some questions about their support of the team (which served to highlight their identification with it), the participants had to walk to another building on campus, allegedly to watch a video for the next part of the study. On the way they encountered a jogger (actually, a confederate) who fell and seemed to be in pain with an injured ankle. For some of the participants, this jogger happened to be wearing the shirt of the participants' favorite team. For others, the jogger was wearing either a shirt of a rival team or a neutral shirt with no team logo. Would the shirt affect how likely the jogger was to be offered help?

As you can see in ● Figure 10.10, the shirt did make a big difference. Participants were much more likely to offer help to a person wearing their favorite team's shirt—a fellow ingroup member—than they were to help a person wearing either a neutral or a rival shirt. In this study, wearing a rival team's shirt did not reduce the jogger's chances of getting help compared to wearing a neutral shirt; it was just that wearing a shirt that signified similar team affiliation led to increased helping.

Intergroup biases in helping can be reduced significantly if the members of the different groups can perceive themselves as members of a common group. Through fostering perceptions of shared identities and highlighting similarities between individuals across groups, an ingroup and an outgroup can begin to see each other as more similar than different, thereby promoting helping and other positive behaviors (Dovidio et al., 2010; Gaertner & Dovidio, 2012).

The effects of similarity and ingroup status on helping suggest that members of the same race should help each other more than they help members of different races. However, in a meta-analysis of more than 30 studies, Donald Saucier and others (2005) found no consistent overall

● **FIGURE 10.10**

**Helping Ingroup Members**

Participants who were fans of a particular British football (soccer) team came across a fallen jogger who seemed to be in pain. They were much more likely to offer the jogger help if he was wearing a shirt of the participants' favorite team than if he was wearing either a rival team's shirt or a neutral shirt.

Based on Levine et al., 2005. © Cengage Learning

*Jogger's Shirt*

■ % who helped

relationship between racial similarity and helping. What accounts for these inconsistencies? First, although helping can be a compassionate response to another, it can also be seen as a sign of superiority over the person who needs help, and this can greatly complicate the decision about helping someone (Halabi et al., 2012; Nadler & Fisher, 1986; Täuber & van Zomeren, 2012; Vorauer & Sasaki, 2009). Given the possibility that helping someone can seem threatening or condescending, it may make it harder to predict when helping as a function of racial ingroup or outgroup will or won't occur. Second, public displays of racial prejudice risk social disapproval, and prejudiced individuals may bend over backward (in public, at least) to avoid revealing their attitudes. As discussed in Chapter 5, however, modern racism relies on more subtle forms of discrimination. Consistent with predictions from theories of modern racism, Saucier et al.'s meta-analysis found that when the situation provides people with excuses or justifications for not helping, racial discrimination in helping is more likely.

## Gender and Helping

Here's a quick, one-question quiz: Who helps more, men or women? Before you answer, consider the following situations:

**A.** Two strangers pass on the street. Suddenly, one of them needs help that might be dangerous to give. Other people are watching.

**B.** Two individuals have a close relationship. Every so often, one of them needs assistance that takes time and energy to provide but is not physically dangerous. No one else is around to notice whether help is given.

Is your answer different for these two situations? It's likely to be. Situation A is a classic male-helper scenario. Because much of the research on helping used to focus on emergency situations, such as in the bystander intervention studies, older reviews tended to find that, on average, men are more helpful than women and women receive more help than men (Eagly & Crowley, 1986). Situation B is the classic female-helper scenario. Every day, millions of people provide support for their friends and loved ones, and some reviews indicate that women are more likely to provide this kind of help than are men (Becker & Eagly, 2004; George et al., 1998; McGuire, 1994). Though it lacks the high drama of an emergency intervention, this type of helping, called "social support," plays a crucial role in the quality of our lives. Chapter 14 reports evidence indicating that social support is associated with better physical and psychological health.

For types of helping that do not easily fit into either of these categories, the evidence for gender differences is not strong or reliable. Overall, then, there does not seem to be a general and consistent gender difference in who is most likely to help others. What about the other side of the coin, though: Is there a difference in who is likely to *seek* help? Have you ever had the experience of getting lost while driving with a member of the opposite sex? Who wanted to stop early on and ask for directions? Who kept insisting that help wasn't necessary? In this case, the stereotype is true: Men ask for help less frequently than do women—a difference replicated in several countries around the world (Chang, 2007; Mackenzie et al., 2006; Murray et al., 2008; Sherer, 2007). Help-seeking is less socially acceptable for men and is more threatening to their self-esteem (Wills & DePaulo, 1991).

**Women seek help more often than men do.** **T**RUE.

"Are you telling me you won't even ask the computerized navigational system for directions?"

**Men are less likely to seek help than women, possibly because it is more threatening to their self-esteem.**

## > Culture and Who Receives Help

As we said earlier in the chapter, compared to individualists, collectivists may be more likely to help ingroup members but less likely to help outgroup members (Conway et al., 2001; Schwartz, 1990).

We also discussed earlier that people are less likely to help if they think the person is responsible for his or her plight. Elizabeth Mullen and Linda Skitka (2009) proposed that this may be a stronger influence on helping in an individualist culture—where individuals may be expected to have more control over their own fates—than in a collectivist one. On the other hand, perceptions of how much the person in need contributes to society might affect the helping decisions of collectivists—who have stronger norms of interdependence—more than of individualists.

To test these ideas, Mullen and Skitka (2009) had participants from the United States and the Ukraine (a more collectivistic society) read about 16 individuals who needed an organ transplant. Information about each individual suggested that some were more responsible for their illness than others (e.g., a person continued to eat unhealthy foods and resist exercise despite warnings versus a person had a genetically defective organ). The researchers also varied information about how much contribution the individuals seemed to make to society (e.g., a person who volunteers for multiple organizations versus a person who does not volunteer). After reading about all 16 people, participants were asked to indicate which of up to six of them should receive a transplant.

In both cultures, people were less likely to help patients who were more responsible for their organ failure or who contributed less to society. However, as can be seen in ● Figure 10.11, the issue of personal responsibility played a bigger role in the decisions

---

● **FIGURE 10.11**

**Who Should Receive Help? A Cross-Cultural Difference**

Americans and Ukrainians were asked to decide which 6 of up to 16 individuals should receive an organ transplant. Participants were given information about the individuals that varied in terms of how personally responsible they seemed to be for their illnesses and how much they seemed to contribute to their society. Although participants in both countries preferred helping individuals who were not responsible for their illness and who made contributions to society, Americans' decisions were affected more by how responsible the person seemed, whereas Ukrainians' decisions were affected more by whether the person made contributions to society. Based on Mullen & Skitka, 2009. © Cengage Learning

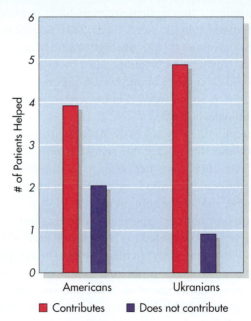

made by the Americans, whereas the issue of contribution to society played a bigger role in the decisions by the Ukrainians.

There also may be cultural differences in seeking help. Heejung Kim and others (2012), for example, observed that Asians and Asian Americans report seeking social support less than European Americans do. This greater resistance to seeking help among Asians and Asian Americans may be due to greater concerns about shame, receiving criticism, and hurting the relationship with the person or people whom they would ask for help. Indeed, Shelley Taylor and others (2007) found that seeking and receiving social support from close others are more stressful—both psychologically and physiologically—to Asian and Asian American students than to European American students. Asian students benefited more from what the researchers called *implicit social support*—support that comes from just thinking about close others but that does not involve actually seeking or receiving their help in coping with stressful events.

## ❭ The Helping Connection

Although whether or not people help others can be quite variable, a consistent theme appears repeatedly in this chapter: a sense of connection. Throughout the chapter, this connection has taken various forms—genetic relatedness, empathic concern, sense of responsibility for someone, perceived similarity, shared group membership, and so on.

In the United States, one of the richest countries on Earth, thousands of men, women, and children are without a home. Many sleep on the street, carry their belongings in grocery carts, and rummage through piles of garbage to find food. In contrast, among some of the poorest people on Earth, no one goes without shelter or remains thirsty as long as anyone has water to drink. How can we account for this difference? Homelessness is, of course, a complex phenomenon affected by many specific economic and political factors. But it may also be a symptom of a profound loss of social connection in American society.

Consider, however, the outpouring of help by Americans after large-scale tragedies, such as the hurricane that destroyed much of the New Jersey shore and parts of New York in 2012, the tsunami in Japan in 2011, or the earthquakes in Haiti in 2010. Families throughout the country, as well as around the world, donated time, money, and resources to help the victims of these catastrophes and to help rebuild the shattered communities. Tragedies such as these can remind people of their common humanity, highlighting their social connection while, temporarily at least, rendering their differences insignificant.

The relationship between helping and interpersonal connection runs like a bright red thread through much of the research on helping. For example:

- People are prone to help their kin, ingroup members, and people with whom they have a close or reciprocal relationship.

- Two kinds of connections lie at the heart of the empathy–altruism hypothesis: the cognitive connection of perspective taking and the emotional connection of empathic concern.

- In an emergency, bystanders who know the victim or know each other are more likely to intervene.

- People who respond empathically to another's suffering and consider the plight of others in their own moral reasoning are more likely to help than are others.

- Perceived similarity increases helping.

Company 6 firefighters are reunited with Josephine Harris, the woman they risked their lives to save in the World Trade Center on September, 11, 2001. The men presented Josephine with a jacket honoring her as their "Guardian Angel"—a reminder of how their selfless act of helping her may have in turn saved their own lives as the 110-story skyscraper collapsed around them.

Taken as a whole, these points suggest that helping requires the recognition of individual human beings with whom we can have a meaningful connection. Which brings us back to Ladder Company 6 and the so many others who risked and even lost their lives that day. Most of the people didn't know the others they were helping. But suddenly, horribly, fate had thrown them together, and suddenly their lives deeply mattered to each other. They felt responsible for each other. Many of those who helped in the face of grave danger may never have read the words that English poet John Donne wrote almost 400 years ago. But they would have understood them:

> No man is an island, entire of itself. Every man is a piece of the continent, a part of the main. If a clod be washed away by the sea, Europe is the less, as well as if a promontory were, as well as if a manor of thy friends or of thine own were. Any man's death diminishes me, because I am involved in mankind. And therefore never send to know for whom the bell tolls; it tolls for thee.

# Review

## Evolutionary and Motivational Factors: Why Do People Help?

### Evolutionary Factors in Helping

- Evolutionary perspectives emphasize two ways that helping could become an innate, universal behavioral tendency: kin selection, in which individuals protect their own genes by helping close relatives, and reciprocal altruism, in which those who give also receive.
- Various primates have been observed to show some relatively elaborate examples of reciprocal altruism and cooperation.

### The Evolution of Empathy

- Empathy involves understanding the emotional experience of another individual and experiencing emotions consistent with what the other is feeling.
- Recent work examines how seemingly higher-order, uniquely human constructs such as morality and empathy are evolved characteristics.
- Many primates seem to exhibit empathy both in laboratory and natural settings.

### Rewards of Helping: Helping Others to Help Oneself

- People are much more likely to help when the potential rewards of helping seem high relative to the potential costs.
- Helping others often makes the helper feel good, it can relieve negative feelings such as guilt, and it is associated with better health. Long-term or high-risk helping, however, can be costly to the health and well-being of the helper.
- People who are feeling bad may be inclined to help others in order to feel relief from their negative mood.

- Some situations call to mind norms that promote particular kinds of self-sacrificing, helpful behaviors.

### Altruism or Egoism: The Great Debate

- Scholars have debated whether egoistic motives are always behind helpful behaviors or whether helping is ever truly altruistic.
- According to the empathy–altruism hypothesis, taking the perspective of a person perceived to be in need creates the other-oriented emotion of empathic concern, which in turn produces the altruistic motive to reduce the other's distress.
- A number of studies have supported the empathy–altruism hypothesis, for example by demonstrating that when people are altruistically motivated, they will help even when escaping from the helping situation is easy. However, there are limits to the role of altruism in helping behavior.
- Longer-term acts of helping, such as volunteerism, reflect both altruistic and egoistic motivations. Self-interested goals in this context can be a good thing because they promote a commitment to helping behavior to the extent that such goals are met.

---

**Putting *Common Sense* to the Test**

**People are more likely to help someone in an emergency if the potential rewards seem high and the potential costs seem low.**
**True.** *For both emergency situations and more long-term, well-planned helping, people's helping behaviors are determined in part by a cost–benefit analysis.*

# Situational Influences: When Do People Help?

## The Bystander Effect

- Research on the bystander effect, in which the presence of others inhibits helping in an emergency, indicates why the five steps necessary for helping—noticing, interpreting, taking responsibility, deciding how to help, and providing help—may not be taken.
- The distractions caused by the presence of other people and by our own self-concerns may impair our ability to notice that someone needs help.
- The presence of others can make bystanders less likely to interpret a situation as an emergency, possibly through the pluralistic ignorance created by everyone trying to appear unconcerned.
- People may fail to take responsibility because they assume that others will do so—a phenomenon called *diffusion of responsibility*.
- Bystanders are less likely to offer direct aid when they do not feel competent to do so.
- Even if people want to help, they may not do so if they fear that behaving in a helpful fashion will make them look foolish.
- The bystander effect occurs even in online contexts, when the bystanders are not physically present.
- The legacy of the bystander effect research and of the Kitty Genovese tragedy that inspired it endures, even as revisions are suggested to some of the research conclusions or to some of the details of the Genovese case.
- The bystander effect has been examined in the context of understanding problems such as sexual assault, bullying, and animal abuse, and it has inspired numerous intervention programs.

## Time Pressure

- When people are in a hurry, they are less likely to notice or choose to help others in need.

## Location and Helping

- Residents of heavily populated areas are less likely to provide spontaneous, informal help to strangers than are residents of smaller or less densely populated communities.

## Culture and Helping

- Cross-cultural research has found variation in the helping rates of people in cities around the world. According to one study, people in cities with relatively low levels of economic well-being were somewhat more likely to help strangers, and people from *simpatía* cultures were more likely to help strangers than people from *non-simpatía* cultures.
- Research concerning the relationship between individualism–collectivism and helping has yielded rather mixed results. According to some analyses, collectivists may be more responsive than individualists to the immediate needs of a particular person but less helpful in more abstract situations.

## Moods and Helping

- A good mood increases helpfulness.
- People in a good mood may help in order to maintain their positive mood or because they have more positive thoughts and expectations about helpful behavior, about the person in need, or about social activities in general.
- A bad mood can often increase helpfulness, for example when people feel guilty about something.
- People in a bad mood may be motivated to help others in order to improve their mood.
- A bad mood is less likely to increase helpfulness if the bad mood is attributed to the fault of others or if it causes the person to become very self-focused.

## Prosocial Media Effects

- Playing video games featuring prosocial content, and watching prosocial television, are both associated with increased prosocial behavior.

## Role Models and Social Norms

- Observing a person modeling helpful behavior increases helping.
- Social norms that promote helping are based on a sense of fairness or on standards about what is right.

---

### Putting *Common Sense* to the Test

**In an emergency, a person who needs help has a much better chance of getting it if three other people are present than if only one other person is present.**

**False.** *In several ways, the presence of others inhibits helping.*

**People are much more likely to help someone when they're in a good mood.**

**True.** *Compared to neutral moods, good moods tend to elicit more helping and other prosocial behaviors.*

**People are much less likely to help someone when they're in a bad mood.**

**False.** *Compared to neutral moods, negative moods often elicit more helping and prosocial behaviors. This effect depends on a number of factors, including whether people take responsibility for their bad mood or blame it on others, but in many circumstances, feeling bad leads to doing good.*

# Personal Influences: Who Is Likely to Help?

### Are Some People More Helpful Than Others?
- There is some evidence of relatively stable individual differences in helping tendencies.
- Recent findings suggest that there may be a genetic, heritable component to helpfulness.

### What Is the Altruistic Personality?
- Some personality traits are associated with helpful behavioral tendencies in some situations, but no one set of traits appears to define the altruistic personality.
- Qualities that do predict helping behaviors are agreeableness, humility, empathy, and advanced moral reasoning.

# Interpersonal Influences: Whom Do People Help?

### Perceived Characteristics of the Person in Need
- Attractive individuals are more likely to receive help than are those who are less attractive.
- People are more willing to help when they attribute a person's need for assistance to uncontrollable causes rather than to events perceived to be under the person's control.

### A Little Help for Our Friends, and Others Like Us
- People in a communal relationship feel mutual responsibility for each others' needs; people in an exchange relationship are more likely to keep track of how reciprocal the relationship is in terms of costs and benefits.
- In general, perceived similarity to a person in need increases willingness to help.
- People are more likely to help members of their ingroups.
- Research on the role of race in helping has yielded inconsistent results.

### Gender and Helping
- Men help strangers in potentially dangerous situations more than women do; women help friends and relations with social support more than men do. The evidence for gender differences is not strong for acts of helping that do not easily fit either of these categories.
- Compared to women, men are more hesitant to seek help, especially for relatively minor problems.

### Culture and Who Receives Help
- Some research has shown that people with a collectivistic orientation may be less likely to help outgroup members or strangers than are those with an individualistic orientation.

- A study found that attributions of how responsible a person in need was for their situation played a stronger role in individualists' decisions to help the person than it did in collectivists' decisions to help. In contrast, perceptions of how much the person in need contributes to society affected collectivists' decisions to help more than it affected individualists' decisions.
- Asian and Asian American students tend to be more hesitant to seek social support than European Americans, and when they do receive social support, they tend to find receiving it more stressful. Asian and Asian American students may prefer social support that is more implicit than explicit.

### The Helping Connection
- Theory and research seem to indicate that helping requires the recognition of meaningful connections among individuals.

---

**Putting *Common Sense* to the Test**

**Attractive people have a better chance than unattractive people of getting help when they need it.**
**True.** *People are more likely to help those who are attractive.*

**Women seek help more often than men do.**
**True.** *At least for relatively minor problems, men ask for help less frequently than women do.*

## KEY TERMS

altruistic (402)

arousal: cost–reward model (400)

audience inhibition (410)

bystander effect (407)

diffusion of responsibility (409)

egoistic (402)

empathy–altruism hypothesis (403)

empathy (398)

kin selection (394)

negative state relief model (401)

pluralistic ignorance (409)

prosocial behaviors (394)

social norm (419)

## MEDIA RESOURCES

Go to CengageBrain.com to access Psychology CourseMate, where you will find an interactive eBook, glossaries, flashcards, quizzes, videos, and more.

# Aggression

In this chapter, we examine a disturbing aspect of human behavior: aggression. First, we ask, "What is aggression?" and consider its definition. After describing how aggression may vary by culture, gender, and individual differences, we examine various theories concerning the origins of aggression. We then explore a variety of situational factors that influence when people are likely to behave aggressively. Next, we focus on media effects on aggression, including the consequences of exposure to media violence and pornography. We conclude by discussing ways of reducing violence.

# 11

**It's a curious quirk of human nature** that so many of us love to go into a darkened room together and get scared. We pay good money to see violence displayed in vivid detail and bold colors in front of us and hear the eardrum-rattling sounds of destruction surrounding us. But when we go to the movies to watch superheroes battle supervillains, we do it with the understanding that we, in fact, are quite safe. It's a vicarious thrill we seek, an escape from our everyday lives into a fictional universe. So when that safe divide between the fictional universe on screen and the real world was shattered shortly after midnight on July 20, 2012, in Aurora, Colorado, the shock and horror would not be soon forgotten.

The third movie in the trilogy of the newest series of *Batman* movies was one of the most highly anticipated movies in years, and so there was tremendous excitement at the packed midnight premiere showing of *The Dark Knight Rises* at the multiplex in the city near Denver. About a half hour into the movie James Holmes, a 24-year-old man in the front row, left the theater through a side exit door—which he propped open, went to his car and changed into protective clothing, retrieved numerous firearms, and returned to the theater, where he proceeded to horrifically and seemingly randomly fire at the people in the theater, killing 12 and wounding 58 others. Details of the attack, and of some of the heroic attempts of several of the victims to shield friends and loved ones from the barrage of gunfire, are heartbreaking.

The magnitude of the deadly attack brought to mind an earlier rampage in Colorado: the massacre at Columbine High School in the town of Littleton. On April 20, 1999, teenagers Dylan Klebold and Eric Harris, armed with a semiautomatic rifle, a semiautomatic handgun, two sawed-off shotguns, and more than 30 homemade bombs, terrorized the school. These boys first shot and killed two students in the school parking lot. Then they entered the cafeteria, where they threw pipe bombs and opened fire, filling the room with bullets. From there, the boys went upstairs, shot a school police officer, and then shot and killed a teacher, ten other students, and themselves.

Almost exactly a year before the Aurora movie theater shootings, on July 22, 2011, Anders Behring Breivik, an anti-Muslim militant, unleashed a series of bomb and gun attacks at government buildings in Oslo, Norway, and at a Labor Party youth camp while posing as a police officer. The series of attacks killed 77 people. And five months after the Aurora shootings, on December 14, 2012, a young man reportedly shot and killed his mother and then drove to an elementary school in Newtown, Connecticut, where he fatally shot 20 young children, ages 6 and 7, and a half dozen adults.

When the safety of a school, a movie theater, a summer camp, or a government building is destroyed by violence, it raises profoundly important questions about the causes of aggression and violence and about how to reduce its prevalence. But while these high-profile incidents get most of the attention, every day there are numerous acts of aggression and violence that should also raise these questions and promote their urgency. For example, there were well more than a *million* violent crimes and almost 15,000 murders in the United States alone in 2011. Multiply each of these crimes by the numbers of friends and loved ones who suffer along with the victims, and you can begin to get a sense of the massive toll that violence brings. And

## Putting *Common Sense* to the Test

*Circle Your Answer*

T  F   In virtually every culture, males are more violent than females.

T  F   For virtually any category of aggression, males are more aggressive than females.

T  F   Children who are spanked or otherwise physically disciplined (but not abused) for behaving aggressively tend to become less aggressive.

T  F   Blowing off steam by engaging in safe but aggressive activities (such as sports) makes people less likely to aggress later.

T  F   Exposure to TV violence in childhood is related to aggression later in life.

**Snapshots of terror.** Eric Harris and Dylan Klebold are seen in the photo on the left as they walk through Columbine High School on the day of their murderous rampage in April 1999. The photo on the right was taken outside the movie theater in Aurora, Colorado after the shootings at the midnight premiere showing of *The Dark Knight Rises* on July 20, 2012.

once you consider those numbers, think about this: These numbers are actually much lower than they were a couple of decades ago.

The suffering caused by aggression is not limited even to these millions of cases a year of violent crime, of course. Every day schoolchildren are bullied, sometimes relentlessly and with tragic outcomes. Every day people spread malicious gossip about others. Every day some parents wound their children with physical or verbal abuse. It is clear, then, that aggression and violence are not limited to a handful of crazed individuals who confuse fiction with reality or whose frustrations with life boil over into explosions of mass violence. It is all the more important, therefore, that we try to understand the root causes and situational triggers of aggression, and that is the goal of this chapter. It focuses primarily on aggression by individuals; aggression by groups, such as rampaging mobs and warring nations, was discussed in Chapter 8. This chapter also discusses factors that reduce aggression.

# What Is Aggression?

Although there are numerous ways one can define **aggression**, the definition that best represents the research today is that aggression is behavior that is intended to harm another individual. Aggressive behaviors come in many forms. Words as well as deeds can be aggressive. Quarreling couples who intend their spiteful remarks to hurt are behaving aggressively. Spreading a vicious rumor about someone is another form of aggression. Even failure to act can be aggressive, if that failure is intended to hurt someone, such as by not helping someone avoid what you know will be a humiliating outcome.

To distinguish them from less harmful behaviors, extreme acts of aggression are called *violence*. Some other terms in the language of aggression refer to emotions and attitudes. *Anger* consists of strong feelings of displeasure in response to a perceived injury; the exact nature of these feelings (for example, outrage, hate, or irritation) depends on the specific situation. *Hostility* is a negative, antagonistic attitude toward another person or group. Anger and hostility are often closely connected to aggression, but not always. People can be angry with others and regard them with great hostility without ever trying to harm them. And aggression can occur without a trace of anger or hostility, as when a contract killer murders a perfect stranger in order to "make a killing" financially.

**aggression** Behavior intended to harm another individual.

A young woman gets blasted in the face with pepper spray by a police officer in Portland, Oregon, during a 2011 protest against the banking industry. Was the officer's use of pepper spray an instance of proactive aggression to restore order and prevent a more violent occurrence? Or was it reactive aggression, in which the officer's frustrations with the protestors boiled over and led to lashing out against some of them? The lines between these two categories of aggression can sometimes be quite blurry.

The aggression of a hired gun is an example of **proactive aggression**, in which harm is inflicted as a means to a desired end. Aggression aimed at harming someone for personal gain, attention, or even self-defense fits this definition. If the aggressor believes that there is an easier way to obtain the goal, aggression will not occur. Some researchers call this type of aggression *instrumental aggression*.

In **reactive aggression**, the means and the end coincide. Harm is inflicted for its own sake. Some researchers call this type of aggression *emotional aggression*. Reactive aggression is often impulsive, carried out in the heat of the moment. The jealous lover strikes out in rage; fans of rival soccer teams go at each other with fists and clubs. Reactive aggression, however, can also be calm, cool, and calculating. Revenge, so the saying goes, is a dish best served cold.

Of course, sometimes it is hard to distinguish between proactive and reactive aggression. Why does a frustrated fighter illegally head butt his opponent—is it a deliberate, sneaky attempt to gain an advantage over a frustrating opponent, or does it simply reflect someone losing control and lashing out unthinkingly in frustration? It can be difficult to know where to draw the line between the two types of aggression and motives. Indeed, some scholars believe that all aggression is fundamentally proactive, serving some need, and still others suggest that proactive and reactive aggression are not distinct categories but endpoints on a continuum (Anderson & Huesmann, 2007; Tedeschi & Bond, 2001).

# Culture, Gender, and Individual Differences

---

**TABLE 11.1**

**The Violent Crime Clock**

Although the rates of violent crimes in the United States have declined in recent years, they are still distressingly high, as these averaged statistics illustrate, and are much higher than they were several decades ago.

In the United States in 2011, there was, on average:

| | |
|---|---|
| One MURDER | every 36 minutes |
| One FORCIBLE RAPE | every 6 minutes |
| One AGGRAVATED ASSAULT | every 42 seconds |
| One VIOLENT CRIME | every 26 seconds |

Based on Federal Bureau of Investigation statistics. © Cengage Learning

**proactive aggression** Aggressive behavior whereby harm is inflicted as a means to a desired end (also called instrumental aggression).

**reactive aggression** Aggressive behavior where the means and the end coincide; harm is inflicted for its own sake.

Just as not all types of aggression are alike, not all groups of people are alike in their attitudes and propensities toward aggression. Before we discuss the causes of aggression and what can be done about it, we need to consider how aggression is similar and different across cultures, gender, and individuals.

## Culture and Aggression

Cultures vary dramatically in how—and how much—their members aggress against each other. We can see this variation across societies and across specific groups, or subcultures, within a society.

**Comparisons Across Societies** The United States has enjoyed recent dramatic decreases in its rates of violent crimes, but it continues to be an exceptionally violent country (see Table 11.1). Its murder rate is one of the highest among politically stable, industrialized nations, far worse than the rates for Canada, Australia, New Zealand, and much of Western Europe. However, several countries in Eastern Europe, Africa, Asia, and the Americas have worse rates than the United States. ● Figure 11.1 illustrates some of the variation in homicide rates around the world.

Murder rates tend to be much higher in Central and South America, the Caribbean, and Southern and Middle Africa than in other regions in the world (United Nations

● **FIGURE 11.1**

**Murder Around the World**

These figures indicate the number of recorded intentional homicides per 100,000 people in each of several countries in 2010, or the most recent year for which statistics are available, according to United Nations statistics published in 2011. Interpret the numbers with great caution, however, because there are large differences in reporting and recording practices in the various countries, but the basic point is clear: There is wide variation in the frequency of murder around the world.

© Cengage Learning

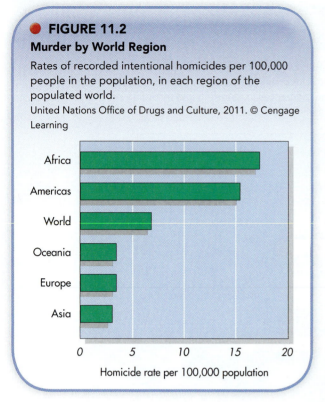

● **FIGURE 11.2**

**Murder by World Region**

Rates of recorded intentional homicides per 100,000 people in the population, in each region of the populated world.

United Nations Office of Drugs and Culture, 2011. © Cengage Learning

Homicide rate per 100,000 population

Office of Drugs and Crime, 2011) (see ● Figure 11.2). A variety of factors contribute to this tendency, including poverty, drug trafficking, availability of guns, political and social unrest, and so on. Countries with wide disparities in income have murder rates almost four times greater than societies more equal income distribution.

Another difference across countries concerns how individualistic or collectivistic cultures tend to be. As discussed throughout this book, individualistic cultures place more emphasis on the values of independence, autonomy, and self-reliance, whereas collectivistic cultures place greater emphasis on the values of interdependence, cooperation, and social harmony. Gordon Forbes and others (2009; 2011) hypothesized that individualistic cultures, which are less concerned with social harmony and the avoidance of open conflict, are most likely to have a relatively high rate of aggression. To examine this idea, they asked college students in China (a highly collectivistic culture) and the United States (a highly individualistic culture) to answer questions about how they would likely respond in a particular conflict situation. The researchers found that men in the United States tended to be significantly more likely to advocate overt aggressive responses compared to men in China; the women tended not to differ in their responses across culture. A more recent study involving 15 countries found that countries high in individualism were associated with greater frequency of school violence (Menzer & Torney-Purta, 2012). In addition, Yan Li and others (2010) found that within a sample of Chinese adolescents, those who were more likely to endorse values associated with individualism tended to be more aggressive—as rated by their teachers and peers—than were adolescents who more strongly endorsed collectivism values. It is important to note, however, that collectivist cultures are not immune from aggression and violence. For example, murder rates in India and Korea (relatively collectivistic cultures) tend to be much higher than in the United Kingdom or France (relatively individualistic cultures).

The forms violence typically takes, and people's attitudes toward various kinds of aggression, also differ internationally. Relative to most of the world, the United States has a tremendous amount of gun-related violence. The prevalence of handguns in the United States is exceptionally high, and even when compared to countries with which it shares much culturally, such as England and Australia, attitudes about guns tend to be much more permissive and positive in the United States, especially among males (Cooke, 2004). Indeed, although the rate of violent crime is actually lower in the United States than in the United Kingdom or Canada, the murder rate is much higher in the United States than in the United Kingdom (Barclay & Tavares, 2003; Slack, 2009). Researchers believe that the higher murder rate in the United States is due to the prevalence of guns. According to one report, the firearm homicide rate was about 20 times higher in the United States than in other high-income countries; for 15 to 24 year olds, the rate was almost 43 times higher (Richardson & Hemenway, 2011)! The ease with which the shooters in the massacres at the *Batman* movie theater and at Columbine High School obtained a massive amount of guns and ammunition led to debates about stronger gun control laws, but no significant changes resulted.

The violence in the United States also tends to involve individuals rather than groups of people. Group attacks against other groups in political, ethnic, tribal, or other institutionalized conflict are seen throughout the world but are particularly associated with the Middle East, Africa, Eastern Europe, and parts of South America. And violent mobs of European football (what Americans call soccer) fans are not uncommon in England and other parts of Europe—behavior rarely seen at American sports events.

Cultures also differ in their attitudes about aggression. In a study involving students at 36 universities in 19 different countries around the world, there was considerable variation in how acceptable the students found different actions, such as a husband slapping a wife or vice versa (Douglas & Straus, 2006). For example, almost 80% of the respondents from a university in India did not strongly disapprove of a husband slapping a wife, compared to only about 24% at a university in the United States. In general, respondents from Europe were more approving of a husband slapping a wife than were respondents from Australia and New Zealand, who in turn tended to be somewhat more approving than respondents from North America. In contrast, these trends were reversed for the question of whether respondents had ever injured a dating partner—on this issue, North American rates tended to be highest. According to a recent UNICEF (2012) report, a majority of adolescent girls and boys in India and in Nepal believe that it is acceptable for a man to beat his wife (Sinha, 2012).

Even within the same region, cultural differences can lead to very different attitudes and behaviors regarding aggression between men and women. A study of Israeli youths revealed that rates of dating violence were much higher among Israeli Arabs than Israeli Jews, apparently reflecting the very different norms between the two cultures (Sherer, 2009).

What is considered to be aggression and unacceptable in relation to children also can differ across cultures. For example, in Japan, it is not uncommon for Japanese adult businessmen to grope schoolgirls on public transportation (Ronzone, 2009), a practice that would be considered aggressive and unacceptable in many other cultures, including the far more violent United States. Indeed, the problem has become so bad that some train companies in Tokyo introduced female-only cars to protect women and girls against this practice, such as on one train line that was formerly considered "a gropers' paradise" because of long gaps between stops and the large number of schoolgirl passengers (Joyce, 2005, p. A6). For similar reasons a program was announced to reserve some subway cars for women in Seoul, South Korea, to protect them from groping, but the plan was scrapped due to an outpouring of criticism (Jung-Yoon, 2011; Kiong, 2011). Exploiting this behavior to more extreme ends, a Japanese 3D video game called *Rape-Lay* has players simulate raping a woman and her two "virgin schoolgirl" daughters in a subway. This game caused an international uproar in February 2009 when it was discovered to be on sale (temporarily) at Amazon.com (Fennelly, 2009). Numerous websites, DVDs, and even fetish clubs in Japan are available for men to watch or act out their fantasies of groping schoolgirls and young women in train cars.

Another example concerns female genital mutilation—any of several procedures in which, according to some estimates, the genitals of approximately 6,000 girls a day are cut in several countries around the world, particularly in parts of Africa and Asia. It is estimated that about 140 *million* females worldwide have undergone this procedure, mostly in childhood and often without anesthesia or sterile techniques (World Health Organization, 2012). The cultures that practice this consider it an important, sacred ritual, but the cultures that condemn it consider it an inhumane and dangerous act of violence and have vigorously called for a worldwide ban (Allam, 2012; Corbett, 2008; Rosenthal, 2006).

**Bullying Around the World**   One form of aggression that is prevalent across virtually all cultures is bullying (Volk et al., 2012). Children and adolescents around the world are physically, sexually, or emotionally bullied by their peers. Bullying involves intentional harm (physically or psychologically), repetition (the victim is targeted a number of times), and a power imbalance (the bully abuses his or her power over the victim). The reported prevalence of bullying varies widely across research studies, with estimates on the low end suggesting that 5% or 10% of schoolchildren are involved in bullying, and estimates on the high end suggesting numbers as high as 70% to 90% (Borntrager et al., 2009; Due & Holstein, 2008; Fleming & Jacobsen, 2010; Olweus, 2004; Rigby & Smith, 2011; Santalahti et al., 2008). When Wendy Craig and her colleagues (2000; Pepler et al., 2004) set up hidden video cameras and microphones to get an unfiltered peek into aggression in schoolyards in Canada, they saw bullying in midsized schools at a rate of 4.5 episodes per hour.

These seemingly ordinary rites of childhood can lead to extraordinary suffering, including feelings of panic, nervousness, and distraction in school; recurring memories of abuse; depression and anxiety that can endure through adulthood; and even suicide (Birkett et al., 2009; Hilton et al., 2010; Jordan & Austin, 2012). It is worth noting that the shooters in most of the instances of school shootings during the past couple of decades reportedly felt that they had been bullied or picked on by peers.

**Nonviolent Cultures**   Although violence seems to be just about everywhere, a handful of societies stand out as nonviolent exceptions. Bruce Bonta, Douglas Fry, and their colleagues have identified a number of societies around the world that are almost completely without violence (Bonta, 1997; Fry, 2012; Miklikawska & Fry, 2010). Bonta (1997) described 25 such societies, and Bonta and Fry (2006) later compiled a list of 40 peaceful societies. For example, the Chewong, who live in the mountains of the Malay Peninsula, do not even have words in their language for quarreling, fighting, aggression, or warfare. The most serious act of aggression noted during a year among the Ifaluk, who live on a small atoll in the Federated States of Micronesia, involved a man who "touched another on the shoulder in anger, an offense which resulted in a stiff fine." The Amish, the Hutterites, and the Mennonites are all societies that reside in the relatively violent United States (as well as in Canada) but remain remarkably nonviolent. Table 11.2 lists some of the other societies that these researchers identified as nonviolent. What makes all of these societies so peaceful? According to Bonta (1997), the large majority of these societies strongly opposes competition and endorses cooperation in all aspects of their lives. This raises the possibility that cooperation and lack of competition may promote nonviolence. Interdependence and having superordinate goals also are evident among the people in many of these societies (Fry, 2012).

The peace of one of these nonviolent communities was shattered, however, on the morning of October 2, 2006. A 32-year-old milk truck driver named Charles Roberts, a father of three, burst into a one-room Amish schoolhouse in Pennsylvania, carrying three firearms, two knives, and up to 600 rounds of ammunition, along with other materials to carry out a horrific attack. He let the boys and a few adults leave, and then lined up the girls—ages 6 to 13—against the blackboard, tied them up, and shot them one by one. After police burst in, Roberts shot and killed himself. Five of the girls were killed, and five more were critically injured.

The details of the massacre were truly nightmarish. At least two of the girls who were shot had asked the killer to shoot them first, in the hope of sparing some of the younger girls. And yet, in a remarkable display of this community's commitment to its principles of peace and forgiveness, families of the slain and injured children offered prayers for the killer and his family. According to some reports, the very night of the killings some Amish "stood in the kitchen of the murderer's family, their arms around his sobbing father, and said, 'We will forgive Charlie.'" One member of the community suggested that the forgiveness displayed by the Amish in this incident could be "a gift to the world. . . . Maybe there's something to learn about how nations might treat other nations" (Dueck, 2006, p. A25).

**Subcultures Within a Country**   There are important variations in aggression within particular societies as a function of age, class, race, and region. For example, teenagers and young adults have a much greater rate of involvement in violent crime—as both offenders and victims—than any other age group. The fact that the American population has been aging in recent years is one of the reasons cited for the sharp drop in violent crime rates over the past couple of decades. (Other factors that are noted frequently include longer jail sentences for criminals, more visible and community-oriented policing, a decline in the market for crack cocaine, and tougher gun-control laws.)

What about race? Despite the stories that get the most attention on the news, the large majority of murders are intraracial rather than interracial. Among incidents when the killer's race was identified in the United States in 2010, 92% of black murder victims were killed by black offenders, and 85% of white murder victims were slain by white offenders. Nevertheless, African Americans live in a much more violent America than do whites. The proportion of African Americans—particularly African American males—who are the perpetrators or victims of homicide is consistently much higher than that of other racial groups. For example, although African Americans represented about 13% of the U.S. population in 2010, they were victims of about half of all murders (U.S. Department of Justice, 2011). Reliable data about homicide rates among other racial or ethnic groups are much more limited.

### TABLE 11.2
#### Nonviolent Societies

In addition to those discussed in the text, this table lists a few of the other societies that researchers identified as nonviolent.

| Society | Comments |
| --- | --- |
| Balinese (Indonesian island of Bali) | A researcher who was there for 4 years never even witnessed two boys fighting. |
| Glwi (Central Kalahari Desert of southern Africa) | They abhor violence and take pleasure from fortunate events only if they are in the company of group members. |
| Inuit (Arctic regions, including those in Siberia, Alaska, Canada, and Greenland) | They use strategies to control anger and prevent violence; they have a strong fear of aggression. |
| Ladakhis (Tibetan Buddhist society in northern India) | Villagers indicate that they have no memory of any fighting in the village. |
| Semai (aboriginal people of the central Malay Peninsula) | People share whatever they can afford and do not expect a "thank you" in return; emotional outbursts almost never occur. |
| Zapotec (Native American society in southern Mexico) | "Several researchers have been fascinated that one community is particularly peaceful, with very strong values that oppose violence, in contrast to other communities nearby where fighting and machismo are comparable with the rest of Mexico" (Bonta, 1997, p. 320). |

Bonta, 1997; Miklikowska & Fry, 2010. © Cengage Learning

Regional differences are also striking. In the United States, the murder rate is consistently highest in the South, followed by the West. Some scholars have attributed the greater violence in the South and West to a *culture of honor* that is prevalent among white males in these regions. The culture of honor encourages violent responses to perceived threats against one's status as an honorable, powerful man (Barnes et al., 2012; Cohen et al., 1998; Hayes & Lee, 2005; Vandello et al., 2013). Other scholars believe that the consistently high rates of murder and violent crime in the South are due to hot weather (Anderson & Anderson, 1996; Anderson & DeLisi, 2011). We will focus more on both the culture of honor and the relationship between heat and aggression later in the chapter.

## Gender and Aggression

Despite all the variation across cultures, one thing is universal: Men are more violent than women. This has been found in virtually all cultures studied around the world. Ninety percent of murderers in the United States in 2010 were male, and 77% of murder victims were male. Despite the significant variation in total violence from one country to another, the gender difference remains remarkably stable over time and place: Men commit the very large majority of homicides, and men constitute the very large majority of murder victims (Buss, 2012; United Nations Office of Drugs and Crime, 2011). In the spate of school shootings discussed at various points in this chapter, all of the perpetrators were males. On the other hand, around the world the vast majority of people killed by an intimate partner—such as a family member or current or former romantic partner—are women.

What about aggression in general, as opposed to violence? In meta-analyses involving hundreds of samples from numerous countries, John Archer (2004) and Noel Card and his colleagues (2008) have found that males are consistently more physically aggressive than females. This was true across all ages and cultures sampled. Females were as likely to feel anger as males, but they were much less likely to act on their anger in aggressive ways. Even among children between 1 and 6 years old, boys show higher rates of physical aggression than girls.

So does all this mean that the stereotype that males are more aggressive than females is correct? Not necessarily. Most of the earlier research on this issue focused on the form of aggression that is typical of males: physical aggression. But think back to our definition of aggression: It concerns intent to harm. There are many ways to harm someone other than through physical means. More recent research has recognized this, and the results challenge the notion that males are more aggressive than females. The findings that emerged can be summarized by a child's remark noted by researchers Britt Galen and Marion Underwood (1997): "Boys may use their fists to fight, but at least it's over with quickly; girls use their tongues, and it goes on forever" (p. 589).

This research reveals that although boys tend to be more *overtly* aggressive than girls, boys do not tend to be more aggressive than girls when it comes to *indirect* or *relational* aggression. Indeed, for these types of aggression, girls sometimes are more aggressive than boys. Indirect forms of aggression include acts such as telling lies to get someone in trouble or shutting a person out of desired activities. Relational aggression is one kind of indirect aggression that particularly targets a person's relationships and social status, such as by threatening to end a friendship, engaging in gossip and backbiting, and trying to get others to dislike the target. Numerous studies conducted in a variety of countries around the world have found that females tend to engage in indirect aggression more often than males, although many others have found only small or no significant gender differences. The results of meta-analyses (Archer, 2004; Card et al., 2008) that have reviewed the very large research literature on the topic have found a very small but statistically significant gender difference, with girls exhibiting somewhat more indirect aggression than boys (see ● Figure 11.3).

Why are girls at least as aggressive as boys on relational (but not physical) forms of aggression? Researchers believe that one reason is because females typically care more about relationships and intimacy than males do and so may see injuring someone socially as particularly effective. Another reason may be that strong norms encourage boys to aggress physically, but these same norms discourage girls from doing so (Crick et al., 1999; McEachern & Snyder, 2012; Spieker et al., 2012).

In addition to gender differences, there may be differences in the types of aggression people exhibit as a function of sexual orientation. Mark Sergeant and others (2006), for example, found that gay men reported significantly lower levels of physical aggression than straight men did, but there was no difference between the two groups on self-reported rates of indirect aggression.

A research finding that is often met with a great deal of surprise and skepticism is that there is no reliable gender difference in the percentage of women and men who physically assault their intimate partners. That is, women are at least as likely to aggress against male partners as men are to aggress against female partners. This has by now been reported in more than 200 studies over the past few decades (Straus, 2011). These

---

In virtually every culture, males are more violent than females. **T**RUE.

---

For virtually any category of aggression, males are more aggressive than females. **F**ALSE.

---

● **FIGURE 11.3**

**Gender and Types of Aggression**

The results of a meta-analysis of 148 studies involving children and adolescents across several countries indicate that the magnitude and direction of gender differences in aggression depend on the type of aggression. The height of the bars in this graph indicates the degree to which boys show more aggression than girls; the higher the bar, the more aggression is shown by boys relative to girls. Boys tended to be much more physically aggressive than girls, as well as to be more verbally aggressive (although this difference was smaller). Regarding indirect aggression, however, girls tended to be more aggressive than boys. This difference was small but statistically reliable across the set of studies. Based on Card et al., 2008. © Cengage Learning

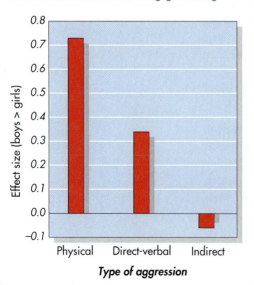

results not only defy most people's expectations and stereotypes, they also do not match up with statistics from the police or agencies involved in helping people suffering from intimate partner violence. Researchers in this area explain that the reason for this difference is that men are far less likely than women to report to the police or various agencies that their partners physically assaulted them. Norms play a role in this, of course, as it is seen by many as far more acceptable for a woman to hit her male partner than it is for a man to hit his female partner. Another, and somewhat related, important reason is that the consequences of aggression and violence are far from equal. Women are more often killed, seriously injured, or sexually assaulted during domestic disputes than are men (Archer, 2000; 2002; Straus & Ramirez, 2005). As Barbara Morse (1995) put it, "Women were more often the victims of severe partner assault and injury not because men strike more often, but because men strike harder" (p. 251). Rates of aggression and violence in the form of sexual assault differ greatly by gender, with males being overwhelmingly more likely to be perpetrators and females to be targets.

The movie *Mean Girls*, starring Lindsay Lohan and Rachel McAdams, depicted high school girls engaged in an escalating battle of indirect, relational aggression.

##  Individual Differences

Although it is clear that aggression can vary across culture and gender, a different question is whether there is consistency in aggression within specific individuals. In other words, do some people simply tend to be more aggressive than others, across time and contexts? The evidence on this point is fairly clear: Although situational variables (as we will see later in this chapter) certainly do influence whether and how someone will aggress, there are some stable individual differences in aggressiveness. Aggression in childhood does predict aggression in adolescence and adulthood, along with adult criminality, alcohol abuse, and other antisocial behaviors. Similarly, low aggression in childhood predicts low aggression well into adulthood (DeWall et al., 2013; Huesmann et al., 2011; Kokko et al., 2009).

What types of personalities tend to be associated with aggressiveness? Researchers often identify individuals' personalities based on what are called the "Big Five" factors—five dimensions that account for a great deal of variability in people's personalities across gender and culture. These five dimensions are (1) agreeableness (good-natured, trustful, cooperative), (2) conscientiousness (responsible, orderly, dependable), (3) openness to experience (intellectual, independent-minded, prefer novelty), (4) extraversion (outgoing, energetic, assertive), and (5) neuroticism (easily upset, emotionally unstable). Of these five factors, being low in agreeableness is a particularly strong predictor of aggression. Being low on the dimension of openness, and high on the dimension of neuroticism, are also associated with aggression (Barlett & Anderson, 2012).

Some traits associated with aggression tend to predict aggression reliably only under conditions of provocation—that is, situations in which the individual feels threatened, insulted, or stressed (Bettencourt et al., 2006). Among these traits are *emotional susceptibility* (the tendency to feel distressed, inadequate, and vulnerable to perceived threats), *Type A personality* (the tendency to be driven by feelings of inadequacy to try to prove oneself through personal accomplishments), and *impulsivity* (being relatively unable to control one's thoughts and behaviors). When not provoked, individuals with these traits are not much more likely than others to behave aggressively. Provocation, however, can light the relatively short fuses of these individuals, leading to the potential explosion of aggression.

Many people assume that individuals—particularly adolescents—with low self-esteem are more likely to aggress than people with average or high self-esteem. The evidence on this is mixed at best (Bushman et al., 2009; Donnellan et al., 2005; Locke,

2009). In fact, recent research suggests not only that low self-esteem does not predict aggression but that people with *high* self-esteem are particularly likely to aggress if (1) they also are high in narcissism, and (2) they have received a threat to their ego, such as from a humiliation or insult (Bushman et al., 2009; Thomaes et al., 2008). Although self-esteem is not a great predictor of aggression, *narcissism* clearly is. Narcissism involves having an inflated sense of self-worth and self-love, having low empathy for others, tending to focus on the self rather than others, and being especially sensitive to perceived insults. Narcissism is consistently and positively correlated with aggression in response to provocation, particularly if the provocation is public rather than private (DeWall et al., 2013; Ferriday et al., 2011; Pauletti et al., 2012).

Unlike self-esteem, one factor that has a very clear and consistent relationship with aggression is self-control (DeWall et al., 2013; Denson, DeWall, & Finkel, 2012). Individuals with strong self-control can resist impulses and act in ways that are consistent with their personal and societal standards for appropriate behavior. Children low in self-control tend to be more aggressive as young adults (Moffitt et al., 2011). Poor self-control predicts aggression toward strangers and romantic partners (DeWall, Finkel, & Denson, 2011; Finkel et al., 2009). Meta-analyses have reported that poor self-control is one of the strongest predictors of crime (Pratt & Cullen, 2000). A recent study involving samples of adolescents and teenagers from 25 European countries found that low self-control was a significant predictor of cyberbullying (Vazsonyi et al., 2012).

# Origins of Aggression

Regardless of these various cultural, gender, and individual differences, aggression has been a prevalent part of human interaction throughout human history and around the world. It is not surprising that many have speculated about the origins of aggression. Where does it come from? Are we *born* aggressive, or are we *taught* to be aggressive? Many have argued for one side or the other of the "nature-nurture" debate—the "nature" side holding that aggression is an innate characteristic of human beings and the "nurture" side holding that aggression is learned through experience. In this section, we look at the theory and research most relevant to tracing the origins of human aggression. In reviewing each perspective, we examine how well it can account for the overall prevalence of aggression as well as for the cultural and gender differences that we have discussed.

##  Is Aggression Innate?

Innate characteristics are not dependent on learning for their development, although they can be influenced by learning, culture, and other factors. Here, we examine two approaches to the issue of whether aggression is innate: (1) evolutionary psychological accounts and (2) biological factors, including genes, hormones, neurotransmitters, and brain and executive functioning.

**Evolutionary Psychology**   Evolutionary psychological accounts of aggression use principles of evolution to understand both the roots and the contemporary patterns of human aggression. For example, in his provocative book *The Most Dangerous Animal: Human Nature and the Origins of War*, David Livingstone Smith (2007) takes an evolutionary psychological perspective in his analysis of the origins of human warfare. This account emphasizes that human warfare originated not only to obtain valuable resources but also to attract mates and forge intragroup bonds. While it might seem that in our evolutionary history it would have been the pacifists who would have been more likely to survive than the warriors, Smith argues that it was the warriors who would have been more likely to attract mates and be accepted as part of a group. Therefore, the individuals who could and would fight had greater chances for reproductive success, and they would pass down these tendencies to their offspring, and so on. The greater reproductive success of warriors over pacifists would result in the tendencies toward aggression and war to evolve to become part of human nature. More recently Anthony Volk and others (2012) have argued the case that the prevalence of bullying across most cultures around the world reflects the fact that bullying is, in part, an evolved adaptive strategy for particular sets of conditions.

Evolutionary social psychology is geared not only to describe the origins of human social behavior but also to generate testable, falsifiable predictions. For example, evolutionary theories emphasize genetic survival rather than the survival of the individual. Because at least some of a person's genes can be transmitted through the reproductive success of genetic relatives, evolution should have favored the inhibition of aggression against those who are genetically related to us. Consistent with that hypothesis, Martin Daly and Margo Wilson (1988; 1996; 2005) report that birth parents are much less likely to abuse or murder their own offspring than stepparents are to harm stepchildren. In two samples studied, preschool children living with a stepparent or foster parent were 70 to 100 times more likely to be fatally abused than were children living with both biological parents.

What can account for the gender differences in aggression? According to an evolutionary perspective, males are competitive with each other because females select high-status males for mating, and aggression is a means by which males traditionally have been able to achieve and maintain status. As researcher Vladas Griskevicius said in an interview about his work on this topic, "For men, fighting for status is akin to fighting for the survival of their genes. Not caring about status, which can be implied by backing away from a fight, can be evolutionary suicide. Aggression can lead to status. A higher status leads to sex, and that leads to more or higher-quality offspring" (*Science Daily*, 2008, December 8). Similarly, Jennifer Bosson and Joseph Vandello (2011) argue that for many men, *manhood* is a status that is precarious. In other words, it must be earned and maintained repeatedly through action. Situations that threaten this status increase the likelihood of aggressive behavior.

In the United States, approximately one-third to one-half of female homicide victims are murdered by a husband or a boyfriend. Of course, partner abuse is not limited to the United States; it is a worldwide phenomenon. Nor is it a new development; it has occurred throughout history. Indeed, evolutionary psychologists point to a number of factors that predict such behavior, including males' uncertainty over whether they are the biological fathers of their children. Behaviors triggered by sexual jealousy, including aggression and the threat of aggression, may be designed to enhance the male's confidence in his paternity of offspring. Consistent with evolutionary reasoning, crime statistics indicate that male-to-male violence is most likely to occur when one male is perceived as challenging the other's status or social power, and male-to-female violence is predominantly triggered by sexual jealousy (Duntley & Buss, 2008; Goetz et al., 2008; Shackelford & Goetz, 2005; Wilson & Daly, 1996).

Of course, as noted earlier, women also aggress. From an evolutionary perspective, reproductive success is dependent on the survival of one's offspring. Because women are much more limited than men in terms of the number of children they can have,

*"The most persistent sound which reverberates through men's history is the beating of war drums."*
—Arthur Koestler

evolution presumably favored those women who were committed to protecting their children. Indeed, much research on aggression by females has focused on maternal aggression, whereby females aggress to defend their offspring against threats by others. For example, females in a variety of species attack male strangers who come too close to their offspring (Ferreira et al., 2000; Gammie et al., 2000). In a similar vein, Anne Campbell (1999) proposes that females tend to place a higher value on protecting their own lives—again, in order to protect their offspring. This hypothesis may explain not only why human males engage more often in risky, potentially self-destructive behaviors but also why human females, when they do aggress, are more likely to use less obvious, and thus less dangerous, means—such as indirect or relational aggression rather than overt physical aggression. Relational aggression also may be particularly effective for women because it can harm the reputations of rival females—which can make men less interested in them (Vaillancourt, 2005).

Vladas Griskevicius and others (2009) propose that men are more likely than women to boost their status (and successfully compete for women) through direct, face-to-face aggression against other men, whereas women are more likely to boost their status (and successfully compete for men) through indirect aggression against other women. In a series of experiments, Griskevicius and others activated either a status motive for some

"It's a guy thing."

of the male and female participants (such as by having them think about competing with same-sex others for a high-status job promotion) or an unrelated motive for other participants. All participants then read about a scenario in which a same-sex person is publicly rude to them, and they were asked to indicate how they would respond. Activating a status motive increased direct aggression responses (e.g., to push or hit the person) in men, whereas it increased indirect aggressive responses (e.g., to talk behind the person's back or exclude the person from a social group) in women.

**Behavior Genetics**    Evolutionary psychology involves tying together evolution, genetic transmission, and behavior. Behavior genetics focuses on the latter two. As we said earlier, aggressiveness is a relatively stable personality characteristic; children relatively high in aggressiveness are more likely to be aggressive later in life. Can this aggressive personality type be due to genes? To answer this question, researchers often use two types of studies in research on humans. In twin studies, monozygotic twins (who are identical in their genetic makeup) are compared with dizygotic twins (who share only part of their genes). On any heritable trait, monozygotic twins will be more similar than dizygotic twins. Adoptee studies are also used in behavior genetics research. On any inherited trait, adopted children will resemble their biological parents more than they resemble their adoptive parents.

The results of twin and adoptee studies have produced somewhat inconsistent results, but the trend in the research supports the heritability of human aggressive behavior to at least some degree (Hines & Saudino, 2002; Miles & Carey, 1997; Rowe et al., 2008; Vierikko et al., 2006). One interesting finding from a study of twins in the Montreal area was that there was much stronger evidence for the role of genes in physical aggression than in indirect, relational aggression (Brendgen et al., 2005). More recent analyses suggest that heritability explains between a quarter and less than half of the variation in aggression in children; genetic differences accounted for a much higher percentage of variation in bullying in another study (Ball et al., 2008; Bezdjian et al., 2011; Tuvblad et al., 2009). Particular genetic variations, such as of the monoamine oxidase A (MAOA) gene, have been linked to aggressive behavior (McDermott et al., 2009). This kind of investigation of genetic variations will no doubt become more common in the next several years.

**The Role of Testosterone** In addition to the question of heritability, researchers have long been interested in determining what specific biological factors influence aggression. Because of the persistent sex differences in physical aggression among humans and other animals, many researchers have wondered if testosterone plays a role. Although men and women both have this "male sex hormone," men usually have much higher levels than women. Research conducted on a variety of animals has found a strong correlation between testosterone levels and aggression. The relationship is far weaker among humans. Even so, a number of studies have documented an association between testosterone and aggression in humans. Using diverse samples of people, such as young boys, prison inmates, college students, and elderly men, these studies tend to show a positive correlation between testosterone levels and physical aggression or violence (Archer, 2006; Book et al., 2001; Dabbs & Dabbs, 2000; Montoya et al., 2012; van Bokhoven et al., 2006).

For example, one study found that college fraternities whose members tended to have higher testosterone levels were more rambunctious and exhibited more crude behavior than other fraternities; fraternities whose members had lower testosterone levels tended to be more academically successful and socially responsible, and their members smiled more (Dabbs et al., 1996). The relationship between testosterone and aggression is not limited to males. Studies have also shown a positive relationship between testosterone and aggression and related behaviors (such as competitiveness) in women (Cashdan, 2003; Dabbs & Dabbs, 2000; von der Pahlen et al., 2002). Recent research suggests that high testosterone is especially likely to be associated with aggression if the individuals are also relatively low in the hormone cortisol (Denson, Mehta, & Ho Tan, 2013; Denson, Ronay et al., 2013; Montoya et al., 2012).

Intriguing as they are, correlational findings cannot prove that testosterone causes aggression. There are alternative explanations. For example, aggression itself can cause temporary increases in testosterone—if the aggression is successful (Gladue et al., 1989; Mazur et al., 1992). Stress may also be involved in the correlation between testosterone and aggression: Stress may simultaneously elevate both testosterone and aggression, resulting in a correlation that may reflect the effects of stress rather than the effects of testosterone.

For ethical reasons, researchers do not manipulate people's levels of testosterone to measure its effects on aggression and other behaviors. But Stephanie Van Goozen and others (1995; Cohen-Ketteinis & Van Goozen, 1997) studied individuals who were voluntarily manipulating their sex hormones—transsexuals undergoing sex reassignment treatments. The researchers administered tests of aggression to 35 female-to-male transsexuals and 15 male-to-female transsexuals shortly before and 3 months after the start of cross-sex hormone treatment in a Dutch hospital. As their levels of male hormones increased, the female-to-male transsexuals exhibited increased aggression-proneness. In contrast, the deprivation of these hormones in the male-to-female group was associated with a decrease in aggression-proneness. It is important to note, however, that these changes in aggressiveness may have been caused not by the hormone treatment per se but rather by indirect factors such as the transsexuals' expectations or other people's reactions to them.

Another line of research that supports the idea that testosterone may predict aggressiveness may strike you as somewhat odd. Look at your index and ring fingers. Which is longer, from tip to where they connect with the hand? Believe it or not, your answer may be a clue to how aggressive you are likely to be! Well, that may be overstating it a bit, but research has shown some intriguing correlations among finger-length ratio, testosterone, and aggression. Men tend to have relatively shorter index fingers relative to ring fingers; shorter ratios (especially on the right hand) are considered more "masculine." Lower ratios (called low *2D:4D* in the literature, with 2D and 4D meaning the second and fourth digits, respectively) are thought to be associated with exposure to higher prenatal testosterone levels. Although one review of this literature suggests the relationship between these ratios and aggression is rather weak (Hönekopp & Watson, 2011), a growing number of studies have found that this finger-length ratio is associated with higher aggression.

For example, studies have shown that for men, lower 2D:4D ratios (that is, more "masculine" ratios) are associated with higher scores for the trait of physical aggression, reports of being more threatening and physically aggressive toward their dating partners, personalities higher in aggressive dominance, and mental toughness and aptitude in sports (Bailey & Hurd, 2005; Cousins et al., 2009; Golby & Meggs, 2011; Hönekopp, 2011; van der Meij et al., 2012). Lower ratios have also been found to predict the success of sumo wrestlers in Japan (Tamiya et al., 2012) and the choice of military service in Korea (Huh, 2012)—in the latter case, Marines (who are commonly believed in Korea to endure the harshest training of the military branches) had significantly lower average 2D:4D ratios than did the members of the Army, Air Force, or Navy (see ● Figure 11.4).

The relationship between finger-length ratios and aggression or aggression-related measures is more mixed for women. Sarah Coyne and others (2007) found that for women this finger-length ratio was not associated with a measure of direct aggression, but it was positively correlated with their indirect aggression.

**The Role of Serotonin**   Testosterone is not the only biological factor linked to human aggression. Many researchers are investigating the role of the neurotransmitter serotonin (Carrillo et al., 2009; Crockett et al., 2008; Montoya et al., 2012; Suarez & Krishnan, 2006; Takahashi et al., 2011). Serotonin appears to work like a braking mechanism to restrain impulsive, reactive acts of aggression. Low levels of serotonin in the nervous systems of humans and many animals are associated with high levels of aggression. Drugs that boost serotonin's activity can dampen aggressiveness, along with a range of other impulsive and socially deviant behaviors. Such drugs have even been used to treat "road rage"—people's impulsive acts of aggression and violence while driving.

**Brain and Executive Functioning**   In addition to hormones and neurotransmitters, the frontal lobe of the brain is another hot topic in research on the biological underpinnings of human aggression. Researchers using a variety of techniques have found evidence linking abnormalities in frontal lobe structures with tendencies toward aggressive and violent behavior (Miczek et al., 2007; Miura, 2009; Raine, 2008). The prefrontal cortex in particular has been implicated. Impaired prefrontal processing can disrupt what is called *executive functioning*, the cognitive abilities and processes that allow humans to plan or inhibit their actions. Executive functioning enables people to respond to situations in a reasoned, flexible manner, as opposed to being driven purely by external stimuli (Hoaken et al., 2007). A growing body of research finds a link between poor executive functioning and high aggression (Ellis et al., 2009; Giancola et al., 2012; Raaijmakers et al., 2008).

● **FIGURE 11.4**

**Finger-Length Ratio and Military Branch in Korea**

According to some research, the shorter one's right index finger is relative to one's right ring finger, the more "masculine" one's finger ratio is said to be, as these ratios are thought to be associated with exposure to higher prenatal testosterone levels. This figure presents the average ratio for a sample of men from each of four branches of the military in the Republic of Korea. The Marines are commonly thought there to have the harshest training, and the men in this study from the Marines had significantly lower finger-length ratios (suggesting higher levels of prenatal testosterone) than did the men from the other branches.

Tamiya et al., 2012. © Cengage Learning

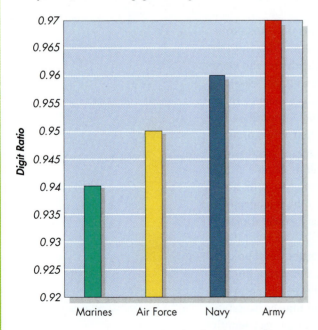

Lower ratios are associated with more prenatal exposure to testosterone.

One noteworthy recent finding is that very aggressive teenagers showed different patterns of brain activity in response to witnessing someone else in pain than did less aggressive youth (Decety et al., 2009). In particular, when watching situations in which someone intentionally inflicted pain on another person, healthy teenagers showed brain activity associated with empathy. The highly aggressive teens, however, exhibited a pattern of brain activity associated with experiencing rewards, suggesting that they enjoyed watching others experience pain that someone intentionally inflicted on them. In addition, the aggressive teenagers showed less activation in areas associated with self-regulation and moral reasoning when seeing someone inflict pain on another than did the nonaggressive teenagers.

These are among the lines of research that demonstrate associations between brain functioning and aggression and other antisocial behaviors. ● Figure 11.5 illustrates some of the brain regions implicated in these studies.

## Is Aggression Learned?

Regardless of the precise contribution of genetic and biological factors, it is clear that aggressive behavior is strongly affected by learning (Bandura, 1973). Rewards obtained by aggression today will increase its use tomorrow. Such rewards come in two flavors: *positive reinforcement*, when aggression produces desired outcomes, and *negative reinforcement*, when aggression prevents or stops undesirable outcomes. The child who gets a toy by hitting the toy's owner is likely to hit again. So, too, the child who can stop other children from teasing by shoving them away has learned the fateful lesson that aggression pays. Children who see aggression producing more good outcomes, and fewer bad outcomes, are more aggressive than other children (Boldizar et al., 1989).

Rewards are one part of the learning equation, but what about punishment? Punishment is often promoted as a way to reduce aggressive behavior. Can people learn not to act aggressively through punishment? Some politicians and police officials in New York City believe that the dramatic

● **FIGURE 11.5**

**Brain Functioning and Aggression**

This figure shows three slices of the brain. Within each slice, the areas highlighted in color have been found in recent research to be impaired in antisocial, violent, and psychopathic populations.

Raine, 2008.

Raine, 2008

reduction in crime in the city in recent years (from 2,245 murders in 1990 to only 515 in 2011—less than a quarter of the 1990 tally!) is due in large part to swift, more effective punishment of all kinds of crimes, even relatively minor crimes such as vandalism, which sends the message that crime will lead to punishment. (Other factors that may be more important in this decline include the reduction in guns and drugs—particularly crack cocaine—and the increase in the age of the population.) Research suggests that punishment is most likely to decrease aggression when it (1) immediately follows the aggressive behavior, (2) is strong enough to deter the aggressor, and (3) is consistently applied and perceived as fair and legitimate by the aggressor. However, such stringent conditions are seldom met, and when they are not met, punishment can backfire. When courts are overburdened and prisons are overcrowded, which is often the case, the relationship between crime and punishment can seem more like a lottery than a rational system in which the punishment fits the crime. In short, the *certainty* of punishment is more important than its *severity* (Berkowitz, 1998).

There are other problems with punishment as well. Punishment perceived as unfair or arbitrary can provoke retaliation, creating an escalating cycle of aggression. Perhaps most troubling is that punishment, especially when delivered in an angry or hostile manner, offers a model to imitate. Murray Straus and his colleagues (Straus, 2000; 2010; Straus & Douglas, 2008) have been outspoken critics of the use of *corporal punishment*: physical force (such as spanking, hitting, and pinching) intended to cause a child pain, but not injury, for the purpose of controlling or correcting the child's behavior. The large majority of children in the United States experience spanking and other forms of corporal punishment. Numerous studies, however, report a positive relationship between corporal punishment and the likelihood of aggression: More corporal punishment now is associated with more aggression later. Elizabeth Gershoff (2002) investigated this issue with a meta-analysis of 88 studies conducted over six decades and involving more than 36,000 participants. Her analysis revealed strong evidence for a positive correlation between corporal punishment and several categories of subsequent antisocial behaviors, such as aggression later as a child, aggression as an adult, and adult criminal behavior. More recent reviews continue to find evidence from countries around the world for the relationship between corporal punishment and later problems of aggression, violence, criminality, drug abuse, and mental health problems (Afifi et al., 2012; Straus, 2010).

The relationship between parental corporal punishment and children's subsequent aggression is influenced by a number of factors, including the overall family environment, the emotions displayed by the parents during the punishment, and cultural and ethnic differences (Benjet & Kazdin, 2003; Pagani et al., 2009; Pinderhughes et al., 2000). For example, corporal punishment may be less likely to increase aggressiveness when it is administered in the context of an overall warm and supportive parent–child relationship (Baumrind, 1997; Deater-Deckard et al., 1998).

**Social Learning Theory**   One of the authors of this book remembers many a late, cold afternoon as a teenager playing informal but competitive games of football and hockey with friends. The way he and his friends played them, both games were played without protective equipment and were quite rough, but football was the more physically brutal of the two. Yet despite the fact that virtually every play culminated in a pile of boys jumping on the flattened body of an opponent, it was very rare that an actual fight would break out. When this same group of friends played hockey, on the other hand, virtually every single game they played featured at least one fight. Why? Although he was years away from his first social psychology class, this future social psychologist was quite sure that he and his friends were basing their behavior on role models. Rarely had they seen professional football players stop and fight on the field. But rarely had they seen a professional hockey game in which that *didn't* happen.

Children who are spanked or otherwise physically disciplined (but not abused) for behaving aggressively tend to become less aggressive. **F**ALSE.

The power of models to modify behavior is a crucial tenet of Albert Bandura's (1977) **social learning theory**. Social learning theory emphasizes that we learn from the example of others as well as from direct experience with rewards and punishments. Models influence the prosocial, helpful behavior described in Chapter 10. They also affect antisocial, aggressive behavior. In a classic study, Bandura and his associates (1961) observed the behavior of mildly frustrated children. Those who had previously watched an adult throw around, punch, and kick an inflatable doll (known as a Bobo doll, named after the character depicted on it) were more aggressive when they later played with the Bobo doll than were those who had watched a quiet, subdued adult. These children followed the adult model's lead not only in degree of aggression but also in the kinds of aggression they exhibited. Subsequent research has amply demonstrated that a wide range of aggressive models can elicit a wide range of aggressive imitations. Furthermore, these models do not have to be present; people on TV—even cartoon characters—can serve as powerful models of aggression (Bandura, 1983; Baron & Richardson, 1994; Berkowitz, 1993).

People learn more than specific aggressive behaviors from aggressive models. They also develop more positive attitudes and beliefs about aggression in general, and they construct aggressive "scripts" that serve as guides for how to behave and solve social problems. These scripts can be activated automatically in various situations, leading to quick, often unthinking aggressive responses that follow the scripts they have learned (Bennett et al., 2005; Huesmann, 1998). Learning these scripts from their parents is one of the reasons that there are positive correlations between witnessing parents behaving aggressively or violently with each other during conflicts and individuals' subsequent aggressiveness as adolescents and adults (Hill & Nathan, 2008; Perkins & Graham-Bermann, 2012; Underwood et al., 2008).

Consider the boys described just above who fought during hockey but not football games. Could their fighting during hockey be due to something about the sport of hockey itself, or did these boys learn aggressive scripts from watching how professional hockey players used their fists to deal with frustrations and provocations? An interesting study by Chris Gee and Larry Leith (2007) supports the social learning hypothesis. Gee and Leith analyzed the penalty records from 200 games of the National Hockey League (NHL). The NHL is the major professional hockey league in North America, and in recent years it has come to include top players from numerous countries around the world. When they were young and developing into hockey players, players born in North America were much more likely to have been exposed to models of aggression and fighting, and to have been rewarded (and not punished severely) for fighting and aggressive play, than were players born in Europe. Subsequently, even though these athletes all were playing the same sport on the same teams in the NHL, Gee and Leith found that the players born in North America were much more likely to be called for aggressive penalties than were players born in Europe (see ● Figure 11.6). Also, of all the infractions that the North Americans committed, more than 32% were for fighting or "roughing," whereas only 16% of the

"I blame all the violent cave paintings."

The idea that aggression may be learned by observing others behaving aggressively may go back a long, long time.

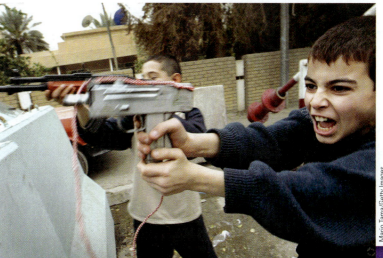

Boys in Baghdad play with toy guns, imitating the adult behavior they have observed in their war-torn country. When U.S. troops patrolled the area regularly, they traded the toy guns for pens to get them off the streets

**social learning theory**   The theory that behavior is learned through the observation of others as well as through the direct experience of rewards and punishments.

● **FIGURE 11.6**

**Social Learning of Aggression in Hockey: North America Versus Europe**

Researchers examined all the penalties called against National Hockey League players born in North America or Europe during 200 games. North American players were likely to have been exposed to more aggressive role models and positive reinforcement for fighting and aggression in hockey than their European counterparts. Consistent with this point, the results depicted here show that the North Americans were much more likely to be called for aggressive (but not for nonaggressive) penalties than the Europeans were.

Based on Gee & Leith, 2007. © Cengage Learning

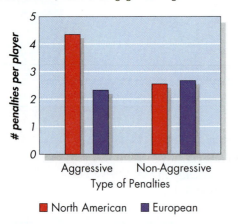

penalties for European players were for these particularly aggressive infractions.

Aggression or violence scripts play important roles in the lives of many young men and women who have committed violent crimes. In a thorough analysis of 416 young violent offenders from two New York City neighborhoods, Deanna Wilkinson and Patrick Carr (2008) found that 93% had seen someone get beaten badly, 75% had seen someone get knifed, 92% had seen someone get shot, and 77% had seen someone get killed. More than three-quarters of these violent offenders reported that a close friend had been killed through violence. Wilkinson and Carr collected chilling interviews with these individuals, many of which illustrated how so much early exposure to violence taught these individuals the unfortunate lesson that violence is the appropriate way to deal with conflicts and to attain a degree of high status in the neighborhood.

Just as aggressive models can increase aggressive behavior, nonaggressive models can decrease it. Observing a nonaggressive response to a provoking situation teaches a peaceful alternative and strengthens existing restraints against aggression. In addition, observing someone who is calm and reasonable may help an angry person settle down rather than strike out. Aggression can spread like wildfire. But nonviolence and prosocial behavior can also be contagious (Donnerstein & Donnerstein, 1976; Gibbons & Ebbeck, 1997).

Consistent with social learning theory and the idea that people learn aggressive scripts is a particularly tragic outcome known as the **cycle of violence**. Children who witness parental violence or who are themselves abused are more likely as adults to inflict abuse on intimate partners or their children, or, perhaps, to be victims of intimate violence (Cochran et al., 2011; Gómez, 2011; Smith et al., 2011; Sunday et al., 2011). There are multiple reasons for this, but one factor is that children and adolescents learn through observation that aggression and violence are how adults deal with problems and try to resolve conflicts or respond to frustrations. This intergenerational transmission of domestic violence is by no means inevitable, however. Most people who witness or experience abuse in their families of origin are not abusive. The cycle of violence refers to a greater tendency, not an absolute certainty.

Bandura's social learning theory has been one of the most important social psychological approaches to the study of human aggression since his classic early experiments in the early 1960s. Its simplicity should not obscure the fact that it can help explain a great amount of human behavior. Daniel Batson and Adam Powell (2003) wrote that social learning theory "has probably come closer to [the goal of accounting for the most facts with the fewest principles] than has any other theory in the history of social psychology" (p. 466).

## ❯ Gender Differences and Socialization: "Boys Will Be Boys"

**cycle of violence** The transmission of domestic violence across generations.

To account for gender differences in aggression, social learning approaches emphasize that males and females are taught different lessons about aggression: They are rewarded and punished differently for aggression and are presented with different models.

Whether or not gender differences in aggressive behavior originated from innate biological factors, today they are maintained and perpetuated through lessons that are passed on from one generation to the next about the acceptability of various kinds and degrees of aggression.

Overt aggression tends to be more socially acceptable in stereotypically male roles than in female roles. Indeed, highly aggressive boys are sometimes (although certainly not always) among the most popular and socially connected children in elementary school (Rodkin et al., 2000; Vaillancourt & Hymel, 2006). Boys who use their fists to deal with conflict are much more likely to be rewarded with increased social status than are girls, who might suffer scorn and ridicule for fighting. As we discussed earlier in the chapter, males often feel that their status as men is precarious and must be repeatedly demonstrated and proven, and direct aggression is an important way to do this (Bosson & Vandello, 2011). On the other hand, a girl who successfully uses relational aggression, such as through social manipulation, can reap social benefits more easily than a boy (Crick & Rose, 2000). One study reported that girls' (but not boys') beliefs about the acceptability of relational aggression correlated significantly with their mothers' attitudes about relational aggression (Werner & Grant, 2009).

## Culture and Socialization: Cultures of Honor

Socialization of aggression also varies from culture to culture. For example, Giovanna Tomada and Barry Schneider (1997) report that adolescent boys in traditional villages in Italy are encouraged to aggress as an indication of their sexual prowess and in preparation for their dominant role in the household. These authors believe that this is why schoolyard bullying among elementary school boys is significantly higher in central and southern Italy than it is in Norway, England, Spain, or Japan. Similarly, some researchers believe that *machismo*—which in its most stereotyped characterization prescribes that challenges, abuse, and even differences of opinion "must be met with fists or other weapons" (Ingoldsby, 1991, p. 57)—contributes to the fact that rates of violence are higher among Latin American men than among European American men (Harris, 1995).

Machismo may represent one form of what anthropologists call a *culture of honor*, which emphasizes honor and social status, particularly for males, and the role of aggression in protecting that honor. Even minor conflicts or disputes are often seen as challenges to social status and reputation and can therefore trigger aggressive responses. Several such subcultures exist around the world (and *Star Trek* fans might recognize the Klingon empire as an intergalactic example of a culture of honor). In an extensive series of studies, Dov Cohen, Richard Nisbett, Joseph Vandello, and their colleagues have examined various cultures of honor. Their original focus was on white men in the American South (Nisbett & Cohen, 1996). Rates of violence are consistently higher in the South than in all other regions of the country. Southerners are more likely than Northerners to agree that "a man has the right to kill" in order to defend his family and house, and they are more accepting of using violence to protect one's honor than are people from other parts of the country. (Note, however, that Southerners are *not* more likely than other Americans to accept violence unrelated to the protection of honor.)

Data from surveys, field experiments, and laboratory experiments suggest that this culture of honor promotes violent behavior. In one series of experiments, Cohen and others (1996) investigated how white male students who had grown up either in the North or in the South responded to insults. The experiments, conducted on a large Midwestern campus, involved an encounter that took place as the participant and the confederate were passing each other in a narrow hallway. The confederate did not give way to the participant, bumped into him, and hurled an insult. Compared with Northerners, Southerners were more likely to think that their masculine reputations had been threatened, exhibited greater physiological signs of being upset, appeared more physiologically primed for aggression (their testosterone levels rose), and engaged in more aggressive and dominant subsequent behavior—such as giving firmer handshakes and being more unwilling to yield to a subsequent confederate as they walked toward each other in a very narrow hallway (see ● Figure 11.7).

More recently Ryan Brown and others (2009) found that cultures of honor are associated with school violence. For example, states in the United States associated with cultures of honor had more than twice as many school shootings per capita as other states, and high-school students from culture-of-honor states were significantly more likely to bring a weapon to school. Lindsay Osterman and Ryan Brown (2011) also found that suicide rates are higher in culture-of-honor states, which the authors speculate may be due in part to greater concern and focus on interpersonal threat and loss of status, and a greater feeling of personal responsibility for failure to protect one's honor. (We should note that in these studies comparing various states or regions, the researchers statistically control for other factors that might be related to these variables, such as differences in economic conditions, so that the results they report are not due to these other factors.)

Institutions support norms about the acceptability of honor-based violence. Cohen and Nisbett (1997) illustrated this in a clever experiment in which they sent letters to employers all over the United States from a fictitious job applicant who admitted that he had been convicted of a felony. To half the employers, the applicant reported that he had impulsively killed a man who had been having an affair with his fiancée and then

● **FIGURE 11.7**

**Insult, Aggression, and the Southern Culture of Honor**

White male participants from either the North or South regions of the United States either were bumped and insulted by a male confederate or they passed the confederate without incident (control condition). As you can see, the incident had a greater effect on Southern participants. Specifically, they thought that they would be seen as less masculine (left); their testosterone levels increased more (center); and they were slower to yield to a confederate who later approached them in a narrow corridor (right).
Cohen et al., 1996. © Cengage Learning

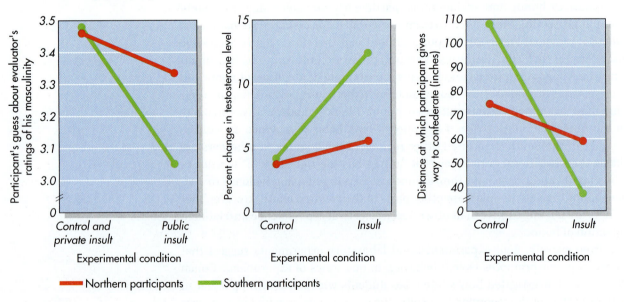

taunted him about it in a crowded bar. To the other half, the applicant reported that he had stolen a car because he needed the money to pay off debts. Employers from the South and the West (which has a culture of honor similar to that of the South) were more likely than their Northern counterparts to respond in an understanding and cooperative way to the letter from the convicted killer—but not to the letter from the auto thief.

Joseph Vandello and Dov Cohen (2003) examined the culture of honor in Brazil in other research. Vandello and Cohen found that a wife's infidelity harmed a man's reputation more in the eyes of Brazilian students than in the eyes of students from the northern United States. In a related study, Vandello, Cohen, and others (2009) had participants from Chile (a culture that emphasizes honor) or Canada (a culture that is neutral concerning honor) listen to a tape of a man describing how he behaved violently toward his wife during a conflict. In one condition, the conflict was triggered when the husband thought she was flirting with another man at a party. In a different condition, the conflict was triggered by something having nothing to do with jealousy or threats to the man's honor. The Chilean participants rated the violence as more acceptable and rated the husband more positively across several dimensions than the Canadian participants did when the conflict was related to jealousy, but there was no cultural difference when the conflict was not related to jealousy or honor (see ● Figure 11.8).

A key to the aggression associated with cultures of honor is the fact that individuals in these cultures perceive aggressive responses to honor-based threats as the norm among their peers. That is, cultures of honor persist because the individuals believe that most people in their peer group have positive attitudes toward aggression (and negative attitudes toward not acting aggressively) in response to threats to one's honor. Consistent with this idea, Vandello, Cohen, and Sean Ransom (2008) found that relative to white men from the northern part of the United States, white men from the South were significantly more likely to overestimate the aggressiveness of their peers and to interpret others' ambiguous advice about how to respond in an interpersonal conflict as encouraging aggression.

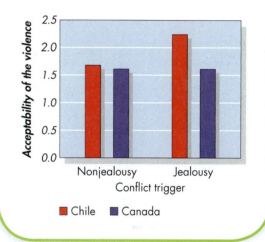

● **FIGURE 11.8**

**Culture of Honor and Attitudes About Domestic Violence**

Participants from Chile (a culture that emphasizes honor) or Canada (a neutral culture regarding honor) listened to a tape of a man describing his violent behavior toward his wife during a conflict. When the conflict was not triggered by an honor-related issue, Chileans and Canadians did not differ in how acceptable they thought the violence was. When the conflict was triggered by the husband perceiving his wife flirting with another man at a party, however, the Chileans were significantly more accepting of the violence than the Canadians were.

Based on Vandello et al., 2009. © Cengage Learning

## Nature Versus Nurture: A False Debate?

The origins of aggression are a source not only of scientific disagreement but also of political controversy. Politicians frequently engage in heated debates about whether to fund research and treatment programs, and they disagree with each other strongly about whether aggression is, to any significant extent, attributable to stable biological characteristics present at birth. However important it may be, this contentious issue should not obscure the considerable agreement that exists on other points. The effects of learning are not disputed; aggression is, at least to some extent, "made" by experience. Nor is there any doubt that in aggression, as in all human behavior, biology and environment interact. Indeed, contemporary research on aggression is paying increasing attention to the interactions of genes and environment (Bezdjian et al., 2011; Boutwell et al., 2011; Rhee & Waldman, 2011; Simons et al., 2012). The debate between nature and nurture may rage on among politicians, but to scientists it is clear that the origins of human aggression represent a profound interaction of evolved mechanisms and environmental and social factors.

# Situational Influences on Aggression

Whatever the ultimate causes of aggression, it is clear that specific, immediate situational factors can promote or inhibit it. In this section, we take a close look at several of these factors: frustration, negative affect, arousal, and factors that influence people's thoughts and information processing.

## The Frustration–Aggression Hypothesis

In 1939, the year that World War II began, John Dollard and his colleagues published *Frustration and Aggression*, one of the most influential books on aggression ever written. This book set forth two major propositions that taken together were called the **frustration–aggression hypothesis**: (1) Frustration—which is produced by interrupting a person's progress toward an expected goal—will always elicit the motive to aggress; and (2) All aggression is caused by frustration.

Dollard and his colleagues claimed that the motive to aggress is a psychological drive that resembles physiological drives like hunger. According to this theory, just as food deprivation elicits a hunger drive, so frustration elicits an aggressive drive. Just as the hunger drive prompts the search for food, so the aggressive drive prompts the attempt to inflict injury. But what if we're unable to aggress against the source of our frustration? After all, we can't hit the boss, nor can we strike out against abstractions such as health problems or financial setbacks. Dollard and his colleagues believed that in such instances the aggressive drive can seep out in the form of **displacement**. Here, the inclination to aggress is deflected from the real target to a substitute. After a bad day at work or at school, do you sometimes come home and yell at the first available target—be it friend, lover, or pet?

Drawing from the ancient idea of **catharsis**, Dollard and his colleagues believed that displacing aggression in these ways can be effective at reducing the drive to aggress further. Since the Dollard group defined aggression quite broadly—to include making hostile jokes, telling violent stories, cursing, and observing the aggression of others, real or fictional—they held out the hope that engaging in some relatively harmless pursuit could drain away energy from more violent tendencies.

**The Frustration–Aggression Hypothesis: Does the Evidence Support It?**    Obviously, there is a connection between frustration and aggression. Break into a line of shoppers at the supermarket or interrupt a student cramming for an exam, and you can see it for yourself. James Holmes, the shooter in *The Dark Knight Rises* movie theater tragedy described in the introduction to the chapter, reportedly bought a high-powered rifle hours after he failed an important exam at the University of Colorado (Harris, 2012).

Soon after the frustration–aggression theory was proposed, however, critics pointed out that the Dollard group had overstated their case. Early on, Neal Miller (1941), one of the originators of the hypothesis, acknowledged that frustration does not always produce aggressive inclinations. The other absolute, that all aggression is caused by frustration, was soon overturned as well. The concepts of displacement and catharsis were also subjected to close scrutiny. Although there were some inconsistent findings concerning displacement over the years, a meta-analysis of 49 published articles found significant evidence for displaced aggression in response to provocation (Marcus-Newhall et al., 2000). Provoked individuals are especially likely to displace aggression toward others they dislike or others who are outgroup members (Pedersen et al., 2008). But what about catharsis?

**frustration–aggression hypothesis** The idea that (1) frustration always elicits the motive to aggress and (2) all aggression is caused by frustration.

**displacement** Aggressing against a substitute target because aggressive acts against the source of the frustration are inhibited by fear or lack of access.

**catharsis** A reduction of the motive to aggress that is said to result from any imagined, observed, or actual act of aggression.

Dollard and his colleagues described catharsis as a two-step sequence. First, aggression reduces the level of physiological arousal. Second, because arousal is reduced, people are less angry and less likely to aggress further. It sounds logical, and many people believe it. But when put to the test, catharsis has not lived up to its advertisement. Most researchers have concluded that the catharsis idea is a myth. It is more counterproductive than effective in reducing subsequent aggression (Bushman, 2002; Geen & Quanty, 1977).

Aggressive behavior may sometimes reduce the likelihood of further immediate aggression, but so can just letting the frustration simply dissipate over time. For that matter, a response incompatible with aggression, such as experiencing sympathy or humor, can be more effective. In the long run, successful aggression sets the stage for more aggression later. In sum, relying on catharsis is dangerous medicine—more likely to inflame aggression than to put it out.

> Blowing off steam by engaging in safe but aggressive activities (such as sports) makes people less likely to aggress later. **F**ALSE.

## Negative Affect

By now it is clear that the original frustration–aggression hypothesis has a lot of flaws. But Leonard Berkowitz (1989) offered a different way to think about frustration as a trigger of aggression that has more merit. Berkowitz proposed that frustration is but one of many unpleasant experiences that can lead to aggression by creating negative, uncomfortable feelings. It is these negative feelings, and not the frustration itself, that can trigger aggression.

A wide variety of noxious stimuli and bad feelings can create negative feelings and increase aggression: noise, crowding, physical pain, threatened self-esteem, feelings of jealousy, social rejection, bad odors, and your home team losing a professional football playoff game (Baumeister et al., 2000; Berkowitz, 1998; De Steno et al., 2006; Leary et al., 2006; Panee & Ballard, 2002; Verona et al., 2002; Warburton et al., 2006). Reactions to a very common unpleasant condition, hot weather, are especially intriguing. Many people assume that temperature and tempers rise together, while others think it's just a myth. Who is right?

*"By far, the worst thing about the firehouse was the heat. It got really, really hot inside there the last few weeks of shooting. We had no air conditioning and the hotter it got, the angrier we got."*
—Jason, one of the people living in the firehouse on MTV's *The Real World: Boston*

**Heat and Aggression: Losing Your Cool** Craig Anderson and others have conducted extensive research on the question of whether heat leads to aggression, and data across time, cultures, and methodologies strongly support the notion that people lose their cool in hot temperatures and behave more aggressively (Anderson, 2001; Anderson et al., 2000; Anderson & DeLisi, 2011; Bushman et al., 2005). More violent crimes occur in the summer than in the winter, in hot years than in cooler years, and in hot cities than in cooler cities at any given time of year. The numbers of political uprisings, riots, homicides, assaults, rapes, and reports of violence peak in the summer months (see ● Figure 11.9).

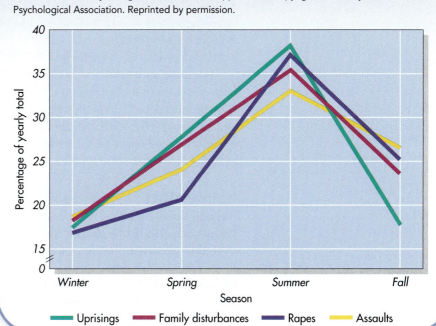

● **FIGURE 11.9**

**The Link Between Heat and Violence**

Worldwide weather records and crime statistics reveal that more violent crimes are committed during the summer than in the other seasons.

From Anderson, C.A. "Temperature and aggression: Ubiquitous effects of heat on occurrence of human violence," *Psychological Bulletin* vol 106 (pp. 74–96). Copyright © 1989 by the American Psychological Association. Reprinted by permission.

Uprisings — Family disturbances — Rapes — Assaults

● **FIGURE 11.10**

**Temper and Temperature in Baseball**

This figure shows the average number of players hit by pitches (HBPs) per game during the 1986 through 1988 Major League Baseball seasons. As the temperature increased, so did the likelihood that pitchers would hit batters (with balls often thrown more than 90 miles per hour and often thrown at a batter's head). Players' general wildness or fatigue, as measured by walks, wild pitches, passed balls, and errors, did not increase with temperature, suggesting that the heat–HBP correlation perhaps was due to hotter temperatures that led to hotter tempers.

From Reifman, A. S., Larrick, R. P., and Fein, S., "Temper and temperature on the diamond: The heat-aggression relationship in major league baseball," *Personality and Social Psychology Bulletin* vol 17 (p. 6). Copyright © 1991 Sage Publications, Inc. Reprinted by permission.

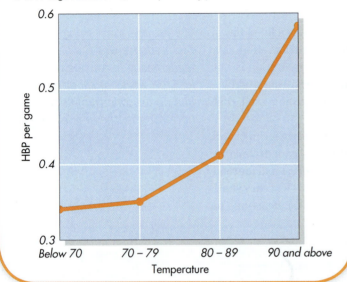

Alan Reifman and others (1991) found that as the temperature rises, Major League Baseball pitchers are more likely to hit batters with a pitch. The pitchers aren't wilder in general (such as in the number of walks they give up or wild pitches they throw)—they are just more likely to hit batters (see ● Figure 11.10).

Given the earlier discussion of the culture of honor and the high incidence of violence in the American South, you may wonder whether it is culture or heat that contributes to the violence. At this point, evidence points to both influences as important. Each probably has independent effects on aggression. In addition, they may interact with each other. For example, the relatively high temperatures of the region may support aggressive norms (Anderson et al., 2000; Nisbett & Cohen, 1996).

**Provocation and Social Rejection** Most aggressive incidents can be directly linked to some type of provocation, and the negative affect caused by the provocation plays a critically important role in triggering aggression. One type of provocation is an insult or threat to one's ego or status. Another type of provocation is social rejection. One of the most unpleasant feelings that people experience is being rejected or ostracized by others. Many experiments have manipulated provocation or social rejection to examine their causal effects on aggression. For example, a participant in an experiment might find himself or herself insulted, or suddenly ignored by the other participants who engage in pleasant interactions only with each other during the experiment. These studies have shown that provocation and social rejection increase the likelihood of aggressive responses (Bettencourt et al., 2006; DeWall et al., 2010; Williams & Wesselmann, 2011). In an interesting correlational study, Richard Larrick and others (2011) replicated the finding we reported earlier of baseball pitchers being more likely to hit opposing batters when it was hot outside, but they found additionally that pitchers were especially likely to hit batters in the heat if their teammates had been hit first—suggesting that provocation strengthened the effect of heat on their likelihood to aggress.

On an extreme level, it was clear that Dylan Klebold and Eric Harris of the Columbine massacre had been feeling extremely frustrated by their exclusion from popular cliques. Indeed, in 13 of the 15 school shootings between 1995 and 2001 that Mark Leary and others (2003) examined, the shooters had apparently been frustrated by social rejection. Social rejection has been cited as the most significant risk factor for adolescent violence (Leary et al., 2006).

**Positive Affect** If negative affect increases the likelihood of aggressing, can positive emotional reactions reduce it? Some evidence suggests that they can. For example, participants in one study were first angered by an experimental confederate. They were then shown funny cartoons or neutral pictures. Presented with an opportunity to retaliate by delivering electric shocks as part of a supposed learning experiment, those who had seen the cartoons delivered fewer shocks (Baron & Ball, 1974). Feeling amused appears to be incompatible with anger and aggression. Feeling concerned about others has similar effects. An empathic response to another person reduces aggression against that individual (Miller & Eisenberg, 1988; Sergeant et al., 2006).

## Arousal

Research on affect clearly indicates that the type of emotion (positive or negative) influences aggression. The intensity of arousal is important as well. In Chapter 9, we described the process of *excitation transfer*, in which the arousal created by one stimulus can intensify an individual's emotional response to another stimulus. For example, men who engaged in vigorous exercise were later more attracted to an attractive female than were those who had barely moved (White et al., 1981). Physical exercise is a highly arousing but emotionally neutral experience. Can it increase aggression as well as attraction? The research of Dolf Zillmann (1983; 2003) suggests that it can. The scope of excitation transfer is not limited to physical exercise. Noise, violent movies, arousing music—all have been shown to increase aggression. Heat has an interesting effect on arousal: Although people believe that heat lowers arousal, it actually increases it. This misperception makes heat a prime candidate for excitation transfer, as people are likely to misattribute arousal caused by heat to something else, such as anger, which can then lead to aggression (Anderson et al., 1996). Later in this chapter, we describe the effects of another arousing stimulus—pornography—on the inclination to aggress.

## Thought: Automatic and Deliberate

Step by step, we have been making our way toward a comprehensive theory of social and situational influences on aggression, particularly reactive aggression. We've examined several kinds of unpleasant experiences (frustration, heat, provocation, and social rejection) that create negative affect. We've considered how arousal can contribute to aggression. The next step is to add cognition. People don't just feel; they also think. These thoughts may be as primitive as automatic, unconscious associations, or they may be higher-order, conscious deliberations. Both automatic and deliberate thoughts play a critically important role in aggressive behavior.

**Aggressive Cues**   As we have already stated, no other stable, relatively wealthy country in the world comes even close to the United States in terms of the prevalence of guns used in violent crime. Guns of course are only an instrument—it's the people who are pulling the trigger. But social psychologist Leonard Berkowitz wondered whether guns were in fact entirely neutral. He hypothesized that the presence of a weapon can act as a situational cue that automatically triggers aggressive thoughts and feelings, thereby increasing the likelihood of aggression. In a classic study designed to test this idea, he and Anthony LePage (1967) had a confederate provoke male participants who could later respond by giving the confederate electric shocks (although in reality the confederate was not shocked). On a table near the shock apparatus just happened to be some objects scattered about, allegedly left there from a previous experiment.

For half of the participants, these objects were a revolver and rifle, and for the other half, they were badminton racquets and shuttlecocks. Berkowitz and LePage found that participants delivered more shocks to the confederate when a revolver and rifle were present than when badminton racquets and shuttlecocks were. In other words, although they didn't use these weapons, their mere presence seemed to make the participants more aggressive. This tendency for the presence of guns to increase aggression came to be known as the **weapons effect**. As Berkowitz put it: "The finger pulls the trigger, but the trigger may also be pulling the finger" (1968, p. 22).

Individuals may differ in what associations they have with various weapons. Bruce Bartholow and others (2005) found that hunters were less likely than nonhunters to associate hunting guns with aggression. Hunters had more positive associations with hunting guns; for example, they linked guns with sport and the pleasurable experiences they had had hunting with friends and family. Nonhunters not only had more negative, aggressive thoughts after exposure to hunting guns than did hunters, but they also behaved more aggressively while doing a subsequent task. However, exposure to assault guns had a very different effect: Hunters had more negative, aggressive associations with assault guns than did nonhunters, and they behaved more aggressively than nonhunters after exposure to them. In other words, hunters cognitively differentiated hunting guns from assault guns more than nonhunters did, and so these two types of weapons triggered very different effects for them.

Jennifer Klinesmith and others (2006) found that weapons had an effect on men's testosterone levels as well as on their aggression. Male college students in this experiment handled either a handgun or a children's game for 15 minutes. Relative to the students who interacted with the game, the students who interacted with the gun showed increased testosterone levels and exhibited greater aggression against another person (by adding a lot of "Frank's Red Hot Sauce" to a cup of water they thought another subject would have to drink!). The greater the increase in testosterone in response to the gun, the more hot sauce the students added to the other person's drink.

More generally, any object or external characteristic that is associated with (1) successful aggression; or (2) the negative affect of pain or unpleasantness can serve as an aggression-enhancing situational cue (Berkowitz, 1993; 1998; 2008). Even brief exposure to words associated with hot temperatures can trigger aggressive thoughts (DeWall & Bushman, 2009).

**Higher-Order Cognition** Situational cues can trigger automatic associations. More complex information about one's situation, however, influences the deliberate, thoughtful consideration that we call higher-order cognitive processing. For example, an angry person might refrain from acting aggressively if the potential costs of fighting seem too high. In this case, the person might choose to flee rather than fight. In addition, people who believe that aggression is inappropriate in a particular situation or whose moral values and principles mandate nonviolent behavior may realize that better alternatives to aggression exist (Huesmann & Guerra, 1997). The behavior of other people in the immediate situation can also influence an individual's considerations. If one or more others in a group are reacting aggressively to the situation, aggression can be contagious (Levy & Nail, 1993).

People's thoughts about the intentions of other people can determine whether they are likely to respond aggressively. Some individuals exhibit a **hostile attribution bias** in that they tend to perceive hostile intent in others. For example, socially maladjusted children who are chronically aggressive and have been rejected by their peers see hostile intent where others don't (Crick & Dodge, 1994). Such perceptions then increase their aggression, and their peers respond by rejecting them further, locking these children into an ever-escalating vicious circle. Chronically aggressive adults, too, tend to expect and perceive hostility in others' motives and behaviors (Dill et al., 1997). Research has found hostile attribution bias to be associated with both physical and relational aggression (Bailey & Ostrov, 2008; Orobio de Castro et al., 2002).

**weapons effect** The tendency that the likelihood of aggression will increase by the mere presence of weapons.

**hostile attribution bias** The tendency to perceive hostile intent in others.

# The Struggle for Self-Control: Rumination, Alcohol, and Other Factors

Not all insults, frustrations, or other situational triggers lead to aggressive behaviors, of course. More often than not we control our aggressive impulses and restrict our fantasies for revenge to our daydreams. It is quite clear that the ability to practice self-control is vital to the inhibition of aggression. It is also quite clear that behind a majority of aggressive and violent acts lies the failure of self-control (Denson, DeWall, & Finkel, 2012; DeWall, Finkel, & Denson, 2011).

One important factor that works against self-control of aggression is **rumination**. In the context of anger and aggression, rumination involves repeatedly thinking about and reliving an anger-inducing event, focusing on angry thoughts and feelings, and perhaps even planning or imagining revenge. Angry rumination can take a minor situational factor that otherwise might have faded away after a few minutes and enable it to retain its force to cause anger and aggression over a long period of time. A rapidly growing set of studies have found that this kind of rumination contributes to direct and displaced aggression, arousal and raised blood pressure, negative affect, and aggressive cognitions (Denson, Moulds, & Grisham, 2012; DeWall, Finkel, & Denson, 2011; Pedersen et al., 2011). Rumination also reduces people's self-control abilities. Therefore this is another way that rumination contributes to aggression—by impairing people's ability to inhibit aggression through regulating themselves against their aggressive impulses (see ● Figure 11.11) (Denson et al., 2011; Denson, DeWall, & Finkel, 2012).

Some other conditions make it more difficult to engage in the higher-order cognition and self-control mechanisms that can inhibit aggressive impulses. High arousal, for example, impairs the cognitive control of aggression (Zillmann et al., 1975). When you are very emotional and angry, it is hard to focus on anything else or to be as reasonable as you might ordinarily like to be. One unusual example of this might be the story of a man in Nepal who was bitten by a cobra in August 2012. He chased the cobra and bit it back! Why did he kill the cobra in this rather intimate and dangerous way? "I could have killed it with a stick but bit it with my teeth instead because I was angry," he explained ("Nepali man bites snake to death in revenge attack," 2012).

Alcohol is a notorious obstacle to self-control. Alcohol is implicated in the majority of violent crimes, suicides, automobile fatalities, and sexually aggressive incidents between college students. The evidence is quite clear about this point: Alcohol consumption often increases aggressive behavior (Bushman et al., 2012; Carr & VanDeusen, 2004;

**rumination** In the context of aggression, rumination involves repeatedly thinking about and reliving an anger-inducing event, focusing on angry thoughts and feelings, and perhaps even planning or imagining revenge.

● **FIGURE 11.11**

**The Path from Provocation to Aggression: The Roles of Rumination and Self-Control**

Research by Thomas Denson and others (2011; Denson, DeWall, & Finkel, 2012) has shown that an anger-inducing provocation, such as an insult or social rejection, can trigger angry rumination, which in turn reduces self-control, which in turn increases the likelihood and severity of aggression.

Denson et al., 2011. © Cengage Learning

Exum, 2006; Graham et al., 2006). But *how* does alcohol increase aggression? As many people who drink alcohol know, alcohol can lower people's inhibitions, and reducing inhibitions against aggression certainly facilitates aggressive behaviors (Ito et al., 1996). Alcohol impairs people's executive functioning, which as we discussed earlier involves cognitive processes that enable people to plan or inhibit actions (Giancola et al., 2012; Weiss & Marksteiner, 2007). This in turn increases aggression. Another way that alcohol can lead to aggression is through what Claude Steele and Robert Josephs (1990) called *alcohol myopia*. That is, alcohol narrows people's focus of attention. Intoxicated people respond to initial, salient information about the situation but often miss later, more subtle indicators. They may therefore focus on a perceived provocation, such as an insult or threat to one's status, and fail to see or think about information that would explain away this provocation or to consider the long-term problems of retaliation, such as injury, guilt, or arrest. This narrowed focus can therefore make aggression much more likely to occur, unless the intoxicated person's narrow focus can be distracted toward something safer (Bushman et al., 2012; Giancola et al., 2010).

The link between alcohol and aggression or violence is so strong that alcohol can serve as an aggressive cue, just as weapons can. For example, participants in some studies were more likely to activate aggressive thoughts and behaviors if they had been exposed briefly to images or words associated with alcohol (e.g., a vodka bottle, or the word *vodka*) than if they had been exposed to neutral images or words (Bartholow & Heinz, 2006; Subra et al., 2010). In addition, alcohol can also affect aggressiveness because of people's *expectations* about alcohol's effects. The more people expect alcohol to affect them and make them more aggressive, the more likely it is that it will have that effect (Bégue et al., 2009; Quigley & Leonard, 2006).

Whereas alcohol reduces people's executive functioning and self-control, nonalcoholic sugar-rich drinks can boost them, especially when people's cognitive resources are already depleted through fatigue or other factors, and this in turn can reduce aggression (Denson, von Hippel, Kemp, & Teo, 2010; DeWall, Deckman, et al., 2011). What about caffeine? Does it give people a boost that might help them control their impulses if their cognitive resources have been depleted? The problem here is that caffeine also significantly increases people's physiological and mental arousal, such as by raising blood pressure and adrenaline—and this in turn can *increase* aggression. Indeed, Thomas Denson, Mandi Jacobson, and others (2012) found that participants who *thought* they had consumed caffeine (but actually did not) showed reduced aggression after they had been cognitively depleted by a long and boring mental task, but those who actually consumed caffeine did not.

> ## Situational Influences: Putting It All Together

We have seen that negative affect, arousal, and aggression-related thoughts can lead to aggression. And a number of factors influence whether one is likely to experience negative affect, arousal, and aggressive thoughts, such as aversive experiences (frustration, heat, provocation), situational cues (guns, violent movies), and individual and cultural differences (chronic hostility, cultures of honor). Craig Anderson and others put all these various factors together to create a model called the General Aggression Model (GAM) (Anderson et al., 1996). ● Figure 11.12 illustrates the basics of this model.

As this figure illustrates, various aversive experiences (such as frustration or heat), situational cues (such as weapons), and individual differences (such as a hostile attribution bias) can create negative affect, high arousal, and/or aggressive thoughts, each of which can lead to aggressive behavior. Whether the affect, arousal, and thoughts translate into aggressive behavior, however, may depend in part on the outcome of higher-order thinking, which can either inhibit aggression (such as by recognizing the

*"I could have killed it with a stick but bit it with my teeth instead because I was angry."*
—A Nepali man explains why he bit to death a cobra that had bitten him in August 2012.

danger of the situation or recognizing that what seemed like a provocation was really just an accident) or facilitate it (such as by perceiving that aggression is encouraged by one's peers in this situation or that a provocation was intentional). More recently Anderson and his colleagues have added elements to this model, such as to integrate more recent research on biological factors, but the basics of the model remain the same and have done an excellent job of capturing the variety of factors that contribute to reactive aggression (Anderson & Bushman, 2002b; Anderson & Carnagey, 2004; DeWall, Anderson, & Bushman, 2011).

Eli Finkel and others (2012; 2013; Denson, DeWall, & Finkel, 2012) recently introduced a new theory of aggression called I$^3$ theory (pronounced "I-cubed theory"). This theory focuses especially on the role of self-control in aggression, which we just discussed in the previous section. The three *I*s in this theory stand for *Instigation* (social factors that often trigger aggressive impulses, such as provocation or social rejection), *Impellance* (personality and situational factors that promote the urge to aggress when encountering instigating factors, such as angry rumination or personality types prone to aggressiveness), and *Inhibition* (the various factors of self-control we described in the previous section). This theory pits the forces of instigation and impellance on the one hand against the power of inhibition on the other to determine the likelihood of aggression. Strong provocation coupled with angry rumination can overpower a person's self-control abilities that have been compromised by alcohol, for example, resulting in an elevated likelihood of aggression.

# Media Effects

Having looked at origins and specific factors that contribute to aggression, we now focus on a special topic that has been a major concern of politicians, families, and social scientists alike for many years: violence in television, film, video games, and other media. Does violence in the media promote real-world aggression and violence? We address this important question, along with another hotly debated question: Does pornography promote real-world aggression?

## Violence in TV, Movies, Music Lyrics, and Video Games

On September 13, 2006, Kimveer Gill, a 25-year-old man, drove up to Dawson College in Montreal, pulled three guns from his car, and started shooting students. In total, Gill shot 20 people. Gill had no apparent connection or dispute with Dawson College or its

● **FIGURE 11.12**

**The General Aggression Model**

This figure represents key aspects of an early version of the General Aggression Model (it has since been updated to include more factors, but the basics are the same). Unpleasant experiences and situational cues can trigger negative affect, high arousal, and aggression-related thoughts. Due to individual differences, some people are more likely than others to experience these feelings and thoughts. Higher-order thinking then shapes these feelings and thoughts into more well-defined emotions and behavioral intentions. Depending on the outcome of this thinking (which can occur beneath the individual's conscious awareness and can be affected by factors such as alcohol or stress), the individual may choose to aggress.

From Anderson, C. A., Anderson, K. B, and Deuser, W. E., "Examining and affective framework: weapon and temperature effects on aggressive thoughts, affect, and attitudes," *Personality and Social Psychology Bulletin* vol 22 (pp. 366–376). Copyright © 1996 Sage Publications, Inc. Reprinted by permission.

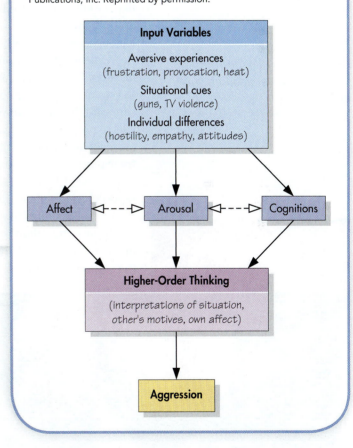

students. Rather, it seemed, he had a tremendous amount of hostility toward the world in general. He had written numerous postings on the Internet about his loathing for humanity and about his fascination with guns, death, and violent video games. On a website popular with Goth culture, he had posted entries about his fantasies of killing people, many of which foreshadowed the events of September 13. "Life is a video game. You've got to die sometime," he wrote in one blog (Struck, 2006, p. A12). These are the same words another young killer had used after killing police officers in Alabama in 2003, in a scene similar to one depicted in the killer's favorite violent video game (Kampis, 2005).

According to one report, when Danny Ledonne heard about the shootings at Dawson College in Montreal, he threw up. Ledonne, living in Colorado, had no connection to Kimveer Gill or his victims, but Ledonne had heard that the killer was a big fan of the extremely violent video game he had posted on the Internet, called *Super Columbine Massacre*. The game was based on the massacre at Columbine High School, and Gill was fascinated by the shootings, both the real event and the video game version. "When I heard about the Dawson shootings," Ledonne said, "people asked me, 'Gosh. How do you feel to have blood on your hands?'" (Gerson, 2006, p. A12).

Despite what Ledonne's physical reaction to the Dawson College news might suggest, Ledonne asserts that he doesn't believe his game promotes real violence. But Gill, like the killers in Columbine and in many other school shootings, was an avid fan of several extremely violent, vicious video games. The question is, then: Do these games—and violence depicted in other popular media—cause real-world aggression and violence?

Violence depicted in the media has been a target of attack and counterattack for decades. But the amount, intensity, and graphic nature of the violence have continued to escalate. According to a 2009 report by the American Academy of Pediatrics, American youth between 8 and 18 spend about 6.5 hours per day using entertainment media, a large proportion of which includes acts of violence. By the age of 18 they will have on average viewed about 200,000 acts of violence on television alone. The video game industry in particular is booming, with an estimated $21 *billion* in sales in 2008 (Gentile, 2011). About 97% of 12 to 17 year-olds in the United States play video games, and the majority report playing violent video games (Willoughby et al., 2012). And all this exposure is not limited to the United States—it is a global phenomenon (Anderson et al., 2010).

If consumers didn't enjoy violence in TV, film, music, videos, and video games, these media would not be featuring it. So can it really be harmful? We explore this question in the sections that follow.

> *"People asked me, 'Gosh. How do you feel to have blood on your hands?'"*
>
> —Danny Ledonne, after learning that the school shooter at Dawson College in 2006 was a fan of the video game he had posted on the Internet

Can playing violent video games cause children and young adults to become more aggressive and violent? A growing body of research suggests that it can.

© David Pearson/Alamy

### Linking Media Violence to Real-World Violence

Does life imitate art? It often seems that way. The night James Holmes opened fire in the Colorado theater showing the latest Batman movie in July 2012, he reportedly referred to himself as "The Joker"—the villain who brought random violence to innocent masses in the previous Batman movie. Dylan Klebold and Eric Harris were big fans of the violent video game *Doom* when they went on their 1999 shooting spree at Columbine High School, and reports indicate that they based their plans for their massacre on the game. Anders Behring Breivik said that when planned his 2011 bombing and shooting attacks in Norway, he played violent video games such as *Call of Duty: Modern Warfare 2* and *World of Warcraft* for training purposes. He claimed that he played these games for about 16 hours a day in 2006, doing little else but playing and sleeping for the entire year (Gibbs & Koranyi, 2012; Pancevski, 2012; Paterson, 2012). Tim Kretschmer, the shooter in a March 2009 rampage at a high school in Winnenden, Germany, had numerous brutally violent video games and videos. This led one of Germany's largest retail chains to stop selling films or games with very violent material (Roxborough, 2009). Indeed, many of the boys and young men involved in the waves of school shootings had consumed a steady diet of violent video games, including the shooter behind the mass killings at the elementary school in Newtown, Connecticut. Each shooting, moreover, was soon followed by additional threats and violent acts. According to one analysis, there were 400 copycat incidents in the United States and Canada in the month after the Columbine shooting (Tobin, 2006). Table 11.3 lists just a few of the many violent incidents that may have been inspired by exposure to violence depicted in popular media. Yet no one can ever prove that a specific fictional depiction was the primary cause of a specific act of violence. There are always other possibilities.

If you ask people whether exposure to media violence causes real aggression, most would probably say that they doubt that it does or that there has never been clear evidence one way or another on this question. When this issue is discussed on the news

> *"According to a national survey of 12- to 17-year-olds in the United States, 99% of boys and 94% of girls play video games."*
> —Lenhart et al., 2008

### TABLE 11.3
#### Copycat Violence?

Although it's impossible to prove that any specific media depiction caused a specific violent action, there have been some close connections.

| Violent Fiction | Subsequent Violent Fact |
| --- | --- |
| *The Matrix* (a trilogy of films starring Keanu Reeves) | Numerous killers have cited the influence of these movies in their violent outbursts. Many of them believed they were in a real-life version of the matrix. |
| *Dexter* (TV series about a serial killer) | A teenager strangled his 10-year-old brother to death, later explaining that he was inspired by the serial killer character Dexter. |
| *Twilight* (series of romance books and movies featuring vampires) | A boy bit at least 11 girls because he was inspired by his love of the movie. |
| *Money Train* (movie starring Wesley Snipes and Woody Harrelson) | In several incidents in New York City, people doused subway token collectors with flammable liquids and burned them, just as had been depicted in the movie. |
| *Natural Born Killers* (movie starring Woody Harrelson and Juliette Lewis) | At least eight murders have been cited as having been inspired by this violent film, including the case of a student who decapitated a classmate because he "wanted to be famous, like the natural born killers" (Brooks, 2002, p. 10). |
| "F*** tha Police" (song by gangsta rap group N.W.A.) | Rifles used in the shooting of a police officer in North Carolina were emblazoned with the letters N.W.A. |
| *Scream* (movie starring Neve Campbell, Courteney Cox, and Drew Barrymore) | Several brutal attacks apparently copied elements of the movie, including the costume worn and the scare tactics used by the fictional killer. For example, a Belgian man put on a *Scream* costume before killing a 15-year-old girl with two kitchen knives. |
| *Fight Club* (movie starring Brad Pitt) | A teen obsessed with *Fight Club* set off a bomb at a Manhattan Starbucks in an act that was similar to an event in the movie. A friend said, "He thought he was Tyler Durden," the lead character from the movie (Gendar et al., 2009, p. 7). |
| Professional wrestling | Mimicking a dangerous wrestling move he had seen on TV, a 7-year-old boy accidentally killed his 3-year-old brother in Dallas. |
| *The Life and Death of Lord Erroll* (a controversial book) | The author's son was killed in an act very similar to the murder that had been described in her book. The author later said, "In some terrible way, I think I pressed the trigger" (Alderson, 2001, p. 6). |
| *Grand Theft Auto* (video game) | Two teenagers in Tennessee fired shotgun blasts at passing cars on a highway, leaving one dead and another wounded. They claimed they didn't mean to kill anyone but simply wanted to emulate *Grand Theft Auto*, their favorite video game. |

The movie *Fight Club*, starring Brad Pitt and Edward Norton, has been linked to numerous copycat acts of aggression and violence, including the 2009 bombing at a Starbucks in New York City by a teenager obsessed with the movie and one of its lead characters, Tyler Durden.

*"I see television's violent content as therapeutic for the population."*
—Jib Fowles, author of *The Case for Television Violence*

or in the media in general, the reports tend to conclude that the relevant scientific evidence is weak and mixed, at best. Defenders of the entertainment industry consistently argue that there is no evidence that viewing media violence causes real-world aggression. Social psychologists and others who study this issue are often confronted by people who assert, "I've played lots of violent video games and I never killed anyone."

But what does the social psychological research *really* say on this matter? Here, we do not need to qualify the answer with "It depends." Enough research evidence has accumulated in the past few decades that six major professional societies in the United States—the American Psychological Association, the American Academy of Pediatrics, the American Academy of Child and Adolescent Psychiatry, the American Medical Association, the American Academy of Family Physicians, and the American Psychiatric Association—together concluded that the research "reveals unequivocal evidence that media violence increases the likelihood of aggressive and violent behavior in both immediate and long-term contexts" (Anderson et al., 2003, p. 81). More recently, the American Academy of Pediatrics, which represents 60,000 child specialists, stated, "Exposure to violence in media, including television, movies, music, and video games, represents a significant risk to the health of children and adolescents. Extensive research indicates that media violence can contribute to aggressive behavior, desensitization to violence, nightmares, and fear of being harmed" (American Academy of Pediatrics, 2009, p. 1495). The general public may not be aware of this, but the scientific community is more convinced than ever.

The magnitude of the relationship is much stronger than most people realize. ● Figure 11.13 illustrates the magnitude of the correlation between TV violence and

● **FIGURE 11.13**

**How Strong Is the Relationship Between Media Violence and Real-World Aggression?**

The correlation between exposure to violence in the media and aggressive behavior is compared here to the correlations of several other well-established relationships. This comparison illustrates the relative magnitude of the link between media violence and aggressive behavior. From Singer, D. G., and Singer, J. L., eds., *Handbook of children and the media* (pp. 223–254). Copyright © 2001 by Sage Publications, Inc. Reprinted by permission of Sage Publications, Inc.

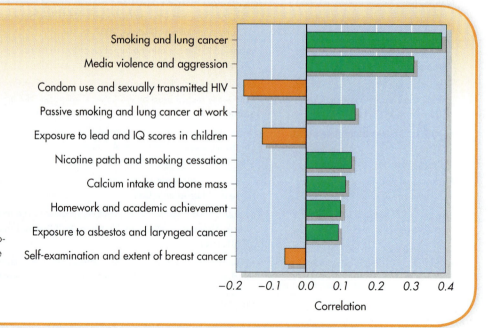

aggression found in one set of research compared to the correlations for other well-established relationships, such as calcium intake and bone mass. It is important to note that media violence is neither a necessary nor a sufficient cause of real-world aggression and violence. In other words, not everyone exposed to media violence will necessarily become more aggressive, and not all acts of aggression are fueled by media violence. Similarly, not everyone who smokes gets lung cancer, and not everyone who gets lung cancer smoked. Rather, frequent exposure to media violence should be seen as an important risk factor for real-world aggression, just as frequent consumption of alcohol is a risk factor for various health problems.

What is the evidence behind these conclusions? The best way to investigate the issue of media violence is to use multiple methods, each of which has different sets of strengths and weaknesses. This is exactly what researchers in this area have done. What is particularly impressive about this research is that the results have been strikingly consistent across methods. Longitudinal research, which examines individuals' exposure to violent media early in life and then examines their real-world aggression years later, has found, for example, that the extent to which 8 year olds watched violent TV predicts their aggressiveness and criminality as adults, even when statistically controlling for other factors such as socioeconomic status and parenting practices (Huesmann et al., 2003) (● Figure 11.14). More recently, a study of more than 1,700 high school students in Germany found that exposure to media violence predicted increases in aggression (based on students' self-reports as well as their teachers' ratings) over a 2-year period (Krahé et al., 2012). A similar result was found in a study of almost 1,500 high school students in Canada over a 4-year period, but this study focused specifically on violent video games rather than media violence more generally (Willoughby et al., 2012). In both of these recent longitudinal studies, other risk factors were statistically controlled for, and nonviolent media or video games play did not predict later aggression.

In experimental research, individuals are randomly assigned to watch or play with violent or nonviolent media, and their aggressive thoughts, feelings, and behaviors are measured immediately after the exposure. In one experiment, for example, adolescent Dutch boys were randomly assigned to play either a violent or a nonviolent video game for 20 minutes. Compared to the boys who played the nonviolent video game, the boys who played the violent game behaved more aggressively after the game by delivering very loud, aversive blasts of noise against an opponent in a reaction-time task. This aggressive effect was especially strong among the boys who reported identifying most strongly with the main character in the video game. Some of these boys chose to blast their opponent with noise so loud that it could—according to the experimenter's instructions—cause permanent hearing loss to the other boy (although, in fact, no one actually received these noise blasts) (Konijn et al., 2007). Another experiment was conducted by a team of researchers in Madrid, who found that 8- to 12-year-old children, particularly boys, were more aggressive after viewing televised bullfights (Graña et al., 2004).

These are just a few examples of the research on this topic. In fact, hundreds of studies have by now been conducted around the world, involving tens of thousands of participants, and extensive reviews have been conducted to test the strength and reliability of the findings. One review examined

*"There's an audience of people who love this genre who are not violent. In fact, they sort of use it to vent their violent nature so they don't have to act it out in real life."*

—Actress Jamie Lee Curtis, star of *Halloween* and some of its sequels, defending horror movie blood and gore

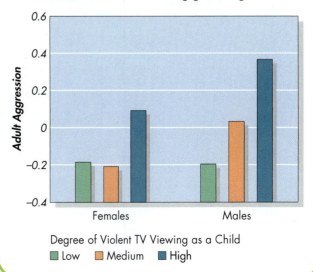

● **FIGURE 11.14**

**Violent TV Viewing and Aggression 15 Years Later**

A longitudinal study tracked individuals over a 15-year period. Based on how much TV violence they viewed as 8 year olds, individuals were categorized as having viewed low (lower 20%), medium (middle 60%), or high (upper 20%) levels of TV violence. Their aggressiveness as adults was measured 15 years later. For both females and males, those who tended to watch the greatest amount of violent TV as children tended to be the most aggressive as adults. Based on Huesmann et al., 2003. © Cengage Learning the relationship between exposure to media violence and real aggression in 46 longitudinal studies, 86 cross-sectional surveys (which look at the relation between individuals' exposure to violent media and their aggressive behavior at a single point in time), 28 field experiments, and 124 laboratory experiments—totaling more than 50,000 participants. The magnitude of the positive relationship between exposure to media violence and real aggressive behavior was consistent across all four types of studies. The laboratory experiments tended to show the strongest effects and the other three types of studies showed only slightly weaker—but still strong—relationships (Anderson & Bushman, 2002a; Anderson et al., 2004).

Violent video games have not been around as long as violent television, but they have become increasingly popular—and more graphically violent—in recent years, and so there has been a corresponding surge in research to examine their potential effects. Craig Anderson and others (2010) conducted a recent meta-analysis of more than 136 research papers, involving more than 130,000 participants in Western countries as well as in Japan and other Eastern countries. This analysis revealed that exposure to violent video games was a significant risk factor for increased aggressive behavior, aggressive cognition, and aggressive affect (e.g., feelings of hostility, anger), and for decreased empathy and prosocial (helpful) behavior (see ● Figure 11.15). Here again the set of studies included longitudinal, cross-sectional, and experimental designs, and the significant relationship between video game violence and aggression was found for both Western and Eastern cultures.

● **FIGURE 11.15**

**Violent Video Games As Risk Factors for Several Outcomes**

A recent meta-analysis of more than 136 research papers, involving more than 130,000 participants in several countries found strong relationships between playing violent video games and a number of outcomes, including higher levels of aggressive behavior, aggressive cognition, aggressive affect, and physiological arousal, along with reduced levels of prosocial behaviors and empathy (and an associated increase in desensitization). (The sizes of the bars in this graph represent the magnitude of the relationships between violent video games and these other variables; bars in a positive direction indicate a positive relationship; bars in a negative direction indicate a negative relationship.)

Based on Anderson et al., 2010; Anderson & Prot, 2011. © Cengage Learning

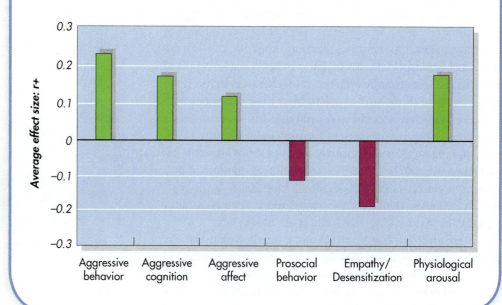

Physical violence is not the only kind of aggression portrayed in the media. Sarah Coyne and John Archer (2004) found examples of indirect aggression in 92% of programs on British television shows that are popular with adolescents, a rate much higher than physical aggression. Compared to physical aggressors, the indirect aggressors portrayed tended to be more rewarded for their aggression, and they were more likely to be female and attractive. In a later experiment, Coyne and her colleagues (2004) found that television exposure to indirect aggression had immediate effects on adolescents' own behavior, such as leading to less helping behavior, more negative evaluations of others, and greater endorsement of using indirect aggression in response to an ambiguous situation.

More recently, Coyne and others (2008) randomly assigned female college students to watch film clips involving physical aggression (from the movie *Kill Bill*), relational aggression (from the movie *Mean Girls*), or no aggression (from the movie *What Lies Beneath*). Although the different clips produced equal degrees of excitement and arousal, the clips showing either physical or relational aggression led the students to become more aggressive (blasting a confederate with painful noise) than did the nonaggressive clip. Other studies have demonstrated that exposure to media violence can lead to later increases in both physical and relational aggression; the relationship between watching media violence and engaging in relational aggression may be stronger for girls than boys (Gentile, Coyne, & Walsh, 2011; Gentile, Mathieson, & Crick, 2011).

### How Does Media Violence Cause These Effects?

The evidence from hundreds of studies makes it clear that media violence can have both immediate and long-term effects. Another question, though, is *how* it can have these effects. Social psychologists have found several paths through which media violence produces real-world aggression. For instance, exposure to media violence can trigger aggressive and hostile thoughts, which in turn can lead individuals to interpret others' actions in hostile ways and promote aggression (Anderson, 2004). Combine these aggressive cognitions with the high arousal caused by these games, and the recipe for aggression becomes more potent.

Media violence influences aggression also by desensitizing individuals to violence. **Desensitization** to violence refers to a reduction in emotion-related physiological reactivity to real violence. Desensitization is one form of *habituation*. A novel stimulus gets our attention, and if it's sufficiently interesting or exciting, it elicits physiological arousal. But when we get used to something, our reactions diminish. Familiarity with violence reduces physiological arousal to new incidents of violence (Geen, 1981). Desensitized to violence, we may become more accepting of it.

Christopher Engelhardt and others (2011) demonstrated this point in an experiment that examined participants' brain activity and aggressiveness after playing either a violent (e.g., *Call of Duty*, *Grand Theft Auto*) or nonviolent (e.g., *Tony Hawk's Pro Skater 4*) video game for 25 minutes. The games were rated by other participants to be equally enjoyable, arousing, and frustrating. The students then viewed a series of neutral (e.g., a man on a bicycle) and violent (e.g., a man holding a gun in another man's mouth) pictures. Consistent with the research we have already summarized, the students who played the violent video game were later more aggressive in blasting an opponent in a competitive reaction time game with loud noise. What's new about this experiment, however, is that through the use of scalp electrodes for electroencephalogram (EEG) recording, the researchers could measure brain activity to indicate how sensitive the students were to seeing the pictures of violence they were shown. The students who had played the violent video games showed reduced neural response to the violent photos compared to the students who had played the nonviolent video game—suggesting that

> Exposure to TV violence in childhood is related to aggression later in life. **T**RUE.

**desensitization** Reduction in emotion-related physiological reactivity in response to a stimulus.

the violent video game desensitized the students to violence. This desensitization, in turn, boosted later aggression. That is, the more desensitized the participants were, the more aggressive they were in their subsequent behavior toward their opponent.

It is also worth noting that the students who had played a lot of violent video games before the study showed desensitization to the violent photographs whether they had just played a violent or a nonviolent video game during the study. In other words, they seemed to already be desensitized to violence before coming to the study. This points to the long-term effects of chronic exposure to violent media.

Another experiment demonstrated that violent video games can desensitize individuals to the needs of a stranger who might be hurt. In one experiment, participants played either a violent or nonviolent video game for 20 minutes. Later, while completing a long questionnaire, they heard someone appear to get injured in a fight outside their lab room. With this person groaning in pain, how long would it take for the participants to leave their lab room and see if they could help? The participants who had played a violent video game took more than 450% longer to help an injured stranger than did participants who played a nonviolent video game. Those who played the violent game also perceived the fight to be less serious than did those who played the nonviolent game (Bushman & Anderson, 2009).

Tom Hummer and others (2010) found intriguing social-neuroscientific evidence, using fMRI procedures, suggesting that playing violent video games impaired players' executive functioning and ability to engage in successful self-control of their impulses. As we have indicated earlier in the chapter, impaired self-control is an important contributor to aggression.

Media violence can also produce long-term effects by influencing people's values and attitudes toward aggression, making it seem more legitimate and even necessary for social interaction and the resolution of social conflicts. Consistent with social learning theory, children may learn that aggression and violence are common, normal ways of dealing with threats or problems and are often rewarded. Frequent exposure to such imagery fuels the aggressive scripts that children and adolescents develop, which they subsequently use to guide their behavior (Anderson & Huesmann, 2007).

The effects of exposure to violence in the media also operate through what George Gerbner and his colleagues (1986) called **cultivation**. Cultivation refers to the capacity of the mass media to construct a social reality that people perceive as true, even if it isn't. The media tend to depict the world as much more violent than it actually is. This can make people become more fearful, more distrustful, more likely to arm themselves, and more likely to behave aggressively in what they perceive as a threatening situation (Morgan & Shanahan, 2010; Riddle, 2010).

**Can Media Cause Positive, Prosocial Effects?** The vast amount of attention and research has focused on the negative effects of media, but can positive media images and messages produce prosocial rather than antisocial effects? Although there is not a great deal of research on this yet, there are some encouraging results. For example, Tobias Greitemeyer (2009) found that listening to music lyrics that promoted socially positive messages caused participants to behave more helpfully. As discussed in Chapter 10, a meta-analysis of 34 studies found a reliable positive effect of prosocial television on children's prosocial behavior, especially when specific acts of altruism were modeled on TV (Mares & Woodard, 2005). Chapter 10 also reported the results of an international set of studies by Douglas Gentile and others (2009) that demonstrated that playing prosocial video games was associated with and can promote prosocial behavior. Indeed, playing prosocial video games has been found not only to increase prosocial behavior, but also to decrease aggressive behavior (Greitemeyer et al., 2012).

**cultivation** The process by which the mass media (particularly television) construct a version of social reality for the public.

# Pornography

Just as the effects of violence in popular media have been discussed and debated for decades, so too have the effects of media displays of sexual material. Defenders and opponents of pornography argue their positions passionately. So what does the social psychological research say?

It is important to recognize the challenges of conducting research on such a controversial and sensitive issue, such as the ethical challenges involved in conducting experiments using pornography. Even defining what is meant by pornography or obscenity is rarely straightforward. Because of the subjectivity involved in such definitions, the term **pornography** is used here to refer to explicit sexual material, regardless of its moral or aesthetic qualities. It is crucial, however, to distinguish between nonviolent and violent pornography in discussing the relationship between pornographic displays and aggression.

**Nonviolent and Violent Pornography**    Earlier in this chapter, we described how both arousal and affect can influence aggression. The results of research on nonviolent pornography confirm the importance of these factors (Donnerstein et al., 1987). For many people, viewing attractive bodies elicits a pleasant emotional response and moderate levels of sexual arousal. This combination of positive affect and only moderate arousal is unlikely to trigger much aggression. Indeed, according to Michael Seto and colleagues (2001), there is little support for a direct causal link between the use of nonviolent pornography and sexual aggression. However, there is more evidence for an association between pornography use and attitudes supporting violence against women (Hald et al., 2010; Malamuth et al., 2012).

Adding violence to pornography greatly increases the possibility of harmful effects. Violent pornography is a triple threat: It brings together high arousal; negative emotional reactions such as shock, alarm, and disgust; and aggressive thoughts. Numerous Internet sites—including many that are free and can be viewed easily by minors—focus specifically on images of sexual violence against women and use depictions of women's pain as a selling point (Gossett & Byrne, 2002). Research suggests that the effects of violent pornography are gender-specific. Male-to-male aggression is no greater after exposure to violent pornography than it is after exposure to highly arousing but nonviolent pornography, but male-to-female aggression is markedly increased (Donnerstein & Malamuth, 1997; Linz et al., 1987; Malamuth & Donnerstein, 1982).

**Individual Differences**    Not everyone is affected by pornography in the same way. Neil Malamuth has developed what he calls the "rapist's profile." Men fit the profile if they have relatively high levels of sexual arousal in response to violent pornography and also express attitudes and opinions indicating acceptance of violence toward women

© Chris Ryan/Corbis

The combination of violence, arousal, and sexual imagery is part of the appeal to many fans of professional wrestling (as in this WWE event in 2009). Research on aggression suggests that this combination can also be particularly potent in contributing to real-world aggression among viewers.

**pornography**    Explicit sexual material.

(see Table 11.4). These individuals report more sexually coercive behavior in the past and more sexually aggressive intentions for the future. Men who score relatively high on scales such as these are more predisposed to sexual aggression than other men. The effects of pornography on aggression or negative attitudes toward women are stronger for these men than they are for other men (Hald et al., 2010; Malamuth et al., 2012). Another risk factor concerns men's family histories. Leslie Gordon Simons and others (2012) reported that men who regularly use pornography and whose parents frequently used harsh corporal punishment were most likely to report engaging in sexually coercive behaviors.

# Reducing Violence

Now that we have explained the many factors that contribute to aggression and violence, and have illustrated the extent of the problem with a variety of grim stories and statistics, a key question must be addressed: What can we do about it? That is, do we have any reason to hope that rates of aggression and violence can be reduced? Are we simply aggressive animals who are destined to go on hurting and killing each other?

Fortunately, there is reason for optimism. Why do we think that rates of aggression and violence can decline? Because they already have.

An intriguing and comprehensive book by psychologist Steven Pinker (2011), called *The Better Angels of Our Nature: Why Violence Has Declined*, is among the recent analyses that makes the case that we are living in a time that is less violent and more peaceful than at any period in human history. He calls this reduction in violence perhaps "the most important thing that has happened in human history" and that "no aspect of life is untouched by the retreat from violence" (p. xxi). This claim flies in the face of how people tend to perceive their contemporary world as extraordinarily violent—reasons for this tendency include our tendency to focus on recent events, the bias to report the most shocking stories on the news, and so on—but Pinker presents chart after chart illustrating a dramatic reduction of violence over the centuries. For example, see ● Figure 11.16 for the rates of homicide in Western Europe from 1300–2000, and in England and New England over several centuries.

So how have we moved away from our inner demons and toward "the better angels of our nature" (the phrase is from the closing of Abraham Lincoln's first inaugural address)? There are numerous causes, as there must be, for such huge changes. Among these are better education and enhanced power of reason, including moral reasoning, that allows us to better see beyond our immediate needs and circumstances and think in more abstract and universal terms. Norms

## TABLE 11.4
### Attitudes About Sex and Aggression

Widely used in research on pornography, these two scales assess attitudes about violence toward women and beliefs about the nature of rape. A few items from each scale are shown here.

**Acceptance of Interpersonal Violence (Toward Women): AIV Scale**

1. Being roughed up is sexually stimulating to many women.

2. Many times a woman will pretend she doesn't want to have intercourse because she doesn't want to seem loose, but she's really hoping the man will force her.

3. A man is never justified in hitting his wife.

*Scoring*: Persons scoring high in acceptance of violence toward women agree with items 1 and 2 but disagree with item 3.

**Rape Myth Acceptance: RMA Scale**

1. If a woman engages in necking or petting and she lets things get out of hand, it is her own fault if her partner forces sex on her.

2. Any female can get raped.

3. Many women have an unconscious wish to be raped, and may then unconsciously set up a situation in which they are likely to be attacked.

4. In the majority of rapes, the victim is promiscuous or has a bad reputation.

*Scoring*: Persons scoring high in acceptance of rape myths agree with items 1, 3, and 4 but disagree with item 2.

Based on Burt, 1980. © Cengage Learning

● **FIGURE 11.16**

**The Decline of Violence: Homicide Rates Over Several Centuries**

The homicide rates per 100,000 people per year in five regions of Western Europe from the year 1300 to 2000 are depicted in the graph on the top. These rates for England (from 1300 to 1925) and New England (from 1630–1914) are presented in the graph on the bottom.

From Pinker, S., *The better angels of our nature: Why violence has declined.* Copyright © 2011 by Steven Pinker. Used by permission of Viking Penguin, a division of Penguin Group (USA) Inc. and Brockman Inc.

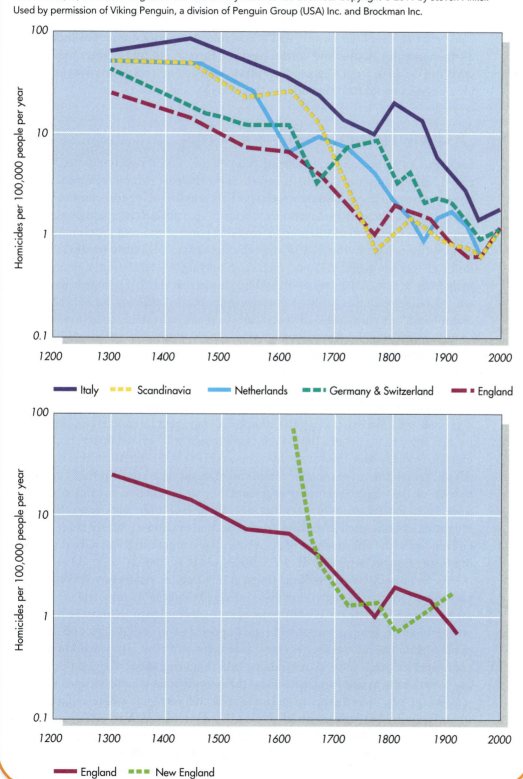

have changed dramatically to discourage aggression. It's no longer acceptable in most modern societies, as it once was, to answer a perceived insult with the challenge of a duel to the death, for example, or to treat fellow humans as property. Pinker and others also argue that people's motivations and abilities to practice self-control of aggressive impulses are stronger today, and as we have seen in this chapter, self-control plays a crucially important role in moderating aggression.

The historical trends, therefore, are encouraging, as are more recent huge drops in the rates of homicide and violent crime in the United States since the early 1990s. But "the better angels of our nature" still have strong competition from our inner demons, as the numerous studies and stories reported throughout this chapter make clear. So what can we do to reduce aggression and violence in our lives today? We turn to examine this question for the remainder of this chapter.

## Changing How We Think and Feel

Let's start with the enhanced education, intelligence, and reasoning that Pinker proposed helped cause the decline in violence over the past several centuries. Continued improvements in these areas clearly can pave the way for more prosocial and less antisocial behaviors. Along with education and reason—particularly moral reasoning—comes empathy. As discussed in Chapter 10, empathy plays a vital role in promoting helpful, cooperative behavior. The lack of empathy similarly contributes greatly to numerous forms of aggression and violence, including bullying, sexual assault, and abuse of animals (Ang & Goh, 2010; Day et al., 2010; Schwartz et al., 2012). Improving education and moral reasoning is likely to improve empathy. In addition, numerous programs and interventions are designed specifically to teach individuals to be more empathic, such as by training them to see things from others' perspectives through various exercises, assignments, and role play. Several of these programs have been very successful at reducing aggression (McGuire, 2008; Sahin, 2012). We will return to this issue at the end of this chapter in a discussion of bullying prevention.

Improved moral reasoning is one part of the formula behind what is known as *aggression replacement training*. The other two components are social competence training and aggression control. These themes are taught with guided instructions and role-playing, typically over the course of twice-weekly sessions for 10 weeks. For example, adolescents in the program go through exercises designed to help them detect when they are on the verge of becoming angry and they are taught how to think and behave in response to those feelings in ways that steer them away from aggression. They are also taught social skills, such as making eye contact and developing interpersonal trust. Several studies of the effectiveness of aggression replacement training have reported very promising results (Hatcher et al., 2008; Holmqvist et al., 2009).

As we have discussed multiple times in this chapter, failure at self-control plays a very important role in aggression and violence. In light of its importance researchers are beginning to study the effectiveness of methods designed to improve people's self-control abilities. Thomas Denson, Miriam Capper, and others (2011) found that participants high in trait aggressiveness were less aggressive after a provocation if they had completed a 2-week self-control training task (requiring them to resist the impulse to use their dominant hand and instead use their nondominant hand between 8 a.m. and 6 p.m. every day!). There has not been enough research yet to know how well such training typically works, but we are confident that that more research on self-control training techniques will be done in the next several years.

Individuals who have unusually severe problems with self-control, aggressive impulses, social skills, lack of empathy, and the other factors we've been discussing are likely to need more than these programs of education and training but instead require

*"Since war begins in the minds of men, it is in the minds of men that the defenses of peace must be constructed."*
—Constitution of UNESCO

Andy Holzman/La Daily News/ZUMA Press/Corbis

Students portray bullying during a skit as part of a bullying prevention program. Many school-wide programs to counter bullying, such as the ones described in the text, have produced very promising results.

more extensive therapy and treatment. Treatments using *behavior modification*, for example, are often used to try to alter individuals' behavior through learning principles that reinforce nonaggressive actions. Medications may also be used, such as to balance serotonin levels to help impulse control.

## Situational and Sociocultural Factors

In addition to educating, training, and treating individuals, what can be done at a broader level? Toward this end, an improved economy, healthier living conditions, and social support are extremely important in reducing the frustration, negative affect and thinking, and provocations that fuel much aggression. Improvements on these fronts would likely have a cascade of positive effects. For example, as Peter Sidebotham and Jon Heron (2006) observed, "The association between poverty and child maltreatment is one of the most consistent observations in the published research" (p. 499). Thus, protecting families from violence also means providing family members with educational and employment opportunities. Furthermore, because abuse of alcohol and other drugs so often leads to family violence, better education about the effects of such substances, as well as support for individuals who need help dealing with them, would be a worthy investment not only for these individuals but also for the people around them.

Because research has shown how the presence of weapons can promote aggressive thoughts, emotions, and actions, reducing the prevalence of guns in society—particularly guns associated strongly with violence rather than sport—may have a number of calming effects. At the same time, teaching and modeling nonviolent responses to frustrations and social problems—and encouraging thoughtful responses that are incompatible with anger, such as humor and relaxation—are among the most effective things we can do for our society's children, and for each other.

Having observed the relative nonviolence of cultures that emphasize cooperation over competitiveness, social psychologists have concluded that cooperation and shared goals across groups are effective methods for reducing intergroup hostilities and aggression. In addition, because communities beset by broken windows and petty crime reveal a loss of control and support—thus possibly signaling to those who live there that aggression and antisocial behavior are left unpunished—police departments in numerous cities have begun to crack down on relatively minor acts of vandalism and aggression in the hope that doing so will prevent more serious acts of violence (Taylor, 2000). Finally, changing the cost–reward payoffs associated with aggression can have profound effects on the aggressive tendencies exhibited within a culture. Socialization practices that reward prosocial rather than antisocial behavior therefore have the potential to greatly reduce the tendency to engage in bullying, fighting, and other aggressive behaviors. Conversely, when overt or even indirect aggression is legitimized, we are all at risk.

The media, of course, play an important role in legitimizing—even glorifying—violence. What, then, can we do about it? Government censorship is one answer, but it is not a very popular one, for a number of reasons. Another alternative is to use public pressure to increase media self-censorship. Of course, the most powerful kind of public pressure would be a commercial boycott. If violence did not sell, the media would not keep producing it. Violence, however, continues to be a moneymaker.

Research on the effects of prosocial song lyrics, television, and video games are quite encouraging in this regard, as discussed earlier in the chapter. If parents can help children select shows and games that provide compelling, vivid prosocial models for their children, the effects may be strong. Parents have also been advised to watch television with their children and to monitor their video game usage, and to teach them how TV and video games differ from real life and how imitating the fictional characters can produce undesirable outcomes. This kind of ongoing parental tutorial takes significant time and effort. But given the extent of media depictions of violence in our society, strengthening children's critical viewing skills is a wise investment.

Lawrence Rosenkoetter and others (2009) implemented a classroom-based intervention along these lines with almost 500 children in more than 30 classrooms (grades 1 to 4) over the course of 7 months. The intervention is based on the concepts and research we have reviewed in this chapter, such as social learning theory and the development of aggressive scripts. Some of the techniques used in this program are designed to help children distinguish between what is pretend and what is real, to encourage them to choose good people to admire and imitate (as opposed to fictional superheroes), and even to get them to talk to the TV in response to bad behaviors that are depicted (to encourage critical thinking). The results thus far from this program have been impressive and include reducing not only the amount of violent TV these children watch but also how much they identify with violent characters.

Similarly, Ingrid Möller and others (2012) conducted a media intervention study involving students from several schools in Berlin, Germany. The students were made to monitor their use of electronic media and to reduce their usage, such as with a "media free weekend," and were encouraged to substitute that time for other activities. In five weekly sessions during school the researchers educated the students about the kinds of issues discussed in this chapter, including how violence is often rewarded in the media or how exposure to violence can lead to desensitization. The students' parents were also given guidelines for sensible media usage and about the harmful effects of exposure to media violence. The results of the program were impressive. The intervention significantly reduced students' use of violent media according to measures taken 7 months after the intervention. In addition, for students whose rates of aggression before the study were relatively high, the intervention significantly reduced their rates of both physical and relational aggression.

Daniel Linz and others (1992) also advocated using educational efforts to increase viewers' critical skills in evaluating media depictions that link violence and sex. A model for such efforts can be found in the debriefing provided to research participants exposed to violent pornography in experiments (Donnerstein et al., 1987). This debriefing emphasizes that rape myths are inaccurate and that violent pornography is unrealistic. Among individuals presented with this information, there are long-term reductions in acceptance of rape myths and increases in sympathy for victims and survivors of rape (Hong, 2000; Proto-Campise et al., 1998).

## Multiple-Level Approaches: Programs to Prevent Violence and Bullying

A variety of factors contribute to aggression and violence—and, as we have seen, the impact of any one factor often involves other factors simultaneously. The link between hot temperatures and aggression, for instance, may involve factors such as arousal, aggressive thoughts, and negative affect. How harmful corporal punishment may be can depend on other family dynamics. The most effective strategies for reducing aggression recognize this complexity and work on multiple levels.

**Multisystemic Therapy**   One of the most successful treatment programs for violent juvenile delinquents is called *multisystemic therapy (MST)*. This approach addresses individuals' problems at several different levels, including the needs of the adolescents and the many contexts in which they are embedded, such as family, peer group, school, and neighborhood (Borduin et al., 2009; Curtis et al., 2009; Henggeler et al., 2009; Letourneau et al., 2009; Timmons-Mitchell & Bender, 2006).

A case study of a 14-year-old boy named Luke illustrates this approach (Wells et al., 2012). Luke was engaging in some serious antisocial behaviors. Rather than just treat Luke with individual therapy, the therapist applying MST wanted to understand the family dynamics in which Luke lived. This enabled the therapist to learn that there was a lack of household routine or rules and that bad behavior was often rewarded (with attention and money) and good behavior was ignored. The therapist therefore worked with Luke's grandmother (his caregiver) and some other nearby family members to help her set up rules, establish routines, determine better and more consistent ways of handing sources of conflict, and to reward positive rather than negative behavior. This approach of learning about and working with his family and environment along with individualized treatment of Luke produced dramatic improvement in Luke's behavior and life.

Multiple studies evaluating the effectiveness of MST have reported very positive results. For example, in one study violent juvenile offenders with an average of almost four felony arrests per person were assigned randomly to either MST or individual therapy during adolescence, and they were assessed more than two decades later. The adolescents were four times less likely to be arrested for a violent felony during the follow-up period if they were treated with MST than with individual therapy (Sawyer & Borduin, 2011). Although this type of multiple-level approach takes a lot of time and resources, the money saved by significantly reducing the rates of violent crimes and in keeping these individuals out of prison far outweighs the costs. For instance, in one study of 176 serious juvenile offenders, MST was estimated to have saved taxpayers and crime victims between $75,000 and $200,000 per MST participant (Klietz et al., 2010).

**Bullying Prevention**   Comprehensive programs that operate on multiple levels have also proven to be effective in reducing the incidence of bullying in many schools around the world. Interest in preventing bullying has skyrocketed in recent years. A generation or so ago bullying was seen by many parents, teachers, school systems, and students as just rites of passage that kids have to go through. Particularly as a consequence of some high-profile cases of young people driven to suicide through bullying, attitudes about bullying have changed dramatically, especially among school administrators.

Anti-bullying programs are being tried in countless schools around the world. Maria Ttofi and David Farrington (2011) conducted a meta-analysis of studies that have examined the effectiveness of a variety of school-based bullying programs, and they found that these programs reduced bullying by an average of more than 20%. Their review suggests that the most successful bullying prevention programs are the more intensive and long-lasting ones that—like multisystemic therapy—involve multiple levels, including parent meetings and training, firm disciplinary methods, better playground supervision, school conferences, classroom management, and individualized work with the students involved in bullying (Ttofi & Farrington, 2009: 2011).

Perhaps the most influential such program is the *Olweus Bullying Prevention Program*. Dan Olweus, a professor of psychology in Norway, is a pioneer in research on bullying and is considered to be one of the world's true experts on the topic. His research on how to reduce and prevent bullying was first implemented in schools in Norway and was a resounding success. The Olweus Bullying Prevention Program has now spread to numerous schools throughout the United States and several other countries, and it has inspired or helped shape other programs as well. Bullying rates in these various schools typically drop by anywhere from 30% to 50% (Olweus & Limber, 2010). Table 11.5 lists some of the important components of the Olweus Bullying Prevention Program.

Whether or not intensive, multiple-level school bullying prevention programs are put in place in a particular school, other more modest strategies can help reduce bullying as well. For example, Mustafa Sahin (2012) found that having bullies in several primary schools in Turkey go through an empathy-training program over the course of 11 weeks significantly reduced their bullying behavior compared to a control group. Another approach that many schools are taking is to specifically target bystanders—students who witness acts of bullying but may not do anything to intervene. Inspired in part by the bystander intervention research on helping behavior discussed in Chapter 10, these programs highlight the important role that peers can play in either allowing or discouraging bullying (Pfetsch et al., 2011).

An interesting line of research by Elizabeth Levy Paluck and Hana Shepherd (2012) targeted *particular* peers. These researchers hypothesized that they could use peer social influence to make students at a high school in Connecticut less accepting of harassment and bullying behavior. To do this the researchers used surveys of the students to identify a set of students who were the most socially connected in the school, and who therefore had the most potential for social influence to spread throughout the student body. A randomly selected subset of them were then recruited to participate in an intervention program. During two training sessions a professional facilitator led these students in discussions of harassment and bullying in school and what roles various students can play in these behaviors (such as an ally to targeted students or a bystander

---

### TABLE 11.5

**The Olweus Bullying Prevention Program**

Some of the components of the very successful bullying prevention program developed by psychologist Dan Olweus are listed here.

*School-Level Components*

- Form a bullying prevention coordinating committee.
- Train committee members and staff.
- Adopt school-wide rules against bullying.
- Develop appropriate positive and negative consequences for students' behavior.
- Hold a school-wide kick-off event to launch the program.
- Involve parents.

*Classroom-Level Components*

- Post and enforce school-wide rules against bullying.
- Hold regular classroom meetings to discuss bullying and related topics.

*Individual-Level Components*

- Ensure that all staff intervene on the spot when bullying is observed.
- Meet with students involved in bullying, and meet with their parents.
- Develop individual intervention plans for involved students.

*Community-Level Components*

- Involve community members on the bullying prevention coordinating committee.
- Adults (in and out of school) should use consistent nonphysical, nonhostile negative consequences when rules are broken and should function as positive role models.

Based on Olweus & Limber, 2010. © Cengage Learning

to the events). These students also prepared to help lead a school-wide assembly on the topic. They performed a skit at the assembly and led a call for tolerance. The researchers found that the socially connected students did in fact change their peers' perceptions of the acceptability of harassment and bullying and led a reduction in many of these behaviors.

Table 11.6 lists some of the possible steps suggested by the research we've reviewed. You may not agree that all of these actions are desirable, and you may prefer others that are not mentioned. What's important is to realize that each of us can do something to reduce aggression. There are many paths to take toward this common goal. And because aggression is caused by multiple factors, it is only through multiple paths that we can reach this goal.

**TABLE 11.6**
**Some Steps to Reduce Aggression and Violence**

Although there may be other reasons to endorse or reject the ideas below, social psychological research on aggression suggests that each has the potential to reduce aggression.

- Reward nonaggressive behavior.
- Provide attractive models of peaceful behavior.
- Reduce all forms of aggression in our society, including physical punishment of children, fighting in sports, violence in the media, and war.
- Reduce frustration by improving the quality of life in housing, health care, employment, and child care.
- Provide fans and air-conditioned shelters when it's hot.
- Reduce access to and display of weapons.
- Apologize when you've angered someone, and regard apologies as a sign of strength—not weakness. Encourage others to do likewise.
- Stop and think when you feel your temper rising. Control it instead of letting it control you.
- Discourage excessive drinking of alcohol and support efforts to provide treatment for alcohol abuse.
- Develop good communication skills in families and relationships, thereby helping to avoid misperceptions, jealousy, and distrust.
- Pay attention and respond to warning signs of trouble in adolescents, including social isolation, talk of violence, and consumption of violence-filled literature and other media.
- Increase education to promote development of skills involving empathy, self-control, and how to solve interpersonal problems with reason rather than emotion.

© Cengage Learning

# Review

## What Is Aggression?

- Aggression is behavior intended to harm another individual.
- Anger is an emotional response to perceived injury; hostility is an antagonistic attitude.
- Proactive aggression is a means to obtain a desired outcome.
- In reactive aggression, harm is inflicted for its own sake.

## Culture, Gender, and Individual Differences

### Culture and Aggression

- The rates of violence and the forms violence takes vary dramatically from one society to another.
- Some research suggests that individualistic cultures tend to have higher rates of aggression than collectivistic cultures.
- The forms that aggression may take and attitudes about whether various practices should be considered aggression vary across cultures.
- Bullying is a persistent and widespread problem that affects a large number of young people in the world.
- Several cultures around the world have virtually no violence. These tend to be very cooperative, interdependent societies with little competition among their members.

- Within a society, different subcultures exhibit different norms concerning aggression.
- Teenagers and young adults, African Americans, and people in the South are the groups most prone to violence in the United States.

### Gender and Aggression

- Men are more violent than women in virtually every culture and time period that has been studied.
- Males tend to be more overtly, physically aggressive than females.
- Females tend to be at least as—and perhaps somewhat more—indirectly or relationally aggressive compared to males.

- There are no reliable gender difference in the percentage of women and men who physically assault their intimate partners, but women are more likely to be killed, seriously injured, or sexually abused by a partner than men.

### Putting *Common Sense* to the Test

**In virtually every culture, males are more violent than females.**

**True.** *In almost all cultures and time periods that have been studied, men commit the large majority of violent crimes.*

**For virtually any category of aggression, males are more aggressive than females.**

**False.** *Girls tend to be somewhat more indirectly, or relationally, aggressive than boys.*

## Origins of Aggression

### Is Aggression Innate?

- Evolutionary psychology views aggression as a universal, innate characteristic that has evolved from natural and sexual selection pressures.
- Evolutionary accounts propose that gender differences in aggression can be traced to competition for status (and the most desirable mates) and sexual jealousy.
- Aggressiveness appears to be a partly heritable trait.
- The sex hormone testosterone and the neurotransmitter serotonin play roles in human aggression.
- Impairments in several areas of the brain, especially to executive functioning, are associated with aggressiveness.

### Is Aggression Learned?

- Aggression is increased when it is rewarded.
- Aggression is decreased by punishment only under specific conditions that are often not met in the real world.
- Physical punishment of children is associated with increases in their subsequent aggressive behavior.
- Social learning theory emphasizes the influence of models on the behavior of observers.
- Aggressive models teach not only specific behaviors but also more general attitudes and ideas about aggression and aggressive "scripts" that guide behavior.
- Growing up in a household or community with a lot of aggression and violence increases the likelihood that one will become an aggressive person.
- Peaceful models can decrease aggressive responses in observers.
- Children who witness parental violence or are themselves abused are more likely as adults to abuse their partners and their own children.

### Individual Differences

- There is some stability in aggression: Aggression in childhood predicts aggression in adulthood.
- Individuals low on the dimensions of agreeableness and openness and high on the dimension of neuroticism are more likely than other people to be aggressive.
- Some other personality traits are associated with aggression only after provocation. These include emotional susceptibility, Type A personality, and impulsivity.
- Narcissism is correlated with aggressiveness in response to provocation.

### Gender Differences and Socialization: "Boys Will Be Boys"

- Gender and cultural differences in human aggression may be due in part to differences in socialization practices—lessons taught, reinforcements and punishments given, models offered, and roles and norms emphasized.

### Culture and Socialization: Cultures of Honor

- A culture of honor promotes status-protecting aggression among white males in the American South and West as well as among men in other parts of the world, such as in Brazil and Chile.

### Nature Versus Nurture: A False Debate?

- Human aggression clearly is affected by learning and experience.
- In aggression, as in all human behavior, biological and environmental influences interact.

### Putting *Common Sense* to the Test

**Children who are spanked or otherwise physically disciplined (but not abused) for behaving aggressively tend to become less aggressive.**

**False.** *Evidence indicates that the use of even a little physical punishment to discipline children is associated with increases in subsequent aggressive and antisocial behavior by the children, even years later, although this relationship may depend on a variety of other factors.*

# Situational Influences on Aggression

## The Frustration–Aggression Hypothesis

- The frustration–aggression hypothesis proposes that frustration produces the motive to aggress and that aggression is caused by frustration.
- But in fact, frustration produces many motives, and aggression is caused by many factors.
- According to the frustration–aggression hypothesis, displacement occurs if aggression against the source of frustration is inhibited.
- The frustration–aggression hypothesis holds that engaging in any aggressive action reduces the motive to engage in further aggression, a process called catharsis.
- Some studies support the idea of displacement of aggression. However, most research does not support the idea of catharsis as an effective means to reduce aggression.

### Putting *Common Sense* to the Test

**Blowing off steam by engaging in safe but aggressive activities (such as sports) makes people less likely to aggress later.**

**False.** *Although people may be less likely to aggress immediately after such activities, initial aggression makes future aggression more—not less—likely.*

## Negative Affect

- A wide variety of noxious stimuli can create negative feelings and increase aggression.
- The negative affect due to provocation is a key factor behind much aggression.
- Hot temperatures are associated with increased aggression and violence.
- Experiencing social rejection is particularly aversive and can increase aggressive responses.
- Positive emotional responses are incompatible with negative affect and reduce retaliatory aggression.

## Arousal

- Highly arousing stimuli increase aggression.

## Thought: Automatic and Deliberate

- Situational cues associated with aggression, such as the presence of a gun, can automatically activate aggression-related thoughts and increase aggressive behavior.
- Individuals differ in what associations they have with different kinds of weapons.
- Deliberate thoughts that affect aggression include the perception of the cost or appropriateness of aggression.
- The extent to which individuals perceive hostile intent in others is an important factor in predicting aggression.

## The Struggle for Self-Control: Rumination, Alcohol, and Other Factors

- Self-control failure is behind most acts of aggression and violence.
- Angry rumination, in which an individual repeatedly thinks about an anger-inducing event, reduces self-control and increases aggression.
- High arousal impairs the cognitive control of aggression, as does alcohol.
- Sugar-rich drinks can boost otherwise depleted self-control; the effects of caffeine are more complex—expectations about caffeine can help self-control, but the arousal caffeine causes can weaken self-control.

## Situational Influences: Putting It All Together

- The General Aggression Model helps explain the relationships among various factors that contribute to aggression, such as the separate and interactive effects of affect, arousal, and cognitions.
- $I^3$ theory focuses on the relative weights of social and personality factors that promote aggression against the factors that promote self-control.

# Media Effects

## Violence in TV, Movies, Music Lyrics, and Video Games

- There is a tremendous amount of violence depicted in the media, and much of it is targeted to children and adolescents.
- A large number of studies, using a variety of different methods, have shown a significant positive relationship between exposure to media violence and real-world aggressive cognitions and behaviors.
- Exposure to TV violence and violent video games in childhood and adolescence is related to aggression later in life.
- In laboratory and field experiments, exposure to media violence increases aggressive behavior among adults and children.
- Exposure to indirect aggression on TV can promote subsequent real-world indirect aggression.
- Exposure to media violence can trigger aggressive cognitions and hostility.
- Because we habituate to familiar stimuli, repeated exposure to violence desensitizes people to violence, reducing physiological arousal to new incidents. This desensitization can increase aggressive behavior and decrease helping behavior.
- Habitual exposure to media violence can suggest that aggression is rewarded, encourage imitation, and promote aggressive scripts, which can guide subsequent behavior.
- Through cultivation of a social reality, the mass media can intensify fear of aggression and encourage aggressive behavior.

- Prosocial song lyrics, TV programs, and video games can increase prosocial behavior.

## Pornography

- In general, the evidence pointing to a causal link between viewing nonviolent pornography and aggressive behavior is weak, although there is stronger evidence that it can promote attitudes more accepting of violence toward women.
- Violent pornography increases aggression, particularly male-to-female aggression.
- Individual differences exist in how likely men's aggressive attitudes or behaviors are affected by pornography.
- Men who fit the "rapist's profile" have relatively high levels of sexual arousal in response to violent pornography and also express attitudes and opinions indicating acceptance of violence toward women. The effects of pornography tend to be stronger among these men.

---

### Putting *Common Sense* to the Test

**Exposure to TV violence in childhood is related to aggression later in life.**

**True.** *Laboratory experiments, field experiments, and correlational research all suggest a link between exposure to violence on TV and subsequent aggressive behavior.*

---

# Reducing Violence

- Rates of violence in much of the world have declined dramatically over the centuries.

## Changing How We Think and Feel

- Improvements in education, intelligence, reasoning, and empathy can reduce aggression.
- Aggression replacement therapy works to reduce aggression by training individuals in social competence, moral reasoning, and aggression control.
- Improving one's self-control abilities is another way to reduce aggression.

## Situational and Sociocultural Factors

- Situational and sociocultural factors that can help reduce violence include reductions in negative affect, aggressive thinking, poverty, the presence of weapons, competitiveness, minor acts of aggression and vandalism, and social rewards for aggressive behavior.

- Models of nonviolent responses to social problems are also useful in reducing violent behavior.
- Teaching individuals to reduce their consumption of violent media and to be aware of the problems associated with media violence has been shown to be effective.

## Multiple-Level Approaches: Programs to Prevent Violence and Bullying

- Recognizing that aggression has multiple levels of causes, multisystemic therapy has been effective in reducing aggressive behaviors among violent adolescents.
- Comprehensive programs that operate on multiple levels to prevent bullying in schools have also proven to be effective in reducing the incidence of bullying in many schools around the world. One of the most influential of these programs is the Olweus Bullying Prevention Program.
- Training students to be more empathic may also help reduce bullying.
- One recent study found promising results of recruiting the most socially connected students to help lead a school-wide bullying prevention program.

## KEY TERMS

aggression (435)
catharsis (456)
cultivation (470)
cycle of violence (452)
desensitization (469)

displacement (456)
frustration–aggression
    hypothesis (456)
hostile attribution bias (460)
pornography (471)

proactive aggression (436)
reactive aggression (436)
rumination (461)
social learning theory (451)
weapons effect (460)

## MEDIA RESOURCES

Go to CengageBrain.com to access Psychology CourseMate, where you will find an interactive eBook, glossaries, flashcards, quizzes, videos, and more.

# Law

This chapter examines applications of social psychology to the law. First, we consider the social psychology of such evidence as eyewitness testimony, confessions, lie-detector tests, and the forensic sciences. Next we examine three stages of a jury trial: jury selection, an often controversial process; the courtroom drama in which jurors are exposed to a combination of evidence and other, possibly biasing, information; and jury deliberation, where the jury reaches a group decision. Next, we consider posttrial factors such as sentencing and prison, the possible result of a guilty verdict. Finally, we discuss people's perceptions of justice both inside and outside the courtroom.

EQUAL·JUSTIC

Brandon Bourdages/Shutterstock

# 12

**Eyewitness Testimony (488)**

Identifying the Culprit

Testifying in Court

Improving Eyewitness Justice

**Confessions (499)**

Suspect Interviews: Psychology of Lie Detection

Police Interrogations: Social Influence Under Pressure

False Confessions: Why Innocent People Confess

Confessions in the Courtroom

**Jury Decision Making (505)**

Jury Selection

The Courtroom Trial

Jury Deliberations

**Posttrial: To Prison and Beyond (520)**

The Sentencing Process

The Prison Experience

**Perceptions of Justice (524)**

Justice as a Matter of Procedure

Culture, Law, and Justice

**Closing Statement (527)**

Review

Key Terms

Media Resources

**It seems that there is always** a high-profile case in the news that spotlights a crime of sex, violence, money, passion, or celebrity and that captures the public's interest. The twenty-first century is still young, and yet we have already witnessed the public trials of corrupt Wall Street executives, celebrities, and terrorists. We even saw two world leaders brought to trial in the Middle East—namely, Saddam Hussein of Iraq and Hosni Mubarek of Egypt. There will be more high-profile trials to come, of course. But few will fascinate and confuse the world quite like the two trials in Italy of Amanda Knox.

On November 2, 2007, British exchange student Meredith Kercher was found raped and murdered in Perugia, Italy. Almost immediately, police suspected 20-year-old Amanda Knox, an American student and one of Kercher's roommates—the only one who stayed in Perugia. Knox had no history of crime or violence and no motive. But something about her demeanor led police to believe she was lying when she said she was with Raffaele Sollecito, her new Italian boyfriend, that night.

On and off for the next 4 days, several police officials interrogated Knox. Her final interrogation started on November 5 a few minutes after 10 p.m. and lasted until November 6 at 6 a.m. In many ways, Knox was a vulnerable suspect—young, far from home, without family, and speaking in a foreign language in which she was not fluent. Knox says she was repeatedly threatened and called a liar. She was told that Sollecito, her boyfriend, had disavowed her alibi, which he then retracted, and that physical evidence placed her at the scene, which was not true. She was then encouraged to imagine how the gruesome crime had occurred, a trauma, she was told, that she had obviously repressed. Eventually, in the wee hours of the morning, Knox broke down and confessed in a "dreamlike vision." Despite a law that requires the recording of suspect interrogations, police and prosecutors said the sessions were not recorded. That morning, the chief of police announced: *Caso chiuso* (case closed).

A few weeks after Knox's confession was taken, DNA found on the victim and throughout the crime scene unequivocally identified a man who had fled to Germany. When he was first arrested he said Knox was not involved. Months later, he changed his story, said that Knox and Raffaele were involved, and received a reduced sentence. Over the ensuing months, police forensic experts concluded that physical evidence put Knox at the crime scene and eyewitnesses, previously silent, came forward with varying claims to have seen Knox in the vicinity that night. One witness said he saw Knox outdoors brandishing a knife.

On December 2009, an eight-person jury convicted Knox and Sollecito of murder. The two were sentenced to 26 and 25 years in prison, respectively. Two years later, on October 3, 2011, having been granted a new trial, they were acquitted. The Italian appeals court released a strongly worded 143-page opinion in which it criticized the prosecution and concluded that there was no credible evidence, motive, or plausible theory of guilt. For the four years of her imprisonment, this story drew international attention (for overviews of the case, see Dempsey, 2010; Burleigh, 2011).

Although this case occurred in Italy, it illustrates the profound relevance of social psychology

## Putting *Common Sense* to the Test

*Circle Your Answer*

T  F  Eyewitnesses find it relatively difficult to recognize members of a race other than their own.

T  F  The more confident an eyewitness is about an identification, the more accurate he or she is likely to be.

T  F  It is not possible to knowingly fool a lie-detector test.

T  F  Without being beaten or threatened, innocent people sometimes confess to crimes they did not commit.

T  F  Contrary to popular opinion, women are harsher as trial jurors than men are.

T  F  One can usually predict a jury's final verdict by knowing where the individual jurors stand the first time they vote.

at work in all legal systems and raises many questions: How reliable are confessions, eyewitnesses, forensic science experts, and other types of evidence presented in court? What kinds of people serve as jurors, and when they do can they set aside their biases? Are jurors influenced by pretrial publicity and other outside information not in evidence? Then, how do they reach a verdict after days, weeks, or months of presentations, often followed by exhausting deliberation? In this chapter, we take social psychology into the courtroom to answer these questions. But first, let's place the trial process in a broader context.

In the U.S. criminal justice system, the trial is just the tip of an iceberg. Once a crime is committed, it must be detected and then reported if it is to receive further attention. Through investigation, the police find a suspect and decide whether to make an arrest. If they do, the suspect is jailed or bail is set and a judge or grand jury decides if there is sufficient evidence for a formal accusation. If there is sufficient evidence, the prosecuting and defense lawyers begin a lengthy process known as "discovery," during which time they gather evidence. At this point, many defendants plead guilty as part of a plea deal negotiated by the lawyers. In cases that do go to trial, the ordeal does not then end with a verdict. After conviction, the trial judge imposes punishment in the form of a sentence and the defendant decides whether to appeal to a higher court. For those in prison, decisions concerning their release are made by parole boards. As ● Figure 12.1 illustrates, the criminal justice apparatus is complex and the actors behind the scenes are numerous. Social psychologists have a lot to say about various aspects of the legal system (Costanzo & Krauss, 2012; Greene & Heilbrun, 2011; Kovera & Borgida, 2010).

The issues that social psychologists are now studying are broad and varied. At present, researchers are looking at a wide range of issues—such as whether police can tell when someone is lying and how they can make these judgments more accurately (Vrij, 2008; Vrij, Granhag, & Porter, 2010); how juries make decisions in civil lawsuits involving large sums of money (Bornstein et al., 2008); why people cooperate with authorities and obey the law (Tyler, 2011); how information can best be gathered in the wake of 9/11 (Loftus, 2011); how the U.S. Supreme Court receives oral arguments and makes decisions (Wrightsman, 2006, 2008); and how social psychology can be used to prevent the wrongful convictions of innocent people (Cutler, 2011). Importantly, much of what social psychologists have discovered with regard to law and justice is not known to judges, lawyers, and laypeople as a matter of common sense (Borgida & Fiske, 2007). In the coming pages, we look at the social psychology of evidence, jury decision making, sentencing and prison, and perceptions of justice.

In a tragedy that captivated the world's attention in 2007, British student Meredith Kircher was brutally murdered while studying in Perugia, Italy (left). Within four days, American student Amanda Knox and her new boyfriend, Raphaelle Solecito, were arrested for the murder (center) after Knox had "confessed." Shortly afterward, physical evidence revealed the guilt of Rudy Guede (right). After four years in jail for a crime they did not commit, Knox and Solecito were acquitted. Guede remains in prison.

# Eyewitness Testimony

Once the commission of a crime is discovered, police investigate in an effort to identify the perpetrator. Eyewitnesses are interviewed, possible suspects are interrogated, and all sorts of physical evidence in the form of fingerprints, shoe prints, hair samples, DNA-rich biological materials, ballistics, and autopsy results are collected and analyzed. Solving crimes is not easy. In this all-too-human enterprise, as we'll see, some of the most critical types of evidence that police gather are subject to social influences and the potential for bias and error.

"I'll never forget that face!" When these words are uttered, police officers, judges, and juries all take notice. Too often, however, eyewitnesses make mistakes. On March 8, 2009, the CBS show *60 Minutes* aired the story of Jennifer Thompson and Ronald Cotton. One night in 1984, in North Carolina, a young man broke into Thompson's apartment, cut the phone wires, and raped her. She described him to the police, helped construct a composite sketch, and then positively identified Ronald Cotton as her assailant. Cotton had alibis for his whereabouts that night, but based on Thompson's eyewitness identification, he was found guilty and sentenced to life in prison. Ten years later, DNA tests of semen stains revealed that Cotton was innocent and that Bobby Poole, a known offender, was the real assailant. In 1995, after ten years in prison, Cotton was released and offered $5,000 in compensation. He has since put the pieces of his life back together. Thompson, upon realizing that she had identified an innocent man, said, "I remember feeling sick, but also I remember feeling just an overwhelming sense of just guilt. . . . I cried and cried and I wept and I was angry at me and I beat myself up for it for a long time." Thompson-Cannino and Cotton (2009) recently wrote a book together entitled, *Picking Cotton: Our Memoir of Injustice and Redemption.*

Every year, thousands of people are charged with crimes solely on the basis of eyewitness evidence. Many of these eyewitness accounts are accurate, but many are not—which is why psychologists have been interested in the topic for more than 100 years

## ● FIGURE 12.1

**Overview of the American Criminal Justice System**

This flow chart presents the movement of cases through different branches of the criminal justice system. As illustrated here, the trial is just one aspect of the criminal justice system.

Adapted from the President's Commission on Law Enforcement and Administration of Justice, 1967.
© Cengage Learning

Crime committed → No arrest

Arrest → Charges dropped or taken to juvenile court

Formal accusation → Case dismissed

Trial → Not guilty verdict

Plea-bargain

Sentencing

- Fine
- Probation
- Other alternatives

Prison

Poole

Cotton

Jennifer Thompson was traumatized twice: the first time when she was raped, the second when she learned that she had identified a man proved to be innocent by DNA tests 10 years later. Here you can see Thompson talking to Ronald Cotton, the man she picked from a lineup. Notice the resemblance between Cotton and Bobby Poole, her actual assailant.

(Doyle, 2005). Several years ago, the National Institute of Justice reported on 28 wrongful convictions in which convicted felons were proved innocent by new tests of old DNA evidence after varying numbers of years in prison. Remarkably, as in Ronald Cotton's case, every one of these convictions involved a mistaken identification (Connors et al., 1996). Now, some 300 DNA exonerations later, it is clear: Eyewitness error is the most common cause of wrongful convictions (Wells, Memon, & Penrod, 2006; Brewer & Wells, 2011).

In 1999, the U.S. Department of Justice took a bold step in response to this problem, assembling a group of police, prosecutors, defense attorneys, and research psychologists to devise a set of "how-to" guidelines. Led by social psychologist Gary Wells, this Technical Working Group went on to publish *Eyewitness Evidence: A Guide for Law Enforcement* (U.S. Department of Justice, 1999; Wells et al., 2000).

As eyewitnesses, people can be called upon to remember just about anything—a face, a weapon, an accident, or a conversation. To date, hundreds of tightly controlled studies of eyewitness testimony have been conducted. Based on this research, three conclusions can be drawn: (1) eyewitnesses are imperfect; (2) certain personal and situational factors can systematically influence their performance, and (3) judges, juries, and lawyers are not adequately informed about these factors (Cutler & Penrod, 1995; Lindsay et al., 2007). It appears that even the U.S. Supreme Court harbors outdated misconceptions about the nature of eyewitness memory (Wells & Quinlivan, 2009).

People tend to think that human memory works like a video camera—that if you turn on the power and focus the lens, all events will be recorded for subsequent playback. Unfortunately, it's not that simple. Over the years, researchers have found it useful to view memory as a three-stage process involving the *encoding, storage*, and *retrieval* of information. The first of these stages, encoding, refers to a witness's perceptions at the time of the event in question. Second, the witness rehearses and stores the information in memory to avoid forgetting. Third, the witness retrieves the information from storage when needed. This model suggests that errors can occur at three different points.

## ▶ Perceiving the Crime

Some kinds of persons and events are more difficult to perceive than others. Common sense tells us that brief exposure time, poor lighting, long distance, physical disguise, and distraction can all limit a witness's perceptions. For example, Rod Lindsay and his colleagues (2008) had approximately 1,300 participants observe a target person, outdoors, at one of various distances ranging from 5 meters (16 feet) to 50 meters (164 feet). They found, first, that the witnesses were not accurate at estimating distance and, second, that the further witnesses were from the target, the less accurate was they were at identifying the target in a lineup shortly afterward.

Research has uncovered other relevant aspects of the witnessing situation. Consider the effects of a witness's emotional state. Often people are asked to recall a bloody shooting, a car wreck, or an assault—emotional events that trigger high levels of stress. In a study that illustrates the debilitating effects of stress, Charles Morgan and others (2004) randomly assigned trainees in a military survival school to undergo a realistic high-stress or low-stress mock interrogation. Twenty-four hours later, he found that those in the high-stress condition had difficulty identifying their interrogators in a lineup. In another study, Tim Valentine and Jan Mesout (2009) fitted adult visitors to the London Dungeon—a house of horrors—with a wireless heart monitor and asked them afterward to describe and identify a scary person they had encountered inside. The more anxious visitors were in the Dungeon, the less accurate they were later at describing and identifying the scary person in a lineup.

It turns out that arousal has a complex effect on memory. Realizing the importance of what they are observing, highly aroused witnesses zoom in on the central features of an event such as the culprit, the victim, or a weapon. As a direct result of this narrowed field of attention, however, arousal impairs a witness's memory for other less central details (Brown, 2003; Christianson, 1992). Alcohol, a drug often involved in crimes, can also cause problems. When participants in one study witnessed a live staged crime, those who had earlier consumed fruit juice were more accurate in their recollections than were those who had been served an alcoholic beverage (Yuille & Tollestrup, 1990). Under the influence of alcohol, people can recognize the perpetrator in a lineup, but they too often make false identifications when the actual perpetrator is absent (Dysart et al., 2002).

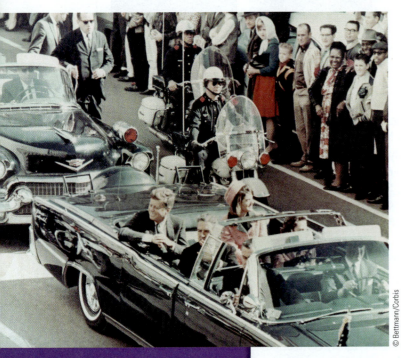

© Bettmann/Corbis

After the tragic assassination of President John F. Kennedy, dozens of eyewitnesses came forward to describe what they saw. Some reported one gunman in the sixth-floor window of a nearby building, others reported two or three gunmen in the building, and still others thought the shots were fired from the ground. Such are the pitfalls of eyewitness testimony.

The **weapon-focus effect** is also an important factor. Across a wide range of settings, research shows that when a criminal pulls out a gun, a razor blade, or a knife, witnesses are less able to identify that culprit than if no weapon is present (Pickel, 1999; Steblay 1992). There are two reasons for this effect. First, people are agitated by the sight of a menacing stimulus, as when participants in one study were approached by an experimenter who was holding a syringe or threatening to administer an injection (Maass & Kohnken, 1989). Second, even in a harmless situation, a witness's eyes lock in on a weapon like magnets, drawing attention away from the face (Hope & Wright, 2007). To demonstrate, Elizabeth Loftus and others (1987) showed people slides of a customer who walked up to a bank teller and pulled out either a pistol or a checkbook. By tracking eye movements, these researchers found that people spent more time looking at the gun than at the checkbook. The net result: An impairment in the ability to identify the criminal in a lineup.

Race is another important consideration. By varying the racial makeup of participants and target persons in laboratory and real-life interactions, researchers discovered that people are more accurate at recognizing members of their own racial group than of a race other than their own—an effect known as the **own-race identification bias** (Malpass & Kravitz, 1969). In one field study, for example, 86 convenience store clerks in El Paso, Texas, were asked to identify three customers—one white, one African American, and one Mexican American—all experimental confederates who had stopped in and

**weapon-focus effect** The tendency for the presence of a weapon to draw attention and impair a witness's ability to identify the culprit.

**own-race identification bias** The tendency for people to be more accurate at recognizing members of their own racial group than of other groups.

made a purchase earlier that day. It turned out that the white, black, and Mexican American clerks were all most likely to accurately identify customers belonging to their own racial or ethnic group (Platz & Hosch, 1988).

The finding that "they all look alike" (referring to members of other groups) is found reliably and in many different racial and ethnic groups. Indeed, Christian Meissner and John Brigham (2001) statistically combined the results of 39 studies involving a total of 5,000 mock witnesses. They found that the witnesses were consistently less accurate and more prone to making false identifications when they tried to recognize target persons from racial and ethnic groups other than their own. Paralleling this research, studies also show that children, young adults, and the elderly have more difficulty recognizing others of an *age* group other than their own (Rhodes & Anastasi, 2012).

> Eyewitnesses find it relatively difficult to recognize members of a race other than their own. **T**RUE.

## Storing the Memory

Can remembrances of the remote past be trusted? As you might expect, memory for faces and events tends to decline with the passage of time. Longer intervals between an event and its retrieval are generally associated with increased forgetting (Shapiro & Penrod, 1986). But not all recollections fade, and time alone does not cause memory slippage. Consider the plight of bystanders who witness firsthand such incidents as terrorist bombings, shootings, plane crashes, or fatal car accidents. Afterward, they may talk about what they saw, read about it, hear what other bystanders have to say, and answer questions from investigators and reporters. By the time witnesses to these events are officially questioned, they are likely to have been exposed to so much postevent information that one wonders if their original memory is still "pure."

According to Loftus (1996), it probably is not. Many years ago, based on her own studies of eyewitness testimony, Loftus proposed a now classic theory of reconstructive memory. After people observe an event, she said, later information about that event—whether the information is true or not—becomes integrated into the fabric of their memory. An initial experiment by Loftus and John Palmer (1974) illustrates the point. Participants viewed a film of a traffic accident and then answered questions, including: "About how fast were the cars going when they *hit* each other?" Other participants answered the same question, except that the verb *hit* was replaced by *smashed*, *collided*, *bumped*, or *contacted*. All participants saw the same accident, yet the wording of the question affected their reports.  Figure 12.2 shows that participants given the "smashed" question estimated the highest average speed and those responding to the "contacted" question estimated the lowest. But there's

**FIGURE 12.2**

**Biasing Eyewitness Reports with Loaded Questions**

Participants viewed a film of a traffic accident and then answered this question: "About how fast were these cars going when they (hit, smashed, or contacted) each other?" As shown, the wording of the question influenced speed estimates (top). One week later, it also caused participants to reconstruct their memory of other aspects of the accident (bottom). From Loftus, G. R., and Loftus, E. F., *Human memory: The processing of information.* Copyright © 1976. Reprinted with permission of Lawrence Erlbaum Associates, Inc.

| Question | Verb | Estimated MPH |
|---|---|---|
| About how fast were the cars going when they _____ each other? | smashed | 40.8 |
| | hit | 34.0 |
| | contacted | 30.8 |

| Original Information | External Information | The "Memory" |
|---|---|---|
| | About how fast were the cars going when they SMASHED into each other? | |

more. One week later, participants were called back for more probing. Had the wording of the questions caused them to reconstruct their memories of the accident? Yes. When asked whether they had seen broken glass at the accident (none was actually present), 32% of the "smashed" participants said they had. As Loftus had predicted, what these participants remembered of the accident was based on two sources: the event itself and postevent information.

This **misinformation effect** has aroused a great deal of controversy. It's clear that eyewitnesses can be compromised when exposed to postevent information—as when they are told, for example, that either the person they identified or someone else had confessed during an interrogation (Hasel & Kassin, 2009). But does this information actually alter a witness's real memory so that it can never be retrieved again? Or do participants merely follow the experimenter's suggestion, leaving their true memory intact for retrieval under other conditions? Either way, whether memory is truly altered or not, it is clear that eyewitness *reports* are hopelessly biased by postevent information and that this effect can be dramatic (Frenda et al., 2011).

In one laboratory study, Craig Stark and others (2010) showed participants a series of slides showing a man stealing a woman's wallet and tucking it into his jacket pocket. These same participants then heard a recorded account of the event that was accurate or misinformed them that the man hid the wallet in his pants pocket. All were later tested about the details of the event while lying in an MRI scanner. Sure enough, a substantial number of misinformation participants incorrectly recalled that the thief put the wallet in his pants, not his jacket—and said that they remembered that detail from the photographs. Interestingly, the neuroimaging data from the MRI scans showed that the true memories—those based on the slides—were accompanied by more activation of the visual cortex of the brain, while false memories—those based on the audio recording—were accompanied by more activation in the auditory cortex.

This phenomenon raises an additional, potentially troubling question. If adults can be misled by postevent information, what about young children? In 1988, Margaret Kelly Michaels, a 26-year-old preschool teacher, was found guilty of 115 counts of sex abuse committed at the Wee Care Nursery School in New Jersey. The charges against her were shocking. For a period of more than 7 months, the jury was told, she danced nude in the classroom, stripped the children, licked peanut butter off their genitals, and raped them with knives, forks, spoons, and Lego blocks.

Were the children's stories accurate? On the one hand, there were some striking consistencies in the testimonies of 19 child witnesses. On the other hand, the social workers and investigators who conducted the interviews often prompted the children with suggestive leading questions, told them that Michaels was a bad person, urged them to describe acts they had initially denied, offered bribes for disclosures, and pressured those who claimed ignorance. Except for this testimony, there was no physical evidence of abuse and no other witnesses even though the acts were supposed to have occurred during school hours in an open classroom. Michaels was found guilty and sentenced to 47 years in prison. After serving five of those years, she was released when the state appeals court overturned the conviction on the ground that the children's testimony could not be trusted. "One day you're getting ready for work and making coffee, minding your business," said Michaels, "and the next minute you are an accused child molester."

Can suggestive interview procedures cause young children to confuse appearance and reality? Over the years, thousands of sex abuse charges have been filed against babysitters, preschool teachers, and family members. Rekindling images of the Salem witch trials of the seventeenth century, some of these suspects were falsely accused of participating in satanic cults (Bottoms & Davis, 1997). In light of these events, judges struggled to decide: Are preschoolers competent to take the witness stand, or are they too suggestible, too prone to confuse reality and fantasy? To provide guidance to the

**misinformation effect** The tendency for false post-event misinformation to become integrated into people's memory of an event.

courts, researchers have studied the factors that influence children's eyewitness memory (Bruck & Ceci, 1999; Lamb et al., 2008).

This research has evolved through several stages. At first, simple laboratory experiments showed that preschoolers were more likely than older children and adults to incorporate misleading "trick" questions into their memories for simple stories (Ceci et al., 1987). Other studies showed that interviewers could get young children to change their memories (or at least their answers) simply by repeating a question over and over—a behavior that implies that the answer given is not good enough (Poole & White, 1991). But are young children similarly suggestible about stressful real-life experiences?

In one study, Leichtman and Ceci (1995) told nursery school children about a clumsy man named Sam Stone who always broke things. A month later, a man visited the school, spent time in the classroom, and left. The next day, the children were shown a ripped book and a soiled teddy bear and asked what had happened. Reasonably, no one said that they saw Stone cause the damage. But then, over the next 10 weeks, they were asked suggestive questions ("I wonder if Sam Stone was wearing long pants or short pants when he ripped the book?"). The result: When a new interviewer asked the children in the class to tell what happened, 72% of the 3 and 4 year olds blamed Stone for the damage and 45% said they saw him do it. One child "recalled" that Stone took a paintbrush and painted melted chocolate on the bear. Others "saw" him spill coffee, throw toys in the air, rip the book in anger, and soak the book in warm water until it fell apart. It's important to realize that false memories in children are not necessarily a byproduct of bad questioning procedures. Even when interviews are fair and neutral, false reports can stem from young children's exposure to misinformation from such outside sources as television (Principe et al., 2000), parents (Poole & Lindsay, 2001), and classmates (Principe & Ceci, 2002), and the use of anatomical dolls and diagrams as props that interviewers sometimes use to get children to demonstrate how they were touched (Poole et al., 2011).

To summarize, research shows that repetition, misinformation, and leading questions can bias a child's memory report and that preschoolers are particularly vulnerable in this regard. The effects can be dramatic. In dozens of studies, these kinds of procedures have led children to falsely report that they were touched, hit, kissed, and hugged; that a thief came into their classroom; that something "yucky" was put into their mouth; and even that a doctor had cut a bone from their nose to stop it from bleeding. Somehow, the courts must distinguish between true and false claims—and do so on a case-by-case basis. To assist in this endeavor, researchers have proposed that clear interviewing guidelines be set so that future child witnesses will be questioned in an objective, nonbiasing manner (Lamb et al., 2008).

"Do you swear to tell your version of the truth as you perceive it, clouded perhaps by the passage of time and preconceived notions?"

© 1989 Sidney Harris

## Identifying the Culprit

For eyewitnesses, testifying is only the last in a series of efforts to retrieve what they saw from memory. Before witnesses reach the courtroom, they are questioned by police and lawyers, view a lineup or mug shots, and even assist in the construction of a facial composite or an artist's sketch of the perpetrator. Yet each of these experiences increases the risk of error and distortion.

Imagine trying to reconstruct a culprit's face by selecting a set of eyes, a nose, a mouth, a hairstyle, and so on, from vast collections of features and then combining them into a composite of the face. Research shows that this process seldom produces a face that resembles the actual culprit (Kovera et al., 1997). To further complicate matters, the face construction process itself may confuse witnesses, making it more difficult for them later to identify the culprit. In one study, for example, participants were asked to select from six pictures a person's face they had seen 2 days earlier. Sixty percent accurately identified the target. When they first tried to reconstruct the face using a computerized facial composite program, however, their identification accuracy dropped to 18% (Wells et al., 2005).

When there are multiple eyewitnesses to a crime, it is common for descriptions of the culprit to vary from one witness to the next. But what if the various descriptions could somehow be averaged into a single face? Is a collection of witnesses better than one witness? To answer this question, Lisa Hasel and Gary Wells (2007) had participants view a series of target faces and construct a sketch for each one, resulting in four sketches per face. Then for each target they used morphing software to create one composite image that combined the four sketches. To see if these morphs resembled the actual faces better than the average of the individual sketches, a new sample of participants rated the similarity of each set of sketches and morphed composite image to the original target. The results were encouraging: On average, the morphs were rated as more similar to the targets than were the individual sketches on which they were based (see ● Figure 12.3).

Nothing an eyewitness does has greater impact than making an identification from a photographic or live lineup. Once police have made an arrest, they often call on their witnesses to view a lineup that includes the suspect and five to seven other individuals. This procedure may take place within days of a crime or months later. Either way, the lineup often results in tragic cases of mistaken identity. Through the application of eyewitness research findings, this risk can be reduced (Wells et al., 1998; Wells et al., 2007).

### ● FIGURE 12.3

#### Morphing Composite Faces to Catch a Thief

Students from Iowa State University volunteered to use morphing software to answer this question: If there are multiple eyewitnesses to a crime, would it help to average their sketches of the perpetrator's face? In this study, participants constructed sketches of target faces of student volunteers they had viewed. Using the morphing software, a single image that combined four sketches was created for each target. Other participants then rated the similarity of each set of sketches and the morphed image to the original target. Overall, the morphs were more similar to targets than were the individual sketches on which they were based.

Hasel & Wells, 2007. © Cengage Learning

Sketch 1

Sketch 2

Sketch 3

Sketch 4

Sketch 5

Target Face

Basically, five factors can affect identification performance at this stage. The first is the lineup *construction*. To be fair, a lineup should contain four to eight innocent persons, or "foils," who match the witness's general description of the culprit. If the witness describes seeing a white male in his 20s with curly hair, for example, foils should not be included that are old, nonwhite, and bald. Also, anything that makes a suspect distinctive compared to the others in the lineup increases his or her chance of being selected (Buckhout, 1974). This is what happened to Steve Titus, who was mistakenly accused of rape when the police showed the victim his photograph alongside those of five other men. Although the foils resembled Titus in appearance, his picture stood out like a sore thumb. It was smaller than the others and was the only one without a border. Titus was also the only man in the group with a smile on his face (Loftus & Ketcham, 1991).

Second, lineup *instructions* to the witness are very important. In a study by Roy Malpass and Patricia Devine (1981), students saw a staged act of vandalism, after which they attended a lineup. Half of the students received "biased" instructions: They were led to believe that the culprit was in the lineup. The others were told that he might or might not be present. Lineups were then presented either with or without the culprit. When the students received biased instructions, they felt compelled to identify *someone* and often picked an innocent person (see Table 12.1). Additional studies have both confirmed and qualified this basic result: When the criminal is present in the lineup, biased instructions are not problematic. When the criminal is not in the lineup, however—which occurs whenever the police suspect is innocent—biased instructions substantially increase the rate of mistaken identifications (Clark, 2005; Steblay, 1997). Again, the story of Steve Titus is a case in point. The police told the victim to pick her assailant from a group of six. After studying the pictures for several minutes and shaking her head in confusion, she was urged to concentrate and make a choice. "This one is the closest," she said. "It has to be this one" (Loftus & Ketcham, 1991, p. 38).

Third, the *format* of a lineup also influences whether a witness feels compelled to make a selection. When witnesses are presented with a *simultaneous* spread of all photographs, they tend to make relative, multiple-choice-like judgments, comparing the different alternatives and picking the one who looks most like the criminal. This strategy increases the tendency to make a false identification. The solution: When the same photos are shown in a *sequential lineup*, one picture at a time, witnesses tend to make absolute judgments by comparing each target person with their memory of the criminal. This situation diminishes the risk of a forced and often false identification of an innocent suspect (Lindsay & Bellinger, 1999; Lindsay et al., 1991; Lindsay & Wells, 1985).

Some researchers are concerned that the benefit of the sequential format will depend on how it is implemented and the extent to which it reduces correct identifications when the actual perpetrator is in the lineup. But the results are clear: In a meta-analysis of 72 comparisons of simultaneous and sequential lineups involving more than 13,000 mock witnesses, identifications were more accurate when the photos were presented in a sequential format (Steblay, Dysart, & Wells, 2011).

The fourth factor is perhaps the most subtle, as it pertains to *familiarity-induced* biases. Research shows that people often remember a face but not the circumstances in which they saw that face. In one study, for example, participants witnessed a staged crime and then looked through mug shots. A few days later, they were asked to view a

---

**TABLE 12.1**

**Effects of Lineup and Instructions on False Identifications**

After witnessing a crime, participants were told either that the culprit was in the lineup (biased instruction) or that he might or might not be present (unbiased instruction). Participants then viewed a lineup in which the real culprit was present or absent. Notice the percentage of participants in each group who identified an innocent person. Those who received the biased instruction were more likely to make a false identification, picking an innocent person rather than no one at all, especially when the real culprit was not in the lineup.

**Percentage of False Identifications**

|  | Unbiased Instructions | Biased Instructions |
|---|---|---|
| Culprit present | 0 | 25 |
| Culprit absent | 33 | 78 |

From Malpass, R., and Devine, P., "Eyewitness identification: Lineup instructions and the absence of the offender," *Journal of Applied Psychology* vol 66 (pp. 482–489). Copyright © 1981 by the American Psychological Association. Reprinted by permission.

lineup. The result was startling: Participants were just as likely to identify an innocent person whose picture was in the mug shots as they were to pick the actual criminal (Brown et al., 1977)! Many different studies have shown that witnesses will often identify from a lineup someone they had seen in another context, including innocent bystanders who also happened to be at the crime scene (Deffenbacher et al., 2006).

A fifth potential influence can be traced to the police officer who administers the lineup—typically a lineup that contains a suspect and some innocent foils. Can a lineup administrator inadvertently steer a witness's identification decision, most likely to the suspect (who may or may not be the culprit)? In a study that specifically addressed this question, Sarah Greathouse and Margaret Bull Kovera (2009) paired student "witnesses" to a staged theft with student "police" who were trained how to administer a simultaneous or sequential photo lineup using either biased or unbiased instructions. In these lineups, a picture of the actual culprit was either present or absent. Half the administrators were *informed* of who the police suspect was in the lineup; the other half was *blind* as to the suspect's identity. The results showed that under relatively biasing conditions (simultaneous photo spreads and biased instructions), witnesses made more suspect identifications—even when the suspect was truly innocent—when the administrator was informed rather than blind. Videotapes of the sessions showed that the informed administrators unwittingly increased identification rates by telling witnesses to look carefully, by asking them to look again when they failed to make a selection, and in some cases by letting on that they knew who the suspect was. Other studies have also shown that comments made by a lineup administrator can influence eyewitness identification decisions (Clark et al., 2009). This research strongly supports a point of reform, recently adopted in several states, that eyewitness researchers have long advocated: the use of a "double-blind" procedure in which neither the suspect nor the police administrator know who the suspect is within the lineup.

## Testifying in Court

Eyewitnesses can be inaccurate, but that's only part of the problem. The other part is that their testimony is not easy to evaluate. To examine how juries view eyewitness testimony, Gary Wells, Rod Lindsay, and others conducted a series of early experiments in which they staged the theft of a calculator in the presence of unsuspecting research participants, who were later cross-examined after trying to pick the culprit from a photo spread. Other participants, who served as mock jurors, observed the questioning and judged the witnesses. The results were sobering: Jurors overestimated how accurate the eyewitnesses were and could not distinguish between witnesses whose identifications were correct and those whose identifications were incorrect (Lindsay et al., 1981; Wells et al., 1979).

There appear to be two problems. First, people do not know about many aspects of human perception and memory through common sense. Brian Cutler and others (1988) found that mock jurors were not sensitive enough to the effects of lineup instructions, weapon focus, and certain other aspects of an eyewitnessing situation, such as the own-race bias, in evaluating the testimony of an eyewitness. People are knowledgeable about some factors but not others (Desmarais & Read, 2011). The second problem is that people tend to base their judgments of an eyewitness largely on how *confident* that witness is, a factor that only is modestly predictive of accuracy. This statement may seem surprising, but studies have shown that the witness who declares "I am absolutely certain" is not necessarily more likely to be right than the one who appears less certain (Penrod & Cutler, 1995; Sporer et al., 1995;

In March of 2009, social psychologist Gary Wells appeared on the CBS news show *60 Minutes*, where he explained how various aspects of a lineup, how photographs are presented, and how witnesses are instructed can influence the tendency for people to make correct or incorrect identifications.

Courtesy of Gary L. Wells

Wells & Murray, 1984). Why are eyewitness confidence and accuracy not more highly related? The reason is that confidence levels can be raised and lowered by factors that do not have an impact on identification accuracy.

To demonstrate, Elizabeth Luus and Wells (1994) staged a theft in front of pairs of participants and then had each separately identify the culprit from a photographic lineup. After the participants made their identifications, the experimenters led them to believe that their partner, a co-witness, either had picked the same person, a similar-looking different person, or a dissimilar-looking different person or had said that the thief was not in the lineup. Participants were then questioned by a police officer who asked, "On a scale from 1 to 10, how confident are you in your identification?" The result: Participants became more confident when told that a co-witness picked the same person or a dissimilar alternative and less confident when told that the co-witness picked a similar alternative or none at all. Other studies as well have demonstrated that eyewitnesses are influenced in this way by the reports of co-witnesses (Gabbert et al., 2003; Shaw et al., 1997; Skagerberg, 2007).

Other studies confirm that a witness's confidence can be influenced by extraneous information. John Shaw (1996) found that mock witnesses who are repeatedly questioned about their observations become more and more confident over time—even though they did not become more accurate. Demonstrating what they called "the dud effect," Steve Charman and his colleagues (2011) found that an eyewitness's confidence in a mistaken identification is inflated by the presence of fillers in the lineup that bear no resemblance to the criminal. By contrast to these duds, the witness's lineup choice seems closer and more correct.

A witness's confidence is not all that can be affected by extraneous information. Gary Wells and Amy Bradfield (1998) found that eyewitnesses who received positive feedback about their false identifications went on to reconstruct their memory of other aspects of the eyewitnessing experience. In a series of studies, they showed participants a security camera videotape of a man who shot a guard followed by a set of photographs that did not contain the actual gunman (in other words, all identifications made were false). The experimenter then said to some witnesses, but not to others, "Oh good. You identified the actual murder suspect." When witnesses were later asked about the whole experience, those given the confirming feedback "recalled" that they had paid more attention to the event, had a better view of the culprit, and found it easier to make the identification (see ● Figure 12.4).

Clearly, an eyewitness's account of the entire experience can be altered by feedback—and this makes confidence even less predictive of accuracy (Bradfield et al.,

● **FIGURE 12.4**

**The Biasing Effects of Post-Identification Feedback**

Participants saw a gunman on videotape and then tried to make an identification from a set of photographs in which he was absent. Afterward, the experimenter gave some witnesses but not others confirming feedback about their selection. As shown, those given the confirming feedback later recalled that they had paid more attention to the event, had a better view of it, could make out details of the culprit's face, and found it easier to make the identification. They were also more willing to testify in court.
Wells & Bradfield, 1998. © Cengage Learning

> The more confident an eyewitness is about an identification, the more accurate he or she is likely to be. **F**ALSE.

2002; Douglass & Steblay, 2006). To make matters worse, research now shows that eyewitnesses who have been tainted by extraneous information are not fully aware of that influence (Charman & Wells, 2008). Also, the witness whose confidence is artificially inflated is more likely to be believed by jurors—even when that witness has identified an innocent person (Douglass et al., 2010).

## > Improving Eyewitness Justice

Having described the problems with information obtained from eyewitnesses, social psychologists are in a position to put their knowledge to use in two important ways: (1) By educating judges and juries about the science so they can better evaluate eyewitnesses who testify in court, and (2) by making eyewitness identification evidence itself more accurate.

To educate juries, psychologists sometimes testify as eyewitness experts at trial. Just like medical doctors who testify about a patient's physical condition, economists who testify on monopolies and other antitrust matters, and architectural engineers who testify on the structural integrity of buildings, psychologists are often called by one party or the other to inform the trial jury about relevant aspects of human perception, memory, and behavior (Cutler, 2009).

What, specifically, do these experts say to the jury? What findings do they present in court? Several years ago, researchers surveyed 64 eyewitness experts, many of whose studies are described in this chapter. The principles listed in Table 12.2 were seen by the vast majority of respondents as highly reliable and worthy of expert testimony (Kassin et al., 2001). Does the jury need to be informed? On some matters, yes. Research shows that there are certain aspects of the psychology of eyewitness testimony (for example, the fact that lineup instructions and presentation format can affect whether eyewitnesses will identify an innocent person) that the average person does not already know as a matter of common sense (Desmarais & Read, 2011). This selective lack of knowledge is not limited to lay people. Surveys show that compared to experts, judges, prosecutors, and defense attorneys also lack awareness of many of the factors described in this chapter that influence eyewitness memory (Benton et al., 2005; Wise & Safer, 2004; Magnussen et al., 2008).

In recent years, psychologists have also helped to improve upon the accuracy of eyewitness identifications. Led by Gary Wells, eyewitness researchers have replicated their laboratory experiments in police departments; they have testified not only in trials but in state legislatures and criminal justice commissions; they have appeared in national news shows; they have submitted briefs to courts; and they have inspired a wave of state-level reforms—all designed to improve the procedures that are used in getting lineup identifications from

---

**TABLE 12.2**

**What Eyewitness Experts Say in Court**

Presented with a list of eyewitness factors, 64 experts were asked what research findings were strong enough to present in court. In order of how much support they elicited, the following are among the most highly regarded topics of expert testimony.

| Eyewitness Factor | Statement |
| --- | --- |
| Wording of questions | An eyewitness's testimony about an event can be affected by how the questions put to the witness are worded. |
| Lineup instructions | Police instructions can affect an eyewitness's willingness to make an identification. |
| Mug shot–induced bias | Exposure to mug shots of a suspect increases the likelihood that the witness will later choose that suspect in a lineup. |
| Confidence malleability | An eyewitness's confidence can be influenced by factors that are unrelated to the accuracy of an identification. |
| Postevent information | Eyewitness testimony about an event often reflects not only what the witness actually saw but also information they obtained later on. |
| Child suggestibility | Young children are more vulnerable than adults to interviewer suggestion, peer pressures, and other social influences. |
| Alcoholic intoxication | Alcoholic intoxication impairs an eyewitness's later ability to recall persons and events. |
| Cross-race bias | Eyewitnesses are more accurate at identifying members of their own race than they are at identifying members of other races. |
| Weapon focus | The presence of a weapon impairs an eyewitness's ability to accurately identify the perpetrator's face. |
| Accuracy confidence | An eyewitness's confidence is not a good predictor of the accuracy of his or her identification. |

From Kassin, S. M., Tubb, V. A., Hosch, H. M., and Memon, A., "On the 'general acceptance' of eyewitness testimony research: A new survey of the experts," *American Psychologist*, May 2001. Copyright © 2001 by the American Psychological Association. Reprinted by permission.

eyewitnesses. At present, for example, a growing number of police departments require the use of double-blind lineups, unbiased instructions, sequential presentation formats, and the immediate assessment of a witness's confidence.

# Confessions

Every now and then, an extraordinary event comes along that shakes the way you think. The Central Park jogger case was one of these events. In 1989, five boys who were 14 to 16 years old were found guilty of a monstrous assault and rape of a female jogger in New York's Central Park after they confessed (four of them did so on videotape) in vivid detail. Thirteen years later, a serial rapist named Matias Reyes stepped forward from prison to admit that he alone, not the boys, had committed the crime. As part of a thorough investigation of Reyes's claim, the district attorney DNA-tested the semen from the crime scene and found that it was a match: Reyes was the rapist. The five boys, now men, were innocent. Their confessions were false, and the convictions were vacated (Burns, 2011).

## Suspect Interviews: The Psychology of Lie Detection

Sometimes police identify a suspect for interrogation by talking to witnesses and informants, obtaining physical evidence from the crime scene, and other methods of investigation. Often, however, police decide to interrogate a particular person based solely on a personal judgment they make by conducting a special pre-interrogation interview that exposes deception. In *Criminal Interrogations and Confessions*, an influential manual on interrogation first published in 1962 and now in its fifth edition, Inbau and others (2013) have proposed a process by which police can distinguish truths from lies. In this approach, police are advised to ask certain non-accusatory questions and then to observe changes in the suspect's verbal and nonverbal behavior—looking, for example, at eye contact, pauses, posture, fidgety movements—to determine whether he or she is telling the truth or lying.

For a person who is under suspicion, a police officer's judgment at this stage is crucial because it can determine whether a suspect is judged deceptive and interrogated or presumed innocent and sent home. In theory, this approach makes sense. As described in Chapter 4 on social perception, however, research has consistently shown that most of the verbal and nonverbal demeanor cues that are suggested do not discriminate at high levels of accuracy between truth-telling and deception (DePaulo et al., 2003; Hartwig & Bond, 2011). At present, it appears that laypeople on average are only 54% accurate; that training produces little if any improvement; and that police officers, judges, psychiatrists, customs inspectors, and other "professionals" tend to perform only slightly better, if at all (Meissner & Kassin, 2004; Vrij, 2008).

That people are notoriously inept at making accurate judgments of truth and deception can be seen every day—which is why Ponzi scheme perpetrators like Bernie Madoff can fool even an affluent and intelligence clientele. Are there more accurate means of lie detection? In part to improve performance, police over the years have used a **polygraph**, or what most of us would call a lie-detector test. A polygraph is an electronic instrument that simultaneously records multiple channels of physiological arousal. The signals are picked up by sensors attached to different parts of the body. For example, rubber tubes are strapped around a suspect's torso to measure breathing, blood-pressure cuffs are wrapped around the upper arm to measure pulse rate, and

**polygraph** A mechanical instrument that records physiological arousal from multiple channels; it is often used as a lie-detector test.

electrodes are placed on the fingertips to record sweat-gland activity, or perspiration. These signals are then boosted by amplifiers and converted into a visual display.

The polygraph is used to detect deception on the assumption that when people lie, they become anxious and physiologically aroused in ways that can be measured. Here's how the test is conducted. After convincing a suspect that the polygraph works and establishing his or her baseline level of arousal, the examiner asks a series of yes–no questions and compares how the suspect reacts to emotionally arousing *crime-relevant questions* ("Did you steal the money?") and *control questions* that are arousing but not relevant to the crime ("Did you take anything that did not belong to you when you were younger?"). In theory, suspects who are innocent—whose denials are truthful—should be more aroused by the control questions, while guilty suspects—whose denials are false—should be more aroused by the crime-relevant questions.

Does the lie-detector test really work? Many laypeople think of it as foolproof, but scientific opinion is split. Some researchers report accuracy rates of up to 80% to 90%. Others believe that such claims are exaggerated. One well-documented problem is that truthful persons too often fail the test. A second problem is that people who understand the test can fake the results. Studies show that you can beat the polygraph by tensing your muscles, squeezing your toes, or using other physical countermeasures while answering the *control* questions. By artificially inflating the responses to "innocent" questions, one can mask the stress that is aroused by lying on the crime-relevant questions (for a comprehensive overview of research, see Honts et al., 2002).

What, then, are we to conclude? The National Research Council (2003) has concluded that there is no simple answer. Under certain conditions—for example, when the suspect is naive and the examiner is competent—it is possible for the polygraph to detect truth and deception at fairly high levels of accuracy. In fact, handheld "pocket" polygraphs have been used for rapid screening of terrorism suspects in the field. Still, the problems identified by research are hard to overcome, which is why the U.S. Supreme Court ruled, in the context of a military court martial, that judges may refuse to admit polygraph test results into evidence (*United States v. Scheffer*, 1998).

Seeking alternatives, researchers are trying to develop tests that distinguish between truth and deception through the use of a modified polygraph test that asks different types of questions (Ben-Shakhar & Elaad, 2003); the measurement of involuntary electrical activity in the brain (Winograd & Rosenfeld, 2011); pupil dilation when the person being tested is asked to lie, which requires more cognitive effort than telling the truth (Dionisio et al., 2001); the Implicit Association Test, or IAT, which shows that people are quicker to respond to true statements than to false statements (Sartori et al., 2008); the use of fMRI to measure blood oxygen levels in areas of the brain that are associated with deception (Kozel et al., 2005; Bhatt et al., 2009); and the use of thermal imaging cameras in airports to detect lying through rises in skin temperature (Warmelink et al., 2011). Especially in light of the post-9/11 need for intelligence gathering from terrorism suspects, prisoners of war, witnesses and informants, researchers are also working to improve the quality of the interviewing methods used in the field (Loftus, 2011).

It is not possible to knowingly fool a lie-detector test. **F**ALSE.

## Police Interrogations: Social Influence Under Pressure

As the events of the Central Park jogger case unfolded, questions mounted: Why would five boys—or anyone else, for that matter—confess to a crime they did not commit? In general, what social influences are brought to bear on suspects interrogated by police?

Many years ago, police detectives would use brute force to get confessions. Among the commonly used coercive methods were prolonged confinement and isolation; explicit threats; deprivations of sleep, food, and other needs; extreme sensory discomfort (for example, by shining a bright, blinding strobe light on a suspect's face); and assorted forms of physical violence (for example, forcing suspects to stand for hours at a time or beating them with a rubber hose, which seldom left visible marks).

Today, the police are required to warn suspects of their Miranda rights to silence and an attorney, and the tactics they use are more psychological in nature. In *Criminal Interrogation and Confessions*, Inbau et al. (2013) advise police, once they have identified a suspect they believe to be lying, to conduct a process of interrogation. This process begins when police put a suspect alone—with no friends or family present—into a small, bare, soundproof room, a physical environment that is designed to arouse feelings of social isolation and discomfort. Next, they present a vivid nine-step procedure designed to get suspects to confess (see Table 12.3).

Once a suspect is isolated, this method of interrogation offers two approaches. One approach is to pressure the suspect into submission by expressing certainty in his or her guilt and even, at times, claiming falsely to have damaging evidence such as fingerprints or an eyewitness. In this way, the accused is led to believe that it is futile to continue in his or her denials. A second approach is to befriend the suspect, offer sympathy and friendly advice, and "minimize" the offense by offering face-saving excuses or blaming the victim. Under stress, feeling trapped, lulled into a false sense of security, and led to expect leniency, many suspects agree to give a confession. This approach is carefully designed to increase the anxiety associated with denial and reduce the anxiety associated with confession. It may sound like interrogation process springs from a *Law & Order* TV script, but in real life these tactics are routinely used.

In an observational study of 182 live and videotaped interrogations, Richard Leo (1996) found that detectives used an average of five to six tactics per suspect. In a survey of 631 police investigators, Kassin and others (2007) found that the most common reported tactics were to physically isolate suspects, identify contradictions in their accounts, establish rapport, and confront them with evidence of their guilt, appeals to self-interests, and offer sympathy and moral justification. Whatever specific methods are used, it is clear that being accused and pointedly questioned about a crime is a very stressful experience. In one study, participants who were accused of cheating on a laboratory task—compared to those who were not accused—were less able to process the rights they were given to remain silent and to have a lawyer present (Scherr & Madon, in press). It is also now clear that physically painful methods of persuasion, often referred to as "enhanced interrogation" techniques, have been used in recent years to interrogate suspected terrorists (Mayer, 2007; McKelvey, 2007; O'Mara, 2009).

**TABLE 12.3**
**The Nine Steps of Interrogation**

1. Confront the suspect with assertions of his or her guilt.
2. Develop "themes" that appear to justify or excuse the crime.
3. Interrupt all statements of innocence and denial.
4. Overcome all of the suspect's objections to the charges.
5. Keep the increasingly passive suspect from tuning out.
6. Show sympathy and understanding and urge the suspect to tell all.
7. Offer the suspect a face-saving explanation for his or her guilty action.
8. Get the suspect to recount the details of the crime.
9. Convert that statement into a full written confession.

Inbau et al., 2001. © Cengage Learning

"I'm neither a good cop nor a bad cop, Jerome. Like yourself, I'm a complex amalgam of positive and negative personality traits that emerge or not, depending on circumstances."

Courtesy ABCNEWS.com

Courtesy of ABCNEWS.com

In 1989, 16-year-old Kharey Wise (left) and four other teenagers confessed to raping a jogger in New York's Central Park. Based solely on his confession, Wise was convicted and sent to prison. Thirteen years later, Matias Reyes (right) admitted that he alone, not the boys, had committed the crime. DNA tests confirmed that Reyes was the rapist. The boys, despite their confessions, were innocent.

*If you're interested in learning more about false confessions, the Innocence Project would be a good place to start (http://www .innocenceproject.org/).*

## False Confessions: Why Innocent People Confess

It could be argued that the use of trickery and deception does not pose a serious problem because only perpetrators confess; innocent people never confess to crimes they did not commit. This assumption, however, is incorrect. As hard as it is to believe, a number of chilling cases of false confessions are on record. Illustrating the point is the story of Amanda Knox, the American college student accused but ultimately acquitted for the tragic murder of her roommate in Italy. Also illustrating the point is the Central Park jogger case in which five false confessions to a rape were taken. In fact, research shows that false confessions were present in 25% of all cases involving prisoners who were convicted and later proved innocent by DNA evidence (Garrett, 2011). Importantly, too, this sample represents just the tip of an iceberg. Although most case studies are based in the United States and England, proven false confessions have been documented in countries all over the world—including Canada, Norway, Finland, Germany, Iceland, Ireland, the Netherlands, Australia, New Zealand, China, and Japan (Kassin et al., 2010).

It seems unimaginable. Why would an innocent person ever confess to police to a crime he or she did not commit? There are two reasons—and two types of false confession.

Sometimes innocent people under police interrogation agree to confess as an act of mere *compliance*—to escape a very stressful situation. Applying basic psychology, Stephanie Madon and her colleagues (2012) point out that human beings in general are influenced more by rewards and punishments that are immediate (now) than by those that are delayed (later). People are particularly short-sighted when they are tired, stressed, or otherwise in need. For a suspect under intense scrutiny and interrogation, stopping the process through confession may feel so urgent that he or she does not fully consider the future consequence of doing so. Madon et al. demonstrated this type of short-sightedness in a series of experiments in which participants were more likely to admit to various transgressions (such as buying alcohol before they were 21, driving without a license, illegally downloading music, shoplifting, or taking credit for someone else's idea) when doing so was in their immediate interest and the negative consequence would come later.

In real life, the process of interrogation can be so stressful that the short-term benefit of confession outweighs the long-term benefit of denial. The experiences of Amanda Knox and the Central Park jogger boys illustrate the point. All had been in custody and interrogated overnight, relentlessly, for several hours, before giving their confessions. Such long periods of time bring fatigue, despair, and a deprivation of sleep and other need states. In both cases, the police and suspects disagree about what happened during these unrecorded hours so it is not possible to know for sure. In both cases, however, the defendants claimed that they felt threatened and uncertain as to what would happen if they refused to confess. In both cases, the defendants then tried to withdraw their confessions as soon as the pressure of interrogation had passed.

In contrast to instances in which innocent people confess as an act of compliance, or obedience to authority, sometimes the process of interrogation can cause innocent people to confess because they become enough to believe that they are guilty of the crime. In these instances, the false confession illustrates a strong form of social influence known as *internalization*. This process was evident in the recent story of three men and three women in Beatrice, Nebraska. In 1989, they were convicted of the murder of a 68-year-old woman. Five of them pled guilty; four gave vividly detailed confessions to police as a result of intense interrogations. Twenty years later, all six defendants were pardoned after DNA testing cleared them and identified the actual culprit. After a reinvestigation, the Nebraska Attorney General's Office concluded that despite all the confessions, these individuals were innocent "beyond all doubt." Yet remarkably, all of them had come to internalize the erroneous belief in their own guilt. One woman stood by her statement until just before she was pardoned, at which point she said, "I guess I was brainwashed" (Hammel, 2008).

Is it really possible to get people to confess to an act they did not commit? Based on the events of actual cases, Kassin and Kiechel (1996) theorized that two factors can increase this risk: (1) a suspect who lacks a clear memory of the event in question and (2) the presentation of false evidence. To test this hypothesis, they recruited pairs of college students to work on a fast- or slow-paced computer task. At one point, the computer crashed and students were accused of having caused the damage by pressing a key they had been specifically instructed to avoid. All students were truly innocent and denied the charge. In half the sessions, however, the second student (who was really a confederate) said that she had seen the student hit the forbidden key. Demonstrating the process of compliance, many students confronted by this false witness agreed to sign a confession handwritten by the experimenter. Further demonstrating the process of internalization, some students later "admitted" guilt to a stranger (also a confederate) after the study was supposedly over and the two were alone. In short, innocent people who are vulnerable to suggestion can be induced to confess and to internalize guilt by the presentation of false evidence (see Table 12.4). This finding has been replicated in a number of experiments (Perillo & Kassin, 2011; Horselenberg et al., 2003; Nash & Wade, 2009).

False evidence is one tactic that can cause innocent people to confess. An offer of leniency can have the same effect. Melissa Russano and others (2005) asked participants to solve a series of problems, sometimes alone and sometimes with a fellow participant (who was actually a confederate). In the alone trials, participants were instructed not to seek or provide assistance. In a guilty condition, the confederate asked for help, inducing most participants to break the rule. In an innocent condition, no such request was made. Moments later, the experimenter returned, accused the pair of participants of cheating—a possible violation of their university honor code—and

## TABLE 12.4
### Factors That Produce False Confessions

As participants worked on a fast- or slow-paced task, the computer crashed, and they were accused of causing the damage. A confederate then said that she had or had not seen the participants hit the forbidden key. As shown, many participants signed a confession (compliance), and some even "admitted" their guilt in private to another confederate (internalization). Despite their innocence, many participants in the fast-false witness condition confessed on both measures.

| | Control | | False Witness | |
| --- | --- | --- | --- | --- |
| | Slow | Fast | Slow | Fast |
| Compliance | 35% | 65% | 89% | 100% |
| Internalization | 0% | 12% | 44% | 65% |

From Kassin, S. M., and Kiechel, K. L., "The social psychology of false confessions: Compliance, internalization, and confabulation," *Psychological Science* vol 7, no 3 (Table 1, p. 127). Copyright © 1996 by Sage Publications, Inc. Reprinted by permission.

● **FIGURE 12.5**

**Interrogation as a Self-Fulfilling Prophecy: Do Guilty Expectations Produce False Confessions?**

Participants were asked to solve a series of problems, sometimes alone and sometimes with a confederate. Half were induced to cheat on the alone task, making them guilty of violating the rule; the other half were not induced to cheat, making them innocent. Eight young men then interrogated participants to determine if they had cheated. In some cases, the interrogators were led to believe the participant was probably guilty; in other cases, that he or she was probably innocent. As shown, interrogators produced confessions from most participants who had cheated. Armed with guilty expectations, however, they also produced a high rate of false confessions from participants who were innocent.

Narchet et al., 2011. © Cengage Learning

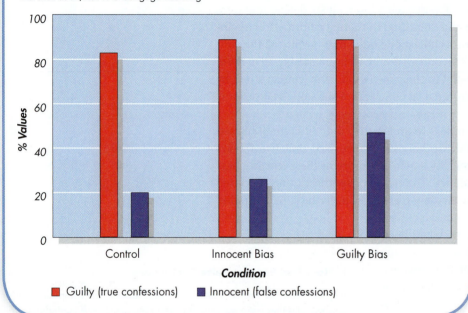

Legend: ■ Guilty (true confessions)   ■ Innocent (false confessions)

then interrogated everyone as to whether they had cheated. As part of this interrogation, the experimenter offered leniency for cooperation to some participants, minimized the seriousness of the violation to others, used both tactics, or used no tactics at all. Would students sign a confession to cheating? Yes. Both promises and minimization increased the number of true confessions among students who broke the rule. But these same tactics also increased the rate of false confessions among students who did nothing wrong.

Everyone agrees that the objective of an interrogation is to draw confessions from people who are guilty but from those who are innocent. In that vein, interrogation tactics that put innocent people at risk should be avoided if possible. There is, however, a basic problem with interrogation: It is a process of social influence that police employ on suspects that they believe to be guilty. Can this expectation of guilt lead police to use tactics that draw false confessions? To test this hypothesis, Fadia Narchet and others (2011) trained eight young men, over 5 weeks, on how to conduct interrogations using various techniques. In a study like the one just described, these trainees were asked to interrogate guilty and innocent participants to determine if they had cheated on the alone task. In some cases, the interrogators were led to believe the participant was probably guilty; in other cases, that he or she was probably innocent. Did expectations influence outcomes? Yes. ● Figure 12.5 shows that interrogators elicited confessions from most participants who had actually cheated regardless of expectations. But when they interrogated participants who did not cheat, interrogators with guilty expectations used more coercive tactics and produced a high rate of false confessions.

## ❭ Confessions in the Courtroom

How does the legal system treat confessions brought out by police interrogations? The process is straightforward. Whenever a suspect confesses but then withdraws the statement, pleads not guilty, and goes to trial, the judge must determine whether the statement was voluntary or coerced. If the confession was clearly coerced—as when a suspect is isolated for long periods of time, deprived of food or sleep, threatened, or abused—it is excluded. If the confession is not coerced, it is admitted into evidence for the jury to evaluate.

In these cases, juries are confronted with a classic attribution dilemma: A suspect's statement may indicate guilt (personal attribution) or it may simply provide the suspect with a way to avoid the unpleasant consequences of silence (situational attribution). According to attribution theory, jurors should reject all confessions made in response to external pressure. But wait. Remember the fundamental attribution error? In Chapter 4, we saw that people tend to overattribute behavior to persons and overlook the influence of situational forces. Is it similarly possible, as in the Amanda Knox and Central Park jogger cases, that jurors view suspects who confess as guilty even if their confessions were coerced during interrogation?

To examine this question, Kassin and Sukel (1997) had mock jurors read one of three versions of a double murder trial. In a control version that did not contain a confession, only 19% voted guilty. In a low-pressure version in which the defendant was said to have confessed immediately upon questioning, the conviction rate rose considerably, to 62%. But there was a third, high-pressure condition in which participants were told that the defendant had confessed out of fear while his hands were cuffed behind his back, causing him pain. How did jurors in this situation react? Reasonably, they judged the confession to be coerced and said it did not influence their verdicts. Yet the conviction rate in this situation increased sharply, this time from 19% to 50%. Apparently, people are powerfully influenced by evidence of a confession, even when they concede that it was coerced. Confessions are powerfully incriminating not only to lay people. The same result was recently found in a study involving judges (Wallace & Kassin, 2012).

The jury's reaction to confession evidence may also depend on how that evidence is presented. Today, many police departments videotape confessions for presentation in court. But could you tell the difference between a true confession and a false confession? Maybe not. Inside prison walls, Kassin, Meissner, and Norwick (2005) videotaped male inmates giving full confessions to the crimes for which they were incarcerated and concocting false confessions to offenses suggested by the researchers that they did not commit. College students and police investigators then watched and judged 10 different inmates, each of whom gave a true or false confession to one of five crimes: aggravated assault, armed robbery, burglary, breaking and entering, and car theft. The results showed that although the police were generally confident in their performance, neither group exhibited high levels of accuracy.

In light of recently discovered false confessions, a number of states are beginning to require that the full interrogations be video recorded. This is an important reform to current practice, in part because it enables judges and juries to see for themselves how a confession came about and the extent to which the suspect was coerced (Kassin et al., 2010). But how should these events be staged for the camera? In a series of experiments, Daniel Lassiter and his colleagues (2001) taped mock confessions from three different camera angles so that either the suspect or the interrogator or both were visible. All participants heard the same exchanges of words, but those who watched the suspects saw the situations as less coercive overall than did those who focused on the interrogators. Follow-up research has shown that even the perceptions of experienced trial judges are influenced by these variations in camera perspective (Lassiter et al., 2007). The practical policy implications are clear: When the camera directs all eyes at the accused, jurors are likely to underestimate the amount of pressure exerted by the "hidden" interrogator.

Without being beaten or threatened, innocent people sometimes confess to crimes they did not commit. **T**RUE.

# Jury Decision Making

The criminal justice system is complex. Yet through it all, the trial—a relatively infrequent but highly dramatic event—is at the heart and soul of the system. The threat of trial is what motivates parties to gather evidence and, later, to negotiate a deal. And when it is over, the trial by judge or jury forms the basis for sentencing and appeals decisions. In this section, we examine the three stages of an American trial: (1) jury selection; (2) the presentation of evidence, arguments, and instructions; and (3) the processes by which juries deliberate to reach a verdict.

## Jury Selection

If you're ever accused of a crime in the United States or involved in a lawsuit, you have a constitutional right to a trial by an impartial jury from your community. This right is considered essential to doing justice within a democracy. Yet whenever a controversial verdict is reached in a high-profile case, people, right or wrong, blame the 12 individuals who constituted the jury. That's why it is important to know how juries are selected.

Jury selection is a three-stage process. First, the court uses voter registration lists, telephone directories, and other sources to compile a master list of eligible citizens who live in the community. Second, so that a representative sample can be obtained, a certain number of people from the list are randomly drawn and summoned for duty. If you've ever been called, you know what happens next. Before people who appear in court are placed on a jury, they are subject to what is known as **voir dire**, a pretrial interview in which the judge and lawyers question the prospective jurors for signs of bias. If someone knows one of the parties, has an interest in the outcome of the case,

"I see jury selection has begun."

or has already formed an opinion, the judge will excuse that person "for cause." In fact, if it can be proven that an entire community is biased, perhaps because of pretrial publicity, then the trial might be postponed or moved to another location.

Although the procedure seems straightforward, there is more to the story. In addition to de-selecting individuals who are clearly biased, the lawyers are permitted to exercise **peremptory challenges**. That is, they can reject a certain limited number of prospective jurors even if they seem fair and open-minded, and they can do so without having to state reasons or win the judge's approval. Why would a lawyer challenge someone who appears to be impartial? What guides lawyers' decisions to accept some jurors and reject others? These questions make the process of voir dire particularly interesting to social psychologists (Vidmar & Hans, 2007).

**Trial Lawyers as Intuitive Psychologists**   Rumor has it that trial lawyers have used some unconventional methods to select juries. Under pressure to make choices quickly and without much information, lawyers rely on implicit personality theories and stereotypes. As described in Chapter 4, an implicit personality theory is a set of assumptions that people make about how certain attributes are related to each other and to behavior. When we believe that all members of a group share the same attributes, these implicit theories are called stereotypes.

As far as trial practice is concerned, how-to books claim that the astute lawyer can predict a juror's verdict by his or her gender, race, age, ethnic background, and other simple demographics. It has been suggested, for example, that athletes lack sympathy for fragile and injured victims, that engineers are unemotional, that men with beards resist authority, and that cabinetmakers are so meticulous in their work that they will never be completely satisfied with the evidence. Clarence Darrow, one of the most prominent trial attorneys of the twentieth century, suggested that jurors of southern European

**voir dire**   The pretrial examination of prospective jurors by the judge or opposing lawyers to uncover signs of bias.

**peremptory challenge**   A means by which lawyers can exclude a limited number of prospective jurors without the judge's approval.

descent favored the defense whereas those from Scandinavia favored the prosecution. Other lawyers have theorized that women are more skeptical as jurors than men, particularly in response to attractive female witnesses. Still others offer selection advice based on faces, facial expressions, body language, and clothing. Perhaps the most interesting rule of thumb is also the simplest: "If you don't like a juror's face, chances are he doesn't like yours either!" (Wishman, 1986, pp. 72–73).

The intuitive approach to jury selection by which lawyers use peremptory challenges may provide for colorful stories from inside the courtroom, but the consequences of this kind of stereotyping for justice can be troubling. For example, what if a prosecutor were to use peremptory challenges to exclude from the jury all whites, blacks, Latinos, or Asians; or all men or all women, possibly stripping the jury of the defendant's peers? In recent years, the U.S. Supreme Court has for the first time limited the use of peremptory challenges to prevent lawyers from systematically excluding prospective jurors on the basis of race. According to the Court, judges can now require lawyers suspected of discriminating in this way to explain the basis of their challenges (*Batson v. Kentucky*, 1986; *Miller-El v. Dretke*, 2005).

Citing social psychological research on stereotyping and prejudice, Sommers and Norton (2008) point to two problems: (1) The influence of conscious and unconscious racial stereotypes on social perceptions is prevalent and likely to influence lawyers in the courtroom; and (2) these racial biases are difficult to identify in specific instances because lawyers, like everyone else, typically do not acknowledge having been influenced by their stereotypes. In a study that illustrated both points, Sommers and Norton (2007) presented college students, law students, and attorneys with a summary of a criminal trial involving a black defendant and asked them to choose between two prospective jurors with various characteristics—one white, the other black. As predicted, all groups were far more likely to challenge the juror who was black rather than the one who was white, yet very few subjects cited race as a factor in their decisions.

The intuitive approach to jury selection sometimes leads to discrimination on the basis of race and other characteristics. This approach is also not very effective. Thus, although some experienced trial attorneys take pride in their jury-selection skills, researchers have found that most lawyers cannot effectively predict how jurors will vote, either on the basis of their intuitive rules of thumb (Olczak et al., 1991) or by relying on how prospective jurors answer questions during the voir dire (Kerr et al., 1991; Zeisel & Diamond, 1978). Apparently, whether a juror characteristic predicts verdicts depends on the specifics of each and every case. Hence a new service industry was born: scientific jury selection.

Contrary to popular opinion, women are harsher as trial jurors than men are. **FALSE.**

**Scientific Jury Selection**    In a movie based on John Grisham's *Runaway Jury*, a ruthless jury consultant named Rankin Fitch, played by Gene Hackman, helps lawyers select jurors through the use of intrusive high-tech surveillance work. Burrowing deep into the lives of prospective jurors, Fitch trails them, investigates them, and even resorts at times to bribery, blackmail, and intimidation. Determined to stack the jury in order to defend gun company defendants against a multimillion-dollar wrongful death lawsuit, Fitch declares, "A trial is too important to be left up to juries."

Grisham's depiction of jury consulting is a work of fiction, not fact. But it is based on a kernel of truth. Instead of relying on hunches, successful stock market investors, baseball managers, and poker players play the odds whenever they can. Now many trial lawyers do too. In recent years, the "art" of jury selection has been transformed into something of a "science" (Lieberman & Sales, 2007).

This use of jury consultants began during the Vietnam War era, when the federal government prosecuted a group of antiwar activists known as the Harrisburg Seven.

The case against the defendants was strong, and the trial was to be held in the conservative city of Harrisburg, Pennsylvania. To help the defense select a jury, sociologist Jay Schulman and his colleagues (1973) surveyed the local community by interviewing 840 residents. Two kinds of information were taken from each resident: demographic (for example, sex, race, age, and education) and attitudes relevant to the trial (for example, attitudes toward the government, the war, and political dissent). By correlating these variables, Schulman's team came up with a profile of the ideal defense juror: "a female Democrat with no religious preference and a white-collar job or a skilled blue-collar job" (p. 40). Guided by this result, the defense selected its jury. The rest is history: Against all odds, the trial ended in a hung jury, split 10 to 2 in favor of acquittal.

Today, the technique known as **scientific jury selection** is used often, especially in high-profile criminal trials and civil trials in which large sums of money are at stake. Research shows, for example, that jurors are differently predisposed when confronted with cases that pit lone individuals against large corporations, with some people favoring big business and others harboring an anti-business prejudice (Hans, 2000). How is scientific jury selection carried out? What are the methods used? The procedure is simple. Because lawyers are often not allowed to ask jurors intrusive and personal questions, they try to determine jurors' attitudes and verdict tendencies from information that is known about their backgrounds. The relevance of this information can be determined through focus groups, mock juries, or community-wide surveys, in which statistical relationships are sought between general demographic factors and attitudes relevant to a particular case. Then, during the voir dire, lawyers ask prospective jurors about their backgrounds and use peremptory challenges to exclude those whose profiles are associated with unfavorable attitudes.

In *Runaway Jury*, a film based on John Grisham's novel, actor Gene Hackman played feared jury consultant Rankin Fitch. In a film that blurred fact and fiction, Fitch not only researched prospective jurors for jury selection purposes but also engaged in jury tampering, blackmail, and other illegal tactics in a desperate but failed effort to win the verdict.

As you might expect, scientific jury selection is a controversial enterprise. By law, consultants are not permitted to communicate with or approach the prospective jurors themselves, despite the tactics portrayed in *Runaway Jury*. But how effective are the techniques that are employed? It's hard to say. On the one hand, trial lawyers who have used scientific jury selection boast an impressive winning percentage. On the other hand, it is impossible to know the extent to which these victories are attributable to the jury-selection surveys (Strier, 1999). So does scientific jury selection work? Although more data are needed to evaluate the claims made, it appears that attitudes can influence verdicts in some cases and that pretrial research can help lawyers identify these attitudes (Lieberman et al., 2011; Seltzer, 2006). As we'll soon see, the linkage between attitudes and verdicts is particularly strong in cases that involve capital punishment.

Before concluding our review of scientific jury selection, let's stop to consider an ethical question: Is justice enhanced or impaired by the intervention of professional jury consultants? Is the real goal for lawyers to eliminate jurors who are biased or to create juries slanted in their favor? Those who practice scientific jury selection argue that picking juries according to survey results is simply a more refined version of what lawyers are permitted to do by intuition. If there's a problem, they say, it is not in the *science* but in the *law* that permits trial attorneys to use peremptory challenges to exclude jurors who are not obviously biased. In response, critics argue that scientific jury selection tips the scales of justice in favor of wealthy clients who can afford the service, an outcome that further widens the socioeconomic gap that exists within the courts. Hence, Neil and Dorit Kressel (2002), authors of *Stack and Sway: The New Science of Jury Consulting*,

**scientific jury selection** A method of selecting juries through surveys that yield correlations between demographics and trial-relevant attitudes.

argue that peremptory challenges, which enable lawyers and their consultants to strike jurors who are not overtly biased, should be abolished.

**Juries in Black and White: Does Race Matter?**  To what extent does a juror's race color his or her decision making? Research suggests that there is no simple answer. In one study, Norbert Kerr and others (1995) tested the most intuitive hypothesis of all, that jurors favor defendants who are similar to themselves. They presented mixed-race groups with a strong or weak case involving a black or white defendant. They found that when the evidence was weak, the participants were more lenient in their verdicts toward the defendant of the same race. Yet when the evidence was strong, they were harsher against that similar defendant, as if distancing themselves from his or her wrongdoing.

In a second study, Sommers and Ellsworth (2001) tested the popular notion that jurors will show preference for others of their racial group when a crime involves race, as when it is a motivated hate crime or when attorneys "play the race card" in arguments to the jury. Yet they found the opposite pattern. When race was not an issue that is "on the radar," white jurors predictably treated the defendant more favorably when he was white than when he was black. Yet when race was made a prominent issue at trial, white jurors bent over backward *not* to appear prejudiced and did not discriminate. Other research has shown that jurors may at times be motivated to watch for racist tendencies in themselves, leading them to process trial information even more carefully when a defendant is black than when he or she is white (Sargent & Bradfield, 2004).

The potential for individual jurors to exhibit racial bias may also depend on the composition of the jury with whom they expect to deliberate. In a courthouse located in Ann Arbor, Michigan, Sommers (2006) showed a *Court TV* summary of a sexual assault trial in which the defendant was African American. A total of 200 locals participated in 29 six-person mock juries after a voir dire that either did or did not make race an issue. Ultimately, the juries that were formed were either all white or heterogeneous, consisting of four whites and two blacks. After the videotaped trial summary but before the groups deliberated, each juror was asked to indicate his or her verdict preference. Look at ● Figure 12.6, and you'll see that jurors were influenced by the racial composition of their groups as a whole. In diverse groups, 34% of white jurors voted guilty compared to 23% of black jurors—a small difference. In the all-white groups, however, 51% of jurors voted guilty, which represented a significant jump compared to both blacks and whites in the more diverse groups.

**Death Qualification**  On September 21, 2011, 43-year-old Troy Davis was executed by lethal injection for the 1989 murder of off-duty police officer Mark MacPhail in Savannah, Georgia. Davis had been convicted at trial on the basis of several eyewitnesses and informants who said they heard him confess. Over the years, however, many witnesses recanted their testimony, saying they were pressured to give it. New evidence seemed to implicate someone else. The courts were unconvinced. Whatever the truth may have been, the Davis execution was highly controversial, drawing protest and criticism from around the world. In his final

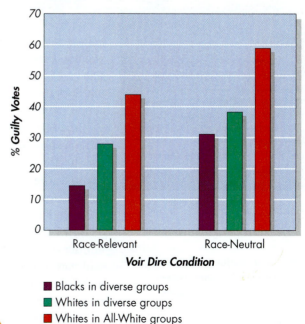

● **FIGURE 12.6**

**Effects of Racial Diversity on the Jury**

Six-person mock juries watched the trial of an African American defendant in groups that were homogeneous (all white) or diverse (four white, two black). In some cases, the issue of race was raised during the voir dire; in others, it was not. Either way, the white jurors in homogeneous groups were more likely to vote guilty than white jurors in diverse groups who, in turn, were more likely to vote guilty than black jurors in diverse groups. It seems that individual jurors are influenced in their decisions by the racial composition of their groups.

Sommers, 2006. © Cengage Learning

dying words, Davis maintained his innocence: "Well, first of all I'd like to address the MacPhail family. I'd like to let you all know, despite the situation—I know all of you are still convinced that I'm the person that killed your father, your son and your brother, but I am innocent."

Over the years, the death penalty has stimulated a heated public debate in America (Bedau & Cassell, 2004). Think about it: If you had to sentence someone to die, could you do it? Not everyone answers this question in the same way. Yet your answer could mean the difference between life and death for a defendant convicted of murder. Today, a majority of American states permit capital punishment. Among those that do, the jury decides not only the verdict but the sentence as well. In these cases, it is not surprising that sentencing decisions are influenced not only by the facts of a specific case but also by jurors' general attitudes toward the death penalty. Kevin O'Neil and his colleagues (2004) found that these attitudes are composed of various beliefs, such as beliefs in the legitimacy of retribution and revenge ("There are some murderers whose death would give me a sense of personal satisfaction"), deterrence ("The death penalty

On September 21, 2011, Troy Davis was executed for the 1989 murder of a Georgia police officer. Davis had been convicted on the basis of eyewitnesses and informants who said they heard him confess. New evidence later cast doubt on his guilt, leading supporters of Davis and opponents of the death penalty to protest his execution. In the United States, the death penalty is both permissible and a recurring source of controversy.

makes criminals think twice before committing murder"), and cost ("Executing a murderer is less expensive than keeping him in jail for the rest of his life"). Monica Miller and David Hayward (2008) found that people who favor the death penalty are more likely to hold fundamentalist religious views and a belief in the literal interpretation of the Bible. Brooke Butler and Gary Moran (2007) found that people who favor the death penalty also tend to harbor authoritarian beliefs and the belief that the world is a just place in which people get what they deserve and deserve what they get.

In cases involving crimes punishable by death and in which the jury makes both decisions, a special jury-selection practice known as **death qualification** is typically used. Through death qualification, judges may exclude all prospective jurors who say that they would refuse to vote for the death penalty. These jurors are excluded for the entire trial. To ensure that *sentencing* decisions are unbiased, it makes sense to exclude those who admit they are close-minded. But does this same selection practice tip the balance toward the prosecution when it comes to the *verdict*? In other words, are death-qualified juries prone to convict?

In a series of studies, Phoebe Ellsworth, Craig Haney, and others have examined this question. Their results have shown that compared to people who oppose the death penalty, those who support it are more prosecution-minded on a host of issues. For example, they are more concerned about crime, more trustful of police, more cynical about defense lawyers, and less tolerant of procedures that are designed to protect the accused (Fitzgerald & Ellsworth, 1984; Haney et al., 1994). When it comes to trial verdicts, the difference can be substantial. In one study, 288 people watched a videotaped murder trial and then participated in mock juries. The results showed that jurors who said they were willing to impose the death penalty were more likely to vote guilty both before and after deliberating than were those who would have been excluded for their refusal to impose a death sentence (Cowan et al., 1984).

Similar results have been found in studies of real jurors (Moran & Comfort, 1986). In fact, Haney (1984) found that hearing death-qualification voir dire questions

**death qualification** A jury-selection procedure used in capital cases that permits judges to exclude prospective jurors who say they would not vote for the death penalty.

themselves is biasing because these questions presume the defendant's guilt and communicate to prospective jurors that the courts consider death a desirable form of punishment. In his studies, even randomly selected mock jurors were more likely to vote for conviction—and for the death penalty—when exposed to such questions during the voir dire than when they were not.

As the research evidence mounted, American courts had to face a sobering prospect. Were hundreds of prisoners on death row tried by juries that were biased against them? In the case of *Lockhart v. McCree* (1986), the U.S. Supreme Court considered the issue. To help to inform the Court, the American Psychological Association submitted an exhaustive review of the literature (Bersoff & Ogden, 1987)—but to no avail. In an opinion that disappointed many social psychologists, the Court rejected the research and ruled that death qualification does not violate a defendant's right to a fair trial.

Should the Supreme Court have been persuaded by the research findings of social psychologists? Some say yes (Ellsworth, 1991); others say no (Elliott, 1991). Either way, it is now important to devise alternative, non-prejudicial methods that can be used to select capital juries. For example, research shows that many people who would be excluded because of a *general* opposition to capital punishment also admit that they would consider the death penalty for *specific* defendants found guilty of committing atrocious acts of violence—suggesting that perhaps these individuals should not be removed from the jury (Cox & Tanford, 1989). This issue continues to spark interest and concern among social psychologists (Costanzo, 1997). It is especially relevant these days, in light of sobering revelations brought about by DNA tests showing that many prisoners, including many on death row, did not commit the crimes for which they were convicted (Baumgartner et al., 2008).

Worldwide, the most common methods of execution are by hanging, shooting, and beheading. In the United States, the most commonly used methods are electrocution, lethal injection, and poisonous gas—as delivered in this gas chamber. For more information on the death penalty, such as up-to-date lists of death-row inmates, visit http://www.deathpenaltyinfo.org/home.

## The Courtroom Trial

Once a jury is selected, the trial officially begins and the evidence previously gathered comes to life. The evidence produced in the courtroom can range far and wide, from eyewitness testimony, informants, and confessions to DNA and other types of physical evidence, medical tests, handwriting samples, diaries, fingerprints, photographs, and business documents. The trial is a well-orchestrated event. Lawyers for both sides make opening statements. Witnesses then answer questions under oath. Lawyers make closing arguments. The judge instructs the jury. Yet there are many problems in this all-too-human enterprise: The evidence may not be accurate or reliable, jurors may harbor misconceptions or bias from extraneous factors, judges' instructions may fall on deaf ears, and the process of deliberation may cause some jurors to vote for a verdict that contradicts their beliefs. The social psychology of jury decision-making is involved and fascinating (see Bornstein & Greene, 2011; Lieberman & Krauss, 2009; Vidmar & Hans, 2007). In this section, we identify some of the problems and possible solutions.

Over the years, psychologists and other social scientists have sought to evaluate the competence of trial juries to reach accurate verdicts. In *The American Jury*, Henry Kalven and Hans Zeisel (1966) surveyed 550 judges who

"Ask the judge whether we can find the defendant not guilty and still execute him."

presided over 3,576 criminal jury trials nationwide. While each jury was deliberating, judges were asked to indicate what their verdict would be. A comparison of their responses to the actual jury verdicts revealed that judges and juries agreed on a verdict in 78% of all cases (in a separate study of civil cases, typically involving disputes over money, a 78% agreement rate was also observed). Among the 22% of cases in which there was a disagreement, it was because the jury voted to acquit a defendant that judges perceived to be guilty. This last result suggests that juries are more lenient than judges.

Are juries competent, objective, and accurate in their verdicts? There is no simple way to answer this question. As a general rule, research has shown that juries are sound decision makers, even in cases containing complex evidence, and that jury verdicts are based largely on the strength of the evidence presented at trial (Diamond & Rose, 2005; Eisenberg et al., 2005; Hans et al., 2011). Still, as we saw earlier, juries tend to accept eyewitness identifications and confessions—often without sufficient scrutiny or concern about the situations and ways in which these types of evidence were taken. To help inform juries in these cases, psychologists sometimes testify as expert witnesses (Cutler & Kovera, 2011).

**Nonevidentiary Influences**    A trial is a well-orchestrated event that follows strict rules of evidence and procedure. The goal is to ensure that juries base their verdicts solely on the evidence and testimony presented in court—not on rumors, newspaper stories, a defendant's physical appearance, and other information. The question is "To what extent is this goal achieved, and to what extent are jury verdicts tainted by non-evidentiary influences?" Before Amanda Knox was tried for murder in Perugia Italy, in 2007, newspapers and social media—not only in Italy, but in the United States, Great Britain, and elsewhere in the world—were saturated with stories about Knox, her past, her Italian boyfriend, her alleged confession, and witnesses who claimed to have seen her near the crime scene. By the time Knox went to trial, her jury had already been exposed to a good deal of information that was not in evidence.

Many high-profile cases find their way into newspapers and other mass media long before they appear in court. In these instances, the legal system struggles with this dilemma: Does exposure to pretrial news stories corrupt the pool of prospective jurors? Public opinion surveys consistently show that the more people know about a case, the more likely they are to presume the defendant guilty, even when they claim to be impartial (Kovera, 2002; Moran & Cutler, 1991). There is nothing mysterious about this result. The information in news reports usually comes from the police or district attorney's office, so it often reveals facts unfavorable to the defense. The question is whether these reports have an impact on juries that go on to hear evidence in court and deliberate to a verdict.

To examine the effects of pretrial publicity, Geoffrey Kramer and his colleagues (1990) played a videotaped reenactment of an armed robbery trial to hundreds of people participating in 108 mock juries. Before watching the tape, participants were exposed to news clippings about the case. Some read news material that was neutral. Others read information that was incriminating—for example, revealing that the defendant had a prior record or implicating the defendant in a hit-and-run accident in which a child was killed. Even though participants were instructed to base their decisions solely on the evidence, pretrial publicity had a marked effect. Among those exposed to neutral material, 33% voted guilty after deliberating in a jury. Among those exposed to the prejudicial material, that figure increased to 48%. What's worse, neither judges nor defense lawyers could identify in a simulated voir dire which jurors had been biased by the publicity. As shown in ● Figure 12.7, 48% of jurors who were questioned and perceived to be impartial—those who said they were unaffected—went on to vote guilty (Kerr et al., 1991).

Pretrial publicity is potentially dangerous in two respects. First, it often divulges information that is not later allowed into the trial record. Second is the matter of timing. Because many news stories precede the actual trial, jurors learn certain facts even before they enter the courtroom. From what is known about the power of first impressions, the implications are clear. If jurors receive prejudicial news information about a defendant before trial, that information will distort the way they interpret the facts of the case (Hope et al., 2004). In fact, an analysis of secretly recorded mock jury deliberations showed that exposure to pretrial publicity completely tainted their discussions of the defendant and evidence—despite the judge's warning to disregard that information (Ruva & LeVasseur, 2012). So, is there a solution? Since the biasing effects persist despite the practices of jury selection, the presentation of hard evidence, cautionary words from the judge, and open jury deliberations, justice may demand that highly publicized cases be postponed or their trials moved to less informed communities (Steblay et al., 1999; Studebaker & Penrod, 1997).

Is it possible that juries are influenced by pretrial publicity of a more general nature that is unrelated to their specific case? Perhaps you have watched the popular television drama *CSI* (which stands for "crime scene investigation"), and focuses on the process by which police investigators collect and analyze fingerprints, bodily fluids, and other types of forensic evidence (the original is set in Las Vegas; spin-offs were later set in Miami and New York). Many legal commentators are speculating that the public's exposure to this show is influencing jury verdicts; they call it the "CSI effect." The fear is that the television programs lead jurors to have unrealistically high expectations that cause them to vote cautiously for acquittal because they find the actual evidence insufficient to support a guilty verdict. If true, then the CSI effect would represent a special type of pretrial publicity potentially influencing an entire population of juries. Tom Tyler (2006a) is quick to note, however, that although the hypothesis is plausible, there is at present no hard evidence to support it. Just as jurors are biased by news stories, they occasionally receive extralegal information within the body of the trial itself. If a witness discloses hearsay that is not considered reliable, or blurts out something about the defendant's past that the courts consider prejudicial—in either case, information the jury is not supposed to hear—then what? What happens next, typically, is that the opposing lawyer will object and the judge will sustain the objection and instruct the jury to disregard the disclosure.

If something seems wrong with this series of events, you should know that it is a script often replayed in the courtroom. But can people really strike information from

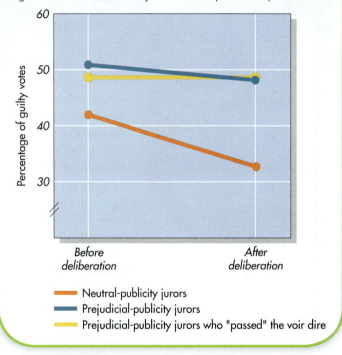

● **FIGURE 12.7**

**Contaminating Effects of Pretrial Publicity**

In this study, participants were exposed to prejudicial or neutral news reports about a defendant, watched a videotaped trial, and voted before and after participating in a mock jury deliberation. As shown, pretrial publicity increased the conviction rate both before and after deliberation, even among participants perceived to be impartial by judges and lawyers.

From Kerr, M. I., Kramer, G. P., Carroll, J. S., and Alfinin, J. J., "On the effectiveness of voir dire in criminal cases with prejudicial pretrial publicity: An empirical study," *American University Law Review* vol 40 (pp. 665–701). Copyright © 1982 American University Law Review. Reprinted with permission.

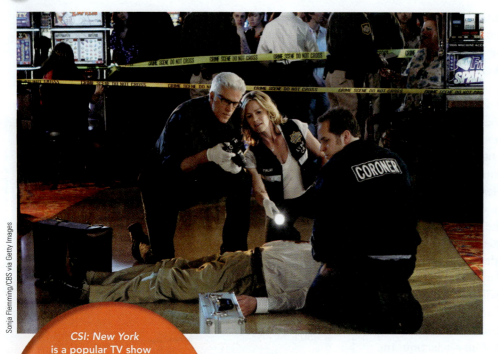

Sonja Flemming/CBS via Getty Images

*CSI: New York* is a popular TV show about police investigators who use science to analyze evidence. Does this show and others like it lead jurors to set unrealistically high expectations for evidence, causing them to acquit criminals? At least for now, there is no evidence to support this "CSI effect" hypothesis.

their minds the way court reporters can strike it from the record? Can people on a jury resist the forbidden fruit of inadmissible testimony? Although common sense suggests they cannot, the research is mixed. In one study, a group of mock jurors read about a murder case based on evidence so weak that not a single juror voted guilty. A second group read the same case, except that the prosecution introduced an illegally obtained tape recording of a phone call made by the defendant: "I finally got the money to pay you off. . . . When you read the papers tomorrow, you'll know what I mean." The defense argued that the illegal tape should not be admissible but the judge disagreed. At this point, the conviction rate increased to 26%. In a third group, as in the second, the tape was brought in and the defense objected. Yet this time, the judge sustained the objection and told jurors to disregard the tape. The result: 35% voted for conviction (Sue et al., 1973). Other studies as well have revealed that jurors are often not deterred by "limiting instructions" (Steblay et al., 2006).

Why do people not follow a judge's order to disregard inadmissible evidence? There are several possible explanations (Lieberman & Arndt, 2000). Imagine yourself in the jury box, and three reasons will become apparent. First, the added instruction draws attention to the information in controversy. It's like being told not to think about white bears. As we saw in Chapter 3, trying to suppress a specific thought increases its tendency to intrude upon our consciousness (Wegner, 1994). A second reason is that a judge's instruction to disregard, much like censorship, restricts a juror's decision-making freedom. As a result, it can backfire by arousing reactance. So, when a judge emphasizes the ruling by *forbidding* jurors from using the information ("You have no choice but to disregard it"), they become even *more* likely to use it (Wolf & Montgomery, 1977). The third reason is the easiest to understand. Jurors want to reach the right decision. If they stumble onto relevant information, they want to use that information whether it satisfies the law's technical rules or not.

To test this third hypothesis, Kassin and Sommers (1997) had mock jurors read a transcript of a double murder trial that was based on weak evidence, leading only 24% to vote guilty. Three other groups read the same case except that the state's evidence included a wiretapped phone conversation in which the defendant confessed to a friend. In all cases, the defense lawyer objected to the disclosure. When the judge ruled to admit the tape into evidence, the conviction rate increased considerably, to 79%. But when the judge excluded the tape and instructed jurors to disregard it, their reaction depended on the reason the tape was excluded. When told to disregard the tape because it was barely audible and could not be trusted, participants mentally erased the information, as they should, and delivered the same 24% conviction rate as in the no-tape control group. But when told to disregard the item because it had been illegally obtained, 55% voted guilty. Despite the judge's warning, these latter participants were unwilling to ignore testimony they saw as highly relevant merely because of a legal technicality.

Additional studies indicate that jurors in this situation may comply with a judge's instruction to disregard when the technicality involves a *serious* violation of the defendant's rights (Fleming et al., 1999) and that the process of deliberation increases compliance, which minimizes the bias (London & Nunez, 2000).

**The Judge's Instructions**    One of the most important rituals in any trial is the judge's instructions to the jury. It is through these instructions that juries are educated about relevant legal concepts, informed of the verdict options, admonished to disregard extralegal factors, and advised on how to conduct their deliberations. To make verdicts adhere to the law, juries are supposed to comply with these instructions. The task seems simple enough, but there are problems.

To begin with, the jury's intellectual competence has been called into question. For years, the courts have doubted whether jurors understood their instructions. One skeptical judge put it bluntly when he said that "these words may as well be spoken in a foreign language" (Frank, 1949, p. 181). He may have been right. When actual instructions are tested with community mock jurors, the results reveal high levels of misunderstanding—a serious problem in light of the fact that jurors seem to have many preconceptions about crimes and the requirements of the law.

Comprehensibility is even problematic when it comes to death penalty instructions that are required in capital cases (Wiener et al., 1995) and for college students as well as ordinary jurors from the community (Rose & Ogloff, 2001). There is, however, reason for hope. Research has shown that when conventional instructions—which are poorly structured, esoteric, and filled with complex legal terms—are rewritten in plain English, comprehension rates increase markedly (Elwork et al., 1982; English & Sales, 1997). Supplementing a judge's instructions with flow charts, computer animations, and other audiovisual aids is also effective (Brewer et al., 2004).

In this Detroit courtroom, Dr. Jack Kevorkian was tried for an assisted suicide. Although physician-assisted suicide is illegal in Michigan, the jury in this case "nullified" the law in favor of its own conceptions of justice and voted not guilty. However, Kevorkian was eventually convicted and sent to prison.

A lack of comprehension is one reason that a judge's instruction may have little impact. But there's a second reason: Sometimes juries disagree with the law, thus raising the controversial issue of **jury nullification**. Because juries deliberate in private, they can choose to disregard, or "nullify," the judge's instructions. The pages of history are filled with poignant examples. Consider the case of someone tried for euthanasia, or "mercy killing." By law, it is murder. But to the defendant, it might be a noble act on behalf of a loved one. Faced with this kind of conflict—an explosive moral issue on which public opinion is sharply divided—juries often evaluate the issue in human terms, use their own notions of common-sense justice, and vote despite the law for acquittal (Finkel, 1995; Horowitz & Willging, 1991; Niedermeier et al., 1999). This nullification tendency is particularly likely to occur when jurors who disagree with the law are told of their right to nullify it (Meissner et al., 2003). In these instances, research suggests the possibility that a nullification instruction may unleash a form of "chaos," liberating jurors to follow their emotions in an emotionally charged case (Horowitz et al., 2006).

**jury nullification**    The jury's power to disregard, or "nullify," the law when it conflicts with personal conceptions of justice.

Jury nullification is what happened in cases pertaining to physician-assisted suicide, as was practiced by the late Jack Kevorkian, a pathologist. During the 1990s, Kevorkian presided over 130 deaths. For three of these incidents, he was tried for murder and the juries, sympathetic to his plight, practiced nullification and acquitted him. Then he injected a terminally ill man with a lethal dose of drugs, videotaped the death, gave the tape to CBS News, and again challenged authorities to take him to court. They did, and in 1999, after having defied the law in the boldest of ways, Kevorkian was found guilty. He was Prisoner #284797 in a Michigan state prison until he was released on parole in June 2007. He died 4 years later at the age of 83.

## Jury Deliberation

Anyone who has seen the original 1957 movie *Twelve Angry Men* can appreciate how colorful and passionate a jury's deliberation can be. This film classic opens with a jury eager to convict a young man of murder—no ifs, ands, or buts. The group selects a foreperson and takes a show-of-hands vote. The result is an 11-to-1 majority, with actor Henry Fonda the lone dissenter. After many tense moments, Fonda manages to convert his peers, and the jury votes unanimously for acquittal.

It is often said that the unique power of the jury stems from the wisdom that emerges when individuals come together privately as one *group*. Is this assumption justified? *Twelve Angry Men* is a work of fiction, but does it realistically portray what transpires in the jury room? And in what ways does the legal system influence the group dynamics? By interviewing jurors after trials and by recruiting people to participate on mock juries and then recording their deliberations, researchers have learned a great deal about how juries make their decisions.

**Leadership in the Jury Room**   In theory, all jurors are created equal. In practice, however, dominance hierarchies tend to develop. As in other decision-making groups, a handful of individuals lead the discussion while others join in at a lower rate or watch from the sidelines, speaking only to cast their votes (Hastie et al., 1983).

It's almost as if there is a jury within the jury. The question is, what kinds of people emerge as leaders?

It is often assumed that the foreperson is the leader. The foreperson, after all, calls for votes, acts as a liaison between the judge and jury, and announces the verdict in court. It seems like a position of importance, yet the selection process is very quick and casual. It's interesting that foreperson selection outcomes do follow a predictable pattern (Stasser et al., 1982). People of higher occupational status or with prior experience on a jury are frequently chosen. Interestingly too, the first person who speaks is often chosen to be the foreperson (Strodtbeck et al., 1957). And when jurors deliberate around a rectangular table, those who sit at the heads of the table are more likely to be chosen than are those seated in the middle (Bray et al., 1978; Strodtbeck & Hook, 1961).

In the classic movie *Twelve Angry Men*, Henry Fonda plays a lone juror who single-handedly converts his 11 guilty-voting peers to vote for acquittal. Sometimes life imitates art; in this case, it does not. Research shows that majorities on the first jury vote usually prevail in the final verdict.

The Everett Collection

If you find such inequalities bothersome, fear not: Forepersons may act as nominal leaders, but they do not exert more than their fair share of influence over the group. In fact, although they spend more time than other jurors talking about procedural matters, they spend less time expressing opinions about the verdict (Hastie et al., 1983). Thus, it may be most accurate to think of the foreperson not as the jury's leader but as its moderator. In *Twelve Angry Men*, actor Martin Balsam—not Henry Fonda—was the foreperson. He was also among the least influential members of the jury.

**The Dynamics of Deliberation**  If the walls of the jury room could talk, they would tell us that the decision-making process typically passes through three stages (Hastie et al., 1983; Stasser et al., 1982). Like other problem-solving groups, juries begin in a relaxed *orientation* period during which they set an agenda, talk in open-ended terms, raise questions, and explore the facts. Then, once differences of opinion are revealed (usually after the first vote is taken), factions develop and the group shifts abruptly into a period of *open conflict*. With the battle lines sharply drawn, discussion takes on a more focused, argumentative tone. Together, jurors scrutinize the evidence, construct stories to account for that evidence, and discuss the judge's instructions (Pennington & Hastie, 1992). If all jurors agree, they return a verdict. If not, the majority tries to achieve a consensus by converting the holdouts through information and social pressure. If unanimity is achieved, the group enters a period of *reconciliation*, during which it smoothes over the conflicts and affirms its satisfaction with the outcome. If the holdouts continue to disagree, the jury declares itself hung. This process is diagrammed in ● Figure 12.8.

When it comes to decision-making *outcomes*, deliberations follow a predictable course first discovered by Kalven and Zeisel (1966). By interviewing the members of 225 juries, they were able to reconstruct how these juries split on their very first vote. Out of 215 juries that opened with an initial majority, 209 reached a final verdict consistent with that first vote. This finding—which was later bolstered by the results of mock jury studies (Kerr, 1981; Stasser & Davis, 1981; see Table 12.5)—led Kalven and Zeisel (1966) to conclude that "the deliberation process might well be likened to what the developer does for an exposed film; it brings out the picture, but the outcome is predetermined" (p. 489). Setting aside Henry Fonda's *Twelve Angry Men* heroics, one can usually predict the final verdict by knowing where the individual jurors stand the first time they vote. Juries are not generally more or less subject to bias than the individuals who constitute the groups (Kerr et al., 1999). Hence, "majority rules" seems to describe what happens not only in juries but in most other small decision-making groups (Hastie & Kameda, 2005).

There is one exception to this majority-wins rule in the jury room. In criminal trials, deliberation tends to produce a **leniency bias** that favors the defendant. All other factors being equal, individual jurors are more likely to vote guilty on their own than they are in a group; they are also more prone to convict before deliberations than they

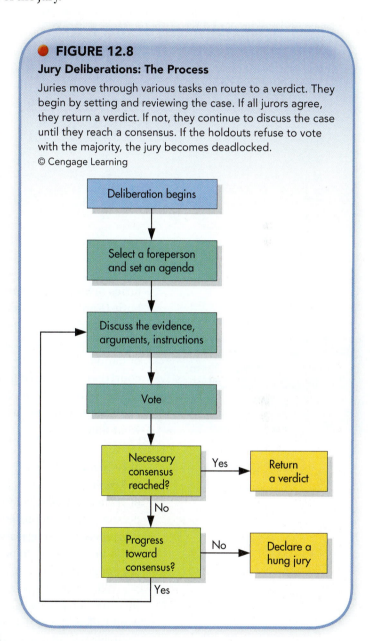

● **FIGURE 12.8**

**Jury Deliberations: The Process**

Juries move through various tasks en route to a verdict. They begin by setting and reviewing the case. If all jurors agree, they return a verdict. If not, they continue to discuss the case until they reach a consensus. If the holdouts refuse to vote with the majority, the jury becomes deadlocked.

© Cengage Learning

**leniency bias**  The tendency for jury deliberation to produce a tilt toward acquittal.

**TABLE 12.5**

**The Road to Agreement: From Individual Votes to a Group Verdict**

Research has shown how verdicts are reached by mock juries that begin with different combinations of initial votes. You can see that the results support the majority-wins rule. But also note the evidence for a leniency bias: When the initial vote is split, juries gravitate toward acquittal (Kerr, 1981, as cited in Stasser et al., 1982).

| Initial Votes (Guilty–Not Guilty) | Final Jury Verdicts (%) | | |
|---|---|---|---|
| | Conviction | Acquittal | Hung |
| 6–0 | 100 | 0 | 0 |
| 5–1 | 78 | 7 | 16 |
| 4–2 | 44 | 26 | 30 |
| 3–3 | 9 | 51 | 40 |
| 2–4 | 4 | 79 | 17 |
| 1–5 | 0 | 93 | 7 |
| 0–6 | 0 | 100 | 0 |

© Cengage Learning

One can usually predict a jury's final verdict by knowing where the individual jurors stand the first time they vote. **T**RUE.

are afterward (MacCoun & Kerr, 1988). Look again at Table 12.5, and you'll see that juries that are equally divided in their initial vote are ultimately likely to return not-guilty verdicts. Perhaps it is easier to raise a "reasonable doubt" in other people's minds than it is to erase all doubt. In this regard, it is interesting to note that in their classic study, as described earlier, Kalven and Zeisel found that juries are more lenient than their judges would have been. Perhaps this disagreement is due, in part, to the fact that juries decide as groups and judges decide as individuals.

Knowing that the majority tends to prevail doesn't tell us how juries manage to resolve disagreements en route to a verdict. From the conformity studies discussed in Chapter 7, we know that there are two possibilities. Sometimes people conform because through a process of *informational influence* they are genuinely persuaded by what others say. At other times, people yield to the pressures of *normative influence* by changing their overt behavior in the majority's direction even though they disagree in private. Justice demands that juries reach a consensus through a vigorous exchange of views and information, not as the result of heavy-handed social pressure. But is that how it works? Research shows that juries achieve unanimity not by one process or the other but by a combination of both (Kaplan & Schersching, 1981). Research also shows that certain factors can upset the delicate balance between informational and normative influences. Social pressure is increased, for example, in juries that vote by a public roll call or show of hands (Davis et al., 1989) and in deadlocked juries that are called back into the courtroom and urged by the judge to resolve their differences (Smith & Kassin, 1993).

Over the years, the U.S. Supreme Court has addressed the decision-making dynamics of the jury in two ways. In the following pages, we look at these important issues and what they mean.

**Jury Size: How Small Is Too Small?**    How many people does it take to form a jury? In keeping with British tradition, twelve has been the magic number. Then, in the case of *Williams v. Florida* (1970), the defendant was convicted of armed robbery by a six-person jury. He appealed the verdict to the U.S. Supreme Court but lost. As a result of this precedent, American courts are now permitted to cut trial costs by using six-person juries in cases that do not involve the death penalty. Juries consisting of fewer than six are not permitted (*Ballew v. Georgia*, 1978).

What is the impact of moving from twelve to six? The Supreme Court approached this question as a social psychologist would. It sought to determine whether the change would affect the decision-making process. Unfortunately, the Court misinterpreted the available research so badly that Michael Saks (1974) concluded that it "would not win a passing grade in a high school psychology class" (p. 18). Consider whether a reduction in size affects the ability of those in the voting minority to resist normative pressures. The Supreme Court did not think it would. Citing Asch's (1956) conformity studies, the Court argued that an individual juror's resistance depends on the *proportional* size of the majority. But is that true? Is the lone dissenter caught in a 5-to-1 bind as well insulated from the group norm as the minority in a 10-to-2 split? The Court argued that these 83%-to-17% divisions are psychologically identical. But wait. Asch's research showed exactly the opposite—that the mere presence of a single ally enables dissenters to keep their independence better than anything else.

Research has shown that the size of a jury has other effects too. Michael Saks and Molli Marti (1997) conducted a meta-analysis of studies involving 15,000 mock jurors who deliberated in over 2,000 six-person or twelve-person juries. Overall, they found that the smaller juries were less likely to represent minority segments of the population. They were also more likely to reach a unanimous verdict and to do so while deliberating for shorter periods of time. Even in civil trials, in which juries have to make complex decisions on how much money to award the plaintiff, six-person groups spend less time discussing the case (Davis et al., 1997).

**Less-Than-Unanimous Verdicts**   The jury's size is not all that has changed. In 1972, the Supreme Court considered whether states may accept jury verdicts that are not unanimous. In one opinion, two defendants had been convicted by jury verdicts that were not unanimous—one by a vote of 11 to 1, the other by 10 to 2 (*Apodaca v. Oregon*, 1972). In a second opinion, a guilty verdict was determined by a 9-to-3 margin (*Johnson v. Louisiana*, 1972). In both decisions, the Supreme Court upheld the convictions.

The Court was divided in its view of these cases. Five justices argued that a rule allowing verdicts that are not unanimous would not adversely affect the jury; four justices believed that it would reduce the intensity of deliberations and undermine the potential for minority influence. Table 12.6 presents these dueling points of view. Which do you find more convincing? Imagine yourself on a jury that needs only a 9-to-3 majority to return a verdict. You begin by polling the group and find that you already have the nine votes needed. What next? According to one script, the group continues to argue vigorously and with open minds. According to the alternative scenario, the group begins to deliberate but the dissenters are quickly cast aside because their votes are not needed. Again, which scenario seems more realistic?

To answer that question, Reid Hastie and others (1983) recruited more than 800 people from the Boston area to take part in 69 mock juries. After watching a reenactment of a murder trial, the groups were instructed to reach a verdict by a 12-to-0, a 10-to-2, or an 8-to-4 margin. The differences were striking. Compared with juries that needed unanimous decisions, the others spent less time discussing the case and more time voting. After reaching the required number of votes, they often rejected the holdouts, terminated discussion, and returned a verdict. Afterward, participants in the non-unanimous juries rated their peers as more close-minded and themselves as less informed and less confident about the verdict. What's worse, Hastie's team saw in tapes of the deliberations that majority-rule juries often adopted "a more forceful, bullying, persuasive style" (1983, p. 112). After being

---

**TABLE 12.6**

### *Johnson v. Louisiana* (1972): Contrasting Views

"Notice the contrasting views in the U.S. Supreme Court's decision to permit jury verdicts that are not unanimous. Justice White wrote the majority opinion and Justice Douglas wrote the dissent. The decision was reached by a vote of 5 to 4."

#### *Mr. Justice White, for the Majority*

"We have no grounds for believing that majority jurors, aware of their responsibility and power over the liberty of the defendant, would simply refuse to listen to arguments presented to them in favor of acquittal, terminate discussion, and render a verdict. On the contrary, it is far more likely that a juror presenting reasoned argument in favor of acquittal could either have his arguments answered or would carry enough other jurors with him to prevent conviction. A majority will cease discussion and outvote a minority only after reasoned discussion has ceased to have persuasive effect or to serve any other purpose—when a minority, that is, continues to insist upon acquittal without having persuasive reasons in support of its position."

#### *Mr. Justice Douglas, for the Minority*

"Non-unanimous juries need not debate and deliberate as fully as most unanimous juries. As soon as the requisite majority is attained, further consideration is not required either by Oregon or by Louisiana even though the dissident jurors might, if given the chance, be able to convince the majority. . . . The collective effort to piece together the puzzle of historical truth . . . is cut short as soon as the requisite majority is reached in Oregon and Louisiana. . . . It is said that there is no evidence that majority jurors will refuse to listen to dissenters whose votes are unneeded for conviction. Yet human experience teaches us that polite and academic conversation is no substitute for the earnest and robust argument necessary to reach unanimity."

© Cengage Learning

permitted to videotape 50 non-unanimous civil juries in Arizona, Shari Diamond and colleagues (2006) similarly observed that thoughtful minorities were sometimes "marginalized" by majorities that had the power to ignore them.

Today, only two states permit less-than-unanimous verdicts in criminal trials. A substantial number do so for civil cases. Yet research has shown that this procedure weakens jurors who are in the voting minority, breeds close-mindedness, short-circuits the discussion, and leaves many jurors uncertain about the decision. Henry Fonda, step aside. The jury has reached its verdict.

# Posttrial: To Prison and Beyond

In Italy, Amanda Knox and her boyfriend were sentenced to 26 and 25 years, respectively, in prison after they were convicted of the murder for which they was ultimately found innocent. In contrast, Rudy Guede—the perpetrator who fled Italy and whose fingerprints, shoe prints, and DNA littered the crime scene—was sentenced to 30 years, but that sentence was reduced to 16 years after he implicated Knox and apologized for his role in the crime. As this case illustrates, sentencing decisions are human judgments of great consequence. The question is "What influences these judgments?"

##  The Sentencing Process

Defendants who are found not guilty are free to go home. For those convicted of crimes, however, the jury's verdict is followed by a second decision to determine the nature and extent of their punishment. Sentencing decisions are usually made by judges, not juries, and they are often controversial. One reason for the controversy is that many people see judges as being too lenient (Stalans & Diamond, 1990). Another is that people disagree on the goals served by imprisonment. For many judges, the goal of a prison sentence is practical: to incapacitate offenders and deter them from committing future crimes. For many citizens, however, there is a more powerful motive at work: to exact retribution, or revenge, against the offender for his or her misdeeds. Research shows that people are driven by this "just deserts" motive, recommending sentences of increasing harshness for crimes of increasing severity, regardless of whether the offender is seen as likely to strike again and regardless of whether such sentences deter crime or serve other useful purposes (Carlsmith et al., 2002; Carlsmith, 2006; Darley et al., 2000; Darley & Pittman, 2003). Interestingly, research also shows that although people think that "sweet revenge" against someone who exploited them will make them feel better, sometimes it has the opposite effect (Carlsmith et al., 2008).

*In 2011, the U.S. Department of Justice's Bureau of Justice Statistics reported that the number of American adults incarcerated in jail or prison was at 2.27 million.*

Judges also disagree about issues related to sentencing. Thus, a recurring public complaint is that there is too much **sentencing disparity**—that punishments for crime are inconsistent from one judge to the next. To document the problem, Anthony Partridge and William Eldridge (1974) compiled identical sets of files from 20 actual cases and sent them to 50 federal judges for sentencing recommendations. They found major disparities in the sentences the judges said they would impose. In one case, for example, judges had read about a man who was convicted of extortion and tax evasion. One judge recommended a three-year prison sentence, while another recommended 20 years in prison and a fine of $65,000. It's hard to believe these two judges read the same case. But other studies have uncovered similar differences.

**sentencing disparity** Inconsistency of sentences for the same offense from one judge to another.

Some judges are unusually creative in their sentencing of convicted felons. For example, a judge in Houston ordered a piano teacher who molested two students to donate his piano to a local school, a South Dakota judge sentenced cattle rustlers to shovel manure for a week, and a Florida judge ordered drunk drivers to display a bumper sticker on their cars that said "Convicted DUI" (Greene et al., 2007). In recent years, the federal government and many state governments have created sentencing guidelines to minimize the disparities and bring greater consistency into the process (Ruback & Wroblewski, 2001).

Still, sentencing decisions can be influenced by irrelevant factors. For example, Birte Englich and others (2006) theorized that judges would be influenced by the well-known "anchoring effect"—the tendency to use one stimulus as an "anchor," or reference point, in judging a second stimulus (Tversky & Kahneman, 1974). In a series of studies conducted in Germany, these researchers presented legal professionals—mostly judges—with materials about a criminal case. All participants received the same file except that some files suggested a low sentencing number (one year) and others suggested a high number (3 years). Regardless of whether the number was presented as a prosecutor's recommendation, a question from a journalist, or a random roll of the dice, those first exposed to the high anchor point assigned harsher sentences than those exposed to the lower anchor point.

Some influences on this human decision-making process are even more disturbing. By combing through U.S. death penalty statistics, researchers long ago discovered that sentencing decisions are consistently biased by race: All else being equal, convicted murderers are more likely to be sentenced to death if they are black or if the victim is white (Baldus et al., 1990). Informed by the racial stereotyping studies we saw in Chapter 5, Jennifer Eberhardt and her colleagues (2006) revisited a number of capital cases involving black defendants, this time looking for an even more subtle effect. For each case, they obtained a photograph of the defendant and had college students rate the degree to which he had a stereotypically black appearance—for example, a broad nose, thick lips, and dark skin. Using these ratings, they found that when the victim was black, the defendant's appearance was unrelated to sentencing. When the victim was white, however, the death penalty odds were predictable by the blackness of the defendant's appearance (24% among the least stereotypical; 58% among the most stereotypical). It seems that there are shades of black that influence whether judges and juries perceive defendants to be "deathworthy."

## > The Prison Experience

It is no secret that the prison population in the United States has grown over the years, that many prisons are overcrowded, and that the situation has worsened as a result of recently toughened sentencing guidelines. It is also no secret that prison life can be cruel, violent, and degrading. The setting is highly oppressive and regimented, many prison guards are abusive, and many inmates fall into a state of despair (Paulus, 1988). Indeed, many are psychologically disturbed and in need of treatment they do not receive (Kupers, 1999). Clearly, prisoners are not representative of the population as a whole. Still it is natural for social psychologists to wonder: Is there something about the prison *situation* that leads guards and prisoners to behave as they do? Would the rest of us react in the same way?

For ethical reasons, one obviously cannot place research participants inside a real prison. So, many years ago, a team of researchers from Stanford University did the next best thing: They constructed a simulated prison in the basement of the psychology department building (Haney et al., 1973; Haney & Zimbardo, 1998; Zimbardo et al.,

1973). Complete with iron-barred cells, a solitary-confinement closet, and a recreation area for guards, the facility housed 21 participants—all healthy and stable men between the ages of 17 and 30 who had answered a newspaper ad promising $15 a day for a 2-week study of prison life. By the flip of a coin, half the participants were designated as guards and the other half became prisoners. Neither group was told specifically how to fulfill its role.

On the first day, each of the participant prisoners was unexpectedly "arrested" at his home, booked, fingerprinted, and driven to the simulated prison by officers of the local police department. These prisoners were then stripped, searched, and dressed in loose-fitting smocks with an identification number, a nylon stocking to cover their hair, and rubber sandals. A chain was bolted to the ankle of each prisoner. The guards were dressed in khaki uniforms and supplied with nightsticks, handcuffs, reflector sunglasses, keys, and whistles. The rules specified that prisoners were to be called by number, routinely lined up to be counted, fed three bland meals, and permitted three supervised toilet visits per day. The stage was set. It remained to be seen just how seriously the participants would take their roles and react to one another in this novel setting.

The events of the next few days were startling. Filled with a sense of power and authority, a few guards became progressively more abusive. They harassed the inmates, forced them into crowded cells, woke them during the night, and subjected them to hard labor and solitary confinement. These guards were particularly cruel when they thought they were alone with a prisoner. The prisoners themselves were rebellious at first, but their efforts were met with retaliation. Soon they all became passive and demoralized. After 36 hours, the experimenters had to release their first prisoner, who was suffering from acute depression. On subsequent days, other prisoners had to be released. By the sixth day, those who remained were so shaken by the experience that the study was terminated. It is reassuring, if not remarkable, that after a series of debriefing sessions, participants seemed to show no signs of lasting distress.

This study was instantly criticized on methodological and ethical grounds (Banuazizi & Movahedi, 1975; Savin, 1973). Still, the results are fascinating. Within a brief period of time, under relatively mild conditions, and with a group of men not prone to violence, the Stanford study recreated some of the prisoner and guard behaviors actually found behind prison walls. But would this occur today, in the twenty-first century? To find out, social psychologists Steve Reicher and Alex Haslam (2006) worked in the spring of 2002 with the British Broadcasting Corporation, or BBC, to create a survivor-like reality TV special called *The Experiment*, modeled after Zimbardo's study. Shown in four episodes, the television special brought together 15 men, all of whom were carefully screened, were warned that they would be exposed to hardships, and were randomly assigned to prisoner and guard roles. Determined to set limits, monitor events closely, and adhere to ethical guidelines for research with human subjects, Haslam and Reicher did not fully recreate the conditions of the original study and did not observe the same kinds of brutality from the guards. In their view, these findings challenge the conclusion that normal people can be dehumanized by the mere assignment to institutional roles. They also note that while the Stanford Prison study demonstrated oppression and abuse of power, it also provided a glimpse into how members of low-status groups can form a shared identity—which provides a basis for the social psychology of resistance (Haslam & Reicher, 2012).

One other profound question has arisen concerning the Stanford prison study, the same question that is often raised about Milgram's obedience experiments: Did the behavior of guards reflect on the power of the situation they were in or were the men who took part in the study uniquely prone to violence? Seeking an answer to this

P. G. Zimbardo, Inc. Stanford, CA

P. G. Zimbardo, Inc. Stanford, CA

P. G. Zimbardo, Inc. Stanford, CA

In this simulation study of prison behavior, subjects were arbitrarily assigned to be prisoners or guards. Local police officers arrested the prisoners, who were brought to a jail constructed at Stanford University. After several days, the guards took on cruel, authoritarian roles that demoralized the prisoners to such an extent that the experiment was terminated.

question, Thomas Carnahan and Sam McFarland (2007) posted two newspaper ads—one, like Zimbardo's, for a study on prison life; the other, identical in every way except that it omitted the words "prison life." Those who volunteered for the prison study scored higher on tests that measure aggressiveness, authoritarianism, and narcissism and lower on tests that measure empathy and altruism. Reflecting on the differences, these researchers suggested that perhaps the Stanford prison study had attracted individuals who were prone to antisocial behavior. In response, Haney and Zimbardo (2009) note that volunteers in the original study were also tested and that no personality differences were found between them and the general population. More importantly, they note, no differences were found between those assigned to prisoner and guard roles within the experiment.

Reiterating his belief in the power of the situation, Zimbardo (2007) points to the striking parallels between the behaviors observed in his simulated prison and the sadistic abuses of real prisoners in 2004, more than 30 years later, by military guards at the Abu Ghraib Prison in Iraq. Noting that various social psychological factors create a "perfect storm" that leads good people to behave in evil ways, Zimbardo refers to this unfortunate transformation as the "Lucifer Effect," named after God's favorite angel, Lucifer, who fell from grace and ultimately became Satan.

# Perceptions of Justice

People tend to measure the success of a legal system by its ability to produce fair and accurate results. But is that all there is to justice? Let's step back for a moment from the specifics and ask if it is possible to define justice in a way that is unrelated to outcomes.

## Justice as a Matter of Procedure

In a book entitled *Procedural Justice* (1975), John Thibaut and Laurens Walker proposed that our satisfaction with the way legal and other disputes are resolved depends not only on outcomes but also on the procedures used to achieve those outcomes. Two aspects of procedure are important in this regard: One is *decision control*—whether a procedure affords the involved parties the power to accept, reject, or otherwise influence the final decision. The other is *process control*—whether it offers the parties an opportunity to present their case to a third-party decision maker. In the courtroom, of course, the disputants are limited in their decision control. Thus, their satisfaction must depend on whether they feel that they had a chance to express their views.

There are two ways to look at the effects of process control on perceptions of justice. Originally, it was thought that people want an opportunity to express their opinions only because having a voice in the process improves the odds of achieving a favorable ruling. In this view, process control is satisfying only because it increases decision control (Thibaut & Walker, 1978). However, research suggests that people value the chance to present their side of a story to an impartial decision maker even when they do not prevail in the ultimate outcome. In other words, process control is more than just an instrumental means to an end. When people believe that they have a voice in the proceedings, are treated with respect, and are judged by an impartial decision maker, process control can be an end in itself (Lind et al., 1990).

This aspect of the legal system is important because it makes the system appear fair and legitimate and foster cooperation—which is why many social psychologists study people's perceptions of justice (Tornblom & Vermunt, 2007; Tyler, 2011). It means, for example, that regardless of whether people agree or disagree with how a case turns out, they can find solace in the fact that both sides had their "day in court," at least when the decision maker is seen as impartial. Yet certain members of the legal community are openly critical of that so-called day in court. As law professor Alan Dershowitz once put it, "Nobody really wants justice. Winning is the only thing to most participants in the criminal justice system, just as it is to professional athletes" (1982, p. xvi).

Dershowitz's skepticism is centered on something that many of us take for granted: the **adversarial model** of justice. In the adversarial system (as practiced in North America, Great Britain, and a handful of other countries), the prosecution and defense oppose each other, each presenting one side of the story in an effort to win a favorable verdict. In contrast, most other countries use an **inquisitorial model**, in which a neutral investigator gathers the evidence from both sides and presents the findings in court. With two such different methods of doing justice, social psychologists could not resist the temptation to make comparisons (van Koppen & Penrod, 2003).

Interested in which approach people prefer, Laurens Walker and others (1974) constructed a business simulation in which two companies competed for a cash prize. Participants who were assigned to the role of president of a company learned that someone on their staff was accused of spying on the competition. To resolve the dispute, a "trial"

**adversarial model**  A dispute–resolution system in which the prosecution and defense present opposing sides of the story.

**inquisitorial model**  A dispute–resolution system in which a neutral investigator gathers evidence from both sides and presents the findings in court.

was held. In some cases, the trial followed an adversarial procedure in which the two sides were presented by law students who were chosen by participants and whose payment was contingent on winning. Other cases followed an inquisitorial model in which a single law student who was appointed by the experimenter and paid regardless of the outcome presented both sides. Regardless of whether they had won or lost the verdict, participants who took part in an adversarial trial were more satisfied than those involved in an inquisitorial trial. Even impartial observers preferred the adversarial proceedings.

Other researchers found similar results, not only in the United States and Great Britain, where citizens are accustomed to the adversarial system, but in France and West Germany as well (Lind et al., 1978). This perception of procedural justice is not limited to adversarial methods of resolving legal disputes. Rather, it seems that any method that offers participants a *voice* in the proceedings, including methods that are nonadversarial, is seen as most fair and just—not only in law, but also in business, politics, school settings, and intimate relationships (Folger & Greenberg, 1985; Sheppard, 1985). It is also important in this regard for people to perceive that they were granted as much "voice" as others were (Van Prooijen et al., 2006) and that the decision maker was open-minded and not acting out of self-interest (De Cremer, 2004). In matters of justice, people all over the world are motivated not only by the desire for personal gain but by their need to be recognized, respected, and treated fairly by others who are impartial. Research thus shows that for people to accept the rule of law and comply with outcomes they do not like, they must see the decision-making procedures as fair (Tyler, 2006b).

## Culture, Law, and Justice

When it comes to the basics of human behavior, much of the research in this chapter can be universally applied. In eyewitness testimony, the problems and limitations of human memory—as seen in our ability to accurately encode, store, and retrieve certain types of information—are universal. In police interviews and interrogations, suspects all over the world, including some who are innocent, are more likely to confess when they are isolated and intensely pressured than when they are not. In courtrooms wherever juries are used, their decision making will invariably reflect the joint influences of their personal dispositions, the information they receive in court, and the conformity dynamics that seize hold of small groups. Finally, recurring stories of prison abuses have shown that prison is a social setting that tends to bring out the worst in guards and their prisoners—wherever they are.

Although the similarities are clear, they should not mask important cross-cultural differences. Because cultures have different norms, customs, and values, they also create different laws to regulate their citizens' behavior. To be sure, certain universal values have evolved among humans and are passed from one generation to the next, such as prohibitions against physical violence, taking someone's property without consent, and deception in important transactions. In other ways, however, the world's cultural and religious groups differ markedly in the behaviors they scorn and seek to regulate. In some countries but not in others, it is against the law to have sex outside of marriage, take more than one husband or wife, assist in a suicide, gamble, eat meat, or drink alcohol. Based on the belief in an afterlife, some religions prohibit autopsies. Others impose strict dress codes, particularly for women.

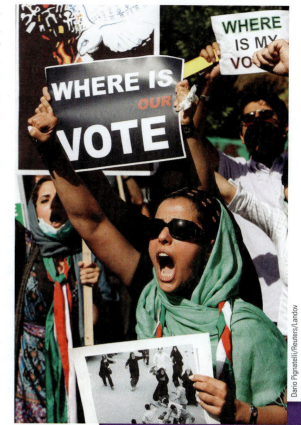

In the summer of 2009, thousands of Iranian men and women took to the streets of Tehran and other major cities to protest the re-election of Mahmoud Ahmadinejad as president. With evidence suggesting that the vote may have been rigged, these protests illustrate how frustrated people get when they don't trust that their voices are being heard in a fair manner—an essential aspect of procedural justice.

Dario Pignatelli/Reuters/Landov

In diverse populations such as the United States, these cultural practices can put governments and cultures into conflict with one another. In one highly publicized case, a Japanese woman living in California was prosecuted for drowning her two children in the Pacific Ocean before being rescued while she was trying to drown herself. At trial, she testified that she had tried to commit *oyaku-shinju*, a Japanese custom of parent–child suicide, after learning that her husband was having an affair. Her motive, she said, was to save her children from the shame that their father had brought to the family. In a second case, a Navajo defendant was prosecuted for using the hallucinogen peyote, an illegal substance in the United States. He argued that the substance is used to achieve spiritual exaltation and should be protected by the freedom of religion. (Immigrants from Yemen, Kenya, and Somalia have similarly been arrested for chewing khat leaves in social gatherings, the way Americans chew tobacco, even though the effect is comparable to drinking three espressos.) In a third case, two Cambodian immigrants were prosecuted for trying to eat a 4-month-old puppy, an acceptable practice in their homeland but not in the United States. As these examples illustrate, judges and juries are sometimes asked to consider *cultural defenses* in their decision making (Renteln, 2004).

Just as nations differ in the crime laws that are set, the study of *comparative law* shows that they also differ in the processes used to enforce these laws. In Great Britain, the United States, Canada, and Australia, the accused has a right to be tried by a jury composed of fellow citizens. In France, Russia, and Brazil, that right is reserved for only the most serious crimes. In India and throughout Asia, all defendants are tried by professional judges, not juries. Yet China recently introduced mixed panels consisting of one judge and two lay jurors. Beginning in 2009, Japan also started to use a quasi-jury system, called *saiban-in*, in which three law-trained judges and six lay citizens chosen by lottery come together to render verdicts and sentencing decisions by a majority vote. Ever since juries were abolished in Japan during World War II, all Japanese defendants have been tried by three-judge panels; almost all have been convicted, typically after confessing to save face and minimize embarrassment to the family.

For people judged guilty of serious crimes, the consequences may also vary from one country to another. As noted earlier, "doing justice" often means punishing those who violate rules as a means of seeking retribution. But whether people are offended enough to seek revenge depends in part on the power of individualist and collectivist norms within the culture. For example, research shows that American college students are offended more when their personal rights are violated—for example, when a co-worker steals the credit for their idea, while Korean students are offended more when their sense of duty and obligation is violated—for example, when a co-worker fails to contribute his or her promised share in a cooperative effort (Shteynberg et al., 2009).

When it comes to punishment, the most notable cultural difference concerns the death penalty. When Iraq's former president Saddam Hussein was executed by hanging in December of 2006, many world leaders, including many of Hussein's enemies, took the opportunity to condemn the execution and, more generally, capital punishment. According to Amnesty International, there are substantial differences of opinion and practice across the world regarding the death penalty (Amnesty International, 2012). Currently, 97 countries prohibit the death penalty for all crimes (Australia, Austria, Belgium, Canada, Colombia, Denmark, England, France, Germany, Greece, Ireland, Italy, Mexico, the Netherlands, Norway, Portugal, Spain, Sweden, Switzerland, Turkey, and Venezuela are prominent examples); 8 ban the death penalty as a general rule but permit it for exceptional crimes, such as espionage, or crimes committed in exceptional circumstances (Brazil, Chile, Israel, and Peru are some examples); 36 countries allow for the death penalty in law but do not execute people as a matter of practice (Algeria, Kenya, Morocco, and Russia are some examples); and 57 countries permit and use the death penalty (in addition to the United States, the others include China, Cuba, Egypt,

Iran, Iraq, India, Japan, Pakistan, Saudi Arabia, and Thailand). On matters of crime and punishment, it is clear that cultural influences are substantial.

# Closing Statement

This chapter focuses on criminal justice, from the gathering of evidence from witnesses and suspects to the various stages of a jury trial, sentencing, and prison. Yet we've only scratched the surface. In recent years, more and more judges, lawyers, and policy makers have come to recognize that social psychology can make important contributions to the legal system. Thus, with increasing frequency, social psychologists are called on for expert advice in and out of court and are cited in the opinions written by judges. Clearly, the collection, presentation, and evaluation of evidence are imperfect human enterprises and subject to bias. Through an understanding of social psychology, however, we can now identify the problems—and even some solutions.

# Review

- The conviction and acquittal of Amanda Knox in Italy illustrates the many ways in which social psychology is relevant to the legal system.

## Eyewitness Testimony

- Mistaken eyewitness identifications are the most frequent cause of wrongful convictions.
- Eyewitness memory is a three-stage process involving encoding, storage, and retrieval.
- During encoding, witnesses who are highly stressed zoom in on the central features of an event but lose memory for peripheral details.
- The presence of a weapon hinders a witness's ability to identify the perpetrator.
- Witnesses have trouble recognizing members of a race other than their own.
- During storage, misleading postevent information biases eyewitness memory.
- Young children are particularly suggestible in this regard.
- Lineups are biased when a suspect is distinctive, when the police hint that the criminal is in the lineup, when witnesses make relative judgments, and when the suspect is familiar for other reasons.

- In court, jurors overestimate eyewitnesses' accuracy and cannot distinguish between accurate and inaccurate witnesses.
- People are too readily persuaded by a witness's confidence—a factor that does not reliably predict identification accuracy.
- Psychologists are sometimes called to testify as experts on eyewitness evidence.
- Through reforms to police practices, social psychologists have also helped to improve the accuracy of eyewitness identifications.

---

**Putting *Common Sense* to the Test**

**Eyewitnesses find it relatively difficult to recognize members of a race other than their own.**

**True.** *Researchers have observed this own-race identification bias in both laboratory and field settings.*

# Confessions

- Police conduct interviews to determine if suspects are telling the truth or if they are lying and should be interrogated.
- These judgments of truth and deception are not highly accurate.
- By recording physiological arousal, the polygraph can also be used as a lie detector.
- Polygraph examiners report high rates of accuracy; however, truthful persons are too often judged guilty, and the test can be fooled.
- The police employ various methods of interrogation designed to get suspects believed to be guilty to confess.
- One method is to befriend the suspect and "minimize" the offense; a second is to scare the suspect into believing that it is futile to deny the charges.
- Under pressure, people sometimes give false confessions to crimes they did not commit.
- Actual cases and laboratory research shows that certain interrogation tactics—such as the presentation of false evidence and offers of leniency—increase false confessions.
- Although judges and juries are supposed to reject coerced confessions, their verdicts are still influenced by such evidence.

---

### Putting *Common Sense* to the Test

**The more confident an eyewitness is about an identification, the more accurate he or she is likely to be.**

**False.** *Studies have shown that the confidence of an eyewitness does not reliably predict accuracy, in part because confidence is influenced by post-identification factors.*

**It is not possible to knowingly fool a lie-detector test.**

**False.** *It is possible to beat a lie-detector test by elevating arousal when "innocent" questions are asked but not by trying to suppress arousal in response to "guilty" questions.*

**Without being beaten or threatened, innocent people sometimes confess to crimes they did not commit.**

**True.** *Innocent suspects sometimes confess, either to escape an unpleasant situation or because they are led to believe they committed a crime they cannot recall.*

---

# Jury Decision Making

## Jury Selection

- Once called for service, prospective jurors are questioned by the judge or lawyers in a process known as voir dire.
- Those who exhibit a clear bias are excluded. Lawyers may also strike a limited number through the use of peremptory challenges.
- Pressured to make juror selections quickly, lawyers rely on implicit personality theories and stereotypes.
- But general demographic factors do not reliably predict how jurors will vote.
- Lawyers sometimes hire psychologists to conduct surveys that identify correlations between demographics and trial-relevant attitudes.
- Scientific jury selection raises ethical issues concerning its effects on justice.
- On the question of whether race influences a juror's decision making, research suggests that there is no simple answer.
- Whether or not jurors are biased by race may depend on the strength of the evidence, the extent to which attention is drawn to race, and the diversity of the jury as a whole.
- In capital cases, prospective jurors who say they would not vote for the death penalty are excluded in a process known as death qualification.
- Jurors who favor the death penalty are more likely to find defendants guilty than are jurors who oppose the death penalty.

---

### Putting *Common Sense* to the Test

**Contrary to popular opinion, women are harsher as trial jurors than men are.**

**False.** *Demographic factors such as gender do not consistently predict juror verdicts; men may be harsher in some cases, women in others.*

---

## The Courtroom Trial

- Once the jury is selected, evidence previously gathered is presented in court.
- Questions are often raised about whether juries are accurate and objective or biased in their decision making.
- The more pretrial knowledge people have about a case, the more likely they are to presume the defendant guilty.
- Research shows that pretrial publicity can bias jury verdicts.
- Once inadmissible testimony leaks out in court, the jury is contaminated by it.
- A judge's cautionary instruction may worsen the situation by drawing attention to the forbidden testimony, arousing reactance, or leading jurors to see the information as relevant.
- The judge's instructions often have little impact, in part because they are often incomprehensible.
- The instructions are usually delivered after the evidence, after many jurors have formed an opinion.
- Jurors may not follow instructions that conflict with their own conceptions of justice, a phenomenon known as jury nullification.

## Jury Deliberations

- Dominance hierarchies develop in the jury room.
- Certain people are more likely than others to be elected foreperson, but the foreperson tends to play the role of moderator rather than group leader.
- Jury deliberations pass through three stages: orientation, open conflict, and reconciliation.
- The period of open conflict is filled with informational and normative pressures.
- When it comes to outcomes, the initial majority typically wins, although deliberation tends to produce a leniency bias.

- The U.S. Supreme Court has ruled that the use of six-person juries is acceptable.
- But these smaller groups do not deliberate for as long as twelve-person juries do and contain less minority representation.
- In some states, juries are permitted to reach verdicts by a less-than-unanimous majority.
- Research shows that once a required majority is reached, these juries reject the holdouts, terminate discussion, and return a verdict.

> **Putting *Common Sense* to the Test**
>
> **One can usually predict a jury's final verdict by knowing where the individual jurors stand the first time they vote.**
> **True.** *As a result of both informational and normative group influences, the preference of the initial voting majority usually prevails.*

## Posttrial: To Prison and Beyond

### The Sentencing Process
- Many people believe that judges are too lenient and that punishments for the same offense are often inconsistent from one case to another.
- Part of the problem is that people have different views of the goals of sentencing and punishment.

### The Prison Experience
- Stanford researchers built a simulated prison and recruited male adults to act as guards and prisoners.
- Some guards were abusive, the prisoners became passive, and the study had to be terminated.
- To this day, the Stanford prison study continues to draw debate concerning the power of the situation and the similarity between these findings and more recent events.

## Perceptions of Justice

### Justice as a Matter of Procedure
- Satisfaction with justice depends not only on winning and losing but also on the procedures used to achieve the outcome.
- People of all cultures prefer models of justice that offer participants a voice in the proceedings and the opportunity to be judged by an impartial decision maker.

### Culture, Law, and Justice
- Reflecting cultural and religious values, countries set different laws in an effort to regulate behavior.
- In diverse populations, differing cultural practices sometimes put governments into conflict with segments of their population.
- Cultures also differ in the processes used to enforce laws and the consequences for those who are convicted.

## Closing Statement

- Increasingly social psychologists have become involved in studying the legal system—identifying the problems and seeking solutions.

## KEY TERMS

adversarial model (524)
death qualification (510)
inquisitorial model (524)
jury nullification (515)
leniency bias (517)

misinformation effect (492)
own-race identification bias (490)
peremptory challenge (506)
polygraph (499)
scientific jury selection (508)

sentencing disparity (520)
voir dire (506)
weapon-focus effect (490)

## MEDIA RESOURCES

Go to CengageBrain.com to access Psychology CourseMate, where you will find an interactive eBook, glossaries, flashcards, quizzes, videos, and more.

# Business

This chapter examines the social side of business—specifically, the role of social factors in the workplace and their influence on economic decisions. First, we look at social influences on personnel selection and performance appraisals made within organizations. Then, we examine the roles of leadership and worker motivation. Finally, we explore economic decision making, the stock market, and other business settings.

# 13

© Unknown/Corbis/Bettmann/Corbis

**Whenever two adults meet for the first time,** the opening line of their conversation is predictable: "So, what do you do?" "Oh, I'm a (social psychologist). And you?" For many people, work is an integral part of their personal identity. Of course, most of us would rather spend next Monday morning lying on a warm and breezy beach, reading a paperback novel, and sipping a tropical fruit drink, but most people spend more time working than playing. In large part, we work to make money. But jobs also provide us with activity, a sense of purpose, and a social community. Imagine that you had just won $10 million in a lottery. Would you continue to work? When pollsters ask this question, typically half of Americans say they would continue, either at their current jobs or elsewhere. Thus, it is important to identify the social influences on this significant human experience.

There is a flip side to the importance of work: unemployment. The financial crisis that struck in 2007 caused the worst job market since the Great Depression. Worldwide, an estimated 210 million people were listed as out of work, with the largest increases found in the United States, New Zealand, Spain, and Taiwan. According to the U.S. Bureau of Labor Statistics, the 2012 unemployment rate in the United States was in the 8% range. Sadly, behind these numbers are real people—men and women who have lost jobs and are unable to find new jobs, often plunging them into a situation, through no fault of their own, that is financially and psychologically devastating. If you have a job, it is an important part of your life; if you don't have a job and want one, that fact too is an important part of your life (to learn more about the individual experience of unemployment, see Wanberg, 2012).

This chapter considers applications of social psychology to business. First, we'll look at **industrial/organizational (I/O) psychology**, the study of human behavior in the workplace. This subdiscipline of psychology is broad and includes in its ranks both social and nonsocial psychologists who do research, teach in business schools or universities, and work in government and private industry. Whatever the setting, I/O psychology raises important practical questions about job interviews, evaluations, and promotions, leadership, motivation, and other aspects of life in the workplace. Next, we'll examine some social influences on economic decision making in the stock market and elsewhere in the business world.

The impact of social psychological factors in the workplace was first recognized many years ago—thanks, oddly enough, to a study of industrial lighting. The year was 1927. Calvin Coolidge was president, baseball legend Babe Ruth hit 60 home runs, Charles Lindbergh flew across the Atlantic for the first time, and the U.S. economy seemed sound, though the stock market would soon crash, triggering the Great Depression. Just outside of Chicago, the Hawthorne plant of the Western Electric Company employed 30,000 men and women who manufactured telephones and central office equipment. As in other companies, management wanted to boost productivity. The bottom line was important.

At first, managers thought that they could make workers at the plant more productive by altering the illumination levels in the factory. Proceeding

**industrial/organizational (I/O) psychology** The study of human behavior in business and other organizational settings.

## Putting *Common Sense* to the Test

*Circle Your Answer*

**T  F**   Although flawed, job interviews consistently make for better hiring decisions.

**T  F**   A problem with having workers evaluate their own job performance is that self-ratings are overly positive.

**T  F**   The most effective type of leader is one who knows how to win support through the use of reward.

**T  F**   People who feel overpaid work harder on the job than those who see their pay as appropriate.

**T  F**   People losing money on an investment tend to cut their losses rather than hang tough.

logically, they increased the lighting for one group of workers in a special test room, kept the same lighting in a control room, and compared the effects. Much to their surprise, productivity rates increased in both rooms. At that point, a team of psychologists was brought in to vary other conditions in the factory. Over the next 5 years, groups of employees from various departments were selected to do their work in a test room where, at different times, they were given more rest periods, coffee breaks, a free mid-morning lunch, shorter work days, shorter weeks, a new location, overtime, financial incentives, dimmer lights, or just a different method of payment. At one point, the researchers even went back and reinstated the original pre-study conditions inside the test room. Yet no matter what changes were made, productivity levels always increased.

The Hawthorne project, described in a classic book entitled *Management and the Worker* (Roethlisberger & Dickson, 1939), has had a great impact on the study of behavior in the workplace. At first, the researchers were puzzled and discouraged. With positive effects observed among all test-room workers (even when the original pretest conditions were in place), it seemed that the project had failed. Ponder the results, however, and you'll see why these studies are so important. With striking consistency, workers became more productive—not because of any of the specific changes made but because they had been singled out for special assignment. Many researchers have criticized the methods used in this study and the ways the results have been interpreted (Adair, 1984; Chiesa & Hobbs, 2008; Parsons, 1974). Still, the phenomenon that has become known as the **Hawthorne effect** laid a foundation for I/O psychology.

The Hawthorne plant no longer exists, but the study that was conducted there helped psychologists understand the profound impact of social influences in the workplace. Interested in the conditions that affect satisfaction, motivation, and performance, today's researchers study all aspects of life in the workplace, including the effects of monitoring workers' activity on the computer (Alge, 2001); the benefits of sabbatical (Davidson et al., 2010); perceptions and realities of sexual harassment (O'Leary-Kelly et al., 2009); the relationship between daylight saving time, sleep, and workplace injuries (Barnes & Wagner, 2009); the perpetrators and targets of bullying in the workplace (Glasø et al., 2009); and the effects of sabotage, revenge, sexist humor, and other forms of insidious behavior in the workplace (Greenberg, 2010).

The three of us who write this textbook all work on college campuses amid students, professors, and administrators. We spend most of our time in classrooms, offices, and research laboratories. For women and men in other occupations—store clerks, taxicab drivers, carpenters, doctors, web designers, farmers, teachers, accountants, firefighters, and airline pilots—the workplace is very different. Yet despite the diversity of roles and settings, certain common concerns arise: How are applicants selected for jobs? How is performance then evaluated? What makes for an effective leader who can influence others and mobilize their support? What motivates people to work hard and feel satisfied with this aspect of their lives? And what factors influence the kinds of economic decisions that people make? Let's enter the workplace and address these important questions.

These women were among the assembly plant workers who took part in the classic Hawthorne studies of productivity in the workplace.

"And the dim fluorescent lighting is meant to emphasize the general absence of hope."

**Hawthorne effect** The finding that workers who were given special attention increased their productivity regardless of what actual changes were made in the work setting.

# Personnel Selection

For all kinds of organizations, especially in a tight economy, the secret to success begins with the recruitment and development of a competent work staff. For that reason, personnel selection is the first important step (Sackett & Lievens, 2008).

## The Typical Job Interview

Anyone who has ever applied for a desirable job knows that sometimes you have to climb hurdles and jump through hoops to land a position that matches your desires. The routine is a familiar one: You submit a résumé or post one online, fill out an application, and perhaps bring in samples of your work or take a standardized test of your abilities, personality traits, or honesty. You may even be placed on the "hot seat" in a face-to-face interview. In a typical interview, a representative of the organization and an applicant meet in person to discuss the job. Interviews thus provide a two-way opportunity for the applicant and employer to evaluate each other. What a social perception dilemma these opportunities present! As an applicant, you have only a half-hour or so to make a favorable impression. As an interviewer, you have the same brief period of time to penetrate the applicant's self-presentation while at the same time presenting the company in a favorable light.

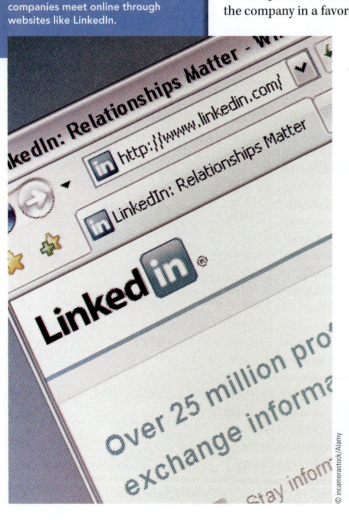

Today, many job seekers and companies meet online through websites like LinkedIn.

© incamerastock/Alamy

Very few employers would consider hiring a complete stranger for a responsible position without an interview. Would *you*? Like most of us, you probably trust your own ability to size people up. But should you? Do interviews promote sound hiring, or do they produce decisions that are biased by job-irrelevant personal characteristics? Civil rights laws explicitly forbid employers to discriminate on the basis of sex, race, age, religion, national origin, or disability. Does the interview process itself intensify or diminish these possible sources of bias? And are interviews valid and predictive of performance?

Focusing on the possibility of race and ethnic background biases in an interview setting, some researchers have reported good news. By statistically combining the results of 31 studies involving more than 11,000 job applicants, Allen Huffcutt and Philip Roth (1998) found that black and Hispanic applicants receive interview ratings only slightly lower on average than those obtained by their white counterparts. Perhaps the face-to-face interactions provided by interviews humanize applicants, bringing to life their interest in the job, their social skills, and other relevant attributes that do not show up on paper. This relative lack of bias also seems to characterize subjective evaluations of job performance—where supervisor (and peer) ratings of black, white, and Hispanic workers are more similar to one another, not less so, than "objective" measures of performance (Roth et al., 2003).

Although most employers have learned to guard against discriminatory hiring practices, there is one possible source of bias that is difficult to regulate: physical appearance. Except for certain types of work (such as modeling), beauty is not relevant to job performance. Yet people in general tend to favor others who are attractive. Does this bias operate in hiring situations? To answer this question, Cynthia Marlowe and others (1996) presented a set of job application folders—including résumés, data sheets, and photographs—to 112 male and female managers of a financial institution. Believing they were evaluating prospective employees, each manager rank-ordered four equivalent and qualified applicants: two men and two women, one of each of whom was highly attractive. Who was selected? Look at ● Figure 13.1, and you'll see that physical appearance had a large impact, with 62% of all managers selecting an attractive applicant as their top choice. Other research has since confirmed that human resource professionals show a preference for applicants who are attractive (Jawahar & Mattsson, 2005). In fact, an applicant may be handicapped merely by a scar or stain on the face—which steals attention, distracts the interviewer, and results in less positive outcomes (Madera & Hebl, 2012).

Although interviews often result in the right selection of new employees, they sometimes lack predictive validity (Eder & Harris, 1999). Part of the problem is that most job applicants use impression management tactics to present themselves in a positive light, as you'd expect, and that some engage in more self-promotion than others—often with positive results (Stevens & Kristof, 1995; Barrick et al., 2010). Some college seniors who enter the job market are also more confident in their interviewing skills than others, and confidence predicts success months later (Tay et al., 2006). Researchers have found that even the quality of an applicant's handshake (as determined by its strength and vigor, firmness of grip, duration, and whether it is accompanied by eye contact) predicts how highly he or she will be rated by an interviewer after an hour-long mock interview (Stewart et al., 2008).

"Faking" in an employment interview—which occurs whenever a job applicant consciously presents himself or herself in distorted ways in order to create a favorable impression—may well compromise the predictive validity of the process. For that reason, researchers have recently sought to develop a questionnaire that measures faking. In a series of studies, Julia Levashina and Michael Campion (2007) asked several hundreds of college seniors who were active on the job market to anonymously rate the degree to which they engaged in various faking behaviors during their most recent interviews. Some of the behaviors involved outright lying ("I claimed that I have skills I do not have"); others involved forms of exaggeration ("I exaggerated my responsibilities on previous jobs"), ingratiation ("I laughed at the interviewer's jokes even when they were not funny"), and image protection ("When asked directly, I did not mention some problems that I had in past jobs"). It will be interesting in future research to see whether applicants' responses on this questionnaire can be used to predict their success or failure—not only during the interview process but also later on the job.

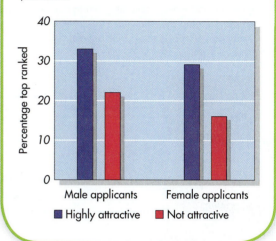

● **FIGURE 13.1**

**The Bias for Beauty in Hiring**

In this study, managers rank-ordered four job applicants, two men and two women. One of each gender was attractive, the other plain. As shown, a majority selected an attractive male or female applicant as their top choice.

From Marlowe, C. M., Schneider, S. L., and Nelson, C. E., "Gender and attractiveness biases in hiring decisions: Are more experienced managers less biased?" *Journal of Applied Psychology* vol 81 (pp. 11–21). Copyright © 1996 by the American Psychological Association. Reprinted by permission.

"Great-looking tie!"

Ingratiation is a strategy often used to curry favor.

Although flawed, job interviews consistently make for better hiring decisions. **F**ALSE.

Even if applicants are completely honest in their self-presentations, another potential problem with interviews is that employers often have preconceptions that can distort the process. In a field study that illustrated the problem, Amanda Phillips and Robert Dipboye (1989) surveyed 34 managers from different branch offices of a large corporation and 164 job applicants that these managers had interviewed. They found that the managers' pre-interview expectations—which were based on written application materials—influenced the kinds of interviews they conducted as well as the outcomes: The higher their expectations, the more time they spent "recruiting" rather than "evaluating" and the more likely they were to make a favorable hiring decision. Similarly, Thomas Dougherty and others (1994) found that interviewers with positive rather than negative expectations sounded warmer, more outgoing, and more cheerful. They also gave more information and spent more time promoting the company. It seems that job interviews can become part of a cycle, or self-fulfilling prophecy. Without realizing it, employers use the opportunity to create realities that bolster their preexisting beliefs (see ● Figure 13.2).

● **FIGURE 13.2**

**Job Interviews: A Self-Fulfilling Prophecy?**

One study indicates that interviewers' expectations influence the kinds of interviews conducted and applicants' performance. The higher the expectations, the more the interviewer tries to impress rather than evaluate the applicant and make a favorable hiring decision. Without realizing it, employers may use job interviews to create a reality that supports their prior beliefs.

Phillips & Dipboye, 1989. © Cengage Learning

## "Scientific" Alternatives to Traditional Interviews

Face-to-face interviews bring to life both job-relevant and not-so-relevant personal characteristics. Given that the process is so variable, should interviews be eliminated? Should they, perhaps, be computerized, leaving applicants to interact with companies through a programmed sequence of questions and answers administered by computer? Online interviews may offer a forum for an initial screening of applicants. Chances are, however, not too many people would feel comfortable making important life decisions in such an impersonal manner. Is it possible, then, to preserve the human touch of an interview while eliminating the bias and error?

Some organizations use the *polygraph*, or lie-detector test, as a screening device. As described in Chapter 12, the polygraph is an instrument that records physiological arousal in different parts of the body. Based on the assumption that lying causes stress, a polygraph examiner conducts an interview and compares the interviewee's level of arousal in response to various questions. Those who administer lie-detector tests argue that it enhances their ability to identify prospective employees who are honest. But opponents argue that the test invades an individual's privacy and that its results are not sufficiently accurate. For these reasons, the U.S. government in 1988 passed a law that prohibits the use of lie-detector tests except in matters involving large sums of money, public safety, and national security, such as for screening FBI agents and scientists who work at nuclear testing facilities (Beardsley, 1999).

**Standardized Tests**  Today, many companies use standardized written tests in the personnel selection process. Three general types of test are used for this purpose.

Tests of intelligence are designed to measure intellectual and cognitive abilities, job-specific knowledge and skills, or "street smarts" and common sense, which all may contribute to success on the job. When it comes to measures of general intelligence, the use of cognitive ability tests in the workplace is a matter of serious debate. On the basis of extensive research, some psychologists believe that cognitive ability tests are useful because they are predictive of job success in high-stakes work settings (Gottfredson, 2002; Schmidt, 2002)—importantly, without discriminating against minorities and others who lack the resources to pay for test preparation courses (Sackett et al., 2008).

The predictive benefits of cognitive ability testing in the workplace have been amply demonstrated. Still, some researchers caution that general intelligence is only one relevant factor and that this focus discriminates against individuals with other abilities who don't happen to score well on these tests (Sternberg & Hedlund, 2002). For this reason, I/O psychologists as a group are ambivalent about the use of intelligence testing in personnel selection. When Kevin Murphy and others (2003) surveyed more than 700 professionals in the field, they found that most agreed that intelligence is not fully captured by standardized tests, that different jobs require different cognitive abilities, and that both cognitive and noncognitive selection measures should be used.

Recently it was estimated that 2,500 U.S. companies also use *personality testing* to measure traits that predict such work-related outcomes as leadership, productivity, helpfulness, absenteeism, and theft (Cha, 2005). For example, research shows that people who score high rather than low in the trait of conscientiousness—which tends to make them more achievement oriented, dependable, orderly, and cautious—are more likely in general to perform well on the job (Dudley et al., 2006). Another example: People who score as extroverted rather than introverted are especially likely to succeed as business managers and salespersons (Hurtz & Donovan, 2000; Salgado, 1997). Research shows that young adults who have high self-esteem, self-confidence, and a sense of control tend to seek out more challenging lines of work and, as a result, are more satisfied with their jobs later in life (Judge et al., 2000). Research also shows that people who have a certain cluster of traits that include emotional stability, conscientiousness, and agreeableness are more likely to exhibit good organizational citizenship behaviors (Chiaburu et al., 2011).

These research findings are clear. But does that mean that companies should test all job applicants and hire those with favorable personalities? Reflecting this trend, one *U.S. News & World Report* writer explains "why a psychologist might be at your next interview" (Wolgemuth, 2009). But is this a sound development in the practical world of personnel selection? Not according to five editors of the research journals that have published much of this personality research. In an article they collectively wrote, these editors concluded that although certain personality factors may well relate to job performance, researchers would need to devise tests that are more predictive—tests that do not rely on the motivated applicant's self-report and therefore cannot easily be faked (Morgeson et al., 2007).

Third, a number of companies have recently begun to administer **integrity tests**—questionnaires designed specifically to assess an applicant's honesty and character by asking direct questions concerning illicit drug use, shoplifting, petty theft, and other transgressions. The tests are easy to administer and the responses are scored by computer. Narrative profiles are provided, and arbitrary cutoff scores are often used to determine if an applicant has passed or failed (Camara & Schneider, 1994).

Are integrity tests useful for predicting job performance? A major concern about integrity tests—and personality tests too, for that matter—is that applicants may be able to fake the tests on their own or with the help of coaching. Specifically, the concern is that applicants will use the tests to present themselves in overly positive ways—for example, as highly stable, conscientious, agreeable, or extroverted (Schmitt & Oswald, 2006). But is this the case with integrity tests? Can they be faked?

Let's consider the two different types of integrity tests that are used: (1) *overt tests*, in which the purpose is obvious to the test-taker, and (2) *covert tests*, in which items measure broad personality characteristics that are not clearly related to the workplace. To examine the susceptibility of these tests to faking, George Alliger and others (1996) gave both overt and covert tests to college students. Some were told to just take the tests, others were

**integrity tests** Questionnaires designed to test a job applicant's honesty and character.

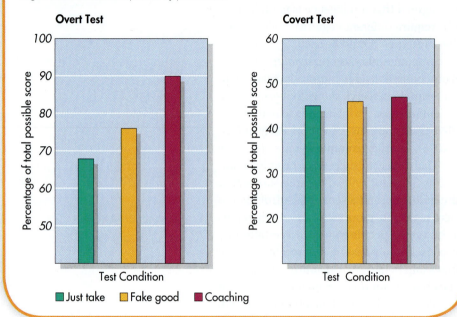

● **FIGURE 13.3**

**Can Integrity Tests Be Faked?**

Alliger and others (1996) gave college students overt and covert integrity tests. Some just took the test; others were told to "fake good"; others were coached. On the overt test, scores increased for subjects who faked good or were coached (left). On the covert test, scores were unaffected by these interventions (right).

From Alliger, G. M., Lillienfield, S. O., and Mitchell, K. E., "The susceptibility of overt and covert integrity tests to coaching and faking," *Psychological Science* vol 7 (pp. 32–39). Copyright © 1996 Sage Publications, Inc. Reprinted by permission.

instructed to "fake good," and still others were coached and given specific strategies for how to beat the tests. ● Figure 13.3 shows how well the students did. On the overt test, the scores increased for those instructed to fake good and then increased again among those who were specifically coached. Yet on the covert personality test, scores were unaffected by these interventions. Other studies, too, reinforce the point: When it comes to faking, the covert tests, quite literally, pass the test (Alliger & Dwight, 2000).

But are such instruments sufficiently valid to be used for personnel selection? This is a source of much debate. Although there is reason for skepticism, research suggests that both types of tests do predict various work-related behaviors (Berry et al., 2007). In one study using overt integrity tests, for example, Michael Cunningham and others (1994) found that actual job applicants scored higher on these tests than did nonmotivated research participants and that their scores matched those obtained from participants specifically instructed to fake good. Does a self-presentation bias compromise a test's validity? Not necessarily. In a second experiment, these same investigators overpaid participants by $5 and found that those with high rather than low test scores were also more likely to return the extra cash. Other researchers have arrived at similar findings (Barrick & Mount, 1996).

How useful are integrity tests in practice? Deniz Ones and others (1993) conducted a meta-analysis of tests taken by thousands of workers and found that test scores were highly predictive of job performance as well as of such counterproductive behaviors as theft, absenteeism, lateness, and other disciplinary problems. When Chad Van Iddekinge and others (2012) revisited the issue in a more recent meta-analysis of 104 separate studies, they also found that integrity test scores were predictive of job performance and counterproductive behaviors but to a lesser degree. At this point, it seems clear that integrity tests have value for use in personnel selection; how much value is not yet clear (Sackett & Schmitt, 2012).

**Structured Interviews**  Another way to improve personnel selection decisions is through the use of **structured interviews**. A structured interview is much like a standardized test in that the same information is obtained in the same situation from all applicants, who are then compared on a common, relevant set of dimensions (Campion et al., 1997; Pettersen & Durivage, 2008). By asking exactly the same set of questions or using the same set of tasks, employers can stop themselves from unwittingly conducting biased interviews that merely confirm their preexisting conceptions.

Over the years, studies have shown that structured interviews are more informative than conventional interviews in the selection of insurance agents, sales clerks, and other workers (Wiesner & Cronshaw, 1988) and are more predictive than

**structured interview**  An interview in which each job applicant is asked a standard set of questions and evaluated on the same criteria.

paper-and-pencil personality tests (Huffcutt et al., 2001)—perhaps because they are more difficult to fake (Van Iddekinge et al., 2005). In fact, structured interviews can be conducted by phone and later scored from a taped transcript, providing information received that can be used to predict a future worker's attendance rate, productivity, and tenure on the job (Schmidt & Rader, 1999).

Does the structured interview completely eliminate the human element that comes with conventional interviews? It appears that the answer is no. Structured interviews typically are preceded by a meet-and-greet session in which the interviewer and applicant engage in small talk to get acquainted before the serious questioning begins. In light of social psychology research showing that people form first impressions quickly on the basis of appearances and a thin slice of behavior, Murray Barrick and his colleagues (2010) examined whether this "pre-interview" predicts the outcomes that follow. In a mock interview study of college-level accounting students, they found that the impressions interviewers formed in the initial meeting—including their sense of the applicants' competence—were highly predictive of post-interview evaluations and of whether the applicants later received internship offers from actual accounting firms.

To create a more structured, multidimensional setting for selection and evaluation purposes, many organizations use **assessment centers**, in which several applicants take part in a group of activities such as written tests, situational tests, and role-playing exercises that are monitored by a group of evaluators. Instead of one method (an interview) and one evaluator (an interviewer), multiple methods and evaluators are used. Assessment centers are widely assumed to be more effective than traditional interviews at identifying applicants who will succeed in a particular position (Thornton & Rupp, 2006). When companies struggle to cut hiring costs, assessments are sometimes streamlined to involve fewer evaluators, fewer exercises, briefer exercises, and other types of shortcuts (Borman et al., 1997). Still, research shows that an assessment center's multidimensional approach is a good way to make hiring decisions that are ultimately quite predictive of job performance (Arthur et al., 2003; Meriac et al., 2008).

**Personnel Selection as a Two-Way Street**  For many years, researchers focused on the ways in which different personnel selection procedures serve employers. As we noted earlier, however, the hiring process is a two-way street in which organizations and applicants size each other up. How do job seekers feel about the methods just described? What is *your* reaction to these methods? In general, people see concrete, job-specific tests and interview situations as the most fair, and they dislike impersonal standardized tests of intelligence, personality, and honesty (Rosse et al., 1994; Rynes & Connerly, 1993). For employers on the lookout for strong recruits, the perceived fairness of the selection process that is used may well influence whether top applicants accept the offers that are made (Bauer et al., 1998).

Even the format of an interview can leave a lasting impression. Flawed as it may be, how does the face-to-face interview compare with computer-mediated sessions? In today's global economy, interviewers and job applicants are often geographically separated, which necessitates either costly travel or the use of technology for computer-mediated interviews, phone interviews, and videoconferencing. If you've ever communicated in these ways, you know how different the interaction can be. But how effective are these media? At the campus recruitment center of a large Canadian university, 970 students who submitted résumés to jobs that were posted on the Internet interviewed with 346 organizations. These were actual interviews. Most were held in person, but some were conducted by telephone or videoconferencing. When questioned about the experience afterward, the students in the in-person interviews saw the process as more fair, saw the outcome as more favorable, and were more likely to accept the job if offered. It may be difficult to replace the connection and caring that are signaled by in-person contact (Chapman et al., 2003).

**assessment center** A structured setting in which job applicants are exhaustively tested and judged by multiple evaluators.

# Affirmative Action

Affirmative action is a policy that gives special consideration to women and members of underrepresented minority groups in recruitment, hiring, admissions, and promotion decisions. This policy is among the most emotional and explosive social issues of our time. On one side of the debate is the argument that preferential treatment is necessary as a way to overcome historical inequities and to bring the benefits of diversity to the workplace. On the other side is the claim that the policy results in unfair reverse discrimination. Surveys show that Americans are sharply divided on the issue: Women are more supportive than men, and African Americans are more supportive than whites (Crosby et al., 2006; Kravitz & Platania, 1993; Parker et al., 1997).

Differences of opinion were apparent during the summer of 2003, just after the U.S. Supreme Court ruled on a pair of historic affirmative action lawsuits filed by students who had been rejected from the University of Michigan. Upholding the law school's policy but not the undergraduate policy, the Court ruled by a 5-to-4 margin that it is proper for a university to take race into account as a way to bring diversity to the campus as long as a specific quota or point system is not used. That day in a Gallup poll of 1,385 Americans, 59% favored affirmative action for women and 49% favored affirmative action for racial minorities. In both cases, women and minorities were more favorable toward the policy (see ● Figure 13.4).

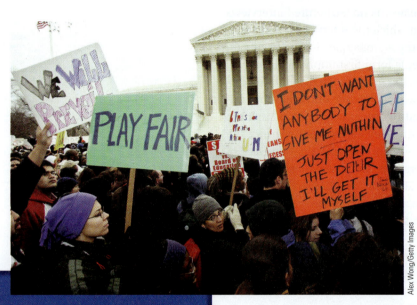

Representing both sides of the debate about affirmative action, Americans demonstrated their passionate opinions outside the U.S. Supreme Court. On June 23, 2003, the Court—by a 5-to-4 margin—upheld a university's right to consider race in admissions in order to create a diverse student body.

Alex Wong/Getty Images

Proponents of affirmative action often accuse opponents of harboring conscious or unconscious prejudice. In contrast, opponents argue that they support a meritocracy, a form of justice in which everyone receives an equal opportunity and then rewards are matched to contributions. In support of this reasoning, Ramona Bobocel and others (1998) studied affirmative action attitudes and found that opposition to it was associated with a strong belief in the principle of merit, not with measures of racial prejudice. So, would these opponents favor preferential selection procedures to rectify the injustice of a workplace contaminated by discrimination? It appears that many would. When opponents of affirmative action were led to see women and minorities as targets of discrimination in a particular workplace, which itself undermines the principle of merit, they became more favorable toward a system of preferential treatment (Son Hing et al., 2002).

Further complicating the question of deservingness is whether all minorities are seen as full-fledged members of their group and equally entitled. In an article entitled "Are You Minority Enough?" Diana Sanchez and George Chavez (2010) describe a study in which they presented research participants with a Latino candidate for a highly selective minority internship. The candidate's resume was strong and included backgrounds in research and business, computer skills, volunteer experience, and a 3.6 college GPA. For some participants, the candidate's resume indicated a fluency in Spanish and English; for others, it indicated a fluency in English only (according to the U.S. Census Bureau, 78% of Latino Americans speak Spanish). In their evaluations, participants saw the Spanish-speaking candidate as more of a Latino minority than the English-only candidate, as more suitable for affirmative action, and as more deserving of the internship. Interestingly, Latino participants in a second study shared these perceptions.

Amidst political debate, many questions are raised. According to Rupert Nacoste (1996), affirmative action affects those the policy is designed to help, those who feel

● **FIGURE 13.4**

**American Attitudes Toward Affirmative Action**

USA Today, 2003. © Cengage Learning

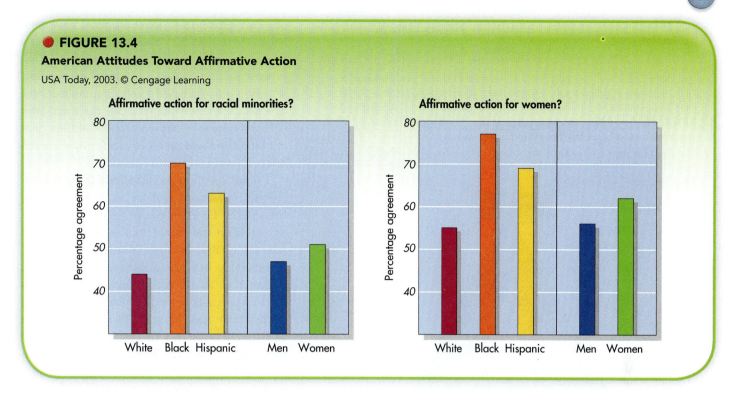

excluded by it, the organizations that implement it, and the interactions among these three interested groups. In addition, Nacoste argues that people react not to the abstract concept of affirmative action but to the procedures that are used to implement the concept and that these reactions can set off "procedural reverberations" within the system. For example, people will be dissatisfied and the system will reverberate to the extent that the policy is set secretly rather than in the open, to the extent that interested parties have no opportunity to express their personal views, and to the extent that group membership considerations are seen as more important than the individual contributions of each applicant. Nacoste's notion of procedural interdependence is diagrammed in ● Figure 13.5.

After years of research on attitudes toward affirmative action, it is now clear that although there are sharp differences of opinion, people's reactions depend—and can be changed by—how the policy is implemented. There is no single approach. Faye Crosby and her colleagues (2006) note that policies have ranged from "soft" forms of affirmative action, such as outreach programs designed to identify, recruit, or specially train applicants from underrepresented groups, to "hard" forms of affirmative action that give preference in hiring to applicants from targeted groups who are equally or less qualified than others. Based on a meta-analysis of 126 studies involving 29,000 respondents, David Harrison and others (2006) found that people are most favorable toward softer forms of affirmative action and least favorable toward quotas and other hard policies that favor some applicants over others regardless of their qualifications. By describing different affirmative action programs to business school students, Ariel Levi and Yitzhak Fried (2008) found not only that participants preferred a soft affirmative action policy but that they were most supportive of a policy that influenced the hiring and training of new employees and least supportive of a policy that affected promotions and layoffs for existing employees.

As you might expect, many people who do not personally benefit from affirmative action react negatively to both the policy and those who benefit from it (Heilman et al., 1996). What about the *recipients* of affirmative action? Does the policy psychologically bolster or undermine those it is intended to help? In an early series of studies, Madeline Heilman and others (1987) selected male and female college students to serve as leaders

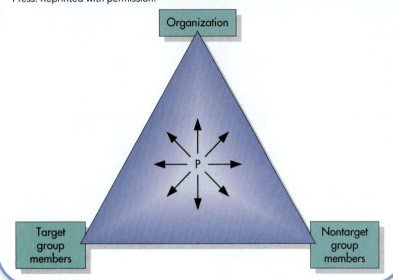

of a two-person task. These students were then led to think that they had been chosen for the leadership role either by a preferential selection process that was based on gender or by a merit selection process based solely on qualifications. The result: The women (but not the men) who believed they were chosen because of their gender later devalued their own performance, even after receiving positive feedback.

There are three explanations for why preferential selection policies may have negative effects. First, people perceive a procedure as unjust to the extent that it excludes those who are qualified simply because of their non-membership in a group (Barnes Nacoste, 1994; Heilman et al., 1996). Second, the recipients become less able to attribute success on the job to their own abilities and efforts, leading them and their co-workers to harbor doubts about their competence (Heilman et al., 1992; Major et al., 1994). Third, preferential selection is seen as a form of assistance, a situation that can lead recipients to feel stigmatized by what they assume to be the negative perceptions of others (Heilman & Alcott, 2001).

Are the recipients of affirmative action doomed to feel stigmatized, like second-class citizens? No. We saw earlier that the way people tend to react to a preferential selection procedure depends on how it is structured and for what purpose it is implemented. A good deal of research shows that people draw negative inferences about themselves and others when employment selections are made *solely* on the basis of sex, skin color, or ethnic background. But would they react more favorably to a preferential selection process if it is clear that merit-based factors also play a role and that the person chosen is competent and qualified for the position?

To find out, Heilman and her colleagues (1998) again brought together male and female participants to take part in a joint two-person task that required a leader and a follower. As in prior experiments, the researchers administered a bogus qualifications test and then assigned each female to the leadership role. Some participants were told that the appointment was based strictly on *merit* (that the person with the higher test score had been selected as the leader). Others were told that the process favored the woman in a way that was *preferential equivalent* (that she was chosen only when her score was similar to that of her male counterpart), *preferential minimum standard* (that she was chosen only if she was minimally qualified), or *preferential absolute* (that she was chosen regardless of merit). The result: Appointed female leaders later rated their own performance and leadership abilities most favorably and saw the process as most fair when their appointment was based on merit, not gender (see ● Figure 13.6). Also important is that they did not devalue their performance or see the selection process as unfair in the preferential equivalent condition, where merit was clearly taken into account. Similarly, neither male co-participants nor observers were troubled by this type of preferential selection process. The key, clearly, is that people need to know that they were selected on the basis of merit (Unzueta et al., 2010). In light of these findings,

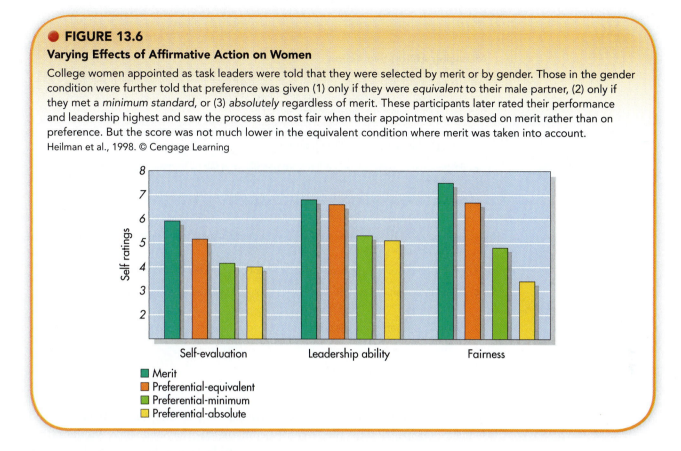

● **FIGURE 13.6**

**Varying Effects of Affirmative Action on Women**

College women appointed as task leaders were told that they were selected by merit or by gender. Those in the gender condition were further told that preference was given (1) only if they were *equivalent* to their male partner, (2) only if they met a *minimum standard*, or (3) *absolutely* regardless of merit. These participants later rated their performance and leadership highest and saw the process as most fair when their appointment was based on merit rather than on preference. But the score was not much lower in the equivalent condition where merit was taken into account.

Heilman et al., 1998. © Cengage Learning

Table 13.1 offers guidelines for managing affirmative action programs in a way that feels just to all concerned.

## Culture and Organizational Diversity

For many years, the study of organizational behavior was "culture blind and culture bound" (Gelfand et al., 2007). As a result of two dramatic historical changes, researchers now look at the workplace through a broader lens. The first change has resulted from affirmative action programs, which increase the number of women and minorities who populate most organizations. The second is the worldwide trend toward globalization, which has brought more and more people from disparate cultures into daily contact with each other as colleagues and co-workers. Georgia Chao and Henry Moon (2005) note that every individual worker has a multidimensional identity that can be characterized within a *cultural mosaic* consisting of the various "tiles" of his or her demographic groups (such as age, gender, race, and ethnic heritage), geographical background (such as country of origin, region, climate, and population density), and personal associations (such as with religion, profession, and political affiliation). In some ways, everyone is similar; in other ways, no two people are alike. For researchers who study organizational behavior, the challenge is to represent the full complexity that comes with a diverse workplace.

As diversity has become a fact of life, researchers have sought to understand what effect this change is having on motivation, morale, and performance in the workplace. On the one hand, a pessimist would predict that diversity would breed division and conflict, making worker teams less effective. In Chapter 5, on "Stereotypes, Prejudice, and Discrimination," we saw that people categorize one another into ingroups and outgroups based on gender, age, race, and other visible characteristics and show

> ### TABLE 13.1
> #### Managing Affirmative Action
>
> Preferential selection practices are often seen as unjust, and they often lead recipients to doubt their own competence. Pratkanis and Turner (1996) recommend that the steps listed here be taken to minimize these negative effects.
>
> 1. Set and communicate clear and explicit qualifications criteria (background, knowledge, skills, etc.) to be used in selection decisions.
>
> 2. Be certain that selection procedures are perceived as fair by targeted applicants and their co-workers.
>
> 3. Provide the target applicant and co-workers with specific feedback about the target's job qualifications.
>
> 4. Develop socialization strategies that keep target applicants from making negative self-attributions.
>
> 5. Emphasize the target applicant's unique contributions to the organization.
>
> 6. Point out that affirmative action does not imply hiring by quotas, since other job-relevant attributes are considered as well.
>
> 7. Recognize that affirmative action is not a panacea and that it cannot be expected to solve all the problems faced by the targeted groups.
>
> © Cengage Learning

*"The globalization of business is a fact of life. More than 63,000 multinational corporations and 821,000 foreign subsidiaries now employ 90 million people around the world."*

—Gabel & Brunner, 2003

a marked preference for "us" over "them." We also saw in Chapter 9, "Attraction and Close Relationships," that people prefer the company of others who have similar rather than dissimilar attitudes and values. If people dislike each other, they will not work well together. On the other hand, an optimist would predict that diversity increases the range of perspectives and skills that are brought to bear on a problem, enhancing productivity and creative problem solving by providing a group with a larger pool of resources to draw from.

What is the net impact of diversity on a group's performance? There is a hint of evidence for both effects. At present, researchers agree that there is no single or simple answer because the effect is likely to depend on the nature of the diversity, whether similarities or differences are accentuated, the proportion of majority to minority members, whether there is a culture of smooth integration within the organization, the type of work to be completed, the group's ability and motivation, and other factors (Mannix & Neale, 2005; van Knippenberg & Schippers, 2007).

A workplace may strive for diversity, but its success may well depend on its philosophy and approach. Reflecting a society-wide debate, many companies struggle with this question: Is it better to acknowledge group differences in the workplace by celebrating multiculturalism, or ignore these differences in an effort to encourage a uniform, colorblind environment? To see if there is a relationship between the beliefs held within a company and how engaged its minority workers feel, Victoria Plaut and others (2009) conducted an online "diversity climate survey" of 5,000 white and minority employees from 18 departments of a large health care organization. By comparing departments, they found that the more multicultural the dominant white employees were in their diversity beliefs (endorsing "employees should recognize and celebrate racial and ethnic differences" rather than "employees should downplay their racial and ethnic differences"), the more engaged their minority workers felt (for example, "I am proud to tell others that I work at this organization").

The real-world correlation is intriguing, but it does not prove that the multicultural beliefs within the organization *caused* minority employees to feel more engaged. To test that hypothesis directly, Valerie Purdie-Vaughns and others (2008) presented African American corporate professionals with a brochure for a fictitious management consulting firm. For participants assigned to a value-diversity condition, the brochure stated: "While other consulting firms mistakenly try to shape their staff into a single mold, we believe that embracing our diversity enriches our culture." For others in a colorblind condition, the brochure stated: "While other firms mistakenly focus on their staff's diversity, we train our diverse workforce to embrace their similarities." Did the African American participants, experienced in the corporate world, feel comfortable with this company? If the brochure photographs depicted a high level of minority representation, they were fine. If the photos depicted a low level of minority representation, however, their comfort level depended on the company's diversity beliefs. In this case, they trusted the multicultural firm that celebrated diversity and difference more than the colorblind firm that sought to minimize it.

Justin Lubin/NBC/NBCU Photo Bank via Getty Images

Interested in satisfaction, motivation, and performance, I/O psychologists study many aspects of social behavior in the workplace. Of course, no two work settings are the same—as seen in the award-winning TV comedy, *The Office*, which parodies the fictional and often dysfunctional Dunder Mifflin Paper Company in Scranton, Pennsylvania.

# Performance Appraisals

Even after a person is hired, the evaluation process continues. Nobody enjoys being scrutinized by a boss or anyone else, for that matter. Still, **performance appraisal**—the process of evaluating an employee's work and communicating the results to that person—is an inevitable fact of life in the workplace. Performance appraisals provide a basis for placement decisions, transfers, promotions, raises and salary cuts, bonuses, and layoffs. They also give feedback to employees about the quality of their work and status within the organization. Performance appraisal is also at times the subject of policy debates as well—as in questions recently raised over how teachers should be evaluated and rewarded (Gollan, 2011). It's no wonder that I/O psychologists have studied this process in great detail (Landy & Farr, 1983; Murphy & Cleveland, 1995).

It would be easy if a worker's performance could be measured by purely *objective* and quantifiable criteria—as when researchers are judged by the number of articles they publish, baseball pitchers by their won–loss percentage and earned run average, car dealers by the number of cars they sell, and sales agents by the number of customers they service. These kinds of quantitative measures are often not available, however, and they do not take into account the quality of work. By necessity, then, performance appraisals are often based on more *subjective* measures such as the perceptions of employees by supervisors, co-workers, and sometimes even the employees themselves.

## Supervisor Ratings

Based on the assumption that supervisors stay informed about the performance of their subordinates, they are most often called on to make evaluations. But are these ratings accurate? And is the process fair? The process has both benefits and drawbacks. On the one hand, research shows that supervisors are influenced more by a worker's on-the-job knowledge, ability, and dependability than by less relevant factors such as friendliness

**performance appraisal** The process of evaluating an employee's work within the organization.

(Borman et al., 1995). On the other hand, as we'll see, evaluators predictably fall prey to the social perception biases described elsewhere in this book.

Over the years, a number of appraisal-related problems have been identified. A good deal of research has identified various types of rating errors. One prominent example is the *halo effect*—a failure to discriminate among different and distinct aspects of a single worker's performance (Cooper, 1981). In Chapter 4, we saw that people's impressions of one another are guided by implicit personality theories—by the preconceptions they have about the relationships among different traits. Believing that someone is warm, we assume that he or she is also generous and good-natured. In a similar manner, supervisors who believe that a worker is unproductive may also rate that worker negatively on teamwork, independence, creativity, and other distinct dimensions. Halo effects are most pronounced when evaluators rate someone they do not know well or when a time delay has caused their memory of performance to fade (Koslowski et al., 1986; Murphy & Balzer, 1986).

A second problem is that evaluators differ in the average numerical ratings they give to others. Because of what is known as the *restriction of range problem*, some people provide uniformly high, lenient ratings; others are inclined to give stingy, low ratings; and still others gravitate toward the center of the numerical scale. In all cases, people who use a restricted range fail to make adequate distinctions. Sometimes the differences among raters are considerable, as was seen in a study of managers employed in numerous organizations (Scullen et al., 2000)—in part, because of differences in their personality. Individuals who have agreeable personalities tend to be lenient in their ratings of others, while those who are highly conscientious tend to be harsher (Bernardin et al., 2000). In a meta-analysis of 25 studies, John Georgesen and Monica Harris (1998) also found that people who are in power, compared to those who are not in power, consistently give lower performance ratings to others who are in subordinate positions.

In addition to problems with rating error and bias, it is now clear that supervisors may also intentionally distort their evaluations depending on their objectives within the organization (Murphy et al., 2004). In a study of students in a human management resources course, for example, raters gave higher ratings overall when their goal was to encourage group harmony, to ensure fairness and accuracy, or to motivate those they were rating, than when the purpose was merely to help members to identify their strengths and weaknesses. (Wang et al., 2010). An obvious but often overlooked fact of life in the workplace is that performance evaluation is not just a measurement process but one that serves social and communication purposes as well.

## Self-Evaluations

Although performance appraisals are typically made by supervisors, input is often sought from co-workers, subordinates, clients, customers, and others whose opinions are relevant. You may not realize it, but by filling out course-evaluation surveys in college, you may have had an influence on tenure and promotion decisions involving your own professors. As when workers are asked to evaluate their managers, these evaluations provide valuable "upward feedback."

One particularly interesting source of information comes from self-evaluations. If you've ever had to describe yourself in a job application, you know that a self-evaluation is not exactly a lesson in modesty. Most people see themselves in overly flattering terms, taking credit for success, denying the blame for failure, having an inflated sense of control, and exhibiting unrealistic optimism about the future. Add the fact that people like to present themselves favorably to others and it comes as no surprise that self-evaluations in the workplace are consistently more positive than the ratings made by supervisors (Campbell & Lee, 1988)—and less predictive of job success (Shore et al., 1992). In a simple illustration of this point, studies have shown that workers tend to underestimate the number of times they had been absent compared with co-workers (Harrison & Shaffer, 1994; Johns, 1994).

Another reason why self-evaluations should be taken with a grain of salt is that individuals differ in the extent to which they tend to present themselves in a positive light. Research shows that the more power people have in an organization, the higher their self-evaluations are (Georgesen & Harris, 1998). Similarly, men in general are more boastful than women and more likely to overestimate their own performance (Beyer, 1990). Insofar as work appraisals are based on self-evaluations, then, these differences put both subordinates and female employees at a disadvantage.

> A problem with having workers evaluate their own job performance is that self-ratings are overly positive. **T**RUE.

## New and Improved Methods of Appraisal

Performance appraisals cannot always be trusted. When more objective measures of work output are not available, however, organizations have no choice but to rely on imperfect and sometimes prejudiced human judges. For researchers, the challenge is to find ways to boost the accuracy of the evaluations that are made.

One solution concerns the timing of evaluations in relation to the observation of performance. Evaluations are less prone to error when made right after performance than when there's a delay of days, weeks, or months. Alternatively, evaluators should take notes and keep clear records of their observations, perhaps using behavioral checklists. Part of the problem is that once memory for details begins to fade, evaluators fall back on stereotypes and other biases (Murphy & Balzer, 1986; Sanchez & De La Torre, 1996).

A second possible solution is to teach raters some of the skills necessary for making accurate appraisals. Over the years, various training programs have been developed, and research suggests that accuracy can be boosted by alerting evaluators to the biases of social perception, focusing their attention on job-relevant behaviors, sharpening their memory skills, informing them of performance norms that serve as a frame of reference within the organization, and providing them with practice and feedback in the use of rating scales (Day & Sulsky 1995; Hedge & Kavanagh, 1988). No system will ever be perfect, but much improvement is possible, particularly when people are motivated to be accurate (Salvemini et al., 1993).

Third, it is now common in most organizations to collect and combine a full circle of ratings from multiple evaluators in a process that is referred to as a 360-degree performance appraisal. As in assessment centers, a multiple-rater system in which a final evaluation represents the average of ratings made by independent sources with different perspectives is more complete than the conventional single-rater approach (Conway & Huffcutt, 1997; Lepsinger & Lucia, 2009). In a typical 360-degree assessment, an employee's performance is rated by superiors, peers, subordinates, the employees themselves, and sometimes even outside stakeholders such as customers, clients, students, and patients. In this way, whatever idiosyncratic bias a single individual brings to his or her ratings can be offset by others. Although there is debate over how to combine, compare, and contrast different sources, research shows that this approach is an improvement over single-rater methods (Craig & Hannum, 2006; Morgeson et al., 2005). In light of globalization trends in the twenty-first century, the presence of multinational corporations, and the reality that every organization is nested within a broader culture, researchers have also become interested in cultural aspects of performance appraisal (Atwater et al., 2009; Peretz & Fried, 2012).

## Due-Process Considerations

In the all-too-human enterprise of performance appraisal, especially in a slow economy in which jobs are at a premium, accuracy is not the only concern. There's also another problem: perceptions of fairness. Is it fair that one professor is tenured while another is not or that one worker is laid off while another is retained? Precisely because the stakes are high in decisions that are made about personnel, performance ratings may be biased and sometimes deliberately distorted by those motivated by political and self-serving agendas within the workplace. Particularly at the executive level, office politics are an organizational fact of life (Gioia & Longnecker, 1994).

To enhance perceptions of fairness, Robert Folger and his colleagues (1992) proposed a "due-process" model of performance appraisal. In general, this model is designed to guard the rights of employees in the same way that the criminal justice system seeks to protect the accused. The model consists of three principles. The first is that there should be *adequate notice*—that is, clear performance standards that employees can understand and ask questions about. The second is that employees should receive a *fair hearing* in which they are evaluated by a supervisor who knows their work and in which they receive timely feedback as well as an opportunity to present their own case. The third principle is that appraisals should be based on *evidence* of job performance, not on prejudice, corruption, or external considerations. As indicated by research on how people react to pay raises, pay cuts, promotions, layoffs, and the implementation of affirmative action policies, procedural fairness (*how* decisions are made) can be just as important to people as a favorable outcome (*what* decisions are made). Thus, workers who are dissatisfied with their pay are more likely to retaliate (for example, by calling in sick, stealing or wasting the company's supplies, or damaging equipment) when they believe the procedures used to determine pay are unfair and were not consulted about the decision (Skarlicki & Folger, 1997).

Recent research has shown that people judge organizational justice according to a large number of criteria—such as the transparency and fairness of the procedures that are used; the extent to which the procedures and the outcomes they produce are explained; the extent to which affected workers are treated with dignity, politeness, and respect; and the decision-making outcomes by which salaries, promotions, and other resources are allocated. Together, the combination of these specific types of justice influences people's satisfaction, commitment, and on-the-job performance within the workplace (Ambrose & Schminke, 2009). In fact, a recent meta-analysis of 83 studies revealed that employees' perceptions of unfairness in the workplace were associated with increases in negative emotional states, stress, burnout, and physical and mental health problems (Robbins et al., 2012).

# Leadership

Regardless of where you're employed, the work experience depends in large part on the quality of the leadership in the organization. A leader is someone who can move a group of people toward a common goal. He or she may be a head of state, the president of a college or university, the principal investigator of a research team, the executive officer of a corporation, or the manager or head coach of a sports team. Across a wide range of settings, researchers have long wondered: What personal and situational factors make for effective leadership? There is no single formula. Some leaders succeed by winning supporters; others lead by mending fences, uniting rivals, negotiating deals, building coalitions, solving problems, or stirring emotions (see Table 13.2). Whatever the strategy, there is one common denominator: Good leadership is about social influence (Avolio, 2011; Bass & Bass, 2008; Goethals et al., 2004; Northouse, 2013).

## The Classic Trait Approach

One approach to the study of leadership is to identify the traits that characterize "natural-born" leaders, those who have the "right stuff." According to the Great Person Theory of history, exceptional individuals rise up to determine the course of human events. This approach has had some support over the years, since certain traits—such as ambition, intelligence, a need for power, self-confidence, a high energy level, and an ability to be flexible and adapt to change—are characteristic of people who go on to become leaders (Hogan et al., 1994; Kenny & Zaccaro, 1983). Even physical height may play a role. In this regard, it is striking that across the entire twentieth century, the tallest candidate for U.S. president won an astonishing 23 out of 25 elections—that's 92% of the time (1972 and 1976 were the only exceptions).

On the basis of past research, Shelley Kirkpatrick and Edwin Locke (1991) argued that certain stable characteristics

**TABLE 13.2**
**Quotable Conceptions of Leadership**

*"The purpose of all rulers is the well-being of those they rule."*
—Saint Augustine

*"The most important quality in a leader is that of being acknowledged as such."*
—Andre Maurois

*"I am a leader by default, only because nature does not allow a vacuum."*
—Bishop Desmond Tutu

*"If one is lucky, a solitary fantasy can totally transform one million realities."*
—Maya Angelou

*"When the effective leader is finished with his work, the people say it happened naturally."*
—Lao Tse

*"Never tell people how to do things. Tell them what to do and they will surprise you with their ingenuity."*
—General George Patton

*"We must become the change we want to see."*
—Mahatma Gandhi

*"The final test of a leader is that he leaves behind him in other men the conviction and will to carry on."*
—Walter J. Lippmann

*"Leadership should be born out of the understanding of the needs of those who would be affected by it."*
—Marian Anderson

*"No man will make a great leader who wants to do it all himself, or to get all the credit for doing it."*
—Andrew Carnegie

*"The task of the leader is to get his people from where they are to where they have not been."*
—Henry Kissinger

© Cengage Learning

are associated with successful leadership among business executives. In particular, they pointed to the importance of *cognitive ability* (intelligence and an ability to quickly process large amounts of information), *inner drive* (a need for achievement, ambition, and a high energy level), *leadership motivation* (a desire to influence others in order to reach a common goal), *expertise* (specific knowledge of technical issues relevant to the organization), *creativity* (an ability to generate original ideas), *self-confidence* (faith in one's own abilities and ideas), *integrity* (reliability, honesty, and an open communication style), and *flexibility* (an ability to adapt to the needs of followers and to changes in the situation). "Regardless of whether leaders are born or made," they say, "it is unequivocally clear that leaders are not like other people" (p. 58). Locke (2000) picked up on this theme in *The Prime Movers*, a book in which he describes the traits that "great wealth creators"—self-made multimillionaires and billionaires—seem to have in common. Zaccaro (2007) adds that various aspects of leadership can best be predicted by unique combinations of attributes rather than by single traits.

In contrast to this approach, more situationally oriented theories were introduced based on the notion that the emergence of a given leader depends on time, place, and

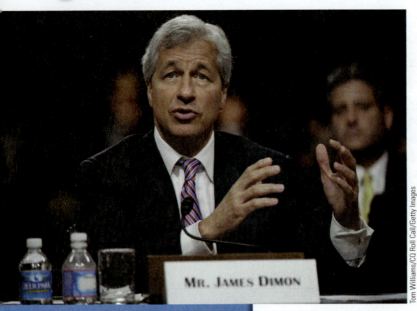

In June 2012, James Dimon, CEO of JP Morgan Chase, testified to Congress about the bank's multibillion dollar trading losses. Coming a few short years after the near collapse and bailout of Wall Street banks, regulators were concerned about risks that were taken. This incident and others like it have stimulated a good deal of discussion of "ethical leadership" in business—a relatively new and unexplored aspect of leadership (see Stouten et al., 2012).

circumstances—that different situations call for different types of leaders (Vroom & Jago, 2007). As the needs, expectations, and resources of a group change, so too will the person best suited to lead it. Studies of presidential leadership in particular can be used to illustrate the point about situations and leadership (Goethals, 2005). For example, David Winter (1987) found that presidential candidates are more likely to be elected and reelected when their primary motive in life—whether it is for achievement, power, or affiliation—matches what Americans want most at that time. An alternative to the classic trait perspective, then, is a view that leadership is the product of a unique interaction between the person and the surrounding situation.

Situations may well dictate the success of a particular leadership style. During the emergence of the dot-com era, for example, the traditional image of a leader who presides from the top down over a hierarchical command structure gave way to a corporate culture in which a leader should be accessible, fluid, lateral, and relationship oriented. But is this situational doctrine necessarily incompatible with the classic trait approach? Maybe not. In *Primal Leadership*, Daniel Goleman, Richard Boyatzis, and Annie McKee (2002) argue that the primary job of leadership is emotional and that great leaders are endowed with *emotional intelligence*, an ability to know how people are feeling and how to use that information to guide their own actions. Great leaders are men and women who exude interest, enthusiasm, and other positive emotions and whose energy is contagious. Precisely because demands change from one time, situation, and organization to the next, however, leaders with emotional intelligence are by nature flexible in their style, serving as visionaries, coaches, pacesetters, and so on as needed.

## Contingency Models of Leadership

Illustrative of this interactional perspective is Fred Fiedler's (1967) **contingency model of leadership**. Fiedler argues that a key difference among leaders is whether they are *primarily task oriented* (single-mindedly focused on the job) or *relations oriented* (concerned about the feelings of employees). The amount of control that a leader has determines which type of leadership is more effective. Leaders enjoy *high situational control* when they have good relations with their staff, a position of power, and a clearly structured task. In contrast, leaders exhibit *low situational control* when they have poor relations with their staff, limited power, and a task that is not clearly defined.

Combining these personal and situational components, studies of various work groups suggest that task-oriented leaders are the most effective in clear-cut situations that are either low or high in control and that relations-oriented leaders perform better in situations that afford a moderate degree of control. In low-control situations, groups need guidance, which task-oriented leaders provide by staying focused on the job. In high-control situations, where conditions are already favorable, these same leaders maintain a relaxed, low profile. Relations-oriented leaders are different. They offer too little guidance in low-control situations and they meddle too much in high-control situations. In ambiguous situations, however, relations-oriented leaders—precisely because of their open, participative, social style—motivate workers to solve problems in creative ways.

Studies of military units, sports teams, schools, hospitals, and other organizations generally support Fiedler's model. While this support is far from unanimous, the main point is well taken: Good leadership requires a match between an individual's personal

**contingency model of leadership** The theory that leadership effectiveness is determined both by the personal characteristics of leaders and by the control afforded by the situation.

Topham/The Image Works, Inc.

Shown at his famous "I have a dream" speech in Washington, D.C., in August 1963, Martin Luther King, Jr., was a transformational leader who inspired massive change by making supporters believe that anything was possible.

style and the demands of a specific situation (Fiedler & Chemers, 1984). A mismatch—that is, the wrong type of person for the situation—can have negative consequences for both the leader and his or her organization. For example, Martin Chemers and others (1985) surveyed college administrators to determine both their leadership style and their situational control. They found that mismatches were associated with increased job stress, stress-related illness, and absence from work, symptoms that diminish a leader's productivity and competence (Fiedler & Garcia, 1987; Fiedler et al., 1992).

Making decisions is one of the most important tasks for any leader. In the two-way street between leaders and followers, however, it is often important to solicit the opinions of others. How much participation should leaders invite? According to the **normative model of leadership** proposed by Victor Vroom and Philip Yetton (1973), leaders vary widely in this regard. Some are highly autocratic and directive (they invite no feedback from workers), while others are highly participative (they frequently seek and use suggestions from workers). For effective long-term leadership, the key is to invite just the right amount of worker participation—not too much (which is often not efficient) and not too little (which can lower morale). As to what constitutes the right amount, Vroom and Yetton argued that it depends on various factors such as the clarity of the problem, the information available to the leader and followers, and whether it's more important that the decision be right or that one have support.

Although the ideal leader is one who adjusts his or her style to meet the situation, people generally prefer leaders who involve them in important decisions. Research shows that participative decision making boosts worker morale, motivation, and productivity and reduces turnover and absenteeism rates. Benefits such as these have been found especially in situations where employees want to have input (Vroom & Jago, 1988) and when they are involved in decision making directly rather than through elected representatives (Rubenowitz et al., 1983).

## >Transactional Leadership

Although contingency models take both the person and situation into account, Edwin Hollander (1985) criticized these "top-down" views of leadership in which workers are

**normative model of leadership** The theory that leadership effectiveness is determined by the amount of feedback and participation that leaders invite from workers.

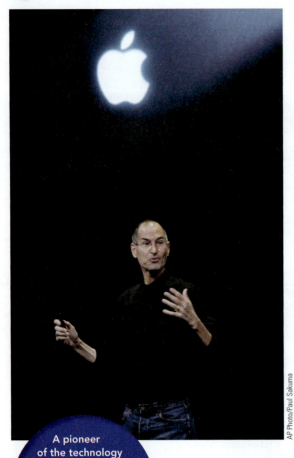

A pioneer of the technology revolution, Steve Jobs, co-founder of Apple, was one of the most forward-looking, transformational business leaders of our time.

AP Photo/Paul Sakuma

portrayed as inert, passive, faceless creatures to be mobilized at the management's discretion. Instead, he sees leadership as a two-way social exchange in which there is mutual and reciprocal influence between a leader and his or her followers. According to Hollander, a good **transactional leader** is one who gains compliance and support from followers by setting clear goals for them, by offering tangible rewards, by providing assistance, and by fulfilling psychological needs in exchange for an expected level of job performance. Transactional leadership thus rests on the leader's willingness and ability to reward subordinates who keep up their end of the bargain and to correct those who do not.

## Transformational Leadership

Think about some of the greatest leaders of the past century, those who were able to transform the status quo by making supporters believe that anything is possible. Martin Luther King Jr. was that kind of leader. So were Franklin D. Roosevelt, Mahatma Gandhi, John F. Kennedy, Ronald Reagan, and Nelson Mandela. In their classic book *In Search of Excellence*, Thomas Peters and Robert Waterman (1982) studied 62 of America's best businesses and found that their success was due largely to the ability of the leaders to elicit extraordinary efforts from ordinary human beings.

Today, two prominent models of such leadership are Microsoft's Bill Gates and Apple's Steven Jobs, both of whom co-founded two of the most important technology companies in the world. In 1975, Gates dropped out of Harvard and co-founded what was then a small company by the name of Microsoft. Long before it seemed possible, he envisioned a day when there would be a PC in every home and office. Then as it was becoming clear that the future resided in cyberspace, he shocked the business world by refocusing Microsoft around the Internet. Retired from Microsoft, he is now one of the richest and most philanthropic people in the world. In 1973, Steven Jobs, like Gates, also dropped out of college. He soon co-founded Apple and helped popularize and innovate the "Mac," bringing to it the mouse, a sleek design, and other creative elements. Until Jobs died in October of 2011, his most recent innovations were the iPod, iPhone, and iPad—the all-in-one gadget. In an industry that demands an ability to anticipate the future, adapt quickly to change, take great risks, and enlist support from others, both Gates and Jobs were world leaders.

What's special about successful leaders? Based on the work of political scientist James MacGregor Burns (1978, 2003), Bernard Bass (1998; Bass & Riggio, 2006) calls them **transformational leaders**. Transformational leaders motivate others to transcend their personal needs in the interest of a common cause, particularly in times of growth, change, and crisis. Through consciousness raising and raw emotional inspiration, they articulate a clear vision for the future and then mobilize others to join in that vision. Over the years, Bass and his colleagues asked people who work for various business managers and executives, military officers, school principals, government bureaucrats, fire chiefs, and store owners to describe the most outstanding leaders they know (Bass & Avolio, 1990). As shown in Table 13.3, the descriptions they gave revealed four attributes: charisma, inspirational motivation, intellectual stimulation, and an individualized consideration of others. Other studies have shown that transformational leaders are also more extroverted than the average person (Bono & Judge, 2004).

To measure the extent to which individuals possess the attributes of transactional and transformational leadership styles, Bass (1985) devised the Multifactor Leader Questionnaire, or MLQ. Using this instrument, researchers have studied leadership in

**transactional leader**    A leader who gains compliance and support from followers primarily through goal setting and the use of rewards.

**transformational leader**    A leader who inspires followers to transcend their own needs in the interest of a common cause.

different cultures and in different types of organizations, including auto manufacturers, express-mail companies, multinational corporations, banks, government agencies, and military groups. Others have varied the use of the different leadership styles in controlled laboratory settings. Indicating that inspiration is universally a more powerful motivator than reward, the results have shown that transformational leaders are more effective than transactional leaders (Bass, 1998; Lowe et al., 1996) and exert influence by getting others to identify with them and the group they represent (Kark et al., 2003). In light of their ability to exert influence, it is not surprising that in a study of 39 managers and 130 employees in six companies, those who emerged as transformational leaders on the MLQ were also more socially networked within their organizations (Bono & Anderson, 2005).

People are drawn like magnets to transformational leaders who have what it takes. But wait. Does this mean that Adolf Hitler and other authoritarian heads of state were leaders of the same stripe as Mahatma Gandhi, Franklin D. Roosevelt, and Nelson Mandela? One would hope not. To separate human evil from virtue, Bass and Steidlmeier (1999) sought to distinguish between what they call pseudo-transformational leaders, who appeal to emotions rather than to reason and manipulate ignorant followers to further their own personal interests, and *authentic* transformational leaders, who morally uplift followers and help them transform their collective visions into realities.

The most effective type of leader is one who knows how to win support through the use of reward.  **F**ALSE.

## Leadership Among Women and Minorities

The fact that Americans elected Barack Obama the first African American president of the United States is remarkable in both historical and current contexts. Look at the leaders of America's Fortune 500 companies at the start of 2012, and you'll find that a mere 3.6% of the CEOs are women—a percentage that is only somewhat higher in the health care industry, government, or educational institutions. Look at the percentage of African Americans, Latinos, and Asians in the top ranks of the same organizations, and you'll see that they don't fare any better. Even today, in the twenty-first century, there are proportionally few U.S. senators who are female or Major League Baseball managers who are black.

Despite progress that has been made in entry- and middle-level positions, working women and minorities who seek positions of leadership have still not fully broken through the "glass ceiling"— a barrier so subtle that it is transparent, yet so strong that it keeps them from reaching the top of the hierarchy (Morrison & Von Glinow, 1990). Indeed, women may also encounter "glass walls" that keep them from moving laterally within an organization—for example, from positions in public relations to those in core areas such as production, marketing, and sales (Lopez, 1992).

Many women are highly qualified for positions of power. Research shows that male and female managers have very similar aspirations, abilities,

**TABLE 13.3**
**Characteristics of Transformational Leaders**

When people are asked to describe the best leaders they know, four characteristics are most often cited: charisma, an ability to inspire others, intellectual stimulation, and individualized consideration. These attributes are evident in the self-descriptions given here.

| Characteristic | Description | Sample Items |
|---|---|---|
| Charisma | Has a vision; gains respect, trust, and confidence; promotes a strong identification of followers. | I have a sense of mission that I communicate to them. They are proud to be associated with me. |
| Inspiration | Gives pep talks, increases optimism and enthusiasm, and arouses emotion in communications. | I present a vision to spur them on. I use symbols and images to focus their efforts. |
| Intellectual stimulation | Actively encourages a reexamination of existing values and assumptions; fosters creativity and the use of intelligence. | I enable them to think about old problems in new ways. I place strong emphasis on careful problem solving before taking action. |
| Individualized consideration | Gives personal attention to all members, acts as adviser and gives feedback in ways that are easy to accept, understand, and use for personal development. | I coach individuals who need it. I express my appreciation when they do a good job. |

Based on Bass & Avolio, 1990. © Cengage Learning

values, and job-related skills. Reviewing what is now a massive amount of research literature on sex differences in leadership, Alice Eagly and Linda Carli (2007) found that female leaders in the workplace are as task oriented as their male counterparts and that male and female leaders in general are equally effective. The only difference seems to be that men are more controlling and women more democratic in their approaches. As a result, men may be more effective as leaders in positions that require a more directive style (for example, in the military), whereas women may be more effective in managerial settings that require openness and cooperation. Indeed, when college students in one study were assigned to participate in long-term work groups, centralized leadership structures emerged over time in all-male groups, while more balanced decentralized leadership structures emerged in all-female groups (Berdahl & Anderson, 2005).

This portrayal of women leaders is consistent with Judy Rosener's (1995) observation that today's leading women draw effectively on qualities traditionally seen as feminine. It is also consistent with Sally Helgesen's (1995) observation that female managers interact more with subordinates, invite them to participate in the decision-making process, share information and power, and spin more extensive networks, or "webs of inclusion"—a leadership style she sees as a feminine advantage. Research shows that men and women differ in their style, not in the capacity for leadership. A meta-analysis of 45 comparative studies suggests that female leaders may even be slightly more transactional and transformational than men (Eagly et al., 2003). Other researchers are quick to caution that all claims of a gender advantage in favor of men or women are based on stereotypes and are overstated (Vecchio, 2002).

If women are competent to serve as leaders, why have so relatively few managed to reach the top in executive positions? For women, the path to power—from their entry into the labor market, to recruitment in an organization, and up the promotion ladder—is something of an obstacle course (Ragins & Sundstrom, 1989)—or, as Eagly & Carli (2007) put it, a labyrinth.

Three sets of impediments have been identified. One is that many women are deeply conflicted about having to juggle a career and family responsibilities and feel as though they have to pick one or the other (Halpern & Cheung, 2008). A second impediment is that some women shy away from competitive, hierarchical positions that offer the potential for leadership in favor of professions that involve helping people (Pratto et al., 1997). Yet a third impediment is societal. Lingering stereotypes portray women as followers, not as having the leadership traits commonly associated with masculinity. As a result, some people are uneasy about women in leadership roles—particularly women who have a task-oriented or who occupy "masculine" positions, as in business (Eagly & Karau, 2002; Koenig et al., 2011).

In a survey of 100 male and female corporate executives, Karen Lyness and Donna Thompson (2000) found that although the men and women were equally successful, the women had overcome more barriers to get where they were going—such as being excluded from informal social networks, being passed over for jobs that required relocating, and not fitting into the corporate culture. To further complicate matters, research shows that people in general exhibit a bias against motherhood when it comes to recommending women with children for promotion (Heilman & Okimoto, 2008).

Statistics show that minorities also fight an uphill battle for leadership positions. President Barack Obama is the most extraordinary exception. In the world of business, in 2009, only six U.S. companies in the Fortune 500 group had an African American CEO, the most notable being Ursula Burns, who became the first black woman to head a Fortune 500 company when she became CEO of the Xerox Corporation. What seems to be the barrier to entry?

Research is mixed on the question of whether employee evaluations are biased by race (Roth et al., 2003; Sackett & DuBois, 1991; Stauffer & Buckley, 2005; Waldman &

*"If you were taking a new job and had your choice of boss, would you prefer to work for a man or woman?' According to a 2006 Gallup poll that asked this question, 34 percent of men preferred a male boss and 10 percent preferred a female boss, and 56 percent had no preference. Among women, 40 percent preferred a male boss, 26 percent preferred a female boss, and 32 percent had no preference."*

Carroll, 2006

Avolio, 1991). Still, in light of what social psychologists have discovered about the subtleties of modern racism, as described in Chapter 5, business leaders should beware of the indirect ways in which minorities are handicapped in the pursuit of leadership. Many years ago, in a study of African Americans in the banking industry, many said that they had felt excluded socially from informal work groups, were not "networked," and lacked the sponsors, role models, and mentors needed for advancing within an organization (Irons & Moore, 1985). Similarly, a study of business school graduates revealed that African American and Hispanic men were less likely than others to have mentoring relationships with the influential white men in their respective companies (Dreher & Cox, 1996).

Overcoming the obstacles, some minorities do manage to break through the racial divide into positions of leadership. How did these individuals, and others who have risen to executive ranks, do it? In *Breaking Through*, David Thomas and John Gabarro (1999) studied the career trajectories and experiences of 54 managers and executives in three large companies. Referring to the corporate career ladder as a tournament, they discovered that the successful African-, Asian-, and Hispanic-American executives they studied climbed slowly at first to positions of middle management but were then fast-tracked relative to their white peers into the executive suite. Minority managers have to build a solid foundation early, they suggested, "because they are promoted only after proving themselves again and again." At every step of this developmental process, they found that mentors played a key role—opening doors, offering challenging assignments, and sponsoring them for recruitment into important, high-profile positions. In *Leading in Black and White*, Ancella Livers and Keith Caver (2003) further suggested, based on surveys and interviews of black professionals, that success involved some common ingredients such as having a distinct identity and a heightened focus on race, office politics, networking, and again, the need for mentors. People need other people, and the corporate world is no exception.

*Courtesy of Xerox Corporation*

When Ursula Burns was named CEO of the Xerox Corporation in 2009, she became the first African American woman ever to serve as the CEO of a Fortune 500 company. Burns is one of the most powerful women in business.

# Motivation at Work

What motivates individuals to work hard, and to work well? What determines your on-the-job satisfaction, attendance, loyalty, and commitment? People's attitudes about their job can positively and negatively affect their productivity and performance (Judge & Kammeyer-Mueller, 2012). Are you driven strictly by economics, or do you have other personal needs to fulfill? There is no single answer. At work, as in the rest of life, our behavior often stems from the convergence of many different motives. Hence, I/O psychologists over the years have found that people's satisfaction at work depends on a host of factors, economic and otherwise—such as leadership quality, a sense of justice, social relationships and comparisons, and the opportunity for advancement. Even the mere newness of a job can prove invigorating. In a longitudinal one-year study of new workers, Wendy Boswell and others (2009) found that satisfaction peaks during an initial honeymoon period before trending downward and settling in.

## Economic Reward Models

Out of necessity, people work to make a living. Yet in strictly economic terms, the issue of payment is more complicated than it may appear. To begin with, someone's overall satisfaction with his or her compensation depends not only on salary (gross income, take-home pay) but also on raises (upward changes in pay, how these changes are determined), how income is distributed (the number of checks received or salary differences within the company), and what benefits an employer offers (stock options, tuition credits, on-site gym facilities, vacation time, sick leave, health insurance, pensions, and other services). Each of these factors constitutes part of a formula for satisfaction (Heneman & Schwab, 1985; Judge & Welbourne, 1994). In fact, many rewards are not monetary but symbolic—such as titles, office size, location, carpeting, furnishings, windows, and the ability to regulate access by others (Sundstrom, 1986).

Perhaps the most basic theory of worker motivation is Victor Vroom's (1964) **expectancy theory**. According to Vroom, people are rational decision makers who analyze the benefits and costs of the possible courses of action. Accordingly, he said, workers become motivated and exert effort when they believe that (1) their effort will result in an improved performance, (2) their performance will be recognized and rewarded, and (3) the monetary and symbolic rewards that are offered are valuable and desirable. Over the years, this theory has been used with some success to predict worker attendance, productivity, and other job-related behaviors (Mitchell, 1974; Van Eerde & Thierry, 1996).

Goal setting is particularly important for motivation. Research shows that people perform better at work and are more productive when they are given specific goals and clear standards for success and failure than when they're simply told to "do your best" (Locke & Latham, 1990). Financial incentives, in particular, can effectively boost worker productivity without compromising the quality of the work (Jenkins et al., 1998). Based on past research, Edwin Locke and Gary Latham (2002) offer a practically useful theory of goal setting. The key, they maintain, is for people to set *specific* and *difficult* goals for themselves or others. This practice increases goal-related choice, effort, and persistence, increases productivity and other aspects of performance, brings reward and satisfaction, and triggers a willingness to take on new challenges and set new goals, thus setting into motion a self-perpetuating cycle of high performance (see ● Figure 13.7).

In February 2012, based on surveys of thousands of employees from hundreds of companies, Fortune named Google the best company to work for in America. Headquartered in Mountain View, California, Google provides its staff with free gourmet meals, onsite doctors, daycare, a spa, laundry service, and time to spend on independent projects. It's no wonder that Google's employees are so motivated—and that the company gets hundreds of résumés a day.

Erin Lubin/Bloomberg via Getty Images

**expectancy theory** The theory that workers become motivated when they believe that their efforts will produce valued outcomes.

● **FIGURE 13.7**
**Goal-Setting and Performance Cycle**
Locke & Latham, 2002. © Cengage Learning

| A specific, difficult goal | Goal-relevant choices, effort, and persistence | Productivity and performance | Reward and satisfaction |

The value of goal setting in the workplace cannot be overstated. In recent years, many organizations have moved from a focus on the individual to work teams. Reflecting this shift in practice, researchers have wondered whether goal setting functions at the group level in the same way that it does for individuals. A recent meta-analysis of this research indicates that it does: For groups as well as for individuals, it is best to set goals that are specific and difficult (Kleingeld et al., 2011).

## Bonuses, Bribes, and Intrinsic Motivation

People may strive for reward, but there's more to money than just economics and more to motivation than the size of a paycheck. Social psychological factors must also be considered. Under certain conditions, reward systems that increase *extrinsic motivation* may undermine *intrinsic motivation*. As we saw in Chapter 3, people are thought to be extrinsically motivated when they engage in an activity for money, recognition, or other tangible rewards. In contrast, people are said to be intrinsically motivated when they perform for the sake of interest, challenge, or sheer enjoyment. Business leaders want employees to feel intrinsically motivated and committed to their work. So where do expectancy theory and incentive programs fit in? Is tangible reward the bottom line or not?

Research shows that when people start getting paid for a task they already enjoy, they sometimes lose interest in it. In the first demonstration of this effect, Edward Deci (1971) recruited college students to work for three one-hour sessions on block-building puzzles they found interesting. During the first and third sessions, all participants were treated in the same manner. In the second session, however, half were paid one dollar for each puzzle they completed. To measure intrinsic motivation, Deci left participants alone during a break in the first and third sessions and recorded the amount of time they spent on the puzzles rather than on other available activities. Compared with participants in the unrewarded group, those who had been paid in the second session later showed less interest in the puzzles when the money was no longer available (see ● Figure 13.8).

This paradoxical finding that rewards undermine intrinsic motivation has been observed for many years in laboratory and field studies (Deci & Ryan, 1985; Lepper & Greene, 1978; Tang & Hall, 1995). By making people feel controlled rather than autonomous, various extrinsic factors commonly found in the workplace—deadlines, punishment, close supervision, evaluation, and competition—also have adverse effects on motivation and performance. Thus, Teresa Amabile (1996) found that people who were paid for artistic activities, compared with others who were not paid, produced work that was later judged to be less creative by independent raters. To be maximally productive, people should feel internally driven, not compelled by outside forces.

But wait. If money undermines intrinsic motivation, should employers *not* use monetary incentives? Are the pay-for-performance programs often used in the workplace doomed to fail, as some have suggested (Kohn,

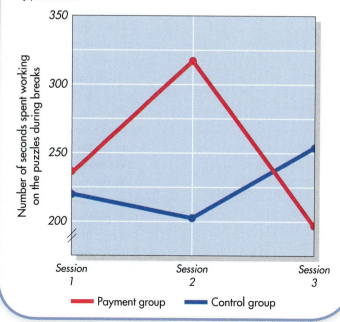

● **FIGURE 13.8**

**The Effect of Payment on Intrinsic Motivation: Turning Play into Work**

In this study, participants worked three times on puzzles they found interesting. After each session, the amount of free time participants spent on the puzzles served as a record of their intrinsic motivation. During the second session, half of the participants were paid for puzzles they completed and half were not. Those paid in the second session later showed less interest in the puzzles when the money was no longer available. From Deci, E. L., "Effects of externally mediated rewards on intrinsic motivation," *Journal of Personality and Social Psychology* vol 18 (pp. 105–115). Copyright © 1971 by the American Psychological Association. Reprinted by permission.

1993)? Not at all. To answer these questions, it's important to realize that any given reward can be interpreted in two ways, depending on how it is presented. On the one hand, being offered payment can make a person feel bribed, bought off, and controlled, which can result in the detrimental effects just described. On the other hand, rewards often provide people with positive feedback about the quality of their performance, as when people earn bonuses, scholarships, and verbal praise from others they respect. Research shows that although controlling rewards tend to lower intrinsic motivation, informational rewards have the opposite positive effect on motivation (Eisenberger & Cameron, 1996) and creativity (Eisenberger & Rhoades, 2001). In fact, for people who are highly focused on the achievement of certain goals at work, or elsewhere, tangible inducements tend to boost intrinsic motivation (Durik & Harackiewicz, 2007; Harackiewicz & Elliot, 1993).

## Equity Considerations

A second aspect of payment that influences motivation is the perception that it is fair. According to *equity theory*, presented in Chapter 9, people want rewards to be equitable. In other words, the ratio between inputs and outcomes should be the same for the self as it is for others. Relative to co-workers, then, the more effort you exert, and the more you contribute, the more money you should earn. If you feel overpaid or underpaid, however, you will experience distress and try to relieve it by (1) restoring actual equity, say, by working less or getting a raise, or (2) convincing yourself that equity already exists (Cropanzano, 1993).

Equity theory has some fascinating implications for behavior in the workplace. Consider Jerald Greenberg's (1988) study of employees in a large insurance firm. To allow for refurbishing, nearly 200 workers had to be moved temporarily from one office to another. The workers were randomly assigned to offices that usually belonged to others who were higher, lower, or equal in rank. Predictably, the usual occupants with the higher rank had a more spacious office, fewer occupants, and a larger desk. Would the random assignments influence job performance? By keeping track of the number of insurance cases processed and by rating the complexity of the cases and the quality of the decisions made, Greenberg was able to derive a measure of job performance for each worker before, during, and after the office switch. To restore equity, he reasoned, workers assigned to higher-status offices would feel overcompensated and improve their job performance and those sent to lower-status offices would feel undercompensated and slow their performance down. That is exactly what happened. ● Figure 13.9 shows that the results offered sound support for equity theory.

Satisfaction depends not only on equity outcomes but also on the belief that the means used to determine those outcomes were fair and clearly communicated (Brockner & Wiesenfeld, 1996; Folger, 1986). For example, Greenberg (1990) studied workers in three manufacturing plants owned by the same parent company. Business was slow, so the company reduced its payroll through temporary pay cuts. Would the cuts make workers feel underpaid? If so, how would the workers restore equity? Concerned that the policy might trigger employee theft, Greenberg randomly varied the conditions in the three plants. In one, the employees were told, without an explanation, that they would receive a 15% pay cut for 10 weeks. In the second plant, the same pay cut was accompanied by an explanation and expressions of regret. In the third plant, salaries were not cut. By keeping track of inventories for the 10 weeks before, during, and after the pay cuts, Greenberg was able to estimate the employee theft rate. The result: Workers whose pay had been cut stole more from the company—presumably to restore equity—but only when they were not provided with an adequate explanation

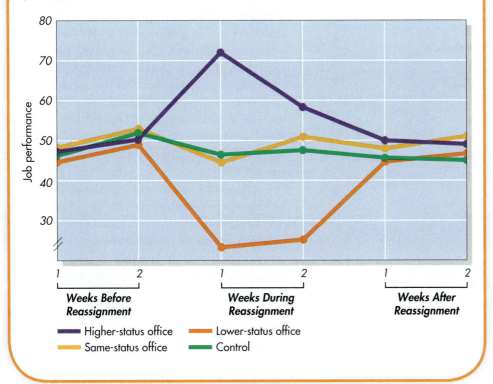

● **FIGURE 13.9**

**Equity in the Workplace**

Insurance company workers were moved temporarily to offices that were the workplaces of those who were higher, lower, or equal in status to their own rank. Supporting equity theory, those assigned to the offices of higher-status individuals increased their job performance, and those sent to offices of lower-status individuals showed a decrease. When workers were reassigned to their original offices, productivity levels returned to normal.

From Greenberg, J., "Equity and workplace status: A field experiment," *Journal of Applied Psychology* vol 73 (pp. 606–613). Copyright © 1988 by the American Psychological Association. Reprinted by permission.

for their loss. When it comes to getting paid, praised, and treated with respect, people are most dedicated to their jobs when they believe they are being treated fairly (Folger & Cropanzano, 1998).

People are so sensitive to unfairness, underpayment, and maltreatment that these feelings can cause stress and compromise their health. In a survey of more than 3,500 workers, Bennett Tepper (2001) discovered that those who felt victimized by injustice in the workplace also reported the most fatigue, anxiety, and depression. Particularly stressful is the combination of feeling underpaid and unfairly treated. Theorizing that people will lose sleep over these concerns, Greenberg (2006) studied 467 nurses at four private hospitals, two of which cut nurses' salaries by 10% and two of which did not. In one hospital from each group, he taught nursing supervisors how to help promote feelings of organizational justice. Across a 6-month period, participants periodically reported on their nighttime sleep patterns. The results showed two interesting patterns: (1) Underpaid nurses reported more symptoms of insomnia than those whose salaries were unchanged; and (2) this problem was reduced among underpaid nurses whose supervisors had been trained to treat them fairly (see ● Figure 13.10).

● **FIGURE 13.10**

**Losing Sleep over Underpayment and Organizational Injustice**

Nurses were studied at four hospitals—two that cut their salaries, two that did not. In one hospital of each group, supervisors were trained to promote feelings of organizational justice. For 6 months, participating nurses reported on their nighttime sleep patterns. As shown, those whose salaries had been cut reported more sleep loss than the others, but the problem was reduced among nurses whose supervisors had been trained to treat them fairly.

Greenberg, 2006. © Cengage Learning

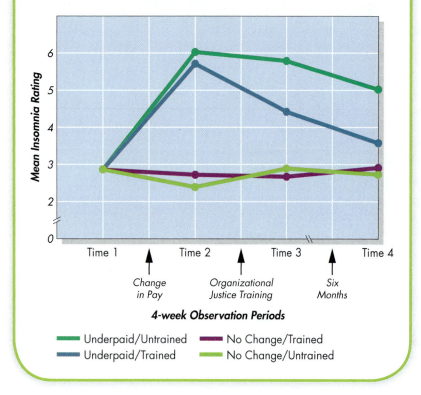

People who feel overpaid work harder on the job than those who see their pay as appropriate. **T**RUE.

Equity in the workplace is important, perhaps more so for men than for women. In studies of reward allocation, people are led to believe that they and a partner are working at a task for which they will be paid. They work separately, receive false feedback on their performance, and then are told that they must decide how to divide a joint reward. In this situation, women typically pay themselves less than men do and react less strongly when they are underpaid by others (Major & Deaux, 1982). Studies of outcomes outside the laboratory reinforced the point. An old study of male and female graduates of an Ivy League business school showed that men were more likely than women to negotiate starting salaries that were higher than the salaries the companies initially offered (Gerhart & Rynes, 1991). Other studies have since confirmed the point: Men negotiate more aggressively than women do—or, to put it another way, "Women don't ask" (Babcock & Laschever, 2003).

The gender wage gap has been narrowing in recent years, but it has not been fully closed. According to the U.S. Bureau of Labor Statistics, American women in 1980 earned only 60 cents for every dollar that men were paid. By 1990, the figure was up slightly, to 72 cents. By 2006, it had climbed to 81 cents. In 2012, it was at 82 cents.

There are many possible explanations for this gender wage gap. One is that women expect less pay than men do, even when they are equally qualified—an expectation that may stem from a long history of discrimination (Major & Konar, 1984). Second, women sometimes care less about money and more about interpersonal relationships (Crosby, 1982). Third, women may be satisfied with less money because they compare themselves with other women instead of with their more highly paid male counterparts (Bylsma et al., 1995; Chesler & Goodman, 1976). Fourth, women on average tend to rate themselves less favorably than do men, so even when they work harder and perform better, they feel less entitled (Major et al., 1984). Whatever the explanation, it is clear that the gender gap in wages is deeply rooted in history (Goldin, 1990). It appears equally clear, however, that today's working women are not content to remain underpaid relative to men. Perhaps the gender wage gap will vanish as successive generations of women become more established in high-paying careers.

## The Progress Principle

A great deal of research has centered on the effects of money and other intrinsic or extrinsic rewards. There is no question that people work primarily to make a living and that money is a powerful motivating force. But is one's compensation the key to job satisfaction? Through a meta-analysis of 92 studies that reported correlations between pay and various aspects of job satisfaction, Timothy Judge and his colleagues (2010) found that although the correlation is greater than zero, people's level of satisfaction at work was only weakly correlated with how much they were paid. With regard to the implications, they concluded that "Given a choice, individuals would be better off weighing other job attributes more heavily than pay" (p. 163).

Clearly, there is more to motivation in the workplace than money—at least for some people. But what is it? In a *Harvard Business Review* article entitled "What Really Motivates Workers," Teresa Amabile and Steven Kramer (2010) surveyed more than 600 managers from dozens of companies to rank the impact of various factors on employee motivation. They ranked "recognition for good work" as number 1—even ahead of financial incentives. "Unfortunately," note Amabile and Kramer, "those managers are wrong."

In a massive multiyear study described in their book *The Progress Principle*, Amabile and Kramer (2011) tracked 238 "knowledge workers" from a variety of settings through entries in a structured diary that they emailed to researchers at the end of every work day (a knowledge worker is someone who thinks for a living—such as software engineers, architects, scientists, writers, and lawyers). Each day, the workers reported on their activities, emotions, and motivation levels. Through nearly 12,000 entries, the results showed that people's sense that they had made meaningful progress in their work was the aspect of their day most frequently associated with a positive mood; feelings of joy, warmth, and pride; a perception of support; a sense of accomplishment; and a high level of motivation. As one computer programmer put it, "I smashed that bug that's been frustrating me for almost a calendar week. That may not be an event to you, but I live a very drab life, so I'm all hyped."

Overall, participants noted progress on 76% of their best days and only 25% of their worst days. The association between making progress and feeling good is a correlation that can be interpreted in different ways. On the basis of this association, however, Amabile and Kramer offer advice on how to set this positive process in motion. Managers, they note, can motivate workers, not only through financial incentives—seldom mentioned in the diary entries—but by facilitating progress. They can do this by providing more time, resources, encouragement, and personal assistance; by removing unnecessary obstacles, distractions, and demands; by keeping a daily progress checklist; and then by celebrating the incremental advances or "small wins" that are made along the way.

"Productivity is up nine percent since I made everyone a vice-president."

# Economic Decision Making

People are intensely focused on money—anxious to have more of it and afraid to be without it. In powerful and symbolic ways, money arouses emotion, activates thought, and motivates action. We ran a Google search on the word *money* in the summer of 2012 and found that there were 3.6 trillion entries, exceeding the 312 million entries generated by the word *happiness*. (Being social psychologists, we were interested to find that *love* conquered all at 6.9 trillion entries.)

*"Money is power, freedom, a cushion, the root of all evil, the sum of blessings."*

—Carl Sandburg

## The Symbolic Power of Money

Although actor and comedian W. C. Fields once said that a rich man is nothing but a poor man with money, common sense and recent research suggest that money can change people in interesting ways.

Think about it. If you had a fortune, you would be financially independent. How would that make you feel? In a series of laboratory experiments, Kathleen Vohs and her colleagues (2006) found that when college students were merely primed to think about money, they became more self-sufficient, more autonomous, and less social in relation to others. In each study, the researchers primed money in some participants but not others in subtle ways—for example, by having them read an essay that mentioned money, by presenting them with scrambled sentences that relate to money, by having them count a large stack of Monopoly money, or by seating them at a computer with a screensaver that featured floating bills. Across the board, those who were exposed to money cues later became more independent. Put into a social situation, they preferred working alone rather than on a team, they put more distance between themselves and a fellow participant, they sought less help on a puzzle they could not solve, and they gave less help to someone who needed it. Reflecting on these findings, Vohs speculates that "money changes people at a core, basic level," that "having money makes people feel less connected and more independent, whereas having little money makes you feel more interdependent with others" (Carpenter, 2005, p. 27).

Let's take this speculation one step further. If money leads us to feel more self-sufficient, does it lessen our need for approval and blunt the pain of social rejection? And following rejection, do we attach greater value to money? Through research conducted in China, Xinyue Zhou and others (2009) sought to answer these questions. In one study, they brought a handful of university students together for a getting-acquainted conversation. The students were then separated and asked to pick someone from the group they'd like to work with. At that point, by random assignment, all students were told that they had to be dismissed—either because everyone selected them (social acceptance) or because no one selected them (social rejection). Afterward, they completed a set of money-related tasks. Here's the interesting part: When asked to draw a Chinese coin from memory, students in the rejection condition drew larger coins. They also said they were more willing to permanently give up such pleasures as chocolate, sunshine, and the beach in exchange for the equivalent of $1.4 million. Rejection had increased the subjective value of money.

In a second study, students engaged in what they thought to be a "finger dexterity" task: They counted out either 80 pieces of paper or 80 $100 bills. Next they played a computerized online ball-tossing game, presumably with three live students. In the normal condition, the game proceeded uneventfully. In a rejection condition, however, the others soon started to exclude the participant from the ball toss. When later asked how they felt about the game, those who had counted paper were more distressed than those who had counted money. Somehow, the money served to buffer students from the distress normally caused by social rejection (see ● Figure 13.11).

"I wish they'd quit sending my financial statements."

Living alone on a deserted island, money would not be necessary to bolster self-sufficiency or protect against social rejection.

## Social Influences in the Stock Market

For all its tangible and symbolic benefits, and although human motivation is complex, money plays a prominent role. In recent years, therefore, social psychologists have become interested in how people make economic decisions, for example when they invest in the stock market. The stock market can be remarkably volatile, as it has been over the past decade—surging up, plummeting down, and inching its way back up in ways that resemble a roller coaster ride. Why does the market fluctuate so much? Are the companies we invest in unpredictable from day to day or are social psychological factors at work? To what extent are day-to-day price movements determined by rational economic indicators such as the gross domestic product, interest rates, budget surpluses and deficits, inflation, employment statistics, company earnings, political uncertainty, consumer confidence, and stock prices that are too high or too low and need correction? To what extent, for that matter, is the stock market influenced by fear, greed, false beliefs, financial experts like CNBC's Jim Cramer who appear on business shows, rumors that spread over the Internet, conformity pressures, and other social influences, all compounded by the speed and volume with which traders can buy and sells stocks online?

The odds of making money are far better in the stock market than in the slot machines found in gambling casinos. Most of the time, most investors come out ahead. In many ways, however, choosing stocks is a form of gambling. In *A Random Walk Down Wall Street*, first published in 1981, economist Burton Malkiel (2007) reported that over the long haul, mutual fund portfolios compiled by experts perform no better than randomly selected groups of stocks. Thus, when *Consumer Reports* evaluated the advice given by professional brokers, it concluded that "a monkey throwing darts at the stock pages . . . could probably do as well in overall investment performance, perhaps even better" (Shefrin & Statman, 1986, p. 52).

But don't some professionals turn a greater profit than others? And if stock prices rise and fall in reaction to market conditions and the success of a company in relation to that of its competitors, can't the astute investor or short-term day trader take advantage of these relationships? The answer to both questions is "not necessarily." It is certainly true that some brokers perform better than others do for a period of time, perhaps even for a few years. But individuals are no more likely to succeed after a string of wins than after a string of losses. Since many investors and traders have access to the same information and since stock prices can change at a moment's notice, short-term price movements in the market cannot be predicted with precision or reliability. The only way to guarantee profit is to use confidential inside information, which is illegal. Yet studies show that the average person has a measure of faith in professional investors, overestimating their rate of success relative to their actual performance (Törngren & Montgomery, 2004).

If stock market decisions are not made on strictly economic grounds, then on what are they based? As described in *Greed and Fear*, Hersh Shefrin's (2006) book on the behavioral finance and the psychology of investing, predictions of the future on Wall Street are heavily influenced by social psychological factors. In October 1987, for example, the U.S. stock market crashed, resulting in an estimated loss of $500 billion. Shortly afterward, economist Robert Shiller sent questionnaires to a large group of active traders to try to determine what caused the crisis. For the 1,000 or so investors who responded, the key event was news about the market itself, including a sharp decline that occurred on the morning of the crash. In other words, price movements in the stock market were triggered not by objective economic information but by other price movements in the market.

● **FIGURE 13.11**

**Links Between Money and Social Rejection**

After counting either blank pieces of paper or money, some research participants but not others were told other players had excluded them from an online ball-tossing game. As seen in terms of how they felt about the game, excluded participants who had counted paper were more distressed than before (right), yet those who had counted money were not (left). It appears that money and the self-sufficiency that it symbolizes can mute the adverse effects of social rejection. Zhou et al., 2009. © Cengage Learning

"I don't buy stocks simply because others are buying them. I buy them because many, many others are buying them."

Does this phenomenon ring a bell? Studies on the processes of social comparison and conformity have shown that when people feel they cannot clearly and concretely measure their own opinion, they turn to others for guidance. Perhaps that is why investors are more influenced by news and stock market tips during periods of rising or falling prices than they are during periods of relative stability (Schachter et al., 1985).

With respect to coin flips and other chance events, gamblers too often assume that hot streaks are due to turn cold and vice versa. Yet when it comes to games of skill, such as basketball, people often make the opposite assumptions that a hot streak forecasts continued success and a cold spell predicts failure. Both assumptions are incorrect. One event does not imply another. But what about the ups and downs of a stock market? Do either of these beliefs color the decisions investors make?

To explore this question, Stanley Schachter and others (1987) presented college students with recent price histories of stocks that had increased, decreased, or remained stable over a 3-week period. The conventional wisdom on Wall Street, of course, is that investors should buy low and sell high. Yet most participants indicated they would buy stocks that had risen and sell stocks that had fallen. In a follow-up study, very similar decisions were made by more sophisticated students attending the business school at Columbia University.

Do people always go with the flow of the marketplace, or do they sometimes buck the trend to buy low and sell high? Paul Andreasson (1987) argued that the answer depends on attributions. According to Andreasson, investors may follow conventional wisdom. But, he asked, what about price changes for which they have a ready explanation? What if a rise in a stock's price is attributed to certain company or world events? As far as the stock market is concerned, attributions such as these can produce self-fulfilling prophecies by leading investors to believe that the changes will persist—that rising prices will continue to climb or that declining prices will continue to fall. To test his hypothesis, Andreasson simulated a stock market on the computer and found that without news stories to explain the fluctuations, research participants assumed that prices would gravitate to previous levels. The result: They bought stocks when the price was low and sold when the price was high. However, those who also received *Wall Street Journal* explanations for the changes pursued the less profitable strategy, buying stocks that were climbing (based on the assumption that they would continue to do so) and selling those that were on the decline (based on the same assumption of continuity).

Even unpublished rumors can have this effect. Nicholas DiFonzo and Prashant Bordia (1997) conducted a stock market simulation in which unconfirmed company rumors were leaked to some participants but not others. Interestingly, the participants said that they felt that the rumors were not credible and thus did not sway their decisions. Yet they traded on these rumors as if they were hard facts. It doesn't stretch the imagination to see how all these findings might relate to actual behavior in the stock market. Faced with upward and downward movements, the financial news media often seize upon current events for a quick explanation. In some cases, the rumors spread like wildfire through the business community. Whether the news is true or false is irrelevant. Either way, it can turn an initial rise into a bull rally and an initial dip into a steep dive. For this reason, researchers are using laboratory simulations to mimic the decision making that causes stock market bubbles, crashes, and other phenomena (Porter & Smith, 2003).

Sometimes emotional factors can lead us astray. Contradicting rational theories of economic decision making, research shows that people fall prey to the **endowment effect**, a tendency to inflate the value of objects they already own (Thaler, 1980). In a study that demonstrates this point, people demanded a higher price for a coffee mug that had been given to them than they did for a comparable mug that they did not yet own (Kahneman et al., 1990). In a second study, researchers observed the orders placed by Australian stock market investors and found that sellers valued their own shares higher than buyers did, regardless of the current market price (Furche & Johnstone, 2006).

As investors, it has long seemed that people also fall prey to the *disposition effect*, a tendency for people to sell stocks that have risen too early and to hold stocks that have declined too long (Shefrin & Statman, 1985). Experiments have confirmed this pattern and have shown that people value gains and losses relative to the price they paid for their shares. Using purchase price as a reference point, we are more likely to take risks in order to avert possible losses than to maximize our gains (Barberis & Xiong, 2009; Weber & Camerer, 1998).

## Commitment, Entrapment, and Escalation

Stock market behavior, like other business decisions that individuals, small groups, and organizations make, is complicated by another social factor. Shefrin and Meir Statman (1985) argued that many investors lack the self-control necessary for sound investment decisions. As we just noted, people who own shares of a stock that is climbing often sell too early so they can enjoy the quick pleasure of making a profit. This tendency is easy to understand. But when people own stock that is falling, they often wait too long before selling in the hope that they might avoid a financial loss. Why do people often continue to hang on in a failing situation—a decision-making disease that Shefrin (2006) calls "Get-Evenitis." When the handwriting is on the wall, why compound the problem by throwing good money after bad?

In *Too Much Invested to Quit*, Alan Teger (1980) described a dollar-auction game that illustrates part of the dilemma. Imagine yourself in this situation: The auctioneer tells you and other participants that a $1 bill is about to be sold. As in a typical auction,

**endowment effect** The tendency for people to inflate the value of objects, goods, or services they already own.

The floor of a stock exchange is a setting fraught with social influence (left). Today's investors are also bombarded by social influences from business shows such as CNBC's *Mad Money*, starring Jim Cramer (right).

the highest bidder will receive the dollar in exchange for the amount bid. Yet contrary to convention, the second highest bidder must also pay the amount bid and will receive nothing in return. You and the other participants are asked not to communicate, and the minimum opening bid is set at five cents. Then, before you know it, the bidding begins. In laboratory experiments, two participants compete in the auction. They are supplied with a small amount of money that is theirs to keep, and they are free to quit the experiment at any time. What happens next might seem startling. Some pairs reasonably choose to take the money and run without making a single bid. Other pairs, however, get involved in escalating bidding wars. According to Teger, bidding for the dollar frequently climbs into the $5 range—more than the amount allocated for play by the experimenter. On one occasion, the auctioneer had to terminate the game after the two participants had bid $24.95 and $25!

The dollar auction helps us to grasp how we can become financially overcommitted in real life. In Chapter 8, we saw that individuals and groups can become *entrapped* by their own initial commitments as they try to justify or salvage investments they have already made. In business, the economic conditions in which an investment is made sometimes justify continued commitment. When there is a reasonable likelihood of success and when potential earnings are high relative to the additional necessary costs, it may pay to persist. With certain long-term investments, sizable up-front costs have to be endured before the delayed benefits are likely to materialize. As in the dollar auction, however, entrapment may occur when economic conditions do not provide a basis for optimism.

Why do investors, business executives, and others losing money on a failing investment so often "hang tough," only to sink deeper and deeper? Why do supervisors who recommend that a worker be hired later overrate that worker's job performance compared with others in the company who were not involved in the hiring (Schoorman, 1988)? Why do NBA teams continue to start players who were selected as top draft picks even though they have not performed well (Staw & Hoang, 1995)? One explanation for these **escalation effects** is that while people ordinarily avoid taking large financial risks to gain money, they are often willing to take risks to keep from losing money. When offered a hypothetical choice between a certain gain of $1,000 and a 50–50 shot at a gain of $2,500, most people choose the smaller guaranteed alternative. Yet when offered a choice between a certain loss of $1,000 and a 50–50 shot at a loss of $2,500, most people roll the dice (Kahneman & Tversky, 1979).

Our aversion to loss accounts for part of the problem, but it's clear that social psychological factors also contribute heavily to the escalation effect. Research has shown that individuals who make the decisions that lead to loss are more likely than others to persist or even to invest further when they feel personally responsible. Why? There are two reasons, both of which are valid (Moon, 2001). One is that people are trained to finish what they have started—a desire for completion that can lead people to throw good money or time after bad (Garland & Conlon, 1998). The second, according to Barry Staw, Joel Brockner, and others, is that people often remain committed to a failing course of action in order to justify their prior decisions, protect their self-esteem, or save face in front of others. Thus, Staw and his colleagues (1997) found that banks were less likely to cut their losses on bad business and real estate loans when the executives who had funded those loans were still with the bank than when they were not. Zhang and Baumeister (2006) found that participants whose self-esteem was threatened were more likely to become entrapped in a failing laboratory game, losing more money as a result.

In organizations, escalation effects can be minimized by removing the individuals who made the initial losing investment from the decision making later on. Fortunately, individual investors can also learn to use various de-escalation strategies designed to make them more responsive to available evidence and keep them from throwing good money after bad (Simonson & Staw, 1992). In one study, for example, Richard Larrick

**escalation effect** The tendency for people to persist in failing investments to avert loss, which causes losses to mount.

and others (1990) found that people often violate the **sunk cost principle** of economics, which states that only future costs and benefits, not past commitments, or "sunk costs," should be considered in making a decision.

To appreciate the practical implications, imagine that you've bought a $40 ticket to a basketball game weeks in advance. Now, on the day of the game, you don't feel well, it's snowing, and your favorite player is injured. Do you still go to the game to make sure you use the ticket? Not wanting to "waste" the money, many of us would go even though the money is already sunk, and even though we would have to bear the added costs of getting sick, driving in bad weather, and sitting through a boring game. To see if there is a more rational economic choice, ask yourself this question: Would you go to the game if someone called on game day and offered you a free ticket? If you said that you would go if you'd paid for the ticket but not if it were free, then—like investors who don't know when to cut their losses—you fell into the sunk cost trap and should have stayed home.

Over and over again, studies have shown that human adults fall prey to the sunk cost effect, allowing their economic decisions to be biased by past investments of time, money, and effort, a maladaptive tendency that, curiously, is *not* exhibited by children or laboratory animals (Arkes & Ayton, 1999). Thankfully, we are trainable. In a study of University of Michigan professors, Larrick and others (1990) found that the economists among them were more likely than their counterparts in other disciplines to use the sunk cost principle—not only in hypothetical problems but also in personal decisions. More important, they found that others can be taught to apply the rule as well. Indeed, a full month after exposure to a brief training session, college students were more likely to report that they were using the rule in their own lives. Even without explicit training, a developmental study that compared people of different ages showed that older adults were less likely to fall into the sunk cost trap than were younger adults (Strough et al., 2008). Mercifully, it appears that people learn this lesson from life experience.

> People losing money on an investment tend to cut their losses rather than hang tough. **F**ALSE.

> **sunk cost principle** The economic rule of thumb that only future costs and benefits, not past commitments, should be considered in making a decision.

# Review

- The classic Hawthorne studies showed that attention paid to workers increased their productivity.

- In the workplace and other business settings, behavior is heavily influenced by social psychological factors.

## Personnel Selection

- Recruiting a competent staff is the first important step in developing a successful organization.

### The Typical Job Interview
- Employment interviews may actually diminish the tendency of employers to make simple stereotyped judgments.
- But interviews often give rise to poor selection decisions, in part because of the self-presentations of applicants and by expectations of the interviewer that bias the interview.

### "Scientific" Alternatives to Traditional Interviews
- Many companies use standardized tests of cognitive ability, personality, and integrity as part of the selection process.

- Although overt integrity tests are easy to fake, covert tests are not, and the results of covert tests are somewhat predictive of job performance.
- A more effective selection method is the structured interview, in which all applicants are evaluated in a standardized manner.
- Many organizations use assessment centers, in which multiple applicants take part in multiple activities monitored by a group of evaluators.

### Affirmative Action
- Affirmative action affects those it is designed to help, those who feel excluded by it, organizations that implement it, and interactions among these three groups.

- Research shows that women devalue their own performance when they think they have been preferentially selected.
- But reactions are more favorable when procedures are seen as fair, as when merit plays a role, and when the recipients are seen as minorities and deserving.

### Culture and Organizational Diversity

- Affirmative action and the globalization of business have combined to increase diversity in the workplace.
- One prediction is that diversity will breed division and conflict, making work teams less effective.
- A more optimistic prediction is that diversity will increase the range of perspectives brought to bear on a problem, enhancing group performance.

- At present, research provides a hint of support for both predictions, suggesting that there is no single or simple effect.

> **Putting *Common Sense* to the Test**
>
> **Although flawed, job interviews consistently make for better hiring decisions.**
> **False.** *Although interviews may lessen the tendency among employers to make simple stereotyped judgments, they often lack predictive validity.*

# Performance Appraisals

- Performance appraisals involve the evaluation of an employee and communication of the results to that person.
- Sometimes objective measures of performance are available, but usually evaluations are based on subjective judgments.

### Supervisor Ratings

- Research shows that supervisor ratings are based largely on job-relevant characteristics.
- These ratings may be biased by halo effects, contrast effects, and individual differences in the tendency to give high, low, or neutral ratings on a numeric scale.

### Self-Evaluations

- Self-evaluations also figure into performance appraisals, but they tend to be self-serving and inflated.
- Self-evaluations are higher among those who have power in an organization. They are also higher among men than among women.

### New and Improved Methods of Appraisal

- Performance appraisals can be improved when ratings are made shortly after observation, careful notes are taken, multiple raters are used, and raters are trained in the necessary skills.

### Due-Process Considerations

- Procedural fairness (not just outcomes) is an important factor in the way people react to evaluations of their performance.

> **Putting *Common Sense* to the Test**
>
> **A problem with having workers evaluate their own job performance is that self-ratings are overly positive.**
> **True.** *Self-evaluations of job performance are not only more positive than ratings made by others but also less predictive of success.*

# Leadership

- Everyone agrees that leadership requires social influence.

### The Classic Trait Approach

- One approach is to identify the traits that characterize people who appear to have leadership qualities.
- Situational theories are based on the notion that different situations call for different types of leaders.

### Contingency Models of Leadership

- In Fiedler's contingency model, task-oriented leaders excel in high- and low-control situations, whereas relations-oriented leaders are effective in moderate-control situations.
- According to the normative model, although leaders range from autocratic to participative, the key to good leadership is to invite the right amount of worker participation.

### Transactional Leadership

- Transactional leaders reward followers who keep up their end of the bargain and correct those who do not.

### Transformational Leadership

- Transformational leaders motivate followers through their charisma, inspiration, intellectual stimulation, and personal concern for others.
- Studies show that transformational leaders are more effective than transactional leaders.

### Leadership Among Women and Minorities

- Despite recent gains, working women and minorities are underrepresented in positions of leadership.
- Many women who are qualified encounter obstacles at home and at work, where people hold stereotypes about women in leadership roles.
- Part of the problem for minorities is that they are excluded from social networks and influential mentors in the workplace.

> **Putting *Common Sense* to the Test**
>
> **The most effective type of leader is one who knows how to win support through the use of reward.**
> **False.** *Great leaders articulate a vision and then inspire others to join in that vision and work for a common cause.*

# Motivation at Work

- Both economic and social factors influence motivation in the workplace.

### Economic Reward Models

- On the economic side, Vroom's expectancy theory states that workers behave in ways designed to produce the most desirable outcome.
- Various incentive programs are thus used to motivate by reward.

### Bonuses, Bribes, and Intrinsic Motivation

- When people perceive a reward as a bribe and a means of controlling their behavior, they lose interest in the work itself.
- But when a reward is presented as a bonus, giving positive information about the quality of work, it can enhance intrinsic motivation.

### Equity Considerations

- Equity theory says that the ratio between inputs and outcomes should be the same for all workers.

- Research shows that workers adjust their productivity levels upward when they feel overpaid and downward when they feel underpaid.
- For various reasons, women accept as equitable a lower level of pay than men do.

### The Progress Principle

- Although money is a powerful motivating force, a study of "knowledge workers" showed that making meaningful progress in their work was the aspect of their day most frequently associated with a good mood and high level of motivation

---

**Putting *Common Sense* to the Test**

**People who feel overpaid work harder on the job than those who see their pay as appropriate.**

(**True.**) *People who feel overpaid work harder to restore their sense of equity.*

---

# Economic Decision Making

### The Symbolic Power of Money

- Research shows that money makes people feel more independent, more self-sufficient, and less in need of others.
- As a result, exposure to money can mute the distressing effects of social rejection.

### Social Influences in the Stock Market

- Economic decisions are often influenced by social psychological factors.
- Sharp changes in the stock market can be triggered by news of what other investors are doing.
- The goal in the stock market is to buy low and sell high, yet various factors can lead investors to follow less-profitable strategies.
- Stock market simulations have shown that investors can be influenced by news stories and unconfirmed rumors, which can set in motion a self-fulfilling prophecy.

### Commitment, Entrapment, and Escalation

- People often become entrapped by their initial commitments and so stick to failing courses of action and throw good money after bad.
- At an organizational level, escalation can be minimized by removing those who made the initial losing investment from later decision making.
- Individually, people can be taught de-escalation strategies, such as the rule that only future costs and benefits, not sunk costs, are relevant to economic decisions.

---

**Putting *Common Sense* to the Test**

**People losing money on an investment tend to cut their losses rather than hang tough.**

(**False.**) *People often remain committed to a failing course of action in order to justify the initial decision to themselves and others.*

---

## KEY TERMS

assessment center (539)

contingency model of leadership (550)

endowment effect (565)

escalation effect (566)

expectancy theory (556)

Hawthorne effect (533)

industrial/organizational (I/O) psychology (532)

integrity tests (537)

normative model of leadership (551)

performance appraisal (545)

structured interview (538)

sunk cost principle (567)

transactional leader (552)

transformational leader (552)

## MEDIA RESOURCES

Go to CengageBrain.com to access Psychology CourseMate, where you will find an interactive eBook, glossaries, flashcards, quizzes, videos, and more.

# Health and Well-Being

This chapter explores the social psychology of physical and mental health. We focus first on the links between stress and health. Four questions are asked in this regard: What causes stress, how does it affect the body, how do we appraise potentially stressful situations, and what are some ways of coping with stress? Next we discuss some of the social influences on treatment and prevention. We then conclude on a positive note, looking at the roots of happiness.

# 14

Richard Price/Getty Images

**When Laurence Sterne**, an eighteenth-century English novelist, weighed the value of good health, he concluded that it was "above all gold and treasure." Most would agree—which is why health care is so important to everyone and why political, economic, and legal debates over health reform in the United States has been such a contentious topic. This long and complex debate clearly illustrates the intensity of feelings on this issue. In matters of life and death, everyone cares deeply, including social psychologists.

The reasons that social psychologists study *mental health* and such disorders as anxiety and depression are obvious. We humans are inherently social creatures, and our psychological well-being can be both damaged and repaired by our relationships with other people. But social psychologists are also interested in *physical health*, a domain normally associated with medicine. Working in universities, medical schools, hospitals, and government agencies, many social psychologists are involved in the relatively new area of **health psychology**—the application of psychology to the promotion of physical health and the prevention and treatment of illness (Straub, 2012; Taylor, 2012a).

You may wonder: What does social psychology have to do with catching a cold, having a heart attack, or being afflicted by cancer? If you could turn the clock back a few years and ask your family doctor, his or her reply would be "nothing." In the past, physical illness was considered a purely biological event. But this narrow medical perspective has given way to a broader model, which holds that health is a joint product of biological, psychological, and social factors.

Part of the reason for this expanded view is that illness patterns over the years have changed in significant ways. In the year 1900, the principal causes of death in the United States were contagious diseases such as polio, smallpox, tuberculosis, typhoid fever, malaria, influenza, and pneumonia. Today, none of these infectious illnesses are leading killers. Instead, Americans are most likely to die (in order of risk) from heart disease, cancers, strokes, respiratory diseases, and accidents (AIDS is twentieth on the list in the United States but fourth worldwide). Interestingly, these diseases can sometimes be prevented through changes in lifestyle, outlook, and behavior. In light of useful research that has been conducted in recent years, this chapter focuses first on stress: what causes it, what it does to the body, and how we appraise stressful situations in order to cope with them. Next, we look at some social influences on the treatment and prevention of illness. Finally, we consider the pursuit of happiness and life satisfaction.

**health psychology**   The study of physical health and illness by psychologists from various areas of specialization.

# Putting *Common Sense* to the Test

*Circle Your Answer*

**T   F**   The accumulation of daily hassles does more to make people sick than catastrophes or major life changes.

**T   F**   Like humans, zebras get ulcers.

**T   F**   Stress can weaken the heart, but it cannot affect the immune system.

**T   F**   When it comes to physical health, research does not support popular beliefs about the power of positive thinking.

**T   F**   People who have lots of friends are healthier and live longer than those who live more isolated lives.

**T   F**   Countries and at all levels of wealth, the more money people have, the happier they are.

# Stress and Health

**Stress** is an unpleasant state of arousal that arises when we perceive that the demands of a situation threaten our ability to cope effectively. Nobody knows the precise extent of the problem, but stress is a potent killer. Regardless of who you are, when you were born, or where you live, you have no doubt experienced stress. Sitting in rush-hour traffic, packing your belongings to move, losing your job and looking for work, getting married or divorced, getting into an argument with a close friend, worrying about the health of a parent or your child, living in a high-crime neighborhood, struggling to make financial ends meet, and caring for a loved one who is sick are examples of stresses and strains we all must live with.

Clearly, what stresses an entire generation or population can be influenced by world events. In a nationwide survey of thousands of men and women commissioned by the American Psychological Association (2008), respondents were asked to indicate the sources of stress in their lives. Four out of five cited money and the economy. In fact, five of the top 10 stressors related to money, the others being work, housing costs, and job stability (see Table 14.1). The effects on a person's health and well-being are clear. Among the symptoms most commonly reported were irritability and anger, fatigue, nervousness, lack of energy and motivation, sadness, depression, headaches, wanting to cry, stomach upset, and muscular tension.

From the standpoint of population demographics, it appears that some types of people are more likely to report feeling stressed than others. Analyzing national surveys that were conducted from 1983 to 2009, Sheldon Cohen and Denise Janicki-Deverts (2012) found that more stress is consistently reported by women than men, minority respondents than whites, people who are unemployed than employed, those who are employed rather than retired, and people in general who are younger, less educated, and have lower incomes.

Whether the stress is short term or long term, serious or mild, and despite these group differences, no one is immune from stress and there is no escape. But there are ways to cope. According to Richard Lazarus and Susan Folkman (1984), the stress-and-coping process is an ongoing transaction between a person and his or her environment. Faced with an event that may prove threatening, our subjective **appraisal** of the situation determines how we will experience the stress and what **coping** strategies we will use—in other words, what thoughts, feelings, and behaviors we will employ to try to reduce the stress. At times, people also take proactive steps to keep a potentially stressful event from occurring in the first place. As we'll see, effective coping helps to maintain good health; ineffective coping can cause harm (Monat et al., 2007; Harrington, 2013).

In the next two sections, we examine two questions that are relevant to health and well-being: (1) What causes stress, and (2) how does stress "get into" the body? Then we look at appraisal and coping, processes that account for why an event that flattens one person can prove harmless to another. As all the pieces come together, we'll see that the answers to these questions provide a broad and useful model of the stress-and-coping process (see ● Figure 14.1).

*According to the World Health Organization, the average life expectancy from birth ranges widely from a low of 47 years in Malawi to a high of 83 in Japan and San Marino. (The average life expectancy is 79 in the United States and 81 in Canada.) For up-to-date health statistics, you can visit online the World Health Organization (www.who.org) and the National Center for Health Statistics (www.cdc.gov/nchs).*

**TABLE 14.1**

**What Americans Cite as Top Stressors**

| Stressors | Percent of Americans |
| --- | --- |
| Money | 81 |
| The economy | 80 |
| Work | 67 |
| Family health problems | 67 |
| Family responsibilities | 64 |
| Housing costs | 62 |
| Relationships | 62 |
| Personal health concerns | 61 |
| Job stability | 56 |
| Personal safety | 48 |

American Psychological Association, 2008. © Cengage Learning

*Anthony Robbins offers a simple two-step formula for handling stress: (1) Don't sweat the small stuff, and (2) remember that it's all small stuff.*

**stress**   An unpleasant state of arousal in which people perceive the demands of an event as taxing or exceeding their ability to satisfy or alter those demands.

**appraisal**   The process by which people make judgments about the demands of potentially stressful events and their ability to meet those demands.

**coping**   Efforts to reduce stress.

## FIGURE 14.1
**The Stress-and-Coping Process**

This process involves a potentially stressful event, the appraisal of that event, and attempts to cope. Played out against a variety of background factors unique to each individual, the stress-and-coping process influences health outcomes.

© Cengage Learning

```
          Personal and Situational
            Background Factors
                    │
                    ▼
         The Stress-and-Coping Process
    ┌──────────┐   ┌──────────┐   ┌──────────┐
    │Potentially│→ │ Appraisal │→ │  Coping  │
    │ stressful │   │          │   │          │
    │   event   │   │          │   │          │
    └──────────┘   └──────────┘   └──────────┘
                    │
                    ▼
              Health Outcomes
```

# What Causes Stress?

Make a list of the stressors in your own life and you'll probably find that the items on your list can be sorted into three major categories: catastrophes, major life events, and daily hassles. Before we consider these causes of psychological stress, however, let's step back and ask a more basic research question: How can a psychologist know how much stress a person is under? How can it be measured? There are many different sources of stress, or **stressors**, and their effects can be defined in different ways (Cohen et al., 2007).

Over years, two different types of approaches have been taken. Using *self-report*, many researchers have asked people to check off life events that have happened to them from a list of known stressors; others have asked people to keep daily diaries in which they report on stressful experiences as they occur; still others conducted live interviews to get more detailed information about the source and extent of the stress. Looking at stress as a bodily response to perceived threat, other researchers use *physiological measures* by analyzing stress hormone levels in blood, urine, or saliva samples; or by recording autonomic arousal through heart rate, respiration rate, blood pressure, or sweat gland activity. It may even be possible to assess the effects of stress on the body over time. In recent years, researchers have observed that accumulated levels of cortisol (a stress hormone) found in hair samples are associated with exposure to stress—suggesting that hair cortisol may provide a "biomarker" for life stress (Russell et al., 2012). In one study, for example, hair cortisol levels were higher in a sample of men and women who were out of work than in a comparison sample of others who were employed (Dettenborn et al., 2010).

## Crises and Catastrophes

> We are running from the wave, and we can see the water right behind us. We run toward the other side of the island. When we get about halfway across, we meet people running and screaming from the other direction. Then we see the water in front of us too. The waves meet, and we are under water. (Dittmann, 2005, p. 36)

On December 26, 2004, one of the worst natural disasters in history spread over Southeast Asia, India, Indonesia, and Africa. It started when a powerful earthquake struck deep under the Indian Ocean, triggering massive tsunamis that obliterated cities, seaside communities, and holiday resorts. Approximately 320,000 people in a dozen countries were killed; thousands of survivors were injured and traumatized in the process.

Eight months later, Hurricane Katrina stampeded through the Gulf Coast of the United States with winds of up to 175 miles per hour, devastating areas in Florida, Mississippi, Alabama, and Louisiana and killing nearly 2,000 people. In New Orleans, the surge breached the levees, ultimately flooding 80% of the city and many neighboring parishes. Causing an estimated $81 billion in damage, Hurricane Katrina quickly became the costliest natural disaster in U.S. history. It was not, of course, the last. Floods, fires, tornadoes, and earthquakes are part of life in many regions of the world.

**stressor** Anything that causes stress.

AP Photo/Gaylon Wampler

AP Photo/Seth Perlman

Natural disasters can devastate entire populations. In the summer of 2012, wild fires spread through the mountains of Colorado, destroying hundreds of thousands of acres and displacing thousands of people. At the same time, drought conditions afflicted more than half of the United States, destroying crops in much of the Midwest and other parts of the country.

The largest natural disaster area ever was declared during the summer of 2012 because of the droughts that afflicted 26 states.

The intense stress that natural catastrophes impose on a population can also be caused by human beings. Sometimes the disaster that strikes is accidental—as in the massive BP oil spill of 2010 that gushed millions of gallons of oil into the Gulf of Mexico, killing wildlife and causing billions of dollars in damage. At other times, human-caused disasters result from malicious motives. The terrorist assault on the World Trade Center and the Pentagon on September 11, 2001, was a different kind of tragedy that no one who was old enough to witness it will ever forget. Americans all over the world took the attack personally and were touched by it, whether they were present or not. In a nationwide telephone survey of 560 adults conducted later that week, 90% said they were experiencing some symptoms of stress and 44% reported "substantial" symptoms such as recurring thoughts, dreams, and memories; difficulty falling or staying asleep; difficulty concentrating on work; and unprovoked outbursts of anger (Schuster et al., 2001). These problems were far more common among New Yorkers than in people living in other areas (Schlenger et al., 2002). Even within Manhattan, researchers found that the closer residents lived to Ground Zero, the more traumatized and depressed they were by the experience. The most profoundly affected were those who worked in the towers or nearby, those who had friends and family in the vicinity, and rescue workers who were called to the scene (Galea et al., 2002).

The harmful effects of catastrophic stressors on health have long been documented. Paul and Gerald Adams (1984) examined the public records in Othello, Washington, before and after the 1980 eruption of the Mount St. Helens volcano, which spewed thick layers of ash all over the area. After the eruption, they observed increases in calls made to a mental health crisis line, police reports of domestic violence, referrals to a local alcohol treatment center, and visits to the emergency room. Then there was an earthquake that shook San Francisco in 1989. Houses collapsed, highways buckled, overpasses fell apart, water mains burst, and fires raged out of control, leaving thousands of people homeless. By coincidence, Susan Nolen-Hoeksema and Jannay Morrow (1991) had administered some trauma-relevant measures to a group of Stanford University students 2 weeks before the earthquake. Follow-up assessments 10 days later and again after 6 weeks provided these investigators with a before and after examination of coping. They found that people who had initially been more distressed and those who had encountered more danger during the quake experienced the most psychological distress afterward.

The scarring effects of large-scale disasters are without dispute. Based on their review of 52 studies, Anthony Rubonis and Leonard Bickman (1991) found that high rates of psychological disorders are common among residents of areas that have been hit by these catastrophic events. In a study of disasters involving 377 counties, a team of researchers found that compared with the years preceding each disaster, the suicide rate increased by 14% after floods, 31% after hurricanes, and 63% after earthquakes (Krug et al., 1998). Other events that can have similarly traumatic effects include war, car accidents, plane crashes, violent crimes, physical or sexual abuse, and the death of a loved one (Kubany et al., 2000).

War in particular leaves deep, permanent psychological scars. Soldiers in combat believe that they have to kill or be killed. They suffer intense anxiety and see horrifying injuries, death, and destruction, all of which leaves them with images and emotions that do not fade. Given this level of stress, it's not surprising that when a war is over, some veterans suffer greatly. In World War I, the problem was called "shell shock." In World War II, it was called "combat fatigue." Now the problem is seen as a specific form of **posttraumatic stress disorder (PTSD)** and is identified by such enduring symptoms as recurring anxiety, sleeplessness, nightmares, intrusive bad thoughts, flashbacks, attention problems, and social withdrawal. What's worse, families are often shattered when a loved one returns from war and seems different, as if still trapped in combat (McCarty-Gould, 2000). Apparently, time alone does not heal the wounds of war-induced PTSD. In a longitudinal study of 88,000 American soldiers who had returned from the war in Iraq, researchers found that soldiers had more mental health problems 3 to 6 months after their return than immediately afterward, with the number of reported PTSD cases rising from 49% to 59% (Milliken et al., 2007).

War can traumatize civilian populations as well. In Israel, 16% of adults had personally been exposed to a terrorist attack, and 37% had a close friend or family member who had been exposed (Bleich et al., 2003). With regard to the mental health consequences of such exposure, a study of 905 Jewish and Palestinian citizens revealed that exposure to terrorism was associated with PTSD symptoms in both groups—more so among the Palestinian citizens, members of an ethnic minority who have fewer coping resources to turn to when in distress (Hobfoll et al., 2006).

**posttraumatic stress disorder (PTSD)** A condition in which a person experiences enduring physical and psychological symptoms after an extremely stressful event.

These soldiers, like thousands of other troops and civilians, have experienced the recent wars in Iraq and Afghanistan firsthand. It has long been recognized that combat leaves psychological scars and increases the risk of posttraumatic stress disorder.

Tyler Hicks/The New York Times/Redux

Over the years, clinical psychologists have studied PTSD and the life experiences that precipitate its onset (Friedman et al., 2007). Based on a nationwide survey of 6,000 Americans aged 15 to 54 years, Ronald Kessler and others (1995) estimated that 8% of the population (5% of men, 10% of women) suffer posttraumatic stress disorder in the course of a lifetime and that the symptoms often persist for many years. Among the experiences that produced these traumas were witnessing a murder or injury, the death of a loved one, life-threatening accidents, serious illness, war, fires and natural disasters, physical and sexual assaults, and prison. From a meta-analysis of 290 studies involving thousands of participants, it is clear that PTSD is more prevalent among women than among men, even though men are more likely to experience potentially traumatic events (Tolin & Foa, 2006).

## Major Life Events

Some people are lucky enough to avoid major catastrophes. But nobody can completely avoid stress. Indeed, change itself may cause stress by forcing us to adapt to new circumstances. This hypothesis was first proposed by Thomas Holmes and Richard Rahe (1967), who interviewed hospital patients and found that their illnesses had often been preceded by major changes in some aspect of their lives. Some of the changes were negative (getting hurt, divorced, or fired), but others were positive (getting married or promoted or having a baby). To measure life stress, Holmes and Rahe then devised the Social Readjustment Rating Scale (SRRS), a checklist of 43 major life events each assigned a numerical value based on the amount of readjustment it requires. Among the events sampled (and the numerical values they were assigned) were the death of a spouse (100), divorce (73), imprisonment (63), marriage (50), job loss (47), pregnancy (40), school transfer (20), and even vacations (13).

The simple notion that change is inherently stressful has an intuitive ring about it. But is change per se, positive or negative, necessarily harmful? There are two problems with this idea. First, although there is a statistical link between negative events and illness, research does not similarly support the claim that positive "stressors" such as taking a vacation, graduating, winning a lottery, starting a new career, or getting married are similarly harmful (Stewart et al., 1986). Happiness is not the absence of distress, nor is distress the absence of happiness. A person can simultaneously experience both emotions (Carver & Scheier, 1990), and the health consequences are different (Taylor, 1991). The second complicating factor is that the impact of any change depends on who the person is and how the change is interpreted. Moving to a new country, for example, is less stressful to immigrants who can speak the new language (Berry et al., 1992); victims of physical assault who keep wondering "what if?" take longer to recover emotionally than those who do not (El Leithy et al., 2006). Pregnant women from diverse backgrounds deliver their infants earlier and at a lower birth weight when they reported pregnancy-specific stress—because of health concerns, parenting concerns, relationship strains, and other related issues—than when they did not (Lobel et al., 2008). To sum up: Change in a person's life may provide a crude estimate of stress and future health, but the predictive equation is not that simple.

## Microstressors: The Hassles of Everyday Life

Think again about the stress in your life, and catastrophes and other exceptional events will spring to mind. Yet the most common source of stress arises from the hassles that irritate us every day. Environmental factors such as population density, loud noise, extreme heat or cold, and cigarette smoke are all sources of stress. Car problems, gas prices, waiting in lines, traffic, losing keys, bad work days, money troubles, and other "microstressors" also place a constant strain on us. Unfortunately, there is nothing "micro" about the impact of these stressors on health and well-being. Studies suggest that the accumulation of daily hassles contributes more to illness than do major life events (Kohn et al., 1991). Interpersonal conflicts are the most upsetting of our daily stressors and have a particularly long-lasting impact (Bolger et al., 1989).

One problem that plagues many people in the workplace is occupational stress (Barling et al., 2005). One type of reaction is *burnout*—a prolonged response to job stress that is characterized by emotional exhaustion, cynicism, disengagement, and a lack of personal accomplishment. Teachers, doctors, nurses, police officers, social workers, and others in human-service professions are especially at risk. Under relentless job pressures, those who are burned out describe themselves as feeling drained, frustrated, hardened, apathetic, and lacking in energy and motivation (Maslach, 1982;

Waiting in line at Chicago's O'Hare Airport, a common occurrence in these days of heightened security, is the kind of microstressor that plagues air travelers on a daily basis (left). The streets of Calcutta, India—a city with 16 million people—are crowded with vendors, pedestrians, and taxis. Today there are 21 "mega cities" in the world with populations over 10 million, most in developing countries, where urban areas absorb the rising population—and stress (right).

Maslach et al., 2001). People are most likely to have this experience when they do not have enough resources at work—such as support from supervisors and friendly relations with co-workers—to meet the demands of the job (Lee & Ashforth, 1996). To make matters worse, people who burn out at work are at greater risk for cardiovascular disease (Melamed et al., 2006).

Over the years, research had suggested that burnout is an experience that afflicts women more than men. It now appears that the role of gender is more complex. A recent analysis of 183 studies has shown both men and women are potentially susceptible to burnout under bad circumstances—but the symptoms are different. Female employees are 8% more likely than men to become *emotionally exhausted* in the workplace, feeling overwhelmed and physically drained. However, men are 14% more likely to become *depersonalized* at work, withdrawing and distancing themselves from clients and co-workers (Purvanova & Muros, 2010).

Another form of daily stress comes from commuting to and from work. At present, more than 120 million Americans commute to work each weekday—by car or by public transportation, for an average of 25 minutes (Rampell, 2011). Research has shown that driving to work can increase stress (Koslowsky et al., 1995). Commuting long distances by train can have the same effect. Studying railroad commuters who traveled regularly from their homes in suburban New Jersey to work in Manhattan, Gary Evans and Richard Wener (2006) found that the longer their commute was, the more stress they reported feeling, the sloppier they were at a simple proofreading task, and the higher was their level of cortisol—a stress hormone that was measured by taking saliva samples after the morning trips.

On the home front, financial pressure is a particularly common and dramatic source of stress (American Psychological Association, 2008). Even before the recent economic crisis in the United States, a 3-year study of more than 400 married American couples showed that those who are strained by a tight budget and have difficulty paying the bills experience more distress and conflict in their marriages (Conger et al., 1999). A follow-up study of African American families showed that economic hardship spells emotional distress for parents and adjustment problems for their children (Conger et al., 2002).

In recent years, health psychologists have come to realize that *socioeconomic status* (SES) is a powerful proxy for the hassles of everyday living. Across a range of health outcomes, individuals who are less educated, have lower status jobs, and earn less or no income are more likely to suffer from health problems relative to others who are better off (Adler et al., 1994). There are two reasons for this association. First, people who live in low-income neighborhoods are invariably subject to more exposure to noise, crowding, crime, poor diet, and other stressors. Second, people of low socio-economic status have fewer tangible, medical, social, and psychological resources to help them meet these daily challenges. For children who grow up in low SES families, the influences can accumulate over time and endure (Matthews & Gallo, 2011).

> The accumulation of daily hassles does more to make people sick than catastrophes or major life changes. **T**RUE.

# How Does Stress Affect the Body?

The term *stress* was first popularized by Hans Selye (1936), an endocrinologist. As a young medical student, Selye noticed that patients who were hospitalized for many different illnesses often had similar symptoms, such as muscle weakness, a loss of weight and appetite, and a lack of ambition. Maybe these symptoms were part of a generalized response to an attack on the body, he thought. In the 1930s, Selye tested this hypothesis by exposing laboratory rats to various stressors, including heat, cold, heavy exercise, toxic substances, food deprivation, and electric shock. As anticipated, the different stressors all produced a similar physiological response: enlarged adrenal glands, shrunken lymph nodes, and bleeding stomach ulcers. Borrowing a term from engineering, Selye called the reaction *stress*—a word that quickly became part of everyday language.

## The General Adaptation Syndrome

According to Selye, the body naturally responds to stress in a three-stage process that he called the **general adaptation syndrome** (see ● Figure 14.2). Sparked by the recognition of a threat—such as a predator, an enemy soldier, a speeding car, or a virus—the body has an initial *alarm* reaction. To meet the challenge, adrenaline and other hormones are poured into the bloodstream, creating physiological arousal. Heart rate, blood pressure, and breathing rates increase, while slower, long-term functions such as growth, digestion, and the operation of the immune system are inhibited. At this stage, the body mobilizes all of its resources to ward off the threat. Next comes a *resistance* stage, during which the body remains aroused and on the alert. There is continued release of stress hormones, and

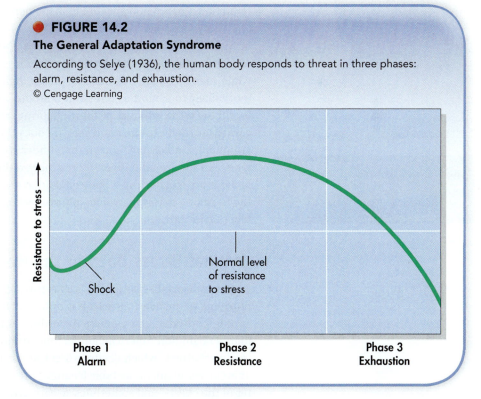

● **FIGURE 14.2**

**The General Adaptation Syndrome**

According to Selye (1936), the human body responds to threat in three phases: alarm, resistance, and exhaustion.

© Cengage Learning

local defenses are activated. But if the stress persists for a prolonged period of time, the body will fall into an *exhaustion* stage. According to Selye, our antistress resources are limited. In fact, however, research has shown that exhaustion occurs not because our stress-fighting resources are limited but because their overuse causes other systems in the body to break down, which puts us at risk for illness and even death. Selye's basic

**general adaptation syndrome** A three-stage process (alarm, resistance, and exhaustion) by which the body responds to stress.

model thus makes an important point: Stress may be an adaptive short-term reaction to threat, but over time it compromises our health and well-being.

A stress response is found in all mammals. So why, asks neuroscientist Robert Sapolsky (2004), don't zebras get ulcers? Sapolsky notes that the physiological stress response is superbly designed through evolution to help animals mobilize to fight or escape in acute emergencies. For the zebra, this occurs when a hungry lion leaps out from a bush and sprints at top speed across the savanna. For humans, it occurs during combat or competitive sports and perhaps even on first dates and in job interviews. But think about the list of situations you find stressful, and you'll see that people become anxious over things that would make no sense to a zebra. "We humans live well enough and long enough, and are smart enough, to generate all sorts of stressful events purely in our heads," says Sapolsky. From the perspective of the evolution of the animal kingdom, he notes, psychological stress is a "recent invention" (p. 5). The reason stress causes ulcers and other illnesses, then, is that the response is designed for acute physical emergencies, yet we turn it on often and for prolonged periods of time as we worry about taxes, mortgages, oral presentations, the job market, marital problems, and the inevitability of death.

All humans respond bodily to stress, which is what enables us to mount a defense. Physiologically, the sympathetic nervous system is activated and more adrenaline is secreted, which increases the heart rate and heightens arousal. Then all at once the liver pours extra sugar into the bloodstream for energy, the pupils dilate to let in more light, breathing speeds up for more oxygen, perspiration increases to cool down the body, blood clots faster to heal wounds, saliva flow is inhibited, and digestion slows down to divert blood to the brain and skeletal muscles. Faced with threat, the body readies itself for action. But what, behaviorally, is the nature of the defense?

Many years ago, Walter Cannon (1932) described the body as prepared for "fight or flight." To be sure, men often lash out aggressively when under siege. But do women respond similarly? In her book *The Tending Instinct*, Shelley Taylor (2002) argues that while men frequently exhibit the classic fight-or-flight reaction to stress, women are more likely to exhibit a "tend-and-befriend" response. Prepared by evolution, in order to enhance the survival of their offspring, she argues, women adapt to hardship by caring for their children and seeking out others who might help. Consistent with this argument, studies have shown that, under stress, women become more nurturing than men—and more affiliative. Interestingly, animal and human studies show that when females are isolated, unsupported, and in social distress, they exhibit elevated levels of the hormone oxytocin, which, in turn, increases their tendency to seek out social contact (Taylor, 2012b).

Like humans, zebras get ulcers.  **FALSE.**

## What Stress Does to the Heart

Coronary heart disease (CHD) is a narrowing of the blood vessels that carry oxygen and nutrients to the heart muscle. It is by far the leading cause of death in the United States among both men and women. According to the American Heart Association, an estimated 80 million American adults (one in three) suffer from CHD. For many, the result is a heart attack, which occurs when the precious blood supply to the heart is blocked. This causes an uncomfortable feeling of pressure, fullness, squeezing, or pain in the center of the chest—and sometimes sweating, dizziness, nausea, fainting, and shortness of breath. Every year, 1.5 million Americans have heart attacks. One-third do not survive. (For more information, you can visit www.americanheart.org.)

Several factors are known to increase the risk of CHD. The three most important are hypertension, or high blood pressure; cigarette smoking; and high cholesterol. (Others include a family history of CHD, a high-fat diet, obesity, and a lack of exercise.) People with one of the three major risk factors are twice as likely to develop CHD, those with two risk factors are three and a half times as likely, and those with all three are six times as likely. These statistics are compelling and should not be taken lightly. Combined, however, these variables account for fewer than half the known cases of CHD. What's missing from the equation is the fourth major risk factor: psychological stress—from work, from marital troubles, and from the negative life events that plague people who lack resources because of low socioeconomic status (Gallo & Matthews, 2003; Matthews, 2005).

In 1956, cardiologists Meyer Friedman and Ray Rosenman were studying the relationship between cholesterol and coronary heart disease. After noticing that husbands were more likely than their wives to have CHD, they speculated that work-related stress might be the reason (at the time, most women did not work outside the home). To test this hypothesis, Friedman and Rosenman interviewed 3,000 healthy middle-aged men. Those who seemed the most hard-driving, competitive, impatient, time-conscious, and quick to anger were classified as having a **Type A personality** (also called coronary-prone behavior pattern—a more optimistic label since it is easier to change a behavior pattern than a personality). Roughly an equal number of men who were easygoing, relaxed, and laid back were classified as having a Type B personality. Interestingly, out of 258 men who went on to have heart attacks over the following 9 years, 69% had been classified as Type A and only 31% as Type B (Rosenman et al., 1975).

The Type A, or coronary-prone, behavior pattern is made up of a cluster of traits, including competitive drive, a sense of time urgency, and a dangerous mix of anger, cynicism, and hostility (Friedman & Booth-Kewley 1987; Matthews, 1988). In interviews and written questionnaires, Type As report that they walk fast, talk fast, work late, interrupt speakers in mid-sentence, detest waiting in lines, race through yellow lights when they drive, lash out at others in frustration, strive to win at all costs, and save time by multitasking. In contrast, "there are those who breeze through the day as pleased as park rangers—despite having deadlines and kids and a broken down car and charity work and scowling Aunt Agnes living in the spare bedroom" (Carey, 1997, p. 75).

By the early 1980s, the influence of the Type A behavior pattern on CHD was widely accepted. A panel of distinguished scientists convened by the National Heart, Lung and Blood Institute concluded that the Type A pattern was a risk factor for CHD, comparable to more traditional risks such as high blood pressure, smoking, high blood cholesterol, and obesity. But science, like time, moves on. Later studies of Type A and CHD obtained weaker results that varied depending on how Type A was measured and the kind of population that was studied (Matthews, 1988). Certainty about the bad effects of "hurry sickness" and "workaholism" began to crumble.

One issue that arose concerned measurement. Specifically, it turns out that the strength of the link between Type A behavior and coronary heart disease depends on how people are diagnosed. In the original study, Friedman and Rosenman classified men by means of a structured interview in which they could observe the men's verbal and nonverbal behavior. Afterward, however, many psychologists—in their haste to pursue this vital line of research—tried to identify Type A people using quick, easy-to-take questionnaires instead of time-consuming interviews. The questionnaires were not nearly as predictive. Apparently, the Type A pattern is more evident from a person's interview *behavior* (whether he or she constantly checks the time, speaks quickly, interrupts the interviewer, and makes restless fidgety movements) than from *self-reports*. When interviews are used to make the diagnosis, 70% of men who have CHD also have a Type A behavior pattern—compared with only 46% of those who are healthy (Miller et al., 1991).

**Type A personality** A pattern of behavior characterized by extremes of competitive striving for achievement, a sense of time urgency, hostility, and aggression.

The Type A behavior pattern was also refined conceptually, and a new line of inquiry sprang up. This research showed the primary toxic ingredient in CHD is *hostility*—as seen in people who are constantly angry, resentful, cynical, suspicious, and mistrustful of others (see Table 14.2). Apparently, people who are always in a negative emotional state and are quick to explode are besieged by stress. Because the heart is just a dumb pump and the blood vessels mere hoses, the health result is predictable: "The cardiovascular stress-response basically consists of making them work harder for a while, and if you do that on a regular basis, they will wear out, just like any pump or hoses you could buy at Sears" (Sapolsky, 1994, p. 42). In the long run, chronic hostility and anger can be lethal (Miller et al., 1996; Siegman & Smith, 1994). In fact, people who have lots of anger and suppress it are as likely to develop high blood pressure as those with anger who express it. It's the emotion that is toxic, not whether you hold it in or let it out (Everson et al., 1998; Everson-Rose & Lewis, 2005).

What else explains the connection between hostility and coronary heart disease? One possibility is that hostile people are less health-conscious—that they tend to smoke more, consume more caffeine and alcohol, exercise less, sleep less, and eat less healthy foods. They are also less likely to comply with advice from doctors (Leiker & Hailey, 1988; Siegler, 1994). A second explanation is that hostile people are physiologically reactive, so in tense social situations they exhibit greater increases in blood pressure, pulse rate, and adrenaline, a hormone that accelerates the buildup of fatty plaques on the artery walls, causing hardening of the arteries (Krantz & McCeney, 2002). In fact, research shows that people who are hostile exhibit more intense cardiovascular reactions not only during the event that makes them angry—say, being involved in a heated argument (Davis et al., 2000)—but long afterward as well, when asked to relive the event (Frederickson et al., 2000).

As a result of all this research and its many offshoots, a whole new subfield has developed that is sure to produce more valuable and practical insights in the years to come. Appropriately enough, this new subfield, which brings together the heart and the mind, has been called *psychocardiology* (Jordan et al., 2007)—or the practice of *cardiac psychology* (Allan & Fisher, 2011).

> ## What Stress Does to the Immune System

Increasingly, it has become clear that psychological stress produces a wide range of effects on the body, including increases in the risk of chronic back pain, diabetes, appendicitis, upper respiratory infections, arthritis, herpes, gum disease, common colds, and some forms of cancer. How can stress have so broad a range of disabling effects? Answer: By compromising the body's immune system, the first line of defense against illness (Ader, 2007).

The **immune system** is a complex surveillance system that fights bacteria, viruses, parasites, fungi, and other "nonself" substances that invade the body. The system contains more than a trillion specialized white blood cells called *lymphocytes* that circulate throughout the bloodstream and secrete chemical antibodies. These shark-like search-and-destroy cells protect us 24 hours a day by patrolling the body and attacking

---

**TABLE 14.2**

**How "Hostile" Is Your Pattern of Behavior?**

- When in the express checkout line at the supermarket, do you often count the items in the baskets of the people ahead of you to be sure they aren't over the limit?
- When an elevator doesn't come as quickly as it should, do your thoughts quickly focus on the inconsiderate behavior of the person on another floor who's holding it up?
- When someone criticizes you, do you quickly begin to feel annoyed?
- Do you frequently find yourself muttering at the television during a news broadcast?
- When you are held up in a slow line in traffic, do you quickly sense your heart pounding and your breath quickening?

Williams, 1993. © Cengage Learning

---

**immune system** A biological surveillance system that detects and destroys "nonself" substances that invade the body.

trespassers. The immune system is also equipped with large scavenger cells that zero in on viruses and cancerous tumors. Serving as a "sixth sense" for foreign invaders, the immune system continually renews itself. For example, during the few seconds it took to read this sentence, your body produced 10 million new lymphocytes.

Today, many health psychologists specializing in **psychoneuroimmunology**, or **PNI** (*psycho* for the mind, *neuro* for the nervous system, and *immunology* for the immune system) study the connections among the brain, behavior, the immune system, health, and illness. Before we get into some of the fascinating results, let's pause for a moment and consider three of the methods these researchers use to spy on the operations of the immune system. One method is to take blood samples from animal or human participants exposed to varying degrees of stress and count the number of lymphocytes and other white blood cells circulating in the bloodstream. A second is to extract blood, add cancerous tumor cells to the mix, and measure the extent to which the natural killer cells destroy the tumors. A third method is to "challenge" the living organism by injecting a foreign agent into the skin and measuring the amount of swelling that arises at the site of the injection. The more swelling there is, the more potent the immune reaction is assumed to be (Ader, 2007; Daruna, 2012; Segerstrom, 2012).

It is now clear that stress can affect the immune system, at least temporarily. The medical community used to reject the idea outright, but no longer. What changed? First, animal experiments showed that rats exposed to noise, overcrowding, or inescapable shocks, and primates separated from their social companions, exhibit a drop in immune cell activity compared with non-exposed animals (Coe, 1993; Moynihan & Ader, 1996). A link was also observed in humans. Intrigued by the fact that people often become sick and die shortly after they are widowed, R. W. Barthrop and others (1977) took blood samples from 26 men and women whose spouses had recently died. Compared with non-widowed controls, these grief-stricken spouses exhibited a weakened immune response. This demonstration was the first of its kind.

Additional studies soon revealed weakened immune responses in NASA astronauts after their reentry into the atmosphere and splashdown, in people deprived of sleep for a prolonged period of time, in students in the midst of final exams, in men and women recently divorced or separated, in people caring for a family member with Alzheimer's disease, in snake-phobic people who are exposed to a live snake, and in workers who

**psychoneuroimmunology (PNI)** A subfield of psychology that examines the links among psychological factors, the brain and nervous system, and the immune system.

Meckes/Ottowa/Photo Researchers

This color-enhanced microscopic image shows two "natural killer" immune cells (in yellow) engulfing and destroying a leukemia cell (in red). The human immune system contains more than a trillion specialized white blood cells.

have just lost their jobs. Even in the laboratory, people who are given complex arithmetic problems to solve or painful stimuli to tolerate exhibit changes in immune cell activity that last for one or more hours after the stress has subsided (Cohen & Herbert, 1996).

In an intriguing study, Arthur Stone and others (1994) paid 48 adult volunteers to take a harmless but novel protein pill every day for 12 weeks—a substance that would lead the immune system to respond by producing an antibody. Every day, the participants completed a diary in which they reported about their moods and experiences at work, at home, in financial matters, in leisure activities, and in social relationships with their friends, spouses, and children. The participants also gave daily saliva samples that were later used to measure the amount of antibody produced. The results were striking, as are their implications: The more positive events participants experienced in a given day, the more antibody was produced. The more negative events they experienced, the less antibody was produced.

In many ways, it is now clear that negative experiences and the emotions they elicit can weaken our immune system's ability to protect us from injuries, infections, and a wide range of illnesses (Kiecolt-Glaser et al., 2002). In an experiment that well illustrates this point in action, researchers brought healthy male and female volunteers into a clinical research laboratory, administered a battery of questionnaires, injected them with a needle in the arm, and then used a vacuum pump to raise a blister. In follow-up visits during the next 8 days, the researchers measured the speed with which the wounds were healing. They found that participants whose questionnaires indicated that they had anger control problems—for example, losing their temper or boiling inside—secreted more of the stress hormone cortisol in response to the blistering procedure and the wound was slower to heal over time (Gouin et al., 2008).

Clearly, psychological states can "get into" the immune system. As illustrated in ● Figure 14.3, there are two possible ways this can happen. First, people who are under intense stress tend to smoke more, ingest more alcohol and drugs, sleep less, exercise less, and have poorer diets, behaviors that tend to compromise the immune system. For example, one study showed that when healthy male adults were kept awake between 3:00 and 7:00 a.m., immune cell activity diminished and returned to normal only after a full night of uninterrupted sleep (Irwin et al., 1994). Second, stress triggers the release of adrenaline and other stress hormones into the bloodstream, and these hormones tend to suppress immune cell activity. The result is a temporary lowering of the body's resistance (Cohen & Williamson, 1991). Either way, hundreds of studies now show that the effects of stress on the immune system are complex. Brief stressors (such as a shark attack, a difficult exam, or an injury) can enhance the immune response in ways that are adaptive in the short term, but chronic life stressors (such as a high-pressure job, a distressed marriage, or a family illness) can suppress the immune response over time, putting the organism at risk (Segerstrom & Miller, 2004).

● **FIGURE 14.3**

**Pathways from Stress to Illness**

Hostility, stress, and other negative emotional states may cause illness in two ways: (1) by promoting unhealthful behaviors (more alcohol, less sleep, and so on) and (2) by triggering the release of hormones that weaken the immune system. © Cengage Learning

## The Links Between Stress and Illness

If chronic stress can weaken the immune system, are people who are stressed in life more likely to become sick? Might some people, for example, be psychologically more susceptible than others to catching the flu? Sheldon Cohen and his colleagues (1993) conducted a fascinating and elaborate study to help answer this question. They paid 420 volunteers to spend 9 days in a medical experiment and risk exposure to a common cold virus. In the first 2 days, participants filled out several questionnaires, including one that measured recent stressful experiences in their lives. They also received a physical examination, including a blood test. Then, to simulate the person-to-person transmission of a virus, the researchers dropped a clear liquid solution into each participant's nose. Those randomly assigned to the control group received a placebo saline solution. Others, less fortunate, received a cold virus in doses that tend to produce illness rates of 20% to 60%.

For the next week, participants were quarantined in large apartments, where they were examined daily by a nurse who took their temperature, extracted mucus samples, and looked for signs of colds, such as sneezing, watery eyes, stuffy nose, and sore throat. (The participants did not realize it, but the nurse also kept track of the number of tissues they used.) All participants were healthy at the start of the project, and not a single one in the saline control group developed a cold. Yet among those exposed to a virus, 82% became infected, and 46% of those who were infected caught a cold, symptoms and all. A virus is a virus, so often there is no escape. Most interesting, however, is that life stress made a difference. Among those who became infected, high-stress participants were more likely to catch a cold than were the low-stress participants—53% compared with 40%. In short, people whose lives are filled with stress are particularly vulnerable to contagious illness.

In a follow-up of this experiment, Cohen and others (1998) interviewed 276 volunteers about recent life stressors, infected them with a cold virus, and then measured whether or not they developed a cold. They found that some types of stress were more toxic than others. Specifically, people who had endured *chronic* stressors that lasted for more than a month (like ongoing marital problems or unemployment) were more likely to catch a cold than those who had experienced *acute* short-term stress (such as a fight with a spouse or a reprimand at work). ● Figure 14.4 shows that the longer a stressor had lasted, the more likely a person was to catch a cold. Over time, stress breaks down the body's immune system.

The effects of stress are clear. But it appears that certain personal characteristics can buffer people against the adverse health effects. In yet another follow-up study, Cohen and his colleagues (2006) found that the more sociable people were in life, the more resistant they were to developing the lab-induced cold. They also found that the more positively people *see themselves* on the SES ladder relative to others in the population—regardless of their *actual* levels of education, occupation, and income—the less likely they were to catch the lab-induced cold (Cohen et al., 2008).

These common-cold studies are important because they demonstrate not only that stress can weaken the immune system but also that it can leave us vulnerable to illness as a result. Does stress have similar effects on more serious illnesses? Can it, for example, hasten the spread of HIV/AIDS or cancer? In an early test of this hypothesis, Madeline Visintainer and others (1982) implanted tumorous cancer cells into laboratory rats, some of which were then exposed repeatedly to shocks they could not escape. After a month, 50% of the animals not shocked died of cancer. Yet relative to that baseline, the death rate climbed to 73% among those subjected to the inescapable shock. This study was among the first to show that psychological states such as a feeling of helplessness can influence the spread of cancer.

● **FIGURE 14.4**

**Stress Duration and Illness**

Two hundred seventy-six volunteers were interviewed about recent life stress, then infected with a cold virus. As shown above, the more months a stressor had lasted, the more likely a person was to catch the cold. Over time, stress breaks down the body's immune system. Cohen et al., 1998. © Cengage Learning

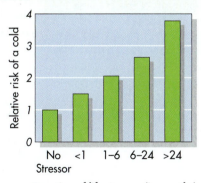

*Duration of life stressor (in months)*

The growth of tumors in helpless white laboratory rats is interesting, but does the same principle apply to people? For obvious ethical reasons, researchers cannot fill humans with despair or inject lethal tumors into their bodies to test the cause-and-effect chain directly. But they can examine the medical records of people whose lives have been struck by tragedy. Investigations of this sort have revealed that cancer appears more often than normal in people who are prone to being in a negative emotional state (Sklar & Anisman, 1981). In one large-scale study, investigators looked up 2,000 male employees of the Western Electric Company in Chicago whose personalities had been assessed in 1958. At that time, test scores had shown that some of the men were low in self-esteem, unhappy, and depressed. The outcome: Some 20 years later, these men were more likely than their coworkers to have died of cancer (Persky et al., 1987).

Let's be clear about what these results mean. Nobody disputes that cancer is caused by exposure to toxic substances and other biological factors. But individuals who are clinically depressed or under great stress have weakened immune systems and a heightened susceptibility to infectious agents, which, in some cases, may result in a higher death rate from cancer and other diseases as well (Cohen et al., 2007; Kiecolt-Glaser, 2009; Miller et al., 2009).

For people who are married, divorce is a particularly gut-wrenching experience. In the United States, approximately 40% of first marriages end in divorce (Tejada-Vera & Sutton, 2009). The process is logistically, financially, socially, and emotionally disruptive. Most people manage the transition and adapt to the change (Amato, 2010). For some men and women, however, divorce is an acute stressor that can have long-lasting effects on their physical and mental health (Lucas, 2005; Sbarra et al., 2009). Can divorce be fatal? In an ambitious meta-analysis, David Sbarra and his colleagues (2011) combined the results of 32 studies of 6.5 million men and women, 755,000 divorces, and 160,000 deaths in 11 countries (the United States, Canada, Great Britain, Japan, Sweden, Germany, Finland, Norway, Russia, Israel, and the Netherlands). Consistent with prior research showing that divorce is associated with increased alcohol consumption, insomnia, and other negative health behaviors, the results were sobering. Relative to their married counterparts, people who were divorced at the start of the prospective studies were later 23% more likely to die early from all causes of death during follow-up assessments. This risk was most elevated for men and those younger than 65 years of age. On questions of cause and effect, and how to interpret these associations, more research is needed. What's clear, however, is that divorce is a stressful life event with consequences for health, life, and well-being.

> Stress can weaken the heart, but it cannot affect the immune system. **F**ALSE.

## Processes of Appraisal

Some 2,500 years ago, an anonymous author wrote an extraordinary poem about human suffering: the Book of Job. A pious and prosperous man when the poem opens, Job is soon beset by great calamities. He loses his property, his children, and his health. Job and his friends try to understand how these terrible things could happen. His friends argue that Job's plight must be a punishment sent by God and tell Job to repent. Because he believes that his sufferings far exceed any wrongdoing on his part, Job cannot accept this explanation. In despair, he doubts his capacity to withstand continued hardship and longs for death. But eventually Job finds strength and peace through trusting in God's will. From the perspective of the stress-and-coping model shown in Figure 14.1, Job and his friends were engaged in the process of appraisal. They considered possible explanations for Job's suffering and formed expectations about his ability to cope with his situation. These same themes are found in research on stress and coping.

## Attributions and Explanatory Styles

Depression is a mood disorder characterized by feelings of sadness, pessimism, and apathy and slowed thought processes. Other symptoms include disturbances in sleeping and eating patterns and a reduced interest in sex. Every year, between 6% and 7% of the U.S. population experiences a major depression. Many more suffer from briefer, milder bouts with the blues. Sometimes called the "common cold" of psychological disorders, depression is universal and widespread (Gotlib & Hammen, 2009).

About twice as many women as men seek treatment for being depressed. During the course of a lifetime, an estimated 12% of American men and 21% of women will suffer from a major depression (Kessler et al., 1994). This sex difference first begins to appear in adolescence, although the disparity is a bit smaller in less developed nations (Culbertson, 1997). While depression has many causes, some researchers have focused on the attributions people make for the positive and negative events of their lives.

In 1975, Martin Seligman argued that depression results from a feeling of **learned helplessness**, the acquired expectation that one cannot control important outcomes. In a classic series of experiments, Seligman found that dogs strapped into a harness and exposed to painful electric shocks soon became passive and gave up trying to escape, even in new situations where escape was possible. In contrast, dogs that had not received uncontrollable shocks quickly learned the escape routine. As applied to humans, this finding suggested that prolonged exposure to uncontrollable events might similarly cause apathy, inactivity, a loss of motivation, and pessimism. In human research participants, those exposed to inescapable bursts of noise thus failed to protect themselves in a later situation where the noise could be easily avoided. Seligman was quick to note that people who are exposed to uncontrollable events become, in many ways, like depressed individuals: discouraged, pessimistic about the future, and lacking in initiative. Thus, he saw depression as a form of learned helplessness.

Lynn Abramson and her colleagues (1989) later proposed that depression is a state of *hopelessness* brought on by the negative self-attributions people make for failure. In fact, some people have a **depressive explanatory style**—a tendency to attribute bad events to factors that are internal rather than external ("It's my fault"), stable rather than unstable ("It will not change"), and global rather than specific ("It spreads to all parts of my life"). Research supports this proposition. Whether people are trying to explain social rejection, a sports defeat, low grades, or their inability to solve an experimenter's puzzle, those who are depressed are more likely than others to blame factors that are within the self, unlikely to change, and broad enough to impair other aspects of life. The result: hopelessness and despair (Abramson et al., 1989; Metalsky et al., 1993). This way of thinking may signal a vulnerability to future depression. Indeed, when Lauren Alloy and her colleagues (2006) measured the explanatory styles of non-depressed newly entered college students and then followed up on these students in their junior year, they found that those with a negative explanatory style in their first year—compared to classmates with a more positive style—were far more likely to have suffered from a major or minor depressive disorder (see ● Figure 14.5).

● **FIGURE 14.5**

**Using Attributional Styles to Predict Depression**

In this study, researchers measured the explanatory styles of first-year college students. As juniors 2 years later, those with a negative rather than positive style in their first year were more likely to suffer from a major or minor depressive disorder. Alloy et al., 2006. © Cengage Learning

■ Positive explanatory style
■ Negative explanatory style

**learned helplessness** A phenomenon in which experience with an uncontrollable event creates passive behavior in the face of subsequent threats to well-being.

**depressive explanatory style** A habitual tendency to attribute negative events to causes that are stable, global, and internal.

## The Human Capacity for Resilience

Stress affects people differently, an observation that first led Suzanne Kobasa and her colleagues (1982) to wonder why some of us are more resilient than others in the face of stress. Kobasa studied some 200 business executives who were under stress. Many said they were frequently sick, affirming the link between stress and illness; others had managed to stay healthy. The two groups were similar in terms of age, education, job status, income, and ethnic and religious background. But it was clear from various tests that they differed in their attitudes toward themselves, their jobs, and the people in their lives. Based on these differences, Kobasa identified a personality style that she called *hardiness* and concluded that hardy people have three characteristics: (1) commitment—a sense of purpose with regard to one's work, family, and other domains; (2) challenge—an openness to new experiences and a desire to embrace change; and (3) control—the belief that one has the power to influence important future outcomes.

Research supports the general point that resilience, or hardiness, serves as a buffer against stress (Funk, 1992). As you might expect, most people are exposed to at least one highly traumatic event during the course of a lifetime. Yet while many react with PTSD, others maintain their equilibrium and mental health: "Roughly 50 percent to 60 percent of the U.S. population is exposed to traumatic stress but only 5 percent to 10 percent develop PTSD" (Ozer et al., 2003, p. 54). Thus, Ann Masten (2001) and George Bonanno (2004) both argue that most human beings are highly resilient and exhibit a remarkable capacity to thrive in the wake of highly aversive events. In fact, Vicki Helgeson and her colleagues (2006) note that many people who confront heart attacks, cancer, divorce, war, family illness, and other traumas will often find ways to accept, benefit, and grow from the experience.

It's clear that people with different personalities cope with stress in different ways (Carver & Connor-Smith, 2010). What are the specific characteristics of hardiness, resilience, and the ability to find benefit in loss? In two-part longitudinal interviews of Israeli Jews and Arabs during a period of intense terrorist and rocket attacks, Steven Hobfoll and others (2009) found that 64% of those interviewed experienced chronic or delayed distress, while 36% were mostly resistant to symptoms or completely resilient. Comparisons of the two groups showed that resilience in this population was more common among men than women; among Jews, who are in the majority of the population, than Arabs, an ethnic minority; and among people in general with more education, more money, and more social support from friends. These findings may be specific to the populations and events of Israel. More likely, however, they tell us something more generally about the characteristics of resilience. Let's see.

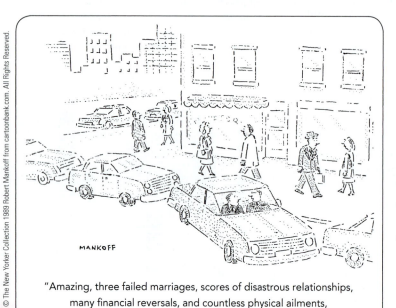

MANKOFF

"Amazing, three failed marriages, scores of disastrous relationships, many financial reversals, and countless physical ailments, but through it all I've always had good luck parking."

**People often have feelings of self-efficacy in some life domains but not others.**

**Self-Efficacy** When Kobasa and others (1982) first identified hardiness as an adaptive trait, they—and other researchers—were quick to notice that the perception of control is an important ingredient (Florian et al., 1995). Early on, research showed that the harmful effects of crowding, noise, heat, and other stressors are reduced when people think they can exert control over these aspects of their environment (Glass & Singer, 1972). The perception of control is especially meaningful for people whose lives are regulated to a large extent by others. For example, elderly residents of nursing homes who were given more control over daily routines became happier and more active (Langer & Rodin, 1976; Schulz, 1976). Other studies showed that patients with heart disease, cancer, and AIDS were better adjusted emotionally when they felt that they could influence the course of their illness (Helgeson, 1992; Rodin, 1986; Thompson et al., 1993).

The perception of control refers to the expectation that our behaviors can produce satisfying outcomes. But people also differ in the extent to which they believe that they can perform these behaviors in the first place. These concepts seem related, but in fact they refer to different beliefs, both of which are necessary for us to feel that we control important outcomes in our lives (Skinner, 1996). According to Albert Bandura (1997), these latter expectations are based on feelings of competence, or **self-efficacy**. Some individuals may be generally more confident than others, says Bandura, but self-efficacy is a state of mind that varies from one specific task and situation to another. In other words, you may have high self-efficacy about meeting new people but not about raising your

grades. Or you may have high self-efficacy about solving a math problem but not about writing a paper.

Research on self-efficacy has shown that the more of it you have at a particular task, the more likely you are to take on that task, try hard, persist in the face of failure, and succeed. The implications for mental and physical health are particularly striking. For example, individuals with high self-efficacy on health-related matters are more likely, if they want, to stay physically fit, abstain from alcohol, and tolerate the pain of arthritis, childbirth, and migraine headaches (Maddux, 1995)—and even to stop smoking (Baldwin et al., 2006) or lose weight (Linde et al., 2006).

At times, having a strong sense of self-efficacy may literally mean the difference between life and death. In one recent study, Urmimala Sarkar and colleagues (2009) recruited 1,024 heart disease patients and tracked their health over time. At the start of the study, all participants completed a Cardiac Self-Efficacy Scale in which they indicated how confident they were in their ability to maintain their usual activities, engage in sexual activity, and get aerobic exercise. Over the ensuing years, 124 of the patients were hospitalized and 235 died. When the patients were sorted into four categories of self-efficacy—from the highest scores to the lowest—the results showed that the higher their self-efficacy at the start of the study, the more likely they were to survive hospitalization years later (see ● Figure 14.6).

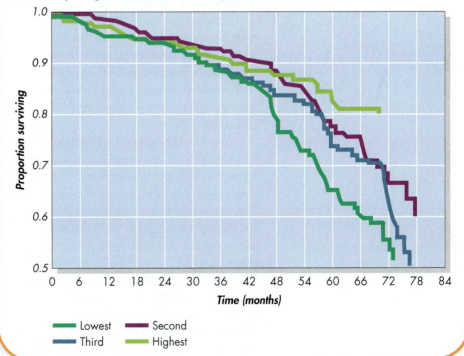

● **FIGURE 14.6**

**Self-Efficacy: A Matter of Life and Death?**

One thousand and twenty-four heart disease patients varying in "cardiac self-efficacy" were tracked over time. As shown, the higher their cardiac self-efficacy scores were at the start of the study, the more likely they were to survive hospitalization up to 78 months later.

From Sarkar, U., Ali, S., & Whooley, M. A., "Self-efficacy as a marker of cardiac function and predictor of heart failure hospitalization and mortality in patients with stable coronary heart disease: Findings from the Heart and Soul Study," *Health Psychology* vol 28 (pp. 166–173). Copyright © 2009 by the American Psychological Association. Reprinted by permission.

**self-efficacy** A person's belief that he or she is capable of the specific behavior required to produce a desired outcome in a given situation.

**Dispositional Optimism** The reason it's important to understand our attributions for past outcomes and our perceptions of control in present situations is that both have implications for our outlook on the future. In *Learned Optimism*, Seligman (1991) argues that a generalized tendency to expect positive outcomes is characterized by a non-depressive explanatory style. According to Seligman, optimists tend to blame failure on factors that are external, temporary, and specific, and to credit success to factors that are internal, permanent, and global. Thankfully, in light of the advantages that optimism brings, Suzanne Segerstrom (2006a), like Seligman, notes that even pessimists can retrain themselves to think in optimistic ways.

Consider your own view of the future. Are you the eternal optimist who looks on the bright side and generally expects good things to happen, or do you tend to believe in Murphy's Law, that if something can go wrong it will? By asking questions such as these, Michael Scheier and Charles Carver (1985) categorized college students along this dimension and found that dispositional optimists reported fewer illness symptoms during the semester than did pessimists. Correlations between optimism and health are common. Studies have shown that optimists are more likely to take an active problem-focused approach in coping with stress (Nes & Segerstrom, 2006). As a result, they are more likely to complete a rehabilitation program for alcoholics; make a quicker, fuller recovery from coronary artery bypass surgery; and, among gay men concerned about AIDS, take a more active approach to the threat (Scheier & Carver, 1992). In a study of 1,306 healthy adult men from the Boston area, those reporting high levels of optimism rather than pessimism were half as likely to have coronary heart disease 10 years later (Kubzansky et al., 2001). In a study of 5,000 municipal workers in Finland, those who were high rather than low in optimism were healthier and missed fewer days from work if they were struck by a death or serious illness in the family over the next 5 years (Kivimäki et al., 2005).

In the course of a lifetime, everyone has setbacks. But an optimistic disposition may help us weather the storms better. There may even be long-term health implications. In one study, researchers collected personal essays written in the 1940s by 99 men who had just graduated from Harvard and then analyzed these materials to determine what each man's explanatory style had been in his youth. Thirty-five years later, those who in their youth had an optimistic outlook were healthier than their more pessimistic peers (Peterson et al., 1988).

How can these results be explained? There are two possibilities: one biological, the other behavioral. In research that supports a biological explanation, investigators analyzing blood samples have found that optimists exhibit a stronger immune response to stress than pessimists do (Kamen-Siegel et al., 1991; Segerstrom et al., 1998). In research that supports a behavioral explanation, Christopher Peterson and others (1988) scored the explanatory styles of 1,528 healthy young adults from questionnaires they had filled out between 1936 and 1940. Astonishingly, after 50 years, the optimists (specifically, those who had made global rather than specific attributions for good events) were less likely to have died an accidental, reckless, or violent death.

There's an old saying: "Where there's life, there's hope." Perhaps the opposite is also true: "Where there's hope, there's life." In a stunning illustration of this possibility, Susan Everson and others (1996) studied 2,428 middle-aged men in Finland. Based on the extent to which they agreed with two simple statements ("I feel that it is impossible to reach the goals I would like to strive for" and "The future seems hopeless, and I can't believe that things are changing for the better"), the men were initially classified as having a high, medium, or low sense of hopelessness. When the investigators checked the death records roughly 6 years later, they found that the more hopeless the men were at the start, the more likely they were to have died of various causes—even when the

*"The optimist proclaims we live in the best of all possible worlds; and the pessimist fears this is true."*

—James Cabell

*"The most important thing in illness is never to lose heart."*

—Nikolai Lenin

men were otherwise equated for their age and prior health status. Compared with those who were low in hopelessness, the highs were more than twice as likely to die from cancer and four times more likely to die of cardiovascular disease (see ● Figure 14.7). These results bring to life what Norman Cousins (1989) described as "the biology of hope," reminding us that "positive expectations can be self-fulfilling" (Peterson, 2000).

## Pollyanna's Health

Pollyanna is the upbeat heroine created by American writer Eleanor Porter. Although she used to get bad press for her boundless belief that even the most ominous cloud has a bright silver lining, the research in this section suggests that Pollyanna should be an extraordinarily healthy person.

Let's be clear about what the research means. The mind is a powerful tool that can be used to hurt, heal, and protect the body (Ray, 2004). Still, no credible scientist believes that our attributions, perceptions of control, optimism, or other sources of resilience are the sole determinants of a

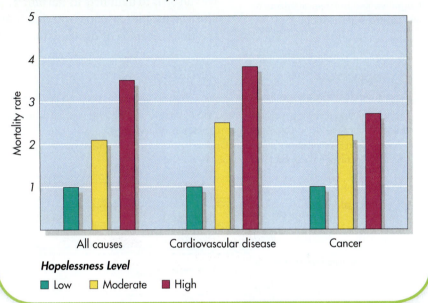

● **FIGURE 14.7**
**Hopelessness and the Risk of Death**
Among middle-aged men in Finland, those who were initially high rather than low in hopelessness were more likely to die within 6 years—overall, from cancer, and from cardiovascular disease. Those who were moderate in hopelessness fell between the two extremes.
From Everson, S. A., et al., "Hopelessness and risk of mortality and incidence of myorcardial infarction and cancer," *Psychosomatic Medicine* vol 58 (pp. 121–133). Copyright © 1996 Wolters Kluwer Health. Reprinted by permission.

long life. A positive outlook cannot guarantee future good health. So although we should appreciate the powers of the mind to influence the body, it would be a cruel mistake to blame victims of illness for having a bad outlook on life. As Howard Friedman (1991) put it in *The Self-Healing Personality*, "We must walk a fine line between blaming patients on the one hand and absolving them of any role in their health on the other" (p. 96).

It's also important to recognize that there may be drawbacks to positive thinking, especially if it leads us to see ourselves and the events around us in ways that are grossly unrealistic. As we saw in Chapter 3, people with overly positive views of themselves are sometimes disliked by their friends and seen as boastful, inconsiderate, and oversensitive to criticism (Colvin et al., 1995; Heatherton & Vohs, 2000). It may also be detrimental for people to believe that they have control over events when they do not. In a study of patients suffering from a loss of kidney function, those who felt that they had control over their health became more depressed, not less, after having a transplant that failed (Christensen et al., 1991). In a study of first-year law students, optimists exhibited a stronger immune response than did pessimists when their transition to law school was easy but a weaker immune response when the transition was difficult (Segerstrom, 2006b). Faced with some setbacks, a sense of control can help us bounce back. But setting control expectations too high can do more harm than good in the wake of negative outcomes.

This brings us back to Job. At the end of this biblical account, Job recovers his health, his property, and his family prosperity. He does not, however, regain the sense of personal control and optimism that he enjoyed prior to being struck by calamity. Instead, Job's hard-won serenity is based on his belief that life has meaning and purpose. Pollyanna has her charm, but Job is a hero of the human condition.

When it comes to physical health, research does not support popular beliefs about the power of positive thinking. **F**ALSE.

# Ways of Coping With Stress

Leaving home. Studying for final exams. Breaking up with a boyfriend or girlfriend. Working long nights—or not at all. Waiting on long security lines at the airport. Feeling squeezed in a tight job market. Having children. Raising children. Struggling to meet the deadline to complete a textbook. Stress is inevitable. No one can prevent it. The best we can do is to minimize its harmful effects on our health. Depending on the person and stressor, people can cope by trying to solve the problem, talking to friends, inviting distractions, sleeping or drinking too much to escape, praying, brooding, venting, lashing out, laughing it off, getting outside help, pretending that all is well—or freaking out. Combining all psychological theories and research, it appears that there are about 400 specific ways to cope with stress (Skinner et al., 2003). In a recent nationwide survey, men and women were asked about how they manage the stress in their lives. As you can see in ● Figure 14.8, people cope in a wide variety of ways—some healthy, others not (American Psychological Association, 2008).

By grouping specific strategies that are similar, researchers study different general types of coping. Based on the self-reports of large numbers of people, Charles Carver and others (1989) constructed a multidimensional questionnaire they called COPE that measures twelve distinct methods of coping (see Table 14.3). While noting that people can use different coping strategies, Lazarus and Folkman (1984) distinguished two general types. The first is **problem-focused coping**, cognitive and behavioral efforts to reduce stress by overcoming the source of the problem. Difficulties in school? Study harder, hire a tutor, or reduce your workload. Marriage on

**problem-focused coping**
Cognitive and behavioral efforts to alter a stressful situation.

● **FIGURE 14.8**

**How Americans Manage Stress**

There is no single way to manage stress. When American men and women were asked to indicate how they do it, the list that emerged was quite varied.
From American Psychological Association (October 7, 2008). *Stress in America*. Copyright © 2009 by the American Psychological Association. Reprinted by permission.

| | |
|---|---|
| Listen to music | |
| Exercise or walk | |
| Read | |
| Spend time with friends or family | |
| Nap | |
| Play video games or surf the Internet | |
| Pray | |
| Eat | |
| Spend time doing a hobby | |
| Go to church or religious services | |
| Drink alcohol | |
| Shop | |
| Smoke | |
| Play sports | |
| Get a massage/go to a spa | |
| Meditation or yoga | |
| See a mental health professional | |
| Gamble | |
| Play with/care for pets | |
| Gardening | |
| Other | |

*Percent* (axis: 0, 10, 20, 30, 40, 50, 60)

the rocks? Talk it out or see a counselor. Problem finding work? Look for an internship, expand your search, or try a new location. As indicated in several of the items in Table 14.3, the goal is to attack the source of stress. A second approach is **emotion-focused coping**, which consists of efforts to manage our emotional reactions to stressors rather than trying to change the stressors themselves. If you struggle at school, at work, or in a romantic relationship, you can keep a stiff upper lip, accept what is happening, tune out, or vent your emotions. According to Lazarus and Folkman, we tend to take an active, problem-focused approach when we think we can overcome a stressor but fall back on an emotion-focused approach when we perceive the problem to be out of our control. Lisa Aspinwall and Shelley Taylor (1997) note that there is a third alternative: **proactive coping**, which consists of up-front efforts to ward off or modify the onset of a stressful event. As we'll see, coping is an ongoing process by which we try to prevent—not just react to—life's bumps and bruises.

 ## Problem-Focused Coping

Problem-focused coping seems like the prime candidate for a starring role in the war against stress. Surely our most active and assertive efforts are associated with better health (Aspinwall & Taylor, 1992). And clearly we often benefit from confronting a stressor head on rather than avoiding it. Consider something we all are guilty of on occasion: procrastination—a purposeful delay in beginning or completing a task, often

**emotion-focused coping** Cognitive and behavioral efforts to reduce the distress produced by a stressful situation.

**proactive coping** Up-front efforts to ward off or modify the onset of a stressful event.

---

**TABLE 14.3**
**Ways of Coping with Stress**

These statements describe some coping strategies that people say they use. The strategies are listed in order from those that are relatively common to those that are less common.

**Planning/Active Coping**

- I try to come up with a strategy about what to do.
- I take additional action to try to get rid of the problem.

**Positive Reinterpretation**

- I look for something good in what is happening.
- I try to make it seem more positive.

**Acceptance**

- I learn to live with it.
- I accept that this has happened and can't be changed.

**Seeking Social Support**

- I talk to someone about how I feel.
- I ask people who had similar experiences what they did.

**Restraint Coping**

- I force myself to wait for the right time to do something.
- I make sure not to make matters worse by acting too soon.

**Focusing on/Venting Emotions**

- I get upset and let my emotions out.
- I let my feelings out.

**Suppression of Competing Activities**

- I put aside other activities to concentrate on this.
- If necessary I let other things slide a little.

**Mental Disengagement**

- I turn to work . . . to take my mind off things.
- I go to the movies or watch TV, to think about it less.

**Turning to Religion**

- I seek God's help.
- I try to find comfort in my religion.

**Behavioral Disengagement**

- I give up the attempt to get what I want.
- I admit to myself that I can't deal with it.

**Denial**

- I refuse to believe that it has happened.
- I pretend that it hasn't really happened.

**Alcohol and Drugs**

- I drink alcohol or take drugs to think about it less.

Carver et al., 1989. © Cengage Learning

accompanied by feelings of discomfort (Ferrari et al., 1995). In a longitudinal study of college students enrolled in a health psychology class, Dianne Tice and Roy Baumeister (1997) administered a questionnaire at the start of the semester that assesses the extent to which people tend to procrastinate. True to their word, those students who were classified from their test scores as procrastinators turned in their term papers later than did their classmates and received lower grades. More interesting was the relationship to daily reports of stress and physical health. Early on, while procrastinators were in the "putting it off" stage of their projects, they were relatively stress-free compared with others. Later in the semester, however, as the deadline neared and passed, procrastinators were under greater stress and reported having more symptoms of illness. In the end, the short-term benefits of avoidance were outweighed by the long-term costs.

In dealing with essential tasks, it is better to confront and control than to avoid. But is this always the more beneficial approach? There are two reasons why sometimes it is not. First, to exert control a person must stay vigilant, alert, and actively engaged, which is physiologically taxing (Light & Obrist, 1980). Second, a controlling orientation can cause problems if it leads us to develop an overcontrolling, stress-inducing, Type A pattern of behavior—whether that means always having the last word in an argument, "driving" from the back seat of a car, or planning every last detail of a leisurely vacation. Not all events are within our control or important enough to worry about. There are times when it's better to just let go (Friedland et al., 1992; Wright et al., 1990).

When we use the word *control*, we usually have in mind active efforts to manage something: win an argument, work out a marital problem, or solve a problem at work. But control comes in many guises. Knowledge, for instance, is a form of control. Knowing why something happens increases your chance of making sure it goes your way—if not now, then the next time. Sometimes we can cope effectively with tragedies such as technological disasters, terrorist acts, and spousal abuse by blaming the perpetrators for their actions. In these situations, holding others responsible can force a helpful response, such as financial compensation or police protection.

But what about self-blame? Is it ever adaptive to cope with a bad situation by blaming oneself? According to Ronnie Janoff-Bulman (1979), it depends on whether you blame your behavior or yourself as a person. People can change their own behavior, she notes, so behavioral self-blame paves the way for control in an effort to reduce current stresses or avoid future ones. But it is not similarly adaptive, she warns, to blame your own enduring personal characteristics, which are harder to change. Janoff-Bulman (1992) later amended this hypothesis, noting that it may take time to realize the mental health benefits of behavioral self-blame. This prediction was tested in studies of how female rape victims adjust to the trauma. Consistently, both behavioral and characterological self-blame were associated with an increase in distress. Contrary to prediction, rape victims who blame their own behavior for what happened do *not* cope better than those who blame their character (Frazier & Schauben, 1994; Hall et al., 2003).

In light of past research, Patricia Frazier (2003) offers a somewhat more complex perspective on blame, control, and coping. Clearly, she notes, it can be adaptive for the victims of rape and other traumas to own a sense of future control (Carver et al., 2000; Frazier et al., 2004). But noting that behavioral self-blame for a past trauma does not guarantee the prevention of future trauma, she distinguishes past, present, and future control—and what each implies about the dreaded possibility of a future recurrence. In a longitudinal study of female rape victims appearing in an emergency room, she assessed attributions of blame and responsibility, perceptions of control, and feelings of distress periodically from 2 weeks up to a year later. Overall, women blamed the rapist more than they blamed themselves, a tendency that strengthened over time. As in other studies, however, those who assigned more blame either to the rapist or to themselves were more distressed. Apparently, the problem with behavioral self-blame, once thought to be adaptive, is that it did not engender feelings of future safety. In this regard, the most useful sense of control was over the *present*: women who believed that they could help themselves get better and facilitate their own recovery were more optimistic about the future and the least distressed.

## Emotion-Focused Coping

Stress is by definition an unpleasant and arousing experience that fills people with negative and unhealthy emotions. Do some coping mechanisms focus on this emotional aspect of adversity?

**Positive Emotions: Building Blocks of Emotion-Focused Coping**  Following the terrorist attacks of 9/11, many Americans reported in public opinion polls that they cried and felt sad, angry, fearful, anxious, and disgusted. Under conditions so tragic, one would not also expect people to feel positive emotions. But it is possible for positive and negative feelings to coexist—as when we find consolation in loss or a silver lining in the dense gray clouds (Folkman & Moskowitz, 2000).

People who cope well and are resilient tend to experience positive emotions in the face of stress—a common capacity that Ann Masten (2001) termed "ordinary magic." How is it that positive emotions work like magic? On the basis of numerous studies, Barbara Frederickson (2009) offers a two-step theory of why our fleeting but pleasant positive emotions are so effective. First, she notes that positive emotions help people to *broaden* their outlook in times of stress so they can cope with adversity—in part by providing a welcome distraction from the anger, fear, and other negative states that increase blood pressure and arousal and narrow the focusing of attention.

To test the hypothesis that positive emotion is adaptive in this way, Frederickson and colleagues (2003) contacted 46 college students days after September 11, 2001, who had previously taken part in a study on stress and coping. Across the board, the students felt angry, sad and fearful; they also felt scorn toward the attackers. But many also expressed positive feelings of gratitude (to be alive), love (a renewed appreciation for loved ones), and interest (in unfolding world events). In fact, those who scored as most resilient before the crisis were later the most likely to have these positive emotions and least likely to suffer depression after the crisis. By coping with positive emotions in one specific situation after another, Frederickson (2009) suggests, people over time *build* personal resources—learning, for example, how to stay calm, focused, in control, and capable of giving and receiving emotional support.

Positive emotions may serve the coping process better than negative emotions, but are all positive emotions equally adaptive? Maybe not. Sarah Pressman and Sheldon Cohen (2012) analyzed the language used by 88 highly influential deceased psychologists in their writings. Specifically, they categorized and counted the words used that were positive or negative and high or low in arousal. These distinctions resulted in four types of emotion words: positive-high arousal (*lively, enthusiastic, energetic*) positive-low arousal (*calm, peaceful, content*), negative-high arousal (*tense, afraid, angry*), and negative-low arousal (*lonely, drowsy, tired*). On average, the psychologists sampled had lived an average of 79 years. Even after controlling for the possible effects of sex, year of birth, and other individual factors, Pressman and Cohen found that the more positive-high arousal emotion words the psychologists had used in their writings, the longer they lived—by an average of 5 years. The use of positive-low arousal emotion words was not similarly associated with longevity.

Research on positive emotions reminds us not to over-intellectualize the coping process and underestimate the value of emotion-focused coping. Look back at Table 14.3, and you will see many instances of emotion-focused coping, such as acceptance, denial, focusing on or venting of emotions, disengaging mentally and behaviorally, or turning to religion. By and large, we will see that there are two other general ways to cope with the emotional aspects of stress: shutting down and opening up. Let's examine the health effects of each of these strategies.

**Shutting Down: Suppressing Unwanted Thoughts**    Often we react to stress by shutting down and trying to deny or suppress the unpleasant thoughts and feelings. One specific form of avoidance coping is distraction. Consider what happens when terrorists take innocent victims hostage. Police surround the site and negotiations begin. Are certain ways of coping with this frightening situation particularly effective? To help answer this question, 57 airline employees voluntarily participated in a remarkable training exercise conducted by the Special Operations and Research Staff of the FBI Academy (Auerbach et al., 1994; Strentz & Auerbach, 1988). Some volunteers were trained in problem-focused coping techniques such as helping each other, interacting with their captors, and gathering intelligence. Others were trained in emotion-focused techniques designed to decrease anxiety—such as distraction, deep breathing, and muscle relaxation. Volunteers in a control condition did not receive any specific instruction.

After the training session, the volunteers were "abducted" by FBI agents acting as terrorists. Automatic weapons were fired (with blanks), and bloody injuries were simulated. The volunteers were then "held captive" in one room and isolated by having pillowcases placed over their heads. A few cooperative "hostages" were released. Four days later, other FBI agents "stormed" the building and "rescued" the remaining hostages. The exercise was conducted in a realistic manner, and the volunteers found it exceedingly stressful. Those who had been instructed in anxiety-management techniques coped better than those given problem-solving training or no training at all. In this kind of situation, where individuals have little actual control over events, distraction and other emotion-focused techniques were more effective in reducing distress than were problem-focused efforts to exert control.

Although potentially effective, suppression of unwanted thoughts from awareness can also have a peculiar, paradoxical effect. As described in Chapter 3, Daniel Wegner (1994, 1997) conducted a series of studies in which he told people not to think of a white bear and found that they could not then keep the image from popping to mind. What's more, he found that among participants who were permitted later to think about the bear, those who had earlier tried to suppress the image were unusually preoccupied with it, providing evidence of a rebound effect. Sometimes, the harder you try not to think about something, the less likely you are to succeed (Wegner et al., 1998). The solution: focused distraction. When participants were told to imagine a tiny red Volkswagen every time the forbidden bear intruded into consciousness, the rebound effect vanished (Wenzlaff & Wegner, 2000).

What do white bears and red cars have to do with coping? A lot. When people try to block stressful thoughts from awareness, the problem may worsen. That's where focused distraction comes in. In a study of pain tolerance, Delia Cioffi and James Holloway (1993) had people put a hand into a bucket of ice-cold water and keep it there until they could no longer bear the pain. One group was instructed to avoid thinking about the sensation. A second group was told to form a mental picture of their home. Afterward, those who had coped through suppression were slower to recover from the pain than were those who had used focused self-distraction. To manage stress—whether it's caused by physical pain, a strained romance, final exams, or problems at work—distraction ("think about lying on the beach") is a better coping strategy than mere suppression ("don't think about the pain").

Keeping secrets and holding in strong emotions may also be physically taxing. In the laboratory, James Gross and Robert Levenson (1997) showed female students funny, sad, and neutral films. Half the time, they told the students to not let their feelings show. From a hidden camera, videotapes confirmed that when they were asked to conceal their feelings, the students were less expressive. But physiological recordings revealed that as they watched the funny and sad films, the students exhibited a greater cardiovascular response when they tried to inhibit their feelings than when they did not. Physiologically, the effort to suppress the display of emotion backfired. Also in the laboratory, Michael Slepian and his colleagues (2012) found that people who harbored and recall important secrets (for example, concerning cheating or sexual orientation) perceived distances to be farther, hills to be steeper, and physical tasks to require more effort—all suggesting that "as with physical burdens, secrets weigh people down" (p. 619).

A real-life study by Steve Cole and his colleagues (1996) pushes this point a profound step further. These investigators identified 80 gay men in the Los Angeles area who were newly infected with the HIV virus but had no symptoms, administered various psychological tests, and monitored their progress every 6 months for 9 years. They found that in men who were partly "in the closet"—compared with those who were open about their homosexuality—the infection spread more rapidly, causing them to die sooner. This provocative correlation does not prove that "coming out" is healthier than "staying in." In a controlled laboratory experiment, however, participants who were instructed to suppress rather than express turbulent emotional thoughts exhibited a temporary decrease in the activity of certain immune cells (Petrie et al., 1998). At least in Western cultures that encourage self-expression, actively concealing your innermost thoughts and feelings can be hazardous to your health.

**Opening Up: Confronting One's Demons**    The research just described suggests that just as shutting down can sometimes have benefits, so too can the opposite form of coping: opening up. There are two aspects to this emotional means of coping with stress. The first is acknowledging and understanding our emotional reactions to important events; the second is expressing these inner feelings to ourselves and others (Stanton et al., 2000).

According to James Pennebaker (1997), psychotherapy, self-help groups, and various religious rituals have something in common: All offer a chance for people to confide in someone, spill their guts, confess, and talk freely about their troubles—maybe for the first time. To test for the healing power of opening up, Pennebaker conducted a series of controlled studies in which he brought college students into a laboratory and asked them to talk into a tape recorder or write for 20 minutes either about past traumas or trivial daily events. While speaking or writing, the students were upset and physiologically aroused. Many tearfully recounted accidents, failures, instances of physical or sexual abuse, loneliness, the death or divorce of their parents, shattered relationships, and their fears about the future. Soon these students felt better than ever. Pennebaker found that when they opened up, their systolic blood pressure levels rose during the disclosures but then later dipped below their pre-experiment levels. The students even exhibited a decline in the number of times they visited the campus health center over the next 6 months. Other studies, too, have shown that keeping personal secrets can be stressful and that "letting it out" and "getting it off your chest" can have true therapeutic effects on mental and physical health. These effects are especially strong when participants are comfortable with disclosure, when the disclosures are made across multiple sessions, and when the events being described are recent and traumatic (Frattaroli, 2006; Lepore & Smyth, 2002).

It appears that confession may be good for the body as well as the soul. But why does it help to open up? Why do *you* sometimes feel the need to talk out your problems? One possibility, recognized a full century ago by Sigmund Freud, is that the experience provides a much-needed *catharsis*, a discharge of tension—like taking the lid off a boiling pot of water to slow the boiling. People who experience trauma—whether it's a bout with cancer, death, an accident, a natural disaster, or exposure to violence—are often haunted by intrusive images of their stressor that pop to mind and cannot be stopped. In these cases, disclosure may bring emotional closure. Another explanation for the benefits of opening up, one favored by Pennebaker, is that talking about a problem can help you to sort out your thoughts, understand the problem better, and gain *insight*, in cognitive terms. Whatever the reason, it's clear that opening up, perhaps to someone else, can be therapeutic—provided that the listener can be trusted. This last point is critical: Despite the potential for gain, opening up can also cause great distress when the people we confide in react with rejection or unwanted advice or, worse, betray what was said to others (Kelly & McKillop, 1996).

Indicating the importance of the "to whom" part of opening up, Stephen Lepore and colleagues (2000) exposed college students to disturbing Nazi Holocaust images. Afterward, the students were randomly divided into groups and asked to talk about their reactions to themselves while alone in a room, to a validating confederate who smiled and agreed, or to an invalidating confederate who avoided eye contact and disagreed. An additional group was given no opportunity to talk. As reported 2 days later, students who talked alone or to a validating confederate—compared to those who did not talk—said they had fewer intrusive Holocaust thoughts in the intervening period and were less stressed when re-exposed to the original images. However, for students who talked to an invalidating confederate the benefits of opening up were muted. This finding supports our earlier conclusion: It is better to discuss one's demons than to conceal them—but the extent of the benefit depends on whether the people we talk to are supportive. It's no wonder, then, that people are more likely to join mutual support groups, both live and online, when they suffer from stigmatizing disorders such as AIDS, alcoholism, breast cancer, and prostate cancer than when they have less embarrassing but equally toxic illnesses such as heart disease and diabetes (Davison et al., 2000).

**Self-Focus: Getting Trapped Versus Getting Out**   In Chapter 3, we saw that people spend little time actually thinking about the self—and when they do, they wish they were doing something else (Csikszentmihalyi & Figurski, 1982). According to self-awareness theory, self-focus brings out our personal shortcomings the way staring in a mirror draws our attention to every blemish on the face. It comes as no surprise, then, that self-focus seems to intensify some of the most undesirable consequences of emotion-focused coping. Here's the script.

The state of self-awareness can be induced in us by external stimuli such as mirrors, cameras, and audiences. Mood, too, plays a role. Peter Salovey (1992) found that, compared with a neutral mood state, both positive and negative moods increase awareness of the self. Thus, when a stressful event occurs, the negative feelings that arise magnify self-focus. What happens next depends on a person's self-esteem, as people with a negative self-concept experience more negative moods when self-focused than do those with a positive self-concept (Sedikides, 1992). The end result is a self-perpetuating feedback loop: Being in a bad mood triggers self-focus, which in people with low self-esteem further worsens the mood. This vicious circle forms the basis for a self-focusing model of depression according to which coping with stress by attending to your own feelings only makes things worse (Mor & Winquist, 2002; Pyszczynski & Greenberg, 1992).

A great deal of research has shown that individuals who respond to distress by rumination and repetitive thought—by constantly fixating on themselves, their feelings, their symptoms, and the source of their distress—are more likely to become anxious and depressed than those who allow themselves to be distracted (Nolen-Hoeksema, 1991; Nolen-Hoeksema et al., 2008). Although some types of self-focus may be useful, as when people react to a stressful event by focusing on the positives or worrying in ways that lead them to plan, problem solve, and alter their expectations in adaptive ways, the adverse effects are clear (Watkins, 2008). Over the years, and across a range of different cultures, research has also shown that girls and women in particular have a tendency to ruminate, confront their negative feelings, and seek treatment for being depressed, while boys and men resort to alcohol and other drugs, physical activity, antisocial behavior, and other means of distraction. As a general rule, it appears that women who are upset tend to brood, while men who are upset are more likely to act out (Culbertson, 1997; Nolen-Hoeksema & Girgus, 1994).

Thankfully, there are healthier alternatives. To redirect attention away from the self, it helps to become absorbed in an activity such as aerobic exercise, gardening, writing, or reading a book. Whatever the activity, it should be difficult, demanding, and fully engaging. Ralph Erber and Abraham Tesser (1992) found that people who were in a bad mood felt better after performing a difficult task than a simple task or none at all. Difficult tasks, it appears, can "absorb" a bad mood. Meditation—which calls on you to focus your attention on a chosen nonself object—can have positive effects for the same reason (Lutz et al., 2008). Referring to techniques of focused relaxation that he had developed, Cardiologist Herbert Benson recommended that people sit comfortably, close their eyes, relax the muscles, breathe deeply, and silently utter some word over and over again. Says Benson (1993), "By practicing two basic steps—the repetition of a sound, word, phrase, prayer, or muscular activity; and a passive return to the repetition whenever distracting thoughts recur—you can trigger a series of physiological changes that offer protection against stress" (p. 256).

Healthy distractions such as exercise are a good way to break out of the trap of self-focused depression. Unhealthy distractions, such as an alcohol binge, reduce self-focus at a self-destructive cost.

Stan Honda/AFP/Getty Images

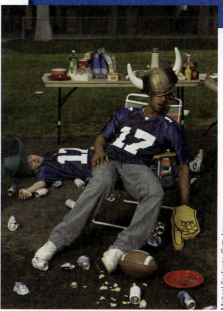

Michael Cogliantry/Getty Images

## > Proactive Coping

According to Lisa Aspinwall and Shelley Taylor (1997), people often benefit from *proactive coping*, which consists of up-front efforts to ward off or modify the onset of a stressful event. As illustrated in ● Figure 14.9, coping can be seen as an ongoing process by which we try to prevent as well as react to the bumps and bruises of daily life. Also as shown, the first line of defense involves the accumulation of resources—personal, financial, social, and otherwise—that can later, if needed, serve as a buffer against stress. In this section, we look at two possible resources: social support and religion.

**● FIGURE 14.9**
**Aspinwall and Taylor's Model of Proactive Coping**

Coping can be seen as an ongoing, multi-step process by which people try to prevent, not just react to, life's daily stressors.

From Aspinwall and Taylor, "A stick in time: self-regulation and proactive coping," *Psychological Bulletin* vol 121 (pp. 417–436). Copyright © 1997 by the American Psychological Association. Reprinted by permission.

**Social Support** If the world is crashing down around you, what do you do? Do you try to stop it? Do you try to manage your emotions? Or do you try to get help from others? Throughout this book, we have seen that no man or woman is an island, that human beings are social animals, that people need people, and that to get by you need a little help from friends. But do our social nature and our connections to others have anything to do with health? Do close family ties, lovers, buddies, online support groups, and relationships at work serve as a buffer against stress? The answer is yes. The evidence is now overwhelming that **social support** has therapeutic effects on our physical and psychological well-being (Cohen, 2004; Uchino, 2009).

David Spiegel, of Stanford University's School of Medicine, came to appreciate the value of social connections many years ago when he organized support groups for women with advanced breast cancer. The groups met weekly in 90-minute sessions to laugh, cry, share stories, and discuss ways of coping. Spiegel had fully expected the women to benefit emotionally from the experience. But he found something else he did not expect: These women lived an average of 18 months longer than did similar others who did not attend the groups. According to Spiegel (1993), "The added survival time was longer than any medication or other known medical treatment could be expected to provide for women with breast cancer so far advanced" (pp. 331–332).

Similar discoveries were then made by other researchers. In one study, Lisa Berkman and Leonard Syme (1979) surveyed 7,000 residents of Alameda County, California, and conducted a 9-year follow-up of mortality rates. They found that the more social contacts people had, the longer they lived. This was true of men and women, young and old, rich and poor, and people from all racial and ethnic backgrounds. James House and others (1988) studied 2,754 adults interviewed during visits to their doctors. He found that the most socially active men were two to three times less likely to die within 9 to 12 years

**social support** The helpful coping resources provided by friends and other people.

than others of similar age who were more isolated. According to House, social isolation was statistically just as predictive of an early death as smoking or high cholesterol.

Research findings like these are common. For example, married people are more likely than those who are single, divorced, or widowed to survive cancer for 5 years (Taylor, 1990), gay men infected with HIV are less likely to contemplate suicide if they have close ties than if they do not (Schneider et al., 1991), people who have a heart attack are less likely to have a second one if they live with someone than if they live alone (Case et al., 1992), and people, once married, who are then separated or divorced for long periods of time, are at an increased risk of early death (Sbarra & Nietert, 2009). Based on this type of research, Bert Uchino and his colleagues (1996) concluded that in times of stress, having social support lowers blood pressure, lessens the secretion of stress hormones, and strengthens immune responses.

On the flip side of the coin, people who are lonely suffer greater age-related increases in blood pressure and have more difficulty sleeping at night (Cacioppo et al., 2002; Hawkley et al., 2003). In fact, a study of first-year college students showed that feelings of loneliness during the semester were associated with elevated levels of the stress hormone cortisol and a weakened immune response to a flu shot they had received at the university health clinic (Pressman et al., 2005). There's no doubt about it: Being isolated from other people can be hazardous to your health.

There is, however, a vital exception to this rule. Of all the social networks that support us, romantic partnerships, as in marriage, are the most powerful. But while men and women who are happily married live longer than those who are single or divorced, marital conflict breeds stress, elevated blood pressure, ulcers, depression, alcohol and drug abuse, changes in immune function, and other unhealthy effects, especially for women (Kiecolt-Glaser & Newton, 2001).

Our social connections are therapeutic for many reasons. Friends may encourage us to get out, eat well, exercise, and take care of ourselves. They also give sympathy, reassurance, someone to talk to, advice, and a second opinion. The value of social support is so basic that people who support us don't need to be physically present. In one study, for example, the physiological responses of research participants were measured as they played a competitive fire-fighting simulation on computer. Via closed-circuit monitor, some participants thought they were being watched, spoken to, and comforted by a friendly person of the same sex, while others were left alone. The result: Social support delivered over a monitor, even from a confederate who was not physically present, had a calming influence on participants. It lowered their heart rate, reduced the level of cortisol in their saliva, and led them to see the task as easier (Thorsteinsson et al., 1998).

The health benefits of social support show just how important it is to connect with others. Are there any drawbacks to an active social life? Is it possible, for example, that the more people we see in a day—such as family, friends, classmates, teammates, co-workers, and neighbors— the more exposed we are to colds or the flu? Natalie Hamrick and others (2002) asked 18- to 30-year-old adults about recent stressful events and about their social lives, then had them keep a health diary for 3 months. Based on past research, they expected that participants who were under high stress would get sick more than those under low stress. But what about people with high versus low levels of social contact? What do you think? Would their social connections make them vulnerable to illness or protect them? It depends. Look at ● Figure 14.10 and you'll see that for people under low stress, social connections did not matter. For people

● **FIGURE 14.10**

**Does Being Popular Always Promote Health?**

Young adults were asked about recent stressful events and about their social lives—and then kept a health diary for 3 months. As you can see, social contact made no difference for people under low stress. For people under high stress, however, those with active social lives were more likely to get sick. Social contact increases exposure to infectious agents—and can bring illness for those whose resistance is compromised by stress.
From Hamrick, N., Cohen, S., and Rodriguez, M. S., "Being popular can be healthy or unhealthy: Stress, social network diversity, and incidence of upper respiratory infection," *Health Psychology* vol 21 (pp. 294–298). Copyright © 2002 by the American Psychological Association. Reprinted by permission.

under high stress, however, those with high levels of social contact were *more* likely to catch a cold or flu. It's healthy to be popular except, perhaps, during flu season.

Precisely because researchers agree that social support is vital to health, they have struggled mightily to come up with ways to measure it (Cohen et al., 2000). In some studies, social support is defined by the sheer *number of social contacts* a person has. This measure can be useful, but a simple social contact model has some limitations. One is that it glosses over the fact that people who are stuck in bad relationships are sometimes more distressed, not less (Rook, 1984). Another problem is that having too many contacts can actually reduce levels of support. Consider the plight of the urban poor in India who are packed into overcrowded residences of up to 11 people per room. They are more stressed than people in less crowded conditions and have *less* social support, in part because they tend to withdraw (Evans & Lepore, 1993).

A second model of social support focuses on the *diversity* of a person's social network, one that consists, for example, of a spouse, close family members, friends, co-workers, and neighbors. Over the years, research has shown that people who are socially "integrated," who have connections to different types of people in different types of relationships, are healthier and live longer lives (Cohen & Janicki-Deverts, 2009).

A third model focuses on the quality of a person's relationships rather than their quantity. This *intimacy model* predicts that the key is to have a close relationship with a significant other who is emotionally on call for late-night conversations. Having one special relationship may be all a person needs. Thus, while many women with breast cancer benefit physically and emotionally from peer discussion groups, these groups are not needed by—and do not help—women who have supportive partners at home (Helgeson et al., 2000).

A fourth approach defines social support by *its perceived availability* (Sarason et al., 1983). Compared with people who are uncertain of what social resources they have, those who believe that ample support is available when needed cope more effectively. In almost any demanding situation you can imagine, perceived support is associated with better adjustment—even when these perceptions are not entirely accurate (Lakey & Cassady, 1990; Lakey & Orehek, 2011).

### The Religious Connection

Finally, it is clear that religion provides a deeply important source of social and emotional support for many people. There are more than 6 billion people on Earth who belong to hundreds of religions—the most populated, in order, being Christianity, Islam, Hinduism, and Buddhism (Judaism and others have many fewer adherents). Only about 15% to 20% of the world's population is unaffiliated with a religious group. In the United States, two-thirds of all adults describe religion as a very important part of their lives. Is there a link between religiosity and health?

This is an interesting but controversial question. On the one hand, population surveys suggest that people who regularly attend religious services live longer than those who do not (McCullough et al., 2000). When you think about it, this correlation makes some intuitive sense. Religious faith may fill people with hope and optimism rather than with despair, offer the physiological benefits of relaxation in prayer, provide a community lifeline of social support to prevent isolation, and promote a safe and healthy way of life by discouraging such toxic habits as drinking and smoking. After analyzing 30 years of health data from 2,600 California adults, for example, William Strawbridge and others (2001) found that men and women who regularly attend religious services drink less, smoke less, and exercise more. On the

> People who have lots of friends are healthier and live longer than those who live more isolated lives. **T**RUE.

Religion provides an important source of support for many people. Here, people meditate in New York's Central Park during "Change Your Mind Day," which consists of yoga, meditation, music, and various spiritual practices from Buddhist traditions.

AP/Wide World Photos

other hand, some researchers caution that the correlations between religiosity and longevity are modest and can be interpreted in other ways. It's possible, for example, that nonsmokers, teetotalers, and others who regularly abstain from unhealthful behaviors are more likely to adopt religion as part of their lives than smokers, drinkers, and risk-takers, and that their survival comes from who they are, not from their attendance at religious services (Sloan et al., 1999).

At this point, the research is suggestive but not conclusive: A religious way of life is associated with physiological benefits, health, and longevity, but the basis for these correlations—and the ultimate causal question of whether becoming religious will increase one's health—is a compelling question that remains to be determined (Miller & Thoresen, 2003; Plante & Thoresen, 2007; Powell et al., 2003; Seeman et al., 2003).

## Culture and Coping

Everyone in the world feels stress during the course of a lifetime. Whether the result of a natural disaster, the death of a loved one, the breakup of a relationship, war, serious illness, an accident, or the chronic microstressors of studying, working, and trying to make ends meet, stress is universal to the human experience. But do people in all cultures solve problems and cope in the same ways?

Most of the research on coping is conducted with people from Western cultures, in which individualism and independence are highly valued. Do people from collectivist cultures that value interdependence use the same coping mechanisms that are listed in Table 14.3? The answer may not be as obvious as it seems. In view of the differences between Eastern and Western cultures, for example, one might predict that Asians are more likely than European Americans to cope with stress by turning to others for support. Yet Shelley Taylor and her colleagues (2004) found that when they asked college students to describe what they do to relieve stress, only 39% of South Koreans (compared to 57% of Americans) said they sought social support. Additional research has confirmed this surprising cultural difference. Regardless of whether the source of stress is social, academic, financial, or health related; across age groups; and in diverse Asian samples that included Chinese, Japanese, Korean, and Vietnamese participants, the result is always the same: People from Asian cultures are less likely to seek out social support in times of stress.

Additional probing has shed light on this difference. In individualistic cultures, people often use others to service their personal goals. Yet in collectivist cultures, where social groups take precedence over the self, people are reluctant to strain relationships by calling on others for support. This being the case, Heejung Kim and her colleagues (2008) distinguished between *explicit social support* (disclosing one's distress to others

| TABLE 14.4 |
| --- |
| **Collectivist Coping Styles** |

The following sample statements describe five common types of coping styles, in order of frequency of usage, that have emerged from studies in Taiwan.

| | |
| --- | --- |
| **Acceptance, Reframing, and Striving** | **91%** |
| • Tried to accept the trauma for what it offered me | |
| • Believed I would grow from surviving the traumatic event | |
| • Realized that the trauma served an important purpose in my life | |
| **Avoidance and Detachment** | **71%** |
| • Saved face by not telling anyone | |
| • Pretended to be okay | |
| • Kept my feelings within myself in order not to worry my parents | |
| **Family Support** | **66%** |
| • Shared my feelings with my family | |
| • Knew that I could ask assistance from my family | |
| • Followed the guidance of my elders | |
| **Religion and Spirituality** | **40%** |
| • Found comfort in my religion or spirituality | |
| • Found guidance from my religion | |
| • Found comfort through prayer or other religious rituals | |
| **Private Emotional Outlets** | **30%** |
| • Saved face by seeking advice from a professional I did not know | |
| • Chatted with people about the trauma on the Internet | |
| • Ate in excess | |

Heppner et al., 2006. © Cengage Learning

and seeking their advice, aid, or comfort) and *implicit social support* (merely thinking about or being with close others without openly asking for help). In a study that asked participants to imagine themselves in one of these two situations, Asian Americans reacted with more stress to the explicit social support situation, while European Americans found the more contained implicit situation more stressful (Taylor et al., 2007).

To better understand the "collectivist coping style," Paul Heppner and others (2006) administered extensive questionnaires to more than 3,000 Asian college students in Taiwan, many of whom had endured the kinds of traumatic events described in this chapter (the three most frequent were breakups, academic pressure, and the death or illness of a loved one). Table 14.4 shows five ways of coping that were identified. In order of how often they are used, the strategies are (1) acceptance, reframing, and striving; (2) avoidance and detachment; (3) family support; (4) religion and spirituality; and (5) private emotional outlets. Of the five strategies, participants rated acceptance as the most helpful. Do these results describe how Taiwanese adults cope with stress? What about Asians from Korea, Japan, China, and elsewhere? Interest is growing in these questions and, more generally, in the intersections of social psychology, culture, and health (Gurung, 2010).

Recent research by Jacqueline Chen and other (2012) sheds some light on these questions. These investigators note that social support can take a variety of forms—most notably, problem-solving support (providing insight, advice, money, and other tangible resources to help resolve the stressor) and emotion-focused support (providing comfort, reassurance, and a boost to self-esteem). In one study, college students from the United States and Japan were asked to describe their most recent social interaction with someone they were close to and then to indicate whether they did something to try to help that person. Overall American participants were twice as likely as the Japanese participants to spontaneously report giving social support in their interactions. But ● Figure 14.11 shows that the two groups also differed in terms of the types of social support they provided: Americans gave more emotion-focused support aimed at helping their close other feel better about himself or herself; Japanese gave more problem-focused support aimed at helping to resolve the stressor.

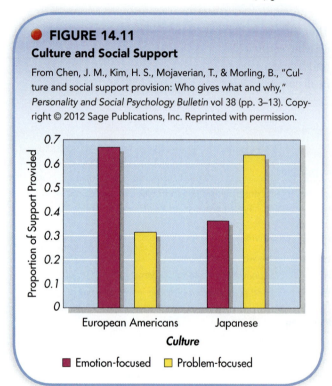

● **FIGURE 14.11**

**Culture and Social Support**

From Chen, J. M., Kim, H. S., Mojaverian, T., & Morling, B., "Culture and social support provision: Who gives what and why," *Personality and Social Psychology Bulletin* vol 38 (pp. 3–13). Copyright © 2012 Sage Publications, Inc. Reprinted with permission.

## Treatment and Prevention

Understanding what social support is and how it operates is important in the study of health because so many of life's problems and prospects occur in a social context and so many of our efforts to cope with stress involve other people. Indeed, as we'll see in this section, health psychologists are actively trying to find ways in which social influences can be used to improve the development of treatment and prevention programs.

### Treatment: The "Social" Ingredients

Often, what ails us can be treated through medical intervention. The treatments vary widely—from a simple change in diet to vitamin supplements, aspirin, antibiotics, surgery, and the like. There's no doubt about it: Medicine is vital to health. In addition, however, treatment has a social component, what the family doctor used to call "bedside manner." What are the active social ingredients?

To begin to answer this question, let's consider research on the benefits of psychotherapy. Over the years, studies have shown that although there are vastly different schools of thought and techniques for doing psychotherapy, all approaches are somewhat effective and, surprisingly, all are generally equivalent (Smith et al., 1980; Wampold et al., 1997). Apparently, despite the surface differences, all psychotherapies have a great deal in common at a deeper level and these common factors—more than the specific techniques used—provide the active ingredients necessary for change. What are some of these factors?

First, all healers—regardless of whether they are medical doctors, psychologists, or others—provide *social support*, a close human relationship characterized by warmth, expressions of concern, a shoulder to cry on, and someone to talk to. Earlier, we discussed the benefits to health and longevity of having social contacts. In psychological therapy, studies have shown that the better the "working alliance" is between a therapist and client, the more favorable the outcome is likely to be (Horvath & Luborsky, 1993). As psychotherapist Hans Strupp (1996) put it, "The simple and incontrovertible truth is that if you are anxious or depressed, or if you are experiencing difficulties with significant people in your life, chances are that you feel better if you talk to someone you can trust" (p. 1017).

Second, all therapies offer a ray of *hope* to people who are sick, demoralized, unhappy, or in pain. In all aspects of life, people are motivated by upbeat, positive expectations. Although some of us are more optimistic than others, optimism is a specific expectation that can be increased or decreased in certain situations (Armor & Taylor, 1998). Indeed, a common aspect of all treatments is that they communicate and instill positive expectations. It has been suggested that high expectations can spark change even when they are not justified (Prioleau et al., 1983). This suggestion is consistent with the well-known placebo effect in medicine, whereby patients improve after being given an inactive drug or treatment. Believing can help make it so, which is how faith healers, shamans, and witch doctors all over the world have managed to perform "miracle cures" with elaborate rituals. Even modern medicine exploits the power of hope. As Walter Brown (1998) puts it, "The symbols and rituals of healing—the doctor's office, the stethoscope, the physical examination—offer reassurance" (p. 91).

A third important ingredient is *choice*. Allowing patients to make meaningful choices, such as deciding on a type of treatment, increases the effectiveness of treatments for alcoholism (Miller, 1985) and obesity (Mendonca & Brehm, 1983). Choosing to undergo an effortful or costly treatment is particularly beneficial in this regard. The person who voluntarily pays in time, money, or discomfort needs to self-justify that investment—a predicament sure to arouse cognitive dissonance. As seen in Chapter 6, one way to reduce dissonance is to become ultra-motivated to succeed: "Why have I chosen to do this? Because I really want to get better." Perhaps because highly motivated individuals are more careful and conscientious about carrying out the prescribed treatment, they tend to improve more.

Danny Axsom (1989) tested this specific proposition in a study of snake phobias. Participants, all of whom were highly snake-phobic, were or were not given an explicit choice about undertaking a treatment that was described as either requiring "extreme exertion" or being "easy." Among the four experimental conditions, participants who were given an explicit choice about continuing an effortful treatment reported the greatest motivation to change their phobic behavior and came closest to the 5-foot-long New Jersey corn snake used to measure approach behavior.

## > Prevention: Getting the Message Across

We live in what could aptly be described as the era of prevention in that many serious health threats are preventable. Just watch TV, leaf through a magazine, or surf the Internet: There are programs for AIDS prevention; campaigns to persuade smokers to break the habit; sunscreens that protect the skin from harmful rays; screening for various types of cancer; warnings about high-sugar foods, high-fat foods, and obesity; and laws that mandate the use of seat belts. To a large extent, we know what to do and what not to do to promote good health and avoid disease and injury. But just how do we convince ourselves and others to translate that knowledge into action?

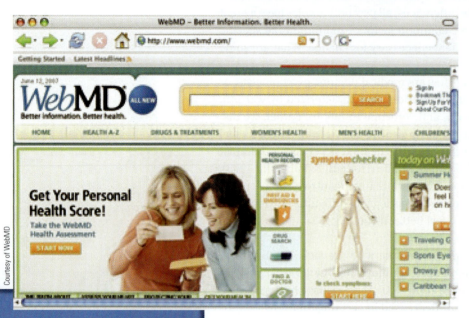

Today, people can find all sorts of information and advice on health-related issues on WebMD and other Internet sites.

Nowhere is this problem more acute than among people who suffer from AIDS. Earlier in the chapter, we noted that heart attacks, cancer, strokes, and accidents are now more common causes of death than infectious diseases. But AIDS, the first truly global epidemic, came along and spread at an alarming rate. Years ago, AIDS was described as a microbiological time bomb. In 1981, five homosexual men in North America were diagnosed with AIDS and were among only 189 cases reported that year. By 1996, the number of cases in North America had skyrocketed to three-quarters of a million and included heterosexual men, women, and children (Mann, 1992). In 2010, the World Health Organization estimated that 34 million people worldwide were infected with HIV; an estimated 1.8 million died in that year alone. Worldwide, both numbers are down from previous years. However, the number of new infections continues to climb in parts of Latin America, sub-Saharan Africa, North Africa, the Middle East, Eastern Europe, and parts of Asia.

The AIDS virus is transmitted from one person to another in infected blood, semen, and vaginal secretions. People who are HIV-positive may have no symptoms for several years and may not even realize they are infected. Eventually, however, the virus will ravage the immune system by destroying lymphocytes that help ward off disease. What's frightening about AIDS is that it appears fatal, that it is increasing at a rate of one new case every few seconds, and despite 25 years of testing, that there is no vaccine that can prevent its occurrence (Stine, 2012).

At present, the most effective way to slow the spread of AIDS is to alter people's beliefs, motivations, and risk-taking behaviors (Fisher & Fisher, 1992; Fisher et al., 1994; Gerrard et al., 1996; Kalichman, 2006)—and that's where social psychology comes in. Across a range of perspectives, several basic steps emerge (see ● Figure 14.12).

For social psychologists, the challenge in addressing the HIV crisis is to convert the science into a practice that works. In an excellent illustration, Jeffrey Fisher and his colleagues (2002) theorized that HIV prevention in city schools, which is essential for controlling the number of newly infected teens, requires a three-pronged attack. In their model, students must be provided with accurate *information* about HIV transmission and how to prevent it, with a personal and social *motivation* to engage in HIV-preventative behaviors, and with the *behavioral skills* necessary to follow through—notably, by using condoms. Armed with this model, these investigators set up HIV prevention programs in four urban high schools, devised a control group that lacked these "active ingredients," and found that the program, when administered by the classroom teachers, changed

### FIGURE 14.12

**Aiming for Good Health**

Several major factors help convince people to engage in healthy practices. Recognition that a threat to health exists is a necessary first step. Positive models and healthy subjective norms encourage people to adopt health-protective behaviors. A sense of self-efficacy about being able to carry out healthy behaviors and the belief that such behaviors will be effective increase the likelihood of active efforts.

© Cengage Learning

| The recognition that a threat to health exists | Imitating the healthy behaviors of others | Conforming to a subjective norm favoring healthy behaviors | A sense of self-efficacy about one's ability to perform healthy behaviors | Accurate beliefs that healthy behaviors will have the desired effect | → | Healthy Behaviors |

HIV-prevention behavior, increasing condom use up to a year later—all for an estimated cost of $2.22 per student. Other similarly oriented efforts have been developed as well, also with good success (Albarracín et al., 2005).

Armed with a theory and various effective techniques, social psychologists are looking to make important strides in the fight against AIDS. There are two caveats, however. First, it is necessary (and not that easy) for prevention programs to attract the kinds of high-risk participants for whom they are designed. Yet this is exactly the group, ironically, that is least likely to attend. In a study of 350 inhabitants of a high-risk community, Allison Earl and her colleagues (2009) found that people who were the most informed, most motivated, and most skilled at using condoms to prevent the spread of HIV were also the most likely to accept an offer to participate in the program. Those who were less informed, less motivated, and less skilled were less receptive. Clearly, for any HIV prevention program to work, it must bring in those members of the community who need it most.

The second caveat is that a focus on educating "healthy" people in the use of condoms addresses the spread of HIV prevention from one perspective. A second approach is to focus prevention efforts on HIV positive individuals who can transmit the virus. To achieve this objective, it is necessary to increase the number of HIV positive individuals who are aware of their infections. It is also necessary to educate the few who know they are infected and yet still engage in behaviors that put sex partners at risk. With an eye on this objective, Ann O'Leary and Richard Wolitski (2009) describe a number of possible ways to encourage those who are knowingly infected to take responsibility, reject rationalization and excuse making, humanize and empathize with their sex partners, and bring their behavior in line with their own moral standards.

# The Pursuit of Happiness

Long before the emergence of social psychology, philosophers regarded happiness as the ultimate state of being. In the U.S. Declaration of Independence, Thomas Jefferson thus cited life, liberty, and "the pursuit of happiness" as the most cherished of human rights. But what is happiness, and how is it achieved? Aristotle said it was the reward of an active life. Freud linked it with both work and love. Others have variously suggested that happiness requires money and power, health and fitness, religion, beauty, the satisfaction of basic needs, and an ability to derive pleasure from the events of everyday life. In recent years, social psychologists have applied their theories and methods to the study of this most basic human motive: the pursuit of happiness (Diener & Biswas-Diener, 2008; Gilbert, 2006; Haidt, 2006; Lyubomirsky, 2013).

To study happiness—or **subjective well-being**, as social psychologists like to call it—one must be able to measure it. How do researchers know whether someone is happy? Simple: They ask. Better yet, they use questionnaires such as the Satisfaction with Life Scale, in which people respond to statements such as "If I could live my life over, I would change almost nothing" (Diener et al., 1984; Pavot & Diener, 1993). As Marcus Aurelius said, "No man is happy who does not think himself so."

Using self-reports, surveys show that 75% of American adults rate themselves as happy and that in 86% of all nations sampled, the ratings are, on average, more often positive than neutral (Diener, 2000). In general, people who are happy also have cheerful moods, high self-esteem, a sense of personal control, more memories of positive as opposed to negative events, and optimism about the future (Myers & Diener, 1995). Even more than physical beauty or material wealth, happiness underlies people's belief that life is worth living (King & Napa, 1998). A meta-analysis of 225 studies revealed that happiness gives rise to many successful life outcomes in the domains of marriage, friendship, health, income, and work performance (Lyubomirsky et al., 2005).

It's no secret that our outlook on life becomes rosy right after you win a big game, fall in love, land a great job, or make money and that the world seems gloomy right after you lose, fall out of love, or suffer a personal tragedy or financial setback. Predictably, the events of everyday life trigger fluctuations in mood. For example, people are most happy on Fridays and Saturdays and least happy on Mondays and Tuesdays (Larsen & Kasimatis, 1990). Even during the day, happiness levels fluctuate like clockwork. For example, David Watson and others (1999) asked college students to rate their mood states once a day for 45 days, always at a different hour. They found, on average, that the students felt best during the middle of the day (noon to 6 p.m.) and worst in the early morning and late evening hours.

But what determines our long-term satisfaction, and why are some of us happier than others? Seeking the roots of happiness, Ed Diener and his colleagues (1999) reviewed many years of research and found that subjective well-being is not meaningfully related to demographic factors such as age, sex, racial and ethnic background, IQ, education level, or physical attractiveness. Contrary to popular belief, people are not less happy during the so-called crisis years of midlife or in old age than during their youth and "peak" young-adult years. Men and women do not differ on this measure, and, in the United States, African and Hispanic Americans are as happy as white Americans. It's clear that people from all walks of life have ways to make themselves happy. In a survey of "online happiness seekers," Acacia Parks and others (in press) found that most cited such activities as engaging in acts of kindness, pursuing important goals, expressing gratitude, staying optimistic, doing physical exercise, and nurturing social relationships. Overall, there are three key predictors of happiness: *social relationships* (people with an active social life, close friends, and a happy marriage are more satisfied than those who lack these intimate connections), *employment status* (regardless of income, employed people are happier than those who are out of work), and *physical and mental health* (people who are healthy are happier than those who are not). Reflecting the impact of these factors, worldwide surveys of more than 100,000 respondents in 55 countries have shown that happiness levels vary from one culture to the next (Diener & Suh, 2000).

The *World Happiness Report* revealed that Denmark ranks as the happiest country in the world. This picturesque image is of Nyhavn Harbor, in the happy city of Copenhagen.

**subjective well-being** One's happiness, or life satisfaction, as measured by self-report.

Although specific rankings fluctuate from one survey to the next, national happiness ratings are consistently higher in some countries than in others. In a study commissioned by the United Nations General Assembly, the *World Happiness Report* revealed that the happiest countries in the world, in polls conducted from 2005 to 2011, are clustered in Northern Europe (Denmark, Norway, Finland, Netherlands; their average life evaluation score is 7.6 on a 0–10 scale). The least happy countries are in Sub-Saharan Africa (Togo, Benin, Central African Republic, Sierra Leone; their average score is 3.4). A partial list is presented in Table 14.5. The Report went on to note that although relative wealth clearly distinguishes the nations on the list, "Political freedom, strong social networks and an absence of corruption are together more important than income in explaining well-being differences between the top and bottom countries" (Helliwell et al., 2012). It comes as no surprise, therefore, that in a poll of 132,516 people from 128 countries, the more satisfied people were with their country as a whole, the happier they were with the state of their own lives (Morrison et al., 2011).

## Does Money Buy Happiness?

Over the years, the most interesting statistical relationship has been between income and subjective well-being. We all know the saying that "money can't buy happiness"—though some people (particularly those who are financially strapped) do not believe it. But is wealth truly a key to happiness? To some extent, yes, but the evidence is complex. Ed Diener and Martin Seligman (2004) note that multimillionaires from the Forbes list of the 400 richest Americans report high levels of life satisfaction (5.8 on a 7-point scale), but so do the Masai, a herding people in East Africa with no electricity or running water who live in huts made with dung (5.7 on the same 7-point scale).

As seen in the huge disparity in wealth between the happiest countries of Northern Europe and the unhappiest countries of Sub-Saharan Africa, cross-national studies reveal a strong positive association between a nation's wealth and the subjective well-being of its people. There are some exceptions. But as a general rule, the more money a country has, the happier its citizens are, at least up to a point. Within any given country, however, the differences between wealthy and middle-income people are modest. In one survey, for example, a group of the wealthiest Americans said they were happy 77% of the time, which was only moderately higher than the 62% figure reported by those of average income. And when comparisons within a single culture are made over time, there is no relationship between affluence and happiness. Americans on average are two to three times richer now than 50 years ago—before we had computers, flat-screen TVs, GPS systems, iPhones, iPads, and digital cameras that fit into the palm of your hand. Yet the number of respondents who said they were "very happy" was 35% in 1957 and only 32% in 1998 (see ● Figure 14.13).

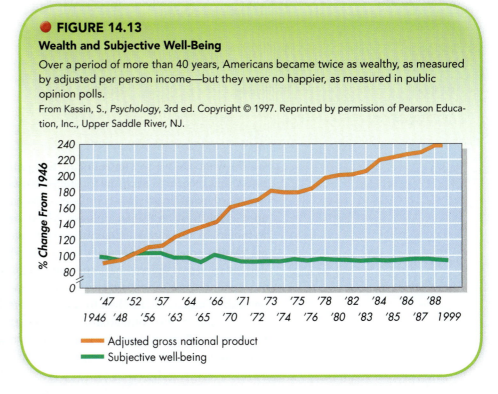

● **FIGURE 14.13**

**Wealth and Subjective Well-Being**

Over a period of more than 40 years, Americans became twice as wealthy, as measured by adjusted per person income—but they were no happier, as measured in public opinion polls.

From Kassin, S., *Psychology*, 3rd ed. Copyright © 1997. Reprinted by permission of Pearson Education, Inc., Upper Saddle River, NJ.

— Adjusted gross national product
— Subjective well-being

**TABLE 14.5**

**National Happiness Rankings**

Based on recent surveys conducted all over the globe, the *World Happiness Report* rank-ordered nations according to their average happiness levels. This table presents the rank ordering of the top 100 on the list (Helliwell et al., 2012).

| | | | |
|---|---|---|---|
| 1. Denmark | 26. Saudi Arabia | 51. Malaysia | 76. Russia |
| 2. Finland | 27. Puerto Rico | 52. Thailand | 77. Peru |
| 3. Norway | 28. Italy | 53. Poland | 78. Turkey |
| 4. Netherlands | 29. Kuwait | 54. Jordan | 79. Uzbekistan |
| 5. Canada | 30. Germany | 55. Slovakia | 80. Romania |
| 6. Switzerland | 31. Qatar | 56. South Korea | 81. Libya |
| 7. Sweden | 32. Turkmenistan | 57. Bolivia | 82. Laos |
| 8. New Zealand | 33. Singapore | 58. Croatia | 83. Indonesia |
| 9. Australia | 34. Belize | 59. Kazakhstan | 84. Iran |
| 10. Ireland | 35. Cyprus | 60. Lithuania | 85. Pakistan |
| 11. United States | 36. Czech Republic | 61. Bahrain | 86. Montenegro |
| 12. Costa Rica | 37. Guatemala | 62. Belarus | 87. Tunisia |
| 13. Austria | 38. Trinidad & Tobago | 63. Honduras | 88. Albania |
| 14. Israel | 39. Argentina | 64. Mauritius | 89. Nicaragua |
| 15. Belgium | 40. Jamaica | 65. Vietnam | 90. South Africa |
| 16. Luxembourg | 41. Colombia | 66. Ecuador | 91. Ukraine |
| 17. United Arab Emirates | 42. Greece | 67. Hong Kong | 92. Lebanon |
| 18. United Kingdom | 43. Chile | 68. Kosovo | 93. Dominican Republic |
| 19. Venezuela | 44. Japan | 69. Cuba | 94. India |
| 20. Iceland | 45. Guyana | 70. Paraguay | 95. Djibouti |
| 21. Panama | 46. Taiwan | 71. Algeria | 96. Hungary |
| 22. Spain | 47. Malta | 72. Estonia | 97. Namibia |
| 23. France | 48. El Salvador | 73. Portugal | 98. Iraq |
| 24. Mexico | 49. Slovenia | 74. Myanmar | 99. Bosnia & Herzegovina |
| 25. Brazil | 50. Uruguay | 75. Moldova | 100. Nigeria |

So what are we to conclude? At this point, it appears that having shelter, food, safety, and security is essential for subjective well-being. But once these basic needs are met, particularly in an already prosperous society, additional increases in wealth do not appreciably raise levels of happiness. Why doesn't money contribute more to subjective well-being? One reason is that our perceptions of wealth are not absolute but, instead, are relative to certain personally set standards (Parducci, 1995). These standards are derived from two sources: other people and our own past.

According to *social comparison theory*, as described in Chapter 3, people tend to naturally compare themselves to others and feel contented or deprived depending on how they fare in this comparison. To demonstrate, Ladd Wheeler and Kunitate Miyake (1992) had college students for 2 weeks keep a written record of every time they mentally compared their own grades, appearance, abilities, possessions, or personality traits to someone else's. Consistently, these diaries revealed that making "upward comparisons" (to others who were better off) sparked negative feelings, while making "downward comparisons" (to others who were worse off) triggered positive feelings. That is why the middle-class worker whose neighbors can't pay their bills feels fortunate but the upper-class social climber who rubs elbows with the rich and famous feels deprived. This relativity may also help explain why there are only modest relationships between happiness and actual income and perceptions of financial status (Johnson & Krueger, 2006).

It is also natural for people to use their own recent past as a basis of comparison. According to *adaptation-level theory*, our satisfaction with the present depends on the level of success to which we are accustomed. Get married, buy a new house or a flashy new car, get the job you were aiming for, or a promotion, and you will surely enjoy a wave of euphoria. Before long, however, the glitter will wear off, and you'll adapt to your better situation and raise your standard of comparison. This phenomenon is known as *hedonic adaptation*. Indeed, when Philip Brickman and others (1978) interviewed 22 people who had won between $50,000 and $1 million in a lottery, they found that these people did not rate themselves as happier than in the past. Compared to others from similar backgrounds, the winners said that they now derived less pleasure from routine activities such as shopping, reading, and talking to a friend. Perhaps the more money you have, the more you need to stay happy. The results of a Chicago public opinion poll suggest that this is the case: Whereas people who earned less than $30,000 a year said that $50,000 would fulfill their dreams, those who earned more than $100,000 said it would take $250,000 to make them happy (Csikszentmihalyi, 1999). Highlighting a dark side of the "American dream," research shows that the more materialistic people are, the less satisfied they seem to be (Nickerson et al., 2003). Economists have thus come to appreciate that our sense of well-being stems in part from the gap between our income and material aspirations (Stutzer, 2004).

It would be a mistake to assume that people "adapt" to gains and losses in money, or other positive and negative life events, in the same way and at the same rate. Recent longitudinal studies that track the same people over time have shown that the effects of some major life events are more persistent than others. For example, people tend to adapt quickly, typically within 2 years, to the initial boost in happiness that comes from marriage—and divorce is often followed by an increase in life satisfaction, as people adapt after the ordeal has ended. Yet the impact of disability, unemployment, and the grief that follows the death of a spouse tend to last longer—and childbirth is followed by a range of conflicting—positive and negative—patterns (Lucas, 2007; Luhmann et al., 2012).

There's one other possible and intriguing explanation for why money, per se, and other major life events, is not more predictive of happiness over time: Perhaps each of us, as a result of both biological and environmental factors, has a set baseline level of happiness, a "set point" toward which we gravitate. This notion is supported by three recent findings. One is that ratings of happiness are higher among pairs of identical twins than among fraternal twins—leading David Lykken (2000) to suggest that there may be a genetic basis for having a certain set level of contentment. A second finding is that the fluctuations in mood that accompany positive and negative life events tend to wear off over time. For example, in a study spanning 2 years, Eunkook Suh and others (1996) studied participants for 2 years and found that only experiences

> *"It matters little whether one is rich or poor, successful or unsuccessful, or beautiful or plain: Happiness is completely relative . . . the pleasantness of any particular experience depends on its relationship to a context of other experiences, real or imagined."*
>
> —Allen Parducci

"Remember how I said I was happiest when we had nothing?"

In all countries and at all levels of wealth, the more money people have, the happier they are. **F**ALSE.

occurring in the last 3 months correlated with reports of subjective well-being. Getting engaged or married, breaking up, starting a new job, and being hospitalized are the kinds of high-impact experiences that people assume have lasting if not permanent effects on happiness levels (Gilbert et al., 1998)—but in fact, the impacts are often temporary. A third finding is that happiness levels, like personality traits, are relatively stable over time and place, which leads to the conclusion that some people are, in general, happier than others (DeNeve & Cooper, 1998).

## Emerging Science on How to Increase Happiness

The pursuit of happiness is a powerful human motive that is still not fully understood. Each of us may well be predisposed by nature toward a particular set point, but it is clear that our happiness is not completely set in stone. In a 17-year study of individuals in Germany, researchers found that 24% of the respondents had significantly higher or lower levels of life satisfaction in the last 5 years of the study than they did in the first 5 years (Fujita & Diener, 2005). In a study of national surveys that spanned from 1981 to 2007, other researchers found that average happiness ratings increased in 45 out of 52 countries in which multiple surveys were administered over time—an increase that was linked to increasing democratization in these countries (Inglehart et al., 2008).

Realizing that happiness is malleable, both for individuals and large populations, social psychologists are now trying to figure out how people can produce sustainable increases in subjective well-being (Lyubomirsky et al., 2005). Consider this question: If you had money to spend, would you rather use it to purchase an experience or a material object? Would one type of purchase make you happier? Leaf Van Boven and Thomas Gilovich (2003) conducted a national telephone survey in which they asked people of varying income levels about a time they purchased an experience (they most often named tickets to a concert, theater, travel, dinner, or spa) or a material object (they most often named clothing, jewelry, a computer, or electronic equipment) to make themselves happy. Respondents were then asked to indicate which purchase, if any, made them happier. ● Figure 14.14 shows that except at the lowest income levels,

● **FIGURE 14.14**

**What Yields More Happiness: Experiences or Material Objects?**

After recalling a time when they spent money on an experience or a material object, people in general said that the experiences they purchased made them happier than the material objects.

From Van Boven, L., "Experientialism, materialism, and the pursuit of happiness," *Review of General Psychology* vol 9 (pp. 132–142). Copyright © 2005 by the American Psychological Association. Reprinted by permission.

where people have to satisfy basic material needs, the experiences they purchased—thanks, in part, to the memories that lingered—made them happier than the material objects (see Van Boven, 2005).

Social psychological research has uncovered other ways to boost happiness levels as well. For example, people who are prompted by random assignment to write gratitude letters, savor a happy memory, or engage in acts of kindness exhibit increases in subjective well-being compared to others in a control group (Sin & Lyubomirsky, 2009). As for the fact that people tend to "adapt" to a positive change in fortune, get used to it, and revert to their own baseline levels, a collateral question comes into play: Once your level of happiness is raised, is there a way to ensure that you stay that way? In answer to this question, researchers are now looking for ways to prevent hedonic adaptation so that the benefits of positive changes will endure over time (Sheldon & Lyubomirsky, 2012).

Quite apart from developments in Western psychological science is the question of how, if at all, governments should try to foster happiness in their citizens. Consider the Kingdom of Bhutan—a small, secluded, landlocked Buddhist country nestled high in the Himalayan Mountains and bordering India and Tibet. In 1972, the King of Bhutan adopted "Gross National Happiness" (GNH) as its national goal instead of the Gross National Product—making a choice of happiness over wealth. Every year since that time, the government has systematically measured GNH and has shaped policies designed to sustain it. In contrast to the Western scientist's measurement focus on people's ratings of their own subjective well-being, happiness in the GNH is a multidimensional concept that measures many aspects of the quality of a person's material, physical, social, and spiritual life. By tracking these indicators over time and in various communities, the GNH is used to advance government policies in ways that increase happiness in people who are "not yet happy." The indicators that comprise the GNH appear in ● Figure 14.15 (for a fascinating case study on the GNH in Bhutan, see Ura et al., 2012).

The research described in this section offers some concrete advice on how people can maximize their levels of happiness. Should social psychologists and nations use this research to seek to maximize levels of happiness within a population? In light of the undisputed benefits of being happy, this hardly seems like a controversial question. But let's stop and ponder the question. Concerned that there is a possible dark side

Bhutan is a small Buddhist country nestled high in the Himalayan Mountains between India and Tibet. In the only program of its kind, designed to prioritize subjective well-being over material wealth, the government has set "Gross National Happiness" (GNH) as its national goal and seeks to increase the GNH of its population.

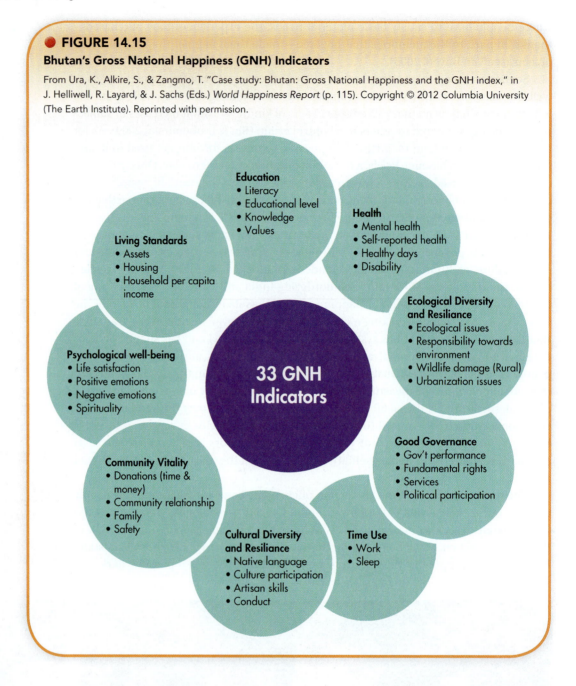

● **FIGURE 14.15**

**Bhutan's Gross National Happiness (GNH) Indicators**

From Ura, K., Alkire, S., & Zangmo, T. "Case study: Bhutan: Gross National Happiness and the GNH index," in J. Helliwell, R. Layard, & J. Sachs (Eds.) *World Happiness Report* (p. 115). Copyright © 2012 Columbia University (The Earth Institute). Reprinted with permission.

the *pursuit* of happiness, Iris Mauss and her colleagues (2011) asked, "Can seeking happiness make people unhappy?" Echoing this concern, June Gruber and others (2011) suggested that sometimes being "too happy" is not adaptive because excessive positive emotions can lead people to engage in risky behaviors and not pay enough attention to possible threats (consuming alcohol, having sex with strangers, driving too fast). What's more, some situations call for fear, anger, or a more sober emotional state for coping purposes. They also note that although most people say they are reasonably happy, many report wanting to be even happier—a state of desire that can have paradoxical effects: "The more people strive for happiness, the more likely it is that they will become disappointed about how they feel" (p. 226). Since people who are happy tend to be content with what they have rather than focused on what they lack, this last point is particularly thought-provoking. Is it possible to be *too focused* on being happy? Is it possible to be *too happy*? Stay tuned for future research on these questions.

# Review

## Stress and Health

- Stress is an unpleasant state that arises when we perceive that the demands of an event strain our ability to cope effectively.
- A person's appraisal of a situation determines how stress is experienced and how he or she copes.

- Coping responses consist of the thoughts, feelings, and behaviors by which people attempt to reduce stress.

## What Causes Stress?

- There are many different causes of stress, or stressors.

### Crises and Catastrophes

- Natural disasters and other catastrophic events can have harmful and long-term effects on mental and physical health.
- People with posttraumatic stress disorder suffer from psychological and physical symptoms long after the event is over.
- Soldiers exposed to combat often suffer from posttraumatic stress.

### Major Life Events

- Early research suggested that all change is stressful.
- However, more recent studies suggest that only negative events are harmful.

### Microstressors: The Hassles of Everyday Life

- The most common sources of stress are minor everyday hassles.
- Constant noise, burnout from job pressures, and commuting are all stressful in this regard.
- Importantly, research shows that low socioeconomic status is a proxy for hassled living and is strongly predictive of negative health outcomes and death.

> **Putting *Common Sense* to the Test**
>
> **The accumulation of daily hassles does more to make people sick than catastrophes or major life changes.**
>
> **True.** *Car problems, arguments with friends, and other "microstressors" contribute more to our levels of stress than larger but less frequent stressors.*

## How Does Stress Affect the Body?

- Selye coined the term *stress* upon observing that different stressors produce similar physiological effects on the body.

### The General Adaptation Syndrome

- The body responds to stress in three stages: alarm, resistance, and exhaustion.
- The stress response is designed for acute emergencies, not for the constant long-term stress that humans often experience.

### What Stress Does to the Heart

- Stress is a major risk factor in coronary heart disease (CHD).
- Early research suggested that the hard-driving Type A personality, also called coronary behavior pattern, is associated with CHD.
- This link was found when the Type A pattern was assessed in structured interviews but not when it was measured by questionnaire.
- Hostility is now known to be the "toxic" element in the Type A behavior pattern.

### What Stress Does to the Immune System

- The immune system contains specialized white blood cells called lymphocytes that detect and destroy foreign substances in the body.

- Laboratory and field research shows that stress affects the activity of these cells, sometimes resulting in a weakened immune response.
- Stress can "get into" the immune system by causing people to behave in unhealthy ways or by triggering the release of stress hormones that suppress immune cell activity.

### The Links Between Stress and Illness

- Stress weakens the immune system, so people under stress are more likely to catch a cold when exposed to a virus.
- There may also be a link between negative emotional states and serious diseases such as cancer, but the evidence is less strong.

> **Putting *Common Sense* to the Test**
>
> **Like humans, zebras get ulcers.**
>
> **False.** *Stress causes ulcers in humans, not zebras. That's because the stress response is designed for acute emergencies; but in people, it is activated often and for long periods of time.*

# Processes of Appraisal

## Attributions and Explanatory Styles

- According to the learned helplessness model of depression, exposure to an uncontrollable event sparks passive, apathetic, depression-like symptoms.
- Research shows that the attributions people make for their lack of control are of central importance.
- The depressive explanatory style is a tendency to make stable, global, internal attributions for bad events; it is associated with depression and perhaps with physical illness.

## The Human Capacity for Resilience

- Some individuals are more resilient than others in the face of stress, a trait called hardiness.
- The key ingredient of hardiness is the belief that one has the power to control future outcomes through one's own behavior.
- Depending on the situation, people may have a high or low self-efficacy—the belief that they can perform the behaviors needed to produce positive outcomes.

- Some individuals are characteristically more optimistic than others, and optimism at one point in time is predictive of later positive health outcomes.

## Pollyanna's Health

- Positive thinking is associated with good health, but the causal relationship is unclear.
- Unrealistic positive illusions may have undesirable interpersonal and health consequences.

> **Putting *Common Sense* to the Test**
>
> **Stress can weaken the heart, but it cannot affect the immune system.**
>
> **False.** *Recent research has shown that stress and other psychological states can alter the activity of white blood cells in the immune system and affect our resistance to illness.*

# Ways of Coping with Stress

## Problem-Focused Coping

- In problem-focused coping, people try to reduce stress by overcoming the source of the problem.
- Problem-focused coping is often effective, but at times there are drawbacks.
- For example, exerting control is physiologically taxing and can increase stress rather than reduce it.
- Also, both behavioral and characterological self-blame are associated with increased distress.

## Emotion-Focused Coping

- In emotion-focused coping, people try to manage the emotional turmoil produced by a stressful situation.
- The best starting point is the experience of positive emotions.
- In situations that one cannot control, mental distraction and avoidance can reduce stress.
- But the suppression from awareness of unwanted thoughts and feelings can backfire, causing us to become preoccupied with them.
- Research shows that opening up and confronting one's feelings about upsetting events improves mental and physical health.
- Among people with low self-esteem, self-focus worsens their mood and heightens their distress.
- In contrast, it is helpful to become absorbed in demanding external activities such as reading, exercise, and gardening.

## Proactive Coping

- As a first line of defense, people can ward off stress through proactive coping efforts such as the accumulation of resources.

- Having many different roles and identities serves as a buffer against stressors in any one domain of life.
- Friendships and other sources of social support have strong beneficial effects on physical health and psychological well-being.
- All researchers agree that social support is healthy, but they measure it in different ways, focusing on such factors as the number of social contacts a person has, the presence of special close relationships, or perceptions that social support is available.
- Social psychologists are also studying the role of religion in reducing stress.

## Culture and Coping

- Stress is universal, but people from collectivist cultures appear to rely less often on social support as a means of coping than do people from individualist cultures.
- Recent research has identified that acceptance, avoidance, family support, religion, and private emotional outlets are the coping styles members of collectivist cultures use.

> **Putting *Common Sense* to the Test**
>
> **When it comes to physical health, research does not support popular beliefs about the power of positive thinking.**
>
> **False.** *Consistently, people who are optimistic—and situations that promote optimism—are associated with better health outcomes.*

# Treatment and Prevention

## Treatment: The "Social" Ingredients

- Medical treatment includes an important social component.
- Doctors, therapists, and other health care workers provide patients with social support and a ray of hope.

- Choice of treatment is also an important factor, particularly when patients choose an effortful treatment, which increases commitment.

## Prevention: Getting the Message Across

- Many causes of death are preventable through changes in lifestyle and behavior, which is where social psychology comes in.
- First, people have to recognize that a threat to their health exists.
- Others serve as important role models and spokespersons for healthy or unhealthy behavior.
- Subjective norms can also encourage healthy or unhealthy behaviors.

# The Pursuit of Happiness

- Most people report being relatively happy, but there are individual differences.
- Three important factors are social relationships, employment, and health.

## Does Money Buy Happiness?

- Evidence that money can buy happiness is mixed. More affluent nations tend to have happier citizens than less affluent nations, but correlations with groups of citizens within nations are modest.
- One reason for the limited association between wealth and happiness is that our perceptions of wealth are relative—to what others and also to what we have become accustomed to.
- Research suggests that each of us has a baseline level of happiness toward which we gravitate over time.

- A sense of self-efficacy enhances a person's adoption and maintenance of healthy behaviors.
- Accurate information is needed to sustain people's commitment to healthy behaviors.

### Putting *Common Sense* to the Test

**People who have lots of friends are healthier and live longer than those who live more isolated lives.**

**True.** *Across a range of studies, researchers have found that social support is strongly associated with positive health outcomes.*

## Emerging Science on How to Increase Happiness

- Research shows that happiness levels are somewhat malleable in individuals and in nations.
- Researchers are starting to test ways that people can use to make themselves happier—for example, by using their money to purchase experiences, not material objects.
- Bhutan provides a case study of a nation that measures and tracks it's people's GNH—Gross National Happiness with an eye toward policies that will make people happy.
- Researchers are starting to wonder: Is it possible that the pursuit of happiness will backfire, or that one can be too happy?

### Putting *Common Sense* to the Test

**In all countries and at all levels of wealth, the more money people have, the happier they are.**

**False.** *Research results are complex, but it is clear that once people have enough money to satisfy basic needs, additional wealth does not produce more happiness.*

## KEY TERMS

appraisal (573)
coping (573)
depressive explanatory style (587)
emotion-focused coping (593)
general adaptation syndrome (579)
health psychology (572)
immune system (582)

learned helplessness (587)
posttraumatic stress disorder (PTSD) (576)
proactive coping (593)
problem-focused coping (592)
psychoneuroimmunology (PNI) (583)

self-efficacy (589)
social support (600)
stress (573)
stressor (574)
subjective well-being (608)
Type A personality (581)

## MEDIA RESOURCES

Go to CengageBrain.com to access Psychology CourseMate, where you will find an interactive eBook, glossaries, flashcards, quizzes, videos, and more.

# GLOSSARY

**adversarial model** A dispute–resolution system in which the prosecution and defense present opposing sides of the story.

**affective forecasting** The process of predicting how one would feel in response to future emotional events.

**aggression** Behavior intended to harm another individual.

**altruistic** Motivated by the desire to improve another's welfare.

**ambivalent sexism** A form of sexism characterized by attitudes about women that reflect both negative, resentful beliefs and feelings and affectionate and chivalrous but potentially patronizing beliefs and feelings.

**applied research** Research whose goals are to enlarge the understanding of naturally occurring events and to find solutions to practical problems.

**appraisal** The process by which people make judgments about the demands of potentially stressful events and their ability to meet those demands.

**arousal: cost–reward model** The proposition that people react to emergency situations by acting in the most cost-effective way to reduce the arousal of shock and alarm.

**assessment center** A structured setting in which job applicants are exhaustively tested and judged by multiple evaluators.

**attachment style** The way a person typically interacts with significant others.

**attitude** A positive, negative, or mixed reaction to a person, object, or idea.

**attitude scale** A multiple-item questionnaire designed to measure a person's attitude toward some object.

**attribution theory** A group of theories that describe how people explain the causes of behavior.

**audience inhibition** Reluctance to help for fear of making a bad impression on observers.

**availability heuristic** The tendency to estimate the likelihood that an event will occur by how easily instances of it come to mind.

**base-rate fallacy** The finding that people are relatively insensitive to consensus information presented in the form of numerical base rates.

**basic research** Research whose goal is to increase the understanding of human behavior, often by testing hypotheses based on a theory.

**bask in reflected glory (BIRG)** To increase self-esteem by associating with others who are successful.

**behavioral economics** An interdisciplinary subfield that focuses on how psychology—particularly social and cognitive psychology—relates to economic decision making.

**behavioral genetics** A subfield of psychology that examines the role of genetic factors in behavior.

**belief in a just world** The belief that individuals get what they deserve in life, an orientation that leads people to disparage victims.

**belief perseverance** The tendency to maintain beliefs even after they have been discredited.

**biased sampling** The tendency for groups to spend more time discussing shared information (information already known by all or most group members) than unshared information (information known by only one or a few group members).

**bogus pipeline** A phony lie-detector device that is sometimes used to get respondents to give truthful answers to sensitive questions.

**bogus pipeline technique** A procedure in which research participants are (falsely) led to believe that their responses will be verified by an infallible lie detector.

**brainstorming** A technique that attempts to increase the production of creative ideas by encouraging group members to speak freely without criticizing their own or others' contributions.

**bystander effect** The effect whereby the presence of others inhibits helping.

**catharsis** A reduction of the motive to aggress that is said to result from any imagined, observed, or actual act of aggression.

**central route to persuasion** The process by which a person thinks carefully about a communication and is influenced by the strength of its arguments.

**central traits** Traits that exert a powerful influence on overall impressions.

**cognitive dissonance theory** The theory holding that inconsistent cognitions arouses psychological tension that people become motivated to reduce.

**collective effort model** The theory that individuals will exert effort on a collective task to the degree that they think their individual efforts will be important, relevant, and meaningful for achieving outcomes that they value.

**collectivism** A cultural orientation in which interdependence, cooperation, and social harmony take priority over personal goals.

**communal relationship** A relationship in which the participants expect and desire mutual responsiveness to each other's needs.

**companionate love** A secure, trusting, stable partnership.

**compliance** Changes in behavior that are elicited by direct requests.

**confederate** Accomplice of an experimenter who, in dealing with the real participants in an experiment, acts as if he or she is also a participant.

**confirmation bias** The tendency to seek, interpret, and create information that verifies existing beliefs.

**conformity** The tendency to change our perceptions, opinions, or behavior in ways that are consistent with group norms.

**confound** A factor other than the independent variable that varies between the conditions of an experiment, thereby calling into question what caused any effects on the dependent variable.

**construct validity** The extent to which the measures used in a study measure the variables they were designed to measure and the manipulations in an experiment manipulate the variables they were designed to manipulate.

**contact hypothesis** The theory that direct contact between hostile groups will reduce intergroup prejudice under certain conditions.

**contingency model of leadership**    The theory that leadership effectiveness is determined both by the personal characteristics of leaders and by the control afforded by the situation.

**coping**    Efforts to reduce stress.

**correlational research**    Research designed to measure the association between variables that are not manipulated by the researcher.

**correlation coefficient**    A statistical measure of the strength and direction of the association between two variables.

**counterfactual thinking**    The tendency to imagine alternative events or outcomes that might have occurred but did not.

**covariation principle**    A principle of attribution theory that holds that people attribute behavior to factors that are present when a behavior occurs and are absent when it does not.

**cross-cultural research**    Research designed to compare and contrast people of different cultures.

**cultivation**    The process by which the mass media (particularly television) construct a version of social reality for the public.

**culture**    A system of enduring meanings, beliefs, values, assumptions, institutions, and practices shared by a large group of people and transmitted from one generation to the next.

**cycle of violence**    The transmission of domestic violence across generations.

**death qualification**    A jury-selection procedure used in capital cases that permits judges to exclude prospective jurors who say they would not vote for the death penalty.

**debriefing**    A disclosure, made to participants after research procedures are completed, in which the researcher explains the purpose of the research, attempts to resolve any negative feelings, and emphasizes the scientific contribution made by the participants' involvement.

**deception**    In the context of research, a method that provides false information to participants.

**deindividuation**    The loss of a person's sense of individuality and the reduction of normal constraints against deviant behavior.

**dependent variable**    In an experiment, a factor that experimenters measure to see if it is affected by the independent variable.

**depressive explanatory style**    A habitual tendency to attribute negative events to causes that are stable, global, and internal.

**desensitization**    Reduction in emotion-related physiological reactivity in response to a stimulus.

**dialecticism**    An Eastern system of thought that accepts the coexistence of contradictory characteristics within a single person.

**diffusion of responsibility**    The belief that others will or should take the responsibility for providing assistance to a person in need.

**discrimination**    Behavior directed against persons because of their membership in a particular group.

**displacement**    Aggressing against a substitute target because aggressive acts against the source of the frustration are inhibited by fear or lack of access.

**distraction–conflict theory**    A theory that the presence of others will produce social facilitation effects only when those others distract from the task and create attentional conflict.

**door-in-the-face technique**    A two-step compliance technique in which an influencer prefaces the real request with one that is so large that it is rejected.

**downward social comparison**    The defensive tendency to compare ourselves with others who are worse off than we are.

**egoistic**    Motivated by the desire to increase one's own welfare.

**elaboration**    The process of thinking about and scrutinizing the arguments contained in a persuasive communication.

**embodied cognition**    An interdisciplinary subfield that examines the close links between our minds and the positioning, experiences, and actions of our bodies.

**emotion-focused coping**    Cognitive and behavioral efforts to reduce the distress produced by a stressful situation.

**empathy–altruism hypothesis**    The proposition that empathic concern for a person in need produces an altruistic motive for helping.

**empathy**    Understanding or vicariously experiencing another individual's perspective and feeling sympathy and compassion for that individual.

**endowment effect**    The tendency for people to inflate the value of objects, goods, or services they already own.

**equity theory**    The theory that people are most satisfied with a relationship when the ratio between benefits and contributions is similar for both partners.

**escalation effect**    The condition in which commitments to a failing course of action are increased to justify investments already made.

**escalation effect**    The tendency for people to persist in failing investments to avert loss, which causes losses to mount.

**evaluation apprehension theory**    A theory that the presence of others will produce social facilitation effects only when those others are seen as potential evaluators.

**evaluative conditioning**    The process by which we form an attitude toward a neutral stimulus because of its association with a positive or negative person, place, or thing.

**evolutionary psychology**    A subfield of psychology that uses the principles of evolution to understand human social behavior.

**exchange relationship**    A relationship in which the participants expect and desire strict reciprocity in their interactions.

**excitation transfer**    The process whereby arousal caused by one stimulus is added to arousal from a second stimulus and the combined arousal is attributed to the second stimulus.

**expectancy theory**    The theory that workers become motivated when they believe that their efforts will produce valued outcomes.

**experiment**    A form of research that can demonstrate causal relationships because (1) the experimenter has control over the events that occur and (2) participants are randomly assigned to conditions.

**experimental realism**    The degree to which experimental procedures are involving to participants and lead them to behave naturally and spontaneously.

**experimenter expectancy effects**    The effects produced when an experimenter's expectations about the results of an experiment affect his or her behavior toward a participant and thereby influence the participant's responses.

**external validity**    The degree to which there can be reasonable confidence that the results of a study would be obtained for other people and in other situations.

**facial electromyograph (EMG)**    An electronic instrument that records facial muscle activity associated with emotions and attitudes.

**facial feedback hypothesis**    The hypothesis that changes in facial expression can lead to corresponding changes in emotion.

**false-consensus effect**   The tendency for people to overestimate the extent to which others share their opinions, attributes, and behaviors.

**foot-in-the-door technique**   A two-step compliance technique in which an influencer sets the stage for the real request by first getting a person to comply with a much smaller request.

**frustration–aggression hypothesis**   The idea that (1) frustration always elicits the motive to aggress and (2) all aggression is caused by frustration.

**fundamental attribution error**   The tendency to focus on the role of personal causes and underestimate the impact of situations on other people's behavior.

**general adaptation syndrome**   A three-stage process (alarm, resistance, and exhaustion) by which the body responds to stress.

**graduated and reciprocated initiatives in tension-reduction (GRIT)**   A strategy for unilateral persistent efforts to establish trust and cooperation between opposing parties.

**group**   A set of individuals who interact over time and have shared fate, goals, or identity.

**group cohesiveness**   The extent to which forces push group members closer together, such as through feelings of intimacy, unity, and commitment to group goals.

**group polarization**   The exaggeration of initial tendencies in the thinking of group members through group discussion.

**group support systems**   Specialized interactive computer programs that are used to guide group meetings, collaborative work, and decision-making processes.

**groupthink**   A group decision-making style characterized by an excessive tendency among group members to seek concurrence.

**hard-to-get effect**   The tendency to prefer people who are highly selective in their social choices over those who are more readily available.

**Hawthorne effect**   The finding that workers who were given special attention increased their productivity regardless of what actual changes were made in the work setting.

**health psychology**   The study of physical health and illness by psychologists from various areas of specialization.

**hostile attribution bias**   The tendency to perceive hostile intent in others.

**hypothesis**   A testable prediction about the conditions under which an event will occur.

**idiosyncrasy credits**   Interpersonal "credits" that a person earns by following group norms.

**illusory correlation**   An overestimate of the association between variables that are only slightly or not at all correlated.

**immune system**   A biological surveillance system that detects and destroys "nonself" substances that invade the body.

**Implicit Association Test (IAT)**   A covert measure of unconscious attitudes derived from the speed at which people respond to pairings of concepts—such as black or white with good or bad.

**implicit attitude**   An attitude, such as prejudice, that one is not aware of having.

**implicit egotism**   A nonconscious form of self-enhancement.

**implicit personality theory**   A network of assumptions people make about the relationships among traits and behaviors.

**implicit racism**   Racism that operates unconsciously and unintentionally.

**impression formation**   The process of integrating information about a person to form a coherent impression.

**independent variable**   In an experiment, a factor that experimenters manipulate to see if it affects the dependent variable.

**individualism**   A cultural orientation in which independence, autonomy, and self-reliance take priority over group allegiances.

**industrial/organizational (I/O) psychology**   The study of human behavior in business and other organizational settings.

**informational influence**   Influence that produces conformity when a person believes others are correct in their judgments.

**information integration theory**   The theory that impressions are based on (1) perceiver dispositions and (2) a weighted average of a target person's traits.

**informed consent**   An individual's deliberate, voluntary decision to participate in research, based on the researcher's description of what will be required during such participation.

**ingroup favoritism**   The tendency to discriminate in favor of ingroups over outgroups.

**ingroups**   Groups with which an individual feels a sense of membership, belonging, and identity.

**inoculation hypothesis**   The idea that exposure to weak versions of a persuasive argument increases later resistance to that argument.

**inquisitorial model**   A dispute–resolution system in which a neutral investigator gathers evidence from both sides and presents the findings in court.

**insufficient deterrence**   A condition in which people refrain from engaging in a desirable activity, even when only mild punishment is threatened.

**insufficient justification**   A condition in which people freely perform an attitude-discrepant behavior without receiving a large reward.

**integrative agreement**   A negotiated resolution to a conflict in which all parties obtain outcomes that are superior to what they would have obtained from an equal division of the contested resources.

**integrity tests**   Questionnaires designed to test a job applicant's honesty and character.

**interactionist perspective**   An emphasis on how both an individual's personality and environmental characteristics influence behavior.

**internal validity**   The degree to which there can be reasonable certainty that the independent variables in an experiment caused the effects obtained on the dependent variables.

**interrater reliability**   The degree to which different observers agree on their observations.

**intimate relationship**   A close relationship between two adults involving emotional attachment, fulfillment of psychological needs, or interdependence.

**jigsaw classroom**   A cooperative learning method used to reduce racial prejudice through interaction in group efforts.

**jury nullification**   The jury's power to disregard, or "nullify," the law when it conflicts with personal conceptions of justice.

**kin selection**   Preferential helping of genetic relatives, which results in the greater likelihood that genes held in common will survive.

**learned helplessness** A phenomenon in which experience with an uncontrollable event creates passive behavior in the face of subsequent threats to well-being.

**leniency bias** The tendency for jury deliberation to produce a tilt toward acquittal.

**loneliness** A feeling of deprivation about existing social relations.

**lowballing** A two-step compliance technique in which the influencer secures agreement with a request but then increases the size of that request by revealing hidden costs.

**matching hypothesis** The proposition that people are attracted to others who are similar in physical attractiveness.

**mere exposure effect** The phenomenon whereby the more often people are exposed to a stimulus, the more positively they evaluate that stimulus.

**mere presence theory** The proposition that the mere presence of others is sufficient to produce social facilitation effects.

**meta-analysis** A set of statistical procedures used to review a body of evidence by combining the results of individual studies to measure the overall reliability and strength of particular effects.

**mind perception** The process by which people attribute human-like mental states to various animate and inanimate objects, including other people.

**minority influence** The process by which dissenters produce change within a group.

**misinformation effect** The tendency for false post-event misinformation to become integrated into people's memory of an event.

**modern racism** A form of prejudice that surfaces in subtle ways when it is safe, socially acceptable, and easy to rationalize.

**multicultural research** Research designed to examine racial and ethnic groups within cultures.

**mundane realism** The degree to which the experimental situation resembles places and events in the real world.

**need for affiliation** The desire to establish and maintain many rewarding interpersonal relationships.

**need for closure** The desire to reduce cognitive uncertainty, which heightens the importance of first impressions.

**need for cognition (NC)** A personality variable that distinguishes people on the basis of how much they enjoy effortful cognitive activities.

**negative state relief model** The proposition that people help others in order to counteract their own feelings of sadness.

**nonverbal behavior** Behavior that reveals a person's feelings without words, through facial expressions, body language, and vocal cues.

**normative influence** Influence that produces conformity when a person fears the negative social consequences of appearing deviant.

**normative model of leadership** The theory that leadership effectiveness is determined by the amount of feedback and participation that leaders invite from workers.

**obedience** Behavior change produced by the commands of authority.

**operational definition** The specific procedures for manipulating or measuring a conceptual variable.

**outgroup homogeneity effect** The tendency to assume that there is greater similarity among members of outgroups than among members of ingroups.

**outgroups** Groups with which an individual does not feel a sense of membership, belonging, or identity.

**overjustification effect** The tendency for intrinsic motivation to diminish for activities that have become associated with reward or other extrinsic factors.

**own-race identification bias** The tendency for people to be more accurate at recognizing members of their own racial group than of other groups.

**passionate love** Romantic love characterized by high arousal, intense attraction, and fear of rejection.

**peremptory challenge** A means by which lawyers can exclude a limited number of prospective jurors without the judge's approval.

**performance appraisal** The process of evaluating an employee's work within the organization.

**peripheral route to persuasion** The process by which a person does not think carefully about a communication and is influenced instead by superficial cues.

**personal attribution** Attribution to internal characteristics of an actor, such as ability, personality, mood, or effort.

**persuasion** The process by which attitudes are changed.

**pluralistic ignorance** The state in which people in a group mistakenly think that their own individual thoughts, feelings, or behaviors are different from those of the others in the group.

**polygraph** A mechanical instrument that records physiological arousal from multiple channels; it is often used as a lie-detector test.

**pornography** Explicit sexual material.

**posttraumatic stress disorder (PTSD)** A condition in which a person experiences enduring physical and psychological symptoms after an extremely stressful event.

**prejudice** Negative feelings toward persons based on their membership in certain groups.

**primacy effect** The tendency for information presented early in a sequence to have more impact on impressions than information presented later.

**priming** The tendency for recently used or perceived words or ideas to come to mind easily and influence the interpretation of new information.

**prisoner's dilemma** A type of dilemma in which one party must make either cooperative or competitive moves in relation to another party. The dilemma is typically designed so that the competitive move appears to be in one's self-interest, but if both sides make this move, they both suffer more than if they had both cooperated.

**private conformity** The change of beliefs that occurs when a person privately accepts the position taken by others.

**private self-consciousness** A personality characteristic of individuals who are introspective, often attending to their own inner states.

**proactive aggression** Aggressive behavior whereby harm is inflicted as a means to a desired end (also called instrumental aggression).

**proactive coping** Up-front efforts to ward off or modify the onset of a stressful event.

**problem-focused coping** Cognitive and behavioral efforts to alter a stressful situation.

**process gain**  The increase in group performance so that the group outperforms the individuals who comprise the group.

**process loss**  The reduction in group performance due to obstacles created by group processes, such as problems of coordination and motivation.

**prosocial behaviors**  Actions intended to benefit others.

**psychological reactance**  The theory that people react against threats to their freedom by asserting themselves and perceiving the threatened freedom as more attractive.

**psychoneuroimmunology (PNI)**  A subfield of psychology that examines the links among psychological factors, the brain and nervous system, and the immune system.

**public conformity**  A superficial change in overt behavior without a corresponding change of opinion that is produced by real or imagined group pressure.

**public self-consciousness**  A personality characteristic of individuals who focus on themselves as social objects, as seen by others.

**racism**  Prejudice and discrimination based on a person's racial background, or institutional and cultural practices that promote the domination of one racial group over another.

**random assignment**  A method of assigning participants to the various conditions of an experiment so that each participant in the experiment has an equal chance of being in any of the conditions.

**random sampling**  A method of selecting participants for a study so that everyone in a population has an equal chance of being in the study.

**reactive aggression**  Aggressive behavior where the means and the end coincide; harm is inflicted for its own sake.

**realistic conflict theory**  The theory that hostility between groups is caused by direct competition for limited resources.

**reciprocity**  A mutual exchange between what we give and receive—for example, liking those who like us.

**relative deprivation**  Feelings of discontent aroused by the belief that one fares poorly compared with others.

**resource dilemmas**  Social dilemmas involving how two or more people will share a limited resource.

**rumination**  In the context of aggression, rumination involves repeatedly thinking about and reliving an anger-inducing event, focusing on angry thoughts and feelings, and perhaps even planning or imagining revenge.

**scientific jury selection**  A method of selecting juries through surveys that yield correlations between demographics and trial-relevant attitudes.

**self-awareness theory**  The theory that self-focused attention leads people to notice self-discrepancies, thereby motivating either an escape from self-awareness or a change in behavior.

**self-concept**  The sum total of an individual's beliefs about his or her own personal attributes.

**self-disclosure**  Revelations about the self that a person makes to others.

**self-efficacy**  A person's belief that he or she is capable of the specific behavior required to produce a desired outcome in a given situation.

**self-esteem**  An affective component of the self, consisting of a person's positive and negative self-evaluations.

**self-fulfilling prophecy**  The process by which one's expectations about a person eventually lead that person to behave in ways that confirm those expectations.

**self-handicapping**  Behaviors designed to sabotage one's own performance in order to provide a subsequent excuse for failure.

**self-monitoring**  The tendency to change behavior in response to the self-presentation concerns of the situation.

**self-perception theory**  The theory that when internal cues are difficult to interpret, people gain self-insight by observing their own behavior.

**self-presentation**  Strategies people use to shape what others think of them.

**self-regulation**  The process by which people control their thoughts, feelings, or behavior in order to achieve a personal or social goal.

**self-schema**  A belief people hold about themselves that guides the processing of self-relevant information.

**sentencing disparity**  Inconsistency of sentences for the same offense from one judge to another.

**sexism**  Prejudice and discrimination based on a person's gender, or institutional and cultural practices that promote the domination of one gender over another.

**sexual orientation**  A person's preference for members of the same sex (homosexuality), opposite sex (heterosexuality), or both sexes (bisexuality).

**situational attribution**  Attribution to factors external to an actor, such as the task, other people, or luck.

**sleeper effect**  A delayed increase in the persuasive impact of a noncredible source.

**social categorization**  The classification of persons into groups on the basis of common attributes.

**social cognition**  The study of how people perceive, remember, and interpret information about themselves and others.

**social comparison theory**  The theory that people evaluate their own abilities and opinions by comparing themselves to others.

**social dilemma**  A situation in which a self-interested choice by everyone will create the worst outcome for everyone.

**social dominance orientation**  A desire to see one's ingroup as dominant over other groups and a willingness to adopt cultural values that facilitate oppression over other groups.

**social exchange theory**  A perspective that views people as motivated to maximize benefits and minimize costs in their relationships with others.

**social facilitation**  A process whereby the presence of others enhances performance on easy tasks but impairs performance on difficult tasks.

**social identity model of deindividuation effects (SIDE)**  A model of group behavior that explains deindividuation effects as the result of a shift from personal identity to social identity.

**social identity theory**  The theory that people favor ingroups over outgroups in order to enhance their self-esteem.

**social impact theory**  The theory that social influence depends on the strength, immediacy, and number of source persons relative to target persons.

**social learning theory**  The theory that behavior is learned through the observation of others as well as through the direct experience of rewards and punishments.

**social loafing**  A group-produced reduction in individual output on tasks where contributions are pooled.

**social neuroscience**  The study of the relationship between neural and social processes.

**social norm**    A general rule of conduct reflecting standards of social approval and disapproval.

**social perception**    A general term for the processes by which people come to understand one another.

**social psychology**    The scientific study of how individuals think, feel, and behave in a social context.

**social role theory**    The theory that small gender differences are magnified in perception by the contrasting social roles occupied by men and women.

**social support**    The helpful coping resources provided by friends and other people.

**stereotype**    A belief or association that links a whole group of people with certain traits or characteristics.

**stereotype content model**    A model proposing that the relative status and competition between groups influence group stereotypes along the dimensions of competence and warmth.

**stereotype threat**    The experience of concern about being evaluated based on negative stereotypes about one's group.

**stigmatized**    Being persistently stereotyped, perceived as deviant, and devalued in society because of membership in a particular social group or because of a particular characteristic.

**stress**    An unpleasant state of arousal in which people perceive the demands of an event as taxing or exceeding their ability to satisfy or alter those demands.

**stressor**    Anything that causes stress.

**structured interview**    An interview in which each job applicant is asked a standard set of questions and evaluated on the same criteria.

**subjective well-being**    One's happiness, or life satisfaction, as measured by self-report.

**subject variable**    A variable that characterizes preexisting differences among the participants in a study.

**subliminal presentation**    A method of presenting stimuli so faintly or rapidly that people do not have any conscious awareness of having been exposed to them.

**sunk cost principle**    The economic rule of thumb that only future costs and benefits, not past commitments, should be considered in making a decision.

**superordinate goal**    A shared goal that can be achieved only through cooperation among individuals or groups.

**system justification theory**    A theory that proposes that people are motivated (at least in part) to defend and justify the existing social, political, and economic conditions.

**Terror Management Theory**    The theory that humans cope with the fear of their own death by constructing worldviews that help to preserve their self-esteem.

**that's-not-all technique**    A two-step compliance technique in which the influencer begins with an inflated request, then decreases its apparent size by offering a discount or bonus.

**theory**    An organized set of principles used to explain observed phenomena.

**theory of planned behavior**    The theory that attitudes toward a specific behavior combine with subjective norms and perceived control to influence a person's actions.

**transactional leader**    A leader who gains compliance and support from followers primarily through goal setting and the use of rewards.

**transactive memory**    A shared system for remembering information that enables multiple people to remember information together more efficiently than they could do so alone.

**transformational leader**    A leader who inspires followers to transcend their own needs in the interest of a common cause.

**triangular theory of love**    A theory proposing that love has three basic components—intimacy, passion, and commitment—that can be combined to produce eight subtypes.

**two-factor theory of emotion**    The theory that the experience of emotion is based on two factors: physiological arousal and a cognitive interpretation of that arousal.

**Type A personality**    A pattern of behavior characterized by extremes of competitive striving for achievement, a sense of time urgency, hostility, and aggression.

**voir dire**    The pretrial examination of prospective jurors by the judge or opposing lawyers to uncover signs of bias.

**weapon-focus effect**    The tendency for the presence of a weapon to draw attention and impair a witness's ability to identify the culprit.

**weapons effect**    The tendency that the likelihood of aggression will increase by the mere presence of weapons.

**what-is-beautiful-is-good stereotype**    The belief that physically attractive individuals also possess desirable personality characteristics.

Abelson, R. P. (1981). Psychological status of the script concept. *American Psychologist, 36,* 715–729.

Abelson, R. P., Aronson, E., McGuire, W. J., Newcomb, T. M., Rosenberg, M. J., & Tannenbaum, P. H. (1968). *Theories of cognitive consistency: A sourcebook.* Chicago: Rand McNally.

Abramson, L. Y., Metalsky, G. I., & Alloy, L. B. (1989). Hopelessness depression: A theory-based subtype of depression. *Psychological Review, 96,* 358–372.

Acevedo, B. P., & Aron, A. (2009). Does a long-term relationship kill romantic love? *Review of General Psychology, 13,* 59–65.

Acevedo, B. P., Aron, A., Fisher, H. E., & Brown, L. L. (2011). Neural correlates of long-term intense romantic love. *Social Cognitive and Affective Neuroscience, 7,* 145–159.

Acker, M., & Davis, M. H. (1992). Intimacy, passion, and commitment in adult romantic relationships: A test of the triangular theory of love. *Journal of Social and Personal Relationships, 9,* 21–50.

Ackerman, J. M., Griskevicius, V., & Li, N. P. (2011). Let's get serious: Communicating commitment in romantic relationships. *Journal of Personality and Social Psychology, 100,* 1079–1094.

Adair, J. G. (1984). The Hawthorne effect: A reconsideration of the methodological artifact. *Journal of Applied Psychology, 69,* 334–345.

Adair, W. L., & Brett, J. M. (2005). The negotiation dance: Time, culture, and behavioral sequences in negotiation. *Organization Science, 16,* 33–51.

Adams, J. S. (1965). Equity in social exchange. *Advances in Experimental Social Psychology, 2,* 267–299.

Adams, P. R., & Adams, G. R. (1984). Mount Saint Helens's ash-fall: Evidence for a disaster stress reaction. *American Psychologist, 39,* 252–260.

Ader, R. (Ed.). (2007). *Psychoneuroimmunology* (4th ed.). Burlington, MA: Elsevier.

Adherents.com. (2012). Major religions of the world ranked by number of adherents. Available at http://www.adherents.com/Religions_By _Adherents.html.

Adla, A. A., Zarate, P. P., & Soubie, J. L. (2011). A proposal of toolkit for GDSS facilitators. *Group Decision and Negotiation, 20,* 57–77.

Adler, N. E., Boyce, T., Chesney, M. A., Cohen, S., Folkman, S., Kahn, R. L., & Syme, S. L. (1994). Socioeconomic status and health: The challenge of the gradient. *American Psychologist, 49,* 15–24.

Adorno, T., Frenkel-Brunswik, E., Levinson, D., & Sanford, R. N. (1950). *The authoritarian personality.* New York: Harper.

Afifi, T. O., Mota, N. P., Dasiewicz, P., MacMillan, H. L., & Sareen, J. (2012). Physical punishment and mental disorders: Results from a nationally representative U.S. sample. *Pediatrics, 130,* 184–192.

Aggarwal, P., & O'Brien, C. L. (2008). Social loafing on group projects: Structural antecedents and effect on student satisfaction. *Journal of Marketing Education, 30,* 255–264.

Aguiar, P., Vala, J., Correia, I., & Pereira, C. (2008). Justice in our world and in that of others: Belief in a just world and reactions to victims. *Social Justice Research, 21,* 50–68.

Aharon, I., Etcoff, N., Ariely, D., Chabris, C. F., O'Connor, E., & Breiter, H. C. (2001). Beautiful faces have variable reward value: fMRI and behavioral evidence. *Neuron, 32,* 537–551.

Ainsworth, M., Blehar, M. C., Waters, E., & Wall, S. (1978). *Patterns of attachment: A psychological study of the strange situation.* Hillsdale, NJ: Erlbaum.

Ajzen, I. (1991). The theory of planned behavior. *Organizational Behavior and Human Decision Processes, 50,* 179–211.

Ajzen, I., & Fishbein, M. (1977). Attitude-behavior relations: A theoretical analysis and review of empirical research. *Psychological Bulletin, 84,* 888–918.

Ajzen, I., & Fishbein, M. (2005). The influence of attitudes on behavior. In D. Albarracín, B. T. Johnson, & M. P. Zanna (Eds.), *The handbook of attitudes* (pp. 173–221). Hillsdale, NJ: Erlbaum.

Akimoto, S. A., & Sanbonmatsu, D. M. (1999). Differences in self-effacing behavior between European and Japanese Americans: Effect on competence evaluations. *Journal of Cross-Cultural Psychology, 30,* 159–177.

Albarracín, D., Gillette, J. C., Earl, A. N., Glasman, L. R., Durantini, M. R., & Ho, M.-H. (2005). A test of major assumptions about behavior change: A comprehensive look at the effects of passive and active HIV-prevention interventions since the beginning of the epidemic. *Psychological Bulletin, 131,* 856–897.

Albarracín, D., Johnson, B. T., Fishbein, M., & Muellerleile, P. A. (2001). Theories of reasoned action and planned behavior as models of condom use: A meta-analysis. *Psychological Bulletin, 127,* 142–161.

Albiero, P., Matricardi, G., Speltri, D., & Toso, D. (2009). The assessment of empathy in adolescence: A contribution to the Italian validation of the 'Basic Empathy Scale.' *Journal of Adolescence, 32,* 393–408.

Alexander, G. M. (2003). An evolutionary perspective of sex-typed toy preferences: Pink, blue, and the brain. *Archives of Sexual Behavior, 32,* 7–14.

Alexander, G. M., & Hines, M. (2002). Sex differences in response to children's toys in nonhuman primates *(Cercopithecus aethiops sabaeus). Evolution and Human Behavior, 23,* 467–479.

Alge, B. J. (2001). Effects of computer surveillance on perceptions of privacy and procedural justice. *Journal of Applied Psychology, 86,* 797–804.

Alicke, M. D., & Largo, E. (1995). The role of the self in the false consensus effect. *Journal of Experimental Social Psychology, 31,* 28–47.

Allam, A. (2012). A toxic mix of tradition and religion; Egypt. *Financial Times (London, England),* p. 3.

Allan, R., & Fisher, J. (Eds.) (2011). *Heart and mind: The practice of cardiac psychology* (2nd edition). Washington, DC: American Psychological Association.

Allen-Arave, W., Gurven, M., & Hill, K. (2008). Reciprocal altruism, rather than kin selection, maintains nepotistic food transfers on an Ache reservation. *Evolution and Human Behavior, 29,* 305–318.

Allen, J. B., Kenrick, D. T., Linder, D. E., & McCall, M. A. (1989). Arousal and attribution: A response-facilitation alternative to misattribution and negative-reinforcement models. *Journal of Personality and Social Psychology, 57,* 261–270.

Allen, V. L. (1965). Situational factors in conformity. In L. Berkowitz (Ed.), *Advances in Experimental Social Psychology, 2,* 133–175.

Allen, V. L., & Levine, J. M. (1969). Consensus and conformity. *Journal of Experimental Social Psychology, 5,* 389–399.

Alliger, G. M., & Dwight, S. A. (2000). A meta-analytic investigation of the susceptibility of integrity tests to faking and coaching. *Educational and Psychological Measurement, 60,* 59–72.

Alliger, G. M., Lilienfeld, S. O., & Mitchell, K. E. (1996). The susceptibility of overt and covert integrity tests to coaching and faking. *Psychological Science, 7,* 32–39.

Alloy, L. B., Abramson, L. Y., Whitehouse, W. G., Hogan, M. E., Panzarella, C., & Rose, D. T. (2006). Prospective incidence of first onsets and recurrences of depression in individuals at high and low cognitive risk for depression. *Journal of Abnormal Psychology, 115,* 145–156.

Allport, F. H. (1924). *Social psychology.* Boston: Houghton Mifflin.

Allport, F. H., et al. (1953). The effects of segregation and the consequences of desegregation: A social science statement. *Minneapolis Law Review, 37,* 429–440.

Allport, G. W. (1954). *The nature of prejudice.* Reading, MA: Addison-Wesley.

Allport, G. W. (1985). The historical background of social psychology. In G. Lindzey & E. Aronson (Eds.), *Handbook of social psychology* (3rd ed., Vol. I, pp. 1–46). New York: Random House.

Allport, G. W., & Postman, L. J. (1947). *The psychology of rumor.* New York: Holt.

Alterovitz, S. S.-R., & Mendelsohn, G. A. (2009). Partner preferences across the life span: Online dating by older adults. *Psychology and Aging, 24,* 513–517.

Altman, I. (1973). Reciprocity of interpersonal exchange. *Journal for Theory of Social Behavior, 3,* 249–261.

Altman, I., & Taylor, D. A. (1973). *Social penetration: The development of interpersonal relationships.* New York: Holt, Rinehart and Winston.

Alvidrez, A., & Weinstein, R. S. (1999). Early teacher perceptions and later student academic achievement. *Journal of Educational Psychology, 91,* 731–746.

Alwin, D. F. (1990). Cohort replacement and changes in parental socialization values. *Journal of Marriage and the Family 52,* 347–360.

Amabile, T. M. (1996). *Creativity in context.* New York: Westview.

Amabile, T. M., & Kramer, S. J. (2010). What really motivates workers. *Harvard Business Review, 88* (1), 44–45.

Amabile, T. M., & Kramer, S. J. (2011). *The Progress Principle: Using small wins to ignite joy, engagement, and creativity at work.* Cambridge, MA: Harvard Business Press.

Amabile, T. M., Hill, K. G., Hennessey, B. A., & Tighe, E. M. (1994). The work preference inventory: Assessing intrinsic and extrinsic motivation orientations. *Journal of Personality and Social Psychology, 66,* 950–967.

Amato, P. R. (1983). Helping behavior in urban and rural environments: Field studies based on a taxonomic organization of helping episodes. *Journal of Personality and Social Psychology, 45,* 571–586.

Amato, P. R. (2010). Research on divorce: Continuing trends and new developments. *Journal of Marriage and Family, 72,* 650–666.

Ambady, N. (2010). The perils of pondering: Intuition and thin slice judgments. *Psychological Inquiry, 21,* 271–278.

Ambady, N., & Rosenthal, R. (1993). Half a minute: Predicting teacher evaluations from thin slices of nonverbal behavior and physical attractiveness. *Journal of Personality and Social Psychology, 64,* 431–441.

Ambrose, M. L., & Schminke, M. (2009). The role of overall justice judgments in organizational justice research: A test of mediation. *Journal of Applied Psychology, 94,* 491–500.

American Academy of Pediatrics (2009). Policy statement—media violence. *Pediatrics, 124,* 1495–1503.

American Psychological Association (2010). Amendments to the 2002 "Ethical principles of psychologists and code of conduct." *American Psychologist, 65,* 493.

American Psychological Association. (2002). Ethical principles of psychologists and code of conduct. *American Psychologist, 57,* 1060–1073.

American Psychological Association. (2008, October 7). *Stress in America 2008 Survey: Executive summary.* Washington, DC: American Psychological Association. Available at http://apahelpcenter.mediaroom.com/index.php?s=pageC.

Amnesty International. (2009). http://www.amnesty.org.

Amnesty International. (2012). *Choice and prejudice: Discrimination against Muslims in Europe.* London: Amnesty International.

Amodio, D. (2008). The social neuroscience of intergroup relations. *European Review of Social Psychology, 19,* 1–54.

Amodio, D. M. (2013). The social neuroscience of prejudice: Then, now, and what's to come. In C. Stangor & C. S. Crandall (Eds.), *Advances in stereotyping and prejudice.* New York: Psychology Press.

Andersen, S. M., & Chen, S. (2002). The relational self: An interpersonal social-cognitive theory. *Psychological Review, 109,* 619–645.

Anderson, C. A. (1989). Temperature and aggression: Ubiquitous effects of heat on occurrence of human violence. *Psychological Bulletin, 106,* 74–96.

Anderson, C. A. (2001). Heat and violence. *Current Directions in Psychological Science, 10,* 33–38.

Anderson, C. A. (2004). An update on the effects of playing violent video games. *Journal of Adolescence, 27,* 113–122.

Anderson, C. A., & Anderson, K. B. (1996). Violent crime rate statistics in philosophical context: A destructive testing approach to heat and southern culture of violence effects. *Journal of Personality and Social Psychology, 70,* 740–756.

Anderson, C. A., & Bushman, B. J. (2002a). The effects of media violence on society. *Science, 295,* 2377–2379.

Anderson, C. A., & Bushman, B. J. (2002b). Human aggression. *Annual Review of Psychology, 53,* 27–51.

Anderson, C. A., & Carnagey, N. L. (2004). Violent evil and the General Aggression Model. In A. G. Miller (Ed.), *The social psychology of good and evil* (pp. 168–192). New York: Guilford.

Anderson, C. A., & DeLisi, M. (2011). Implications of global climate change for violence in developed and developing countries. In J. P. Forgas, A. W. Kruglanski, & K. D. Williams (Eds.) , *The psychology of social conflict and aggression* (pp. 249–265). New York: Psychology Press.

Anderson, C. A., & Huesmann, L. R. (2007). Human aggression: A social-cognitive review. In M. A. Hogg & J. Cooper (Eds.), *The Sage handbook of social psychology* (pp. 259–287). London: Sage.

Anderson, C. A., & Prot, S. (2011). Effects of playing violent video games. In M. Paludi (Ed.), *The psychology of teen violence and victimization* (Vols 1 and 2: From bullying to cyberstalking to assault and sexual violation; Prevention strategies for families and schools), pp. 41–70. Santa Barbara, CA: Praeger.

Anderson, C. A., & Sechler, E. S. (1986). Effects of explanation and counter-explanation on the development and use of social theories. *Journal of Personality and Social Psychology, 50,* 24–34.

Anderson, C. A., Anderson, K. B., & Deuser, W. E. (1996). Examining an affective framework: Weapon and temperature effects on aggressive thoughts, affect, and attitudes. *Personality and Social Psychology Bulletin, 22,* 366–376.

Anderson, C. A., Anderson, K. B., Dorr, N., DeNeve, K. M., & Flanagan, M. (2000). Temperature and aggression. In M. P. Zanna (Ed.), *Advances in experimental social psychology* (Vol. 32, pp. 63–133). San Diego, CA: Academic Press.

Anderson, C. A., Berkowitz, L., Donnerstein, E., Huesmann, L. R., Johnson, J. D., Linz, D., Malamuth, N. M., & Wartella, E. (2003). The influence of media violence on youth. *Psychological Science in the Public Interest, 4,* 81–110.

Anderson, C. A., Carnagey, N. L., Flanagan, M., Benjamin, A. J., Eubanks, J., & Valentine, J. C. (2004). Violent video games: Specific effects of violent content on aggressive thoughts and behavior. *Advances in Experimental Social Psychology, 36,* 199–249.

Anderson, C. A., Lepper, M. R., & Ross, L. (1980). Perseverance of social theories: The role of explanation in the persistence of discredited information. *Journal of Personality and Social Psychology, 39,* 1037–1049.

Anderson, C. A., Shibuya, A., Ihori, N., et al. (2010). Violent video game effects on aggression, empathy, and prosocial behavior in Eastern and Western countries: A meta-analytic review. *Psychological Bulletin, 136,* 151–173.

Anderson, J. L., Crawford, C. B., Nadeau, J., & Lindberg, T. (1992). Was the Duchess of Windsor right? A cross-cultural review of the socioecology of ideals of female body shape. *Ethology and Sociobiology, 13,* 197–227.

Anderson, N. H. (1965). Averaging versus adding as a stimulus combination rule in impression formation. *Journal of Experimental Social Psychology, 70,* 394–400.

Anderson, N. H. (1968). Likableness ratings of 555 personality-trait words. *Journal of Personality and Social Psychology, 9,* 272–279.

Anderson, N. H. (1981). *Foundations of Information Integration Theory.* New York: Academic Press.

Anderson, N. H., & Hubert, S. (1963). Effects of concomitant verbal recall on order effects in personality impression formation. *Journal of Verbal Learning and Verbal Behavior, 2,* 379–391.

Andreasson, P. B. (1987). On the social psychology of the stock market: Aggregate attributional effects and the regressiveness of prediction. *Journal of Personality and Social Psychology, 53,* 490–496.

Ang, R. P., & Goh, D. H. (2010). Cyberbullying among adolescents: The role of affective and cognitive empathy, and gender. *Child Psychiatry and Human Development, 41,* 387–397.

Anti-Defamation League. (2012). *Attitudes toward Jews in ten European countries.* Available at www.adl.org.

Antonio, A. L., Chang, M. J., Hakuta, K., Kenny, D. A., Levin, S., & Milem, J. F. (2004). Effects of racial diversity on complex thinking in college students. *Psychological Science, 15,* 507–510.

Apfelbaum, E. P., Pauker, K., Ambady, N., Sommers, S. R., & Norton, M. I. (2008). Learning (not) to talk about race: When older children underperform in social categorization. *Developmental Psychology, 44,* 1513–1518.

Apodaca v. Oregon, 406 U.S. 404 (1972).

Archer, J. (2000). Sex differences in aggression between heterosexual partners: A meta-analytic review. *Psychological Bulletin, 126,* 651–680.

Archer, J. (2002). Sex differences in physically aggressive acts between heterosexual partners: A meta-analytic review. *Aggression and Violent Behavior: A Review Journal, 7,* 313–351.

Archer, J. (2004). Sex differences in aggression in real-world settings: A meta-analytic review. *Review of General Psychology, 8,* 291–322.

Archer, J. (2006). Testosterone and human aggression: An evaluation of the challenge hypothesis. *Neuroscience and Biobehavioral Reviews, 30,* 319–345.

Archibald, F. S., Bartholomew, K., & Marx, R. (1995). Loneliness in early adolescence: A test of the cognitive discrepancy model of loneliness. *Personality and Social Psychology Bulletin, 21,* 296–301.

Arendt, H. (1963). *Eichmann in Jerusalem: A report on the banality of evil.* New York: Viking.

Argote, L., & Ren, Y. (2012). Transactive memory systems: Micro foundations of dynamic capabilities. *Journal of Management Studies.*

Arkes, H. R., & Ayton, P. (1999). The sunk cost and Concorde effects: Are humans less rational than lower animals? *Psychological Bulletin, 125,* 591–600.

Arkin, R. M. (1981). Self-presentation styles. In J. T. Tedeschi (Ed.), *Impression management theory and social psychological research* (pp. 311–333). New York: Academic Press.

Arluke, A. (2012). Interpersonal barriers to stopping animal abuse: Exploring the role of adolescent friendship norms and breeches. *Journal of Interpersonal Violence,* in press.

Armor, D. A., & Taylor, S. E. (1998). Situated optimism: Specific outcome expectancies and self-regulation. *Advances in Experimental Social Psychology, 30,* 309–379.

Aron, A., & Westbay L. (1996). Dimensions of the prototype of love. *Journal of Personality and Social Psychology, 70,* 535–551.

Aron, A., Aron, E. N., & Smollan, D. (1992). Inclusion of Other in the Self Scale and the structure of interpersonal closeness. *Journal of Personality and Social Psychology, 63,* 596–612.

Aron, A., Dutton, D. G., Aron, E. N., & Iverson, A. (1989). Experiences of falling in love. *Journal of Social and Personal Relationships, 6,* 243–257.

Aron, A., Norman, C. C., Aron, E. N., McKenna, C., & Heyman, R. E. (2000). Couples' shared participation in novel and arousing activities and experienced relationship quality. *Journal of Personality and Social Psychology, 78,* 273–284.

Aronson, E. (1969). The theory of cognitive dissonance: A current perspective. *Advances in Experimental Social Psychology, 4,* 1–34.

Aronson, E. (1992). Stateways can change folkways. In R. M. Baird & S. E. Rosenbaum (Eds.), *Bigotry, prejudice, and hatred: Definitions, causes, and solutions* (pp. 185–201). Buffalo, NY: Prometheus.

Aronson, E. (1999). Dissonance, hypocrisy, and the self-concept. In E. Harmon-Jones & J. Mills (Eds.), *Cognitive dissonance: Progress on a pivotal theory in social psychology* (pp. 103–126). Washington, DC: American Psychological Association.

Aronson, E. (2004). Reducing hostility and building compassion: Lessons from the jigsaw classroom. In A. G. Miller (Ed.), *The social psychology of good and evil* (pp. 469–488). New York: Guilford.

Aronson, E., & Carlsmith, J. M. (1963). Effect of severity of threat on the devaluation of forbidden behavior. *Journal of Abnormal and Social Psychology, 66,* 584–588.

Aronson, E., & Carlsmith, J. M. (1968). Experimentation in social psychology. In G. Lindzey & E. Aronson (Eds.), *Handbook of social psychology* (2nd ed., Vol. 2, pp. 1–79). Reading, MA: Addison-Wesley.

Aronsom, E., & Cope, V. (1968). My enemy's enemy is my friend. *Journal of Personality and Social Psychology, 8,* 8–12.

Aronson, E., & Linder, D. (1965). Gain and loss of esteem as determinants of interpersonal attractiveness. *Journal of Experimental Social Psychology, 1,* 156–172.

Aronson, E., & Mills, J. (1959). The effect of severity of initiation on liking for a group. *Journal of Abnormal and Social Psychology, 59,* 177–181.

Aronson, E., Blaney, N., Stephan, C., Sikes, J., & Snapp, M. (1978). *The jigsaw classroom.* Beverly Hills, CA: Sage.

Aronson, J., & Inzlicht, M. (2004). The ups and downs of attributional ambiguity: Stereotype vulnerability and the academic self-knowledge of African American college students. *Psychological Science, 15,* 829–836.

Aronson, J., Lustina, M. J., Good, C., Keough, K., Steele, C. M., & Brown, J. (1999). When white men can't do math: Necessary and sufficient factors in stereotype threat. *Journal of Experimental Social Psychology, 35,* 29–46.

Arora, P., Peterson, N. D., Krantz, D. H., Hardisty, D. J., & Reddy, K. S. (2012). To cooperate or not to cooperate: Using new methodologies and frameworks to understand how affiliation influences cooperation in the present and future. *Journal of Economic Psychology, 33,* 842–853.

Arthur, W., Day, E. D., McNelly, T. L., & Edens, P. S. (2003). A meta-analysis of the criterion-related validity of assessment center dimensions. *Personnel Psychology, 56,* 125–154.

Asch, S. E. (1946). Forming impressions of personality. *Journal of Abnormal and Social Psychology, 41,* 258–290.

Asch, S. E. (1951). Effects of group pressure upon the modification and distortion of judgments. In H. Guetzkow (Ed.), *Groups, leadership, and men.* Pittsburgh: Carnegie Press.

Asch, S. E. (1955, November). Opinions and social pressure. *Scientific American,* pp. 31–35.

Asch, S. E. (1956). Studies of independence and conformity: A minority of one against a unanimous majority. *Psychological Monographs, 70,* 416.

Asch, S. E., & Zukier, H. (1984). Thinking about persons. *Journal of Personality and Social Psychology, 46,* 1230–1240.

Ashton-James, C. E., Maddux, W. W., Galinsky, A. D., & Chartrand, T. L. (2009). Who I am depends on how I feel: The role of affect in the expression of culture. *Psychological Science, 20,* 340–346.

Askenasy, H. (1978). *Are we all Nazis?* Secaucus, NJ: Lyle Stuart.

Aspinwall, L. G., & Taylor, S. E. (1992). Modeling cognitive adaptation: A longitudinal investigation of the impact of individual differences and coping on college adjustment and performance. *Journal of Personality and Social Psychology, 63,* 989–1003.

Aspinwall, L. G., & Taylor, S. E. (1993). The effects of social comparison direction, threat, and self-esteem on affect, self-evaluation, and expected success. *Journal of Personality and Social Psychology, 64,* 708–722.

Aspinwall, L. G., & Taylor, S. E. (1997). A stitch in time: Self-regulation and proactive coping. *Psychological Bulletin, 121,* 417–436.

Associated Press (2012, March 22). French terror suspect shot in head by police, filmed shootings of children, paratroopers.

Associated Press. (2009, July 4). Man who tried to rescue suicidal OC woman dies. The Associated Press State and Local Wire.

Atran, S., & Norenzayan, A. (2004). Religion's evolutionary landscape: Counterintuition, commitment, compassion, communion. *Behavioral and Brain Sciences, 27,* 713–770.

Atwater, L., Wang, M., Smither, J. W., & Fleenor, J. W. (2009). Are cultural characteristics associated with the relationship between self and others' ratings of leadership? *Journal of Applied Psychology, 94,* 876–886.

Auerbach, S. M., Kiesler, D. J., Strentz, T., Schmidt, J. A., & Serio, C. D. (1994). Interpersonal impacts and adjunctment to the stress of simulated captivity: An empirical test of the Stockholm Syndrome. *Journal of Social and Clinical Psychology, 13,* 207–221.

Aviezer, H., Hassin, R. R., Ryan, J., Grady, C., Susskind, J., Anderson, A., & Bentin, S. (2008). Angry, disgusted, or afraid? Studies on the malleability of emotion perception. *Psychological Science, 19,* 724–732.

Avolio, B. J. (2011). *Full range leadership development.* Thousand Oaks, CA: Sage.

Axsom, D. (1989). Cognitive dissonance and behavior change in psychotherapy. *Journal of Experimental Social Psychology, 25,* 234–252.

Axsom, D., & Cooper, J. (1985). Cognitive dissonance and psychotherapy: The role of effort justification in inducing weight loss. *Journal of Experimental Social Psychology, 21,* 149–160.

Axtell, R. E. (1993). *Do's and taboos around the world* (3rd ed.). New York: John Wiley.

Babcock, L., & Laschever, S. (2003). *Women don't ask: Negotiation and the gender divide.* Princeton, NJ: Princeton University Press.

Back, M. D., Schmukle, S. C., & Egloff, B. (2008). Becoming friends by chance. *Psychological Science, 19,* 439–440.

Back, M. D., Stopfer, J. M.,Vazire, S., Gaddis, S., Schmukle, S. C., Egloff, B., & Gosling, S. D. (2010). Facebook profiles reflect actual personality, not self-idealization. *Psychological Science, 21,* 372–374.

Bagemihl, B. (1999). *Biological exuberance: Animal homosexuality and natural diversity.* New York: St. Martin's Press.

Bahrick, H. P., Hall, L. K., & Berger, S. A. (1996). Accuracy and distortion in memory for high school grades. *Psychological Science, 7,* 265–271.

Bailenson, J. N., & Yee, N. (2005). Digital chameleons: Automatic assimilation of nonverbal gestures in immersive virtual environments. *Psychological Science, 16,* 814–819.

Bailey, A. A., & Hurd, P. L. (2005). Finger length ratio (2D:4D) correlates with physical aggression in men but not in women. *Biological Psychology, 68,* 215–222.

Bailey, C. A., & Ostrov, J. M. (2008). Differentiating forms and functions of aggression in emerging adults: Associations with hostile attribution biases and normative beliefs. *Journal of Youth and Adolescence, 37,* 713–722.

Bailey, J. M., & Pillard, R. C. (1991). A genetic study of male sexual orientation. *Archives of General Psychiatry, 48,* 1089–1096.

Bailey, J. M., & Zucker, K. J. (1995). Childhood sex-typed behavior and sexual orientation: A conceptual analysis and quantitative review. *Developmental Psychology, 31,* 43–55.

Bailey, J. M., Dunne, M. P., & Martin, N. G. (2000). Genetic and environmental influences on sexual orientation and its correlates in an Australian twin sample. *Journal of Personality and Social Psychology 78,* 524–536.

Bailey, J. M., Pillard, R. C., Neale, M. C., & Agyei, Y. (1993). Heritable factors influence sexual orientation in women. *Archives of General Psychiatry, 50,* 217–223.

Balcetis, E., & Dunning, D. (2006). See what you want to see: Motivational influences on visual perception. *Journal of Personality and Social Psychology, 91,* 612–625.

Balcetis, E., & Dunning, D. (2007). Cognitive dissonance and the perception of natural environments. *Psychological Science, 18,* 917–921.

Balcetis, E., & Dunning, D. (2010). Wishful seeing: more desired objects are seen as closer. *Psychological Science, 21,* 147–152.

Baldus, D. C., Woodworth, G., & Pulaski, C. A. (1990). *Equal justice and the death penalty: A legal and empirical analysis.* Boston: Northeastern University Press.

Baldwin, A. S., Rothman, A. J., Hertel, A. W., Linde, J. A., Jeffery, R. W., Finch, E. A., & Lando, H. A. (2006). Specifying the determinants of the initiation and maintenance of behavior change: An examination of self-efficacy, satisfaction, and smoking cessation. *Health Psychology, 25,* 626–634.

Baldwin, M. W., & Sinclair, L. (1996). Self-esteem and "if . . . then" contingencies of interpersonal acceptance. *Journal of Personality and Social Psychology, 71,* 1130–1141.

Bales, R. F. (1958). Task roles and social roles in problem-solving groups. In E. E. Maccoby, T. M. Newcomb, & E. L. Hartley (Eds.), *Readings in social psychology* (3rd ed., pp. 437–447). New York: Holt.

Ball, H. A., Arseneault, L., Taylor, A., Maughan, B., Caspi, A., & Moffitt, T. E. (2008). Genetic and environmental influences on victims, bullies and bully-victims in childhood. *Journal of Child Psychology and Psychiatry, 49,* 104–112.

Ballew v. Georgia, 435 U.S. 223 (1978).

Balliet, D., Li, N. P., Macfarlan, S. J., & Van Vugt, M. (2011). Sex differences in cooperation: A meta-analytic review of social dilemmas. *Psychological Bulletin, 137,* 881–909.

Balliet, D., Parks, C., & Joireman, J. (2009). Social value orientation and cooperation in social dilemmas: A meta-analysis. *Group Processes & Intergroup Relations, 12,* 533–547.

Banaji, M. R., & Steele, C. M. (1989). Alcohol and self-evaluation: Is a social cognition approach beneficial? *Social Cognition, 7,* 137–151.

Bandler, J., & Varchaver, N. (2009, May 11). How Bernie did it. *Fortune, 159*(10). Bandura, A. (1973). *Aggression: A social learning analysis.* Englewood Cliffs, NJ: Prentice-Hall.

Bandura, A. (1977). *Social learning theory.* Englewood Cliffs, NJ: Prentice-Hall.

Bandura, A. (1983). Psychological mechanisms of aggression. In R. G. Geen & E. I. Donnerstein (Eds.), *Aggression: Theoretical and empirical reviews: Vol. l. Theoretical and methodological issues* (pp. 1–40). New York: Academic Press.

Bandura, A. (1997). *Self-efficacy: The exercise of control.* New York: W. H. Freeman.

Bandura, A. (1999). A sociocognitive analysis of substance abuse: An agentic perspective. *Psychological Science, 10,* 214–218.

Bandura, A., Ross, R., & Ross, S. (1961). Transmission of aggression through imitation of aggressive models. *Journal of Abnormal and Social Psychology, 63,* 575–582.

Banuazizi, A., & Movahedi, S. (1975). Interpersonal dynamics in a simulated prison: A methodological analysis. *American Psychologist, 30,* 152–160.

Banyard, V. L. (2011). Who will help prevent sexual violence: Creating an ecological model of bystander intervention. *Psychology of Violence, 1,* 216–229.

Barberis, N., & Xiong, W. (2009). What drives the disposition effect? An analysis of a long-standing preference-based explanation." *Journal of Finance, 64,* 751–784.

Barclay, G., & Tavares, C. (2003). *International comparisons of criminal justice statistics 2001.* London: Home Office Statistical Bulletin.

Barden, J., & Petty, R. E. (2008). The mere perception of elaboration creates attitude certainty: Exploring the thoughtfulness heuristic. *Journal of Personality and Social Psychology, 95,* 489–509.

Bargh, J. A., & Chartrand, T. L. (2000). The mind in the middle: A practical guide for priming and automaticity research. In H. T. Reis and C. M. Judd (Eds.), *Handbook of research methods in social and personality psychology* (pp. 253–285). New York: Cambridge University Press.

Bargh, J. A., & McKenna, K. Y. A. (2004). The internet and social life. *Annual Review of Psychology, 55,* 1–20.

Bargh, J. A., & Pietromonaco, P. (1982). Automatic information processing and social perception: The influence of trait information presented outside of conscious awareness on impression formation. *Journal of Personality and Social Psychology, 43,* 437–449.

Bargh, J. A., Chaiken, S., Govender, R., & Pratto, F. (1992). The generality of the automatic attitude activation effect. *Journal of Personality and Social Psychology, 62,* 893–912.

Bargh, J. A., Chaiken, S., Raymond, P., & Hymes, C. (1996). The automatic evaluation effect: Unconditional automatic attitude activation with a pronunciation task. *Journal of Experimental Social Psychology, 31,* 104–128.

Bargh, J. A., Chen, M., & Burrows, L. (1996). Automaticity of social behavior: Direct effects of trait construct and stereotype activation on action. *Journal of Personality and Social Psychology, 71,* 230–244.

Bargh, J. A., Lombardi, W. J., & Higgins, E. T. (1988). Automaticity of chronically accessible constructs in person x situation effects on person perception: It's just a matter of time. *Journal of Personality and Social Psychology, 55,* 599–605.

Barlett, C. P., & Anderson, C. A. (2012). Direct and indirect relations between the Big 5 personality traits and aggressive and violent behavior. *Personality and Individual Differences,* in press.

Barlett, C. P., Vowels, C. L., & Saucier, D. A. (2008). Meta-analyses of the effects of media images on men's body-image concerns. *Journal of Social and Clinical Psychology, 27,* 279–310.

Barling, J., Kelloway, K., & Frone, M. (2005). *Handbook of occupational stress.* Los Angeles: Sage.

Barnes Nacoste, R. (1994). If empowerment is the goal . . . : Affirmative action and social interaction. *Basic and Applied Social Psychology, 15,* 87–112.

Barnes, C. D., Brown, R. P., & Tamborski, M. (2012). Living dangerously: Culture of honor, risk-taking, and the nonrandomness of "accidental" deaths. *Social Psychological and Personality Science, 3,* 100–107.

Barnes, C. M., & Wagner, D. T. (2009). Changing to daylight saving time cuts into sleep and increases workplace injuries. *Journal of Applied Psychology, 94,* 1305–1317.

Barnes, R. D., Ickes, W., & Kidd, R. F. (1979). Effects of the perceived intentionality and stability of another's dependency on helping behavior. *Personality and Social Psychology Bulletin, 5,* 367–372.

Baron, A. S., & Banaji, M. R. (2006). The development of implicit attitudes: Evidence of race evaluations from ages 6 and 10 and adulthood. *Psychological Science, 17,* 53–58.

Baron, R. A. (1997). The sweet smell of helping: Effects of pleasant ambient fragrance on prosocial behavior in shopping malls. *Journal of Personality and Social Psychology, 23*(5), 498–503.

Baron, R. A., & Ball, R. L. (1974). The aggression-inhibiting influence of nonhostile behavior. *Journal of Experimental Social Psychology, 10,* 23–33.

Baron, R. A., & Richardson, D. R. (1994). *Human aggression* (2nd ed.). New York: Plenum.

Baron, R. S. (1986). Distraction-conflict theory: Progress and problems. In L. Berkowitz (Ed.), *Advances in experimental social psychology* (Vol. 19, pp. 1–40). Orlando, FL: Academic Press.

Baron, R. S. (2005). So right it's wrong: Groupthink and the ubiquitous nature of polarized group decision making. In M. P. Zanna (Ed.), *Advances in experimental social psychology* (pp. 219–253). San Diego: Elsevier Academic Press.

Baron, R. S., Hoppe, S. I., Kao, C. F., Brunsman, B., Linneweh, B., & Rogers, D. (1996). Social corroboration and opinion extremity. *Journal of Experimental Social Psychology, 32,* 537–560.

Barreto, M., Ryan, M. K., & Schmitt, M. T. (2009). *The glass ceiling in the 21st century: Understanding barriers to gender equality.* Washington, DC: American Psychological Association.

Barrett, H. C., Todd, P. M., Miller, G. F., & Blythe, P. W. (2005). Accurate judgments of intention from motion cues alone: A cross-cultural study. *Evolution and Human Behavior, 26,* 313–331.

Barrett, L. F., & Mesquita, B., & Gendron, M. (2011). Emotion perception in context. *Current Directions in Psychological Science, 20,* 286–290.

Barrick, M. R., & Mount, M. K. (1996). Effects of impression management and self-deception on the predictive validity of personality constructs. *Journal of Applied Psychology, 81,* 261–272.

Barrick, M. R., Swider, B. W., & Stewart, G. L. (2010). Initial evaluations in the interview: Relationships with subsequent interviewer evaluations and employment offers. *Journal of Applied Psychology, 95,* 1163–1172.

Bartholow, B. D., & Heinz, A. (2006). Alcohol and aggression without consumption: Alcohol cues, aggressive thoughts, and hostile perception bias. *Psychological Science, 17,* 30–37.

Bartholow, B. D., Anderson, C. A., Carnagey, N. L., & Benjamin, A. J., Jr. (2005). Interactive effects of life experience and situational cues on aggression: The weapons priming effect in hunters and nonhunters. *Journal of Experimental Social Psychology, 41,* 48–60.

Bartholow, B. D., Dickter, C. L., & Sestir, M. A. (2006). Stereotype activation and control of race bias: Cognitive control of inhibition and its impairment by alcohol. *Journal of Personality and Social Psychology, 90,* 272–287.

Barthrop, R. W., Lazarus, L., Luckhurst, E., Kiloh, L. G., & Penny, R. (1977). Depressed lymphocyte function after bereavement. *Lancet, 1,* 834–839.

Bartlett, T. (2011). The fraud who fooled (almost) everyone. *The Chronicle of Higher Education,* November 3.

Bartlett, T. (2012). Is psychology about to come undone? *The Chronicle of Higher Education,* April 17.

Baruah, J., & Paulus, P. B. (2011). Category assignment and relatedness in the group ideation process. *Journal of Experimental Social Psychology, 47,* 1070–1077.

Bass, B. M. (1985). *Leadership and performance beyond expectations.* New York: Free Press.

Bass, B. M. (1998). *Transformational leadership: Industry, military, and educational impact.* Mahwah, NJ: Erlbaum.

Bass, B. M., & Avolio, B. J. (1990). *Manual: The multifactor leadership questionnaire.* Palo Alto, CA: Consulting Psychologists Press.

Bass, B. M., & Bass, R. (2008). *The Bass handbook of leadership: Theory, research, and managerial applications* (4th edition). New York: The Free Press.

Bass, B. M., & Riggio, R. E. (2006). *Transformational leadership* (2nd ed.). Mahwah, NJ: Erlbaum.

Bass, B. M., & Steidlmeier, P. (1999). Ethics, character, and the authentic transformational leadership behavior. *Leadership Quarterly, 10,* 181–217.

Bassili, J. N. (2003). The minority slowness effect: Subtle inhibitions in the expression of views not shared by others. *Journal of Personality and Social Psychology, 84,* 261–276.

Bassili, J. N., & Provencal, A. (1988). Perceiving minorities: A factor-analytic approach. *Personality and Social Psychology Bulletin, 14,* 5–15.

Bateson, M., Nettle, D., & Roberts, G. (2006). Cues of being watched enhance cooperation in a real-world setting. *Biology Letters, 2,* 412–414.

Batson v. Kentucky, 476 U.S. 79 (1986).

Batson, C. D. (1991). *The altruism question.* Hillsdale, NJ: Erlbaum.

Batson, C. D. (2009a). Empathy and altruism. In C. R. Snyder & S. J. Lopez (Eds.), *Oxford handbook of positive psychology* (2nd ed., pp. 417–426). New York: Oxford University Press.

Batson, C. D. (2009b). These things called empathy: Eight related but distinct phenomena. In J. Decety & W. Ickes (Eds.), *The social neuroscience of empathy* (pp. 3–15). Cambridge, MA: MIT.

Batson, C. D. (2011). *Empathy in humans.* New York: Oxford University Press.

Batson, C. D. (2012). A history of prosocial behavior research. In A. W. Kruglanski, & W. Stroebe (Eds.), *Handbook of the history of social psychology* (pp. 243–264). New York: Psychology Press.

Batson, C. D., & Powell, A. A. (2003). Altruism and prosocial behavior. In T. Millon & M. J. Lerner (Eds.), *Handbook of psychology: Personality and social psychology* (Vol. 5, pp. 463–484). New York: Wiley.

Batson, C. D., Ahmad, N., Powell, A. A., & Stocks, E. L. (2013). Prosocial motivation. In J. Shah & W. Gardner (Eds.), *Handbook of motivation science.* New York: Guilford.

Batson, C. D., Cochran, P. J., Biederman, M. F., Blosser, J. L., Ryan, M. J., & Vogt, B. (1978). Failure to help when in a hurry: Callousness or conflict? *Personality and* Batson, C. D., Lishner, D. A., Cook, J., & Sawyer, S. (2005). Similarity and nurturance: Two possible sources of empathy for strangers. *Basic and Applied Social Psychology, 27,* 15–25.

Batson, C. D., O'Quin, K., Fultz, J., Vanderplas, M., & Isen, A. M. (1983). Influence of self-reported distress and empathy on egoistic versus altruistic motivation to help. *Journal of Personality and Social Psychology, 45,* 706–718.

Batson, C., Ahmad, N., Powell, A. A., & Stocks, E. L. (2008). Prosocial motivation. In J. Y. Shah & W. L. Gardner (Eds.), *Handbook of motivation science* (pp. 135–149). New York: Guilford.

Bauer, I., Wrosch, C., & Jobin, J. (2008). I'm better off than most other people: The role of social comparisons for coping with regret in young adulthood and old age. *Psychology and Aging, 23,* 800–811.

Bauer, T. N., Maertz, C. P., Dolen, M. R., & Campion, M. A. (1998). Longitudinal assessment of applicant reactions to employment testing and test outcome feedback. *Journal of Applied Psychology, 83,* 892–903.

Baum, A. (Ed.). (1984). Social psychology and cigarette smoking [Special issue]. *Journal of Applied Social Psychology, 14*(3).

Baumeister, R. F. (1982). A self-presentational view of social phenomena. *Psychological Bulletin, 91,* 3–26.

Baumeister, R. F. (1984). Choking under pressure: Self-consciousness and paradoxical effects of incentives on skillful performance. *Journal of Personality and Social Psychology, 46,* 610–620.

Baumeister, R. F. (1991). *Escaping the self.* New York: Basic Books.

Baumeister, R. F. (2000). Gender differences in erotic plasticity: The female sex drive as socially flexible and responsive. *Psychological Bulletin, 126,* 347–374.

Baumeister, R. F. (2012). Self-control—The moral muscle. *The Psychologist, 25,* 112–115.

Baumeister, R. F., & Leary, M. R. (1995). The need to belong: Desire for interpersonal attachments as a fundamental human motivation. *Psychological Bulletin, 117,* 497–529.

Baumeister, R. F., & Scher, S. J. (1988). Self-defeating behavior patterns among normal individuals: Review and analysis of common self-destructive tendencies. *Psychological Bulletin, 104,* 3–22.

Baumeister, R. F., & Tice, D. M. (1984). Role of self-presentation and choice in cognitive dissonance under forced compliance: Necessary or sufficient causes? *Journal of Personality and Social Psychology, 46,* 5–13.

Baumeister, R. F., & Vohs, K. D. (Eds.). (2004). *Handbook of self-regulation: Research, theory, and applications*. New York: Guilford.

Baumeister, R. F., Bratslavsky, E., Finkenauer, C., & Vohs, K. D. (2001). Bad is stronger than good. *Review of General Psychology, 5*, 323–370.

Baumeister, R. F., Bushman, B. J., & Campbell, W. K. (2000). Self-esteem, narcissism, and aggression: Does violence result from low self-esteem or from threatened egotism? *Current Directions in Psychological Science, 9*, 26–29.

Baumeister, R. F., Campbell, J. D., Krueger, J. I., & Vohs, K. D. (2003). Does high self-esteem cause better performance, interpersonal success, happiness, or healthier lifestyles? *Psychological Science in the Public Interest, 4*, 1–44.

Baumeister, R. F., Chesner, S. P., Sanders, P. S., & Tice, D. M. (1988). Who's in charge here? Group leaders do lend help in emergencies. *Personality and Social Psychology Bulletin, 14*, 17–22.

Baumeister, R., Stillwell, A. M., & Hetherington, T. F. (1994). Guilt: An interpersonal approach. *Psychological Bulletin, 115*, 243–267.

Baumgartner, F. R., De Bouf, S. L., & Boydstun, A. E. (2008). *The decline of the death penalty and the discovery of innocence*. New York: Cambridge University Press.

Baumrind, D. (1997). Necessary distinctions. *Psychological Inquiry, 8*, 176–229.

Baxter, L. A. (1987). Self-disclosure and disengagement. In V. J. Derleg & J. H. Berg (Eds.), *Self-disclosure: Theory, research, and therapy* (pp. 155–174). New York: Plenum.

Bazerman, M. H., & Neale, M. A. (1992). *Negotiating rationally*. New York: Free Press.

Beal, D. J., Cohen, R. R., Burke, M. J., & McLendon, C. L. (2003, December). Cohesion and performance in groups: A meta-analytic clarification of construct relations. *Journal of Applied Psychology, 88*, 989–1004.

Beaman, A. L., Klentz, B., Diener, E., & Svanum, S. (1979). Objective self-awareness and transgression in children: A field study. *Journal of Personality and Social Psychology, 37*, 1835–1846.

Beaman, A., Barnes, P., Klentz, B., & McQuirk, B. (1978). Increasing helping rates through information dissemination: Teaching pays. *Personality and Social Psychology Bulletin, 4*, 406–411.

Beardsley, T. (1999, October). Truth or consequences. *Scientific American*, pp. 21, 24.

Beaton, E. A., Schmidt, L. A., Schulkin, J., Antony, M. M., Swinson, R. P., & Hall, G. B. (2008). Different neural responses to stranger and personally familiar faces in shy and bold adults. *Behavioral Neuroscience, 122*, 704–709.

Becker, J. C., & Swim, J. K. (2011). Seeing the unseen: Attention to daily encounters with sexism as way to reduce sexist beliefs. *Psychology of Women Quarterly, 35*, 227–242.

Becker, S. W., & Eagly, A. H. (2004). The heroism of women and men. *American Psychologist, 59*, 163–178.

Beckerman, S., & Valentine, P. (Eds.). (2002). *Cultures of multiple fathers: The theory and practice of partible paternity in lowland South America*. Gainesville: University Press of Florida.

Bedau, H., & Cassell, P. (Eds.). (2004). *Debating the death penalty: Should America have capital punishment?* New York: Oxford University Press.

Beedie, C. J., & Lane, A. M. (2012). The role of glucose in self-control: Another look at the evidence and an alternative conceptualization. *Personality and Social Psychology Review, 16*, 143–153.

Beer, J. S. (2012). This time with motivation: The implications of social neuroscience for research on motivated self- and other-perception (and vice versa). *Motivation and Emotion, 36*, 38–45.

Bègue, L., Subra, B., Arvers, P., Muller, D., Bricout, V., & Zorman, M. (2009). A message in a bottle: Extrapharmacological effects of alcohol on aggression. *Journal of Experimental Social Psychology, 45*, 137–142.

Beidel, D. C., & Turner, S. M. (1998). *Shy children, phobic adults: Nature and treatment of social phobia*. Washington, DC: American Psychological Association.

Beilock, S. L., & Carr, T. H. (2001). On the fragility of skilled performance: What governs choking under pressure? *Journal of Experimental Psychology: General, 130*, 701–725.

Bell, A. P., Weinberg, M. S., & Hammersmith, S. K. (1981). *Sexual preference: Its development in men and women*. Bloomington: Indiana University Press.

Bell, D. C. (2001). Evolution of parental caregiving. *Personality and Social Psychology Review, 5*, 216–229.

Bell, J., Grekul, J., Lamba, N., Minas, C., & Harrell, W. A. (1995). The impact of cost on student helping behavior. *Journal of Social Psychology, 135*, 49–56.

Belmore, S. M. (1987). Determinants of attention during impression formation. *Journal of Experimental Psychology: Learning, Memory, and Cognition, 13*, 480–489.

Bem, D. J. (1965). An experimental analysis of self-persuasion. *Journal of Experimental Social Psychology, 1*, 199–218.

Bem, D. J. (1967). Self-perception: An alternative interpretation of cognitive dissonance phenomena. *Psychological Review, 74*, 183–200.

Bem, D. J. (1996). Exotic becomes erotic: A developmental theory of sexual orientation. *Psychological Review, 103*, 320–335.

Bem, D. J. (2000). Exotic becomes erotic: Interpreting the biological correlates of sexual orientation. *Archives of Sexual Behavior, 29*, 531–548.

Bem, D. J. (2011). Feeling the future: Experimental evidence for anomalous retroactive influences on cognition and affect. *Journal of Personality and Social Psychology, 100*, 407–425.

Ben-Ami Bartal, I., Decety, J., & Mason, P. (2011). Empathy and pro-social behavior in rats. *Science, 334*, 1427–1439.

Ben-Shakhar, G., & Elaad, E. (2003). The validity of psychophysiological detection of information with the Guilty Knowledge Test: a meta-analytic review. *Journal of Applied Psychology, 88*, 131–151.

Ben-Zeev, T., Fein, S., & Inzlicht, M. (2005). Arousal and stereotype threat. *Journal of Experimental Social Psychology, 41*, 174–181.

Benjamin, L. T., & Simpson, J. A. (2009). The power of the situation: The impact of Milgram's obedience studies on personality and social psychology. *American Psychologist, 64*, 12–19.

Benjet, C., & Kazdin, A. E. (2003). Spanking children: The controversies, findings and new directions. *Clinical Psychology Review, 23*, 197–224.

Bennett, S., Farrington, D. P., & Huesmann, L. R. (2005). Explaining gender differences in crime and violence: The importance of social cognitive skills. *Aggression and Violent Behavior, 10*, 263–288.

Benson, H. (1993). The relaxation response. In D. Goleman & J. Gurin (Eds.), *Mind body medicine: How to use your mind for better health* (pp. 233–257). Yonkers, NY: Consumer Reports Books.

Benson, P. L., Karabenick, S. A., & Lerner, R. M. (1976). Pretty pleases: The effects of physical attractiveness, race, and sex on receiving help. *Journal of Experimental Social Psychology, 12*, 409–415.

Benton, R. B., Ross, D. F., Bradshaw, E., Thomas, W. N., & Bradshaw, G. S. (2005). Eyewitness memory is still not common sense: Comparing jurors, judges, and law enforcement to eyewitness experts. *Applied Cognitive Psychology, 20*, 115–129.

Berdahl, J. L., & Anderson, C. (2005). Men, women, and leadership centralization in groups over time. *Group Dynamics: Theory, Research, and Practice, 9*, 45–57.

Berg, J. H., & McQuinn, R. D. (1986). Attraction and exchange in continuing and noncontinuing dating relationships. *Journal of Personality and Social Psychology, 50*, 942–952.

Berglas, S., & Jones, E. E. (1978). Drug choice as a self-handicapping strategy in response to noncontingent success. *Journal of Personality and Social Psychology, 36*, 405–417.

Berkman, L., & Syme, S. L. (1979). Social networks, host resistance, and mortality: A nine-year follow-up study of Alameda County residents. *American Journal of Epidemiology, 109*, 186–204.

Berkowitz, L. (1968). Impulse, aggression, and the gun. *Psychology Today, 2*(4), 18–22.

Berkowitz, L. (1993). *Aggression: Its causes, consequences, and control*. New York: McGraw-Hill.

Berkowitz, L. (1998). Affective aggression: The role of stress, pain, and negative affect. In R. G. Geen & E. Donnerstein (Eds.), *Human aggression: Theories, research, and implications for social policy* (pp. 49–72). San Diego: Academic Press.

Berkowitz, L. (2008). On the consideration of automatic as well as controlled psychological processes in aggression. *Aggressive Behavior, 34,* 117–129.

Berkowitz, L., & Donnerstein, E. (1982). External validity is more than skin deep: Some answers to criticisms of laboratory experiments. *American Psychologist, 37,* 245–257.

Berkowitz, L., & LePage, A. (1967). Weapons as aggression-eliciting stimuli. *Journal of Personality and Social Psychology, 7,* 202–207.

Bermeitinger, C., Goelz, R., Johr, N., Neumann, M., Ecker, U., & Doerr, R. (2009). The hidden persuaders break into the tired brain. *Journal of Experimental Social Psychology, 45,* 320–326.

Bernardin, H. J., Cooke, D. K., & Villanova, P. (2000). Conscientiousness and agreeableness as predictors of rating leniency. *Journal of Applied Psychology, 85,* 232–236.

Bernhard, H., Fischbacher, U., & Fehr, E. (2006). Parochial altruism in humans. *Nature, 442,* 912–915.

Berns, G. S., Chappelow, J., Zink, C. F., Pagnoni, G., Martin-Skurski, M. E., & Richards, J. (2005). Neurobiological correlates of social conformity and independence during mental rotation. *Biological Psychiatry, 58,* 245–253.

Bernstein, M. J., & Claypool, H. M. (2012). Social exclusion and pain sensitivity: Why exclusion sometimes hurts and sometimes numbs. *Personality and Social Psychology Bulletin, 38,* 185–196.

Bernstein, M. J., Young, S. G., Brown, C. M., Sacco, D. F., & Claypool, H. M. (2008). Adaptive responses to social exclusion: Social rejection improves detection of real and fake smiles. *Psychological Science, 19,* 981–983.

Bernsten, D. (2009). *Involuntary autobiographical memories: An introduction to the unbidden past.* New York: Cambridge University Press.

Berry, C. M., Sackett, P. R., & Wiemann, S. (2007). A review of recent developments in integrity test research. *Personnel Psychology, 60,* 271–301.

Berry, D. S., & Zebrowitz-McArthur, L. (1986). Perceiving character in faces: The impact of age-related craniofacial changes in social perception. *Psychological Bulletin, 100,* 3–18.

Berry, J. W. (1979). A cultural ecology of social behavior. *Advances in Experimental Social Psychology, 12,* 177–206.

Berry, J. W., Poortinga, Y. H., Segall, M. H., & Dasen, P. R. (1992). *Cross-cultural psychology: Research and application.* Cambridge: Cambridge University Press.

Berscheid, E. (1966). Opinion change and communicator-communicatee similarity and dissimilarity. *Journal of Personality and Social Psychology, 4,* 670–680.

Berscheid, E. (2010). Love in the fourth dimension. *Annual Review of Psychology, 61,* 1–25.

Berscheid, E., & Meyers, S. A. (1996). A social categorical approach to a question about love. *Personal Relationships, 3,* 19–43.

Berscheid, E., & Regan, P. (2004). *The psychology of interpersonal relationships.* Upper Saddle River, NJ: Prentice-Hall.

Berscheid, E., & Reis, H. T. (1998). Attraction and close relationships. In D. Gilbert, S. Fiske, & G. Lindzey (Eds.), *Handbook of social psychology* (4th ed.). New York: McGraw-Hill.

Berscheid, E., & Walster, E. (1974). A little bit about love. In T. Huston (Ed.), *Foundations of interpersonal attraction* (pp. 355–381). New York: Academic Press.

Berscheid, E., Dion, K., Walster, E., & Walster, G. W. (1971). Physical attractiveness and dating choice: A test of the matching hypothesis. *Journal of Experimental Social Psychology, 7,* 173–189.

Berscheid, E., Snyder, M., & Omoto, A. M. (1989). The relationship closeness inventory: Assessing the closeness of interpersonal relationships. *Journal of Personality and Social Psychology, 57,* 792–807.

Berscheid, E., Walster, E., & Campbell, R. (1972). *Grow old along with me.* Unpublished manuscript, Department of Psychology, University of Minnesota.

Bersoff, D. N., & Ogden, D. W. (1987). In the Supreme Court of the United States: *Lockhart v. McCree. American Psychologist, 42,* 59–68.

Bessenoff, G. R. (2006). Can the media affect us? Social comparison, self-discrepancy, and the thin ideal. *Psychology of Women Quarterly, 30,* 239–251.

Bettencourt, B. A., & Dorr, N. (1998). Cooperative interaction and intergroup bias: Effects of numerical representation and cross-cut role assignment. *Personality and Social Psychology Bulletin, 24,* 1276–1293.

Bettencourt, B. A., Molix, L., Talley, A. E., Sheldon, K. M. (2006). Psychological need satisfaction through social roles. In T. Postmes & J. Jetten (Eds.), *Individuality and the group: Advances in social identity* (pp. 196–214). Thousand Oaks, CA: Sage.

Bettencourt, B. A., Talley, A., Benjamin, A. J., & Valentine, J. (2006). Personality and aggressive behavior under provoking and neutral conditions: A meta-analytic review. *Psychological Bulletin, 132,* 751–777.

Betts, L., & Hartley, J. (2012). The effects of changes in the order of verbal labels and numerical values on children's scores on attitude and rating scales. *British Educational Research Journal, 38,* 319–331.

Beu, D. S., & Buckley, M. R. (2004). This is war: How the politically astute achieve crimes of obedience through the use of moral disengagement. *Leadership Quarterly, 15,* 551–568.

Beyer, S. (1990). Gender differences in the accuracy of self-evaluations of performance. *Journal of Personality and Social Psychology, 59,* 960–970.

Bezdjian, S., Tuvblad, C., Raine, A., & Baker, L. A. (2011). The genetic and environmental covariation among psychopathic personality traits, and reactive and proactive aggression in childhood. *Child Development, 82,* 1267–1281.

Bhatt, S., Mbwana, J., Adeyemo, A., Sawyer, A., Hailu, A., & VanMeter, J. (2009). Lying about facial recognition: An fMRI study. *Brain and Cognition, 69,* 382–390.

Bickman, L. (1974). The social power of a uniform. *Journal of Applied Social Psychology, 4,* 47–61.

Biesanz, J. C. Human, L. J. (2010). The cost of forming more accurate impressions: Accuracy motivated perceivers see the personality of others more distinctively but less normatively. *Psychological Science, 21,* 589–594.

Bijleveld, E., Scheepers, D., & Ellemers, N. (2012). The cortisol response to anticipated intergroup interactions predicts self-reported prejudice. *Plos ONE, 7,* 0033681.

Birkett, M., Espelage, D. L., & Koenig, B. (2009). LGB and questioning students in schools: The moderating effects of homophobic bullying and school climate on negative outcomes. *Journal of Youth and Adolescence, 38,* 989–1000.

Bishara, A. J., & Payne, B. K. (2009). Multinomial process tree models of control and automaticity in weapon misidentification. *Journal of Experimental Social Psychology, 45,* 524–534.

Bizer, G., Krosnick, J., Holbrook, A., Wheeler, S., Rucker, D., & Petty, R. E. (2004). The impact of personality on cognitive, behavioral, and affective political processes: The effects of need to evaluate. *Journal of Personality, 72,* 995–1027.

Blair, I. V., Park, B., & Bachelor, J. (2003). Understanding intergroup anxiety: Are some people more anxious than others? *Group Processes and Intergroup Relations, 6,* 151–169.

Blanchard, A. L., & Henle, C. A. (2008). Correlates of different forms of cyberloafing: The role of norms and external locus of control. *Computers in Human Behavior, 24,* 1067–1084.

Blanchard, B. (2011). Chinese girl dies in hit-and-run that sparked outrage. *Reuters,* October 21.

Blandon-Gitlin, I., Sperry, K., & Leo, R. A. (2010). Jurors believe interrogation tactics are not likely to elicit false confessions: Will expert witness testimony inform them otherwise? *Psychology, Crime, & Law, 17,* 239–260.

Blank, H., Ziegler, R., & de Bloom, J. (2012). Self-monitoring and linguistic adaptation. *Social Psychology, 43,* 67–80.

Blanton, H., & Jaccard, J. (2006). Arbitrary metrics in psychology. *American Psychologist, 61,* 27–41.

Blanton, H., & Jaccard, J. (2008). Unconscious racism: A concept in pursuit of a measure. *Annual Review of Sociology, 34,* 277–297.

Blanton, H., Jaccard, J., Gonzales, P. M., & Christie, C. (2006). Decoding the implicit association test: Implications for criterion prediction. *Journal of Experimental Social Psychology, 42,* 192–212.

Blanton, H., Jaccard, J., Klick, J., Mellers, B., Mitchell, G., & Tetlock, P. E. (2009). Strong claims and weak evidence: Reassessing the predictive validity of the IAT. *Journal of Applied Psychology, 94*, 567–582.

Blascovich, J., & McCall, C. (2010). Attitudes in virtual reality. In J. P. Forgas, J. Cooper, & W. D. Crano (Eds.), *The psychology of attitudes and attitude change* (pp. 283–297). New York: Psychology Press.

Blass, T. (1991). Understanding behavior in the Milgram obedience experiment: The role of personality, situations, and their interactions. *Journal of Personality and Social Psychology, 60*, 398–413.

Blass, T. (1992). The social psychology of Stanley Milgram. *Advances in Experimental Social Psychology, 25*, 227–329.

Blass, T. (1999). The Milgram paradigm after 35 years: Some things we now know about obedience to authority. *Journal of Applied Social Psychology, 25*, 955–978.

Blass, T. (2004). *The man who shocked the world.* New York: Basic Books.

Blass, T. (2009). From New Haven to Santa Clara: A historical perspective on the Milgram obedience experiments. *American Psychologist, 64*, 37–45.

Blass, T. (2012). A cross-cultural comparison of studies of obedience using the Milgram paradigm: A review. *Social and Personality Psychology Compass, 6*, 196–205.

Bleich, A., Gelkopf, M., & Solomon, Z. (2003). Exposure to terrorism, stress-related mental health symptoms, and coping behaviors among a nationally representative sample in Israel. *Journal of the American Medical Association, 290*, 612–620.

Bloom, A. (1981). *The linguistic shaping of thought.* Hillsdale, NJ: Erlbaum.

Bobocel, D. R., Son Hing, L. S., Davey, L. M., Stanley, D. J., & Zanna, M. P. (1998). Justice-based opposition to social policies: Is it genuine? *Journal of Personality and Social Psychology, 75*, 653–669.

Bochner, S., & Insko, C. A. (1966). Communicator discrepancy, source credibility, and opinion change. *Journal of Personality and Social Psychology, 4*, 614–621.

Bodenhausen, G. V. (1990). Stereotypes as judgmental heuristics: Evidence of circadian variations in discrimination. *Psychological Science, 1*, 319–322.

Bogart, L. M., & Helgeson, V. S. (2000). Social comparisons among women with breast cancer: A longitudinal investigation. *Journal of Applied Social Psychology, 30*, 547–575.

Bohner, G., & Dickel, N. (2011). Attitudes and attitude change. *Annual Review of Psychology, 62*, 391–417.

Boldero, J., & Francis, J. (2000). The relation between self-discrepancies and emotion: The moderating roles of self-guide importance, location relevance, and social self-domain centrality. *Journal of Personality and Social Psychology, 78*, 38–52.

Boldizar, J. P., Perry, D. G., & Perry, L. (1989). Outcome values and aggression. *Child Development, 60*, 571–579.

Bolger, N., DeLongis, A., Kessler, R. C., & Schilling, E. A. (1989). Effects of daily stress and negative mood. *Journal of Personality and Social Psychology, 57*, 808–818.

Bonanno, G. A. (2004). Loss, trauma, and human resilience: Have we underestimated the human capacity to thrive after extremely aversive events? *American Psychologist, 59*, 20–28.

Bond, C. F., Jr., & Titus, L. T. (1983). Social facilitation: A metaanalysis of 241 studies. *Psychological Bulletin, 94*, 265–292.

Bond, C., & DePaulo, B. (2006). Accuracy of deception judgments. *Personality and Social Psychology Review, 10*, 214–234.

Bond, R., & Smith, P. B. (1996). Culture and conformity: A metaanalysis of studies using Asch's (1952b, 1956) line judgment task. *Psychological Bulletin, 119*, 111–137.

Boninger, D. S., Brock, T. C., Cook, T. D., Gruder, C. L., & Romer, D. (1990). Discovery of reliable attitude change persistence resulting from a transmitter tuning set. *Psychological Science, 1*, 268–271.

Boninger, D. S., Krosnick, J. A., & Berent, M. K. (1995). Origins of attitude importance: Self-interest, social identification, and value relevance. *Journal of Personality and Social Psychology, 68*, 61–80.

Bono, J. E., & Anderson, M. H. (2005). The advice and influence networks of transformational leaders. *Journal of Applied Psychology, 90*, 1306–1314.

Bono, J. E., & Judge, T. A. (2004). Personality and transformational and transactional leadership: A meta-analysis. *Journal of Applied Psychology, 89*, 901–910.

Bonta, B. D. (1997). Cooperation and competition in peaceful societies. *Psychological Bulletin, 121*, 299–320.

Bonta, B. D., & Fry, D. P. (2006). Lessons for the rest of us: Learning from peaceful societies. In M. Fitzduff & C. Stout (Eds.), *The psychology of resolving global conflicts: From war to peace: Vol. 1. Nature vs. nurture* (pp. 175–210). Westport, CT: Praeger.

Book, A. S., Starzyk, K. B., & Qunisey, V. L. (2001). The relationship between testosterone and aggression: A meta-analysis. *Aggression and Violent Behavior, 6*, 579–599.

Borders, A., & Giancola, P. R. (2011). Trait and state hostile rumination facilitate alcohol-related aggression. *Journal of Studies on Alcohol and Drugs, 72*, 545–554.

Borduin, C. M., Schaeffer, C. M., & Heiblum, N. (2009). A randomized clinical trial of multisystemic therapy with juvenile sexual offenders: Effects on youth social ecology and criminal activity. *Journal of Consulting and Clinical Psychology, 77*, 26–37.

Borgida, E., & Fiske, S. T. (Eds.). (2007). *Psychological science in court: Beyond common knowledge.* Oxford, UK: Blackwell.

Borkenau, P., Mauer, N., Riemann, R., Spinath, F. M., & Angleitner, A. (2004). Thin slices of behavior as cues of personality and intelligence. *Journal of Personality and Social Psychology, 86*, 599–614.

Borman, W. C., Hanson, M. A., & Hedge, J. W. (1997). Personnel selection. *Annual Review of Psychology, 48*, 299–337.

Borman, W. C., White, L. A., & Dorsey, D. W. (1995). Effects of ratee task performance and interpersonal factors on supervisor and peer performance ratings. *Journal of Applied Psychology, 80*, 168–177.

Bornman, E. (2010). Emerging patterns of social identification in post-apartheid South Africa. *Journal of Social Issues, 66*, 237–254.

Bornstein, B. H., & Greene, E. (2011). Jury decision making: Implications for and from psychology. *Current Directions in Psychological Science, 20*, 63–67.

Bornstein, B. H., Wiener, R. L., Schopp, R., & Willborn, S. L. (Eds.). (2008). *Civil juries and civil justice: Psychological and legal perspectives.* New York: Springer.

Bornstein, R. F. (1989). Exposure and affect: Overview and metaanalysis of research, 1968–1987. *Psychological Bulletin, 106*, 265–289.

Bornstein, R. F., & D'Agostino, P. R. (1992). Stimulus recognition and the mere exposure effect. *Journal of Personality and Social Psychology, 63*, 545–552.

Borntrager, C., Davis, J. L., Bernstein, A., & Gorman, H. (2009). A cross-national perspective on bullying. *Child and Youth Care Forum, 38*, 121–134.

Bosson, J. K., & Swann, W. B. Jr. (2009). Self-esteem. In M. R. Leary, R. H. Hoyle (Eds.), *Handbook of individual differences in social behavior* (pp. 527–546). New York: Guilford.

Bosson, J. K., & Vandello, J. A. (2011). Precarious manhood and its links to action and aggression. *Current Directions in Psychological Science, 20*, 82–86.

Bosson, J. K., Johnson, A. B., Niederhoffer, K., & Swann, W. B., Jr. (2006). Interpersonal chemistry through negativity: Bonding by sharing negative attitudes about others. *Personal Relationships, 13*, 135–150.

Boswell, W. R., Shipp, A. J., Payne, S. C., & Culbertson, S. S. (2009). Changes in newcomer job satisfaction over time: Examining the pattern of honeymoons and hangovers. *Journal of Applied Psychology, 94*, 844–858.

Bottoms, B. L., & Davis, S. L. (1997). The creation of satanic ritual abuse. *Journal of Social and Clinical Psychology, 16*, 112–132.

Boucher, H. C., Peng, K., Shi, J., & Wang, L. (2009). Culture and implicit self-esteem: Chinese are 'good' and 'bad' at the same time. *Journal of Cross-Cultural Psychology, 40*, 24–45.

Boutwell, B. B., Franklin, C. A., Barnes, J. C., & Beaver, K. M. (2011). Physical punishment and childhood aggression: The role of gender and gene–environment interplay. *Aggressive Behavior, 37*, 559–568.

Bowlby, J. (1988). *A secure base.* New York: Basic Books.

Boysen, S. T., & Himes, G. T. (1999). Current issues and emerging theories in animal cognition. *Annual Review of Psychology, 50*, 683–705.

Bradbury, T. N. (Ed.). (1998). *The developmental course of marital dysfunction.* New York: Cambridge University Press.

Bradbury, T. N., & Fincham, F. D. (1992). Attributions and behavior in marital interaction. *Journal of Personality and Social Psychology, 63*, 613–628.

Brader, T. (2006). *Campaigning for hearts and minds: How emotional appeals in political ads work.* Chicago: University of Chicago Press.

Bradfield, A. L., Wells, G. L., & Olson, E. A. (2002). The damaging effect of confirming feedback on the relation between eyewitness certainty and identification accuracy. *Journal of Applied Psychology, 87*, 112–120.

Bradley, K. I., & Kennison, S. M. (2012). The effect of mortality salience on weapon bias. *International Journal of Intercultural Relations, 36*, 403–408.

Brauchli, R., Bauer, G. F., & Hämmig, O. (2011). Relationship between time-based work-life conflict and burnout: A cross-sectional study among employees in four large Swiss enterprises. *Swiss Journal of Psychology/Schweizerische Zeitschrift Für Psychologie/Revue Suisse De Psychologie, 70*, 165–173.

Brauer, M., & Er-rafiy, A. (2011). Increasing perceived variability reduces prejudice and discrimination. *Journal of Experimental Social Psychology, 47*, 871–881.

Brauer, M., Er-rafiy, A., Kawakami, K., & Phills, C. E. (2012). Describing a group in positive terms reduces prejudice less effectively than describing it in positive and negative terms. *Journal of Experimental Social Psychology, 48*, 757–761.

Bray, R. M., Johnson, D., & Chilstrom, J. T., Jr. (1982). Social influence by group members with minority opinions: A comparison of Hollander & Moscovici. *Journal of Personality and Social Psychology, 43*, 78–88.

Bray, R. M., Struckman-Johnson, C., Osborne, M., McFarlane, J., & Scott, J. (1978). The effects of defendant status on decisions of student and community juries. *Social Psychology, 41*, 256–260.

Brean, H. (1958, March 31). What hidden sell is all about. *Life,* pp. 104–114.

Brehm, J. W. (1956). Post-decision changes in desirability of alternatives. *Journal of Abnormal and Social Psychology, 52*, 384–389.

Brehm, S. S., & Brehm, J. W. (1981). *Psychological reactance: A theory of freedom and control.* New York: Academic Press.

Brendgen, M., Dionne, G., Girard, A., Boivin, M., Vitaro, F., & Pérusse, D. (2005). Examining genetic and environmental effects on social aggression: A study of 6-year-old twins. *Child Development, 76*, 930–946.

Brescoll, V. L., Dawson, E., & Uhlmann, E. (2010). Hard won and easily lost: The fragile status of leaders in gender-stereotype-incongruent occupations. *Psychological Science, 21*, 1640–1642.

Bressan, P., & Martello, M. F. D. (2002). Talis Pater, Talis Filius: Perceived resemblance and the belief in genetic relatedness. *Psychological Science, 13*, 213–218.

Brett, J. M., & Gelfand, M. (2006). A cultural analysis of the underlying assumptions of negotiation theory. In L. L. Thompson (Ed.), *Negotiation theory and research* (pp. 173–201). Madison, CT: Psychological Press.

Brett, J. M., Shapiro, D. L., & Lytle, A. L. (1998). Breaking the bonds of reciprocity in negotiations. *Academy of Management Journal, 41*, 410–424.

Brewer, M. B., & Caporael, L. R. (2006). An evolutionary perspective on social identity: Revisiting groups. In M. Schaller (Ed.), *Evolution and social psychology* (pp. 143–161). Madison, CT: Psychosocial Press.

Brewer, M. B., & Feinstein, A. S. H. (1999). Dual processes in the cognitive representation of persons and social categories. In S. Chaiken & Y. Trope (Eds.), *Dual-process theories in social psychology* (pp. 255–270). New York: Guilford.

Brewer, M. B., & Gaertner, S. L. (2004). Toward reduction of prejudice: Intergroup contact and social categorization. In M. B. Brewer & M. Hewstone (Eds.), *Self and social identity* (pp. 298–318). Malden, MA: Blackwell.

Brewer, N., & Wells, G. L. (2011). Eyewitness identification. *Current Directions in Psychological Science, 20*, 24–27.

Brewer, N., Harvey, S., & Semmler, C. (2004). Improving comprehension of jury instructions with audio-visual presentation. *Applied Cognitive Psychology, 18*, 765–776.

Brickman, P., Coates, D., & Janoff-Bulman, R. J. (1978). Lottery winners and accident victims: Is happiness relative? *Journal of Personality and Social Psychology, 36*, 917–927.

Briñol , P. Petty , R. E. (2009). Persuasion: Insights from the self-validation hypothesis. *Advances in Experimental Social Psychology, 41*, 69–118.

Briñol, P., & Petty , R. (2003). Overt head movements and persuasion: A self-validation analysis. *Journal of Personality and Social Psychology, 84*, 1123–1139.

Briñol, P., Petty, R. E. & Wagner, B. C. (2011). Embodied attitude change: A self validation perspective. *Social and Personality Psychology Compass, 5*, 1039 1050.

Brochu, P. M., & Esses, V. M. (2011). What's in a name? The effects of the labels "fat" versus "overweight" on weight bias. *Journal of Applied Social Psychology, 41*, 1981–2008.

Brockner, J. (1983). Low self-esteem and behavioral plasticity: Some implications. In L. Wheeler & P. Shaver (Eds.), *Review of personality and social psychology* (Vol. 4, pp. 237–271). Beverly Hills, CA: Sage.

Brockner, J., & Wiesenfeld, B. M. (1996). An integrative frame-work for explaining reactions to decisions: Interactive effects of outcomes and procedures. *Psychological Bulletin, 120*, 189–208.

Brodish, A. B., Cogburn, C. D., Fuller-Rowell, T. E., Peck, S., Malanchuk, O., & Eccles, J. S. (2011). Perceived racial discrimination as a predictor of health behaviors: The moderating role of gender. *Race and Social Problems, 3*, 160–169.

Brody, G. H., Kogan, S. M., & Chen, Y. (2012). Perceived discrimination and longitudinal increases in adolescent substance use: Gender differences in mediational pathways. *American Journal of Public Health, 102*, 1006–1011.

Broesch, T., Callaghan, T., Henrich, J., Murphy, C., & Rochat, P. (2011). Cultural variations in children's mirror self-recognition. *Journal of Cross-Cultural Psychology, 42*, 1018–1029.

Bronfenbrenner, U. (1961). The mirror-image in Soviet-American relations. *Journal of Social Issues, 17*, 45–56.

Brooks, R., & Meltzoff, A. N. (2002). The importance of eyes: How infants interpret adult looking behavior. *Developmental Psychology, 38*, 958–966.

Brown, E., Deffenbacher, K., & Sturgill, W. (1977). Memory for faces and the circumstances of encounter. *Journal of Applied Psychology, 62*, 311–318.

Brown, J. D. (2003). The self-enhancement motive in collectivistic cultures: The rumors of my death have been greatly exaggerated. *Journal of Cross-Cultural Psychology, 34*, 603–605.

Brown, J. D. (2012). Understanding the better than average effect: Motives (still) matter. *Personality and Social Psychology Bulletin, 38*, 209–219.

Brown, J. D., & Dutton, K. A. (1995). The thrill of victory, the complexity of defeat: Self-esteem and people's emotional reactions to success and failure. *Journal of Personality and Social Psychology, 68*, 712–722.

Brown, J. M. (2003). Eyewitness memory for arousing events: Putting things into context. *Applied Cognitive Psychology, 17*, 93–106.

Brown, P. (2012). Bilic rages at his racist fans. *The Express,* June 18, p. 58.

Brown, R. (1986). *Social psychology* (2nd ed.). New York: Free Press.

Brown, R. A. (2010). Perceptions of psychological adjustment, achievement outcomes, and self-esteem in Japan and America. *Journal of Cross-Cultural Psychology, 31*, 51–61.

Brown, R. P., Osterman, L. L., & Barnes, C. D. (2009). School violence and the culture of honor. *Psychological Science, 20*, 1400–1405.

Brown, R., & Kulik, J. (1977). Flashbulb memories. *Cognition, 5*, 73–99.

Brown, W. A. (1998, January). The placebo effect. *Scientific American,* pp. 90–95.

Brownstein, A., Read, S. J., & Simon, D. (2004). Bias at the racetrack: Effects of individual expertise and task importance on predecision reevaluation of alternatives. *Personality and Social Psychology Bulletin, 30*, 891–904.

Bruch, M. A., Gorsky, J. M., Collins, T. M., & Berger, P. A. (1989). Shyness and sociability examined: A multicomponent analysis. *Journal of Personality and Social Psychology, 57*, 904–915.

Bruck, M., & Ceci, S. J. (1999). The suggestibility of children's memory. *Annual Review of Psychology, 50*, 419–439.

Bruner, J. S., & Potter, M. C. (1964). Interference in visual recognition. *Science, 144,* 424–425.

Bruner, J. S., & Tagiuri, R. (1954). Person perception. In G. Lindzey (Ed.), *Handbook of social psychology* (Vol. 2, pp. 634–654). Reading, MA: Addison-Wesley.

Buckhout, R. (1974, December). Eyewitness testimony. *Scientific American,* pp. 23–31.

Bucolo, D.O., & Cohn, E.S. (2010). Playing the race card: Making race salient in defense opening and closing statements. *Legal and Criminological Psychology, 15,* 293–303.

Buhrmester, M., Kwang, T., & Gosling, S. D. (2011). Amazon's Mechanical Turk: A new source of inexpensive, yet high-quality, data? *Perspectives on Psychological Science, 6,* 3–5.

Buhs, E. S., Ladd, G. W., & Herald-Brown, S. L. (2010). Victimization and exclusion: Links to peer rejection, classroom engagement, and achievement. In S. R. Jimerson, S. M. Swearer, & D. L. Espelage (Eds.), *Handbook of bullying in schools: An international perspective* (pp. 163–172). New York: Routledge/Taylor & Francis.

Buhs, E. S., Ladd, G. W., & Herald, S. L. (2006). Peer exclusion and victimization: Processes that mediate the relation between peer group rejection and children's classroom engagement and achievement. *Journal of Educational Psychology, 98,* 1–13.

Burger, J. M. (1986). Increasing compliance by improving the deal: The that's-not-all technique. *Journal of Personality and Social Psychology, 51,* 277–283.

Burger, J. M. (1999). The foot-in-the-door compliance procedure: A multiple-process analysis and review. *Personality and Social Psychology Review, 3,* 303–325.

Burger, J. M. (2009). Replicating Milgram: Would people still obey today? *American Psychologist, 64,* 1–11.

Burger, J. M., & Caldwell, D. F. (2003). The effects of monetary incentives and labeling on the foot-in-the-door effect: Evidence for a self-perception process. *Basic and Applied Social Psychology, 25,* 235–241.

Burger, J. M., & Cornelius, T. (2003). Raising the price of agreement: Public commitment and the low-ball compliance procedure. *Journal of Applied Social Psychology, 33,* 923–934.

Burger, J. M., & Petty, R. E. (1981). The low-ball compliance technique: Task or person commitment? *Journal of Personality and Social Psychology, 40,* 492–500.

Burger, J. M., Horita, M., Kinoshita, L., Roberts, K., & Vera, C. (1997). Effects of time on the norm of reciprocity. *Basic and Applied Social Psychology, 19,* 91–100.

Burger, J. M., Messian, N., Patel, S., del Prado, A., & Anderson, C. (2004). What a coincidence! The effects of incidental similarity on compliance. *Personality and Social Psychology Bulletin, 30,* 35–43.

Burleigh, N. (2011). *The fatal gift of beauty: The trials of Amanda Knox.* New York: Broadway Books.

Burn, S. (2009). A situational model of sexual assault prevention through bystander intervention. *Sex Roles, 60,* 779–792.

Burns, J. M. (1978). *Leadership.* New York: Harper & Row.

Burns, J. M. (2003). *Transformational leadership.* New York: Atlantic Monthly Press.

Burns, S. (2011). *The Central Park Five: A Chronicle of a City Wilding.* New York: Knopf.

Burnstein, E., & Schul, Y. (1982). The informational basis of social judgments: The operations in forming an impression of another person. *Journal of Experimental Social Psychology, 18,* 217–234.

Burnstein, E., Crandall, C., & Kitayama, S. (1994). Some neo-Darwinian decision rules for altruism: Weighing cues for inclusive fitness as a function of the biological importance of the decision. *Journal of Personality and Social Psychology, 67,* 773–789.

Burt, M. C. (1980). Cultural myths and supports for rape. *Journal of Personality and Social Psychology, 38,* 217–230.

Bushman, B. J. (1988). The effects of apparel on compliance: A field experiment with a female authority figure. *Personality and Social Psychology Bulletin, 14,* 459–467.

Bushman, B. J. (1996). Individual differences in the extent and development of aggressive cognitive-associative networks. *Personality and Social Psychology Bulletin, 22,* 811–819.

Bushman, B. J. (1998). Priming effects of violent media on the accessibility of aggressive constructs in memory. *Personality and Social Psychology Bulletin, 24,* 537–545.

Bushman, B. J. (2002). Does venting anger feed or extinguish the flame? Catharsis, rumination, distraction, anger, and aggressive responding. *Personality and Social Psychology Bulletin, 28,* 724–731.

Bushman, B. J., & Anderson, C. A. (2009). Comfortably numb: Desensitizing effects of violent media on helping others. *Psychological Science, 20,* 273–277.

Bushman, B. J., & Huesmann, L. (2010). Aggression. In S. T. Fiske, D. T. Gilbert, & G. Lindzey (Eds.), *Handbook of social psychology* (5th ed., Vol. 2, pp. 833–863). Hoboken, NJ: Wiley.

Bushman, B. J., Baumeister, R. F., Thomaes, S., Ryu, E., Begeer, S., & West, S. G. (2009). Looking again, and harder, for a link between low self-esteem and aggression. *Journal of Personality, 77,* 427–446.

Bushman, B. J., Giancola, P. R., Parrott, D. J., & Roth, R. M. (2012). Failure to consider future consequences increases the effects of alcohol on aggression. *Journal of Experimental Social Psychology, 48,* 591–595.

Bushman, B. J., Wang, M. C., & Anderson, C. A. (2005). Is the curve relating temperature to aggression linear or curvilinear? Assaults and temperature in Minneapolis reexamined. *Journal of Personality and Social Psychology, 89,* 62–66.

Buss, A. H. (1980). *Self-consciousness and social anxiety.* San Francisco: Freeman.

Buss, D. (2011). *Evolutionary psychology: The new science of the mind* (4th edition).New York: Prentice-Hall.

Buss, D. M. (1989). Sex differences in human mate preferences: Evolutionary hypotheses tested in 37 cultures. *Behavioral and Brain Sciences, 12,* 1–14.

Buss, D. M. (2000). *The dangerous passion: Why jealousy is as necessary as love and sex.* New York: Free Press.

Buss, D. M. (2003). *The evolution of desire: Strategies of human mating* (rev. ed.). New York: Basic Books.

Buss, D. M. (2012). *Evolutionary psychology: The new science of the mind* (4th ed.). Boston: Allyn & Bacon.

Buss, D. M., & Schmitt, D. P. (1993). Sexual strategies theory: An evolutionary perspective on human mating. *Psychological Review, 100,* 204–232.

Buss, D. M., & Shackelford, T. K. (1997). From vigilance to violence: Mate retention tactics in married couples. *Journal of Personality and Social Psychology, 72,* 346–361.

Buss, D. M., Larsen, R. J., Westen, D., & Semmelroth, J. (1992). Sex differences in jealousy: Evolution, physiology, and psychology. *Psychological Science, 3,* 251–255.

Butler, B., & Moran, G. (2007). The impact of death qualification, belief in a just world, legal authoritarianism, and locus of control on venirepersons' evaluations of aggravating and mitigating circumstances in capital trials. *Behavioral Sciences and the Law, 25,* 57–68.

Butz, D. A., & Yogeeswaran, K. (2011). A new threat in the air: Macroeconomic threat increases prejudice against Asian Americans. *Journal of Experimental Social Psychology, 47,* 22–27.

Bylsma, W. H., Major, B., & Cozzarelli, C. (1995). The influence of legitimacy appraisals on the determinants of entitlement beliefs. *Basic and Applied Social Psychology, 17,* 223–237.

Byrne, D. (1971). *The attraction paradigm.* New York: Academic Press.

Byrne, D. (1997). An overview (and underview) of research and theory within the attraction paradigm. *Journal of Social and Personal Relationships, 14,* 417–431.

Byrne, D., & Clore, G. L. (1970). A reinforcement model of evaluative processes. *Personality: An International Journal, 1,* 103–128.

Byrne, D., Clore, G. L., & Smeaton, G. (1986). The attraction hypothesis: Do similar attitudes affect anything? *Journal of Personality and Social Psychology, 51,* 1167–1170.

Byrne, R. M. J., & McEleney, A. (2000). Counterfactual thinking about actions and failures to act. *Journal of Experimental Psychology: Learning, Memory, and Cognition, 26,* 1318–1331.

Cacioppo, J. T., & Patrick, W. (2008). *Loneliness: Human nature and the need for social connection.* New York: Norton.

Cacioppo, J. T., & Petty, R. E. (1981). Electromyograms as measures of extent and affectivity of information processing. *American Psychologist, 36,* 441–456.

Cacioppo, J. T., & Petty, R. E. (1982). The need for cognition. *Journal of Personality and Social Psychology, 42,* 116–131.

Cacioppo, J. T., Crites, S. L., Berntson, G. G., & Coles, M. G. H. (1993). If attitudes affect how stimuli are processed, should they not affect the event-related brain potential? *Psychological Science, 4,* 108–112.

Cacioppo, J. T., Gardner, W. L., & Bernston, G. G. (1997). Beyond bipolar conceptualizations and measures: The case of attitudes and evaluative space. *Personality and Social Psychology Review, 1,* 3–25.

Cacioppo, J. T., Hawkley, L. C., Berntson, G. G., Ernst, J. M., Gibbs, A. C., Stickgold, R., & Hobson, J. A. (2002). Lonely days invade the nights: Social modulation of sleep efficiency. *Psychological Science, 13,* 385–388.

Cacioppo, J. T., Hughes, M. E., Waite, L. J., Hawkley, L. C., & Thisted, R. A. (2006). Loneliness as a specific risk factor for depressive symptoms: Cross-sectional and longitudinal analyses. *Psychology and Aging, 21,* 140–151.

Cacioppo, J. T., Petty, R. E., & Morris, K. (1983). Effects of need for cognition on message evaluation, recall, and persuasion. *Journal of Personality and Social Psychology, 45,* 805–818.

Cacioppo, J. T., Petty, R. E., Feinstein, J. A., & Jarvis, W. B. G. (1996). Dispositional differences in cognitive motivation: The life and times of individuals varying in need for cognition. *Psychological Bulletin, 119,* 197–253.

Cacioppo, J. T., Petty, R. E., Losch, M. E., & Kim, H. S. (1986). Electromyographic activity over facial muscle regions can differentiate the valence and intensity of affective reactions. *Journal of Personality and Social Psychology, 50,* 260–268.

Calogero, R. M., Tantleff-Dunn, S., & Thompson, J. (2011). *Self-objectification in women: Causes, consequences, and counteractions.* Washington, DC: American Psychological Association.

Camara, W. J., & Schneider, D. L. (1994). Integrity tests: Facts and unresolved issues. *American Psychologist, 49,* 112–119.

Cameron, J. J., Stinson, D. A., Gaetz, R., & Balchen, S. (2010). Acceptance is in the eye of the beholder: Self-esteem and motivated perceptions of acceptance from the opposite sex. *Journal of Personality and Social Psychology, 99,* 513–529.

Cameron, J., & Pierce, W. D. (1994). Reinforcement, reward, and intrinsic motivation: A meta-analysis. *Review of Educational Research, 64,* 363–423.

Cameron, J., Pierce, W. D., Banko, K. M., & Gear, A. (2005). Achievement-based rewards and intrinsic motivation: A test of cognitive mediators. *Journal of Educational Psychology, 97,* 641–655.

Cameron, L., Rutland, A., Hossain, R., & Petley, R. (2011). When and why does extended contact work? The role of high quality direct contact and group norms in the development of positive ethnic intergroup attitudes amongst children. *Group Processes & Intergroup Relations, 14,* 193–206.

Campbell, A. (1999). Staying alive: Evolution, culture, and women's intrasexual aggression. *Behavioral and Brain Sciences, 22,* 203–252.

Campbell, D. J., & Lee, C. (1988). Self-appraisal in performance evaluation: Development versus evaluation. *Academy Management Review, 13,* 302–313.

Campion, M. A., Palmer, D. K., & Campion, J. E. (1997). A review of structure in the selection interview. *Personnel Psychology, 50,* 655–703.

Candiotti, S., & Levitt, R. (2012, July 2). Purported e-mails suggest Paterno may have altered decision not to report abuse. Retrieved from cnn.com.

Cannon, W. B. (1932). *The wisdom of the body.* New York: Norton.

Capozza, D., & Brown, R. (2000). *Social identity processes: Trends in theory and research.* London: Sage.

Capozza, D., Voci, A., & Licciardello, O. (2000). Individualism, collectivism, and social identity theory. In D. Capozza & R. Brown (Eds.), *Social identity processes: Trends in theory and research.* London: Sage.

Caprara, G., Alessandri, G., & Eisenberg, N. (2012). Prosociality: The contribution of traits, values, and self-efficacy beliefs. *Journal of Personality and Social Psychology, 102,* 1289–1303.

Caprariello, P. A., Cuddy, A. J. C., & Fiske, S. T. (2009). Social structure shapes cultural stereotypes and emotions: A causal test of the stereotype content model. *Group Processes & Intergroup Relations, 12,* 147–155.

Card, N. A., Stucky, B. D., Sawalani, G. M., & Little, T. D. (2008). Direct and indirect aggression during childhood and adolescence: A meta-analytic review of gender differences, intercorrelations, and relations to maladjustment. *Child Development, 79,* 1185–1229.

Cárdenas, R. A., & Harris, L. J. (2006). Symmetrical decorations enhance the attractiveness of faces and abstract designs. *Evolution and Human Behavior, 27,* 1–18.

Carey, B. (1997, April). Don't face stress alone. *Health,* pp. 74–76, 78.

Carey, H. R., & Laughlin, P. R. (2012). Groups perform better than the best individuals on letters-to-numbers problems: Effects of induced strategies. *Group Processes & Intergroup Relations, 15*(2), 231–242.

Carlo, G., Knight, G. P., McGinley, M., & Hayes, R. (2011). The roles of parental inductions, moral emotions, and moral cognitions in prosocial tendencies among Mexican American and European American early adolescents. *The Journal of Early Adolescence, 31,* 757–781.

Carlo, G., Okun, M. A., Knight, G. P., & de Guzman, M. R. T. (2005). The interplay of traits and motives on volunteering: Agreeableness, extraversion and prosocial value motivation. *Personality and Individual Differences, 38,* 1293–1305.

Carlsmith, K. M. (2006). The roles of retribution and utility in determining punishment. *Journal of Experimental Social Psychology, 42,* 437–451.

Carlsmith, K. M., Darley, J. M., & Robinson, P. H. (2002). Why do we punish? Deterrence and just deserts as motives for punishment. *Journal of Personality and Social Psychology, 83,* 284–299.

Carlsmith, K. M., Wilson, T. D., & Gilbert, D. T. (2008). The paradoxical consequences of revenge. *Journal of Personality and Social Psychology, 95,* 1316–1324.

Carlson, E. N., Vazire, S., & Furr, R. M. (2011). Meta-insight: Do people really know how others see them? *Journal of Personality and Social Psychology, 101,* 831–841.

Carlson, M. (2008). I'd rather go along and be considered a man: Masculinity and bystander intervention. *Journal of Men's Studies, 16,* 3–17.

Carnaghi, A., & Yzerbyt, V. Y. (2007). Subtyping and social consensus: The role of the audience in the maintenance of stereotypic beliefs. *European Journal of Social Psychology, 37,* 902–922.

Carnahan, T., & McFarland, S. (2007). Revisiting the Stanford Prison Experiment: Could participant self-selection have led to the cruelty? *Personality and Social Psychology Bulletin, 33,* 603–614.

Carnegie, D. (1936). *How to win friends and influence people.* New York: Simon & Schuster.

Carpenter, S. (2005). The rich science of economic choice. *APS Observer, 18,* No. 4, 21–27.

Carr, J. L., & VanDeusen, K. M. (2004). Risk factors for male sexual aggression on college campuses. *Journal of Family Violence, 19,* 279–289.

Carr, P. B., Dweck, C. S., & Pauker, K. (2012). "Prejudiced" behavior without prejudice? Beliefs about the malleability of prejudice affect interracial interactions. *Journal of Personality and Social Psychology.*

Carrillo, M., Ricci, L. A., Coppersmith, G. A., & Melloni, R. H., Jr. (2009). The effect of increased serotonergic neurotransmission on aggression: A critical meta-analytic review of preclinical studies. *Psychopharmacology, 205,* 349–368.

Carroll, J. (2006, September 1). Americans prefer male boss to a female boss. Gallup News Service (http://www.gallup.com/poll/24346/americans-prefer-male-boss-female-boss.aspx#).

Carroll, J. M., & Russell, J. A. (1996). Do facial expressions signal specific emotions? Judging emotion from face in context. *Journal of Personality and Social Psychology, 70,* 205–218.

Carron, A. V., Colman, M. M., Wheeler, J., & Stevens, D. (2002). Cohesion and performance in sport: A meta analysis. *Journal of Sport and Exercise Psychology, 24,* 168–188.

Cartwright, D., & Zander, A. (1960). Group cohesiveness: Introduction. In D. Cartwright & A. Zander (Eds.), *Group dynamics: Research and theory* (2nd ed., pp. 69–94). Evanston, IL: Row, Peterson.

Carver, C. S., & Connor-Smith, J. (2010). Personality and coping. *Annual Review of Psychology, 61,* 679–704.

Carver, C. S., & Scheier, M. F. (1981). *Attention and self-regulation: A control-theory approach to human behavior.* New York: Springer-Verlag.

Carver, C. S., & Scheier, M. F. (1990). Origins and functions of positive and negative affect: A control-process view. *Psychological Review, 97,* 19–35.

Carver, C. S., & Scheier, M. F. (1998). *On the self-regulation of behavior.* New York: Cambridge University Press.

Carver, C. S., Harris, S. D., Lehman, J. M., Durel, L. A., Antoni, M. H., Spencer, S. M., & Pozo-Kaderman, C. (2000). How important is the perception of personal control? Studies of early stage breast cancer patients. *Personality and Social Psychology Bulletin, 26,* 139–149.

Carver, C. S., Scheier, M. F., & Weintraub, J. K. (1989). Assessing coping strategies: A theoretically based approach. *Journal of Personality and Social Psychology, 56,* 267–283.

Case, R. B., Moss, A. J., Case, N., McDermott, M., & Eberly, S. (1992). Living alone after myocardial infarction: Impact on prognosis. *Journal of the American Medical Association, 267,* 515–519.

Casey, E. A., & Ohler, K. (2012). Being a positive bystander: Male anti-violence allies' experiences of "stepping up." *Journal of Interpersonal Violence, 27,* 62–83.

Cashdan, E. (2003). Hormones and competitive aggression in women. *Aggressive Behavior, 29,* 107–115.

Caspi, A. (2000). The child is the father of man: Personality continuities from childhood to adulthood. *Journal of Personality and Social Psychology, 78,* 158–172.

Cassidy, J., & Shaver, P. R. (Eds.). (1999). *Handbook of attachment: Theory, research, and clinical applications.* New York: Guilford Press.

Cassidy, J., Kirsh, S. J., Scolton, K. L., & Parke, R. D. (1996). Attachment and representations of peer relationships. *Developmental Psychology, 32,* 892–904.

Castelli, L., Zogmaister, C., & Tomelleri, S. (2009). The transmission of racial attitudes within the family. *Developmental Psychology, 45,* 586–591.

Ceci, S. J., Ross, D. F., & Toglia, M. P. (1987). Suggestibility of children's memory: Psycholegal implications. *Journal of Experimental Psychology, 116,* 38–49.

Cesarani, D. (2004). *Eichmann: His life and crimes.* London: Heinemann.

Cesario, J., & Higgins, E. T. (2008). Making message recipients "feel right": How nonverbal cues can increase persuasion. *Psychological Science, 19,* 415–420.

Cesario, J., Grant, H., & Higgins, E. T. (2004). Regulatory fit and persuasion: Transfer from "feeling right." *Journal of Personality and Social Psychology, 86,* 388–404.

Cesario, J., Plaks, J. E., & Higgins, E. T. (2006). Automatic social behavior as motivated preparation to interact. *Journal of Personality and Social Psychology, 90,* 893–910.

Cha, A. E. (2005, March 27). Employers relying on personality tests to screen applicants. *Washington Post,* p. A01.

Chaiken, S. (1979). Communicator physical attractiveness and persuasion. *Journal of Personality and Social Psychology, 37,* 1387–1397.

Chaiken, S. (1980). Heuristic versus systematic information processing and the use of source versus message cues in persuasion. *Journal of Personality and Social Psychology, 39,* 752–766.

Chaiken, S. (1987). The heuristic model of persuasion. In M. P. Zanna, J. M. Olson, & C. P. Herman (Eds.), *Social influence: The Ontario symposium* (Vol. 5, pp. 3–39). Hillsdale, NJ: Erlbaum.

Chaiken, S., & Baldwin, M. W. (1981). Affective-cognitive consistency and the effect of salient behavioral information on the self-perception of attitudes. *Journal of Personality and Social Psychology, 41,* 1–12.

Chan, D. K., & Fishbein, M. (1993). Determinants of college women's intentions to tell their partners to use condoms. *Journal of Applied Social Psychology, 23,* 1455–1470.

Chandrashekaran, M., Walker, B. A., Ward, J. C., & Reingen, P. H. (1996). Modeling individual preference evolution and choice in a dynamic group setting. *Journal of Marketing Research, 33,* 211–223.

Chang, H. (2007). Psychological distress and help-seeking among Taiwanese college students: Role of gender and student status. *British Journal of Guidance & Counselling, 35,* 347–355.

Chao, G. T., & Moon, H. (2005). The cultural mosaic: A metatheory for understanding the complexity of culture. *Journal of Applied Psychology, 90,* 1128–1140.

Chapdelaine, A., Kenny, D. A., & LaFontana, K. M. (1994). Matchmaker, matchmaker, can you make me a match? Predicting liking between two unacquainted persons. *Journal of Personality and Social Psychology, 67,* 83–91.

Chapman, D. S., Uggerslev, K. L., & Webster, J. (2003). Applicant reactions to face-to-face and technology-mediated interviews: A field investigation. *Journal of Applied Psychology, 88,* 944–953.

Charman, S. D., & Wells, G. L. (2008). Can eyewitnesses correct for external influences on their lineup identifications? The actual/counterfactual assessment paradigm. *Journal of Experimental Psychology: Applied, 14,* 5–20.

Charman, S. D., Wells, G. L., & Joy, S. W. (2011). The dud effect: Adding highly dissimilar fillers increases confidence in lineup identifications. *Law and Human Behavior, 35,* 479–500.

Chartrand, T. L., & Bargh, J. A. (1999). The chameleon effect: The perception-behavior link and social interaction. *Journal of Personality and Social Psychology, 76,* 893–910.

Chartrand, T. L., & van Baaren, R. (2009). Human mimicry. *Advances in Experimental Social Psychology, 41,* 219–274.

Chasteen, A. L., Bhattacharyya, S., Horhota, M., Tam, R., & Hasher, L. (2005). How feelings of stereotype threat influence older adults' memory performance. *Experimental Aging Research, 31,* 235–260.

Chatard, A., & Selimbegović, L. (2011). When self-destructive thoughts flash through the mind: Failure to meet standards affects the accessibility of suicide-related thoughts. *Journal of Personality and Social Psychology, 100,* 587–605.

Cheek, J. M., & Melchior, L. A. (1990). Shyness, self-esteem, and self-consciousness. In H. Leitenberg (Ed.), *Handbook of social and evaluation anxiety.* New York: Plenum.

Chemers, M. M., Hays, R. B., Rhodewalt, F., & Wysocki, J. (1985). A person-environment analysis of job stress: A contingency model explanation. *Journal of Personality and Social Psychology, 49,* 628–635.

Chen, F. F., & Kenrick, D. T. (2002). Repulsion or attraction: Group membership and assumed attitude similarity. *Journal of Personality and Social Psychology, 83,* 111–125.

Chen, J. M., Kim, H. S., Mojaverian, T., & Morling, B. (2012). Culture and social support provision: Who gives what and why. *Personality and Social Psychology Bulletin, 38,* 3–13.

Chen, S., & Chaiken, S. (1999). The heuristic-systematic model in its broader context. In S. Chaiken & Y. Trope (Eds.), *Dual-process theories in social psychology* (pp. 73–96). New York: Guilford.

Chen, S., Langner, C. A., & Mendoza-Denton, R. (2009). When dispositional and role power fit: Implications for self-expression and self–other congruence. *Journal of Personality and Social Psychology, 96,* 710–727.

Chen, Y.-R., Brockner, J., & Chen, X.-P. (2002). Individual-collective primacy and ingroup favoritism: Enhancement and protection effects. *Journal of Experimental Social Psychology, 38,* 482–491.

Cheng, C. M., & Chartrand, T. L. (2003). Self-monitoring without awareness: Using mimicry as a nonconscious affiliation strategy. *Journal of Personality and Social Psychology, 85,* 1170–1179.

Cheng, P. W., & Novick, L. R. (1990). A probabilistic contrast model of causal induction. *Journal of Personality and Social Psychology, 58,* 545–567.

Cherry, E. C. (1953). Some experiments on the recognition of speech, with one and with two ears. *Journal of the Acoustical Society of America, 25,* 975–979.

Chesler, P., & Goodman, E. J. (1976). *Women, money, and power.* New York: Morrow.

Chiaburu, D. S., Oh, I.-S., Berry, C. M., Li, N., & Gardner, R. G. (2011). The five-factor model of personality traits and organizational citizenship behaviors: A meta analysis. *Journal of Applied Psychology, 96,* 1140–1166.

Chiao, J. Y. (2011). Towards a cultural neuroscience of empathy and prosociality. *Emotion Review, 3,* 111–112.

Chiesa, M., & Hobbs, S. (2008). Making sense of social research: How useful is the Hawthorne Effect? *European Journal of Social Psychology, 38,* 67–74.

Chiocchio, F., & Essiembre, H. (2009). Cohesion and performance: A meta-analytic review of disparities between project teams, production teams, and service teams. *Small Group Research, 40,* 382–420.

Chivers, M. L., Rieger, G., Latty, E., & Bailey, J. M. (2004). A sex difference in the specificity *of sexual arousal. Psychological Science, 15,* 736–744.

Choi, J. N., & Kim, M. U. (1999). The organizational application of group-think and its limitations in organizations. *Journal of Applied Psychology, 84,* 297–306.

Choi, S. M., Lee, W.-N., & Kim, H.-J. (2005). Lessons from the rich and famous: A cross-cultural comparison of celebrity endorsement in advertising. *Journal of Advertising, 34,* 85–98.

Christensen, A. J., Turner, C. W., Smith, T. W., Holman, J. M., Jr., & Gregory, M. C. (1991). Health locus of control and depression in end-stage renal disease. *Journal of Counseling and Clinical Psychology, 59,* 419–424.

Christensen, A., & Heavey, C. L. (1993). Gender differences in marital conflict: The demand/withdraw interaction pattern. In S. Oskamp & M. Costanzo (Eds.), *Gender issues in contemporary society* (pp. 113–141). Newbury Park, CA: Sage.

Christensen, T. C., Wood, J. V., & Barrett, L. F. (2003). Remembering everyday experience through the prism of self-esteem. *Personality and Social Psychology Bulletin, 29,* 51–62.

Christianson, S. (1992). Emotional stress and eyewitness memory: A critical review. *Psychological Bulletin, 112,* 284–309.

Chua, R. J., Morris, M. W., & Mor, S. (2012). Collaborating across cultures: Cultural metacognition and affect-based trust in creative collaboration. *Organizational Behavior and Human Decision Processes, 118,* 116–131.

Cialdini, R. B. (2003). Crafting normative messages to protect the environment. *Current Directions in Psychological Science, 12,* 105–109.

Cialdini, R. B. (2007). *Influence: The psychology of persuasion.* New York: HarperCollins.

Cialdini, R. B., & Ascani, K. (1976). Test of a concession procedure for inducing verbal, behavioral, and further compliance with a request to give blood. *Journal of Applied Psychology, 61,* 295–300.

Cialdini, R. B., & De Nicholas, M. E. (1989). Self-presentation by association. *Journal of Personality and Social Psychology, 57,* 626–631.

Cialdini, R. B., & Goldstein, N. J. (2004). Social influence: Compliance and conformity. *Annual Review of Psychology, 55,* 591–621.

Cialdini, R. B., Baumann, D. J., & Kenrick, D. T. (1981). Insights from sadness: A three-step model of the development of altruism as hedonism. *Developmental Review, 1,* 207–223.

Cialdini, R. B., Borden, R. J., Thorne, A., Walker, M. R., Freeman, S., & Sloan, L. R. (1976). Basking in reflected glory: Three (football) field studies. *Journal of Personality and Social Psychology, 34,* 366–375.

Cialdini, R. B., Cacioppo, J. T., Bassett, R., & Miller, J. A. (1978). Low-ball procedure for producing compliance: Commitment then cost. *Journal of Personality and Social Psychology, 36,* 463–476.

Cialdini, R. B., Kallgren, C. A., & Reno, R. R. (1991). A focus theory of normative conduct: A theoretical refinement and reevaluation of the role of norms in human behavior. *Advances in Experimental Social Psychology, 24,* 201–234.

Cialdini, R. B., Reno, R. R., & Kallgren, C. A. (1990). A focus theory of normative conduct: Recycling the concept of norms to reduce littering in public places. *Journal of Personality and Social Psychology, 58,* 1015–1026.

Cialdini, R. B., Schaller, M., Houlihan, D., Arps, K., Fultz, J., & Beaman, A. L. (1987). Empathy-based helping: Is it selflessly or selfishly motivated? *Journal of Personality and Social Psychology, 52,* 749–758.

Cialdini, R. B., Trost, M. R., & Newsom, J. T. (1995). Preference for consistency: The development of a valid measure and the discovery of surprising behavioral implications. *Journal of Personality and Social Psychology, 69,* 318–328.

Cialdini, R. B., Vincent, J. E., Lewis, S. K., Catalan, J., Wheeler, D., & Darby, B. L. (1975). Reciprocal concessions procedure for inducing compliance: The door-in-the-face technique. *Journal of Personality and Social Psychology, 31,* 206–215.

Cialdini, R.B. (2009). *Influence: Science and Practice* (5th edition). Boston: Allyn & Bacon.

Cioffi, D., & Holloway, J. (1993). Delayed costs of suppressed pain. *Journal of Personality and Social Psychology, 64,* 274–282.

Claidiere, N., & Whiten, A. (2012). Integrating the study of conformity and culture in humans and nonhuman animals. *Psychological Bulletin, 138,* 126–145.

Clark, J. K., Wegener, D. T., Habashi, M. M., & Evans, A. T. (2012). Source expertise and persuasion: The effects of perceived opposition or support on message scrutiny. *Personality and Social Psychology Bulletin, 38*(1), 90–100.

Clark, M. S. (1984). Record keeping in two types of relationships. *Journal of Personality and Social Psychology, 47,* 549–557.

Clark, M. S., & Mills, J. (1979). Interpersonal attraction in exchange and communal relationships. *Journal of Personality and Social Psychology, 37,* 12–24.

Clark, M. S., & Mills, J. (1993). The difference between communal and exchange relationships: What it is and is not. *Personality and Social Psychology Bulletin, 19,* 684–691.

Clark, R. D., III, & Maass, A. (1990). The effects of majority size on minority influence. *European Journal of Psychology, 20,* 99–117.

Clark, R. D., III, & Word, L. E. (1972). Why don't bystanders help? Because of ambiguity? *Journal of Personality and Social Psychology, 24,* 392–400.

Clark, R. D., III. (2001). Effects of majority defection and multiple minority sources on minority influence. *Group Dynamics, 5,* 57–62.

Clark, S. E. (2005). A re-examination of the effects of biased lineup instructions in eyewitness identification. *Law and Human Behavior, 29,* 395–424.

Clark, S. E., Marshall, T. E., & Rosenthal, R. (2009). Lineup administrator influences on eyewitness identification decisions. *Journal of Experimental Psychology: Applied, 15,* 63–75.

Clifford, M. M., & Walster, E. H. (1973). The effect of physical attractiveness on teacher expectations. *Sociology of Education, 46,* 248–258.

Cochran, J. K., Sellers, C. S., Wiesbrock, V., & Palacios, W. R. (2011). Repetitive intimate partner victimization: An exploratory application of social learning theory. *Deviant Behavior, 32,* 790–817.

Cochran, S. D., Mays, V. M., Ciarletta, J., Caruso, C., & Mallon, D. (1992). Efficacy of the theory of reasoned action in predicting AIDS-related sexual risk reduction among gay men. *Journal of Applied Social Psychology, 22,* 1481–1501.

Coe, C. L. (1993). Psychosocial factors and immunity in nonhuman primates: A review. *Psychosomatic Medicine, 55,* 298–308.

Cohen-Ketteinis, P. T., & Van Goozen, S. H. M. (1997). Sex reassignment of adolescent transsexuals: A follow-up study. *Journal of the American Academy of Child and Adolescent psychiatry, 36,* 263–271.

Cohen, D., & Nisbett, R. E. (1997). Field experiments examining the culture of honor: The role of institutions in perpetuating norms about violence. *Personality and Social Psychology Bulletin, 23,* 1188–1199.

Cohen, D., Nisbett, R. E., Bowdle, B. F., & Schwarz, N. (1996). Insult, aggression, and the southern culture of honor: An "experimental ethnography." *Journal of Personality and Social Psychology, 70,* 945–960.

Cohen, D., Vandello, J., & Rantilla, A. K. (1998). The sacred and the social: Cultures of honor and violence. In P. Gilbert & B. Andrews (Eds.), *Shame: Interpersonal behavior, psychopathology, and culture* (pp. 261–282). Cambridge: Oxford University Press.

Cohen, G. L. (2003). Party over policy: The dominating impact of group influence on political beliefs. *Journal of Personality and Social Psychology, 85,* 808–822.

Cohen, G. L., & Garcia, J. (2008). Identity, belonging, and achievement: A model, interventions, implications. *Current Directions in Psychological Science, 17,* 365–369.

Cohen, G. L., Garcia, J., Apfel, N., & Master, A. (2006). Reducing the racial achievement gap: A social-psychological intervention. *Science, 313,* 1307–1310.

Cohen, G. L., Garcia, J., Purdie-Vaughns, V., Apfel, N., & Brzustoski, P. (2009). Recursive processes in self-affirmation: Intervening to close the minority achievement gap. *Science, 324,* 400–403.

Cohen, G. L., Steele, C. M., & Ross, L. D. (1999). The mentor's dilemma: Providing critical feedback across the racial divide. *Personality and Social Psychology Bulletin, 25,* 1302–1318.

Cohen, J. B., & De La Torre, V. (2009, May 16). A year later, would bystanders lend hand? *Hartford Courant,* p. A1.

Cohen, L. J., & DeBenedet, A. T. (2012). Penn State Cover-up: Groupthink in action. *Time.com,* July 17. http://ideas.time.com/2012/07/17/penn-state-cover-up-group-think-in-action/.

Cohen, S. (2004). Social relationships and health. *American Psychologist, 59,* 676–684.

Cohen, S., & Herbert, T. (1996). Health psychology: Psychological factors and physical disease from the perspective of human psychoneuroimmunology. *Annual Review of Psychology, 47,* 113–142.

Cohen, S., & Janicki-Deverts, D. (2009). Can we improve our physical health by altering our social networks? *Perspectives on Psychological Science, 4,* 375–378.

Cohen, S., & Janicki-Deverts, D. (2012). Who's stressed? Distributions of psychological stress in the United States in probability samples from 1983, 2006, and 2009. *Journal of Applied Social Psychology, 42,* 1320–1334.

Cohen, S. Janicki-Deverts, D., & Miller, G. E. (2007). Psychological stress and disease. *Journal of the American Medical Association 298,* 1685–1687.

Cohen, S., & Williamson, G. (1991). Stress and infectious disease in humans. *Psychological Bulletin, 109,* 5–24.

Cohen, S., Alper, C. M., Doyle, W. J., Adler, N. E., Treanor, J. J., & Turner, R. B. (2008). Objective and subjective socioeconomic status and susceptibility to the common cold. *Health Psychology, 27,* 268–274.

Cohen, S., Doyle, W. J., Turner, R., Alper, C. M., & Skoner, D. P. (2006). Sociability and susceptibility to the common cold. *Psychological Science, 14,* 389–395.

Cohen, S., Frank, E., Doyle, W. J., Skoner, D. P., Rabin, B. S., & Gwaltney, J. M. (1998). Types of stressors that increase susceptibility to the common cold in healthy adults. *Health Psychology, 17,* 214–223.

Cohen, S. Janicki-Deverts, D., & Miller, G. E. (2007). Psychological stress and disease. *Journal of the American Medical Association 298,* 1685–1687.

Cohen, S., Kessler, R. C., & Gordon, L. U. (1995). *Measuring stress: A guide for health and social scientists.* New York: Oxford University Press.

Cohen, S., Tyrrell, D. A. J., & Smith, A. P. (1993). Negative life events, perceived stress, negative affect, and susceptibility to the common cold. *Journal of Personality and Social Psychology, 64,* 131–140.

Cohen, S., Underwood, L. G., & Gottlieb, B. H. (Eds.). (2000). *Social support measurement and intervention: A guide for health and social scientists.* New York: Oxford University Press.

Cole, S. W., Kemeny, M. E., Taylor, S. E., Visscher, B. R., & Fahey, J. L. (1996). Accelerated course of human immunodeficiency virus infection in gay men who conceal their homosexual identity. *Psychosomatic Medicine, 58,* 219–231.

Collins, N. L., & Feeney, B. C. (2000). A safe haven: An attachment theory perspective on support seeking and caregiving in intimate relationships. *Journal of Personality and Social Psychology, 78,* 1053–1073.

Collins, N. L., & Miller, L. C. (1994). Self-disclosure and liking: A meta-analytic review. *Psychological Bulletin, 116,* 457–475.

Columb, C., & Plant, E. (2011). Revisiting the Obama Effect: Exposure to Obama reduces implicit prejudice. *Journal of Experimental Social Psychology, 47,* 499–501.

Colvin, C. R., Block, J., & Funder, D. C. (1995). Overly positive self-evaluations and personality: Negative implications for mental health. *Journal of Personality and Social Psychology, 68,* 1152–1162.

Conger, R. D., Reuter, M. A., & Elder, G. H., Jr. (1999). Couple resilience to economic pressure. *Journal of Personality and Social Psychology, 76,* 54–71.

Conger, R. D., Wallace, L. E., Sun, Y., Simons, R. L., McLoyd, V. C., & Brody, G. H. (2002). Economic pressure in African American families: A replication and extension of the family stress model. *Developmental Psychology, 38,* 179–193.

Conner, M., Godin, G., Sheeran, P., & Germain, M. (in press). Some feelings are more important: Cognitive attitudes, affective attitudes, anticipated affect, and blood donation. *Health Psychology.*

Connors, E., Lundregan, T., Miller, N., & McEwen, T. (1996). *Convicted by juries, exonerated by science: Case studies in the use of DNA evidence to establish innocence after trial.* Washington, DC: U.S. Department of Justice.

Conway, J. M., & Huffcutt, A. I. (1997). Psychometric properties of multisource performance ratings: A meta-analysis of subordinate, supervisor, peer, and self-ratings. *Human Performance, 10,* 331–360.

Conway, L. G., III, & Schaller, M. (2005). When authorities' commands backfire: Attributions about consensus and effects on deviant decision making. *Journal of Personality and Social Psychology, 89,* 311–326.

Conway, M. A. (1995). *Flashbulb memories.* Mahwah, NJ: Erlbaum.

Conway, M. A., & Pleydell-Pearce, C. W. (2000). The construction of autobiographical memories in the self-memory system. *Psychological Review, 107,* 261–288.

Conway, M. A., Wang, Q., Hanyu, K., & Haque, S. (2005). A cross-cultural investigation of autobiographical memory: On the universality and cultural variation of the "Reminiscence Bump." *Journal of Cross-Cultural Psychology, 36,* 739–749.

Cook, J. E., Purdie-Vaughns, V., Garcia, J., & Cohen, G. L. (2012). Chronic threat and contingent belonging: Protective benefits of values affirmation on identity development. *Journal of Personality and Social Psychology, 102,* 479–496.

Cook, T. D., & Campbell, D. T. (1979). *Quasi-experimentation: Design and analysis issues for field settings.* Chicago: Rand McNally.

Cooke, C. A. (2004). Young people's attitudes towards guns in America, Great Britain, and Western Australia. *Aggressive Behavior, 30,* 93–104.

Cooley, C. H. (1902). *Human nature and the social order.* New York: Schocken Books.

Cooper, J. (2007). *Cognitive dissonance: Fifty years of classic theory.* London: Sage.

Cooper, J., & Fazio, R. H. (1984). A new look at dissonance theory. In L. Berkowitz (Ed.), *Advances in experimental social psychology* (Vol. 17, pp. 229–267). New York: Academic Press.

Cooper, J., & Hogg, M. (2007). Feeling the anguish of others: A theory of vicarious dissonance. *Advances in Experimental Social Psychology, 39,* 359–403.

Cooper, J., & Neuhaus, I. M. (2000). The "hired gun" effect: Assessing the effect of pay, frequency of testifying, and credentials on the perception of expert testimony. *Law and Human Behavior, 24* Cooper, J., Zanna, M. P., & Goethals, G. R. (1974). Mistreatment of an esteemed other as a consequence affecting dissonance reduction. *Journal of Experimental Social Psychology, 10,* 224–233.

Cooper, L. A., Roter, D. L., Carson, K. A., Beach, M., Sabin, J. A., Greenwald, A. G., & Inui, T. S. (2012). The associations of clinicians' implicit attitudes about race with medical visit communication and patient ratings of interpersonal care. *American Journal of Public Health, 102,* 979–987.

Cooper, M. L., Frone, M. R., Russell, M., & Mudar, P. (1995). Drinking to regulate positive and negative emotions: A motivational model of alcohol use. *Journal of Personality and Social Psychology, 69,* 990–1005.

Cooper, W. H. (1981). Ubiquitous halo. *Psychological Bulletin, 90,* 218–224.

Coopersmith, S. (1967). *The antecedents of self-esteem.* San Francisco: Freeman.

Copeland, J. T. (1994). Prophecies of power: Motivational implications of social power for behavioral confirmation. *Journal of Personality and Social Psychology, 67,* 264–277.

Corbett, S. (2008, January 20). A cutting tradition. *New York Times,* p. 44.

Cordery, J. L., & Soo, C. (2008). Overcoming impediments to virtual team effectiveness. *Human Factors and Ergonomics in Manufacturing, 18,* 487–500.

Correll, J., Lemoine, C., & Ma, D. S. (2011). Hemispheric asymmetry in cross-race face recognition. *Journal of Experimental Social Psychology, 47,* 1162–1166.

Correll, J., Park, B., Judd, C. M., & Wittenbrink, B. (2002). The police officer's dilemma: Using ethnicity to disambiguate potentially threatening individuals. *Journal of Personality and Social Psychology, 83,* 1314–1329.

Correll, J., Park, B., Judd, C. M., & Wittenbrink, B. (2007a). The influence of stereotypes on decisions to shoot. *European Journal of Social Psychology, 37,* 1102–1117.

Correll, J., Park, B., Judd, C. M., Wittenbrink, B., Sadler, M. S., & Keesee, T. (2007b). Across the Thin Blue Line: Police officers and racial bias in the decision to shoot. *Journal of Personality and Social Psychology, 92,* 1006–1023.

Correll, J., Wittenbrink, B., Park, B., Judd, C. M., & Goyle, A. (2011). Dangerous enough: Moderating racial bias with contextual threat cues. *Journal of Experimental Social Psychology, 47,* 184–189.

Corriveau, K. H., & Harris, P. L. (2010). Preschoolers (sometimes) defer to the majority in making simple perceptual judgments. *Developmental Psychology, 46,* 437–445.

Corriveau, K. H., Fusaro, M., & Harris, P. L. (2009). Going with the flow: Preschoolers prefer nondissenters as informants. *Psychological Science, 20,* 372–377.

Coscarelli, J. (2012). Jonah Lehrer's self-plagiarizing issues are snowballing. http://nymag.com/daily/intel/2012/06/jonah-lehrer-plagiarism-new-yorker-examples-pile-up.html.

Cose, E. (1997). *Color-blind: Seeing beyond race in a race-obsessed world.* New York: HarperCollins.

Costanzo, M. (1997). *Just revenge: Costs and consequences of the death penalty.* New York: St. Martin's Press.

Costanzo, M., & Krauss, D. (2012). *Forensic and legal psychology.* New York: Worth.

Cottle, M. (2012). Race baiting: All the rage; a loud backfire in Michigan. *Newsweek,* February 20, p. 5.

Cousins, A. J., Fugére, M. A., & Franklin, M. (2009). Digit ratio (2D:4D), mate guarding, and physical aggression in dating couples. *Personality and Individual Differences, 46,* 709–713.

Cousins, N. (1989). *Head first: The biology of hope.* New York: Dutton.

Cowan, C. L., Thompson, W. C., & Ellsworth, P. C. (1984). The effects of death qualification on jurors' predisposition to convict and on the quality of deliberation. *Law and Human Behavior, 8,* 53–80.

Cowley, G. (1996, June 3). The biology of beauty. *Newsweek,* pp. 61–69.

Cox, M., & Tanford, S. (1989). An alternative method of capital jury selection. *Law and Human Behavior, 13,* 167–183.

Coyne, S. M., & Archer, J. (2004). Indirect aggression in the media: A content analysis of British television programs. *Aggressive Behavior, 30,* 254–271.

Coyne, S. M., Archer, J., & Eslea, M. (2004). Cruel intentions on television and in real life: Can viewing indirect aggression increase viewers' subsequent indirect aggression? *Journal of Experimental Child Psychology, 88,* 234–253.

Coyne, S. M., Manning, J. T., Ringer, L., & Bailey, L. (2007). Directional asymmetry (right-left differences) in digit ratio (2D:4D) predict indirect aggression in women. *Personality and Individual Differences, 43,* 865–872.

Coyne, S. M., Nelson, D. A., Lawton, F., Haslam, S., Rooney, L., Titterington, L., et al. (2008). The effects of viewing physical and relational aggression in the media: Evidence for a cross-over effect. *Journal of Experimental Social Psychology, 44,* 1551–1554.

Craig, S. B., & Hannum, K. (2006). Research update: 360-degree performance assessment. *Consulting Psychology Journal: Practice and Research, 58,* 117–124.

Craig, W. M., Pepler, D., & Atlas, R. (2000). Observations of bullying in the playground and in the classroom. *School Psychology International, 21,* 22–36.

Cramer, R. E., McMaster, M. R., Bartell, P. A., & Dragna, M. (1988). Subject competence and the minimization of the bystander effect. *Journal of Applied Social Psychology, 18,* 1133–1148.

Crandall, C. S., & Eshleman, A. (2003). A justification-suppression model of the expression and experience of prejudice. *Psychological Bulletin, 129,* 414–446.

Crandall, C. S., Merman, A., & Hebl, M. (2009). Anti-fat prejudice. In T. D. Nelson (Ed.), *Handbook of prejudice, stereotyping, and discrimination* (pp. 469–487). New York: Psychology Press.

Crano, W. D. (2000). Milestones in the psychological analysis of social influence. *Group Dynamics: Theory, Research, and Practice, 4,* 68–80.

Crano, W. D., & Prislin, R. (Eds.). (2008). *Attitudes and attitude change.* New York: Psychology Press.

Crano, W. D., & Seyranian, V. (2009). How minorities prevail: The context/comparison -leniency contract model. *Journal of Social Issues, 65,* 335–363.

Crawford, M. T., & Salaman, L. (2012). Entitativity, identity, and the fulfillment of psychological needs. *Journal of Experimental Social Psychology, 48,* 726–730.

Crick, N. R., & Dodge, K. A. (1994). A review and reformulation of social information-processing mechanisms in children's social adjustment. *Psychological Bulletin, 115,* 74–101.

Crick, N. R., & Rose, A. J. (2000). Toward a gender-balanced approach to the study of social-emotional development: A look at relational aggression. In R. G. Geen & E. Donnerstein (Eds.), *Human aggression: Theories, research, and implications for social policy* (pp. 153–168). San Diego: Academic Press.

Crick, N. R., Werner, N. E., Casas, J. F., O'Brien, K. M., Nelson, D. A., Grotpeter, J. K., & Markon, K. (1999). Childhood aggression and gender: A new look at an old problem. In D. Bernstein (Ed.), *Gender and motivation* (pp. 75–141). Lincoln, NE: University of Nebraska Press.

Crocker, J., & Park, L. E. (2004). The costly pursuit of self-esteem. *Psychological Bulletin, 130,* 392–414.

Crocker, J., Canevello, A., Breines, J. G., & Flynn, H. (2010). Interpersonal goals and change in anxiety and dysphoria in first-semester college students. *Journal of Personality and Social Psychology, 98,* 1009–1024.

Crocker, J., Voelkl, K., Testa, M., & Major, B. (1991). Social stigma: The affective consequences of attributional ambiguity. *Journal of Personality and Social Psychology, 60,* 218–228.

Crockett, M. J., Clark, L., Tabibnia, G., Lieberman, M. D., & Robbins, T. W. (2008). Serotonin modulates behavioral reactions to unfairness. *Science, 320,* 1739.

Croizet, J. C., & Claire, T. (1998). Extending the concept of stereotype and threat to social class: The intellectual underperformance of students from low socioeconomic backgrounds. *Personality and Social Psychology Bulletin, 24,* 588–594.

Cronbach, L. J. (1955). Processes affecting scores on "understanding of others" and "assumed similarity." *Psychological Bulletin, 52,* 177–193.

Cronin, P., & Reicher, S. (2009). Accountability processes and group dynamics: A SIDE perspective on the policing of an anti-capitalist riot. *European Journal of Social Psychology, 39,* 237–254.

Cropanzano, R. (Ed.). (1993). *Justice in the workplace: Approaching fairness in human resource management.* Hillsdale, NJ: Erlbaum.

Crosby, F. (1982). *Relative deprivation and working women.* New York: Oxford University Press.

Crosby, F. J., Iyer, A., & Sincharoen, S. (2006). Understanding affirmative action. *Annual Review of Psychology, 57,* 585–611.

Crosby, J. R., Monin, B., & Richardson, D. (2008). Where do we look during potentially offensive behavior? *Psychological Science, 19,* 226–228.

Crotty, S. K., & Brett, J. M. (2012). Fusing creativity: Cultural metacognition and teamwork in multicultural teams. *Negotiation and Conflict Management Research, 5,* 210–234.

Croyle, R., & Cooper, J. (1983). Dissonance arousal: Physiological evidence. *Journal of Personality and Social Psychology, 45,* 782–791.

Crozier, W. R. (Ed.). (2001). *Shyness: Development, consolidation, and change.* London: Routledge.

Crozier, W. R., & Alden, L. E. (Eds.). (2005). *The essential handbook of social anxiety for clinicians.* New York: John Wiley & Sons.

Crutchfield, R. S. (1955). Conformity and character. *American Psychologist, 10,* 195–198.

Cryder, C. E., Springer, S., & Morewedge, C. K. (2012). Guilty feelings, targeted actions. *Personality and Social Psychology Bulletin, 38,* 607–618.

Csikszentmihalyi, M. (1999). If we are so rich, why aren't we happy? *American Psychologist, 54,* 821–827.

Csikszentmihalyi, M., & Figurski, T. J. (1982). Self-awareness and aversive experience in everyday life. *Journal of Personality, 50,* 15–28.

Cuddy, A. J. C., Fiske, S. T., & Glick, P. (2008). Warmth and competence as universal dimensions of social perception: The Stereotype Content Model and the BIAS Map. In M. P. Zanna (Ed.), *Advances in Experimental Social Psychology* (Vol. 40, pp. 61–149). New York: Academic Press.

Cuddy, A. J. C., Rock, M. S., & Norton, M. I. (2007). Aid in the aftermath of Hurricane Katrina: Inferences of secondary emotions and intergroup helping. *Group Processes & Intergroup Relations, 10,* 107–118.

Cuddy, A. J., Fiske, S. T., Kwan, V., S. Y. Glick, P., Demoulin, S., Leyens, J. P., et al. (2009). Stereotype content model across cultures: Towards universal similarities and some differences. *British Journal of Social Psychology, 48,* 1–33.

Cue, M. (2012). Uefa probes claims banana thrown at Balotelli. *The Times (London),* June 15, thetimes.co.uk.

Culbertson, F. M. (1997). Depression and gender: An international review. *American Psychologist, 52,* 25–31.

Cunningham, J. H. (2009, May 11). Doctor shares 3 steps to save lives; Shows workers Heimlich moves. *The Record* (Bergen County, NJ), p. L6.

Cunningham, M. R. (1979). Weather, mood, and helping behavior: Quasi experiments with the sunshine Samaritan. *Journal of Personality and Social Psychology, 37,* 1947–1956.

Cunningham, M. R., Roberts, A. R., Wu, C., Barbee, A. P., & Druen, P. B. (1995). "Their ideas of beauty are, on the whole, the same as ours": Consistency and variability in the cross-cultural perception of female physical attractiveness. *Journal of Personality and Social Psychology, 68,* 261–279.

Cunningham, M. R., Wong, D. T., & Barbee, A. P. (1994). Self-presentation dynamics on overt integrity tests: Experimental studies of the Reid Report. *Journal of Applied Psychology, 79,* 643–658.

Cunningham, W. A., Johnson, M. K., Gatenby, J. C., Gore, J. C., & Banaji, M. R. (2003). Neural components of social evaluation. *Journal of Personality and Social Psychology, 85,* 639–649.

Cunningham, W. A., Johnson, W. A., Raye, C. L., Gatenby, J. C., Gore, J. C., & Banaji, M. R. (2004). Separable neural components in the processing of black and white faces. *Psychological Science, 15,* 806–813.

Curtis, N. M., Ronan, K. R., Heiblum, N., & Crellin, K. (2009). Dissemination and effectiveness of multisystemic treatment in New Zealand: A benchmarking study. *Journal of Family Psychology, 23,* 119–129.

Curtis, R. C., & Miller, K. (1986). Believing another likes or dislikes you: Behaviors making the beliefs come true. *Journal of Personality and Social Psychology, 51,* 284–290.

Cutler, B. L. (Ed.). (2009). *Expert testimony on the psychology of eyewitness identification.* New York: Oxford University Press.

Cutler, B. L. (Ed.). (2011). *Convictions of the innocent: Lessons from psychological research.* Washington, DC: American Psychological Association.

Cutler, B. L., & Kovera, M. B. (2011). Expert psychological testimony. *Current Directions in Psychological Science, 20,* 53–57.

Cutler, B. L., & Penrod, S. D. (1995). *Mistaken identification: The eyewitness, psychology, and the law.* New York: Cambridge University Press.

Cutler, B. L., Penrod, S. D., & Stuve, T. E. (1988). Juror decision making in eyewitness identification cases. *Law and Human Behavior, 12,* 41–55.

Dabbs, J. M., & Dabbs, M. G. (2000). *Heroes, rogues, and lovers: Testosterone and behavior.* New York: McGraw-Hill.

Dabbs, J. M., Jr., Hargrove, M. F., & Heusel, C. (1996). Testosterone differences among college fraternities: Well-behaved vs. rambunctious. *Personality and Individual Differences, 20,* 157–161.

Dailey, D. E., & Humphreys, J. C. (2011). Social stressors associated with antepartum depressive symptoms in low-income African American women. Public Health Nursing, 28, 203–212.

Daly, M., & Wilson, M. (1988). *Homicide.* New York: Aldine de Gruyter.

Daly, M., & Wilson, M. (1996). Violence against stepchildren. *Current Directions in Psychological Science, 5,* 77–81.

Daly, M., & Wilson, M. (2005). The 'Cinderella effect' is no fairy tale: Comment. *Trends in Cognitive Sciences, 9,* 507–508.

Darke, P. R., & Chaiken, S. (2005). The pursuit of self-interest: Self-interest bias in attitude judgment and persuasion. *Journal of Personality and Social Psychology, 89,* 864–883.

Darley, J. M., & Batson, C. D. (1973). From Jerusalem to Jericho: A study of situational and dispositional variables in helping behavior. *Journal of Personality and Social Psychology, 27,* 100–108.

Darley, J. M., & Fazio, R. (1980). Expectancy confirmation processes arising in the social interaction sequence. *American Psychologist, 35,* 867–881.

Darley, J. M., & Gross, P. H. (1983). A hypothesis-confirming bias in labeling effects. *Journal of Personality and Social Psychology, 44,* 20–33.

Darley, J. M., & Latané, B. (1968). Bystander intervention in emergencies: Diffusion of responsibility. *Journal of Personality and Social Psychology, 8,* 377–383.

Darley, J. M., & Latané, B. (1970). Norms and normative behavior: Field studies of social interdependence. In J. Macauley & L. Berkowitz (Eds.), *Altruism and helping behavior* (pp. 83–101). New York: Academic Press.

Darley, J. M., & Pittman, T. S. (2003). The psychology of compensatory and retributive justice. *Personality and Social Psychology Review, 7,* 324–336.

Darley, J. M., Carlsmith, K. M., & Robinson, P. H. (2000). Incapacitation and just deserts as motives for punishment. *Law and Human Behavior, 24,* 659–684.

Daruna, J. H. (2012). *Introduction to psychoneuroimmunology* (2nd ed.). San Diego: Academic Press.

Darwin, C. (1872). *The expression of the emotions in man and animals.* London: John Murray.

Dasgupta, N. (2009). Mechanisms underlying the malleability of implicit prejudice and stereotypes: The role of automaticity and cognitive control. In T. D. Nelson (Ed.), *Handbook of prejudice, stereotyping, and discrimination* (pp. 267–284). New York: Psychology Press.

David, N., Bewernick, B. H., Cohen, M. X., Newen, A., Lux, S., Fink, G. R., Shah, N. J., & Vogeley, K. (2006). Neural representations of self versus other: Visual-spatial perspective taking and agency in a virtual ball-tossing game. *Journal of Cognitive Neuroscience, 18,* 898–910.

Davidson, A. R., & Jaccard, J. J. (1979). Variables that moderate the attitude-behavior relation: Results of a longitudinal survey. *Journal of Personality and Social Psychology, 37,* 1364–1376.

Davidson, A. R., Yantis, S., Norwood, M., & Montano, D. E. (1985). Amount of information about the attitude object and attitude-behavior consistency. *Journal of Personality and Social Psychology, 49,* 1184–1198.

Davidson, O. B., Eden, D., Westman, M., Cohen-Charash, Y., Hammer, L. B., Kluger, A. N., & Spector, P. E. (2010). Sabbatical leave: Who gains and how much? *Journal of Applied Psychology, 95,* 953–964.

Davies, K., Tropp, L. R., Aron, A., Pettigrew, T. F., & Wright, S. C. (2011). Cross-group friendships and intergroup attitudes: A meta-analytic review. *Personality and Social Psychology Review, 15,* 332–351.

Davies, P. G., Spencer, S. J., Quinn, D. M., & Gerhardstein, R. (2002). Consuming images: How television commercials that elicit stereotype threat can restrain women academically and professionally. *Personality and Social Psychology Bulletin, 28,* 1615–1628.

Davis, B. P., & Knowles, E. S. (1999). A Disrupt-Then-Reframe technique of social influence. *Journal of Personality and Social Psychology, 76,* 192–199.

Davis, J. H., Au, W. T., Hulbert, L., Chen, X., & Zarnoth, P. (1997). Effects of group size and procedural influence on consensual judgments of quantity: The example of damage awards and mock civil juries. *Journal of Personality and Social Psychology, 73,* 703–718.

Davis, J. H., Kameda, T., Parks, C., Stasson, M., & Zimmerman, S. (1989). Some social mechanics of group decision-making: The distribution of opinion, polling sequence, and implications for consensus. *Journal of Personality and Social Psychology, 57,* 1000–1012.

Davis, J. L., & Rusbult, C. E. (2001). Attitude alignment in close relationships. *Journal of Personality and Social Psychology, 81,* 65–84.

Davis, J. P., & Hall, J. W. (2003). A software-supported process for assembling evidence and handling uncertainty in decisionmaking. *Decision Support Systems, 35,* 415–433.

Davis, M. C., Matthews, K. A., & McGrath, C. (2000). Hostile attitudes predict elevated vascular resistance during interpersonal stress in men and women. *Psychosomatic Medicine, 62,* 17–25.

Davis, M. D., & Stephan, W. G. (2011). Electromyographic analyses of responses to intergroup threat. *Journal of Applied Social Psychology, 41,* 196–218.

Davis, S. (1990). Men as success objects and women as sex objects: A study of personal advertisements. *Sex Roles, 23,* 43–50.

Davison, K. P., Pennebaker, J. W., & Dickerson, S. S. (2000). Who talks? The social psychology of illness support groups. *American Psychologist, 55,* 205–217.

Dawes, R. M. (1980). Social dilemmas. *Annual Review of Psychology, 31,* 169–193.

Dawkins, R. (1989). *The selfish gene* (2nd ed.). Oxford: Oxford University Press.

Day, A., Casey, S., & Gerace, A. (2010). Interventions to improve empathy awareness in sexual and violent offenders: Conceptual, empirical, and clinical issues. *Aggression and Violent Behavior, 15,* 201–208.

Day, D. D., & Sulsky, L. M. (1995). Effects of frame-of-reference training and information configuration on memory organization and rating accuracy. *Journal of Applied Psychology, 80*, 158–167.

Day, D. V., Shleicher, D. J., Unckless, A. L., & Hiller, N. J. (2002). Self-monitoring personality at work: A meta-analytic investigation of construct validity. *Journal of Applied Psychology, 87*, 390–401.

De Cremer, D. (2004). The influence of accuracy as a function of leader's bias: The role of trustworthiness in the psychology of procedural justice. *Personality and Social Psychology Bulletin, 30*, 293–304.

De Dreu, C. K. W. (2010). Social conflict: The emergence and consequences of struggle and negotiation. In S. T. Fiske, D. T. Gilbert, & G. Lindzey (Eds.), *Handbook of social psychology* (5th ed.). New York: Wiley.

De Dreu, C. K. W., Beersma, B., Steinel, W., Van Kleef, G. A. (2007). The psychology of negotiation: Principles and basic processes (pp. 608–629). In A. W. Kruglanski & E. T. Higgins (Eds.), *Social psychology: Handbook of basic principles* (2nd ed.). New York: Guilford.

De Dreu, C. K. W., Beersma, B., Stroebe, K., & Euwema, M. C. (2006). Motivated information processing, strategic choice, and the quality of negotiated agreement. *Journal of Personality and Social Psychology, 90*, 927–943.

De Dreu, C. W. (2012). Oxytocin modulates the link between adult attachment and cooperation through reduced betrayal aversion. *Psychoneuroendocrinology, 37*, 871–880.

De Dreu, C. W., Nijstad, B. A., Bechtoldt, M. N., & Baas, M. (2011). Group creativity and innovation: A motivated information processing perspective. *Psychology of Aesthetics, Creativity, and The Arts, 5*, 81–89.

De Dreu, C., & De Vries, N. (Eds.). (2001). *Group consensus and minority influence: Implications for innovation.* London: Blackwell.

de Hoog, N., Stroebe, W., & de Wit, J. B. F. (2007). The impact of vulnerability to and severity of a health risk on processing and acceptance of fear-arousing communications: A meta-analysis. *Review of General Psychology, 11*, 258–285.

De Houwer, J., Teige-Mocigemba, S., Spruyt, A., & Moors, A. (2009). Implicit measures: A normative analysis and review. *Psychological Bulletin, 135*, 347–368.

de Paula Couto, M., & Koller, S. (2012). Warmth and competence: Stereotypes of the elderly among young adults and older persons in Brazil. *International Perspectives In Psychology: Research, Practice, Consultation, 1*, 52–62.

De Raad, B. (2000). *The big five personality factors: Theory and applications.* Germany: Hogrefe & Huber.

De Steno, D. A., & Salovey, P. (1996). Evolutionary origins of sex differences in jealousy? Questioning the "fitness" model. *Psychological Science, 7*, 367–372.

De Steno, D. M., Valdesolo, P., & Bartlett, M. Y. (2006). Jealousy and the threatened self: Getting to the heart of the green-eyed monster. *Journal of Personality and Social Psychology, 91*, 626–641.

De Veer, M. W., Gallup, G. G., Theall, L. A., van den Bos, R., & Povinelli, D. J. (2003). An 8-year longitudinal study of mirror self-recognition in chimpanzees *(Pan troglodytes). Neuropsychologia, 41*, 229–234.

de Waal, F. B. M. (1996). *Good natured: The origins of right and wrong in humans and other animals.* Cambridge, MA: Harvard University Press.

de Waal, F. B. M. (2003). The chimpanzee's service economy: Evidence for cognition-based reciprocal exchange. In E. Ostrom & J. Walker (Eds.), *Trust and reciprocity: Interdisciplinary lessons from experimental research* (pp. 128–143). New York: Russell Sage.

de Waal, F. B. M. (2006). Joint ventures require joint pay-offs: Fairness among primates. *Social Research, 73*, 349–364.

de Waal, F. B. M. (2008). Putting the altruism back into altruism: The evolution of empathy. *Annual Review of Psychology, 59*, 279–300.

de Waal, F. B., & Berger, M. L. (2000). Payment for labor in monkeys. *Nature, 404*, 563.

de Waal, F. M. (2008). How selfish an animal? The case of primate cooperation. In P. J. Zak (Ed.), *Moral markets: The critical role of values in the economy* (pp. 63–76). Princeton, NJ: Princeton University Press.

de Waal, F. M., & Ferrari, P. (Eds.) (2012). *The primate mind: Built to connect with other minds. Cambridge,* MA: Harvard University Press.

Deater-Deckard, K., Dodge, K. A., Bates, J. E., & Pettit, G. S. (1998). Multiple-risk factors in the development of externalizing behavior problems: Group and individual differences. *Development and Psychopathology, 10*, 469–493.

Deaux, K., & Emswiller, T. (1974). Explanations for successful performance on sex-linked tasks: What is skill for the male is luck for the female. *Journal of Personality and Social Psychology, 29*, 80–85.

DeBono, K. G., Leavitt, A., & Backus, J. (2003). Product packaging and product evaluation: An individual difference approach. *Journal of Applied Social Psychology, 33*, 513–521.

Decety, J. (2011). Dissecting the neural mechanisms mediating empathy. *Emotion Review, 3*, 92–108.

Decety, J., Echols, S., & Correll, J. (2010). The blame game: The effect of responsibility and social stigma on empathy for pain. *Journal of Cognitive Neuroscience, 22*, 985–997.

Decety, J., Michalska, K. J., Akitsuki, Y., & Lahey, B. B. (2009). Atypical empathic responses in adolescents with aggressive conduct disorder: A functional MRI investigation. *Biological Psychology, 80*(2), 203–211.

Decety, J., & Svetlova, M. (2012). Putting together phylogenetic and ontogenetic perspectives on empathy. *Developmental Cognitive Neuroscience, 2*, 1–24.

Deci, E. L. (1971). Effects of externally mediated rewards on intrinsic motivation. *Journal of Personality and Social Psychology, 18*, 105–115.

Deci, E. L., & Ryan, R. M. (1985). *Intrinsic motivation and self-determination in human behavior.* New York: Plenum.

Deer, B. (2011). How the case against the MMR vaccine was fixed. *British Medical Journal, 342*, 77–82.

Deffenbacher, K. A., Bornstein, B. H., & Penrod, S. D. (2006). Mugshot exposure effects: Retroactive interference, mugshot commitment, source confusion, and unconscious transference. *Law and Human Behavior, 30*, 287–307.

DelPriore, D. J., Hill, S. E., & Buss, D. M. (2012). Envy: Functional specificity and sex-differentiated design features. *Personality and Individual Differences, 53*, 317–322.

Demoulin, S., Pozo, B. C., & Leyens, J.-P. (2009). Infrahumanization: The differential interpretation of primary and secondary emotions. In S. L. Demoulin, J.-P. Leyens, & J. F. Dovidio (Eds.), *Intergroup misunderstandings: Impact of divergent social realities* (pp. 153–171). New York: Psychology Press.

Dempsey, C. (2010). *Murder in Italy: The shocking slaying of a British student, the accused American girl, and an international scandal.* New York: Berkley Books.

DeNeve, K. M., & Cooper, H. (1998). The happy personality: A meta-analysis of 137 personality traits and subjective well-being. *Psychological Bulletin, 124*, 197–229.

Denissen, J. A., Penke, L., & Schmitt, D. P. (2008). Self-esteem reactions to social interactions: Evidence for sociometer mechanisms across days, people, and nations. *Journal of Personality and Social Psychology, 95*, 181–196.

Denrell, J. (2005). Why most people disapprove of me: Experience sampling in impression formation. *Psychological Review, 112*, 951–978.

Denson, T. F., Capper, M. M., Oaten, M., Friese, M., & Schofield, T. P. (2011). Self-control training decreases aggression in response to provocation in aggressive individuals. *Journal of Research in Personality, 45*, 252–256.

Denson, T. F., DeWall, C., & Finkel, E. J. (2012). Self-control and aggression. *Current Directions in Psychological Science, 21*, 20–25.

Denson, T. F., Jacobson, M., von Hippel, W., Kemp, R. I., & Mak, T. (2012). Caffeine expectancies but not caffeine reduce depletion-induced aggression. *Psychology of Addictive Behaviors, 26*, 140–144.

Denson, T. F., Mehta, P. H., & Ho Tan, D. (2013). Endogenous testosterone and cortisol jointly influence reactive aggression in women. *Psychoneuroendocrinology,* in press.

Denson, T. F., Moulds, M. L., & Grisham, J. R. (2012). The effects of analytical rumination, reappraisal, and distraction on anger experience. *Behavior Therapy, 43*, 355–364.

Denson, T. F., Pedersen, W. C., Friese, M., Hahm, A., & Roberts, L. (2011). Understanding impulsive aggression: Angry rumination and reduced self-control capacity are mechanisms underlying the provocation-aggression relationship. *Personality and Social Psychology Bulletin, 37*, 850–862.

Denson, T. F., Ronay, R., von Hippel, W., & Schira, M. M. (2013). Risk for aggression: Endogenous testosterone and cortisol modulate neural responses to induced anger control. *Social Neuroscience,* in press.

Denson, T. F., von Hippel, W., Kemp, R. I., & Teo, L. S. (2010). Glucose consumption decreases impulsive aggression in response to provocation in aggressive individuals. *Journal of Experimental Social Psychology, 46,* 1023–1028.

DePaulo, B. (2011). Living single: Lightening up those dark, dopey myths. In W. R. Cupach, & B. H. Spitzberg (Eds.), *The dark side of close relationships II* (pp. 409–439). New York: Routledge/Taylor & Francis Group.

DePaulo, B. M., Lindsay, J. J., Malone, B. E., Muhlenbruck, L., Charlton, K., & Cooper, H. (2003). Cues to deception. *Psychological Bulletin, 129,* 74–112.

Derlega, V. J., Metts, S., Petronio, S., & Margulis, S. T. (1993). *Self-disclosure.* Newbury Park, CA: Sage.

Derlega, V. J., Wilson, M., & Chaikin, A. L. (1976). Friendship and disclosure reciprocity. *Journal of Personality and Social Psychology, 34,* 578–587.

DeRosa, D. M., Smith, C. L., & Hantula, D. A. (2007). The medium matters: Mining the long-promised merit of group interaction in creative idea generation tasks in a meta-analysis of the electronic group brainstorming literature. *Computers in Human Behavior, 23,* 1549–1581.

Dershowitz, A. M. (1982). *The best defense.* New York: Vintage Books.

Desmarais, S. L., & Read, J. D. (2011). After 30 years, what do we know about what jurors know? A meta-analytic review of lay knowledge regarding eyewitness factors. *Law and Human Behavior, 35,* 200–210.

Dettenborn, L., Tietze, A., Bruckner, F., & Kirschbaum, C. (2010). Higher cortisol content in hair among long-term unemployed individuals compared to controls. *Psychoneuroendocrinology, 35,* 1404–1409.

Deutsch, F. M. (1989). The false consensus effect: Is the self-justification hypothesis justified? *Basic and Applied Social Psychology, 10,* 83–99.

Deutsch, M., & Gerard, H. B. (1955). A study of normative and informational social influences upon individual judgment. *Journal of Abnormal and Social Psychology, 51,* 629–636.

Devine, D. J., Buddenbaum J., Houp S., Studebaker N., & Stolle D. (2009). Strength of evidence, extraevidentiary influence, and the liberation hypothesis: Data from the field. *Law and Human Behavior, 33,* 136–148.

Devine, P. G. (1989). Stereotypes and prejudice: Their automatic and controlled components. *Journal of Personality and Social Psychology, 56,* 5–18.

Devos, T., Gavin, K., & Quintana, F. J. (2010). Say "adios" to the American dream? The interplay between ethnic and national identity among Latino and Caucasian Americans. *Cultural Diversity and Ethnic Minority Psychology, 16,* 37–49.

DeWall, C. N., & Bushman, B. J. (2009). Hot under the collar in a lukewarm environment: Words associated with hot temperature increase aggressive thoughts and hostile perceptions. *Journal of Experimental Social Psychology, 45,* 1045–1047.

DeWall, C. N., Anderson, C. A., & Bushman, B. J. (2013). Aggression and violence. In I. Weiner (Ed.), *Comprehensive handbook of psychology* (2nd Ed.); H. Tenn & J Suls (Eds.), Volume 5: *Personality and social psychology.* New York: Wiley.

DeWall, C. N., Maner, J. K., & Rouby, D. A. (2009). Social exclusion and early-stage interpersonal perception: Selective attention to signs of acceptance. *Journal of Personality and Social Psychology, 96,* 729–741.

DeWall, C., & Bushman, B. J. (2009). Hot under the collar in a lukewarm environment: Words associated with hot temperature increase aggressive thoughts and hostile perceptions. *Journal of Experimental Social Psychology, 45,* 1045–1047.

DeWall, C., Anderson, C. A., & Bushman, B. J. (2011). The general aggression model: Theoretical extensions to violence. *Psychology of Violence, 1,* 245–258.

DeWall, C., Deckman, T., Gailliot, M. T., & Bushman, B. J. (2011). Sweetened blood cools hot tempers: Physiological self-control and aggression. *Aggressive Behavior, 37,* 73–80.

DeWall, C., Finkel, E. J., & Denson, T. F. (2011). Self-control inhibits aggression. *Social and Personality Psychology Compass, 5,* 458–472.

DeWall, C., Lambert, N. M., Pond, R. R., Kashdan, T. B., & Fincham, F. D. (2012). A grateful heart is a nonviolent heart: Cross-sectional, experience sampling, longitudinal, and experimental evidence. *Social Psychological and Personality Science, 3,* 232–240.

DeWall, C., Twenge, J. M., Bushman, B., Im, C., & Williams, K. (2010). A little acceptance goes a long way: Applying social impact theory to the rejection-aggression link. *Social Psychological and Personality Science, 1,* 168–174.

Diamond, L. M. (2003). Was it a phase? Young women's relinquishment of lesbian/bisexual identities over a 5-year period. *Journal of Personality and Social Psychology, 84,* 352–364.

Diamond, L. M. (2007). A dynamical systems approach to female same-sex sexuality. *Perspectives on Psychological Science, 2,* 142–161.

Diamond, M. (1993). Homosexuality and bisexuality in different populations. *Archives of Sexual Behavior, 22,* 291–310.

Diamond, S. S., & Rose, M. R. (2005). Real juries. *Annual Review of Law and Social Science, 1,* 255–284.

Diamond, S. S., Rose, M. R., & Murphy, B. (2006). Revisiting the unanimity requirement: The behavior of the non-unanimous civil jury. *Northwestern Law Review, 100,* 201–230.

Diehl, M., & Stroebe, W. (1987). Productivity loss in brainstorming groups: Toward the solution of a riddle. *Journal of Personality and Social Psychology, 53,* 497–509.

Diener, E. (1979). Deindividuation, self-awareness, and disinhibition. *Journal of Personality and Social Psychology, 37,* 1160–1171.

Diener, E. (1980). Deindividuation: The absence of self-awareness and self-regulation in group members. In P. B. Paulus (Ed.), *Psychology of group influence* (pp. 209–242). Hillsdale, NJ: Erlbaum.

Diener, E. (2000). Subjective well-being: The science of happiness, and a proposal for a national index. *American Psychologist, 55,* 34–43.

Diener, E., & Biswas-Diener, R. (2008). *Happiness: Unlocking the mysteries of psychological wealth.* Malden, MA: Blackwell.

Diener, E., & Seligman, M. E. P. (2004). Beyond money: Toward an economy of well-being. *Psychological Science in the Public Interest, 5,* whole No. 1.

Diener, E., & Suh, E. M. (Eds.). (2000). *Culture and subjective well-being.* Cambridge, MA: MIT Press.

Diener, E., Emmons, R. A., Larsen, R. J., & Griffin, S. (1984). The Satisfaction with Life Scale. *Journal of Personality Assessment, 49,* 71–75.

Diener, E., Fraser, S. C., Beaman, A. L., & Kelem, R. T. (1976). Effects of deindividuation variables on stealing among Halloween trick-or-treaters. *Journal of Personality and Social Psychology, 33,* 178–183.

Diener, E., Suh, E. M., Lucas, R. E., & Smith, H. L. (1999). Subjective well-being: Three decades of progress. *Psychological Bulletin, 125,* 276–302.

Diener, E., Wolsic, B., & Fujita, F. (1995). Physical attractiveness and subjective well-being. *Journal of Personality and Social Psychology, 69,* 120–129.

Dietz-Uhler, B. (1996). The escalation of commitment in political decision-making groups: A social identity approach. *European Journal of Social Psychology, 26,* 611–629.

DiFonzo, N., & Bordia, P. (1997). Rumor and prediction: Making sense (but losing dollars) in the stock market. *Organizational Behavior and Human Decision Processes, 71,* 329–353.

Dijksterhuis, A., & Aarts, H. (2003). Of wildebeests and humans: The preferential detection of negative stimuli. *Psychological Science, 14,* 14–18.

Dijksterhuis, A., & Bargh, J. A. (2001). The perception-behavior expressway: Automatic effects of social perception on social behavior. *Advances in Experimental Social Psychology, 33,* 1–40.

Dill, K. E., Anderson, C. A., Anderson, K. B., & Deuser, W. E. (1997). Effects of aggressive personality on social expectations and social perceptions. *Journal of Research in Personality, 31,* 272–292.

Dillard, A. J., Schiavone, A., & Brown, S. L. (2008). Helping behavior and positive emotions: Implications for health and well-being. In S. J. Lopez (Ed.), *Positive psychology: Exploring the best in people: Vol. 2. Capitalizing on emotional experiences* (pp. 101–114). Westport, CT: Praeger.

Dimberg, U., & Ohman, A. (1996). Behold the wrath: Psychophysiological responses to facial stimuli. *Motivation and Emotion, 20,* 149–181.

Dimberg, U., & Söderkvist, S. (2011). The voluntary facial action technique: a method to test the facial feedback hypothesis. *Journal of Nonverbal Behavior, 35,* 17–33.

Dimberg, U., Thunberg, M., & Elmehed, K. (2000). Unconscious facial reactions to emotional facial expressions. *Psychological Science, 11,* 86–89.

Dindia, K., & Allen, M. (1992). Sex differences in self-disclosure: A meta-analysis. *Psychological Bulletin, 112,* 106–124.

Dinero, R. E., Conger, R. D., Shaver, P. R., Widaman, K. F., & Larsen-Rife, D. (2008). The influence of family of origin and adult romantic partners on romantic attachment security. *Journal of Family Psychology, 22,* 622–632.

Dion, K. K., & Dion, K. L. (1996). Cultural perspectives on romantic love. *Personal Relationships, 3,* 5–17.

Dion, K. K., Berscheid, E., & Walster, E. (1972). What is beautiful is good. *Journal of Personality and Social Psychology, 24,* 285–290.

Dion, K. L. (2000). Group cohesion: From "field of forces" to multidimensional construct. *Group Dynamics, 4,* 7–26.

Dion, K. L., & Dion, K. K. (1976). Love, liking and trust in heterosexual relationships. *Personality and Social Psychology Bulletin, 2,* 187–190.

Dionisio, D. P., Granholm, E., Hillix, W. A., & Perrine, W. F. (2001). Differentiation of deception using pupillary responses as an index of cognitive processing. *Psychophysiology 38,* 205–211.

Dittmann, M. (2005). After the wave. *APA Monitor on Psychology, 36,* No. 3, p. 36.

Dizikes, C., & Sobol, R. R. (2012). Pediatric surgeon raced to save boys in lake despite his kids' concerns. *Chicago Tribune,* August 6. http://articles.chicagotribune.com/2012-08-06/news/chi-pediatric-surgeon-dies-saving-two-children-from-drowning-in-lake-michigan-20120805_1_compassionate-surgeon-and-one-pediatric-surgeon-liu.

Dolinski, D. (2000). On inferring one's beliefs from one's attempt and consequences for subsequent compliance. *Journal of Personality and Social Psychology, 78,* 260–272.

Dollard, J., Doob, L. W., Miller, N. E., Mowrer, O. H., & Sears, R. R. (1939). *Frustration and aggression.* New Haven, CT: Yale University Press.

Dominus, S. (2012). What happened to the girls in Le Roy. *The New York Times Magazine* March 7, 2012, p. 28.

Donnellan, M. B., Trzesniewski, K. H., Robins, R. W., Moffitt, T. E., & Caspi, A. (2005). Low self-esteem is related to aggression, antisocial behavior, and delinquency. *Psychological Science, 16,* 328–335.

Donnerstein, E., & Berkowitz, L. (1981). Victim reactions in aggressive erotic films as a factor in violence against women. *Journal of Personality and Social Psychology, 41,* 710–724.

Donnerstein, E., & Donnerstein, M. (1976). Research in the control of interracial aggression. In R. G. Geen and E. C. O'Neal (Eds.), *Perspectives on aggression* (pp. 133–168). New York: Academic Press.

Donnerstein, E., & Malamuth, N. (1997). Pornography: Its consequences on the observer. In L. B. Schlesinger & E. Revitch (Eds.), *Sexual dynamics of anti-social behavior* (2nd ed., pp. 30–49). Springfield, IL: Charles C Thomas.

Donnerstein, E., Linz, D., & Penrod, S. (1987). *The question of pornography.* New York: Free Press.

Dooley, P. A. (1995). Perceptions of the onset controllability of AIDS and helping judgments: An attributional analysis. *Journal of Applied Social Psychology, 25,* 858–869.

Dornburg, C. C., Stevens, S. M., Hendrickson, S. L., & Davidson, G. S. (2009). Improving extreme-scale problem solving: Assessing electronic brainstorming effectiveness in an industrial setting. *Human Factors, 51,* 519–527.

Dornbusch, S. M., Hastorf, A. H., Richardson, S. A., Muzzy, R. E., & Vreeland, R. S. (1965). The perceiver and the perceived: Their relative influence on categories of interpersonal perception. *Journal of Personality and Social Psychology, 1,* 434–440.

Dougherty, T. W., Turban, D. B., & Callender, J. C. (1994). Confirming first impressions in the employment interview: A field study of interviewer behavior. *Journal of Applied Psychology, 79,* 659–665.

Douglas, E. M., & Straus, M. A. (2006). Assault and injury of dating partners by university students in 19 countries and its relation to corporal punishment experienced as a child. *European Journal of Criminology, 7,* 293–318.

Douglass, A. B., & Steblay, N. (2006). Memory distortion in eyewitnesses: A meta-analysis of the post-identification feed-back effect. *Applied Cognitive Psychology, 20,* 859–869.

Douglass, A. B., Neuschatz, J. S., Imrich, J., & Wilkinson, M. (2010). Does post—identification feedback affect evaluations of eyewitness testimony and identification procedures? *Law and Human Behavior, 34,* 282–294.

Dovidio, J. F. (1984). Helping behavior and altruism: An empirical and conceptual overview. In L. Berkowitz (Ed.), *Advances in experimental social psychology* (Vol. 17, pp. 361–427). New York: Academic Press.

Dovidio, J. F., & Gaertner, S. L. (2004). Aversive racism. In M. P. Zanna (Ed.), *Advances in experimental social psychology* (Vol. 36, pp. 1–52). San Diego, CA: Elsevier.

Dovidio, J. F., Brigham, J. C., Johnson, B. T., & Gaertner, S. L. (1996). Stereotyping, prejudice, and discrimination: Another look. In C. N. Macrae, C. Stangor, & M. Hewstone (Eds.), *Stereotypes and stereotyping* (pp. 276–319). New York: Guilford.

Dovidio, J. F., Eller, A., & Hewstone, M. (2011). Improving intergroup relations through direct, extended and other forms of indirect contact. *Group Processes & Intergroup Relations, 14,* 147–160.

Dovidio, J. F., Gaertner, S. E., Kawakami, K., & Hodson, G. (2002). Why can't we just get along? Interpersonal biases and interracial distrust. *Cultural Diversity and Ethnic Minority Psychology, 8,* 88–102.

Dovidio, J. F., Gaertner, S. L., Shnabel, N., Saguy, T., & Johnson, J. (2010). Recategorization and prosocial behavior: Common in-group identity and a dual identity. In S. Stürmer & M. Snyder (Eds.), *The psychology of prosocial behavior: Group processes, intergroup relations, and helping* (pp. 191–207). Wiley-Blackwell.

Dovidio, J. F., Kawakami, K., Johnson, C., Johnson, B., & Howard, A. (1997). On the nature of prejudice: Automatic and controlled processes. *Journal of Experimental Social Psychology, 33,* 510–540.

Dovidio, J. F., Piliavin, J., Schroeder, D. A., & Penner, L. (2006). *The social psychology of prosocial behavior.* Mahwah, NJ: Erlbaum.

Dovidio, J. F., Saguy, T., Gaertner, S. L., & Thomas, E. L. (2013). From attitudes to (in)action: The darker side of "we." In J. Dixon & M. Levine (Eds.), *Beyond the "prejudice problematic": Extending the social psychology of intergroup conflict, inequality, and social change.* Cambridge: Cambridge University Press.

Downs, A. C., & Lyons, P. M. (1991). Natural observations of the links between attractiveness and initial legal judgments. *Personality and Social Psychology Bulletin, 17,* 541–547.

Doyle, J. M. (2005). *True witness: Cops, courts, science, and the battle against misidentification.* New York: Palgrave MacMillan.

Dreher, G. F., & Cox, T. H., Jr. (1996). Race, gender, and opportunity: A study of compensation attainment and the establishment of mentoring relationships. *Journal of Applied Psychology, 81,* 297–308.

Drigotas, S. M., & Rusbult, C. E. (1992). Shall I stay or should I go? A dependence model of breakups. *Journal of Personality and Social Psychology, 62,* 62–87.

Drigotas, S. M., Rusbult, C. E., & Verette, J. (1999). Level of commitment, mutuality of commitment, and couple well-being. *Personal Relationships, 6,* 389–409.

Druckman, D. (1994). Determinants of compromising behavior in negotiation: A meta-analysis. *Journal of Conflict Resolution, 38,* 507–556.

Duck, S., & Wright, P. H. (1993). Reexamining gender differences in same-gender friendships: A close look at two kinds of data. *Sex Roles, 28,* 709–727.

Duckitt, J., & Mphuthing, T. (1998). Group identification and intergroup attitudes: A longitudinal analysis in South Africa. *Journal of Personality and Social Psychology, 74,* 80–85.

Duclos, S. E., Laird, J. D., Schneider, E., Sexter, M., Stern, L., & Van Lighten, O. (1989). Emotion-specific effects of facial expressions and postures on emotional experience. *Journal of Personality and Social Psychology, 57,* 100–108.

Dudley, N. M., Orvis, K. A., Lebiecki, J. E., & Cortina, J. M. (2006). A meta-analytic investigation of conscientiousness in the prediction of job performance: Examining the intercorrelations and the incremental validity of narrow traits. *Journal of Applied Psychology, 91,* 40–57.

Due, P., & Holstein, B. (2008). Bullying victimization among 13 to 15 year old school children: Results from two comparative studies in 66 countries and regions. *International Journal of Adolescent Medicine and Health, 20,* 209–221.

Dueck, L. (2006, November 3). There's a lot we can learn from the Amish. *The Globe and Mail* (Canada), p. A25.

Dunbar, R. M. (2012). The social brain meets neuroimaging. *Trends in Cognitive Sciences, 16,* 101–102.

Dunham, Y., Baron, A. S., & Banaji, M. R. (2008). The development of implicit intergroup cognition. *Trends in Cognitive Sciences, 12,* 248–253.

Dunning, D. (2005). *Self-insight: Roadblocks and detours on the path to knowing thyself.* New York: Psychology Press.

Dunning, D., & Sherman, D. A. (1997). Stereotypes and tacit inference. *Journal of Personality and Social Psychology, 73,* 459–471.

Dunning, D., Griffin, D. W., Milojkovic, J. D., & Ross, L. (1990). The overconfidence effect in social prediction. *Journal of Personality and Social Psychology, 58,* 568–581.

Dunning, D., Heath, C., & Suls, J. M. (2004). Flawed self-assessment: Implications for health, education, and the workplace. *Psychological Science in the Public Interest, 5,* 69–106.

Dunning, D., Johnson, K., Ehrlinger, J., & Kruger, J. (2003). Why people fail to recognize their own incompetence. *Current Directions in Psychological Science, 12,* 83–87.

Duntley, J., & Buss, D. (2008). The origins of homicide. In J. D. Duntley & T. K. Shackelford (Eds.), *Evolutionary forensic psychology: Darwinian foundations of crime and law* (pp. 41–63). New York: Oxford University Press.

Dunton, B. C., & Fazio, R. H. (1997). An individual difference measure of motivation to control prejudiced reactions. *Personality and Social Psychology Bulletin, 23,* 316–326.

Durán, M., Moya, M., & Megías, J. L. (2011). It's his right, it's her duty: Benevolent sexism and the justification of traditional sexual roles. *Journal of Sex Research, 48,* 470–478.

Durantini, M. R., Albarracín, D., Mitchell, A. L., Earl, A. N., & Gillette, J. C. (2006). Conceptualizing the influence of social agents of behavior change: A meta-analysis of the effectiveness of HIV-prevention interventionists for different groups. *Psychological Bulletin, 132,* 212–248.

Durik, A. M., & Harackiewicz, J. M. (2007). Different strokes for different folks: Individual interest as a moderator of the effects of situational factors on task interest. *Journal of Educational Psychology, 99,* 597–610.

Dutton, D. G., & Aron, A. P. (1974). Some evidence for heightened sexual attraction under conditions of high anxiety. *Journal of Personality and Social Psychology, 30,* 510–517.

Dutton, K. (2010). *Split-second persuasion: The ancient art and new science of changing minds.* New York: Houghton Mifflin Harcourt.

Duval, S., & Wicklund, R. A. (1972). *A theory of objective self-awareness.* New York: Academic Press.

Duval, S., Duval, V. H., & Mulilis, J. P. (1992). Effects of self-focus, discrepancy between self and standard, and outcome expectancy favorability on the tendency to match self to standard or to withdraw. *Journal of Personality and Social Psychology, 62,* 340–348.

Dweck, C. S. (2012). Implicit theories. In P. M. Van Lange, A. W. Kruglanski, & E. Higgins (Eds.), *Handbook of theories of social psychology* (Vol. 2, pp. 43–61). Thousand Oaks, CA: Sage.

Dysart, J. E., Lindsay, R. C. L., MacDonald, T. K., & Wicke, C. (2002). The intoxicated witness: Effects of alcohol on identification accuracy from showups. *Journal of Applied Psychology, 87,* 170–175.

Eagly, A. H. (1987). *Sex differences in social behavior: A social-role interpretation.* Hillsdale, NJ: Erlbaum.

Eagly, A. H. (2004). Few women at the top: How role incongruity produces prejudice and the glass ceiling. In D. van Knippenberg & M. A. Hogg (Eds.), *Leadership and power: Identity processes in groups and organizations* (pp. 79–93). London: Sage Publications.

Eagly, A. H., & Carli, L. L. (1981). Sex of researchers and sex-typed communications as determinants of sex differences in influenceability: A meta-analysis of social influence studies. *Psychological Bulletin, 90,* 1–20.

Eagly, A. H., & Carli, L. L. (2007). *Through the labyrinth: The truth about how women become leaders.* Boston: Harvard Business School Publishing.

Eagly, A. H., & Crowley, M. (1986). Gender and helping behavior: A meta-analytic review of the social psychological literature. *Psychological Bulletin, 100,* 283–308.

Eagly, A. H., & Karau, S. J. (2002). Role congruity theory of prejudice toward female leaders. *Psychological Review, 109,* 573–598.

Eagly, A. H., & Wood, W. (2012). *Social role theory.* In P. M. Van Lange, A. W. Kruglanski, & E. T. Higgins (Eds.), *Handbook of theories of social psychology* (Vol. 2, pp. 458–476). Thousand Oaks, CA: Sage.

Eagly, A. H., Ashmore, R. D., Makhijani, M. G., & Longo, L. C. (1991). What is beautiful is good, but . . . : A meta-analytic review of research on the physical attractiveness stereotype. *Psychology Bulletin, 110,* 107–128.

Eagly, A. H., Johannesen-Schmidt, M. C., & van Engen, M. L. (2003). Transformational, transactional, and laissez-faire leadership styles: A meta-analysis comparing women and men. *Psychological Bulletin, 129,* 569–591.

Eagly, A. H., Mladinic, A., & Otto, S. (1994). Are women evaluated more favorably than men? An analysis of attitudes, beliefs, and emotions. *Psychology of Women Quarterly, 15,* 203–216.

Eagly, A. H., Wood, W., & Chaiken, S. (1978). Causal inferences about communicators and their effect on opinion change. *Journal of Personality and Social Psychology, 36,* 424–435.

Earl, A., Albarracín, D., Durantini, M., Gunnoe, J., Leeper, J., & Levitt, J. (2009). Participation in counseling programs: High-risk participants are reluctant to accept HIV-prevention counseling. *Journal of Consulting and Clinical Psychology, 77,* 668–679.

Earle, A., & Heymann, J. (2012). The cost of caregiving: Wage loss among caregivers of elderly and disabled adults and children with special needs. *Community, Work & Family, 15,* 357–375.

Easton, J., Schipper, L., & Shackelford, T. (2007). Morbid jealousy from an evolutionary psychological perspective. *Evolution and Human Behavior, 28,* 399–402.

Eastwick, P. W., & Finkel, E. J. (2008). Sex differences in mate preferences revisited: Do people know what they initially desire in a romantic partner? *Journal of Personality and Social Psychology, 94,* 245–264.

Eastwick, P. W., Finkel, E. J., Mochon, D., & Ariely, D. (2007). Selective versus unselective romantic desire: Not all reciprocity is created equal. *Psychological Science, 18,* 317–319.

Eberhardt, J. L., Davies, P. G., Purdie-Vaughns, V. J., & Johnson, S. L. (2006). Looking deathworthy: Perceived stereotypicality of black defendants predicts capital-sentencing outcomes. *Psychological Science, 17,* 383–386.

Ebstein, R. P., Israel, S., Chew, S. H., Zhong, S., & Knafo, A. (2010). Genetics of human social behavior. *Neuron, 65,* 831–844.

Eden, D. (1990). Pygmalion without interpersonal contrast effects: Whole groups gain from raising manager expectations. *Journal of Applied Psychology, 75,* 394–398.

Eder, R. W., & Harris, M. M. (Eds.). (1999). *The employment interview handbook* (2nd ed.). Thousand Oaks, CA: Sage.

Edwards, K., & Smith, E. E. (1996). A disconfirmation bias in the evaluation of arguments. *Journal of Personality and Social Psychology, 71,* 5–24.

Effron, D., Miller, D. T., & Monin, B. (2012). Inventing racist roads not taken: The licensing effect of immoral counterfactual behaviors. *Journal of Personality and Social Psychology,* in press.

Ehrlichman, H., & Eichenstein, R. (1992). Private wishes: Gender similarities and differences. *Sex Roles, 26,* 399–422.

Ehrlinger, J., Gilovich, T., & Ross, L. (2005). Peering into the bias blind spot: People's assessments of bias in themselves and others. *Personality and Social Psychology Bulletin, 31,* 680–692.

Eichstaedt, J., & Silvia, P. J. (2003). Noticing the self: Implicit assessment of self-focused attention using word recognition latencies. *Social Cognition, 21,* 349–361.

Eidelman, S., Crandall, C. S., & Pattershall, J. (2009). The existence bias. *Journal of Personality and Social Psychology, 97,* 765–775.

Eisenberg, N., Eggum, N. D., & Di Giunta, L. (2010). Empathy-related responding: Associations with prosocial behavior, aggression, and intergroup relations. *Social Issues and Policy Review, 4,* 143–180.

Eisenberg, N., Eggum, N. D., & Edwards, A. (2010). Empathy-related responding and moral development. In W. F. Arsenio & E. A. Lemerise (Eds.), *Emotions, aggression, and morality in children: Bridging development and psychopathology* (pp. 115–135). Washington, DC: American Psychological Association.

Eisenberg, N., Guthrie, I. K., Cumberland, A., Murphy, B. C., Shepard, S. A., Zhou, Q., & Carlo, G. (2002). Prosocial development in early adulthood: A longitudinal study. *Journal of Personality and Social Psychology, 82,* 993–1006.

Eisenberg, T., Hannaford-Agor, P. L., Hans, V. P., Mott, N. L., Munsterman, G. T., Schwab, S. J., & Wells, M. T. (2005). Judge-jury agreement in criminal cases: A partial replication of Kalven & Zeisel's *The American Jury. Journal of Empirical Legal Studies, 2,* 171–206.

Eisenberger, N. I. (2012). Broken hearts and broken bones: A neural perspective on the similarities between social and physical pain. *Current Directions In Psychological Science, 21,* 42–47.

Eisenberger, N. I., & Cole, S. W. (2012). Social neuroscience and health: Neurophysiological mechanisms linking social ties with physical health. *Nature Neuroscience, 15,* 1–6.

Eisenberger, N. I., Inagaki, T. K., Muscatell, K. A., Haltom, K. E. B., & Leary, M. R. (2011). The neural sociometer: brain mechanisms underlying state self-esteem. *Journal of Cognitive Neuroscience, 23,* 3448–3455.

Eisenberger, N. I., Lieberman, M. I., & Williams, K. D. (2003). Does rejection hurt? An fMRI study of social exclusion. *Science, 302,* 290–292.

Eisenberger, N. I., Way, B. M., Taylor, S. E., Welch, W. T., & Lieberman, M. D. (2007). Understanding genetic risk for aggression: Clues from the brain's response to social exclusion. *Biological Psychiatry, 61,* 1100–1108.

Eisenberger, R., & Cameron, J. (1996). Detrimental effects of reward: Reality or myth? *American Psychologist, 51,* 1153–1166.

Eisenberger, R., & Rhoades, L. (2001). Incremental effects of reward on creativity. *Journal of Personality and Social Psychology, 81,* 728–741.

Eisenberger, R., Cotterell, N., & Marvel, J. (1987). Reciprocation ideology. *Journal of Personality and Social Psychology, 53,* 743–750.

Ekman, P., & Friesen, W. V. (1974). Detecting deception from the body or face. *Journal of Personality and Social Psychology, 29,* 288–298.

Ekman, P., & O'Sullivan, M. (1991). Who can catch a liar? *American Psychologist, 46,* 913–920.

Ekman, P., Friesen, W. V., O'Sullivan, M., Chan, A., Diacoyanni-Tarlatzis, I., Heider, K., Krause, R., LeCompte, W. A., Pitcairn, T., Ricci-Bitti, P., Scherer, K., Tomita, M., & Tzavaras, A. (1987). Universals and cultural differences in the judgments of facial expressions of emotion. *Journal of Personality and Social Psychology, 53,* 712–717.

El Leithy, S., Brown, G. P., & Robbins, I. (2006). Counterfactual thinking and posttraumatic stress reactions. *Journal of Abnormal Psychology, 115,* 629–635.

Elder, M. (2012). St Petersburg bans "homosexual propaganda." http://www.guardian.co.uk/world/2012/mar/12/st-petersburg-bans-homosexual-propaganda.

Elfenbein, H. A., & Ambady N. (2002). On the universality and cultural specificity of emotion recognition: A meta-analysis. *Psychological Bulletin, 128,* 203–235.

Elfenbein, H. A., & Ambady, N. (2003). When familiarity breeds accuracy: Cultural exposure and facial emotion recognition. *Journal of Personality and Social Psychology, 85,* 276–290.

Elkin, R. A., & Leippe, M. R. (1986). Physiological arousal, dissonance, and attitude change: Evidence for a dissonance-arousal link and a "don't remind me" effect. *Journal of Personality and Social Psychology, 51,* 55–65.

Ellemers, N., & Haslam, S. (2012). Social identity theory. In P. M. Van Lange, A. W. Kruglanski, & E. T. Higgins (Eds.), *Handbook of theories of social psychology* (Vol. 2, pp. 379–398). Thousand Oaks, CA: Sage.

Elliot, A. J., & Devine, P. G. (1994). On the motivational nature of cognitive dissonance: Dissonance as psychological discomfort. *Journal of Personality and Social Psychology, 67,* 382–394.

Elliot, A. J., & Niesta, D. (2008). Romantic red: Red enhances men's attraction to women. *Journal of Personality and Social Psychology, 95,* 1150–1164.

Elliott, M. A., Armitage, C. J., & Baughan, C. J. (2003). Drivers' compliance with speed limits: An application of the theory of planned behavior. *Journal of Applied Psychology, 88,* 964–972.

Elliott, R. (1991). Social science data and the APA: The Lockhart brief as a case in point. *Law and Human Behavior, 15,* 59–76.

Ellis, M. L., Weiss, B., & Lochman, J. E. (2009). Executive functions in children: Associations with aggressive behavior and appraisal processing. *Journal of Abnormal Child Psychology, 37,* 945–956.

Ellsworth, P. C. (1991). To tell what we know or wait for Godot? *Law and Human Behavior, 15,* 77–90.

Elms, A. C. (2009). Obedience lite. *American Psychologist, 64,* 32–36.

Elms, A., & Milgram, S. (1966). Personality characteristics associated with obedience and defiance toward authoritative command. *Journal of Experimental Research in Personality, 1,* 282–289.

Elwork, A., Sales, B. D., & Alfini, J. J. (1982). *Making jury instructions understandable.* Charlottesville, VA: Miche.

Emerson, M. O., Kimbro, R., & Yancey, G. (2002). Contact theory extended: The effects of prior racial contact on current social ties. *Social Science Quarterly, 83,* 745–761.

Emonds, G., Declerck, C. H., Boone, C., Vandervliet, E. M., & Parizel, P. M. (2011). Comparing the neural basis of decision making in social dilemmas of people with different social value orientations, a fMRI study. *Journal of Neuroscience, Psychology, and Economics, 4,* 11–24.

Engelhardt, C. R., Bartholow, B. D., Kerr, G. T., & Bushman, B. J. (2011). This is your brain on violent video games: Neural desensitization to violence predicts increased aggression following violent video game exposure. *Journal of Experimental Social Psychology, 47,* 1033–1036.

Englich, B., Mussweiler, T., & Strack, F. (2006). Playing dice with criminal sentences: The influence of irrelevant anchors on experts' judicial decision making. *Personality and Social Psychology Bulletin, 32,* 188–200.

English, P. W., & Sales, B. D. (1997). A ceiling or consistency effect for the comprehension of jury instructions. *Psychology, Public Policy, and Law, 3,* 381–401.

English, T., & Chen, S. (2007). Culture and self-concept stability: Consistency across and within contexts among Asian Americans and European Americans. *Journal of Personality and Social Psychology, 93,* 478–490.

Eply, N., & Whitchurch, E. (2008). Mirror, mirror on the wall: Enhancement in self—recognition. *Personality and Social Psychology Bulletin, 34,* 1159–1170.

Erber, R., & Tesser, A. (1992). Task effort and the regulation of mood: The absorption hypothesis. *Journal of Experimental Social Psychology, 28,* 339–359.

Ericksen, J. A., & Steffen, S. A. (1999). *Kiss and tell: Surveying sex in the twentieth century.* Cambridge, MA: Harvard University Press.

Eskine, K. J., Kacinic, N. A., & Prinz, J. J.(2011). A bad taste in the mouth: Gustatory influences on moral judgment. *Psychological Science, 22,* 295–299.

Esser, J. K. (1998). Alive and well after 25 years: A review of groupthink research. *Organizational Behavior and Human Decision Processes, 73,* 116–141.

Esses, V. M., Veenvliet, S., Hodson, G., & Mihic, L. (2008). Justice, morality, and the dehumanization of refugees. *Social Justice Research, 21,* 4–25.

Evans, A. T., & Clark, J. K. (2012). Source characteristics and persuasion: The role of self-monitoring in self-validation. *Journal of Experimental Social Psychology, 48,* 383–386.

Evans, G. W., & Lepore, S. J. (1993). Household crowding and social support: A quasiexperimental analysis. *Journal of Personality and Social Psychology, 65,* 308–316.

Evans, G. W., & Wener, R. E. (2006). Rail commuting duration and passenger stress. *Health Psychology, 25,* 408–412.

Evans, H., & Bartholomew, R. (2009). *Outbreak! The Encyclopedia of Extraordinary Social Behavior.* San Antonio, TX: Anomalist Books.

Evans, R. I., Smith, C. K., & Raines, B. E. (1984). Deterring cigarette smoking in adolescents: A psychosocial-behavioral analysis of an intervention strategy. In A. Baum, S. E. Taylor, & J. E. Singer (Eds.), *Handbook of psychology and health: Vol. 4. Social psychological aspects of health* (pp. 301–318). Hillsdale, NJ: Erlbaum.

Everly, B. A., Shih, M. J., & Ho, G. C. (2012). Don't ask, don't tell? Does disclosure of gay identity affect partner performance? *Journal of Experimental Social Psychology, 48,* 407–410.

Everson-Rose, S. A., & Lewis, T. T. (2005). Psychosocial factors in cardiovascular diseases. *Annual Review of Public Health, 26,* 469–500.

Everson, S. A., Goldberg, D. E., Kaplan, G. A., Cohen, R. D., Pukkala, E., Tuomiletho, P., & Salonen, J. T.. (1996). Hopelessness and risk of mortality and incidence of myorcardial infarction and cancer. *Psychosomatic Medicine, 58,* 113–121.

Everson, S. A., Goldberg, D. E., Kaplan, G. A., Julkunen, J., & Salonen, J. T. (1998). Anger expression and incident hypertension. *Psychosomatic Medicine, 60,* 730–735.

Exum, M. L. (2006). Alcohol and aggression: An integration of findings from experimental studies. *Journal of Criminal Justice, 34,* 131–145.

Fagin-Jones, S., & Midlarsky, E. (2007). Courageous altruism: Personal and situational correlates of rescue during the Holocaust. *Journal of Positive Psychology, 2,* 136–147.

Fairburn, C. G., & Brownell, K. D. (Eds.). (2002). *Eating disorders and obesity: A comprehensive handbook.* New York: Guilford Press.

Falk, C. F., Heine, S. J., Yuki, M., & Takemura, K. (2009). Why do Westerners self-enhance more than East Asians? *European Journal of Personality, 23*(3), 183–203.

Farrelly, D., Lazarus, J., & Roberts, G. (2007). Altruists attract. *Evolutionary Psychology, 5,* 313–329.

Fay, R. E., Turner, C. F., Klassen, A. D., & Gagnon, J. H. (1989). Prevalence and patterns of same-gender sexual contact among men. *Science, 243,* 343–348.

Fazio, R. H. (1990). Multiple processes by which attitudes guide behavior: The MODE model as an integrative framework. In M. P. Zanna (Ed.), *Advances in experimental social psychology* (Vol. 23, pp. 75–109). New York: Academic Press.

Fazio, R. H., & Olson, M. A. (2003). Implicit measures in social cognition research: Their meaning and use. *Annual Review of Psychology, 54,* 297–327.

Fazio, R. H., & Petty, R. E. (Eds.). (2008). *Attitudes: Their structure, function, and consequences.* New York: Psychology Press.

Fazio, R. H., & Towles-Schwen, T. (1999). The MODE model of attitude-behavior processes. In S. Chaiken & Y Trope (Eds.), *Dual-process theories in social psychology* (pp. 97–116). New York: Guilford.

Fazio, R. H., & Zanna, M. P. (1981). Direct experience and attitude-behavior consistency. In L. Berkowitz (Ed.), *Advances in experimental social psychology* (Vol. 14, pp. 162–202). New York: Academic Press.

Fazio, R. H., Ledbetter, J. E., & Towles-Schwen, T. (2000). On the costs of accessible attitudes: Detecting that the attitude object has changed. *Journal of Personality and Social Psychology, 78,* 197–210.

Fazio, R. H., Zanna, M. P., & Cooper, J. (1977). Dissonance and self perception: An integrative view of each theory's proper domain of application. *Journal of Experimental Social Psychology, 13,* 464–479.

Fehr, B., & Russell, J. A. (1991). The concept of love viewed from a prototype perspective. *Journal of Personality and Social Psychology, 60,* 425–438.

Fein, E., & Schneider, S. (1996). *The rules: Time-tested secrets for capturing the heart of Mr. Right.* New York: Warner Books.

Fein, S., & Spencer, S. J. (1997). Prejudice as self-image maintenance: Affirming the self through derogating others. *Journal of Personality and Social Psychology, 73,* 31–44.

Fein, S., Goethals, G. R., & Kugler, M. B. (2007). Social influence on political judgments: The case of presidential debates. *Political Psychology, 28,* 165–192.

Fein, S., Hoshino-Browne, E., Davies, P. G., & Spencer, S. J. (2003). Self-image maintenance goals and sociocultural norms in motivated social perception. In S. J. Spencer, S. Fein, M. P. Zanna, & J. M. Olson (Eds.), *Motivated social perception: The Ontario symposium* (Vol. 9, pp. 21–44). Mahwah, NJ: Erlbaum.

Fein, S., Morgan, S. J., Norton, M. I., & Sommers, S. R. (1997). Hype and suspicion: The effects of pretrial publicity, race, and suspicion on jurors' verdicts. *Journal of Social Issues, 53,* 487–502.

Feinberg, T. E., & Keenan, J. P. (Eds.). (2005). *The lost self: Pathologies of the brain and identity.* New York: Oxford University Press.

Feingold, A. (1988). Matching for attractiveness in romantic partners and same-sex friends: A meta-analysis and theoretical critique. *Psychological Bulletin, 104,* 226–235.

Feingold, A. (1992a). Gender differences in mate selection preferences: A test of the parental investment model. *Psychological Bulletin, 112,* 125–139.

Feingold, A. (1992b). Good-looking people are not what we think. *Psychological Bulletin, 111,* 304–341.

Fenigstein, A., & Abrams, D. (1993). Self-attention and the egocentric assumption of shared perspectives. *Journal of Experimental Social Psychology, 29,* 287–303.

Fenigstein, A., Scheier, M. F., & Buss, A. H. (1975). Public and private self-consciousness: Assessment and theory. *Journal of Consulting and Clinical Psychology, 43,* 522–527.

Fennelly, G. (2009, February 12). Amazon selling rape simulation game. *Belfast Telegraph.*

Ferguson, E., Farrell, K., & Lawrence, C. (2008). Blood donation is an act of benevolence rather than altruism. *Health Psychology, 27,* 327–336.

Ferguson, M. (2007). On the automatic evaluation of end-states. *Journal of Personality and Social Psychology, 92,* 596–611.

Ferrari, J. R. (1998). Procrastination. In H. S. Friedman (Ed.), *Encyclopedia of mental health* (pp. 5.1–5.7). San Diego: Academic Press.

Ferrari, J. R., Diaz-Morales, J. F., O'Callaghan, J., Diaz, K., & Argumedo, D. (2007). Frequent behavioral delay tendencies by adults: International prevalence rates of chronic procrastination. *Journal of Cross-Cultural Psychology, 38,* 458–464.

Ferrari, J. R., Johnson, J. A., & McCowan, W. G. (1995). *Procrastination and task avoidance: Theory, research, and treatment.* New York: Plenum.

Ferreira, A., Picazo, O., Uriarte, N., Pereira, M., & Fernandez-Guasti, A. (2000). Inhibitory effect of buspirone and diazepam, but not of 8-OH-DPAT, on maternal behavior and aggression. *Pharmacology, Biochemistry and Behavior, 66,* 389–396.

Ferriday, C., Vartanian, O., & Mandel, D. R. (2011). Public but not private ego threat triggers aggression in narcissists. *European Journal of Social Psychology, 41,* 564–568.

Festinger, L. (1950). Informal social communication. *Psychological Review, 57,* 271–282.

Festinger, L. (1954). A theory of social comparison processes. *Human Relations, 7,* 117–140.

Festinger, L. (1957). *A theory of cognitive dissonance.* Stanford, CA: Stanford University Press.

Festinger, L., & Carlsmith, J. M. (1959). Cognitive consequences of forced compliance. *Journal of Abnormal and Social Psychology, 58,* 203–210.

Festinger, L., Pepitone, A., & Newcomb, T. (1952). Some consequences of de-individuation in a group. *Journal of Abnormal and Social Psychology, 47,* 382–389.

Festinger, L., Schachter, S., & Back, K. W. (1950). *Social pressures in informal groups: A study of human factors in housing.* New York: Harper.

Fiedler, F. E. (1967). *A theory of leadership effectiveness.* New York: McGraw-Hill.

Fiedler, F. E., & Chemers, M. M. (1984). *Improving leadership effectiveness: The leader match concept* (2nd ed.). New York: Wiley.

Fiedler, F. E., & Garcia, J. E. (1987). *Leadership: Cognitive resources and performance.* New York: Wiley.

Fiedler, F. E., Murphy, S. E., & Gibson, F. W. (1992). Inaccurate reporting and inappropriate variables: A reply to Vecchio's (1990) examination of cognitive resource theory. *Journal of Applied Psychology, 77,* 372–374.

Fincham, F. D. (2003). Marital conflict, correlates, structure, and context. *Current Directions in Psychological Science, 12,* 23–27.

Fincham, F. D., Harold, G. T., & Gano-Phillips, S. (2000). The longitudinal association between attributions and marital satisfaction: Direction of effects and role of efficacy expectations. *Journal of Family Psychology, 14,* 267–285.

Fincham, F., Beach, S., & Davila, J. (2007). Longitudinal relations between forgiveness and conflict resolution in marriage. *Journal of Family Psychology, 21,* 542–545.

Fine, M. A., & Harvey, J. H. (Eds.). (2006). *Handbook of divorce and relationship dissolution.* Hillsdale, NJ: Erlbaum.

Fine, M. A., & Sacher, J. A. (1997). Predictors of distress following relationship termination among dating couples. *Journal of Social and Clinical Psychology, 16,* 381–388.

Finkel, E. J., & Eastwick, P. W. (2008). Speed-dating. *Current Directions in Psychological Science, 17,* 193–197.

Finkel, E. J., & Eckhardt, C. I. (2013). Intimate partner violence. In J. A.Simpson & L.Campbell (Eds.), *The Oxford handbook of close relationships.* New York: Oxford University Press.

Finkel, E. J., DeWall, C., Slotter, E. B., McNulty, J. K., Pond, R. R., & Atkins, D. C. (2012). Using I³ theory to clarify when dispositional aggressiveness predicts intimate partner violence perpetration. *Journal of Personality and Social Psychology, 102,* 533–549.

Finkel, E. J., DeWall, C., Slotter, E. B., Oaten, M., & Foshee, V. A. (2009). Self-regulatory failure and intimate partner violence perpetration. *Journal of Personality and Social Psychology, 97,* 483–499.

Finkel, E. J., Eastwick, P. W., Karney, B. R., Reis, H. T., & Sprecher, S. (2012). Online dating: A critical analysis from the perspective of psychological science. *Psychological Science in the Public Interest, 13,* 3–66.

Finkel, E. J., Rusbult, C. E., Kumashiro, M., & Hannon, P. A. (2002). Dealing with betrayal in close relationships: Does commitment promote forgiveness? *Journal of Personality and Social Psychology, 82,* 956–974.

Finkel, N. J. (1995). *Commonsense justice: Jurors' notions of the law.* Cambridge, MA: Harvard University Press.

Finkelstein, M. A. (2009). Intrinsic vs. extrinsic motivational orientations and the volunteer process. *Personality and Individual Differences, 46,* 653–658.

Fischer, P., Krueger, J. I., et al. (2011). The bystander-effect: A meta-analytic review on bystander intervention in dangerous and non-dangerous emergencies. *Psychological Bulletin, 137,* 517–537.

Fishbein, M. (1980). A theory of reasoned action: Some applications and implications. In H. E. Howe & M. M. Page (Eds.), *Nebraska Symposium on Motivation* (Vol. 27, pp. 65–116). Lincoln: University of Nebraska Press.

Fishbein, M., & Ajzen, I. (1972). Attitudes and opinions. In P. H. Mussen & M. R. Rosenzweig (Eds.), *Annual Review of Psychology, 23,* 487–544.

Fisher, H. E. (2004). *Why we love: The nature and chemistry of romantic love.* New York: Henry Holt.

Fisher, J. D., & Fisher, W. A. (1992). Changing AIDS-risk behavior. *Psychological Bulletin, 111,* 455–474.

Fisher, J. D., Fisher, W. A., Bryan, A. D., & Misovich, S. J. (2002). Information-motivation-behavioral skills model-based HIV risk behavior change intervention for inner-city high school youth. *Health Psychology, 21,* 177–186.

Fisher, J. D., Fisher, W. A., Williams, S. S., & Malloy, T. E. (1994). Empirical tests of an information-motivation-behavioral skills model of AIDS-preventive behavior with gay men and heterosexual university students. *Health Psychology, 13,* 238–250.

Fiske, A. P. (1992). The four elementary forms of sociality: Framework for a unified theory of social relations. *Psychological Review, 99,* 689–723.

Fiske, S. T. (2012). The continuum model and the stereotype content model. In P. M. Van Lange, A. W. Kruglanski, & E. T. Higgins (Eds.), *Handbook of theories of social psychology* (Vol. 1, pp. 267–288). Thousand Oaks, CA: Sage.

Fiske, S. T., & Neuberg, S. L. (1990). A continuum model of impression formation: From category-based to individuating processes: Influence of information and motivation on attention and interpretation. In M. P. Zanna (Ed.), *Advances in experimental social psychology* (Vol. 23, pp. 1–74). San Diego, CA: Academic Press.

Fiske, S. T., Bersoff, D. N., Borgida, E., Deaux, K., & Heilman, M. E. (1991). Social science research on trial: Use of sex stereotyping research in *Price Waterhouse v. Hopkins. American Psychologist, 46,* 1049–1060.

Fiske, S. T., Cuddy, A., & Glick, P. (2007). Universal dimensions of social cognition: Warmth and competence. *Trends in Cognitive Sciences, 11,* 77–83.

Fiske, S. T., Lin, M., & Neuberg, S. L. (1999). The continuum model: Ten years later. In S. Chaiken & Y. Trope (Eds.), *Dual-process theories in social psychology* (pp. 231–254). New York: Guilford.

Fitzgerald, C. J. (2009). Altruism and reproductive limitations. *Evolutionary Psychology, 7,* 234–252.

Fitzgerald, C. J., & Colarelli, S. M. (2009). Altruism and reproductive limitations. *Evolutionary Psychology, 7,* 234–252.

Fitzgerald, C. J., & Colarelli, S. M. (2009). Altruism and reproductive limitations. *Evolutionary Psychology, 7,* 234–252.

Fitzgerald, J. M. (1988). Vivid memories and the reminiscence phenomenon: The role of self-narrative. *Human Development, 31,* 261–273.

Fitzgerald, R., & Ellsworth, P. C. (1984). Due process vs. crime control: Death qualification and jury attitudes. *Law and Human Behavior, 8,* 31–52.

Fivush, R., Haden, C. A., & Dimmick, J. W. (Eds.). (2003). *Autobiographical memory and the construction of a narrative self: Developmental and cultural perspectives.* Mahwah, NJ: Erlbaum.

Flack, W. F., Jr., Laird, J. D., & Cavallaro, L. A. (1999). Separate and combined effects of facial expressions and bodily postures on emotional feelings. *European Journal of Social Psychology, 29,* 203–217.

Fleming, L. C., & Jacobsen, K. H. (2010). Bullying among middle-school students in low and middle income countries. *Health Promotion International, 25,* 73–84.

Fleming, M. A., Wegener, D. T., & Petty, R. E. (1999). Procedural and legal motivations to correct for perceived judicial biases. *Journal of Experimental Social Psychology, 35,* 186–203.

Florian, V., Mikulincer, M., & Taubman, O. (1995). Does hardiness contribute to mental health during a stressful real-life situation? The roles of appraisal and coping. *Journal of Personality and Social Psychology, 68,* 687–695.

Flory, J. D., Raikkonen, K., Matthews, K. A., & Owens, J. F. (2000). Self-focused attention and mood during everyday social interactions. *Personality and Social Psychology Bulletin, 26,* 875–883.

Folger, R. (1986). Rethinking equity theory: A referent cognitions model. In H. W. Bierhoff, R. L. Cohen, & J. Greenberg (Eds.), *Justice in social relations* (pp. 145–162). New York: Plenum.

Folger, R., & Cropanzano, R. (1998). *Organizational justice and human resource management.* Thousand Oaks, CA: Sage.

Folger, R., & Greenberg, J. (1985). Procedural justice: An interpretive analysis of personnel systems. In K. Rowland & G. Ferris (Eds.), *Research in personnel and human resource management* (Vol. 3, pp. 141–183). Greenwich, CT: JAI Press.

Folger, R., Konovsky, M. A., & Cropanzano, R. (1992). A due process metaphor for performance appraisal. *Research in Organizational Behavior, 14,* 129–177.

Folkman, S., & Moskowitz, J. T. (2000). Positive affect and the other side of coping. *American Psychologist, 55,* 647–654.

Follett, M. P. (1942). Constructive conflict. In H. C. Metcalf & L. Urwick (Eds.), *Dynamic administration: The collected papers of Mary Parker Follett* (pp. 30–49). New York: Harper.

Forbes, G. B., Adams-Curtis, L. E., Pakalka, A. H., & White, K. B. (2006). Dating aggression, sexual coercion, and aggression-supporting atti-tudes among college men as a function of participation in aggressive high school sports. *Violence Against Women, 12,* 441–455.

Forbes, G. B., Collinsworth, L. L., Zhao, P., Kohlman, S., & LeClaire, J. (2011). Relationships among individualism–collectivism, gender, and ingroup/outgroup status, and responses to conflict: A study in China and the United States. *Aggressive Behavior, 37,* 302–314.

Forbes, G., Zhang, X., Doroszewicz, K., & Haas, K. (2009). Relationships between individualism-collectivism, gender, and direct or indirect aggression: A study in China, Poland, and the US. *Aggressive Behavior, 35,* 24–30.

Ford, T. E., Ferguson, M. A., Brooks, J. L., & Hagadone, K. M. (2004). Coping sense of humor reduces effects of stereotype threat on women's math performance. *Personality and Social Psychology Bulletin, 30,* 643–653.

Forgas, J. P. (2011). Can negative affect eliminate the power of first impressions? Affective influences on primacy and recency effects in impression formation. *Journal of Experimental Social Psychology, 47,* 425–429.

Forgas, J. P. (Ed.). (2000). *Feeling and thinking: Affective influences on social cognition.* New York: Cambridge University Press.

Forgas, J. P., & Bower, G. H. (1987). Mood effects on person perception judgments. *Journal of Personality and Social Psychology, 53,* 53–60.

Forgas, J. P., & East, R. (2008a). How real is that smile? Mood effects on accepting or rejecting the veracity of emotional facial expressions. *Journal of Nonverbal Behavior, 32,* 157–170.

Forgas, J. P., & East, R. (2008b). On being happy and gullible: Mood effects on skepticism and the detection of deception. *Journal of Experimental Social Psychology, 44,* 1362–1367.

Forgas, J. P., & Locke, J. (2005). Affective influences on causal inferences: The effects of mood on attributions for positive and negative interpersonal episodes. *Cognition and Emotion, 19,* 1071–1081.

Forgas, J. P., Baumeister, R. F., & Tice, D. M. (Eds.). (2009). *Psychology of self-regulation: Cognitive, affective, and motivational processes.* New York: Psychology Press.

Forgas, J. P., Cooper, J., & Crano, W. D. (Eds.) (2010). *The psychology of attitudes and attitude change.* New York: Psychology Press.

Forgas, J. P., Dunn, E., & Granland, S. (2008). Are you being served . . . ? An unobtrusive experiment of affective influences on helping in a department store. *European Journal of Social Psychology, 38,* 333–342.

Forgas, J. P., & Rebekah, E. (2008). On being happy and gullible: Mood effects on skepticism and the detection of deception. *Journal of Experimental Social Psychology, 44,* 1362–1367.

Foster, C. A., & Campbell, W. K. (2005). The adversity of secret relationships. *Personal Relationships, 12,* 125–143.

Foster, C. A., Witcher, B. S., Campbell, W. K., & Green, J. D. (1998). Arousal and attraction: Evidence for automatic and controlled processes. *Journal of Personality and Social Psychology, 74,* 86–101.

Fosterling, F. (1992). The Kelley model as an analysis of variance analogy: How far can it be taken? *Journal of Experimental Social Psychology, 28,* 475–490.

Fox, E., Russo, R., & Dutton, K. (2002). Attentional bias for threat: Evidence for delayed disengagement from emotional faces. *Cognition and Emotion, 16,* 355–379.

Franck, K. A. (1980). Friends and strangers: The social experience of living in urban and non-urban settings. *Journal of Social Issues, 36*(3), 52–71.

Frank, J. (1949). *Courts on trial.* Princeton, NJ: Princeton University Press.

Frantz, C. M., Cuddy, A. J. C., Burnett, M., Ray, H., & Hart, A. (2004). A threat in the computer: The race Implicit Association Test as a stereotype threat experience. *Personality and Social Psychology Bulletin, 30,* 1611–1624.

Frattaroli, J. (2006). Experimental disclosure and its moderators: A meta-analysis. *Psychological Bulletin, 132,* 823–865.

Frazier, P. A. (2003). Perceived control and distress following sexual assault: A longitudinal test of a new model. *Journal of Personality and Social Psychology, 84,* 1257–1269.

Frazier, P., & Schauben, L. (1994). Causal attributions and recovery from rape and other stressful events. *Journal of Social and Clinical Psychology, 13,* 1–14.

Frazier, P., Steward, J., & Mortensen, H. (2004). Perceived control and adjustment to trauma: A comparison across events. *Journal of Social and Clinical Psychology, 23,* 303–324.

Frederickson, B. L., Maynard, K. E., Helms, M. J., Haney, T. L., Siegler, I. C., & Barefoot, J. C. (2000). Hostility predicts magnitude and duration of blood pressure response to anger. *Journal of Behavioral Medicine, 23,* 229–243.

Fredrickson, B. L. (2009). *Positivity: Groundbreaking research reveals how to embrace the hidden strength of positive emotions, overcome negativity, and thrive.* New York: Crown Books.

Fredrickson, B. L., Roberts, T., Noll, S. M., Quinn, D. M., & Twenge, J. M. (1998). That swimsuit becomes you: Sex differences in self-objectification, restrained eating, and math performance. *Journal of Personality and Social Psychology, 75,* 269–284.

Fredrickson, B. L., Tugade, M. M., Waugh, C. E., & Larkin, G. R. (2003). What good are positive emotions in crisis? A prospective study of resilience and emotions following the terrorist attacks on the United States on September 11th, 2001. *Journal of Personality and Social Psychology, 84,* 365–376.

Freedman, J. L., & Fraser, S. C. (1966). Compliance without pressure: The foot-in-the-door technique. *Journal of Personality and Social Psychology, 4,* 195–202.

Freedman, J. L., & Sears, D. O. (1965). Warning, distraction, and resistance to influence. *Journal of Personality and Social Psychology, 1,* 262–266.

Frenda , S. J. Nichols , R. M. Loftus , E. F. (2011). Current issues and advances in misinformation research. *Current Directions in Psychological Science, 20,* 20–23.

Freud, S. (1905). Fragments of an analysis of a case of hysteria. *Collected papers* (Vol. 3). New York: Basic Books. (Reprinted in 1959).

Frey, K. S., Hirschstein, M. K., Edstrom, L. V., & Snell, J. L. (2009). Observed reductions in school bullying, nonbullying aggression, and destructive bystander behavior: A longitudinal evaluation. *Journal of Educational Psychology, 101,* 466–481.

Friedland, N., Keinan, G., & Regev, Y. (1992). Controlling the uncontrollable: Effects of stress on illusory perceptions of controllability. *Journal of Personality and Social Psychology, 63,* 923–931.

Friedman, H. S. (1991). *The self-healing personality.* New York: Henry Holt.

Friedman, H. S., & Booth-Kewley, S. (1987). The "disease-prone personality": A meta-analytic view of the construct. *American Psychologist, 42,* 539–555.

Friedman, M. J., Keane, T. M., & Resick, P. A. (Eds.). (2007). *Handbook of PTSD: Science and Practice.* New York: Guilford.

Friedrich, J., Fethersonhaugh, D., Casey, S., & Gallagher, D. (1996). Argument integration and attitude change: Suppression effects in the integration of one-sided arguments that vary in persuasiveness. *Personality and Social Psychology Bulletin, 22,* 179–191.

Friend, R., Rafferty, Y., & Bramel, D. (1990). A puzzling misinterpretation of the Asch "conformity" study. *European Journal of Social Psychology, 20,* 29–44.

Fritzsche, B. A., Finkelstein, M. A., & Penner, L. A. (2000). To help or not to help: Capturing individuals' decision policies. *Social Behavior and Personality, 28,* 561–578.

Fry, D. P. (2012). Life without war. *Science, 336,* 879–884.

Frye, N. E., & Karney, B. R. (2006). The context of aggressive behavior in marriage: A longitudinal study of newlyweds. *Journal of Family Psychology, 20,* 12–20.

Fujino, N., & Okamura, H. (2009, April). Factors affecting the sense of burden felt by family members caring for patients with mental illness. *Archives of Psychiatric Nursing, 23*(2), 128–137.

Fujita, F., & Diener, E. (2005). Life satisfaction set point: Stability and change. *Journal of Personality and Social Psychology, 88,* 158–164.

Funk, S. C. (1992). Hardiness: A review of theory and research. *Health Psychology, 11,* 335–345.

Furche, A., & Johnstone, D. (2006). Evidence of the endowment effect in stock market order placement. *Journal of Behavioral Finance, 7,* 145–154.

Furnham, A. (2003). Belief in a just world: Research progress over the past decade. *Personality and Individual Differences, 34,* 795–817.

Furnham, A., & Paltzer, S. (2010). The portrayal of men and women in television advertisements: An updated review of 30 studies published since 2000. *Scandinavian Journal of Psychology, 51,* 216–236.

Furnham, A., Simmons, K., & McClelland, A. (2000). Decisions concerning the allocation of scarce medical resources. *Journal of Social Behavior and Personality, 15,* 185–200.

Gabbert, F., Memon, A., & Allan, K. (2003). Memory conformity: Can eyewitnesses influence each other's memories for an event? *Applied Cognitive Psychology, 17,* 533–543.

Gabel, M., & Brunner, H. (2003). *Global Inc.: An atlas of the multinational corporation.* New York: New Press.

Gaertner, S. L., & Dovidio, J. F. (1986). The aversive form of racism. In J. F. Dovidio & S. L. Gaernter (Eds.), *Prejudice, discrimination, and racism* (pp. 61–89). San Diego, CA: Academic Press.

Gaertner, S. L., & Dovidio, J. F. (2009). A common intergroup identity: A categorization-based approach for reducing intergroup bias. In T. D. Nelson (Ed.), *Handbook of prejudice, stereotyping, and discrimination* (pp. 489–505). New York: Psychology Press.

Gaertner, S. L., & Dovidio, J. F. (2012). The common ingroup identity model. In P. M. Van Lange, A. W. Kruglanski, & E. T. Higgins (Eds.), *Handbook of theories of social psychology* (Vol. 2, pp. 439–457). Thousand Oaks, CA: Sage.

Gagne, F. M., & Lydon, J. E. (2001). Mindset and relationship illusions: The moderating effects of domain specificity and relationship commitment. *Personality and Social Psychology Bulletin, 27,* 1144–1155.

Gailliot, M. T., Peruche, B. M., Plant, E. A., & Baumeister, R. F. (2009). Stereotypes and prejudice in the blood: Sucrose drinks reduce prejudice and stereotyping. *Journal of Experimental Social Psychology, 45,* 288–290.

Gailliot, M., Baumeister, R., DeWall, C., Maner, J., Plant, E., Tice, D., Brewer, L., & Schmeichel, B. (2007). Self-control relies on glucose as a limited energy source: Willpower is more than just a metaphor. *Journal of Personality and Social Psychology, 92,* 325–336.

Galanter, M. (1999). *Cults: Faith, healing, and coercion* (2nd ed.). New York: Oxford University Press.

Galea, S., Ahern, J., Resnick, H., Kilpatrick, D., Bucuvalas, M., Gold, J., & Vlahov, D. (2002). Psychological sequelae of the September 11 terrorist attacks in New York City. *New England Journal of Medicine, 346,* 982–987.

Galen, B. R., & Underwood, M. K. (1997). A developmental investigation of social aggression among children. *Developmental Psychology, 33,* 589–600.

Galinsky, A. D., & Kray, L. J. (2004). From thinking about what might have been to sharing what we know: The role of counterfactual mind-sets in information sharing in groups. *Journal of Experimental Social Psychology, 40,* 606–618.

Galinsky, A. D., Stone, J., & Cooper, J. (2000). The reinstatement of dissonance and psychological discomfort following failed affirmations. *European Journal of Social Psychology, 30,* 123–147.

Galinsky, A. D., Wang, C. S., & Ku, G. (2008). Perspective-takers behave more stereotypically. *Journal of Personality and Social Psychology, 95,* 404–419.

Gallo, L. C., & Matthews, K. A. (2003). Understanding the association between socioeconomic status and physical health: Do negative emotions play a role? *Psychological Bulletin, 129,* 10–51.

Gallup Poll Editors. (2002). *Gallup poll of the Islamic world: Subscriber report.* Princeton, NJ: Gallup Press.

Gallup, G. G., Jr. (1977). Self-recognition in primates: A comparative approach to the bidirectional properties of consciousness. *American Psychologist, 32,* 329–337.

Gallup. (2008). Americans evenly divided on morality of homosexuality. htttp://www.gallup.com/poll/108115/Americans-Evenly-Divided-Morality-Homosexuality.aspx (June 18).

Gallup. (2011). http://www.gallup.com/poll/148187/Americans-Prefer-Boys-Girls-1941.aspx.

Gallup. (2012). http://www.gallup.com/poll/154634/Acceptance-Gay-Lesbian-Relations-New-Normal.aspx.

Game, F., Carchon, I., & Vital-Durand, F. (2003). The effect of stimulus attractiveness on visual tracking in 2- to 6-month-old infants. *Infant Behavior & Development, 26,* 135–150.

Gammie, S. C., Olaghere-da-Silva, U. B., & Nelson, R. J. (2000). 3-Bromo-7-nitroindazole, a neuronal nitric oxide synthase inhibitor, impairs maternal aggression and citrulline immunoreactivity in prairie voles. *Brain Research, 870,* 80–86.

Gamson, W. A., Fireman, B., & Rytina, S. (1982). *Encounters with unjust authority.* Homewood, IL: Dorsey.

Gangestad, S. W. (1993). Sexual selection and physical attractiveness: Implications for mating dynamics. *Human Nature, 4,* 205–235.

Gangestad, S. W., & Simpson, J. A. (2000). The evolution of human mating: Trade-offs and strategic pluralism. *Behavioral and Brain Sciences, 23,* 573–587.

Gangestad, S. W., & Snyder, M. (1991). Taxonomic analysis redux: Some statistical considerations for testing a latent class model. *Journal of Personality and Social Psychology, 61,* 141–146.

Gangestad, S. W., & Snyder, M. (2000). Self-monitoring: Appraisal and reappraisal. *Psychological Bulletin, 126,* 530–555.

Garcia, M. (2012). Student president loses title after gay-inclusive prom pitch. *Advocate.com,* March 22.

Garcia, S. M., Weaver, K., Moskowitz, G. B., & Darley, J. M. (2002). Crowded minds: The implicit bystander effect. *Journal of Personality and Social Psychology, 83,* 843–853.

Gardikiotis, A. (2011). Minority influence. *Social and Personality Psychology Compass, 5,* 679–693.

Gardner, W. L., & Knowles, M. L. (2008). Love makes you real: Favorite television characters are perceived as "real" in a social facilitation paradigm. *Social Cognition, 26,* 156–168.

Garland, H., & Conlon, D. E. (1998). Too close to quit: The role of project completion in maintaining commitment. *Journal of Applied Social Psychology, 28,* 2025–2048.

Garrett, B. L. (2011). *Convicting the innocence: When criminal prosecutions go wrong.* Cambridge, MA: Harvard University Press.

Garris, C. P., Ohbuchi, K., Oikawa, H., & Harris, M. J. (2011). Consequences of interpersonal rejection: A cross-cultural experimental study. *Journal of Cross-Cultural Psychology, 42,* 1066–1083.

Gaucher, D., Friesen, J., & Kay, A. C. (2011). Evidence that gendered wording in job advertisements exists and sustains gender inequality. *Journal of Personality and Social Psychology, 101,* 109–128.

Gawronski, B., & Bodenhausen, G. V. (2006). Associative and propositional processes in evaluation: An integrative review of implicit and explicit attitude change. *Psychological Bulletin, 132,* 692–731.

Gawronski, B., Peters, K. R., Brochu, P. M., & Strack, F. (2008). Understanding the relations between different forms of racial prejudice: A cognitive consistency perspective. *Personality and Social Psychology Bulletin, 34,* 648–665.

Geary, D. C. (2000). Evolution and proximate expression of human paternal investment. *Psychological Bulletin, 126,* 55–77.

Geary, D. C. (2005). Evolution of life-history trade-offs in mate attractiveness and health: Comment on Weeden and Sabini. *Psychological Bulletin, 131,* 654–657.

Gee, C. J., & Leith, L. M. (2007). Aggressive behavior in professional ice hockey: A cross-cultural comparison of North American and European born NHL players. *Psychology of Sport and Exercise, 8,* 567–583.

Geen, R. G. (1981). Behavioral and physiological reactions to observed violence: Effects of prior exposure to aggressive stimuli. *Journal of Personality and Social Psychology, 40,* 868–875.

Geen, R. G. (1991). Social motivation. *Annual Review of Psychology, 42,* 377–399.

Geen, R. G., & Quanty, M. B. (1977). The catharsis of aggression: An evaluation of a hypothesis. In L. Berkowitz (Ed.), *Advances in experimental social psychology* (Vol. 10, pp. 1–37). New York: Academic Press.

Geis, F. L., Brown, V., Jennings (Walstedt), J., & Porter, N. (1984). TV commercials as achievement scripts for women. *Sex Roles, 10,* 513–525.

Geiselman, R. E., Haight, N. A., & Kimata, L. G. (1984). Context effects in the perceived physical attractiveness of faces. *Journal of Experimental Social Psychology, 20,* 409–424.

Gelfand, M. J., Erez, M., & Aycan, Z. (2007). Cross-cultural organizational behavior. *Annual Review of Psychology, 58,* 479–514.

Gendar, A., Burke, K., & McShane, L. (2009, July 16). "Fight Club" bomber: Teen nabbed in Memorial Day blast at East Side Starbucks. *New York Daily News,* p. 7.

Gentile, D. A. (2011). The multiple dimensions of video game effects. *Child Development Perspectives, 5,* 75–81.

Gentile, D. A., Anderson, C. A., Yukawa, S., Ihori, N., Saleem, M., Ming, L. M., et al. (2009). The effects of prosocial video games on prosocial behaviors: International evidence from correlational, longitudinal, and experimental studies. *Personality and Social Psychology Bulletin, 35,* 752–763.

Gentile, D. A., Coyne, S., & Walsh, D. A. (2011). Media violence, physical aggression, and relational aggression in school age children: A short-term longitudinal study. *Aggressive Behavior, 37,* 193–206.

Gentile, D. A., Mathieson, L. C., & Crick, N. R. (2011). Media violence associations with the form and function of aggression among elementary school children. *Social Development, 20,* 213–232.

George, D. M., Carroll, P., Kersnick, R., & Calderon, K. (1998). Gender-related patterns of helping among friends. *Psychology of Women Quarterly, 22,* 685–704.

Georgesen, J. C., & Harris, M. J. (1998). Why's my boss always holding me down? A meta-analysis of power effects on performance evaluations. *Personality and Social Psychology Review, 2,* 184–195.

Gerard, H. B., Whilhelmy, R. A., & Connolley, R. S. (1968). Conformity and group size. *Journal of Personality and Social Psychology, 8,* 79–82.

Gerber, J., & Wheeler, L. (2009). On being rejected: A meta-analysis of experimental research on rejection. *Perspectives on Psychological Science, 4,* 468–488.

Gerbner, G., Gross, L., Morgan, M., & Signorielli, N. (1986). Living with television: The dynamics of the cultivation process. In J. Bryant & D. Zillmann (Eds.), *Perspectives on media effects* (pp. 17–40). Hillsdale, NJ: Erlbaum.

Gergen, K. J. (1973). Social psychology as history. *Journal of Personality and Social Psychology, 26,* 309–320.

Gerhart, B., & Rynes, S. (1991). Determinants and consequences of salary negotiations by male and female MBA graduates. *Journal of Applied Psychology, 76,* 256–262.

Gerrard, M., Gibbons, F. X., & Bushman, B. J. (1996). Relation between perceived vulnerability in HIV and precautionary sexual behavior. *Psychological Bulletin, 119,* 390–409.

Gershoff, E. T. (2002). Corporal punishment by parents and associated child behaviors and experiences: A meta-analytic and theoretical review. *Psychological Bulletin, 128,* 539–579.

Gerson, J. (2006, September 21). Montreal shootings disturb Columbine game creator. *Toronto Star,* p. A12.

Gervais, W. M., & Norenzayan, A. (2012). Like a camera in the sky? Thinking about God increases public self-awareness and socially desirable responding. *Journal of Experimental Social Psychology, 48,* 298–302.

Gervais, W. M., Shariff, A. F., & Norenzayan, A. (2011). Do you believe in atheists? Distrust is central to anti-atheist prejudice. *Journal of Personality and Social Psychology, 101,* 1189–1206.

Giancola, P. R., Godlaski, A. J., & Roth, R. M. (2012). Identifying component-processes of executive functioning that serve as risk factors for the alcohol-aggression relation. *Psychology of Addictive Behaviors, 26,* 201–211.

Giancola, P. R., Josephs, R. A., Parrott, D. J., & Duke, A. A. (2010). Alcohol myopia revisited: Clarifying aggression and other acts of disinhibition through a distorted lens. *Perspectives on Psychological Science, 5,* 265–278.

Gibbons, F. X., & McCoy, S. B. (1991). Self-esteem, similarity, and reactions to active versus passive downward comparison. *Journal of Personality and Social Psychology, 60,* 414–424.

Gibbons, F. X., Lane, D. J., Gerrard, M., Reis-Bergan, M., Lautrup, C., Pexa, N., & Blanton, H. (2002). Comparison level preferences after performance: Is downward comparison theory still useful? *Journal of Personality and Social Psychology, 83,* 865–880.

Gibbons, F. X., O'Hara, R. E., Stock, M. L., Gerrard, M., Weng, C., & Wills, T. A. (2012). The erosive effects of racism: Reduced self-control mediates the relation between perceived racial discrimination and substance use in African American adolescents. *Journal of Personality and Social Psychology, 102,* 1089–1104.

Gibbons, S. L., & Ebbeck, V. (1997). The effect of different teaching strategies on the moral development of physical education students. *Journal of Teaching in Physical Education, 17,* 85–98.

Gibbs, W., & Koranyi, B. (2012). Mass killer planned bigger attack; Tells court he prepared by playing World of Warcraft "a lot." *The Gazette* (Montreal), April 20, p. A17.

Gibson, B., & Sachau, D. (2000). Sandbagging as a self-presentational strategy: Claiming to be less than you are. *Personality and Social Psychology Bulletin, 26,* 56–70.

Gidycz, C. A., Orchowski, L. M., & Berkowitz, A. D. (2011). Preventing sexual aggression among college men: An evaluation of a social norms and bystander intervention program. *Violence Against Women, 17,* 720–742.

Giebels, E., & Taylor, P. J. (2009). Interaction patterns in crisis negotiations: Persuasive arguments and cultural differences. *Journal of Applied Psychology, 94,* 5–19.

Giesler, R. B., Josephs, R. A., & Swann, W. B., Jr. (1996). Self-verification in clinical depression: The desire for negative evaluation. *Journal of Abnormal Psychology, 105,* 358–368.

Gilbert, & G. Lindzey (Eds.), *Handbook of Social Psychology* (Volume 1), pp.1343–1385. . New York: Wiley.

Gilbert, D. (2006). *Stumbling on happiness.* New York: Alfred A. Knopf.

Gilbert, D. T., & Jones, E. E. (1986). Perceiver-induced constraint: Interpretations of self-generated reality. *Journal of Personality and Social Psychology, 50,* 269–280.

Gilbert, D. T., & Malone, P. S. (1995). The correspondence bias. *Psychological Bulletin, 117,* 21–38.

Gilbert, D. T., McNulty, S. E., Giuliano, T. A., & Benson, J. E. (1992). Blurry words and fuzzy deeds: The attribution of obscure behavior. *Journal of Personality and Social Psychology, 62,* 18–25.

Gilbert, D. T., Morewedge, C. K., Risen, J. L., & Wilson, T. D. (2004). Looking forward to looking backward: The misprediction of regret. *Psychological Science, 15,* 346–350.

Gilbert, D. T., Pelham, B. W., & Krull, D. S. (1988). On cognitive busyness: When person perceivers meet persons perceived. *Journal of Personality and Social Psychology, 54,* 733–740.

Gilbert, D. T., Pinel, E. C., Wilson, T. D., Blumberg, S. J., & Wheatley, T. (1998). Immune neglect: A source of durability bias in affective forecasting. *Journal of Personality and Social Psychology, 75,* 617–638.

Gilbert, S. J. (1981). Another look at the Milgram obedience studies: The role of the gradated series of shocks. *Personality and Social Psychology Bulletin, 7,* 690–695.

Gillig, P. M., & Greenwald, A. G. (1974). Is it time to lay the sleeper effect to rest? *Journal of Personality and Social Psychology, 29,* 132–139.

Gilovich, T., Griffin, D., & Kahneman, D. (Eds.). (2002). *Heuristics and biases: The psychology of intuitive judgment.* New York: Cambridge University Press.

Gilovich, T., Medvec, V. H., & Savitsky, K. (2000). The spotlight effect in social judgment: An egocentric bias in estimates of the salience of one's own actions and appearance. *Journal of Personality and Social Psychology, 78,* 211–222.

Giner-Sorolla, R., & Chaiken, S. (1997). Selective use of heuristic and systematic processing under defensive motivation. *Personality and Social Psychology Bulletin, 23,* 84–97.

Gioia, D. A., & Longnecker, C. O. (1994). Delving into the dark side: The politics of executive appraisal. *Organizational Dynamics, 22,* 47–58.

Gladue, B. A., Boechler, M., & McCaul, K. D. (1989). Hormonal response to competition in human males. *Aggressive Behavior, 15,* 409–422.

Gladwell, M. (2005). *Blink: The power of thinking without thinking.* New York: Little, Brown, and Company.

Glanz, J., & Schwartz, J. (September 26, 2003). Dogged engineer's effort to assess shuttle damage. *New York Times,* p. A1.

Glasman, L. R., & Albarracín, D. (2006). Forming attitudes that predict future behavior: A meta-analysis of the attitude-behavior relation. *Psychological Bulletin, 132,* 778–822.

Glasø, L., Nielsen, M. B., & Einarsen, S. (2009). Interpersonal problems among perpetrators and targets of workplace bullying. *Journal of Applied Social Psychology, 39,* 1316–1333.

Glass, D. C., & Singer, J. E. (1972). *Urban stress.* New York: Academic Press.

Gleicher, F., & Petty, R. E. (1992). Expectations of reassurance influence the nature of fear-stimulated attitude change. *Journal of Experimental Social Psychology, 28,* 86–100.

Glick, P., & Fiske, S. T. (2001). Ambivalent sexism. In M. P. Zanna (Ed.), *Advances in experimental social psychology* (Vol. 33, pp. 115–188). San Diego, CA: Academic Press.

Glick, P., & Fiske, S. T. (2011). Ambivalent sexism revisited. *Psychology of Women Quarterly, 35,* 530–535.

Glick, P., Fiske, S. T., et al. (2000). Beyond prejudice as simple antipathy: Hostile and benevolent sexism across cultures. *Journal of Personality and Social Psychology, 79,* 763–775.

Global Deception Research Team. (2006). A world of lies. *Journal of Cross-Cultural Psychology, 37,* 60–74.

Godfrey, D. K., Jones, E. E., & Lord, C. G. (1986). Self-promotion is not ingratiating. *Journal of Personality and Social Psychology, 50,* 106–115.

Goethals, G. R. (2005). Presidential leadership. *Annual Review of Psychology, 56,* 545–570.

Goethals, G. R., & Darley, J. (1977). Social comparison theory: An attributional approach. In J. M. Suls & R. L. Miller (Eds.), *Social comparison processes: Theoretical and empirical perspectives* (pp. 259–278). Washington, DC: Hemisphere.

Goethals, G. R., Cooper, J., & Naficy, A. (1979). Role of foreseen, foreseeable, and unforeseeable behavioral consequences in the arousal of cognitive dissonance. *Journal of Personality and Social Psychology, 37,* 1179–1185.

Goethals, G. R., Sorensen, G., & Burns, J. M. (Eds.). (2004). *Encyclopedia of leadership.* Thousand Oaks, CA: Sage.

Goetz, A. T., Shackelford, T. K., Romero, G. A., Kaighobadi, F., & Miner, E. J. (2008). Punishment, proprietariness, and paternity: Men's violence against women from an evolutionary perspective. *Aggression and Violent Behavior, 13,* 481–489.

Goff, P. A., Eberhardt, J. L., Williams, M. J., & Jackson, M. C. (2008). Not yet human: Implicit knowledge, historical dehumanization, and contemporary consequences. *Journal of Personality and Social Psychology, 94,* 292–306.

Goff, P. A., Steele, C. M., & Davies, P. G. (2008). The space between us: Stereotype threat and distance in interracial contexts. *Journal of Personality and Social Psychology, 94,* 91–107.

Goffman, E. (1955). On face-work: An analysis of ritual elements in social interaction. *Psychiatry, 18,* 213–231.

Goffman, E. (1959). *The presentation of self in everyday life.* Garden City: Doubleday.

Golby, J., & Meggs, J. (2011). Exploring the organizational effect of prenatal testosterone upon the sporting brain. *Journal of Sports Science and Medicine, 10,* 445–451.

Goldberg, A. B., & Dooley, S. (2011). Disappearing daughters: Women pregnant with girls pressured into abortions. December 9. http://news.yahoo.com/video/tech-15749651/india-s-deadly-secret-27566497.html.

Goldberg, P. (1968). Are women prejudiced against women? *Transaction, 5,* 28–30.

Goldhagen, D. J. (1996). *Hitler's willing executioners: Ordinary Germans and the Holocaust.* New York: Knopf.

Goldin, C. (1990). *Understanding the gender gap: An economic history of American women.* New York: Oxford University Press.

Goldstein, N. J., & Cialdini, R. B. (2007). The spyglass self: A model of vicarious self-perception. *Journal of Personality and Social Psychology, 92,* 402–417.

Goleman, D., Boyatzis, R., & McKee, A. (2002). *Primal leadership: Realizing the power of emotional intelligence.* Cambridge, MA: Harvard Business School Press.

Gollan, J. (2011, January 21). Rethinking evaluations when almost every teacher gets an "A." *The New York Times.* Available at http://www.nytimes.com.

Golombok, S., & Hines, M. (2002). Sex differences in social behavior. In P. K. Smith & C. H. Hart (Eds.), *Blackwell handbook of childhood social development* (pp. 117–136). Malden, MA: Blackwell.

Gómez, A. (2011). Testing the cycle of violence hypothesis: Child abuse and adolescent dating violence as predictors of intimate partner violence in young adulthood. *Youth & Society, 43,* 171–192.

Gonzaga, G., Campos, B., & Bradbury, T. (2007). Similarity, convergence, and relationship satisfaction in dating and married couples. *Journal of Personality and Social Psychology, 93,* 34–48.

Gonzalez, A. Q., & Koestner, R. (2006). What Valentine announcements reveal about the romantic emotions of men and women. *Sex Roles, 55,* 767–773.

Good, C., Rattan, A., & Dweck, C. S. (2012). Why do women opt out? Sense of belonging and women's representation in mathematics. *Journal of Personality and Social Psychology, 102,* 700–717.

Goodwin, S. A., Fiske, S. T., Rosen, L. D., & Rosenthal, A. M. (2002). The eye of the beholder: Romantic goals and impression biases. *Journal of Experimental Social Psychology, 38,* 232–241.

Gopnik, A., Meltzoff, A. N., & Kuhl, P. K. (1999). *The scientist in the crib: Minds, brains, and how children learn.* New York: Morrow.

Gorchoff, S., John, O., & Helson, R. (2008). Contextualizing change in marital satisfaction during middle age: An 18-year longitudinal study. *Psychological Science, 19,* 1194–1200.

Gorman, E. H., & Kmec, J. A. (2009). Hierarchical rank and women's organizational mobility: Glass ceilings in corporate law firms. *American Journal of Sociology, 114,* 1428–1474.

Gosling, P., Denizeau, M., & Oberlé, D. (2006). Denial of responsibility: A new mode of dissonance reduction. *Journal of Personality and Social Psychology, 90,* 722–733.

Gosling, S. (2008). *Snoop: What your stuff says about you.* New York: Basic Books.

Gossett, J. L., & Byrne, S. (2002). "CLICK HERE": A content analysis of Internet rape sites. *Gender and Society, 16,* 689–709.

Gotlib, I. H., & Hammen, C. L. (Eds.). (2009). *Handbook of depression* (2nd ed.). New York: Guilford.

Gottfredson, L. S. (2002). Where and why *g* matters: Not a mystery. *Human Performance, 15,* 25–46.

Gottfried, M. (2007, August 23). A rape witnessed, a rape ignored. *St. Paul Pioneer Press.*

Gottfried, M. (2008, July 18). Man gets 12 years for hallway rape captured on video. *St. Paul Pioneer Press.*

Gottman, J. M. (1994). *What predicts divorce?* Hillsdale, NJ: Erlbaum.

Gottman, J. M. (1998). Psychology and the study of marital processes. *Annual Review of Psychology, 49,* 169–197.

Gottman, J. M., & Levenson, R. W. (1992). Marital processes predictive of later dissolution: Behavior, physiology, and health. *Journal of Personality and Social Psychology, 63,* 221–233.

Gouin, J., Kiecolt-Glaser, J., Malarkey, W., & Glaser, R. (2008). The influence of anger expression on wound healing. *Brain, Behavior, and Immunity, 22,* 699–708.

Gouldner, A. W. (1960). The norm of reciprocity: A preliminary statement. *American Sociological Review, 25,* 161–178.

Gracia, E., García, F., & Lila, M. (2009). Public responses to intimate partner violence against women: The influence of perceived severity and personal responsibility. *The Spanish Journal of Psychology, 12,* 648–656.

Graham, K., Osgood, D. W., Wells, S., & Stockwell, T. (2006). To what extent is intoxication associated with aggression in bars? A multilevel analysis. *Journal of Studies on Alcohol, 67,* 382–390.

Grammer, K., & Thornhill, R. (1994). Human facial attractiveness and sexual selection: The role of averageness and symmetry. *Journal of Comparative Psychology, 108,* 233–242.

Grammer, K., Fink, B., Moller, A. P., & Manning, J. T. (2005). Physical attractiveness and health: Comment on Weeden and Sabini. *Psychological Bulletin, 131,* 658–661.

Graña, J. L., Cruzado, J. A., Andreu, J. M., Muñoz-Rivas, M. J., Peña, M. E., & Brain, P. F. (2004). Effects of viewing videos of bullfights on Spanish children. *Aggressive Behavior, 30,* 16–28.

Granberg, D., & Bartels, B. (2005). On being a lone dissenter. *Journal of Applied Social Psychology, 35,* 1849–1858.

Granhag, P. A., & Strömwall. L. A. (Eds.). (2004). *Deception detection in forensic contexts.* Cambridge: Cambridge University Press.

Grant, F., & Hogg, M. A. (2012). Self-uncertainty, social identity prominence and group identification. *Journal of Experimental Social Psychology, 48,* 538–542.

Gray-Little, B., & Hafdahl, A. R. (2000). Factors influencing racial comparisons of self-esteem: A quantitative review. *Psychological Bulletin, 126,* 26–54.

Gray, H. M., Gray, K., & Wegner, D. M. (2007, February 2). Dimensions of mind perception. *Science, 315,* 619.

Gray, J. (1997). *Men are from Mars, women are from Venus.* New York: HarperCollins.

Gray, R. (2004). Attending to the execution of a complex sensorimotor skill: Expertise differences, choking, and slumps. *Journal of Experimental Psychology: Applied, 10,* 42–54.

Greathouse, S. M., & Kovera, M. B. (2009). Instruction bias and lineup presentation moderate the effects of administrator knowledge on eyewitness identification. *Law and Human Behavior, 33,* 70–82.

Green, J. D., Sedikides, C., & Gregg, A. P. (2008). Forgotten but not gone: The recall and recognition of self-threatening memories. *Journal of Experimental Social Psychology, 44,* 547–561.

Greenberg, J. (1988). Equity and workplace status: A field experiment. *Journal of Applied Psychology, 73,* 606–613.

Greenberg, J. (1990). Employee theft as a reaction to underpayment inequity: The hidden costs of pay cuts. *Journal of Applied Psychology, 75,* 561–568.

Greenberg, J. (2006). Losing sleep over organizational injustice: Attenuating insomniac reactions to underpayment inequity with supervisory training in interactional justice. *Journal of Applied Psychology, 91,* 58–69.

Greenberg, J. (Ed). (2010). *Insidious workplace behavior.* New York: Routledge / Taylor & Francis.

Greenberg, J., & Arndt, J. (2012). Terror management theory. In P. M. Van Lange, A. W. Kruglanski, & E. T. Higgins (Eds.), *Handbook of theories of social psychology* (Vol. 1, pp. 398–415). Thousand Oaks, CA: Sage.

Greenberg, J., Landau, M., Kosloff, S., & Solomon, S. (2009). How our dreams of death transcendence breed prejudice, stereotyping, and conflict: Terror Management Theory. In T. D. Nelson (Ed.), *Handbook of prejudice, stereotyping, and discrimination* (pp. 309–332). New York: Psychology Press.

Greenberg, J., Solomon, S., & Pyszczynski, T. (1997). Terror management theory of self-esteem and cultural worldviews: Empirical assessments and conceptual refinements. *Advances in Experimental Social Psychology, 29,* 61–139.

Greenberg, M. S., & Westcott, D. R. (1983). Indebtedness as a mediator of reactions to aid. In J. D. Fisher, A. Nadler, & B. M. DePaulo (Eds.), *New directions in helping: Vol. 1. Recipient reactions to aid* (pp. 85–112). New York: Academic Press.

Greene, E., & Heilbrun, K. (2011). *Wrightsman's psychology in the legal system* (7th ed.). Belmont, CA: Wadsworth.

Greene, E., Heilbrun, K., Fortune, W. H., & Nietzel, M. T. (2007). *Wrightsman's psychology and the legal system* (6th ed.). Belmont, CA: Wadsworth.

Greenland, K., Xenias, D., & Maio, G. (2012). Intergroup anxiety from the self and other: Evidence from self-report, physiological effects, and real interactions. *European Journal of Social Psychology, 42,* 150–163.

Greenwald, A. G. (1968). Cognitive learning, cognitive responses to persuasion, and attitude change. In A. Greenwald, T. Brock, & T. Ostrom (Eds.), *Psychological Foundations of Attitudes* (pp. 147–170). New York: Academic Press.

Greenwald, A. G. (1980). The totalitarian ego: Fabrication and revision of personal history. *American Psychologist, 35,* 603–618.

Greenwald, A. G. (1992). New look 3: Unconscious cognition reclaimed. *American Psychologist, 47,* 766–779.

Greenwald, A. G., & Farnham, S. D. (2000). Using the Implicit Association Test to measure self-esteem and self-concept. *Journal of Personality and Social Psychology, 79,* 1022–1038.

Greenwald, A. G., McGhee, D. E., & Schwartz, J. L. K. (1998). Measuring individual differences in implicit cognition: The implicit association test. *Journal of Personality and Social Psychology, 74,* 1464–1480.

Greenwald, A. G., Oakes, M. A., & Hoffman, H. G. (2003). Targets of discrimination: Effects of race on responses to weapons holders. *Journal of Experimental Social Psychology, 39,* 399–405.

Greenwald, A. G., Poehlman, T. A., Uhlmann, E. L., & Banaji, M. R. (2009). Understanding and using the Implicit Association Test: III. Meta-analysis of predictive validity. *Journal of Personality and Social Psychology, 97,* 17–41.

Greenwald, A. G., Pratkanis, A. R., Leippe, M. R., & Baumgardner, M. H. (1986). Under what conditions does theory obstruct research progress? *Psychological Review, 93,* 216–229.

Greenwald, A. G., Spangenberg, E. R., Pratkanis, A. R., & Eskenazi, J. (1991). Double-blind tests of subliminal self-help audiotapes. *Psychological Science, 2,* 119–122.

Gregory, A. M., Light-Häusermann, J. H., Rijsdijk, F., & Eley, T. C. (2009). Behavioral genetic analyses of prosocial behavior in adolescents. *Developmental Science, 12,* 165–174.

Greitemeyer, T., Agthe, M., Turner, R., & Gschwendtner, C. (2012). Acting prosocially reduces retaliation: Effects of prosocial video games on aggressive behavior. *European Journal of Social Psychology, 42,* 235–242.

Greitemeyer, T., Schulz-Hardt, S., & Frey, D. (2009). The effects of authentic and contrived dissent on escalation of commitment in group decision making. *European Journal of Social Psychology, 39,* 639–647.

Greitemeyer, T., Schulz-Hardt, S., Brodbeck, F. C., & Frey, D. (2006). Information sampling and group decision making: The effects of an advocacy decision procedure and task experience. *Journal of Experimental Psychology: Applied, 12,* 31–42.

Griskevicius, V., Goldstein, N. J., Mortensen, C. R., Cialdini, R. B., & Kenrick, D. T. (2006). Going along versus going alone: When fundamental motives facilitate strategic nonconformity. *Journal of Personality and Social Psychology, 91,* 281–294.

Griskevicius, V., Tybur, J. M., Ackerman, J. M., Delton, A. W., Robertson, T. E., & White, A. E. (2012). The financial consequences of too many men: Sex ratio effects on saving, borrowing, and spending. *Journal of Personality and Social Psychology, 102,* 69–80.

Griskevicius, V., Tybur, J. M., Gangestad, S. W., Perea, E. F., Shapiro, J. R., & Kenrick, D. T. (2009). Aggress to impress: Hostility as an evolved context-dependent strategy. *Journal of Personality and Social Psychology, 96,* 980–994.

Gross, J. J., & Levenson, R. W. (1997). Hiding feelings: The acute effects of inhibiting negative and positive emotion. *Journal of Abnormal Psychology, 106,* 95–103.

Grossman, M., & Wood, W. (1993). Sex differences in intensity of emotional experience: A social role interpretation. *Journal of Personality and Social Psychology, 65,* 1010–1020.

Grote, N. K., & Clark, M. S. (2001). Perceiving unfairness in the family: Cause or consequence of marital distress? *Journal of Personality and Social Psychology, 80,* 281–293.

Grover, K. W., & Miller, C. T. (2012). Does expressed acceptance reflect genuine attitudes? A bogus pipeline study of the effects of mortality salience on acceptance of a person with AIDS. *The Journal of Social Psychology, 152,* 131–135.

Gruber, J., Mauss, I. B., & Tamir, M. (2011). A dark side of happiness? How, when, and why happiness is not always good. *Perspectives on Psychological Science, 6,* 222–233.

Gudjonsson, G. H. (2003). *The psychology of interrogations and confessions.* London: Wiley.

Gudykunst, W., & Bond, M. H. (1997). Intergroup relations across cultures. In J. W. Berry, M. H. Segall, & C. Kagitçibasi (Eds.), *Handbook of cross-cultural psychology: Social behavior and applications* (2nd ed., Vol. 3, pp. 119–161). Needham Heights, MA: Allyn & Bacon.

Guéguen, N. (2007). Bust size and hitchhiking: A field study. *Perceptual and Motor Skills, 105,* 1294–1298.

Guéguen, N. (2012). The sweet smell of . . . implicit helping: Effects of pleasant ambient fragrance on spontaneous help in shopping malls. *The Journal of Social Psychology, 152,* 397–400.

Guéguen, N., & Fischer-Lokou, J. (2004). Hitchhikers' smiles and receipt of help. *Psychological Reports, 94,* 756–760.

Guéguen, N., & Lamy, L. (2009). Hitchhiking women's hair color. *Perceptual and Motor Skills, 109,* 941–948.

Guéguen, N., & Martin, A. (2009). Incidental similarity facilitates behavioral mimicry. *Social Psychology, 40,* 88–92.

Guerin, B. (2003). Social behaviors as determined by different arrangements of social consequences: Diffusion of responsibility effects with competition. *Journal of Social Psychology, 143,* 313–329.

Guerrero, L. K., La Valley, A. G., & Farinelli, L. (2008). The experience and expression of anger, guilt, and sadness in marriage: An equity theory explanation. *Journal of Social and Personal Relationships, 25,* 699–724.

Gully, S. M., Devine, D. J., & Whitney, D. J. (1995). A meta-analysis of cohesion and performance: Effects of level of analysis and task interdependence. *Small Group Research, 26,* 497–520.

Gump, B. B., & Kulik, J. A. (1997). Stress, affiliation, and emotional contagion. *Journal of Personality and Social Psychology, 72,* 305–319.

Günaydin, G., Zayas, V., Selcuk, E., & Hazan, C. (2012). I like you but I don't know why: Objective facial resemblance to significant others influences snap judgments. *Journal of Experimental Social Psychology, 48,* 350–353.

Gunia, B. C., Sivanathan, N., & Galinsky, A. D. (2009). Vicarious entrapment: Your sunk costs, my escalation of commitment. *Journal of Experimental Social Psychology, 45,* 1238–1244.

Gurtner, A.,Tschan, F., Semmer, N. K., & Nägele, C. (2007). Getting groups to develop good strategies: Effects of reflexivity interventions on team process, team performance, and shared mental models. *Organizational Behavior and Human Decision Processes, 102,* 127–142.

Gurung, R. A. R. (2010). *Health psychology: A cultural approach* (2nd ed.). Belmont, CA: Wadsworth.

Hackman, J. R., & Katz, N. (2010). Group behavior and performance. In S. T. Fiske, D. T. Gilbert, & G. Lindzey (Eds.), *Handbook of social psychology* (5th ed.). New York: McGraw-Hill.

Haddock, G., Maio, G., Arnold, K., & Huskinson, T. (2008). Should persuasion be affective or cognitive? The moderating effects of need for affect and need for cognition. *Personality and Social Psychology Bulletin, 34,* 769–778.

Hafer, C. L. (2000). Do innocent victims threaten the belief in a just world? Evidence from a modified Stroop task. *Journal of Personality and Social Psychology, 79,* 165–173.

Hafer, C. L., & Bègue, L. (2005). Experimental research on just-world theory: Problems, developments, and future challenges. *Psychological Bulletin, 131,* 128–167.

Haidt, J. (2006). *The happiness hypothesis: Finding modern truth in ancient wisdom.* New York: Basic Books.

Haines, H., & Vaughan, G. M. (1979). Was 1898 a "great date" in the history of experimental social psychology? *Journal of the History of the Behavioral Sciences, 15,* 323–332.

Halabi, S., Dovidio, J. F., & Nadler, A. (2012). Responses to intergroup helping: Effects of perceived stability and legitimacy of intergroup relations on Israeli Arabs' reactions to assistance by Israeli Jews. *International Journal of Intercultural Relations, 36,* 295–301.

Halberstadt, J., & Rhodes, G. (2000). The attractiveness of non-face averages: Implications for an evolutionary explanation of the attractiveness of average faces. *Psychological Science, 11,* 285–289.

Halberstadt, J., & Rhodes, G. (2003). It's not just average faces that are attractive: Computer-manipulated averageness makes birds, fish, and automobiles attractive. *Psychonomic Bulletin and Review, 10,* 149–156.

Hald, G., Malamuth, N. M., & Yuen, C. (2010). Pornography and attitudes supporting violence against women: Revisiting the relationship in non-experimental studies. *Aggressive Behavior, 36,* 14–20.

Hall, J. A., Coats, E. J., & LeBeau, L. S. (2005). Nonverbal behavior and the vertical dimension of social relations: A metaanalysis. *Psychological Bulletin, 131,* 898–924.

Hall, S., French, D. P., & Marteau, T. M. (2003). Causal attributions following serious unexpected negative events: A systematic review. *Journal of Social and Clinical Psychology, 22,* 515–536.

Halloran, M., & Chambers, G. (2011). The effects of a common in-group prime on intentions to help indigenous and homeless Australians. Australian Psychologist, 46, 163–170.

Halpern, D. F., & Cheung, F. M. (2008). *Women at the top: Powerful leaders tell us how to combine work and family.* New York: Wiley-Blackwell.

Hamer, D. H., Rice, G., Risch, N., & Ebers, G. (1999). Genetics and male sexual orientation. *Science, 285,* 803.

Hamermesh, D. S., & Biddle, J. E. (1994). Beauty and the labor market. *American Economic Review, 84,* 1174–1195.

Hamilton, D. L., & Rose, T. L. (1980). Illusory correlation and the maintenance of stereotypic beliefs. *Journal of Personality and Social Psychology, 39,* 832–845.

Hamilton, D. L., Chen, J. M., & Way, N. (2011). Dynamic aspects of entitativity: From group perceptions to social interaction. In R. M. Kramer, G. J. Leonardelli, & R. W. Livingston (Eds.), *Social cognition, social identity, and intergroup relations: A Festschrift in honor of Marilynn B. Brewer* (pp. 27–52). New York: Psychology Press.

Hamilton, W. D. (1964). The genetical evolution of social behavior: I and II. *Journal of Theoretical Biology, 7,* 1–52.

Hammel, P. (2008, November 29). Psychologist had dual role in confessions of Beatrice 6. *Omaha World-Herald.*

Hammersla, J. F., & Frease-McMahan, L. (1990). University students' priorities: Life goals vs. relationships. *Sex Roles, 23,* 1–14.

Hampson, R. B. (1984). Adolescent prosocial behavior: Peer-group and situational factors associated with helping. *Journal of Personality and Social Psychology, 46,* 153–162.

Hamrick, N., Cohen, S., & Rodriguez, M. S. (2002). Being popular can be healthy or unhealthy: Stress, social network diversity, and incidence of upper respiratory infection. *Health Psychology, 21,* 294–298.

Han, S., & Shavitt, S. (1994). Persuasion and culture: Advertising appeals in individualistic and collectivistic societies. *Journal of Experimental Social Psychology, 30,* 326–350.

Hanc, J. (2006, September 12). Muscle men: Today's culture has produced fitness buffs obsessed with becoming muscular. But how much is too much? *Newsday* (New York), p. B12.

Haney, C. (1984). On the selection of capital juries: The biasing effects of the death-qualification process. *Law and Human Behavior, 8,* 121–132.

Haney, C., & Zimbardo, P. G. (1998). The past and future of U.S. prison policy: Twenty-five years after the Stanford Prison Experiment. *American Psychologist, 53,* 709–727.

Haney, C., & Zimbardo, P. G. (2009). Persistent dispositionalism in interactionist clothing: Fundamental attribution error in explaining prison abuse. *Personality and Social Psychology Bulletin, 35,* 807–814.

Haney, C., Banks, C., & Zimbardo, P. (1973). Interpersonal dynamics in a simulated prison. *International Journal of Criminology and Penology, 1,* 69–97.

Haney, C., Hurtado, A., & Vega, L. (1994). "Modern" death qualification: New data on its biasing effects. *Law and Human Behavior, 18,* 619–633.

Hans, V. P. (2000). *Business on trial: The civil jury and corporate responsibility.* New Haven, CT: Yale University Press.

Hans, V. P., Kaye, D. H., Dann, B. M., Farley, E. J., & Albertson, S. (2011). Science in the jury box: Jurors' comprehension of mitochondrial DNA evidence. *Law and Human Behavior, 35,* 60–71.

Hansen, C. H., & Hansen, R. D. (1988). Finding the face in the crowd: An anger superiority effect. *Journal of Personality and Social Psychology, 54,* 917–924.

Harackiewicz, J. M., & Elliot, A. J. (1993). Achievement goals and intrinsic motivation. *Journal of Personality and Social Psychology, 65,* 904–915.

Hardin, C., & Banaji, M. R. (1993). The influence of language on thought. *Social Cognition, 11,* 277–308.

Hardin, G. (1968). The tragedy of the commons. *Science, 162,* 1243–1248.

Haritos-Fatouros, M. (2002). *Psychological origins of institutionalized torture.* London: Routledge.

Harkins, S. G., & Petty, R. E. (1981). Effects of source magnification of cognitive effort on attitudes: An information processing view. *Journal of Personality and Social Psychology, 40,* 401–413.

Harkins, S. G., & Petty, R. E. (1987). Information utility and the multiple source effect. *Journal of Personality and Social Psychology, 52,* 260–268.

Harmon-Jones, E., & Mills, J. (Eds.). (1999). *Cognitive dissonance: Progress on a pivotal theory in social psychology.* Washington, DC: American Psychological Association.

Harmon-Jones, E., Brehm, J. W., Greenberg, J., Simon, L., & Nelson, D. E. (1996). Evidence that the production of aversive consequences is not necessary to create cognitive dissonance. *Journal of Personality and Social Psychology, 70,* 5–16.

Harrington, R. (2013). *Stress, health & well-being: Thriving in the 21st century.* Belmont, CA: Wadsworth, Cengage Learning.

Harris, C. R. (2002). Sexual and romantic jealousy in heterosexual and homosexual adults. *Psychological Science, 13,* 7–12.

Harris, C. R. (2003). A review of sex differences in sexual jealousy, including self-report data, psychophysiological responses, interpersonal violence, and morbid jealousy. *Personality and Social Psychology Review, 7,* 102–128.

Harris, C. R. (2005). Male and female jealousy: Still more similar than different: Reply to Sagarin. *Personality and Social Psychology Review, 9,* 76–86.

Harris, C. R., & Christenfeld, N. (1996). Gender, jealousy, and reason. *Psychological Science, 7,* 364–366.

Harris, D. (2012). James Holmes bought rifle after failing oral exam at University of Colorado. *ABC News,* July 25.

Harris, L. T., & Fiske, S. T. (2006). Dehumanizing the lowest of the low: Neuroimaging responses to extreme out-groups. *Psychological Science, 17,* 847–853.

Harris, L. T., & Fiske, S. T. (2009). Social neuroscience evidence for dehumanised perception. *European Review of Social Psychology, 20,* 192–231.

Harris, M. B. (1995). Ethnicity, gender, and evaluations of aggression. *Aggressive Behavior, 21,* 343–357.

Harris, M. J., & Perkins, R. (1995). Effects of distraction on interpersonal expectancy effects: A social interaction test of the cognitive busyness hypothesis. *Social Cognition, 13,* 163–182.

Harris, M. J., & Rosenthal, R. (1985). Mediation of interpersonal expectancy effects. *Psychological Bulletin, 97,* 363–386.

Harrison, D. A., & Shaffer, M. A. (1994). Comparative examinations of self-reports and perceived absenteeism norms: Wading through Lake Wobegon. *Journal of Applied Psychology, 79,* 240–251.

Harrison, D. A., Kravitz, D. A., Mayer, D. M., Leslie, L. M., & Lev-Arey, D. (2006). Understanding attitudes toward affirmative action programs in employment: Summary and meta-analysis of 35 years of research. *Journal of Applied Psychology, 91,* 1013–1036.

Hart, A. J., Whalen, P. J., Shin, L. M., McInerney, S. C., Fischer, H., & Rauch, S. L. (2000). Differential response in the human amygdala to racial outgroup vs ingroup face stimuli. *Neuro-Report, 11,* 2351–2355.

Hart, W., Albarracín, D., Eagly, A. H., Lindberg, M., Lee, K. H., & Brechan, I. (2009). Feeling validated vs. being correct: A meta-analysis of exposure to information. *Psychological Bulletin, 135,* 555–588.

Hartwig, M., & Bond, C. F. (2011). Why do lie-catchers fail? A lens model meta-analysis of human lie judgments. *Psychological Bulletin, 137,* 643–659.

Hartwig, M., Granhag, P. A., Strömwall, L. A., & Vrij, A. (2005). Detecting deception via strategic disclosure of evidence. *Law and Human Behavior, 29,* 469–484.

Harvey, J. H., & Manusov, V. L. (Eds.). (2001). *Attribution, communication behavior, and close relationships.* New York: Cambridge University Press.

Harvey, J. H., & Omarzu, J. (2000). *Minding the close relationship: A theory of relationship enhancement.* New York: Cambridge University Press.

Hasel, L. E., & Kassin, S. M. (2009). On the presumption of evidentiary independence: Can confessions corrupt eyewitness identifications? *Psychological Science, 20,* 122–126.

Hasel, L. E., & Wells, G. L. (2007). Catching the bad guy: Morphing composite faces helps. *Law and Human Behavior, 31,* 193–207.

Haslam, N., & Loughnan, S. (2012). Prejudice and dehumanization. In J. Dixon & M. Levine (Eds.), *Beyond prejudice: Extending the social psychology of conflict, inequality and social change* (pp. 89–104). New York: Cambridge University Press.

Haslam, S. A., & Reicher, S. (2007). Beyond the banality of evil: Three dynamics of an interactionist social psychology of tyranny. *Personality and Social Psychology Bulletin, 33,* 615–622.

Haslam, S. A., & Reicher, S. D. (2012). When prisoners take over the prison: A social psychology of resistance. *Personality and Social Psychology Review, 16,* 154–179.

Haslam, S. A., Ryan, M. K., Postmes, T., Spears, R., Jetten, J., & Webley, P. (2006). Sticking to our guns: Social identity as a basis for the maintenance of commitment to faltering organizational projects. *Journal of Organizational Behavior, 27,* 607–628.

Hass, R. G. (1981). Effects of source characteristics on the cognitive processing of persuasive messages and attitude change. In R. Petty, T. Ostrom, & T. Brock (Eds.), *Cognitive responses in persuasion* (pp. 141–172). Hillsdale, NJ: Erlbaum.

Hass, R. G. (1984). Perspective taking and self-awareness: Drawing an E on your forehead. *Journal of Personality and Social Psychology, 46,* 788–798.

Hass, R. G., & Eisenstadt, D. (1990). The effects of self-focused attention on perspective-taking and anxiety. *Anxiety Research, 2,* 165–176.

Hass, R. G., & Grady, K. (1975). Temporal delay, type of forewarning, and resistance to influence. *Journal of Experimental Social Psychology, 11,* 459–469.

Hass, R. G., Katz, I., Rizzo, N., Bailey, J., & Moore, L. (1992). When racial ambivalence evokes negative affect, using a disguised measure of mood. *Personality and Social Psychology Bulletin, 18,* 786–797.

Hassin, R., & Trope, Y. (2000). Facing faces: Studies on the cognitive aspects of physiognomy. *Journal of Personality and Social Psychology, 78,* 837–852.

Hastie, R., & Kameda, T. (2005). The robust beauty of majority rules in group decisions. *Psychological Review, 112,* 494–508.

Hastie, R., Penrod, S. D., & Pennington, N. (1983). *Inside the jury.* Cambridge, MA: Harvard University Press.

Hatcher, R. M., Palmer, E. J., McGuire, J., Hounsome, J. C., Bilby, C. L., & Hollin, C. R. (2008). Aggression replacement training with adult male offenders within community settings: A reconviction analysis. *Journal of Forensic Psychiatry & Psychology, 19,* 517–532.

Hatemi, P. K., Hibbing, J. R., Medland, S. E., Keller, M. C., Alford, J. R., Smith, K. B., Martin, N. G., & Eaves, L. J. (2010). Not by twins alone: Using the extended family design to investigate genetic influence on political beliefs. *American Journal of Political Science, 54,* 798–814.

Hatfield, E. (1988). Passionate and companionate love. In R. J. Sternberg & M. L. Barnes (Eds.), *The psychology of love* (pp. 191–217). New Haven, CT: Yale University Press.

Hatfield, E., & Rapson, R. L. (1993). *Love, sex, and intimacy: Their psychology, biology, and history.* New York: HarperCollins.

Hatfield, E., Greenberger, E., Traupmann, J., & Lambert, P. (1982). Equity and sexual satisfaction in recently married couples. *Journal of Sex Research, 18,* 18–32.

Hatfield, E., Rapson, R. L., & Aumer-Ryan, K. (2008). Social justice in love relationships: Recent developments. *Social Justice Research, 21,* 413–431.

Hatfield, E., Rapson, R. L., & Martel, L. D. (2007). Passionate love. In S. Kitayama & D. Cohen (Eds.), *Handbook of cultural psychology.* New York: Guilford.

Hauge, L., Einarsen, S., Knardahl, S., Lau, B., Notelaers, G., & Skogstad, A. (2011). Leadership and role stressors as departmental level predictors of workplace bullying. *International Journal of Stress Management, 18,* 305–323.

Hawkins, D. L., Pepler, D. J., & Craig, W. M. (2001). Naturalistic observations of peer interventions in bullying. *Social Development, 10,* 512–527.

Hawkley, L. C., & Cacioppo, J. T. (2013). Social connectedness and health. In C. Hazan & M. Campa (Eds.), *Human Bonding.* New York: Guilford.

Hawkley, L. C., Burleson, M. H., Berntson, G. G., & Cacioppo, J. T. (2003). Loneliness in everyday life: Cardiovascular activity, psychosocial context, and health behaviors. *Journal of Personality and Social Psychology, 85,* 105–120.

Hay, D. F., & Cook, K. V. (2007). The transformation of prosocial behavior from infancy to childhood. In C. A. Brownell & C. B. Kopp (Eds.), *Socioemotional development in the toddler years: Transitions and transformations* (pp. 100–131). New York: Guilford.

Hayes, T. C., & Lee, M. R. (2005). The southern culture of honor and violent attitudes. *Sociological Spectrum, 25,* 593–617.

Hays, G. (2008). Central Washington offers the ultimate act of sportsmanship. Available at http://sports.espn.go.com/ncaa/columns/story?columnist=hays_graham&id=3372631.

Hays, R. B. (1985). A longitudinal study of friendship development. *Journal of Personality and Social Psychology, 48,* 909–924.

Hazan, C., & Diamond, L. M. (2000). The place of attachment in human mating. *Review of General Psychology, 4,* 186–204.

Hazan, C., & Shaver, P. (1987). Romantic love conceptualized as an attachment process. *Journal of Personality and Social Psychology, 52,* 511–524.

Hearold, S. (1986). A synthesis of 1043 effects of television on social behavior. In G. Comstock (Ed.), *Public communication and behavior* (Vol. 1, pp. 65–133). Orlando, FL: Academic Press.

Hearst, P. C. (1982). *Every secret thing.* New York: Doubleday.

Heatherton, T. F. (2011). Neuroscience of self and self-regulation. *Annual Review of Psychology, 62,* 363–390.

Heatherton, T. F., & Polivy, J. (1991). Development and validation of a scale for measuring state self-esteem. *Journal of Personality and Social Psychology, 60,* 895–910.

Heatherton, T. F., & Vohs, K. D. (2000). Interpersonal evaluations following threats to self: Role of self-esteem. *Journal of Personality and Social Psychology, 78,* 725–736.

Hebl, M. R., & Heatherton, T. F. (1998). The stigma of obesity in women: The difference is black and white. *Personality and Social Psychology Bulletin, 24,* 417–426.

Hebl, M. R., & Turchin, J. M. (2005). The stigma of obesity: What about men? *Basic and Applied Social Psychology, 27,* 267–275.

Hebl, M. R., King, E. B., & Perkins, A. (2009). Ethnic differences in the stigma of obesity: Identification and engagement with a thin ideal. *Journal of Experimental Social Psychology, 45,* 1165–1172.

Hebl, M., Dovidio, J. F., Richeson, J. A., Shelton, J. N., Gaertner, S. L., & Kawakami, K. (2009). Interpretation of interaction: Responsiveness to verbal and nonverbal cues. In S. Demoulin, J. P. Leyens, & J. F. Dovidio (Eds.), *Intergroup misunderstandings: Impact of divergent social realities* (pp. 101–116). New York: Psychology Press.

Hedge, J. W., & Kavanagh, M. J. (1988). Improving the accuracy of performance evaluations: Comparison of three methods of performance appraiser training. *Journal of Applied Psychology, 73,* 68–73.

Hedges, C. (2008, December 8). The best and the brightest led America off a cliff. Available at Truthdig.com.

Hehman, E., Gaertner, S. L., & Dovidio, J. F. (2011). Evaluations of presidential performance: Race, prejudice, and perceptions of Americanism. *Journal of Experimental Social Psychology, 47,* 430–435.

Heider, F. (1958). *The psychology of interpersonal relations.* New York: Wiley.

Heilman, M. E., & Alcott, V. B. (2001). What I think you think of me: Women's reactions to being viewed as beneficiaries of preferential selection. *Journal of Applied Psychology, 86,* 574–582.

Heilman, M. E., & Okimoto, T. G. (2008). Motherhood: A potential source of bias in employment decisions. *Journal of Applied Psychology, 93,* 189–198.

Heilman, M. E., Battle, W. S., Keller, C. E., & Lee, R. A. (1998). Type of affirmative action policy: A determinant of reactions to sex-based preferential selection? *Journal of Applied Psychology, 83,* 190–205.

Heilman, M. E., Block, C. J., & Lucas, J. A. (1992). Presumed incompetent? Stigmatization and affirmative action efforts. *Journal of Applied Psychology, 77,* 536–544.

Heilman, M. E., McCullough, W. F., & Gilbert, D. (1996). The other side of affirmative action: Reactions of nonbeneficiaries to sex-based preferential selection. *Journal of Applied Psychology, 81,* 346–357.

Heilman, M. E., Simon, M. C., & Repper, D. P. (1987). Intentionally favored, unintentionally harmed? Impact of sex-based preferential selection on self-perceptions and self-evaluations. *Journal of Applied Psychology, 72,* 62–68.

Heine, S. J. (2005). Where is the evidence for pancultural self-enhancement? A reply to Sedikides, Gaertner, & Toguchi (2003). *Journal of Personality and Social Psychology, 89,* 531–538.

Heine, S. J. (2007). Culture and motivation. In S. Kitayama & D. Cohen (Eds.), *Handbook of cultural psychology.* New York: Guilford.

Heine, S. J., & Hamamura, T. (2007). In search of East Asian self-enhancement. *Personality and Social Psychology Review, 11,* 1–24.

Heine, S. J., Kitayama, S., Lehman, D. R., Takata, T., Ide, E., Leung, C., & Matsumoto, H. (2001). Divergent consequences of success and failure in Japan and North America: An investigation of self-improving motivations and malleable selves. *Journal of Personality and Social Psychology, 81,* 599–615.

Heine, S. J., Lehman, D. R., Markus, H. R., & Kitayama, S. (1999). Is there a universal need for positive self-regard? *Psychological Review, 106,* 756–794.

Heine, S. J., Takata, T., & Lehman, D. R. (2000). Beyond self-presentation: Evidence for self-criticism among Japanese. *Personality and Social Psychology Bulletin, 26,* 71–78.

Heine, S. J., Takemoto, T., Moskalenko, S., Lasaleta, J., & Henrich, J. (2008). Mirrors in the head: Cultural variation in objective self-awareness. *Personality and Social Psychology Bulletin, 34,* 879–887.

Helgesen, S. (1995). *Web of inclusion: A new architecture for building great organizations.* New York: Doubleday.

Helgeson, V. S. (1992). Moderators of the relation between perceived control and adjustment to chronic illness. *Journal of Personality and Social Psychology, 63,* 652–666.

Helgeson, V. S., Cohen, S., Schulz, R., & Yasko, J. (2000). Group support interventions for women with breast cancer: Who benefits from what? *Health Psychology, 19,* 107–114.

Helgeson, V. S., Reynolds, K. A., & Tomich, P. L. (2006). A meta-analytic review of benefit finding and growth. *Journal of Consulting and Clinical Psychology, 74,* 797–816.

Heller, J. F., Pallak, M. S., & Picek, J. M. (1973). The interactive effects of intent and threat on boomerang attitude change. *Journal of Personality and Social Psychology, 26,* 273–279.

Helliwell, J., Layard, R., & Sachs, J. (Eds.) (2012). *World Happiness Report.* New York: Columbia University: The Earth Institute.

Henchy, T., & Glass, D. C. (1968). Evaluation apprehension and the social facilitation of dominant and subordinate responses. *Journal of Personality and Social Psychology, 10,* 446–454.

Henderlong, J., & Lepper, M. R. (2002). The effects of praise on children's intrinsic motivation: A review and synthesis. *Psychological Bulletin, 128,* 774–795.

Henderson-King, D., Henderson-King, E., & Hoffman, L. (2001). Media images and women's self-evaluations: Social context and importance of attractiveness as moderators. *Personality and Social Psychology Bulletin, 27,* 1407–1416.

Henderson-King, E., & Henderson-King, D. (1997). Media effects on women's body esteem: Social and individual differences factors. *Journal of Applied Social Psychology, 27,* 399–417.

Henderson, L., & Zimbardo, P. (1998). Shyness. In H. S. Friedman (Ed.), *Encyclopedia of mental health.* San Diego: Academic Press.

Henderson, M. D. (2011). Mere physical distance and integrative agreements: When more space improves negotiation outcomes. *Journal of Experimental Social Psychology, 47,* 7–15.

Henderson, M. D., Huang, S., & Chang, C. (2012). When others cross psychological distance to help: Highlighting prosocial actions toward outgroups encourages philanthropy. *Journal of Experimental Social Psychology, 48,* 220–225.

Hendren, A., & Blank, H. (2009). Prejudiced behavior toward lesbians and gay men: A field experiment on everyday helping. *Social Psychology, 40,* 234–238.

Hendrick, C., & Hendrick, S. S. (Eds.). (2000). *Close relationships: A sourcebook.* Thousand Oaks, CA: Sage.

Hendrick, S. S., & Hendrick, C. (1995). Gender differences and similarities in sex and love. *Personal Relationships, 2,* 55–65.

Heneman, H. G., & Schwab, D. P. (1985). Pay satisfaction: Its multidimensional nature and measurement. *International Journal of Psychology, 20,* 129–141.

Henggeler, S. W., Letourneau, E. J., Chapman, J. E., Borduin, C. M., Schewe, P. A., & McCart, M. R. (2009). Mediators of change for multisystemic therapy with juvenile sexual offenders. *Journal of Consulting and Clinical Psychology, 77,* 451–462.

Henle, C. A., Kohut, G., & Booth, R. (2009). Designing electronic use policies to enhance employee perceptions of fairness and to reduce cyberloafing: An empirical test of justice theory. *Computers in Human Behavior, 25,* 902–910.

Henley, N. M. (1977). *Body politics: Power, sex, and nonverbal communication.* Englewood Cliffs, NJ: Prentice-Hall.

Henningsen, D. D., Henningsen, M. L. M., Eden, J., & Cruz, M. G. (2006). Examining the symptoms of groupthink and retrospective sensemaking. *Small Group Research, 37,* 36–64.

Henry, D. B., Kobus, K., & Schoeny, M. E. (2011). Accuracy and bias in adolescents' perceptions of friends' substance use. *Psychology of Addictive Behaviors, 25,* 80–89.

Heppner, P. P., Heppner, M. J., Lee, D., Wang, Y., Park, H., & Wang, L. (2006). Development and validation of a collectivist coping styles inventory. *Journal of Counseling Psychology, 53,* 107–125.

Herdt, G. (1998). *Same sex, different cultures: Exploring gay and lesbian lives.* Boulder, CO: Westview Press.

Herek, G. M. (2006). Legal recognition of same-sex relationships in the United States: A social science perspective. *American Psychologist, 61,* 607–621.

Herring, C. (2009). Does diversity pay? Race, gender, and the business case for diversity. *American Sociological Review, 74,* 208–224.

Hertel, G. (2011). Synergetic effects in working teams. *Journal of Managerial Psychology, 26,* 176–184.

Hertwig, R., & Ortmann, A. (2008). Deception in experiments: Revisiting the arguments in its defense. *Ethics & Behavior, 18,* 59–92.

Hewitt, P. L., Flett, G. L., Sherry, S. B., Habke, M., Parkin, M., Lam, R., McMurtry, B., Ediger, E., Fairlie, P., & Stein, M. B. (2003). The interpersonal expression of perfection: Perfectionistic self-presentation and psychological distress. *Journal of Personality and Social Psychology, 84,* 1303–1325.

Hewstone, M., & Lord, C. G. (1998). Changing intergroup cognitions and intergroup behavior: The role of typicality. In C. Sedikides, J. Schopler, & C. A. Insko (Eds.), *Intergroup cognition and intergroup behavior* (pp. 367–392). Mahwah, NJ: Erlbaum.

Hewstone, M., Clare, A., Newheiser, A., & Voci, A. (2011). Individual and situational predictors of religious prejudice: Impact of religion, social dominance orientation, intergroup contact, and mortality salience. *TPM-Testing, Psychometrics, Methodology In Applied Psychology, 18,* 143–155.

Heyes, C. (2011). Automatic imitation. *Psychological Bulletin, 137,* 463–483.

Higgins, C. A., & Judge, T. A. (2004). The effect of applicant influence tactics on recruiter perceptions of fit and hiring recommendations: A field study. *Journal of Applied Psychology, 89,* 622–632.

Higgins, E. T. (1989). Self-discrepancy theory: What patterns of self-beliefs cause people to suffer? In L. Berkowitz (Ed.), *Advances in experimental social psychology* (Vol. 22, pp. 93–136). New York: Academic Press.

Higgins, E. T. (1999). Self-discrepancy: A theory relating self and affect. In R. F. Baumeister (Ed.), *The self in social psychology* (pp. 150–181). Philadelphia, PA: Psychology Press/Taylor & Francis.

Higgins, E. T., & Rholes, W. S. (1978). "Saying is believing": Effects of message modification on memory and liking for the person described. *Journal of Experimental Social Psychology, 14,* 363–378.

Higgins, E. T., King, G. A., & Mavin, G. H. (1982). Individual construct accessibility and subjective impressions and recall. *Journal of Personality and Social Psychology, 43,* 35–47.

Higgins, E. T., Rholes, C. R., & Jones, C. R. (1977). Category accessibility and impression formation. *Journal of Experimental Social Psychology, 13,* 141–154.

Higgins, L. T., Zheng, M., Liu, Y., & Sun, C. H. (2002). Attitudes to marriage and sexual behaviors: A survey of gender and culture differences in China and the United Kingdom. *Sex Roles, 46,* 75–89.

Higgins, R. L., & Harris, R. N. (1988). Strategic "alcohol" use: Drinking to self-handicap. *Journal of Social and Clinical Psychology, 6,* 191–202.

Hill, C. A. (1987). Affiliation motivation: People who need people . . . but in different ways. *Journal of Personality and Social Psychology, 52,* 1008–1018.

Hill, C., Memon, A., & McGeorge, P. (2008). The role of confirmation bias in suspect interviews: A systematic evaluation. *Legal and Criminological Psychology, 13,* 357–371.

Hill, J., & Nathan, R. (2008). Childhood antecedents of serious violence in adult male offenders. *Aggressive Behavior, 34,* 329–338.

Hilmert, C. J., Kulik, J. A., & Christenfeld, N. J. S. (2006). Positive and negative outcome modeling: The influence of another's similarity and dissimilarity. *Journal of Personality and Social Psychology, 90,* 440–452.

Hilton, J. L., & Darley, J. M. (1985). Constructing other persons: A limit on the effect. *Journal of Experimental Social Psychology, 21,* 1–18.

Hilton, J. L., & Darley, J. M. (1991). The effects of interaction goals on person perception. *Advances in Experimental Social Psychology, 24,* 235–267.

Hilton, J. L., & Fein, S. (1989). The role of typical diagnosticity in stereotype-based judgments. *Journal of Personality and Social Psychology, 57,* 201–211.

Hilton, J. M., Anngela-Cole, L., & Wakita, J. (2010). A cross-cultural comparison of factors associated with school bullying in Japan and the United States. *The Family Journal, 18,* 413–422.

Hines, D. A., & Saudino, K. J. (2002). Intergenerational transmission of intimate partner violence: A behavioral genetic perspective. *Trauma Violence and Abuse, 3,* 210–225.

Hinsz, V. B., Tindale, R. S., & Vollrath, D. A. (1997). The emerging conceptualization of groups as information processors. *Psychological Bulletin, 121,* 43–64.

Hinsz, V. B., Tindale, R. S., Nagao, D. H., Davis, J. H., & Robertson, B. A. (1988). The influence of the accuracy of individuating information on the use of base rate information in probability judgment. *Journal of Experimental Social Psychology, 24,* 127–145.

Hinsz, V. B., Tindale, R., & Nagao, D. H. (2008). Accentuation of information processes and biases in group judgments integrating base-rate and case-specific information. *Journal of Experimental Social Psychology, 44,* 116–126.

Hirsch, A. (2012) Moroccan legal system under fire over women's rights after teenager's suicide: Court ordered marriage of girl, 16, to alleged rapist. *The Guardian (London),* April 4, p. 18.

Hirt, E. R., Deppe, R. K., & Gordon, L. J. (1991). Self-reported versus behavioral self-handicapping: Empirical evidence for a theoretical distinction. *Journal of Personality and Social Psychology, 61,* 981–991.

Hitler, A. (1933). *Mein Kampf* (E. T. S. Dugdale, Trans.). Cambridge, MA: Riverside.

Hoaken, P. N. S., Allaby, D. B., & Earle, J. (2007). Executive cognitive functioning and the recognition of facial expressions of emotion in incarcerated violent offenders, non-violent offenders, and controls. *Aggressive Behavior, 33,* 412–421.

Hobfoll, S. E., Canetti-Nisim, D., & Johnson, R. J. (2006). Exposure to terrorism, stress-related mental health symptoms, and defensive coping among Jews and Arabs in Israel. *Journal of Consulting and Clinical Psychology, 74,* 207–218.

Hobfoll, S. E., Palmieri, P. A., Johnson, R. J., Canetti-Nisim, D., Hall, B. J., & Galea, S. (2009). Trajectories of resilience, resistance, and distress during ongoing terrorism: The case of Jews and Arabs in Israel. *Journal of Consulting and Clinical Psychology, 77,* 138–148.

Hobza, C. L., & Rochlen, A. B. (2009). Gender role conflict, drive for muscularity, and the impact of ideal media portrayals on men. *Psychology of Men and Masculinity, 10,* 120–130.

Hodges, B. H., & Geyer, A. L. (2006). A nonconformist account of the Asch experiments: Values, pragmatics, and moral dilemmas. *Personality and Social Psychology Review, 10,* 2–19.

Hodson, G., Dovidio, J. F., & Gaertner, S. L. (2010). The aversive form of racism. In J. Chin (Ed.), *The psychology of prejudice and discrimination: A revised and condensed edition* (pp. 1–13). Santa Barbara, CA: Praeger/ABC-CLIO.

Hoever, I. J., van Knippenberg, D., van Ginkel, W. P., & Barkema, H. G. (2012). Fostering team creativity: Perspective taking as key to unlocking diversity's potential. *Journal of Applied Psychology.*

Hofling, C. K., Brotzman, E., Dalrymple, S., Graves, N., & Pierce, C. (1966). An experimental study of nurse-physician relations. *Journal of Nervous and Mental Disease, 143,* 171–180.

Hofmann, W., Baumeister, R. F., Förster, G., & Vohs, K. D. (2012). Everyday temptations: An experience sampling study of desire, conflict, and self-control. *Journal of Personality and Social Psychology, 102,* 1318–1335.

Hofmann, W., De Houwer, J., Perugini, M., Baeyens, F., & Crombez, G. (2010). Evaluative conditioning in humans: A meta-analysis. *Psychological Bulletin, 136,* 390–421.

Hofstede, G. (1980). *Culture's consequences.* Beverly Hills, CA: Sage.

Hogan, R., Curphy, G. J., & Hogan, J. (1994). What we know about leadership: Effectiveness and personality. *American Psychologist, 49,* 493–504.

Hoigaard, R., & Ommundsen, Y. (2007). Perceived social loafing and anticipated effort reduction among young football (soccer) players: An achievement goal perspective. *Psychological Reports, 100,* 857–875.

Hollander, E. P. (1958). Conformity, status, and idiosyncrasy credit. *Psychological Review, 65,* 117–127.

Hollander, E. P. (1985). Leadership and power. In G. Lindzey & E. Aronson (Eds.), *Handbook of social psychology* (3rd ed., Vol. 2, pp. 485–537). New York: Random House.

Hollén, L. I., & Radford, A. N. (2009). The development of alarm call behaviour in mammals and birds. *Animal Behaviour, 78,* 791–800.

Holloway, R. A., Waldrip, A. M., & Ickes, W. (2009). Evidence that a simpático self-schema accounts for differences in the self-concepts and social behavior of Latinos versus Whites (and Blacks). *Journal of Personality and Social Psychology, 96,* 1012–1028.

Holmes, T. H., & Rahe, R. H. (1967). The Social Readjustment Rating Scale. *Journal of Psychosomatic Research, 11,* 213–218.

Holmqvist, R., Hill, T., & Lang, A. (2009). Effects of aggression replacement training in young offender institutions. *International Journal of Offender Therapy and Comparative Criminology, 53,* 74–92.

Holoien, D. S., & Shelton, J. N. (2012). You deplete me: The cognitive costs of colorblindness on ethnic minorities. *Journal of Experimental Social Psychology, 48,* 562–565.

Homans, G. C. (1961). *Social behavior.* New York: Harcourt, Brace & World.

Hönekopp, J. (2006). Once more: Is beauty in the eye of the beholder? Relative contributions of private and shared taste to judgments of facial attractiveness. *Journal of Experimental Psychology: Human Perception and Performance, 32,* 199–209.

Hönekopp, J. (2011). Relationships between digit ratio 2D:4D and self-reported aggression and risk taking in an online study. *Personality and Individual Differences, 51,* 77–80.

Hönekopp, J., & Watson, S. (2011). Meta-analysis of the relationship between digit-ratio 2D:4D and aggression. *Personality and Individual Differences, 51,* 381–386.

Honeycutt, J. M., Woods, B. L., & Fontenot, K. (1993). The endorsement of communication conflict rules as a function of engagement, marriage and marital ideology. *Journal of Social and Personal Relationships, 10,* 285–304.

Hong, L. (2000). Toward a transformed approach to prevention: Breaking the link between masculinity and violence. *Journal of American College Health, 48,* 269–279.

Hong, Y.-y., Wyer, R. S., Jr., & Fong, C. P. S. (2008). Chinese working in groups: Effort dispensability versus normative influence. *Asian Journal of Social Psychology, 11,* 187–195.

Hong, Y., Morris, M. W., Chiu, C., & Benet-Martinez, V. (2000). Multicultural minds: A dynamic constructivist approach to culture and cognition. *American Psychologist, 55,* 709–720.

Honts, C. R., Raskin, D. C., & Kircher, J. C. (1994). Mental and physical countermeasures reduce the accuracy of polygraph tests. *Journal of Applied Psychology, 79,* 252–259.

Honts, C. R., Raskin, D. C., & Kircher, J. C. (2002). The scientific status of research on polygraph techniques: The case for polygraph tests (pp. 446–483). In D. L. Faigman, D. Kaye, M. J. Saks, & J. Sanders (Eds.), *Modern scientific evidence: The law and science of expert testimony.* St. Paul, MN: West.

Hoorens, V., & Nuttin, J. M. (1993). Overvaluation of own attributes: Mere ownership or subjective frequency? *Social Cognition, 11,* 177–200.

Hope, L., & Wright, D. (2007). Beyond unusual? Examining the role of attention in the weapon focus effect. *Applied Cognitive Psychology, 21,* 951–962.

Hope, L., Memon, A., & McGeorge, P. (2004). Understanding pretrial publicity: Predecisional distortion of evidence by mock jurors. *Journal of Experimental Psychology: Applied, 10,* 111–119.

Horner, V., Carter, J., Suchak, M., & de Waal, F. M. (2011). Spontaneous prosocial choice by chimpanzees. *PNAS Proceedings of the National Academy of Sciences of the United States of America, 108,* 13847–13851.

Hornsey, M. J., & Jetten, J. (2004). The individual within the group: Balancing the need to belong with the need to be different. *Personality and Social Psychology Review, 8,* 248–264.

Horowitz, I. A., & Willging, T. E. (1991). Changing views of jury power: The nullification debate, 1787–1988. *Law and Human Behavior, 15,* 165–182.

Horowitz, I. A., Kerr, N. L., Park, E. S., & Gockel, C. (2006). Chaos in the courtroom reconsidered: Emotional bias and juror nullification. *Law and Human Behavior, 30,* 163–181.

Horry, R., Palmer, M. A., Sexton, M. L., & Brewer, N. (2012). Memory conformity for confidently recognized items: The power of social influence on memory reports. *Journal of Experimental Social Psychology, 48,* 783–786.

Horselenberg, R., Merckelbach, H., & Josephs, S. (2003). Individual differences and false confessions: A conceptual replication of Kassin and Kiechel (1996). *Psychology, Crime and Law, 9,* 1–18.

Horstmann, G., & Bauland, A. (2006). Search asymmetries with real faces: Testing the anger-superiority effect. *Emotion, 6,* 193–207.

Horvath, A. O., & Luborsky, L. (1993). The role of the therapeutic alliance in psychotherapy. *Journal of Consulting and Clinical Psychology, 61,* 561–573.

Hoshino-Browne, E., Zanna, A. S., Spencer, S. J.; Zanna, M. P., Kitayama, S., & Lackenbauer, S. (2005). On the cultural guises of cognitive dissonance: The case of Easterners and Westerners. *Journal of Personality and Social Psychology, 89,* 294–310.

Hosoda, M., Stone-Romero, E. F., & Coats, G. (2003). The effects of physical attractiveness on job-related outcomes: A metaanalysis of experimental studies. *Personnel Psychology, 56,* 431–462.

Houghton, D. P. (2008). Invading and occupying Iraq: Some insights from political psychology. *Peace and Conflict: Journal of Peace Psychology, 14,* 169–192.

Houldsworth, C., & Mathews, B. P. (2000). Group composition, performance and educational attainment. *Education and Training, 42,* 40–53.

House, J. S., Landis, K. R., & Umberson, D. (1988). Social relationships and health. *Science, 241,* 540–545.

Hovland, C. I., & Weiss, W. (1951). The influence of source credibility on communication effectiveness. *Public Opinion Quarterly, 15,* 635–650.

Hovland, C. I., Janis, I. L., & Kelley, H. H. (1953). *Communication and persuasion: Psychological studies of opinion change.* New Haven, CT: Yale University Press.

Hovland, C. I., Lumsdaine, A. A., & Sheffield, F. D. (1949). *Experiments on mass communication.* Princeton, NJ: Princeton University Press.

Howard, D. J. (1990). The influence of verbal responses to common greetings on compliance behavior: The foot-in-the-mouth effect. *Journal of Applied Social Psychology, 20,* 1185–1196.

Howard, P. N., & Hussain, M. (2011). Digital media and the Arab Spring. *Journal of Democracy, 22,* 35–48.

Huang, C., & Dong, N. (2012). Factor structures of the Rosenberg Self-Esteem Scale: A meta-analysis of pattern matrices. *European Journal of Psychological Assessment, 28,* 132–138.

Huesmann, L. R. (1998). The role of social information processing and cognitive schema in the acquisition and maintenance of habitual aggressive behavior. In R. G. Geen & E. Donnerstein (Eds.), *Human aggression: Theories, research, and implications for social policy* (pp. 73–109). San Diego: Academic Press.

Huesmann, L. R., & Guerra, N. G. (1997). Children's normative beliefs about aggression and aggressive behavior. *Journal of Personality and Social Psychology, 72,* 408–419.

Huesmann, L. R., Moise-Titus, J., Podolski, C. P., & Eron, L. D. (2003). Longitudinal relations between children's exposure to TV violence and their aggressive and violent behavior in young adulthood: 1977–1992. *Developmental Psychology, 39,* 201–229.

Huesmann, L., Dubow, E. F., & Boxer, P. (2011). The transmission of aggressiveness across generations: Biological, contextual, and social learning processes. In P. R. Shaver & M. Mikulincer (Eds.), *Human aggression and violence: Causes, manifestations, and consequences* (pp. 123–142). Washington, DC: American Psychological Association.

Huffcutt, A. I., & Roth, P. L. (1998). Racial group differences in employment interview evaluations. *Journal of Applied Psychology, 83,* 179–189.

Huffcutt, A. I., Conway, J. M., Roth, P. L., & Stone, N. J. (2001). Identification and meta-analytic assessment of psychological constructs measured in employment interviews. *Journal of Applied Psychology, 86,* 897–913.

Hugenberg, K., & Bodenhausen, G. V. (2003). Facing prejudice: Implicit prejudice and the perception of facial threat. *Psychological Science, 14,* 640–643.

Hugenberg, K., & Bodenhausen, G. V. (2004). Ambiguity in social categorization: The role of prejudice and facial affect in race categorization. *Psychological Science, 15,* 342–345.

Hugenberg, K., & Corneille, O. (2009). Holistic processing is tuned for in-group faces. *Cognitive Science, 33,* 1173–1181.

Huh, H. (2012). Born to be a Marine: Digit ratios and military service. *Personality and Individual Differences,* in press.

Hull, J. G., & Young, R. D. (1983). Self-consciousness, self-esteem, and success-failure as determinants of alcohol consumption in male social drinkers. *Journal of Personality and Social Psychology, 44,* 1097–1109.

Human, L. J., & Biesanz, J. C. (2011). Through the looking glass clearly: Accuracy and assumed similarity in well-adjusted individuals' first impressions. *Journal of Personality and Social Psychology, 100,* 349–364.

Hummer, T. A., Wang, Y., et al. (2010). Short-term violent video game play by adolescents alters prefrontal activity during cognitive inhibition. *Media Psychology, 13,* 136–154.

Hung, T., Chi, N., & Lu, W. (2009). Exploring the relationships between perceived coworker loafing and counterproductive work behaviors: The mediating role of a revenge motive. *Journal of Business and Psychology, 24,* 257–270.

Huntsinger, J. R., Lun, J., Sinclair, S., & Clore, G. L. (2009). Contagion without contact: Anticipatory mood matching in response to affiliative motivation. *Personality and Social Psychology Bulletin, 35,* 909–922.

Hur, M. H. (2006). Exploring the motivation factors of charitable giving and their value structure: A case study of Seoul, Korea. *Social Behavior and Personality, 34,* 661–680.

Hurtz, G. M., & Donovan, J. J. (2000). Personality and job performance: The Big Five revisited. *Journal of Applied Psychology, 85,* 869–879.

Huston, T. L., & Vangelisti, A. L. (1991). Socioemotional behavior and satisfaction in marital relationships: A longitudinal study. *Journal of Personality and Social Psychology, 61,* 721–733.

Hutchings, P. B., & Haddock, G. (2008). Look black in anger: The role of implicit prejudice in the categorization and perceived emotional intensity of racially ambiguous faces. *Journal of Experimental Social Psychology, 44,* 1418–1420.

Hutchison, P., Jetten, J., & Gutierrez, R. (2011). Deviant but desirable: Group variability and evaluation of atypical group members. *Journal of Experimental Social Psychology, 47,* 1155–1161.

Huynh, Q., Devos, T., & Dunbar, C. M. (2012). The psychological costs of painless but recurring experiences of racial discrimination. *Cultural Diversity and Ethnic Minority Psychology, 18,* 26–34.

Huynh, Q., Devos, T., & Smalarz, L. (2011). Perpetual foreigner in one's own land: Potential implications for identity and psychological adjustment. *Journal of Social and Clinical Psychology, 30,* 133–162.

Hyde, M. K., & White, K. M. (2009). To be a donor or not to be? Applying an extended theory of planned behavior to predict posthumous organ donation intentions. *Journal of Applied Social Psychology, 39,* 880–900.


Igou, E. R. (2008). "How long will I suffer?" versus "How long will you suffer?" A self-other effect in affective forecasting. *Journal of Personality and Social Psychology, 95,* 899–917.

Imada, T. (2012). Cultural narratives of individualism and collectivism: A content analysis of textbook stories in the United States and Japan. *Journal of Cross-Cultural Psychology, 43,* 576–591,

Inbau, F. E., Reid, J. E., Buckley, J. P., & Jayne, B. C. (2001). *Criminal interrogation and confessions* (4th ed.). Gaithersburg, MD: Aspen.

Inbau, F. E., Reid, J. E., Buckley, J. P., & Jayne, B. C. (2013). *Criminal interrogation and confessions* (5th ed.). Burlington, MA: Jones & Bartlett.

Ingham, A. G., Levinger, G., Graves, J., & Peckham, V. (1974). The Ringelmann effect: Studies of group size and group performance. *Journal of Experimental Social Psychology, 10,* 371–384.

Inglehart, R., Foa, R., Peterson, C., & Welzel, C. (2008). Development, freedom, and rising happiness: A global perspective (1981–2007). *Current Perspectives on Psychological Science, 3,* 264–285.

Ingoldsby, B. B. (1991). The Latin American family: Familism vs. machismo. *Journal of Comparative Family Studies, 23,* 47–62.

Innocence Project. (2009). Know the causes. Available at http://www.innocenceproject.org/understand/.

Insko, C. A., Sedlak, A. J., & Lipsitz, A. (1982). A two-valued logic or two-valued balance resolution of the challenge of agreement and attraction effects in p-o-x triads, and a theoretical perspective on conformity and hedonism. *European Journal of Social Psychology, 12,* 143–167.

International Labour Office. (2008). LABORSTA Internet. Available at http://laborsta.ilo.org/.

Internet World Stats. (2011). Internet usage statistics: The big picture. Available at http://www.internetworldstats.com/stats.htm.

Inzlicht, M., & Schmader, T. (Eds.) (2012). *Stereotype threat: Theory, process, and application.* New York: Oxford University Press.

Ireland, M. E., & Pennebaker, J. W. (2010). Language style matching in writing: Synchrony in essays, correspondence, and poetry. *Journal of Personality and Social Psychology, 99,* 549–571.

Irons, E. D., & Moore, G. W. (1985). *Black managers: The case of the banking industry.* New York: Praeger.

Irwin, M., Mascovich, S., Gillin, J. C., Willoughby, R., Pike, J., & Smith, T. L. (1994). Partial sleep deprivation reduces natural killer cell activity in humans. *Psychosomatic Medicine, 56,* 493–498.

Isen, A. M. (1984). Toward understanding the role of affect in cognition. In R. S. Wyer & T. K. Srull (Eds.), *Handbook of social cognition* (Vol. 3, pp. 179–236). Hillsdale, NJ: Erlbaum.

Ishii, K., & Kurzban, R. (2008). Public goods games in Japan: Cultural and individual differences in reciprocity. *Human Nature, 19,* 138–156.

Ishii, K., Reyes, J., & Kitayama, S. (2003). Spontaneous attention to word content versus emotional tone: Differences among three cultures. *Psychological Science, 14,* 39–46.

Israel, S., Weisel, O., Ebstein, R. P., & Bornstein, G. (2012). Oxytocin, but not vasopressin, increases both parochial and universal altruism. *Psychoneuroendocrinology, 37,* 1341–1344.

Ito, T. A., & Urland, G. R. (2003). Race and gender on the brain: Electrocortical measures of attention to the race and gender of multiply categorizable individuals. *Journal of Personality and Social Psychology, 85,* 616–626.

Ito, T. A., Larsen, J. T., Smith, N. K., & Cacioppo, J. T. (1998). Negative information weighs more heavily on the brain: The negativity bias in evaluative categorizations. *Journal of Personality and Social Psychology, 75,* 887–900.

Ito, T. A., Miller, N., & Pollock, V. E. (1996). Alcohol and aggression: A meta-analysis on the moderating effects of inhibitory cues, triggering events, and self-focused attention. *Psychological Bulletin, 120,* 60–82.

Izard, C. E. (1990). Facial expressions and the regulation of emotions. *Journal of Personality and Social Psychology, 58,* 487–498.


Jacks, J. Z., & Cameron, K. A. (2003). Strategies for resisting persuasion. *Basic and Applied Social Psychology, 25,* 145–161.

Jackson, J. M. (1986). In defense of social impact theory: Comment on Mullin. *Journal of Personality and Social Psychology, 50,* 511–513.

Jackson, L. M., Esses, V. M., & Burris, C. T. (2001). Contemporary sexism and discrimination: The importance of respect for men and women. *Personality and Social Psychology Bulletin, 27,* 48–61.

Jackson, T., Chen, H., Guo, C., & Gao, X. (2006). Stories we love by: Conceptions of love among couples from People's Republic of China and the United States. *Journal of Cross-Cultural Psychology, 4,* 446–464.

Jackson, T., Fritch, A., Nagasaka, T., & Gunderson, J. (2002). Towards explaining the association between shyness and loneliness: A path analysis with American college students. *Social Behavior and Personality, 30,* 263–270.

James, W. (1890). *Principles of psychology* (Vols. 1–2). New York: Holt.

Jamjoom, M. (2009, May 10). Saudi judge: It's OK to slap spendthrift wives. *CNN.com.*

Janis, I. L. (1968). Attitude change via role playing. In R. Abelson, E. Aronson, W. McGuire, T. Newcomb, M. Rosenberg, & P. Tennenbaum (Eds.), *Theories of cognitive consistency: A sourcebook* (pp. 810–818). Chicago: Rand McNally.

Janis, I. L. (1982). *Groupthink* (2nd ed.). Boston: Houghton Mifflin.

Janis, I. L., & Feshbach, S. (1953). Effects of fear arousing communications. *Journal of Abnormal and Social Psychology, 48,* 78–92.

Janis, I. L., & King, B. T. (1954). The influence of role playing on opinion change. *Journal of Abnormal and Social Psychology, 49,* 211–218.

Janis, I. L., Kaye, D., & Kirschner, P. (1965). Facilitating effects of "eating while reading" on responsiveness to persuasive communications. *Journal of Personality and Social Psychology, 1,* 181–186.

Jankowiak, W. R., & Fischer, E. F. (1992). A cross-cultural perspective on romantic love. *Ethnology, 31,* 149–155.

Janoff-Bulman, R. (1979). Characterological versus behavioral self-blame: Inquiries into depression and rape. *Journal of Personality and Social Psychology, 37,* 1798–1809.

Janoff-Bulman, R. (1992). *Shattered assumptions: Towards a new psychology of trauma.* New York: Free Press.

Jansari, A., & Parkin, A. J. (1996). Things that go bump in your life: Explaining the reminiscence bump in autobiographical memory. *Psychology and Aging, 11,* 85–91.

Janssen, L., Fennis, B. M., & Pruyn, A. (2010). Forewarned is forearmed: Conserving self-control strength to resist social influence. *Journal of Experimental Social Psychology, 46,* 911–921.

Jarvis, W. B. G., & Petty, R. E. (1996). The need to evaluate. *Journal of Personality and Social Psychology, 70,* 172–194.

Jawahar, I. M., & Mattsson, J. (2005). Sexism and beautyism effects in selection as a function of self-monitoring level of decision maker. *Journal of Applied Psychology, 90,* 563–573.

Jawahar, I. M., Kisamore, J. L., Stone, T. H., & Rahn, D. L. (2012). Differential effect of inter-role conflict on proactive individual's experience of burnout. *Journal of Business and Psychology, 27,* 243–254.

Jenkins, A. C., & Mitchell, J. P. (2011). How has cognitive neuroscience contributed to social psychological theory? In A. Todorov, S. T. Fiske, & D. A. Prentice (Eds.), *Social neuroscience: Toward understanding the underpinnings of the social mind* (pp. 3–13). New York: Oxford University Press.

Jenkins, G. D., Jr., Mitra, A., Gupta, N., & Shaw, J. D. (1998). Are financial incentives related to performance? A meta-analytic review of empirical research. *Journal of Applied Psychology, 83,* 777–787.

Jennings (Walstedt), J., Geis, F. L., & Brown, V. (1980). Influence of television commercials on women's self-confidence and independent judgment. *Journal of Personality and Social Psychology, 38,* 203–210.

Jepson, C., & Chaiken, S. (1990). Chronic issue-specific fear inhibits systematic processing of persuasive communications. *Journal of Social Behavior and Personality, 5,* 61–84.

Jetten, J., Hornsey, M. J., & Adarves-Yorno, I. (2006). When group members admit to being conformist: The role of relative intragroup status in conformity self-reports. *Personality and Social Psychology Bulletin, 32,* 162–173.

Jetten, J., Hornsey, M. J., Spears, R., Haslam, S., & Cowell, E. (2010). Rule transgressions in groups: The conditional nature of newcomers' willingness to confront deviance. *European Journal of Social Psychology, 40,* 338–348.

Johansson, G., von Hofsten, C., & Jansson, G. (1980). Event perception. *Annual Review of Psychology, 31,* 27–53.

John, L. K., Lowenstein, G., & Prelec, D. (2012). Measuring the prevalence of questionable research practices with incentives for truth telling. *Psychological Science, 23,* 524–532.

Johns, G. (1994). Absenteeism estimates by employees and managers: Divergent perspectives and self-serving perceptions. *Journal of Applied Psychology, 79,* 229–239.

Johns, M., Schmader, T., & Martens, A., (2005). Knowing is half the battle: Teaching stereotype threat as a means of improving women's math performance. *Psychological Science, 16,* 175–179.

Johnson v. Louisiana, 406 U.S. 356 (1972).

Johnson, D. J., & Rusbult, C. E. (1989). Resisting temptation: Devaluation of alternative partners as a means of maintaining commitment in close relationships. *Journal of Personality and Social Psychology, 57,* 967–980.

Johnson, J. T. (2009). The once and future self: Beliefs about temporal change in goal importance and goal achievement. *Self and Identity, 8,* 94–112.

Johnson, R. D., & Downing, L. L. (1979). Deindividuation and valance of cues: Effects on prosocial and antisocial behavior. *Journal of Personality and Social Psychology, 37,* 1532–1538.

Johnson, R. W., Kelly, R. J., & LeBlane, B. A. (1995). Motivational basis of dissonance: Aversive consequences or inconsistency. *Personality and Social Psychology Bulletin, 21,* 850–855.

Johnson, W., & Krueger, R. F. (2006). How money buys happiness: Genetic and environmental processes linking finances and life satisfaction. *Journal of Personality and Social Psychology, 90,* 680–691.

Johnston, K. E., & Jacobs, J. E. (2003). Children's illusory correlations: The role of attentional bias in group impression formation. *Journal of Cognition and Development, 4,* 129–160.

Jones, B. C., DeBruine, L. M., & Little, A. C. (2007). The role of symmetry in attraction to average faces. *Perception & Psychophysics, 69,* 1273–1277.

Jones, E. E. (1964). *Ingratiation: A social psychological analysis.* New York: Appleton-Century-Crofts.

Jones, E. E. (1990). *Interpersonal perception.* New York: Freeman.

Jones, E. E., & Davis, K. E. (1965). From acts to dispositions: The attribution process in person perception. *Advances in Experimental Psychology, 2,* 219–266.

Jones, E. E., & Harris, V. A. (1967). The attribution of attitudes. *Journal of Experimental Social Psychology, 3,* 1–24.

Jones, E. E., & Pittman, T. S. (1982). Toward a general theory of strategic self presentation. In J. Suls (Ed.), *Psychological perspectives on the self.* Hillsdale, NJ: Erlbaum.

Jones, E. E., & Sigall, H. (1971). The bogus pipeline: A new paradigm for measuring affect and attitude. *Psychological Bulletin, 76,* 349–364.

Jones, E. E., Davis, K. E., & Gergen, K. (1961). Role playing variations and their informational value for person perception. *Journal of Abnormal and Social Psychology, 63,* 302–310.

Jones, E. E., Rhodewalt, F., Berglas, S., & Skelton, J. A. (1981). Effects of strategic self-presentation on subsequent self-esteem. *Journal of Personality and Social Psychology, 41,* 407–421.

Jones, E. E., Rock, L., Shaver, K. G., Goethals, G. R., & Ward, L. M. (1968). Pattern of performance and ability attribution: An unexpected primary effect. *Journal of Personality and Social Psychology, 10,* 317–340.

Jones, E., & Sigall, H. (1971). "The Bogus Pipeline: A new paradigm for measuring affect and attitude." *Psychological Bulletin, 76,* 349–364.

Jones, J. H. (1997a). *Alfred C. Kinsey: A public/private life.* New York: Norton.

Jones, J. M. (1997b). *Prejudice and racism* (2nd ed.). New York: McGraw-Hill.

Jones, J. T., Pelham, B. W., Carvallo, M., & Mirenberg, M. C. (2004). How do I love thee? Let me count the Js: Implicit egotism and interpersonal attraction. *Journal of Personality and Social Psychology, 87,* 665–683.

Jones, S. S. (2007). Imitation in infancy: The development of mimicry. *Psychological Science, 18,* 593–599.

Jones, T. F., Craig, A. S., Hoy, D., Gunter, E. W., Ashley, D. L., Barr, D. B., Brock, J. W., & Schaffner, W. (2000). Mass psychogenic illness attributed to toxic exposure at a high school. *New England Journal of Medicine, 342,* 96–100.

Jordan, J., Bardé, B., & Zeiher, A. M. (Eds.). (2007). *Contributions toward evidence-based psychocardiology: A systematic review of the literature.* Washington, DC: American Psychological Association.

Jordan, K., & Austin, J. (2012). A review of the literature on bullying in U.S. schools and how a parent–educator partnership can be an effective way to handle bullying. *Journal of Aggression, Maltreatment and Trauma, 21,* 440–458.

Josephs, R. A., Bosson, J. K., & Jacobs, C. G. (2003). Self-esteem maintenance processes: When low self-esteem may be resistant to change. *Personality and Social Psychology Bulletin, 29,* 920–933.

Jost, J. T. (2011). System justification theory as compliment, complement, and corrective to theories of social identification and social dominance. In D. Dunning (Ed.), *Social motivation* (pp. 223–263). New York: Psychology Press.

Jost, J. T., & Amodio, D. M. (2012). Political ideology as motivated social cognition: Behavioral and neuroscientific evidence. *Motivation and Emotion, 36,* 55–64.

Jost, J. T., & van der Toorn, J. (2012). System justification theory. In P. M. van Lange, A. W. Kruglanski, & E. T. Higgins (Eds.), *Handbook of theories of social psychology* (Vol. 2, pp. 313–343). London: Sage.

Joyce, C. (2005, May 16). Japanese women escape subway gropers: Transit officials tackle problems with women-only cars. *Ottawa Citizen*, p. A6.

Judge, T. A., & Kammeyer-Mueller, J. D. (2012). Job attitudes. *Annual Review of Psychology, 63*, 341–367.

Judge, T. A., & Welbourne, T. M. (1994). A confirmatory investigation of the dimensionality of the Pay Satisfaction Questionnaire. *Journal of Applied Psychology, 79*, 461–466.

Judge, T. A., Bono, J. E., & Locke, E. A. (2000). Personality and job satisfaction: The mediating role of job characteristics. *Journal of Applied Psychology, 85*, 237–249.

Judge, T. A., Hurst, C., & Simon, L. S. (2009). Does it pay to be smart, attractive, or confident (or all three)? Relationships among general mental ability, physical attractiveness, core self-evaluations, and income. *Journal of Applied Psychology, 94*, 742–755.

Judge, T. A., Piccolo, R. F., & Kosalka, T. (2009). The bright and dark sides of leader traits: A review and theoretical extension of the leader trait paradigm. *Leadership Quarterly, 20*, 855–875.

Judge, T. A., Piccolo, R. F., Podsakoff, N. P., Shaw, J. C., & Rich, B. L. (2010). The relationship between pay and job satisfaction: A meta-analysis of the literature. *Journal of Vocational Behavior, 77*, 157–167.

Jung-Yoon, C. (2011). Seoul offers women-only subway cars; effort to reduce cases of abuse draws mixed reviews from potential users. *The Vancouver Sun*, August 24, p. B9.

Jussim, L. (2012). *Social perception and social reality: Why accuracy dominates bias and self-fulfilling prophecy.* New York: Oxford University Press.

Juvonen, J., Nishina, A., & Graham, S. (2006). Ethnic diversity and perceptions of safety in urban middle schools. *Psychological Science, 17*, 393–400.

Kagan, J. (1994). *Galen's prophecy: Temperament in human nature.* New York: Basic Books.

Kahneman, D. (2011). *Thinking, Fast and Slow.* New York: Farrar, Straus, & Giroux.

Kahneman, D., & Miller, D. T. (1986). Norm theory: Comparing reality to its alternatives. *Psychological Review, 93*, 136–153.

Kahneman, D., & Tversky A. (1979). Prospect theory: An analysis of decisions under risk. *Econometrika, 47*, 263–291.

Kahneman, D., Knetsch, J. L., & Thaler, R. H. (1990). Experimental tests of the endowment effect and the coase theorem. *Journal of Political Economy, 98*, 1325–1348.

Kahneman, D., Slovic, P., & Tversky, A. (Eds.). (1982). *Judgment under uncertainty: Heuristics and biases.* New York: Cambridge University Press.

Kaholokula, J., Grandinetti, A., Keller, S., Nacapoy, A. H., Kingi, T., & Mau, M. K. (2012). Association between perceived racism and physiological stress indices in native Hawaiians. *Journal of Behavioral Medicine, 35*, 27–37.

Kalichman, S. C. (Ed.). (2006). *Positive prevention: Reducing HIV transmission among people living with HIV/AIDS.* New York: Springer.

Kallgren, C. A., & Wood, W. (1986). Access to attitude-relevant information in memory as a determinant of attitude-behavior consistency. *Journal of Experimental Social Psychology, 22*, 328–338.

Kalven, H., & Zeisel, H. (1966). *The American jury.* Boston: Little, Brown.

Kamen-Siegel, L., Rodin, J., Seligman, M. E. P., & Dwyer, J. (1991). Explanatory style and cell-mediated immunity in elderly men and women. *Health Psychology, 10*, 229–235.

Kampis, J. (2005, February 15). Lawsuit claims video violence precipitated Fayetteville shootings. *Tuscaloosa News* (Alabama).

Kandler, C., Bleidorn, W., & Riemann, R. (2012). Left or right? Sources of political orientation: The roles of genetic factors, cultural transmission, assortative mating, and personality. *Journal of Personality and Social Psychology, 102*, 633–645.

Kane, H. S., McCall, C., Collins, N. L., & Blascovich, J. (2012). Mere presence is not enough: Responsive support in a virtual world. *Journal of Experimental Social Psychology, 48*, 37–44.

Kaplan, M. F., & Schersching, C. (1981). Juror deliberation: An information integration analysis. In B. Sales (Ed.), *The trial process* (pp. 235–262). New York: Plenum.

Karau, S. J., & Williams, K. D. (1993). Social loafing: A meta-analytic review and theoretical integration. *Journal of Personality and Social Psychology, 65*, 681–706.

Karau, S. J., & Williams, K. D. (2001). Understanding individual motivation in groups: The collective effort model. In M. E. Turner (Ed.), *Groups at work: Theory and research. Applied social research* (pp. 113–141). Mahwah, NJ: Erlbaum.

Kark, R., Shamir, B., & Chen, G. (2003). The two faces of transformational leadership: Empowerment and dependency. *Journal of Applied Psychology, 88*, 246–255.

Karney, B. R., & Bradbury, T. N. (1995). The longitudinal course of marital quality and stability: A review of theory, method, and research. *Psychological Bulletin, 118*, 3–34.

Karney, B. R., & Bradbury, T. N. (2000). Attributions in marriage: State or trait? A growth curve analysis. *Journal of Personality and Social Psychology, 78*, 295–309.

Karpinski, A. T., & von Hippel, W. (1996). The role of the linguistic intergroup bias in expectancy maintenance. *Social Cognition, 14*, 141–163.

Karremans, J. C., Stroebe, W., & Claus, J. (2006). Beyond Vicary's fantasies: The impact of subliminal priming and brand choice. *Journal of Experimental Social Psychology, 42*, 792–798.

Kashima, Y., & Kerekes, A. R. Z. (1994). A distributed memory model of averaging phenomena in person impression formation. *Journal of Experimental Social Psychology, 30*, 407–455.

Kassin, S. M. (2012). Why confessions trump innocence. *American Psychologist, 67*, 431–445.

Kassin, S. M., & Kiechel, K. L. (1996). The social psychology of false confessions: Compliance, internalization, and confabulation. *Psychological Science, 7*, 125–128.

Kassin, S. M., & Sommers, S. R. (1997). Inadmissible testimony, instructions to disregard, and the jury: Substantive versus procedural considerations. *Personality and Social Psychology Bulletin, 23*, 1046–1054.

Kassin, S. M., & Sukel, H. (1997). Coerced confessions and the jury: An experimental test of the "harmless error" rule. *Law and Human Behavior, 21*, 27–46.

Kassin, S. M., Drizin, S. A., Grisso, T., Gudjonsson, G. H., Leo, R. A., & Redlich, A. D. (2010). Police-induced confessions: Risk factors and recommendations. *Law and Human Behavior, 34*, 3–38.

Kassin, S. M., Goldstein, C. J., & Savitsky, K. (2003). Behavioral confirmation in the interrogation room: On the dangers of presuming guilt. *Law and Human Behavior, 27*, 187–203.

Kassin, S. M., Leo, R. A., Meissner, C. A., Richman, K. D., Colwell, L. H., Leach, A.-M., & LaFon, D. (2007). Police interviewing and interrogation: A self-report survey of police practices and beliefs. *Law and Human Behavior, 31*, 381–400.

Kassin, S. M., Meissner, C. A., & Norwick, R. J. (2005). "I'd know a false confession if I saw one": A comparative study of college students and police investigators. *Law and Human Behavior, 29*, 211–227.

Kassin, S. M., Tubb, V. A., Hosch, H. M., & Memon, A. (2001). On the "general acceptance" of eyewitness testimony research: A new survey of the experts. *American Psychologist, 56*, 405–416.

Kaufman, D. Q., Stasson, M. F., & Hart, J. W. (1999). Are the tabloids always wrong or is that just what we think? Need for cognition and perceptions of articles in print media. *Journal of Applied Social Psychology, 29*, 1984–1997.

Kavanagh, L. C., Suhler, C. L., Churchland, P. S., & Winkielman, P. (2011). When it's an error to mirror: The surprising reputational costs of mimicry. *Psychological Science, 22*, 1274–1276.

Kawakami, K., Dion, K. L., & Dovidio, J. F. (1998). Racial prejudice and stereotype activation. *Personality and Social Psychology Bulletin, 24*, 407–416.

Kawakami, K., Dovidio, J. F., & van Kamp, S. (2007). The impact of naïve theories related to strategies to reduce biases and correction processes on the application of stereotypes. *Group Processes and Intergroup Relations, 10*, 139–156.

Kawakami, K., Dovidio, J. F., Moll, J., Hermsen, S., & Russin, A. (2000). Just say no (to stereotyping): Effects of training in the negation of stereotypic association on stereotype activation. *Journal of Personality and Social Psychology, 78,* 871–888.

Kay, A. C., & Jost, J. T. (2003). Complementary justice: Effects of "poor but happy" and "poor but honest" stereotype exemplars on system justification and implicit activation of the justice motive. *Journal of Personality and Social Psychology, 85,* 823–837.

Kay, A. C., Jost, J. T., & Young, S. (2005). Victim derogation and victim enhancement as alternate routes to system justification. *Personality and Social Psychology Bulletin, 16,* 240–246.

Keenan, J. P. Gallup, G. G. Falk, D. (2003). *The face in the mirror: The search for the origins of consciousness.* New York: HarperCollins/Ecco.

Keil, M., Depledge, G., & Rai, A. (2007). Escalation: The role of problem recognition and cognitive bias. *Decision Sciences, 38,* 391–421.

Keillor, J. M., Barrett, A. M., Crucian, G. P., Kortenkamp, S., & Heilman, K. M. (2003). Emotional experience and perception in the absence of facial feedback. *Journal of the International Neurological Society, 8,* 130–135.

Keller, P. A. (1999). Converting the unconverted: The effect of inclination and opportunity to discount health-related fear appeals. *Journal of Applied Psychology, 84,* 403–415.

Kelley, H. H. (1950). The warm-cold variable in first impressions of persons. *Journal of Personality, 18,* 431–439.

Kelley, H. H. (1967). Attribution in social psychology. *Nebraska Symposium on Motivation, 15,* 192–238.

Kelly, A. E., & McKillop, K. J. (1996). Consequences of revealing personal secrets. *Psychological Bulletin, 120,* 450–465.

Kelly, A. E., & Rodriguez, R. R. (2006). Publicly committing oneself to an identity. *Basic and Applied Social Psychology, 28,* 185–191.

Kelman, H. C. (1961). Processes of opinion change. *Public Opinion Quarterly, 25,* 57–78.

Kelman, H. C. (1967). Human use of human subjects: The problem of deception in social psychology experiments. *Psychological Bulletin, 67,* 1–11.

Kelman, H. C., & Hamilton, V. L. (1989). *Crimes of obedience: Toward a social psychology of authority and responsibility.* New Haven, CT: Yale University Press.

Kelman, H. C., & Hovland, C. I. (1953). "Reinstatement" of the communicator in delayed measurement of opinion change. *Journal of Abnormal and Social Psychology, 48,* 327–335.

Kemmelmeier, M., Jambor, E. E., & Letner, J. (2006). Individualism and good works: Cultural variation in giving and volunteering across the United States. *Journal of Cross-Cultural Psychology, 37,* 327–344.

Kemp, J., & Lemire, J. (2012). Yer out! Detroit Tigers slugger in hate attack. *New York Daily News,* April 28, p. 7.

Kenny, D. A. (1994). *Interpersonal perception: A social relations analysis.* New York: Guilford.

Kenny, D. A., & Acitelli, L. K. (2001). Accuracy and bias of perceptions of the partner in close relationships. *Journal of Personality and Social Psychology, 80,* 439–448.

Kenny, D. A., & Zaccaro, S. J. (1983). An estimate of variance due to traits in leadership. *Journal of Applied Psychology, 68,* 678–685.

Kenny, D. A., Albright, L., Malloy, T. E., & Kashy, D. A. (1994). Consensus in interpersonal perception: Acquaintance and the Big Five. *Psychological Bulletin, 116,* 245–258.

Kenny, D. A., Snook, A., Boucher, E. M., & Hancock, J. T. (2010). Interpersonal sensitivity, status, and stereotype accuracy. *Psychological Science, 21,* 1735–1739.

Kenrick, D. T., & Keefe, R. C. (1992). Age preferences in mates reflect sex differences in human reproductive strategies. *Behavioral and Brain Sciences, 15,* 75–133.

Kenrick, D. T., Gabrielidis, C., Keefe, R. C., & Cornelius, J. S. (1996). Adolescents' age preferences for dating partners: Support for an evolutionary model of life-history strategies. *Child Development, 67,* 1499–1511.

Kenrick, D. T., Goldstein, N. J., & Braver, S. L. (2012). *Six degrees of social influence: Science, application, and the psychology of Robert Cialdini.* New York: Oxford.

Kernis, M. H., & Waschull, S. B. (1995). The interactive roles of stability and level of self-esteem: Research and theory. *Advances in Experimental Social Psychology, 27,* 93–141.

Kerr, N. L. (1981). Social transition schemes: Charting the group's road to agreement. *Journal of Personality and Social Psychology, 41,* 684–702.

Kerr, N. L. (1983). Motivation losses in small groups: A social dilemma analysis. *Journal of Personality and Social Psychology, 45,* 819–828.

Kerr, N. L., Harmon, D. L., & Graves, J. K. (1982). Independence of multiple verdicts by jurors and juries. *Journal of Applied Social Psychology, 12,* 12–29.

Kerr, N. L., Hymes, R. W., Anderson, A. B., & Weathers, J. E. (1995). Defendant-juror similarity in mock juror judgments. *Law and Human Behavior, 19,* 545–567.

Kerr, N. L., Kramer, G. P., Carroll, J. S., & Alfini, J. J. (1991). On the effectiveness of voir dire in criminal cases with prejudicial pretrial publicity: An empirical study. *American University Law Review, 40,* 665–701.

Kerr, N. L., Niedermeier, K. E., & Kaplan, M. F. (1999). Bias in jurors vs. bias in juries: New evidence from the SDS perspective. *Organizational Behavior and Human Decision Processes, 80,* 70–86.

Kersten, G. E., & Lai, H. (2007). Negotiation support and E-negotiation systems: An overview. *Group Decision and Negotiation, 16,* 553–586.

Kervyn, N. Bergsieker, H. B., & Fiske, S. T. (2012). The innuendo effect: Hearing the positive but inferring the negative. *Journal of Experimental Social Psychology, 48,* 77–85.

Kessler, R. C., et al. (1994). Lifetime and 12-month prevalence of DSM-III-R psychiatric disorders in the United States. *Archives of General Psychiatry, 51,* 8–19.

Kessler, R. C., Sonnega, A., Bromet, E., Hughes, M., & Nelson, C. B. (1995). Posttraumatic stress disorder in the National Comorbidity Survey. *Archives of General Psychiatry, 52,* 1048–1060.

Key, W. B. (1973). *Subliminal seduction.* Englewood Cliffs, NJ: Signet.

Key, W. B. (1989). *The age of manipulation.* New York: Holt.

Keysar, B., & Henly, A. S. (2002). Speakers' overestimation of their effectiveness. *Psychological Science, 13,* 207–212.

Kiecolt-Glaser, J. K. (2009). Psychoneuroimmunology: Psychology's gateway to the biomedical future. *Perspectives on Psychological Science, 4,* 367–369.

Kiecolt-Glaser, J. K., & Newton, T. L. (2001). Marriage and health: His and hers. *Psychological Bulletin, 127,* 472–503.

Kiecolt-Glaser, J. K., McGuire, L., Robles, T., & Glaser, R. (2002). Psychoneuroimmunology: Psychological influences on immune function and health. *Journal of Consulting and Clinical Psychology, 70,* 537–547.

Kierein, N. M., & Gold, M. A. (2000). Pygmalion in work organizations: A meta-analysis. *Journal of Organizational Behavior, 21,* 913–928.

Kiesler, C. A. (1971). *The psychology of commitment.* New York: Academic Press.

Kiesler, C. A., & Kiesler, S. B. (1969). *Conformity.* Reading, MA: Addison-Wesley.

Kilbourne, J. (2003). Mass media: Shaping the self-concept: Beauty and the beast of advertising. In J. M. Henslin (Ed.), *Down to earth sociology: Introductory readings* (12th ed.) (pp. 421–424). New York: Free Press.

Kilham, W., & Mann, L. (1974). Level of destructive obedience as a function of transmitter and executant roles in the Milgram obedience paradigm. *Journal of Personality and Social Psychology, 29,* 696–702.

Kilianski, S. E. (2008). Who do you think I am? Accuracy in perceptions of others' self-esteem. *Journal of Research in Personality, 42,* 386–398.

Kilianski, S. E., & Rudman, L. A. (1998). Wanting it both ways: Do women approve of benevolent sexism? *Sex Roles, 39,* 333–352.

Kim, H. S., Mojaverian, T., & Sherman, D. K. (2012). Culture and genes: Moderators of the use and effect of social support. In O. Gillath, G. Adams, & A. Kunkel (Eds.), *Relationship science: Integrating evolutionary, neuroscience, and sociocultural approaches* (pp. 73–90). Washington, DC: American Psychological Association.

Kim, H. S., Sherman, D. K., Taylor, S. (2008). Culture and social support. *American Psychologist, 63,* 518–526.

Kim, H., & Markus, H. R. (1999). Deviance or uniqueness, harmony or conformity? A cultural analysis. *Journal of Personality and Social Psychology, 77,* 785–800.

Kim, Y. (2009). *Handbook of behavior genetics*. New York: Springer.

Kimmel, A. J. (2012). Deception in research. In S. J. Knapp, M. C. Gottlieb, M. M. Handelsman, & L. D. VandeCreek (Eds.), *APA handbook of ethics in psychology: Vol 2. Practice, teaching, and research* (pp. 401–421). Washington, DC: American Psychological Association.

Kimmel, P. R. (1994). Cultural perspectives on international negotiations. *Journal of Social Issues, 50,* 179–196.

Kimmel, P. R. (2000). Culture and conflict. In M. Deutsch & P. T. Coleman (Eds.), *The handbook of conflict resolution: Theory and practice* (pp. 453–474). San Francisco, CA: Jossey-Bass.

King, L. A., & Napa, C. K. (1998). What makes a life good? *Journal of Personality and Social Psychology, 75,* 156–165.

Kingston, D. A., Malamuth, N. M., Fedoroff, P., & Marshall, W. L. (2009). The importance of individual differences in pornography use: Theoretical perspectives and implications for treating sexual offenders. *Journal of Sex Research, 46,* 216–232.

Kinsey, A. C., Pomeroy, W. B., & Martin, C. E. (1948). *Sexual behavior in the human male*. Philadelphia: Saunders.

Kinsey, A. C., Pomeroy, W. B., Martin, C. E., & Gebhard, P. H. (1953). *Sexual behavior in the human female*. Philadelphia: Saunders.

Kinzer, S. (1999, September 13). A sudden friendship blossoms between Greece and Turkey. *New York Times*.

Kiong, L. C. (2011). Moves to protect women rebuffed in some cities. *The Straits Times* (Singapore), December 17.

Kirkman, B. L., Rosen, B., Gibson, C. B., Tesluk, P., & McPherson, S. O. (2002). Five challenges to virtual team success: Lessons from Sabre, Inc. *Academy of Management Executive, 16,* 67–79.

Kirkpatrick, L. A., & Hazan, C. (1994). Attachment styles and close relationships: A four-year prospective study. *Personal Relationships, 1,* 123–142.

Kirkpatrick, S. A., & Locke, E. A. (1991). Leadership: Do traits matter? *Academy of Management Executive, 5,* 48–60.

Kitayama, S., & Uchida, Y. (2003). Explicit self-criticism and implicit self-regard: Evaluating self and friend in two cultures. *Journal of Experimental Social Psychology, 39,* 476–482.

Kitayama, S., Duffy, S., Kawamura, T., & Larsen, J. T. (2003). Perceiving an object and its context in different cultures: A cultural look at New Look. *Psychological Science, 14,* 201–206.

Kitayama, S., Snibbe, A. C., Markus, H. R., & Suzuki, T. (2004). Is there any "free" choice? Self and dissonance in two cultures. *Psychological Science, 15,* 527–533.

Kite, M. E. (1992). Age and the spontaneous self-concept. *Journal of Applied Social Psychology, 22,* 1828–1837.

Kivimäki, M., Vahtera, J., Elovainio, M., Helenius, H., Singh-Manoux, A., & Pentti, J. (2005). Optimism and pessimism as predictors of change in health after death or onset of severe illness in family. *Health Psychology, 24,* 413–421.

Klapwijk, A., & Van Lange, P. A. M. (2009). Promoting cooperation and trust in 'noisy' situations: The power of generosity. *Journal of Personality and Social Psychology, 96,* 83–103.

Klauer, K., Voss, A., & Stahl, C. (2011). *Cognitive methods in social psychology*. New York: Guilford.

Klein, O., Spears, R., & Reicher, S. (2007). Social identity performance: Extending the strategic side of SIDE. *Personality and Social Psychology Review, 11,* 1–18.

Klein, W. M. (1997). Objective standards are not enough: Affective, self-evaluative, and behavioral responses to social comparison information. *Journal of Personality and Social Psychology, 72,* 763–774.

Klein, W. P., Harris, P. R., Ferrer, R. A., & Zajac, L. E. (2011). Feelings of vulnerability in response to threatening messages: Effects of self-affirmation. *Journal Of Experimental Social Psychology, 47,* 1237–1242.

Kleingeld, A., van Mierlo, H., & Arends, L. (2011). The effect of goal setting on group performance: A meta-analysis. *Journal of Applied Psychology, 96,* 1289–1304.

Kleinke, C. L. (1986). Gaze and eye contact: A research review. *Psychological Bulletin, 100,* 78–100.

Kleinke, C. L., Paterson, T. R., & Rutledge, T. R. (1998). Effects of self-generated facial expressions of mood. *Journal of Personality and Social Psychology, 74,* 272–279.

Klietz, S. J., Borduin, C. M., Schaeffer, C. M. (2010). Cost-benefit analysis of multisystemic therapy with serious and violent juvenile offenders. *Journal of Family Psychology, 24,* 657–666.

Klinesmith, J., Kasser, T., & McAndrew, F. T. (2006). Guns, testosterone, and aggression: An experimental test of a mediational hypothesis. *Psychological Science, 17,* 568–571.

Kling, K. C., Hyde, J. S., Showers, C. J., & Buswell, B. N. (1999). Gender differences in self-esteem: A meta-analysis. *Psychological Bulletin, 125,* 470–500.

Kmec, J. A. (2005). Setting occupational sex segregation in motion: Sex traditional employment. *Work and Occupations, 32,* 322–354.

Knafo, A., & Plomin, R. (2006). Prosocial behavior from early to middle childhood: Genetic and environmental influences on stability and change. *Developmental Psychology, 42,* 771–786.

Kniffin, K., & Wilson, D. S. (2004). The effect of nonphysical traits on the perception of physical attractiveness: Three naturalistic studies. *Evolution and Human Behavior, 25,* 88–101.

Knobloch, S., Callison, C., Chen, L., Fritzsche, A., & Zillmann, D. (2005). Children's sex-stereotyped self-socialization through selective exposure to entertainment: Cross-cultural experiments in Germany, China, and the United States. *Journal of Communication, 55,* 122–138.

Knowles, E. D., Lowery, B. S., & Schaumberg, R. L. (2010). Racial prejudice predicts opposition to Obama and his health care reform plan. *Journal of Experimental Social Psychology, 46,* 420–423.

Knowles, E. S. (1983). Social physics and the effects of others: Tests of the effects of audience size and distance on social judgments and behavior. *Journal of Personality and Social Psychology, 45,* 1263–1279.

Knox, R. E., & Inskter, J. A. (1968). Postdecision dissonance at post-time. *Journal of Personality and Social Psychology, 8,* 319–323.

Ko, S. J., Judd, C. M., & Blair, I. V. (2006). What the voice reveals: Within- and between-category stereotyping on the basis of voice. *Personality and Social Psychology Bulletin, 32,* 806–819.

Kobasa, S. C., Maddi, S. R., & Kahn, S. (1982). Hardiness and health: A prospective study. *Journal of Personality and Social Psychology, 42,* 168–177.

Koenig, A. M., Eagly, A. H., Mitchell, A. A., & Ristikari, T. (2011). Are leader stereotypes masculine? A meta-analysis of three research paradigms. *Psychological Bulletin, 137,* 616–642.

Kogut, T., & Ritov, I. (2007). 'One of us': Outstanding willingness to help save a single identified compatriot. *Organizational Behavior and Human Decision Processes, 104,* 150–157.

Kohn, A. (1993). *Punished by rewards*. Boston: Houghton Mifflin.

Kohn, P. M., Lafreniere, K., & Gurevich, M. (1991). Hassles, health, and personality. *Journal of Personality and Social Psychology, 61,* 478–482.

Kokko, K., Pulkkinen, L., Huesmann, L. R., Dubow, E. F., & Boxer, P. (2009). Intensity of aggression in childhood as a predictor of different forms of adult aggression: A two-country (Finland and the United States) analysis. *Journal of Research on Adolescence, 19,* 9–34.

Kolditz, T. A., & Arkin, R. M. (1982). An impression management interpretation of the self-handicapping strategy. *Journal of Personality and Social Psychology, 43,* 492–502.

Konijn, E. A., Nije Bijvank, M., & Bushman, B. J. (2007). I wish I were a warrior: The role of wishful identification in the effects of violent video games on aggression in adolescent boys. *Developmental Psychology, 43,* 1038–1044.

Kopelman, S. (2009). The effect of culture and power on cooperation in commons dilemmas: Implications for global resource management. *Organizational Behavior and Human Decision Processes, 108,* 153–163.

Kopelman, S., & Rosette, A. S. (2008). Cultural variation in response to strategic emotions in negotiations. *Group Decision and Negotiation, 17,* 65–77.

Korchmaros, J. D., Kenny, D. A., & Flory, K. (2006). An evolutionary and close-relationship model of helping. *Journal of Social and Personal Relationships, 23,* 21–43.

Korte, C. (1980). Urban-nonurban differences in social behavior and social psychological models of urban impact. *Journal of Social Issues, 36*(3), 29–51.

Koslowski, S. W., Kirsch, M. P., & Chao, G. T. (1986). Job knowledge, ratee familiarity, conceptual similarity, and halo error: An exploration. *Journal of Applied Psychology, 71,* 45–49.

Koslowsky, M., Kluger, A., & Reich, M. (1995). *Commuting stress: Causes, effects, and methods of coping.* New York: Plenum Press.

Kovacs, L. (1983). A conceptualization of marital development. *Family Therapy, 3,* 183–210.

Kovera, M. B. (2002). The effects of general pretrial publicity on juror decisions: An examination of moderators and mediating mechanisms. *Law and Human Behavior, 26,* 43–72.

Kovera, M. B., & Borgida, E. (2010). *Social psychology and law.* In S. T. Fiske, D. T.

Kovera, M. B., Penrod, S. D., Pappas, C., & Thill, D. L. (1997). Identification of computer-generated facial composites. *Journal of Applied Psychology, 82,* 235–246.

Kowalski, R. M. (1993). Inferring sexual interest from behavioral cues: Effects of gender and sexually relevant attitudes. *Sex Roles, 29,* 13–36.

Kowalski, R. M. (1996). Complaints and complaining: Functions, antecedents, and consequences. *Psychological Bulletin, 119,* 179–196.

Kozak, M. N., Marsh, A. A., & Wegner, D. M. (2006). What do I think you're doing? Action identification and mind attribution. *Journal of Personality and Social Psychology, 90,* 543–555.

Kozel, F., Johnson, K., Mu, Q., Grenesko, E., Laken, S., & George, M. (2005). Detecting deception using functional magnetic resonance imaging. *Biological Psychiatry, 58,* 605–613.

Krahé, B., Busching, R., & Möller, I. (2012). Media violence use and aggression among German adolescents: Associations and trajectories of change in a three-wave longitudinal study. *Psychology of Popular Media Culture, 1,* 152–166.

Kramer, G. P., Kerr, N. L., & Carroll, J. S. (1990). Pretrial publicity, judicial remedies, and jury bias. *Law and Human Behavior, 14,* 409–438.

Kramer, R. M. (1998). Revisiting the Bay of Pigs and Vietnam decisions 25 years later: How well has the groupthink hypothesis stood the test of time? *Organizational Behavior and Human Decision Processes, 73,* 236–271.

Krantz, D. S., & McCeney, M. K. (2002). Effects of psychological and social factors on organic disease: A critical assessment of research on coronary heart disease. *Annual Review of Psychology, 53,* 341–369.

Kraus, S. J. (1995). Attitudes and the prediction of behavior: A meta-analysis of the empirical literature. *Personality and Social Psychology Bulletin, 21,* 58–75.

Kravitz, D. A., & Martin, B. (1986). Ringelmann rediscovered: The original article. *Journal of Personality and Social Psychology, 50,* 936–941.

Kravitz, D. A., & Platania, J. (1993). Attitudes and beliefs about affirmative action: Effects of target and of respondent sex and ethnicity. *Journal of Applied Psychology, 78,* 928–938.

Kray, L. J., Galinsky, A. D., & Thompson, L. (2002). Reversing the gender gap in negotiations: An exploration of stereotype regeneration. *Organizational Behavior and Human Decision Processes, 87,* 386–409.

Kray, L. J., George, L. G., Liljenquist, K. A., Galinsky, A. D., Tetlock, P. E., & Roese, N. J. (2010). From what might have been to what must have been: Counterfactual thinking creates meaning. *Journal of Personality and Social Psychology, 98,* 106–118.

Krebs, D. (1987). The challenge of altruism in biology and psychology. In C. Crawford, M. Smith, & D. Krebs (Eds.), *Sociobiology and psychology: Ideas, issues, and applications* (pp. 81–118). Hillsdale, NJ: Erlbaum.

Krendl, A. C., Magoon, N. S., Hull, J. G., & Heatherton, T. F. (2011). Judging a book by its cover: The differential impact of attractiveness on predicting one's acceptance to high or low status social groups. *Journal of Applied Social Psychology, 41,* 2538–2550.

Kressel, N. J., & Kressel, D. F. (2002). *Stack and sway: The new science of jury consulting.* Boulder, CO: Westview Press.

Kringelbach, M. L., et al. (2008). A specific and rapid neural signature for parental instinct. *PLoS ONE, 3*(2): 1–7.

Krizan, Z., & Windschitl, P. D. (2007). The influence of outcome desirability on optimism. *Psychological Bulletin, 133,* 95–121.

Kroon, M. B. R., t'Hart, P., & van Kreveld, D. (1991). Managing group decision making processes: Individual versus collective accountability and groupthink. *International Journal of Conflict Management, 2,* 91–115.

Krueger, J. (1998). On the perception of social consensus. *Advances in Experimental Social Psychology, 30,* 163–240.

Krueger, J. (2000). The projective perception of the social world: A building block of social comparison processes. In J. Suls & L. Wheeler (Eds.), *Handbook of social comparison: Theory and research* (pp. 323–351). New York: Plenum/Kluwer.

Krueger, J. I., & DiDonato, T. E. (2008). Social categorization and the perception of groups and group differences. *Social and Personality Psychology Compass, 2,* 733–750.

Krug, E. G., Kresnow, M., Peddicord, J. P., Dahlberg, L. L., Powell, K. E., Crosby, A. E., & Annest, J. L. (1998). Suicide after natural disasters. *New England Journal of Medicine, 338,* 373–378.

Kruger, J., Wirtz, D., & Miller, D. T. (2005). Counterfactual thinking and the first instinct fallacy. *Journal of Personality and Social Psychology, 88,* 725–735.

Kruglanski, A. W., & Freund, T. (1983). The freezing and unfreezing of lay-inferences: Effects of impressional primacy, ethnic stereotyping, and numerical anchoring. *Journal of Experimental Social Psychology, 19,* 448–468.

Kruglanski, A. W., & Webster, D. M. (1996). Motivated closing of the mind: "Seizing" and "freezing." *Psychological Review, 103,* 263–283.

Kteily, N., Ho, A. K., & Sidanius, J. (2012). Hierarchy in the mind: The predictive power of social dominance orientation across social contexts and domains. *Journal of Experimental Social Psychology, 48,* 543–549.

Kubany, E. S., Leisen, M. B., Kaplan, A. S., Watson, S. B., Haynes, S. N., Owens, J. A., & Burns, K. (2000). Development and preliminary validation of a brief broad-spectrum measure of trauma exposure: The Traumatic Life Events Questionnaire. *Psychological Assessment, 12,* 210–224.

Kubzansky, L. D., Sparrow, D., Vokonas, P., & Kawachi, I. (2001). Is the glass half empty or half full? A prospective study of optimism and coronary heart disease in the Normative Aging Study. *Psychosomatic Medicine, 63,* 910–916.

Kugihara, N. (1999). Gender and social loafing in Japan. *Journal of Social Psychology, 139,* 516–526.

Kulik, J. A., & Mahler, H. I. M. (1989). Stress and affiliation in a hospital setting: Preoperative roommate preferences. *Personality and Social Psychology Bulletin, 15,* 183–193.

Kulik, J. A., Mahler, H. I. M., & Earnest, A. (1994). Social comparison and affiliation under threat: Going beyond the affiliate-choice paradigm. *Journal of Personality and Social Psychology, 66,* 301–309.

Kulik, J. A., Mahler, H. I. M., & Moore, P. J. (1996). Social comparison and affiliation under threat: Effects of recovery from major surgery. *Journal of Personality and Social Psychology, 71,* 967–979.

Kumkale, G. T., & Albarracín, D. (2004). The sleeper effect in persuasion: A meta-analytic review. *Psychological Bulletin, 130,* 143–172.

Kunda, Z., Adams, B., Davies, P. G., Hoshino-Browne, E., & Jordan, C. (2003). The impact of comprehension goals on the ebb and flow of stereotype activation during interaction. In Spencer, S. J., Fein, S., Zanna, M. P., & Olson, J. M. (Eds.), *Motivated social perception: The Ontario symposium* (Vol. 9, pp. 1–20). Mahwah, NJ: Erlbaum.

Kunda, Z., Sinclair, L., & Griffin, D. (1997). Equal ratings but separate meanings: Stereotypes and the construal of traits. *Journal of Personality and Social Psychology, 72,* 720–734.

Kuntz-Wilson, W., & Zajonc, R. B. (1980). Affective discrimination of stimuli that cannot be recognized. *Science, 207,* 557–558.

Kupers, T. A. (1999). *Prison madness: The mental health crisis behind bars and what we must do about it.* New York: Jossey-Bass.

Kurbat, M. A., Shevell, S. K., & Rips, L. J. (1998). A year's memories: The calendar effect in autobiographical recall. *Memory and Cognition, 26,* 532–552.

Kurdek, L. (2008). Change in relationship quality for partners from lesbian, gay male, and heterosexual couples. *Journal of Family Psychology, 22,* 701–711.

Kurdek, L. A. (1991a). Correlates of relationship satisfaction in cohabiting gay and lesbian couples: Interpretation of contextual, investment, and problem-solving models. *Journal of Personality and Social Psychology, 61,* 910–922.

Kurdek, L. A. (1991b). The dissolution of gay and lesbian couples. *Journal of Social and Personal Relationships, 8,* 265–278.

Kurdek, L. A. (1999). The nature and predictors of the trajectory of change in marital quality for husbands and wives over the first 10 years of marriage. *Developmental Psychology, 35,* 1283–1296.

Kurdek, L. A. (2005). What do we know about gay and lesbian couples? *Current Directions in Psychological Science, 14,* 251–254.

Kwan, V. S. Y., & Fiske, S. T. (2008). Missing links in social cognition: The continuum from nonhuman agents to dehumanized humans. *Social Cognition, 26,* 125–128.

LaBouff, J., Rowatt, W. C., Johnson, M. K., Tsang, J., & Willerton, G. (2012). Humble persons are more helpful than less humble persons: Evidence from three studies. *The Journal of Positive Psychology, 7,* 16–29.

Laird, J. D. (1974). Self-attribution of emotion: The effects of expressive behavior on the quality of emotional experience. *Journal of Personality and Social Psychology, 29,* 475–486.

Lakey, B., & Cassady, P. B. (1990). Cognitive processes in perceived social support. *Journal of Personality and Social Psychology, 59,* 337–343.

Lakey, B., & Orehek, E. (2011). Relation regulation theory: A new approach to explain the link between perceived social support and mental health. *Psychological Review, 118,* 482–495.

Lakin, J. L., Chartrand, T. L., & Arkin, R. M. (2008). I am too just like you: Nonconscious mimicry as an automatic behavioral response to social exclusion. *Psychological Science, 19,* 816–822.

Lakoff, G., & Johnson, M. (1999). *Philosophy in the flesh: The embodied mind and its challenge to western thought.* New York: Basic Books.

Laland, K. N., & Galef, B. G. (Eds.) (2009). *The question of animal culture.* Cambridge, MA: Harvard University Press.

Lalwani, A. K., Shavitt, S., & Johnson, T. (2006). What is the relation between cultural orientation and socially desirable responding? *Journal of Personality and Social Psychology, 90,* 165–178.

Lamb, M. E., Hershkowitz, I., Orbach, Y., & Esplin, P. W. (2008). *Tell me what happened: Structured investigative interviews of child victims and witnesses.* West Sussex, England: Wiley.

Lambert, A. J., Payne, B. K., Jacoby, L. L., Shaffer, L. M., Chasteen, A. L., & Khan, S. R. (2003). Stereotypes as dominant responses: On the "social facilitation" of prejudice in anticipated public contexts. *Journal of Personality and Social Psychology, 84*(2), 277–295.

Lamm, C., Decety, J., & Singer, T. (2011). Meta-analytic evidence for common and distinct neural networks associated with direct experienced pain and empathy for pain. *Neuroimage, 54,* 2492–2502.

Lamm, H., & Myers, D. G. (1978). Group-induced polarization of attitudes and behavior. In L. Berkowitz (Ed.), *Advances in experimental social psychology* (Vol. 11, pp. 145–195). New York: Academic Press.

Landau, M. J., Solomon, S., Greenberg, J., Cohen, F., Pyszczynski, T., Arndt, J., Miller, C. H., Ogilvie, D. M., & Cook, A. (2004). Deliver us from evil: The effects of mortality salience and reminders of 9/11 on support for President George W. Bush. *Personality and Social Psychology Bulletin, 30,* 1136–1150.

Landau, M. J., Sullivan, D., Keefer, L. A., Rothschild, Z. K., & Osman, M. R. (2012). Subjectivity uncertainty theory of objectification: Compensating for uncertainty about how to positively relate to others by downplaying their subjective attributes. *Journal of Experimental Social Psychology.*

Landau, T. (1989). *About faces: The evolution of the human face.* New York: Anchor Books.

Landy, F. J., & Farr, J. L. (1983). *The measurement of work performance: Methods, theory, and applications.* New York: Academic Press.

Lane, C. (2007). *Shyness: How normal behavior became a sickness.* New Haven, CT: Yale University Press.

Lane, K. A., Kang, J., & Banaji, M. R. (2007). Implicit social cognition and law. *Annual Review of Law and Social Science, 3,* 427–451.

Lane, L. W., Groisman, M., & Ferreira, V. S. (2006). Don't talk about pink elephants! Speakers' control over leaking private information during language production. *Psychological Science, 17,* 273–277.

Lange, N. D., Thomas, R. P., Dana, J., & Dawes, R. M. (2011). Contextual biases in the interpretation of auditory evidence. *Law and Human Behavior, 35,* 178–187.

Langer, E. J. (1975). The illusion of control. *Journal of Personality and Social Psychology, 32,* 311–328.

Langer, E. J. (1989). *Mindfulness.* Reading, MA: Addison-Wesley.

Langer, E. J., & Rodin, J. (1976). The effects of choice and enhanced personal responsibility for the aged: A field experiment in an institutional setting. *Journal of Personality and Social Psychology, 34,* 191–198.

Langer, E. J., Blank, A., & Chanowitz, B. (1978). The mindlessness of ostensibly thoughtful action. *Journal of Personality and Social Psychology, 36,* 635–642.

Langlois, J. H., & Roggman, L. A. (1990). Attractive faces are only average. *Psychological Science, 1,* 115–121.

Langlois, J. H., Kalakanis, L., Rubenstein, A. J., Larson, A., Hallam, M., & Smoot, M. (2000). Maxims or myths of beauty? A meta-analytic and theoretical review. *Psychological Bulletin, 126,* 390–423.

Langlois, J. H., Ritter, J. M., Roggman, L. A., & Vaughn, L. S. (1991). Facial diversity and infant preferences for attractive faces. *Developmental Psychology, 27,* 79–84.

Langlois, J. H., Roggman, L. A., & Musselman, L. (1994). What is average and what is not average about attractive faces? *Psychological Science, 5,* 214–220.

Langton, S. R. H., Watt, R. J., & Bruce, V. (2000). Do the eyes have it? Cues to the direction of social attention. *Trends in Cognitive Sciences, 4,* 50–59.

LaPiere, R. T. (1934). Attitudes vs. action. *Social Forces, 13,* 230–237.

Larrick, R. P., Morgan, J. N., & Nisbett, R. E. (1990). Teaching the use of cost-benefit reasoning in everyday life. *Psychological Science, 1,* 362–370.

Larrick, R. P., Timmerman, T. A., Carton, A. M., & Abrevaya, J. (2011). Temper, temperature, and temptation: Heat-related retaliation in baseball. *Psychological Science, 22,* 423–428.

Larsen, J. T., Noms, C. J., & Cacioppo, J. T. (2003). Effects of positive and negative affect on electromyographic activity over zygomaticus major and corrugator supercilii. *Psychophysiology, 40,* 776–785.

Larsen, R. J., & Kasimatis, M. (1990). Individual differences in entrainment of mood to the weekly calendar. *Journal of Personality and Social Psychology, 58,* 164–171.

Larson, J. R., Jr., Foster-Fishman, P. G., & Franz, T. M. (1998). Leadership style and the discussion of shared and unshared information in decision-making groups. *Personality and Social Psychology Bulletin, 24,* 482–495.

Lassiter, G. D., & Meissner, C. A. (Eds.) (2010). *Police interrogations and false confessions: Current research, practice, and policy recommendations.* Washington, DC: American Psychological Association.

Lassiter, G. D., Diamond, S. S., Schmidt, H. C., & Elek, J. K. (2007). Evaluating videotaped confessions: Expertise provides no defense against the camera-perspective effect. *Psychological Science, 18,* 224–226.

Lassiter, G. D., Geers, A. L., Munhall, P. J., Handley, I. M., & Beers, M. J. (2001). Videotaped confessions: Is guilt in the eye of the camera? *Advances in Experimental Social Psychology, 33,* 189–254.

Lassiter, G. D., Stone, J. I., & Rogers, S. L. (1988). Memorial consequences of variation in behavior perception. *Journal of Experimental Social Psychology, 24,* 222–239.

Latané, B. (1981). The psychology of social impact. *American Psychologist, 36,* 343–356.

Latané, B., & Darley, J. M. (1968). Group inhibition of bystander intervention. *Journal of Personality and Social Psychology, 10,* 215–221.

Latané, B., & Darley, J. M. (1970). *The unresponsive bystander: Why doesn't he help?* New York: Appleton-Century-Crofts.

Latané, B., & L'Herrou, T. (1996). Spatial clustering in the conformity game: Dynamic social impact in electronic groups. *Journal of Personality and Social Psychology, 70,* 1218–1230.

Latané, B., & Nida, S. (1981). Ten years of research on group size and helping. *Psychological Bulletin, 89,* 308–324.

Latané, B., & Werner, C. (1978). Regulation of social contact in laboratory rats: Time, not distance. *Journal of Personality and Social Psychology, 36,* 1128–1137.

Latané, B., & Wolf, S. (1981). The social impact of majorities and minorities. *Psychological Review, 88,* 438–453.

Latané, B., Liu, J. H., Nowak, A., Bonevento, M., & Zheng, L. (1995). Distance matters: Physical space and social impact. *Personality and Social Psychology Bulletin, 21,* 795–805.

Latané, B., Williams, K., & Harkins, S. (1979). Many hands make light the work: The causes and consequences of social loafing. *Journal of Personality and Social Psychology, 37,* 822–832.

Latham, G. P., & Locke, E. A. (2007). New developments in and directions for goal-setting research. *European Psychologist, 12,* 290–300.

Lau, R. L., & Rovner, I. B. (2009). Negative campaigning. *Annual Review of Political Science, 12,* 285–306.

Laughlin, P. R., Carey, H. R., & Kerr, N. L. (2008). Group-to-individual problem-solving transfer. *Group Processes and Intergroup Relations, 11,* 319–330.

Laughlin, P. R., Hatch, E. C., Silver, J. S., & Boh, L. (2006). Groups perform better than the best individuals on letters-to-numbers problems: Effects of group size. *Journal of Personality and Social Psychology, 90,* 644–651.

Laurin, K., Kay, A. C., & Fitzsimons, G. M. (2012). Divergent effects of activating thoughts of God on self-regulation. *Journal of Personality and Social Psychology, 102,* 4–21.

Lawrence, E., Rothman, A., Cobb, R., Bradbury, T., & Rothman, M. (2008). Marital satisfaction across the transition to parenthood. *Journal of Family Psychology, 22,* 41–50.

Lazarus, R. S., & Folkman, S. (1984). *Stress, appraisal, and coping.* New York: Springer.

Le Bon, G. (1895). *Psychologie des foules.* Paris: Félix Alcan.

Le, B., & Agnew, C. R. (2003). Commitment and its theorized determinants: A meta-analysis of the investment model. *Personal Relationships, 10,* 37–57.

Leary, M. R. (Ed.). (2001). *Interpersonal rejection.* New York: Oxford University Press.

Leary, M. R., & Baumeister, R. F. (2000). The nature and function of self-esteem: Sociometer theory. *Advances in Experimental Social Psychology, 32,* 1–62.

Leary, M. R., & Kowalski, R. M. (1995). *Social anxiety.* New York: Guilford Press.

Leary, M. R., & Tangney, J. P. (Eds.). (2003). *Handbook of self and identity.* New York: Guilford.

Leary, M. R., Kowalski, R. M., Smith, L., & Phillips, S. (2003). Teasing, rejection, and violence: Case studies of the school shootings. *Aggressive Behavior, 29,* 202–214.

Leary, M. R., Tchividjian, L. R., & Kraxberger, B. E. (1994). Self-presentation can be hazardous to your health: Impression management and health risk. *Health Psychology, 13,* 461–470.

Leary, M. R., Twenge, J. M., & Quinlivan, E. (2006). Interpersonal rejection as a determinant of anger and aggression. *Personality and Social Psychology Review, 10,* 111–132.

LeDoux, J. (2002). *The synaptic self: How our brains become who we are.* New York: Penguin Books.

LeDoux, J. E. (1996). *The emotional brain: The mysterious underpinnings of emotional life.* New York: Simon & Schuster.

Lee, E.-J. (2008). When are strong arguments stronger than weak arguments? Deindividuation effects on message elaboration in computer-mediated communication. *Communication Research, 35,* 646–665.

Lee, J. A. (1988). Love-styles. In R. J. Sternberg & M. L. Barnes (Eds.), *The psychology of love* (pp. 38–67). New Haven, CT: Yale University Press.

Lee, L., Loewenstein, G., Ariely, D., Hong, J., & Young, J. (2008). If I'm not hot, are you hot or not? Physical-attractiveness evaluations and dating preferences as a function of one's own attractiveness. *Psychological Science, 19,* 669–677.

Lee, M. J. (2012). Geraldo Rivera: Trayvon Martin killed due to "hoodie." Retrieved from http://www.politico.com/news/stories/0312/74392_Page2.html

Lee, P., Gillespie, N., Mann, L., & Wearing, A. (2010). Leadership and trust: Their effect on knowledge sharing and team performance. *Management Learning, 41,* 473–491.

Lee, R. T., & Ashforth, B. E. (1996). A meta-analytic examination of the correlates of the three dimensions of job burnout. *Journal of Applied Psychology, 81,* 123–133.

Legault, L., Gutsell, J. N., & Inzlicht, M. (2011). Ironic effects of antiprejudice messages: How motivational interventions can reduce (but also increase) prejudice. *Psychological Science, 22,* 1472–1477.

Lehman, D. R., Chiu, C.-Y., & Schaller, M. (2004). Psychology and culture. *Annual Review of Psychology, 55,* 689–714.

Lehman, D. R., Lempert, R. O., & Nisbett, R. E. (1988). The effects of graduate training on reasoning: Formal discipline and thinking about everyday-life events. *American Psychologist, 43,* 431–442.

Leicht, K. T. (2008). Broken down by race and gender? Sociological explanations of new sources of earnings inequality. *Annual Review of Sociology, 34,* 237–255.

Leichtman, M. D., & Ceci, S. J. (1995). The effects of stereotypes and suggestions on preschoolers' reports. *Developmental Psychology, 31,* 568–578.

Leigh, B. C., & Stacy, A. W. (1993). Alcohol outcome expectancies: Scale construction and predictive utility in higher-order confirmatory models. *Psychological Assessment, 5,* 216–229.

Leiker, M., & Hailey, B. J. (1988). A link between hostility and disease: Poor health habits? *Behavioral Medicine, 14,* 129–133.

Leinbach, M. D., & Fagot, B. I. (1993). Categorical habituation to male and female faces: Gender schematic processing in infancy. *Infant Behavior and Development, 16,* 317–332.

Leippe, M. R., & Eisenstadt, D. (1994). Generalization of dissonance reduction: Decreasing prejudice through induced compliance. *Journal of Personality and Social Psychology, 67,* 395–413.

Leland, J. (1995, December 11). "Copycat" crimes in New York's subways reignite the debate: Do TV and movies cause actual mayhem? *Newsweek,* p. 46.

Lench, H. C. (2009). Automatic optimism: The affective basis of judgments about the likelihood of future events. *Journal of Experimental Psychology: General, 138,* 187–200.

Lenhart, A., Kahne, J., Middaugh, E., Macgill, A. R., Evans, C., & Vitak, J. (2008, September 16). *Teens, video games, and civics.* Washington, DC: Pew Internet and American Life Project.

Leo, R. A. (1996). Inside the interrogation room. *Journal of Criminal Law and Criminology, 86,* 266–303.

Leo, R. A. (2008). *Police interrogation and American justice.* Cambridge, MA: Harvard University Press.

Lepore, L., & Brown, R. (1997). Category and stereotype activation: Is prejudice inevitable? *Journal of Personality and Social Psychology, 72,* 275–287.

Lepore, L., & Brown, R. (2002). The role of awareness: Divergent automatic stereotype activation and implicit judgment correction. *Social Cognition, 20,* 321–351.

Lepore, S. J., & Smyth, J. M. (2002). *The writing cure: How expressive writing promotes health and emotional well-being.* Washington, DC: American Psychological Association.

Lepore, S. J., Ragan, J. D., & Jones, S. (2000). Talking facilitates cognitive-emotional processes of adaptation to an acute stressor. *Journal of Personality and Social Psychology, 78,* 499–508.

Lepper, M. R., & Greene, D. (Eds.). (1978). *The hidden costs of reward.* Hillsdale, NJ: Erlbaum.

Lepper, M. R., Greene, D., & Nisbett, R. E. (1973). Undermining children's intrinsic interest with extrinsic reward: A test of the "overjustification" hypothesis. *Journal of Personality and Social Psychology, 28,* 129–137.

Lepsinger, R., & Lucia, A. D. (2009). *The art and science of 360–degree feedback* (2nd ed.). New York: Wiley.

Lerner, M. J. (1980). *The belief in a just world: A fundamental delusion.* New York: Plenum.

Lerner, M. J. (1998). The two forms of belief in a just world: Some thoughts on why and how people care about justice. In L. Montada, & M. J. Lerner (Eds.), *Responses to victimization and belief in a just world: Critical issues in social justice* (pp. 247–269). New York: Plenum.

Lerner, M. J., & Simmons, C. H. (1966). Observers' reaction to the "innocent victim": Compassion or rejection? *Journal of Personality and Social Psychology, 4*, 203–210.

Leshowitz, B., Eignor DiCerbo, K., & Okun, M. A. (2002). Effects of instruction in methodical reasoning on information evaluation. *Teaching of Psychology, 29*, 5–10.

Letourneau, E. J., Henggeler, S. W., Borduin, C. M., Schewe, P. A., McCart, M. R., Chapman, J. E., & Saldana, L. (2009). Multisystemic therapy for juvenile sexual offenders: 1-year results from a randomized effectiveness trial. *Journal of Family Psychology, 23*, 89–102.

Levashina, J., & Campion, M. A. (2007). Measuring faking in the employment interview: Development and validation of an interview faking behavior scale. *Journal of Applied Psychology, 92*, 1638–1656.

LeVay, S. (1991). A difference in hypothalamic structure between heterosexual and homosexual men. *Science, 253*, 1034–1037.

Leventhal, H. (1970). Findings and theory in the study of fear communications. In L. Berkowitz (Ed.), *Advances in experimental social psychology* (Vol. 5, pp. 119–186). New York: Academic Press.

Leventhal, H., Watts, J. C., & Pagano, F. (1967). Effects of fear and instructions on how to cope with danger. *Journal of Personality and Social Psychology, 6*, 313–321.

Levesque, M. J. (1997). Meta-accuracy among acquainted individuals: A social relations analysis of interpersonal perception and metaperception. *Journal of Personality and Social Psychology, 72*, 66–74.

Levesque, M. J., Nave, C. S., & Lowe, C. A. (2006). Toward an understanding of gender differences in inferring sexual interest. *Psychology of Women Quarterly, 30*, 150–158.

Levi, A. S., & Fried, Y. (2008). Differences between African Americans and Whites in reactions to affirmative action programs in hiring, promotion, training, and layoffs. *Journal of Applied Psychology, 93*, 1118–1129.

Levin, D. T., & Banaji, M. R. (2006). Distortions in the perceived lightness of faces: The role of race categories. *Journal of Experimental Psychology: General, 135*, 501–512.

Levin, S., Matthews, M., Guimond, S., Sidanius, J., Pratto, F., Kteily, N., & . . . Dover, T. (2012). Assimilation, multiculturalism, and colorblindness: Mediated and moderated relationships between social dominance orientation and prejudice. *Journal of Experimental Social Psychology, 48*, 207–212.

Levin, S., Taylor, P. L., & Caudle, E. (2007). Interethnic and interracial dating in college: A longitudinal study of social psychological predictors and outcomes. *Journal of Social and Personal Relationships, 24*, 323–341.

Levine, J. M. (1989). Reaction to opinion deviance in small groups. In P. B. Paulus (Ed.), *Psychology of group influence* (2nd ed., pp. 187–231). Hillsdale, NJ: Erlbaum.

Levine, J. M., & Choi, H.-S. (2010). Newcomers as change agents: Minority influence in task groups. In R. Martin & M. Hewstone (Eds.), *Minority influence and innovation: Antecedents, processes, and consequences.* New York: Psychology Press.

Levine, M., & Cassidy, C. (2010). Groups, identities, and bystander behavior: How group processes can be used to promote helping. In S. Stürmer & M. Snyder (Eds.), *The psychology of prosocial behavior: Group processes, intergroup relations, and helping* (pp. 209–222). Wiley-Blackwell.

Levine, M., & Crowther, S. (2008). The responsive bystander: How social group membership and group size can encourage as well as inhibit bystander intervention. *Journal of Personality and Social Psychology, 95*, 1429–1439.

Levine, M., Prosser, A., Evans, D., & Reicher, S. (2005, April). Identity and emergency intervention: How social group membership and inclusiveness of group boundaries shape helping behavior. *Personality and Social Psychology Bulletin, 31*, 443–453.

Levine, R. A., & Campbell, D. T. (1972). *Ethnocentrism: Theories of conflict, ethnic attitudes, and group behavior.* New York: Wiley.

Levine, R. V., Norenzayan, A., & Philbrick, K. (2001). Cross-cultural differences in helping strangers. *Journal of Cross-Cultural Psychology, 32*, 543–560.

Levine, R. V., Reysen, S., & Ganz, E. (2008). The kindness of strangers revisited: A comparison of 24 US cities. *Social Indicators Research, 85*, 461–481.

Levine, R., Sato, S., Hashimoto, T., & Verma, J. (1995). Love and marriage in eleven cultures. *Journal of Cross-Cultural Psychology, 26*, 554–571.

Levine, T. R., Kim, R. K., & Blair, J. P. (2010). (In) accuracy at detecting true and false confessions and denials: An initial test of a projected motive model of veracity judgments. *Human Communication Research, 36*, 81–101.

Levy, D. A., & Nail, P. R. (1993). Contagion: A theoretical and empirical review and reconceptualization. *Genetic, Social, and General Psychology Monographs, 119*, 233–284.

Levy, S. R., Chiu, C.-Y., & Hong, Y.-Y. (2006). Lay theories and intergroup relations. *Group Processes and Intergroup Relations, 9*, 5–24.

Levy, S. R., Rosenthal, L., & Herrera-Alcazar, A. (2010). Racial and ethnic prejudice among children. In J. Chin (Ed.) , *The psychology of prejudice and discrimination: A revised and condensed edition* (pp. 37–49). Santa Barbara, CA: Praeger/ABC-CLIO.

Lewin, K. (1935). *A dynamic theory of personality.* New York: McGraw-Hill.

Lewin, K. (1947). Group decision and social change. In T. M. Newcomb & E. L. Hartley (Eds.), *Readings in social psychology* (pp. 330–344). New York: Holt.

Lewin, K. (1951). Problems of research in social psychology. In D. Cartwright (Ed.), *Field theory in social science* (pp. 155–169). New York: Harper & Row.

Lewis, B. P., & Linder, D. E. (1997). Thinking about choking? Attentional processes and paradoxical performance. *Personality and Social Psychology Bulletin, 23*, 937–944.

Lewis, K., & Herndon, B. (2011). Transactive memory systems: Current issues and future research directions. *Organization Science, 22*, 1254–1265.

Lewis, M., & Brooks-Gunn, J. (1979). *Social cognition and the acquisition of self.* New York: Plenum.

Li, N. P., & Kenrick, D. T. (2006). Sex similarities and differences in preferences for short-term mates: What, whether, and why. *Journal of Personality and Social Psychology, 90*, 468–489.

Li, N. P., Bailey, J. M., Kenrick, D. T., & Linsenmeier, J. A. W. (2002). The necessities and luxuries of mate preferences: Testing the tradeoffs. *Journal of Personality and Social Psychology, 82*, 947–955.

Li, Y., Wang, M., Wang, C., & Shi, J. (2010). Individualism, collectivism, and Chinese adolescents' aggression: Intracultural variations. *Aggressive Behavior, 36*, 187–194.

Liao, J., Jimmieson, N. L., O'Brien, A. T., & Restubog, S. D. (2012). Developing transactive memory systems: Theoretical contributions from a social identity perspective. *Group & Organization Management, 37*, 204–240.

Libby, L. K., & Eibach, R. P. (2002). Looking back in time: Self-concept change affects visual perspective in autobiographical memory. *Journal of Personality and Social Psychology, 82*, 167–179.

Libby, L. K., Valenti, G., Pfent, A., & Eibach, R. P. (2011). Seeing failure in your life: Imagery perspective determines whether self-esteem shapes reactions to recalled and imagined failure. *Journal of Personality and Social Psychology, 101*, 1157–1173.

Liden, R. C., Wayne, S. J., Jaworski, R. A., & Bennett, N. (2004). Social loafing: A field investigation. *Journal of Management, 30*, 285–304.

Lieberman J., & Krauss D. (2009). *Jury psychology: Social aspects of the trial process.* Burlington, VT: Ashgate.

Lieberman, J. D., & Arndt, J. (2000). Understanding the limits of limiting instructions. *Psychology, Public Policy, and Law, 6*, 677–711.

Lieberman, J., & Sales, B. (2007). *Scientific jury selection.* Washington, DC: American Psychological Association.

Lieberman, M. D., Gaunt, R., Gilbert, D. T., & Trope, Y. (2004). Reflection and reflexion: A social cognitive neuroscience approach to attributional inference. In M. P. Zanna (Ed.), *Advances in experimental social psychology* (Vol. 34, pp. 199–249). San Diego, CA: Academic Press.

Lifton, R. J. (1986). *The Nazi doctors: Medical killing and the psychology of genocide.* New York: Basic Books.

Light, K. C., & Obrist, P. A. (1980). Cardiovascular response to stress: Effects of opportunity to avoid shock experience, and performance feedback. *Psychophysiology, 17,* 243–252.

Likert, R. (1932). A technique for the measurement of attitudes. *Archives of Psychology, 140,* 1–55.

Lim, J., & Guo, X. (2008). A study of group support systems and the inter-group setting. *Decision Support Systems, 45,* 452–460.

Lind, E. A., Erickson, B. E., Friedland, N., & Dickenberger, M. (1978). Reactions to procedural models for adjudicative conflict resolution: A cross national study. *Journal of Conflict Resolution, 22,* 318–341.

Lind, E. A., Kanfer, R., & Farley, P. C. (1990). Voice, control, and procedural justice: Instrumental and noninstrumental concerns in fairness judgments. *Journal of Personality and Social Psychology, 59,* 952–959.

Linde, J. A., Rothman, A. J., Baldwin, A. S., & Jeffery, R. W. (2006). The impact of self-efficacy on behavior change and weight change among overweight participants in a weight loss trial. *Health Psychology, 25,* 282–291.

Linder, D. E., Cooper, J., & Jones, E. E. (1967). Decision freedom as a determinant of the role of incentive magnitude in attitude change. *Journal of Personality and Social Psychology, 6,* 245–254.

Lindsay, R. C. L., & Bellinger, K. (1999). Alternatives to the sequential lineup: The importance of controlling the pictures. *Journal of Applied Psychology, 84,* 315–321.

Lindsay, R. C. L., & Wells, G. L. (1985). Improving eyewitness identifications from lineups: Simultaneous versus sequential lineup presentations. *Journal of Applied Psychology, 70,* 556–564.

Lindsay, R. C. L., Lea, J. A., & Fulford, J. A. (1991). Sequential lineup presentation: Technique matters. *Journal of Applied Psychology, 76,* 741–745.

Lindsay, R. C. L., Ross, D. F., Read, J. D., & Toglia, M. P. (Eds.). (2007). *The handbook of eyewitness psychology: Vol. 2. Memory for people.* Mahwah, NJ: Erlbaum.

Lindsay, R. C. L., Semmler, C., Weber, N., Brewer, N., & Lindsay, M. R. (2008). How variations in distance affect eyewitness reports and identification accuracy. *Law and Human Behavior, 32,* 526–535.

Lindsay, R. C. L., Wells, G. L., & Rumpel, C. M. (1981). Can people detect eyewitness-identification accuracy within and across situations? *Journal of Applied Psychology, 66,* 79–89.

Lindskold, S., & Han, G. (1988). GRIT as a foundation for integrative bargaining. *Personality and Social Psychology Bulletin, 14,* 335–345.

Linville, P. W., & Jones, E. E. (1980). Polarized appraisals of out-group members. *Journal of Personality and Social Psychology, 38,* 689–703.

Linville, P. W., Fischer, G. W., & Fischoff, B. (1992). Perceived risk and decision making involving AIDS. In J. B. Pryor & G. D. Reeder (Eds.), *The social psychology of HIV infection.* Hillsdale, NJ: Erlbaum.

Linz, D., Donnerstein, E., & Penrod, S. (1987). The findings and recommendations of the Attorney General's Commission on Pornography: Do the psychological "facts" fit the political fury? *American Psychologist, 42,* 946–953.

Linz, D., Wilson, B. J., & Donnerstein, E. (1992). Sexual violence in the mass media: Legal solutions, warnings, and mitigation through education. *Journal of Social Issues, 48,* 145–171.

Lippa, R. A. (2006). Is high sex drive associated with increased sexual attraction to both sexes? *Psychological Science, 17,* 46–52.

Lishner, D. A., Batson, C., & Huss, E. (2011). Tenderness and sympathy: Distinct empathic emotions elicited by different forms of need. *Personality and Social Psychology Bulletin, 37,* 614–625.

Liu, L., Chua, C., & Stahl, G. K. (2010). Quality of communication experience: Definition, measurement, and implications for intercultural negotiations. *Journal of Applied Psychology, 95,* 469–487.

Liu, M., & Wilson, S. R. (2011). The effects of interaction goals on negotiation tactics and outcomes: A dyad-level analysis across two cultures. *Communication Research, 38,* 248–277.

Livers, A. B., & Caver, K. A. (2003). *Leading in black and white: Working across the racial divide in corporate America.* San Francisco: Jossey-Bass.

Lo Sasso, A. T., Richards, M. R., Chou, C. F., & Gerber, S. E. (2011). The $16,819 pay gap for newly trained physicians: The unexplained trend of men earning more than women. *Health Affairs, 30,* 193–201.

Lobchuk, M. M., McClement, S. E., McPherson, C., & Cheang, M. (2008). Does blaming the patient with lung cancer affect the helping behavior of primary caregivers? *Oncology Nursing Forum, 35,* 681–689.

Lobel, M., Cannella, D. L., Graham, J. E., DeVincent, C., Schneider, J., & Meyer, B. A. (2008). Pregnancy-specific stress, prenatal health behaviors, and birth outcomes. *Health Psychology, 27,* 604–615.

Locke, E. A. (2000). *The prime movers: Traits of the great wealth creators.* New York: Amacomb.

Locke, E. A., & Latham, G. P. (1990). *A theory of goal setting and task performance.* Englewood Cliffs, NJ: Prentice Hall.

Locke, E. A., & Latham, G. P. (2002). Building a practically useful theory of goal setting and task motivation: A 35-year odyssey. *American Psychologist, 57,* 705–717.

Locke, K. (2009). Aggression, narcissism, self-esteem, and the attribution of desirable and humanizing traits to self versus others. *Journal of Research in Personality, 43,* 99–102.

Lockhart v. McCree, 54 U.S.L.W. 4449 (1986).

Loewenstein, G. F., Weber, E. U., Hsee, C. K., & Welch, N. (2001). Risk as feelings. *Psychological Bulletin, 127,* 267–286.

Loftus, E. F. (1996). *Eyewitness testimony* (reprint ed.). Cambridge, MA: Harvard University Press.

Loftus, E. F. (2011). Intelligence gathering post 9/11. *American Psychologist, 66,* 532–541.

Loftus, E. F., & Ketcham, K. (1991). *Witness for the defense: The accused, the eyewitness, and the expert who puts memory on trial.* New York: St. Martin's Press.

Loftus, E. F., & Palmer, J. C. (1974). Reconstruction of automobile destruction: An example of the interaction between language and memory. *Journal of Verbal Learning and Verbal Behavior, 13,* 585–589.

Loftus, E. F., Loftus, G. R., & Messo, J. (1987). Some facts about "weapon focus." *Law and Human Behavior, 11,* 55–62.

Loken, B. (2006). Consumer psychology: Categorization, inferences, affect, and persuasion. *Annual Review of Psychology, 57,* 453–485.

London, K., & Nunez, N. (2000). The effect of jury deliberations on jurors' propensity to disregard inadmissible evidence. *Journal of Applied Psychology, 85,* 932–939.

Long, E. C. J., & Andrews, D. W. (1990). Perspective taking as a predictor of marital adjustment. *Journal of Personality and Social Psychology, 59,* 126–131.

Lopez, J. A. (1992, March 3). Study says women face glass walls as well as ceilings. *Wall Street Journal,* pp. B1, B8.

Lortie-Lussier, M. (1987). Minority influence and idiosyncrasy credit: A new comparison of the Moscovici and Hollander theories of innovation. *European Journal of Social Psychology, 17,* 431–446.

Losch, M. E., & Cacioppo, J. T. (1990). Cognitive dissonance may enhance sympathetic tonus, but attitudes are changed to reduce negative affect rather than arousal. *Journal of Experimental Social Psychology, 26,* 289–304.

Lott, A. J., & Lott, B. E. (1974). The role of reward in the formation of positive interpersonal attitudes. In T. L. Huston (Ed.), *Foundations of interpersonal attraction* (pp. 171–189). New York: Academic Press.

Lott, B. (1985). The devaluation of women's competence. *Journal of Social Issues, 41,* 43–60.

Loula, F., Prasad, S., Harber, K., & Shiffrar, M. (2005). Recognizing people from their movement. *Journal of Experimental Psychology: Human Perception & Performance, 31,* 210–220.

Lowe, K., Kroeck, K., & Sivasubramaniam, N. (1996). Effectiveness correlates of transformational and transactional leadership: A meta-analytic review of the MLQ literature. *Leadership Quarterly, 7,* 385–425.

Lu, H., While, A. E., & Barriball, K. L. (2008). Role perceptions and reported actual role content of hospital nurses in Mainland China. *Journal of Clinical Nursing, 17,* 1011–1022.

Lucas, R. E. (2005). Time does not heal all wounds: A longitudinal study of reaction and adaptation to divorce. *Psychological Science, 16,* 945–950.

Lucas, R. E. (2007). Adaptation and the set-point model of subjective well-being: Does happiness change after major life events? *Current Directions in Psychological Science, 16,* 945–950.

Luhmann, M., Hofmann, W., Eid, M., & Lucas, R. E. (2012). Subjective well-being and adaptation to life events: A meta-analysis. *Journal of Personality and Social Psychology, 102,* 592–615.

Luo, S., & Klohnen, E. C. (2005). Assortative mating and marital quality in newlyweds: A couple-centered approach. *Journal of Personality and Social Psychology, 88,* 304–326.

Luo, Y., Hawkley, L. C., Waite, L. J., & Cacioppo, J. T. (2012). Loneliness, health, and mortality in old age: A national longitudinal study. *Social Science & Medicine, 74,* 907–914.

Lutz, A., Slagter, H. A., Dunne, J. D., & Davidson, R. J. (2008). Attention regulation and monitoring in meditation. *Trends in the Cognitive Sciences, 12,* 163–169.

Luus, C. A. E., & Wells, G. L. (1994). The malleability of eyewitness confidence: Co-witness and perseverance effects. *Journal of Applied Psychology, 79,* 714–723.

Lybarger, J. E., & Monteith, M. J. (2011). The effect of Obama saliency on individual-level racial bias: Silver bullet or smokescreen? *Journal of Experimental Social Psychology, 47,* 647–652.

Lydon, J. E. (2010). How to forego forbidden fruit: The regulation of attractive alternatives as a commitment mechanism. *Social and Personality Psychology Compass, 4,* 635–644.

Lykken, D. T. (2000). *Happiness: The nature and nurture of joy and contentment.* New York: St. Martin's Press.

Lykken, D. T., & Tellegen, A. (1993). Is human mating adventitious or the result of lawful choice? A twin study of mate selection. *Journal of Personality and Social Psychology, 65,* 56–68.

Lyness, K. S., & Thompson, D. E. (2000). Climbing the corporate ladder: Do female and male executives follow the same route? *Journal of Applied Psychology, 85,* 86–101.

Lyons, A., & Kashima, Y. (2001). The representation of culture: Communication processes tend to maintain cultural stereotypes. *Social Cognition, 19,* 372–394.

Lysiak, M., & Boyle, C. (2012). Hero dad dives into waters off Coney Island in bid to save suicidal man. *New York Daily News,* June 23, p. 12.

Lyubomirsky , S., King, L., & Diener , E. (2005). The benefits of frequent positive affect: Does happiness lead to success? *Psychological Bulletin, 131,* 803–855.

Lyubomirsky, S. (2013). *The myths of happiness: What should make you happy, but doesn't, what shouldn't make you happy, but does.* New York: Penguin.

Lyubomirsky, S., Sheldon, K. M., & Schkade, D. (2005). Pursuing happiness: The architecture of sustainable change. *Review of General Psychology, 9,* 111–131.

Ma, D. S., & Correll, J. (2011). Target prototypicality moderates racial bias in the decision to shoot. *Journal of Experimental Social Psychology, 47,* 391–396.

Maass, A., & Clark, R. D., III. (1984). Hidden impact of minorities: Fifteen years of minority influence research. *Psychological Bulletin, 95,* 428–450.

Maass, A., & Kohnken, G. (1989). Eyewitness identification: Simulating the "weapon effect." *Law and Human Behavior, 13,* 397–408.

Maass, A., D'Ettole, C., & Cadinu, M. (2008). Checkmate? The role of gender stereotypes in the ultimate intellectual sport. *European Journal of Social Psychology, 38,* 231–245.

Maass, A., Volpato, C., & Mucchi-Faina, A. (1996). Social influence and the verifiability of the issue under discussion: Attitudinal versus objective items. *British Journal of Social Psychology, 35,* 15–26.

MacCoun, R. J., & Kerr, N. L. (1988). Asymmetric influence in mock jury deliberation: Jurors' bias for leniency. *Journal of Personality and Social Psychology, 54,* 21–33.

MacDonald, G., & Leary, M. R. (2005). Why does social exclusion hurt? The relationship between social and physical pain. *Psychological Bulletin, 131,* 202–223.

Macionis, J. J. (2012). *Sociology* (14th ed.). Englewood Cliffs, NJ: Prentice Hall.

Mackay, N., & Barrowclough, C. (2005). Accident and emergency staff's perceptions of deliberate self-harm: Attributions, emotions, and willingness to help. *British Journal of Clinical Psychology, 44,* 255–267.

Mackenzie, C. S., Gekoski, W. L., & Knox, V. J. (2006). Age, gender, and the underutilization of mental health services: The influence of help-seeking attitudes. *Aging & Mental Health, 10,* 574–582.

Mackie, D. M., & Worth, L. T. (1989). Processing deficits and the mediation of positive affect in persuasion. *Journal of Personality and Social Psychology, 57,* 27–40.

Mackie, D. M., Asuncion, A. G., & Rosselli, F. (1992). Impact of positive affect on persuasion processes. *Review of Personality and Social Psychology, 14,* 247–270.

Mackie, D. M., Worth, L. T., & Asuncion, A. G. (1990). Processing of persuasive in-group messages. *Journal of Personality and Social Psychology, 58,* 812–822.

MacLean, P. D. (1985). Brain evolution relating to family, play, and the separation call. *Archives of General Psychiatry, 42,* 405–417.

MacLeod, C., & Campbell, L. (1992). Memory accessibility and probability judgments: An experimental evaluation of the availability heuristic. *Journal of Personality and Social Psychology, 63,* 890–902.

MacNeil, S., & Byers, E. S. (2009). Role of sexual self-disclosure in the sexual satisfaction of long-term heterosexual couples. *Journal of Sex Research, 46,* 3–14.

Maddux, J. E. (1995). *Self-efficacy, adaptation, and adjustment: Theory, research, and application.* New York: Perseus.

Madera, J. M., & Hebl, M. R. (2012). Discrimination against facially stigmatized applicants in interviews: An eye-tracking and face-to-face investigation. *Journal of Applied Psychology, 97,* 317–330.

Madey, S. F., Simo, M., Dillworth, D., Kemper, D., Toczynski, A., & Perella, A. (1996). They do get more attractive at closing time, but only when you are not in a relationship. *Basic and Applied Social Psychology, 18,* 387–393.

Madon, S., Guyll, M., Aboufadel, K., Montiel, E., Smith, A., Palumbo, P., & Jussim, L. (2001). Ethnic and national stereotypes: The Princeton trilogy revisited and revised. *Personality and Social Psychology Bulletin, 27,* 996–1010.

Madon, S., Guyll, M., Scherr, K., Greathouse, S., & Wells, G. L. (2012). Temporal discounting: The differential effect of proximal and distal consequences on confession decisions. *Law and Human Behavior, 36,* 13–20.

Madon, S., Guyll, M., Spoth, R., Cross, S. E., & Hilbert, S. J. (2003). The self-fulfilling influence of mother expectations on children's underage drinking. *Journal of Personality and Social Psychology, 84,* 1188–1205.

Madon, S., Jussim, L., Keiper, S., Eccles, J., Smith, A., & Palumbo, P. (1998). The accuracy and power of sex, social class, and ethnic stereotypes: A naturalistic study in person perception. *Personality and Social Psychology Bulletin, 24,* 1304–1318.

Madon, S., Willard, J., Guyll, M., & Scherr, K. C. (2011). Self-fulfilling prophecies: Mechanisms, power, and links to social problems. *Social and Personality Psychology Compass, 5,* 578–590.

Madon, S., Willard, J., Guyll, M., Trudeau, L., & Spoth, R. (2006). Self-fulfilling prophecy effects of mothers' beliefs on children's alcohol use: Accumulation, dissipation, and stability over time. *Journal of Personality and Social Psychology, 90,* 911–926.

Madsen, E. A., Tunney, R. J., Fieldman, G., Plotkin, H. C., Dunbar, R. I. M., Richardson, J. M., & McFarland, D. (2007). Kinship and altruism: A cross-cultural experimental study. *British Journal of Psychology, 98,* 339–359.

Magnussen, S., Wise, R. A., Raja, A. Q., Safer, M. A., Pawlenko, N., & Stridbeck, U. (2008). What judges know about eyewitness testimony: A comparison of Norwegian and US judges. *Psychology, Crime & Law, 14,* 177–188.

Maio, G., & Olson, J. M. (Eds.). (2000). *Why we evaluate: Functions of attitudes.* Mahwah, NJ: Erlbaum.

Major, B., & Crocker, J. (1993). Social stigma: The affective consequences of attributional ambiguity. In D. M. Mackie & D. L. Hamilton (Eds.), *Affect, cognition, and stereotyping: Interactive processes in intergroup perception* (pp. 345–370). New York: Academic Press.

Major, B., & Deaux, K. (1982). Individual differences in justice behavior. In J. Greenberg & R. L. Cohen (Eds.), *Equity and justice in social behavior* (pp. 13–76). New York: Academic Press.

Major, B., & Konar, E. (1984). An investigation of sex differences in pay expectations and their possible causes. *Academy of Management Journal, 27,* 777–792.

Major, B., Carrington, P. I., & Carnevale, P. J. D. (1984). Physical attractiveness and self-esteem: Attributions for praise from an other-sex evaluator. *Personality and Social Psychology Bulletin, 10,* 43–50.

Major, B., Feinstein, J., & Crocker, J. (1994). Attributional ambiguity of affirmative action. *Basic and Applied Social Psychology, 15,* 113–142.

Major, B., McFarlin, D. B., & Gagnon, D. (1984). Overworked and underpaid: On the nature of gender differences in personal entitlement. *Journal of Personality and Social Psychology, 47,* 1399–1412.

Malamuth, N. M. (1996). The confluence model of sexual aggression: Feminist and evolutionary perspectives. In D. M. Buss & N. M. Malamuth (Eds.), *Sex, power, conflict: Evolutionary and feminist perspectives* (pp. 269–295). New York: Oxford University Press.

Malamuth, N. M., & Donnerstein, E. I. (1982). The effects of aggressive-pornographic mass media stimuli. In L. Berkowitz (Ed.), *Advances in experimental social psychology* (Vol. 15, pp. 103–136). New York: Academic Press.

Malamuth, N. M., Hald, G., & Koss, M. (2012). Pornography, individual differences in risk and men's acceptance of violence against women in a representative sample. *Sex Roles, 66,* 427–439.

Malhotra, D., & Bazerman, M. H. (2008). Psychological influence in negotiation: An introduction long overdue. *Journal of Management, 34*(3), 509–531.

Malkiel, B. G. (2007). *A random walk down Wall Street: The time-tested strategy for successful investing* (9th ed.). New York: Norton.

Malle, B. F., & Knobe, J. (1997). Which behaviors do people explain? A basic actor-observer asymmetry. *Journal of Personality and Social Psychology, 72,* 288–304.

Malle, B. F., Knobe, J. M., & Nelson, S. E. (2007). Actor-observer asymmetries in explanations of behavior: New answers to an old question. *Journal of Personality and Social Psychology, 93,* 491–514.

Malle, B. F., Knobe, J., O'Laughlin, M. J., Pearce, G. E., & Nelson, S. E. (2000). Conceptual structure and social functions of behavior explanations: Beyond person-situation attributions. *Journal of Personality and Social Psychology, 79,* 309–326.

Malloy, T. E., & Albright, L. (1990). Interpersonal perception in a social context. *Journal of Personality and Social Psychology, 58,* 419–428.

Malpass, R. S., & Devine, P. G. (1981). Eyewitness identification: Lineup instructions and the absence of the offender. *Journal of Applied Psychology, 66,* 482–489.

Malpass, R. S., & Kravitz, J. (1969). Recognition for faces of own and other race. *Journal of Personality and Social Psychology, 13,* 330–334.

Malti, T., Gasser, L., & Gutzwiller-Helfenfinger, E. (2010). Children's interpretive understanding, moral judgments, and emotion attributions: Relations to social behaviour. *British Journal of Developmental Psychology, 28,* 275–292.

Man, D. C., & Lam, S. K. (2003). The effects of job complexity and autonomy on cohesiveness in collectivistic and individualistic work groups: A cross-cultural analysis. *Journal of Organizational Behavior, 24,* 979–1001.

Manago, A. M., Taylor, T., & Greenfield, P. M. (2012). Me and my 400 friends: The anatomy of college students' Facebook networks, their communication patterns, and well-being. *Developmental Psychology, 48,* 369–380.

Maner, J. K., Miller, S. L., Moss, J. H., Leo, J. L., & Plant, E. (2012). Motivated social categorization: Fundamental motives enhance people's sensitivity to basic social categories. *Journal of Personality and Social Psychology, 103,* 70–83.

Maner, J., Gailliot, M., Rouby, D., & Miller, S. (2007). Can't take my eyes off you: Attentional adhesion to mates and rivals. *Journal of Personality and Social Psychology, 93,* 389–401.

Mann, J. M. (1992). AIDS—The second decade: A global perspective. *Journal of Infectious Diseases, 165,* 245–250.

Mann, N. H., & Kawakami, K. (2012). The long, steep path to equality: Progressing on egalitarian goals. *Journal of Experimental Psychology: General, 141,* 187–197.

Manning, R., Levine, M., & Collins, A. (2008). The legacy of the 38 witnesses and the importance of getting history right. *American Psychologist, 63,* 562–563.

Mannix, E., & Neale, M. A (2005). What differences make a difference? The promise and reality of diverse teams in organizations. *Psychological Science in the Public Interest, 6,* 31–55.

Maoz, I., & McCauley, C. (2008). Threat, dehumanization, and support for retaliatory aggressive policies in asymmetric conflict. *Journal of Conflict Resolution, 52,* 93–116.

Marcon, J. L., Meissner, C. A., Frueh, M., Susa, K. J., & MacLin, O. H. (2010). Perceptual identification and the cross-race effect. *Visual Cognition, 18,* 767–779.

Marcus-Newhall, A., Pedersen, W. C., Carlson, M., & Miller, N. (2000). Displaced aggression is alive and well: A meta-analytic review. *Journal of Personality and Social Psychology, 78,* 670–689.

Mares, M.-L., & Woodard, E. (2005). Positive effects of television on children's social interactions: A meta-analysis. *Media Psychology, 7,* 301–322.

Margolin, G., & Wampold, B. E. (1981). A sequential analysis of conflict and accord in distressed and nondistressed marital partners. *Journal of Consulting and Clinical Psychology, 49,* 554–567.

Markey, P. M. (2000). Bystander intervention in computer-mediated communication. *Computers in Human Behavior, 16,* 183–188.

Marks, J. (2011). *The alternative introduction to biological anthropology.* New York: Oxford.

Markus, H. (1977). Self-schemata and processing information about the self. *Journal of Personality and Social Psychology, 35,* 63–78.

Markus, H. R. (2008). Pride, prejudice, and ambivalence: Toward a unified theory of race and ethnicity. *American Psychologist, 63,* 651–670.

Markus, H. R., & Kitayama, S. (1991). Culture and the self: Implications for cognition, emotion, and motivation. *Psychological Review, 98,* 224–253.

Markus, H. R., & Lin, L. R. (1999). Conflictways: Cultural diversity in the meanings and practices of conflict. In D. A. Prentice & D. T. Miller (Eds.), *Cultural divides: Understanding and overcoming group conflict* (pp. 302–333). New York: Russell Sage.

Markus, H. R., Uchida, Y., Omoregie, H., Townsend, S. M., & Kitayama, S. (2006). Going for the gold: Models of agency in Japanese and American contexts. *Psychological Science, 17,* 103–112.

Markus, H., Hamill, R., & Sentis, K. P. (1987). Thinking fat: Self-schemas for body weight and the processing of weight-relevant information. *Journal of Applied Social Psychology, 17,* 50–71.

Marlowe, C. M., Schneider, S. L., & Nelson, C. E. (1996). Gender and attractiveness biases in hiring decisions: Are more experienced managers less biased? *Journal of Applied Psychology, 81,* 11–21.

Martin, J., & Govender, K. (2011). 'Making muscle junkies': Investigating traditional masculine ideology, body image discrepancy, and the pursuit of muscularity in adolescent males. *International Journal of Men's Health, 10,* 220–239.

Maslach, C. (1979). Negative emotional biasing of unexplained arousal. *Journal of Personality and Social Psychology, 37,* 953–969.

Maslach, C. (1982). *Burnout: The cost of caring.* Englewood Cliffs, NJ: Prentice-Hall.

Maslach, C., Schaufeli, W. B., & Leiter, M. P. (2001). Job burnout. *Annual Review of Psychology, 52,* 397–422.

Mason, M. F., Tatkow, E. P., & Macrae, C. N. (2005). The look of love: Gaze shifts and person perception. *Psychological Science, 16,* 236–239.

Mason, W., & Suri, S. (2012). Conducting behavioral research on Amazon's Mechanical Turk. *Behavior Research Methods, 44,* 1–23.

Masser, B., Lee, K., & McKimmie, B. M. (2010). Bad woman, bad victim? Disentangling the effects of victim stereotypicality, gender stereotypicality and benevolent sexism on acquaintance rape victim blame. *Sex Roles, 62,* 494–504.

Masten, A. S. (2001). Ordinary magic: Resilience processes in development. *American Psychologist, 56,* 227–238.

Masuda, T., & Nisbett, R. E. (2001). Attending holistically vs. analytically: Comparing the context sensitivity of Japanese and Americans. *Journal of Personality and Social Psychology, 81,* 922–934.

Matheson, K., & Anisman, H. (2012). Biological and psychosocial responses to discrimination. In J. Jetten, C. Haslam, & S. Haslam (Eds.), *The social cure: Identity, health and well-being* (pp. 133–153). New York: Psychology Press.

Mathieu, J., Maynard, M. T., Rapp, T., & Gilson, L. (2008). Team effectiveness 1997–2007: A review of recent advancements and a glimpse into the future. *Journal of Management, 34,* 410–476.

Mathur, M., & Chattopadhyay, A. (1991). The impact of moods generated by TV programs on responses to advertising. *Psychology and Marketing, 8,* 59–77.

Matthews, K. A. (1988). Coronary heart disease and Type A behaviors: Update on and alternative to the Booth-Kewley and Friedman (1987) quantitative review. *Psychological Bulletin, 104,* 373–380.

Matthews, K. A. (2005). Psychological perspectives on the development of coronary heart disease. *American Psychologist, 60,* 783–796.

Matthews, K. A., & Gallo, L. C. (2011). Psychological perspectives on pathways linking socioeconomic status and physical health. *Annual Review of Psychology, 62,* 501-530.

Matz, D. C., & Wood, W. (2005). Cognitive dissonance in groups: The consequences of disagreement. *Journal of Personality and Social Psychology, 88,* 22–37.

Mauss, I. B., Tamir, M., Anderson, C. L., & Savino, N. S. (2011). Can seeking happiness make people unhappy? Paradoxical effects of valuing happiness. *Emotion, 11,* 807–815.

Mayer, J. (2007, August 13). The black sites: A rare look into the CIA's secret interrogation program. *The New Yorker,* pp. 1–24.

Mazur, A., Booth, A., & Dabbs, J. M. (1992). Testosterone and chess competition. *Social Psychology Quarterly, 55,* 70–77.

McAdams, D. P. (1989). *Intimacy: The need to be close.* New York: Doubleday.

McArthur, L. A. (1972). The how and what of why: Some determinants and consequences of causal attribution. *Journal of Personality and Social Psychology, 22,* 171–193.

McAuliffe, B. J., Jetten, J., Hornsey, M. J., & Hogg, M. A. (2003). Individualist and collectivist norms: When it's ok to go your own way. *European Journal of Social Psychology, 33,* 57–70.

McCabe, J., Fairchild, E., Grauerholz, L., Pescosolido, B. A., & Tope, D. (2011). Gender in twentieth-century children's books: Patterns of disparity in titles and central characters. *Gender & Society, 25,* 197–226.

McCarthy, E. (2009, April 24). On dating: Shared qualities for a successful relationship. *The Washington Post.*

McCarty-Gould, C. (2000). *Crisis and chaos: Life with the combat veteran.* New York: Nova Kroshka Books.

McClam, E. (2009, January 17). Pilot's life had prepared him for "miracle" flight. *Associated Press.*

McCrae, R. R., & Costa, P. T., Jr. (2003). *Personality in adulthood: A five-factor theory perspective* (2nd ed.). New York: Guilford Press.

McCreary, D. R. (2011). Body image and muscularity. In T. F. Cash & L. Smolak (Eds.), *Body image: A handbook of science, practice, and prevention* (2nd ed.) (pp. 198–205). New York: Guilford Press.

McCullough, M. E., Hoyt, W. T., Larson, D. B., Koenig, H. G., & Thoresen, C. (2000). Religious involvement and mortality: A meta-analytic review. *Health Psychology, 19,* 211–222.

McCullough, M. E., Kimeldorf, M. B., & Cohen, A. D. (2008). An adaptation for altruism? The social causes, social effects, and social evolution of gratitude. *Current Directions in Psychological Science, 17,* 281–285.

McDermott, R., Tingley, D., Cowden, J., Frazzetto, G., & Johnson, D. P. (2009). Monoamine oxidase A gene (MAOA) predicts behavioral aggression following provocation. *PNAS Proceedings of the National Academy of Sciences of the United States of America, 106,* 2118–2123.

McDougall, W. (1908). *An introduction to social psychology.* London: Methuen.

McEachern, A. D., & Snyder, J. (2012). Gender differences in predicting antisocial behaviors: Developmental consequences of physical and relational aggression. *Journal of Abnormal Child Psychology, 40,* 501–512.

McElwee, R. O., Dunning, D., Tan, P. L., & Hollmann, S. (2001). Evaluating others: The role of who we are versus what we think traits mean. *Basic and Applied Social Psychology, 23,* 123–136.

McGarty, C., Turner, J. C., Hogg, M. A., David, B., et al. (1992). Group polarization as conformity to the prototypical group member. *British Journal of Social Psychology, 31,* 1–19.

McGuire, A. M. (1994). Helping behaviors in the natural environment: Dimensions and correlates of helping. *Personality and Social Psychology Bulletin, 20,* 45–56.

McGuire, J. (2008). A review of effective interventions for reducing aggression and violence. *Philosophical Transactions of the Royal Society B,* 1–21.

McGuire, W. J. (1964). Inducing resistance to persuasion. In L. Berkowitz (Ed.), *Advances in experimental social psychology* (Vol. 1, pp. 192–229). New York: Academic Press.

McGuire, W. J. (1967). Some impending reorientations in social psychology: Some thoughts provoked by Kenneth Ring. *Journal of Experimental Social Psychology, 3,* 124–139.

McGuire, W. J. (1968). Personality and susceptibility to social influence. In E. F. Borgatta & W. W. Lambert (Eds.), *Handbook of personality theory and research* (pp. 1130–1187). Chicago: Rand McNally.

McGuire, W. J. (1969). The nature of attitudes and attitude change. In G. Lindzey & E. Aronson (Eds.), *Handbook of social psychology* (2nd ed., Vol. 3, pp. 136–314). Reading, MA: Addison-Wesley.

McGuire, W. J., & McGuire, C. V. (1988). Content and process in the experience of self. In L. Berkowitz (Ed.), *Advances in experimental social psychology* (Vol. 20, pp. 97–144). New York: Academic Press.

McGuire, W. J., McGuire, C. V., & Winton, W. (1979). Effects of household sex composition on the salience of one's gender in the spontaneous self-concept. *Journal of Experimental Social Psychology 15,* 77–90.

McIntyre, R. B., Paulson, R. M., & Lord, C. G. (2003). Alleviating women's mathematics stereotype threat through salience of group achievements. *Journal of Experimental Social Psychology, 39,* 83–90.

McKelvey, T. (2007). *Monstering: Inside America's policy of secret interrogations and torture in the terror war.* New York: Basic Books.

McKenna, K. Y. A., & Bargh, J. A. (1998). Coming out in the age of the Internet: "Demarginalization" through virtual group participation. *Journal of Personality and Social Psychology, 75,* 681–694.

McKimmie, B. M., Terry, D. J., & Hogg , M. A. (2009). Dissonance reduction in the context of group membership: The role of metaconsistency. *Group Dynamics: Theory, Research, and Practice, 13,* 103–119.

McLeish, K. N., & Oxoby, R. J. (2011). Social interactions and the salience of social identity. *Journal of Economic Psychology, 32,* 172–178.

McNatt, D. B. (2000). Ancient Pygmalion joins contemporary management: A meta-analysis of the result. *Journal of Applied Psychology, 85,* 314–322.

McPherson, M., Smith-Lovin, L., & Cook, J. M. (2001). Birds of a feather: Homophily in social networks. *Annual Review of Sociology, 27,* 415–444.

Mead, G. H. (1934). *Mind, self, and society.* Chicago: University of Chicago Press.

Mealey, L., Bridgstock, R., & Townsend, G. C. (1999). Symmetry and perceived facial attractiveness: A monozygotic co-twin comparison. *Journal of Personality and Social Psychology, 76,* 151–158.

Medvec, V. H., & Savitsky, K. (1997). When doing better means feeling worse: The effects of categorical cutoff points on counterfactual thinking and satisfaction. *Journal of Personality and Social Psychology, 72,* 1284–1296.

Medvec, V. H., Madey, S. F., & Gilovich, T. (1995). When less is more: Counterfactual thinking and satisfaction among Olympic medalists. *Journal of Personality and Social Psychology, 69,* 603–610.

Meeus, W. H. J., & Raaijmakers, Q. A. W. (1995). Obedience in modern society: The Utrecht studies. *Journal of Social Issues, 51,* 155–175.

Meier, B. P., Schnall, S., Schwarz, N., & Bargh, J. A. (2012). Embodiment in social psychology. *Topics in Cognitive Science.*

Meiser, T., & Hewstone, M. (2006). Illusory and spurious correlations: Distinct phenomena or joint outcomes of exemplar-based category learning? *European Journal of Social Psychology, 36,* 315–336.

Meissner, C. A., & Brigham, J. C. (2001). 30 years of investigating the own-race bias in memory for faces: A meta-analytic review. *Psychology, Public Policy, and Law, 7,* 3–35.

Meissner, C. A., & Kassin, S. M. (2002). "He's guilty!" Investigator bias in judgments of truth and deception. *Law and Human Behavior, 26,* 469–480.

Meissner, C. A., Brigham, J. C., & Butz, D. A. (2005). Memory for own- and other-race faces: A dual-process approach. *Applied Cognitive Psychology, 19,* 545–567.

Meissner, C. A., Brigham, J. C., & Pfeifer, J. E. (2003). Jury nullification: The influence of judicial instruction on the relationship between attitudes and juridic decision-making. *Basic and Applied Social Psychology, 25,* 243–254.

Melamed, S., Shirom, A., Toker, S., Berliner, S., & Shapira, I. (2006). Burnout and risk of cardiovascular disease: Evidence, possible causal paths, and promising research directions. *Psychological Bulletin, 132,* 327–353.

Meltzoff, A. N., & Moore, M. K. (1977). Imitation of facial and manual gestures by human neonates. *Science, 198,* 75–78.

Mendel, R., Traut-Mattausch, E., Jonas, E., Leucht, S., Kane, J. M., Maino, K., Kissling, W., & Hamann, J. (2011). Confirmation bias: why psychiatrists stick to wrong preliminary diagnoses. *Psychological Medicine, 41,* 2651–2659.

Mendes, W. B., Blascovich, J., Lickel, B., & Hunter, S. (2002). Challenge and threat during social interaction with white and black men. *Personality and Social Psychology Bulletin, 28,* 939–952.

Mendes, W. B., & Jamieson, J. (2012). Embodied stereotype threat: Exploring brain and body mechanisms underlying performance impairment. In M. Inzlicht & T. Schmader (Eds.), *Stereotype threat: Theory, process, and application* (pp. 51–68). New York: Oxford University Press.

Mendonca, P. J., & Brehm, S. S. (1983). Effects of choice on behavioral treatment of overweight children. *Journal of Social and Clinical Psychology, 1,* 343–358.

Mendoza-Denton, R., & Page-Gould, E. (2008). Can cross-group friendships influence minority students' well-being at historically white universities? *Psychological Science, 19,* 933–939.

Menzer, M. M., & Torney-Purta, J. (2012). Individualism and socioeconomic diversity at school as related to perceptions of the frequency of peer aggression in fifteen countries. *Journal of Adolescence, 35,* 1285–1294.

Mereish, E. H., Liu, M. M., & Helms, J. E. (2012). Effects of discrimination on Chinese, Pilipino, and Vietnamese Americans' mental and physical health. *Asian American Journal of Psychology, 3,* 91–103.

Meriac, J. P., Hoffman, B. J., Woehr, D. J., & Fleisher, M. S. (2008). Further evidence for the validity of assessment center dimensions: A meta-analysis of the incremental criterion-related validity of dimension ratings. *Journal of Applied Psychology, 93,* 1042–1052.

Merikle, P., & Skanes, H. E. (1992). Subliminal self-help audiotapes: A search for placebo effects. *Journal of Applied Psychology, 77,* 772–776.

Merritt, A. C., Effron, D. A., & Monin, B. (2010). Moral self-licensing: When being good frees us to be bad. *Social and Personality Psychology Compass, 4,* 344–357.

Merritt, A. C., Effron, D. A., Fein, S., Savitsky, K. K., Tuller, D. M., & Monin, B. (2012). The strategic pursuit of moral credentials. *Journal of Experimental Social Psychology, 48,* 774–777.

Mesmer-Magnus, J., & DeChurch, L. (2009). Information sharing and team performance: A meta-analysis. *Journal of Applied Psychology, 94,* 535–546.

Messick, D. M., & Cook, K. S. (Eds.). (1983). *Equity theory: Psychological and sociological perspectives.* New York: Praeger.

Meston, C. M., & Frohlich, P. F. (2003). Love at first sight: Partner salience moderates roller-coaster-induced excitation transfer. *Archives of Sexual Behavior, 32,* 537–544.

Metalsky, G. I., Joiner, T. E., Hardin, T. S., & Abramson, L. Y. (1993). Depressive reactions to failure in a naturalistic setting: A test of the hopelessness and self-esteem theories of depression. *Journal of Abnormal Psychology, 102,* 101–109.

Meyers-Levy, J., Zhu, R., & Jiang, L. (2010). Context effects from bodily sensations: examining bodily sensations induced by flooring and the moderating role of product viewing distance. *Journal of Consumer Research, 37,* 1–14.

Mezulis, A. H., Abramson, L. Y., Hyde, J. S., & Hankin, B. L. (2004). Is there a universal positivity bias in attributions? A meta-analytic review of individual, developmental, and cultural differences in the self-serving attributional bias. *Psychological Bulletin, 130,* 711–747.

Mezzacappa, E. S., Katkin, E. S., & Palmer, S. N. (1999). Epinephrine, arousal, and emotion: A new look at two-factor theory. *Cognition and Emotion, 13,* 181–199.

Michelle, C. (2012). Co-constructions of gender and ethnicity in New Zealand television advertising. *Sex Roles, 66,* 21–37.

Mickelson, K. D., Kessler, R. C., & Shaver, P. R. (1997). Adult attachment in a nationally representative sample. *Journal of Personality and Social Psychology, 73,* 1092–1106.

Miczek, K. A., de Almeida, R. M. M, Kravitz, E. A., Rissman, E. F., de Boer, S. F., & Raine, A. (2007). Neurobiology of escalated aggression and violence. *Journal of Neuroscience, 27,* 11803–11806.

Midlarsky, E., Fagan Jones, S., & Corley, R. P. (2005). Personality correlates of heroic rescue during the Holocaust. *Journal of Personality, 73,* 907–934.

Miklikowska, M., & Fry, D. P. (2010). Values for peace: Ethnographic lessons from the Mardu of Australi and the Semai of Malaysia. *Beliefs and Values, 2,* 124–137.

Mikulincer, M., & Shaver, P. R. (2007). *Attachment patterns in adulthood: Structure, dynamics, and change.* New York: Guilford.

Miles, D. R., & Carey, G. (1997). Genetic and environmental architecture on human aggression. *Journal of Personality and Social Psychology, 72,* 207–217.

Miles, J. A., & Greenberg, J. (1993). Using punishment threats to attenuate social loafing effects among swimmers. *Organizational Behavior and Human Decision Processes, 56,* 246–265.

Milgram, S. (1963). Behavioral study of obedience. *Journal of Abnormal and Social Psychology, 67,* 371–378.

Milgram, S. (1970). The experience of living in cities. *Science, 167,* 1461–1468.

Milgram, S. (1974). *Obedience to authority: An experimental view.* New York: Harper & Row.

Milgram, S., & Toch, H. (1969). Collective behavior: Crowds and social movements. In G. Lindzey & E. Aronson (Eds.), *The handbook of social psychology* (2nd ed., Vol. 4, pp. 507–610). Reading, MA: Addison-Wesley.

Milgram, S., & Sabini, J. (1978). On maintaining urban norms: A field experiment in the subway. In A. Baum, J. E. Singer, & S. Valins (Eds.), *Advances in environmental psychology* (Vol. 1). Hillsdale, NJ: Erlbaum.

Milgram, S., Bickman, L., & Berkowitz, L. (1969). Note on the drawing power of crowds of different size. *Journal of Personality and Social Psychology, 13,* 79–82.

Millar, M. (2002). Effects of guilt induction and guilt reduction on door in the face. *Communication Research, 29,* 666–680.

Miller-El v. Dretke, 545 U.S. 231 (2005).

Miller, A. G. (1986). *The obedience experiments: A case study of controversy in social science.* New York: Praeger.

Miller, A. G. (2009). Reflections on "Replicating Milgram" (Burger, 2009). *American Psychologist, 64,* 20–27.

Miller, A. G., Gordon, A. K., & Buddie, A. M. (1999). Accounting for evil and cruelty: Is to explain to condone? *Personality and Social Psychology Review, 3,* 254–268.

Miller, A. G., Jones, E. E., & Hinkle, S. (1981). A robust attribution error in the personality domain. *Journal of Experimental Social Psychology, 17,* 587–600.

Miller, E. (2011). 'There are no words that can possibly express how we feel': Toward an understanding of the social-psychological experiences of caregivers of the mentally ill. *Illness, Crisis, & Loss, 19,* 381–386.

Miller, G., Chen, E., & Cole, S. W. (2009). Health psychology: Developing biologically plausible models linking the social world and physical health. *Annual Review of Psychology, 60,* 501–524.

Miller, G. F. (2009). *Spent: Sex, evolution and consumer behavior.* New York: Penguin/Putnam.

Miller, J. G. (1984). Culture and the development of everyday social explanation. *Journal of Personality and Social Psychology, 46,* 961–978.

Miller, J. G., Das, R., & Chakravarthy, S. (2011). Culture and the role of choice in agency. *Journal of Personality and Social Psychology, 101,* 46–61.

Miller, M. K., & Hayward, R. D. (2008). Religious characteristics and the death penalty. *Law and Human Behavior, 32,* 113–123.

Miller, N. E. (1941). The frustration-aggression hypothesis. *Psychological Review, 48,* 337–342.

Miller, N., & Campbell, D. T. (1959). Recency and primacy in persuasion as a function of the timing of speeches and measurements. *Journal of Abnormal and Social Psychology, 59,* 1–9.

Miller, P. A., & Eisenberg, N. (1988). The relation of empathy to aggressive and externalizing/antisocial behavior. *Psychological Bulletin, 103,* 324–344.

Miller, R., & Perlman, D. (2009). *Intimate relationships* (5th ed.). New York: McGraw-Hill.

Miller, S. L., Maner, J. K., & Becker, D. (2010). Self-protective biases in group categorization: Threat cues shape the psychological boundary between "us" and "them." *Journal of Personality and Social Psychology, 99,* 62–77.

Miller, T. Q., Smith, T. W., Turner, C. W., Guijarro, M. L., & Hallet, A. J. (1996). A meta-analytic review of research on hostility and physical health. *Psychological Bulletin, 119,* 322–348.

Miller, T. Q., Turner, C. W., Tindale, R. S., Posavac, E. J., & Dugon, B. L. (1991). Reasons for the trend toward null findings in research on Type A behavior. *Psychological Bulletin, 110,* 469–485.

Miller, W. R. (1985). Motivation for treatment: A review with special emphasis on alcoholism. *Psychological Bulletin, 98,* 84–107.

Miller, W. R., & Thoresen, C. E. (2003). Spirituality, religion, and health: An emerging research field. *American Psychologist, 58,* 24–35.

Milliken, C. S., Auchterlonie, J. L., & Hoge, C. W. (2007). Longitudinal assessment of mental health problems among active and reserve component soldiers returning from the Iraq war. *JAMA: Journal of the American Medical Association, 298,* 2141–2148.

Milton, A. C., & Mullan, B. A. (2012). An application of the theory of planned behavior—A randomized controlled food safety pilot intervention for young adults. *Health Psychology, 31,* 250–259.

Minson, J. A., & Mueller, J. S. (2012). The cost of collaboration: Why joint decision making exacerbates rejection of outside information. *Psychological Science, 23,* 219–224.

Mioshi, E., Bristow, M., Cook, R., & Hodges, J. R. (2009). Factors underlying caregiver stress in frontotemporal dementia and Alzheimer's disease. *Dementia and Geriatric Cognitive Disorders, 27,* 76–81.

Miranda, S. M. (1994). Avoidance of groupthink: Meeting management using group support systems. *Small Group Research, 25,* 105–136.

Mita, T. H., Dermer, M., & Knight, J. (1977). Reversed facial images and the mere exposure hypothesis. *Journal of Personality and Social Psychology, 35,* 597–601.

Mitchell, T. R. (1974). Expectancy models of job satisfaction, occupational preference, and effort: A theoretical, methodological, and empirical appraisal. *Psychological Bulletin, 81,* 1096–1112.

Miura, H. (2009). Differences in frontal lobe function between violent and nonviolent conduct disorder in male adolescents. *Psychiatry and Clinical Neurosciences, 63,* 161–166.

Miyamoto, Y., & Kitayama, S. (2002). Cultural variation in correspondence bias: The critical role of attitude diagnosticity of socially constrained behavior. *Journal of Personality and Social Psychology, 83,* 1239–1248.

Mobius, M. M., & Rosenblat, T. S. (2006). Why beauty matters. *American Economic Review, 96,* 222–235.

Moffitt, T. E., Arseneault, L., et al. (2011). A gradient of childhood self-control predicts health, wealth, and public safety. *PNAS Proceedings of The National Academy of Sciences of The United States of America, 108,* 2693–2698.

Mojza, E. J., Sonnentag, S., & Bornemann, C. (2011). Volunteer work as a valuable leisure-time activity: A day-level study on volunteer work, non-work experiences, and well-being at work. *Journal of Occupational and Organizational Psychology, 84,* 123–152.

Molden, D. C., & Hui, C. M. (2011). Promoting de-escalation of commitment: The regulatory focus perspective on sunk costs. *Psychological Science, 22,* 8–12.

Molden, D. C., Hui, C. M., Scholer, A. A., Meier, B. P., Noreen, E. E., D'Agostino, P. R., & Martin, V. (2012). The motivational versus metabolic effects of carbohyrdates on self-control. *Psychological Science,* in press.

Moll, J., Krueger, F., Zahn, R., Pardini, M., de Oliveira-Souza, R., & Grafman, J. (2006). Human fronto-mesolimbic networks guide decisions about charitable donation. *PNAS Proceedings of The National Academy of Sciences of the United States of America, 103,* 15623–15628.

Möller, I., & Krahé, B. (2009, January). Exposure to violent video games and aggression in German adolescents: A longitudinal analysis. *Aggressive Behavior, 35,* 75–89.

Möller, I., Krahé, B., Busching, R., & Krause, C. (2012). Efficacy of an intervention to reduce the use of media violence and aggression: An experimental evaluation with adolescents in Germany. *Journal of Youth and Adolescence, 41,* 105–120.

Monat, A., Lazarus, R. S., & Reevy, G. (Eds.). (2007). *The Praeger handbook on stress and coping.* New York: Praeger.

Mondschein, E. R., Adolph, K. E., & Tamis-LeMonda, C. S. (2000). Gender bias in mothers' expectations about infant crawling. *Journal of Experimental Child Psychology, 77,* 304–316.

Montañés, P., de Lemus, S., Bohner, G., Megías, J. L., Moya, M., & Garcia-Retamero, R. (2012). Intergenerational transmission of benevolent sexism from mothers to daughters and its relation to daughters' academic performance and goals. *Sex Roles, 66,* 468–478.

Monteith, M. J., & Mark, A. Y. (2009). The self-regulation of prejudice. In T. D. Nelson (Ed.), *Handbook of prejudice, stereotyping, and discrimination* (pp. 507–523). New York: Psychology Press.

Monteith, M. J., Ashburn-Nardo, L., Voils, C. I., & Czopp, A. M. (2002). Putting the brakes on prejudice: On the development and operation of cues for control. *Journal of Personality and Social Psychology, 83,* 1029–1050.

Monteith, M. J., Mark, A. Y., & Ashburn-Nardo, L. (2010). The self-regulation of prejudice: Toward understanding its lived character. *Group Processes & Intergroup Relations, 13,* 183–200.

Montoya, E. R., Terburg, D., Bos, P. A., & van Honk, J. (2012). Testosterone, cortisol, and serotonin as key regulators of social aggression: A review and theoretical perspective. *Motivation and Emotion, 36,* 65–73.

Montoya, R. M., Horton, R. S., & Kirchner, J. (2008). Is actual similarity necessary for attraction? A meta-analysis of actual and perceived similarity. *Journal of Social and Personal Relationships, 25,* 889–922.

Moon, H. (2001). Looking forward and looking back: Integrating completion and sunk-cost effects within an escalation-of-commitment progress decision. *Journal of Applied Psychology, 86,* 104–113.

Moore, C., Detert, J. R., Treviño, L. K., Baker, V. L., & Mayer, D. M. (2012). Why employees do bad things: Moral disengagement and unethical organizational behavior. *Personnel Psychology, 65,* 1–48.

Moore, D. A. (2005). Myopic biases in strategic social prediction: Why deadlines put everyone under more pressure than everyone else. *Personality and Social Psychology Bulletin, 31,* 668–679.

Moore, T. E. (1982). Subliminal advertising: What you see is what you get. *Journal of Marketing, 46,* 38–47.

Mor, N., & Winquist, J. (2002). Self-focused attention and negative affect: A meta-analysis. *Psychological Bulletin, 128,* 638–662.

Moradi, B., Dirks, D., & Matteson, A. V. (2005). Roles of sexual objectification experiences and internalization of standards of beauty in eating disorder symptomatology: A test and extension of objectification theory. *Journal of Counseling Psychology, 52,* 420–428.

Moran, G., & Comfort, C. (1986). Neither "tentative" nor "fragmentary": Verdict preference of impaneled felony jurors as a function of attitude toward capital punishment. *Journal of Applied Psychology, 71,* 146–155.

Moran, G., & Cutler, B. L. (1991). The prejudicial impact of pretrial publicity. *Journal of Applied Social Psychology, 21,* 345–367.

Moran, J. M., Heatherton, T. F., & Kelley, W. M. (2009). Modulation of cortical midline structure by implicit and explicit self-relevance evaluation. *Social Neuroscience, 4,* 197–211.

Moreland, R. L., & Beach, S. R. (1992). Exposure effects in the classroom: The development of affinity among students. *Journal of Experimental Social Psychology, 28,* 255–276.

Moreland, R. L., & Levine, J. M. (2002). Socialization and trust in work groups. *Group Processes and Intergroup Relations, 5,* 185–201.

Morewedge, C. K., Preston, J., & Wegner, D. M. (2007). Timescale bias in the attribution of mind. *Journal of Personality and Social Psychology, 93,* 1–11.

Morgan, C. A., Hazlett, G., Doran, A., Garrett, S., Hoyt, G., Thomas, P., et al. (2004). Accuracy of eyewitness memory for persons encountered during exposure to highly intense stress. *International Journal of Law and Psychiatry, 27,* 265–279.

Morgan, M., & Shanahan, J. (2010). The state of cultivation. *Journal of Broadcasting & Electronic Media, 54,* 337–355.

Morgeson, F. P., Campion, M. A., Dipboye, R. L., Hollenbeck, J. R., Murphy, K., & Schmitt, N. (2007). Reconsidering the use of personality tests in personnel contexts. *Personnel Psychology, 60,* 683–729.

Morgeson, F. P., Mumford, T. V., & Campion, M. A. (2005). Coming full circle: Using research and practice to address 27 questions about 360-degree feedback programs. *Consulting Psychology Journal: Practice and Research, 57,* 196–209.

Moriarty, T. (1975). Crime, commitment, and the responsive bystander: Two field experiments. *Journal of Personality and Social Psychology, 31,* 370–376.

Morr Serewicz, M. C., & Gale, E. (2008). First-date scripts: Gender roles, context, and relationship. *Sex Roles, 58,* 149–164.

Morrison, A. M., & Von Glinow, M. A. (1990). Women and minorities in management. *American Psychologist, 45,* 200–208.

Morrison, K., & Chung, A. H. (2011). "White" or "European American"? Self-identifying labels influence majority group members' interethnic attitudes. *Journal of Experimental Social Psychology, 47,* 165–170.

Morrison, K., & Ybarra, O. (2008). The effects of realistic threat and group identification on social dominance orientation. *Journal of Experimental Social Psychology, 44,* 156–163.

Morrison, M., Tay, L., & Diener, E. (2011). Subjective well-being and national satisfaction: Findings from a worldwide survey. *Psychological Science, 22,* 166–171.

Morrongiello, B. A., & Dawber, T. (2000). Mothers' responses to sons and daughters engaging in injury-risk behaviors on a playground: Implications for sex differences in injury rates. *Journal of Experimental Child Psychology, 76,* 89–103.

Morrongiello, B. A., Midgett, C., & Stanton, K. L. (2000). Gender biases in children's appraisals of injury risk and other children's risk-taking behaviors. *Journal of Experimental Child Psychology, 77,* 317–336.

Morse, B. J. (1995). Beyond the Conflict Tactics Scale: Assessing gender differences in partner violence. *Violence and Victims, 10,* 251–272.

Moscovici, S. (1980). Toward a theory of conversion behavior. In L. Berkowitz (Ed.), *Advances in Experimental Social Psychology, 6,* 149–202.

Moscovici, S., & Personnaz, B. (1991). Studies in social influence VI: Is Lenin orange or red? Imagery and social influence. *European Journal of Social Psychology, 21,* 101–118.

Moscovici, S., & Zavalloni, M. (1969). The group as a polarizer of attitudes. *Journal of Personality and Social Psychology, 12,* 125–135.

Moscovici, S., Lage, E., & Naffrechoux, M. (1969). Influence of a consistent minority on the responses of a majority in a color perception task. *Sociometry, 32,* 365–380.

Moscovici, S., Mugny, G., & Van Avermaet, E. (Eds.). (1985). *Perspectives on minority influence.* New York: Cambridge University Press.

Moskalenko, S., & Heine, S. J. (2003). Watching your troubles away: Television viewing as a stimulus for subjective self-awareness. *Personality and Social Psychology Bulletin, 29,* 76–85.

Moskowitz, G. B. (1996). The mediational effects of attributions and information processing in minority social influence. *British Journal of Social Psychology, 35,* 47–66.

Moskowitz, G. B., Li, P., Ignarri, C., & Stone, J. (2011). Compensatory cognition associated with egalitarian goals. *Journal of Experimental Social Psychology, 47,* 365–370.

Mostofsky, E., Maclure, M., Sherwood, J. B., Tofler, G. H., Muller, J. E., & Mittleman, M. A. (2012). Risk of acute myocardial infarction after the death of a significant person in one's life: The determinants of myocardial infarction onset study. *Circulation, 125,* 491–496.

Mouton, J., Blake, R., & Olmstead, J. (1956). The relationship between frequency of yielding and the disclosure of personal identity. *Journal of Personality, 24,* 339–347.

Moynihan, J. A., & Ader, R. (1996). Psychoneuroimmunology: Animal models of disease. *Psychosomatic Medicine, 58,* 546–558.

Mueller, J. H. (1982). Self-awareness and access to material rated as self-descriptive and nondescriptive. *Bulletin of the Psychonomic Society, 19,* 323–326.

Mugny, G. (1982). *The power of minorities.* London: Academic Press.

Mugny, G., & Perez, J. A. (1991). *Social psychology of minority influence.* Cambridge: Cambridge University Press.

Mulder, L. B. (2008). Undermining trust and cooperation: The paradox of sanctioning systems in social dilemmas. *Journal of Experimental Social Psychology, 42,* 147–162.

Mullen, B. (1983). Operationalizing the effect of the group on the individual: A self-attention perspective. *Journal of Experimental Social Psychology, 19,* 295–322.

Mullen, B. (1985). Strength and immediacy of sources: A meta-analytic evaluation of the forgotten elements of social impact theory. *Journal of Personality and Social Psychology, 48,* 1458–1466.

Mullen, B., & Copper, C. (1994). The relation between group cohesiveness and performance: An integration. *Psychological Bulletin, 115,* 210–227.

Mullen, B., Anthony, T., Salas, E., & Driskell, J. E. (1994). Group cohesiveness and quality of decision making: An integration of tests of the group-think hypothesis. *Small Group Research, 25,* 189–204.

Mullen, B., Johnson, C., & Salas, E. (1991). Productivity loss in brainstorming groups: A meta-analytic integration. *Basic and Applied Social Psychology, 12,* 3–23.

Mullen, E., & Skitka, L. J. (2009). Comparing Americans' and Ukrainians' allocations of public assistance: The role of affective reactions in helping behavior. *Journal of Cross-Cultural Psychology, 40,* 301–318.

Muraven, M., & Baumeister, R. F. (1998). Self-control as a limited resource: Regulatory depletion patterns. *Journal of Personality and Social Psychology, 74,* 774–789.

Muraven, M., & Baumeister, R. F. (2000). Self-regulation and depletion of limited resources: Does self-control resemble a muscle? *Psychological Bulletin, 126,* 247–259.

Murphy, K. R., & Balzer, W. K. (1986). Systematic distortions in memory-based behavior ratings and performance evaluation: Consequences for rating accuracy. *Journal of Applied Psychology, 71,* 39–44.

Murphy, K. R., & Cleveland, J. N. (1995). *Understanding performance appraisal: Social, organizational, and goal-based perspectives.* Thousand Oaks, CA: Sage.

Murphy, K. R., Cronin, B. E., & Tam, A. P. (2003). Controversy and consensus regarding the use of cognitive ability testing in organizations. *Journal of Applied Psychology, 88,* 660–671.

Murphy, K., Cleveland, J., Skattebo, A., & Kinney, T. (2004). Raters who pursue different goals give different ratings. *Journal of Applied Psychology, 89,* 158–164.

Murphy, M. C., & Taylor, V. (2012). The role of situational cues in signaling and maintaining stereotype threat. In M. Inzlicht & T. Schmader (Eds.), *Stereotype threat: Theory, process, and application* (pp. 17–33). New York: Oxford University Press.

Murphy, S. P. (2008, July 17). Big Dig's red ink engulfs state; Cost spirals to $22b. *Boston Globe,* p. A1.

Murphy, V. (2012). Woman dies during chat on Facebook. *The Mirror,* March 28, p. 14.

Murray, G., Judd, F., Jackson, H., Komiti, A., Wearing, A., Robins, G., et al. (2008). Big boys don't cry: An investigation of stoicism and its mental health outcomes. *Personality and Individual Differences, 44,* 1369–1381.

Murray, S. L., & Holmes, J. G. (1999). The (mental) ties that bind: Cognitive structures that predict relationship resilience. *Journal of Personality and Social Psychology, 77,* 1228–1244.

Murray, S. L., & Holmes, J. G. (2008). The commitment insurance system: Self-esteem and the regulation of connection in close relationships. *Advances in Experimental Social Psychology, 40,* 1–60.

Murray, S. L., Aloni, M., Holmes, J. G., Derrick, J. L., Stinson, D. A., & Leder, S. (2009). Fostering partner dependence as trust insurance: The implicit contingencies of the exchange script in close relationships. *Journal of Personality and Social Psychology, 96,* 324–348.

Murray, S. L., Holmes, J. G., & Collins, N. L. (2006). Optimizing assurance: The risk regulation system in relationships. *Psychological Bulletin, 132,* 641–666.

Murray, S. L., Holmes, J. G., & Griffin, D. W. (1996). The benefits of positive illusions: Idealization and the construction of satisfaction in close relationships. *Journal of Personality and Social Psychology, 70,* 79–98.

Murstein, B. I. (1986). *Paths to marriage*. Beverly Hills, CA: Sage.

Mussweiler, T., & Damisch, L. (2008). Going back to Donald: How comparisons shape judgmental priming effects. *Journal of Personality and Social Psychology, 95*, 1295–1315.

Mussweiler, T., & Rüter, K. (2003). What friends are for! The use of routine standards in social comparison. *Journal of Personality and Social Psychology, 85*, 467–481.

Mussweiler, T., & Strack, F. (2000). The "relative self": Informational and judgmental consequences of comparative self-evaluation. *Journal of Personality and Social Psychology, 79*, 23–38.

Mussweiler, T., Rüter, K., & Epstude, K. (2004). The man who wasn't there: Subliminal social comparison standards influence self-evaluation. *Journal of Experimental Social Psychology, 40*, 689–696.

Myers, D. G., & Diener, E. (1995). Who is happy? *Psychological Science, 6*, 10–19.

Myers, D. G., & Lamm, H. (1976). The group polarization phenomenon. *Psychological Bulletin, 83*, 602–627.

Myers, E. M., & Zeigler-Hill, V. (2012). How much do narcissists really like themselves? Using the bogus pipeline procedure to better understand the self-esteem of narcissists. *Journal of Research In Personality, 46*, 102–105.


Na, J., & Kitayama, S. (2011). Spontaneous trait inference is culture-specific: Behavioral and neural evidence. *Psychological Science, 22*, 1025–1032.

Nacoste, R. W. (1996). Social psychology and the affirmative action debate. *Journal of Social and Clinical Psychology, 15*, 261–282.

Nadler, A., & Fisher, J. D. (1986). The role of threat to self-esteem and perceived control in recipient reactions to help: Theory development and empirical validation. In L. Berkowitz (Ed.), *Advances in experimental social psychology* (Vol. 19, pp. 81–122). New York: Academic Press.

Nakashima, K., Isobe, C., & Ura, M. (2008). Effect of self-construal and threat to self-esteem on ingroup favouritism: Moderating effect of independent/interdependent self-construal on use of ingroup favouritism for maintaining and enhancing self-evaluation. *Asian Journal of Social Psychology, 11*, 286–292.

Naquin, C. E., & Kurtzberg, T. R. (2009). Team negotiation and perceptions of trustworthiness: The whole versus the sum of the parts. *Group Dynamics: Theory, Research, and Practice, 13*, 133–150.

Narchet, F. M., Meissner, C. A., & Russano, M. B. (2011). Modeling the influence of investigator bias on the elicitation of true and false confessions. *Law and Human Behavior, 35*, 452–465.

Narvaez, D., & Lapsley, D. K. (2009). Moral identity, moral functioning, and the development of moral character. In D. M. Bartels, C. W. Bauman, L. J. Sktika, & D. L. Medin (Eds.), *Moral judgment and decision making* (pp. 237–274). San Diego, CA: Elsevier Academic Press.

Nash, R. A., & Wade, K. A. (2009). Innocent but proven guilty: Using false video evidence to elicit false confessions and create false beliefs. *Applied Cognitive Psychology, 23*, 624–637.

*National Law Journal.* (1990, September 10). Rock group not liable for deaths. p. 33.

National Research Council, Committee to Review the Scientific Evidence on the Polygraph, Division of Behavioral and Social Sciences and Education. (2003). *The polygraph and lie detection*. Washington, DC: National Academies Press.

Nattinger, A. B., et al. (1998). Celebrity medical care decisions can influence others. *Journal of the American Medical Association, 279*, 788–789.

Nederveen Pieterse, A., van Knippenberg, D., & Van Dierendonck, D. (2013). Cultural diversity and team performance: The role of team member goal orientation. *Academy of Management Journal*, in press.

Neel, R., & Shapiro, J. R. (2012). Is racial bias malleable? Whites' lay theories of racial bias predict divergent strategies for interracial interactions. *Journal of Personality and Social Psychology, 103*, 101–120.

Neff, L. A., & Karney, B. R. (2005). To know you is to love you: The implications of global adoration and specific accuracy for marital relationships. *Journal of Personality and Social Psychology, 88*, 480–497.

Neisser, U. (1981). John Dean's memory: A case study. *Cognition, 9*, 1–22.

Nelson, J. (2012). On day to honor Yucapia soldier, I. E. looking to drown out extreme group planning to picket funeral. *San Bernardino County Sun* (California). June 21.

Nelson, J. K., Dunn, K. M., & Paradies, Y. (2011). Bystander anti-racism: A review of the literature. *Analyses of Social Issues and Public Policy (ASAP), 11*, 263–284.

Nelson, T. D. (2009). Ageism. In T. D. Nelson (Ed.), *Handbook of prejudice, stereotyping, and discrimination* (pp. 431–440). New York: Psychology Press.

Nemeth, C. (1986). Differential contributions of majority and minority influence. *Psychological Review, 93*, 23–32.

Nemeth, C. J., Connell, J. B., Rogers, J. D., & Brown, K. S. (2001). Improving decision making by means of dissent. *Journal of Applied Social Psychology, 31*, 48–58.

Nemeth, C., & Kwan, J. (1987). Minority influence, divergent thinking, and detection of correct solutions. *Journal of Applied Social Psychology, 17*, 788–799.

Nemeth, C., Mayseless, O., Sherman, J., & Brown, Y. (1990). Exposure to dissent and recall of information. *Journal of Personality and Social Psychology, 58*, 429–437.

"Nepali man bites snake to death in revenge attack" (2012). *Reuters*, August 23.

Nes, L. S., & Segerstrom, S. C. (2006). Dispositional optimism and coping: A meta-analytic review. *Personality and Social Psychology Review, 10*, 235–251.

Neuman, W. R., Marcus, G. E., Crigler, A. N., & MacKuen, M. (Eds.). (2007). *The affect effect: Dynamics of emotion in political thinking and behavior*. Chicago: University of Chicago Press.

Neumann, R., & Strack, F. (2000). "Mood contagion": The automatic transfer of mood between persons. *Journal of Personality and Social Psychology, 79*, 211–223.

Newby-Clark, I. R., McGregor, I., & Zanna, M. P. (2002). Thinking and caring about cognitive inconsistency: When and from whom does attitudinal ambivalence feel uncomfortable? *Journal of Personality and Social Psychology, 82*, 157–166.

Newcomb, T. M. (1943). *Personality and social change: Attitude formation in a student community*. Ft. Worth, TX: Dryden Press.

Newcomb, T. M. (1961). *The acquaintance process*. New York: Holt, Rinehart and Winston.

Newheiser, A., & Olson, K. R. (2012). White and Black American children's implicit intergroup bias. *Journal of Experimental Social Psychology, 48*, 264–270.

Newman, C. (2000, January). The enigma of beauty. *National Geographic*, pp. 94–121.

Newman, L. S., & Uleman, J. S. (1989). Spontaneous trait inference. In J. S. Uleman & J. A. Bargh (Eds.), *Unintended thought* (pp. 155–188). New York: Guilford.

Newman, R. S. (2005). The cocktail party effect in infants revisited: Listening to one's name in noise. *Developmental Psychology, 41*, 352–362.

Newtson, D. (1974). Dispositional inference from effects of actions: Effects chosen and effects foregone. *Journal of Experimental Social Psychology, 10*, 487–496.

Newtson, D., Hairfield, J., Bloomingdale, J., & Cutino, S. (1987). The structure of action and interaction. *Social Cognition, 5*, 191–237.

Nezlek, J. B., Wesselmann, E. D., Wheeler, L., & Williams, K. D. (2012). Ostracism in everyday life. *Group Dynamics: Theory, Research, and Practice, 16*, 91–104.

Ng, K. Y., & Van Dyne, L. (2005). Antecedents and performance consequences of helping behavior in work groups: A multilevel analysis. *Group and Organization Management, 30*, 514–540.

Nibler, R., & Harris, K. L. (2003). The effects of culture and cohesiveness in collectivistic and individualistic work groups: A cross-cultural analysis. *Journal of Organizational Behavior, 24*, 979–1001.

Nickerson, C., Schwarz, N., Diener, E., & Kahneman, D. (2003). Zeroing in on the dark side of the American dream: A closer look at the negative consequences of the goal for financial success. *Psychological Science, 14*, 531–536.

Niedenthal, P. M., Barsalou, L. W., Winkielman, P., Krauth-Gruber, S. & Ric, F. (2005). Embodiment in attitudes, social perception, and emotion. *Personality and Social Psychology Review, 9*, 184–211.

Niedermeier, K. E., Horowitz, I. A., & Kerr, N. L. (1999). Informing jurors of their nullification power: A route to a just verdict or judicial chaos? *Law and Human Behavior, 23,* 331–351.

Niesta Kayser, D., Greitemeyer, T., Fischer, P., & Frey, D. (2010). Why mood affects help giving, but not moral courage: Comparing two types of pro-social behaviour. *European Journal of Social Psychology, 40,* 1136–1157.

Nieva, V. F., & Gutek, B. A. (1981). *Women and work: A psychological perspective.* New York: Praeger.

Nijstad, B. A., & Stroebe, W. (2006). How the group affects the mind: A cognitive model of idea generation in groups. *Personality and Social Psychology Review, 10,* 186–213.

Nisbett, R. E. (2003). *The geography of thought: How Asians and Westerners think differently . . . and why.* New York: Free Press.

Nisbett, R. E., & Cohen, D. (1996). *Culture of honor: The psychology of violence in the South.* Boulder, CO: Westview.

Nisbett, R. E., & Ross, L. (1980). *Human inference: Strategies and shortcomings of social judgment.* Englewood Cliffs, NJ: Prentice-Hall.

Nisbett, R. E., & Wilson, T. D. (1977). Telling more than we can know: Verbal reports on mental processes. *Psychological Review, 84,* 231–259.

Nock, M., Park, J., Finn, C., Deliberto, T., Dour, H., & Banaji, M. (2010). Measuring the suicidal mind: Implicit cognition predicts suicidal behavior. *Psychological Science, 21,* 511–517.

Nolen-Hoeksema, S. (1991). Responses to depression and their effects on the duration of depressive episodes. *Journal of Abnormal Psychology, 100,* 569–582.

Nolen-Hoeksema, S., & Girgus, J. S. (1994). The emergence of gender differences in depression during adolescence. *Psychological Bulletin, 115,* 424–443.

Nolen-Hoeksema, S., & Morrow, J. (1991). A prospective study of depression and posttraumatic stress symptoms after a natural disaster: The 1989 Loma Prieta earthquake. *Journal of Personality and Social Psychology, 61,* 115–121.

Nolen-Hoeksema, S., Wisco, B. E., & Lyubomirsky, S. (2008). Rethinking rumination. *Perspectives on Psychological Science, 3,* 400–424.

Norenzayan, A., & Nisbett, R. E. (2000). Culture and causal cognition. *Current Directions in Psychological Science, 9,* 132–135.

North, A. C., Hargreaves, D. J., & McKendrick, J. (1999). The influence of in-store music on wine selections. *Journal of Applied Psychology, 84,* 271–276.

North, M. S., & Fiske, S. T. (2012). An inconvenienced youth? Ageism and its potential intergenerational roots. *Psychological Bulletin,* in press.

Northoff, G., & Panksepp, J. (2008). The trans-species concept of self and the subcortical-cortical midline system. *Trends in Cognitive Sciences, 12,* 259–264.

Northouse, P. G. (2013). *Leadership: Theory and practice* (6th edition). Thousand Oaks, CA: Sage.

Norton, K. I., Olds, T. S., Olive, S., & Dank, S. (1996). Ken and Barbie at life size. *Sex Roles, 34,* 287–294.

Norton, M. I., Sommers, S. R., Apfelbaum, E. P., Pura, N., & Ariely, D. (2006). Color blindness and interracial interaction: Playing the political correctness game. *Psychological Science, 17,* 949–953.

Norton, M. I., Sommers, S. R., Vandello, J. A., & Darley, J. M. (2006). Mixed motives and racial bias: The impact of legitimate and illegitimate criteria on decision making. *Psychology, Public Policy, and Law, 12,* 36–55.

Nosek, B. A., & Smyth, F. L. (2011). Implicit social cognitions predict sex differences in math engagement and achievement. *American Educational Research Journal, 48,* 1124–1154.

Nosek, B. A., Banaji, M. R., & Greenwald, A. G. (2002). Harvesting implicit attitudes and stereotype data from the Implicit Association Test website. *Group Dynamics, 6,* 101–115.

Nosek, B. A., Hawkins, C. B., & Frazier, R. S. (2011). Implicit social cognition: From measures to mechanisms. *Trends in Cognitive Sciences, 15,* 152–159.

Nosko, A., Tieu, T.-T., Lawford, H., & Pratt, M. W. (2011). How do I love thee? Let me count the ways: Parenting during adolescence, attachment styles, and romantic narratives in emerging adulthood. *Developmental Psychology, 47,* 645–657.

O'Brien, B. (2009). Prime suspect: An examination of factors that aggravate and counteract confirmation bias in criminal investigations. *Psychology, Public Policy, and Law, 15,* 315–334.

O'Connor, S. C., & Rosenblood, L. K. (1996). Affiliation motivation in everyday experience: A theoretical comparison. *Journal of Personality and Social Psychology, 70,* 513–522.

O'Keefe, D. J., & Figge, M. (1997). A guilt-based explanation of the door-in-the-face influence strategy. *Human Communication Research, 42,* 64–81.

O'Gorman, R., Sheldon, K. M., & Wilson, D. S. (2008). For the good of the group? Exploring group-level evolutionary adaptations using multilevel selection theory. *Group Dynamics: Theory, Research, and Practice, 12,* 17–26.

O'Leary-Kelly, A. M., Bowes-Sperry, L., Bates, C. A., & Lean, E. R. (2009). Sexual harassment at work: A decade (plus) of progress. *Journal of Management, 35,* 503–536.

O'Leary, A., & Wolitski, R. J. (2009). Moral agency and the sexual transmission of HIV. *Psychological Bulletin, 135*(3): 478–494.

O'Leary, K. D., & Smith, D. A. (1991). Marital interaction. *Annual Review of Psychology, 42,* 191–212.

O'Mara, E. M., McNulty, J. K., & Karney, B. R. (2011). Positively biased appraisals in everyday life: When do they benefit mental health and when do they harm it? *Journal of Personality and Social Psychology, 101,* 415–432.

O'Mara, S. (2009). Torturing the brain. *Trends in the Cognitive Sciences, 13,* 497–500.

O'Neil, K. M., Patry, M. W., & Penrod, S. D. (2004). Exploring the effects of attitudes toward the death penalty on capital sentencing verdicts. *Psychology, Public Policy, and Law, 10,* 443–470.

O'Neill, A. M., Green, M., & Cuadros, P. (1996, September 2). *People,* 72.

Oetzel, J., Garcia, A. J., & Ting-Toomey, S. (2008). An analysis of the relationships among face concerns and facework behaviors in perceived conflict situations: A four-culture investigation. *International Journal of Conflict Management, 19,* 382–403.

Ogilvy, D. (1985). *Ogilvy on advertising.* New York: Vintage Books.

Olczak, P. V., Kaplan, M. F., & Penrod, S. (1991). Attorneys' lay psychology and its effectiveness in selecting jurors: Three empirical studies. *Journal of Social Behavior and Personality, 6,* 431–452.

Oleson, E., (2009, July 9). A defibrillator in every building; Pappases want devices for public. *Telegram & Gazette* (Worcester, MA), p. 3.

Oliver, M. G., & Hyde, J. S. (1993). Gender differences in sexuality: A meta-analysis. *Psychological Bulletin, 114,* 29–51.

Olson, J. M., Vernon, P. A., Harris, J. A., & Jang, K. L. (2001). The heritability of attitudes: A study of twins. *Journal of Personality and Social Psychology, 80,* 845–860.

Olson, M. A., & Fazio, R. H. (2001). Implicit attitude formation through classical conditioning. *Psychological Science, 12,* 413–417.

Olson, M. A., & Fazio, R. H. (2006). Reducing automatically activated racial prejudice through implicit evaluative conditioning. *Personality and Social Psychology Bulletin, 32,* 421–433.

Olweus, D. (2004). The Olweus Bullying Prevention Programme: Design and implementation issues and a new national initiative in Norway. In P. K. Smith, D. Pepler, & K. Rigby (Eds.), *Bullying in schools: How successful can interventions be?* (pp. 13–36). New York: Cambridge University Press.

Olweus, D., & Limber, S. P. (2010). Bullying in school: Evaluation and dissemination of the Olweus Bullying Prevention Program. *American Journal of Orthopsychiatry, 80,* 124–134.

Omarzu, J. (2000). A disclosure decision model: Determining how and when individuals will self-disclose. *Personality and Social Psychology Review, 4,* 174–185.

Omoto, A. M., & Snyder, M. (1995). Sustained helping without obligation: Motivation, longevity of service, and perceived attitude change among AIDS volunteers. *Journal of Personality and Social Psychology, 68,* 671–686.

Omoto, A. M., Malsch, A. M., & Barraza, J. A. (2009). Compassionate acts: Motivations for and correlates of volunteerism among older adults. In B. Fehr, S. Sprecher, & L. G. Underwood (Eds.), *The science of compassionate love: Theory, research, and applications.* Malden, MA: Wiley-Blackwell.

Ones, D. S., Viswesvaran, C., & Schmidt, F. L. (1993). Comprehensive meta-analysis of integrity test validities: Findings and implications for personnel selection and theories of job performance. *Journal of Applied Psychology, 78,* 679–703.

Orenstein, P. (1994). *Schoolgirls: Young women, self-esteem, and the confidence gap.* New York: Anchor Books.

Orobio de Castro, B., Veerman, J. W., Koops, W., Bosch, J. D., & Monshouwer, H. J. (2002). Hostile attribution of intent and aggressive behavior: A meta-analysis. *Child Development, 73,* 916–934.

Orwell, G. (1942). Looking back on the Spanish War. In S. Orwell & I. Angus (Eds.), *The collected essays, journalism and letters of George Orwell: Vol. 2. My country right or left, 1940–1943* (pp. 249–267). New York: Harcourt, Brace & World.

Osborn, A. F. (1953). *Applied imagination.* New York: Scribner.

Osgood, C. E. (1962). *An alternative to war or surrender.* Urbana: University of Illinois Press.

Oshri, I., van Fenema, P., & Kotlarsky, J. (2008). Knowledge transfer in globally distributed teams: The role of transactive memory. *Information Systems Journal, 18,* 593–616.

Osterman, L. L., & Brown, R. P. (2011). Culture of honor and violence against the self. *Personality and Social Psychology Bulletin, 37,* 1611–1623.

Oxley, D. R., Smith, K., Alford, J., Hibbing, M., Miller, J., Scalora, M., Hatemi, P., & Hibbing, J. (2008). Political attitudes vary with physiological traits. *Science, 321,* 667–1670.

Oxley, N. L., Dzindolet, M. T., & Paulus, P. B. (1996). The effects of facilitators on the performance of brainstorming groups. *Journal of Social Behavior and Personality, 11,* 633–646.

Oyamot, C. M., Fisher, E. L., Deason, G., & Borgida, E. (2012). Attitudes toward immigrants: The interactive role of the authoritarian predisposition, social norms, and humanitarian values. *Journal of Experimental Social Psychology, 48,* 97–105.

Oyserman, D., & Lee, S. W. (2008). Does culture influence what and how we think? Effects of priming individualism and collectivism. *Psychological Bulletin, 134,* 311–342.

Oyserman, D., Coon, H. M., & Kemmelmeier, M. (2002). Rethinking individualism and collectivism: Evaluation of theoretical assumptions and meta-analyses. *Psychological Bulletin, 128,* 3–72.

Ozer, E. J., Best, S. R., Lipsey, T. L., & Weiss, D. S. (2003). Predictors of post-traumatic stress disorder and symptoms in adults: A meta-analysis. *Psychological Bulletin, 129,* 52–71.

Özgen, E. (2004). Language, learning, and color perception. *Current Directions in Psychological Science, 13,* 95–98.

Packard, V. (1957). *The hidden persuaders.* New York: Pocket Books.

Packer, D. J. (2008). Identifying systematic disobedience in Milgram's obedience experiments. *Perspectives on Psychological Science, 3,* 301–304.

Packer, D. J., & Chasteen, A. L. (2010). Loyal deviance: Testing the normative conflict model of dissent in social groups. *Personality and Social Psychology Bulletin, 36,* 5–18.

Packer, D. J., & Miners, C. H. (2012). At the first sign of trouble or through thick and thin? When nonconformity is and is not disengagement from a group. *Journal of Experimental Social Psychology, 48,* 316–322.

Pagani, L., Tremblay, R. E., Nagin, D., Zoccolillo, M., Vitaro, F., & McDuff, P. (2009). Risk factor models for adolescent verbal and physical aggression toward fathers. *Journal of Family Violence, 24,* 173–182.

Page-Gould, E. (2012). To whom can I turn? Maintenance of positive intergroup relations in the face of intergroup conflict. *Social Psychological and Personality Science, 3,* 462–470.

Page-Gould, E., & Mendoza-Denton, R. (2011). Friendship and social interaction with outgroup members. In L. R. Tropp, & R. K. Mallett (Eds.), *Moving beyond prejudice reduction: Pathways to positive intergroup relations* (pp. 139–158). Washington, DC: American Psychological Association.

Page-Gould, E., Mendoza-Denton, R., & Tropp, L. R. (2008). With a little help from my cross-group friend: Reducing anxiety in intergroup contexts through cross-group friendship. *Journal of Personality and Social Psychology, 95,* 1080–1094.

Page-Gould, E., Mendoza-Denton, R., Alegre, J., & Siy, J. (2010). Understanding the impact of cross-group friendship on interactions with novel outgroup members. *Journal of Personality and Social Psychology, 98,* 775–793.

Pager, D., & Shepherd, H. (2008). The sociology of discrimination: Racial discrimination in employment, housing, credit, and consumer markets. *Annual Review of Sociology, 34,* 181–209.

Paluck, E. L. (2009). Reducing intergroup prejudice and conflict using the media: A field experiment in Rwanda. *Journal of Personality and Social Psychology, 96,* 574–587.

Paluck, E. L. (2011). Peer pressure against prejudice: A high school field experiment examining social network change. *Journal of Experimental Social Psychology, 47,* 350–358.

Paluck, E. L., & Shepherd, H. (2012). The salience of social referents: A field experiment on collective norms and harassment behavior in a school social network. *Journal of Personality and Social Psychology.*

Pancevski, B. (2012). Breivik trial exposes mass killer as a lonely loser addicted to tall tales and screen games. *The Australian,* April 24, p. 9.

Panee, C. D., & Ballard, M. E. (2002). High versus low aggressive priming during video-game training: Effects on violent action during game play, hostility, heart rate, and blood pressure. *Journal of Applied Social Psychology, 32,* 2458–2474.

Parducci, A. (1995). *Happiness, pleasure, and judgment: The contextual theory and its applications.* Mahwah, NJ: Erlbaum.

Park, B. (1986). A method for studying the development of impressions of real people. *Journal of Personality and Social Psychology, 51,* 907–917.

Park, S., & Catrambone, R. (2007). Social facilitation effects of virtual humans. *Human Factors, 49,* 1054–1060.

Parker, C. P., Baltes, B. B., & Christiansen, N. D. (1997). Support for affirmative action, justice perceptions, and work attitudes: A study of gender and racial-ethnic group differences. *Journal of Applied Psychology, 82,* 376–389.

Parks, A. C., Della Porta, M. D., Pierce, R. S., Zilca, R., & Lyubomirsky, S. (in press). Pursuing happiness in everyday life: The characteristics and behaviors of online happiness seekers. *Emotion.*

Parsons, C. A., Sulaeman, J., Yates, M. C., & Hamermesh, D. S. (2009). *Strike three: Discrimination, incentives, and evaluation.* University of North Carolina.

Parsons, H. M. (1974). What happened at Hawthorne? *Science, 183,* 922–932.

Partridge, A., & Eldridge, W. B. (1974). *The second circuit sentencing study: A report to the judges of the second circuit.* Washington, DC: Federal Judicial Center.

Pascoe, E. A., & Smart Richman, L. (2009). Perceived discrimination and health: A meta-analytic review. *Psychological Bulletin, 135,* 531–554.

Paterson, T. (2012). Psychotic or not? The experts are still divided; Tony Paterson explained what we've learnt about the man who killed 77 people. *The Independent (London),* June 23, p. 24.

Patzer, G. L. (2006). *The power and paradox of physical attractiveness.* Boca Raton, FL: Brown Walker Press.

Pauletti, R. E., Menon, M., Menon, M., Tobin, D. D., & Perry, D. G. (2012). Narcissism and adjustment in preadolescence. *Child Development, 83,* 831–837.

Paulhus, D. L. (1998). Interpersonal and intrapsychic adaptiveness of trait self-enhancement: A mixed blessing? *Journal of Personality and Social Psychology, 74,* 1197–1208.

Paulus, P. B. (1988). *Prison crowding: A psychological perspective.* New York: Springer-Verlag.

Paulus, P. B., & Brown, V. R. (2007). Toward more creative and innovative group idea generation: A cognitive-social-motivational perspective of brainstorming. *Social and Personality Psychology Compass, 1,* 248–265.

Paulus, P. B., Nakui, T., Putman, V. L., & Brown, V. (2006). Effects of task instructions and brief breaks on brainstorming. *Group Dynamics: Theory, Research, and Practice, 10,* 206–219.

Pavitt, C. (1994). Another view of group polarizing: The "reasons for" one-sided oral argumentation. *Communication Research, 21,* 625–642.

Pavlov, I. P. (1927). *Conditioned Reflexes:An investigation of the physiological activity of the cerebral cortex.* Translated and edited by G. V. Anrep. London: Oxford University Press.

Pavot, W., & Diener, E. (1993). Review of the Satisfaction with Life Scale. *Psychological Assessment, 5,* 164–172.

Pawlowski, B., Dunbar, R. I. M., & Lipowicz, A. (2000). Evolutionary fitness: Tall men have more reproductive success. *Nature, 403,* 156.

Payne, B. (2001). Prejudice and perception: The role of automatic and controlled processes in misperceiving a weapon. *Journal of Personality and Social Psychology, 81,* 181–192.

Payne, B., & Iannuzzi, J. (2012). Automatic and controlled decision making: A process dissociation perspective. In J. I. Krueger (Ed.) , *Social judgment and decision making* (pp. 41–58). New York: Psychology Press.

Pazda, A. D., Elliot, A. J., & Greitemeyer, T. (2012). Sexy red: Perceived sexual receptivity mediates the red-attraction relation in men viewing woman. *Journal of Experimental Social Psychology, 48,* 787–790.

Pedersen, W. C., Bushman, B. J., Vasquez, E. A., & Miller, N. (2008). Kicking the (barking) dog effect: The moderating role of target attributes on triggered displaced aggression. *Personality and Social Psychology Bulletin, 34,* 1382–1395.

Pedersen, W. C., Denson, T. F., Goss, R., Vasquez, E. A., Kelley, N. J., & Miller, N. (2011). The impact of rumination on aggressive thoughts, feelings, arousal, and behaviour. *British Journal of Social Psychology, 50,* 281–301.

Pedersen, W. C., Miller, L. C., Putch-Bhagavatula, A. D., & Yang, Y. (2002). Evolved sex differences in the number of partners desired? The long and the short of it. *Psychological Science, 13,* 157–161.

Pelham, B. W. (1995). Self-investment and self-esteem: Evidence for a Jamesian model of self-worth. *Journal of Personality and Social Psychology, 69,* 1141–1150.

Pelham, B. W., Carvallo, M., & Jones, J. T. (2005). Implicit egotism. *Current Directions in Psychological Science, 14,* 106–110.

Pelham, B. W., Mirenberg, M. C., & Jones, J. T. (2002). Why Susie sells seashells by the seashore: Implicit egotism and major life decisions. *Journal of Personality and Social Psychology, 82,* 469–487.

Peng, K., & Nisbett, R. E. (1999). Culture, dialectics, and reasoning about contradiction. *American Psychologist, 54,* 741–754.

Pennebaker, J. W. (1997). Writing about emotional experiences as a therapeutic process. *Psychological Science, 8,* 162–166.

Pennebaker, J. W., Dyer, M. A., Caulkins, R. J., Litowitz, D. L., Ackreman, P. L., Anderson, D. B., & McGraw, K. M. (1979). Don't the girls get prettier at closing time: A country and western application to psychology. *Personality and Social Psychology Bulletin, 5,* 122–125.

Penner, L. A. (2004). Volunteerism and social problems: Making things better or worse? *Journal of Social Issues, 60,* 645–666.

Penner, L. A., Dovidio, J. F., Piliavin, J. A., & Schroeder, D. A. (2005). Prosocial behavior: Multiple perspectives. *Annual Review of Psychology, 56,* 365–392.

Penner, L. A., Dovidio, J. F., West, T. V., Gaertner, S. L., Albrecht, T. L., Dailey, R. K., & Markova, T. (2010). Aversive racism and medical interactions with Black patients: A field study. *Journal of Experimental Social Psychology, 46,* 436–440.

Pennington, N., & Hastie, R. (1992). Explaining the evidence: Tests of the story model for juror decision making. *Journal of Personality and Social Psychology, 62,* 189–206.

Penrod, S. D., & Cutler, B. (1995). Witness confidence and witness accuracy: Assessing their forensic relation. *Psychology, Public Policy, and Law, 1,* 817–845.

*People.* (1996, December 30). She gave a helping hand to a distant—very distant—relation. p. 66.

Peplau, L. A. (2003). Human sexuality: How do men and women differ? *Current Directions in Psychological Science, 12,* 37–40.

Peplau, L. A., & Fingerhut, A. W. (2007). The close relationships of lesbians and gay men. *Annual Review of Psychology, 58,* 405–424.

Peplau, L. A., & Perlman, D. (Eds.). (1982). *Loneliness: A sourcebook of current theory, research, and therapy.* New York: Wiley.

Peplau, L. A., Garnets, L. D., Spalding, L. R., Conley, T. D., & Veniegas, R. C. (1998). A critique of Bem's "Exotic becomes erotic" theory of sexual orientation. *Psychological Review, 105,* 387–394.

Pepler, D., Craig, W., Yuile, A., & Connolly, J. (2004). Girls who bully: A developmental and relational perspective. In M. Putallaz & K. L. Bierman (Eds.), *Aggression, antisocial behavior, and violence among girls: A developmental perspective* (pp. 90–109). New York: Guilford.

Peralta, E. (2012). Southern Miss band hurls "Where's your green card?" chant at Latino player. http://www.npr.org/blogs/thetwo-way/2012/03/15/148703015/southern-miss-band-hurls-wheres-your-green-card-chant-at-latino-player.

Peretz, H., & Fried, Y. (2012). National cultures, performance appraisal practices, and organizational absenteeism and turnover: A study across 21 countries. *Journal of Applied Psychology, 97,* 448–459.

Perillo, J. T., & Kassin , S. M. (2011). Inside interrogation: The lie, the bluff, and false confessions. *Law and Human Behavior, 35,* 327–337.

Perilloux, C., Duntley, J. D., & Buss, D. M. (2012). The costs of rape. *Archives of Sexual Behavior.*

Perilloux, C., Easton, J. A., & Buss, D. M. (2012). The misperception of sexual interest. *Psychological Science, 23,* 146–151.

Perkins, S., & Graham-Bermann, S. (2012). Violence exposure and the development of school-related functioning: Mental health, neurocognition, and learning. *Aggression and Violent Behavior, 17,* 89–98.

Perloff, R. M. (2010). *The dynamics of persuasion: Communication and attitudes in the 21st century* (4th edition). New York: Taylor & Francis.

Persky, V. W., Kempthorne-Rawson, J., & Shekelle, R. B. (1987). Personality and risk of cancer: 20-year follow-up of the Western Electric Study. *Psychosomatic Medicine, 49,* 435–449.

Peruche, B. M., & Plant, E. A. (2006). The correlates of law enforcement officers' automatic and controlled race-based responses to criminal suspects. *Basic and Applied Social Psychology, 28,* 193–199.

Peters, T. J., & Waterman, R. H. (1982). *In search of excellence: Lessons from America's best-run companies.* New York: Warner.

Peterson, C. (2000). The future of optimism. *American Psychologist, 55,* 44–55.

Peterson, K. S. (1997, November 3). For today's teens, race "not an issue anymore." *USA Today,* p. 1A.

Peterson, R. S., Owens, P. D., Tetlock, P. E., Fan, E. T., & Martorana, P. (1998). Group dynamics in top management teams: Groupthink, vigilance, and alternative models of organizational failure and success. *Organizational Behavior and Human Decision Processes, 73,* 272–305.

Petrie, K. J., Booth, R. J., & Pennebaker, J. W. (1998). The immunological effects of thought suppression. *Journal of Personality and Social Psychology, 75,* 1264–1272.

Pettersen, N., & Durivage, A. (2008). *The structured interview.* Quebec: Presses de l'Université du Québec.

Pettigrew, T. F., & Tropp, L. R. (2000). Does intergroup contact reduce prejudice: Recent meta-analytic findings. In S. Oskamp (Ed.), *Reducing prejudice and discrimination: The Claremont Symposium on Applied Social Psychology* (pp. 93–114). Mahwah, NJ: Erlbaum.

Pettigrew, T. F., & Tropp, L. R. (2006). A meta-analytic test of intergroup contact theory. *Journal of Personality and Social Psychology, 90,* 751–783.

Pettigrew, T. F., & Tropp, L. R. (2008). How does intergroup contact reduce prejudice? Meta-analytic tests of three mediators. *European Journal of Social Psychology, 38,* 922–934.

Pettigrew, T. F., Christ, O., Wagner, U., van Dick, R., Zick, A., & Meertens, R. W. (2008). Relative deprivation and intergroup prejudice. *Journal of Social Issues, 64,* 385–401.

Pettigrew, T. F., Tropp, L. R., Wagner, U., & Christ, O. (2011). Recent advances in intergroup contact theory. *International Journal of Intercultural Relations, 35,* 271–280.

Pettit, N. C., & Sivanathan, N. (2011). The plastic trap: Self-threat drives credit usage and status consumption. *Social Psychological and Personality Science, 2,* 146–153.

Petty, R. E., & Cacioppo, J. T. (1983). The role of bodily responses in attitude measurement and change. In J. Cacioppo & R. Petty (Eds.), *Social psychophysiology: A sourcebook* (pp. 51–101). New York: Guilford.

Petty, R. E., & Cacioppo, J. T. (1984). The effects of involvement on response to argument quantity and quality: Central and peripheral routes to persuasion. *Journal of Personality and Social Psychology, 46,* 69–81.

Petty, R. E., & Cacioppo, J. T. (1986). *Communication and persuasion: Central and peripheral routes to attitude change.* New York: Springer-Verlag.

Petty, R. E., & Fazio, R. H., & Brinol, P. (Eds.). (2009). *Attitudes: Insights from the new implicit measures.* New York: Psychology Press.

Petty, R. E., & Krosnick, J. A. (Eds.). (1995). *Attitude strength: Antecedents and consequences.* Mahwah, NJ: Erlbaum.

Petty, R. E., & Wegener, D. T. (1998). Attitude change: Multiple roles for persuasion variables. In D. Gilbert, S. Fiske, & G. Lindzey (Eds.), *The handbook of social psychology* (4th ed., pp. 323–390). New York: McGraw-Hill.

Petty, R. E., Cacioppo, J. T., & Goldman, R. (1981). Personal involvement as a determinant of argument-based persuasion. *Journal of Personality and Social Psychology, 41,* 847–855.

Petty, R. E., Schumann, D. W., Richman, S. A., & Strathman, A. J. (1993). Positive mood and persuasion: Different roles for affect under high- and low-elaboration conditions. *Journal of Personality and Social Psychology, 64,* 5–20.

Petty, R. E., Wegener, D. T., & Fabrigar, L. R. (1997). Attitudes and attitude change. *Annual Review of Psychology, 48,* 609–647.

Petty, R. E., Wegener, D. T., & White, P. (1998). Flexible correction processes in persuasion. *Social Cognition, 16,* 93–113.

Pew Research Center for People & the Press. (2009). Trends in political values and core attitudes: 1987–2009. Available at http://people-press. org/report/?reportid=312.

Pew Research Center for People and the Press. (2012). *American values survey.* http://www.people-press.org/values-questions/.

Pfau, M., Kenski, H. C., Nitz, M., & Sorenson, J. (1990). Efficacy of inoculation strategies in promoting resistance to political attack messages: Application to direct mail. *Communication Monographs, 57,* 25–43.

Pfetsch, J., Steffgen, G., Gollwitzer, M., & Ittel, A. (2011). Prevention of aggression in schools through a bystander intervention training. *International Journal of Developmental Science, 5,* 139–149.

Pfetsch, J., Steffgen, G., Gollwitzer, M., & Ittel, A. (2011). Prevention of aggression in schools through a bystander intervention training. *International Journal of Developmental Science, 5,* 139–149.

Phelan, J. E., Moss-Racusin, C. A., & Rudman, L. A. (2008). Competent yet out in the cold: Shifting criteria for hiring reflect backlash toward agentic women. *Psychology of Women Quarterly, 32,* 406–413.

Phelps, E. A., O'Connor, K. J., Cunningham, W. A., Funayama, E. S., Gatenby, J. C., Gore, J. C., & Banaji, M. R. (2000). Performance on indirect measures of race evaluation predicts amygdala activation. *Journal of Cognitive Neuroscience, 12,* 729–738.

Phillips, A. G., & Silvia, P. J. (2005). Self-awareness and the emotional consequences of self-discrepancies. *Personality and Social Psychology Bulletin, 31,* 703–713.

Phillips, A. P., & Dipboye, R. L. (1989). Correlational tests of predictions from a process model of the interview. *Journal of Applied Psychology, 74,* 41–52.

Phillips, K. W. (Ed.). (2008). *Diversity and groups.* Stamford, CT: JAI Press.

Pickel, K. L. (1999). The influence of context on the "weapon focus" effect. *Law and Human Behavior, 23,* 299–311.

Piferi, R. L., Jobe, R. L., Jones, W. H., & Gaines, S. O., Jr. (2006). Giving to others during national tragedy: The effects of altruistic and egoistic motivations on long-term giving. *Journal of Social and Personal Relationships, 23,* 171–184.

Piliavin, J. A. (2003). Doing well by doing good: Benefits for the benefactor. In C. L. M. Keyes & J. Haidt (Eds.), *Flourishing: Positive psychology and the life well-lived* (pp. 227–247). Washington, DC: American Psychological Association.

Piliavin, J. A., & Callero, P. L. (1991). *Giving blood: The development of an altruistic identity.* Baltimore: Johns Hopkins.

Piliavin, J. A., & Siegl, E. (2008). Health benefits of volunteering in the Wisconsin Longitudinal Study. *Journal of Health and Social Behavior, 48,* 450–464.

Piliavin, J. A., Dovidio, J. F., Gaertner, S. L., & Clark, R. D., III. (1981). *Emergency intervention.* New York: Academic Press.

Pillemer, D. B., Picariello, M. L., Law, A. B., & Reichman, J. S. (1996). Memories of college: The importance of educational episodes. In D. C. Rubin (Ed.), *Remembering our past: Studies in autobiographical memory* (pp. 318–337). New York: Cambridge University Press.

Pinderhughes, E. E., Dodge, K. A., Bates, J. E.. Pettit, G. S., & Zelli, A. (2000). Discipline responses: Influences of parents' socioeconomic status, ethnicity, beliefs about parenting, stress, and cognitive-emotional processes. *Journal of Family Psychology, 14,* 380–400.

Pinel, E. C., & Long, A. E. (2012). When I's meet: Sharing subjective experience with someone from the outgroup. *Personality and Social Psychology Bulletin, 38,* 296–307.

Pinel, E. C., Long, A. E., Landau, M. J., Alexander, K., & Pyszczynski, T. (2006). Seeing I to I: A pathway to interpersonal connectedness. *Journal of Personality and Social Psychology, 90,* 243–257.

Pinker, S. (2011). *The better angels of our nature: Why violence has declined.* New York: Viking.

Pinker, S. (2012). The false allure of group selection. *Edge,* Aug 6. http://edge.org/conversation/the-false-allure-of-group-selection#ednref9.

Pinter, B., & Greenwald, A. G. (2011). A comparison of minimal group induction procedures. *Group Processes & Intergroup Relations, 14,* 81–98.

Pinter, B., & Wildschut, T. (2012). Self-interest masquerading as ingroup beneficence: Altruistic rationalization and interindividual–intergroup discontinuity. *Small Group Research, 43*(1), 105–123.

Pittman, T. S. (1975). Attribution of arousal as a mediator of dissonance reduction. *Journal of Experimental Social Psychology, 11,* 53–63.

Pittman, T. S., & Heller, J. F. (1987). Social motivation. *Annual Review of Psychology, 38,* 461–489.

Plaks, J. E., & Higgins, E. T. (2000). Pragmatic use of stereotyping in teamwork: Social loafing and compensation as a function of inferred partner-situation fit. *Journal of Personality and Social Psychology, 79,* 962–974.

Plaks, J. E., Malahy, L., Sedlins, M., & Shoda, Y. (2012). Folk beliefs about human genetic variation predict discrete versus continuous racial categorization and evaluative bias. *Social Psychological and Personality Science, 3,* 31–39.

Plant, E. A., & Butz, D. A. (2006). The causes and consequences of an avoidance-focus for interracial interactions. *Personality and Social Psychology Bulletin, 32,* 833–846.

Plant, E. A., & Devine, P. G. (1998). Internal and external motivation to respond without prejudice. *Journal of Personality and Social Psychology, 75,* 811–832.

Plant, E. A., & Devine, P. G. (2009). The active control of prejudice: Unpacking the intentions guiding control efforts. *Journal of Personality and Social Psychology, 96,* 640–652.

Plant, E. A., Peruche, B. M., & Butz, D. A. (2005). Eliminating automatic racial bias: Making race non-diagnostic for responses to criminal suspects. *Journal of Experimental Social Psychology, 41,* 141–156.

Plante, T. G., & Thoresen, C. E. (Eds.). (2007). *Spirit, science, and health: How the spiritual mind fuels physical wellness.* Westport, CT: Praeger.

Platek, S. M., Wathne, K., Tierney, N. G., & Thomson, J. W. (2008). Neural correlates of self-face recognition: An effect-location meta-analysis. *Brain Research, 1232,* 173–184.

Platz, S. J., & Hosch, H. M. (1988). Cross-racial/ethnic eyewitness identification: A field study. *Journal of Applied Social Psychology, 18,* 972–984.

Plaut, V. C., Garnett, F. G., Buffardi, L. E., & Sanchez-Burks, J. (2011). "What about me?" Perceptions of exclusion and Whites' reactions to multiculturalism. *Journal of Personality and Social Psychology, 101,* 337–353.

Plaut, V. C., Thomas, K. M., & Goren, M. J. (2009). Is multiculturalism or color blindness better for minorities? *Psychological Science, 20,* 444–446.

Plotnik, J. M., de Waal, F. B. M., & Reiss, D. (2006). Self-recognition in an Asian elephant. *Proceedings of the National Academy of Sciences, 103,* 17053–17057.

Polivy, J., Garner, D. M., & Garfinkel, P. E. (1986). Causes and consequences of the current preference for thin female physiques. In C. P. Herman, M. P. Zanna, & E. T. Higgins (Eds.), *The Ontario symposium: Vol. 3. Physical appearance, stigma, and social behavior* (pp. 89–112). Hillsdale, NJ: Erlbaum.

Pontari, B. A., & Schlenker, B. R. (2000). The influence of cognitive load on self-presentation: Can cognitive busyness help as well as harm social performance? *Journal of Personality and Social Psychology, 78,* 1092–1108.

Poole, D. A., & White, L. T. (1991). Effects of question repetition on the eyewitness testimony of children and adults. *Developmental Psychology, 27,* 975–986.

Poole, D. A., Bruck, M., & Pipe, M. E. (2011). Forensic interviewing aids: Do props help children answer questions about touching? *Current Directions in Psychological Science, 20,* 11–15.

Poole, D., & Lindsay, D. S. (2001). Children's eyewitness reports after exposure to misinformation from parents. *Journal of Experimental Psychology: Applied, 7,* 27–50.

Pornpitakpan, C. (2004). The persuasiveness of source credibility: A critical review of five decades' evidence. *Journal of Applied Social Psychology, 34,* 243–281.

Porter, D. P., & Smith, V. L. (2003). Stock market bubbles in the laboratory. *Journal of Behavioral Finance, 4,* 7–20.

Posavac, H. D., Posavac, S. S., & Posavac, E. J. (1998). Exposure to media images of female attractiveness and concern with body weight among young women. *Sex Roles, 38,* 187–201.

Post, J. (2011). Crimes of obedience: "Groupthink" at Abu Ghraib. *International Journal of Group Psychotherapy, 61,* 49–66.

Post, S. G. (2005). Altruism, happiness, and health: It's good to be good. *International Journal of Behavioral Medicine, 12,* 66–77.

Postmes, T., & Branscombe, N. R. (2010). *Rediscovering social identity.* New York: Psychology Press.

Postmes, T., & Spears, R. (1998). Deindividuation and antinormative behavior: A meta-analysis. *Psychological Bulletin, 123,* 238–259.

Postmes, T., Spears, R., & Cihangir, S. (2001). Quality of decision making and group norms. *Journal of Personality and Social Psychology, 80,* 918–930.

Povinelli, D. J., Gallup, G. G., Jr., Eddy, T. J., Bierschwale, D. T., Engstrom, M. C., Perilloux, H. K., & Toxopeus, I. B. (1997). Chimpanzees recognize themselves in mirrors. *Animal Behaviour, 53,* 1083–1088.

Powell, L. H., Shahabi, L., & Thoresen, C. E. (2003). Religion and spirituality: Linkages to physical health. *American Psychologist, 58,* 36–52.

Powers, S. I., Pietromonaco, P. R., Gunlicks, M., & Sayer, A. (2006). Dating couples' attachment styles and patterns of cortisol reactivity and recovery in response to a relationship conflict. *Journal of Personality and Social Psychology, 90,* 613–628.

Pratkanis, A. R. (1992). The cargo-cult science of subliminal persuasion. *Skeptical Inquirer, 16,* 260–272.

Pratkanis, A. R., & Turner, M. E. (1994). Nine principles of successful affirmative action: Mr. Branch Rickey, Mr. Jackie Robinson, and the integration of baseball. *Nine: A Journal of Baseball History and Social Policy Perspectives, 3,* 36–65.

Pratkanis, A. R., & Turner, M. E. (1996). The proactive removal of discriminatory barriers: Affirmative action as effective help. *Journal of Social Issues, 52,* 111–132.

Pratkanis, A. R., Greenwald, A. G., Leippe, M. R., & Baumgardner, M. H. (1988). In search of reliable persuasion effects: III. The sleeper effect is dead. Long live the sleeper effect. *Journal of Personality and Social Psychology, 54,* 203–218.

Pratt, T. C., & Cullen, F. T. (2000). The empirical status of Gottfredson and Hirschi's general theory of crime: A meta-analysis. *Criminology, 38,* 931–964.

Pratto, F., & John, O. P. (1991). Automatic vigilance: The attention-grabbing power of negative social information. *Journal of Personality and Social Psychology, 61,* 380–391.

Pratto, F., Stallworth, L. M., Sidanius, J., & Sieres, B. (1997). The gender gap in occupational attainment: A social dominance approach. *Journal of Personality and Social Psychology, 72,* 37–53.

Prentice-Dunn, S., & Rogers, R. W. (1982). Effects of public and private self-awareness on deindividuation and aggression. *Journal of Personality and Social Psychology, 43,* 503–513.

Prentice-Dunn, S., & Rogers, R. W. (1983). Deindividuation in aggression. In R. G. Geen & E. I. Donnerstein (Eds.), *Aggression: Theoretical and empirical reviews: Vol. 2. Issues in research* (pp. 155–171). New York: Academic Press.

Prentice, D. A., & Carranza, E. (2002). What women should be, shouldn't be, are allowed to be, and don't have to be: The contents of prescriptive gender stereotypes. *Psychology of Women Quarterly, 26,* 269–281.

Prentice, D. A., & Miller, D. T. (1996). Pluralistic ignorance and the perpetuation of social norms by unwitting actors. *Advances in Experimental Social Psychology, 28,* 161–209.

President's Commission on Law Enforcement and Administration of Justice. (1967). *The challenge of crime in a free society.* Washington, DC: U.S. Government Printing Office.

Presidential Commission on the Space Shuttle Challenger Accident. (1986). *Report of the Presidential Commission on the Space Shuttle Challenger Accident.* Washington, DC: U.S. Government Printing Office.

Pressman, S. D., & Cohen, S. (2012). Positive emotion word use and longevity in famous deceased psychologists. *Health Psychology, 31,* 297–305.

Pressman, S. D., Cohen, S., Miller, G. E., Barkin, A., Rabin, B. S., & Treanor, J. J. (2005). Loneliness, social network size, and immune response to influenza vaccination in college freshmen. *Health Psychology, 24,* 297–306.

Prestwich, A., Conner, M. T., Lawton, R. J., Ward, J. K., Ayres, K., & McEachan, R. C. (2012). Randomized controlled trial of collaborative implementation intentions targeting working adults' physical activity. *Health Psychology, 31,* 486–495.

Price, M. E. (2008). The resurrection of group selection as a theory of human cooperation. *Social Justice Research, 21,* 228–240.

Prichard, J. S., & Ashleigh, M. J. (2007). The effects of team-skills training on transactive memory and performance. *Small Group Research, 38,* 696–726.

Priester, J. R., & Petty, R. E. (1995). Source attributions and persuasion: Perceived honesty as a determinant of message scrutiny. *Personality and Social Psychology Bulletin, 21,* 637–654.

Priester, J. R., Cacioppo, J. T., & Petty, R. E. (1996). The influence of motor processes on attitudes toward novel versus familiar semantic stimuli. *Personality and Social Psychology Bulletin, 22,* 442–447.

Principe, G. F., & Ceci, S. J. (2002). "I saw it with my own ears": The effects of peer conversations on preschoolers' reports of nonexperienced events. *Journal of Experimental Child Psychology, 83,* 1–25.

Principe, G. F., Ornstein, P. A., Baker-Ward, L., & Gordon, B. N. (2000). The effects of intervening experiences on children's memory for a physical examination. *Applied Cognitive Psychology 14,* 59–80.

Prioleau, L., Murdock, M., & Brody, N. (1983). An analysis of psychotherapy versus placebo studies. *Behavioral and Brain Sciences, 6,* 275–310.

Prokosch, M., Coss, R., Scheib, J., & Blozis, S. (2009). Intelligence and mate choice: Intelligent men are always appealing. *Evolution and Human Behavior, 30,* 11–20.

Pronin, E., Berger, J., & Molouki, S. (2007). Alone in a crowd of sheep: Asymmetric perceptions of conformity and their roots in an introspection illusion. *Journal of Personality and Social Psychology, 92,* 585–595.

Pronin, E., Gilovich, T., & Ross, L. (2004). Objectivity in the eye of the beholder: Divergent perceptions of bias in self versus others. *Psychological Review, 111,* 781–799.

Pronin, E., Wegner, D. M., McCarthy, K., & Rodriguez, S. (2006). Everyday magical powers: The role of apparent mental causation in the overestimation of personal influence. *Journal of Personality and Social Psychology, 91,* 218–231.

Proto-Campise, L., Belknap, J., & Wooldredge, J. (1998). High school students' adherence to rape myths and the effectiveness of high school rape-awareness programs. *Violence Against Women, 4,* 308–328.

Pruetz, J. D., & Lindshield, S. (2012). Plant-food and tool transfer among savanna chimpanzees at Fongoli, Senegal. *Primates, 53,* 133–145.

Pruitt, D. G. (1998). Social conflict. In D. T. Gilbert, S. T. Fiske, & G. Lindzey (Eds.), *The handbook of social psychology* (4th ed., Vol. 2, pp. 410–503). New York: McGraw-Hill.

Pryor, J. B., & Merluzzi, T. V. (1985). The role of expertise in processing social interaction scripts. *Journal of Experimental Social Psychology, 21,* 362–379.

Pryor, J. B., Reeder, G. D., & Monroe, A. E. (2012). The infection of bad company: Stigma by association. *Journal of Personality and Social Psychology, 102,* 224–241.

Purdie-Vaughns, V., Steele, C. M., Davies, P. G., Ditlmann, R., & Crosby, J. R. (2008). Social identity contingencies: How diversity cues signal threat or safety for African Americans in mainstream institutions. *Journal of Personality and Social Psychology, 94,* 615–630.

Purvanova, R. K., & Muros, J. P. (2010). Gender differences in burnout: A meta-analysis. *Journal of Vocational Behavior, 77,* 168–185.

Putnam, R. D. (2001). *Bowling alone: The collapse and revival of American community.* New York: Simon & Schuster.

Putnam, R. D. (2006, July 3). You gotta have friends. *Time,* 36.

Pyszczynski, T. A., Solomon, S., & Greenberg, J. (2002). *In the wake of 9/11: The psychology of terror.* Washington, DC: American Psychological Association.

Pyszczynski, T., & Greenberg, J. (1987). Self-regulatory preservation and the depressive self-focusing style: A self-awareness theory of reactive depression. *Psychological Bulletin, 201,* 122–138.

Pyszczynski, T., & Greenberg, J. (1992). *Hanging on and letting go.* New York: Springer-Verlag.

Pyszczynski, T., Greenberg, J., Solomon, S., Arndt, J., & Schimel, J. (2004). Why do people need self-esteem? A theoretical and empirical review. *Psychological Bulletin, 130,* 435–468.

Pyszczynski, T., Henthorn, C., Motyl, M., & Gerow, K. (2010). Is Obama the Anti-Christ? Racial priming, extreme criticisms of Barack Obama, and attitudes toward the 2008 US presidential candidates. *Journal of Experimental Social Psychology, 46,* 863–866.

Qualter, T. H. (1962). *Propaganda and psychological warfare.* New York: Random House.

Quigley, B. M., & Leonard, K. E. (2006). Alcohol expectancies and intoxicated aggression. *Aggression and Violent Behavior, 11,* 484–496.

Quinn, D. M., Kahng, S. K., & Crocker, J. (2004). Discreditable: Stigma effects of revealing a mental illness history on test performance. *Personality and Social Psychology Bulletin, 30,* 803–815.

Raaijmakers, M. A. J., Smidts, D. P., Sergeant, J. A., Maassen, G. H., Posthumus, J. A., van Engeland, H., et al. (2008). Executive functions in preschool children with aggressive behavior: Impairments in inhibitory control. *Journal of Abnormal Child Psychology, 36,* 1097–1107.

Radel, R., & Clement-Guillotin, C. (2012). Evidence of motivational influences in early visual perception: Hunger modulates conscious access. *Psychological Science, 23,* 232–234.

Ragins, B. R., & Sundstrom, E. (1989). Gender and power in organizations: A longitudinal perspective. *Psychological Bulletin, 105,* 51–88.

Raine, A. (2008). From genes to brain to antisocial behavior. *Current Directions in Psychological Science, 17,* 323–328.

Rains, S. A. (2005). Leveling the organizational playing field—virtually: A meta-analysis of experimental research assessing the impact of group support system use on member influence behaviors. *Communication Research, 32,* 193–234.

Rajecki, D. W., Bledsoe, S. B., & Rasmussen, J. L. (1991). Successful personal ads: Gender differences and similarities in offers, stipulations, and outcomes. *Basic and Applied Social Psychology, 12,* 457–469.

Ramírez-Esparza, N., Gosling, S. D., & Pennebaker, J. W. (2008). Paradox lost: Unraveling the puzzle of Simpatía. *Journal of Cross-Cultural Psychology, 39,* 703–715.

Rampell, C. (2011). Commuter Nation. *The New York Times,* September 11, 2011. http://economix.blogs.nytimes.com/2011/09/22/commuter-nation/

Rattan, A., & Ambady, N. (2012). Diversity ideologies and intergroup relations: An examination of colorblindness and multiculturalism. *European Journal of Social Psychology.*

Rattan, A., & Eberhardt, J. L. (2010). The role of social meaning in inattentional blindness: When the gorillas in our midst do not go unseen. *Journal of Experimental Social Psychology, 46,* 1085–1088.

Rattan, A., Levine, C. S., Dweck, C. S., & Eberhardt, J. L. (2012). Race and the fragility of the legal distinction between juveniles and adults. *PLoS ONE, 7,* e36680.

Ray, D. G., Mackie, D. M., Rydell, R. J., & Smith, E. R. (2008). Changing categorization of self can change emotions about outgroups. *Journal of Experimental Social Psychology, 44,* 1210–1213.

Ray, E., & Heyes, C. (2010). Imitation in infancy: The wealth of the stimulus. *Developmental Science,* 1–14.

Ray, O. (2004). How the mind hurts and heals the body. *American Psychologist, 59,* 29–40.

Rayner, R. (2010). Channeling Ike. *The New Yorker,* April 26.

Read, S. J. (1987). Constructing causal scenarios: A knowledge structure approach to causal reasoning. *Journal of Personality and Social Psychology, 52,* 288–302.

Reeder, G. D. (1993). Trait-behavior relations and dispositional inference. *Personality and Social Psychology Bulletin, 19,* 586–593.

Reeder, G. D., & Brewer, M. B. (1979). A schematic model of dispositional attribution in interpersonal perception. *Psychological Review, 86,* 61–79.

Reeder, G. D., Davison, D. M., Gipson, K. L., & Hesson-McInnis, M. S. (2001). Identifying the motivations of African American volunteers working to prevent HIV/AIDS. *AIDS Education and Prevention, 13,* 343–354.

Regan, D. T. (1971). Effects of a favor and liking on compliance. *Journal of Experimental Social Psychology, 7,* 627–639.

Regan, D. T., & Kilduff, M. (1988). Optimism about elections: Dissonance reduction at the ballot box. *Political Psychology, 9,* 101–107.

Regan, P. (2011). *Close relationships.* New York: Routledge.

Regan, P. C., & Berscheid, E. (1997). Gender differences in characteristics desired in a potential sexual and marriage partner. *Journal of Psychology and Human Sexuality, 9,* 25–37.

Regan, P. C., & Berscheid, E. (1999). *Lust: What we know about human sexual desire.* Thousand Oaks, CA: Sage.

Regan, P. C., Kocan, E. R., & Whitlock, T. (1998). Ain't love grand! A prototype analysis of the concept of romantic love. *Journal of Social and Personal Relationships, 15,* 411–420.

Reicher, S. D., & Haslam, S. A. (2006). Rethinking the psychology of tyranny: The BBC prison study. *British Journal of Social Psychology, 45,* 1–40.

Reifman, A. S., Larrick, R. P., & Fein, S. (1991). Temper and temperature on the diamond: The heat-aggression relationship in major-league baseball. *Personality and Social Psychology Bulletin, 17,* 580–585.

Reifman, A., Klein, J. G., & Murphy, S. T. (1989). Self-monitoring and age. *Psychology and Aging, 4,* 245–246.

Riek, B. M., Mania, E. W., Gaertner, S. L., McDonald, S. A., & Lamoreaux, M. J. (2010). Does a common ingroup identity reduce intergroup threat? *Group Processes & Intergroup Relations, 13,* 403–423.

Reinhard, M.-A., Messner, M., & Sporer, S. L. (2006). Explicit persuasive intent and its impact on success at persuasion: The determining roles of attractiveness and likeableness. *Journal of Consumer Psychology, 16,* 249–259.

Reis, H. T., Maniaci, M. R., Caprariello, P. A., Eastwick, P. W., & Finkel, E. J. (2011). Familiarity does indeed promote attraction in live interaction. *Journal of Personality and Social Psychology, 101,* 557–570.

Reisenzein, R. (1983). The Schachter theory of emotion: Two decades later. *Psychological Bulletin, 94,* 239–264.

Reiss, D., & Marino, L. (2001). Mirror self-recognition in the bottlenose dolphin: A case of cognitive convergence. *Proceedings of the National Academy of the Sciences, 98,* 5937–5942.

Remley, A. (1988, October). The great parental value shift: From obedience to independence. *Psychology Today,* 56–59.

Rendell, L., & Whitehead, H. (2001). Culture in whales and dolphins. *Behavioral and Brain Sciences, 24,* 309–382.

Renteln, A. D. (2004). *The cultural defense.* New York: Oxford University Press.

Responsible citizenship. (2002, December 31). *Ottawa Citizen,* p. A14.

Rhatigan, D. L., & Axsom, D. K. (2006). Using the investment model to understand battered women's commitment to abusive relationships. *Journal of Family Violence, 21,* 153–162.

Rhee, E., Uleman, J. S., Lee, H. K., & Roman, R. J. (1995). Spontaneous self-descriptions and ethnic identities in individualistic and collectivistic cultures. *Journal of Personality and Social Psychology, 69,* 142–152.

Rhee, S., & Waldman, I. D. (2011). Genetic and environmental influences on aggression. In P. R. Shaver & M. Mikulincer (Eds.), *Human aggression and violence: Causes, manifestations, and consequences* (pp. 143–163). Washington, DC: American Psychological Association.

Rhodes, G. (2006). The evolutionary psychology of facial beauty. *Annual Review of Psychology, 57,* 199–226.

Rhodes, G., Simmons, L. W., & Peters, M. (2005). Attractiveness and sexual behavior: Does attractiveness enhance mating success? *Evolution and Human Behavior, 26,* 186–201.

Rhodes, G., Sumich, A., & Byatt, G. (1999). Are average facial configurations attractive only because of their symmetry? *Psychological Science, 10,* 52–58.

Rhodes, G., Zebrowitz, L. A., Clark, A., Kalick, S. M., Hightower, A., & McKay, R. (2001). Do facial averageness and symmetry signal health? *Evolution and Human Behavior, 22,* 31–46.

Rhodes, M. G., & Anastasi, J. S. (2012). The own-age bias in face recognition: A meta-analytic and theoretical review. *Psychological Bulletin, 138,* 146–174.

Rhodes, N., & Wood, W. (1992). Self-esteem and intelligence affect influenceability: The mediating role of message reception. *Psychological Bulletin, 111,* 156–171.

Rhodewalt, F. (1990). Self-handicappers: Individual differences in the preference for anticipatory, self-protective acts. In R. L. Higgins, C. R. Synder, & S. Berglas (Eds.), *Self-handicapping: The paradox that isn't* (pp. 69–106). New York: Plenum.

Rhodewalt, F., & Agustsdottir, S. (1986). Effects of self-presentation on the phenomenal self. *Journal of Personality and Social Psychology, 50,* 47–55.

Rhodewalt, F., Sandonmatsu, D. M., Tschanz, B., Feick, D. L., & Waller, A. (1995). Self-handicapping and interpersonal tradeoffs: The effects of claimed self-handicaps on observers' performance evaluations and feedback. *Personality and Social Psychology Bulletin, 21,* 1042–1050.

Rholes, W. S., & Simpson, J. A. (Eds.). (2004). *Adult attachment: Theory, research, and clinical implications.* New York: Guilford.

Richardson, E. G., & Hemenway, D. (2011). Homicide, suicide, and unintentional firearm fatality: Comparing the United States with other high-income countries, 2003. *The Journal of Trauma, 70,* 238–243.

Richardson, M. J., Marsh, K. L., & Schmidt, R. C. (2005). Effects of visual and verbal interaction on unintentional interpersonal coordination. *Journal of Experimental Psychology: Human Perception and Performance, 31,* 62–79.

Richeson, J. A., & Shelton, J. (2012). Stereotype threat in interracial interactions. In M. Inzlicht, & T. Schmader (Eds.), *Stereotype threat: Theory, process, and application* (pp. 231–245). New York: Oxford University Press.

Richeson, J. A., & Shelton, J. N. (2010). Prejudice and bias in intergroup interactions. In J. F. Dovidio, M. Hewstone, P. Glick, & V. M. Esses (Eds.), *Handbook of prejudice, stereotyping, and discrimination* (pp. 276–293). London: Sage.

Richeson, J. A., & Trawalter, S. (2005). Why do interracial interactions impair executive function? A resource depletion account. *Journal of Personality and Social Psychology, 88,* 934–947.

Richeson, J. A., Todd, A. R., Trawalter, S., & Baird, A. A. (2008). Eye-gaze direction modulates race-related amygdala activity. *Group Processes & Intergroup Relations, 11,* 233–246.

Riddle, K. (2010). Always on my mind: Exploring how frequent, recent, and vivid television portrayals are used in the formation of social reality judgments. *Media Psychology, 13,* 155–179.

Rieger, G., Chivers, M. L., & Bailey, J. M. (2005). Sexual arousal patterns of bisexual men. *Psychological Science, 16,* 579–584.

Rieger, G., Linsenmeier, J. A. W., Gygax, L., & Bailey, J. M. (2008). Sexual orientation and childhood gender nonconformity: Evidence from home videos. *Developmental Psychology, 44,* 46–58.

Rigby, K., & Smith, P. K. (2011). Is school bullying really on the rise? *Social Psychology of Education, 14,* 441–455.

Rilling, J. K., & Sanfey, A. G. (2011). The neuroscience of social decision-making. *Annual Review of Psychology, 6,* 223–248.

Rilling, J. K., Gutman, D. A., Zeh, T. R., Pagnoni, G., Berns, G. S., & Kilts, C. D. (2002). A neural basis for social cooperation. *Neuron, 35,* 395–405.

Rimal, R. N., & Real, K. (2005). Assessing the perceived importance of skin cancer: How question-order effects are influenced by issue involvement. *Health Education & Behavior, 32,* 398–412.

Rind, B., & Strohmetz, D. B. (2001). Effect on restaurant tipping of a helpful message written on the back of customers' checks. *Journal of Applied Social Psychology, 31,* 1379–1384.

Ringelmann, M. (1913). Recherches sur les moteurs animés: Travail de l'homme. *Annales de l'Institut National Agronomique,* 2e série, tom XII, 1–40.

Riniolo, T. C., Johnson, K. C., Sherman, T. R., & Misso, J. A. (2006). Hot or not: Do professors perceived as physically attractive receive higher student evaluations? *Journal of General Psychology, 133,* 19–35.

Risen, J. L., Gilovich, T., & Dunning, D. (2007). One-shot illusory correlations and stereotype formation. *Personality and Social Psychology Bulletin, 33,* 1492–1502.

Roach, M. (2008). *Bonk: The curious coupling of science and sex.* New York: Norton.

Roane, K. R. (2000, February 28). Boston's big-bucks highway to hell. *U.S. News and World Report,* p. 34.

Robbins, J. M., Ford, M. T., & Tetrick, L. E. (2012). Perceived unfairness and employee health: A meta-analytic integration. *Journal of Applied Psychology, 97,* 235–272.

Robins, R. W., Mendelsohn, G. A., Connell, J. B., & Kwan, V. S. Y. (2004). Do people agree about the causes of behavior? A social relations analysis of behavior ratings and causal attributions. *Journal of Personality and Social Psychology, 86,* 334–344.

Robinson, J. P., Shaver, P. R., & Wrightsman, L. S. (Eds.). (1991). *Measures of personality and social psychological attitudes.* New York: Academic Press.

Robinson, J. P., Shaver, P. R., & Wrightsman, L. S. (Eds.). (1998). *Measures of political attitudes.* New York: Academic Press.

Rockloff, M. J., & Dyer, V. (2007). An experiment on the social facilitation of gambling behavior. *Journal of Gambling Studies, 23,* 1–12.

Rodin, J. (1986). Aging and health: Effects of the sense of control. *Science, 233,* 1271–1276.

Rodkin, P. C., & Ryan, A. M. (2012). Child and adolescent peer relations in educational context. In K. R. Harris, S. Graham, T. Urdan, S. Graham, J. M. Royer, & M. Zeidner (Eds.), *APA educational psychology handbook: Vol 2. Individual differences and cultural and contextual factors* (pp. 363–389). Washington, DC: American Psychological Association.

Rodkin, P. C., Farmer, T. W., Pearl, R., & van Acker, R. (2000). Heterogeneity of popular boys: Antisocial and prosocial configurations. *Developmental Psychology, 36,* 14–24.

Rodrigues, A., Assmar, E. M. L., & Jablonski, B. (2005). Social-psychology and the invasion of Iraq. *Revista de Psicologia Social, 20,* 387–398.

Rodriguez Mosquera, P. M., Fischer, A. H., & Manstead, A. S. R. (2004). Inside the heart of emotion. On culture and relational concerns. In L. Z. Tiedens & C. W. Leach (Eds.), *The social life of emotions* (pp. 187–202). Cambridge: Cambridge University Press.

Rodriguez Mosquera, P. M.., Fischer, A. H., Manstead, A. S. R., & Zaalberg, R. (2008). Attack, disapproval, or withdrawal? The role of honour in anger and shame responses to being insulted. *Cognition & Emotion, 22,* 1471–1498.

Roese, N. J. (1997). Counterfactual thinking. *Psychological Bulletin, 121,* 133–148.

Roese, N. J., & Olson, J. M. (Eds.). (1995). *What might have been: The social psychology of counterfactual thinking.* Hillsdale, NJ: Erlbaum.

Roese, N. J., & Summerville, A. (2005). What we regret most . . . and why. *Personality and Social Psychology Bulletin, 31,* 1273–1285.

Roethlisberger, F. J., & Dickson, W. J. (1939). *Management and the worker.* Cambridge, MA: Harvard University Press.

Rofé, Y. (1984). Stress and affiliation: A utility theory. *Psychological Review, 91,* 235–250.

Rogers, M., Miller, N., Mayer, F. S., & Duval, S. (1982). Personal responsibility and salience of the request for help: Determinants of the relation between negative affect and helping behavior. *Journal of Personality and Social Psychology, 43,* 956–970.

Rogers, R. W. (1983). Cognitive and psychological processes in fear appeals and attitude change: A revised theory of protection motivation. In J. Cacioppo & R. Petty (Eds.), *Social psychophysiology: A sourcebook* (pp. 153–176). New York: Guilford.

Rogers, R. W., & Mewborn, R. C. (1976). Fear appeals and attitude change: Effects of a threat's noxiousness, probability of occurrence, and the efficacy of coping responses. *Journal of Personality and Social Psychology, 34,* 54–61.

Rohrer, J. H., Baron, S. H., Hoffman, E. L., & Swander, D. V. (1954). The stability of autokinetic judgments. *Journal of Abnormal and Social Psychology, 49,* 595–597.

Ronquillo, J., Denson, T., Lickel, B., Nandy, A., Maddox, K., & Lu, Z. (2007). The effects of skin tone on race-related amygdala activity: An fMRI investigation. *Social Cognitive and Affective Neuroscience, 2,* 39–44.

Ronzone, R. (2009, April 2). Video games not just children's play. *The Villanovan.*

Rook, K. S. (1984). The negative side of social interaction: Impact on psychological well-being. *Journal of Personality and Social Psychology, 46,* 1097–1108.

Rook, K. S. (1987). Reciprocity of social exchange and social satisfaction among older women. *Journal of Personality and Social Psychology, 52,* 145–154.

Rook, K. S., & Peplau, L. A. (1982). Perspectives on helping the lonely. In L. A. Peplau & D. Perlman (Eds.), *Loneliness: A sourcebook of current theory, research and therapy* (pp. 351–378). New York: Wiley.

Rose, V. G., & Ogloff, J. R. P. (2001). Evaluating the comprehensibility of jury instructions: A method and an example. *Law and Human Behavior, 25,* 409–431.

Rosenbaum, M. E. (1986). The repulsion hypothesis: On the nondevelopment of relationships. *Journal of Personality and Social Psychology, 51,* 1156–1166.

Rosenberg, S., Nelson, C., & Vivekananthan, P. S. (1968). A multidimensional approach to the structure of personality impressions. *Journal of Personality and Social Psychology, 9,* 283–294.

Rosenbloom, T., Shahr, A., Perlman, A., Estreich, D., & Kirzner, E. (2007). Success on a practical driver's license test with and without the presence of another testee. *Accident Analysis and Prevention, 39,* 1296–1301.

Rosener, J. B. (1995). *America's competitive secret: Utilizing women as a management strategy.* New York: Oxford University Press.

Rosenfeld, M. J., & Thomas, R. J. (2012). Searching for a mate: The rise of the Internet as a social intermediary. *American Sociological Review, 77,* 523–547.

Rosenkoetter, L. I., Rosenkoetter, S. E., & Acock, A. C. (2009). Television violence: An intervention to reduce its impact on children. *Journal of Applied Developmental Psychology, 30,* 381–397.

Rosenman, R. H., Brand, R. J., Jenkins, C. D., Friedman, M., Strau, R., & Wurm, M. (1975). Coronary heart disease in the Western Collaborative Group Study: Final follow-up experience of 8 1/2 years. *Journal of the American Medical Association, 233,* 872–877.

Rosenthal, A. M., Sylva, D., Safron, A., & Bailey, M. J. (2012). The male bisexuality debate revisited: Some bisexual men have bisexual arousal patterns. *Archives of Sexual Behavior, 41,* 135–147.

Rosenthal, E. (2006, June 2). Genital cutting raises by 50% likelihood mothers or their newborns will die, study finds. *New York Times,* p. A10.

Rosenthal, H. E. S., & Crisp, R. J. (2006). Reducing stereotype threat by blurring intergroup boundaries. *Personality and Social Psychology Bulletin, 32,* 501–511.

Rosenthal, R. (1976). *Experimenter effects in behavioral research.* New York: Irvington.

Rosenthal, R. (1985). From unconscious experimenter bias to teacher expectancy effects. In J. B. Dusek, V. C. Hall, & W. J. Meyer (Eds.), *Teacher expectancies* (pp. 37–65). Hillsdale, NJ: Erlbaum.

Rosenthal, R. (2002). Covert communication in classrooms, clinics, courtrooms, and cubicles. *American Psychologist, 57,* 839–849.

Rosenthal, R., & Jacobson, L. (1968). *Pygmalion in the classroom: Teacher expectation and pupils' intellectual development.* New York: Holt, Rinehart and Winston.

Rosh, L., Offermann, L. R., & Van Diest, R. (2012). Too close for comfort? Distinguishing between team intimacy and team cohesion. *Human Resource Management Review, 22,* 116–127.

Rosnow, R. L., & Rosenthal, R. (1993). *Beginning behavioral research: A conceptual primer.* New York: Macmillan.

Ross, E. A. (1908). *Social psychology: An outline and source book.* New York: Macmillan.

Ross, J., & Staw, B. M. (1986). Expo 86: An escalation prototype. *Administrative Science Quarterly, 31,* 274–297.

Ross, L. (1977). The intuitive psychologist and his shortcomings: Distortions in the attribution process. In L. Berkowitz (Ed.), *Advances in experimental social psychology* (Vol. 10, pp. 174–221). New York: Academic Press.

Ross, L., Amabile, T. M., & Steinmetz, J. L. (1977). Social roles, social control, and biases in social-perception processes. *Journal of Personality and Social Psychology, 35,* 485–494.

Ross, L., Bierbrauer, G., & Hoffman, S. (1976). The role of attribution processes in conformity and dissent. *American Psychologist, 31,* 148–157.

Ross, L., Greene, D., & House, P. (1977). The false consensus phenomenon: An attributional bias in self-perception and social-perception processes. *Journal of Experimental Social Psychology, 13,* 279–301.

Rosse, J. G., Miller, J. L., & Stecher, M. D. (1994). A field study of job applicants' reactions to personality and cognitive ability testing. *Journal of Applied Psychology, 79,* 987–992.

Roth-Hanania, R., Davidov, M., & Zahn-Waxler, C. (2011). Empathy development from 8 to 16 months: Early signs of concern for others. *Infant Behavior & Development, 34,* 447–458.

Roth, P. L., Huffcutt, A. I., & Bobko, P. (2003). Ethnic group differences in measures of job performance: A new metaanalysis. *Journal of Applied Psychology, 88,* 694–706.

Rothbaum, F., & Tsang, B. Y. (1998). Lovesongs in the United States and China: On the nature of romantic love. *Journal of Cross-Cultural Psychology, 29,* 306–319.

Rowatt, W. C., Cunningham, M. R., & Druen, P. B. (1999). Lying to get a date: The effect of facial physical attractiveness on the willingness to deceive prospective dating partners. *Journal of Social and Personal Relationships, 16,* 209–223.

Rowe, R., Rijsdijk, F. V., Maughan, B., Hosang, G. M., & Eley, T. C. (2008). Heterogeneity in antisocial behaviours and comorbidity with depressed mood: A behavioural genetic approach. *Journal of Child Psychology and Psychiatry, 49,* 526–534.

Roxborough, S. (2009, March 19). German retailer pulls violent DVDs, games. *Reuters.* Available at http://www.reuters.com/article/filmNews/idUSTRE52I7WC20090319.

Rozin, P., & Fallon, A. E. (1987). A perspective on disgust. *Psychological Review, 94,* 23–41.

Rozin, P., & Royzman, E. B. (2001). Negativity bias, negativity dominance, and contagion. *Personality and Social Psychology Review, 5,* 296–320.

Ruback, R. B., & Wroblewski, J. (2001). The federal sentencing guidelines: Psychological and policy reasons for simplification. *Psychology, Public Policy, and Law, 7,* 739–775.

Rubenowitz, S., Norrgren, F., & Tannenbaum, A. S. (1983). Some social psychological effects of direct and indirect participation in ten Swedish companies. *Organization Studies, 4,* 243–259.

Rubin, D. C. (Ed.). (1996). *Remembering our past: Studies in autobiographical memory.* New York: Cambridge University Press.

Rubin, J. Z., Provenzano, F. J., & Luria, Z. (1974). The eye of the beholder: Parents' views on sex of newborns. *American Journal of Orthopsychiatry, 44,* 512–519.

Rubin, J. Z., Pruitt, D. G., & Kim, S. H. (1994). *Social conflict: Escalation, stalemate, and settlement.* New York: McGraw-Hill.

Rubin, Z. (1973). *Liking and loving.* New York: Holt, Rinehart and Winston.

Ruble, D. N., & Martin, C. L. (1998). Gender development. In W. Damon & N. Eisenberg (Eds.), *Handbook of child psychology, 5th edition: Volume 3: Social, emotional, and personality development* (pp. 933–1016). Hoboken, NJ: Wiley.

Rubonis, A. V., & Bickman, L. (1991). Psychological impairment in the wake of disaster: The disaster-psychopathology relationship. *Psychological Bulletin, 109,* 384–399.

Rudman, L. A., & Glick, P. (2001). Prescriptive gender stereotypes and backlash toward agentic women. *Journal of Social Issues, 57,* 743–762.

Rudman, L. A., Moss-Racusin, C. A., Phelan, J. E., & Nauts, S. (2012). Status incongruity and backlash effects: Defending the gender hierarchy motivates prejudice against female leaders. *Journal of Experimental Social Psychology, 48,* 165–179.

Ruffle, B. J., & Sosis, R. (2006). Cooperation and the in-group-out-group bias: A field test on Israeli kibbutz members and city residents. *Journal of Economic Behavior and Organization, 60,* 147–163.

Rule, N. O., & Ambady, N. (2008). The face of success: Inferences from chief executive officers' appearance predict company profits. *Psychological Science, 19,* 109–111.

Rusbult, C. E., & Buunk, B. P. (1993). Commitment processes in close relationships: An interdependence analysis. *Journal of Social and Personal Relationships, 10,* 175–204.

Rusbult, C. E., Agnew, C. R., & Arriaga, X. B. (2012). The investment model of commitment processes. In P. Van Lange, A. Kruglanski, & E. T. Higgins (Eds.), *Handbook of theories of social psychology* (Vol. 2, pp. 218–231). Thousand Oaks, CA: Sage.

Rusbult, C. E., Martz, J. M., & Agnew, C. R. (1998). The investment model scale: Measuring commitment level, satisfaction level, quality of alternatives, and investment size. *Personal Relationships, 5,* 357–391.

Rushton, J. P. (1981). The altruistic personality. In J. P. Rushton & R. M. Sorrentino (Eds.), *Altruism and helping behavior: Social, personality, and developmental perspectives* (pp. 251–266). Hillsdale, NJ: Erlbaum.

Russano, M. B., Meissner, C. A., Narchet, F. M., & Kassin, S. M. (2005). Investigating true and false confessions within a novel experimental paradigm. *Psychological Science, 16,* 481–486.

Russell, E., Koren, G., Rieder, M., & Van Uum, S. (2012). Hair cortisol as a biological marker of chronic stress: Current status, future directions and unanswered questions. *Psychoneuroendocrinology, 37,* 589–601.

Russell, J. A. (1994). Is there universal recognition of emotion from facial expression? A review of cross-cultural studies. *Psychological Bulletin, 115,* 102–141.

Rutchick, A. M., Hamilton, D. L., & Sack, J. D. (2008). Antecedents of entitativity in categorically and dynamically construed groups. *Journal of Social Psychology, 38,* 905–921.

Ruva, C. L., & LeVasseur, M. A. (2012). Behind closed doors: The effect of pretrial publicity on jury deliberations. *Psychology, Crime & Law, 18,* 431–452.

Rydell, R. J., Hamilton, D. L., & Devos, T. (2010). Now they are American, now they are not: Valence as a determinant of the inclusion of African Americans in the American identity. *Social Cognition, 28,* 161–179.

Rydell, R. J., McConnell, A. R., & Beilock, S. L. (2009). Multiple social identities and stereotype threat: Imbalance, accessibility, and working memory. *Journal of Personality and Social Psychology, 96,* 949–966.

Rydell, R. J., Sherman, S. J., Boucher, K. L., & Macy, J. T. (2012). The role of motivational and persuasive message factors in changing implicit attitudes toward smoking. *Basic and Applied Social Psychology, 34,* 1–7.

Rynes, S. L., & Connerly, M. L. (1993). Applicant reactions to alternative selection procedures. *Journal of Business and Psychology, 4,* 261–277.

Saad, G. (2007). *The evolutionary bases of consumption.* Mahwah, NJ: Erlbaum.

Sabin, J. A., & Greenwald, A. G. (2012). The influence of implicit bias on treatment recommendations for 4 common pediatric conditions: Pain, urinary tract infection, attention deficit hyperactivity disorder, and asthma. *American Journal of Public Health, 102,* 988–995.

Sackett, P. R., & DuBois, C. L. Z. (1991). Rater-ratee race effects on performance evaluation: Challenging meta-analytic conclusions. *Journal of Applied Psychology, 76,* 873–877.

Sackett, P. R., & Leivens, F. (2008). Personnel selection. *Annual Review of Psychology, 59,* 419–450.

Sackett, P. R., & Schmitt, N. (2012). On reconciling conflicting meta-analytic findings regarding integrity test validity. *Journal of Applied Psychology, 97,* 550–556.

Sackett, P. R., Borneman, M. J., & Connelly, B. S. (2008). High-stakes testing in higher education and employment: Appraising the evidence for validity and fairness. *American Psychologist, 63,* 215–227.

Sacks, O. (1985). *The man who mistook his wife for a hat.* New York: Summit.

Sagar, H. A., & Schofield, J. W. (1980). Racial and behavioral cues in black and white children's perceptions of ambiguously aggressive acts. *Journal of Personality and Social Psychology, 39,* 590–598.

Sagarin, B. J. (2005). Reconsidering evolved sex differences in jealousy: Comment on Harris (2003). *Personality and Social Psychology Review, 9,* 62–75.

Saguy, T., Quinn, D. M., Dovidio, J. F., & Pratto, F. (2010). Interacting like a body: Objectification can lead women to narrow their presence in social interactions. *Psychological Science, 21,* 178–182.

Sahin, M. (2012). An investigation into the efficiency of empathy training program on preventing bullying in primary schools. *Children and Youth Services Review, 34,* 1325–1330.

Saks, M. J. (1974). Ignorance of science is no excuse. *Trial, 10,* 18–20.

Saks, M. J., & Marti, M. W. (1997). A meta-analysis of the effects of jury size. *Law and Human Behavior, 21,* 451–468.

Salas, E., Nichols, D. R., & Driskell, J. E. (2007). Testing three team training strategies in intact teams: A meta-analysis. *Small Group Research, 38,* 471–488.

Salgado, J. F. (1997). The five factor model of personality and job performance in the European community. *Journal of Applied Psychology, 82,* 30–43.

Salovey, P. (1992). Mood-induced focus of attention. *Journal of Personality and Social Psychology, 62,* 699–707.

Salovey, P., Mayer, J. D., & Rosenhan, D. L. (1991). Mood and helping: Mood as a motivator of helping and helping as a regulator of mood. In M. S. Clark (Ed.), *Prosocial behavior* (Vol. 12, pp. 215–237). Newbury Park, CA: Sage.

Salvemini, N. J., Reilly, R. R., & Smither, J. W. (1993). The influence of rater motivation on assimilation effects and accuracy in performance ratings. *Organizational Behavior and Human Decision Processes, 55,* 41–60.

Sampson, E. E. (2000). Reinterpreting individualism and collectivism: Their religious roots and monologic versus dialogic person-other relationship. *American Psychologist, 55,* 1425–1432.

Sanchez-Burks, J., Nisbett, R. E., & Ybarra, O. (2000). Relational schemas, cultural styles, and prejudice against outgroups. *Journal of Personality and Social Psychology, 79,* 174–189.

Sanchez, D. T., & Chavez, G. (2010). Are you minority enough? Language ability affects targets' and perceivers' assessments of a candidate's appropriateness for affirmative action. *Basic and Applied Social Psychology, 32,* 99–107.

Sanchez, D. T., & Garcia, J. A. (2009). When race matters: Racially stigmatized others and perceiving race as a biological construction affect biracial people's daily well-being. *Personality and Social Psychology Bulletin, 35,* 1154–1164.

Sanchez, D. T., & Garcia, J. A. (2012). Putting race in context: Socioeconomic status predicts racial fluidity. In S. T. Fiske & H. R. Markus (Eds.), *Facing social class: How societal rank influences interaction* (pp. 216–233). New York: Russell Sage Foundation.

Sanchez, J. I., & De La Torre, P. (1996). A second look at the relationship between rating and behavioral accuracy in performance appraisal. *Journal of Applied Psychology, 81*, 3–10.

Sanders, G. S. (1981). Driven by distraction: An integrative review of social facilitation theory and research. *Journal of Experimental Social Psychology, 17*, 227–251.

Sanderson, C. A., & Evans, S. M. (2001). Seeing one's partner through intimacy-colored glasses: An examination of the processes underlying the intimacy goals-relationship satisfaction link. *Personality and Social Psychology Bulletin, 27*, 463–473.

Sanderson, D. W. (1997). *Smileys.* Sebastopol, CA: O'Reilly.

Sandstrom, M. J., & Bartini, M. (2010). Do perceptions of discrepancy between self and group norms contribute to peer harassment at school? *Basic and Applied Social Psychology, 32*, 217–225.

Santalahti, P., Sourander, A., Aromaa, M., Helenius, H., Ikäheimo, K., & Piha, J. (2008). Victimization and bullying among 8-year-old Finnish children: A 10-year comparison of rates. *European Child and Adolescent Psychiatry, 17*, 463–472.

Santos, M. D., Leve, C., & Pratkanis, A. R. (1994). Hey buddy, can you spare seventeen cents? Mindful persuasion and the pique technique. *Journal of Applied Social Psychology, 24*, 755–764.

Sapolsky, R. M. (1994). *Why zebras don't get ulcers: A guide to stress, diseases, and coping.* New York: Freeman.

Sapolsky, R. M. (2004). *Why zebras don't get ulcers* (3rd ed.). New York: Owl Books.

Sarason, I. G., Levine, H. M., Basham, R. B., & Sarason, B. R. (1983). Assessing social support: The social support questionnaire. *Journal of Personality and Social Psychology, 44*, 127–139.

Sarat, A. (Ed.). (2005). *Dissent in dangerous times.* Ann Arbor: University of Michigan Press.

Sargent, M. J., & Bradfield, A. L. (2004). Race and information processing in criminal trials: Does the defendant's race affect how the facts are evaluated? *Personality and Social Psychology Bulletin, 30*, 995–1008.

Sarkar, U., Ali, S., & Whooley, M. A. (2009). Self-efficacy as a marker of cardiac function and predictor of heart failure hospitalization and mortality in patients with stable coronary heart disease: Findings from the Heart and Soul Study. *Health Psychology, 28*, 166–173.

Sarnoff, I., & Zimbardo, P. (1961). Anxiety, fear, and social affiliation. *Journal of Abnormal and Social Psychology, 62*, 356–363.

Sartori, G. Agosta, S. Zogmaister, C. Ferrara, S. D., & Castiello, U. (2008). How to accurately assess autobiographical events. *Psychological Science, 19*, 772–780.

Saucier, D. A., Miller, C. T., & Doucet, N. (2005). Differences in helping whites and blacks: A meta-analysis. *Personality and Social Psychology Review, 9*, 2–16.

Savin, H. B. (1973). Professors and psychological researchers: Conflicting values in conflicting roles. *Cognition, 2*, 147–149.

Savitsky, K., Epley, N., & Gilovich, T. (2001). Do others judge us as harshly as we think? Overestimating the impact of our failures, shortcomings, and mishaps. *Journal of Personality and Social Psychology, 81*, 44–56.

Savitsky, K., Gilovich, T., Berger, G., & Medvec, V. H. (2003). Is our absence as conspicuous as we think? Overestimating the salience and impact of one's absence from a group. *Journal of Experimental Social Psychology, 39*, 386–392.

Sawyer, A. M., & Borduin, C. M. (2011). Effects of multisystemic therapy through midlife: A 21.9-year follow-up to a randomized clinical trial with serious and violent juvenile offenders. *Journal of Consulting and Clinical Psychology, 79*, 643–652.

Sawyer, P. J., Major, B., Casad, B. J., Townsend, S. M., & Mendes, W. (2012). Discrimination and the stress response: Psychological and physiological consequences of anticipating prejudice in interethnic interactions. *American Journal of Public Health, 102*(5), 1020–1026.

Sbarra, D. A., & Nietert, P. J. (2009). Divorce and death: Forty years of the Charleston Heart Study. *Psychological Science, 20*, 107–113.

Sbarra, D. A., Law, R. W., & Portley, R. M. (2011). Divorce and death: A meta-analysis and research agenda for clinical, social, and health psychology. *Perspectives on Psychological Science, 6*, 454–474.

Schachter, S. (1951). Deviation, rejection, and communication. *Journal of Abnormal and Social Psychology, 46*, 190–207.

Schachter, S. (1959). *The psychology of affiliation: Experimental studies of the sources of gregariousness.* Stanford, CA: Stanford University Press.

Schachter, S. (1964). The interaction of cognitive and physiological determinants of emotional state. In L. Berkowitz (Ed.), *Advances in experimental social psychology* (Vol. 1, pp. 49–80). New York: Academic Press.

Schachter, S., & Singer, J. (1962). Cognitive, social, and physiological determinants of the emotional state. *Psychological Review, 69*, 379–399.

Schachter, S., & Singer, J. (1979). Comments on the Maslach and Marshall-Zimbardo experiments. *Journal of Personality and Social Psychology, 37*, 989–995.

Schachter, S., Hood, D., Gerin, W., Andreasson, P. B., & Rennert, M. (1985). Some causes and consequences of dependence and independence in the stock market. *Journal of Economic Behavior and Organization, 6*, 339–357.

Schachter, S., Ouellette, R., Whittle, B., & Gerin, W. (1987). Effects of trends and of profit or loss on the tendency to sell stock. *Basic and Applied Social Psychology, 8*, 259–271.

Schafer, M. H., & Ferraro, K. F. (2011). The stigma of obesity: Does perceived weight discrimination affect identity and physical health? *Social Psychology Quarterly, 74*(1), 76–97.

Schafer, R. B., & Keith, P. M. (1981). Equity and marital roles across the family life cycle. *Journal of Marriage and the Family, 43*, 359–367.

Schaller, M., & Neuberg, S. L. (2012). Danger, disease, and the nature of prejudice(s). In J. M. Olson & M. P. Zanna (Eds.), *Advances in Experimental Social Psychology* (Vol. 46), pp. 1–54. San Diego: Academic Press.

Schaller, M., & Park, J. H. (2011). The behavioral immune system (and why it matters). *Current Directions in Psychological Science, 20*, 99–103.

Schaller, M., Park, J. H., & Faulkner, J. (2003). Prehistoric dangers and contemporary prejudices. *European Review of Social Psychology, 14*, 105–137.

Schaller, M., Simpson, J. A., & Kenrick, D. T. (Eds.). (2006). *Evolution and social psychology.* New York: Taylor & Francis.

Scheepers, D., Spears, R., Doosje, B., & Manstead, A. S. R. (2006). The social functions of ingroup bias: Creating, confirming, or changing social reality. *European Review of Social Psychology, 17*, 359–396.

Scheier, M. F., & Carver, C. S. (1983). Two sides of the self: One for you and one for me. In J. Suls and A. G. Greenwald (Eds.), *Psychological perspectives on the self* (Vol. 2, pp. 123–157). Hillsdale, NJ: Erlbaum.

Scheier, M. F., & Carver, C. S. (1985). Optimism, coping, and health: Assessment and implications of generalized outcome expectancies. *Health Psychology, 4*, 219–247.

Scheier, M. F., & Carver, C. S. (1992). Effects of optimism on psychological and physical well-being: Theoretical overview and empirical update. *Cognitive Therapy and Research, 16*, 201–228.

Schel, A. M., Tranquilli, S., & Zuberbühler, K. (2009). The alarm call system of two species of black-and-white colobus monkeys (Colobus polykomos and Colobus guereza). *Journal of Comparative Psychology, 123*, 136–150.

Scher, S. J., & Cooper, J. (1989). Motivational basis of dissonance: The singular role of behavioral consequences. *Journal of Personality and Social Psychology, 56*, 899–906.

Scherr, K. C., & Madon, S. (in press). You have the right to understand: The deleterious effect of stress on suspect's ability to comprehend *Miranda. Law and Human Behavior.*

Schimel, J., Arndt, J., Pyszczynski, T., & Greenberg, J. (2001). Being accepted for who we are: Evidence that social validation of the intrinsic self reduces general defensiveness. *Journal of Personality and Social Psychology, 80*, 35–52.

Schimmack, U., Oishi, S., & Diener, E. (2005). Individualism: A valid and important dimension of cultural differences between nations. *Personality and Social Psychology Review, 9*, 17–31.

Schino, G. (2007). Grooming and agonistic support: A meta-analysis of primate reciprocal altruism. *Behavioral Ecology, 18*, 115–120.

Schlagman, S., Schulz, J., & Kvavilashvili, L. (2006). A content analysis of involuntary autobiographical memories: Examining the positivity effect in old age. *Memory, 14*, 161–175.

Schlauch, R. C., Lang, A. R., Plant, E. A., Christensen, R., & Donohue, K. F. (2009). Effect of alcohol on race-biased responding: The moderating role of internal and external motivations to respond without prejudice. *Journal of Studies on Alcohol and Drugs, 70*, 328–336.

Schlenger, W. E., et al. (2002). Psychological reactions to terrorist attacks: Findings from the National Study of Americans' Reactions to September 11. *Journal of the American Medical Association, 288*, 581–588.

Schlenker, B. R. (1982). Translating actions into attitudes: An identity-analytic approach to the explanation of social conduct. In L. Berkowitz (Ed.), *Advances in experimental social psychology* (Vol. 15, pp. 193–247). New York: Academic Press.

Schlenker, B. R. (2003). Self-presentation. In M. R. Leary & J. P. Tangney (Eds.), *Handbook of self and identity* (pp. 492–518). New York: Guilford.

Schlenker, B. R., & Trudeau, J. V. (1990). The impact of self-presentations on private self-beliefs: Effects of prior self-beliefs and misattribution. *Journal of Personality and Social Psychology, 58*, 22–32.

Schlenker, B. R., Weigold, M. F., & Hallam, J. R. (1990). Self-serving attributions in social context: Effects of self-esteem and social pressure. *Journal of Personality and Social Psychology, 58*, 855–863.

Schmader, T., & Beilock, S. (2012). An integration of processes that underlie stereotype threat. In M. Inzlicht, & T. Schmader (Eds.), *Stereotype threat: Theory, process, and application* (pp. 34–50). New York: Oxford University Press.

Schmader, T., Johns, M., & Forbes, C. (2008). An integrated process model of stereotype threat effects on performance. *Psychological Review, 115*, 336–356.

Schmeichel, B. J., & Vohs, K. (2009). Self-affirmation and self-control: Affirming core values counteracts ego depletion. *Journal of Personality and Social Psychology, 96*, 770–782.

Schmeichel, B. J., Gailliot, M. T., Filardo, E.-A., McGregor, I., Gitter, S., & Baumeister, R. F. (2009). Terror management theory and self-esteem revisited: The roles of implicit and explicit self-esteem in mortality salience effects. *Journal of Personality and Social Psychology, 96*, 1077–1087.

Schmidt, F. L. (2002). The role of general cognitive ability and job performance: Why there cannot be a debate. *Human Performance, 15*, 187–210.

Schmidt, F. L., & Rader, M. (1999). Exploring the boundary conditions for interview validity: Meta-analytic validity findings for a new interview type. *Personnel Psychology, 52*, 445–464.

Schmidt, K., & Nosek, B. A. (2010). Implicit (and explicit) racial attitudes barely changed during Barack Obama's presidential campaign and early presidency. *Journal of Experimental Social Psychology, 46*, 308–314.

Schmitt, D. P. (2003). Universal sex differences in the desire for sexual variety: Tests from 52 nations, 6 continents, and 13 islands. *Journal of Personality and Social Psychology, 85*, 85–104.

Schmitt, M. T., Branscrombe, N. R., Kobrynowicz, D., & Owen, S. (2002). Perceiving discrimination against one's gender group has different implications for well-being in women and men. *Personality and Social Psychology Bulletin, 28*, 197–210.

Schmitt, N., & Oswald, F. L. (2006). The impact of corrections for faking on the validity of noncognitive measures in selection settings. *Journal of Applied Psychology, 91*, 613–621.

Schneider, D. J. (1973). Implicit personality theory: A review. *Psychological Bulletin, 79*, 294–309.

Schneider, S. G., Taylor, S. E., Hammen, C., Kemeny, M. E., & Dudley, J. (1991). Factors influencing suicide intent in gay and bisexual suicide ideators: Differing models for men with and without human immunodeficiency virus. *Journal of Personality and Social Psychology, 61*, 776–778.

Schneiderman, R. M. (2008, October 30). Do Americans still hate welfare? *New York* Schoorman, F. D. (1988). Escalation bias in performance appraisals: An unintended consequence of supervisor participation in hiring decisions. *Journal of Applied Psychology, 73*, 58–62.

Schoorman, F. D. (1988). Escalation bias in performance appraisals: An unintended consequence of supervisor participation in hiring decisions. *Journal of Applied Psychology, 73*, 58–62.

Schott, J., Scherer, L. D., & Lambert, A. J. (2011). Casualties of war and sunk costs: Implications for attitude change and persuasion. *Journal of Experimental Social Psychology, 47*, 1134–1145.

Schreiner, B. (2012). Fans burn couches, flip cars after Kentucky's win. *Associated Press*, April 1, 2012.

Schuldt, J. P., Konrath, S. H., & Schwarz, N. (2011). "Global warming" or "climate change"? Whether the planet is warming depends on question wording. *Public Opinion Quarterly, 75*, 115–124.

Schulman, J., Shaver, P., Colman, R., Emrick, B., & Christie, R. (1973, May). Recipe for a jury. *Psychology Today*, pp. 37–44, 77, 79–84.

Schultz, B., Ketrow, S. M., & Urban, D. M. (1995). Improving decision quality in the small group: The role of the reminder. *Small Group Research, 26*, 521–541.

Schultz, M. (2012). Hoekstra on defense as he's urged to pull ad. *The Detroit News*, February 7, p. A1.

Schulz, R. (1976). Effects of control and predictability on the physical and psychological well-being of the institutionalized aged. *Journal of Personality and Social Psychology, 33*, 563–573.

Schuster, M. A., Stein, B. D., Jaycox, L. H., Collins, R. L., Marshall, G. N., Elliott, M. N., Zhou, A. J., Kanouse, D. E., Morrison, J. L., & Berry, S. H. (2001). A national survey of stress reactions after the September 11, 2001, terrorist attacks. *New England Journal of Medicine, 345*, 1507–1512.

Schützwohl, A. (2004). Which infidelity type makes you more jealous? Decision strategies in a forced-choice between sexual and emotional infidelity. *Evolutionary Psychology, 2*, 121–128.

Schwartz, C. E., Wright, C. I., Shin, L. M., Kagan, J., & Rauch, S. L. (2003). Inhibited and uninhibited infants "grow up": Adult amygdalar response to novelty. *Science, 300*, 1952–1953.

Schwartz, R. L., Fremouw, W., Schenk, A., & Ragatz, L. L. (2012). Psychological profile of male and female animal abusers. *Journal of Interpersonal Violence, 27*, 846–861.

Schwartz, S. H. (1990). Individualism-collectivism: Critique and proposed refinements. *Journal of Cross-Cultural Psychology, 21*, 139–157.

Schwartz, S. H., & Gottlieb, A. (1980). Bystander anonymity and reaction to emergencies. *Journal of Personality and Social Psychology, 39*, 418–430.

Schwarz, N. (1990). Feelings as information: Information and motivational functions as affective states. In E. T. Higgins et al. (Eds.), *Handbook of motivation and cognition: Foundations of social behavior* (Vol. 2, pp. 527–561). New York: Guilford.

Schwarz, N., & Oyserman, D. (2011). Asking questions about behavior: Self-reports in evaluation research. In M. M. Mark, S. I. Donaldson, & B. Campbell (Eds.), *Social psychology and evaluation* (pp. 243–264). New York: Guilford.

Schwarz, N., Bless, H., & Bohner, G. (1991). Mood and persuasion: Affective states influence the processing of persuasive communications. In M. P. Zanna (Ed.), *Advances in experimental social psychology* (Vol. 24, pp. 161–199). New York: Academic Press.

Schwarz, N., Oyserman, D., & Peytcheva, E. (2010). Cognition, communication, and culture: Implications for the survey response process. In J. Harkness et al. (Eds.), *Survey methods in multinational, multiregional and multicultural contexts* (pp. 177–190). New York: Wiley.

Schwarzwald, J., Raz, M., & Zvibel, M. (1979). The applicability of the door-in-the-face technique when established behavioral customs exist. *Journal of Applied Social Psychology, 9*, 576–586.

Schweber, N. (2011, November 10). Penn State students clash with police in unrest after announcement. *New York Times*.

*Science Daily.* (2008, December 8). Why do people make "a mountain out of a molehill?" Aggression, status, and sex. Retrieved from http://www.sciencedaily.com/releases/2008/12/081208140156.htm

Scullen, S. E., Mount, M., & Goff, M. (2000). Understanding the latent structure of job performance ratings. *Journal of Applied Psychology, 85*, 956–970.

Seacat, J. D., & Mickelson, K. D. (2009). Stereotype threat and the exercise/dietary health intentions of overweight women. *Journal of Health Psychology, 14*, 556–567.

Sears, D. O., & Henry, P. J. (2005). Over thirty years later: A contemporary look at symbolic racism. In M. P. Zanna (Ed.), *Advances in experimental social psychology* (Vol. 37, pp. 95–150). San Diego: Elsevier.

Sechrist, G. B., & Milford, L. R. (2007). The influence of social consensus information on intergroup helping behavior. *Basic and Applied Social Psychology, 29,* 365–374.

Sedikides, C. (1992). Attentional effects on mood are moderated by chronic self-conception valence. *Personality and Social Psychology Bulletin, 18,* 580–584.

Sedikides, C., & Anderson, C. A. (1994). Causal perceptions of intertrait relations: The glue that holds person types together. *Personality and Social Psychology Bulletin, 20,* 294–302.

Sedikides, C., & Gregg, A. P. (2008). Self-enhancement: Food for thought. *Perspectives on Psychological Science, 3,* 102–116.

Sedikides, C., & Jackson, J. M. (1990). Social impact theory: A field test of source strength, source immediacy and number of targets. *Basic and Applied Social Psychology, 11,* 273–281.

Sedikides, C., & Spencer, S. J. (Eds.). (2007). *The self.* New York: Psychology Press.

Sedikides, C., Gaertner, L., & Toguchi, Y. (2003). Pancultural self-enhancement. *Journal of Personality and Social Psychology, 84,* 60–79.

Sedikides, C., Gaertner, L., & Vevea, J. L. (2005). Pancultural self-enhancement reloaded: A meta-analytic reply to Heine (2005). *Journal of Personality and Social Psychology, 89,* 539–551.

Seeman, T. E., Dubin, L. F., & Seeman, M. (2003). Religiosity/spirituality and health: A critical review of the evidence for biological pathways. *American Psychologist, 58,* 53–63.

Segerstrom, S. C. (2006a). *Breaking Murphy's law: How optimists get what they want from life and pessimists can too.* New York: Guilford Press.

Segerstrom, S. C. (2006b). How does optimism suppress immunity? Evaluation of three affective pathways. *Health Psychology, 25,* 653–657.

Segerstrom, S. C. (Ed.). (2012). *The Oxford Handbook of Psychoneuroimmunology.* New York: Oxford University Press.

Segerstrom, S. C., & Miller, G. E. (2004). Psychological stress and the human immune system: A meta-analytic study of 30 years of inquiry. *Psychological Bulletin, 130,* 601–630.

Segerstrom, S. C., Taylor, S. E., Kemeny, M. E., & Fahey, J. L. (1998). Optimism is associated with mood, coping, and immune change in response to stress. *Journal of Personality and Social Psychology, 74,* 1646–1655.

Seib, C. (2009, March 16). Storm gathers as propped-up AIG plans to pay 'outrageous' bonuses. *London Times,* p. 38.

Seibert, S. E., & Goltz, S. M. (2001). Comparison of allocations by individuals and interacting groups in an escalation of commitment situation. *Journal of Applied Social Psychology, 31,* 134–156.

Seijts, G. H., & Latham, G. P. (2000). The effects of goal setting and group size on performance in a social dilemma. *Canadian Journal of Behavioural Science, 32,* 104–116.

Sekaquaptewa, D., & Thompson, M. (2003). Solo status, stereotype threat, and performance expectancies: Their effects on women's performance. *Journal of Experimental Social Psychology, 39,* 68–74.

Seligman, M. E. P. (1975). *On depression, development, and death.* San Francisco: Freeman.

Seligman, M. E. P. (1991). *Learned optimism.* New York: Knopf.

Selterman, D., Apetroaia, A., & Waters, E. (2012). Script-like attachment representations in dreams containing current romantic partners. *Attachment and Human Development,* in press.

Seltzer, R. (2006). Scientific jury selection: Does it work? *Journal of Applied Social Psychology, 36,* 2417–2435.

Selye, H. (1936). A syndrome produced by diverse nocuous agents. *Nature, 138,* 32.

Senju, A., & Johnson, M. (2009). The eye contact effect: Mechanisms and development. *Trends in Cognitive Sciences, 13,* 127–134.

Sergeant, M. J. T., Dickins, T. E., Davies, M. N. O., & Griffiths, M. D. (2006). Aggression, empathy and sexual orientation in males. *Personality and Individual Differences, 40,* 475–486.

Seto, M. C., Marc, A., & Barbaree, H. E. (2001). The role of pornography in the etiology of sexual aggression. *Aggression and Violent Behavior, 6,* 35–53.

Severson, K. (2012). Number of U.S. hate groups is rising, report says. *New York Times,* March 8, p. 17.

Seyle, D. C., & Newman, M. L. (2006). A house divided? The psychology of red and blue America. *American Psychologist, 61,* 571–580.

Shackelford, T. K., & Goetz, A. T. (2005). When we hurt the ones we love: Predicting violence against women from men's mate retention tactics. In S. M. Platek & T. K. Shackelford (Eds.), *Human paternal uncertainty and anti-cuckoldry tactics: How males deal with female infidelity.* Cambridge: Cambridge University Press.

Shackelford, T. K., & Larsen, R. J. (1999). Facial attractiveness and physical health. *Evolution and Human Behavior, 20,* 71–76.

Shackelford, T. K., Goetz, A. T., Liddle, J. R., & Bush, L. S. (2012). Sexual conflict in humans. In T. K. Shackelford, A. T. Goetz (Eds.), *The Oxford handbook of sexual conflict in humans* (pp. 3–14). New York: Oxford University.

Shackelford, T. K., Voracek, M., Schmitt, D. P., Buss, D. M., Weekes-Shackelford, V. A., & Michalski, R. L. (2004). Romantic jealousy in early adulthood and later life. *Human Nature, 15,* 283–300.

Shackelford, T. K., Weekes-Shackelford, V. A., & Schmitt, D. P. (2005). An evolutionary perspective on why some men refuse or reduce their child support payments. *Basic and Applied Social Psychology, 27,* 297–306.

Shapiro, P. N., & Penrod, S. (1986). Meta-analysis of facial identification studies. *Psychological Bulletin, 100,* 139–156.

Shariff, A. F., & Norenzayan, A. (2007). God is watching you: Priming God concepts increases prosocial behavior in an anonymous economic game. *Psychological Science, 18,* 803–809.

Shaver, K. G. (1970). Defensive attribution: Effects of severity and relevance on the responsibility assigned for an accident. *Journal of Personality and Social Psychology, 14,* 101–113.

Shavers, V. L., Klein, W. M. P., & Fagan, P. (2012). Research on race/ethnicity and health care discrimination: Where we are and where we need to go. *American Journal of Public Health, 102,* 930–932.

Shaw, J. S., Garven, S., & Wood, J. M. (1997). Co-witness information can have immediate effects on eyewitness memory reports. *Law and Human Behavior, 5,* 503–521.

Shaw, J. S., III. (1996). Increases in eyewitness confidence resulting from postevent questioning. *Journal of Experimental Psychology: Applied, 2,* 126–146.

Shefrin, H. (2006). *Greed and fear: Understanding behavioral finance and the psychology of investing.* New York: Oxford University Press.

Shefrin, H. M., & Statman, M. (1985). The disposition to sell winners too early and ride losers too long: theory and evidence. *Journal of Finance, 40,* 777–790.

Shefrin, H. M., & Statman, M. (1986, February). How not to make money in the stock market. *Psychology Today,* pp. 52–57.

Sheldon, K. M., & Lyubomirsky, S. (2012). The challenge of staying happier: Testing the hedonic adaptation prevention model. *Personality and Social Psychology Bulletin, 38,* 670–680.

Sheldon, W. H. (1954). *Atlas of men: A guide for somatotyping the adult male at all ages.* New York: Harper & Brothers.

Shelton, J. N., & Richeson, J. A. (2005). Intergroup contact and pluralistic ignorance. *Journal of Personality and Social Psychology, 88,* 91–107.

Shelton, J., West, T. V., & Trail, T. E. (2010). Concerns about appearing prejudiced: Implications for anxiety during daily interracial interactions. *Group Processes & Intergroup Relations, 13,* 329–344.

Shen, H., Wan, F., & Wyer, R. S. (2011). Cross-cultural differences in the refusal to accept a small gift: The differential influence of reciprocity norms on Asians and North Americans. *Journal of Personality and Social Psychology, 100,* 271–281.

Shepela, S. T., Cook, J., Horlitz, E., Leal, R., Luciano, S., Lutfy, E., Miller, C., Mitchell, G., & Worden, E. (1999). Courageous resistance: A special case of altruism. *Theory and Psychology, 9,* 787–805.

Sheppard, B. H. (1985). Justice is no simple matter: Case for elaborating our model of procedural fairness. *Journal of Personality and Social Psychology, 49,* 953–962.

Shepperd, J. A. (1993a). Productivity loss in performance groups: A motivation analysis. *Psychological Bulletin, 113,* 67–81.

Shepperd, J. A. (1993b). Student derogation of the Scholastic Aptitude Test: Biases in perceptions and presentations of college board scores. *Basic and Applied Social Psychology, 14,* 455–473.

Shepperd, J. A., & Taylor, K. M. (1999). Social loafing and expectancy-value theory. *Personality and Social Psychology Bulletin, 25,* 1147–1158.

Sherer, M. (2007). Advice and help-seeking intentions among youth in Israel: Ethnic and gender differences. *Journal of Sociology & Social Welfare, 34,* 53–76.

Sherer, M. (2009). The nature and correlates of dating violence among Jewish and Arab youths in Israel. *Journal of Family Violence, 24,* 11–26.

Sherif, M. (1936). *The psychology of social norms.* New York: Harper.

Sherif, M. (1966). *In common predicament: Social psychology of intergroup conflict and cooperation.* Boston: Houghton Mifflin.

Sherif, M., Harvey, L. J., White, B. J., Hood, W. R., & Sherif, C. W. (1961). *The Robbers Cave experiment: Intergroup conflict and cooperation.* Middletown, CT: Wesleyan University Press.

Sherman, J. W., Stroessner, S. J., Conrey, F. R., & Azam, O. A. (2005). Prejudice and stereotype maintenance processes: Attention, attribution, and individuation. *Journal of Personality and Social Psychology, 89,* 607–622.

Shih, M. J., Pittinsky, T. L., & Ho, G. C. (2012). Stereotype boost: Positive outcomes from the activation of positive stereotypes. In M. Inzlicht & T. Schmader (Eds.), *Stereotype threat: Theory, process, and application* (pp. 141–156). New York: Oxford University Press.

Shih, M., Bonam, C., Sanchez, D., & Peck, C. (2007). The social construction of race: Biracial identity and vulnerability to stereotypes. *Cultural Diversity and Ethnic Minority Psychology, 13,* 125–133.

Shore, T. H., Shore, L. M., & Thornton, G. C., III. (1992). Construct validity of self- and peer evaluations of performance dimensions in an assessment center. *Journal of Applied Psychology, 77,* 42–54.

Shotland, R. L., & Heinold, W. D. (1985). Bystander response to arterial bleeding: Helping skills, the decision-making process, and differentiating the helping response. *Journal of Personality and Social Psychology, 49,* 347–356.

Shotland, R. L., & Stebbins, C. A. (1980). Bystander response to rape: Can a victim attract help? *Journal of Applied Social Psychology, 10,* 510–527.

Shteynberg, G., Gelfand, M. J., & Kim, K. (2009). Peering into the "magnum mysterium" of culture: The explanatory power of descriptive norms. *Journal of Cross-Cultural Psychology, 40,* 46–69.

Shuffler, M. L., DiazGranados, D., & Salas, E. (2011). There's a science for that: Team development interventions in organizations. *Current Directions In Psychological Science, 20,* 365–372.

Sidanius, J., & Pratto, F. (2012). Social dominance theory. In P. M. Van Lange, A. W. Kruglanski, E. T. Higgins (Eds.), *Handbook of theories of social psychology* (Vol. 2, pp. 418–438). Thousand Oaks, CA: Sage.

Sidebotham, P., & Heron, J. (2006). Child maltreatment in the 'children of the nineties': A cohort study of risk factors. *Child Abuse and Neglect, 30,* 497–522.

Siegler, I. C. (1994). Hostility and risk: Demographic and lifestyle variables. In A. W. Siegman & T. W. Smith (Eds.), *Anger, hostility, and the heart* (pp. 199–214). Hillsdale, NJ: Erlbaum.

Siegman, A. W., & Smith, T. W. (1994). *Anger, hostility, and the heart.* Hillsdale, NJ: Erlbaum.

Silverstein, B., Perdue, L., Peterson, B., & Kelly, E. (1986). The role of the mass media in promoting a thin standard of bodily attractiveness for women. *Sex Roles, 14,* 519–532.

Silvia, P. (2006). Reactance and the dynamics of disagreement: Multiple paths from threatened freedom to resistance to persuasion. *European Journal of Social Psychology, 36,* 673–685.

Silvia, P. J., & Duval, T. S. (2001). Objective self-awareness theory: Recent progress and enduring problems. *Personality and Social Psychology Review, 5,* 230–241.

Simons, L., Simons, R. L., Lei, M., & Sutton, T. E. (2012). Exposure to harsh parenting and pornography as explanations for males' sexual coercion and females' sexual victimization. *Violence and Victims, 27,* 378–395.

Simons, R. L., Lei, M., Stewart, E. A., Beach, S. H., Brody, G. H., Philibert, R. A., & Gibbons, F. X. (2012). Social adversity, genetic variation, street code, and aggression: A genetically informed model of violent behavior. *Youth Violence and Juvenile Justice, 10,* 3–24.

Simonsohn, U. (2011). Spurious? Name similarity effects (implicit egotism) in marriage, job, and moving decisions. *Journal of Personality and Social Psychology, 101,* 1–24.

Simonson, I., & Staw, B. W. (1992). Deescalation strategies: A comparison of techniques for reducing commitment to losing courses of action. *Journal of Applied Psychology, 77,* 419–426.

Simpson, J. A. (1987). The dissolution of romantic relationships: Factors involved in relationship stability and emotional distress. *Journal of Personality and Social Psychology, 53,* 683–692.

Simpson, J. A., Campbell, B., & Berscheid, E. (1986). The association between romantic love and marriage: Kephart (1967) twice revisited. *Personality and Social Psychology Bulletin, 12,* 363–372.

Simpson, J. A., Gangestad, S. W., & Lerma, M. (1990). Perception of physical attractiveness: Mechanisms involved in the maintenance of romantic relationships. *Journal of Personality and Social Psychology, 59,* 1192–1201.

Simpson, J. A., Rholes, W. S., & Phillips, D. (1996). Conflicts in close relationships: An attachment perspective. *Journal of Personality and Social Psychology, 71,* 899–914.

Sin, N. L., & Lyubomirsky, S. (2009). Enhancing well-being and alleviating depressive symptoms with positive psychology interventions: A practice-friendly meta-analysis. *Journal of Clinical Psychology, 65,* 467–487.

Sinclair, R. C., Hoffman, C., Mark, M. M., Martin, L. M., & Pickering, T. L. (1994). Construct accessibility and the misattribution of arousal: Schachter and Singer revisited. *Psychological Science, 5,* 15–19.

Singelis, T. M. (1994). The measurement of independent and interdependent self-construals. *Personality and Social Psychology Bulletin, 20,* 580–591.

Singh, D. (1993). Adaptive significance of female physical attractiveness: Role of waist-to-hip ratio. *Journal of Personality and Social Psychology, 65,* 293–307.

Singh, D. (1995). Female judgment of male attractiveness and desirability for relationships: Role of waist-to-hip ratio and financial status. *Journal of Personality and Social Psychology, 69,* 1089–1101.

Singh, D., & Randall, P. K. (2007). Beauty is in the eye of the plastic surgeon: Waist-hip ratio (WHR) and women's attractiveness. *Personality and Individual Differences, 43,* 329–340.

Singh, E. (2009). *Caste system in India: A historical perspective.* New Delhi: Kalpaz Publications.

Sinha, K. (2012). 57% of boys, 53% of girls think wife beating is justified. *The Times of India,* April 25.

Sinnott-Armstrong, W. (Ed.). (2008). *Moral psychology: Vol. 1. The evolution of morality.* Cambridge, MA: MIT Press.

Siris, P. (2009, January 19). Survivors of the storm. *New York Daily News,* p. 2.

Sistrunk, F., & McDavid, J. W. (1971). Sex variable in conforming behavior. *Journal of Personality and Social Psychology, 17,* 200–207.

Siu, A. M. H., Cheng, H. C. H., & Leung, M. C. M. (2006). Pro-social norms as a positive youth development construct: Conceptual bases and implications for curriculum development. *International Journal of Adolescent Medicine and Health, 18,* 451–457.

Skagerberg, E. M. (2007). Co-witness feedback in line-ups. *Applied Cognitive Psychology, 21,* 489–497.

Skarlicki, D. P., & Folger, R. (1997). Retaliation in the workplace: The roles of distributive, procedural, and interactional justice. *Journal of Applied Psychology, 82,* 434–443.

Skinner, E. A. (1996). A guide to constructs of control. *Journal of Personality and Social Psychology, 71,* 549–570.

Skinner, E. A., Edge, K., Altman, J., & Sherwood, H. (2003). Searching for the structure of coping: A review and critique of category systems for classifying ways of coping. *Psychological Bulletin, 129,* 216–269.

Skitka, L. J., Mullen, E., Griffin, T., Hutchinson, S., & Chamberlin, B. (2002). Dispositions, scripts, or motivated correction? Understanding ideological differences in explanations for social problems. *Journal of Personality and Social Psychology, 83,* 470–487.

Sklar, L. S., & Anisman, H. (1981). Stress and cancer. *Psychological Bulletin, 89,* 369–406.

Skowronski, J. J., & Carlston, D. E. (1989). Negativity and extremity biases in impression formation: A review of explanations. *Psychology Bulletin, 105,* 131–142.

Slack, J. (2009). The most violent country in Europe: Britain is also worse than South Africa and U.S. *The Daily Mail Online*, July 2.

Slamecka, N. J., & Graff, P. (1978). The generation effect: Delineation of a phenomenon. *Journal of Experimental Psychology: Human Learning and Memory, 4,* 592–604.

Slepian, M. L., Young, S. G., Rule, N. O., Weisbuch, M., & Ambady, N. (2012). Embodied impression formation: Social judgments and motor cues to approach and avoidance. *Social Cognition, 30,* 232–240.

Sloan, R., Bagiella, E., & Powell, T. (1999). Religion, spirituality, and medicine. *Lancet, 353,* 664–667.

Slovic, P. (2000). *The perception of risk.* London: Earthscan.

Smart Richman, L., & Leary, M. R. (2009). Reactions to discrimination, stigmatization, ostracism, and other forms of interpersonal rejection: A multimotive model. *Psychological Review, 116,* 365–383.

Smeaton, G., Byrne, D., & Murnen, S. K. (1989). The repulsion hypothesis revisited: Similarity irrelevance or dissimilarity bias? *Journal of Personality and Social Psychology, 56,* 54–59.

Smedley, B. D. (2012). The lived experience of race and its health consequences. *American Journal of Public Health, 102,* 933–935.

Smidt, K. E., & DeBono, K. G. (2011). On the effects of product name on product evaluation: An individual difference perspective. *Social Influence, 6,* 131–141.

Smith, A., & Williams, K. D. (2004). RU there? Ostracism by cell phone text messages. *Group Dynamics: Theory, Research, and Practice, 8,* 291–301.

Smith, A., Jussim, L., & Eccles, J. (1999). Do self-fulfilling prophecies accumulate, dissipate, or remain stable over time? *Journal of Personality and Social Psychology, 77,* 548–565.

Smith, C. (2012a). Pittsburgh basketball game marred by horrible racist banana suited monkey chants. http://sports.yahoo.com/blogs/highschool-prep-rally/pittsburgh-basketball-game-marred-horrible-racist-banana-suited-131740578.html.

Smith, C. (2012b). San Antonio prep hoops fans accused of racism over "USA, USA" chant. http://sports.yahoo.com/blogs/highschool-prep-rally/san-antonio-prep-hoops-fans-accused-racismabover-usa-123930890.html.

Smith, C. A., Ireland, T. O., Park, A., Elwyn, L., & Thornberry, T. P. (2011). Intergenerational continuities and discontinuities in intimate partner violence: A two-generational prospective study. *Journal of Interpersonal Violence, 26,* 3720–3752.

Smith, C. T., Ratiiff, K. A., & Nosek, B. A. (2012). Rapid assimilation: Automatically integrating new information with existing beliefs. *Social Cognition, 30,* 199–219.

Smith, D. L. (2007). *The most dangerous animal: Human nature and the origins of war.* New York: St. Martin's.

Smith, H. J., Spears, R., & Hamstra, I. J. (1999). Social identity and the context of relative deprivation. In N. Ellemers, R. Spears, & I. J. Hamstra (Eds.), *Social identity: Context, commitment, content* (pp. 205–229). Oxford, UK: Blackwell.

Smith, L., & Redington, R. M. (2010). Class dismissed: Making the case for the study of classist microaggressions. In D. Sue (Ed.), *Microaggressions and marginality: Manifestation, dynamics, and impact* (pp. 269–285). Hoboken, NJ: Wiley.

Smith, M. L., Glass, G. V., & Miller, T. I. (1980). *The benefits of psychotherapy.* Baltimore: Johns Hopkins University Press.

Smith, N. K., Cacioppo, J. T., Larsen, J. T., & Chartrand, T. L. (2003). May I have your attention, please: Electrocortical responses to positive and negative stimuli. *Neuropsychologia, 41,* 171–183.

Smith, P. B., & Bond, M. H. (1993). *Social psychology across cultures: Analysis and perspective.* New York: Harvester/Wheatsheaf.

Smith, S. S., & Richardson, D. (1983). Amelioration of deception and harm in psychological research: The important role of debriefing. *Journal of Personality and Social Psychology, 44,* 1075–1082.

Smith, T. W., Snyder, C. R., & Perkins, S. C. (1983). The self-serving function of hypochondriacal complaints: Physical symptoms as self-handicapping strategies. *Journal of Personality and Social Psychology, 44,* 787–797.

Smith, V. L., & Kassin, S. M. (1993). Effects of the dynamite charge on the deliberations of deadlocked mock juries. *Law and Human Behavior, 17,* 625–643.

Smolak, L., & Thompson, J. K. (Eds.). (2009). *Body image, eating disorders, and obesity in youth: Assessment, prevention, and treatment* (2nd ed.). Washington, DC: American Psychological Association.

Snibbe, A. C., Kitayama, S., Markus, H. R., & Suzuki, T. (2003). They saw a game: A Japanese and American (football) field study. *Journal of Cross-Cultural Psychology, 34,* 581–595.

Snyder, C. R., & Higgins, R. L. (1988). Excuses: Their effective role in the negotiation of reality. *Psychological Bulletin, 104,* 23–35.

Snyder, C. R., Lassegard, M. A., & Ford, C. E. (1986). Distancing after group success and failure: Basking in reflected glory and cutting off reflected failure. *Journal of Personality and Social Psychology, 51,* 382–388.

Snyder, M. (1974). The self-monitoring of expressive behavior. *Journal of Personality and Social Psychology, 30,* 526–537.

Snyder, M. (1987). *Public appearances/private realities: The psychology of self-monitoring.* New York: Freeman.

Snyder, M. (1993). Basic research and practical problems: The promise of a "functional" personality and social psychology. *Personality and Social Psychology Bulletin, 19,* 251–264.

Snyder, M., & DeBono, K. (1985). Appeals to image and claims about quality: Understanding the psychology of advertising. *Journal of Personality and Social Psychology, 49,* 586–597.

Snyder, M., & Gangestad, S. (1986). On the nature of self-monitoring: Matters of assessment, matters of validity. *Journal of Personality and Social Psychology, 51,* 125–139.

Snyder, M., & Monson, T. C. (1975). Persons, situations, and the control of social behavior. *Journal of Personality and Social Psychology, 32,* 637–644.

Snyder, M., & Omoto, A. (2008). Volunteerism: Social issues perspectives and social policy implications. *Social Issues and Policy Review, 2,* 1–36.

Snyder, M., & Stukas, A. A. (1999). Interpersonal processes: The interplay of cognitive, motivational, and behavioral activities in social interaction. *Annual Review of Psychology, 50,* 273–303.

Snyder, M., & Swann, W. B., Jr. (1978). Behavioral confirmation in social interaction: From social perception to social reality. *Journal of Personality and Social Psychology, 36,* 1202–1212.

Snyder, M., Tanke, E. D., & Berscheid, E. (1977). Social perception and interpersonal behavior: On the self-fulfilling nature of social stereotypes. *Journal of Personality and Social Psychology, 35,* 656–666.

Soll, J. B., & Larrick, R. P. (2009). Strategies for revising judgment: How (and how well) people use others' opinions. *Journal of Experimental Psychology: Learning, Memory, and Cognition, 35,* 780–805.

Sommers, S. (2006). On racial diversity and group decision making: Identifying multiple effects of racial composition on jury deliberations. *Journal of Personality and Social Psychology, 90,* 597–612.

Sommers, S. (2011). *Situations matter: Understanding how context transforms your world.* New York: Riverhead Books.

Sommers, S. R., & Ellsworth, P. C. (2001). White juror bias: An investigation of racial prejudice against Black defendants in the American courtroom. *Psychology, Public Policy, and Law, 7,* 201–229.

Sommers, S. R., & Ellsworth, P. C. (2009). 'Race salience' in juror decision-making: Misconceptions, clarifications, and unanswered questions. *Behavioral Sciences and The Law, 27,* 599–609.

Sommers, S. R., & Norton, M. I. (2007). Race-based judgments, race-neutral justifications: Experimental examination of peremptory use and the Batson challenge procedure. *Law and Human Behavior, 31,* 261–273.

Sommers, S. R., & Norton, M. I. (2008). Race and jury selection: Psychological perspectives on the peremptory challenge debate. *American Psychologist, 63,* 527–539.

Sommers, S. R., Warp, L. S., & Mahoney, C. C. (2008). Cognitive effects of racial diversity: White individuals' information processing in heterogeneous groups. *Journal of Experimental Social Psychology, 44,* 1129–1136.

Son Hing, L. S., Bobocel, D. R., & Zanna, M. P. (2002). Meritocracy and opposition to affirmative action: Making concessions in the face of discrimination. *Journal of Personality and Social Psychology, 83,* 493–509.

Son Hing, L. S., Chung-Yan, G. A., Hamilton, L. K., & Zanna, M. P. (2008). A two-dimensional model that employs explicit and implicit attitudes to characterize prejudice. *Journal of Personality and Social Psychology, 94,* 971–987.

Song, H., & Schwarz, N. (2009). If it's difficult to pronounce, it must be risky: Fluency, familiarity, and risk perception. *Psychological Science, 20,* 135–138.

Song, H., Vonasch, A. J., Meier, B. P., & Bargh, J. A. (2012). Brighten up: Smiles facilitate perceptual judgment of facial lightness. *Journal of Experimental Social Psychology, 48,* 450–452.

Sovacool, B. K. (2008). Exploring scientific misconduct: Isolated individuals, impure institutions, or an inevitable idiom of modern science? *Bioethical Inquiry, 5,* 271–282.

Spears, R. (2011). Group identities: The social identity perspective. In S. J. Schwartz, K. Luyckx, & V. L. Vignoles (Eds.), *Handbook of identity theory and research* (Vols 1 and 2) (pp. 201–224). New York: Springer.

Spencer-Rodgers, J., Boucher, H. C., Mori, S. C., Wang, L., & Peng, K. (2009). The dialectical self-concept: Contradiction, change, and holism in East Asian cultures. *Personality and Social Psychology Bulletin, 35,* 29–44.

Spencer-Rodgers, J., Williams, M. J., & Peng, K. (2012). Culturally based lay beliefs as a tool for understanding intergroup and intercultural relations. *International Journal of Intercultural Relations, 36,* 169–178.

Spencer, B., & Castano, E. (2007). Social class is dead. Long live social class! Stereotype threat among low socioeconomic status individuals. *Social Justice Research, 20,* 418–432.

Spencer, S. J., Fein, S., Wolfe, C. T., Fong, C., & Dunn, M. A. (1998). Automatic activation of stereotypes: The role of self-image threat. *Personality and Social Psychology Bulletin, 24,* 1139–1152.

Spencer, S. J., Fein, S., Zanna, M., & Olson, J. M. (Eds.). (2003). *Motivated social perception: The Ontario symposium* (Vol. 9). Mahwah, NJ: Erlbaum.

Spencer, S. J., Steele, C. M., & Quinn, D. M. (1999). Stereotype threat and women's math performance. *Journal of Experimental Social Psychology, 35,* 4–28.

Spiegel, D. (1993). Social support: How friends, family, and groups can help. In D. Goleman & J. Gurin (Eds.), *Mind body medicine: How to use your mind for better health* (pp. 331–350). Yonkers, NY: Consumer Reports Books.

Spieker, S. J., Campbell, S. B., Vandergrift, N., Pierce, K. M., Cauffman, E., Susman, E. J., & Roisman, G. I. (2012). Relational aggression in middle childhood: Predictors and adolescent outcomes. *Social Development, 21,* 354–375.

Spivey, C. B., & Prentice-Dunn, S. (1990). Assessing the directionality of deindividuated behavior: Effects of deindividuation, modeling, and private self-consciousness on aggressive and prosocial responses. *Basic and Applied Social Psychology, 11,* 387–403.

Sporer, S. L., Penrod, S. D., Read, J. D., & Cutler, B. L. (1995). Choosing, confidence, and accuracy: A meta-analysis of the confidence-accuracy relation in eyewitness identification studies. *Psychological Bulletin, 118,* 315–327.

Spradley, J., & McCurdy, D. W. (2009). *Conformity and conflict: Readings in cultural anthropology* (13th ed.). Boston: Allyn & Bacon.

Spradley, J., & McCurdy, D. W. (2012). *Conformity and conflict. Readings in cultural Anthropology* (14th edition). Upper Saddle River, NJ: Pearson.

Sprecher, S. (1994). Two sides to the breakup of dating relationships. *Personal Relationships, 1,* 199–222.

Sprecher, S. (1999). "I love you more today than yesterday": Romantic partners' perceptions of changes in love and related affect over time. *Journal of Personality and Social Psychology, 76,* 46–53.

Sprecher, S. (2001). Equity and social exchange in dating couples: Associations with satisfaction, commitment, and stability. *Journal of Marriage and the Family, 63,* 599–613.

Sprecher, S., & Hendrick, S. S. (2004). Self-disclosure in intimate relationships: Associations with individual and relationship characteristics over time. *Journal of Social and Clinical Psychology, 23,* 857–877.

Sprecher, S., & Regan, P. C. (1998). Passionate and companionate love in courting and young married couples. *Sociological Inquiry, 68,* 163–185.

Sprecher, S., Sullivan, Q., & Hatfield, E. (1994). Mate selection preferences: Gender differences examined in a national sample. *Journal of Personality and Social Psychology, 66,* 1074–1080.

Sprecher, S., Wenzel, A., & Harvey, J. (Eds.). (2008). *Handbook of relationship initiation.* New York: Psychology Press.

Staats, A. W., & Staats, C. K. (1958). Attitudes established by classical conditioning. *Journal of Abnormal and Social Psychology, 57,* 37–40.

Ståhl, T., Van Laar, C., & Ellemers, N. (2012). The role of prevention focus under stereotype threat: Initial cognitive mobilization is followed by depletion. *Journal of Personality and Social Psychology, 102,* 1239–1251.

Stalans, L. J., & Diamond, S. S. (1990). Formation and change in lay evaluations of criminal sentencing: Misperception and discontent. *Law and Human Behavior, 14,* 199–214.

Stangor, C., Sechrist, G. B., & Jost, J. T. (2001). Changing racial beliefs by providing consensus information. *Personality and Social Psychology Bulletin, 27,* 486–496.

Stankiewicz, J. M., & Rosselli, F. (2008). Women as sex objects and victims in print advertisements. *Sex Roles, 58,* 579–589.

Stanton, A. L., Kirk, S. B., Cameron, C. L., & Danoff-Berg, S. (2000). Coping through emotional approach: Scale construction and validation. *Journal of Personality and Social Psychology, 78,* 1150–1169.

Stark, C.E.L., Okado, Y., & Loftus, E.F. (2010). Imaging the reconstruction of true and false memories using sensory reactivation and the misinformation paradigms. *Learning and Memory, 17,* 485–488.

Starzyk, K., Fabrigar, L., Soryal, A., & Fanning, J. (2009). A painful reminder: The role of level and salience of attitude importance in cognitive dissonance. *Personality and Social Psychology Bulletin, 35,* 126–137.

Stasser, G. (1992). Pooling of unshared information during group discussions. In S. Worchel, W. Wood, & J. A. Simpson (Eds.), *Group process and productivity* (pp. 48–67). Newbury Park, CA: Sage.

Stasser, G., & Davis, J. H. (1981). Group decision making and social influence: A social interaction sequence model. *Psychological Review, 88,* 523–551.

Stasser, G., & Titus, W. (2003). Hidden profiles: A brief history. *Psychological Inquiry, 14,* 304–313.

Stasser, G., Kerr, N. L., & Bray, R. M. (1982). The social psychology of jury deliberations: Structure, process, and product. In N. Kerr & R. Bray (Eds.), *The psychology of the courtroom* (pp. 221–256). New York: Academic Press.

Stasser, G., Stewart, D. D., & Wittenbaum, G. M. (1995). Expert roles and information exchange during discussion: The importance of knowing who knows what. *Journal of Experimental Social Psychology, 31,* 244–265.

Staub, E. (2004). Understanding and responding to group violence: Genocide, mass killing, and terrorism. In F. M. Moghaddam & A. J. Marsella (Eds.), *Understanding terrorism: Psychosocial roots, consequences, and interventions* (pp. 151–168). Washington, DC: American Psychological Association.

Staub, E., & Vollhardt, J. (2008). Altruism born of suffering: The roots of caring and helping after victimization and other trauma. *American Journal of Orthopsychiatry, 78,* 267–280.

Stauffer, J. M., & Buckley, M. R. (2005). The existence and nature of racial bias in supervisory ratings. *Journal of Applied Psychology, 90,* 586–591.

Staw, B. M. (1997). The escalation of commitment: An update and appraisal. In Z. Shapira (Ed.), *Organizational decision making. Cambridge series on judgement and decision making* (pp. 191–215). New York: Cambridge University Press.

Staw, B. M., & Hoang, H. (1995). Sunk costs in the NBA: Why draft order affects playing time and survival in professional basketball. *Administrative Science Quarterly, 40,* 474–493.

Staw, B. M., Barsade, S. G., & Koput, K. W. (1997). Escalation at the credit window: A longitudinal study of bank executives' recognition and write-off of problem loans. *Journal of Applied Psychology, 82,* 130–142.

Steblay, N. K. Dysart , J. E. Wells , G. L. (2011). Seventy-two tests of the sequential lineup superiority effect: A meta-analysis and policy discussion. *Psychology, Public Policy, and Law, 17,* 99–139.

Steblay, N. M. (1987). Helping behavior in rural and urban environments: A meta-analysis. *Psychological Bulletin, 102,* 346–356.

Steblay, N. M. (1992). A meta-analytic review of the weapon-focus effect. *Law and Human Behavior, 16,* 413–424.

Steblay, N. M. (1997). Social influence in eyewitness recall: A meta-analytic review of lineup instruction effects. *Law and Human Behavior, 21,* 283–297.

Steblay, N., Besirevic, J., Fulero, S., & Jiminez-Lorente, B. (1999). The effects of pretrial publicity on juror verdicts: A meta-analytic review. *Law and Human Behavior, 23,* 219–235.

Steblay, N., Hosch, H. M., Culhane, S. E., & McWethy, A. (2006). The impact on juror verdicts of judicial instruction to disregard inadmissible evidence: A meta-analysis. *Law and Human Behavior, 30,* 469–492.

Steele, C. M. (1988). The psychology of self-affirmation: Sustaining the integrity of the self. In L. Berkowitz (Ed.), *Advances in experimental social psychology* (Vol. 21, pp. 261–302). New York: Academic Press.

Steele, C. M. (1997). A threat in the air: How stereotypes shape intellectual identity and performance. *American Psychologist, 52,* 613–629.

Steele, C. M. (1999). Thin ice: "Stereotype threat" and black college students. *Atlantic Monthly, 284,* 44–47, 50–54.

Steele, C. M. (2010). *Whistling Vivaldi: How stereotypes affect us and what we can do.* New York: Norton.

Steele, C. M., & Aronson, J. (1995). Stereotype vulnerability and the intellectual test performance of African Americans. *Journal of Personality and Social Psychology, 69,* 797–811.

Steele, C. M., & Josephs, R. A. (1990). Alcohol myopia: Its prized and dangerous effects. *American Psychologist, 45,* 921–933.

Steele, C. M., Spencer, S. J., & Aronson, J. (2002). Contending with group image: The psychology of stereotype and social identity threat. In M. P. Zanna (Ed.), *Advances in experimental social psychology* (Vol. 34, pp. 379–440). San Diego, CA: Academic Press.

Steele, C. M., Spencer, S. J., & Lynch, M. (1993). Self-image resilience and dissonance: The role of affirmational resources. *Journal of Personality and Social Psychology, 64,* 885–896.

Stein, M. B., Walker, J. R., & Forde, D. R. (1996). Public-speaking fears in a community sample. *Archives of General Psychiatry, 53,* 169–174.

Steiner, I. D. (1972). *Group process and productivity.* New York: Academic Press.

Stephan, W. G. (1986). The effects of school desegregation: An evaluation 30 years after Brown. In M. J. Saks & L. Saxe (Eds.), *Advances in applied social psychology* (Vol. 3, pp. 181–206). Hillsdale, NJ: Erlbaum.

Stephan, W. G., Renfro, C. L., Esses, V. M., Stephan, C. W., & Martin, T. (2005). The effects of feeling threatened on attitudes toward immigrants. *International Journal of Intercultural Relations, 29,* 1–19.

Stephan, W. G., Ybarra, O., & Morrison, K. (2009). Intergroup threat theory. In T. D. Nelson (Ed.), *Handbook of prejudice, stereotyping, and discrimination* (pp. 43–59). New York: Psychology Press.

Stepper, S., & Strack, F. (1993). Proprioceptive determinants of emotional and nonemotional feelings. *Journal of Personality and Social Psychology, 64,* 211–220.

Sternberg, R. J. (1986). A triangular theory of love. *Psychological Review, 93,* 119–135.

Sternberg, R. J. (1997). *Successful intelligence: How practical and creative intelligence determine success in life.* New York: Plume.

Sternberg, R. J. (1999). *Cupid's arrow: The course of love through time.* New York: Cambridge University Press.

Sternberg, R. J., & Hedlund, J. (2002). Practical intelligence, *g,* and work psychology. *Human Performance, 15,* 143–160.

Sternberg, R. J., & Weis, K. (Eds.). (2006). *The new psychology of love.* New Haven, CT: Yale University Press.

Sternglanz, R. W., & DePaulo, B. M. (2004). Reading nonverbal cues to emotions: Advantages and liabilities of relationship closeness. *Journal of Nonverbal Behavior, 28,* 245–266.

Stevens, C. K., & Kristof, A. L. (1995). Making the right impression: A field study of applicant impression management during job interviews. *Journal of Applied Psychology, 80,* 587–606.

Stewart-Williams, S. (2007). Altruism among kin vs. nonkin: Effects of cost of help and reciprocal exchange. *Evolution and Human Behavior, 28,* 193–198.

Stewart-Williams, S. (2008). Human beings as evolved nepotists: Exceptions to the rule and effects of cost of help. *Human Nature, 19,* 414–425.

Stewart, A. J., Sokol, M., Healy, J. M., Jr., & Chester, N. L. (1986). Longitudinal studies of psychological consequences of life changes in children and adults. *Journal of Personality and Social Psychology, 50,* 143–151.

Stewart, B. D., & Payne, B. K. (2008). Bringing automatic stereotyping under control: Implementation intentions as efficient means of thought control. *Personality and Social Psychology Bulletin, 34,* 1332–1345.

Stewart, D. (2012). Racist Hunger Games fans are very disappointed. http://jezebel.com/5896408/racist-hunger-games-fans-dont-care-how-much-money-the-movie-made. March 26.

Stewart, G. L., Dustin, S. L., Barrick, M. R., & Darnold, T. C. (2008). Exploring the handshake in employment interviews. *Journal of Applied Psychology, 93,* 1139–1146.

Stewart, L. H., Ajina, S., Getov, S., Bahrami, B., Todorov, A., & Rees, G. (2012). Unconscious evaluation of faces on social dimensions. *Journal of Experimental Psychology: General,* April 2, 2012.

Steyn, R., & Mynhardt, J. (2008) Factors that influence the forming of self-evaluation and self-efficacy perceptions. *South African Journal of Psychology, 38,* 563–573.

Stine, G. J. (2007). *AIDS Update 2007.* New York: McGraw-Hill Science.

Stine, G. J. (2012). *AIDS Update 2012* (21st edition). New York: McGraw-Hill/Dushkin.

Stinson, D. A., Cameron, J. J., Wood, J. V., Gaucher, G., & Holmes, J. G. (2009). Deconstructing the "reign of error": Interpersonal warmth explains the self-fulfilling prophecy of anticipated acceptance. *Personality and Social Psychology Bulletin, 35,* 1165–1168.

Stinson, D. A., Logel, C., Shepherd, S., & Zanna. M. P. (2011). Rewriting the self—fulfilling prophecy of social rejection: Self-affirmation improves relational security and social behavior up to 2 months later. *Psychological Science, 22,* 1145–1149.

Stoltzfus, N. (1996). *Resistance of the heart: Intermarriage and the Rosenstrasse protest in Nazi Germany.* New York: Norton.

Stone, A. A., Neale, J. M., Cox, D. S., Napoli, A., Valdimarsdottir, H., & Kennedy-Moore, E. (1994). Daily events are associated with a secretory immune response to an oral antigen in men. *Health Psychology, 13,* 440–446.

Stone, J. (2003). Self-consistency for low self-esteem in dissonance processes: The role of self-standards. *Personality and Social Psychology Bulletin, 29,* 846–858.

Stone, J., Lynch, C. I., Sjomeling, M., & Darley, J. M. (1999). Stereotype threat effects on black and white athletic performance. *Journal of Personality and Social Psychology, 77,* 1213–1227.

Stone, J., Perry, Z. W., & Darley, J. M. (1997). "White men can't jump": Evidence for the perceptual confirmation of racial stereotypes following a basketball game. *Basic and Applied Social Psychology, 19,* 291–306.

Stone, J., Wiegand, A. W., Cooper, J., & Aronson, E. (1997). When exemplification fails: Hypocrisy and the motive for self-integrity. *Journal of Personality and Social Psychology, 72,* 54–65.

Stone, W. F., Lederer, G., & Christie, R. (Eds.). (1993). *Strength and weakness: The authoritarian personality today.* New York: Springer-Verlag.

Stout, J. G., Dasgupta, N., Hunsinger, M., & McManus, M. A. (2011). STEMing the tide: Using ingroup experts to inoculate women's self-concept in science, technology, engineering, and mathematics (STEM). *Journal of Personality and Social Psychology, 100,* 255–270.

Stouten, J., van Dijke, M., & De Cremer, D. (2012). Ethical leadership: An overview and future perspectives. *Journal of Personnel Psychology, 11,* 1–6.

Strahan, E. J., Spencer, S. J., & Zanna, M. P. (2002). Subliminal priming and persuasion: Striking while the iron is hot. *Journal of Experimental Social Psychology, 38,* 556–568.

Straub, R. O. (2012). *Health psychology: A Biosocial approach* (3rd ed.). New York: Worth Publishers.

Strauman, T. J. (1992). Self-guides, autobiographical memory, and anxiety and dysphoria: Toward a cognitive model of vulnerability to emotional distress. *Journal of Abnormal Psychology, 101,* 87–95.

Strauman, T. J., Lemieux, A. M., & Coe, C. L. (1993). Self-discrepancy and natural killer cell activity: Immunological consequences of negative self-evaluation. *Journal of Personality and Social Psychology, 64,* 1042–1052.

Strauman, T. J., Woods, T. E., Schneider, K. L., Kwapil, L., & Coe, C. L. (2004). Self-regulatory cognition and immune reactivity: Idiographic success and failure feedback effects on the natural killer cell. *Brain, Behavior and Immunity, 18,* 544–554.

Straus, M. A. (2000). *Beating the devil out of them: Corporal punishment in American families and its effects on children* (2nd ed.). New Brunswick, NJ: Transaction Publishers.

Straus, M. A. (2010). Criminogenic effects of corporal punishment by parents. In M. Herzog-Evans & I. Dréan-Rivette (Eds.), *Transnational criminology manual* (Vol. 1, pp. 373–390). Amsterdam: Wolf Legal Publishing.

Straus, M. A. (2011). Gender symmetry and mutuality in perpetration of clinical-level partner violence: Empirical evidence and implications for prevention and treatment. *Aggression and Violent Behavior, 16,* 279–288.

Straus, M. A., & Douglas, E. M. (2008). Research on spanking by parents: Implications for public policy. *The Family Psychologist: Bulletin of the Division of Family Psychology, 43,* 18–20.

Straus, M. A., & Ramirez, I. L. (2005). Gender symmetry in prevalence, severity, and chronicity of physical aggression against dating partners by university students in Mexico and the USA. In S. Fein, G. R. Goethals, & M. J. Sandstrom (Eds.), *Gender and aggression: Interdisciplinary perspectives.* Mahwah, NJ: Erlbaum.

Straus, S. G., Parker, A. M., Bruce, J. B., & Dembosky, J. W. (2009). *The group matters: A review of the effects of group interaction on processes and outcomes in analytic teams.* Report WR-580-USG. Arlington, VA: Rand Corporation.

Strawbridge, W. J., Shema, S. J., Cohen, R. D., & Kaplan, G. A. (2001). Religious attendance increases survival by improving and maintaining good health behaviors, mental health, and social relationships. *Annals of Behavioral Medicine, 23,* 68–74.

Strentz, T., & Auerbach, S. M. (1988). Adjustment to the stress of simulated captivity: Effects of emotion-focused versus problem-focused preparation on hostages differing in locus of control. *Journal of Personality and Social Psychology, 55,* 652–660.

Strick, M., van Baaren, R. B., Holland, R. W., & van Knippenberg, A. (2009). Humor in advertisements enhances product liking by mere association. *Journal of Experimental Psychology: Applied, 15,* 35–45.

Strier, F. (1999). Wither trial consulting: Issues and projections. *Law and Human Behavior, 23,* 93–115.

Strodtbeck, F. L., & Hook, L. (1961). The social dimensions of a twelve-man jury table. *Sociometry, 24,* 397–415.

Strodtbeck, F. L., James, R., & Hawkins, C. (1957). Social status in jury deliberations. *American Sociological Review, 22,* 713–719.

Stroebe, W. (2012). The truth about Triplett (1898), but nobody seems to care. *Perspectives on Psychological Science, 7,* 54–57.

Stroessner, S. J., & Plaks, J. E. (2001). Illusory correlation and stereotype formation: Tracing the arc of research over a quarter century. In G. B. Moskowitz (Ed.), *Cognitive social psychology: The Princeton symposium on the legacy and future of social cognition* (pp. 247–259). Mahwah, NJ: Erlbaum.

Strohmetz, D. B., Rind, B., Fisher, R., & Lynn, M. (2002). Sweetening the till: The use of candy to increase restaurant tipping. *Journal of Applied Social Psychology, 32,* 300–309.

Strough, J., Mehta, C. M., McFall, J. P., & Schuller, K. L. (2008). Are older adults less subject to the sunk-cost fallacy than younger adults? *Psychological Science, 19,* 650–652.

Strube, M. J. (2005). What did Triplett really find? A contemporary analysis of the first experiment in social psychology. *American Journal of Psychology, 118,* 271–286.

Struck, D. (2006, September 15). Gunman's writings presaged rampage; blog described fascination with death, laid out events that would unfold in Montreal. *Washington Post,* p. A12.

Strupp, H. H. (1996). The tripartite model and the Consumer Reports study. *American Psychologist, 51,* 1017–1024.

Studebaker, C. A., & Penrod, S. D. (1997). Pretrial publicity: The media, the law, and common sense. *Psychology, Public Policy, and Law, 3,* 428–460.

Stürmer, S., Snyder, M., & Omoto, A. M. (2005). Prosocial emotions and helping: The moderating role of group membership. *Journal of Personality and Social Psychology, 88,* 532–546.

Stürmer, S., Snyder, M., Kropp, A., & Siem, B. (2006). Empathy-motivated helping: The moderating role of group membership. *Personality and Social Psychology Bulletin, 32,* 943–956.

Stutzer, A. (2004). The role of income aspirations in individual happiness. *Journal of Economic Behavior and Organization, 54,* 89–109.

Suarez, E. C., & Krishnan, K. R. R. (2006). The relation of free plasma tryptophan to anger, hostility, and aggression in a nonpatient sample of adult men and women. *Annals of Behavioral Medicine, 31,* 254–260.

Subra, B., Muller, D., Bègue, L., Bushman, B. J., & Delmas, F. (2010). Automatic effects of alcohol and aggressive cues on aggressive thoughts and behaviors. *Personality and Social Psychology Bulletin, 36,* 1052–1057.

Sudman, S., Bradburn, N. M., & Schwarz, N. (2010). *Thinking about answers: The application of cognitive processes to survey methodology.* New York: Jossey-Bass.

Sue, S., Smith, R. E., & Caldwell, C. (1973). Effects of inadmissible evidence on the decisions of simulated jurors: A moral dilemma. *Journal of Applied Social Psychology, 3,* 345–353.

Suh, E., Diener, E., & Fujita, F. (1996). Events and subjective well-being: Only recent events matter. *Journal of Personality and Social Psychology, 70,* 1091–1102.

Suls, J. M., & Wheeler, L. (Eds.). (2000). *Handbook of social comparison: Theory and research.* New York: Plenum.

Sunday, S., Kline, M., Labruna, V., Pelcovitz, D., Salzinger, S., & Kaplan, S. (2011). The role of adolescent physical abuse in adult intimate partner violence. *Journal of Interpersonal Violence, 26,* 3773–3789.

Sundie, J. M., Kenrick, D. T., Griskevicius, V., Tybur, J. M., Vohs, K. D., & Beal, D. J. (2011). Peacocks, Porsches, and Thorstein Veblen: Conspicuous consumption as a sexual signaling system. *Journal of Personality and Social Psychology, 100,* 664–680.

Sundstrom, E. (1986). *Work places.* New York: Cambridge University Press.

Supple, A. J., & Plunkett, S. W. (2011). Dimensionality and validity of the Rosenberg Self-Esteem Scale for use with Latino adolescents. *Hispanic Journal of Behavioral Sciences, 33,* 39–53.

Surowiecki, J. (2005). *The wisdom of crowds.* New York: Anchor Books.

Susskind, J. (2003). Children's perception of gender-based illusory correlations: Enhancing preexisting relationships between gender and behavior. *Sex Roles, 48,* 483–494.

Swami, V., & Furnham, A. (2008). *The psychology of physical attraction.* New York: Routledge/Taylor & Francis.

Swann, W. B. Jr., Jetten, J., Gómez, Á., Whitehouse, H., & Bastian, B. (2012). When group membership gets personal: A theory of identity fusion. *Psychological Review, 119,* 441–456.

Swann, W. B., Jr. (1984). Quest for accuracy in person perception: A matter of pragmatics. *Psychological Review, 91,* 457–477.

Swann, W. B., Jr. (1987). Identity negotiation: Where two roads meet. *Journal of Personality and Social Psychology, 53,* 1038–1051.

Swann, W. B., Jr., & Bosson, J. K. (2010). Self and identity. In S. T. Fiske, D. T. Gilbert, & G. Lindzey (Eds.), *Handbook of social psychology* (5th ed.). New York: McGraw-Hill.

Swann, W. B., Jr., & Ely, R. J. (1984). A battle of wills: Self-verification versus behavioral confirmation. *Journal of Personality and Social Psychology, 46,* 1287–1302.

Swann, W. B., Jr., & Hill, C. A. (1982). When our identities are mistaken: Reaffirming self-conceptions through social interaction. *Journal of Personality and Social Psychology, 43,* 59–66.

Swann, W. B., Jr., Chang-Schneider, C. S., & McClarty, K. L. (2007). Do our self-views matter? Self-concept and self-esteem in everyday life. *American Psychologist, 62,* 84–94.

Swann, W. B., Jr., Hixon, J. G., & De La Ronde, C. (1992). Embracing the bitter "truth": Negative self-concepts and marital commitment. *Psychological Science, 3,* 118–121.

Sweldens, S., van Osselaer, S. M. J., Janiszewski, C. (2010). Evaluative conditioning procedures and the resilience of conditioned brand attitudes. *Journal of Consumer Research, 37,* 473–489.

Swider, B. W., Barrick, M. R., Harris, T. B., & Stoverink, A. C. (2011). Managing and creating an image in the interview: The role of interviewee initial impressions. *Journal of Applied Psychology, 96*, 1275–1288.

Swim, J. K., & Hyers, L. L. (2009). Sexism. In T. D. Nelson (Ed.), *Handbook of prejudice, stereotyping, and discrimination* (pp. 407–430). New York: Psychology Press.

Swim, J. K., & Sanna, L. J. (1996). He's skilled, she's lucky: A meta-analysis of observers' attributions for women's and men's successes and failures. *Personality and Social Psychology Bulletin, 22*, 507–519.

Swim, J. K., Mallett, R., Russo-Devosa, Y., & Stangor, C. (2005). Judgments of sexism: A comparison of sexism measures and sources of variability in judgments of sexism. *Psychology of Women Quarterly, 29*, 406–411.

t'Hart, P. (1998). Preventing groupthink revisited: Evaluating and reforming groups in government. *Organizational Behavior and Human Decision Processes, 73*, 306–326.

t'Hart, P., Stern, E., & Sundelius, B. (1995). *Beyond groupthink*. Stockholm: Stockholm Center for Organizational Research.

Tajfel, H. (1982). Social psychology of intergroup relations. *Annual Review of Psychology, 33*, 1–39.

Tajfel, H., Billig, M. G., Bundy, R. P., & Flament, C. (1971). Social categorization and intergroup behavior. *European Journal of Social Psychology, 1*, 149–178.

Takahashi, A., Quadros, I. M., de Almeida, R. M., & Miczek, K. A. (2011). Brain serotonin receptors and transporters: Initiation vs. termination of escalated aggression. *Psychopharmacology, 213*(2–3), 183–212.

Takemura, K., & Yuki, M. (2007). Are Japanese groups more competitive than Japanese individuals? A cross-cultural validation of the interindividual-intergroup discontinuity effect. *International Journal of Psychology, 42*, 27–35.

Talarico, J. M., & Rubin, D. C. (2007). Flashbulb memories are special after all; in phenomenology, not accuracy. *Applied Cognitive Psychology, 21*, 557–578.

Tamiya, R., Lee, S., & Ohtake, F. (2012). Second to fourth digit ratio and the sporting success of sumo wrestlers. *Evolution And Human Behavior, 33*(2), 130–131.

Tan, H. H., & Tan, M.-L. (2008). Organizational citizenship behavior and social loafing: The role of personality, motives, and contextual factors. *Journal of Psychology: Interdisciplinary and Applied, 142*, 89–108.

Tanford, S., & Penrod, S. (1984). Social influence model: A formal integration of research on majority and minority influence processes. *Psychological Bulletin, 95*, 189–225.

Tang, J-H., & Wang, C-C. (2012). Self-disclosure among bloggers: Re-examination of Social Penetration theory. *Cyberpsychology, Behavior, and Social Networking, 15*, 245–250.

Tang, S., & Hall, V. C. (1995). The overjustification effect: A meta-analysis. *Applied Cognitive Psychology, 9*, 365–404.

Tassinary, L. G., & Cacioppo, J. T. (1992). Unobservable facial actions and emotion. *Psychological Science, 3*, 28–33.

Täuber, S., & van Zomeren, M. (2012). Refusing intergroup help from the morally superior: How one group's moral superiority leads to another group's reluctance to seek their help. *Journal of Experimental Social Psychology, 48*, 420–423.

Tay, C., Ang, S., & Linn, V. (2006). Personality, biographical characteristics, and job interview success: A longitudinal study of the mediating effects of interviewing self-efficacy and the moderating effects of internal locus of causality. *Journal of Applied Psychology, 91*, 446–454.

Taylor, K. A., Mesmer-Magnus, J., & Burns, T. M. (2008). Teaching the art of negotiation: Improving students' negotiating confidence and perceptions of effectiveness. *Journal of Education for Business, 83*, 135–140.

Taylor, L. S., Fiore, A. T., Mendelsohn, G. A., & Cheshire, C. (2011). "Out of my league": A real-world test of the matching hypothesis. *Personality and Social Psychology Bulletin, 37*, 942–954.

Taylor, R. B. (2000). *Breaking away from broken windows: Baltimore neighborhoods and the nationwide fight against crime, grime, fear, and decline.* Boulder, CO: Westview Press.

Taylor, S. E. (1989). *Positive illusions: Creative self-deceptions and the healthy mind.* New York: Basic Books.

Taylor, S. E. (1990). Health psychology: The science and the field. *American Psychologist, 45*, 40–50.

Taylor, S. E. (1991). Asymmetrical effects of positive and negative events: The mobilization-minimization hypothesis. *Psychological Bulletin, 110*, 67–85.

Taylor, S. E. (2002). *The tending instinct: Women, men, and the biology of nurturing.* New York: Times Books.

Taylor, S. E. (2012a). *Health Psychology* (8th ed.). New York: McGraw-Hill.

Taylor, S. E. (2012b). Tend and befriend theory. In P. Van Lange, A. Kruglanski, & E. T. Higgins (Eds.), *Handbook of theories of social psychology* (Volume 1), pp. 32–49. Thousand Oaks, CA: Sage.

Taylor, S. E., & Brown, J. D. (1988). Illusion and well-being: A social psychological perspective on mental health. *Psychological Bulletin, 103*, 193–210.

Taylor, S. E., & Fiske, S. T. (1975). Point of view and perceptions of causality. *Journal of Personality and Social Psychology, 32*, 439–445.

Taylor, S. E., & Lobel, M. (1989). Social comparison activity under threat: Downward evaluation and upward contacts. *Psychological Review, 96*, 569–575.

Taylor, S. E., Lerner, J. S., Sherman, D. K., Sage, R. M., & McDowell, N. K. (2003). Portrait of the self-enhancer: Well adjusted and well liked or maladjusted and friendless? *Journal of Personality and Social Psychology, 84*, 165–176.

Taylor, S. E., Sherman, D. K., Kim, H. S., Jarcho, J., Takgi, K., & Dunagan, M. S. (2004). Culture and social support: Who seeks it and why? *Journal of Personality and Social Psychology, 87*, 354–362.

Taylor, S. E., Welch, W. T., Kim, H. S., & Sherman, D. K. (2007). Cultural differences in the impact of social support on psychological and biological stress responses. *Psychological Science, 18*, 831–837.

Taylor, V., & Walton, G. M. (2011). Stereotype threat undermines academic learning. *Personality and Social Psychology Bulletin, 37*, 1055–1067.

Tedeschi, J. T., & Bond, M. H. (2001). Aversive behavior and aggression in cultural perspective. In R. M. Kowalski (Ed.), *Behaving badly: Aversive behaviors in interpersonal relationships* (pp. 257–293). Washington, DC: American Psychological Association.

Tedeschi, J. T., Schlenker, B. R., & Bonoma, T. V. (1971). Cognitive dissonance: Private ratiocination or public spectacle? *American Psychologist, 26*, 685–695.

Teger, A. (1980). *Too much invested to quit.* New York: Pergamon Press.

Tejada-Vera, B., & Sutton, P. (2009). *Births, marriages, divorces, and deaths: Provisional data for July 2008* (National Vital Statistics Reports No. 57). Hyattsville, MD: National Center for Health Statistics.

Tekleab, A. G., Quigley, N. R., & Tesluk, P. E. (2009). A longitudinal study of team conflict, conflict management, cohesion, and team effectiveness. *Group & Organization Management, 34*, 170–205.

Tenenbaum, H. R., & Leaper, C. (2002). Are parents' gender schemas related to their children's gender-related cognitions? A meta-analysis. *Developmental Psychology, 38*, 615–630.

Tepper, B. J. (2001). Health consequences of organizational injustice: Tests of main and interactive effects. *Organizational Behavior and Human Decision Processes, 86*, 197–215.

Tesser, A. (1978). Self-generated attitude change. In L. Berkowitz (Ed.), *Advances in experimental social psychology* (Vol. 11, pp. 288–338). New York: Academic Press.

Tesser, A. (1993). The importance of heritability in psychological research: The case of attitudes. *Psychological Review, 100*, 129–142.

Tetlock, P. E. (1998). Social psychology and world politics. In D. T. Gilbert, S. T. Fiske, & G. Lindzey (Eds.), *The handbook of social psychology* (4th ed., Vol. 2, pp. 868–912). New York: McGraw-Hill.

Thaler, R. (1980). Toward a positive theory of consumer choice. *Journal of Economic Behavior and Organization, 1*, 39–60.

Thibaut, J. W., & Kelley, H. H. (1959). *The social psychology of groups.* New York: Wiley.

Thibaut, J., & Walker, L. (1975). *Procedural justice: A psychological analysis.* Hillsdale, NJ: Erlbaum.

Thibaut, J., & Walker, L. (1978). A theory of procedure. *California Law Review, 66,* 541–566.

Thomaes, S., Bushman, B. J., Stegge, H., & Olthof, T. (2008). Trumping shame by blasts of noise: Narcissism, self-esteem, shame, and aggression in young adolescents. *Child Development, 79,* 1792–1801.

Thomaes, S., Reijntjes, A., Orobio de Castro, B., & Bushman, B. J. (In press). Do inflated self-views buffer or fuel the negative impact of threatening events? *Psychological Science.*

Thomas, D. A., & Gabarro, J. J. (1999). *Breaking through: The making of minority executives in corporate America.* Cambridge, MA: Harvard Business School Press.

Thomas, E. F., Mavor, K. I., & McGarty, C. (2012). Social identities facilitate and encapsulate action-relevant constructs: A test of the social identity model of collective action. *Group Processes & Intergroup Relations, 15,* 75–88.

Thomas, K. D., & Levant, R. F. (2012). Does the endorsement of traditional masculinity ideology moderate the relationship between exposure to violent video games and aggression? *The Journal of Men's Studies, 20,* 47–56.

Tomasello, M. (2008). *Developmental Psychology, 44,* 1785–1788.

Thompson-Cannino, J., & Cotton, R. (2009). *Picking cotton: Our memoir of injustice and redemption.* New York: St. Martin's Press.

Thompson, C. P., Herrmann, D. J., Read, J. D., Bruce, D., Payne, D. G., & Toglia, M. P. (Eds.). (1998). *Eyewitness memory: Theoretical and applied perspectives.* Mahwah, NJ: Erlbaum.

Thompson, J. K. (Ed.). (2003). *Handbook of eating disorders and obesity.* New York: Wiley.

Thompson, L. (1990). Negotiation behavior and outcomes: Empirical evidence and theoretical issues. *Psychological Bulletin, 108,* 515–532.

Thompson, L. L., Wang, J., & Gunia, B. C. (2010). Negotiation. *Annual Review of Psychology, 61,* 491–515.

Thompson, L., & Hrebec, D. (1996). Lose-lose agreements in interdependent decision making. *Psychological Bulletin, 120,* 396–409.

Thompson, L., Wang, J., & Gunia, B. (2010, January). Negotiation. In S. Fiske (Ed.), *Annual Review of Psychology, 61,* 491–515.

Thompson, S. C. (1999). Illusions of control: How we overestimate our personal influence. *Current Directions in Psychological Science, 8,* 187–190.

Thompson, S. C., Sobolew-Shubin, A., Galbraith, M. E., Schwankovsky, L., & Cruzen, D. (1993). Maintaining perceptions of control: Finding perceived control in low-control circumstances. *Journal of Personality and Social Psychology, 64,* 293–304.

Thornhill, R., & Gangestad, S. W. (1993). Human facial beauty: Averageness, symmetry, and parasite resistance. *Human Nature, 4,* 237–269.

Thornton, B. (1992). Repression and its mediating influence on the defensive attribution of responsibility. *Journal of Research in Personality, 26,* 44–57.

Thornton, G. C., & Rupp, D. E. (2006). *Assessment centers in human resource management: Strategies for prediction, diagnosis, and development.* Mahwah, NJ: Erlbaum.

Thorpe, V. (2012). Richard Dawkins in furious row with EO Wilson over theory of evolution: Book review sparks war of words between grand old man of biology and Oxford's most high-profile Darwinist. *The Guardian,* June 23.

Thorsteinsson, E. B., James, J. E., & Gregg, M. E. (1998). Effects of video-relayed social support on hemodynamic reactivity and salivary cortisol during laboratory-based behavioral challenge. *Health Psychology, 17,* 436–444.

Thurstone, L. L. (1928). Attitudes can be measured. *American Journal of Sociology, 33,* 529–544.

Tice, D. M. (1991). Esteem protection or enhancement? Self-handicapping motives and attributions differ by trait self-esteem. *Journal of Personality and Social Psychology, 60,* 711–725.

Tice, D. M., & Baumeister, R. F. (1997). Longitudinal study of procrastination, performance, stress, and health: The costs and benefits of dawdling. *Psychological Science, 8,* 454–458.

Tiddi, B., Aureli, F., & Schino, G. (2010). Grooming for infant handling in tufted capuchin monkeys: A reappraisal of the primate infant market. *Animal Behaviour, 79,* 1115–1123.

Tiddi, B., Aureli, F., di Sorrentino, E., Janson, C. H., & Schino, G. (2011). Grooming for tolerance? Two mechanisms of exchange in wild tufted capuchin monkeys. *Behavioral Ecology, 22,* 663–669.

Tierney, J. (2011). Social scientist sees bias within. *New York Times,* February 8, D1.

Tiggemann, M., & Williams, E. (2012). The role of self-objectification in disordered eating, depressed mood, and sexual functioning among women: A comprehensive test of objectification theory. *Psychology of Women Quarterly, 36,* 66–75.

Tilcsik, A. (2011). Pride and prejudice: Employment discrimination against openly gay men in the United States. *American Journal of Sociology, 117,* 586–626.

Tilker, H. A. (1970). Socially responsible behavior as a function of observer responsibility and victim feedback. *Journal of Personality and Social Psychology, 14,* 95–100.

*Time* (1994, June 27). p. 26.

Timmons-Mitchell, J., Bender, M. B., Kishna, M. A., & Mitchell, C. C. (2006). An independent effectiveness trial of multisystemic therapy with juvenile justice youth. *Journal of Clinical Child and Adolescent Psychology, 35,* 227–236.

Tjosvold, D., Hui, C., & Sun, H. (2004). Can Chinese discuss conflicts openly? Field and experimental studies of face dynamics in China. *Group Decision and Negotiation, 13,* 351–373.

Tobin, A. M. (2006, October 3). "Copycat effect" may explain cluster. *Toronto Star,* p. A7.

Tobin, S. J., & Raymundo, M. M. (2009). Persuasion by causal arguments: The motivating role of perceived causal expertise. *Social Cognition, 27,* 105–127.

Todd, A. R., Galinsky, A. D., & Bodenhausen, G. V. (2012). Perspective taking undermines stereotype maintenance processes: Evidence from social memory, behavior explanation, and information solicitation. *Social Cognition, 30,* 94–108.

Todorov, A., & Uleman, J. S. (2004). The person reference process in spontaneous trait inferences. *Journal of Personality and Social Psychology, 87,* 482–493.

Todorov, A., Said, C. P., Engell, A. D., & Oosterhof, N. A. (2008). Understanding evaluation of faces on social dimensions. *Trends in Cognitive Sciences, 12,* 455–460.

Tolin, D. F., & Foa, E. B. (2006). Sex differences in trauma and posttraumatic stress disorder: A quantitative review of 25 years of research. *Psychological Bulletin, 132,* 959–992.

Tolstedt, B. E., & Stokes, J. P. (1984). Self-disclosure, intimacy, and the depenetration process. *Journal of Personality and Social Psychology, 46,* 84–90.

Tomada, G., & Schneider, B. H. (1997). Relational aggression, gender, and peer acceptance: Invariance across culture, stability over time, and concordance among informants. *Developmental Psychology, 33,* 601–609.

Toosi, N. R., Babbitt, L. G., Ambady, N., & Sommers, S. R. (2012). Dyadic interracial interactions: A meta-analysis. *Psychological Bulletin, 138,* 1–27.

Toosi, N. R., Sommers, S. R., & Ambady, N. (2012). Getting a word in groupwise: Effects of racial diversity on gender dynamics. *Journal of Experimental Social Psychology,* in press.

Top, T. J. (1991). Sex bias in the evaluation of performance in the scientific, artistic, and literary professions: A review. *Sex Roles, 24,* 73–106.

Tormala, Z. L., & Petty, R. E. (2002). What doesn't kill me makes me stronger: The effects of resisting persuasion on attitude certainty. *Journal of Personality and Social Psychology, 83,* 1298–1313.

Tormala, Z. L., Brinol, P., & Petty, R. E. (2006). When credibility attacks: The reverse impact of source credibility on persuasion. *Journal of Experimental Social Psychology, 42,* 684–691.

Tornblom, K., & Vermunt, R. (Eds.) (2007). *Distributive and procedural justice: Research and social applications.* Burlington, VT: Ashgate.

Törngren, G., & Montgomery, H. (2004). Worse than chance? Performance and confidence among professionals and lay-people in the stock market. *Journal of Behavioral Finance, 5,* 148–153.

Torres-Harding, S. R., Andrade, A. r., & Romero Diaz, C. E. (2012). The Racial Microaggressions Scale (RMAS): A new scale to measure experiences of racial microaggressions in people of color. *Cultural Diversity and Ethnic Minority Psychology, 18,* 153–164.

Tórrez, L., Robles, N., González, A., & Crofoot, M. C. (2012). Risky business? Lethal attack by a jaguar sheds light on the costs of predator mobbing for capuchins (*Cebus capucinus*). *International Journal of Primatology, 33*, 440–446.

Tourangeau, R., Rips, L. J., & Rasinksi, K. (2000). *The psychology of survey response*. New York: Cambridge University Press.

Tourangeau, R., Smith, T. W., & Rasinski, K. A. (1997). Motivation to report sensitive behaviors on surveys: Evidence from a bogus pipeline experiment. *Journal of Applied Social Psychology, 27*, 209–222.

Trafimow, D., Silverman, E. S., Fan, R. M. T., & Law, J. S. F. (1997). The effects of language and priming on the relative accessibility of the private self and collective self. *Journal of Cross-Cultural Psychology, 28*, 107–123.

Trafimow, D., Triandis, H. C., & Goto, S. G. (1991). Some tests of the distinction between the private and collective self. *Journal of Personality and Social Psychology, 60*, 649–655.

Trawalter, S., & Shapiro, J. R. (2010). Racial bias and stereotyping: Interpersonal processes. In B. Gawronski & B. Payne (Eds.), *Handbook of implicit social cognition: Measurement, theory, and applications* (pp. 375–391). New York: Guilford.

Trawalter, S., Adam, E. K., Chase-Lansdale, P., & Richeson, J. A. (2012). Concerns about appearing prejudiced get under the skin: Stress responses to interracial contact in the moment and across time. *Journal of Experimental Social Psychology, 48*, 682–693.

Trawalter, S., Todd, A. R., Baird, A. A., & Richeson, J. A. (2008). Attending to threat: Race-based patterns of selective attention. *Journal of Experimental Social Psychology, 44*, 1322–1327.

Triandis, H. C. (1994). *Culture and social behavior*. New York: McGraw-Hill.

Triandis, H. C. (1995). *Individualism and collectivism*. Boulder, CO: Westview.

Triandis, H., Chen, X. P., & Chan, D. K. (1998). Scenarios for the measurement of collectivism and individualism. *Journal of Cross-Cultural Psychology, 29*, 275–289.

Triplett, N. (1897–1898). The dynamogenic factors in pacemaking and competition. *American Journal of Psychology, 9*, 507–533.

Tripp, C., Jensen, T. D., & Carlson, L. (1994). The effects of multiple product endorsements by celebrities on consumers' attitudes and intentions. *Journal of Consumer Research, 20*, 535–547.

Trivers, R. L. (1971). The evolution of reciprocal altruism. *Quarterly Review of Biology, 46*, 35–57.

Trivers, R. L. (1972). Parental investment and sexual selection. In B. Campbell (Ed.), *Sexual selection and the descent of man* (pp. 136–179). Chicago: Aldine-Atherton.

Trivers, R. L. (1985). *Social evolution*. Menlo Park, CA: Benjamin/ Cummings.

Troll, L. E., & Skaff, M. M. (1997). Perceived continuity of self in very old age. *Psychology and Aging, 12*, 162–169.

Trope, Y. (1986). Identification and inferential processes in dispositional attribution. *Psychological Review, 93*, 239–257.

Trope, Y., & Alfieri, T. (1997). Effortfulness and flexibility of dispositional judgment processes. *Journal of Personality and Social Psychology, 73*, 662–674.

Tropp, L. R. (2013). *Handbook of intergroup conflict*. Oxford: Oxford University Press.

Tropp, L. R., & Page-Gould, E. (2013). Contact between groups. In J. Dovidio & J. Simpson (Eds.), *APA handbook on personality and social psychology: Vol. 2. Interpersonal relationships and group processes*. Washington, DC: American Psychological Association.

Trzesniewski, K. H., Donnellan, M. B., & Robins, R. W. (2003). Stability of self-esteem across the life span. *Journal of Personality and Social Psychology, 84*, 205–220.

Tsapelas, I., Aron, A., & Orbuch, T. (2009). Marital boredom now predicts less satisfaction 9 years later. *Psychological Science, 20*, 543–545.

Tsukiura, T., & Cabeza, R. (2011). Shared brain activity for aesthetic and moral judgments: implications for the beauty-is-good stereotype. *Social Cognitive and Affective Neuroscience.6*, 138–148.

Ttofi, M. M., & Farrington, D. P. (2009). What works in preventing bullying: Effective elements of anti-bullying programmes. *Journal of Aggression, Conflict and Peace Research, 1*, 13–24.

Ttofi, M. M., Farrington, D. P., & Lösel, F. (2012). School bullying as a predictor of violence later in life: A systematic review and meta-analysis of prospective longitudinal studies. *Aggression and Violent Behavior*, in press.

Tubre, T. C., & Collins, J. M. (2000). Jackson and Schuler (1985) revisited: A meta-analysis of the relationships between role ambiguity, role conflict, and job performance. *Journal of Management, 26*, 155–169.

Tuckman, B. W. (1965). Developmental sequence in small groups. *Psychological Bulletin, 63*, 384–399.

Turner, J. C. (1987). *Rediscovering the social group: A self-categorization theory*. Oxford, UK: Basil Blackwell.

Turner, J. C. (1991). *Social influence*. Pacific Grove, CA: Brooks/ Cole.

Tuvblad, C., Raine, A., Zheng, M., & Baker, L. A. (2009). Genetic and environmental stability differs in reactive and proactive aggression. *Aggressive Behavior, 35*, 437–452.

Tversky, A., & Kahneman, D. (1973). Availability: A heuristic for judging frequency and probability. *Cognitive Psychology, 5*, 207–232.

Tversky, A., & Kahneman, D. (1974). Judgment under uncertainty: Heuristics and biases. *Science, 185*, 1124–1131.

Twenge, J. M. (2006). *Generation me: Why today's young Americans are more confident, assertive, entitled—and more miserable than ever before*. New York: Free Press.

Twenge, J. M. (2009). Change over time in obedience: The jury's still out, but it might be decreasing. *American Psychologist, 64*, 28–31.

Twenge, J. M., & Crocker, J. (2002). Race and self-esteem: Metaanalyses comparing Whites, Blacks, Hispanics, Asians, and American Indians. *Psychological Bulletin, 128*, 371–408.

Twenge, J. M., Campbell, W. K., & Freeman, E. C. (2012). Generational differences in young adults' life goals, concern for others, and civic orientation, 1966–2009. *Journal of Personality and Social Psychology, 102*, 1045–1062.

Tyler, T. R. (2006a). Viewing *CSI* and the threshold of guilt: Managing truth and justice in reality and fiction. *Yale Law Journal, 115*, 1050–1085.

Tyler, T. R. (2006b). *Why people obey the law*. Princeton, NJ: Princeton University Press.

Tyler, T. R. (2011). *Why people cooperate: The role of social motivations*. Princeton, NJ: Princeton University Press.

U.S. Department of Justice (1999). *Eyewitness evidence: A guide for law enforcement*. Washington, DC: U.S. Department of Justice.

Uchino, B. N. (2006). Social support and health: A review of physiological processes potentially underlying links to disease outcomes. *Journal of Behavioral Medicine, 29*, 377–387.

Uchino, B. N. (2009). Understanding the links between social support and physical health: A life-span perspective with emphasis on the separability of perceived and received support. *Perspectives on Psychological Science, 4*, 236–255.

Uchino, B. N., Cacioppo, J. T., & Kiecolt-Glaser, J. K. (1996). The relationship between social support and physiological processes: A review with emphasis on underlying mechanisms and implications for health. *Psychological Bulletin, 119*, 488–531.

Underwood, J., & Pezdek, K. (1998). Memory suggestibility as an example of the sleeper effect. *Psychonomic Bulletin and Review, 5*, 449–453.

Underwood, M. K., Beron, K. J., Gentsch, J. K., Galperin, M. B., & Risser, S. D. (2008). Family correlates of children's social and physical aggression with peers: Negative interparental conflict strategies and parenting styles. *International Journal of Behavioral Development, 32*, 549–562.

UNICEF. (2012). *Progress for children: A report card on adolescents*. New York: United Nations Children's Fund.

United Nations Office on Drugs and Crime (2011). *Global study on homicide*. Vienna.

United States v. Scheffer, 523 U.S. 303 (1998).

Unkelbach, C., Forgas, J. P., & Denson, T. F. (2008). The turban effect: The influence of Muslim headgear and induced affect on aggressive responses in the shooter bias paradigm. *Journal of Experimental Social Psychology, 44*, 1409–1413.

Unzueta, M. M., Gutiérrez, A. S., & Ghavami, N. (2010). How believing in affirmative action quotas affects White women's self-image. *Journal of Experimental Social Psychology, 46*, 120–126.

Ura, K., Alkire, S., & Zangmo, T. (2012). Case study: Bhutan: Gross National Happiness and the GNH index. In J. Helliwell, R. Layard, & J. Sachs (Eds.) *World Happiness Report* (pp. 108–145). New York: Columbia University: The Earth Institute.

USA Today. (2003, June 23). Gallup Poll results. Available at http://www.usatoday.com/news/polls/tables/live/0623.htm.

Uziel, L. (2007). Individual differences in the social facilitation effect: A review and meta-analysis. *Journal of Research in Personality, 41*, 579–601.

Vaillancourt, T. (2005). Indirect aggression among humans: Social construct or evolutionary adaptation? In R. E. Tremblay, W. W. Hartup, & J. Archer (Eds.), *Developmental origins of aggression* (pp.158–177). New York: Guilford.

Vaillancourt, T., & Hymel, S. (2006). Aggression and social status: The moderating roles of sex and peer-valued characteristics. *Aggressive Behavior, 32*, 396–408.

Vaish, A., Grossmann, T., & Woodward, A. (2008). Not all emotions are created equal: The negativity bias in social-emotional development. *Psychological Bulletin, 134*, 383–403.

Valdesolo, P., Ouyang, J., & DeSteno, D. (2010). The rhythm of joint action: Synchrony promotes cooperative activity. *Journal of Experimental Social Psychology, 46*, 693–695.

Valentine, T., & Mesout, J. (2009). Eyewitness identification under stress in the London Dungeon. *Applied Cognitive Psychology, 23*, 151–161.

Vallacher, R. R., Read, S. J., & Nowak, A. (2002). The dynamical perspective in personality and social psychology. *Personality and Social Psychology Review, 6*, 264–273.

Van Bavel, J. J., & Cunningham, W. A. (2009). Self-categorization with a novel mixed-race group moderates automatic social and racial biases. *Personality and Social Psychology Bulletin, 35*, 321–335.

Van Bavel, J. J., & Cunningham, W. A. (2010). A social neuroscience approach to self and social categorisation: A new look at an old issue. *European Review Of Social Psychology, 21*, 237–284.

Van Bavel, J. J., Packer, D. J., & Cunningham, W. A. (2011). Modulation of the fusiform face area following minimal exposure to motivationally relevant faces: Evidence of in-group enhancement (not out group disregard). *Journal of Cognitive Neuroscience, 23*, 3343–3354.

Van Bavel, J. J., Swencionis, J. K., O'Connor, R. C., & Cunningham, W. A. (2012). Motivated social memory: Belonging needs moderate the own-group bias in face recognition. *Journal of Experimental Social Psychology, 48*, 707–713.

van Bokhoven, I., van Goozen, S. H. M., van Engeland, H., Schaal, B., Arseneault, L., Séguin, J. R., Assaad, J.-M., Nagin, D. S., Vitaro, F., & Tremblay, R. E. (2006). Salivary testosterone and aggression, delinquency, and social dominance in a population-based longitudinal study of adolescent males. *Hormones and Behavior, 50*, 118–125.

Van Boven, L. (2005). Experientialism, materialism, and the pursuit of happiness. *Review of General Psychology, 9*, 132–142.

Van Boven, L., & Gilovich, T. (2003). To do or to have? That is the question. *Journal of Personality and Social Psychology, 85*, 1193–1202.

van der Meij, L., Almela, M., Buunk, A. P., Dubbs, S., & Salvador, A. (2012). 2D:4D in men is related to aggressive dominance but not to sociable dominance. *Aggressive Behavior, 38*, 208–212.

Van Dijk, E., De Kwaadsteniet, E. W., & De Cremer, D. (2009). Tacit coordination in social dilemmas: The importance of having a common understanding. *Journal of Personality and Social Psychology, 96*, 665–678.

Van Dyne, L., & Saavedra, R. (1996). A naturalistic minority influence experiment: Effects on divergent thinking, conflict, and originality in work-groups. *British Journal of Social Psychology, 35*, 151–167.

Van Eerde, W., & Thierry, H. (1996). Vroom's expectancy models and work-related criteria: A meta-analysis. *Journal of Applied Psychology, 81*, 575–586.

van Ginkel, W. P., & van Knippenberg, D. (2008). Group information elaboration and group decision making: The role of shared task representations. *Organizational Behavior and Human Decision Processes, 105*, 82–97.

van Ginkel, W. P., & van Knippenberg, D. (2012). Group leadership and shared task representations in decision making groups. *The Leadership Quarterly, 23*, 94–106.

van Ginkel, W., Tindale, R., & van Knippenberg, D. (2009). Team reflexivity, development of shared task representations, and the use of distributed information in group decision making. *Group Dynamics: Theory, Research, and Practice, 13*, 265–280.

Van Goozen, S. H. M., Cohen-Kettenis, P. T., Gooren, L. J. G., & Frijda, N. H., et al. (1995). Gender differences in behaviour: Activating effects of cross-sex hormones. *Psychoneuroendocrinology 20*, 343–363.

Van Iddekinge, C. H., Raymark, P. H., & Roth, P. L. (2005). Assessing personality with a structured employment interview: Construct-related validity and susceptibility to response inflation. *Journal of Applied Psychology, 90*, 536–552.

Van Iddekinge, C. H., Roth, P. L., Raymark, P. H., & Odle-Dusseau, H. N. (2012). The criterion-related validity of integrity tests: An updated meta-analysis. *Journal of Applied Psychology, 97*, 499–530.

van Knippenberg, D., & Schippers, M. C. (2007). Work group diversity. *Annual Review of Psychology, 58*, 515–541.

van Koppen, P. J., & Penrod, S. D. (Eds.). (2003). *Adversarial versus inquisitorial justice: Psychological perspectives on criminal justice systems.* New York: Kluwer Academic/Plenum.

Van Prooijen, J.-W., Van den Bos, K., Lind, E. A., & Wilke, H. (2006). How do people react to negative procedures? On the moderating role of authority's biased attitudes. *Journal of Experimental Social Psychology, 42*, 632–645.

van Straaten, I., Engels, R., Finkenauer, C., & Holland, R. W. (2009). Meeting your match: Attractiveness similarity affects approach behavior in mixed-sex dyads. *Personality and Social Psychology Bulletin, 35*, 685–697.

Van Vugt, M. (2012). The missing link: Leadership, identity, and the social brain. *British Journal of Psychology, 103*, 177–179.

Van Vugt, M., & Schaller, M. (2008). Evolutionary approaches to group dynamics: An introduction. *Group Dynamics: Theory, Research, and Practice, 12*, 1–6.

van Zomeren, M., Postmes, T., & Spears, R. (2008). Toward an integrative social identity model of collective action: A quantitative research synthesis of three socio-psychological perspectives. *Psychological Bulletin, 134*, 504–535.

Vandello, J. A., & Cohen, D. (2003). Male honor and female fidelity: Implicit cultural scripts that perpetuate domestic violence. *Journal of Personality and Social Psychology, 84*, 997–1010.

Vandello, J. A., Cohen, D., & Ransom, S. (2008). U.S. Southern and Northern differences in perceptions of norms about aggression: Mechanisms for the perpetuation of a culture of honor. *Journal of Cross-Cultural Psychology, 39*, 162–177.

Vandello, J. A., Cohen, D., Grandon, R., & Franiuk, R. (2009). Stand by your man: Indirect prescriptions for honorable violence and feminine loyalty in Canada, Chile, and the United States. *Journal of Cross-Cultural Psychology, 40*, 81–104.

Vandello, J. A., Hettinger, V. E., & Michniewicz, K. (2013). Region as culture. In A. Cohen (Ed.), *New directions in the psychology of culture*. Washington, DC: American Psychological Association.

VanderStoep, S. W., & Shaughnessy, J. J. (1997). Taking a course in research methods improves reasoning about real-life events. *Teaching of Psychology, 24*, 122–124.

Vasconcelos-Raposo, J., Fernandes, H., Teixeira, C. M., & Bertelli, R. (2012). Factorial validity and invariance of the Rosenberg Self-Esteem Scale among Portuguese youngsters. *Social Indicators Research, 105*, 483–498.

Vathanophas, V., & Liang, S. Y. (2007). Enhancing information sharing in group support systems (GSS). *Computers in Human Behavior, 23*, 1675–1691.

Vazire, S. (2010). Who knows what about a person? The self–other knowledge asymmetry (SOKA) model. *Journal of Personality and Social Psychology, 98*, 281–300.

Vazire, S., & Carlson, E. N. (2011). Others sometimes know us better than we know ourselves. *Current Directions in Psychological Science, 20,* 104–108.

Vazsonyi, A. T., Machackova, H., Sevcikova, A., Smahel, D., & Cerna, A. (2012). Cyberbullying in context: Direct and indirect effects by low self-control across 25 European countries. *European Journal of Developmental Psychology, 9,* 210–227.

Vecchio, R. P. (2002). Leadership and the gender advantage. *Leadership Quarterly, 13,* 643–671.

Verona, E., Patrick, C. J., & Lang, A. R. (2002). A direct assessment of the role of state and trait negative emotion in aggressive behavior. *Journal of Abnormal Psychology, 111,* 249–258.

Vetlesen, A. J. (2005). *Evil and human agency.* Cambridge: Cambridge University Press.

Vezzali, L., Capozza, D., Stathi, S., & Giovannini, D. (2012). Increasing outgroup trust, reducing infrahumanization, and enhancing future contact intentions via imagined intergroup contact. *Journal of Experimental Social Psychology, 48,* 437–440.

Vidmar, N., & Hans, V. P. (2007). *American juries: The verdict.* Amherst, NY: Prometheus.

Vierikko, E., Pulkkinen, L., Kaprio, J., & Rose, R. J. (2006). Genetic and environmental sources of continuity and change in teacher-rated aggression during early adolescence. *Aggressive Behavior, 32,* 308–320.

Viglione, J., Hannon, L., & DeFina, R. (2011). The impact of light skin on prison time for Black female offenders. *The Social Science Journal, 48,* 250–258.

Viki, G. T., Abrams, D., & Masser, B. (2004). Evaluating stranger and acquaintance rape: The role of benevolent sexism in perpetrator blame and recommended sentence length. *Law and Human Behavior, 28,* 295–303.

Vinokur, A., & Burnstein, E. (1974). Effects of partially shared persuasive arguments on group-induced shifts: A group-problem-solving approach. *Journal of Personality and Social Psychology, 29,* 305–315.

Visintainer, M., Volpicelli, J., & Seligman, M. (1982). Tumor rejection in rats after inescapable or escapable shock. *Science, 216,* 437–439.

Visser, P. S., & Mirabile, R. R. (2004). Attitudes in the social context: The impact of social network composition on individual-level attitude strength. *Journal of Personality and Social Psychology, 87,* 779–795.

Vittengl, J. R., & Holt, C. S. (2000). Getting acquainted: The relationship of self-disclosure and social attraction to positive affect. *Journal of Social and Personal Relationships, 17,* 53–66.

Vogel, D. L., Wester, S. R., & Heesacker, M. (1999). Dating relationships and the demand/withdraw pattern of communication. *Sex Roles, 41,* 297–306.

Vohs, K. D., & Finkel, E. J. (Eds.). (2006). *Self and relationships: Connecting intrapersonal and interpersonal processes.* New York: Guilford.

Vohs, K. D., & Heatherton, T. F. (2000). Self-regulatory failure: A resource-depletion approach. *Psychological Science, 11,* 249–252.

Vohs, K. D., Baumeister, R. F., & Ciarocco, N. J. (2005). Self-regulation and self-presentation: Regulatory resource depletion impairs impression management and effortful self-presentation depletes regulatory resources. *Journal of Personality and Social Psychology, 88,* 632–657.

Vohs, K. D., Baumeister, R. F., & Schmeichel, B. J. (2012). Motivation, personal beliefs, and limited resources all contribute to self-control. *Journal of Experimental Social Psychology.*

Vohs, K. D., Mead, N. L., & Goode, M. R. (2006). The psychological consequences of money. *Science, 314,* 1154–1156.

Volk, A. A., Camilleri, J. A., Dane, A. V., & Marini, Z. A. (2012). Is adolescent bullying an evolutionary adaptation? *Aggressive Behavior, 38,* 222–238.

Vollhardt, J. R. (2009). Altruism born of suffering and prosocial behavior following adverse life events: A review and conceptualization. *Social Justice Research, 22,* 53–97.

Vollhardt, J. R., & Staub, E. (2011). Inclusive altruism born of suffering: The relationship between adversity and prosocial attitudes and behavior toward disadvantaged outgroups. *American Journal of Orthopsychiatry, 81,* 307–315.

von der Pahlen, B., Lindman, R., Sarkola, T., Maekisalo, H., & Eriksson, C. J. P. (2002). An exploratory study on self-evaluated aggression and androgens in women. *Aggressive Behavior, 28,* 273–280.

von Hippel, C., Wiryakusuma, C., Bowden, J., & Shochet, M. (2011). Stereotype threat and female communication styles. *Personality and Social Psychology Bulletin, 37,* 1312–1324.

von Hippel, W., & Henry, J. D. (2011). Aging and self-regulation. In K. D. Vohs, & R. F. Baumeister (Eds.), *Handbook of self-regulation: Research, theory, and applications* (2nd ed.) (pp. 321–335). New York: Guilford.

von Hippel, W., & Trivers, R. (2011). The evolution and psychology of self-deception. *Behavioral and Brain Sciences, 34,* 1–16.

von Hippel, W., Lakin, J. L., & Shakarchi, R. J. (2005). Individual differences in motivated social cognition: The case of self-serving information processing. *Personality and Social Psychological Bulletin, 31,* 1347–1357.

Von Lang, J., & Sibyll, C. (Eds.). (1983). *Eichmann interrogated* (R. Manheim, Trans.). New York: Farrar, Straus & Giroux.

Vonk, R. (1998). The slime effect: Suspicion and dislike of likeable behavior toward superiors. *Journal of Personality and Social Psychology, 74,* 849–864.

Voracek, M., & Fisher, M. L. (2002). Shapely centrefolds? Temporal change in body measures: Trend analysis. *British Medical Journal, 325,* 1447–1448.

Vorauer, J. D. (2003). Dominant group members in intergroup interaction: Safety or vulnerability in numbers? *Personality and Social Psychology Bulletin, 29,* 498–511.

Vorauer, J. D., & Claude, S. D. (1998). Perceived versus actual transparency of goals in negotiation. *Personality and Social Psychology Bulletin, 24,* 371–385.

Vorauer, J. D., & Sasaki, S. J. (2009). Helpful only in the abstract? Ironic effects of empathy in intergroup interaction. *Psychological Science, 20,* 191–197.

Vorauer, J. D., Cameron, J. J., Holmes, J. G., & Pearce, D. G. (2003). Invisible overtures: Fears of rejection and the signal amplification bias. *Journal of Personality and Social Psychology, 84,* 793–812.

Vorauer, J. D., Martens, V., & Sasaki, S. (2009). When trying to understand detracts from trying to behave: Effects of perspective taking in intergroup interaction. *Journal of Personality and Social Psychology, 96,* 811–827.

Vrij, A. (2008). *Detecting lies and deceit: Pitfalls and opportunities.* Chichester, UK: Wiley.

Vrij, A. Granhag , P. Mann , S., & Leal , S. (2011). Outsmarting the liars: Toward a cognitive lie detection approach. *Current Directions in Psychological Science, 20,* 28–32.

Vrij, A., & Granhag, P. A. (2012). Eliciting cues to deception and truth: What matters are the questions asked. *Journal of Research in Memory and Cognition, 1,* 110–117.

Vrij, A., Granhag, P. A., Porter, S. (2010). Pitfalls and opportunities in nonverbal and verbal lie detection. *Psychological Science in the Public Interest, 11,* 89–121.

Vrij, A., Mann, S., Fisher, R., Leal, S., Milne, R., & Bull, R. (2008). Increasing cognitive load to facilitate lie detection: The benefit of recalling an event in reverse order. *Law and Human Behavior, 32,* 253–265.

Vrij, A., Mann, S., Leal, S., & Fisher, R. (2010). "Look into my eyes": Can instruction to maintain eye contact facilitate lie detection? *Psychology, Crime & Law, 16,* 327–348.

Vroom, V. H. (1964). *Work and motivation.* New York: Wiley.

Vroom, V. H., & Jago, A. G. (1988). *Managing participation in organizations.* Englewood Cliffs, NJ: Prentice-Hall.

Vroom, V. H., & Jago, A. G. (2007). The role of the situation in leadership. *American Psychologist, 62,* 17–24.

Vroom, V. H., & Yetton, P. W. (1973). *Leadership and decisionmaking.* Pittsburgh: University of Pittsburgh Press.

Wageman, R., Fisher, C. M., & Hackman, J. R. (2009). Leading teams when the time is right: Finding the best moments to act. *Organizational Dynamics, 38,* 192–203.

Wagner, D. T., Barnes, C. M., Lim, V. G., & Ferris, D. (2012). Lost sleep and cyberloafing: Evidence from the laboratory and a daylight saving time quasi-experiment. *Journal of Applied Psychology.*

Waldman, D. A., & Avolio, B. J. (1991). Race effects in performance evaluations: Controlling for ability, education, and experience. *Journal of Applied Psychology, 76,* 897–901.

Walker, I., & Smith, H. J. (2002). *Relative deprivation: Specification, development, and integration.* Cambridge: Cambridge University Press.

Walker, L., LaTour, S., Lind, E. A., & Thibaut, J. (1974). Reactions of participants and observers to modes of adjudication. *Journal of Applied Social Psychology, 4,* 295–310.

Wallace, D. B., & Kassin S. M. (2012). Harmless error analysis: How do judges respond to confession errors? *Law and Human Behavior, 36,* 151–157.

Wallis, C. (2011). Performing gender: A content analysis of gender display in music videos. *Sex Roles, 64,* 160–172.

Walster, E. (1966). Assignment of responsibility for important events. *Journal of Personality and Social Psychology, 3,* 73–79.

Walster, E., & Festinger, L. (1962). The effectiveness of "overheard" persuasive communications. *Journal of Abnormal and Social Psychology, 65,* 395–402.

Walster, E., Aronson, V., Abrahams, D., & Rottman, L. (1966). The importance of physical attractiveness in dating behavior. *Journal of Personality and Social Psychology, 4,* 508–516.

Walster, E., Walster, G. W., & Berscheid, E. (1978). *Equity: Theory and research.* Boston: Allyn & Bacon.

Walster, E., Walster, G. W., Piliavin, J., & Schmidt, L. (1973). "Playing hard-to-get": Understanding an elusive phenomenon. *Journal of Personality and Social Psychology, 26,* 113–121.

Walther, E., Weil, R., & Düsing, J. (2011). The role of evaluative conditioning in attitude formation. *Current Directions in Psychological Science, 20,* 192–196.

Walton, G. M., & Carr, P. B. (2012). Social belonging and the motivation and intellectual achievement of negatively stereotyped students. In M. Inzlicht & T. Schmader (Eds.), *Stereotype threat: Theory, process, and application* (pp. 89–106). New York: Oxford University Press.

Walton, G. M., & Cohen, G. L. (2007). A question of belonging: Race, social fit, and achievement. *Journal of Personality and Social Psychology, 92,* 82–96.

Walton, G. M., & Cohen, G. L. (2011). A brief social-belonging intervention improves academic and health outcomes of minority students. *Science, 331,* 1447–1451.

Walton, G. M., Cohen, G. L., Cwir, D., & Spencer, S. J. (2012). Mere belonging: The power of social connections. *Journal of Personality and Social Psychology, 102,* 513–532.

Wampold, B. E., Mondin, G. W., Moody, M., Stich, F., Benson, K., & Ahn, H. (1997). A meta-analysis of outcome studies comparing bona fide psychotherapies: Empirically, "all must have prizes." *Psychological Bulletin, 122,* 203–215.

Wanberg, C. R. (2012). The individual experience of unemployment. *Annual Review of Psychology, 63,* 369–396.

Wang, Q. (2006). Culture and the development of self-knowledge. *Current Directions in Psychological Science, 15,* 182–187.

Wang, S. (2006). Contagious behavior. *APS Observer, 19,* 2.

Wang, X. M., Wong, K. F. E., & Kwong, J. Y. Y. (2010). The roles of rater goals and ratee performance levels in the distortion of performance ratings. *Journal of Applied Psychology, 95,* 546–561.

Warburton, W. A., Williams, K. D., & Cairns, D. R. (2006). When ostracism leads to aggression: The moderating effects of control deprivation. *Journal of Experimental Social Psychology, 42,* 213–220.

Ward, L. M., & Friedman, K. (2006). Using TV as a guide: Associations between television viewing and adolescents' sexual attitudes and behavior. *Journal of Research on Adolescence, 16,* 133–156.

Ware, A., & Kowalski, G. S. (2012). Sex identification and love of sports: BIRGing and CORFing among sport fans. *Journal of Sport Behavior, 35,* 223–237.

Warmelink, L. Vrij , A. Mann , S. Leal , S. Forrester , D. Fisher , R. (2011). Thermal imaging as a lie detection tool at airports. *Law and Human Behavior, 35,* 40–48.

Warneken, F., & Tomasello, M. (2006). Altruistic helping in human infants and young chimpanzees. *Science, 311,* 1301–1303.

Warren, B. L. (1966). A multiple variable approach to the assortive mating phenomenon. *Eugenics Quarterly, 13,* 285–298.

Watkins, E. R. (2008). Constructive and unconstructive repetitive thought. *Psychological Bulletin, 134,* 163–206.

Watson, D., Wiese, D., Vaidya, J., & Tellegen, A. (1999). The two general activation systems of affect: Structural findings, evolutionary considerations, and psychobiological evidence. *Journal of Personality and Social Psychology, 76,* 820–838.

Wax, E. (2008, November 22). Can love conquer caste? *Washington Post.*

Wayment, H. A. (2004). It could have been me: Vicarious victims and disaster-focused distress. *Personality and Social Psychology Bulletin, 30,* 515–528.

Waytz, A., & Epley, N. (2012). Social connection enables dehumanization. *Journal of Experimental Social Psychology, 48,* 70–76.

Waytz, A., Gray, K., Epley, N., & Wegner, D. M. (2010). Causes and consequences of mind perception. *Trends in the Cognitive Sciences, 14,* 383–388.

Weary, G., & Edwards, J. A. (1994). Individual differences in causal uncertainty. *Journal of Personality and Social Psychology, 67,* 308–318.

Weaver, J. R., & Bosson, J. K. (2011). I feel like I know you: Sharing negative attitudes of others promotes feelings of familiarity. *Personality and Social Psychology Bulletin, 37,* 481–491.

Weber, M., & Camerer, C. (1998). The disposition effect in securities trading: An experimental analysis. *Journal of Economic Behavior and Organization, 33,* 167–184.

Webster, D. M., Richter, L., & Kruglanski, A. W. (1996). On leaping to conclusions when feeling tired: Mental fatigue effects on impressional primacy. *Journal of Experimental Social Psychology, 32,* 181–195.

Webster, R. J., & Saucier, D. A. (2011). The effects of death reminders on sex differences in prejudice toward gay men and lesbians. *Journal of Homosexuality, 58,* 402–426.

Weeden, J., & Sabini, J. (2005). Physical attractiveness and health in Western societies: A review. *Psychological Bulletin, 131,* 635–653.

Wegener, D. T., & Petty, R. E. (1994). Mood management across affective states: The hedonic contingency hypothesis. *Journal of Personality and Social Psychology, 66,* 1034–1048.

Wegener, D. T., Petty, R. E., & Smith, S. M. (1995). Positive mood can increase or decrease message scrutiny: The hedonic contingency view of mood and message processing. *Journal of Personality and Social Psychology, 69,* 5–15.

Wegge, J., Bipp, T., & Kleinbeck, U. (2007). Goal setting via videoconferencing. *European Journal of Work and Organizational Psychology, 16,* 169–194.

Wegner, D. M. (1994). Ironic processes of mental control. *Psychological Review, 101,* 34–52.

Wegner, D. M. (1997). When the antidote is the poison: Ironic mental control processes. *Psychological Science, 8,* 148–153.

Wegner, D. M., Ansfield, M., & Pilloff, D. (1998). The putt and the pendulum: Ironic effects of the mental control of action. *Psychological Science, 9,* 196–199.

Wegner, D. M., Erber, R., & Raymond, P. (1991). Transactive memory in close relationships. *Journal of Personality and Social Psychology, 61,* 923–929.

Wegner, D. M., Lane, J. D., & Dimitri, S. (1994). The allure of secret relationships. *Journal of Personality and Social Psychology, 66,* 287–300.

Weiner, B. (1985). "Spontaneous" causal thinking. *Psychological Bulletin, 97,* 74–84.

Weiner, B. (2008). Reflections on the history of attribution theory and research. *Social Psychology, 39,* 151–156.

Weinstein, N. D. (1980). Unrealistic optimism about future life events. *Journal of Personality and Social Psychology, 39,* 806–820.

Weinstein, N. D. (1989). Effects of personal experience on self-protective behavior. *Psychological Bulletin, 105,* 31–50.

Weiss, E., & Marksteiner, J. (2007). Alcohol-related cognitive disorders with a focus on neuropsychology. *International Journal on Disability and Human Development, 6,* 337–342.

Weldon, M. S., Blair, C., & Huebsch, D. (2000). Group remembering: Does social loafing underlie collaborative inhibition? *Journal of Experimental Psychology: Learning, Memory, and Cognition, 26,* 1568–1577.

Wells, B. M., & Skowronski, J. J. (2012). Evidence of choking under pressure on the PGA Tour. *Basic and Applied Social Psychology, 34,* 175–182.

Wells, C., Adhyaru, J., Cannon, J., Lamond, M., & Baruch, G. (2010). Multisystemic therapy (MST) for youth offending, psychiatric disorder and substance abuse: Case examples from a UK MST team. *Child and Adolescent Mental Health, 15,* 142–149.

Wells, C., Adhyaru, J., Cannon, J., Lamond, M., & Baruch, G. (2010). Multisystemic therapy (MST) for youth offending, psychiatric disorder and substance abuse: Case examples from a UK MST team. *Child and Adolescent Mental Health, 15,* 142–149.

Wells, G. L., & Bradfield, A. L. (1998). "Good, you identified the suspect": Feedback to eyewitnesses distorts their reports of the witnessing experience. *Journal of Applied Psychology, 83,* 360–376.

Wells, G. L., & Murray, D. M. (1984). Eyewitness confidence. In G. Wells & E. Loftus (Eds.), *Eyewitness testimony: Psychological perspectives* (pp. 155–170). New York: Cambridge University Press.

Wells, G. L., & Petty, R. E. (1980). The effects of overt head-movements on persuasion: Compatibility and incompatibility of responses. *Basic and Applied Social Psychology, 1,* 219–230.

Wells, G. L., & Quinlivan, D. S. (2009). Suggestive eyewitness identification procedures and the Supreme Court's reliability test in light of eyewitness science: 30 years later. *Law and Human Behavior, 33,* 1–24.

Wells, G. L., Charman, S. D., & Olson, E. A. (2005). Building face composites can harm lineup identification performance. *Journal of Experimental Psychology: Applied, 11,* 147–156.

Wells, G. L., Lindsay, R. C. L., & Ferguson, T. J. (1979). Accuracy, confidence, and juror perceptions in eyewitness identification. *Journal of Applied Psychology, 64,* 440–448.

Wells, G. L., Malpass, R. S., Lindsay, R. C. L., Fisher, R. P., Turtle, J. W., & Fulero, S. M. (2000). From the lab to the police station: A successful application of eyewitness research. *American Psychologist, 55,* 581–598.

Wells, G. L., Memon, A., & Penrod, S. (2007). Eyewitness evidence: Improving its probative value. *Psychological Science in the Public Interest, 7,* 45–75.

Wells, G. L., Small, M., Penrod, S., Malpass, R. S., Fulero, S. M., & Brimacombe, C. A. E. (1998). Eyewitness identification procedures: Recommendations for lineups and photospreads, *Law and Human Behavior, 22,* 603–648.

Wells, R. (2011). Social network acts to reduce suicide. *The Age (Melbourne, Australia).* p. 5.

Wenzlaff, R. M., & Wegner, D. M. (2000). Thought suppression. *Annual Review of Psychology, 51,* 59–91.

Werner, N. E., & Grant, S. (2009). Mothers' cognitions about relational aggression: Associations with discipline responses, children's normative beliefs, and peer competence. *Social Development, 18,* 77–98.

West, S. G., & Brown, T. J. (1975). Physical attractiveness, the severity of the emergency and helping: A field experiment and interpersonal simulation. *Journal of Experimental Social Psychology, 11,* 531–538.

West, T. V., & Kenny, D. A. (2011). The truth and bias model of judgment. *Psychological Review, 118,* 357–378.

Westen, D. (2007). *The political brain: The role of emotion in deciding the fate of the nation.* New York: Public Affairs.

Westen, D., Kilts, C., Blagov, P., Harenski, K., & Hamann, S. (2006). The neural basis of motivated reasoning: An fMRI study of emotional constraints on political judgment during the U.S. presidential election of 2004. *Journal of Cognitive Neuroscience, 18,* 1947–1958.

Wheelan, S. A. (2009). Group size, group development, and group productivity. *Small Group Research, 40,* 247–262.

Wheeler, B. C. (2008). Selfish or altruistic? An analysis of alarm call function in wild capuchin monkeys, Cebus apella nigritus. *Animal Behaviour, 76,*1465–1475.

Wheeler, L., & Kim, Y. (1997). What is beautiful is culturally good: The physical attractiveness stereotype has different content in collectivist cultures. *Personality and Social Psychology Bulletin, 23,* 795–800.

Wheeler, L., & Miyake, K. (1992). Social comparison in everyday life. *Journal of Personality and Social Psychology, 62,* 760–773.

Wheeler, L., Koestner, R., & Driver, R. E. (1982). Related attributes in the choice of comparison others. *Journal of Experimental Social Psychology, 18,* 489–500.

Wheeler, M. E., & Fiske, S. T. (2005). Controlling racial prejudice: Social-cognitive goals affect amygdala and stereotype activation. *Psychological Science, 16,* 56–63.

Whitaker, J. L., & Bushman, B. J. (2012). "Remain calm. Be kind." Effects of relaxing video games on aggressive and prosocial behavior. *Social Psychological and Personality Science, 3,* 88–92.

Whitbeck, L. B., & Hoyt, D. R. (1994). Social prestige and assortive mating: A comparison of students from 1956 and 1988. *Journal of Social and Personal Relationships, 11,* 137–145.

Whitchurch, E. R., Wilson, T. D., & Gilbert, D. T. (2011). "He loves me, he loves me not . . .": Uncertainty can increase romantic attraction. *Psychological Science, 22,* 172–175.

White, G. L., Fishbein, S., & Rutstein, J. (1981). Passionate love: The misattribution of arousal. *Journal of Personality and Social Psychology, 41,* 56–62.

Whittaker, J. O., & Meade, R. D. (1967). Social pressure in the modification and distortion of judgment: A cross-cultural study. *International Journal of Psychology, 2,* 109–113.

Whorf, B. L. (1956). Science and linguistics. In J. B. Carroll (Ed.), *Language, thought, and reality: Selected writings of Benjamin Lee Whorf* (pp. 207–219). Cambridge, MA: MIT Press.

Whyte, G. (1998). Recasting Janis's groupthink model: The key role of collective efficacy in decision fiascoes. *Organizational Behavior and Human Decision Processes, 73,* 185–209.

Wicker, B., Keysers, C., Plailly, J., Royet, J. P., Gallese, V., & Rizzolatti, G. (2003). Both of us disgusted in *my* insula: The common neural basis of seeing and feeling disgust. *Neuron, 40,* 655–664.

Wicklund, R. A. (1975). Objective self-awareness. In L. Berkowitz (Ed.), *Advances in experimental social psychology* (Vol. 8, pp. 233–275). New York: Academic Press.

Widmeyer, W. N., & Loy, J. W. (1988). When you're hot, you're hot! Warm-cold effects in first impressions of persons and teaching effectiveness. *Journal of Educational Psychology, 80,* 118–121.

Wiener, R. L., Prichard, C. C., & Weston, M. (1995). Comprehesibility of approved jury instructions in capital murder cases. *Journal of Applied Psychology, 80,* 455–467.

Wiesner, W. H., & Cronshaw, S. F. (1988). A meta-analytic investigation of the impact of interview format and degree of structure on the validity of the employment interview. *Journal of Occupational Psychology, 61,* 275–290.

Wiggins, J. S. (Ed.). (1996). *The five-factor model of personality: Theoretical perspectives.* New York: Guilford.

Wilder, D. A. (1977). Perception of groups, size of opposition, and social influence. *Journal of Experimental Social Psychology, 13,* 253–268.

Wilder, D. A., Simon, A. F., & Myles, F. (1996). Enhancing the impact of counterstereotypic information: Dispositional attributions for deviance. *Journal of Personality and Social Psychology, 71,* 276–287.

Wildschut, T., Pinter, B., Vevea, J. L., Insko, C. A., & Schopler, J. (2003). Beyond the group mind: A quantitative review of the interindividual-intergroup discontinuity effect. *Psychological Bulletin, 129,* 698–722.

Wilkinson, D. L., & Carr, P. J. (2008). Violent youths' response to high levels of exposure to community violence: What violent events reveal about youth violence. *Journal of Community Psychology, 36,* 1026–1051.

Willard, G. & Gramzow, R. H. (2008). Exaggeration in memory: Systematic distortion of self-evaluative information under reduced accessibility. *Journal of Experimental Social Psychology, 44,* 246–259.

Willer, R. (2004). The effects of government-issued terror warnings on presidential approval ratings. *Current Research in Social Psychology, 10,* 1–12.

Williams v. Florida, 399 U.S. 78 (1970).

Williams, E. F., Gilovich, T., & Dunning, D. (2012). Being all that you can be: How potential performances influence assessments of self and others. *Personality and Social Psychology Bulletin, 38,* 143–154.

Williams, K. D. (2012). Ostracism: The impact of being rendered meaningless. In P. R. Shaver, & M. Mikulincer (Eds.), *Meaning, mortality, and choice: The social psychology of existential concerns* (pp. 309–323). Washington, DC: American Psychological Association.

Williams, K. D., & Wesselmann, E. D. (2011). The link between ostracism and aggression. In J. P. Forgas, A. W. Kruglanski, & K. D. Williams (Eds.), *The psychology of social conflict and aggression* (pp. 37–51). New York: Psychology Press.

Williams, K. D., Cheung, C., & Choi, W. (2000). Cyberostracism: Effects of being ignored over the internet. *Journal of Personality and Social Psychology, 79,* 748–762.

Williams, K. D., Govan, C. L., Croker, V., Tynan, D., Cruickshank, M., & Lam, A. (2002). Investigations into differences between social- and cyberostracism. *Group Dynamics: Theory, Research, and Practice, 6,* 65–77.

Williams, L. E., & Bargh, J. A. (2008). Experiencing physical warmth promotes interpersonal warmth. *Science, 322,* 606–607.

Williams, M. J., & Eberhardt, J. L. (2008). Biological conceptions of race and the motivation to cross racial boundaries. *Journal of Personality and Social Psychology, 94,* 1033–1047.

Williams, R. (1993). *Anger kills.* New York: Times Books.

Williams. K. D., & Nida, S. A. (2011). Ostracism: Consequences and coping. *Current Directions in Psychological Science, 20,* 71–75.

Williamson, G. M., Clark, M. S., Pegalis, L. J., & Behan, A. (1996). Affective consequences of refusing to help in communal and exchange relationships. *Personality and Social Psychology Bulletin, 22,* 34–47.

Willis, J., & Todorov, A. (2006). First impressions: Making up your mind after a 100-ms exposure to a face. *Psychological Science, 17,* 592–598.

Willoughby, T., Adachi, P. C., & Good, M. (2012). A longitudinal study of the association between violent video game play and aggression among adolescents. *Developmental Psychology, 48,* 1044–1057.

Wills, T. A. (1981). Downward comparison principles in social psychology. *Psychological Bulletin, 90,* 245–271.

Wills, T. A., & DePaulo, B. M. (1991). Interpersonal analysis of the help-seeking process. In C. R. Snyder & D. R. Forsyth (Eds.), *Handbook of social and clinical psychology: The health perspective* (pp. 350–375). New York: Pergamon Press.

Wilson, A. E., & Ross, M. (2000). The frequency of temporal and social comparisons in people's personal appraisals. *Journal of Personality and Social Psychology, 78,* 928–942.

Wilson, D. W. (1978). Helping behavior and physical attractiveness. *Journal of Social Psychology, 104,* 313–314.

Wilson, E. O. (2012). *The social conquest of Earth.* New York: Norton.

Wilson, M. I., & Daly, M. (1996). Male sexual proprietariness and violence against wives. *Current Directions in Psychological Science, 5,* 2–7.

Wilson, T. D. (2002). *Strangers to ourselves: Discovering the adaptive unconscious.* Cambridge, MA: Belknap Press.

Wilson, T. D., & Gilbert, D. T. (2003). Affective forecasting. *Advances in Experimental Social Psychology, 35,* 345–411.

Wilson, T. D., & Gilbert, D. T. (2005). Affective forecasting: Knowing what to want. *Current Directions in Psychological Science, 14,* 131–134.

Wilson, T. D., Lindsey, S., & Schooler, T. Y. (2000). A model of dual attitudes. *Psychological Review, 107,* 101–126.

Wilson, T. D., Wheatley, T., Meyers, J. M., Gilbert, D. T., & Axsom, D. (2000). Focalism: A source of durability bias in affective forecasting. *Journal of Personality and Social Psychology, 78,* 821–836.

Wiltermuth, S. S. (2012). Synchronous activity boosts compliance with requests to aggress. *Journal of Experimental Social Psychology, 48,* 453–456.

Wiltermuth, S. S., & Heath, C. (2010). Synchrony and cooperation. *Psychological Science, 20,* 1–5.

Winch, R. F., Ktsanes, T., & Ktsanes, V. (1954). The theory of complementary needs in mate selection: An analytic and descriptive study. *American Sociological Review, 19,* 241–249.

Winograd, M. R., & Rosenfeld, J. P. (2011), Mock crime application of the Complex Trial Protocol (CTP) P300-based concealed information test. *Psychophysiology, 48,* 155–161.

Winter, D. G. (1987). Leader appeal, leader performance, and the motive profiles of leaders and followers: A study of American presidents and elections. *Journal of Personality and Social Psychology, 52,* 41–46.

Wise, R. A., & Safer, M. A. (2004). What U.S. judges know and believe about eyewitness testimony. *Applied Cognitive Psychology, 18,* 427–443.

Wishman, S. (1986). *Anatomy of a jury: The system on trial.* New York: Times Books.

Wittenbrink, B., Judd. C. M., & Park, B. (1997). Evidence for racial prejudice at the implicit level and its relationship with questionnaire measures. *Journal of Personality and Social Psychology, 72,* 262–274.

Wolf, S., & Montgomery, D. A. (1977). Effects of inadmissible evidence and level of judicial admonishment to disregard on the judgments of mock jurors. *Journal of Applied Social Psychology, 7,* 205–219.

Wolgemuth, L. (2009, June 17). Why a psychologist might be at your next interview. *U.S. News & World Report.*

Wong, R. Y.-m., & Hong, Y.-y. (2005). Dynamic influences of culture on cooperation in the prisoner's dilemma. *Psychological Science, 16,* 429–434.

Wood, J. V. (1989). Theory and research concerning social comparisons of personal attributes. *Psychological Bulletin, 106,* 231–248.

Wood, N., & Cowan, N. (1995). The cocktail party phenomenon revisited: How frequent are attention shifts to one's name in an irrelevant auditory channel? *Journal of Experimental Psychology: Learning, Memory, and Cognition, 21,* 255–260.

Wood, W., & Quinn, J. M. (2003). Forewarned and forearmed? Two meta-analysis syntheses of forewarnings of influence appeals. *Psychological Bulletin, 129,* 119–138.

Wood, W., Kallgren, C. A., & Preisler, R. M. (1985). Access to attitude-relevant information in memory as a determinant of persuasion: The role of message attributes. *Journal of Experimental Social Psychology, 21,* 73–85.

Wood, W., Lundgren, S., Ouellette, J. A., Busceme, S., & Blackstone, T. (1994). Minority influence: A meta-analytic review of social influence processes. *Psychological Bulletin, 115,* 323–345.

Wood, W., Pool, G. J., Leck, K., & Purvis, D. (1996). Self-definition, defensive processing, and influence: The normative impact of majority and minority groups. *Journal of Personality and Social Psychology, 71,* 1181–1193.

Woolley, A. W., Gerbasi, M. E., Chabris, C. F., Kosslyn, S. M., & Hackman, J. R. (2008). Bringing in the experts: How team composition and collaborative planning jointly shape analytic effectiveness. *Small Group Research, 39,* 352–371.

Woolley, A. W., Hackman, J. R., Jerde, T. E., Chabris, C. F., Bennett, S. L., & Kosslyn, S. M. (2007). Using brain-based measures to compose teams: How individual capabilities and team collaboration strategies jointly shape performance. *Social Neuroscience, 2,* 96–105.

Word, C. O., Zanna, M. P., & Cooper, J. (1974). The nonverbal mediation of self-fulfilling prophecies in interracial interaction. *Journal of Experimental Social Psychology, 10,* 109–120.

World Health Organization. (2012). *Female genital mutilation.* Retrieved from http://www.who.int/mediacentre/factsheets/fs241/en/.

Worth, L. T., & Mackie, D. M. (1987). Cognitive mediation of positive affect in persuasion. *Social Cognition, 5,* 76–94.

Wright, L., von Bussman, K., Friedman, A., Khoury, M., & Owens, F. (1990). Exaggerated social control and its relationship to the Type A behavior pattern. *Journal of Research in Personality, 24,* 258–269.

Wright, N. S., & Drewery, G. P. (2006). Forming cohesion in culturally heterogeneous teams differences in Japanese, Pacific Islander and Anglo experiences. *Cross Cultural Management, 13,* 43–53.

Wright, P. H. (1982). Men's friendships, women's friendships and the alleged inferiority of the latter. *Sex Roles, 8,* 1–20.

Wright, R. A., & Contrada, R. J. (1986). Dating selectivity and interpersonal attraction: Toward a better understanding of the "elusive phenomenon." *Journal of Social and Personal Relationships, 3,* 131–148.

Wright, S. C., Aron, A., & Brody, S. M. (2008). Extended contact and including others in the self: Building on the Allport/Pettigrew legacy. In U. Wagner, L. R. Tropp, G. Finchilescu, & C. Tredoux (Eds.), *Improving intergroup relations: Building on the legacy of Thomas F. Pettigrew* (pp. 143–159). Malden: Blackwell.

Wrightsman, L. S. (2006). *The psychology of the Supreme Court.* New York: Oxford University Press.

Wrightsman, L. S. (2008). *Oral arguments before the Supreme Court: An empirical approach.* New York: Oxford University Press.

Wyer, N. A., Sadler, M. S., & Judd, C. M. (2002). Contrast effects in stereotype formation and change: The role of comparative context. *Journal of Experimental Social Psychology, 38,* 443–458.

Wyer, R. S., Jr. (2012). A theory of social information processing. In P. M. Van Lange, A. W. Kruglanski, & E. T. Higgins (Eds.), *Handbook of theories of social psychology* (Vol 1, pp. 156–177). Thousand Oaks, CA: Sage.

Xu, H., Bègue, L., & Shankland, R. (2011). Guilt and guiltlessness: An integrative review. *Social and Personality Psychology Compass, 5,* 440–457.

Xu, X., Zuo, X., Wang, X., & Han, S. (2009). Do you feel my pain? Racial group membership modulates empathic neural responses. *Journal of Neuroscience, 29,* 8525–8529.

Yablo, P. D., & Field, N. P. (2007). The role of culture in altruism: Thailand and the United States. *Psychologia: An International Journal of Psychology in the Orient, 50,* 236–251.

Yamagishi, T., Makimura, Y., Foddy, M., Matsuda, M., Kiyonari, T., & Platow, M. J. (2005). Comparisons of Australians and Japanese on group-based cooperation. *Asian Journal of Social Psychology, 8,* 173–190.

Yantz, C. L., & McCaffrey, R. J. (2007). Social facilitation effect of examiner attention or inattention to computer-administered neuro-psychological testing: First sign that the examiner may affect result. *Clinical Neuropsychologist, 21,* 663–671.

Yen, H. (2012). Many resist census race labels. *Associated Press,* January 31.

Yeung, N. C. J., & von Hippel, C. (2008). Stereotype threat increases the likelihood that female drivers in a simulator run over jaywalkers. *Accident Analysis and Prevention, 40,* 667–674.

Yopyk, D. J. A., & Prentice, D. A. (2005). Am I an athlete or a student? Identity salience and stereotype threat in student-athletes. *Basic and Applied Social Psychology, 27,* 329–336.

Yoshida, E., Peach, J. M., Zanna, M. P., & Spencer, S. J. (2012). Not all automatic associations are created equal: How implicit normative evaluations are distinct from implicit attitudes and uniquely predict meaningful behavior. *Journal of Experimental Social Psychology, 48,* 694–706.

Young, E. (2012). Bad copy: In the wake of high-profile controversies, psychologists are facing up to problems with replication. *Nature, 485,* 298–300.

Young, R. K., Kennedy, A. H., Newhouse, A., Browne, P., & Thiessen, D. (1993). The effects of names on perceptions of intelligence, popularity, and competence. *Journal of Applied Social Psychology, 23,* 1770–1788.

Young, S. G., Hugenberg, K., Bernstein, M. J., & Sacco, D. F. (2012). Perception and motivation in face recognition: A critical review of theories of the cross-race effect. *Personality and Social Psychology Review, 16,* 116–142.

Yu, D. W., & Shepard, G. H. (1998). Is beauty in the eye of the beholder? *Nature, 296,* 321–322.

Yuille, J. C., & Tollestrup, P. A. (1990). Some effects of alcohol on eyewitness memory. *Journal of Applied Psychology, 75,* 268–273.

Yuki, M. (2003). Intergroup comparison versus intragroup relationships: A cross-cultural examination of social identity theory in North American and East Asian cultural contexts. *Social Psychology Quarterly, 66,* 166–183.

Yzerbyt, V. Y., Dardenne, B., & Leyens, J.-Ph. (1998). Social judgeability concerns in impression formation. In V. Y. Yzerbyt, G. Lories, & B. Dardenne (Eds.), *Metacognition: Cognitive and social dimensions* (pp. 126–156). London: Sage.

Yzerbyt, V., & Demoulin, S. (2010). Intergroup relations. In S. T. Fiske, D. T. Gilbert, & G. Lindzey (Eds.), *The handbook of social psychology* (5th ed.). New York: McGraw-Hill.

Zaccaro, S. J. (2007). Trait-based perspectives of leadership. *American Psychologist, 62,* 6–16.

Zajonc, R. B. (1965). Social facilitation. *Science, 149,* 269–274.

Zajonc, R. B. (1968). Attitudinal effects of mere exposure. *Journal of Personality and Social Psychology Monograph Supplement, 9*(2), 1–27.

Zajonc, R. B. (1980). Compresence. In P. B. Paulus (Ed.), *Psychology of group influence* (pp. 35–60). Hillsdale, NJ: Erlbaum.

Zajonc, R. B. (1993). Brain temperature and subjective emotional experience. In M. Lewis & J. M. Haviland (Eds.), *Handbook of emotions* (pp. 209–220). New York: Guilford.

Zajonc, R. B. (2001). Mere exposure: A gateway to the subliminal. *Current Directions in Psychological Science, 10,* 224–228.

Zajonc, R. B., Heingartner, A., & Herman, E. M. (1969). Social enhancement and impairment of performance in the cockroach. *Journal of Personality and Social Psychology, 13,* 82–92.

Zajonc, R. B., Murphy, S. T., & Inglehart, M. (1989). Feeling and facial efference: Implications of the vascular theory of emotion. *Psychological Review, 96,* 395–416.

Zanna, M. P., & Cooper, J. (1974). Dissonance and the pill: An attribution approach to studying the arousal properties of dissonance. *Journal of Personality and Social Psychology, 29,* 703–709.

Zárate, M. A., Garcia, B., Garza, A. A., & Hitlan, R. T. (2004). Cultural threat and perceived realistic group conflict as dual predictors of prejudice. *Journal of Experimental Social Psychology, 40,* 99–105.

Zebrowitz, L. A., & Montepare, J. M. (2005). Appearance DOES Matter. *Science, 308,* 1565–1566.

Zebrowitz, L. A., Luevano, V. X., Bronstad, P. M., & Aharon, I. (2009). Neural activation to babyfaced men matches activation to babies. *Social Neuroscience, 4,* 1–10.

Zebrowitz, L. A., Wang, R., Bronstad, P. M., Eisenberg, D., Undurraga, E., Reyes-García, V., & Godoy, R. (2012). First impressions from faces among U.S. and culturally isolated Tsimane' people in the Bolivian rainforest. *Journal of Cross-Cultural Psychology, 43,* 119–134.

Zeigler-Hill, V., Besser, A., & King, K. (2011). Contingent self-esteem and anticipated reactions to interpersonal rejection and achievement failure. *Journal of Social and Clinical Psychology, 30,* 1069–1096.

Zeisel, H., & Diamond, S. (1978). The effect of peremptory challenges on jury and verdict: An experiment in a federal district court. *Stanford Law Review, 30,* 491–531.

Zell, E., & Alicke, M. D. (2009). Self-evaluative effects of temporal and social comparison. *Journal of Experimental Social Psychology, 45,* 223–227.

Zemack-Rugar, Y., Bettman, J. R., & Fitzsimons, G. J. (2007). The effects of nonconsciously priming emotion concepts on behavior. *Journal of Personality and Social Psychology, 93,* 927–939.

Zentall, T. R. (2012). Perspectives on observational learning in animals. *Journal of Comparative Psychology.*

Zhang, J., & Shavitt, S. (2003). Cultural values in advertisements to the Chinese X-generation. *Journal of Advertising, 32,* 23–33.

Zhang, L., & Baumeister, R. F. (2006). Your money or your self-esteem: Threatened egotism promotes costly entrapment in losing endeavors. *Personality and Social Psychology Bulletin, 32,* 881–893.

Zhang, S., & Kline, S. L. (2009). Can I make my own decision? A cross-cultural study of perceived social network influence in mate selection. *Journal of Cross-Cultural Psychology, 40,* 3–23.

Zhong, C. B., & Liljenquist, K. (2006). Washing away your sins: Threatened morality and physical cleansing. *Science, 313,* 1451–1452.

Zhong, X., Huang, Q., Davison, R. M., Yang, X., & Chen, H. (2012). Empowering teams through social network ties. *International Journal of Information Management, 32,* 209–220.

Zhou, X., Vohs, K. D., & Baumeister, R. F. (2009). The symbolic power of money: Reminders after money alter social distress and physical pain. *Psychological Science, 20,* 700–706.

Zhu, Y., McKenna, B., & Sun, Z. (2007a). Negotiating with Chinese: Success of initial meetings is key. *Cross Cultural Management: An International Journal, 14,* 354–364.

Zhu, Y., Zhang, L., Fan, J., & Han, S. (2007b). Neural basis of cultural influence on self-representation. *Neuroimage, 34*, 1310–1316.

Zillmann, D. (1983). Arousal and aggression. In R. G. Geen & E. I. Donnerstein (Eds.), *Aggression: Theoretical and empirical reviews: Vol. l. Theoretical and methodological issues* (pp. 75–101). New York: Academic Press.

Zillmann, D. (1984). *Connections between sex and aggression.* Hillsdale, NJ: Erlbaum.

Zillmann, D. (2003). Theory of affective dynamics: Emotions and moods. In J. Bryant, D. Roskos-Ewoldsen, & J. Cantor (Eds.), *Communication and emotion: Essays in honor of Dolf Zillmann* (pp. 533–567). Mahwah, NJ: Erlbaum.

Zillmann, D., Bryant, J., Cantor, J. R., & Day, K. D. (1975). Irrelevance of mitigating circumstances in retaliatory behavior at high levels of excitation. *Journal of Research in Personality, 9,* 282–293.

Zimbardo, P. G. (1969). The human choice: Individuation, reason, and order versus deindividuation, impulse, and chaos. *Nebraska Symposium on Motivation, 17,* 237–307.

Zimbardo, P. G. (1985, June). Laugh where we must, be candid where we can. *Psychology Today,* pp. 43–47.

Zimbardo, P. G. (2007). *The Lucifer effect: How good people turn evil.* New York: Random House.

Zimbardo, P. G., Banks, W. C., Haney, C., & Jaffe, D. (1973, April 8). The mind is a formidable jailer: A Pirandellian prison. *New York Times Magazine,* pp. 38–60.

Zimbardo, P. G., LaBerge, S., & Butler, L. D. (1993). Psychophysiological consequences of unexplained arousal: A posthypnotic suggestion paradigm. *Journal of Abnormal Psychology, 102,* 466–473.

Zuckerman, M., DePaulo, B. M., & Rosenthal, R. (1981). Verbal and nonverbal communication of deception. In L. Berkowitz (Ed.), *Advances in experimental social psychology* (Vol. 14, pp. 1–59). New York: Academic Press.

Zuckerman, M., Knee, C. R., Hodgins, H. S., & Miyake, K. (1995). Hypothesis confirmation: The joint effect of positive test strategy and acquiescence response set. *Journal of Personality and Social Psychology, 68,* 52–60.

Zuwerink, J. R., & Devine, P. G. (1996). Attitude importance and resistance to persuasion: It's not just the thought that counts. *Journal of Personality and Social Psychology, 70,* 931–944.

# NAME INDEX

John, L. K., 49
John, O. P., 134
Johns, G., 547
Johnson, D. J., 351, 368
Johnson, J. T., 84
Johnson, M., 113, 132, 220
Johnson, R. D., 310
Johnson, R. W., 244
Johnson, W., 611
Johnston, K. E., 184
Johnstone, D., 565
Jones, B. C., 349
Jones, E. E., 31, 59, 86–87, 93, 94,
    117–18, 123, 137, 172, 208, 278
Jones, J. H., 379
Jones, J. M., 155
Jones, J. T., 84, 85
Jones, S. S., 256
Jones, T. F., 254
Jordan, J., 582
Jordan, K., 440
Josephs, R. A., 74, 78, 462
Jost, J. T., 10, 20, 130, 174
Joyce, C., 439
Judge, T. A., 93, 93f, 348, 537, 552, 555,
    556, 561
Jung-Yoon, C., 439
Jussim, L., 142, 183
Juvonen, J., 325

Kagan, J., 382
Kahneman, D., 120, 122, 521, 565, 566
Kaholokula, J., 17
Kalichman, S. C., 606
Kallgren, C. A., 216
Kalven, H., 511–12, 517, 518
Kameda, T., 517
Kamen-Siegel, L., 590
Kammeyer-Mueller, J. D., 555
Kampis, J., 464
Kane, H. S., 20
Kaplan, M. F., 518
Karau, S. J., 306, 307, 554
Kark, R., 553
Karney, B. R., 369, 384, 385
Karpinski, A. T., 185
Karremans, J. C., 233
Kashima, Y., 131, 184
Kasimatis, M., 608
Kassin, S. M., 115, 142, 256f, 492,
    498, 498t, 499, 501, 502, 503, 505,
    514, 518
Katz, D., 155
Katz, N., 319, 324, 325
Kaufman, D. Q., 234
Kavanagh, M. J., 547
Kawakami, K., 31, 186
Kay, A. C., 130
Kazdin, A. E., 450
Keefe, R. C., 361
Keenan, J. P., 55, 56
Keil, M., 318
Keillor, J. M., 61
Keith, P. M., 370
Keller, P. A., 230
Kelley, H. H., 118, 136, 368
Kelly, A. E., 59, 598

Kelman, H. C., 15, 221, 225, 226f,
    262, 279
Kemmelmeier, M., 415
Kemp, J., 152
Kemp, R. I., 462
Kennison, S. M., 188
Kenny, D. A., 134, 145, 146, 549
Kenrick, D. T., 273, 356, 361, 365
Kerekes, A. R. Z., 131
Kernis, M. H., 73
Kerr, N. L., 307, 507, 509, 513, 517,
    518, 518t
Kersten, G. E., 332
Kervyn, N., 134
Kessler, R. C., 576, 587
Ketcham, K., 495
Key, W. B., 231
Keysar, B., 84
Kiechel, K. L., 503
Kiecolt-Glaser, J. K., 584, 586, 601
Kierein, N. M., 142
Kiesler, C. A., 255, 275
Kiesler, S. B., 255
Kilbourne, J., 162
Kilduff, M., 242
Kilham, W., 283–84
Kilianski, S. E., 90
Kim, H. S., 70, 71f, 237, 427, 603–4
Kim, M. U., 318
Kim, Y., 17, 352
Kimmel, A. J., 45
Kimmel, P. R., 333t
King, B. T., 238
King, L. A., 608
Kinsey, A. C., 379
Kinzer, S., 176
Kiong, L. C., 439
Kirkman, B. L., 324
Kirkpatrick, L. A., 372
Kirkpatrick, S. A., 549
Kitayama, S., 68, 69, 69f, 91, 126,
    127, 248
Kite, M. E., 64
Kivimäki, M., 590
Klapwijk, A., 328
Klauer, K., 33
Klein, O., 310
Klein, W. M., 65
Kleingeld, A., 557
Kleinke, C. L., 61, 113
Klietz, S. J., 477
Kline, S. L., 378
Klinesmith, J., 460
Kling, K. C., 75
Klohnen, E. C., 355, 357
Knafo, A., 420
Kniffin, K., 351
Knobe, J., 117
Knobloch, S., 181
Knowles, E. D., 20, 159
Knowles, E. S., 263, 272
Knowles, M. L., 304
Knox, R. E., 242
Ko, S. J., 106–7
Kobasa, S. C., 588
Koenig, A. M., 554

Koestner, R., 363
Kogan, S. M., 167
Kogut, T., 424
Kohn, A., 63, 557–58
Kohnken, G., 490
Kohut, A., 154f
Kokko, K., 443
Kolditz, T. A., 87
Koller, S., 175
Konar, E., 353f, 560
Konijn, E. A., 467
Kopelman, S., 329, 333, 334f
Koranyi, B., 465
Korchmaros, J. D., 395
Korte, C., 413
Koslowski, S. W., 546
Koslowsky, M., 578
Kovacs, S., 383
Kovera, M. B., 487, 493, 496, 512
Kowalski, G. S., 88
Kowalski, R. M., 86, 341, 343, 380
Kozak, M. N., 109
Kozel, F., 500
Krahé, B., 467
Kramer, G. P., 512
Kramer, R. M., 318
Kramer, S. J., 561
Krantz, D. S., 582
Kraus, S. J., 214
Krauss, D., 487, 511
Kravitz, D. A., 305, 540
Kravitz, J., 490
Kray, L. J., 122, 169
Krebs, D., 396
Krendl, A. C., 348
Kressel, D. F., 508–9
Kressel, N. J., 508–9
Kringelbach, M. L., 107
Krishnan, K. R. R., 448
Kristof, A. L., 93, 93f, 535
Krizan, Z., 86
Kroon, M. B. R., 318
Krosnick, J. A., 215
Krueger, J. I., 121, 145, 171, 410
Krueger, R. F., 611
Krug, E. G., 576
Kruger, J., 122
Kruglanski, A. W., 137, 146
Kubany, E. S., 576
Kubzansky, L. D., 590
Kugihara, N., 306
Kulik, J. A., 67, 343
Kumkale, G. T., 226
Kunda, Z., 183
Kuntz-Wilson, W., 346
Kupers, T. A., 521
Kurbat, M. A., 67
Kurdek, L., 345, 368, 383, 384f, 385
Kurtzberg, T. R., 328
Kurzban, R., 329
Kwan, J., 268

LaBouff, J., 421
Ladd, G. W., 4
Lai, H., 332
Laird, J. D., 61

Lakey, B., 602
Lakin, J. L., 256
Lakoff, G., 132, 220
Laland, K. N., 256
Lalwani, A. K., 91
Lam, S. K., 302
Lamb, M. E., 493
Lambert, A. J., 303
Lamm, C., 399
Lamm, H., 314, 315
Lamy, L., 423
Landau, M. J., 173, 229
Landau, T., 350
Landy, F. J., 545
Lane, A. M., 197
Lane, C., 343
Lane, K. A., 211
Lane, L. W., 83
Lange, N. D., 139
Langer, E. J., 86, 271, 589
Langlois, J. H., 348, 349, 350,
    350c, 353
Langton, S. R. H., 113
LaPiere, R. T., 214
Lapsley, D. K., 398
Largo, E., 129
Larrick, R. P., 311, 458, 566–67
Larsen, J. T., 209
Larsen, R. J., 349, 608
Larson, J. R., Jr., 320
Laschever, S., 560
Lassiter, G. D., 109, 505
Latané, B., 263, 268, 289–90, 306, 342,
    346, 407, 408f, 409, 411, 412, 420
Latham, G. P., 322, 328, 556
Lau, R. L., 229
Laughlin, P. R., 312
Laurin, K., 79
Lawrence, E., 383
Lazarus, R. S., 573, 592
Le, B., 369
Leaper, C., 181
Leary, M. R., 7, 54, 73, 94, 261, 340–41,
    343, 457, 458
LeDoux, J. E., 55, 229
Lee, C., 547
Lee, E.-J., 310
Lee, J. A., 373
Lee, L., 348
Lee, M. J., 153
Lee, M. R., 441
Lee, P., 320
Lee, R. T., 578
Lee, S. W., 127
Lee, W.-N., 237
Legault, L., 197
Lehman, D. R., 27, 179
Leicht, K. T., 164
Leichtman, M. D., 493
Leigh, B. C., 78
Leiker, M., 582
Leinbach, M. D., 181
Leippe, M. R., 240, 244
Leith, L. M., 451, 452f
Leivens, F., 534
Lemire, J., 152
Lemoine, C., 172

# SUBJECT INDEX

2